14th Workshop on Innovative Use of NLP for Building Educational Applications 2019

Florence, Italy
2 August 2019

ISBN: 978-1-5108-9101-2

ACL 2019

Innovative Use of NLP for Building Educational Applications

Proceedings of the 14th Workshop

August 2, 2019
Florence, Italy

Gold Sponsors

Silver Sponsors

Bronze Sponsors

Jonathan Gordon, Vassar College
Cyril Goutte, National Research Council Canada
Iryna Gurevych, UKP Lab, TU Darmstadt
Binod Gyawali, Educational Testing Service
Na-Rae Han, University of Pittsburgh
Jiangang Hao, Educational Testing Service
Homa Hashemi, Microsoft
Trude Heift, Simon Fraser University
Derrick Higgins, American Family Insurance
Heiko Holz, LEAD Graduate School & Research Network at the University of Tübingen
Andrea Horbach, University Duisburg-Essen
Chung-Chi Huang, Frostburg State University
Yi-Ting Huang, Academia Sinica
Radu Tudor Ionescu, University of Bucharest
Lifeng Jin, The Ohio State University
Pamela Jordan, University of Pittsburgh
Taraka Kasicheyanula, University of Oslo
Elma Kerz, RWTH Aachen
Mamoru Komachi, Tokyo Metropolitan University
Lun-Wei Ku, Academia Sinica
Chong Min Lee, Educational Testing Service
Ji-Ung Lee, UKP Lab, Technische Universität Darmstadt
John Lee, City University of Hong Kong
Lung-Hao Lee, National Central University
Ben Leong, Educational Testing Service
James Lester, North Carolina State University
Chen Liang, Facebook
Diane Litman, University of Pittsburgh
Yang Liu, Laix
Peter Ljunglöf, University of Gothenburg
Anastassia Loukina, Educational Testing Service
Xiaofei Lu, Pennsylvania State University
Luca Lugini, University of Pittsburgh
Nabin Maharjan, University of Memphis
Jean Maillard, University of Cambridge
Shervin Malmasi, Harvard Medical School
Montse Maritxalar, University of the Basque Country
Ditty Mathew, IIT Madras
Julie Medero, Harvey Mudd College
Beata Megyesi, Uppsala University
Detmar Meurers, Universität Tübingen
Margot Mieskes, University of Applied Sciences, Darmstadt
Elham Mohammadi, CLaC Laboratory, Concordia University
Maria Moritz, German Research Center for Artificial Intelligence
William Murray, Pearson
Courtney Napoles, Grammarly
Diane Napolitano, LCSR, Rutgers University
Hwee Tou Ng, National University of Singapore
Huy Nguyen, LingoChamp
Rodney Nielsen, University of North Texas
Nobal Niraula, Boeing Research and Technology

Yoo Rhee Oh, Electronics and Telecommunications Research Institute (ETRI)
Constantin Orasan, University of Wolverhampton
Ulrike Pado, HFT Stuttgart
Alexis Palmer, University of North Texas
Martí Quixal, Universität Tübingen
Vipul Raheja, Grammarly
Zahra Rahimi, University of Pittsburgh
Lakshmi Ramachandran, Amazon Search
Vikram Ramanarayanan, Educational Testing Service
Hanumant Redkar, Indian Institute of Technology Bombay
Marek Rei, University of Cambridge
Robert Reynolds, Brigham Young University
Brian Riordan, Educational Testing Service
Andrew Rosenberg, Google
Mark Rosenstein, Pearson
Alla Rozovskaya, City University of New York
C. Anton Rytting, University of Maryland
Keisuke Sakaguchi, Allen Institute for Artificial Intelligence
Allen Schmaltz, Harvard University
Serge Sharoff, University of Leeds
Swapna Somasundaran, Educational Testing Service
Richard Sproat, Google
Helmer Strik, Radboud University Nijmegen
Jan Švec, NTIS, University of West Bohemia
Anaïs Tack, UCLouvain & KU Leuven
Joel Tetreault, Grammarly
Yuen-Hsien Tseng, National Taiwan Normal University
Giulia Venturi, Institute for Computational Linguistics "A. Zampolli", Italy
Aline Villavicencio, Federal University of Rio Grande do Sul and University of Essex
Carl Vogel, Trinity College Dublin
Elena Volodina, University of Gothenburg
Shuting Wang, Facebook Inc
Xinhao Wang, Educational Testing Service
Michael White, The Ohio State University
Michael Wojatzki, LTL, University of Duisburg-Essen
Magdalena Wolska, Eberhard Karls Universität Tübingen
Huichao Xue, LinkedIn
Victoria Yaneva, National Board of Medical Examiners / University of Wolverhampton
Zheng Yuan, University of Cambridge
Marcos Zampieri, University of Wolverhampton (UK)
Klaus Zechner, Educational Testing Service
Fan Zhang, Google
Haoran Zhang, University of Pittsburgh
Ramon Ziai, University of Tübingen

Table of Contents

Workshop Program

Friday, August 2, 2019

8:30–9:00   ***Loading of Oral Presentations***

9:00–9:15   **Opening Remarks**

9:15–10:30   **Oral Presentations 1**

9:15–9:40   *The many dimensions of algorithmic fairness in educational applications*
Anastassia Loukina, Nitin Madnani and Klaus Zechner

9:40–10:05   *Predicting the Difficulty of Multiple Choice Questions in a High-stakes Medical Exam*
Le An Ha, Victoria Yaneva, Peter Baldwin and Janet Mee

10:05-10:30   **Ambassador paper: Effects of the self-view window during video-mediated survey interviews: An eye-tracking study, Shelley Feuer**

10:30–11:00   **Coffee Breaks**

11:00–12:30   **Oral Presentations 2**

11:00–11:25   *An Intelligent Testing Strategy for Vocabulary Assessment of Chinese Second Language Learners*
Wei Zhou, Renfen Hu, Feipeng Sun and Ronghuai Huang

11:25–11:50   *Computationally Modeling the Impact of Task-Appropriate Language Complexity and Accuracy on Human Grading of German Essays*
Zarah Weiss, Anja Riemenschneider, Pauline Schröter and Detmar Meurers

11:50–12:10   *Analysing Rhetorical Structure as a Key Feature of Summary Coherence*
Jan Šnajder, Tamara Sladoljev-Agejev and Svjetlana Kolić Vehovec

Neural Grammatical Error Correction Systems with Unsupervised Pre-training on Synthetic Data
Roman Grundkiewicz, Marcin Junczys-Dowmunt and Kenneth Heafield

14:45–15:30   Poster Session B

Evaluation of automatic collocation extraction methods for language learning
Vishal Bhalla and Klara Klimcikova

Anglicized Words and Misspelled Cognates in Native Language Identification
Ilia Markov, Vivi Nastase and Carlo Strapparava

Linguistically-Driven Strategy for Concept Prerequisites Learning on Italian
Alessio Miaschi, Chiara Alzetta, Franco Alberto Cardillo and Felice Dell'Orletta

Grammatical-Error-Aware Incorrect Example Retrieval System for Learners of Japanese as a Second Language
Mio Arai, Masahiro Kaneko and Mamoru Komachi

Toward Automated Content Feedback Generation for Non-native Spontaneous Speech
Su-Youn Yoon, Ching-Ni Hsieh, Klaus Zechner, Matthew Mulholland, Yuan Wang and Nitin Madnani

Analytic Score Prediction and Justification Identification in Automated Short Answer Scoring
Tomoya Mizumoto, Hiroki Ouchi, Yoriko Isobe, Paul Reisert, Ryo Nagata, Satoshi Sekine and Kentaro Inui

Content Customization for Micro Learning using Human Augmented AI Techniques
Ayush Shah, Tamer Abuelsaad, Jae-Wook Ahn, Prasenjit Dey, Ravi Kokku, Ruhi Sharma Mittal, Aditya Vempaty and Mourvi Sharma

Curio SmartChat : A system for Natural Language Question Answering for Self-Paced K-12 Learning
Srikrishna Raamadhurai, Ryan Baker and Vikraman Poduval

Supporting content evaluation of student summaries by Idea Unit embedding
Marcello Gecchele, Hiroaki Yamada, Takenobu Tokunaga and Yasuyo Sawaki

On Understanding the Relation between Expert Annotations of Text Readability and Target Reader Comprehension
Sowmya Vajjala and Ivana Lucic

The many dimensions of algorithmic fairness in educational applications

Anastassia Loukina, Nitin Madnani, Klaus Zechner
Educational Testing Service
Princeton, NJ, USA
`aloukina,nmadnani,kzechner@ets.org`

Abstract

The issues of algorithmic fairness and bias have recently featured prominently in many publications highlighting the fact that training the algorithms for maximum performance may often result in predictions that are biased against various groups. Educational applications based on NLP and speech processing technologies often combine multiple complex machine learning algorithms and are thus vulnerable to the same sources of bias as other machine learning systems. Yet such systems can have high impact on people's lives especially when deployed as part of high-stakes tests. In this paper we discuss different definitions of fairness and possible ways to apply them to educational applications. We then use simulated and real data to consider how test-takers' native language backgrounds can affect their automated scores on an English language proficiency assessment. We illustrate that total fairness may not be achievable and that different definitions of fairness may require different solutions.

1 Introduction

The issues of algorithmic fairness and bias have recently featured prominently in many publications highlighting the fact that training the algorithms for maximum performance may often result in predictions that are biased against various groups (Kamiran and Calders, 2009; Kamishima et al., 2012; Luong et al., 2011; Zemel et al., 2013; Feldman et al., 2015; Friedler et al., 2016). Like any algorithm, NLP systems are not immune to such bias (Hovy and Spruit, 2016; Caliskan et al., 2017). These days it is hardly necessary to justify the importance of ensuring algorithmic fairness, especially in applications that can have a substantial impact on users' lives.

Automated test scoring is one such application, and the educational measurement community has been concerned with the fairness of automated scoring since long before this topic gained wide popularity. There exist a variety of standard measures generally recommended for evaluating fairness of the automated scoring systems (Clauser et al., 2002; Williamson et al., 2012; Ramineni and Williamson, 2013) as well as open-source tools for computing such measures (Madnani et al., 2017).

In this paper we use the data from an operational spoken language proficiency assessment and an automated speech scoring engine to show that the application of these measures may sometimes lead to seemingly contradictory results. We apply the insight from the machine learning community that there are different ways to formally define algorithmic fairness, and propose a framework which leverages work from both educational measurement and machine learning to formalize these definitions in the context of automated scoring.

2 Fairness in educational applications and beyond

2.1 Fairness metrics for automated scoring

Fairness research has a long tradition in educational measurement where "fairness" has been defined with reference to "construct". A construct is defined as a set of related knowledge, skills, and other abilities that a test is designed to measure (Zieky, 2016). A fair test is one where differences in test scores between the test-takers are due *only* to differences in skills which are part of the construct. Any consistent differences in scores between different *non-random* groups of test-takers that result from other factors *not* immediately related to the construct (i.e., "construct-irrelevant") may indicate that the test is unfair (Xi, 2010; Zieky, 2016). Notably such "construct-

Proceedings of the Fourteenth Workshop on Innovative Use of NLP for Building Educational Applications, pages 1–10
Florence, Italy, August 2, 2019. ©2019 Association for Computational Linguistics

irrelevant" factors include not only protected attributes often considered in studies on algorithmic bias but also other factors that can affect predefined groups of test-takers, such as screen resolution on the computers used to administer an assessment (Bridgeman et al., 2001). It follows that a fair automated scoring system should not introduce additional construct-irrelevant group-related variance or disadvantage any group of test-takers in comparison to human scores (Penfield, 2016).

Several standard measures have been used to evaluate the fairness of the automated scoring systems across different groups, for example speakers of different languages or test-takers with disabilities (Burstein and Chodorow, 1999; Bridgeman et al., 2012; Wang and von Davier, 2014; Wang et al., 2016; An et al., 2016; Loukina and Buzick, 2017). The two most common analyses are standardized mean score differences and overall model performance for different groups with human scores (predictive ability) (Ramineni and Williamson, 2013; Williamson et al., 2012). More recently other measures have been used such as differential feature functioning (Zhang et al., 2017) to analyze the performance of individual features or variance in mean model residual across groups (Yao et al., 2019). The approach taken in many previous studies on the fairness of automated scores has been that substantial between-groups differences in human and automated scores in *any* of the measures indicate that the system might not be fair.

2.2 Algorithmic fairness

There are two key conclusions that emerged from general research on algorithmic fairness that are most relevant for this paper. First, there are many different ways to formally define algorithmic fairness. Second, it may be impossible to achieve fairness according to each and every one of these definitions at the same time (Friedler et al., 2016; Berk et al., 2018).

In their review of algorithmic bias in the context of criminal justice risk assessment, Berk et al. (2018) offer five definitions of fairness: (1) Overall accuracy equality: overall classification accuracy is the same for all groups; (2) Statistical parity: the marginal distribution of predicted classes is the same for all groups; (3) Conditional procedure accuracy equality: the prediction is equally accurate for all groups when conditioned on a known outcome; (4) Conditional use accuracy equality: the prediction is equally accurate for all groups when conditioned on a predicted outcome; (5) Treatment equality: the ratio of false negatives and false positives is the same for both groups. Total fairness is achieved when all five definitions are met. As Berk et al. (2018) show, in practice total fairness cannot be achieved, except for trivial cases.

3   Data

The analyses in this paper are based on actual responses collected during a large-scale assessment of English language speaking proficiency. For this assessment all test-takers answered 6 questions that elicited spontaneous speech. Depending on the question, the speakers were given 45 seconds or 1 minute to record their responses.

We will focus on whether automated scoring might disadvantage test-takers depending on their native language (L1), a common concern in automated scoring contexts. Learners with different L1 might have different linguistic profile and it has been shown that it is possible to identify learner L1 from their written or spoken response (Malmasi et al., 2017). Therefore there is a danger that the scoring engine might inadvertently assign different scores to speakers of different L1 even when there is no difference in English proficiency, the actual construct measured by the test. In other words the system would introduce group-related construct-irrelevant differences.

In an actual operational scenario there are many additional factors that can introduce bias to the performance of an automated scoring system: some L1s might be over- or under-represented in the data used for model training and evaluation; sometimes different versions of the test are administered in different countries for security reasons, introducing further scope for conflation between native language and prompt.

For this study we constructed a corpus of responses designed to control for these factors. Using the information about the native language reported by test-takers when taking the test, we selected responses from native speakers of the 6 most frequently languages among the test-taker population[1]: Chinese (CHI), Korean (KOR), Japanese (JPN), Spanish (SPA), Arabic (ARA) and

---

[1]The metadata does not differentiate between different linguistic varieties.

German (GER). All test-takers responded to one of the two versions of the test that were administered across all these regions.

We then created a corpus with uniform distribution of native languages by randomly sampling a similar number of test-takers for each version of the test. The final corpus included 26,710 responses from 4,452 test-takers (742 for each language, about 370 test-takers per version). The corpus was split into a training set (75%) and a test set (25%), with 19,942 responses from 3,324 test-takers (554 from each group) allocated to the former, and the remaining 6,768 responses from 1,128 test-takers (188 from each group) allocated to the latter.

All responses had been scored by trained human raters on a scale from 1-4. The raters assigned a single holistic score to each response using a scoring rubric that covered different aspects of language proficiency including delivery, language use and content. Most responses were scored by a single rater. About 6% of responses were double-scored. Human-human agreement for responses in the test set is Pearson's $r = 0.66$. The scoring process was set up following best practices in order to minimize any possible bias (Wang and von Davier, 2014; Penfield, 2016). Multiple raters took part in this process and in no instance did a given rater score multiple responses from the same test-taker. All raters were monitored throughout the process using both exemplar responses with known scores and random back-scoring. Despite all these measures, there is still some possibility that the human scores contained bias which would then be learnt by the model. For the sake of simplicity, however, in this paper we will ignore such a possibility and treat the human scores as a gold standard measure.

3.1 Simulated models

When looking at algorithmic fairness, it is often helpful to look at extreme simulated cases. In all four models discussed in this section, the 'system' scores were produced by training a linear regression on the training set and using the regression parameters to generate predictions for the test set. All evaluations were done on the test set. The models were trained using the human score as the dependent variable and four different types of features described below.

Random model: The RANDOM model was based on a single feature: a random sample drawn from a normal distribution with mean and standard deviation equal to those of human scores on the training set. This feature by definition is blind to a test-taker's L1 and any properties of their response. This model is not valid as it does not differentiate test-takers on any construct-relevant dimension but it is not expected to consistently differentiate based on any construct-irrelevant factors. To further make sure that no bias is introduced by chance, we repeated the whole procedure from feature generation to analysis 10 times with different random states. All reported results are average values of the corresponding metrics across these 10 repetitions. As expected, the model failed to predict human scores on the test set with no correlation between the predicted and observed scores (average $r = -0.004$)

A perfect model: The PERFECT model also contained a single feature, but this time the feature was equal to the human score with the addition of random noise. Random noise was also sampled from a normal distribution with mean = 0 and $\sigma = 0.2$. Like the RANDOM model, this procedure was applied to the whole data set without using any information about a test-taker's L1 or any properties of their response beyond the human score. We expect this model to be fair because it distinguishes test-takers primarily based on their human scores which are implicitly taken as proxies for language proficiency. As in case of the RANDOM model, we repeated the whole procedure 10 times to ensure no bias had been introduced accidentally during random sampling. Unsurprisingly, these models achieved an almost perfect performance on the test set with average $r = 0.97$.

An almost perfect model: The ~PERFECT model was identical to the PERFECT model, except that the random noise added to the human score when generating the "feature" was sampled from a normal distribution with $\sigma = 0.5$, that is the model was less accurate. Like the PERFECT model, this model also distinguishes test-takers primarily based on their language proficiency. This model achieved a good performance on the test set with average $r = 0.83$.

Metadata-based model: While RANDOM and PERFECT models were designed to be blind to any L1-effects, the META model only relied on demographic information. It included two features: the native country of the test-taker and the country where they took the test. While this model did not directly make use of L1, it used two closely related features (in our data, L1 was closely related to the native country and test country). The model achieved a moderate performance of $r = 0.44$. Since this model differentiates test-takers based on their geographic location and not on their language proficiency, we expect that this model should not be deemed fair.

4 Fairness evaluations

4.1 Standardized mean differences

We first computed standardized mean difference (SMD) a standard measure used to evaluate the fairness of automated scoring engines (Williamson et al., 2012). To do so, both human and system scores were converted to z-scores using their respective means and standard deviations. SMD for each group is the average difference between such standardized human and system scores within this group (System score - human score). Absolute values above 0.1 are considered an issue of concern and require further evaluation (Williamson et al., 2012).

	RANDOM	PERFECT	∼PERFECT	META
ARA	0.02	-0.00	0.00	**0.14**
CHI	**0.22**	0.01	0.03	**-0.40**
GER	**-0.78**	-0.02	**-0.13**	**0.93**
JPN	**0.63**	0.02	**0.11**	**-0.70**
KOR	**0.17**	0.00	0.03	**-0.30**
SPA	**-0.20**	-0.01	-0.02	**0.27**

Table 1: Standardized mean difference (system-human) for 6 languages in our corpus for scores generated by different models. Absolute values above 0.1 threshold are highlighted in bold

Table 1 shows SMDs for the four models. As we predicted, the speakers of all languages would be disadvantaged by using the META model. Yet surprisingly, even in the case of the ∼PERFECT model two of the languages, GER and JPN, show absolute SMDs slightly above the recommended 0.1 threshold. In other words, the evaluation suggests that speakers of these two languages are not treated fairly by the model: GER speakers are underscored while JPN speakers are over-scored.

Yet we know that the ∼PERFECT model by design is blind to test-taker's L1. Why then do we see relatively large SMDs? The reason is the unusual score distribution for these two groups of test-takers and consequently the large difference in their mean scores. As shown in Table 2, the scores are not distributed uniformly: the propor-

	1	2	3	4	Mean
ARA	0.05	0.29	0.51	0.14	2.74
CHI	0.03	0.37	0.55	0.04	2.60
GER	0.00	0.05	0.54	0.41	3.35
JPN	0.11	0.52	0.34	0.02	2.29
KOR	0.05	0.36	0.49	0.10	2.63
SPA	0.02	0.23	0.58	0.17	2.92

Table 2: Proportion of responses assigned each of the four possible human scores for test-takers with each L1 and mean human score for each group

tion of '2' and '3' is much higher (80% of all scores) than the proportion of '1' and '4'. Furthermore, proficiency levels as measured by human scores vary greatly across the 6 groups in our study: GER speakers have a very high proportion of score 4 responses (40.9%) and a mean score of 3.35, while JPN speakers have a high number of responses scored as '1' or '2' (63%) and a mean score of 2.286. The very uneven score distribution in the training set, in combination with the noise we introduced to the 'feature', resulted in greater prediction error at the edges of the scale: mean standardized score differences is 0.35 for responses scored 1 and -0.29 for responses scored 4 vs. 0.17 for responses scored 2 and -0.05 for responses scored 3. This in combination with the unusual score distribution lead to higher absolute SMDs for GER and JPN speakers.

To confirm that the observed differences are due to score distribution and are not an artefact of the model-training process, we sampled from the test set a subset of 2,700 responses (450 responses per group) with identical (but not uniform) distributions of human scores in each group: the sample sizes for each score level were determined by the maximum number of responses available for this score level from all L1s. As a result, 80% in this sample received a score of '3', 13% received a score of '2', 5% received a score of '4' and 1% received a score of '1'. The mean human score for all subgroups was 2.9. We then recomputed SMDs using only this subset. While SMDs for the META model remained high, the absolute SMDs for the other three models were all below 0.02.

4.2 Measuring different dimensions of fairness

In this section we propose a set of measures that capture different definitions of fairness. Note that not all definitions of fairness considered in Berk et al. (2018) are applicable to automated scoring in assessment: thus we do not expect *statistical parity* that is the same marginal score distribution for all groups. The unequal distribution of social, economic, and educational resources means that some differences in performance across groups are to be expected (AERA, 1999).

The three definitions that we will consider in this paper are: (1) Overall score accuracy; (2) Overall score difference; (3) Conditional score difference.[2]

The *overall score accuracy* (OSA) measures whether automated scores are equally accurate for each group by looking at differences in squared error $(S - H)^2$ (where H is the human score for a given response and S is the system score). This measure is essentially the same as predictive accuracy for different groups considered in previous studies on automated scoring (Ramineni and Williamson, 2013; Yao et al., 2019). To get a numeric estimate we fit a linear regression with squared error as a dependent variable and test-taker L1 as an independent variable, used the R^2 from this model as a measure of model fairness: larger R^2 indicates high impact of L1 on score accuracy.[3]

The *overall score difference* (OSD) considers whether automated scores are consistently different from human scores for members of a certain group. Since we are interested in the sign of difference we are using actual error $S - H$ for each response rather than squared error. This measure is generally similar to what is evaluated by SMDs and similar in spirit to the 'Treatment equality' in Berk et al. (2018). To get a numeric estimate we fit a linear regression with error as a dependent variable and test-taker L1 as an independent variable, and used the R^2 from this model as a measure of model fairness: larger R^2 values indicate high impact of L1 on score differences.

The *conditional score difference* (CSD) shows whether automated scoring engines assign different scores to speakers from different groups despite their having the same language proficiency.

This is similar to conditional procedure equality in Berk et al. (2018). In educational measurement, a similar approach has been applied to feature analysis and is known as "differential feature functioning" (Zhang et al., 2017). Using human scores as a proxy for language proficiency, we can estimate this metric by fitting a linear regression with error $S - H$ as a dependent variable, and both test-taker L1 and human score as independent variables. To evaluate the impact of L1 beyond human scores, we first fit the model with human scores only and then compared the difference in R^2 values between the two models. We use analysis of variance to establish whether the difference is significant. As with overall score difference, larger R^2 values indicate higher impact of L1 on automatic scores[4].

	Actual			Equal		
	OSA	OSD	CSD	OSA	OSD	CSD
RANDOM	.020	.189	ns	ns	ns	ns
PERFECT	ns	.012	ns	ns	ns	ns
∼PERFECT	.003	.058	ns	ns	ns	ns
META	.011	.002	.207	.050	.352	.354

Table 3: Adjusted R^2 showing the percentage of variance in scoring error attributed to L1 for different models and score distributions (equal and actual score distribution). Larger values correspond to the greater impact of L1 on scoring error. Cells marked 'ns' mean that the effect of L1 was not significant at α=0.01. See section 4.2 for further explanation.

4.3 Evaluation on simulated models

Table 3 shows the results of these evaluations for the four models considered in this section. Since based on the results in previous section we expect the overall difference to be dependent on score distribution, we conducted all analyses twice: once using the whole test set ("actual score distribution") and once using the subset with identical score distribution across all groups described in 4.1.

As expected, Table 3 shows a striking difference in results between the two samples. When the score distribution is held constant across the groups, we see the results we expect from the design of the model: L1 was observed to have a significant effect on only the META model. For all

---

[2] For the sake of simplicity we will not consider the fifth definition of fairness: conditional use equality, that is do the same automated scores assigned to different group members correspond to the same proficiency level? This is another important dimension of fairness that affects score use and interpretation and we will return to it in future work.

[3] We treat all responses as independent since mixed linear model analysis showed no clustering by speaker in our data. This assumption may not hold for all data sets in which case mixed models might be necessary.

[4] The code used to compute these metrics is open-sourced as part of RSMTool: https://github.com/EducationalTestingService/rsmtool (Madnani et al., 2017)

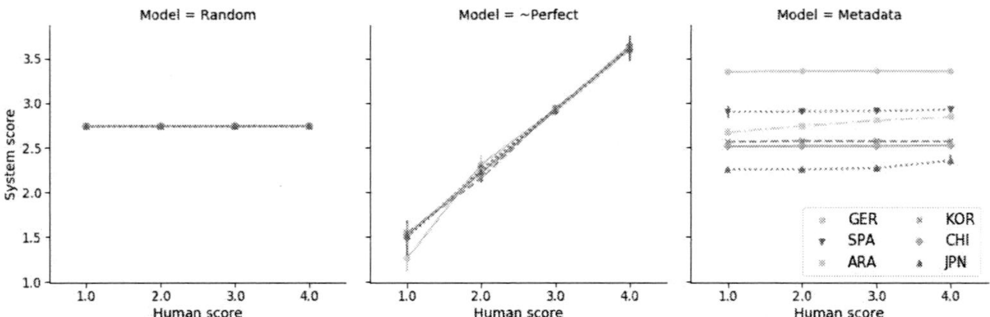

Figure 1: Average system score conditioned on human score for different models and native languages

other models, there was no significant impact of L1 on scores.

A different picture emerges when we consider results on the actual score distribution. As we already observed for SMDs, we saw a significant impact of L1 on the OSD. It was particularly large for the RANDOM and ~PERFECT models, but we also saw a consistent, albeit small, effect for the PERFECT model. In addition, there was a difference in OSA for both RANDOM and ~PERFECT models. As expected, no CSD was observed for any of the models other than META. We will return to this finding in the discussion.

5 Application to automated speech scoring

5.1 Automated scoring engine

We will now now apply these evaluations to the actual scores produced by an automated speech scoring engine similar to the one described in Chen et al. (2018). The ASR system was trained using the Kaldi toolkit (Povey et al., 2011) on a proprietary corpus consisting of 800 hours of non-native speech from 8,700 speakers of more than 100 native languages. There was no overlap of speakers or questions between the ASR training corpus and the corpus used in this paper. We did not additionally adapt the ASR to the speakers or responses in this study.

For each response, we extracted 77 non-sparse continuous features which covered two of the three aspects of language proficiency considered by the human raters: delivery (i.e., prosody, pronunciation, fluency) and language use (i.e., grammar, vocabulary). The correlation between different features and human scores varied between r=0.05 and r=0.63. For this study we did not use any features

that cover the content of the response.

5.2 Scoring models

Baseline model: As a baseline (BASE) we used a model which included all 77 features. The model was fitted using Ridge regression available via RSMTool, an open-source tool for training automated scoring models (Madnani et al., 2017). The model coefficients were estimated using all responses in the training set with human score as the dependent variable and features as independent variables. The model parameters were used to generate predictions on the test set. The correlation between automated and human scores was r = 0.71.

L1-specific model: We also trained a separate L1 model for each native language using only responses from test-takers from this group and the same general procedure as for the BASE model and then pooled together predictions from these six models for evaluation. The overall correlation for all pooled predictions was r = 0.72, similar to the BASE model. We expect that this model might reduce the score error for each L1 but will likely increase CSD as it makes use of speaker L1 in the scoring process.

Model with "fairer" feature subset: Some of the features in our model showed greater differential feature performance; in other words, feature values differed across groups even for the same score level. This, in turn, could result in different scores for different groups. To identify such features, we repeated the same analysis as used to compute conditional procedure accuracy but using each feature as a dependent variable. The amount of variance attributed to native language for different features varied between <0.1% and 11% with median at 3.4%. We used 3% as a threshold and excluded features where more than 3% of feature variance could be attributed to native language. This left us with 34 out of 77 features. These analyses were done using the training set. We then used this subset of 34 features to re-fit the Ridge regression to the training set and to generate predictions for the test set. This FAIR(ER) model achieved $r = 0.67$, a small loss in performance considering that we removed more than half of all features. This model was optimized to reduce CSD but it might do so at the cost of other measures.

5.3 Model fairness

The fairness evaluations for these three models are summarized in Table 4. For the BASE model, test-taker L1 explained 1.7% of variance in OSD and 6.2% of variance in CSD. There also was a small difference in OSA. In other words, these evaluations pointed towards a small but significant bias in model performance.

	Actual			Equal		
	OSA	OSD	CSD	OSA	OSD	CSD
BASE	.002	.017	.062	.008	.112	.112
L1	.003	ns	.135	.014	.222	.223
FAIR(ER)	.004	.045	.030	.004	.054	.055

Table 4: Adjusted R^2 showing percentage of variance in scoring error attributed to L1 for different models and score distributions. See caption to Table 3 and section 4.2 for further explanation

To further understand the nature of these differences, we can look at the estimates for each group produced by the model in Table 5. For estimates computed on the actual score distribution we see that not only the size but also the direction of differences differs depending on whether we look at the overall or conditional difference. Thus, for example, the overall difference for GER speakers suggests lower overall automated scores relative to human scores than for the reference group (SPA), while the conditional difference implies that the automated scores are higher relative to human ratings than for the reference group when speaker language proficiency is held constant.

Since we already saw that overall differences may be affected by the score distributions, Table 5 also shows the estimates for the model fitted to the subset of responses where the score distribution is held constant across all groups. In this case, OSA and OSD estimates are identical and show that given the same level of profi-

ciency the model in fact assigns higher scores to GER speakers relative to human scores and lower scores to JPN speakers relative to human scores. In other words, in the actual data this difference for GER speakers is compensated by the score distribution effects. Conditional score differences for the three models are illustrated in Figure 2. For comparison, Figure 1 shows the same plots for simulated models.

	Actual			Equal		
	OSA	OSD	CSD	OSA	OSD	CSD
ARA	ns	0.06	ns	ns	ns	ns
CHI	ns	0.09	-0.10	ns	-0.12	-0.12
GER	ns	-0.11	0.16	0.06	0.20	0.20
JPN	ns	ns	-0.33	0.08	-0.31	-0.31
KOR	ns	0.06	-0.11	ns	-0.10	-0.10

Table 5: Model estimates for 6 languages in our corpus for scores generated by the BASE model. SPA is used as a reference category.

For the other two models the evaluations in Table 4 are consistent with our predictions: FAIR(ER) model has the lowest CSD (0.03) while for the L1 model CSD more than doubled and reached 0.135. At the same time OSD shows the reverse pattern with the L1 model outperforming both BASE and FAIR(ER) model. All three models show small but significant OSA.

Finally, we compared these results with the standardized mean differences in Table 6. As in the case of simulated models, SMDs allowed us to reach the same general conclusion: L1 model is the least fair and FAIR(ER) model is probably the most fair of the three models. Yet in this case SMDs also obscure the fact that both BASE and FAIR(ER) model might be over-scoring GER speakers: in fact the SMDs for the two models have the opposite sign.

	BASE	FAIR(ER)	L1
ARA	0.07	0.08	-0.01
CHI	0.04	**0.10**	**-0.13**
GER	0.08	-0.07	**0.35**
JPN	**-0.26**	**-0.18**	**-0.24**
KOR	0.00	0.05	**-0.11**
SPA	0.06	0.02	**0.11**

Table 6: Standardized mean difference for 6 languages in our corpus for scores generated by different models. Absolute values above the 0.1 threshold are highlighted in bold

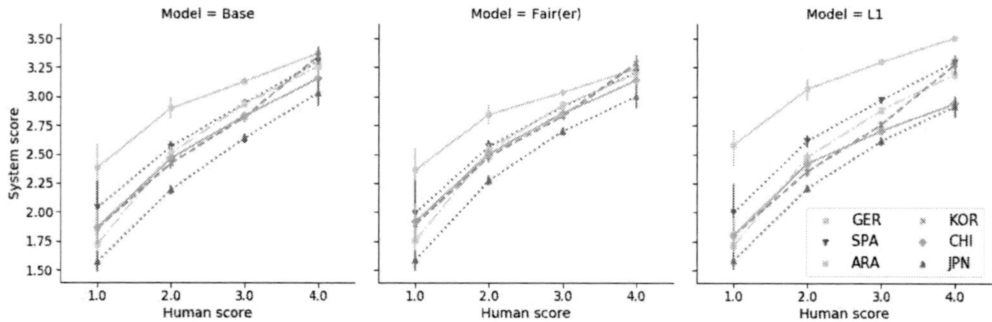

Figure 2: Average system score conditioned on human score for different models and native languages

6   Discussion

In this paper we considered three definitions of fairness in the context of automated scoring: (1) Overall score accuracy - are automated scores equally accurate for all groups of interest? (2) Overall score difference - are automated scores consistently higher or lower than human scores for members of different groups? (3) Conditional score difference - are automated scores consistently higher or lower for members of different groups despite them having the same language proficiency? These three metrics capture different dimensions of fairness and answer different questions.

Ideally, automated scores should be fair along all of these dimensions and as we showed it is possible if the automated scores are a perfect prediction of human scores (error = 0 for all scores) or if the human score distributions are the same across all groups. Yet in practice, achieving such total fairness may not be possible. Thus, even scores from the PERFECT model (r=0.97) failed to achieve overall score difference equality. The scores from the ∼PERFECT model, with slightly less accurate automated scores than the PERFECT model, failed to achieve both overall score accuracy equality and overall score difference equality when evaluated on the data with actual score distribution.

Notably when the score distributions differ across groups, the three different dimensions of fairness are not necessarily aligned with each other. Thus the META model based on metadata only was better than the PERFECT model in terms of the overall score difference equality: there was almost no variation between the groups. Yet as expected, it failed the conditional score difference

equality test since the scores were assigned based on test-taker geographic location rather than language proficiency.

Similarly for actual models, the model trained separately for each native language is most fair in terms of overall score differences since the predictions for each group are centered around the group mean. Yet this model is the worst of the three we considered in terms of conditional score difference which is unsurprising given that test-taker native language is considered when assigning the score.

None of these definitions of fairness is in principle more important than another. Overall score accuracy equality might be more desirable if a system is deployed independently in many countries and the scores are never compared across countries. At the same time a system that achieves high overall score accuracy equality but fails to achieve conditional score difference equality would not be acceptable in a high-stakes international assessment context.

In automated scoring model fairness issues have often been interpreted as emerging from particular linguistic patterns exhibited by a group in question or implicit use of group membership in scoring procedure. As we have shown throughout this paper, not all measures of fairness are good indicators of such group awareness. Thus overall score accuracy was in fact higher for the META model than for the RANDOM model. It also did not differentiate between generic and L1-specific models. It is also not the case that group unaware models will be more fair across all dimensions: the RANDOM model was blind to group membership and yet it was not deemed totally fair. And indeed a system that assigns a random score would clearly disadvantage a very proficient speaker but might be advantageous for a low proficiency speaker. If proficiency is aligned with group membership, this can mean that the model favors certain groups over others.

Finally, the distinction between different aspects of fairness is crucial for fine-tuning the automated scoring models, especially the ones that do not lend themselves easily to interpretation. Thus for example the model optimized to minimize the overall score differences might in fact learn to "hold the thumb on the scale" by indirectly using group membership as was the case with our L1 model. On the other hand, the model optimized for minimal conditional score differences may not be equally accurate for all groups. Unlike SMDs, that conflate different aspects of fairness into the same dimension, different measures discussed in this paper provide different information that helps better understand subgroup differences in the performance of an automated scoring engines. Thus for example in a hypothetical scenario where the ∼PERFECT model is deployed for scoring, SMDs rightly point out that German speakers as a group would see a reduction in their scores: the mean score for this group would decrease from 3.35 to 3.16. This could be a problem if old and new scores are ever compared at individual or group levels. Yet it would be counterproductive to search for solutions by looking for idiosyncrasies in the way the scoring engine handles the responses from German speakers. To resolve this problem the engine developers would need to focus on generally improving model performance, especially at scale edges.

7 Conclusion

We considered different definitions of fairness of an automated scoring system and argued that achieving all of them simultaneously may not be possible as long as the automated scores are not in perfect agreement with human scores and the score distributions vary across groups. In this paper we considered human scores to be the true 'gold standard' measure of language proficiency. Yet in most practical applications human scores are likely to contain a certain amount of error and possibly even bias which brings additional complexity to fairness evaluations. At the same time, at least in some contexts, automated scoring can improve overall score reliability and consistency which benefits all takers. Ultimately, both the magnitude and the nature of the impact of auto-mated scores on score differences between groups needs to be weighed against other benefits of using automated scoring in a particular educational application and the consequences for the final user.

Acknowledgements

Mo Zhang was instrumental in creating the corpus for this study. Matt Mulholland extracted the features used in this study. We thank Keelan Evanini, Aoife Cahill, Dan McCaffrey and three anonymous BEA reviewers for their comments and suggestions.

References

AERA. 1999. *Standards for Educational and Psychological Testing*. American Educational Research Association.

Ji An, Vincent Kieftenbeld, and Raghuveer Kanneganti. 2016. Fairness in automated scoring: Screening features for subgroup differences. Presented at the Annual Meeting of the National Council on Measurement in Education, Washington DC.

Richard Berk, Hoda Heidari, Shahin Jabbari, Michael Kearns, and Aaron Roth. 2018. Fairness in criminal justice risk assessments. *Sociological Methods & Research*, page 004912411878253.

Brent Bridgeman, Mary Louise Lennon, and Altamese Jackenthal. 2001. Effects of screen size, screen resolution, and display rate on computer-based test performance. Technical Report October 2001, Educational Testing Service.

Brent Bridgeman, Catherine Trapani, and Yigal Attali. 2012. Comparison of human and machine scoring of essays: Differences by gender, ethnicity, and country. *Applied Measurement in Education*, 25(1):27–40.

Jill Burstein and Martin Chodorow. 1999. Automated essay scoring for nonnative English speakers. In *Proceedings of a Symposium on Computer Mediated Language Assessment and Evaluation in Natural Language Processing*, pages 68–75, Stroudsburg, PA, USA.

Aylin Caliskan, Joanna J. Bryson, and Arvind Narayanan. 2017. Semantics derived automatically from language corpora contain human-like biases. *Science*, 356(6334):183–186.

Lei Chen, Klaus Zechner, Su-Youn Yoon, Keelan Evanini, Xinhao Wang, Anastassia Loukina, Jidong Tao, Lawrence Davis, Chong Min Lee, Min Ma, Robert Mundkowsky, Chi Lu, Chee Wee Leong, and Binod Gyawali. 2018. Speechrater 5.0. *ETS Research Report Series*.

Brian E. Clauser, Michael T. Kane, and David B. Swanson. 2002. Validity issues for performance-based tests scored with computer-automated scoring systems. *Applied Measurement in Education*, 15(4):413–432.

Michael Feldman, Sorelle A. Friedler, John Moeller, Carlos Scheidegger, and Suresh Venkatasubramanian. 2015. Certifying and removing disparate impact. *Proceedings of the 21th ACM SIGKDD International Conference on Knowledge Discovery and Data Mining*, pages 259–268.

Sorelle A. Friedler, Carlos Scheidegger, and Suresh Venkatasubramanian. 2016. On the (im)possibility of fairness. *Arxiv preprint*, (609.07236):1–16.

Dirk Hovy and L Shannon Spruit. 2016. The social impact of natural language processing. *Proceedings of ACL*, pages 591–598.

Faisal Kamiran and Toon Calders. 2009. Classifying without discriminating. In *Proceedings of the IEEE International Conference on Computer, Control and Communication*, pages 1–6.

Toshihiro Kamishima, Shotaro Akaho, Hideki Asoh, and Jun Sakuma. 2012. Fairness-aware classifier with prejudice remover regularizer. In *Proceedings of the Joint European Conference on Machine Learning and Knowledge Discovery in Databases*, pages 35–50.

Anastassia Loukina and Heather Buzick. 2017. Use of automated scoring in spoken language assessments for test takers with speech impairments. *ETS Research Report Series*, RR-17-42.

Binh Thanh Luong, Salvatore Ruggieri, and Franco Turini. 2011. k-NN as an implementation of situation testing for discrimination discovery and prevention. In *Proceedings of the 17th ACM SIGKDD international conference on Knowledge discovery and data mining*, pages 502–510.

Nitin Madnani, Anastassia Loukina, Alina Von Davier, Jill Burstein, and Aoife Cahill. 2017. Building better open-source tools to support fairness in automated scoring. In *Proceedings of the First Workshop on ethics in Natural Language Processing, Valencia, Spain, April 4th, 2017*, pages 41–52, Valencia, Spain. Association for Computational Linguistics.

Shervin Malmasi, Keelan Evanini, Aoife Cahill, Joel Tetreault, Robert Pugh, Christopher Hamill, Diane Napolitano, and Yao Qian. 2017. A report on the 2017 Native Language Identification shared task. In *Proceedings of the 12th Workshop on Innovative Use of NLP for Building Educational Applications*, pages 62–75, Copenhagen, Denmark. Association for Computational Linguistics.

Randall D. Penfield. 2016. Fairness in test scoring. In Neil J. Dorans and Linda L. Cook, editors, *Fairness in Educational Assessment and Measurement*, pages 55–76. Routledge.

D. Povey, A. Ghoshal, G. Boulianne, L. Burget, O. Glembek, N. Goel, M. Hannemann, P. Motlicek, Y. Qian, P. Schwarz, J. Silovsky, G. Stemmer, and K. Vesely. 2011. The Kaldi speech recognition toolkit. *IEEE Workshop on Automatic Speech Recognition and Understanding*, pages 1–4.

Chaitanya Ramineni and David M. Williamson. 2013. Automated essay scoring: Psychometric guidelines and practices. *Assessing Writing*, 18(1):25–39.

Zhen Wang and Alina von Davier. 2014. Monitoring of scoring using the e-rater automated scoring system and human raters on a writing test. *ETS Research Report Series*, 2014(1):1–21.

Zhen Wang, Klaus Zechner, and Yu Sun. 2016. Monitoring the performance of human and automated scores for spoken responses. *Language Testing*, pages 1–20.

David M. Williamson, Xiaoming Xi, and F. Jay Breyer. 2012. A framework for evaluation and use of automated scoring. *Educational Measurement: Issues and Practice*, 31(1):2–13.

Xiaoming Xi. 2010. How do we go about investigating test fairness? *Language Testing*, 27(2):147–170.

Lili Yao, Shelby J. Haberman, and Mo Zhang. 2019. Penalized best linear prediction of true test scores. *Psychometrika*, 84(1):186–211.

Richard S Zemel, Yu Wu, Kevin Swersky, Toniann Pitassi, and Cynthia Dwork. 2013. Learning fair representations. In *Proceedings of ICML*, pages 325–333.

Mo Zhang, Neil J. Dorans, Chen Li, and Andre A. Rupp. 2017. Differential feature functioning in automated essay scoring. In H. Jiao and R.W. Lissitz, editors, *Test fairness in the new generation of large-scale assessment*.

Michael J. Zieky. 2016. Fairness in test design and development. In Neil J. Dorans and Linda L. Cook, editors, *Fairness in Educational Assessment and Measurement*, pages 9–32. Routledge.

Predicting the Difficulty of Multiple Choice Questions in a High-stakes Medical Exam

Le An Ha[1]   Victoria Yaneva[2]   Peter Baldwin[2]   Janet Mee[2]

[1]Research Group in Computational Linguistics, University of Wolverhampton, UK
`ha.l.a@wlv.ac.uk`
[2]National Board of Medical Examiners, Philadelphia, USA
`{vyaneva, pbaldwin, jmee}@nbme.org`

Abstract

Predicting the construct-relevant difficulty of Multiple-Choice Questions (MCQs) has the potential to reduce cost while maintaining the quality of high-stakes exams. In this paper, we propose a method for estimating the difficulty of MCQs from a high-stakes medical exam, where all questions were deliberately written to a common reading level. To accomplish this, we extract a large number of linguistic features and embedding types, as well as features quantifying the difficulty of the items for an automatic question-answering system. The results show that the proposed approach outperforms various baselines with a statistically significant difference. Best results were achieved when using the full feature set, where embeddings had the highest predictive power, followed by linguistic features. An ablation study of the various types of linguistic features suggested that information from all levels of linguistic processing contributes to predicting item difficulty, with features related to semantic ambiguity and the psycholinguistic properties of words having a slightly higher importance. Owing to its generic nature, the presented approach has the potential to generalize over other exams containing MCQs.

1   Introduction

For many years, approaches from Natural Language Processing (NLP) have been applied to estimating reading difficulty, but relatively fewer attempts have been made to measure conceptual difficulty or question difficulty beyond linguistic complexity. In addition to expanding the horizons of NLP research, estimating the construct-relevant difficulty of test questions has a high practical value because ensuring that exam questions are appropriately difficult is both one of the most important and one of the most costly tasks within the testing industry. For example, test questions

that are too easy or too difficult are less able to distinguish between different levels of examinee ability (or between examinee ability and a defined cut-score of some kind – e.g., pass/fail). This is especially important when scores are used to make consequential decisions such as those for licensure, certification, college admission, and other high-stakes applications[1]. To address these issues, we propose a method for predicting the difficulty of multiple choice questions (MCQs) from a high-stakes medical licensure exam, where questions of varying difficulty may not necessarily vary in terms of reading levels.

Owing to the criticality of obtaining difficulty estimates for items (exam questions) prior to their use for scoring, current best practices require newly-developed items to be pretested. Pretesting typically involves administering new items to a representative sample of examinees (usually between a few hundred and a few thousand), and then using their responses to estimate various statistical characteristics. Ideally, pretest data are collected by embedding new items within a standard live exam, although sometimes special data collection efforts may also be needed. Based on the responses, items that are answered correctly by a proportion of examinees below or above certain thresholds (i.e. items that are too easy or too difficult for almost all examinees) are discarded. While necessary, this procedure has a high financial and administrative cost, in addition to the time required to obtain the data from a sufficiently large sample of examinees.

Here, we propose an approach for estimating the difficulty of expert-level MCQs, where the

---

[1]Examples of well-known high-stakes exams include the TOEFL (Test of English as a Foreign Language) (https://www.ets.org/toefl), the SAT (Scholastic Assessment Test) (https://collegereadiness.collegeboard.org/sat), and the USMLE (United States Medical Licensing Examination) (https://www.usmle.org/).

Proceedings of the Fourteenth Workshop on Innovative Use of NLP for Building Educational Applications, pages 11–20
Florence, Italy, August 2, 2019. ©2019 Association for Computational Linguistics

A 55-year-old woman with small cell carcinoma of the lung is admitted to the hospital to undergo chemotherapy. Six days after treatment is started, she develops a temperature of 38C (100.4F). Physical examination shows no other abnormalities. Laboratory studies show a leukocyte count of 100/mm3 (5% segmented neutrophils and 95% lymphocytes). Which of the following is the most appropriate pharmacotherapy to increase this patient's leukocyte count? (A) Darbepoetin (B) Dexamethasone (C) Filgrastim (D) Interferon alfa (E) Interleukin-2 (IL-2) (F) Leucovorin

Table 1: An example of a practice item

gold standard of item difficulty is defined through large-scale pretesting and is based on the responses of hundreds of highly-motivated examinees. Being able to automatically predict item difficulty from item text has the potential to save significant resources by eliminating or reducing the need to pretest the items. These savings are of even greater importance in the context of some automatic item generation strategies, which can produce tens of thousands of items with no feasible way to pretest them or identify which items are most likely to succeed. Furthermore, understanding what makes an item difficult other than manipulating its reading difficulty has the potential to aid the item-writing process and improve the quality of the exam. Last but not least, automatic difficulty prediction is relevant to automatic item generation as an evaluation measure of the quality of the produced output.

Contributions i) We develop and test the predictive power of a large number of different types of features (e.g. embeddings and linguistic features), including innovative metrics that measure the difficulty of MCQs for an automatic question-answering system. The latter produced empirical evidence on whether parallels exist between question difficulty for humans and machines. ii) The results outperform a number of baselines, showing that the proposed approach measures a notion of difficulty that goes beyond linguistic complexity. iii) We analyze the most common errors produced by the models, as well as the most important features, providing insight into the effects that various item characteristics have on the success of predicting item difficulty. iv) Owing to the generic nature of the features, the presented approach is potentially generalizable to other MCQ-based exams. We make our code available[2] at: `https://bit.ly/2EaTFNN`.

2 Related Work

The vast majority of previous work on difficulty prediction has been concerned with estimating readability (Flesch, 1948; Dubay, 2004; Kintsch and Vipond, 2014; François and Miltsakaki, 2012; McNamara et al., 2014; Yaneva et al., 2017). Various complexity-related features have been developed in readability research (see Dubay (2004) and Kintsch and Vipond (2014) for a review), starting from ones utilising surface lexical features (e.g. Flesch (1948)) to NLP-enhanced models (François and Miltsakaki, 2012) and features aimed at capturing cohesion (McNamara et al., 2014).

There have also been attempts to estimate the difficulty of questions for humans. This has been mostly done within the realm of language learning, where the difficulty of reading comprehension questions is strongly related to their associated text passages (Huang et al., 2017; Beinborn et al., 2015; Loukina et al., 2016). Another area where question-difficulty prediction is discussed is the area of automatic question generation, as a form of evaluation of the output (Alsubait et al., 2013; Ha and Yaneva, 2018). In many cases such evaluation is conducted through some form of automatic measure of difficulty (e.g., the semantic similarity between the question and answer options as in (Ha

---

[2]The questions cannot be made available because of test security.

and Yaneva, 2018)) rather than through extensive evaluation with humans. Past research has also focused on estimating the difficulty of open-ended questions in community question-answering platforms (Wang et al., 2014; Liu et al., 2013); however, these questions were generic in nature and did not require expert knowledge. Other studies use taxonomies representing knowledge dimensions and cognitive processes involved in the completion of a test task to predict the difficulty of short-answer questions (Padó, 2017) and identify skills required to answer school science questions (Nadeem and Ostendorf, 2017). We build upon previous work by implementing a large number of complexity-related features, as well as testing various prediction models (Section 4).

While relevant in a broad sense, the above works are not directly comparable to the current task. Unlike community question answering, the questions used in this study were developed by experts and require the application of highly specialized knowledge. Reading exams, where comprehension difficulty is highly associated with text complexity, are also different from our medical MCQs, which are deliberately written to a common reading level (see Section 3). Therefore, the models needed to capture difficulty in this context that goes beyond linguistic complexity.

3 Data

Data comprises 12,038 MCQs from the Clinical Knowledge component of the United States Medical Licensing Examination®. An example of a test item is shown in Table 1. The part describing the case is referred to as the *stem*, the correct answer option is called the *key* and the incorrect answer options are known as *distractors*. The majority of the items in the data set used here had five or six answer options.

Item writing All items tested medical knowledge and were designed to emulate real-life scenarios wherein examinees must first identify the relevant findings and then, based on these findings, make a diagnosis or take a clinical action. Items were written by experienced item-writers following a set of guidelines. These guidelines stipulated that the writers adhere to a standard structure and avoid excessive verbosity, "window dressing" (extraneous material not needed to answer the item), "red herrings" (information designed to mislead the test-taker), overly long or complicated stems

or options, and grammatical cues (e.g., correct answers that are longer, more specific, or more complete than the other options; or the inclusion of the same word or phrase in both the stem and the correct answer). Item writers had to ensure that the produced items did not have flaws related to various aspects of validity. For example, flaws related to irrelevant difficulty include: *Stems or options are overly long or complicated, Numeric data not stated consistently* and *Language or structure of the options is not homogeneous.* Flaws related to "testwiseness" are: *Grammatical cues; The correct answer is longer, more specific, or more complete than the other options;* and *A word or phrase is included both in the stem and in the correct answer.* Finally, stylistic rules concerning preferred usage of terms, formatting, abbreviations, conventions, drug names, and alphabetization of option sets were also enforced. The goal of standardizing items in this manner is to produce items that vary in difficulty and discriminating power due only to differences in the medical content they assess. This practice, while sensible, makes modeling difficulty very challenging.

Item administration The questions in our data set were pretested by embedding them within live exams. In practice, the response data collected during pretesting is used to filter out items that are misleading, too easy, or too difficult based on various criteria. Only those items satisfying these criteria are eligible for use during scoring on subsequent test forms. The current set of items contains pretest data administered for four standard annual cycles between 2012 and 2015. The questions were embedded within a standard nine-hour exam and test-takers had no way of knowing which items were used for scoring and which were being pretested. Examinees were medical students from accredited[3] US and Canadian medical schools taking the exam for the first time as part of a multistep examination sequence required for medical licensure in the US.

Determining item difficulty On average, each item was answered by 328 examinees ($SD = 67.17$). The difficulty of an item is defined by the proportion of its responses that are correct, which is commonly referred to in the educational-testing literature as its *P-value*[4]. The P-value is calculated

---

[3] Accredited by the Liaison Committee on Medical Education (LCME).

[4] We adopt this convention here but care should be taken not to confuse this usage with a p-value indicating statistical

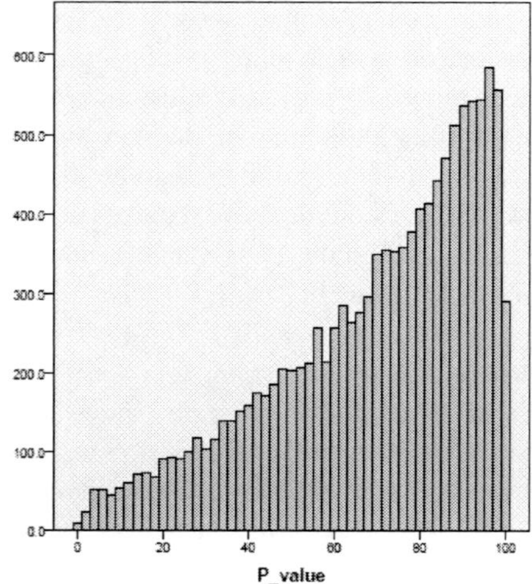

Figure 1: Distribution of the P-value variable

in the following way:

$$P_i = \frac{\sum_{n=1}^{N} U_n}{N},$$

where Pi is the p-value for item i, Un is the 0-1 score (correct-incorrect) on item i earned by examinee n , and N is the total number of examinees in the sample. As an example, a P-value of .3 means that the item was answered correctly by 30% of the examinees. The distribution of P-values for the data set is presented in Figure 1.

4   Features

A number of features were modeled for P-value prediction and can be roughly divided into three classes. First, we extract embeddings, which have been found to have predictive power in many different applications. The second class of features included more than one hundred linguistic characteristics, which account for differences in the way the items are written. Finally, a third class of features were based on the difficulty an item posed to an automated question-answering system under the working hypothesis that this system difficulty had a positive relationship with the difficulty an item poses to human respondents. Information about each type of feature is presented below. Additional details can be found in the available code.

4.1   Embeddings

We experiment with two types of embeddings: Word2Vec (300 dimensions) (Mikolov et al.,

2013) and ELMo (1,024 dimensions) (Peters et al., 2018).   The embeddings were generated using approximately 22,000,000 MEDLINE abstracts,[5], which were found to outperform other versions of the embeddings extracted from generic corpora (Google News Corpus[6] for Word2Vec and 1B Word (Chelba et al., 2013) for ELMo).   Embeddings were aggregated at item level using mean pooling, where an average item embedding is generated from the embeddings of all words.

4.2   Linguistic features

This class of features includes the following subcategories.

Lexical Features Previous research has found surface lexical features to be very informative in predicting text readability (Dubay, 2004). Lexical features in our experiments include counts, incidence scores and ratios for *ContentWord, Noun, Verb, Adjective,* and *Adverb*; *Numeral Count; Type-Token Ratio; Average Word Length In Syllables*; and *Complex Word Count* ($>$ 3 syllables).

Syntactic Features: These were implemented using information from the Stanford NLP Parser (Manning et al., 2014) and include: *Average Sentence Length (words); Average Depth Of Tree; Negation Count; Negation In Stem; Negation In the Lead-In Question; NP Count; NP Count With Embedding* (the number of noun phrases derived by counting all the noun phrases present in an item, including embedded NPs); *Average NP Length; PP and VP Count; Proportion Passive VPs; Agentless Passive Count; Average Number of Words Before Main Verb;* and *Relative Clauses* and *Conditional Clauses Count*.

Semantic Ambiguity Features: This subcategory concerns the semantic ambiguity of word concepts according to WordNet (WN), as well as medical concepts according to the UMLS (Unified Medical Language System) Meta-thesaurus (Schuyler et al., 1993). The features include *Polysemic Word Index; Average Number of Senses of: Content Words, Nouns, Verbs, Adjectives, Adverbs; Average Distance To WN Root for: Nouns, Verbs, Nouns and Verbs; Total No Of UMLS Concepts; Average No Of UMLS Concepts; and Average No Of Competing Concepts Per Term* (average number of UMLS concepts that each medical term can refer to).

significance.

[5]https://www.nlm.nih.gov/bsd/medline.html
[6]https://news.google.com

Readability Formulae: *Flesch Reading Ease* (Flesch, 1948); *Flesch Kincaid Grade Level* (Kincaid et al., 1975); *Automated Readability Index (ARI)* (Senter and Smith, 1967); *Gunning Fog index* (Gunning, 1952); *Coleman-Liau* (Coleman, 1965); and *SMOG* index (McLaughlin, 1969).

Cognitively-Motivated Features: These are calculated based on information from the MRC Psycholinguistic Database (Coltheart, 1981), which contains cognitive measures based on human ratings for a total of 98,538 words. These features include *Imagability*, which indicates the ease with which a mental image of a word is constructed; *Familiarity* of the word for an adult; *Concreteness*; *Age Of Acquisition*; and finally *Meaningfulness Ratio Colorado* and *Meaningfulness Ratio Paivio*. The meaningfulness rating assigned to a word indicates the extent to which the word is associated with other words.

Word Frequency Features: These include *Average Word Frequency*, as well as threshold frequencies such as words not included in the most frequent words on the BNC frequency list (*Not In First 2000/ 3000/ 4000 or 5000 Count*).

Text Cohesion Features: These include counts of *All Connectives*, as well as *Additive, Temporal*, and *Causal* Connectives, and *Referential Pronoun Count*.

4.3 Information Retrieval (IR) features

The working hypothesis behind this group of features is that there is a positive correlation between the difficulty of questions for humans and for machines. To quantify machine-difficulty, we develop features based on information retrieval that capture how difficult it is for an automatic question-answering (QA) system to answer the items correctly. This was accomplished following the approaches to QA presented in Clark and Etzioni (2016).

First, we use Lucene[7] with its default options to index the abstracts of medical articles contained in the MEDLINE[8] database. Then for each test item we build several queries, corresponding to the stem and one answer option. We use three different settings: i) All words, ii) Nouns only, and iii) Nouns, Verbs, and Adjectives (NVA). We then get the top 5 MEDLINE documents returned by Lucene as a result of each query and calculate the

---

[7]https://lucene.apache.org/
[8]https://www.nlm.nih.gov/bsd/medline.html

	r	RMSE
Random Forests	**0.24**	**23.15**
Linear Regression	0.17	25.65
SVM	0.17	25.41
Gaussian Processes	0.2	23.87
Dense NN (3 layers)	0.16	25.85

Table 2: Results for algorithm selection (validation set)

sum of the retrieval scores. These scores represent the content of the IR features (*Stem Only, Stem + Correct Answer*, and *Stem + Options*, where for each of these configurations we have a different feature for All words, Nouns only, and NVA.). The scores reflect how difficult it is for a QA system to choose the correct answer. Specifically, if the IR scores of Stem + Correct Answer are much higher than those of Stem + Options, then the QA system is more confident in its answer choice and the item is deemed relatively easy. This information can then be used to predict item difficulty.

5 Experiments

In this section we present our experiments on predicting the P-value.

First, we randomly divide the full data set into training (60%), validation (20%) and test (20%) sets for the purpose of evaluating a number of different algorithms[9] on the validation set. This was done using all features. The most notable results on algorithm selection are presented in Table 2. As can be seen from the table, the best results are obtained using the Random Forests (RF) algorithm (Breiman, 2001), which was selected for use in subsequent experiments.

5.1 Baselines

Five baselines were computed to evaluate model performance. The first baseline is the output of the ZeroR algorithm, which simply assigns the mean of the P-value variable in the training set as a prediction for every instance. Each of the four remaining baselines was based on a common feature known to be a strong predictor of reading difficulty: *Word Count, Average Sentence Length, Average Word Length in Syllables*, and the *Flesch Reading Ease*[10] formula (Flesch, 1948). These

---

[9]Parameters for the Neural Network algorithm: 3 dense layers of size 100, activation function: RELU, loss function: MSE, weight initialization Xavier and learning rate = 0.001. Trained for 500 epochs with early stopping after 10 epochs with no improvement.

[10]While readability formulae are used as features in the models and their predictive power is assessed, it is acknowl-

simple baselines allow us to assess whether the difficulty of the items in our data set can be reliably predicted using heuristics such as "longer items are more difficult" or "items using longer words and sentences are more difficult". The performances of the baselines as single features in an RF model (except ZeroR, which is an algorithm of its own) are presented in Table 3. In terms of Root Mean Squared Error (RMSE), the strongest baseline was ZeroR, with *Average Word Length in Syllables* producing somewhat similar results. All other baselines performed worse than ZeroR, showing that item length (*Word Count*), as well as *Average Sentence Length* and especially *Flesch readability*, are rather weak predictors of item difficulty for our data. These results provide an empirical evidence in support of the claim that easy and difficult items do not differ in terms of surface readability, commonly measured through word and sentence length.

5.2 P-value Prediction

We use various combinations of the features presented in Section 4 as input to an RF model to predict P-value. The results are presented in Table 4. As can be seen from the table, using the full feature set performs best and is a statistically significant improvement over the strongest baseline (ZeroR) with an RMSE reduction of approximately one point (Training set (10-fold CV): $p = 7.684^{e-10}$ with 95% Confidence Intervals (CI) from 10,000 bootstrap replicates: -0.9170, -0.4749. Test set: $p = 2.20^{e-16}$ with 95% CI from 10,000 bootstrap replicates: -1.423, -0.952).

In terms of individual feature groups, Linguistic, W2V, and ELMo achieved comparable performance (RMSE $\approx$ 22.6 for Test Set). The IR features performed notably worse, (RMSE = 23.4 for Test set), which is also the only result that does *not* outperform the ZeroR baseline ($p = 0.08$, 95% CI: -0.5336, 0.0401). For reference, the next "worst" result is obtained by combining the IR and Linguistic features (RMSE = 22.63); nevertheless, this is a significant improvement over ZeroR ($p = 5.517^{e-14}$ with 95% CI: -1.279, -0.756). Combining the Linguistic, W2V and ELMo features leads to a slight improvement in performance over their individual use, indicating that the signals captured

by the different feature groups do not overlap entirely.

5.3 Error Analysis

Analysis of the 500 test-set items with largest error residuals between predicted and actual values (the bottom 20% of the test-set predictions) revealed that the largest errors occur for items with very low P-values ($\mu = 32$, SD = 13.39, min = 0, max = 62). This was expected given the skewness of the P-value variable towards the high end of the scale. These items (P-value < 62) account for 34.5% of the full data. Therefore, one possible explanation for these large errors is the fact that these items are underrepresented as training examples.

As a follow-up study, we looked into items with P-values under .20, which account for only 4.5% of the full data. These items are considered to be either highly misleading and/or very difficult, as test-takers systematically chose incorrect answer options and performed worse than chance (the majority of items had five or six answer options). Excluding this small percentage of items from the training and test sets resulted in substantial improvements in RMSE (20.04 after excluding the items compared to 22.45 before excluding them), and outperformed ZeroR again a similar margin (20.98). This result shows that the success of the proposed approach would be higher for test samples with fewer extremely difficult or misleading items. It is acknowledged, however, that which items are too difficult or misleading can rarely be known a priori.

5.4 Feature Importance

Understanding the contributions of individual feature classes from the Linguistic set is useful for interpreting the models, as well as for informing future item-writing guidelines. To address this, we perform an ablation study where we remove one feature class at a time from the model using all Linguistic features.

As shown in Table 5, the removal of individual classes does *not* lead to dramatic changes in RMSE, suggesting that the predictive power of the Linguistic model is not dependent on a particular feature type (e.g. lexical, syntactic, semantic, etc). Nevertheless, removal of the Semantic Ambiguity and the Cognitively-motivated features led to a slightly lower performance for both cross-validation on the training set and for the test set. Indeed, a correlation analysis between individual

edged that the various formulae were validated on different types of texts than the MCQs in our data. Therefore, their performance is expected to be lower compared to applications which use the intended types of materials.

	Training set (10-fold CV)			Test set		
	r	MAE	RMSE	r	MAE	RMSE
ZeroR	-0.02	19.9	24.09	0	19.67	23.65
Word Count	0.01	20.13	24.5	0.05	19.81	23.87
Av. Sent. Length	-0.006	20.76	25.52	0.04	20.2	24.58
Av. Word Length	0.05	19.89	24.14	0.07	19.6	23.63
Flesch Reading Ease	0.02	22.05	27.53	-0.01	22.27	27.61

Table 3: Baseline results using 10-fold cross validation on the training set and evaluating the models on the test set (r = correlation coefficient, MAE = Mean Absolute Error, RMSE = Root Mean Squared Error).

	Training set (10-fold CV)			Test set		
	r	MAE	RMSE	r	MAE	RMSE
All	0.27	18.88	23.15	**0.32**	**18.53**	**22.45**
Linguistic	0.26	19	23.22	0.29	18.73	22.62
IR	0.17	19.58	23.91	0.18	19.28	23.4
W2V	0.27	18.94	23.18	0.3	18.61	22.58
ELMo	0.27	18.95	23.18	0.29	18.77	22.64
Ling + IR	0.26	19.04	23.25	0.29	18.75	22.63
Ling + ELMo	0.27	19.08	23.19	0.3	18.79	22.61
Ling + W2Vec	0.28	18.9	23.14	0.31	18.65	22.54
IR + W2V	0.27	18.94	23.18	0.3	18.67	22.56
IR + ELMo	0.26	18.95	23.26	0.31	18.53	22.55
W2V + ELMo	0.28	18.84	23.13	0.32	18.51	22.5
IR + W2V + ELMo	0.27	18.88	23.18	0.3	18.56	22.56
IR + Ling + W2V	**0.289**	**18.9**	**23.11**	0.31	18.6	22.52
IR + Ling + ELMO	0.27	19	23.2	0.327	18.64	22.48

Table 4: Results for the training (10-fold CV) and test sets for various feature combinations.

	CV RMSE	Test RMSE
All Linguistic	23.22	22.62
Without Lexical	23.3	22.49
Without Syntactic	23.23	22.66
Without Sem. ambiguity	23.31	22.89
Without Readability	23.22	22.59
Without Word Frequency	23.27	22.63
Without Cognitive	23.3	22.74
Without Cohesion	23.29	22.51

Table 5: Changes in RMSE after removing individual feature classes

features and the P-value variable reveals that the top three features with highest correlations are Age of Acquisition (-.11), Familiarity (.1038) and Referential Pronoun Incidence (.1035). Since the texts are domain-specific and contain a great deal of medical terminology, it is likely that the Age of Acquisition and Familiarity indices reflect the use of terms, however, further analysis is needed to confirm this.

6 Discussion

The experiments presented in the previous section provided empirical evidence that the difficulty of expert-level[11] multiple-choice questions can be predicted with accuracy significantly higher than various baselines. It was shown that simple metrics of complexity such as item length or average word and sentence length performed poorer than the ZeroR baseline, indicating that the difficulty of the items could not be predicted using surface readability measures. Best results were achieved when combining all types of available features (Linguistic, IR, Word2Vec, and ELMo), which showed a statistically significant improvement over the baselines. In terms of individual feature classes, the IR features performed poorly and were outperformed by the Linguistic, Word2Vec, and ELMo features – with the latter two being the strongest classes of predictors. Nevertheless, the fact that the combination of all the feature classes performed best supports the idea that the signals from the different feature groups did not overlap entirely and instead complemented each other. To understand whether the way the items were written had an effect on difficulty prediction and to gain insight into how item-writing could be improved, we analyzed the performance of the different types of Linguistic features. It was shown that the strength of the predictions were *not* due to a single linguistic feature; however, the strongest predictors were features related to semantic ambiguity and cognitively-motivated features (espe-

---

[11]Requiring expert knowledge as opposed to general knowledge

cially Age of Acquisition and Familiarity). Errors were largest for items at the lower end of the P-value scale, potentially because these items were underrepresented as training examples. Further experiments are needed to corroborate this.

In terms of generalizability, the presented approach is not test-specific and can therefore be applied to other exams containing MCQs. The results are, however, highly dependent on the population of test-takers. In fact, predicting the P-value in our particular case was arguably more challenging than for other exams owing to the homogeneity of the test-taker population. The majority of items were answered correctly by the majority of examinees because the test-takers were highly-able and highly-motivated medical students, who had already passed many other competitive high-stakes exams, including those for medical school admission. All else being equal, the expectation is that the performance of these models would improve for exams administered to, for example, examinees from K-12, where the ability of the test-takers has a higher variance and the distribution of P-values is less-skewed. However, all else is not equal and K-12 exams have substantially different test questions, the effects of which is unknown. Further research is needed here.

The presented approach is a first step toward predicting item difficulty and, therefore, there are a number of avenues for future work that could lead to better results. One of these relates to having separate embeddings for the stem and answer options as opposed to item-level embeddings. Another interesting approach would be to divide the items by content category (e.g. psychiatric, cardiac, etc). Content categories are not used as features in the current approach because there was no practical value in learning that, say, cardiac items are more difficult than psychiatric ones. However, it might be worthwhile to build content-specific models that predict item difficulty within-category (e.g., what are the relative item difficulties within the pool of psychiatric items). Finally, the performance of the IR features could be improved if the information is extracted from corpora that are more relevant (such as textbooks and examinee study materials) as opposed to medical abstracts.

The results presented in this paper have both practical and theoretical importance. Being able to predict the P-value of an MCQ reduces the cost of pretesting while maintaining exam quality. From a theoretical perspective, assessing difficulty beyond readability is an exciting new frontier that has implications for language understanding and cognition. Last but not least, such an application could also potentially be useful for assessing the performance of question-answering systems by predicting the difficulty of the questions for humans.

7 Conclusion

The paper presented an approach for predicting the construct-relevant difficulty of multiple-choice questions for a high-stakes medical licensure exam. Three classes of feature were developed: linguistic features, embeddings (ELMo and Word2Vec), and features quantifying the difficulty of items for an automatic question-answering system (IR features). A model using the full feature set outperformed five different baselines (ZeroR, Word Count, Average Sentence Length, Average Word Length in Syllables, and the Flesch Reading Ease formula) with a statistically significant reduction of RMSE of approximately one point. Embeddings had the highest predictive power, followed by linguistic features, while the IR features were ranked least useful. Largest errors occurred for very difficult items, possibly due to the skewness of the data distribution towards items with a higher proportion of correct responses. Amongst the linguistic features, all classes contributed to predicting item difficulty, with the semantic-ambiguity and cognitively-motivated features having a slightly higher predictive power.

These results indicate the usefulness of NLP for predicting the difficulty of MCQs. While this study is an early attempt toward the goal of automatic difficulty prediction for MCQs, it has both theoretical and practical importance in that it goes beyond predicting linguistic complexity and in that it has the potential to reduce cost in the testing industry. Next steps include the application of the approach to other exam content administered to a different population of examinees, as well as various improvements in the methodology.

References

Tahani Alsubait, Bijan Parsia, and Ulrike Sattler. 2013. A similarity-based theory of controlling mcq difficulty. In *e-Learning and e-Technologies in Education (ICEEE), 2013 Second International Conference on*, pages 283–288. IEEE.

Lisa Beinborn, Torsten Zesch, and Iryna Gurevych. 2015. Candidate evaluation strategies for improved difficulty prediction of language tests. In *Proceedings of the Tenth Workshop on Innovative Use of NLP for Building Educational Applications*, pages 1–11.

Leo Breiman. 2001. Random forests. *Machine learning*, 45(1):5–32.

Ciprian Chelba, Tomas Mikolov, Mike Schuster, Qi Ge, Thorsten Brants, Phillipp Koehn, and Tony Robinson. 2013. One billion word benchmark for measuring progress in statistical language modeling. *arXiv preprint arXiv:1312.3005*.

Peter Clark and Oren Etzioni. 2016. My computer is an honor student - but how intelligent is it? standardized tests as a measure of ai. *AI Magazine*, 37:5–12.

E. B. Coleman. 1965. *On understanding prose: some determiners of its complexity.* National Science Foundation, Washington, D.C.

Max Coltheart. 1981. The mrc psycholinguistic database. *The Quarterly Journal of Experimental Psychology Section A*, 33(4):497–505.

William H. Dubay. 2004. *The Principles of Readability.* Impact Information.

R. Flesch. 1948. A New Readability Yardstick. *Journal of Applied Psychology*, 32(3):221–233.

Thomas François and Eleni Miltsakaki. 2012. Do nlp and machine learning improve traditional readability formulas? In *Proceedings of the First Workshop on Predicting and Improving Text Readability for target reader populations*, pages 49–57. Association for Computational Linguistics.

Robert Gunning. 1952. *The technique of clear writing.* McGraw-Hill, New York.

Le An Ha and Victoria Yaneva. 2018. Automatic distractor suggestion for multiple-choice tests using concept embeddings and information retrieval. In *Proceedings of the Thirteenth Workshop on Innovative Use of NLP for Building Educational Applications*, pages 389–398.

Zhenya Huang, Qi Liu, Enhong Chen, Hongke Zhao, Mingyong Gao, Si Wei, Yu Su, and Guoping Hu. 2017. Question difficulty prediction for reading problems in standard tests. In *AAAI*, pages 1352–1359.

J. Peter Kincaid, Robert P. Fishburne, Richard L. Rogers, and Brad S. Chissom. 1975. *Derivation of new readability formulas (Automatic Readability Index, Fog Count and Flesch Reading Ease Formula) for Navy enlisted personnel*, 8-75 edition. CN-TECHTRA.

Walter Kintsch and Douglas Vipond. 2014. Reading comprehension and readability in educational practice and psychological theory. *Perspectives on learning and memory*, pages 329–365.

Jing Liu, Quan Wang, Chin-Yew Lin, and Hsiao-Wuen Hon. 2013. Question difficulty estimation in community question answering services. In *Proceedings of the 2013 Conference on Empirical Methods in Natural Language Processing*, pages 85–90.

Anastassia Loukina, Su-Youn Yoon, Jennifer Sakano, Youhua Wei, and Kathy Sheehan. 2016. Textual complexity as a predictor of difficulty of listening items in language proficiency tests. In *Proceedings of COLING 2016, the 26th International Conference on Computational Linguistics: Technical Papers*, pages 3245–3253.

Christopher D Manning, Mihai Surdeanu, John Bauer, Jenny Rose Finkel, Steven Bethard, and David McClosky. 2014. The stanford corenlp natural language processing toolkit. In *ACL (System Demonstrations)*, pages 55–60.

Harry G. McLaughlin. 1969. SMOG grading - a new readability formula. *Journal of Reading*, pages 639–646.

Danielle S McNamara, Arthur C Graesser, Philip M McCarthy, and Zhiqiang Cai. 2014. *Automated evaluation of text and discourse with Coh-Metrix.* Cambridge University Press.

Tomas Mikolov, Kai Chen, Greg Corrado, and Jeffrey Dean. 2013. Efficient estimation of word representations in vector space. *arXiv preprint arXiv:1301.3781*.

Farah Nadeem and Mari Ostendorf. 2017. Language based mapping of science assessment items to skills. In *Proceedings of the 12th Workshop on Innovative Use of NLP for Building Educational Applications*, pages 319–326.

Ulrike Padó. 2017. Question difficulty–how to estimate without norming, how to use for automated grading. In *Proceedings of the 12th Workshop on Innovative Use of NLP for Building Educational Applications*, pages 1–10.

Matthew E Peters, Mark Neumann, Mohit Iyyer, Matt Gardner, Christopher Clark, Kenton Lee, and Luke Zettlemoyer. 2018. Deep contextualized word representations. *arXiv preprint arXiv:1802.05365*.

Peri L Schuyler, William T Hole, Mark S Tuttle, and David D Sherertz. 1993. The umls metathesaurus: representing different views of biomedical concepts. *Bulletin of the Medical Library Association*, 81(2):217.

R. J. Senter and E. A. Smith. 1967. Automated Readability Index. Technical Report AMRL-TR-6620, Wright-Patterson Air Force Base.

Quan Wang, Jing Liu, Bin Wang, and Li Guo. 2014.
A regularized competition model for question diffi-
culty estimation in community question answering
services. In *Proceedings of the 2014 Conference on
Empirical Methods in Natural Language Processing
(EMNLP)*, pages 1115–1126.

Victoria Yaneva, Constantin Orasan, Richard Evans,
and Omid Rohanian. 2017. Combining multiple corpora for readability assessment for people with cognitive disabilities. In *Proceedings of the 12th Workshop on Innovative Use of NLP for Building Educational Applications*, pages 121–132.

An Intelligent Testing Strategy for Vocabulary Assessment of Chinese Second Language Learners

Wei Zhou[1,3]   Renfen Hu[1,2,✉]   Feipeng Sun[1,3]   Ronghuai Huang[1,3]

{zhouwei, irishu, huangrh}@bnu.edu.cn
sunfeipeng@blcu.edu.cn

[1] National Engineering Laboratory for Cyberlearning and Intelligent Technology,
Beijing Normal University
[2] Institute of Chinese Information Processing, Beijing Normal University
[3] Faculty of Education, Bejing Normal University

Abstract

Testing is an important tool to monitor learning effects. However, it usually costs a large amount of time and human labor to build an item bank and to test large number of students. In this paper, we propose a novel testing strategy by combining automatic item generation (AIG) and computerized adaptive testing (CAT) in vocabulary assessment for Chinese L2 learners. Firstly, we generate three types of vocabulary questions by modeling both the vocabulary knowledge and learners' writing error data. After evaluation and calibration, we construct a balanced item pool with automatically generated items, and implement a three-parameter computerized adaptive test. We conduct manual item evaluation and online student tests in the experiments. The results show that the combination of AIG and CAT can construct test items efficiently and reduce test cost significantly. Also, the test result of CAT can provide valuable feedback to AIG algorithms.

1 Introduction

Vocabulary is one of the most important parts of language competence (Cook, 2016). Testing of vocabulary knowledge is central to research on reading and language (Brown et al., 2005). However, it usually costs a large amount of time and human labor to build an item bank and to test large number of students.

To enhance the testing efficiency and convenience, we propose a novel testing strategy by combining automatic item generation (AIG) and computerized adaptive testing (CAT). Based on this strategy, we build an online testing system to evaluate vocabulary knowledge of Chinese second language learners: `http://test.aihanyu.org`. The pipeline of our method is illustrated in Figure 1:

Step 1. Generate vocabulary questions automatically by modeling both the vocabulary knowledge and learners' writing error data.

Step 2. Construct a balanced item pool by sampling questions from different difficulty levels, and implement an online vocabulary test with these items.

Step 3. Conduct student tests in which students with different language proficiencies take both the online AIG test and a traditional student placement test developed by experts.

Step 4. Build an improved three-parameter CAT model with these items, and estimate the students' abilities.

In the experiments, the student tests demonstrate desirable results. Firstly, the scores of the online AIG test are strongly correlated with that of the placement test (ρ=0.8395). Secondly, the student abilities estimated by our CAT model reaches even stronger correlation with the placement test (ρ=0.8715). Meanwhile, the average test length decreases greatly by 81% (from 140 to 26).

The experiments show that our strategy can construct test items efficiently and reduce test cost significantly for both test developers and test takers. Also, the test result of CAT can provide valuable feedback to question generation and selection algorithms.

2 Related Work

2.1 Automatic Item Generation

Automatic item generation (AIG) is a promising approach to reduce the cost of test development. AIG methods have been used in generating different types of questions, such as reading comprehen-

Proceedings of the Fourteenth Workshop on Innovative Use of NLP for Building Educational Applications, pages 21–29
Florence, Italy, August 2, 2019. ©2019 Association for Computational Linguistics

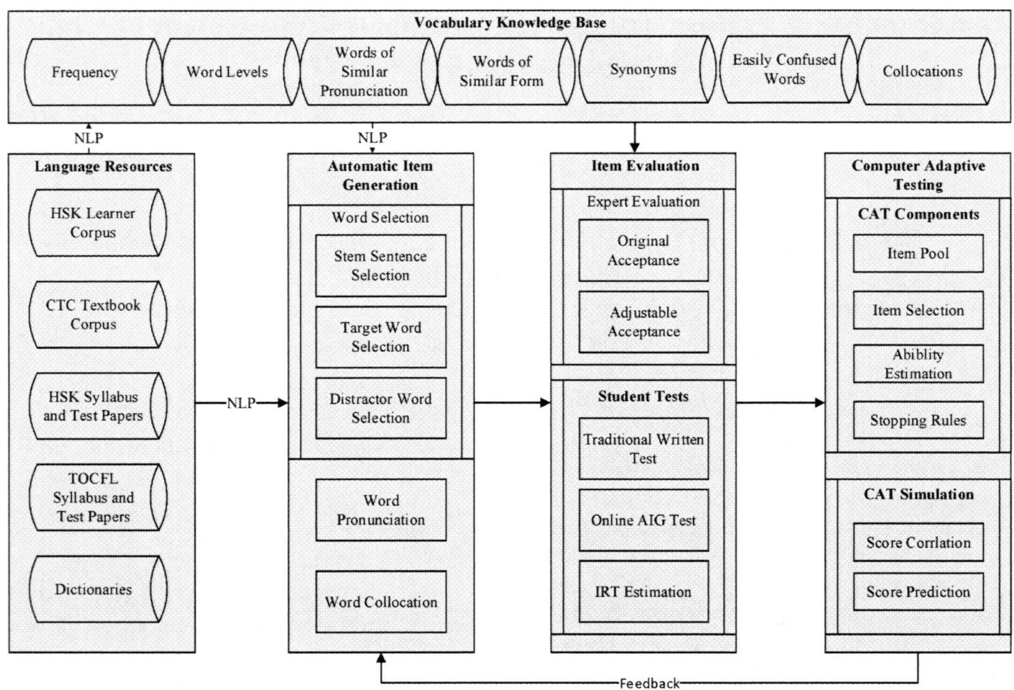

Figure 1: The pipeline of our testing strategy that combines AIG and CAT.

sion (Rus et al., 2007; Mostow et al., 2017) and vocabulary assessment (Mitkov et al., 2006, 2009; Aldabe and Maritxalar, 2014). Due to its high efficiency and controllability, automatic item generation has been used to create solutions and rationales for Computerized Formative Testing (Gierl and Lai, 2018).

For vocabulary testing, researchers have made a lot of efforts in generating vocabulary questions for ESL (English as a second language) learners (Mitkov and An Ha, 2003; Singh Bhatia et al., 2013; Correia et al., 2010; Takuya et al., 2010). It is well known that lexical knowledge vary a lot among different languages. For example, Chinese is a typical analytic language that lacks inflection. It mainly uses function words and word order to express grammatical information.

In the area of Chinese item generation, some methods have been proposed to generate factual questions and character questions (Liu et al., 2017; Ding and Gu, 2010; Liu et al., 2018). Different from existing work, this paper focuses on the generation of vocabulary questions, and utilizes them in vocabulary assessment of CSL (Chinese as a second language) learners. To enhance the test efficiency, we also integrate these automatically generated items into a computerized adaptive testing (CAT) model.

2.2 Computerized Adaptive Testing

With the development of language testing technologies, computerized adaptive testing (CAT) has attracted considerable attention in language testing area and has been successfully applied to large-scale standardized language tests, such as GRE and GMAT (Chang, 2015). Instead of giving all the examinees the same fixed test, CAT selects items that are tailored to each examinee's ability. Compared with traditional computer based or paper-pencil based tests, CAT can greatly shorten the test length by 50% while maintaining good test reliability and increasing the test security (Wainer, 2000; Weiss and Kingsbury, 1984).

However, one of the main challenges in CAT is the item pool development which requires not only large numbers of high-quality test items, but also a careful calibration of these items. In this study, we propose to construct the item pool with automatically generated questions. It can reduce the test cost significantly for both test developers and test takers.

3 Automatic Generation of Vocabulary Questions

To test the vocabulary knowledge of CSL learners, we generate three types of multiple-choice questions which account for different dimensions of vocabulary knowledge. The question examples can be seen in Figure 2.

(1) Word selection: Select a word that can fill in the blank of the sentence. It involves the knowledge of word form, meaning and how it is used in the context.

(2) Word pronunciation: Select a word that has an incorrect pinyin label. It focuses on the pronunciation part.

(3) Word collocation: Select a word that can collocate with the given word. It addresses the syntactic behaviors and collocational knowledge of words.

The generation of the vocabulary questions involves two stages: (1) Build a vocabulary knowledge base by extracting features from learner corpus, textbook corpus, test papers and dictionaries. (2) Generate different types of questions via stem selection, target word selection and distractor selection.

3.1 Vocabulary Knowledge Base

The knowledge base contains totally 8,400 word entries, which are collected from the syllabuses of two official Chinese language proficiency tests: HSK[1] and TOCFL[2]. We build a list of attributes for each entry in the knowledge base, and the attribute values are automatically extracted from large-scale language resources with multiple natural language processing (NLP) methods:

- Word frequency: It is calculated from CTC[3], a text corpus for Chinese L2 learners.

- Word level: The 8400 target words are scaled to 14 difficulty levels according to their frequencies in CTC, i.e. 600 words at each level.

- Words of similar pronunciation: They are extracted with the pronunciation similarity model proposed by Hu (2013).

- Words of similar form: If two words are of equal length in Chinese characters (hanzi) and have at least one same character, we count them as words of similar form.

- Synonyms: They are retrieved from Yang and Jia (2005)'s synonym dictionary.

- Easily confused words: They are extracted from leaners' writing error, as collected and manually labeled in HSK learner corpus[4]. If word a is involved in word selection error for at least 10 times in the learner corpus, and it is mistakenly used as word b for over 20% of the error cases, we identify word b as an easily confused word of a.

- Collocations: Nine types of collocations are retrieved from the collocation knowledge base built by Hu et al. (2016)[5].

3.2 Item Generation

3.2.1 Word Selection Question

The model generate the word selection questions via four steps: preprocessing, stem sentence selection, target word selection and question generation.

Firstly, all the texts in CTC are preprocessed via word segmentation, POS tagging and dependency parsing with LTP-Cloud (Che et al., 2010), a Chinese NLP toolkit. We obtain 2.4 million words and 154,023 dependency trees after the preprocessing.

Secondly, sentences are selected based on the NLP preprocessing results if they can satisfy multiple conditions, including sentence length, sentence independence and difficulty levels. We limit the sentence length to 10-30 words. For independence analysis, we target at sentences whose meanings are context independent, i.e. a complete declarative sentence which is not from a dialogue, and does not involve a pronoun that refers to someone or something in the previous context. We compile 3 rules based on POS tags and dependency relations to exclude unqualified sentences. For difficulty levels, we check if each word of the sentence is in our 8400-word vocabulary for L2 learners, and the percent of OOV (out-of-vocabulary) words should not exceed 10%.

Thirdly, we locate candidate target words in the stem sentences. Each candidate word should appear only once in the sentence and have at least three distractors in the vocabulary knowledge base. The distractors include words of similar pronunciation and form, as well as easily confused words. If more than one candidate target words are

---

[1] http://www.chinesetest.cn/godownload.do
[2] http://www.tw.org/tocfl/
[3] http://www.aihanyu.org/basic_v2/index.html
[4] http://bcc.blcu.edu.cn/hsk
[5] http://cca.xingtanlu.cn/

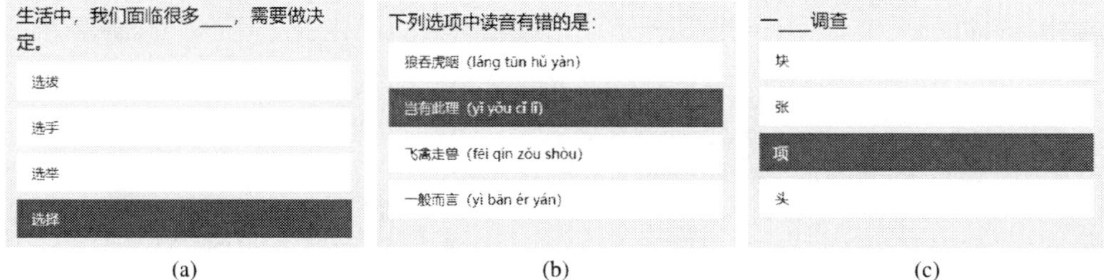

Figure 2: Examples of automatically generated items as they shown in the online testing application. (a) Word Selection, (b) Word Pronunciation, (c) Word Collocation. The highlighted option is the correct answer.

retrieved, we choose the one with higher difficulty, i.e. lower frequency. If a target word has more than three distractors, we choose the distractors that have the most similar difficulty levels with the target words.

At last, the target word is removed to generate a fill-in-blank question. Three distractors and the target word are shuffled to construct four options.

3.2.2 Word Pronunciation Question

A target word is firstly selected if one of its characters has an easily confused pronunciation determined by the pronunciation similarity model (Hu, 2013). We replace the correct pinyin with an easily confused one, and choose three other words from the same difficulty level that have correct pinyin labels and the same length. The item stem is *"Select the word that has an incorrect pinyin label"*.

3.2.3 Word Collocation Question

For word collocation question, we firstly retrieve the collocations of frequency > 3 and mutual information > 0 for each target word. Given a target word and its collocation, we obtain candidate distractors from the vocabulary knowledge base. To ensure there is only one correct answer in the multiple-choice question, we replace the target word with each candidate distractor to constitute a new combination. If the new combination does not appear in our collocation data, this candidate distractor is accepted. If more than three distractors are accepted, we choose the ones that have the most similar difficulty levels with the target word. At last, the target word is removed and we generate the question similarly to the word selection question.

Three types and totally 93764 test items are successfully generated with our method, including 75689 items for word selection, 6697 items for word pronunciation and 11378 items for word

collocation. After that, we sample questions for manual evaluation. The results will be discussed in Section 5.

4 Computerized Adaptive Testing

This paper aims at building a CAT model to evaluate vocabulary knowledge of CSL learners. We use the automatically generated questions for item calibration. The advantage is we can directly sample questions from different difficulty levels, so as to build a balanced item bank. In this study, item response theory (IRT) with three-parameter is used for calibration.

4.1 Theoretical Basis

Let $p_i(\theta)$ be the probability of a correct response to item i from a examinee with ability θ, thus $q_i(\theta) = 1 - p_i(\theta)$ is the probability of a incorrect response.

Let $u = (u_1, u_2, ..., u_n), u_i \in \{0, 1\}$ is the responses of n items. The likelihood function L is given by Equation 1.

$$L(u|\theta) = \prod_{i=1}^{n} p_i(\theta)^{u_i} q_i(\theta)^{1-u_i} \qquad (1)$$

Equation 2 gives the probability of a correct response to item i, where a_i is discrimination parameter, b_i is difficulty parameter, and c_i is the guessing parameter.

$$p_i(\theta) = c_i + \frac{1 - c_i}{1 + e^{-a_i(\theta - b_i)}} \qquad (2)$$

Solving $L'(\theta) = 0$ can find the value of $\hat{\theta}$ that maximize the likelihood function L. To simplify, we transform it to a log-likelihood function $l(u|\theta) = ln(L(u|\theta))$ as shown in Equation 3. The logarithm function could convert the product of factors to a sum of log factors, which makes it much easier to get the derivative.

$$l(u|\theta) = \sum_{i=1}^{n}(u_i \ln p_i(\theta) + (1 - u_i)\ln q_i(\theta)) \quad (3)$$

Thus, to find the $\hat{\theta}$ that maximize L, it is equivalent to solve $l'(\theta) = 0$. It can be computed by the Newton-Raphson method: $\theta_{t+1} = \theta_t - \frac{l'(\theta)}{l''(\theta)}$, which is an iterative algorithm with termination criterion ϵ, t_{max} s.t. $\Delta = \theta_{t+1} - \theta_t < \epsilon \lor t > t_{max}$. A simplified iterative formula is given by Equation 4 (Baker, 2001).

$$\theta_{t+1} = \theta_t + \frac{\sum_{i=1}^{n} a_i(u_i - p_i(\theta_t))}{\sum_{i=1}^{n} a_i^2 p_i(\theta_t)q_i(\theta_t)} \quad (4)$$

The information function is given by Equation 5. $I_i(\theta)$ is the amount of information for item i at ability θ.

$$I_i(\theta) = a_i^2 \frac{(p_i(\theta) - c_i)^2}{(1 - c_i)^2} \frac{q_i(\theta)}{p_i(\theta)} \quad (5)$$

The test information function is given by Equation 6. It is the sum of information for all items in the test.

$$TI(\theta) = \sum_{i=1}^{n} I_i(\theta) \quad (6)$$

The standard error function is given by Equation 7. A higher test information TI implies the higher precision of estimated ability which can not be observed directly. Thus, the smaller SE is, the better estimation is. A threshold of SE acts as a termination criteria in the test.

$$SE(\theta) = \frac{1}{\sqrt{TI(\theta)}} \quad (7)$$

4.2 Adaptive Algorithm

There are four important components in an adaptive testing algorithm: the item pool, the item selection, the ability estimation and stopping rules (Weiss and Kingsbury, 1984).

Item Pool. The success of CAT is highly dependent on the item pool with sufficient items of different difficulty levels. Our AIG method enables the system to select as many items as the test needs from different levels. Thus, a balanced item pool can be easily sampled for calibration.

Item Selection. The item selection is to select an item with the highest information I at the estimated ability $\hat{\theta}$. The test normally starts with an item of medium difficulty. And items can not be repeated during the test.

Ability Estimation. After each item is answered, the examinee's ability is estimated and used by the item selection to select the next item. The most commonly used estimation method is maximum likelihood estimation (MLE). Maximum likelihood is asymptotically unbiased, but it can not provide an ability estimate for a homogeneous set of responses (all correct or all incorrect) (Weiss and Kingsbury, 1984). To address this problem, we set a bound of ability $[\theta_{min}, \theta_{max}]$ to enable Newton-Raphson method to convergence to the bound. The iterative ability estimation process is shown in Algorithm 1.

Stopping Rules. After the ability is estimated, the standard error SE is calculated to determine whether a new item must be selected or the test should be terminated. We implement three stopping rules: the test reaches the maximum length n_{max}, the ability reaches the boundary $[\theta_{min}, \theta_{max}]$ for five consecutive questions when more than 15 items are administrated, or the examinee's standard error SE falls below the threshold s.

5 Experimental Analysis

We evaluate our method via three experiments: (1) Evaluate the automatically generated items manually. (2) Conduct student test with both an online AIG test and a traditional written test developed by CSL teachers. (3) Use CAT model to estimate the students' abilities.

5.1 Expert Evaluation of AIG

To assess the students' vocabulary knowledge, we generate three types and totally 93764 test items. After that, we randomly sample 100 items for each type of question, resulting in 300 items in total. These questions are used for manual evaluation. Original Acceptance Rate (OAR) and Adjustable Acceptance Rate (AAR) are calculated. An item can be originally accepted if two professional CSL teachers both agree that this item can be directly used in a vocabulary test. And it can be an adjustable item if the teachers both agree that it only needs a few simple modifications, i.e. the replacement or deletion of less than 2 words.

The evaluation results are shown in Table 1. The question generation method performs well with the average OAR of 53% and the AAR of 81.67%.

It is noteworthy that the acceptance rate varies a lot among three types of questions. Word pro-

---

Algorithm 1 Estimate($B, \theta_0, s, n_{max}, \theta_{min}, \theta_{max}, t_{max}, \epsilon$)

Set $n = 0$
Set $A = \emptyset$
Set $T = []$
Set $U = []$
Set $\hat{\theta} = \theta_0$
while $n < n_{max} \wedge SE(\hat{\theta}) \geq s$ **do**
   Set $n = n + 1$
   Find item x st. $x \in B \wedge x \notin A \wedge I_x(\hat{\theta}) = \max_{y \notin A} I_y(\hat{\theta})$
   Add(A, x)
   if test taker's answer to item x is correct **then**
      Add($U, 1$)
   else
      Add($U, 0$)
   end if
   Set $t = 0$
   repeat
      Set $t = t + 1$
      Set $\theta_{tmp} = \hat{\theta}$
      Update $\hat{\theta}$ using Equation 4
      Set $\Delta = \left| \hat{\theta} - \theta_{tmp} \right|$
   until $\Delta < \epsilon \vee t > t_{max} \vee \theta_t \notin [\theta_{min}, \theta_{max}]$
   Set $\hat{\theta} = \max(\min(\hat{\theta}, \theta_{max}), \theta_{min})$
   Add($T, \hat{\theta}$)
   if $n > 15 \wedge (\min(\text{Last}(T, 5)) = \theta_{max} \vee \max(\text{Last}(T, 5)) = \theta_{min})$ **then**
      break while
   end if
end while
return $\hat{\theta}$

---

nunciation question performs best since it focuses only on the pinyin label, and its generation module is very simple. The generation of word selection questions is much more complicated. It involves appropriate selection of sentences, target words and distractors. Word collocation question can be considered as a simplified version of word selection question. We further analyze the feedback of the teachers, and find that the distractor selection works very well, indicating that our vocabulary knowledge base has a high quality. Meanwhile, the stem sentence selection and target word selection algorithms needs further improvement on both difficulty control and semantic analysis.

5.2 Online AIG Test

We build an online vocabulary test with accepted vocabulary questions of three types. Specifically, we select 140 questions from 14 word levels, i.e. 10 questions at each level. These questions are manually reviewed and adjusted to ensure they can be used in the student test. The score for each question is one point, thus, the test score equals the number of questions answered correctly. The vocabulary size of each student can be estimated with the method proposed by Beglar and Nation (2007). Since each level has 600 words, a student's test score will be multiplied by 60 to get their total receptive vocabulary size. The interfaces of the online testing system can be seen in Figure 3.

155 international students of different language proficiencies are organized to take a traditional written test of 90 minutes and the AIG online test of 30 minutes. The written test is a student placement test including listening, reading and writing questions constructed by professional CSL teachers. And the online test only includes vocabulary questions. These two tests are administered on the same day to ensure the examinees' language

Table 1: Results of Expert Evaluation

Result	Word Selection	Word Pronunciation	Word Collocation	Average
OAR	19%	100%	40%	53%
AAR	65%	100%	80%	81.67%

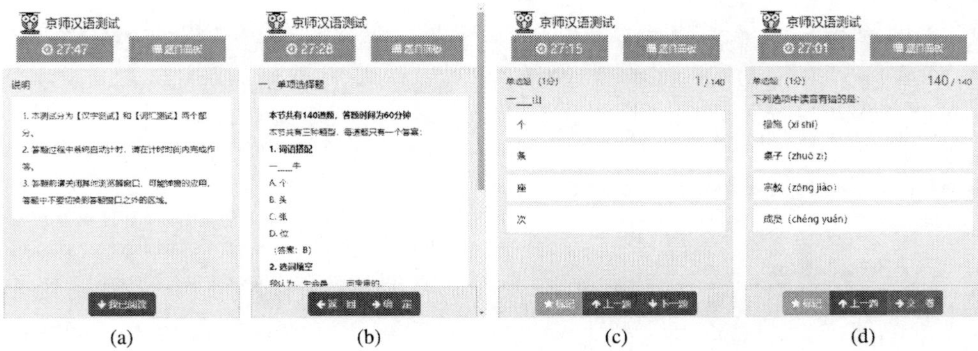

Figure 3: The online testing system on mobile devices (a) description of the test, (b) examples of test items, (c) the first item, (d) the last item.

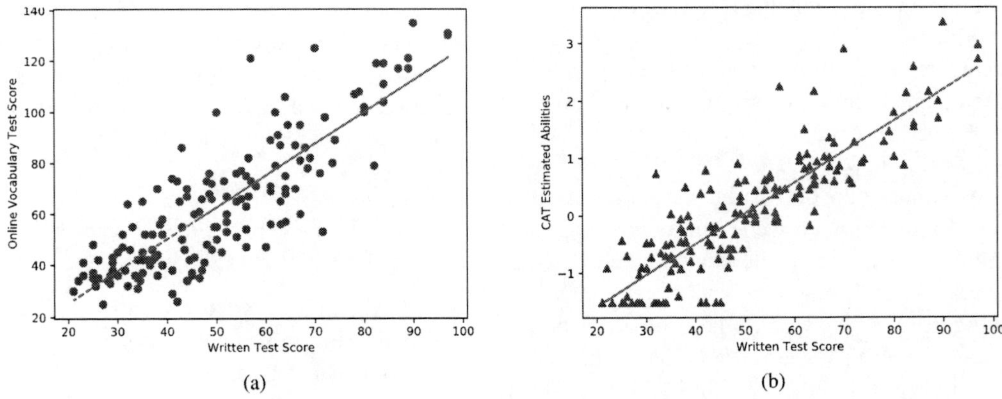

Figure 4: Score Correlations. (a) Written test score and online AIG test score, $\rho = 0.8395$; (b) Written test score and CAT estimated ability, $\rho = 0.8715$.

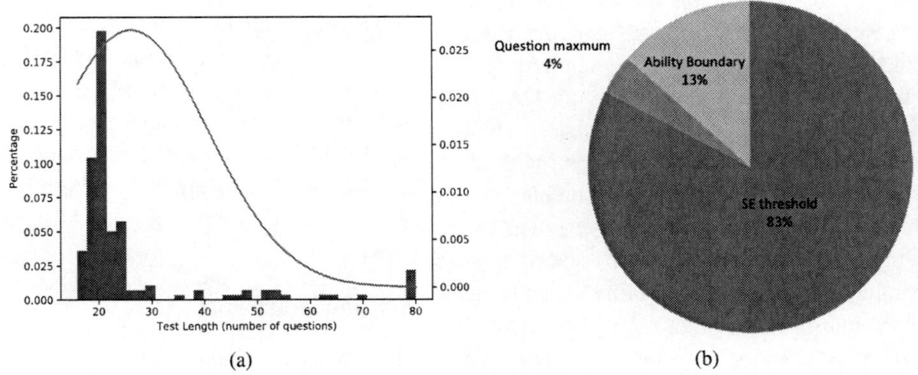

Figure 5: CAT Simulation Results. (a) Test Length, the average length is 26; (b) Percentage of different stopping rules.

proficiencies are stable.

After the tests, we compute the correlation scores of them. As shown in Figure 4(a), the result is very inspiring that the scores are strongly correlated with Pearson correlation coefficient of 0.8395, given we only use AIG based vocabulary questions. Furthermore, the test time is greatly reduced from 90 minutes to 30 minutes. The online AIG test promisingly indicates that:

- Vocabulary knowledge is indeed a core part of second language proficiency, as stated in previous works (Nation, 2001; Cook, 2016).

- AIG is an effective tool for vocabulary assessment.

5.3 CAT Simulation

After the online test, we collect students' answer data, and estimate three parameters for each item, including difficulty parameter b, discrimination parameter a and guessing parameter c. The estimation is based on 3PL item response theory (IRT) and implemented with the R package ltm.

With this calibrated item pool, we implement the adaptive algorithm illustrated in Algorithm 1. The detailed parameter settings are as following: $\theta_0 = 0.2$, $s = 0.3$, $n_{max} = 80$, $[\theta_{min}, \theta_{max}] = [-1.5, 4.5]$, $t_{max} = 80$, $\epsilon = 0.0001$.

We simulate the CAT based vocabulary test with the 155 students' answers, and output estimated abilities when one of the stopping rules is triggered.

Figure 4(b) shows that the estimated abilities reaches an even higher correlation coefficient of $\rho = 0.8715$ than the fixed online AIG test. Meanwhile, the average test length is only 26, which decreases greatly by 81% compared to 140 of the AIG test.

Figure 5 further illustrates the CAT simulation result. Regarding the triggered stopping rules, 83% of the students end with the standard deviation threshold, which indicates that our CAT algorithm has a desirable estimate precision. However, there are still 13% of students end with the lower ability boundary, and 4% of students stop with maximum test length. These cases reflect that our item pool needs improvement by adding more very simple questions for low ability students and very hard questions for high ability students. It is an important feedback to the AIG algorithm, especially on the difficulty control and sampling method.

5.4 Vocabulary Size and Score Prediction

After estimating students' vocabulary abilities with CAT, we train a linear regression model to predict a student's vocabulary size and the written test score.

The vocabulary size vs is predicted with Equation 8.

$$vs = 60 \times (22.37\,\theta + 61.43), R^2 = 0.8505 \quad (8)$$

It has been implemented on our online testing system http://test.aihanyu.org. Users can quickly estimate their vocabulary sizes after taking a CAT test in a few minutes.

The written test score sc can be computed with Equation 9. The result could serve as an effective tool for student placement.

$$sc = 14.10\,\theta + 49.46, R^2 = 0.7594 \quad (9)$$

6 Conclusions and Future Work

In this paper, we propose a novel testing strategy by combining automatic item generation (AIG) and computerized adaptive testing (CAT) in vocabulary assessment. Experiments show that it is a promising and highly effective path to evaluate language proficiency. The advantages are obvious as below:

- AIG is an effective method to construct a balanced CAT item pool.

- CAT is also a good evaluation tool of AIG, since it can provide important feedback to AIG which is hard to be given by manual evaluation.

- The combination of AIG and CAT can reduce the test cost significantly.

We believe that this testing strategy can serve as a good basis for research of language testing, as well as various intelligent learning applications that need students' proficiencies for user modeling. In the future, we aim at enhancing the AIG algorithms and exploring the generation algorithms of more question types, as well as in more disciplines.

Acknowledgments

This work is supported by the Fundamental Research Funds for the Central Universities, National Social Science Fund of China

(No. 18CYY029) and China Postdoctoral Science Foundation funded project (No. 2018M630095).

References

Itziar Aldabe and Montse Maritxalar. 2014. Semantic similarity measures for the generation of science tests in basque. *IEEE transactions on Learning Technologies*, 7(4):375–387.

Frank B Baker. 2001. *The basics of item response theory*. ERIC.

David Beglar and P Nation. 2007. A vocabulary size test. *The Language Teacher*, 31(7):9–13.

Jonathan C Brown, Gwen A Frishkoff, and Maxine Eskenazi. 2005. Automatic question generation for vocabulary assessment. In *Proceedings of the conference on Human Language Technology and Empirical Methods in Natural Language Processing*, pages 819–826. Association for Computational Linguistics.

Hua-Hua Chang. 2015. Psychometrics behind computerized adaptive testing. *Psychometrika*, 80(1):1–20.

Wanxiang Che, Zhenghua Li, and Ting Liu. 2010. Ltp: A chinese language technology platform. In *Proceedings of the 23rd International Conference on Computational Linguistics: Demonstrations*, pages 13–16. Association for Computational Linguistics.

Vivian Cook. 2016. *Second language learning and language teaching*. Routledge.

Rui Correia, Jorge Baptista, Nuno Mamede, Isabel Trancoso, and Maxine Eskenazi. 2010. Automatic generation of cloze question distractors. In *Proceedings of the Interspeech Satellite Workshop on Second Language Studies:Acquisition,Learning,Education and Technology*, Waseda University,Tokyo,Japan.

Xiang-Min Ding and Hong-Bin Gu. 2010. Automatic generation technology of chinese multiple-choice items based on ontology. *Computer Engineering and Design*, 31(6):1397–1400.

Mark J Gierl and Hollis Lai. 2018. Using automatic item generation to create solutions and rationales for computerized formative testing. *Applied psychological measurement*, 42(1):42–57.

Renfen Hu. 2013. Research on phonetic symbols of phonograms in chinese mandarin. *Journal of Chinese Information Processing*, 27(3):41–47.

Renfen Hu, Jiayong Chen, and Kuang-hua Chen. 2016. The construction of a chinese collocational knowledge resource and its application for second language acquisition. In *Proceedings of COLING 2016, the 26th International Conference on Computational Linguistics: Technical Papers*, pages 3254–3263.

Ming Liu, Vasile Rus, and Li Liu. 2017. Automatic chinese factual question generation. *IEEE Transactions on Learning Technologies*, 10(2):194–204.

Ming Liu, Vasile Rus, and Li Liu. 2018. Automatic chinese multiple choice question generation using mixed similarity strategy. *IEEE Transactions on Learning Technologies*, 11(2):193–202.

Ruslan Mitkov and Le An Ha. 2003. Computer-aided generation of multiple-choice tests. volume 2, pages 17–22.

Ruslan Mitkov, Le An Ha, Andrea Varga, and Luz Rello. 2009. Semantic similarity of distractors in multiple-choice tests: extrinsic evaluation. In *Proceedings of the Workshop on Geometrical Models of Natural Language Semantics*, pages 49–56. Association for Computational Linguistics.

Ruslan Mitkov, Ha Le An, and Nikiforos Karamanis. 2006. A computer-aided environment for generating multiple-choice test items. *Natural language engineering*, 12(2):177–194.

Jack Mostow, Yi-Ting Huang, Hyeju Jang, Anders Weinstein, Joe Valeri, and Donna Gates. 2017. Developing, evaluating, and refining an automatic generator of diagnostic multiple choice cloze questions to assess children's comprehension while reading. *Natural Language Engineering*, 23(2):245–294.

Paul Nation. 2001. *Learning Vocabulary in Another Language*. Cambridge University Press.

Vasile Rus, Zhiqiang Cai, and Arthur C Graesser. 2007. Experiments on generating questions about facts. In *International Conference on Intelligent Text Processing and Computational Linguistics*, pages 444–455. Springer.

Arjun Singh Bhatia, Manas Kirti, and Sujan Kumar Saha. 2013. Automatic generation of multiple choice questions using wikipedia. In *Pattern Recognition and Machine Intelligence*, pages 733–738, Berlin, Heidelberg. Springer Berlin Heidelberg.

Goto Takuya, Kojiri Tomoko, Toyohide Watanabe, Iwata Tomoharu, and Yamada Takeshi. 2010. Automatic generation system of multiple-choice cloze questions and its evaluation. *Knowledge Management & E-Learning : an International Journal*, 2.

Howard Wainer. 2000. *Computerized Adaptive Testing: A Primer*. Lawrence Erlbaum Associates.

David J Weiss and G Gage Kingsbury. 1984. Application of computerized adaptive testing to educational problems. *Journal of Educational Measurement*, 21(4):361–375.

Jizhou Yang and Yongfen Jia. 2005. *The usage comparisons of 1700 pairs of synonyms*. Beijing Language and Culture University, Beijing, China.

Computationally Modeling the Impact of Task-Appropriate Language Complexity and Accuracy on Human Grading of German Essays

Zarah Weiss[a]   **Anja Riemenschneider**[b]   **Pauline Schröter**[b]   **Detmar Meurers**[a,b]

[a] Dept. of Linguistics & LEAD   [b] Institute for Educational Quality Improvement
University of Tübingen   Humboldt-Universität zu Berlin
`zweiss@sfs.uni-tuebingen.de`   `riemenan@iqb.hu-berlin.de`
`dm@sfs.uni-tuebingen.de`   `schrotpa@iqb.hu-berlin.de`

Abstract

Computational linguistic research on the language complexity of student writing typically involves human ratings as a gold standard. However, educational science shows that teachers find it difficult to identify and cleanly separate accuracy, different aspects of complexity, contents, and structure. In this paper, we therefore explore the use of computational linguistic methods to investigate how task-appropriate complexity and accuracy relate to the grading of overall performance, content performance, and language performance as assigned by teachers.

Based on texts written by students for the official school-leaving state examination (*Abitur*), we show that teachers successfully assign higher language performance grades to essays with higher task-appropriate language complexity and properly separate this from content scores. Yet, accuracy impacts teacher assessment for all grading rubrics, also the content score, overemphasizing the role of accuracy.

Our analysis is based on broad computational linguistic modeling of German language complexity and an innovative theory- and data-driven feature aggregation method inferring task-appropriate language complexity.

1 Introduction

Official state education standards highlight the relevance of language complexity for the evaluation of text readability and reading skills (CCSSO, 2010) and academic writing proficiency in students first and second language (KMK, 2014a,b). The highly assessment-driven U.S. public education system has long recognized the benefits of automating the evaluation of student learning outcomes, including very substantial research, development, and commercial applications targeting automatic essay scoring (AES, Shermis and Burstein, 2013; Vajjala, 2018; Yannakoudakis et al., 2018). This situation is not transferable to other education systems, such as the German one, where so far there is hardly any discussion of automating the assessment of learning outcomes and no high-stakes testing industry. In the German *Abitur* examination, the official school-leaving state examination that qualifies students for admission to university, teachers grade language performance and content in essays without technical assistance, using grading templates that specify content and language expectations. In the language arts and literacy subject-matters (German, English, French, etc.), language performance is a crucial component of the overall grade across all states. Yet, unlike content, language requirements are only loosely specified in the education standards, mentioning complex and diverse syntax and lexis, and a coherent argumentation structure as indicators of high-quality language performance (KMK, 2014b). The exact implementation of these language requirements is left to the discretion of the teachers. Educational science has questioned to which extent teachers are biased by construct-irrelevant text characteristics while grading. There is evidence that mechanical accuracy over-proportionally influences grades and even affects the evaluation of unrelated concepts such as content (Cumming et al., 2002; Rezaei and Lovorn, 2010). Differences in lexical sophistication and diversity have been shown to impact teachers' evaluation of grammar and essay structure (Vögelin et al., 2019). This is a potentially severe issue for the German education system.

We pick up on this issue by investigating which role language complexity and accuracy play in teachers' grading of German *Abitur* essays. For this, we build upon previous work on complexity and accuracy in the context of the Complexity, Accuracy, and Fluency (CAF) framework (Wolfe-Quintero et al., 1998; Bulté and Housen, 2012) employed in Second Language Acquisition (SLA) research to model different types of language per-

Proceedings of the Fourteenth Workshop on Innovative Use of NLP for Building Educational Applications, pages 30–45
Florence, Italy, August 2, 2019. ©2019 Association for Computational Linguistics

formance (McNamara et al., 2010; Vajjala and Meurers, 2012; Bulté and Housen, 2014). We establish an automatically obtained measure of task-appropriate overall language complexity. With this, we identify texts of more and less appropriate language complexity, which we then manually assess for their accuracy. We use this to experimentally examine teaching experts' grading behaviour and how it is influenced by accuracy and complexity. Our results show that while teachers seem to successfully identify language complexity and include it in their grading when appropriate, they are heavily biased by accuracy even when it is construct-irrelevant.

Our work innovates in exploiting computational linguistic methods to address questions of broader relevance from the domain of educational science by using sophisticated language complexity modeling. This is the first computational linguistic analysis of German *Abitur* essays and their human grading, illustrating the potential of cross-disciplinary work bringing together computational linguistics and empirical educational science. The novel approach presented for the assessment of appropriate overall language complexity also provides valuable insights into the task- or text type-dependence of complexity features. This is of direct relevance for the current discussion of task-effects in CAF research (Alexopoulou et al., 2017; Yoon, 2017).

The article is structured as follows: We briefly review related work on complexity assessment and insights from educational science into human grading behavior. We then present our data set and how we automatically extract language complexity measures. Section 5 elaborates on the construction of appropriate overall language complexity including a qualitative analysis of task-wise differences between document vectors. Section 6 reports our experiment on teacher grading behavior. We close in Section 7 with an outlook.

2   Related Work

Language complexity, commonly defined as "[t]he extent to which the language produced in performing a task is elaborate and varied" (Ellis, 2003, p. 340), has been studied extensively in the context of second language development and proficiency and text readability in particular with regard to the English language (Vajjala and Meurers, 2012; Guo et al., 2013; Bulté and Housen, 2014; Chen

and Meurers, 2019). Complexity has also been investigated in relation to (academic) writing proficiency of native speakers (Crossley et al., 2011; McNamara et al., 2010). Research on languages other than English, remains rather limited, with some work on German, Russian, Swedish, Italian, and French (Weiss and Meurers, 2018; Reynolds, 2016; Pilán et al., 2015; Dell'Orletta et al., 2014; François and Fairon, 2012).

Recently, research has increasingly focused on the influence of task effects on language complexity in writing quality and language proficiency assessment, both in terms of their influence on CAF development in the context of the two main frameworks (Robinson, 2001; Skehan, 1996) as well as its implications for AES systems and other forms of language proficiency modeling (Yannakoudakis et al., 2018; Dell'Orletta et al., 2014). Alexopoulou et al. (2017) show that task complexity and task type strongly affect English as a Foreign Language (EFL) essay writing complexity. Topic and text type, too, have been found to impact CAF constructs in EFL writing and in particular language complexity (Yoon and Polio, 2016; Yoon, 2017; Yang et al., 2015). Vajjala (2018) demonstrates task effects across EFL corpora to the extent that text length strongly impacts essay quality negatively on one and positively on the other data set. Her results further corroborate the importance of accuracy for essay quality across data sets. Accuracy has overall received considerably less attention in SLA research than complexity (Larsen-Freeman, 2006; Yoon and Polio, 2016).

An orthogonal strand of research investigates the quality of human judgments of writing quality and how complexity and accuracy impact them. It has been demonstrated that teachers are biased by accuracy and in particular spelling even when it is irrelevant for the construct under evaluation such as content quality (Rezaei and Lovorn, 2010; Cumming et al., 2002; Scannell and Marshall, 1966). Other studies showed that characteristics such as syntactic complexity, text length, and lexical sophistication impact inter-rater agreement (Lim, 2019; Wind et al., 2017; Wolfe et al., 2016). Vögelin et al. (2019) experimentally manipulate the lexical diversity and sophistication of EFL learners' argumentative essays and let Swiss English teachers rate them for their overall quality, grammar, and essay frame. Their findings show that when the lexical diversity and sophistication of an essay was manually reduced, it received lower grades not only for its overall quality but also for grammar and the essay's frame, i.e., the structured presentation of the writing objective through introduction and conclusion.

3 The *Abitur* Data

We analyzed 344 essays that were written during the German literature and language examination of the German *Abitur* in 2017. The essays were elicited across German states and collected and digitized by the Institute for Educational Quality Improvement (IQB).[1] For each essay, the final overall grade that was assigned to it in the *Abitur* serves as meta information. All essays respond to one of four task prompts.[2] Two tasks require the interpretation of literature (IL): IL-1 and IL-2. The other two elicit material-based argumentative (MA) essays based on several additional materials provided with the task: MA-1 and MA-2.[3]

Topic and task differences may substantially impact the linguistic characteristics of the resulting language (Alexopoulou et al., 2017; Yoon and Polio, 2016). For our data, this is even more the case given that MA task prompts include a recommended essay length (around 1,000 for one, around 800 words for the other), but IL task prompts do not. The effect this has on the relationship between text length and overall essay grade is shown in Figure 1. Texts elicited by MA tasks are overall shorter than answers to IL tasks and exhibit a lesser variation in length. While for IL tasks we observe a weak linear correlation between overall grade and text length, clear deviations from the expected text length seem to have a negative impact on the overall grade for MA tasks. To address this issue, we split our data for the following analyses in four data sets, one per task prompt. The data sets are henceforth referred to by the id of the respective task prompt (IL-1, IL-2, MA-1, MA-2).

4 Automatic Complexity Assessment

Our system automatically extracts 320 measures of language complexity covering a broad range of linguistic features. We include features from

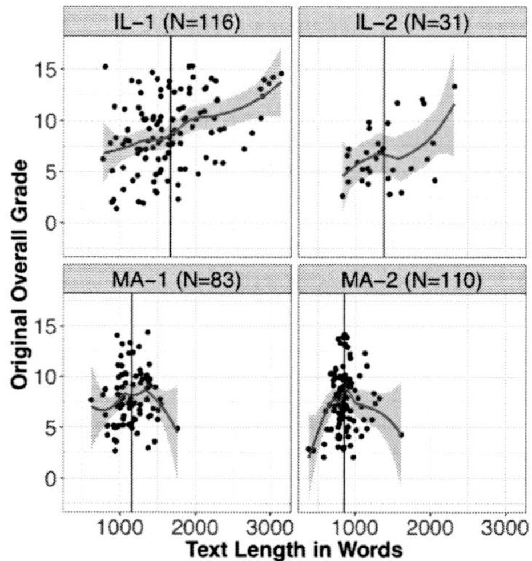

Figure 1: Text length across overall grades split by task prompts. The vertical line marks the mean length.

two main research strands on text complexity in our system: measures of the linguistic system and psycho-linguistic measures of language use and cognitive processing. An overview of all features can be found in Table 1.

Our procedure is based on our implementation of a broad range of complexity features for German which we have successfully used for the assessment of German readability of media captions for adults and children (Weiss and Meurers, 2018), German L2 proficiency (Weiss, 2017; Weiss and Meurers, in press), and German L1 writing development (Weiss and Meurers, 2019). However, for the research presented here, we altered the segmenter for sentences and tokens. Due to the specific abbreviations for line and page references systematically used in our data, we found that a rule-based segmenter combined with a customized list of abbreviations typical for German *Abitur* essays outperformed the segmentation by OpenNLP (Bohnet and Nivre, 2012).[4]

As mentioned earlier, language complexity is an important component of the German curriculum for German arts and literacy (KMK, 2014b). While it lacks a full operationalization of language complexity, it names some examples of language complexification strategies that students' writings should exhibit. Based on this, we identified a set of 75 complexity features, which implement the lan-

---

[1] The IQB is an academic institute that monitors if schools across Germany states adhere to the educational standards set by the Standing Conference of the Ministers of Education and Cultural Affairs of the States in Germany.

[2] Figure 4 in the Appendix shows the distribution of documents and grades across task prompts.

[3] Table 6 in the Appendix describes the task prompts.

[4] We used the segmenter by Stefanie Dipper available at https://www.linguistics.ruhr-uni-bochum.de/~dipper/resources/tokenizer.html

Feature Set	Description
Lexical complexity	measures lexical density, variation, sophistication, and relatedness; e.g., type token ratio
Discourse complexity	measures use of cohesive devices; e.g., connectives per sentence
Phrasal complexity	measures phrase modification; e.g., NP modifiers per NP
Clausal complexity	measures clausal elaboration; e.g., subordinate clauses per sentence
Morphological complexity	measures inflection, derivation, and composition; e.g., average compound depth per compound noun
Language Use	measures word frequencies based on frequency data bases; e.g., mean word frequency in SUBTLEX-DE (Brysbaert et al., 2011)
Language Processing	measures cognitive load during human sentence processing, mostly based on Dependency Locality Theory (Gibson, 2000) e.g., average total integration cost at the finite verb

Table 1: Overview over the feature sets used to capture language complexity

guage requirements that were pre-defined for our data. These may be grouped into three categories:

Argumentation Structure Texts should be structured coherently, clearly, be compelling and provide clear guidance for the reader. The author's reasoning should be made explicit. Both, the text's general structure as well as the language used should facilitate this (KMK, 2014b, p. 17). We operationalized these aspects by measuring various uses of connectives and the local and global co-occurrence of arguments, nouns, and word stems.

Lexical Complexity Texts should be lexically elaborate and varied. Stylistically, vocabulary choice should adhere to a task-appropriate written register (KMK, 2014b, e.g., pp. 42, 52). We cover this by including a range of measures of lexical diversity and density.

Syntactic Complexity Texts should be syntactically elaborate and varied and include connected and subordinated clauses to reflect a coherent structure. Stylistically, they should adhere to a task-appropriate written register. Students should also make appropriate use of tenses (KMK, 2014b, e.g., pp. 42, 52). To measure syntactic complexity, we include sentence length and several clause to sentence ratios, e.g., complex t-units per sentence and relative clauses per sentence.

Due to the repeatedly named focus on stylistically and norm-appropriate writing (KMK, 2014b, p. 16f), we also include prominent measures of German academic language which constitutes the appropriate written register for all four tasks represented in our data. There is a broad consensus that in particular complex noun phrases are a prominent feature of academic language (Hennig and Niemann, 2013; Morek and Heller, 2012; Schleppengrell, 2001), thus we include a series of measures of noun phrase elaboration and the variability of noun complexity. Another prominent aspect of academic language is deagentivization (Hennig and Niemann, 2013; Snow and Uccelli, 2009; Bailey, 2007), which entails passivization, verb modification and verb cluster. Hence, we specifically include measures of verb complexity and the variation of verb clusters as well as the coverage of deagentivization patterns in general. Finally, we include measures of tense usage to cover the specific request for appropriate tense usage across text types. Note that while across tasks the notions of what constitutes appropriate tense use may differ, within tasks these are fixed, e.g., favoring the use of past tense over present tense or vice versa.[5]

5 Complexity-Based Essay Selection

In order to evaluate how language complexity impacts grading behavior, we first needed to identify texts of high and low language complexity for our experiment (Section 6). For this, we followed a two-step approach: First, we transformed each student essay into a vector representation of relevant features of language complexity (Section 5.1). Then, we ranked them with regard to

---

[5]The complete list of theoretically motivated features may be found in Table 7 in the Appendix.

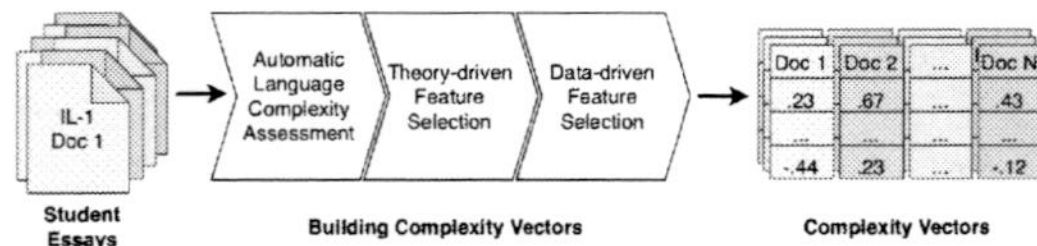

Figure 2: Task-wise transformation of essays to language complexity vector representations.

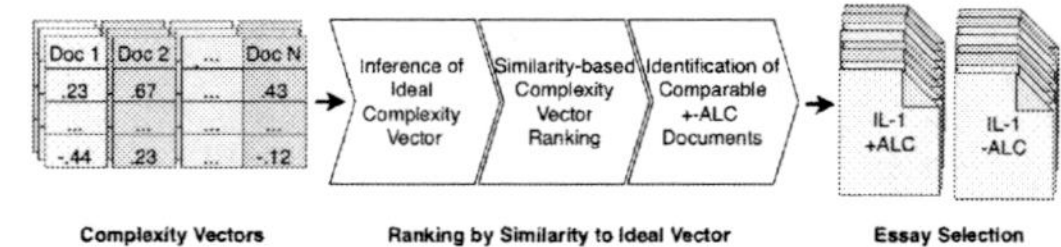

Figure 3: Selection of essays with more and less task-appropriate overall language complexity.

their similarity to an artificial ideal vector and selected for each task two essays of high and two of low language complexity (Section 5.2).

5.1 Building Complexity Vectors

Figure 2 outlines the procedure used to build language complexity vectors tailored towards the individual task prompts. We extracted the 320 measures of language complexity from the *Abitur* data as discussed in Section 4. We then removed all outliers that deviated more than two standard deviations from the mean and calculated the z-score of each feature. Based on this, we identified which of the dimensions of linguistic complexity that we measured are relevant for a given task.

We defined relevance in terms of correlation with the overall grade an essay received. These grades represent teachers' judgments of essay quality under consideration of language performance in a high stakes testing situation. We used a hybrid approach combining theory-driven and data-driven feature selection. First, we calculated the Pearson correlation between the z-scores of 75 theoretically relevant features and the overall grade each essay had received in the *Abitur* examination. We did so separately for each data set. Features with a significant ($p < .05$) absolute correlation of $r \geq .2$ were included in the complexity vector if they did not correlate more than $r = .8$ with another feature in the vector. For highly correlated features, we only kept the feature most highly correlated with the overall grade.

We augmented this feature selection with the remaining features of linguistic complexity in our document vector that had a significant ($p < .05$) absolute Pearson correlation with the overall grade of $r \geq .3$. Features were required to correlate less than $r = .8$ with other features selected for the complexity vector. For highly inter-correlated features, the feature with the highest correlation with the overall grade or the theoretically motivated feature was favored. This lead to complexity vectors of size 33 for IL-1, 45 for IL-2, and 13 for MA-1 and 13 for MA-2.[6, 7]

5.2 Ranking by Similarity to Ideal Vector

We selected essays for our experiment using the similarity of complexity vectors to a reference vector representing the artificial ideal use of each complexity feature as illustrated in Figure 3. We assigned the values 1 for feature dimensions with a positive correlation with the original overall grade and 0 for those with a negative correlation with the original overall grade. Conceptually, this represents the ideal language complexity for a given task: Features that are associated with low performance are not present and features associated with high performance are maximally represented.

For each feature in the complexity vector, we replaced the previously introduced z-scores with a min-max normalization to enforce a scale from 0 to 1. We calculated the similarity between each essay and the reference vector using Manhattan distance and ranked all essays based on their distance to the artificial ideal document vector.

Based on this ranking, we chose four essays per task which were comparable with each other in terms of their text length: two from the top of our ranking, i.e. closer to the ideal vector, and two from the bottom of our ranking, i.e. more distant to the ideal vector. We limited our choice to essays that had received a medium overall grade between 7 and 9 points in the German grading system for the final three years of German high school. This corresponds to essays with a point percentage between 55% and 69% (KMK, 2018, p. 22).[8] This restriction ensures on the one hand that essays are comparable in terms of their overall and content performance. On the other hand, it prevents ceiling and floor effects in teachers' grades.

---

[6]The final feature selection for all four vector representations and the correlation of all features with the original overall grade may be found in Table 8 in the Appendix.

[7]Table 9 in the Appendix shows for each task how many features were selected using the theory-driven and the data-driven selection step.

[8]An overview relating this system to percentage points may be found in Table 10 in the Appendix.

We labeled the resulting eight texts close to the ideal vector as essays with more appropriate language complexity (+ALC) and the eight texts relatively distant from the ideal vector as essays with less appropriate language complexity (-ALC).

5.3 Task-Wise Vector Differences

Comparing the features that were selected for the vector representations across tasks reveals some interesting structures which are relevant for the ongoing discussion of task effects on language performance. Overall, 75 unique features are included across all vectors. Table 2 shows a selection of 10 features chosen to illustrate patterns across vectors.[9]

Nearly a quarter of features (18 of 75) re-occurs in at least three of the four vectors. We take this as an indication of generalizable characteristics of language performance. This group is predominantly comprised of features of lexical sophistication in form of lexical diversity and verb variation (6/18), clausal elaboration in form of words, clauses, dependent clauses, and dependent clauses with conjunctions per sentence as well as the overall use of connectives (6/18), and nominal writing style in form of post-nominal modifiers, genitives, and nominalization strategies (4/18), all of which are positively correlated with the overall grade. These groups are represented in Table 2 by MTLD, dependent clauses per sentence, and the percentage of derived nouns. Taken together, they represent important markers of German academic language (Hennig and Niemann, 2013; Morek and Heller, 2012). Lexical sophistication has also repeatedly been observed as an important indicator of English first and second language writing performance (Guo et al., 2013; Crossley et al., 2011). Evidence that the relevance of these features for writing performance persists across task contexts is highly relevant as it provides empirical underpinning to the mostly theoretical concept of German academic language.

Aside from this general overlap across task prompts, we observe considerable similarities between both IL task prompts indicating that the features represent a coherent subgroup of appropriate linguistic complexity for interpretative writing rather than idiosyncratic properties of the specific task prompts. Of 26 features that are relevant across two tasks, 21 are shared between the IL tasks. This is a remarkable overlap given the respective vector sizes. Characteristic for IL tasks are especially features of phrasal modification (9/21), predominantly but not exclusively with regard to noun phrase modification, and clausal elaboration resulting in higher cognitive load in form of integration cost and dependency lengths (5/21). All of these are positively correlated with the overall grade. The two groups are represented in Table 2 by the percentage of complex noun phrases and the average total integration cost. Several of the features not shared across both IL tasks relate to different realizations of clausal elaboration: while for IL-2 several subtypes of subordination are relevant, such as interrogative clauses, conjunctional clauses, clauses without conjunction, various types of connectives, for IL-1 only relative clauses occur as specific type of clausal elaboration. Table 2 displays this contrast for relative clauses, dependent clauses without conjunction, and conjunctional clauses per sentence. Material-based argumentation does not exhibit such a pattern which may be due to the fact that both MA prompts request different text types, once a commentary (MA-2) and once an essay (MA-1), while both IL tasks share not only a task objective (interpretation) but also the same text type (essay).

6 Experiment

6.1 Set-Up

We recruited 33 teachers (14 female, 19 male) from different schools across German states.[10] Their teaching experience ranges from 5 to 38 years ($\mu = 19.9; SD = 9.1$). All of them have participated in grading German subject-matter *Abitur* tasks at least twice, most of them more than eight times. We asked them to grade essays for their language, content, and overall performance using the grading scale used for the German *Abitur* ranging from 0 to 15 points. Teachers were provided with a grading template for each task prompt, which is a standard feature in the German *Abitur*. The template states the expectations of students' answers with regard to content and language. Each teacher received 8 texts from over-

---

[9] The selection was taken from the aforementioned full table displaying all 75 features relevant for the vector representations in Table 8 in the Appendix.

[10] We recruited 32 teachers plus one replacement teacher to cover an anticipated drop-out. Since all teachers completed the study, eight texts were graded by an additional teacher (i.e. 17 instead of 16 teachers).

Feature	IL-1	IL-2	MA-1	MA-2
MTLD	.2014	.4358	.2876	.3361
Dependent clauses per sentence	*.3040*	.2528	.2046	-.0380
Derived nouns per noun phrase	*.2394*	.4751	.1604	.3301
Average total integration cost at finite verb	.4093	*.4909*	.0708	.0308
Complex noun phrases per noun phrase	.4177	*.3186*	.1316	-.0353
Relative clauses per sentence	.3027	.1814	.1381	-.0077
Dep. clauses w/o conjunction per sentence	.1414	.2460	.0744	.0058
Conjunctional clauses per sentence	.1632	.2433	.0744	-.0285

Table 2: Selection of features in the complexity vectors and their correlation with the original overall grade. Gray font marks uncorrelated features. Italics mark correlated but redundant features.

all 2 tasks: 4 +ALC and 4 -ALC texts. Each text was graded by 16 teachers independently. Teachers did not know the original grades that their texts had received, neither were they aware of the ranking-based selection. This grading situation was maximally familiar to our subjects, because it mimics teachers' real-life experience for essay grading in the context of German *Abitur*.

For each of the three grades (overall, content, and language performance), we built a linear mixed regression model fitted by REML. The respective grade served as response variable and we included task prompt as random effect. Each model had two predictor variables: $\pm$ALC and error rate. We included error rate (in form of z-scores) as a predictor, because accuracy is an important criterion for the evaluation of students' language performance and thus overall performance in the German *Abitur* and to investigate its influence on teachers' grading. We manually extracted spelling mistakes, punctuation errors, and grammatical errors from each essay and aggregated them into one overall error score by dividing the total number of errors by the number of words.

6.2 Results

Tables 3, 4, and 5 show the respective model fits for each grade. For all three models, the residuals were homoscedasticly distributed around a zero mean. Table 3 shows that +ALC affects language performance grades by raising it about 1.37 points ($\pm$ 0.37 SE) for essays with more appropriate linguistic complexity. Error rate, too, clearly affects the grade, lowering it about -1.99 points ($\pm$ 0.21 SE). The model overall explains 37.5% of the variance, 29.3% of which are attributed to both error rate and $\pm$ALC. Although error rate is the stronger of the two predictors, $\pm$ALC does significantly

improve the model fit ($\chi^2 = 1277.7, p < 0.001$). The random intercept for the four tasks accounts for 1.0% of the variance ($\pm$1.0 SD). The residuals account for 7.6% of the variance ($\pm$2.8 SD).

Table 4 shows the fit for the content grades the teachers assigned. We do not see evidence that the content grade is affected by +ALC in our ratings. Error rate, however, influences the grade negatively, lowering it about -1.265 points ($\pm$ 0.227 SE). The model overall explains 29.1% of the variance. 11.9% are attributed to error rate and $\pm$ALC but complexity does not make a significant contribution to the overall model fit. The random intercept for the four tasks accounts for 2.1% of the variance ($\pm$1.4 SD). The residuals account for 8.8% of the variance ($\pm$2.9 SD). In order to rule out that this influence of error rate on the content grade is caused by certain errors obstructing understanding, we refitted the content grade model with each of the individual error types instead of overall error rate. We find that all three error types impact content grade. Spelling significantly lowers it ($t = -4.651, p = 0.000$) about -1.197 points ($\pm$ 0.257 SE). Punctuation significantly lowers it ($t = -3.078, p = 0.002$) about -0.597 points ($\pm$ 0.194 SE). Grammar significantly lowers it ($t = -7.836, p = 0.000$) about -1.560 points ($\pm$ 0.199 SE).

Table 5 shows the fit for the overall grades assigned by the teachers. The overall grade is marginally affected by +ALC . The overall grade is about 0.703 points higher ($\pm$ 0.359 SE) for text with more appropriate linguistic complexity. As for the other grades, error rate strongly influences the overall rating lowering it about -1.518 points ($\pm$ 0.208 SE). The model overall explains 31.1% of the variance. Of this, 17.3% are attributed to

	Estimate	SE	t-value	p-value
(Inter.)	6.989	0.561	12.468	< 0.001
+ALC	1.374	0.368	3.732	< 0.001
Error	-1.992	0.211	-9.459	< 0.001

Table 3: Estimates for language performance grade.

	Estimate	SE	t-value	p-value
(Inter.)	6.138	0.772	7.948	0.003
Error	-1.265	0.227	-5.586	< 0.001
+ALC	0.614	0.393	1.562	0.120

Table 4: Estimates for content grade.

	Estimate	SE	t-value	p-value
(Inter.)	6.460	0.696	9.278	0.002
+ALC	0.703	0.359	1.962	0.051
Error	-1.518	0.208	-7.316	< 0.001

Table 5: Estimates for re-assigned overall grade.

+ALC and error rate. Again, error rate is the stronger predictor and ±ALC does not make a significant contribution to the overall model fit. The random intercept for the four task accounts for 1.7% of the variance (±1.3 SD). The residuals account for 7.3% of the variance (±2.7 SD).

6.3 Discussion

Our results show that the language performance grades based on criteria stated in the grading template reflect differences between essays exhibiting more and less appropriate language complexity (±ALC). This result is not trivial, because previous research suggests that the assessment of quantitative aspects of text complexity is not a key competence of teachers (CCSSO, 2010). We do not find evidence that teachers are unduly influenced by differences in language complexity when assigning content grades. This is an encouraging finding in light of Vögelin et al. (2019)'s study on the effect of differences in lexical complexity on construct-unrelated grades. Our study differs in several aspects from their set-up: We asked experienced teachers rather than pre-service teachers, and we used the set-up of the *Abitur* they are familiar with. We provided them with texts that differed not only in terms of their lexical complexity (although these dimensions are represented in each of the document vector representations) but rather across various linguistic domains. While they altered texts experimentally, we used essays that are ecologically valid. We find that teachers include language complexity to a limited extent in the overall grades they assign. This is in line with the grading template stating that language performance should account for 30% of the overall performance.

As for accuracy, our results clearly show that all three grades are heavily influenced by error rate. For the language performance grade, this is motivated insofar as correctness is one of the criteria named in the corresponding grading template. Similarly, accuracy may be reflected in the overall grade as it is part of the overall evaluation. However, its weighting in both models is disproportionate. For content grading, accuracy is conceptually irrelevant, which is also stated in the grading template. Yet, teachers are clearly biased against essays with higher error rates, which is in line with previous research findings (Rezaei and Lovorn, 2010; Cumming et al., 2002). All three individual error types (punctuation, spelling, and grammar) show the same kind of influence on the content grade as the overall error rate. This demonstrates that the effect is not restricted to error types that may impede understanding, such as grammar errors. All error types affect content grading. Essays with a lower overall error rate receive higher content grades. This strong bias for a construct-irrelevant characteristic that is already included in another grading component, namely language performance, is highly problematic. Note, however, that we cannot rule out the possibility that students with better spelling in fact coincidentally also produce texts with better content. This is one of the limitations of our research design, which focuses on ecological validity. We will address this issue in a follow-up study, in which we will include corrected versions of the texts studied here. This way, we can keep essay content fixed while varying error rate. Overall our results indicate that although teachers can successfully capture different dimensions of language performance, such as complexity, accuracy, and content, they fail to modularize them clearly into separate grades.

7 Outlook

We addressed the question to which extent German teachers are able to identify differences in appropriate language complexity across tasks and how complexity and accuracy bias grading when they are construct-relevant or -irrelevant. For this, we proposed a novel similarity-based approach for the identification of task-appropriate language complexity in student essays. This also yielded some interesting insights in task differences between writing objectives and task prompts confirming common but so far empirically not sufficiently validated assumptions about German academic language. While our results indicate that teachers successfully identify and modularize the concept of language complexity, we show a clear bias for higher language accuracy across all grades. Teachers not only consider accuracy over-proportionally for the grading of language performance, it also influences their assessment of construct-irrelevant aspects such as content. This is in line with previous research findings (Rezaei and Lovorn, 2010; Cumming et al., 2002).

We see our work as a first step towards the analysis of the grading behaviour in the German education system using computational linguistic methods. In future work, we plan to build on this by exploring the grading behavior of teachers in greater depth, clustering teachers in terms of their characteristics and grading behavior. In particular, there is evidence that teachers' personal evaluation of the complexity of a text impacts their perception and, consequently, their grading of its language quality. We will explore this in a follow-up study. We will also follow-up on the question to which extent better accuracy and content quality coincide in ecologically valid texts by studying the link between content grades and writing accuracy in a more controlled setting with experimentally manipulated texts with corrected errors.

References

Theodora Alexopoulou, Marije Michel, Akira Murakami, and Detmar Meurers. 2017. Task effects on linguistic complexity and accuracy: A large-scale learner corpus analysis employing natural language processing techniques. *Language Learning*, 67:181–209.

Allison L. Bailey, editor. 2007. *The Language Demands of School. Putting Academic English to the Test*. Yale University Press, New Haven and London.

Bernd Bohnet and Joakim Nivre. 2012. A transition-based system for joint part-of-speech tagging and labeled non-projective dependency parsing. In *Proceedings of the 2012 Joint Conference on Empirical Methods in Natural Language Processing and Computational Natural Language Learning*, pages 1455–1465, Jeju Island, Korea. Association for Computational Linguistics.

Marc Brysbaert, Matthias Buchmeier, Markus Conrad, Arthur M. Jacobs, Jens Bölte, and Andrea Böhl. 2011. The word frequency effect: A review of recent developments and implications for the choice of frequency estimates in German. *Experimental Psychology*, 58:412–424.

Bram Bulté and Alex Housen. 2012. Defining and operationalising L2 complexity. In Alex Housen, Folkert Kuiken, and Ineke Vedder, editors, *Dimensions of L2 Performance and Proficiency*, pages 21–46. John Benjamins.

Bram Bulté and Alex Housen. 2014. Conceptualizing and measuring short-term changes in L2 writing complexity. *Journal of Second Language Writing*, 26(0):42 – 65. Comparing perspectives on L2 writing: Multiple analyses of a common corpus.

CCSSO. 2010. Common core state standards for English language arts & literacy in history/social studies, science, and technical subjects. Technical report, National Governors Association Center for Best Practices, Council of Chief State School Officers, Washington D.C.

Xiaobin Chen and Detmar Meurers. 2019. Linking text readability and learner proficiency using linguistic complexity feature vector distance. *Computer-Assisted Language Learning*.

Scott A. Crossley, Jennifer L. Weston, Susan T. McLain Sullivan, and Danielle S. McNamara. 2011. The development of writing proficiency as a function of grade level: A linguistic analysis. *Written Communication*, 28(3):282–311.

Alister Cumming, Robert Kantor, and Donald E. Powers. 2002. Decision making while rating ESL/EFL writing tasks: A descriptive framework. *The Modern Language Journal*, 86(1):67–96.

Felice Dell'Orletta, Simonetta Montemagni, and Giulia Venturi. 2014. Assessing document and sentence readability in less resourced languages and across textual genres. *Recent Advances in Automatic Readability Assessment and Text Simplification. Special issue of the International Journal of Applied Linguistics*, 165(2):163–193.

Rod Ellis. 2003. *Task-based Language Learning and Teaching*. Oxford University Press, Oxford, UK.

Thomas François and Cedrick Fairon. 2012. An "AI readability" formula for French as a foreign language. In *Proceedings of the 2012 Joint Conference on Empirical Methods in Natural Language Processing and Computational Natural Language Learning*.

Edward Gibson. 2000. The dependency locality theory: A distance-based theory of linguistic complexity. *Image, language, brain*, pages 95–126.

Liang Guo, Scott A Crossley, and Danielle S. McNamara. 2013. Predicting human judgments of essay quality in both integrated and independent second language writing samples: A comparison study. *Assessing Writing*, 18:218–238.

Mathilde Hennig and Robert Niemann. 2013. Unpersönliches Schreiben in der Wissenschaft. *Informationen Deutsch als Fremdsprache*, 4:439–455.

KMK. 2014a. *Bildungsstandards für die fortgeführte Fremdsprache (Englisch/Französisch) für die Allgemeine Hochschulre*. Sekretariat der Ständigen Konferenz der Kultusminister der Länder in der Bundesrepublik Deutschland (KMK), Wolters Kluwer Deutschland GmbH, Köln.

KMK. 2014b. *Bildungsstandards im Fach Deutsch für die Allgemeine Hochschulreife*. Ständige Konferenz der Kultusminister der Länder in der Bundesrepublik Deutschland (KMK), Wolters Kluwer Deutschland GmbH, Köln.

KMK. 2018. *Vereinbarung zur Gestaltung der gymnasialen Oberstufe und der Abiturprüfung. Beschluss der Kultusministerkonferenz vom 07.07.1972 i.d.F. vom 15.02.2018*. Sekretariat der Ständigen Konferenz der Kultusminister der Länder in der Bundesrepublik Deutschland (KMK), Wolters Kluwer Deutschland GmbH.

Diane Larsen-Freeman. 2006. The emergence of complexity, fluency, and accuracy in the oral and written production of five Chinese learners of English. *Applied Linguistics*, 27(4):590–619.

Jungmin Lim. 2019. An investigation of the text features of discrepantly-scored ESL essays: A mixed methods study. *Assessing Writing*, 39:1–13.

Danielle S. McNamara, Scott A. Crossley, and Philip M. McCarthy. 2010. Linguistic features of writing quality. *Written Communication*, 27(1):57–86.

Miriam Morek and Vivien Heller. 2012. Bildungssprache – kommunikative, epistemische, soziale und interaktive Aspekte ihres Gebrauchs. *Zeitschrift für angewandte Linguistik*, pages 67–101.

Ildikó Pilán, Sowmya Vajjala, and Elena Volodina. 2015. A readable read: Automatic assessment of language learning materials based on linguistic complexity. In *Proceedings of CICLING 2015- Research in Computing Science Journal Issue (to appear)*.

Robert Reynolds. 2016. *Russian natural language processing for computer-assisted language learning: capturing the benefits of deep morphological analysis in real-life applications*. Ph.D. thesis, UiT - The Arctic University of Norway.

Ali Reza Rezaei and Michael Lovorn. 2010. Reliability and validity of rubrics for assessment through writing. *Assessing Writing*, 15:18–39.

Peter Robinson. 2001. Task complexity, task difficulty, and task production: exploring interactions in a componential framework. *Applied Linguistics*, 22(1):27–57.

Dale P. Scannell and Jon C. Marshall. 1966. The effect of selected composition errors on grades assigned to essay examinations. *American Educational Research Journal*, 3(2):125–130.

Mary J. Schleppengrell. 2001. Linguistic features of the language of schooling. *Linguistics and Education*, 12(4):431–459.

Mark D. Shermis and Jill Burstein, editors. 2013. *Handbook on Automated Essay Evaluation: Current Applications and New Directions*. Routledge, Taylor & Francis Group, London and New York.

Peter Skehan. 1996. A framework for the implementation of task-based instruction. *Applied Linguistics*, 17(1):38.

Catherine E. Snow and Paola Uccelli. 2009. The challenge of academic language. In David R. Olson and Nancy Torrance, editors, *The Camebridge Handbook of Literacy*, pages 112–133. Cambridge Univerisity Press, Camebridge.

Sowmya Vajjala. 2018. Automated assessment of nonnative learner essays: Investigating the role of linguistic features. *International Journal of Artificial Intelligence in Education*, 28(1):79–105.

Sowmya Vajjala and Detmar Meurers. 2012. On improving the accuracy of readability classification using insights from second language acquisition. In *Proceedings of the 7th Workshop on Innovative Use of NLP for Building Educational Applications (BEA)*, pages 163–173, Montréal, Canada. ACL.

Cristina Vögelin, Thorben Jansen, Stefan D. Keller, Nils Machts, and Jens Möller. 2019. The influence of lexical features on teacher judgements of ESL argumentative essays. *Assessing Writing*, 39:50–63.

Zarah Weiss. 2017. Using measures of linguistic complexity to assess German L2 proficiency in learner corpora under consideration of task-effects. Master's thesis, University of Tübingen, Germany.

Zarah Weiss and Detmar Meurers. 2018. Modeling the readability of German targeting adults and children: An empirically broad analysis and its cross-corpus validation. In *Proceedings of the 27th International Conference on Computational Linguistics (COLING)*, Santa Fe, New Mexico, USA. International Committee on Computational Linguistic.

Zarah Weiss and Detmar Meurers. 2019. Analyzing linguistic complexity and accuracy in academic language development of German across elementary and secondary school. In *Proceedings of the 14th Workshop on Innovative Use of NLP for Building Educational Applications (BEA)*, Florence, Italy. Association for Computational Linguistics.

Zarah Weiss and Detmar Meurers. in press. Broad linguistic modeling is beneficial for German L2 proficiency assessment. In *Widening the Scope of Learner Corpus Research. Selected Papers from the Fourth Learner Corpus Research Conference*, Louvain-La-Neuve. Presses Universitaires de Louvain.

Stefanie A. Wind, Catanaya Stager, and Yogendra J. Patil. 2017. Exploring the relationship between textual characteristics and rating quality in rater-mediated writing assessments: An illustration with l1 and l2 writing assessments. *Assessing Writing*, 34:1–15.

Edward W. Wolfe, Tian Song, and Hong Jiao. 2016. Features of difficult-to-score essays. *Assessing Writing*, 27:1–10.

Kate Wolfe-Quintero, Shunji Inagaki, and Hae-Young Kim. 1998. *Second Language Development in Writing: Measures of Fluency, Accuracy & Complexity*. Second Language Teaching & Curriculum Center, University of Hawaii at Manoa, Honolulu.

Weiwei Yang, Xiaofei Lu, and Sara Cushing Weigle. 2015. Different topics, different discourse: Relationships among writing topic, measures of syntactic complexity, and judgments of writing quality. *Journal of Second Language Writing*, 28:53–67.

Helen Yannakoudakis, Øistein E. Andersen, Ardeshir Geranpayeh, Ted Briscoe, and Diane Nicholls. 2018. Developing an automated writing placement system for ESL learners. *Applied Measurement in Education*, 31(3):251–267.

Hyung-Jo Yoon. 2017. Linguistic complexity in L2 writing revisited: Issues of topic, proficiency, and construct multidimensionality. *System*, 66:130–141.

Hyung-Jo Yoon and Charlene Polio. 2016. The linguistic development of students of English as a second language in two written genres. *TESOL Quarterly*, pages 275–301.

A Appendix

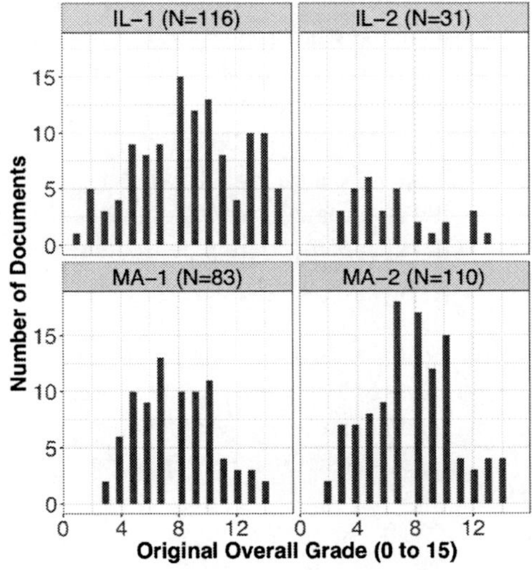

Figure 4: Original overall grades split by task prompt.

Task	Text Type	Description
IL-1	Interpretation of literature	Interpret poem *A* written in the 1950s and compare it with poem *B* written in the 1980s.
IL-2	Interpretation of literature	Interpret the given excerpt from novel *A*. Focus on the conflicts with which the protagonist struggles.
MA-1	Material-based argumentation	Write a newspaper essay on the influence social media has on our communication. Use around 1,000 words. Include the following materials in your argumentation: 6 essays, 1 poem, 1 statistic.
MA-2	Material-based argumentation	Write a newspaper commentary on the influence of dialects and sociolects on success in society. Use around 800 words. Include the following materials in your argumentation: 4 essays, 1 interview, 2 graphics.

Table 6: Overview of the four task prompts used to elicit the *Abitur* data.

Domain	Feature
Argumentation structure	Number of Paragraphs
	Adversative and concessive connectives (Breindl) per sentence
	Additive connectives (Breindl) per sentence
	Adversative connectives (Breindl) per sentence
	All connectives (Breindl) per sentence
	All multi word connectives (Breindl) per sentence
	All single word connectives (Breindl) per sentence
	Causal connectives (Breindl) per sentence
	Concessive connectives (Breindl) per sentence
	Other connectives (Breindl) per sentence
	Temporal connectives (Breindl) per sentence
	Adversative and concessive connectives (Eisenberg) per sentence
	Additive connectives (Eisenberg) per sentence,

41

	Adversative connectives (Eisenberg) per sentence
	All connectives (Eisenberg) per sentence
	All multi word connectives (Eisenberg) per sentence
	All single word connectives (Eisenberg) per sentence
	Causal connectives (Eisenberg) per sentence
	Concessive connectives (Eisenberg) per sentence
	Other connectives (Eisenberg) per sentence
	Temporal connectives (Eisenberg) per sentence
	Global argument overlap per sentence
	Global content overlap per sentence
	Global noun overlap per sentence
	Global stem overlap per sentence
	Local argument overlap per sentence
	Local content overlap per sentence
	Local noun overlap per sentence
	Local stem overlap per sentence
Lexical complexity	HDD
	MTLD
	TTR
	Bilogarithmic TTR
	Corrected TTR
	Root TTR
	Uber index
	Yule's K
	Adjectives and adverbs per lexical word
	Adjectives per lexical word
	Adverbs per lexical word
	Corrected lexical verb type per lexical per token
	haben instanced per verb
	Lexical types per lexical token
	Lexical types per token
	Lexical verb type per lexical token
	Lexical verb type per lexical verb token
	Lexical verb per token
	Nouns per lexical verb
	Lexical verbs per word
	Nouns per lexical word
	Nouns per word
	sein instances per verb
	Squared lexical verb types per lexical verb
	Verbs per noun
Syntactic complexity	Clauses per sentence
	Conjunctional clauses per sentence
	Dependent clauses per sentence
	Relative clauses per sentence
	Dependent clauses with conjunction per sentence
	Dependent clauses without conjunction per sentence
	Interrogative clauses per sentence
	Words per sentence
	Complex t-units per sentence
	Complex nominals per sentence

Postnominal modifiers per noun phrase
Prenominal modifiers per noun phrase
Noun phrase modifiers per noun phrase
Coverage of noun phrase modifier types
Verb modifiers per verb phrase
Coverage of verb modifier types
Coverage of verb cluster sizes
Coverage of verb cluster types
Standard deviation of verb cluster sizes
Mean verb cluster size
Coverage of Periphrastic tenses
Coverage of tenses
Coverage of deagentivization patterns

Table 7: List of all complexity features that are theoretically motivated by the German curriculum (KMK, 2014b).

Feature	IL-1	IL-2	MA-1	MA-2
MTLD	.2014	.4358	.2876	.3361
Root type token ratio	.3140	.3361	.3355	.2179
Corrected lexical verb types per lexical verb	*.2338*	.3103	.2105	*.2294*
Squared lexical verb types per lexical verb	.2588	*.3022*	.1998	.2458
Lexical verb types per lexical verb	.0587	.2257	.2291	.2446
Uber Index	.1153	.2412	.3131	*.2281*
Lexical word types found in dlexDB	-.3367	*-.4004*	-.1795	-.2597
Lexical word types not found in KCT	*.3901*	.4959	*.2770*	.1495
Clauses per sentence	*.2198*	.4681	.2304	-.0623
Dep. clauses per sentence	*.3040*	.2528	.2046	-.0380
Dep. clauses with conjunction per sentence	.3055	*.2013*	.2029	-.0484
Words per sentence	.3546	.4698	.2197	-.0403
Additive conn. per sentence (Breindl)	.2974	.2319	.2073	.1500
1-word conn. per sentence (Breindl)	*.2131*	.2855	*.2044*	.0745
Genitive case per noun phrase	.2853	.4689	.1869	*.2044*
-ung nominalizations per word	*.2080*	.4286	.1122	*.2339*
Derived nouns per noun phrase	*.2394*	.4751	.1604	.3301
Postnominal modifiers per noun phrase	.3064	.4510	.2031	.1113
Probability(other→other) per sentence	.1194	*.2077*	.1152	.3054
Probability(object→object) per sentence	-.1419	-.4929	.0545	*-.2068*
Global noun overlap per sentence	.2686	*.3072*	.1066	-.1590
Local content overlap per sentence	-.1359	-.2527	-.1725	-.3631
Global stem overlap per sentence	*.2587*	.4042	-.1162	-.0647
Temporal conn. per sentence (Breindl)	.2769	-.0185	.2206	.0408
Causal conn. per sentence (Eisenberg)	.3096	.3876	.0485	.0761
1-word conn. per sentence (Eisenberg)	*.2733*	.5241	.1068	.0275
Maximal total integration cost at finite verb (C)	*.2739*	.5062	-.0398	.0514
Average total integration cost at finite verb	.4093	*.4909*	.0708	.0308
Syll. between non-adjacent 1. argument & VFIN	.3158	*.2757*	.0210	.0815
Syllables in middle field per MF	.4244	.4286	.0351	.1092
Longest dependency in words	.3929	*.3207*	.0146	.1740
Prenominal modifiers per noun phrase	.2442	.5263	.0229	.1039
Possessive noun modifiers per NP	.2378	.4167	.1802	-.0308
Complex noun phrases per noun phrase	.4177	*.3186*	.1316	-.0353

43

Noun modifiers per noun phrase	.3357	*.2045*	.0689	.0648
NP deps. per NP with dependents	*.2855*	.4180	.1321	-.0798
Complex noun phrases per sentence	*.4177*	.3186	.1316	-.0353
Verb modifiers per verb phrase	.3565	.4219	.1761	.0375
Prepositional verb modifier per sentence	*.2184*	.4347	.0658	-.1204
Coordinated phrases per sentence	.3413	*.3299*	.0465	.1603
Average log type frequency in Google Books '00	-.4396	*-.4289*	-.1903	-.0994
Accusative case per noun phrase	-.3169	*-.2909*	-.0131	.0996
Lexical types per token	.2413	.1043	.0050	*.2446*
Verbs per noun	-.2213	-.3284	-.1294	-.1475
Nouns per lexical word	*-.2667*	.1709	.1916	.2415
Temporal conn. per sentence (Eisenberg)	.2225	.2244	.1665	-.2012
Determiners per noun phrase	-.3139	*.3066*	-.0006	.0023
Lexical verb types per lexical word	-.3142	-.0391	.1019	.0736
Yule's K	-.1144	-.2352	-.1663	-.0534
Lexical verbs per token	-.2667	-.1414	-.1022	-.0588
Adverbs per lexical word	-.0281	-.2781	-.0311	-.0401
Adjectives per lexical word	.1259	.3089	.1534	.0970
Dative case per noun phrase	-.1291	.1071	-.0440	-.3914
Third person markings per VFIN	-.0097	-.4361	-.1556	-.0727
-ist nominalizations per word	.0128	.4197	-.1266	.0122
Local argument overlap per sentence	.0547	-.1601	-.0256	-.2787
Local noun overlap per sentence	-.0007	-.0650	-.1356	-.2188
Causal conn. per sentence (Breindl)	.1512	.0658	.2936	-.0194
Concessive conn. per sentence (Eisenberg)	.0984	.2497	.0855	.0136
Other conn. per sentence (Breindl)	.1757	.2458	-.0343	.0181
Connectives per sentence (Eisenberg)	.1989	.3342	-.0400	.0386
Relative clauses per sentence	.3027	.1814	.1381	-.0077
Dep. clauses w/o conjunction per sentence	.1414	.2460	.0744	.0058
Conjunctional clauses per sentence	.1632	.2433	.0744	-.0285
Interrogative clauses per sentence	.0982	.4078	.0506	-.0574
Auxiliary verb cluster per verb cluster	.0460	.0569	-.0375	-.3221
haben instances per word	-.1818	-.2031	-.0251	-.1989
Coverage of verb cluster sizes	.1617	-.2824	-.1325	-.0088
Non-modal VP deps. per verb with dependents	.3219	.1250	.1804	.1116
Coverage of verb modifier types	.0758	.2216	.1706	.0119
Coverage of deagentivization patterns	.0763	.0227	.2020	-.0097
Passives per sentence	.1879	.4329	-.1692	-.0660
Average lemma frequency in dlexDB	-.4126	-.1037	-.1461	.0255
Average log lemma frequency in dlexDB	-.3890	-.1767	.0589	.0042
Hyponyms per type in GermaNet	-.3018	-.0741	-.1354	-.0926

Table 8: Features used in at least one of the four complexity document vectors and their correlation with the original overall grade across tasks. Gray font marks uncorrelated features. Italics mark relevant features that were excluded from the respective vector due to redundancy.

Task	Theory-Driven	Data-Driven	Total
IL-1	20	13	33
IL-2	32	13	45
MA-1	13	0	13
MA-2	9	4	13

Table 9: Contribution of theory- and data-driven feature selection to each language complexity vector.

Grade	Points	Percentage
excellent +	15	100–95
excellent	14	94–90
excellent -	13	89–85
good +	12	84–80
good	11	79–75
good -	10	74–70
satisfying +	9	69–65
satisfying	8	64–60
satisfying -	7	59–55
sufficient +	6	54–50
sufficient	5	49–45
sufficient -	4	44–40
insufficient +	3	39–33
insufficient	2	32–27
insufficient -	1	26–20
failed	0	19–0

Table 10: German *Abitur* Grading System (KMK, 2018, p. 22).

Analysing Rhetorical Structure as a
Key Feature of Summary Coherence

Jan Šnajder[1]   **Tamara Sladoljev-Agejev**[2]   **Svjetlana Kolić-Vehovec**[3]

[1] University of Zagreb, Faculty of Electrical Engineering and Computing, TakeLab
[2] University of Zagreb, Faculty of Economics and Business
[3] University of Rijeka, Faculty of Humanities and Social Sciences, Department of Psychology

`jan.snajder@fer.hr, tagejev@efzg.hr, skolic@ffri.hr`

Abstract

We present a model for automatic scoring of coherence based on comparing the rhetorical structure (RS) of college student summaries in L2 (English) against expert summaries. Coherence is conceptualised as a construct consisting of a rhetorical relation and its arguments. Comparison with expert-assigned scores shows that RS scores correlate with both cohesion and coherence. Furthermore, RS scores improve the accuracy of a regression model for cohesion score prediction.

1 Introduction

Assessment of text quality may benefit from automatic scoring as it is cognitively demanding and often requires much expertise (Rahimi et al., 2017), especially in college-level expository writing. One of the key aspects of text quality is writing coherence (Crossley and McNamara, 2010) which reflects students' ability to connect ideas in their mind and to convey the same message in essays or summaries (Halliday and Hasan, 2014).

Existing approaches to text quality predominantly focus on surface measures for assessment (e.g., number of cohesive devices), which sometimes have little relation either to human judgment, e.g., text length (Mintz et al., 2014), or to text-specific meaning (Rahimi et al., 2017). However, automatic scoring of coherence should ideally provide clear and reliable feedback (Burstein et al., 2013) based on features with cognitive validity, e.g., (Loukina et al., 2015).

One way to meet such requirements is to define coherence as the identification of relations between the text's ideas (Rapp et al., 2007). Such a definition may best be analysed in summaries in which the key ideas of the source text are integrated into a *rhetorical structure* (RS).

In cognitive terms, writing summaries is an exercise in *reading-for-understanding* (RU) (Sabatini et al., 2013) and gist reasoning (Chapman and Mudar, 2013). The result of such processes is the macrostructure of the source text constructed in the reader's mind (Louwerse and Graesser, 2005), which consists of concepts and propositions, their mutual relations (Sanders and Noordman, 2000), and relations with prior knowledge. Coherent summaries should express the intention of the source text (Hobbs, 1993) using linguistic devices (cohesion), which makes summarisation also a *reading-to-write* (RW) task (Delaney, 2008). Moreover, summaries have a distinctive feature for annotation: a largely shared knowledge base, i.e., the source text(s) known both to the writer and to the rater(s), which assists raters in their judgment and helps develop a reliable text-specific scoring tool.

In this paper we present a model for automatic scoring of summaries based on analysing a rhetorical structure of a student's summary compared to that of reference summaries. Our starting point is coherence conceptualized as a construct consisting of three elements: a rhetorical relation and its two arguments. We posit that expository text has a rhetorical structure (RS) consisting of a series of text-specific rhetorical segments, the majority of which will be conveyed in a coherent summary if full text-level comprehension is achieved. The model uses a discourse parser to extract rhetorical structures of summaries, and then compares similarity of these structures. We show that the scores produced by the model correlate with the expert-assigned cohesion and coherence scores as well as with surface indices of cohesion. We also show that the model-produced scores can be used to improve cohesion score prediction.

2 Related Work

Automatic assessment of text quality can include content, language accuracy, sophistication and style

Proceedings of the Fourteenth Workshop on Innovative Use of NLP for Building Educational Applications, pages 46–51
Florence, Italy, August 2, 2019. ©2019 Association for Computational Linguistics

as well as sometimes overlapping features such as topic similarity, focus, coherence, cohesion, readability, or text organisation and development, e.g., (Pitler et al., 2010; Yannakoudakis and Briscoe, 2012; Guo et al., 2013; Rahimi et al., 2015; Gao et al., 2018). Coherence is a broad concept assessed by different automatic tools, e.g., (Higgins et al., 2004; Yannakoudakis and Briscoe, 2012; Burstein et al., 2013). Scoring measures may include surface features such as word or text length or the number of pronouns and connectives, e.g., (Yannakoudakis and Briscoe, 2012; MacArthur et al., 2018), which may also be contextualised, e.g., (Pitler et al., 2010). Source overlaps may also be used in scoring such as overlapping n-grams in summaries (Madnani et al., 2013), and semantic similarity (e.g,. LSA) may provide information on relatedness between words, e.g., lexical chaining (Somasundaran et al., 2014), sentences (Foltz et al., 1998; Higgins et al., 2004; Higgins and Burstein, 2007), or larger text sections (Crossley and McNamara, 2010). Both types of features (surface and LSA) are encompassed by Coh-Metrix (Graesser et al., 2004; McNamara et al., 2014), a comprehensive computational tool using a range of measures to grasp cognitive aspects of text analysis. Moreover, inter-sentential coherence can be measured using syntax-based entity grids (Barzilay and Lapata, 2008), for example, to distinguish between high- and low-coherence essays (Burstein et al., 2010), or analysing discourse relations (Pitler and Nenkova, 2008; Skoufaki, 2009).

In order to improve the predictive value of automatic assessment, scoring measures are often combined. For example, Pitler and Nenkova (2008) use entity grids, syntactic features, discourse relations (Prasad et al., 2008), vocabulary, and length features. Yannakoudakis and Briscoe (2012) examine different measures and find that semantic similarity is the best addition to lexical and grammatical features. Somasundaran et al. (2014) combine lexical chains, grammar, word usage, mechanics, and RST discourse relations (Mann and Thompson, 1988) in L1 and L2 texts, while Higgins et al. (2004) use semantic similarity together with discourse structure to measure relatedness to the essay question and between discourse segments. More recently, Sladoljev-Agejev and Šnajder (2017) combine reference-based and linguistic features (e.g., Coh-Metrix, BLEU, ROUGE) to predict coherence and cohesion in college student summaries in L2.

The coherence assessment model presented here relies on summaries as a RU/RW task which consists of detecting and conveying the RS of the source text. Similar to Higgins et al. (2004), we use semantic similarity and rhetorical structure to assess coherence of student summaries against summaries written by experts. While Higgins et al. measured the coherence of functional discourse segments (e.g., thesis, conclusion) via semantic similarity between their respective sentences, in our study coherence is measured via similarity between rhetorical structures. Our intuition relies on the establishment of source macrostructure as a coherence-building exercise during reading. Such an approach appears to be cognitively valid and may ensure meaningful feedback both in terms of comprehension and writing skills development or assessment. Our model is constrained by the source content, so we also compare its performance to cohesion features provided by Coh-Metrix in (Sladoljev-Agejev and Šnajder, 2017) to assess generic RW skills.

3 Summary Scoring Model

The summary scoring model works by comparing the RS of a student summary against the rhetorical structures of one or more reference summaries. The model produces a score that indicates to what extent the two structures overlap.

Discourse parsing. To extract the rhetorical relations and their arguments, we use the PDTB-style parser of Lin et al. (2014), a state-of-the-art, end-to-end parser which labels instances of both implicit and explicit relations as well as their argument spans. The PDTB relation labels are organized in a three-level hierarchy of "sense tags" (Prasad et al., 2008). The parser recognizes the first two levels: relation Category (e.g., *Comparison*) and Type (e.g., *Contrast*). The end-to-end performance of the parser, measured as F1-score under partial argument matching, is 48%. The output of this step is, for each summary S, a set of rhetorical relations $\{r_i\}_i$, where $r_i = (l_i, a_i^1, a_i^2)$ is a relation of class/type label l_i, while a_i^1 and a_i^2 are text segments corresponding to its arguments.

Comparing rhetorical structures. When comparing the similarity of summaries' rhetorical structures, we want the model to assign high scores to pairs of summaries that have many rhetorical relations in common. Of course, we cannot expect the arguments of rhetorical relations to be literally the same, but, if two relations of the same label are to be considered equivalent, their corresponding arguments should be highly semantically similar. We formalize this intuition by defining the weight w_{ij} between a pair of rhetorical relations $r_i = (l_i, a_i^1, a_i^2)$ and $r_j = (l_j, a_j^1, a_j^2)$ as:

$$w_{ij} = \begin{cases} \frac{1}{2}\big(s(a_i^1, a_j^1) + s(a_i^2, a_j^2)\big) & \text{if } l_i = l_j, \\ 0 & \text{otherwise.} \end{cases}$$

where $s(\cdot, \cdot)$ is the semantic similarity between two text segments. In line with much of recent work, we rely on additive compositionality of word embeddings, and compute the semantic similarity as the cosine similarity between averaged word embeddings of the two segments. We use the 300-dimensional skip-gram word embeddings built on the Google-News corpus (Mikolov et al., 2013).[1]

To compute the overlap score between a pair of summaries S_1 and S_2, each consisting of a set of rhetorical relations, we use the maximum bipartite graph matching algorithm (Kuhn, 1955). The graph edges represent pairs of relations (r_i, r_j), $r_i \in S_1$, $r_j \in S_2$, weighted by w_{ij}. Let $n_1 = |S_1|$ and $n_2 = |S_2|$ be the number of rhetorical relations in S_1 and S_2, respectively, and m the maximum matching score between S_1 and S_2. We define the precision (P) and recall (R) of the match as:

$$P = \frac{m - \max(0, n_1 - n_2)}{n_1}$$
$$R = \frac{m - \max(0, n_2 - n_1)}{n_2}$$

The intuition is that precision is maximized if all relations from S_1 are perfectly matched to some relations from S_2, and conversely for recall. The F1-score is the harmonic mean of P and R. Finally, we compute the F1-score of a student's summary S as the mean of pairwise F1-scores between S and both reference summaries.

4 Evaluation

Dataset. For model evaluation, we adopt the dataset of (Sladoljev-Agejev and Šnajder, 2017). The dataset consists of a total of 225 text-present summaries (c. 300 words) of two articles written by 114 first-year business undergraduates in English as L2 (mostly upper intermediate and advanced). Both articles (c. 900 words each) were taken from The Economist, a business magazine. Two expert

raters used a 4-point analytic scale (grades 0–3) to assess the summaries in terms of coherence (RU) and cohesion (RW). The scales were quantified by defining the number of coherence and cohesion breaks. Descriptors for each grade included expressions such as "meaningfully related ideas" and "logical sequencing" (for coherence) and "linguistically connected text segments" (for cohesion). Inter-rater reliability (weighted kappas) was 0.69 for coherence and 0.83 for cohesion. The raters discussed and agreed on all the grades although reliability was adequate. As expected, we observe a strong correlation between coherence and cohesion scores (Spearman correlation coefficient of 0.64). All the summaries were checked for spelling and basic grammar. For the two articles from The Economist, two experts with considerable experience with business texts in English wrote 300-word summaries following the same instruction as the students.

Comparison with expert-assigned scores. To assess the validity of the summary scoring model, we measure the correlations of P, R, and F1 scores produced by the model against expert-provided coherence and cohesion scores, considering both Class and Type levels of PDTB relations. Table 1 shows the results. We can make several observations. First, while all the scores correlate positively with both cohesion and coherence, correlation for coherence is consistently lower, possibly due to the role of the raters' prior knowledge, which is unavailable to the model (also note that inter-annotator agreement is lower for coherence than for cohesion). Second, correlation for Type level is consistently lower than for Class level, which can probably be traced to the PDTB parser being less accurate on Type-level relations. Lastly, we note that the highest correlation with both cohesion and coherence is achieved with the F1-score of the Class level model. These results suggest that the proposed summary scoring model is at least partially successful in modeling both cohesion and coherence – and this in spite of the unavoidable errors of the PDTB parser and errors in similarity computations.

Comparison with Coh-Metrix indices. As mentioned in the introduction, a number of studies have used Coh-Metrix cohesion indices as predictors of both cohesion and coherence. In particular, Sladoljev-Agejev and Šnajder (2017) found

---

[1] https://code.google.com/archive/p/word2vec/

	Class Level			Type Level		
	P@C	R@C	F1@C	P@T	R@T	F1@T
Chs	0.218	0.320	**0.444**	0.207	0.295	0.426
Chr	*0.105*	0.297	**0.381**	*0.071*	0.257	0.337

Table 1: Spearman correlation coefficients between expert-assigned cohesion (Chs) and coherence (Chr) scores and model-produced scores (P, R, and F1) for Class and Type levels of PDTB connectives. The highest correlations for cohesion and correlation are shown in boldface. All correlations except those shown in italics are statistically significant (p<0.05).

	Expert scores		Model scores	
Coh-Metrix index	Chs	Chr	F1@C	F1@T
CNCAdd	0.375	0.229	**0.545**	**0.495**
CNCLogic	**0.453**	0.330	0.492	0.409
CNCAll	0.408	0.289	0.477	0.421
CRFAOa	0.430	**0.405**	0.342	0.320
CRFCWOa	0.416	0.364	0.278	0.278

Table 2: Spearman correlation coefficients between Coh-Metrix indices (connectives – CNC, referential cohesion – CRF) and expert-assigned cohesion (Chs) and coherence (Chr) scores as well as model-produced F1 scores at Class level (F1@C) and Type level (F1@T) of PDTB connectives. The highest correlations in each column are shown in boldface. All correlations are statistically significant (p<0.05).

modest correlation between expert-assigned coherence/cohesion and indices for connectives (additive connectives – CNCAdd, logical connectives – CNCLogic, and all connectives – CNCAll) and referential cohesion indices (mean of noun/pronoun overlaps between two sentences – CRFAOa, and content word overlap – CRFCWOA). It is therefore interesting to investigate to what extent these surface-level predictors correlate with the scores of our model. Table 2 gives Spearman correlation coefficients between the Coh-Metrix indices and expert-provided scores as well as the Class- and Type-level F1-scores of the model. The Coh-Metrix indices correlate positively with both the expert-assigned scores and the scores of our model. However, while CNCLogic and CRFOAo indices mostly correlate with the expert-assigned cohesion and coherence scores, respectively, the scores of our model mostly correlate with the CNCAdd index.

Supervised scoring. Following Sladoljev-Agejev and Šnajder (2017), we frame the automated

Model / Features	Chs	Chr
Baseline	0.369	0.361
Ridge / CM	0.489	0.409
Ridge / RS	0.476*	**0.419**
Ridge / CM+RS	**0.511***	0.414

Table 3: Accuracy of cohesion (Chs) and coherence (Chr) scores predictions for the baseline and ridge regression models with Coh-Metrix (CM), rhetorical structure (RS), and combined (CM+RS) feature sets. The best results are shown in bold. The "*" indicates a statistically significant difference to baseline (p<0.05, Wilcoxon signed-rank test). The differences between regression models with the CM feature set and models with RS and CM+RS feature sets are not statistically significant.

scoring as a multivariate regression task and use two regression models, one for cohesion and the other for coherence, each trained to predict the expert-assigned score on a 0–3 scale. We use an L2-regularized linear regression model (ridge regression)[2] and consider three sets of features: (1) five Coh-Metrix CNC and CRF indices ("CM"), (2) the F1-scores of the summary scoring model computed at Class and Type levels ("RS"), and (3) a combination of the two ("CM+RS"). We evaluate the models using a nested 10×5 cross-validation: the models' performance is measured in terms of accuracy averaged over the five outer folds, after rounding the predictions to closest integers and limiting the scores to the 0–3 range. All the features are z-scored on the train set, and the same transformation is applied on the test set. As baselines, we use the rounded average of the expert-assigned scores.

Table 3 shows the results. We can make three main observations. Firstly, cohesion models outperform the corresponding coherence models. Secondly, the only two models for which the differences against the baseline are statistically significant are the two cohesion models that use RS. This suggests that our model does provide useful signals for predicting expert-assigned cohesion scores. In the absence of statistical significance, the results for coherence are inconclusive, though we observe a similar trend.

5 Conclusion

We have described a model for coherence scoring based on a simple definition of coherence in line

---

[2]We use the implementation of Pedregosa et al. (2011).

with cognitive theories of text comprehension. The model produces scores that correlate with expert-assigned scores and improve the cohesion prediction of a regression model: a model that uses rhetorical structure scores as features yields a statistically significant improvement over the baseline of averaged expert-assigned scores. The proposed model could provide a basis for meaningful feedback in summaries and other similar tasks, and may also be used for measuring gist reasoning in case of a shared knowledge base between the rater and the examinee.

Acknowledgments

We thank Višnja Kabalin-Borenić for her contribution in the assessment of summaries analysed in this work.

References

Regina Barzilay and Mirella Lapata. 2008. Modeling local coherence: An entity-based approach. *Computational Linguistics*, 34(1):1–34.

Jill Burstein, Joel Tetreault, and Slava Andreyev. 2010. Using entity-based features to model coherence in student essays. In *Human language technologies: The 2010 annual conference of the North American chapter of the Association for Computational Linguistics*, pages 681–684.

Jill Burstein, Joel Tetreault, and Martin Chodorow. 2013. Holistic discourse coherence annotation for noisy essay writing. *Dialogue & Discourse*, 4(2):34–52.

Sandra Bond Chapman and Raksha Anand Mudar. 2013. Discourse gist: A window into the brains complex cognitive capacity. *Discourse Studies*, 15(5):519–533.

Scott Crossley and Danielle McNamara. 2010. Cohesion, coherence, and expert evaluations of writing proficiency. In *Proceedings of the Annual Meeting of the Cognitive Science Society*, volume 32.

Yuly Asencion Delaney. 2008. Investigating the reading-to-write construct. *Journal of English for Academic Purposes*, 7(3):140–150.

Peter W Foltz, Walter Kintsch, and Thomas K Landauer. 1998. The measurement of textual coherence with latent semantic analysis. *Discourse processes*, 25(2-3):285–307.

Yanjun Gao, Patricia M Davies, and Rebecca J Passonneau. 2018. Automated content analysis: A case study of computer science student summaries. In *Proceedings of the Thirteenth Workshop on Innovative Use of NLP for Building Educational Applications*, pages 264–272.

Arthur C. Graesser, Danielle S. McNamara, Max M. Louwerse, and Zhiqiang Cai. 2004. Coh-Metrix: Analysis of text on cohesion and language. *Behavior Research Methods*, 36(2):193–202.

Liang Guo, Scott A. Crossley, and Danielle S. McNamara. 2013. Predicting human judgments of essay quality in both integrated and independent second language writing samples: A comparison study. *Assessing Writing*, 18(3):218–238.

Michael Alexander Kirkwood Halliday and Ruqaiya Hasan. 2014. *Cohesion in English*. Routledge.

Derrick Higgins and Jill Burstein. 2007. Sentence similarity measures for essay coherence. In *Proceedings of the 7th International Workshop on Computational Semantics*, pages 1–12.

Derrick Higgins, Jill Burstein, Daniel Marcu, and Claudia Gentile. 2004. Evaluating multiple aspects of coherence in student essays. In *Proceedings of the Human Language Technology Conference of the North American Chapter of the Association for Computational Linguistics: HLT-NAACL 2004*.

Jerry R Hobbs. 1993. Intention, information, and structure in discourse: A first draft. In *Burning Issues in Discourse, NATO Advanced Research Workshop*, pages 41–66. Citeseer.

Harold W Kuhn. 1955. The hungarian method for the assignment problem. *Naval research logistics quarterly*, 2(1-2):83–97.

Ziheng Lin, Hwee Tou Ng, and Min-Yen Kan. 2014. A PDTB-styled end-to-end discourse parser. *Natural Language Engineering*, 20(2):151–184.

Anastassia Loukina, Klaus Zechner, Lei Chen, and Michael Heilman. 2015. Feature selection for automated speech scoring. In *Proceedings of the Tenth Workshop on Innovative Use of NLP for Building Educational Applications*, pages 12–19.

M. M. Louwerse and A. C. Graesser. 2005. Macrostructure. *Encyclopedia of Language and Linguistics*.

Charles A MacArthur, Amanda Jennings, and Zoi A Philippakos. 2018. Which linguistic features predict quality of argumentative writing for college basic writers, and how do those features change with instruction? *Reading and Writing*, pages 1–22.

Nitin Madnani, Jill Burstein, John Sabatini, and Tenaha O'Reilly. 2013. Automated scoring of a summary-writing task designed to measure reading comprehension. In *Proceedings of the Eighth Workshop on Innovative Use of NLP for Building Educational Applications*, pages 163–168. Association for Computational Linguistics.

William C Mann and Sandra A Thompson. 1988. Rhetorical structure theory: Toward a functional theory of text organization. *Text-Interdisciplinary Journal for the Study of Discourse*, 8(3):243–281.

Danielle S. McNamara, Arthur C. Graesser, Philip M. McCarthy, and Zhiqiang Cai. 2014. *Automated evaluation of text and discourse with Coh-Metrix*. Cambridge University Press.

Tomas Mikolov, Ilya Sutskever, Kai Chen, Greg S Corrado, and Jeff Dean. 2013. Distributed representations of words and phrases and their compositionality. In *Advances in neural information processing systems*, pages 3111–3119.

Lisa Mintz, Dan Stefanescu, Shi Feng, Sidney D'Mello, and Arthur Graesser. 2014. Automatic assessment of student reading comprehension from short summaries. In *Educational Data Mining 2014*.

Fabian Pedregosa, Gaël Varoquaux, Alexandre Gramfort, Vincent Michel, Bertrand Thirion, Olivier Grisel, Mathieu Blondel, Peter Prettenhofer, Ron Weiss, Vincent Dubourg, Jake Vanderplas, Alexandre Passos, David Cournapeau, Matthieu Brucher, Matthieu Perrot, and Edouard Duchesnay. 2011. Scikit-learn: Machine learning in Python. *Journal of Machine Learning Research*, 12(Oct):2825–2830.

Emily Pitler, Annie Louis, and Ani Nenkova. 2010. Automatic evaluation of linguistic quality in multi-document summarization. In *Proceedings of the 48th annual meeting of the Association for Computational Linguistics*, pages 544–554. Association for Computational Linguistics.

Emily Pitler and Ani Nenkova. 2008. Revisiting readability: A unified framework for predicting text quality. In *Proceedings of the conference on empirical methods in natural language processing*, pages 186–195. Association for Computational Linguistics.

Rashmi Prasad, Nikhil Dinesh, Alan Lee, Eleni Miltsakaki, Livio Robaldo, Aravind K Joshi, and Bonnie L Webber. 2008. The Penn discourse treebank 2.0. In *LREC*. Citeseer.

Zahra Rahimi, Diane Litman, Richard Correnti, Elaine Wang, and Lindsay Clare Matsumura. 2017. Assessing students' use of evidence and organization in response-to-text writing: Using natural language processing for rubric-based automated scoring. *International Journal of Artificial Intelligence in Education*, 27(4):694–728.

Zahra Rahimi, Diane J Litman, Elaine Wang, and Richard Correnti. 2015. Incorporating coherence of topics as a criterion in automatic response-to-text assessment of the organization of writing. In *Proceedings of the Tenth Workshop on Innovative Use of NLP for Building Educational Applications*, pages 20–30. Association for Computational Linguistics.

David N Rapp, Paul van den Broek, Kristen L McMaster, Panayiota Kendeou, and Christine A Espin. 2007. Higher-order comprehension processes in struggling readers: A perspective for research and intervention. *Scientific studies of reading*, 11(4):289–312.

John Sabatini, Tenaha O'Reilly, and Paul Deane. 2013. Preliminary reading literacy assessment framework: Foundation and rationale for assessment and system design. *ETS Research Report Series*, 2013(2).

Ted JM Sanders and Leo GM Noordman. 2000. The role of coherence relations and their linguistic markers in text processing. *Discourse processes*, 29(1):37–60.

Sophia Skoufaki. 2009. An exploratory application of rhetorical structure theory to detect coherence errors in L2 English writing: Possible implications for automated writing evaluation software. *International Journal of Computational Linguistics & Chinese Language Processing, Volume 14, Number 2, June 2009-Special Issue on Computer Assisted Language Learning*, 14(2).

Tamara Sladoljev-Agejev and Jan Šnajder. 2017. Using analytic scoring rubrics in the automatic assessment of college-level summary writing tasks in l2. In *Proceedings of the Eighth International Joint Conference on Natural Language Processing (Volume 2: Short Papers)*, pages 181–186.

Swapna Somasundaran, Jill Burstein, and Martin Chodorow. 2014. Lexical chaining for measuring discourse coherence quality in test-taker essays. In *Proceedings of COLING 2014, the 25th International conference on computational linguistics: Technical papers*, pages 950–961.

Helen Yannakoudakis and Ted Briscoe. 2012. Modeling coherence in ESOL learner texts. In *Proceedings of the Seventh Workshop on Building Educational Applications Using NLP*, pages 33–43. Association for Computational Linguistics.

The BEA-2019 Shared Task on Grammatical Error Correction

Christopher Bryant   **Mariano Felice**   **Øistein E. Andersen**   **Ted Briscoe**
ALTA Institute
Computer Laboratory
University of Cambridge
Cambridge, UK
`{cjb255,mf501,oa223,ejb}@cam.ac.uk`

Abstract

This paper reports on the BEA-2019 Shared Task on Grammatical Error Correction (GEC). As with the CoNLL-2014 shared task, participants are required to correct all types of errors in test data. One of the main contributions of the BEA-2019 shared task is the introduction of a new dataset, the Write&Improve+LOCNESS corpus, which represents a wider range of native and learner English levels and abilities. Another contribution is the introduction of tracks, which control the amount of annotated data available to participants. Systems are evaluated in terms of ERRANT $F_{0.5}$, which allows us to report a much wider range of performance statistics. The competition was hosted on Codalab and remains open for further submissions on the blind test set.

1 Introduction

The Building Educational Applications (BEA) 2019 Shared Task on Grammatical Error Correction (GEC) continues the tradition of the previous Helping Our Own (HOO) and Conference on Natural Language Learning (CoNLL) shared tasks (Dale and Kilgarriff, 2011; Dale et al., 2012; Ng et al., 2013, 2014) and was motivated by the need to re-evaluate the field after a five year hiatus. Although significant progress has been made since the end of the last CoNLL-2014 shared task, recent systems have been trained, tuned and tested on different combinations of metrics and corpora (Sakaguchi et al., 2017; Yannakoudakis et al., 2017; Chollampatt and Ng, 2018a; Ge et al., 2018; Grundkiewicz and Junczys-Dowmunt, 2018; Junczys-Dowmunt et al., 2018; Lichtarge et al., 2018; Zhao et al., 2019). Thus one of the main aims of the BEA-2019 shared task is to once again provide a platform where systems can be re-evaluated under more controlled conditions.

With this in mind, another significant contribution of the BEA-2019 shared task is the introduction of a new annotated dataset, the Cambridge English Write & Improve (W&I) and LOCNESS corpus, which is designed to represent a much wider range of English levels and abilities than previous corpora. This is significant because systems have traditionally only been tested on the CoNLL-2014 test set, which only contains 50 essays (1,312 sentences) on 2 different topics written by 25 South-East Asian undergraduates (Ng et al., 2014). In contrast, the W&I+LOCNESS test set contains 350 essays (4,477 sentences) on approximately 50 topics written by 334 authors from around the world (including native English speakers). We hope that this diversity will encourage the development of systems that can generalise better to unseen data.

Another difference to the previous shared tasks is the introduction of tracks; namely the Restricted, Unrestricted and Low Resource track. While annotated data was comparatively scarce five years ago, it has since become more available, so we can now control what resources participants have access to. The Restricted track is closest to the original shared tasks, in that we specify precisely which annotated learner datasets participants should use, while the Unrestricted track allows use of any and all available datasets. The Low Resource track, in contrast, significantly limits the amount of annotated data available to participants and encourages development of systems that do not rely on large quantities of human-annotated sentences. A goal of the Low Resource track is thus to facilitate research into GEC for languages where annotated training corpora do not exist.

Like CoNLL-2014, the main evaluation metric was $F_{0.5}$, which weights precision twice as much as recall. Unlike CoNLL-2014 however, this

Proceedings of the Fourteenth Workshop on Innovative Use of NLP for Building Educational Applications, pages 52–75
Florence, Italy, August 2, 2019. ©2019 Association for Computational Linguistics

	A	B	C	N	Total
Train					
Texts	1,300	1,000	700	-	3,000
Sentences	10,493	13,032	10,783	-	34,308
Tokens	183,684	238,112	206,924	-	628,720
Dev					
Texts	130	100	70	50	350
Sentences	1,037	1,290	1,069	998	4,384
Tokens	18,691	23,725	21,440	23,117	86,973
Test					
Texts	130	100	70	50	350
Sentences	1,107	1,330	1,010	1,030	4,477
Tokens	18,905	23,667	19,953	23,143	85,668
Total					
Texts	1,560	1,200	840	100	3,700
Sentences	12,637	15,652	12,862	2,018	43,169
Tokens	221,280	285,504	248,317	46,260	801.361

Table 2: W&I (A, B, C) and LOCNESS (N) corpus statistics.

Input	Travel by bus is exspensive , bored and annoying .
Output	Travelling by bus is expensive , boring and annoying .

Table 1: An example input and output sentence.

is calculated using the ERRANT scorer (Bryant et al., 2017), rather than the M^2 scorer (Dahlmeier and Ng, 2012), because the ERRANT scorer can provide much more detailed feedback, e.g. in terms of performance on specific error types. Official evaluation is carried out on the Codalab competition platform, where a separate competition is created for each track. More details and links can be found on the official shared task website.[1]

The remainder of this report is structured as followed. Section 2 first summarises the task instructions and lists exactly what participants are asked to do. Section 3 next introduces the new W&I+LOCNESS corpus and describes how it was compiled. Section 3 also describes the other corpora that allowed in the shared task, including their formats and how they were standardised, and reports on a cross-corpora error type comparison for the first time. Section 4 next outlines each of the tracks and their restrictions, while Section 5 discusses the evaluation procedure. Section 6 next introduces the shared task participants and summarises each of their approaches, before Section 7 presents and analyses the final results. Appendix A contains more details about corpora and results.

2 Task Instructions

Participants are required to correct all grammatical, lexical and orthographic errors in written plain text files, one tokenised sentence per line, and are asked to produce equivalent corrected text files as output (Table 1). All text is tokenised using spaCy v1.9.0 and the `en_core_web_sm-1.2.0` model.[2]

Having produced a corrected text file, participants can then upload it to Codalab where it is automatically evaluated and a score returned. This procedure is the same for all tracks.

3 Data

This shared task introduces new annotated datasets: the Cambridge English Write & Improve (W&I) and LOCNESS corpus.

3.1 Cambridge English Write & Improve

Write & Improve[3] is an online web platform that assists non-native English students with their writing (Yannakoudakis et al., 2018). Specifically, students from around the world submit letters, stories, articles and essays in response to various prompts, and the W&I system provides automated feedback. Since 2014, W&I annotators have manually annotated some of these submissions with corrections and CEFR ability levels (Little, 2006).

3.1.1 Corpus Compilation

Although users can submit any kind of text to the Write & Improve system, texts are first filtered before they are sent to the annotators to remove, for example, essay fragments, technical essays, copied website text, and non-English text. Although different versions of the same essays may be annotated to build up an annotated essay revision history, we only selected final revisions for inclusion in the W&I corpus.

We also ignored essays that met at least one of the following conditions:

- The text contained fewer than 33 words.

- More than 1.5% of all characters in the text were non-ASCII.

- More than 60% of all non-empty lines were both shorter than 150 characters and did not end with punctuation.

[1] https://www.cl.cam.ac.uk/research/nl/bea2019st/

[2] https://spacy.io/

[3] https://writeandimprove.com/

The precise values of these conditions were tuned manually such that they prioritised 'cleaner' texts while maintaining a large enough pool at each CEFR level. The last condition was designed to filter out texts that had been formatted to fit within a certain page width and so contained explicit new lines; e.g. "This is a \n broken sentence." Such sentences were often tokenised incorrectly.

Since evaluation in GEC is typically carried out at the sentence level, we also wanted to make sure there was an even distribution of sentences at each CEFR level. We thus split the data on this basis, taking into account the fact that beginner essays tend to be shorter than more advanced essays. As CEFR levels are originally assigned at the essay level, sentence level CEFR labels are an approximation, and it is possible that the same sentence might receive a different label in a different text.

We ultimately selected 3,600 annotated submissions from W&I, which we distributed across training, development and test sets as shown in Table 2. We additionally annotated the test set a total of 5 times to better account for alternative corrections (cf. Bryant and Ng, 2015).

3.2 LOCNESS

Since most GEC research has traditionally focused on non-native errors, we also wanted to incorporate some native errors into the shared task. To do this, we used the LOCNESS corpus, a collection of approximately 400 essays written by native British and American undergraduates on various topics (Granger, 1998).[4]

Since these essays were typically much longer than the texts submitted to Write & Improve, we first filtered them to remove essays longer than 550 words. We also removed essays that contained transcription issue XML tags, such as `<quotation>` and `<illegible>`.

There are not enough essays to create an annotated LOCNESS training set, so we extracted a development and test set which was annotated by the W&I annotators. Like the W&I corpus, we also controlled the amount of native data in each set in terms of sentences to ensure a roughly even distribution at all levels. The test split was again annotated a total of 5 times to match the W&I test

---

	Sentences	Tokens
FCE-train	28,350	454,736
FCE-dev	2,191	34,748
FCE-test	2,695	41,932
Lang-8	1,037,561	11,857,938
NUCLE	57,151	1,161,567

Table 3: FCE, Lang-8 and NUCLE corpus statistics.

set. The statistics of this dataset are also shown in Table 2.

3.3 Other Corpora

We allow the use of several existing learner corpora in the Restricted track of the shared task. Since these corpora were previously only available in different formats, we make new standardised versions available with the shared task (Table 3).

FCE The First Certificate in English (FCE) corpus is a subset of the Cambridge Learner Corpus (CLC) that contains 1,244 written answers to FCE exam questions (Yannakoudakis et al., 2011).

Lang-8 Corpus of Learner English Lang-8 is an online language learning website which encourages users to correct each other's grammar. The Lang-8 Corpus of Learner English is a somewhat-clean, English subset of this website (Mizumoto et al., 2012; Tajiri et al., 2012). It is distinct from the raw, multilingual Lang-8 Learner Corpus.

NUCLE The National University of Singapore Corpus of Learner English (NUCLE) consists of 1,400 essays written by mainly Asian undergraduate students at the National University of Singapore (Dahlmeier et al., 2013). It is the official training corpus for the CoNLL-2013 and CoNLL-2014 shared tasks.

3.4 Corpus Standardisation

Since FCE and NUCLE were annotated according to different error type frameworks and Lang-8 and W&I+LOCNESS were not annotated with error types at all, we re-annotated all corpora automatically using ERRANT (Bryant et al., 2017). Specifically, we:

1. Tokenised the FCE and W&I+LOCNESS using spaCy v1.9.0. Lang-8 and NUCLE were pre-tokenised.

---

[4]https://uclouvain.be/en/
research-institutes/ilc/cecl/locness.
html

2. Used ERRANT to automatically classify the human edits in parallel FCE, NUCLE and W&I+LOCNESS sentences.

3. Used ERRANT to automatically extract and classify the edits in parallel Lang-8 sentences.

Note that as Lang-8 is not annotated with explicit edits, it only consists of parallel sentence pairs. We consequently used ERRANT to align the sentences and extract the edits automatically. While we could have also done the same for the other corpora, we instead chose to preserve and re-classify the existing human edits. Table 4 thus shows the ERRANT error type distributions for all these corpora, and makes them comparable for the first time.

In terms of edit operations, all corpora are fairly consistent with respect to the distribution of Missing (M) Replacement (R) and Unnecessary (U) word edits. Replacement edits are by far the most frequent category and account for roughly 60-65% of all edits in all datasets. Missing word edits account for roughly 20-25% of remaining edits, although this figure is noticeably lower in FCE and NUCLE. Unnecessary word edits account for 10-15% of all edits, although this figure rises to almost 20% in NUCLE. One possible explanation for this is that the NUCLE corpus also has more determiner (DET) errors, which are known to be problematic for Asian learners. Each corpus also contains roughly 2-3% of Unknown (UNK) edits that annotators identified but were unable to correct. UNK edits do not exist in Lang-8 because it was never annotated with edit spans.

NUCLE contains more than twice the proportion of noun number (NOUN:NUM) errors compared to the other corpora. This is possibly because noun number was one of the five error types targeted in the CoNLL-2013 shared task. Annotator focus might also account for the slightly higher proportion of determiner and subject-verb agreement (SVA) errors, which were also among the five targeted error types.

There is a significant difference in the proportion of punctuation (PUNCT) errors across corpora. Punctuation errors account for just 5% of all errors in NUCLE, but almost 20% in W&I. This is possibly because W&I contains data from a much wider range of learners than the other corpora. A similar pattern is observed with other (OTHER) errors, which account for over 25% of all errors

```
S This are a sentence .
A 1 2|||R:VERB:SVA|||is|||-REQUIRED-|||NONE|||0
A 3 3|||M:ADJ|||good|||-REQUIRED-|||NONE|||0
A 1 2|||R:VERB:SVA|||is|||-REQUIRED-|||NONE|||1
A -1 -1|||noop|||-NONE-|||REQUIRED|||-NONE-|||2
```

Figure 1: Example M2 format with multiple annotators.

in NUCLE and Lang-8, but roughly 13% of all errors in the FCE and W&I+LOCNESS. We surmise this is because edits are longer and noisier in the first two corpora (cf. Felice et al., 2016) and so do not fit into a more discriminative ERRANT error category.

3.5 Data Formats

All the above corpora are released in M2 format, the standard format for annotated GEC files since the CoNLL-2013 shared task. The FCE and W&I+LOCNESS corpora are additionally released in an untokenised JSON format in case researchers want to inspect the raw data.

In M2 format (Figure 1), a line preceded by S denotes an original sentence while a line preceded by A indicates an edit annotation. Each edit line consists of the start and end token offsets of the edit, the error type, the tokenised correction string, a flag indicating whether the edit is required or optional, a comment field, and a unique annotator ID. The penultimate two fields are rarely used in practice however.

A 'noop' edit explicitly indicates when an annotator/system made no changes to the original sentence. If there is only one annotator, noop edits are optional, otherwise a noop edit should be included whenever at least 1 out of n annotators considered the original sentence to be correct. This is something to be aware of when combining individual M2 files, as missing noops can affect results.

Figure 1 can thus be interpreted as follows:

- Annotator 0 changed "are" to "is" and inserted "good" before "sentence" to produce the correction: "This is a good sentence ."

- Annotator 1 changed "are" to "is" to produce the correction: "This is a sentence ."

- Annotator 2 thought the original was correct and made no changes to the sentence: "This are a sentence ."

Type	FCE (all) %	Lang-8 %	NUCLE %	W&I+LOCNESS Train %	W&I+LOCNESS Dev %	W&I+LOCNESS Test %
M	21.00	26.41	19.09	25.29	26.32	24.86
R	64.39	59.99	59.04	61.43	61.23	63.40
U	11.47	13.60	19.31	10.69	10.21	10.34
UNK	3.13	0.00	2.57	2.59	2.24	1.41
ADJ	1.36	1.25	1.58	1.52	1.48	1.05
ADJ:FORM	0.28	0.19	0.27	0.24	0.21	0.18
ADV	1.94	3.37	1.95	1.51	1.51	1.45
CONJ	0.67	0.98	0.71	0.51	0.58	0.75
CONTR	0.32	0.99	0.11	0.30	0.39	0.32
DET	10.86	11.93	15.98	11.25	10.43	10.41
MORPH	1.90	1.62	3.14	1.85	2.07	2.50
NOUN	4.57	4.51	3.80	4.36	4.30	2.89
NOUN:INFL	0.50	0.18	0.12	0.12	0.13	0.28
NOUN:NUM	3.34	4.28	8.13	4.05	3.29	4.07
NOUN:POSS	0.51	0.35	0.61	0.60	0.87	0.93
ORTH	2.94	3.99	1.62	4.77	4.61	8.03
OTHER	13.26	26.62	25.65	12.76	12.84	15.69
PART	0.29	0.50	0.46	0.84	0.79	0.49
PREP	11.21	8.00	7.69	9.79	9.70	8.33
PRON	3.51	2.72	1.26	2.64	2.33	2.45
PUNCT	9.71	6.06	5.16	17.16	19.37	16.73
SPELL	9.59	4.45	0.26	3.74	5.07	4.63
UNK	3.13	0.00	2.57	2.59	2.24	1.41
VERB	7.01	6.52	4.31	5.86	5.27	5.09
VERB:FORM	3.55	2.56	3.49	3.56	3.09	3.10
VERB:INFL	0.19	0.15	0.01	0.04	0.07	0.12
VERB:SVA	1.52	1.58	3.47	2.23	1.94	2.28
VERB:TENSE	6.04	6.03	7.01	6.07	6.20	5.43
WO	1.82	1.18	0.66	1.64	1.25	1.40
Total Edits	52,671	1,400,902	44,482	63,683	7,632	-

Table 4: The ERRANT error type distributions of the FCE, Lang-8, NUCLE and W&I+LOCNESS corpora. See Bryant et al. (2017) for more information about each error type. The distribution of the W&I+LOCNESS test data is averaged across all 5 annotators.

4 Tracks

As parallel training data is now more readily available, a new feature of the BEA-2019 shared task is the introduction of three tracks: Restricted, Unrestricted and Low Resource. Each track controls the amount of *annotated* data that is available to participants. We place no restriction on the amount of *unannotated* data (e.g. for language modelling) or NLP tools (e.g. POS taggers, parsers, spellcheckers, etc.), provided the resources are publicly available.

4.1 Restricted Track

The Restricted Track is most similar to the previous shared tasks in that participants are limited to using only the official datasets as annotated training data (i.e. the FCE, Lang-8, NUCLE and W&I+LOCNESS). Since we do not limit unannotated data however, system submissions are still not entirely comparable given that they might use, for example, different amounts of monolingual or artificially-generated data.

4.2 Unrestricted Track

The Unrestricted Track is the same as the Restricted Track except participants may use any and all datasets and resources to build systems, including proprietary datasets and software. The main aim of this track is to determine how much better a system can do if it has access to potentially much larger amounts of data and/or resources.

4.3 Low Resource Track

The Low Resource Track is the same as the Restricted Track, except participants are only allowed to use the W&I+LOCNESS development set as annotated learner data. Since current GEC systems exploit as much annotated data as possible to reach the best performance, we hope this track will motivate work in GEC for other languages. We place no restriction on how participants use the W&I+LOCNESS development set; e.g. as a seed corpus to generate artificial data or to tune parameters to the shared task.

5 Evaluation

Systems are evaluated on the W&I+LOCNESS test set using the ERRANT scorer (Bryant et al., 2017), an improved version of the MaxMatch scorer (Dahlmeier and Ng, 2012) that was previously used in the CoNLL shared tasks. As in the previous shared tasks, this means that system performance is primarily measured in terms of span-based correction using the $F_{0.5}$ metric, which weights precision twice as much as recall.

In span-based correction, a system is only rewarded if a system edit exactly matches a reference edit in terms of both its token offsets and correction string. If more than one set of reference edits are available (there were 2 in CoNLL-2014 and 5 in BEA-2019), ERRANT chooses the reference that maximises the global $F_{0.5}$ score, or else maximises true positives and minimises false positives and false negatives. ERRANT is also able to report performance in terms of span-based detection and token-based detection (Table 5).

Although the W&I+LOCNESS training and development sets are released as separate files for each CEFR level, the test set texts are combined and shuffled such that the sentence order in each essay is preserved, but the order of the CEFR levels is random. This is done because systems should not expect to know the CEFR level of an input text in advance and should hence be prepared to handle all levels and abilities. In Section 7, we nevertheless also report system performance in terms of different CEFR and native levels, as well as in terms of detection and error types.

5.1 Metric Justification

Since robust evaluation is still a hot topic in GEC (cf. Asano et al., 2017; Choshen and Abend, 2018), we also wanted to provide some additional evidence that ERRANT $F_{0.5}$ is as reliable as MaxMatch $F_{0.5}$ and other popular metrics (Felice and Briscoe, 2015; Napoles et al., 2015). We evaluated ERRANT in relation to human judgements on the CoNLL-2014 test set using the same setup as Chollampatt and Ng (2018b), and found similar correlation coefficients (Table 6). Although this table shows that no metric is superior in all settings, the main advantage of ERRANT is that it can also provide much more detailed feedback than the alternatives; e.g. in terms of error types. We hope that researchers can make use of this information to build better systems.

6 Participants and Approaches

A total of 24 different teams took part in the BEA-2019 shared task across all 3 tracks. Of these, 21 submitted to the Restricted Track, 7 submitted to the Unrestricted Track, and 9 submitted to the Low Resource Track. This also meant 7 teams submitted to 2 separate tracks while 3 teams submitted to all 3 tracks.

Only 14 teams submitted system description papers however, with a further 4 sending short descriptions by email. The full list of teams, their approaches, and the data and resources they used in each track are shown in Table 8 (Appendix A.1). We refer the reader to the system description papers (where available) for more detailed information. Additionally: i) although Buffalo submitted to all 3 tracks, their paper does not describe their Low Resource system, ii) LAIX submitted exactly the same system to both the Restricted and Unrestricted Track, and iii) TMU submitted 2 separate papers about their respective Restricted and Low Resource Track systems.

While past GEC systems have employed different approaches, e.g. rules, classifiers, and statistical machine translation (SMT), in contrast, approximately two-thirds of all teams in the BEA-2019 shared task[5] used transformer-based neural machine translation (NMT) (Vaswani et al., 2017), while the remainder used convolutional neural networks (CNN), or both. Although they were most likely inspired by Junczys-Dowmunt et al. (2018) and Chollampatt and Ng (2018a), who previously reported state-of-the-art results on the CoNLL-2014 test set, the main consequence of this is that systems could only be differentiated based on lower-level system properties, such as:

- How much artificial data was used, if any, and how it was generated.

- How much over-sampled data was used, if any, and in what proportion.

- How many models were combined or ensembled.

- Whether system output was re-ranked.

- Whether the system contained an error detection component.

---

[5]Based on those that submitted system descriptions.

Original	I often look at TV	**Span-based**	**Span-based**	**Token-based**
Reference	[2, 4, watch]	**Correction**	**Detection**	**Detection**
Hypothesis 1	[2, 4, watch]	Match	Match	Match
Hypothesis 2	[2, 4, see]	No match	Match	Match
Hypothesis 3	[2, 3, watch]	No match	No match	Match

Table 5: Different types of evaluation in ERRANT.

	Corpus		**Sentence**
Metric	**Pearson r**	**Spearman** ρ	**Kendall** τ
ERRANT	0.64	0.626	0.623
M^2	0.623	0.687	0.617
GLEU	0.691	0.407	0.567
I-measure	-0.25	-0.385	0.564

Table 6: Correlation between various evaluation metrics and human judgements.

For example, Shuyao, UEDIN-MS and Kakao&Brain respectively trained their systems on 145 million, 100 million and 45 million artificial sentences, while CAMB-CUED instead concentrated on optimising the ratio of official to artificial sentences. TMU meanwhile focused entirely on re-ranking in their Restricted Track system, and AIP-Tohoku, CAMB-CLED, Web-SpellChecker and YDGEC each incorporated sentence and/or token based detection components into their systems. Since most systems used different combinations of similar techniques, it is difficult to determine which were most successful. For example, several teams used artificial data, but they each generated it using different methods and corpora, so it is unclear which method performed best with respect to all the other uncontrolled system variables.

For the Low Resource track, many teams submitted the same Restricted Track systems except trained with the WikEd Corpus (Grundkiewicz and Junczys-Dowmunt, 2014) or other Wikipedia-based revision data. Notable exceptions include CAMB-CUED, who used Finite State Transducers (FST) to rank confusion sets with a language model; LAIX, who augmented their transformer NMT model with a series of 8 error-type specific classifiers; and TMU, who mapped 'cross-lingual' word embeddings to the same space to induce a phrase table for a SMT system. These systems hence represent promising alternatives in a heavily transformer NMT dominated shared task.

7   Results

All system output submitted to Codalab during the test phase was automatically annotated with ERRANT and compared against the gold standard references. Although this meant there was a mismatch between the automatically annotated hypotheses and the human annotated gold references, we deliberately chose this setting to remain faithful to the gold-standard training data and previous shared tasks. See Appendix A.7 for more on comparing gold and automatic references.

We also set a limit of a maximum of 2 submissions during the test phase to prevent teams from optimising on the test set. The best results, in terms of span-based correction ERRANT $F_{0.5}$, are used for the official BEA-2019 shared task results, and all scores are presented in Table 7.

7.1   Restricted Track - Overall

Since many teams used very similar approaches, it may be unsurprising that many of the Restricted Track scores were very similar. For example, the $F_{0.5}$ difference between the teams that ranked 3-5 was 0.17%, and the precision difference between the teams that ranked 4-6 was 0.47%. We thus carried out significance tests between all teams in each track using the bootstrap method (Efron and Tibshirani, 1993) based on $F_{0.5}$ (1,000 iterations, $p > .05$), and grouped systems that were not significantly different. The resulting groups showed that, for example, there was no significant difference between the top 2 teams and that the top 11 teams fit into 4 statistically significant groups. Groups were defined such that all teams in each group were statistically similar. This means, for example, that although ML@IITB was similar to YDGEC, it was different from Shuyao and the other teams in Group 2, and so was placed in Group 3 instead.

The top 2 teams in Group 1 scored significantly higher than all the teams in Group 2 most likely because both these teams 1) trained their systems on artificial data generated using error type distri-

Restricted

Group	Rank	Teams	TP	FP	FN	P	R	$F_{0.5}$
1	1	UEDIN-MS	3127	1199	**2074**	72.28	60.12	**69.47**
	2	Kakao&Brain	2709	894	2510	**75.19**	51.91	69.00
2	3	LAIX	2618	960	2671	73.17	49.50	66.78
	4	CAMB-CLED	2924	1224	2386	70.49	55.07	66.75
	5	Shuyao	2926	1244	2357	70.17	55.39	66.61
	6	YDGEC	2815	1205	2487	70.02	53.09	65.83
3	7	ML@IITB	**3678**	1920	2340	65.70	**61.12**	64.73
	8	CAMB-CUED	2929	1459	2502	66.75	53.93	63.72
4	9	AIP-Tohoku	1972	902	2705	68.62	42.16	60.97
	10	UFAL	1941	942	2867	67.33	40.37	59.39
	11	CVTE-NLP	1739	811	2744	68.20	38.79	59.22
5	12	BLCU	2554	1646	2432	60.81	51.22	58.62
6	13	IBM	1819	1044	3047	63.53	37.38	55.74
7	14	TMU	2720	2325	2546	53.91	51.65	53.45
	15	qiuwenbo	1428	854	2968	62.58	32.48	52.80
8	16	NLG-NTU	1833	1873	2939	49.46	38.41	46.77
	17	CAI	2002	2168	2759	48.01	42.05	46.69
	18	PKU	1401	1265	2955	52.55	32.16	46.64
9	19	SolomonLab	1760	2161	2678	44.89	39.66	43.73
10	20	Buffalo	604	**350**	3311	63.31	15.43	39.06
11	21	Ramaiah	829	7656	3516	9.77	19.08	10.83

Unrestricted

Group	Rank	Teams	TP	FP	FN	P	R	$F_{0.5}$
1	1	LAIX	2618	960	2671	**73.17**	49.50	**66.78**
	2	AIP-Tohoku	2589	1078	2484	70.60	51.03	65.57
2	3	UFAL	2812	1313	2469	68.17	53.25	64.55
3	4	BLCU	**3051**	2007	**2357**	60.32	**56.42**	59.50
4	5	Aparecium	1585	1077	2787	59.54	36.25	52.76
5	6	Buffalo	699	**374**	3265	65.14	17.63	42.33
6	7	Ramaiah	1161	8062	3480	12.59	25.02	13.98

Low Resource

Group	Rank	Teams	TP	FP	FN	P	R	$F_{0.5}$
1	1	UEDIN-MS	2312	982	**2506**	70.19	47.99	**64.24**
2	2	Kakao&Brain	**2412**	1413	2797	63.06	46.30	58.80
3	3	LAIX	1443	**884**	3175	62.01	31.25	51.81
	4	CAMB-CUED	1814	1450	2956	55.58	38.03	50.88
4	5	UFAL	1245	1222	2993	50.47	29.38	44.13
5	6	Siteimprove	1299	1619	3199	44.52	28.88	40.17
	7	WebSpellChecker	2363	3719	3031	38.85	43.81	39.75
6	8	TMU	1638	4314	3486	27.52	31.97	28.31
7	9	Buffalo	446	1243	3556	26.41	11.14	20.73

Table 7: Official BEA-2019 results for all teams in all tracks using the main overall span-based correction ER-RANT $F_{0.5}$. The highest values (lowest for False Positives and False Negatives) are shown in bold.

butions and confusion sets, and 2) re-ranked their system output. In contrast, Shuyao used a similar method to generate artificial data, but did not re-rank, while CAMB-CLED used back-translation to generate artificial data, but did re-rank. This suggests that confusion set approaches to artificial data generation are more successful than back-translated approaches.

7.2 Unrestricted Track - Overall

Since participants were allowed to use any and all datasets in the Unrestricted Track, we expected scores to be higher, but the highest scoring team actually submitted exactly the same system to the Unrestricted Track as they did to the Restricted Track. The top 2 teams in the Restricted Track could thus also have scored highest on this track if they did the same.

Of the remaining teams, AIP-Tohoku and UFAL increased their scores by approximately 5 $F_{0.5}$ using non-public Lang-8 and parallel Wikipedia data respectively, BLCU added a more modest 1 $F_{0.5}$ similarly using non-public Lang-8 data, and Buffalo added roughly 3 $F_{0.5}$ using artificial data generated from a subsection of the English Gigaword corpus (Graff and Cieri, 2003). While it is unsurprising that larger quantities of training data tended to lead to higher scores, these results help quantify the extent to which performance can be improved by simply adding more data.

7.3 Low Resource Track - Overall

The teams that came top of the Restricted Track also dominated in the Low Resource Track. The UEDIN-MS system even outperformed 14 of the Restricted Track submissions despite the limited training data. This is most likely because UEDIN-MS and Kakao&Brain both made effective use of artificial data.

The CAMB-CUED system also achieved a fairly competitive score despite not using any parallel training data. This contrasts with LAIX, who scored higher by 1 $F_{0.5}$ using a complicated system of classifiers, CNNs and transformer NMT models. The TMU system is also notable for applying techniques from unsupervised SMT to GEC for the first time (cf. Artetxe et al., 2018). Although it performed poorly overall, it took several years to adapt supervised SMT to GEC (Junczys-Dowmunt and Grundkiewicz, 2016), so we hope researchers will continue to explore unsupervised SMT in future work.

8 Conclusion

It is undeniable that significant progress has been made since the last shared task on grammatical error correction five years ago. Transformer based neural machine translation proved effective, and teams generally scored significantly higher in BEA-2019 than in the previous CoNLL-2014 shared task. This is significant because we also introduced a new corpus, the Cambridge English Write & Improve + LOCNESS corpus, which contains a much wider range of texts at different ability levels than previous corpora, yet systems still generalised well to this much more diverse dataset.

Overall, the most successful systems were submitted by UEDIN-MS (Grundkiewicz et al., 2019) and Kakao&Brain (Choe et al., 2019) who respectively ranked first and second in both the Restricted and Low Resource Tracks. UEDIN-MS additionally scored just 5 $F_{0.5}$ lower in the Low Resource Track (64.24) than the Restricted Track (69.47), which shows that it is possible to build a competitive GEC system without large quantities of human annotated training data.

Finally, we note that the appendix contains a much more fine-grained analysis of system performance in terms of CEFR levels, edit operations, error types, single vs. multi token errors, detection vs. correction, and a comparison with other metrics. Some key findings include:

- There was a clear indication that different systems performed better at different CEFR levels.

- All systems still struggle most with content word errors.

- Systems are significantly better at correcting multi token errors than they were 5 years ago.

- The GLEU metric (Napoles et al., 2015) strongly correlates with recall and seems to be less discriminative than other metrics.

We ultimately hope that the results and corpus statistics we report will serve as useful benchmarks and guidance for future work.

Acknowledgements

We are extremely grateful to Diane Nicholls and her team of annotators for annotating the entire W&I+LOCNESS corpus. Our work was supported by Cambridge Assessment, University of Cambridge.

References

Mikel Artetxe, Gorka Labaka, and Eneko Agirre. 2018. Unsupervised statistical machine translation. In *Proceedings of the 2018 Conference on Empirical Methods in Natural Language Processing*, pages 3632–3642, Brussels, Belgium. Association for Computational Linguistics.

Hiroki Asano, Tomoya Mizumoto, and Kentaro Inui. 2017. Reference-based metrics can be replaced with reference-less metrics in evaluating grammatical error correction systems. In *Proceedings of the Eighth International Joint Conference on Natural Language Processing (Volume 2: Short Papers)*, pages 343–348. Asian Federation of Natural Language Processing.

Hiroki Asano, Tomoya Mizumoto, and Masato Mita. 2019. The AIP-Tohoku System at the BEA-2019 Shared Task. In *Proceedings of the 14th Workshop on Innovative Use of NLP for Building Educational Applications*. Association for Computational Linguistics.

Christopher Bryant, Mariano Felice, and Ted Briscoe. 2017. Automatic annotation and evaluation of error types for grammatical error correction. In *Proceedings of the 55th Annual Meeting of the Association for Computational Linguistics (Volume 1: Long Papers)*, pages 793–805, Vancouver, Canada. Association for Computational Linguistics.

Christopher Bryant and Hwee Tou Ng. 2015. How far are we from fully automatic high quality grammatical error correction? In *Proceedings of the 53rd Annual Meeting of the Association for Computational Linguistics and the 7th International Joint Conference on Natural Language Processing (Volume 1: Long Papers)*, pages 697–707, Beijing, China. Association for Computational Linguistics.

Yo Joong Choe, Jiyeon Ham, Kyubyong Park, and Yeoil Yoon. 2019. A Neural Grammatical Error Correction System Built On Better Pre-training and Sequential Transfer Learning. In *Proceedings of the 14th Workshop on Innovative Use of NLP for Building Educational Applications*. Association for Computational Linguistics.

Shamil Chollampatt and Hwee Tou Ng. 2018a. A Multilayer Convolutional Encoder-Decoder Neural Network for Grammatical Error Correction. In *Proceedings of the Thirty-Second AAAI Conference on Artificial Intelligence*.

Shamil Chollampatt and Hwee Tou Ng. 2018b. A reassessment of reference-based grammatical error correction metrics. In *Proceedings of the 27th International Conference on Computational Linguistics*, pages 2730–2741. Association for Computational Linguistics.

Leshem Choshen and Omri Abend. 2018. Inherent biases in reference-based evaluation for grammatical error correction. In *Proceedings of the 56th Annual Meeting of the Association for Computational Linguistics (Volume 1: Long Papers)*, pages 632–642. Association for Computational Linguistics.

Daniel Dahlmeier and Hwee Tou Ng. 2012. Better evaluation for grammatical error correction. In *Proceedings of the 2012 Conference of the North American Chapter of the Association for Computational Linguistics: Human Language Technologies*, pages 568–572. Association for Computational Linguistics.

Daniel Dahlmeier, Hwee Tou Ng, and Siew Mei Wu. 2013. Building a large annotated corpus of learner English: The NUS corpus of learner english. In *Proceedings of the Eighth Workshop on Innovative Use of NLP for Building Educational Applications*, pages 22–31, Atlanta, Georgia. Association for Computational Linguistics.

Robert Dale, Ilya Anisimoff, and George Narroway. 2012. HOO 2012: A Report on the Preposition and Determiner Error Correction Shared Task. In *Proceedings of the Seventh Workshop on Building Educational Applications Using NLP*, pages 54–62. Association for Computational Linguistics.

Robert Dale and Adam Kilgarriff. 2011. Helping Our Own: The HOO 2011 Pilot Shared Task. In *Proceedings of the 13th European Workshop on Natural Language Generation*, pages 242–249. Association for Computational Linguistics.

Bohdan Didenko and Julia Shaptala. 2019. Multi-headed Architecture Based on BERT for Grammar Error Correction. In *Proceedings of the 14th Workshop on Innovative Use of NLP for Building Educational Applications*. Association for Computational Linguistics.

B. Efron and R.J. Tibshirani. 1993. *An Introduction to the Bootstrap*. Chapman & Hall, New York.

Mariano Felice and Ted Briscoe. 2015. Towards a standard evaluation method for grammatical error detection and correction. In *Proceedings of the 2015 Conference of the North American Chapter of the Association for Computational Linguistics: Human Language Technologies*, pages 578–587. Association for Computational Linguistics.

Mariano Felice, Christopher Bryant, and Ted Briscoe. 2016. Automatic extraction of learner errors in ESL sentences using linguistically enhanced alignments. In *Proceedings of COLING 2016, the 26th International Conference on Computational Linguistics: Technical Papers*, pages 825–835, Osaka, Japan. The COLING 2016 Organizing Committee.

Tao Ge, Furu Wei, and Ming Zhou. 2018. Fluency boost learning and inference for neural grammatical error correction. In *Proceedings of the 56th Annual Meeting of the Association for Computational Linguistics (Volume 1: Long Papers)*, pages 1055–1065, Melbourne, Australia. Association for Computational Linguistics.

David Graff and Christopher Cieri. 2003. English gigaword ldc2003t05.

Sylviane Granger. 1998. The computer learner corpus: A versatile new source of data for SLA research. In Sylviane Granger, editor, *Learner English on Computer*, pages 3–18. Addison Wesley Longman, London and New York.

Roman Grundkiewicz and Marcin Junczys-Dowmunt. 2014. The wiked error corpus: A corpus of corrective wikipedia edits and its application to grammatical error correction. In *Advances in Natural Language Processing*, pages 478–490, Cham. Springer International Publishing.

Roman Grundkiewicz and Marcin Junczys-Dowmunt. 2018. Near human-level performance in grammatical error correction with hybrid machine translation. In *Proceedings of the 2018 Conference of the North American Chapter of the Association for Computational Linguistics: Human Language Technologies, Volume 2 (Short Papers)*, pages 284–290, New Orleans, Louisiana. Association for Computational Linguistics.

Roman Grundkiewicz, Marcin Junczys-Dowmunt, and Kenneth Heafield. 2019. Neural Grammatical Error Correction Systems with Unsupervised Pre-training on Synthetic Data. In *Proceedings of the 14th Workshop on Innovative Use of NLP for Building Educational Applications*. Association for Computational Linguistics.

Marcin Junczys-Dowmunt and Roman Grundkiewicz. 2016. Phrase-based machine translation is state-of-the-art for automatic grammatical error correction. In *Proceedings of the 2016 Conference on Empirical Methods in Natural Language Processing*, pages 1546–1556, Austin, Texas. Association for Computational Linguistics.

Marcin Junczys-Dowmunt, Roman Grundkiewicz, Shubha Guha, and Kenneth Heafield. 2018. Approaching neural grammatical error correction as a low-resource machine translation task. In *Proceedings of the 2018 Conference of the North American Chapter of the Association for Computational Linguistics: Human Language Technologies, Volume 1 (Long Papers)*, pages 595–606, New Orleans, Louisiana. Association for Computational Linguistics.

Masahiro Kaneko, Kengo Hotate, Satoru Katsumata, and Mamoru Komachi. 2019. TMU Transformer System Using BERT for Re-ranking at BEA 2019 Grammatical Error Correction on Restricted Track. In *Proceedings of the 14th Workshop on Innovative Use of NLP for Building Educational Applications*. Association for Computational Linguistics.

Yoav Kantor, Yoav Katz, Leshem Choshen, Edo Cohen-Karlik, Naftali Liberman, Assaf Toledo, Amir Menczel, and Noam Slonim. 2019. Learning to combine Grammatical Error Corrections. In *Proceedings of the 14th Workshop on Innovative Use of NLP for Building Educational Applications*. Association for Computational Linguistics.

Satoru Katsumata and Mamoru Komachi. 2019. (Almost) Unsupervised Grammatical Error Correction using a Synthetic Comparable Corpus. In *Proceedings of the 14th Workshop on Innovative Use of NLP for Building Educational Applications*. Association for Computational Linguistics.

Ophélie Lacroix, Simon Flachs, and Anders Søgaard. 2019. Noisy Channel for Low Resource Grammatical Error Correction. In *Proceedings of the 14th Workshop on Innovative Use of NLP for Building Educational Applications*. Association for Computational Linguistics.

Ruobing Li, Chuan Wang, Yefei Zha, Yonghong Yu, Shiman Guo, Qiang Wang, Yang Liu, and Hui Lin. 2019. The LAIX Systems in the BEA-2019 GEC Shared Task. In *Proceedings of the 14th Workshop on Innovative Use of NLP for Building Educational Applications*. Association for Computational Linguistics.

Jared Lichtarge, Christopher Alberti, Shankar Kumar, Noam Shazeer, and Niki Parmar. 2018. Weakly supervised grammatical error correction using iterative decoding. *CoRR*, abs/1811.01710.

David Little. 2006. The common european framework of reference for languages: Content, purpose, origin, reception and impact. *Language Teaching*, 39(3):167190.

Tomoya Mizumoto, Yuta Hayashibe, Mamoru Komachi, Masaaki Nagata, and Yuji Matsumoto. 2012. The effect of learner corpus size in grammatical error correction of ESL writings. In *Proceedings of COLING 2012: Posters*, pages 863–872. The COLING 2012 Organizing Committee.

Jakub Náplava and Milan Straka. 2019. CUNI System for the Building Educational Applications 2019 Shared Task: Grammatical Error Correction. In *Proceedings of the 14th Workshop on Innovative Use of NLP for Building Educational Applications*. Association for Computational Linguistics.

Courtney Napoles, Keisuke Sakaguchi, Matt Post, and Joel Tetreault. 2015. Ground truth for grammatical error correction metrics. In *Proceedings of the 53rd Annual Meeting of the Association for Computational Linguistics and the 7th International Joint Conference on Natural Language Processing (Volume 2: Short Papers)*, pages 588–593. Association for Computational Linguistics.

Hwee Tou Ng, Siew Mei Wu, Ted Briscoe, Christian Hadiwinoto, Raymond Hendy Susanto, and Christopher Bryant. 2014. The CoNLL-2014 Shared Task on Grammatical Error Correction. In *Proceedings of the Eighteenth Conference on Computational Natural Language Learning: Shared Task*, pages 1–14. Association for Computational Linguistics.

Hwee Tou Ng, Siew Mei Wu, Yuanbin Wu, Christian Hadiwinoto, and Joel Tetreault. 2013. The CoNLL-2013 Shared Task on Grammatical Error Correction. In *Proceedings of the Seventeenth Conference on Computational Natural Language Learning: Shared Task*, pages 1–12. Association for Computational Linguistics.

Mengyang Qiu, Xuejiao Chen, Maggie Liu, Krishna Parvathala, Apurva Patil, and Jungyeul Park. 2019. Improving Precision of Grammatical Error Correction with Cheat Sheet. In *Proceedings of the 14th Workshop on Innovative Use of NLP for Building Educational Applications*. Association for Computational Linguistics.

Keisuke Sakaguchi, Courtney Napoles, Matt Post, and Joel Tetreault. 2016. Reassessing the goals of grammatical error correction: Fluency instead of grammaticality. *Transactions of the Association for Computational Linguistics*, 4:169–182.

Keisuke Sakaguchi, Matt Post, and Benjamin Van Durme. 2017. Grammatical error correction with neural reinforcement learning. In *Proceedings of the Eighth International Joint Conference on Natural Language Processing (Volume 2: Short Papers)*, pages 366–372, Taipei, Taiwan. Asian Federation of Natural Language Processing.

Felix Stahlberg and Bill Byrne. 2019. The CUED's Grammatical Error Correction Systems for BEA-2019. In *Proceedings of the 14th Workshop on Innovative Use of NLP for Building Educational Applications*. Association for Computational Linguistics.

Toshikazu Tajiri, Mamoru Komachi, and Yuji Matsumoto. 2012. Tense and aspect error correction for ESL learners using global context. In *Proceedings of the 50th Annual Meeting of the Association for Computational Linguistics (Volume 2: Short Papers)*, pages 198–202. Association for Computational Linguistics.

Ashish Vaswani, Noam Shazeer, Niki Parmar, Jakob Uszkoreit, Llion Jones, Aidan N Gomez, Ł ukasz Kaiser, and Illia Polosukhin. 2017. Attention is all you need. In I. Guyon, U. V. Luxburg, S. Bengio, H. Wallach, R. Fergus, S. Vishwanathan, and R. Garnett, editors, *Advances in Neural Information Processing Systems 30*, pages 5998–6008. Curran Associates, Inc.

Felix Wu, Angela Fan, Alexei Baevski, Yann Dauphin, and Michael Auli. 2019. Pay less attention with lightweight and dynamic convolutions. In *International Conference on Learning Representations*.

Shuyao Xu, Jiehao Zhang, Jin Chen, and Long Qin. 2019. Singsound System for GEC-2019. In *Proceedings of the 14th Workshop on Innovative Use of NLP for Building Educational Applications*. Association for Computational Linguistics.

Liner Yang and Chencheng Wang. 2019. The BLCU System in the BEA 2019 Shared Task. In *Proceedings of the 14th Workshop on Innovative Use of NLP for Building Educational Applications*. Association for Computational Linguistics.

Helen Yannakoudakis, Øistein E. Andersen, Ardeshir Geranpayeh, Ted Briscoe, and Diane Nicholls. 2018. Developing an automated writing placement system for esl learners. *Applied Measurement in Education*, 31(3):251–267.

Helen Yannakoudakis, Ted Briscoe, and Ben Medlock. 2011. A new dataset and method for automatically grading ESOL texts. In *Proceedings of the 49th Annual Meeting of the Association for Computational Linguistics: Human Language Technologies*, pages 180–189, Portland, Oregon, USA. Association for Computational Linguistics.

Helen Yannakoudakis, Marek Rei, Øistein E. Andersen, and Zheng Yuan. 2017. Neural sequence-labelling models for grammatical error correction. In *Proceedings of the 2017 Conference on Empirical Methods in Natural Language Processing*, pages 2795–2806, Copenhagen, Denmark. Association for Computational Linguistics.

Zheng Yuan, Felix Stahlberg, Marek Rei, Bill Byrne, and Helen Yannakoudakis. 2019. Neural and FST-based approaches to grammatical error correction. In *Proceedings of the 14th Workshop on Innovative Use of NLP for Building Educational Applications*. Association for Computational Linguistics.

Wei Zhao, Liang Wang, Kewei Shen, Ruoyu Jia, and Jingming Liu. 2019. Improving grammatical error correction via pre-training a copy-augmented architecture with unlabeled data. *CoRR*, abs/1903.00138.

A Appendix

A.1 Participants and Approaches

Team	Track	Approach	Data	Resources
AIP-Tohoku (Asano et al., 2019)	R	Multi-task learning was used to predict the CEFR level of a sentence and whether it contained any errors. Flagged sentences were then corrected by a transformer NMT model trained on official and back-translated data.	Artificial data, ASAP, ICLE, ICNALE, TOEFL11, Simple Wiki$_{en}$	BERT, Fairseq
	U	The same as above, except the official data was augmented with EFCAMDAT and Lang-8$_{priv}$.	EFCAMDAT, Lang-8$_{priv}$	
Aparecium	U	-	-	-
BLCU (Yang and Wang, 2019)	R	Spelling errors were corrected by a context sensitive spellchecker and the output was pipelined to an ensemble of eight transformer NMT systems. The NMT systems were trained on artificial data and fine-tuned on official data. The artificial data was generated by uniformly inserting/replacing/deleting 30% of all tokens in monolingual sentences.	Artificial data, 1BW	CyHunspell, Fairseq, KenLM
	U	The same as above, except the official data was augmented with ∼6 million non-public Lang-8 sentences.	Lang-8$_{priv}$	
Buffalo (Qiu et al., 2019)	R	An SMT and CNN encoder-decoder system were respectively trained on official data that had been augmented with repetitions of phrase pair edits in context.	-	GIZA++, KenLM, Moses
	U	The same as above, except the system was additionally trained on artificial data that targeted six error types.	Artificial data, AFP News (English Gigaword)	
	LR	-	-	-
CAI	R	-	-	-
CAMB-CLED (Yuan et al., 2019)	R	A CNN encoder-decoder with auxiliary token-based and sentence-based detection functions was combined with an ensemble of four transformer NMT and language models trained on official and back-translated data. The n-best lists from each system were combined using an FST and then re-ranked.	Artificial data, 1BW, BNC, ukWaC, Wiki$_{en}$	ELMo, fastText, GloVe, Hunspell, Jamspell, KenLM, OpenFST, SGNMT, Stanford Parser, Tensor2Tensor
CAMB-CUED (Stahlberg and Byrne, 2019)	R	An ensemble of four transformer NMT models were trained on different combinations of over-sampled official data and back-translated artificial data. The best result came from a ratio of approx. 1:8 official to artificial sentences.	Artificial data, English News Crawl	SGNMT, Tensor2Tensor
	LR	Confusion sets were generated using CyHunspell, a database of morphological inflections, and manual rules. The confusion sets were combined in a cascade of FSTs that were weighted by edit type. The resulting FST was finally constrained by a transformer language model.	English News Crawl	AGID, CyHunspell, OpenFST, SGNMT, Tensor2Tensor
CVTE-NLP Email	R	A CNN encoder-decoder based on Chollampatt and Ng (2018a).	-	-
IBM (Kantor et al., 2019)	R	A novel spellchecker, a language model based confusion set replacement system, and four transformer NMT systems trained on over-sampled official and artificial data were all combined using a system combination technique. The new spellchecker performed better than other popular alternatives. The artificial data was generated based on the error distribution in the W&I+LOCNESS development set.	Project Gutenberg,	BERT, LibreOffice dictionaries, Nematus

Team		Approach	Additional data	Tools
Kakao&Brain (Choe et al., 2019)	R	Spelling and orthography errors were corrected by a context sensitive spellchecker and the output was pipelined to an ensemble of five transformer NMT systems trained on official and artificial data. The artificial data was generated by applying edits that occurred more than four times in the W&I+LOCNESS dev set, or else occurred in a POS-based confusion set, to several native corpora (45 million sentences) based on the edit probability. The output was then re-ranked and type-filtered.	Artificial data, Gutenberg, Tatoeba, WikiText-103	Fairseq, Hunspell, SentencePiece
	LR	The same as above, except the artificial data was only generated from the W&I+LOCNESS dev set and the system was not fine-tuned.		
LAIX (Li et al., 2019)	R, U	An ensemble of four CNN-based systems and an ensemble of eight transformer NMT models were combined using different system combination techniques.	Common Crawl	-
	LR	Eight bi-directional GRU classifiers were trained to correct eight different error types. An ensemble of CNN and transformer NMT models were also trained on the WikEd corpus. The systems were combined and augmented with some rules and a spellchecker.	Common Crawl, WikEd, Wiki$_{en}$	Enchant
ML@IITB Email	R	A sequence labelling model proposed edits in-place rather than regenerating the whole sentence. In-place edits were restricted to the top 500 most common insertions and replacements in the training data, as well as a set of morphological transformations and spelling errors.	-	autocorrect, BERT
NLG-NTU Email	R	A CNN encoder-decoder based on Wu et al. (2019).	-	Fairseq
PKU	R	-	-	-
qiuwenbo	R	-	-	-
Ramaiah	R, U	-	-	-
Shuyao (Xu et al., 2019)	R	A comprehensive collection of confusion sets were designed and used to generate artificial data based on various properties of the official data. An ensemble of four transformer NMT models were trained on the artificial data and fine-tuned on the official data.	Artificial data, 1BW, English News Crawl	NLTK, Tensor2Tensor
Siteimprove (Lacroix et al., 2019)	LR	Confusion sets were generated from the WikEd corpus and filtered to remove noise. Each candidate in each confusion set was then evaluated by two pretrained language models (BERT and GPT-2) in a noisy channel model. Beam search was used to account for interacting errors.	WikEd, Wiki$_{en}$	BERT, Enchant, GPT-2, Spacy, Unimorph, Wiktionary, Wordnet
SolomonLab	R	-	-	-
TMU (Kaneko et al., 2019; Katsumata and Komachi, 2019)	R	An ensemble of three transformer NMT models were trained on the official data, and the output was re-ranked using the same features as Chollampatt and Ng (2018a) along with a new BERT feature.	Common Crawl, Wiki$_{en}$	BERT, Fairseq, fastText, pyspellchecker
	LR	Finnish News Crawl was translated to English using Google Translate (source data). Word embeddings were spearately trained on this and native English News Crawl (target data). The source and target word embedding were then mapped to the same 'cross-lingual' space, which was used to induce a phrase table for a SMT system.	1BW, English News Crawl, Finnish News Crawl	FastAlign, Google Translate, KenLM, Moses, pyspellchecker
UEDIN-MS (Grundkiewicz et al., 2019)	R	Artificial errors generated from Aspell confusion sets were introduced to 100 million English News Crawl sentences based on the error distribution of the W&I+LOCNESS development set. An ensemble of eight transformer NMT systems were trained on over-sampled official and artificial data and the output was re-ranked.	Artificial data, English News Crawl	Aspell, Enchant, KenLM, Marian, SentencePiece
	LR	Similar to the above, except the official data was substituted with a filtered version of the WikEd corpus.	WikEd	

Team	Track	Approach	Data	Resources
UFAL (Náplava and Straka, 2019)	R	A transfomer NMT model was trained on over-sampled official data and fine-tuned with dropout, checkpoint averaging and iterative decoding.	-	Tensor2Tensor
	U	The same as the low resource track system, except fine-tuned on the over-sampled official data.	$Wiki_{en}$	
	LR	The same as the restricted track system, except the official data was substituted for consecutive English Wikipedia snapshots with added character perturbation.		
WebSpellChecker (Didenko and Shaptala, 2019)	LR	A transformer model is used to detect errors based on edit operation, error type, or predicted correction method. The model predicts a start and end offset for an edit, and a correction model predicts the most likely correction for this span from a LM vocabulary.	-	BERT
YDGEC Email	R	A pipeline of: 1. A spelling correction model, 2. A sentence-level detection model to filter out correct sentences, 3. Three error type models for each of missing articles, punctuation and SVA, 4. An ensemble of four transformer NMT models trained on different combinations of over-sampled training data. 5. Re-ranking.	$Wiki_{en}$	BERT, Marian

Table 8: This table shows all the teams that participated in the BEA-2019 shared task and attempts to summarise their approaches in each track. R, U ad LR respectively denote the Restricted, Unrestricted and Low Resource tracks. All teams used the permitted official datasets in all their submissions, so this information is not included in the Data column. See each system paper (where available) for more information about each of the other datasets and/or resources used by each team. A dash (-) indicates either that there is no information for the given cell, or else no additional datasets or resources were used.

A.2 CEFR Levels

Since one of the main contributions of the BEA-2019 shared task was the introduction of new data annotated for different proficiency levels, we analysed each team in terms of their CEFR and Native level performance. The $F_{0.5}$ results for each team and level are thus plotted in Figure 2.

The top 10 teams in the Restricted Track all performed best on C level texts, while the bottom 11 systems typically performed best on A level texts: a clear indication that some systems are more biased towards different learner levels than others. Different systems may also be differently suited to correcting different error types. For example, while punctuation errors are fairly rare at levels A and B, they are much more common at levels C and N. Conversely, noun number errors are common at levels A and B, but are rarer at levels C and N. Consequently, system performance at different CEFR levels is affected by each system's ability to correct specific error types.

The bottom 13 teams in the Restricted Track also typically struggled most with the native level texts. For example, there is an almost 15 $F_{0.5}$ gap between AIP-Tohoku's N level result and their next lowest CEFR level. Since we did not release any native level training data, we note that some systems failed to generalise to the levels and domains that they could not train on. In contrast, Low Resource Track submissions tended to score highest on native level texts, perhaps because several were trained on corrupted native data which may be more similar to the N level texts than the genuine learner data.

A.3 Edit Operation

Results for each team in terms of Missing, Replacement and Unnecessary word errors are shown in Table 9. These results mainly provide a high level overview of the types of errors systems were able to correct, but can also be used to help identify different system strengths and weaknesses. For example, UEDIN-MS only ranked 7th in terms of correcting missing word errors, but made up for this by scoring much higher at replacement and unnecessary word errors, suggesting their system could be improved by paying more attention to missing word errors.

In contrast, Kakao&Brain scored highest at missing word errors, but came 2nd in terms of replacement word errors and 7th in terms of unnec-

essary word errors. Although they also achieved the highest precision out of all teams in terms of unnecessary word errors, they did so at the cost of almost half the recall of the UEDIN-MS system. This suggest that Kakao&Brain should instead focus on improving unnecessary word error correction. That said, it is also worth reiterating that approximately 65% of all errors are replacement word errors, compared to 25% missing and 10% unnecessary, and so it is arguably more important to focus on replacement word errors more than any other category.

In the Restricted Track, ML@IITB and BLCU respectively scored highest in terms of recall on missing and unnecessary word errors. This perhaps suggests that ML@IITB's strategy of only paying attention to the top 500 most frequent missing word errors paid off, while BLCU's artificial data generation method treated all edit operations equally, and so was perhaps more highly optimised for unnecessary word errors.

In the Low Resource Track, UEDIN-MS was again the dominant system in terms of replacement and unnecessary word errors, although Kakao&Brain again came top in terms of missing word errors. There was also a larger discrepancy between certain teams' operation scores and, for example, UFAL scored 43.36 and 50.91 $F_{0.5}$ on missing and replacement word errors, but just 14.89 $F_{0.5}$ on unnecessary word errors, while WebSpellChecker scored 60.40 $F_{0.5}$ on missing word errors, but just 34.13 and 28.63 on replacement and unnecessary word errors. These results suggest that some systems are more heavily biased towards some edit operations than others, but researchers can hopefully use this information to overcome their system's weaknesses.

A.4 Single vs. Multi Token Edits

In addition to error types, we also examined system performance in terms of single and multi token edits, where a multi token edit is defined as any edit that contains 2 or more tokens on at least one side of the edit; e.g. [*eat* → *has eaten*] or [*only can* → *can only*]. Systems were evaluated in this setting mainly because Sakaguchi et al. (2016) previously advocated fluent, rather than simply grammatical, edits in GEC, yet fluency edits often involve multi token corrections. When Bryant et al. (2017) evaluated the CoNLL-2014 systems in terms of multi token edits however, they found

Restricted	M			R			U		
Team	P	R	$F_{0.5}$	P	R	$F_{0.5}$	P	R	$F_{0.5}$
UEDIN-MS	70.20	64.38	68.95	**73.10**	**58.42**	**69.60**	73.10	60.23	**70.11**
Kakao&Brain	**79.39**	65.70	**76.22**	72.51	47.83	65.73	**76.33**	33.91	61.05
LAIX	79.01	58.79	73.93	70.22	46.67	63.78	73.68	40.66	63.39
CAMB-CLED	73.30	64.32	71.31	69.88	50.27	64.82	66.05	59.51	64.63
Shuyao	75.53	61.14	72.14	67.36	53.13	63.94	72.61	53.62	67.81
YDGEC	75.72	59.99	71.95	69.60	47.86	63.80	60.92	64.17	61.54
ML@IITB	74.05	**73.37**	73.91	63.87	53.36	61.45	53.78	67.98	56.13
CAMB-CUED	67.81	66.84	67.62	66.35	47.59	61.50	65.40	56.47	63.39
AIP-Tohoku	71.56	48.63	65.39	69.26	37.73	59.34	61.56	54.70	60.05
UFAL	71.02	47.76	64.72	66.11	36.73	56.99	64.72	45.31	59.61
CVTE-NLP	68.50	40.22	60.05	68.96	38.55	59.56	62.91	37.20	55.27
BLCU	63.86	50.21	60.57	63.16	48.36	59.52	50.48	**68.02**	53.23
IBM	71.88	48.40	65.52	59.56	33.58	51.58	61.70	31.59	51.82
TMU	63.85	57.26	62.42	52.55	49.32	51.87	42.79	52.94	44.50
qiuwenbo	58.94	25.99	47.01	64.64	34.34	54.95	56.04	33.63	49.45
NLG-NTU	56.68	41.46	52.80	48.74	36.09	45.55	41.80	45.66	42.52
CAI	55.59	48.01	53.89	46.81	39.45	45.12	39.64	44.04	40.45
PKU	66.60	35.43	56.64	49.39	30.16	43.80	48.15	38.41	45.82
SolomonLab	53.18	25.38	43.62	45.62	44.18	45.33	33.72	38.26	34.54
Buffalo	57.43	7.38	24.37	64.24	17.62	42.01	62.24	16.22	39.71
Ramaiah	47.31	28.04	41.59	6.23	14.71	7.04	11.69	27.50	13.21

Unrestricted	M			R			U		
Team	P	R	$F_{0.5}$	P	R	$F_{0.5}$	P	R	$F_{0.5}$
LAIX	**79.01**	**58.79**	**73.93**	70.22	46.67	63.78	**73.68**	40.66	**63.39**
AIP-Tohoku	72.23	54.83	67.92	**72.70**	47.38	**65.68**	60.47	63.59	61.07
UFAL	69.21	54.28	65.60	69.47	51.38	64.90	61.03	61.23	61.07
BLCU	64.61	53.85	62.13	63.27	**54.50**	61.30	47.26	**70.93**	50.64
Aparecium	63.61	38.29	56.18	58.89	37.36	52.80	53.33	24.02	42.87
Buffalo	70.64	9.49	30.87	65.03	19.65	44.49	61.24	20.26	43.60
Ramaiah	55.06	31.99	48.12	9.14	22.02	10.35	11.53	28.48	13.09

Low Resource	M			R			U		
Team	P	R	$F_{0.5}$	P	R	$F_{0.5}$	P	R	$F_{0.5}$
UEDIN-MS	69.65	55.92	66.39	**71.56**	**46.77**	**64.70**	**61.16**	33.11	**52.30**
Kakao&Brain	70.12	**61.76**	**68.27**	59.00	41.10	54.28	60.98	31.45	51.33
LAIX	68.19	41.30	60.33	59.11	27.03	47.77	59.07	31.32	50.18
CAMB-CUED	55.05	22.13	42.42	57.65	41.97	53.64	46.46	45.30	46.22
UFAL	57.82	21.68	43.36	58.43	33.61	50.91	14.64	16.01	14.89
Siteimprove	**80.10**	17.16	46.21	42.76	33.33	40.47	34.78	22.71	31.44
WebSpellChecker	60.72	59.14	60.40	33.96	34.80	34.13	25.65	**53.63**	28.63
TMU	35.25	58.81	38.32	21.78	18.53	21.04	18.74	26.72	19.93
Buffalo	27.22	11.94	21.67	26.22	11.95	21.16	25.00	3.05	10.24

Table 9: This table shows the performance of each team in each track in terms of Missing, Replacement and Unnecessary token edits. In terms of frequency, approximately 25% of all edits are M, 65% are R, and 10% are U (cf. Table 4). The highest scores for each column are shown in bold.

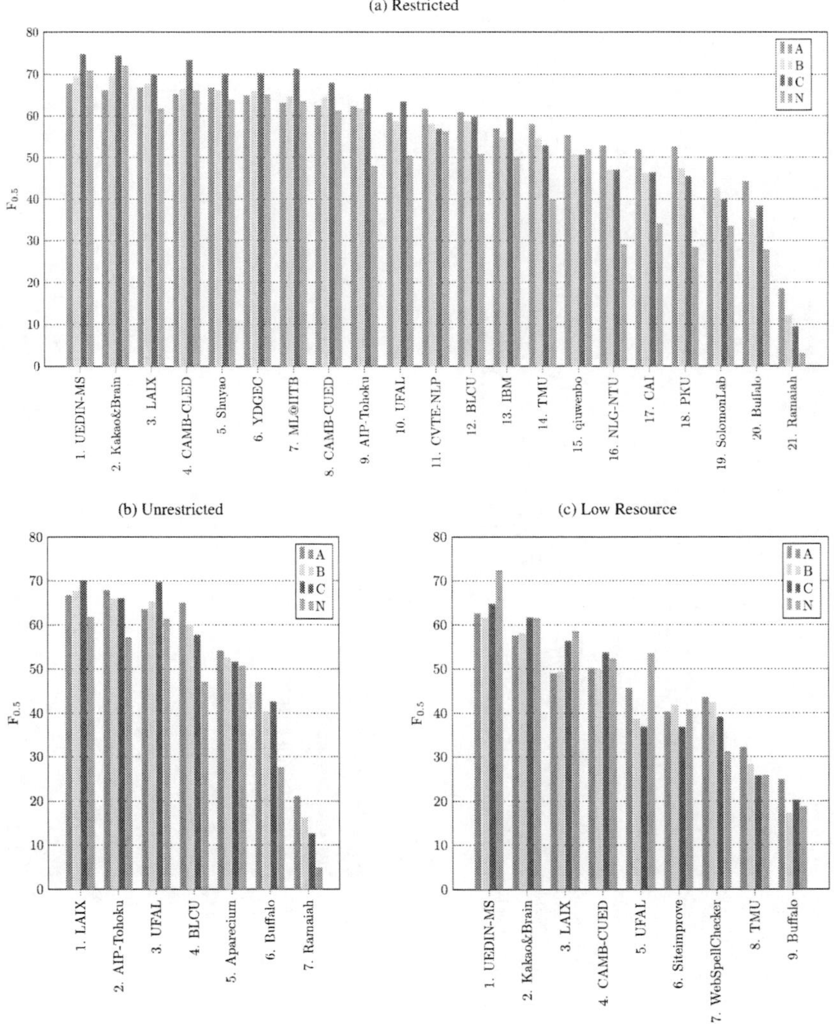

Figure 2: The $F_{0.5}$ scores for each team in each track in terms of CEFR and native levels: A (beginner), B (intermediate), C (advanced) and N (native).

that only 3 out of 12 teams achieved scores higher than 10 $F_{0.5}$, prompting them to conclude that significant progress must be made before fluency corrections become a viable option.

With this in mind, we are pleased to report that Figure 3 shows systems have indeed made significant progress in terms of correcting multi token edits, and in fact almost all teams scored higher than 20 $F_{0.5}$, with an average of 42 $F_{0.5}$. While systems still scored higher in terms of single token errors overall, this is most likely because single token errors are not only typically easier to correct than multi token errors, but are also much more frequent and tend to account for roughly 70-80% of all edits.

It is also noteworthy that Kakao&Brain actually surpassed UEDIN-MS in terms of single token error performance in the Restricted Track, but fell much shorter in terms of multi token edits. Shuyao was also particularly adept at correcting multi token errors, coming second after UEDIN-MS overall. In the Low Resource track meanwhile, Siteimprove is notable for not correcting any multi token errors at all, however this was because their system only targeted a limited number of single token error types by design.

A.5 Detection vs. Correction

One aspect of system performance that is seldom reported in the literature is that of error detection;

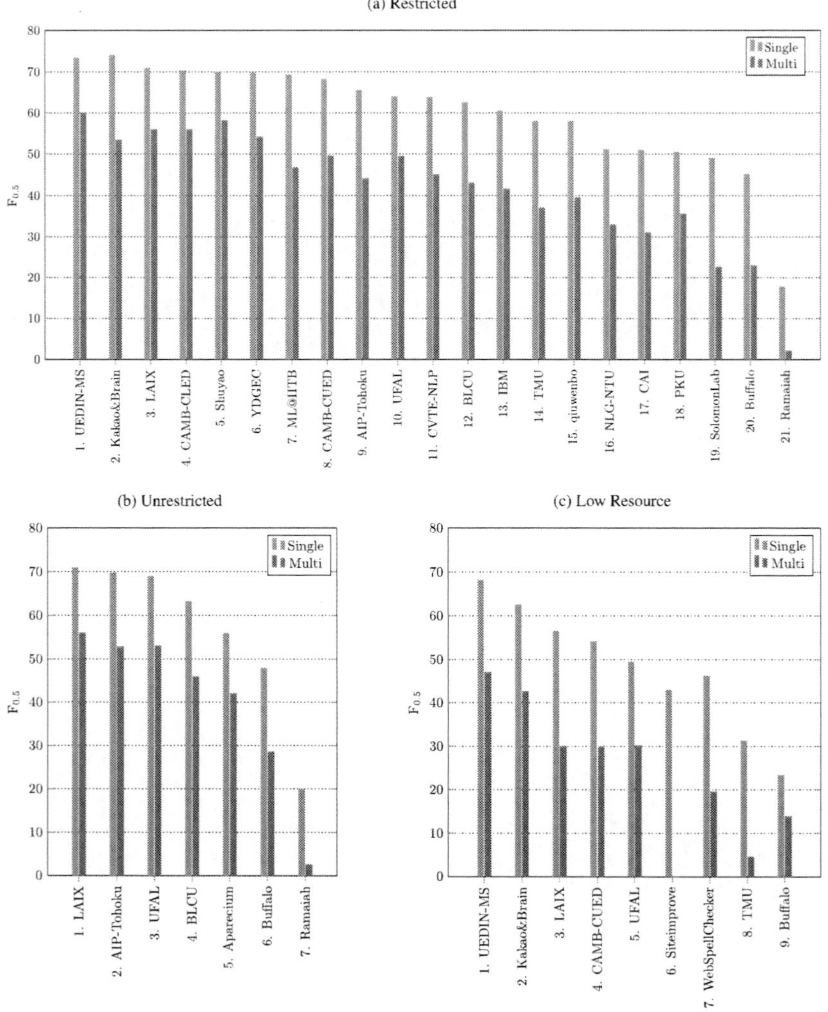

Figure 3: The $F_{0.5}$ scores for each team in each track in terms of single and multi token edits. A multi token is defined as any edit that has 2 or more tokens on at least one side of the edit.

i.e. the extent to which a system can identify errors. This is significant because detection is an important task in its own right as well as the first step in GEC. Figure 4 compares each team in terms of span based detection, span based detection and token based correction $F_{0.5}$.

In general, all systems were fairly consistent in terms of the difference between their detection and correction scores, with most teams scoring approximately 12-17 $F_{0.5}$ higher on token based detection than correction. CAMB-CLED and ML@IITB are noteworthy for achieving the 2nd and 3rd highest scores in terms of token detection, although the former can be explained by the fact that CAMB-CLED explicitly modelled detection in their approach. One of the main applica-

tions of this graph is thus to inform teams whether they should focus on improving the correction of errors they can already detect, or else extend their systems to detect new errors.

A.6 Main Error Types

The overall $F_{0.5}$ scores for each of the main 24 ER-RANT error types for each team in the Restricted Track are shown in Table 10, while similar results for the Unrestricted and Low Resource Tracks are shown in Table 11. The cells in these tables have also been shaded such that a darker red indicates a lower score. This makes it easier to see at a glance which error types were the hardest for all systems to correct.

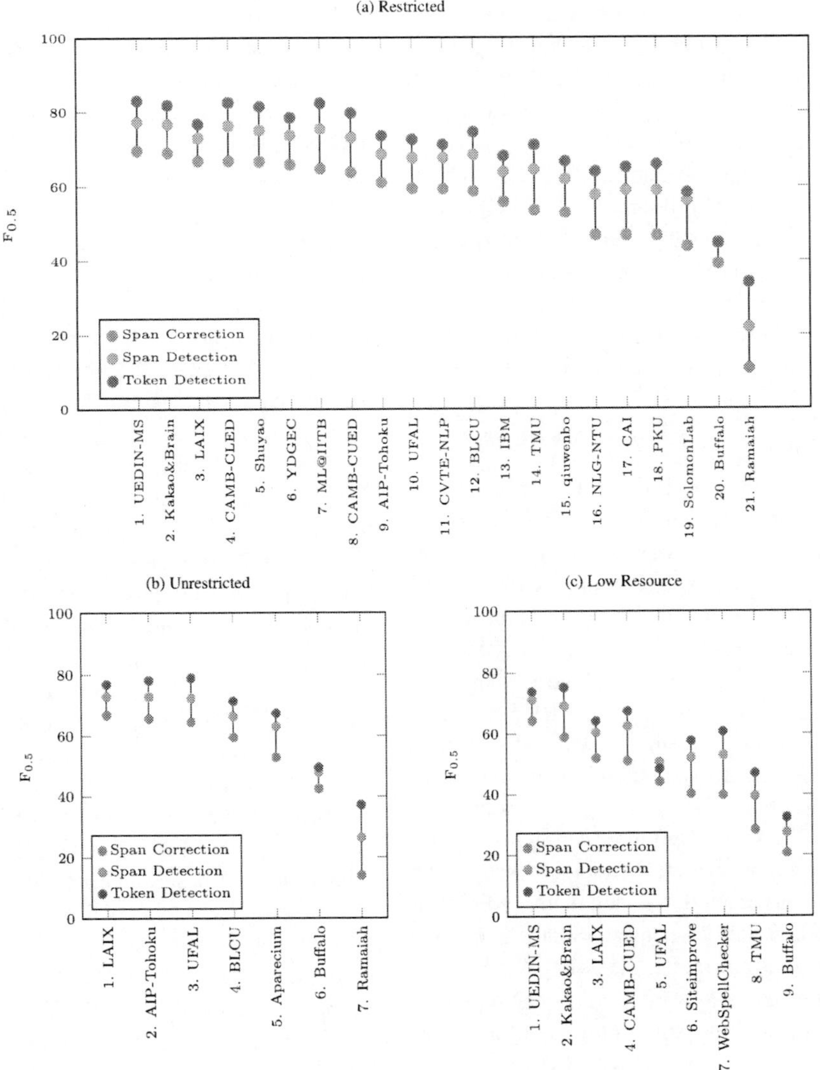

Figure 4: The difference in $F_{0.5}$ scores in terms of span based correction, span based detection, and token based detection (as defined in Section 5) for each team in each track.

With this in mind, the darkest columns in these tables include adjectives (ADJ), adverbs (ADV), conjunctions (CONJ), nouns (NOUN), other (OTHER), verbs (VERB) and word order (WO) errors. It should be made clear however, that these categories mainly contain word choice errors, such as [*eat* → *consume*], and that morphological errors, such as [*eat* → *eating*], are variously subsumed under other categories. The results indicate that while systems are fairly adept at correcting morphological and function word errors, they struggle with content word errors. Content word errors require a deeper understanding of the text compared to morphological and function word errors. Such errors should not be ignored however, and ADJ, ADV, NOUN and VERB errors collectively account for over 10% of all errors, which is equal to the 3rd most frequent error type.

In terms of error types overall, UEDIN-MS was the most successful team and scored highest on 15/24 error types in the Restricted Track and 20/24 in the Low Resource Track. YDGEC meanwhile came 2nd in the Restricted Track, scoring highest on 3/24 error types, while a handful of other teams did best at 1 or 2 types. YDGEC is also notable for scoring much better at adjective and adverb errors than UEDIN-MS; it would be interesting to determine why. In contrast, UEDIN-MS performed significantly better on content word errors in the Low Resource Track than their nearest competitors, which suggests that their artificial data generation method might also be proficient at simulating content word errors.

Finally, the team that came 5th overall, Shuyao, came last in terms of orthography (ORTH) errors, even though they constitute the 5th most frequent error type. This not only indicates a straightforward way for them to improve system, but also demonstrates how an ERRANT error type analysis can help guide the system development process.

A.7 All Metrics

As mentioned at the start of this section, we chose to use gold annotated references as the official references in the shared task even though all system hypotheses were annotated automatically by ERRANT. One consequence of this however, is that systems are unlikely to reach 100 $F_{0.5}$ even if they produce exactly the same corrected sentences as the references. This is because ERRANT computes scores in terms of edit overlap, yet automatic edit spans do not always match human edit spans; for example ERRANT will merge edits such as [$\epsilon \rightarrow has$] and [$eat \rightarrow eaten$] into [$eat \rightarrow has\ eaten$], but human annotators may choose to keep them separate. Consequently, although the edits ultimately produce the same correction, the automatic hypothesis does not match the gold reference and so the system is not rewarded. This explains why some teams found that submitting the official corrected development sentences to Codalab during the development phase only scored $\sim$86 $F_{0.5}$.

In this section, we additionally report system performance using automatic references instead of gold references. While it may seem unorthodox to use automatic references instead of gold references, the main advantage of this setting is that all the edits in the hypothesis and reference files are classified under exactly the same conditions. This not only means hypothesis edits are more likely to match the reference edits, but also that the official corrected sentences will score the maximum 100 $F_{0.5}$ on the development and test sets. Table 12 hence shows that the ERRANT $F_{0.5}$ scores of almost all teams in all tracks increased when compared against the automatic references, which indicates that systems are now rewarded for valid edits that were previously overlooked.

In addition to evaluating systems using gold and automatic references with ERRANT, we also evaluated systems using the other most popular metrics in GEC; namely MaxMatch (Dahlmeier and Ng, 2012), the I-measure (Felice and Briscoe, 2015), and GLEU (Napoles et al., 2015). The results, as well as how they affect each team's ranking, are also shown in Table 12. Note that the I-measure and GLEU are unaffected by the differences between gold and auto references and so are only reported once in this table.

Although we see that the rankings do change depending on the metric and type of reference, UEDIN-MS still came top in all settings in both the Restricted and Low Resource Tracks. While Kakao&Brain also consistently came second in almost all metrics, the exception was GLEU in the Restricted Track where they dropped to 5th. The overall GLEU rankings deviate significantly from the other metrics and also strongly correlate with recall. For example, ML@IITB, BLCU and TMU all ranked much better under GLEU, on account of their higher recall, while LAIX dropped from 3rd to 9th because their system emphasised precision. We additionally note that the range in scores for the top 19 teams in the Restricted Track was less than 7.5 using GLEU, but over 25 $F_{0.5}$ for both ERRANT and MaxMatch and 40 in terms of the I-measure. We thus conclude that GLEU is less discriminative than other metrics.

Finally, although MaxMatch $F_{0.5}$ scores tended to be higher than ERRANT $F_{0.5}$ scores in both the gold and auto reference settings, we note that MaxMatch exploits a dynamic alignment to artificially minimise the false positive rate and hence produces slightly inflated scores (Bryant et al., 2017). We also note that despite previous research that suggested MaxMatch correlates more strongly with human judgements than the I-measure (cf. Section 5), the I-measure still ranked the top 10 Restricted Track systems in exactly the same order as MaxMatch $F_{0.5}$. We hope that these results will encourage researchers to investigate further and perhaps develop better evaluation practices.

Restricted

Teams	ADJ	ADJ FORM	ADV	CONJ	CONTR	DET	MORPH	NOUN	NOUN INFL	NOUN NUM	NOUN POSS	ORTH
UEDIN-MS	43.48	83.33	49.41	48.67	84.75	75.67	79.31	41.17	91.95	79.92	83.68	82.10
Kakao&Brain	42.68	74.07	47.41	19.23	98.21	70.24	70.45	31.82	77.78	75.32	68.97	75.77
LAIX	46.05	54.05	45.11	16.67	76.92	70.07	74.16	34.09	81.52	67.40	63.32	73.02
CAMB-CLED	41.94	78.95	51.65	28.46	77.92	71.87	76.47	34.75	67.31	71.12	69.05	80.69
Shuyao	47.37	83.33	56.64	40.00	91.67	73.10	70.54	33.33	72.29	73.90	66.67	50.41
YDGEC	53.10	76.92	55.02	32.26	75.47	70.42	67.46	25.84	77.59	73.42	64.63	71.08
ML@IITB	19.90	53.57	46.04	58.14	68.97	72.53	63.62	17.73	23.62	72.52	68.63	67.29
CAMB-CUED	50.30	65.22	53.69	36.08	74.47	68.33	72.48	34.05	52.08	71.21	69.31	78.61
AIP-Tohoku	41.67	90.91	51.92	28.17	81.82	68.09	58.69	29.96	69.77	69.64	58.59	65.85
UFAL	43.48	74.07	50.00	32.79	83.33	63.23	72.29	25.24	60.61	65.02	52.63	75.68
CVTE-NLP	46.73	83.33	43.86	45.45	86.54	59.56	62.37	29.24	86.96	68.54	61.22	72.46
BLCU	50.00	83.33	44.12	29.70	61.64	64.30	65.53	22.29	68.42	66.69	58.14	75.63
IBM	28.30	66.67	0.00	0.00	65.22	57.64	51.37	12.58	0.00	62.19	24.75	53.35
TMU	24.62	58.14	32.29	39.82	79.37	61.65	63.69	22.32	72.92	60.53	73.30	74.76
qiuwenbo	38.14	62.50	43.15	16.13	54.05	53.78	57.32	23.32	86.96	64.57	45.00	70.18
NLG-NTU	12.82	41.67	34.74	36.04	70.00	53.09	49.38	9.38	58.82	55.78	60.13	69.15
CAI	19.48	45.45	31.25	28.46	90.16	49.31	54.01	14.60	58.82	52.21	64.71	70.28
PKU	35.97	62.50	34.19	25.32	81.40	59.79	58.46	13.00	60.00	63.66	40.54	69.94
SolomonLab	17.42	62.50	52.08	23.44	77.78	53.23	36.62	12.82	87.63	57.58	57.02	59.15
Buffalo	36.76	58.82	26.32	0.00	50.00	37.13	49.36	18.63	57.14	52.90	18.52	53.55
Ramaiah	3.26	55.56	12.86	3.40	41.67	23.10	33.86	0.80	0.00	40.61	17.24	58.60
Freq. (%)	1.05	0.18	1.45	0.75	0.32	10.41	2.50	2.89	0.28	4.07	0.93	8.03

Teams	OTHER	PART	PREP	PRON	PUNCT	SPELL	VERB	VERB FORM	VERB INFL	VERB SVA	VERB TENSE	WO
UEDIN-MS	45.59	66.90	71.81	68.47	67.87	82.71	59.27	79.52	97.22	86.74	66.20	54.27
Kakao&Brain	34.36	73.53	65.56	67.12	78.17	76.12	43.33	71.65	96.77	83.11	63.08	47.69
LAIX	23.99	68.42	62.85	62.99	75.66	72.82	30.30	75.80	86.21	78.95	56.92	47.32
CAMB-CLED	38.95	74.07	65.40	64.55	75.02	77.51	39.80	75.63	93.75	80.08	60.82	52.71
Shuyao	40.49	69.54	65.86	67.68	76.41	77.22	53.52	78.02	97.22	80.37	60.55	59.47
YDGEC	37.13	75.76	65.53	54.69	70.01	77.37	49.28	77.11	100.00	78.37	62.04	50.65
ML@IITB	31.75	65.84	67.35	62.86	75.89	67.93	49.19	75.93	86.96	84.40	58.82	60.14
CAMB-CUED	35.50	72.25	59.85	61.57	72.64	73.44	40.13	73.43	89.29	79.21	55.60	52.56
AIP-Tohoku	34.77	69.67	60.59	51.17	70.42	70.77	42.19	71.51	62.50	75.55	54.39	46.75
UFAL	29.79	54.35	55.82	57.74	70.44	63.32	44.75	74.36	71.43	77.81	51.48	47.52
CVTE-NLP	24.79	67.01	51.16	54.57	64.36	75.73	40.60	69.26	94.59	72.97	49.13	47.62
BLCU	30.36	58.06	59.17	48.11	66.72	66.39	45.57	71.29	96.77	76.06	50.66	61.92
IBM	15.10	51.02	48.95	43.40	66.81	66.80	21.38	62.50	0.00	70.82	51.66	36.89
TMU	23.84	52.88	54.62	45.32	70.83	63.17	32.94	63.64	94.59	73.85	49.16	43.00
qiuwenbo	22.16	58.82	41.19	52.63	48.94	74.36	30.94	66.19	86.21	71.68	44.19	44.60
NLG-NTU	16.41	62.50	45.43	47.39	62.23	53.64	32.44	60.40	73.53	66.06	42.04	41.81
CAI	17.98	48.00	43.71	42.24	60.57	56.14	25.22	56.58	94.59	66.36	33.83	28.07
PKU	14.73	63.73	49.96	52.56	61.46	60.00	27.23	69.90	80.00	71.43	44.38	45.70
SolomonLab	16.20	62.91	48.73	37.38	26.38	66.67	29.32	50.71	89.29	59.27	38.80	39.80
Buffalo	7.68	47.62	21.01	31.03	30.17	50.00	11.47	65.32	38.46	65.29	34.05	12.05
Ramaiah	0.73	38.46	21.90	22.85	51.28	5.63	3.95	48.78	58.82	52.97	32.32	34.38
Freq. (%)	15.69	0.49	8.33	2.45	16.73	4.63	5.09	3.10	0.12	2.28	5.43	1.40

Table 10: Main error type ERRANT $F_{0.5}$ scores for each team in the Restricted Track. Darker red indicates a lower score. The percent frequency of each type in the test set is also shown.

Unrestricted

Teams	ADJ	ADJ FORM	ADV	CONJ	CONTR	DET	MORPH	NOUN	NOUN INFL	NOUN NUM	NOUN POSS	ORTH
LAIX	46.05	54.05	45.11	16.67	76.92	70.07	74.16	34.09	81.52	67.40	63.32	73.02
AIP-Tohoku	53.96	83.33	49.08	51.14	92.31	68.74	68.38	38.37	89.04	74.74	71.43	71.02
UFAL	50.96	69.77	46.03	37.74	82.19	66.86	70.72	37.91	78.57	71.43	76.04	81.37
BLCU	50.76	78.43	42.57	43.62	68.42	59.67	66.39	33.52	53.85	67.11	59.81	75.79
Aparecium	37.74	43.48	39.53	32.61	30.77	55.87	52.42	18.78	44.44	65.93	50.56	70.69
Buffalo	10.87	53.57	37.04	0.00	66.67	43.26	56.16	13.23	49.02	53.15	33.33	51.75
Ramaiah	1.98	9.26	11.59	0.00	52.63	30.30	30.75	1.20	0.00	41.30	9.90	54.82
Freq. (%)	1.05	0.18	1.45	0.75	0.32	10.41	2.50	2.89	0.28	4.07	0.93	8.03

Teams	OTHER	PART	PREP	PRON	PUNCT	SPELL	VERB	VERB FORM	VERB INFL	VERB SVA	VERB TENSE	WO
LAIX	23.99	68.42	62.85	62.99	75.66	72.82	30.30	75.80	86.21	78.95	56.92	47.32
AIP-Tohoku	44.05	71.97	62.37	67.71	72.34	79.40	45.58	76.09	89.29	77.31	59.75	57.18
UFAL	36.50	75.76	61.79	57.29	70.49	84.80	49.45	72.61	89.29	78.91	59.83	43.41
BLCU	34.98	63.16	58.68	61.15	65.86	77.81	43.27	70.85	97.22	74.70	55.41	61.29
Aparecium	18.63	64.71	47.44	49.85	57.17	61.71	31.20	68.29	93.75	75.04	44.64	34.81
Buffalo	10.70	52.63	30.16	34.29	31.54	50.32	17.39	72.44	38.46	71.78	35.50	32.00
Ramaiah	0.84	32.26	31.67	26.47	55.82	4.23	3.88	47.82	41.67	47.17	20.71	32.89
Freq. (%)	15.69	0.49	8.33	2.45	16.73	4.63	5.09	3.10	0.12	2.28	5.43	1.40

Low Resource

Teams	ADJ	ADJ FORM	ADV	CONJ	CONTR	DET	MORPH	NOUN	NOUN INFL	NOUN NUM	NOUN POSS	ORTH
UEDIN-MS	46.39	83.33	39.39	25.42	51.72	64.01	72.25	41.13	92.59	77.23	79.21	79.23
Kakao&Brain	0.00	50.00	6.10	0.00	44.64	58.17	52.40	16.51	75.58	56.61	18.29	65.14
LAIX	0.00	31.25	9.43	0.00	0.00	51.35	61.71	19.42	80.00	57.36	35.85	51.16
CAMB-CUED	0.00	17.86	0.00	19.13	35.71	40.91	37.18	13.51	93.02	59.71	47.39	73.31
UFAL	32.11	33.33	24.00	10.64	7.69	26.20	48.28	30.49	93.41	66.33	64.52	70.56
Siteimprove	8.20	0.00	9.80	2.48	0.00	18.63	35.71	20.83	40.00	47.18	0.00	4.59
WebSpellChecker	9.98	0.00	16.47	8.33	33.33	54.43	38.67	10.58	37.04	56.07	49.50	67.47
TMU	1.66	36.59	6.99	19.44	0.00	26.50	24.75	1.82	32.05	38.71	10.20	45.95
Buffalo	17.54	0.00	22.47	0.00	21.43	10.64	23.29	7.97	22.73	19.59	17.24	49.28
Freq. (%)	1.05	0.18	1.45	0.75	0.32	10.41	2.50	2.89	0.28	4.07	0.93	8.03

Teams	OTHER	PART	PREP	PRON	PUNCT	SPELL	VERB	VERB FORM	VERB INFL	VERB SVA	VERB TENSE	WO
UEDIN-MS	38.51	73.53	62.01	62.26	62.85	84.09	49.12	78.17	97.22	76.59	50.56	29.97
Kakao&Brain	17.61	51.02	47.22	49.00	74.64	73.82	20.72	61.11	96.77	74.35	47.36	11.81
LAIX	4.16	32.79	41.18	11.63	64.42	60.64	0.00	55.18	0.00	67.31	0.00	0.00
CAMB-CUED	9.09	52.45	50.45	22.14	51.88	68.49	4.89	60.22	97.22	85.25	39.21	4.03
UFAL	21.73	42.86	27.03	24.19	33.17	80.25	27.86	58.46	93.75	72.18	21.02	19.05
Siteimprove	13.31	37.23	39.58	30.63	50.88	76.22	8.23	48.55	96.77	76.06	23.10	0.00
WebSpellChecker	8.38	41.67	37.97	33.42	66.74	42.91	17.89	54.26	33.33	71.73	35.21	42.15
TMU	2.51	30.00	18.12	19.30	46.16	65.50	9.27	28.43	75.00	30.22	14.96	18.07
Buffalo	5.19	29.41	11.74	14.04	36.23	6.35	7.50	8.17	66.67	12.82	6.24	28.00
Freq. (%)	15.69	0.49	8.33	2.45	16.73	4.63	5.09	3.10	0.12	2.28	5.43	1.40

Table 11: Main error type ERRANT $F_{0.5}$ scores for each team in the Unrestricted and Low Resource Track. Darker red indicates a lower score. The percent frequency of each type in the test set is also shown.

| | ERRANT | | | | | | MaxMatch | | | | | | | | |
| Restricted | Gold | | | | Auto | | Gold | | Auto | | | | | | |
Teams	P	R	$F_{0.5}$	#	$F_{0.5}$	#	$F_{0.5}$	#	$F_{0.5}$	#	I	#	GLEU	#
UEDIN-MS	77.87	62.29	69.47	1	74.16	1	76.48	1	76.62	1	38.92	1	77.93	1
Kakao&Brain	80.18	53.28	69.00	2	72.83	2	74.09	2	74.17	2	36.84	2	75.87	5
LAIX	77.03	50.19	66.78	3	69.59	5	70.78	7	70.79	7	28.20	7	74.33	9
CAMB-CLED	74.59	56.53	66.75	4	70.11	3	72.51	3	72.48	3	34.10	3	76.62	3
Shuyao	74.41	56.31	66.61	5	69.91	4	72.22	4	72.37	4	33.22	4	76.55	4
YDGEC	74.50	54.49	65.83	6	69.41	6	71.60	6	71.20	6	29.21	6	75.39	7
ML@IITB	69.69	63.29	64.73	7	68.30	7	71.97	5	71.75	5	30.75	5	77.89	2
CAMB-CUED	71.49	55.63	63.72	8	67.63	8	70.37	8	70.44	8	26.37	8	75.82	6
AIP-Tohoku	72.79	43.05	60.97	9	63.95	9	65.95	9	65.84	9	19.22	9	73.16	11
UFAL	71.56	41.21	59.39	10	62.37	10	65.70	10	65.19	10	17.46	10	72.79	12
CVTE-NLP	72.12	39.12	59.22	11	61.71	12	63.04	12	63.17	12	16.71	11	72.51	13
BLCU	65.11	52.54	58.62	12	62.14	11	64.82	11	65.05	11	13.04	12	74.33	8
IBM	66.19	37.45	55.74	13	57.38	13	59.47	14	58.79	14	8.84	14	71.48	15
TMU	57.69	53.15	53.45	14	56.72	14	61.44	13	61.60	13	-0.54	17	73.96	10
qiuwenbo	66.56	32.84	52.80	15	55.22	15	57.70	15	57.22	15	8.94	13	71.30	16
LG-NTU	52.54	39.20	46.77	16	49.19	17	53.38	17	53.15	17	-1.45	18	71.13	17
CAI	51.49	42.61	46.69	17	49.43	16	53.68	16	53.56	16	-1.49	19	71.68	14
PKU	54.84	32.17	46.64	18	48.06	18	52.84	18	52.30	18	-0.32	15	71.06	18
SolomonLab	47.05	39.69	43.73	19	45.37	19	50.00	19	50.40	19	-3.50	20	70.56	19
Buffalo	65.09	15.08	39.06	20	39.14	20	40.95	20	40.13	20	-0.32	15	68.32	20
Ramaiah	10.29	19.04	10.83	21	11.33	21	18.68	21	18.49	21	-21.78	21	56.31	21

| | ERRANT | | | | | | MaxMatch | | | | | | | | |
| Unrestricted | Gold | | | | Auto | | Gold | | Auto | | | | | | |
Teams	P	R	$F_{0.5}$	#	$F_{0.5}$	#	$F_{0.5}$	#	$F_{0.5}$	#	I	#	GLEU	#
LAIX	77.03	50.19	66.78	1	69.59	1	70.78	3	70.79	3	28.20	3	74.33	3
AIP-Tohoku	75.45	52.59	65.57	2	69.41	2	70.93	2	70.98	2	28.65	2	74.83	2
UFAL	73.35	55.14	64.55	3	68.81	3	71.74	1	71.48	1	29.65	1	75.83	1
BLCU	64.56	58.17	59.50	4	63.17	4	65.42	4	65.74	4	7.08	4	74.11	4
Aparecium	61.87	36.09	52.76	5	54.14	5	55.61	5	55.80	5	5.57	5	71.96	5
Buffalo	66.17	17.19	42.33	6	42.15	6	44.33	6	43.09	6	4.25	6	68.77	6
Ramaiah	13.09	24.94	13.98	7	14.46	7	22.10	7	22.00	7	-20.13	7	57.50	7

| | ERRANT | | | | | | MaxMatch | | | | | | | | |
| Low Resource | Gold | | | | Auto | | Gold | | Auto | | | | | | |
Teams	P	R	$F_{0.5}$	#	$F_{0.5}$	#	$F_{0.5}$	#	$F_{0.5}$	#	I	#	GLEU	#
UEDIN-MS	72.97	47.86	64.24	1	66.04	1	67.34	1	67.39	1	16.06	1	74.30	1
Kakao&Brain	65.75	46.73	58.80	2	60.80	2	63.51	2	63.04	2	15.23	2	73.98	2
LAIX	63.86	30.93	51.81	3	52.65	3	53.84	4	53.64	4	4.73	3	70.76	4
CAMB-CUED	56.77	37.42	50.88	4	51.45	4	54.32	3	54.09	3	-0.16	4	71.86	3
UFAL	52.82	29.23	44.13	5	45.48	5	49.28	5	49.34	5	-3.24	7	69.39	6
Siteimprove	45.34	28.26	40.17	6	40.45	7	42.59	7	42.99	7	-1.48	5	69.29	7
WebSpellChecker	40.79	44.08	39.75	7	41.41	6	48.88	6	48.08	6	-4.58	8	69.76	5
TMU	28.21	31.61	28.31	8	28.83	8	32.09	8	32.20	8	-6.98	9	65.50	9
Buffalo	25.87	10.37	20.73	9	19.92	9	22.55	9	21.63	9	-2.39	6	65.82	8

Table 12: ERRANT $F_{0.5}$ scores on the official gold references are compared against automatic references and other popular metrics. The differences in how these metrics would rank each team are also shown, where a darker red indicates a lower rank.

A Benchmark Corpus of English Misspellings
and a Minimally-supervised Model for Spelling Correction

Michael Flor
Educational Testing Service
Princeton
NJ 08541, USA
mflor@ets.org

Michael Fried
Queens College
City University of New York
NY 11367, USA
mjf314@gmail.com

Alla Rozovskaya
Queens College
City University of New York
NY 11367, USA
arozovskaya@qc.cuny.edu

Abstract

Spelling correction has attracted a lot of attention in the NLP community. However, models have been usually evaluated on artificially-created or proprietary corpora. A publicly-available corpus of authentic misspellings, annotated in context, is still lacking. To address this, we present and release an annotated data set of 6,121 spelling errors in context, based on a corpus of essays written by English language learners. We also develop a minimally-supervised context-aware approach to spelling correction. It achieves strong results on our data: 88.12% accuracy. This approach can also train with a minimal amount of annotated data (performance reduced by less than 1%). Furthermore, this approach allows easy portability to new domains. We evaluate our model on data from a medical domain and demonstrate that it rivals the performance of a model trained and tuned on in-domain data.

1 Introduction

This paper addresses automatic correction of spelling errors where the misspelled string is not a valid word in the language. Correcting non-word spelling errors has a long history in the natural language processing research (Kukich, 1992). Earlier approaches were evaluated on spelling errors from proprietary corpora of native English texts or artificially generated errors in well-formed texts. While spell checkers today are essential and ubiquitous, dealing with data in a variety of "noisy" domains poses particular challenges to traditional spell checkers. Thus, spelling research has shifted focus primarily to correcting spelling errors in social media data, biomedical texts, and texts written by non-native English writers.

Non-native English speakers account for the majority of people writing in English today, and spelling errors are some of the most frequent error types for these writers (Ng et al., 2014). In some grammatical error correction approaches researchers apply a spell checker prior to running a grammar-oriented correction model (Chollampatt and Ng, 2018; Chollampatt et al., 2016; Rozovskaya and Roth, 2016). In addition to writing-assistance feedback, spelling correction for non-native writers is also utilized in computer-aided language learning applications and in automatic scoring systems (Sukkarieh and Blackmore, 2009; Dikli, 2006; Warschauer and Ware, 2006; Leacock and Chodorow, 2003).

Spelling correction in learner texts is particularly challenging. Non-native writers have higher spelling error rates than native writers (Flor et al., 2015). The types of misspellings produced by these writers typically differ from errors produced by native speakers. While the majority of spelling errors produced by native speakers involve single-character edits (Damerau, 1964), multi-character edits are a lot more common among non-native writers (Flor et al., 2015). Finally, learner data is more likely to contain other errors or non-standard usage in context, which may further complicate error correction (Flor and Futagi, 2012).

Several recent works have specifically addressed spelling correction in learner texts. However, they evaluated either on small data sets (Nagata et al., 2017) or on proprietary corpora (Flor, 2012). Despite several decades of research on spelling, there is still no publicly available large-scale corpus, explicitly and exhaustively annotated for spelling errors. Without such data, it is difficult to compare and track research progress in the field.

This paper makes the following contributions:

- We present a corpus of learner essays, TOEFL-Spell, annotated for spelling errors. This corpus can be used as a benchmark corpus to develop state-of-the-art models for spelling correction (Section 3).

Proceedings of the Fourteenth Workshop on Innovative Use of NLP for Building Educational Applications, pages 76–86
Florence, Italy, August 2, 2019. ©2019 Association for Computational Linguistics

- We develop a minimally-supervised approach to spelling correction that combines contextual and non-contextual information (Section 4). We show that inclusion of word embeddings provides information complementary to other contextual features.

- The proposed model is shown to be robust, evaluated on TOEFL-Spell and on an out-of-domain data set of clinical notes. The performance of our model on the clinical data set rivals that of the model trained on a corpus of clinical notes (Section 5).

- Evaluation of the contribution of contextual features shows that contextual information provides an error reduction of about 45%, improving the correction accuracy by 10 points on TOEFL-Spell and by 7 points on the clinical data set.

- Error analysis of the system on TOEFL-Spell and on the clinical data is presented in Section 6.

2 Related Work

A non-word misspelling is a spelling error, such that the produced string is not a valid word in the language. This is different from real-word (context-sensitive) errors, for example confusing "their" and "there" (Wilcox-O'Hearn et al., 2008). This section provides an overview of prior work on correction of non-word spelling errors and availability of corpora for such research.

2.1 Data Sets for Spelling Research

Traditionally, three areas of research have been particularly interested in spelling errors: information retrieval - for misspellings in queries, English language learning - for misspellings made by language learners, and medical information processing - for misspellings in medical documents. Previous work used either proprietary data sets or artificially generated errors. Flor (2012) evaluated on a large corpus of student essays, but the corpus is not publicly available. Toutanova and Moore (2002) and Brill and Moore (2000) similarly evaluated on proprietary data sets of typos collected from native English texts.

Query spelling correction has been an important aspect of research in the domain of information retrieval (Hasan et al., 2015; Chen et al., 2007; Li et al., 2006). The MSR-Bing Web Scale Speller Challenge (Wang and Pedersen, 2011) presented 5500 short queries, with about 10% of them containing typographical errors. Recently, Hagen et al. (2017) presented a large corpus of query misspellings - about 54K queries, with about 9K potential spelling errors. Errors were not explicitly marked; annotators provided alternative formulations, so spelling errors are deduced from comparing the original and revised formulations.

For non-native spelling errors, Nagata et al. (2011, 2017) describe a small corpus (25K words) annotated for various errors, with only 438 spelling error tokens. Mizumoto and Nagata (2017) refer to a newer version of that corpus, with 30K words and 654 spelling errors.

The NUCLE corpus (Dahlmeier et al., 2013) contains 1400 essays written by students at the National University of Singapore, and annotated using twenty seven error codes. In this corpus, spelling errors were included in the *Mechanical errors* category that lumps together quite different types of low-level errors - 'punctuation, capitalization, spelling and typos'. Thus, spelling errors are marked explicitly, but not distinctively.

Heilman et al. (2014) released a corpus of 1511 learner sentences (28K words), judged for grammaticality on an ordinal scale. The JFLEG corpus (Napoles et al., 2017) built on top of that data – for each sentence they added three holistic fluency edits (sentence rewrites) to correct the grammar and also make the original text more fluent. In this corpus, spelling (or other errros) are not explicitly annotated, which makes it difficult to isolate them for spelling correction research. Moreover, the size of this corpus is rather small, and there is no context beyond the sentence level.

The Cambridge Learner Corpus First Certificate in English (FCE) has about 2500 essays (500K words), written by learners taking the English proficiency exam (Yannakoudakis et al., 2011). It was annotated for 80 error types (Nicholls, 2003), including an explicit category for spelling mistakes. However, on closer analysis, one can find that many spelling errors are tagged with other error categories. Thus, its annotation is not directly suitable for spelling correction research.

In the biomedical domain, the largest corpus annotated for spelling errors is a recently released data set of clinical notes (Fivez et al., 2017a), with 873 annotated misspellings in sentence context.

2.2 Approaches to Spelling Correction

Approaches to correcting non-word spelling errors can be broken down into those that only consider the characteristics of the target token when ranking correction candidates, and those that also include the surrounding context. Among the former are those that compute edit distance (Levenshtein, 1966; Damerau, 1964) and phonetic similarity between the misspelling and a candidate correction (Toutanova and Moore, 2002).

A standard approach to correcting non-word spelling errors follows the noisy channel model formulation (Shannon, 1948). It uses edit distance and phonetic similarity between the misspelling and the candidate correction, and the candidate frequency (Kernighan et al., 1990; Church and Gale, 1991; Toutanova and Moore, 2002). Weights for different edit operations are estimated from large training sets of annotated spelling errors. This approach requires a lot of supervision: thousands of annotated errors paired with their corrections are used to estimate probabilities associated with different edits.

The noisy channel model can also incorporate contextual information. For instance, Brill and Moore (2000) ranked candidate corrections by language model scores and reduced the error rate by 73% on correcting artificially-generated errors in the Brown corpus. However, in general, adding new features from a variety of sources is not straightforward in the noisy channel approach.

Contextual features have been used for correcting simulated non-word errors and real-word errors. Carlson and Fette (2007) use a memory-based model with context features estimated from the Google Web1T n-gram corpus (Brants and Franz, 2006). Use of data from the Web for spelling correction was described by Whitelaw et al. (2009) and Chen et al. (2007).

Flor (2012) introduced an approach to ranking candidate corrections that combines edit distance and phonetic distance with contextual cues, and evaluated it on errors made by non-native English speakers. For instance, given *'forst'*, candidate corrections could include *first, forest, frost,* and even *forced*. In a context like *"forst fires in Yellowstone"*, *forest* is a likely candidate. For *"forst in line"*, *first* seems more adequate. That study demonstrated that contextual features significantly improve spelling correction accuracy on an annotated corpus of spelling errors collected from TOEFL and GRE exam essays. It significantly outperformed popular spellers like Aspell and the speller in MS Word (Flor and Futagi, 2012).

3 The TOEFL-Spell Corpus

We base our data set on the publicly available ETS Corpus of Non-Native Written English (Blanchard et al., 2013, 2014), a.k.a. TOEFL11. It consists of essays written for the TOEFL® iBT test, which is used internationally as a measure of academic English proficiency at institutions of higher learning where English is the language of instruction. TOEFL11 contains 12,100 essays from 11 first language backgrounds; 1,100 essays per language, sampled evenly from eight prompts (topics), along with score levels (low/medium/high) for each essay. Each prompt poses a proposition and asks to write an argumentative essay, stating arguments for or against the proposition.

We sampled 883 essays, selecting among those that received medium or high score (low-scored essays are difficult to understand and to annotate). The data set has 296,141 words. Essay length ranges from 168 to 672 words, with an average of 335 words per essay.

The selected essays were annotated by two annotators with linguistic background and prior experience with linguistic annotation. For each essay, an automatic dictionary lookup system highlighted strings that were not found in dictionary. For each highlighted string, the annotator had to determine whether it was indeed misspelled, and to provide an appropriate correction. To ensure the annotation is exhaustive, annotators were also instructed to check for additional misspellings, beyond those highlighted.

The resulting annotation contains **6,121** spelling errors of non-word type, which gives a word error rate of 2.07%. 35 essays had no spelling errors, while the rest had between one and ten errors per essay. The number of unique misspellings is 3,958, and the number of unique correction replacements is 4,016. In most cases, the same error has the same correction; the average number of unique corrections per error is 1.015.

The distribution of misspellings by edit distance to the correct word is presented in Table 1. The majority (82.8%) of errors differ from the correct word by just one character, and an additional 12.6% differ from the correct form by two characters. This is similar to results reported by Flor

Edit distance	Count	Percentage (%)
1	5,066	82.76
2	769	12.56
3	198	3.23
> 3	88	1.45
Total	6,121	100

Table 1: Distribution of errors by edit distance to correct form, in TOEFL-Spell.

et al. (2015) on a different corpus of learner English. Although the majority of errors constitute single-token edits, about 5% (296) are fusion errors (e.g. *'atleast' for 'at least'*).

Randomly chosen, 76 essays were doubly annotated for calculating inter-annotator agreement. A strict criterion was applied for agreement: two annotations had to cover exactly the same segment of text and to specify the same correction. Inter-Annotator Agreement was 95.6%. (Note that Kappa statistic cannot be applied to error correction, as there are too many different responses).

The full set of annotations for TOEFL-Spell is released and made available for research.[1]

4   The Spelling Correction Model

In this section, we present our benchmark model of spelling correction, which extends the model of Flor (2012). The spelling correction task consists of three subtasks: detection, generating candidate corrections, and ranking of the candidates.

4.1   Error Detection

Detection of non-word misspellings is performed using a dictionary (lexicon). Tokens that are not in the lexicon are considered to be misspelled. We use a dictionary that consists of 140,000 single words (including inflections), 100,000 multi-word terms, and 130,000 names (including names and surnames from various countries). The dictionary includes both American and British spelling variants, common acronyms, and foreign words. The dictionary includes lexica from WordNet,[2] the SCOWL project,[3] names from US Census Data,[4], Wikipedia lists[5], and various sources on the Web.

Feature name	Description
Non-contextual features	
Orthographic similarity	Inverse edit distance
Phonetic similarity	Inverse edit distance of phonetic representations
Word frequency	Candidate word frequency in language
Contextual features	
N-gram support	N-gram counts in a 4-word window (from corpus)
Dejavu	Is the candidate found elsewhere in same essay
DejavuSM	Is the candidate found as candidate for other errors in same essay
Word embeddings	Using word embeddings to estimate candidate word's relatedness to context

Table 2: Description of all the features used in the candidate ranking module.

4.2   Candidate Generation

Candidates are generated using the dictionary described above. Candidates include all dictionary words within edit distance that does not exceed half of the length of the misspelled string, with a maximum distance of 6 characters. Both single-token and multi-token candidates are generated, to allow for correction of fusion errors. For each misspelled token, hundreds of correction candidates are generated, using the Ternary Search Tree data structure (Bentley and Sedgewick, 1997).

4.3   Ranking of Candidate Corrections

The ranking step is the most challenging one and is the focus of the most work on non-word spelling correction (Fivez et al., 2017b). Our model uses both the features of the misspelling+candidate pair and the contextual information. The former include orthographic similarity, phonetic similarity, and candidate word frequency. The contextual information includes n-gram support, an estimate of potential re-use of words in text, and word embeddings. The features are listed in Table 2.

Orthographic similarity is computed as inverse edit distance, $1/(eDist + 1)$, where $eDist$ is the edit distance (including transpositions) between the misspelling and the correction candidate (Levenshtein, 1966; Damerau, 1964).

Phonetic similarity reflects the intuition that a good correction should be phonetically similar to the misspelling. It is computed as $1/(eDistPh + 1)$, where $eDistPh$ is the edit distance between the phonetic representation of the misspelling and the phonetic representation of the candidate. Phonetic representations are computed using the Double-Metaphone algorithm (Philips, 2000).

Candidate frequency. A more frequent word is more likely to be the intended word than a rare word (Kernighan et al., 1990). Unigram word frequency is computed for each candidate using the English Wikipedia corpus.

N-gram support. For each correction candidate, all n-grams in the window of four context words on each side are taken into account by the n-gram support feature. We use co-occurrence counts computed from the English Wikipedia corpus and weighted as the Positive Normalized PMI scores (PNPMI). Normalized PMI was introduced by Bouma (2009), we adapt it as:

$$log_2 \frac{p(c, ngram)}{p(c)p(ngram)} \Big/ (-log_2 p(c, ngram)) \quad (1)$$

PNPMI maps all negative values to zero. For each candidate c, all n-grams of lengths 2-to-4 words in the context window are generated, and the PNPMI values of each $c, ngram$ pair are added.

Dejavu. This feature considers essay-wide context and rewards a candidate that appears in the same essay. Each occurrence of the candidate (or its inflection) in the text strengthens the candidate by the amount $1/sqrt(1 + distance)$, where distance is the number of tokens between the misspelling and the position of the candidate in text.

DejavuSM is a feature that caters for systematic misspellings, when a word is misspelled throughout the essay (Flor, 2012). For each candidate correction, we search in the lists of candidate corrections of other misspelled tokens in the text. Each time the candidate or its inflection is found in another list, the candidate is strengthened with a score of $S_{CC}/sqrt(1 + distance)$, where S_{CC} is the current rescaled overall strength of the corresponding candidate in the other list.

Word embeddings have shown a lot of success in many NLP applications, especially for estimation of semantic relatedness (Levy and Goldberg, 2014). We use word embeddings to score the contextual fit of correction candidates in the local context of a misspelling. The idea is that for a misspelling like *"roat"*, a correction to *"road"* should be strengthened if a word like *"drive"* is found in the vicinity. Given a misspelled token, we define a window of ± 15 tokens around it. For every candidate, we compute the cosine similarity between the embedding vector of the candidate and the vector of each context word, and sum those values. This is the vector-based contextual fit score for the candidate. We use the *word2vec* vectors with 300 dimensions, pre-trained on 100 billion words of Google News (Mikolov et al., 2013).[6]

Ranking of candidates. For each misspelled token, the feature scores of its candidate corrections are *normalized*, by dividing the score of the candidate feature by the highest-scoring candidate on that given feature. The final score for each candidate correction is computed as a weighted sum of the feature scores for the candidate:

$$CandidateScore = \sum_f w_f \cdot S_f$$

where f ranges over the seven feature types used, S_f is the normalized score of the current candidate by feature f, and w_f is the predefined weight of the feature. Learning of weights is described in Section 5.

Our *baseline* system implements all the features, with the exception of word embeddings. Due to the feature formulation, each feature group (e.g. orthographic similarity) requires only one weight. Feature weights for the baseline model are adopted from Flor (2012), where they were manually tuned. In the present work, feature weights are automatically learned with a linear machine learning algorithm. We use two linear classifiers – Logistic Regression and Averaged Perceptron.

5 Experiments

We address the following research questions:

- How does the model compare to a *baseline* system?

- What is the contribution of individual features, especially those that provide contextual information?

- How much training data is needed to learn a robust model?

- How does the model behave on out-of-domain data?

---

[6]`https://code.google.com/archive/p/word2vec`

5.1 Experiments on TOEFL-Spell

First, we present results on error detection. The system detected all 6,121 misspellings and flagged 43 additional words (false positives). Thus, the detection recall is 100%, precision is 99.3% and F1 score is 99.65%. This result applies to all experiments with the TOEFL-Spell data set. The candidate generation performance is over 99%, i.e. for over 99% of the errors a valid correction is generated in the list of candidates. Note that in the candidate generation stage, an average of 213 candidate corrections is generated for each misspelling in the TOEFL-Spell corpus.

We now evaluate the performance of the candidate ranking component, checking whether the top-ranked candidate is indeed the gold correction. The *baseline* system implements all the features, except word embeddings, and uses weights from Flor (2012). For the new approach we add the feature computed with word-embeddings. Feature weights are learned automatically, using linear classifiers – Logistic Regression and Averaged Perceptron.

We address the first research question above, using the TOEFL-Spell corpus in a five-fold cross-validation. Results are presented in Table 3. Each of the classifiers outperforms the baseline, and the differences are statistically significant (by two-proportions z-Test). The difference between Perceptron and Logistic Regression is not significant. The Perceptron algorithm is the best model, with over 2 points of absolute improvement, which is an error reduction of 15%.

Contribution of contextual and non-contextual features. To assess the contribution of individual information sources, we perform feature ablation, by removing one feature at a time. Results are presented in Table 4. The top part of the table shows feature ablation for non-contextual features. The most useful is the orthographic similarity: its removal results in a drop of almost 10 points. Among the contextual features, n-gram support and word2vec prove to be the most useful. Notably, n-gram features and word2vec supply complementary information, and removing each one of those results in a drop in performance. Interestingly, the dejavu and dejavuSM features provide almost no improvement; this result contradicts the finding by Flor (2012). Eliminating all contextual features lowers the performance by more than 10 points, to 77.93%. This demonstrates that contex-

Model	Accuracy
Baseline (Flor, 2012)	85.97
Logistic Regression (this work)	87.83
Perceptron (this work)	88.12

Table 3: Error correction results for the baseline model and two linear classifiers on the TOEFL-Spell data set. Classifiers outperform the baseline (p<0.002).

Feature set	Accuracy
Without *orthographic sim.*	79.84[*]
Without *phonetic sim.*	86.47[*]
Without *word freq.*	88.07
Without *dejavu*	88.07
Without *dejavuSM*	88.01
Without *word2vec*	86.65[*]
Without *ngram support*	82.62[*]
Without contextual features	77.93[*]
Without non-contextual features	65.63[*]
All features	**88.12**

Table 4: Feature ablation performance (error correction accuracy %) on TOEFL-Spell. All models are trained with the Perceptron algorithm in 5-fold cross-validation. Values marked by * differ significantly from the value for *All features*, with $p < 0.003$.

tual features have a substantial contribution. Overall, about 45% of the inadequate corrections produced by the non-contextual model can be corrected by adding context information.

How much training data is needed for a robust model. We train the Perceptron classifier, varying the amounts of training data between 5% and 75% of the entire data set. We similarly perform experiments using 5-fold cross-validation, with the exception that we use less data for training each time. 5% of the training data corresponds to about 240 spelling errors in training. Table 5 demonstrates that even with the smallest training set the

Amount of training data	Accuracy
5%	87.67
10%	87.73
20%	87.86
50%	88.04
75%	88.07
100%	88.12

Table 5: Error correction performance (accuracy %) of the Perceptron classifier trained on different amounts of data, on TOEFL-Spell in 5-fold cross-validation.

drop in performance is less than 1%. In fact, the differences between the models are not significant.

We emphasize that the noisy-channel model requires thousands of examples to estimate the weights of individual edits. In this paper, orthographic similarity is represented as a single feature; thus only one weight is estimated (as opposed to about 1000 weights for character pairs). The same is done for our other features, which allows us to train with a small amount of supervision, couple of hundred of errors.

5.2 Out-of-domain Evaluation

We evaluate the model on a data set from a very different content domain – clinical medical records. The genre of clinical free text poses an interesting challenge to the spelling correction task, since it is notoriously noisy (Fivez et al., 2017a; Lai et al., 2015).

Clinical corpora typically contain higher spelling error rates of 7% to 10%, while in native English text error rates usually range between 0.1% and 0.4% (Ruch et al., 2003). Clinical text contains domain-specific terminology and language conventions. Clinical data, in addition to highly domain-specific vocabulary, can also be characterized by a large amount of noise, e.g. the use of non-standard phrases and abbreviations and is thus particularly challenging (Fivez et al., 2017a). These properties can render traditional spell checkers less effective (Patrick et al., 2010).

We use a data set of clinical notes extracted from the large MIMIC-III medical corpus (Johnson et al., 2016). The data set contains 873 manually annotated misspellings (Fivez et al., 2017a). The distribution of errors in this data set in terms of the edit distance is very similar to that in TOEFL-Spell (see Table 1). In particular, 83% of errors have edit distance of 1 to the correction, while another 15% have an edit distance of 2.

The state-of-the-art results on this data set are reported by Fivez et al. (2017a). Their model is tuned on artificially generated spelling errors and trained on word and character embeddings from MIMIC-III (note that MIMIC-III is the superset of the annotated clinical data set). Their model outperforms off-the-shelf spelling correction tools (Aspell) and the noisy channel model. Similarly to (Fivez et al., 2017a), we accommodate to the medical domain by enhancing the dictionary with a comprehensive medical lexicon (the

Model	Accuracy *off-the-shelf*	Accuracy *completed*
Fivez et al. (2017a)	88.21	93.02
Logistic Regression	87.40	89.35
Perceptron	87.63	89.00

Table 6: Clinical corpus: Performance (accuracy %) of the state-of-the-art system that uses in-domain data, and of the models proposed in this work.

Features	Accuracy
Without *orthographic sim.*	58.88
Without *phonetic sim.*	85.68
Without *word freq.*	87.51
Without *dejavu*	87.06
Without *dejavuSM*	87.74
Without *word2vec*	84.88
Without *ngram support*	85.22
Without contextual feats	80.18
Without non-contextual feats	31.73
All features	**87.63**

Table 7: Feature ablation performance (accuracy %) on the clinical data set. All models are trained with the Perceptron algorithm on TOEFL-Spell data.

UMLS® SPECIALIST Lexicon.[7])

Fivez et al. (2017a) note that some of the required rare corrections were not available even in the medical lexicon. For this reason, they report two versions of results: *off-the-shelf* (using general+medical dictionaries), and *completed lexicon* (where additional rare terms from the annotations were added to the dictionary).

Results for off-the-shelf evaluation are reported in Table 6. Our models were trained on TOEFL-Spell (the same models reported in Table 3). Note that our n-gram and embedding features are also not from the clinical domain. In the off-the-shelf evaluation, our models achieve performance that is comparable to the state-of-the-art system that used in-domain data and was tuned on the clinical corpus. In the completed lexicon evaluation, the Fivez et al. system is better: it obtained a score of 93.02 vs. 89.35 for our Perceptron algorithm. We believe that the off-the-shelf performance reflects a more realistic scenario, as manually adding candidates to the dictionary introduces bias. We further discuss this in the next section.

---

[7] `https://lexsrv3.nlm.nih.gov/ LexSysGroup/Projects/lexicon/current/ web/index.html`

Finally, we evaluate the contribution of each information source on the clinical data (Table 7). Orthographic similarity is the most useful feature, just as it is in the TOEFL-Spell data set, and removing it results in a very big performance drop (almost 30 points). Unsurprisingly, the orthographic similarity feature works well cross-domain. The least helpful features are word frequency, dejavu, and dejavuSM. This is consistent across the two data sets. The word2vec feature provides a slightly better improvement on the clinical data (3 points vs. 2 on TOEFL-Spell), while the n-gram feature performs slightly worse (only 2 points improvement, compared to 6 on TOEFL-Spell). Overall, contextual features contribute 7 points here versus 10 on TOEFL-Spell. This result is expected given that contextual features are estimated on out-of-domain data.

In sum, the experiments on the clinical data set demonstrate that our model is robust and competitive on out-of-domain data. This also stresses the value of the TOEFL-Spell data set, on which our model was trained.

6 Error Analysis

We perform error analysis on both data sets. We first consider cases where the gold correction was not selected as the top candidate. For the TOEFL-Spell data set, our best system places the gold correction at the top of the ranked list in 88% of the cases. If we consider the top five candidates, the system finds the gold correction in 96.7% of the cases. We investigate the cases where the top candidate is different from the gold. In 15.25% of the cases, the top candidate and the gold are inflectional variants of the same lemma (e.g. error: *updations*, gold: *updates*, system-best: *updating*). In 11.4% of cases, the top candidate and the gold are derivationally related (e.g. error: *elastico*, gold: *elasticity*, system-best: *elastic*). In 4% of cases, the top candidate is a close variant of the gold (e.g. error: *donot*, gold: *do not*, system-best: *don't*), or a US/UK spelling variant (e.g. error: *bahaviours*, gold: *behaviours*, system-best: *behaviors*).

For the clinical data set, the system's top suggestion is correct in 87.6% of the cases. The gold correction appears among the top five candidates in 96.7% of the cases (with off-the-shelf dictionaries). In 29.6% of the cases with an incorrect top candidate, the top candidate and the gold correction are inflectional variants of the same lemma, in

14.4% of the cases they are derivationally related, and in 3% of the cases, the top candidate simply has an alternative spelling (e.g. *cyclosporin* and *ciclosporin*). Overall, in 43% of the cases the system selects a morphological variant of the gold correction. This number is lower for the TOEFL-Spell corpus (25%).

We also checked why, in the completed lexicon evaluation on clinical data, our model does not perform as well as the one by Fivez et al. (2017a). It turns out that our model has poor accuracy on the specially added words (41.38%). Further inspection shows that these manually added words are extremely rare medical terms. As a result, contextual features do not fire on them. We expect that adding medical corpora to train word embeddings will solve this issue.

Finally, we provide some examples of errors that our system managed to correct with contextual information but failed to correct without context. An example from the clinical data set: *"was thought to be cold agglutin hemolytic anemia..."*. Without context, the system chooses *agglutin* → *gluten*. With context, the system chooses *agglutin* → *agglutinin*, because *"cold agglutinin"* happens to be a strong collocation. An example from the TOEFL-Spell data set: *"countries such as england, fance and the usa are..."*. Without context, the system prefers *fance* → *fence*, but with context, it correctly chooses *fance* → *france*.

7 Conclusions

This paper addressed the problem of correcting non-word spelling errors, with a focus on errors occurring in noisy natural data. We presented TOEFL-Spell, a publicly-available large data set of authentic misspellings annotated in context. This data set should facilitate further research on spelling correction for noisy data.

We also presented a minimally-supervised model for spelling correction that utilizes non-contextual and contextual features, and does not require a lot of training data. The model demonstrated a state-of-the-art performance on data sets from two noisy domains: learner data and clinical notes. On the latter, competitive performance was achieved, compared to a model developed specifically for the medical domain and trained on in-domain clinical data. We plan to extend this model for handling real-word spelling errors.

Acknowledgments

We thank the anonymous reviewers for valuable comments that helped us to improve this paper.

References

Jon L. Bentley and Robert Sedgewick. 1997. Fast algorithms for sorting and searching strings. In *Proceedings of the 8th Annual ACM-SIAM Symposium on Discrete Algorithms, SODA97*, pages 360–399. ACM.

Daniel Blanchard, Joel Tetreault, Derrick Higgins, Aoife Cahill, and Martin Chodorow. 2013. *TOEFL11: A Corpus of Non-Native English. Research Report ETS RR13-24*. Educational Testing Service, Princeton, NJ, USA.

Daniel Blanchard, Joel Tetreault, Derrick Higgins, Aoife Cahill, and Martin Chodorow. 2014. *ETS Corpus of Non-Native Written English, Catalog No. LDC2014T06*. Linguistic Data Consortium, Philadelphia, PA, USA.

Gerlof Bouma. 2009. Normalized (pointwise) mutual information in collocation extraction. In *From Form to Meaning: Processing Texts Automatically, Proceedings of the Biennial GSCL Conference*, pages 31–40, Tbingen. Gunter Narr Verlag.

Thorsten Brants and Alex Franz. 2006. *Web 1T 5-gram Version 1*. Linguistic Data Consortium.

Eric Brill and Robert C. Moore. 2000. An improved error model for noisy channel spelling correction. In *Proceedings of the 38th Annual Meeting of the Association for Computational Linguistics*, pages 286–293.

Andrew Carlson and Ian Fette. 2007. Memory-based context-sensitive spelling correction at web scale. In *Proceedings of the IEEE International Conference on Machine Learning and Applications (ICMLA)*.

Qing Chen, Mu Li, and Ming Zhou. 2007. Improving query spelling correction using web search results. In *Proceedings of the 2007 Joint Conference on Empirical Methods in Natural Language Processing and Computational Natural Language Learning (EMNLP-CoNLL)*, pages 181–189, Prague, Czech Republic. Association for Computational Linguistics.

Shamil Chollampatt and Hwee Tou Ng. 2018. A multilayer convolutional encoder-decoder neural network for grammatical error correction. In *Proceedings The Thirty-Second AAAI Conference on Artificial Intelligence (AAAI-18)*. Association for the Advancement of Artificial Intelligence.

Shamil Chollampatt, Kaveh Taghipour, and Hwee Tou Ng. 2016. Neural network translation models for grammatical error correction. In *Proceedings of the Twenty-Fifth International Joint Conference on Artificial Intelligence, IJCAI'16*, pages 2768–2774, New York, NY, USA. AAAI Press.

Kenneth W. Church and William A. Gale. 1991. Probability scoring for spelling correction. *Statistics and Computing*, 1:93–103.

Daniel Dahlmeier, Hwee Tou Ng, and Siew Mei Wu. 2013. Building a large annotated corpus of learner English: The NUS Corpus of Learner English. In *Proceedings of the Eighth Workshop on Innovative Use of NLP for Building Educational Applications*, pages 22–31, Atlanta, Georgia. Association for Computational Linguistics.

Frederick Damerau. 1964. A technique for computer detection and correction of spelling errors. *Communications of the ACM*, 7(3):659–664.

Semire Dikli. 2006. An overview of automated scoring of essays. *Journal of Technology, Learning, and Assessment*, 5:4–35.

Pieter Fivez, Simon Suster, and Walter Daelemans. 2017a. Unsupervised Context-Sensitive Spelling Correction of Clinical Free-Text with Word and Character N-Gram Embeddings. In *BioNLP 2017*, pages 143–148, Vancouver, Canada,. Association for Computational Linguistics.

Pieter Fivez, Simon Łuster, and Walter Daelemans. 2017b. Unsupervised Context-Sensitive Spelling Correction of English and Dutch Clinical Free-Text with Word and Character N-Gram Embeddings. In *Arxiv*.

Michael Flor. 2012. Four types of context for automatic spelling correction. *Traitement Automatique des Langues (TAL)*, 53(3):61–99.

Michael Flor and Yoko Futagi. 2012. On using context for automatic correction of non-word misspellings in student essays. In *Proceedings of the Seventh Workshop on Building Educational Applications Using NLP*, pages 105–115, Montréal, Canada. Association for Computational Linguistics.

Michael Flor, Yoko Futagi, Melissa Lopez, and Matthew Mulholland. 2015. Patterns of misspellings in L2 and L1 English: a view from the ETS Spelling Corpus. In *Learner Corpus Research: LCR2013 Conference Proceedings*, volume 6 of *Bergen Language and Linguistic Studies (BeLLS)*, pages 107–132.

Matthias Hagen, Martin Potthast, Marcel Gohsen, Anja Rathgeber, and Benno Stein. 2017. A Large-Scale Query Spelling Correction Corpus. In *40th International ACM Conference on Research and Development in Information Retrieval (SIGIR 17)*, pages 1261–1264. ACM.

Saša Hasan, Carmen Heger, and Saab Mansour. 2015. Spelling correction of user search queries through statistical machine translation. In *Proceedings of the*

2015 Conference on Empirical Methods in Natural Language Processing, pages 451–460, Lisbon, Portugal. Association for Computational Linguistics.

Michael Heilman, Aoife Cahill, Nitin Madnani, Melissa Lopez, Matthew Mulholland, and Joel Tetreault. 2014. Predicting grammaticality on an ordinal scale. In *Proceedings of the 52nd Annual Meeting of the Association for Computational Linguistics (Volume 2: Short Papers)*, pages 174–180, Baltimore, Maryland. Association for Computational Linguistics.

Alistair E. W. Johnson, Tom J. Pollard, Lu Shen, Liwei H. Lehman, Mengling Feng, Mohammad Ghassemi, Benjamin Moody, Peter Szolovits, Leo A. Celi, and Roger G. Mark. 2016. MIMIC-III, a freely accessible critical care database. *Scientific Data*, 3:160035+.

Mark D. Kernighan, Kenneth W. Church, and William A. Gale. 1990. A spelling correction program based on a noisy channel model. In *Papers presented to the 13th International Conference on Computational Linguistics (COLING 1990)*, volume 2, pages 205–210.

Karen Kukich. 1992. Techniques for automatically correcting words in text. *ACM Computing Surveys*, 24:377–439.

Kenneth H. Lai, Maxim Topaz, Foster R. Goss, and Li Zhou. 2015. Automated misspelling detection and correction in clinical free-text records. *Journal of Biomedical Informatics*, 15:188–195.

Claudia Leacock and Martin Chodorow. 2003. C-rater: Automated scoring of short-answer questions. *Computers and Humanities*, 37:389–405.

Vladimir Levenshtein. 1966. Binary codes capable of correcting deletions, insertions and reversals. *Soviet Physics Doklady*, 10:707–710.

Omer Levy and Yoav Goldberg. 2014. Linguistic regularities in sparse and explicit word representations. In *Proceedings of the Eighteenth Conference on Computational Natural Language Learning*, pages 171–180, Ann Arbor, Michigan. Association for Computational Linguistics.

Mu Li, Muhua Zhu, Yang Zhang, and Ming Zhou. 2006. Exploring distributional similarity based models for query spelling correction. In *Proceedings of the 21st International Conference on Computational Linguistics and 44th Annual Meeting of the Association for Computational Linguistics*, pages 1025–1032, Sydney, Australia. Association for Computational Linguistics.

Tomas Mikolov, Ilya Sutskever, Kai Chen, Greg S. Corrado, and Jeff Dean. 2013. Distributed representations of words and phrases and their compositionality. In *Advances in Neural Information Processing Systems*, pages 3111–3119.

Tomoya Mizumoto and Ryo Nagata. 2017. Analyzing the Impact of Spelling Errors on POS-Tagging and Chunking in Learner English. In *Proceedings of the 4th Workshop on Natural Language Processing Techniques for Educational Applications (NLPTEA 2017)*, pages 54–58, Taipei, Taiwan. Asian Federation of Natural Language Processing.

Ryo Nagata, Hiroya Takamura, and Graham Neubig. 2017. Adaptive Spelling Error Correction Models for Learner English. *Procedia Computer Science*, 112:474–483.

Ryo Nagata, Edward Whittaker, and Vera Sheinman. 2011. Creating a manually error-tagged and shallow-parsed learner corpus. In *Proceedings of the 49th Annual Meeting of the Association for Computational Linguistics: Human Language Technologies*, pages 1210–1219, Portland, Oregon, USA. Association for Computational Linguistics.

Courtney Napoles, Keisuke Sakaguchi, and Joel Tetreault. 2017. JFLEG: A Fluency Corpus and Benchmark for Grammatical Error Correction. In *Proceedings of the 15th Conference of the European Chapter of the Association for Computational Linguistics: Volume 2, Short Papers*, pages 229–234, Valencia, Spain. Association for Computational Linguistics.

Hwee Tou Ng, Siew Mei Wu, Ted Briscoe, Christian Hadiwinoto, Raymond Hendy Susanto, and Christopher Bryant. 2014. The CoNLL-2014 Shared Task on Grammatical Error Correction. In *Proceedings of the Eighteenth Conference on Computational Natural Language Learning: Shared Task*, pages 1–14, Baltimore, Maryland. Association for Computational Linguistics.

Diane Nicholls. 2003. The Cambridge Learner Corpus – error coding and analysis for lexicography and ELT. In *Proceedings of the Corpus Linguistics 2003 conference*, pages 572–581.

Jon Patrick, Mojtaba Sabbagh, Suvir Jain, and Haifeng Zheng. 2010. Spelling correction in clinical notes with emphasis on first suggestion accuracy. In *2nd Workshop on Building and Evaluating Resources for Biomedical Text Mining*, pages 2–8.

Lawrence Philips. 2000. The double-metaphone search algorithm. *Dr. Dobb's Journal*.

Alla Rozovskaya and Dan Roth. 2016. Grammatical error correction: Machine translation and classifiers. In *Proceedings of the 54th Annual Meeting of the Association for Computational Linguistics (Volume 1: Long Papers)*, pages 2205–2215, Berlin, Germany. Association for Computational Linguistics.

Patrick Ruch, Robert Baud, and Antoine Geissbuhler. 2003. Using lexical disambiguation and namedentity recognition to improve spelling correction in the electronic patient record. *Artificial Intelligence in Medicine*, 29:169–184.

Claude Shannon. 1948. A mathematical theory of communications. *Bell Systems Technical Journal*, 27:623–656.

Jana Sukkarieh and John Blackmore. 2009. C-rater: Automatic content scoring for short constructed responses. In *Proceedings of the 22nd International Florida Artificial Intelligence Research Society Conference*, pages 290–295.

Kristina Toutanova and Robert Moore. 2002. Pronunciation modeling for improved spelling correction. In *Proceedings of 40th Annual Meeting of the Association for Computational Linguistics*, pages 144–151, Philadelphia, Pennsylvania, USA. Association for Computational Linguistics.

Kuansan Wang and Jan Pedersen. 2011. Review of MSR-Bing web scale speller challenge. In *Proceedings of the 34th international ACM SIGIR conference on Research and development in Information Retrieval (SIGIR 2011)*, pages 1339–1340.

Mark Warschauer and Paige Ware. 2006. Automated writing evaluation: Defining the classroom research agenda. *Language Teaching Research*, 10(2):157–180.

Casey Whitelaw, Ben Hutchinson, Grace Y Chung, and Ged Ellis. 2009. Using the Web for language independent spellchecking and autocorrection. In *Proceedings of the 2009 Conference on Empirical Methods in Natural Language Processing*, pages 890–899, Singapore. Association for Computational Linguistics.

Amber Wilcox-O'Hearn, Graeme Hirst, and Alexander Budanitsky. 2008. Real-word Spelling Correction with Trigrams: A Reconsideration of the Mays, Damerau, and Mercer Model. In *Proceedings of CICLing-2008*, pages 605–616.

Helen Yannakoudakis, Ted Briscoe, and Ben Medlock. 2011. A New Dataset and Method for Automatically Grading ESOL Texts. In *Proceedings of the 49th Annual Meeting of the Association for Computational Linguistics: Human Language Technologies*, pages 180–189, Portland, Oregon, USA. Association for Computational Linguistics.

Artificial Error Generation with Fluency Filtering

Mengyang Qiu[††]   **Jungyeul Park**[†]
[†] Department of Linguistics
[‡] Department of Communicative Disorders and Sciences
State University of New York at Buffalo
{mengyang, jungyeul}@buffalo.edu

Abstract

The quantity and quality of training data plays a crucial role in grammatical error correction (GEC). However, due to the fact that obtaining human-annotated GEC data is both time-consuming and expensive, several studies have focused on generating artificial error sentences to boost training data for grammatical error correction, and shown significantly better performance. The present study explores how fluency filtering can affect the quality of artificial errors. By comparing artificial data filtered by different levels of fluency, we find that artificial error sentences with low fluency can greatly facilitate error correction, while high fluency errors introduce more noise.

1 Introduction

Grammatical Error Correction (GEC), a NLP task of automatically detecting and correcting grammatical errors in text, has received much attention in the past few years, because of an ever-growing demand for reliable and quick feedback to facilitate the progress of English learners. In a typical GEC task, an error sentence such as *I follows his advice* needs to be corrected to a grammatical sentence *I follow his advice*, while a grammatical sentence *She follows his advice* should output the same sentence without any modification. Currently, neural machine translation (NMT) systems using sequence-to-sequence (seq2seq) learning (Sutskever et al., 2014) that "translate" incorrect sentences into correct ones, have shown to be promising in grammatical error correction, and several recent NMT approaches have obtained the state-of-the-art results in GEC (e.g., Chollampatt and Ng, 2018; Ge et al., 2018; Zhao et al., 2019).

While designing a GEC-oriented seq2seq architecture is one important aspect to achieve high performance in grammatical error correction, the quantity and quality of data also plays a crucial

role in the NMT approach to GEC, as NMT parameters cannot learn and generalize well with limited training data. Due to the fact that obtaining human-annotated GEC data is both time-consuming and expensive, several studies have focused on generating artificial error sentences to boost training data for grammatical error correction. One main approach is to extract errors and their surrounding context (the context window approach) from available annotated data, and then apply the errors to error-free sentences naively or probabilistically (Yuan and Felice, 2013; Felice, 2016). The other approach uses machine back-translation, which switches the source-target sentence pairs in GEC and learns to "translate" correct sentences into their incorrect counterparts (Kasewa et al., 2018). While the first approach may not generalize well to unseen errors, and the second one may have no control over what kind of error is produced, artificial error sentences generated from both approaches contribute to better performance in grammatical error correction.

In this paper, we do not focus on which approach is superior in artificial error generation. Rather, given that both approaches can generate multiple error candidates for each correct sentence, we investigate how to select the best ones that can boost GEC performance the most. Although previous studies have shown that artificial errors that match the real error distributions tend to generate better results (Felice, 2016; Xie et al., 2018), we propose an alternative framework that incorporates fluency filtering based on language models. We evaluate four strategies of artificial error selection using different fluency ranges (from lowest to highest) on the recent W&I+LOCNESS test set. Our results show that three of the four strategies lead to evident improvement over the original baseline, which is in line with previous findings that in general GEC benefits from artifi-

Proceedings of the Fourteenth Workshop on Innovative Use of NLP for Building Educational Applications, pages 87–91
Florence, Italy, August 2, 2019. ©2019 Association for Computational Linguistics

cial error data. The model trained with artificial error sentences with the lowest fluency obtains the highest recall among the four settings, while the one trained with error sentences with the median fluency achieves the highest performance in terms of $F_{0.5}$, with an absolute increase of 5.06% over the baseline model.

2   Related Work

Our work mainly builds on the context window approach to artificial error generation. In this approach, all the possible error fragments (errors and their surrounding context) and their corresponding correct fragments are first extracted from GEC annotated corpora. For example, *I follows his* and *I follow his* are the fragments extracted from the example sentences in the first paragraph. With these correct-incorrect fragments, for each error-free sentence, if we find the same correct fragment in the sentence, we can inject errors by replacing that fragment with the incorrect one. Felice (2016) has shown that a context window size of one, that is, one token before and after the error words or phrases, is able to generate a decent amount of error sentences while maintaining the plausibility of the errors. Thus, the current study also adopts this context window size in extracting fragments.

The current work is also inspired by the fluency boost learning proposed in Ge et al. (2018). In their study, sentence fluency is defined as the inverse of the sentence's cross entropy. During fluency boost training, the fluency of candidate sentences generated by their GEC seq2seq model is monitored. Candidate sentences with less than perfect fluency compared to the correct ones are appended as additional error-contained data for subsequent training. Fluency is also used during multi-round GEC inference, in that inference continues as long as the fluency of the output sentences keeps improving. The present study uses fluency measure in an opposite way. We examine how the decrease of fluency in artificial error sentences influences the performance of grammatical error correction.

3   Proposed Methods

To filter candidate error sentences based on fluency, our first step is to generate all the candidate sentences. With correct-incorrect fragment pairs extracted from GEC annotated corpora, we replace all correct fragments found in each error-free sentence with their incorrect counterparts exhaustively. Unlike a method described in Felice (2016) that multiple errors can apply to one sentence at the same time, we only allow one error at a time. Table 1 shows an example of an error-free sentence and the candidate sentences after applying all the possible error replacements. There is only one error in each candidate sentence, and the same position in the correct sentence can have multiple different replacements (*e.g.*, *effects* $\rightarrow$ *impacts|effect|dealing*). We then calculate the fluency score of each candidate sentence and select the ones with the highest fluency, lowest fluency and median fluency. Fluency score is measured by sentence perplexity, the inverse probability of the sentence based on a language model, normalized by the number of words in that sentence. A sentence's fluency score is negatively related to its perplexity. Our prediction is that low sentence fluency (high perplexity) can facilitate error detection and correction by maximizing and highlighting the difference between correct and incorrect sentences. Conversely, artificial error sentences of high fluency can be confusing to the model as the difference between correct and incorrect sentences may be subtle.

4   Experiments and Results

4.1   Dataset and evaluation

We used the four datasets — FCE, NUCLE, W&I+LOCNESS and Lang-8 — provided in the BEA 2019 Shared Task on GEC[1] as the training data for our baseline model (in total about 1.1M sentence pairs). Table 2 shows the summary of the four datasets. There are slightly over half a million error-contained sentences in these datasets, where we extracted 1.3M correct-incorrect fragments. We applied our artificial error injection procedure to the remaining 0.6M error-free sentences, and over 0.4M of them received replacements. We trained a 3-gram language model on all the correct-side sentences using KenLM (Heafield, 2011). The language model was used to calculate perplexity of artificial error sentences. From the 0.4M sentences with error injections, we created four different artificial datasets: one with the highest fluency error sentences among the candidates of each correct sentence, one with the lowest, one with the median, and the last one was

---

[1]`https://www.cl.cam.ac.uk/research/nl/bea2019st/`

	Sentence	Fluency
Correct	the **effects** of **the use** of biometric identification are obvious .	
Candidates:	the effects of **the used** of biometric identification are obvious .	
	the effects of **use** of biometric identification are obvious .	Median
	the effects of **the using** of biometric identification are obvious .	
	the **impacts** of the use of biometric identification are obvious .	
	the **effect** of the use of biometric identification are obvious .	Highest
	...	
	the **dealing** of the use of biometric identification are obvious .	Lowest

Table 1: An example of an error-free sentence and its error injected candidate sentences with three levels of fluency.

Corpus	# Sent Pairs
FCE (Train)	28,346
NUCLE	57,113
W&I+LOCNESS (Train)	34,304
LANG-8	1,037,561
Total	1,157,324
Correct	601,958
Error Injection to Correct	444,521

Table 2: Summary of training data.

randomly selected. Each version was then combined with the original error-contained sentences and the remaining unchanged correct sentences so that all these settings had the same number of sentence pairs as in our baseline model (1.1M). The goal of the experiment was to compare the GEC performance trained with these four settings to the baseline. The W&I+LOCNESS development set of 4,382 sentences was used as validation, and the W&I+LOCNESS test set of 4,477 sentences as evaluation[2]. All these settings were run for three times. Performance was evaluated in terms of precision, recall and $F_{0.5}$ using ERRANT (Bryant et al., 2017).

4.2 Experimental settings

We used the 7-layer convolutional seq2seq model[3] proposed in Chollampatt and Ng (2018) for grammatical error correction with minimal modification. The only difference to Chollampatt and Ng (2018) is that the word embedding dimensions in both encoders and decoders were set to 300 rather than 500, and the word embeddings were trained

separately using the error and correct side training data instead of external corpora. Other parameters were set as recommended in Chollampatt and Ng (2018), including the top 30K BPE tokens as the vocabularies of input and output, $1,024 \times 3$ hidden layers in the encoders and decoders, Nesterov Accelerated Gradient as the optimizer with a momentum of 0.99, dropout rate of 0.2, initial learning rate of 0.25, and minimum learning rate of 10^{-4}. A beam size of 10 was used during model inference. No spell checker was incorporated in the present study, either as pre-processing or post-processing.

4.3 Experimental results

Table 3 shows the results for our baseline and models trained with different fluency-filtered artificial errors. The model trained on the baseline data, which include 0.6M correct sentence pairs, performs the worst in terms of recall (18.85%), because the large proportion of the same sentences makes the model too conservative to make corrections. Indeed, true positive for the baseline model is only 749, which is about half of that in the lowest fluency condition. All the four models with artificial errors obtain higher recall (over 26%), but at the expense of precision. The model with error sentences that have the highest fluency among candidate sentences, in particular, drops over 15% in precision compared to the baseline, making it the worst model in terms of $F_{0.5}$ (42.86%). Error sentences with the lowest fluency lead to the highest recall (32.96%) and second highest $F_{0.5}$ (48.68%) among all the models, while the model in the median fluency condition achieves a good balance between precision drop and recall gain, resulting in the highest $F_{0.5}$ (49.03%).

---

[2]https://competitions.codalab.org/competitions/21922

[3]https://github.com/pytorch/fairseq

	Prec.	Recall	$F_{0.5}$
Original (Baseline)	**65.93**	18.85	43.97
Random	55.67	27.61	46.26
Highest	50.44	26.77	42.86
Median	**57.69**	30.64	**49.03**
Lowest	55.27	**32.96**	48.68

Table 3: Performance of multi-layer CNNs for GEC on W&I+LOCNESS test set with different error data from different fluency filtering.

5 Conclusions and Future Work

The goal of the current study was to explore how the fluency of artificial error sentences can affect the performance of grammatical error correction. We greedily generated all possible error sentences using the similar context window approach as in Felice (2016), and then selected among candidate sentences based on fluency score (sentence perplexity). As predicted, the model trained with artificial error sentences of highest fluency performed even worse than the baseline model with a large proportion of correct sentence pairs. Models in both lowest and median fluency conditions performed significantly better than the other three models. The former one achieved the highest recall, while the latter one was more balanced with the highest $F_{0.5}$. These results indicate that fluency filtering can be used a means to select high-quality artificial error sentences for grammatical error detection and correction.

Although the present study just focused on fluency and ignored error probability, the two factors are not mutually exclusive. Rather, combining the two approaches may generate even better artificial errors. Additionally, fluency filtering is not restricted to the context window approach to error generation, it can be part of the machine back-translation approach to help select among the N best translations.

One limitation of the current study is that we only generated one error at a time for each sentence. In the training data, the 0.5M error sentences contain 1.3M errors, which means that on average each sentence has 2.4 errors. Our next step is to explore using fluency filtering to ensure the quality of artificial multi-error sentences and to see if this can boost GEC performance even further.

References

Christopher Bryant, Mariano Felice, and Ted Briscoe. 2017. Automatic Annotation and Evaluation of Error Types for Grammatical Error Correction. In *Proceedings of the 55th Annual Meeting of the Association for Computational Linguistics (Volume 1: Long Papers)*, pages 793–805, Vancouver, Canada. Association for Computational Linguistics.

Shamil Chollampatt and Hwee Tou Ng. 2018. A Multilayer Convolutional Encoder-Decoder Neural Network for Grammatical Error Correction. In *Proceedings of The Thirty-Second AAAI Conference on Artificial Intelligence (AAAI-18)*, New Orleans, Louisiana.

Mariano Felice. 2016. Artificial error generation for translation-based grammatical error correction. Technical Report UCAM-CL-TR-895, University of Cambridge, Computer Laboratory.

Tao Ge, Furu Wei, and Ming Zhou. 2018. Fluency Boost Learning and Inference for Neural Grammatical Error Correction. In *Proceedings of the 56th Annual Meeting of the Association for Computational Linguistics (Volume 1: Long Papers)*, pages 1055–1065, Melbourne, Australia. Association for Computational Linguistics.

Kenneth Heafield. 2011. KenLM: Faster and Smaller Language Model Queries. In *Proceedings of the Sixth Workshop on Statistical Machine Translation*, pages 187–197, Edinburgh, Scotland. Association for Computational Linguistics.

Sudhanshu Kasewa, Pontus Stenetorp, and Sebastian Riedel. 2018. Wronging a Right: Generating Better Errors to Improve Grammatical Error Detection. In *Proceedings of the 2018 Conference on Empirical Methods in Natural Language Processing*, pages 4977–4983, Brussels, Belgium. Association for Computational Linguistics.

Ilya Sutskever, Oriol Vinyals, and Quoc V. Le. 2014. Sequence to Sequence Learning with Neural Networks. In Z. Ghahramani, M. Welling, C. Cortes, N. D. Lawrence, and K. Q. Weinberger, editors, *Advances in Neural Information Processing Systems 27*, pages 3104–3112. Curran Associates, Inc.

Ziang Xie, Guillaume Genthial, Stanley Xie, Andrew Ng, and Dan Jurafsky. 2018. Noising and Denoising Natural Language: Diverse Backtranslation for Grammar Correction. In *Proceedings of the 2018 Conference of the North American Chapter of the Association for Computational Linguistics: Human Language Technologies, Volume 1 (Long Papers)*, pages 619–628, New Orleans, Louisiana. Association for Computational Linguistics.

Zheng Yuan and Mariano Felice. 2013. Constrained grammatical error correction using statistical machine translation. In *Proceedings of the Seventeenth Conference on Computational Natural Language Learning: Shared Task*, pages 52–61, Sofia,

Bulgaria. Association for Computational Linguistics.

Wei Zhao, Liang Wang, Kewei Shen, Ruoyu Jia, and Jingming Liu. 2019. Improving Grammatical Error Correction via Pre-Training a Copy-Augmented Architecture with Unlabeled Data. In *Proceedings of the 2019 Conference of the North {A}merican Chapter of the Association for Computational Linguistics: Human Language Technologies, Volume 1 (Long and Short Papers)*, pages 156–165, Minneapolis, Minnesota. Association for Computational Linguistics.

Regression or classification? Automated Essay Scoring for Norwegian

Stig Johan Berggren
Department of Informatics
University of Oslo
stigjb@gmail.com

Taraka Rama
Department of Informatics
University of Oslo
taraka.kasi@gmail.com

Lilja Øvrelid
Department of Informatics
University of Oslo
liljao@ifi.uio.no

Abstract

In this paper we present first results for the task of Automated Essay Scoring for Norwegian learner language. We analyze a number of properties of this task experimentally and assess (i) the formulation of the task as either regression or classification, (ii) the use of various non-neural and neural machine learning architectures with various types of input representations, and (iii) applying multi-task learning for joint prediction of essay scoring and native language identification. We find that a GRU-based attention model trained in a single-task setting performs best at the AES task.

1 Introduction

Automated essay scoring (AES), in the literature also referred to as Assessment of Proficiency or Automated Text Scoring (ATS), considers the task of assigning a grade to a free form text, often responding to a specific prompt. Automation of this assessment task has clear applications in language education, where second language learners can receive feedback as to which proficiency level they might be on, for instance in relation to the Common European Framework of Reference (CEFR) level. This may help learners who want to take language examination to find the appropriate timing and level of testing, since an examination can be both an economical and logistical inconvenience. Automation also allows students to receive feedback quicker and more frequently.[1]

Recent work on the AES task has used both non-neural, feature-rich approaches that make use of a variety of linguistic features (Briscoe et al., 2010; Yannakoudakis et al., 2011; Vajjala, 2017), and neural end-to-end architectures (Taghipour and Ng, 2016; Alikaniotis et al., 2016). Previous work has furthermore adopted different formulations of the task, either as a regression problem (Phandi et al., 2015; Taghipour and Ng, 2016) or a classification task (Rudner and Liang, 2002; Briscoe et al., 2010; Vajjala and Rama, 2018). Most previous work however, with a few noteworthy exceptions (Hancke, 2013; Vajjala and Loo, 2014; Pilán et al., 2016), has been focused on English learner language.

In this paper we present first results for automated essay scoring of Norwegian learner language. We make use of the ASK corpus of learner language (Tenfjord et al., 2006), with added CEFR labels (Carlsen, 2012), and compare and contrast different formulations of the task, a number of different machine learning architectures and different input representations and further experiment with a multi-task setting with Native Language Identification as auxiliary task.

The rest of the paper is structured as follows. We present related work in section 2 and go on to describe the Norwegian learner corpus (ASK) in section 3. We describe the aims of this paper in section 4.1 and describe the data preprocessing and the creation of training, development, and test datasets in section 4.2. We present the results of non-neural linear models in section 5 and CNNs and Gated-RNNs on the development dataset in section 6. Then, we briefly describe the results of our experiments with native language identification in section 7 and the subsequent results of multitask experiments in section 8. Finally, we report the results of the best linear and neural models on the held-out test data in section 9. We summarize and conclude the paper in section 10.

---

[1] This work was performed when the first author was a Masters student with the Language Technology Group at University of Oslo. Similarly, the second author took part in the BigMed project https://bigmed.no/ hosted at University of Oslo.

Proceedings of the Fourteenth Workshop on Innovative Use of NLP for Building Educational Applications, pages 92–102
Florence, Italy, August 2, 2019. ©2019 Association for Computational Linguistics

2 Related work

Yannakoudakis et al. (2011) present the CLC First Certificate of English (FCE) corpus as well as a system that makes use of deep linguistic features, such as PoS-tags and syntactic information and further employ a discriminative ranker that is shown to outperform a regression approach on the FCE corpus.

Vajjala (2017) trains linear classifiers over the TOEFL11 corpus of non-native English (Blanchard et al., 2013) and the FCE corpus and makes use of a number of linguistic features for the task, including several different measures for lexical diversity, distribution of POS tags, and syntactic complexity, as well as features capturing discourse properties. Several of these features were based on previous work on measuring syntactic complexity in L2 writing by (Lu, 2010).

Alikaniotis et al. (2016) and Taghipour and Ng (2016) both present neural systems trained and evaluated on the ASAP Kaggle dataset of student essays. Both formulate the AES task as a regression task and experiment with several types of neural architectures applied to the same dataset, showing the best results using a bidirectional LSTM with pre-trained embeddings.

Whereas much previous work has been focused on English learner language, there has also been some work on AES using the CEFR scale for languages other than English, viz. Hancke (2013) for German, Vajjala and Loo (2014) for Estonian and Pilán et al. (2016) for Swedish learner texts. All these papers take a very similar approach to the task, modeling essay scoring as SVM classification using a large number of lexical, morphological, syntactic and semantic features. Finally, Vajjala and Rama (2018) present results for mono-lingual, cross-lingual and multi-lingual CEFR classification using the MERLIN corpus (Boyd et al., 2014).

The ASK corpus (Tenfjord et al., 2006) employed in the current study, and further described in section 3, has been used in several linguistic studies on features of Norwegian learner language and transfer effects from different L1 (Pepper, 2012; Golden, 2016; Vigrestad, 2016). The ASK corpus has also been used in previous work to train machine learning systems for Native Language Identification (NLI). The task of NLI for English language learners has been the subject of several shared tasks (Tetreault et al., 2013; Schuller et al.,

2016; Malmasi et al., 2017). Norwegian NLI has been studied by Malmasi et al. (2015), using the ASK corpus. In their methodology, they create artificial documents to train on by segmenting the learner texts into sentences, then putting all the sentences from learners with the same L1 into a bag and sampling sentences from the bag to create the new documents. Their rationale for the methodology is that all the resulting documents are of similar length, and that they eliminate the variation between individual writers that otherwise might present a stronger signal than the writer's L1 alone.

In a later study, Malmasi and Dras (2017) perform an NLI experiment on several corpora, namely TOEFL11, the Norwegian ASK corpus and the Jinan Chinese Learner corpus. For Norwegian, they use the features such as function word uni-/bigrams and part-of-speech n-grams. By combining a selection of base classifiers using a LDA meta-classifier trained with bootstrap aggregation (bagging), they achieve an accuracy of 0.818 on the artificially Norwegian essay corpus. The authors' methodology also involves generating artificial essays which discard the discourse properties of a text that could help in improving the system performance at NLI task. Therefore, we do not replicate their experiments but chose to test our best models tuned on development split and then report the best model on a separate test split.

In this paper, we test several RNN models were implemented based on the architecture described in Taghipour and Ng (2016). We made necessary changes to the architectures in order to accommodate our data. For instance, Taghipour and Ng (2016) modelled the task as a regression problem, where the output layer consists of a single node with a value constrained to $(0, 1)$ by the sigmoid function. This layer was replaced with a softmax layer which is described further in section 6.

3 Dataset

The ASK corpus (*AndreSpråksKorpus*; Tenfjord et al., 2006) contains Norwegian learner essays from two different language tests: *Språkprøven i norsk for voksne innvandrere* and *Test i norsk – høyere nivå*,[2] which test proficiency at the B1 and B2 levels, respectively. Following the naming in

---

[2]Translated to as "Language testing in Norwegian for adult immigrants" and "Test in upper Norwegian levels".

Carlsen (2012), we will refer to these tests as the *IL test* (Intermediate Level, "Språkprøven") and the *AL test* (Advanced Level, "Høyere nivå").

First language	AL test	IL test	Total
English	100	100	200
Polish	100	100	200
Russian	100	100	200
Somali	7	100	107
Spanish	100	100	200
German	100	100	200
Vietnamese	5	100	105
Subtotal (included languages)	512	700	1212
(Albanian)	24	100	124
(Bosnian-Croatian-Serbian)	100	100	200
(Dutch)	100	100	200
(Norwegian nynorsk)	21	11	32
(Norwegian bokmål)	79	89	168
Subtotal (excluded languages)	324	400	724
Total (all languages)	836	1100	1936

Table 1: Distributions of first languages for each test level in ASK. Texts in each test level for all L1. Languages which are not included in our CEFR-labeled dataset are listed in parentheses.

The corpus contains 1736 texts and each document includes metadata such as the writer's L1: one of German, Dutch, English, Spanish, Russian, Polish, Bosnian-Croatian-Serbian, Albanian, Vietnamese, and Somali. All texts from seven of these language backgrounds, 1212 in total, have been assigned a *CEFR* score at a later stage (Carlsen, 2012), and these texts comprise the subcorpus we will be working with. In particular, all texts except those written by learners with Dutch, Bosnian-Croatian-Serbian or Albanian as L1 have a CEFR score. The CEFR labels are available since work by Carlsen (2012), and were not included in the initial release of the corpus. Table 1 shows the number of texts in the corpus for each native language and at each test level.

Restricting the corpus size to only 1212 documents with CEFR scores, the number of tokens amounted to approximately 487,000 in total. Other types of metadata, apart from L1 and CEFR score, include, but are not limited to: the test level the essay was written for, what topic the essay is about, and the learner's country of origin, age, and gender. The CEFR scores in the ASK corpus range between A2 and C1, and also include intermediate labels between the canonical proficiency scores, such as A2/B1 and B1/B2. Thus, the total number of distinct CEFR scores is seven, which is more fine-grained than the TOEFL11 corpus (Blanchard

et al., 2013), which only uses three distinct proficiency categories, or the corpus used in Vajjala and Rama (2018), the MERLIN corpus, where the CEFR scores range between A1 and C1, but without any intermediate levels.

When examining the correlation between various types of metadata and proficiency scores in the corpus, there are several noteworthy properties. First of all, we observe that test levels have different distributions of proficiency. We find that the distribution of CEFR scores corresponds to the similarity of the various L1 to Norwegian. The Germanic languages—German and English—have the fewest number of essays below B1 level in the IL test. Two non-Indo-European languages—Vietnamese and Somali—rarely score above B1 level in the IL test, and their mode is A2/B1 compared to B1 for all the Indo-European languages.

4 Methods

4.1 Aims

In this section, we describe the objectives of the experiments reported in the paper. Apart from an extensive analysis of the ASK corpus using linear and neural models, we investigate whether AES based on ASK should be modelled as a classification task or a regression task (given that both the approaches are common in the literature, see section 2). We approach this question by testing three different models namely: Logistic regression, Support Vector Regression, and SVM classification for a wide range of linguistic representation combinations. We then go on to assess the level of performance at the AES task using neural methods? Finally, we combine both the AES task and the NLI task under a single multi-tasking model to check if joint training of a neural model with two different objectives can improve the performance at the AES task.

4.2 Preprocessing

The data files in the ASK corpus are in XML format, and contain information about tags, mistakes and corrections, paragraphs, sentences and more. First, the files were converted to plain text files where all the tags or correction labels were stripped of. The text files have one sentence per line, consisting of space-separated tokens, and an empty line separating paragraphs. These raw text files were then processed using the

UDPipe pipeline (Straka and Straková, 2017) for PoS-tagging and dependency parsing, with pretrained models trained on the Norwegian UD treebank (Øvrelid and Hohle, 2016).

Two different sets of output labels are used in the experiments: The original seven CEFR labels, and a collapsed set where the intermediate classes, such as 'A2/B1', are rounded up to the nearest canonical class, i.e., the CEFR label after the slash. This step yields only four different labels in the *collapsed* set: 'A2', 'B1', 'B2' and 'C1'.

4.3 Reported metrics

We report both the macro and micro F_1-scores for all experiments. The metrics are reported for two different modes: The first utilizing the full set of classes, and the second mode involved training and evaluating on the collapsed classes. A third option, namely to train on the full set of classes and reduce the predictions to the collapsed set of classes, was also attempted, however, in practice the best performers on the collapsed labels turned out to be the models that were also trained on the collapsed tags.

4.4 Data split

Since this paper reports the first results for AES on the ASK corpus, care was taken to create well-defined splits of the data for training, development and final held-out testing. In an ideal scenario, the training and testing datasets would typically have the same distribution of classes, but the limited amount of data makes this difficult; and, as many as 15 combinations of language and proficiency label have fewer than three documents. Moreover, we also took care to create splits in such a manner such that there is no overlap of topics between the splits. The reason for this split is to perform our experiments in a real-world setting where the model needs to be tested on topics not seen in the training data. The final data splits follow a 8:1:1 distribution and we tried to ensure that the joint distribution of proficiency and native language is similar across the splits and that topics do not recur across training, development, and test splits.

5 Linear models

In this section, we train and evaluate the performance of three different linear models on the development dataset. We use the results of this experiment to establish if AES is best modelled as a regression or classification task for the ASK dataset.

Classification vs. Regression As mentioned earlier, AES can be modelled both as a classification task and as a regression task. A disadvantage with using regression for the AES task is that while we know the correct order of classes, it is not obvious if the distance between the adjacent classes is always the same. For instance, we do not know if the distance from CEFR score 'A2/B1' to 'B1' is just as 'B1' to 'B1/B2'. However, we need to be aware of this when we transform the labels into numeric values for regression. This challenge of quantifying distance between classes does not apply to the classification approach, but it does come with another problem. The multi-class approach does not take the order of classes into consideration which is an intrinsic property of the class label in AES tasks.

Implementation All models in this section were implemented using the scikit-learn (Pedregosa et al., 2011) library. The logistic regression model was trained with the 'lgbfs' solver to minimize multinomial loss. The linear regression model was a support vector regressor also chosen from scikit-learn with default parameters. We experiment with different types of input and use both tokens, character ngrams, mixed POS and function word ngrams, and POS ngrams as inputs.

Results In order to report classification based metrics for a regression model, we transformed the predicted scores, which are continuous, into discrete scores equivalent to the given classes. This was done by rounding the raw regression scores to the nearest integer. The output from the support vector regression model is not constrained to any interval, making it necessary to additionally clip the output values to the range of scores: $[0, 6]$ in our full set of labels and $[0, 3]$ in the collapsed set. All the macro and micro F_1 scores for the linear models, for both the full and collapsed sets of classes, are reported in table 2. The Support Vector Regression model is the best performing model at both all labels and collapsed labels tasks. The best model turns to the one trained using UPOS ngrams. The results suggest that treating the AES as a regression problem is a better approach than the classification approach, at least for ASK dataset.

	All labels		Collapsed labels	
Model	Macro F_1	Micro F_1	Macro F_1	Micro F_1
Majority	0.040	0.163	0.127	0.341
LogReg BOW	0.199	0.317	0.384	0.626
LogReg Char	0.221	0.317	0.399	0.602
LogReg POS	0.190	0.301	0.312	0.569
LogReg Mix	0.213	0.341	0.337	0.577
SVC BOW	0.210	0.317	0.391	0.610
SVC Char	0.189	0.293	0.347	0.537
SVC POS	0.157	0.244	0.336	0.618
SVC Mix	0.215	0.350	0.319	0.585
SVR BOW	**0.444**	0.415	0.429	0.659
SVR Char	0.252	0.317	0.440	0.602
SVR POS	0.334	0.358	**0.476**	0.593
SVR Mix	0.312	0.350	0.441	0.659

Table 2: F_1-scores of various classifiers. LogReg is logistic regression, SVC is support vector classification, and SVR is support vector regression.

6 Neural models

In this section, we train and evaluate a wide range of convolutional networks and gated RNNs for the AES task. We further experiment with the use of pre-trained word embeddings which are fine-tuned for the task. The embedding models have been trained on a large Norwegian corpus, the combination of Norsk aviskorpus (The Norwegian Newspaper Corpus) and NoWaC (Norwegian Web As Corpus; Stadsnes, 2018) using the FastText software (Bojanowski et al., 2017) and are available from the NLPL vector repository (Fares et al., 2017).[3]

6.1 Convolutional Networks

We train a number of models which are variants of the convolutional architecture described in Kim (2014). Here, documents are represented as sequences of token IDs and fed into an embedding lookup layer. We pad short documents (length < 700) and use a word frequency cutoff to model out-of-vocabulary words. All models were implemented using Keras (Chollet et al., 2015) and TensorFlow (Abadi et al., 2015) as backend.

The central part of the architecture is a set of convolutional filter banks that are applied to sequences of embeddings. The default architecture from (Kim, 2014) uses 300 convolutional filters: 100 each of window size 3, 4 and 5. After applying the convolutions, the output is max pooled along the time axis. This selects the highest output each filter computed across all windows in the document. In practice, three pooling operations

---

[3]http://vectors.nlpl.eu/repository/

are included in the computational graph, one for each filter bank. This is a technical consideration, necessary because of the different window sizes.

The pooled vectors for each of the filter banks are concatenated into a single vector, representing the document as a whole. This vector has as many elements as there are filters in all the filter banks combined. This representation vector is fed to a final softmax layer to produce a classification output. During training, we apply dropout to the final softmax layer.

	All labels		Collapsed labels	
Model	Macro F_1	Micro F_1	Macro F_1	Micro F_1
Randomly initialized embeddings				
CNN	0.168	**0.398**	0.388	0.732
CNN+POS	0.146	0.374	0.398	0.748
CNN Mix	0.201	**0.398**	0.383	0.724
CNN Reg	0.230	0.382	0.439	0.724
CNN Reg+POS	0.236	0.341	0.383	0.724
CNN Reg Mix	**0.258**	**0.398**	0.412	0.642
CNN Rank	0.177	0.374	0.392	0.740
CNN Rank+POS	0.187	0.382	0.397	0.748
CNN Rank Mix	0.231	0.382	0.379	0.715
Pre-trained, fine tuned embeddings				
CNN	0.208	0.382	0.384	0.724
CNN+POS	0.161	0.366	0.402	**0.756**
CNN Reg	0.242	0.341	**0.463**	0.724
CNN Reg+POS	0.232	0.366	0.411	0.715
CNN Rank	0.198	0.350	0.384	0.724
CNN Rank+POS	0.181	0.325	0.401	**0.756**

Table 3: F_1 scores of CNN classifiers on AES. +POS: Multi-channel input with both words and UPOS tags. Reg: Regression model. Rank: Ordinal regression.

We employ both pre-trained and randomly initialized embeddings and fine-tune the embeddings in the training step. The results of this experiment are given in table 3. In the case of all label prediction, the best results are obtained with a CNN regression model with mixed POS tags as input. The best model in the case of collapsed label prediction is a CNN ordinal rank regression with POS tags as input.

6.2 Recurrent Networks

In this section, we tested a wide range of recurrent models for the AES task by modeling the problem as a regression problem. Taghipour and Ng (2016) test multiple recurrent architectures such as LSTM, GRU, and attention model in their paper. We made some changes to the architectures and added more experiments which are described in the following. The embedding layer in Taghipour and Ng (2016) was of 50 dimensions and randomly initialized. We increased the embedding dimensions size to 100 and experimented with randomly initialized embeddings and with pre-trained ones as in the experiments with CNN. Due to the long essay length, we chose to work with gated RNNs since they are known to capture long-distance dependencies. We experimented with the following settings in the case of gated RNNs:

- Long Short Term Memory network (LSTM) vs. Gated Recurrent Unit (GRU)

- Bidirectional vs. unidirectional

- Attention mechanisms: Mean, maximum of the hidden states over all the time steps, and a weighted version of attention involving a feed-forward network (Pappas and Popescu-Belis, 2017).

Model	All labels		Collapsed labels	
	Macro F_1	Micro F_1	Macro F_1	Micro F_1
Random init, unidirectional GRU				
Mean	0.264	0.374	0.455	0.675
Max	0.219	0.325	0.487	0.683
Attn	0.434	0.431	**0.806**	0.805
+POS Mean	0.348	0.398	0.450	0.642
+POS Max	0.230	0.374	0.500	0.748
+POS Attn	0.434	0.423	0.718	0.813
Mix Mean	0.225	0.333	0.388	0.634
Mix Max	0.200	0.398	0.398	0.756
Mix Attn	0.302	**0.455**	0.509	0.780
Random init, BiGRU				
Mean	0.314	0.333	0.444	0.667
Max	0.160	0.325	0.460	0.691
Attn	0.459	0.447	0.805	0.805
+POS Mean	0.373	0.333	0.425	0.683
+POS Max	0.175	0.309	0.503	0.748
+POS Attn	**0.460**	0.447	0.687	**0.821**
Mix Mean	0.231	0.350	0.395	0.642
Mix Max	0.200	0.382	0.405	0.764
Mix Attn	0.275	**0.455**	0.617	0.707
Pre-trained, unidirectional GRU				
Mean	0.274	0.366	0.463	0.715
Max	0.185	0.350	0.401	0.756
Attn	0.414	0.431	0.678	0.797
+POS Mean	0.282	0.382	0.477	0.699
+POS Max	0.193	0.382	0.405	0.764
+POS Attn	0.409	0.423	0.746	0.789
Pre-trained, BiGRU				
Mean	0.266	0.390	0.435	0.707
Max	0.187	0.398	0.393	0.740
Attn	0.454	0.447	0.773	0.797
+POS Mean	0.281	0.382	0.480	0.724
+POS Max	0.183	0.341	0.397	0.748
+POS Attn	0.433	0.439	0.758	0.805

Table 4: F_1 scores of GRU classifiers on AES. BiGRU is birectional GRU; Attn is attention model.

The results of our experiments are given in table 4. Although we experimented with both LSTM and GRUs we found that the GRU architectures performed better than the LSTM architectures at different metrics and label sets with wide variety of settings. Therefore, we report only the results from our GRU classifier. The results show that a combination of embeddings trained separately on words and POS tags give better results at both the full label set and the collapsed label set. Throughout the experiments the document attention model performed the best with randomly initialized embeddings.

7 Native language identification

In contrast to the proficiency labels in ASK where the number of higher level classes are so few, the distribution of L1 labels is more even across the documents. Regression as such is not applicable to NLI since there is no natural ordering among the L1 languages. Therefore, we model the NLI task as a classification problem. We train both CNN, LSTM, and GRU architectures to predict the native language of the writers of the essays. We found that the RNN models performed better than CNN models and among the RNN models, GRU architectures performed better than their LSTM counterparts. Therefore, we report only the results of our best GRU model in table 5. The best model is a GRU model which employs pretrained embeddings and takes mean of the hidden states over the time steps to perform classification using a softmax layer. This model achieves a best accuracy of 0.537 which is lower than the score of 0.542 reported by Malmasi and Dras (2018) on the original essays.

Model	Macro F_1	Micro F_1
Mean	**0.520**	**0.537**
Max	0.401	0.390
Attn	0.447	0.480
+POS Mean	0.467	0.480
+POS Max	0.406	0.431
+POS Attn	0.454	0.463

Table 5: F_1 scores of Pre-trained, BiGRU classifier at the NLI task consisting of 7 classes.

Note however that we cannot compare our results to the previous work for the following reasons. First, our subset of the ASK dataset corresponds to the seven L1 languages which has been assigned CEFR scores, as compared to the full set of ten L1 languages used by Malmasi et al. (2015). Second, Malmasi et al. (2015) used simulated data sets and not the actual raw essays to perform NLI experiments. Third, unlike the previous studies we do not evaluate our results in a cross-validation fashion.

8 Multi-task learning

Until now, we treated AES and NLI as independent tasks and performed experiments on both the tasks separately. We will now attempt to train a joint model to predict both the tasks jointly.

We selected four models for the multi-task experiments—two convolutional and two recurrent neural networks—based on the macro F_1 results on the development set. The top two models (two each for CNN and RNN) had the highest macro F_1 on the full set of labels on the development set. The multi-task model that we use in this paper has two outputs with different loss functions: one for CEFR prediction and the other for NLI task. The loss function for CEFR output is mean squared loss and for NLI is categorical cross-entropy loss. The losses from both the models are linearly weighted with weights summing up to 1. We searched for the best loss weight by searching over the range of $[0, 1]$ where each weight is separated by an interval of 0.1.

Hyperparameter	CNN1	CNN2
Word embeddings	Dynamic	
Embedding size	100	
L_2 constraint	3	
Windows	3,4,5	
Embedding init	Random	Pre-trained
Input representation	Mixed UPOS	Tokens
Hyperparameter	RNN1	RNN2
Word embeddings	Dynamic	
Embedding size	100	
RNN cell	GRU	
Pooling method	Attention	
Bidirectional	Yes	
Embedding init	Random	Pre-trained
Input representation	Tokens+UPOS	Tokens

Table 6: Descriptions of the CNN and RNN models showing different settings.

The hyperparameters for the four models are summarized in table 6. All our word embeddings are based on the FastText model. We also tested the variability of the models by training and evaluating each model five times with different random seeds to estimate the variance of the results.

Results We show the results of all the models with all the auxiliary weight combinations in figure 1. When the auxiliary task loss weight is zero, the model reduces to the original single task model of CEFR prediction. The RNN models show the highest macro F_1 scores on the full label set. There is some variablity in the performance of the RNN models in accordance with the loss weight. In each panel, we show the F_1 scores for the five models trained with different random seeds. The CNN models do not benefit from including the NLI task as additional task. The five highest macro-F_1 scores are in the range of 0.468 and 0.483 and were achieved using auxiliary loss weights in the range from 0 to 0.5. Although, the highest score was achieved in single-task mode the auxiliary task results are also competitive as shown in the figure. In fact, the variability due to the initial random seed allows us to conclude that the macro-F_1 scores for a multi-task model is almost the same as the single task mode (auxiliary loss weight set to zero).

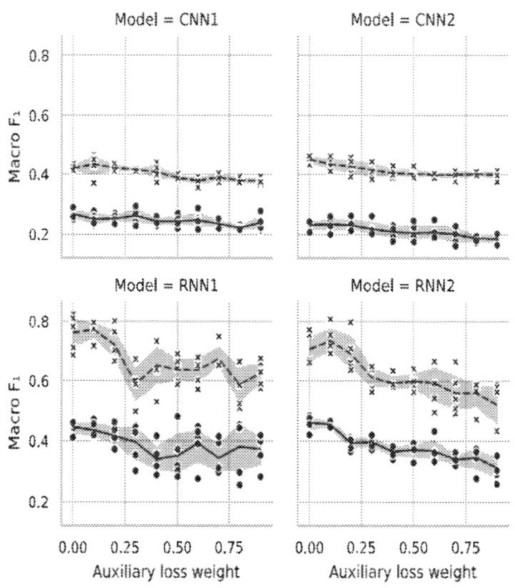

Figure 1: Lines follow the mean of macro F_1 scores. Shaded areas show 95% confidence interval for the mean. Results for the collapsed set of classes are plotted with cross symbols and dashed lines.

The same trend can be observed with RNN2 model also which shows a decreasing trend in the macro-F_1 scores. The macro-F_1 scores' trends for both the RNN models are not similar at the task of collapsed label set classification. The RNN1 model shows a high variation with changes in the auxiliary loss weights. Similar to the full label set classification, the collapsed label set classification does not show worse performance but shows competitive results when the auxiliary loss weight is set to 0.1. We conclude from these experiments that including the NLI task as auxiliary task, at least, does not hurt the performance at AES task.

9 Results

Until now, we evaluated the performance of our models on the development dataset. We now go on to report the performance of our best models from development on the held-out test dataset in table 7. In the case of the neural architectures, we employed the model showing the best macro-F_1 during development.

	All labels		Collapsed labels	
Model	Macro	Micro	Macro	Micro
Majority	0.045	0.187	0.127	0.341
SVR BOW	0.231	0.285	0.420	0.602
SVR POS	0.271	0.350	0.422	0.602
RNN1	0.291	0.439	0.478	**0.724**
RNN2	**0.388**	**0.480**	**0.511**	0.724
Multi-RNN1	0.266	0.398	0.509	0.707
Multi-RNN2	0.356	0.447	0.443	**0.724**

Table 7: Results from evaluation on the held-out test set. SVR is support vector regression. Hyperparameters for RNN1 and RNN2 are found in table 6. Multitask models use an auxiliary task weight of 0.1.

We report the results for SVR, RNNs, and Multi-task RNN models. In terms of micro-F_1 scores, the RNN models are the best across both the collapsed labels and full label sets. Across all the models, both the micro- and macro-F_1 scores are lower than the scores reported on the development split. The Multi-RNN2 model performs the best in terms of micro-F_1 score at collapsed labels. The multi-tasking model shows poor performance in terms of macro-F_1 score across all the tasks when compared to the single task model. The linear models show worse performance than the neural models across all the label sets and evaluation measures. We further observe that a multi-task setup with NLI as auxiliary task does not show competitive results. In conclusion, a fine-tuned embedding BiGRU model augmented with attention and initiated with FastText word embeddings performs the best.

We further examine the confusion matrices for our best multi-task model, 'RNN2 Multi', on the test set. The plot is given in figure 2. We see in the confusion matrix that we can identify a diagonal running from the top-left to the bottom-right, with zeros in the top-right and bottom-left corners. Furthermore, mis-classifications are mostly close to the true value, with no predictions being more than two classes away from the gold label.

In the confusion matrix for L1, we see that all languages are predicted to be Spanish at some point. German is predicted with 100% precision, however a lot of German texts are wrongly classified as English. This seems reasonable since English and German are similar languages in the same language family. However, the Slavic languages are not confused for each other, as one might expect, but rather Russian and Polish are both commonly mistaken for Spanish.

10 Conclusion

In this paper, we analyzed the ASK corpus for the first time at the AES task with neural and non-linear models. We addressed the question of modeling AES as regression vs. classification task using three different non-neural models. We find that the AES task is best modeled as regression, at least in the case of the ASK corpus. We tested different input representations such as word, character, and POS n-grams for training the non-neural models. We find that the best results are obtained when using Support Vector Regression algorithm.

In the case of neural models, we tested both convolutional networks and recurrent neural networks (LSTM and GRU) both at AES and NLI tasks. We augmented the neural models with different models of attention such as mean-over-time, max-over-time, and attention learned through a feed-forward network. We find in our experiments that attention augmented BiGRU perform the best at AES task. In contrast, the simpler mean-over-time BiGRU model performed the best at NLI task.

We performed an extensive evaluation of four multitasking models where NLI is an auxiliary task. We tuned the auxiliary loss weight over the development split and found that the weight of 0.1 is best suited for joint modeling of AES and NLI tasks. Although the joint model does not yield results that are better than the single task AES models, we conclude that the joint model yields results that are competitive with the single task model setting. We conclude that multi-task models do not help improve the performance of AES task. We

Figure 2: Confusion matrices for RNN2 Multi on the held-out test set. AES task on the left, NLI task on the right. The numbers are counts.

also tested if initializing the embeddings with the FastText model improves the AES results. Although the results on development dataset are ambiguous about the choice of pretrained vs. random initialized embeddings, the results on the test set show that the RNN2 model (fine-tuned) works best at AES classification. Therefore, we suggest that any future neural system for AES should use pretrained embeddings to achieve the best results.

As future work, we intend to analyze the errors made by the model and compare them with the errors marked by the human annotators which are available in the ASK corpus. We believe that such an analysis would be the first that would be useful for designing better models and understanding where the neural models make mistakes. Another direction of future work is to use a hierarchical RNN where each sentence within an essay is encoded by a RNN that would be stacked with an additional RNN layer to handle possible loss of signal in extremely long documents.

Acknowledgments

The authors thank the anonymous reviewers for the comments that helped improve the paper. This work is supported by different projects awarded to the Language Technology Group with the University of Oslo.

References

Martín Abadi, Ashish Agarwal, Paul Barham, Eugene Brevdo, Zhifeng Chen, Craig Citro, Greg S. Corrado, Andy Davis, Jeffrey Dean, Matthieu Devin, Sanjay Ghemawat, Ian Goodfellow, Andrew Harp, Geoffrey Irving, Michael Isard, Yangqing Jia, Rafal Jozefowicz, Lukasz Kaiser, Manjunath Kudlur, Josh Levenberg, Dandelion Mané, Rajat Monga, Sherry Moore, Derek Murray, Chris Olah, Mike Schuster, Jonathon Shlens, Benoit Steiner, Ilya Sutskever, Kunal Talwar, Paul Tucker, Vincent Vanhoucke, Vijay Vasudevan, Fernanda Viégas, Oriol Vinyals, Pete Warden, Martin Wattenberg, Martin Wicke, Yuan Yu, and Xiaoqiang Zheng. 2015. TensorFlow: Large-scale machine learning on heterogeneous systems. Software available from tensorflow.org.

Dimitrios Alikaniotis, Helen Yannakoudakis, and Marek Rei. 2016. Automatic text scoring using neural networks. *arXiv preprint arXiv:1606.04289*.

Daniel Blanchard, Joel Tetreault, Derrick Higgins, Aoife Cahill, and Martin Chodorow. 2013. Toefl11: A corpus of non-native english. *ETS Research Report Series*, 2013(2):i–15.

Piotr Bojanowski, Edouard Grave, Armand Joulin, and Tomas Mikolov. 2017. Enriching word vectors with subword information. *Transactions of the Association for Computational Linguistics*, 5:135–146.

Adriane Boyd, Jirka Hana, Lionel Nicolas, Detmar Meurers, Katrin Wisniewski, Andrea Abel, Karin Schone, Barbora Stindlova, and Chiara Vettori. 2014. The MERLIN corpus: Learner language and the CEFR. In *Proceedings of LREC*.

Ted Briscoe, B. Medlock, and O. Andersen. 2010. Automated assessment of ESOL free text examinations. Technical report, University of Cambridge Computer Laboratory.

Cecilie Carlsen. 2012. Proficiency level—a fuzzy variable in computer learner corpora. *Applied Linguistics*, 33(2):161–183.

François Chollet et al. 2015. Keras. `https://keras.io`.

Murhaf Fares, Andrey Kutuzov, Stephan Oepen, and Erik Velldal. 2017. Word vectors, reuse, and replicability: Towards a community repository of large-text resources. In *Proceedings of the 21st Nordic Conference on Computational Linguistics, NoDaLiDa, 22-24 May 2017, Gothenburg, Sweden*, 131, pages 271–276, Linköping, Sweden. Linköping University Electronic Press, Linköpings universitet.

Anne Golden. 2016. Ask-korpuset gjør andrespråksforskningen enda morsommere. men hva gjør voksne innlærere med verbet gjøre i ask? *NOA-Norsk som andrespråk*, 30(1-2):77–120.

Julia Hancke. 2013. Automatic prediction of CEFR proficiency levels based on linguistic features of learner language. Master's thesis, University of Tubingen, Germany.

Yoon Kim. 2014. Convolutional neural networks for sentence classification. *arXiv preprint arXiv:1408.5882*.

Xiaofei Lu. 2010. Automatic analysis of syntactic complexity in second language writing. *International journal of corpus linguistics*, 15(4):474–496.

Shervin Malmasi and Mark Dras. 2017. Native language identification using stacked generalization. *arXiv preprint arXiv:1703.06541*.

Shervin Malmasi and Mark Dras. 2018. Native language identification with classifier stacking and ensembles. *Computational Linguistics*, 44(3):403–446.

Shervin Malmasi, Mark Dras, and Irina Temnikova. 2015. Norwegian native language identification. In *Proceedings of the International Conference Recent Advances in Natural Language Processing*, pages 404–412, Hissar, Bulgaria.

Shervin Malmasi, Keelan Evanini, Aoife Cahill, Joel Tetreault, Robert Pugh, Christopher Hamill, Diane Napolitano, and Yao Qian. 2017. A report on the 2017 native language identification shared task. In *Proceedings of the 12th Workshop on Innovative Use of NLP for Building Educational Applications*, pages 62–75, Copenhagen, Denmark. Association for Computational Linguistics.

Lilja Øvrelid and Petter Hohle. 2016. Universal Dependencies for Norwegian. In *Proceedings of the Tenth International Conference on Language Resources and Evaluation*, Portorož, Slovenia.

Nikolaos Pappas and Andrei Popescu-Belis. 2017. Multilingual hierarchical attention networks for document classification. *arXiv preprint arXiv:1707.00896*.

F. Pedregosa, G. Varoquaux, A. Gramfort, V. Michel, B. Thirion, O. Grisel, M. Blondel, P. Prettenhofer, R. Weiss, V. Dubourg, J. Vanderplas, A. Passos, D. Cournapeau, M. Brucher, M. Perrot, and E. Duchesnay. 2011. Scikit-learn: Machine learning in Python. *Journal of Machine Learning Research*, 12:2825–2830.

Steve Pepper. 2012. Lexical transfer in norwegian interlanguage. Master's thesis, Oslo, Norway.

Peter Phandi, Kian Ming A. Chai, and Hwee Tou Ng. 2015. Flexible domain adaptation for automated essay scoring using correlated linear regression. In *Proceedings of the 2015 Conference on Empirical Methods in Natural Language Processing*, Lisbon, Portugal.

Ildiko Pilán, David Alfter, and Elena Volodina. 2016. Coursebook texts as a helping hand for classifying linguistic complexity in language learners' writings. In *Proceedings of the Workshop on Computational Linguistics for Linguistic Complexity*, Osaka, Japan.

Lawrence M. Rudner and Tahung Liang. 2002. Automated essay scoring using Bayes' theorem. *Journal of Technology, Learning and Assessment*, 1(2).

Björn W Schuller, Stefan Steidl, Anton Batliner, Julia Hirschberg, Judee K Burgoon, Alice Baird, Aaron C Elkins, Yue Zhang, Eduardo Coutinho, and Keelan Evanini. 2016. The INTERSPEECH 2016 Computational Paralinguistics Challenge: Deception, Sincerity & Native Language. In *INTERSPEECH 2016*, pages 2001–2005, San Francisco, CA, USA.

Cathrine Stadsnes. 2018. Evaluating Semantic Vectors for Norwegian. Master's thesis, Oslo, Norway.

Milan Straka and Jana Straková. 2017. Tokenizing, POS Tagging, Lemmatizing and Parsing UD 2.0 with UDPipe. In *Proceedings of the CoNLL 2017 Shared Task: Multilingual Parsing from Raw Text to Universal Dependencies*, pages 88–99, Vancouver, Canada. Association for Computational Linguistics.

Kaveh Taghipour and Hwee Tou Ng. 2016. A neural approach to automated essay scoring. In *Proceedings of the 2016 Conference on Empirical Methods in Natural Language Processing*, pages 1882–1891, Austin, TX, USA.

Kari Tenfjord, Paul Meurer, and Knut Hofland. 2006. The ASK corpus: A language learner corpus of Norwegian as a second language. In *Proceedings of the 5th International Conference on Language Resources and Evaluation (LREC)*, pages 1821–1824, Genoa, Italy.

Joel Tetreault, Daniel Blanchard, and Aoife Cahill. 2013. A report on the first native language identification shared task. In *Proceedings of the eighth workshop on innovative use of NLP for building educational applications*, pages 48–57, Atlanta, GA, USA.

Sowmya Vajjala. 2017. Automated assessment of nonnative learner essays: Investigating the role of linguistic features. *International Journal of Artificial Intelligence in Education*, pages 1–27.

Sowmya Vajjala and Kaidi Loo. 2014. Automatic CEFR level prediction for Estonian learner text. In *Proceedings of the third workshop on NLP for computer-assisted language learning*, Uppsala, Sweden.

Sowmya Vajjala and Taraka Rama. 2018. Experiments with Universal CEFR Classification. In *Proceedings of the Thirteenth Workshop on Innovative Use of NLP for Building Educational Applications*, pages 147–153, New Orleans, LA, USA. Association for Computational Linguistics.

Tone Vigrestad. 2016. Ortografi i norsk som andrespråk. Master's thesis, Oslo, Norway.

Helen Yannakoudakis, Ted Briscoe, and Ben Medlock. 2011. A new dataset and method for automatically grading ESOL texts. In *Proceedings of the 49th Annual Meeting of the Association for Computational Linguistics: Human Language Technologies-Volume 1*, pages 180–189, Portland, OR, USA. Association for Computational Linguistics.

A   Supplemental Material

The data and code for these experiments is available here: `https://github.com/PhyloStar/NorskASK`

Context is Key: Grammatical Error Detection with Contextual Word Representations

Samuel Bell[♠◇]   **Helen Yannakoudakis**[◇♣]   **Marek Rei**[◇♣]
♠Department of Psychology, University of Cambridge, United Kingdom
◇Dept. of Computer Science & Technology, University of Cambridge, United Kingdom
♣ALTA Institute, University of Cambridge, United Kingdom
sjb326@cam.ac.uk, {helen.yannakoudakis,marek.rei}@cl.cam.ac.uk

Abstract

Grammatical error detection (GED) in non-native writing requires systems to identify a wide range of errors in text written by language learners. Error detection as a purely supervised task can be challenging, as GED datasets are limited in size and the label distributions are highly imbalanced. Contextualized word representations offer a possible solution, as they can efficiently capture compositional information in language and can be optimized on large amounts of unsupervised data. In this paper, we perform a systematic comparison of ELMo, BERT and Flair embeddings (Peters et al., 2017; Devlin et al., 2018; Akbik et al., 2018) on a range of public GED datasets, and propose an approach to effectively integrate such representations in current methods, achieving a new state of the art on GED. We further analyze the strengths and weaknesses of different contextual embeddings for the task at hand, and present detailed analyses of their impact on different types of errors.

1   Introduction

Detecting errors in text written by language learners is a key component of pedagogical applications for language learning and assessment. Supervised learning approaches to the task exploit public error-annotated corpora (Yannakoudakis et al., 2011; Ng et al., 2014; Napoles et al., 2017) that are, however, limited in size, in addition to having a biased distribution of labels: the number of correct tokens in a text far outweighs the incorrect (Leacock et al., 2014). As such, Grammatical Error Detection (GED) can be considered a low-/mid-resource task.

The current state of the art explores error detection within a semi-supervised, multi-task learning framework, using a neural sequence labeler optimized to detect errors as well as predict their

surrounding context (Rei, 2017). To further improve GED performance, recent work has investigated the use of artificially generated training data (Rei et al., 2017; Kasewa et al., 2018). On the related task of grammatical error correction (GEC), Junczys-Dowmunt et al. (2018) explore transfer learning approaches to tackle the low-resource bottleneck of the task and, among others, find substantially improved performance when incorporating pre-trained word embeddings (Mikolov et al., 2013), and importing network weights from a language model trained on a large unlabeled corpus.

Herein, we extend the current state of the art for error detection (Rei, 2017) to effectively incorporate *contextual embeddings*: word representations that are constructed based on the context in which the words appear. These embeddings are typically the output of a set of hidden layers of a large language modelling network, trained on large volumes of unlabeled and general domain data. As such, they are able to capture detailed information regarding language and composition from a wide range of data sources, and can help overcome resource limitations for supervised learning.

We evaluate the use of contextual embeddings in the form of Bidirectional Encoder Representations from Transformers (BERT) (Devlin et al., 2018), embeddings from Language Models (ELMo) (Peters et al., 2018) and Flair embeddings (Akbik et al., 2018). To the best of our knowledge, this is the first evaluation of the use of contextual embeddings for the task of GED. Our contributions are fourfold:

- We present a systematic comparison of different contextualized word representations for the task of GED;

- We describe an approach for effectively integrating contextual representations to error detection models, achieving a new state of the

Proceedings of the Fourteenth Workshop on Innovative Use of NLP for Building Educational Applications, pages 103–115
Florence, Italy, August 2, 2019. ©2019 Association for Computational Linguistics

art on a number of public GED datasets, and make our code and models publicly available online;

- We demonstrate that our approach has particular benefits for transferring to out-of-domain datasets, in addition to overall improvements in performance;

- We perform a detailed analysis of the strengths and weaknesses of different contextual representations for the task of GED, presenting detailed results of their impact on different types of errors in order to guide future work.

2 Related work

In this section, we describe previous work on GED and on the related task of GEC. While error correction systems can be used for error detection, previous work has shown that standalone error detection models can be complementary to error correction ones, and can be used to further improve performance on GEC (Yannakoudakis et al., 2017).

Early approaches to GED and GEC relied upon handwritten rules and error grammars (e.g. Foster and Vogel (2004)), while later work focused on supervised learning from error-annotated corpora using feature engineering approaches and often utilizing maximum entropy-based classifiers (e.g. Chodorow et al. (2007); De Felice and Pulman (2008)). A large range of work has focused on the development of systems targeting specific error types, such as preposition (Tetreault and Chodorow, 2008; Chodorow et al., 2007), article usage (Han et al., 2004, 2006), and verb form errors (Lee and Seneff, 2008). Among others, error-type agnostic approaches have focused on generating synthetic ungrammatical data to augment the available training sets, or learning from native English datasets; for example, Foster and Andersen (2009) investigate rule-based error generation methods, while Gamon (2010) trains a language model (LM) on a large, general domain corpus, from which features (e.g. word likelihoods) are derived for use in error classification.

As a distinct task, GEC has been formulated as a naïve-bayes classification (Rozovskaya et al., 2013, 2014; Rozovskaya and Roth, 2016) or a monolingual (statistical or neural) machine translation (MT) problem (where uncorrected text is treated as the source "language" and the corrected text as its target counterpart) (Felice et al., 2014; Junczys-Dowmunt and Grundkiewicz, 2014; Rozovskaya and Roth, 2016; Yuan and Briscoe, 2016).

Recently, Rei and Yannakoudakis (2016) presented the first approach towards neural GED, training a sequence labeling model based on word embeddings processed by a bidirectional LSTM (bi-LSTM), outputting a probability distribution over labels informed by the entire sentence as context. This approach achieves strong results when trained and evaluated on in-domain data, but shows weaker generalization performance on out-of-domain data. Rei et al. (2016) extended this model to include character embeddings in order to capture morphological similarities such as word endings. Rei (2017) subsequently added a secondary LM objective to the neural sequence labeling architecture, operating on both word and character-level embeddings. This was found to be particularly useful for GED – introducing an LM objective allows the network to learn more generic features about language and composition. At the same time, Rei and Yannakoudakis (2017) investigated the effectiveness of a number of auxiliary (morpho-syntactic) training objectives for the task of GED, finding that predicting part-of-speech tags, grammatical relations or error types as auxiliary tasks yields improvements in performance over the single-task GED objective (though not as high as when utilizing an LM objective).

The current state of the art on GED is based on augmenting neural approaches with artificially generated training data. Rei et al. (2017) showed improved GED performance using the bi-LSTM sequence labeler, by generating artificial errors in two different ways: 1) learning frequent error patterns from error-annotated corpora and applying these to error-free text; 2) using a statistical MT approach to "translate" correct text to its incorrect counterpart using parallel corpora. Recently, Kasewa et al. (2018) applied the latter approach using a neural MT system instead, and achieved a new state of the art on GED using the neural model of Rei (2017).

3 Data

In this section, we describe the different public datasets we use to train our models.

The First Certificate in English (FCE) dataset

(Yannakoudakis et al., 2011) is a publicly-released set of essays written by non-native learners of English taking a language assessment exam. Each essay is annotated by professional annotators with the spans of language errors committed, the types of errors, and suggested corrections. In addition, the CoNLL 2014 shared task on GEC (Ng et al., 2014) used a dataset of English essays written by advanced undergraduate students at the National University of Singapore. Each essay is annotated by two experienced annotators and has error annotations similarly to the FCE, though using a different error taxonomy. The Johns Hopkins University (JHU) FLuency-Extended GUG Corpus (JFLEG) dataset (Napoles et al., 2017) contains essays written by a range of English learners with different first languages and proficiency levels. Each essay is corrected by four annotators with native-level proficiency and annotated with fluency and grammar edits.

The 2019 Building Educational Applications (BEA) shared task on GEC (Bryant et al., 2019) released two new datasets: the Cambridge English Write & Improve (W&I) corpus, which is a collection of texts written by learners of English of varying levels of proficiency and submitted for assessment to the Write & Improve system (Yannakoudakis et al., 2018), an automated online tool for writing feedback; and the LOCNESS corpus (Granger, 1998), originally compiled at the Centre for English Corpus Linguistics at the University of Louvain, and comprising essays written by native English students. Both datasets are annotated for corrections by the W&I annotators.

In this work, we use the FCE training set as training data, and evaluate our models on the FCE test set, the CoNLL-2014 test set, the JFLEG test set, and the BEA 2019 shared task development and test sets. This setup allows us to investigate the extent to which our models and the use of contextualized representations transfer to out-of-domain data.

We follow Rei and Yannakoudakis (2016) and convert the span-based annotations in these datasets to binary error detection labels at the token level (i.e. is a token correct or incorrect). Performance is evaluated using precision, recall, and $F_{0.5}$ at the token level. $F_{0.5}$ places twice the weight on precision than recall: systems that incorrectly penalize correct language can have a much more negative impact to language learning compared to systems that miss to detect some errors (Ng et al., 2014). We note that performance on the BEA shared task test set is conducted using the official evaluation tool in CodaLab.

We also perform detailed analyses in order to evaluate the performance of our models per error type. As the datasets above either have their own error type taxonomy or they are not annotated with error types at all, we follow the 2019 BEA shared task and induce error types for all datasets automatically using the ERRor ANnotation Toolkit (ERRANT) (Bryant et al., 2017). ERRANT automatically annotates parallel uncorrected and corrected sentences with error types using a universal error taxonomy and hence allowing for comparisons across datasets. The system uses distance-based alignment followed by rule-based error categorization. An error type is hence assigned to every incorrect token in each dataset, with the exception of the BEA 2019 shared task test set, for which the corrected versions are not yet publicly available.

4 Error detection model

In this section, we extend the current state of the art (neural) architecture for GED (Rei, 2017), which we use as our baseline system. This model is a bi-LSTM sequence labeler over token embeddings where, for each token, the model is trained to output a probability distribution over binary correct/incorrect labels using a softmax layer (i.e. predicting whether a token is correct or incorrect in context). The model is additionally trained with a secondary bidirectional LM objective, predicting the surrounding context of the target token in the sequence. Specifically, the model uses a forward LM to predict the next token in the sequence, and a backward LM to predict the previous token. Rei (2017) also makes use of a character-level bi-LSTM, as opposed to solely conditioning on tokens, in order to benefit from sub-word morphological units, of particular use in the case of unknown or incorrectly spelled words. The outputs of the character-level LSTMs are concatenated to the word embeddings and given as input to the word-level bi-LSTM.

The model learns 300-dimensional word embeddings, initialized with pre-trained Google News embeddings (Mikolov et al., 2013),[1] and

---

[1] https://code.google.com/archive/p/word2vec/

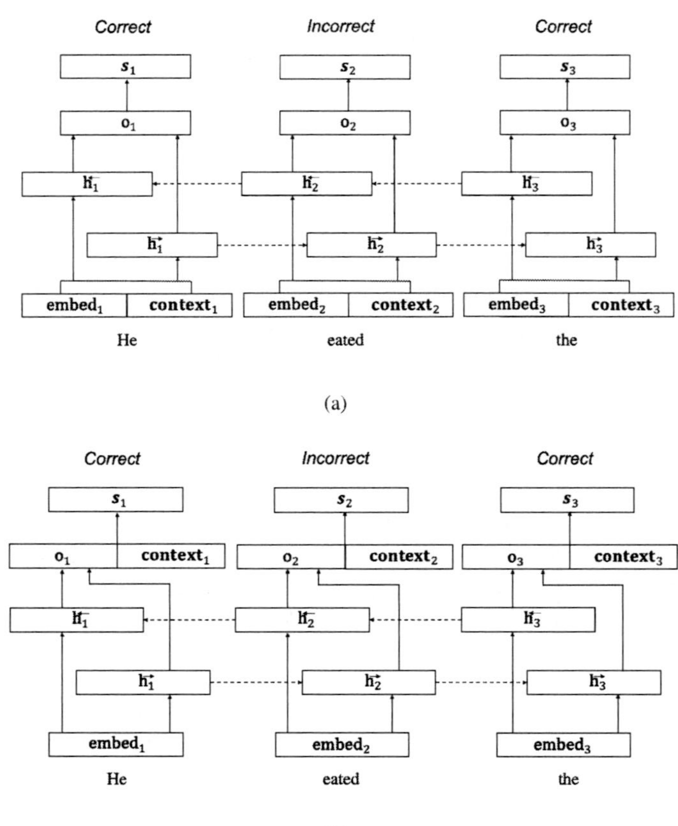

Figure 1: Simplified bi-LSTM sequence labeler with: **(a)** contextual embeddings (**context**) concatenated to the input word embeddings (**embed**), before being passed through the bi-LSTM (**h**); **(b)** contextual embeddings (**context**) concatenated to the LSTM output (**o**) before being passed through a softmax layer (**s**).

100-dimensional character embeddings. The hidden states of the word- and character-level LSTMs are also of 300 and 100 dimensions respectively. The outputs of each LSTM are passed through a 50-dimensional hidden layer with a $tanh$ activation function. Dropout is applied to the inputs and outputs of each LSTM with a probability of 0.5. The model is trained with a cross-entropy loss function for the error detection objective that minimizes the negative log probability of the gold label. As the model is also trained with a secondary LM objective, a second bipartite cross-entropy loss function is used, minimizing the negative log probability of the next word in the sequence for the forward LM, and the previous word for the backward LM. A hyperparameter $\gamma = 0.1$ weights the combination of the two loss functions, assigning more importance to the main task of error detection over the auxiliary task of language modelling. Optimization is performed with the AdaDelta optimizer (Zeiler, 2012), using an initial learning rate of 1.0, and batches of 32 sentences. Training is terminated when validation performance does not improve for 7 epochs.

In this work, we extend the above model by incorporating contextualized word embeddings, produced by three different approaches (BERT, ELMo and Flair; each described in more detail in Section 5). Specifically, we concatenate the contextual embeddings either to the input word embeddings before being passed through the word-level bi-LSTM (Figure 1a), or to the bi-LSTM's output (Figure 1b). Peters et al. (2018) find that the best point to integrate ELMo vectors varies by task and, as such, we continue that line of analysis here.

We make a TensorFlow (Abadi et al., 2016) implementation of our code and models publicly available online.[2]

5 Contextualized embeddings

Three types of contextual embeddings are considered in this work: BERT, ELMo and Flair embeddings (Peters et al., 2017; Devlin et al., 2018; Akbik et al., 2018). In each case, we use the publicly-available pre-trained models released by the authors.

BERT embeddings are extracted from the highest layers of a transformer architecture trained with a masked LM objective: rather than predicting the next or previous word in a sequence, a percentage of input tokens are masked and then the network learns to predict the masked tokens. BERT is also trained with a second objective predicting whether one sentence directly follows another, given two input sentences. BERT pre-trained embeddings are available in two variants: *base* embeddings, which are the concatenation of the four highest 768-dimension hidden layers, yielding a $3,072$-dimension embedding; *large* embeddings, which are the concatenation of the four highest 1024-dimension hidden layers, yielding a $4,096$-dimension embedding (Devlin et al., 2018). BERT embeddings are trained on the BooksCorpus (0.8 billion words) of books written by unpublished authors (Zhu et al., 2015) and English Wikipedia (2.5 billion words).

ELMo embeddings are a weighted element-wise sum of the outputs of three-layered stacked bi-LSTM LMs, trained to predict both the next and previous token in the sequence. Using a task-specific scalar per layer, the outputs of the three LSTMs are reduced to a single $1,024$-dimension embedding (Peters et al., 2018). This task-specific weighting is learned by our sequence labeler during training. ELMo is trained on the One Billion Word Benchmark corpus (0.8 billion words), composed primarily of online news articles (Chelba et al., 2014a).

Flair embeddings are the concatenated output of a single (i.e. unstacked) character-level bi-LSTM. We use the concatenation of both the $2,048$-dimension "news-forward" and "news-backward" embeddings, each produced by a forward and backward bi-LSTM respectively, and both trained on the One Billion Word Benchmark (Chelba et al., 2014b). This yields a $4,096$-dimensional

embedding (Akbik et al., 2018).

6 Results

Table 1 and Table 2 present the results of integrating different contextual embeddings with the current state-of-the-art model described by Rei (2017).[3] The experiments in this section are based on models with contextual representations concatenated to the word embeddings; Section 6.1 includes a more detailed investigation of different integration points. For comparison, we also report the results of Rei et al. (2017) and Kasewa et al. (2018), who improve error detection performance by additionally augmenting Rei (2017)'s model with artificial training data.

The experiments demonstrate a substantial improvement in precision, recall and $F_{0.5}$ for every model incorporating contextual embeddings, across every dataset considered. On the FCE test set, even our lowest performing model (Flair, $F_{0.5} = 49.97$) outperforms the baseline ($F_{0.5} = 42.15$), with a relative improvement of 18.55%. Our best performing model (BERT base, $F_{0.5} = 57.28$) outperforms the baseline by a relative 35.9%. This is also the new state-of-the-art result on the FCE test set, without using additional manually-annotated training data.

The best performance on the CoNLL-2014 test set is achieved by BERT large ($F_{0.5} = 36.94$) and BERT base ($F_{0.5} = 46.29$) for the first and second annotator respectively. These scores show more than 30% relative improvement over the previous best results by Kasewa et al. (2018), even without using additional artificial training data, for both annotators. On the JFLEG test set (Table 2), and both the BEA 2019 GEC Shared Task development and test sets, BERT base yields the highest performance. The improvement on the BEA shared task datasets is particularly large, with BERT base achieving 69.70% relative improvement on the development set and 63.30% relative improvement on the test set, compared to the baseline model.

These experiments demonstrate that contextual embeddings provide a very beneficial addition for GED systems, achieving a new state of the art across all datasets. Learning to compose language

---

[2]https://github.com/samueljamesbell/sequence-labeler

[3]We include the results reported by Rei (2017) along with our re-trained baseline. We note that the differences in performance are due to a re-processing of the data in order to align parallel original–corrected sentences and derive fine-grained error type labels for later analyses (see Section 6.2).

	CoNLL Test 1			CoNLL Test 2			FCE test		
	P	R	$F_{0.5}$	P	R	$F_{0.5}$	P	R	$F_{0.5}$
Rei (2017)	17.68	19.07	17.86	27.6	21.18	25.88	58.88	28.92	48.48
Rei et al. (2017)	23.28	18.01	21.87	35.28	19.42	30.13	60.67	28.08	49.11
Kasewa et al. (2018)	-	-	28.3	-	-	35.5	-	-	55.6
Baseline	20.82	16.31	19.73	31.91	17.81	27.55	46.55	30.58	42.15
Flair	29.53	17.11	25.79	44.12	18.22	34.35	58.36	31.72	49.97
ELMo	30.83	23.90	29.14	46.66	25.77	40.15	58.50	38.01	52.81
BERT base	37.62	29.65	35.70	**53.52**	30.05	**46.29**	64.96	**38.89**	**57.28**
BERT large	**38.04**	**33.12**	**36.94**	51.40	**31.89**	45.80	**64.51**	38.79	56.96

Table 1: Error detection precision, recall, and $F_{0.5}$ on the FCE and CoNLL-2014 test sets: test 1 and test 2 refer to the two different CoNLL annotators. 'Baseline' refers to our own re-training of the model by Rei (2017).

	JFLEG Test			Shared Task Dev			Shared Task Test		
	P	R	$F_{0.5}$	P	R	$F_{0.5}$	P	R	$F_{0.5}$
Baseline	72.84	22.83	50.65	31.31	21.18	28.58	40.05	34.99	38.93
Flair	75.65	25.26	54.08	41.80	24.10	36.45	53.40	39.84	50.00
ELMo	74.95	31.21	58.54	47.90	30.41	42.96	58.72	47.79	56.15
BERT base	**79.51**	32.94	**61.98**	**53.31**	35.65	**48.50**	**66.47**	**54.11**	**63.57**
BERT large	76.47	**34.52**	61.52	51.54	**36.90**	47.75	63.35	54.10	61.26

Table 2: Error detection precision, recall, and $F_{0.5}$ on the JFLEG test set and BEA 2019 GEC Shared Task development and test sets.

representations on large unsupervised datasets allows the models to access a wider range of useful information. While our error detection models are optimized on the FCE training set, we observe particularly large improvements on the CoNLL-2014 and BEA shared task datasets, indicating that contextual embeddings allow the models to generalize better and capture errors in out-of-domain texts. Overall, we found BERT base to provide the highest improvements across all datasets. The slightly lower performance of BERT large could be attributed to the larger embedding sizes requiring more parameters to be optimized on our limited GED dataset.

6.1 Integration method

We performed additional experiments to investigate the optimal method for integrating contextual embeddings into the error detection model. The embeddings are either concatenated to the standard word embeddings at the input level (reported in our results as 'input'), or to the output of the word-level bi-LSTM (reported as 'output'). In all experiments, contextual embeddings are not fine-tuned.

Table 3 compares the $F_{0.5}$ of these two strategies for each model, across all the datasets. We observe that, although performance varies across datasets and models, integration by concatena-

tion to the word embeddings yields the best results across the majority of datasets for all models (BERT: 3/5 datasets; ELMo: 4/5 datasets; Flair: 5/5 datasets). The lower integration point allows the model to learn more levels of task-specific transformations on top of the contextual representations, leading to an overall better performance.

6.2 Error type performance

Using ERRANT (Bryant et al., 2017), we analyze the performance on different types of errors and specifically focus on two error type taxonomies: one that uses part-of-speech (POS) based error types (i.e. the type is based on the POS tag of the incorrect token), and another based on edit operations (i.e. is it a missing token, an unnecessary token, or a replace token error). This allows us to yield insights into how different types of contextual embeddings and the data in which they were trained may impact performance on specific errors. Since identifying type-specific false positives is not possible in this setting, we follow Ng et al. (2014) and report recall on each error type.

Figure 2 presents the performance on POS-based error types, showing the change in error type recall of each contextual embedding model compared to our baseline, averaged over all datasets. While all models yield an improvement in aggregate performance metrics ($P, R, F_{0.5}$), when bro-

		Shared Task Dev	CoNLL Test 1	CoNLL Test 2	FCE test	JFLEG test
Flair	Input	36.45	25.79	34.35	49.97	54.08
	Output	33.47	24.52	33.18	48.50	52.10
ELMo	Input	42.96	29.14	40.15	52.81	58.54
	Output	37.33	27.33	38.10	52.99	54.86
BERT base	Input	**48.50**	35.70	46.29	**57.28**	**61.98**
	Output	46.33	37.04	46.50	55.32	60.97
BERT large	Input	47.75	36.94	45.80	56.96	61.52
	Output	46.72	**39.07**	**46.96**	55.10	60.56

Table 3: Error detection $F_{0.5}$ of different embedding integration strategies ('input' vs. 'output') per model on all datasets.

ken down by POS-based error type, some trends emerge. BERT base, BERT large and ELMo each show strong improvements in recall of errors relating to nouns, particles, prepositions and morphology. In comparison, relatively weak improvements are achieved for errors of conjugation, orthography and spelling. As such words/errors are less likely to occur frequently in general-purpose corpora of English (i.e. spelling mistakes are less frequent in news articles compared to learner essays), contextual embeddings trained on such corpora are also less helpful for these error types.

We also note the sharp decline in recall of the BERT base model on contraction errors. This error type occurs quite infrequently (see Figure 1 in the Appendix) and we do not observe this issue with BERT large.

Compared to BERT and ELMo, Flair offers very little improvement on POS-based error type recall or even actively degrades recall (e.g. conjugation, punctuation or spelling errors). While the purely character-based representations of Flair could potentially offer more flexibility in the model, these results suggest that the limited vocabulary of our learner data may be better captured with word-level approaches.

Figure 3 presents the differences between models when looking at error types based on the necessary edit operation: missing token, replace token or unnecessary token. While BERT improves overall performance compared to ELMo, this improvement appears to be limited to replacement and unnecessary error types. On missing word errors, BERT base performs comparably to ELMo and BERT large even decreases performance. We discuss the possible reasons for this in Section 7.

We include the full results table for different error types in the Appendix (Table 1, Table 2). Our analysis shows that focusing more on punctu-

ation, determiner and preposition errors might be the most beneficial avenue for improving the overall performance on GED. For example, punctuation errors are the third most common error type, but even with contextual embeddings the models only achieve 27.7% recall across all datasets.

Overall, our results suggest that, while contextual embeddings always improve aggregate performance on GED, error type specific properties of models should also be considered.

7 Discussion

The previous section has demonstrated consistent improvement in precision, recall and $F_{0.5}$ across a range of GED datasets, including many examples of transfer to different domains, irrespective of the choice of contextual embedding. Contextual embeddings bring the possibility of leveraging information learned in an unsupervised manner from high volumes of unlabeled data, by large and complex models, trained for substantial periods of time. For these reasons, they are a particularly appropriate addition to a low-resource task such as GED. While each choice of contextual embedding yields improved performance, BERT base and BERT large consistently outperform ELMo and Flair embeddings. Here, we suggest that details of the BERT architecture and training process may be responsible for its specific performance profile.

One difference between contextual embedding models is the choice of training corpora. While both ELMo and Flair embeddings are trained using the One Billion Word Benchmark, BERT is trained on the BooksCorpus, and English Wikipedia. It is likely that the usage and distribution of English varies across these corpora, yielding different results on downstream tasks. We might expect a corpus of books to exhibit a greater

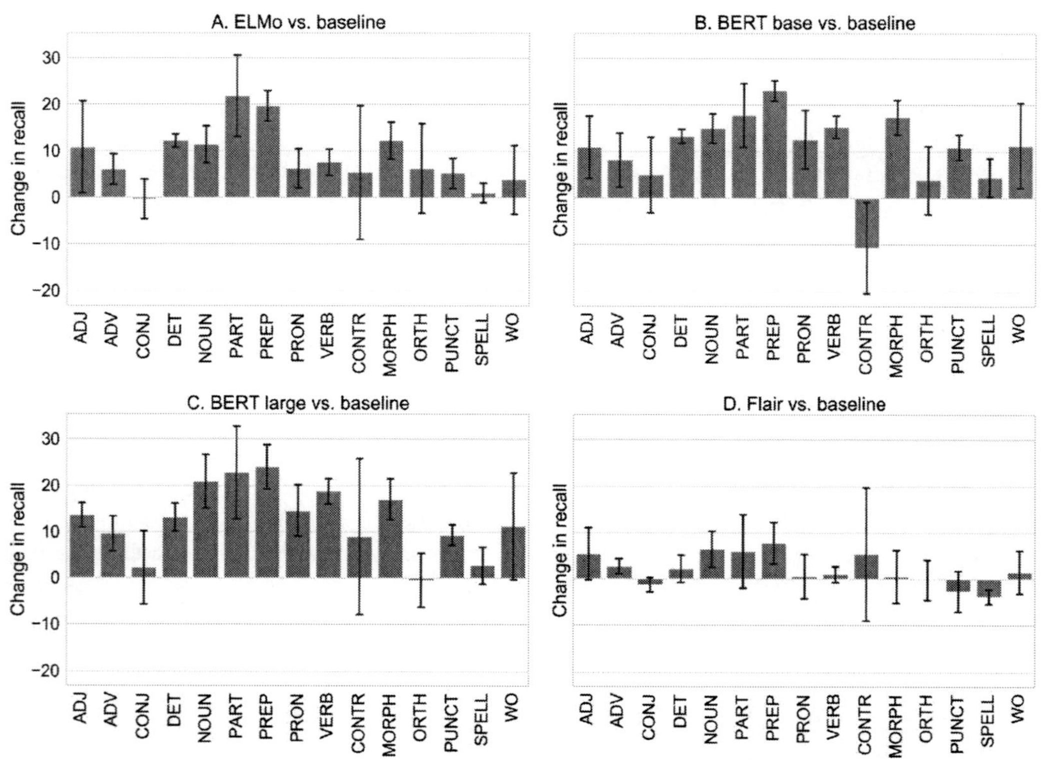

Figure 2: Mean change in recall of ERRANT-induced POS-based error types over all datasets when adding contextual embeddings at the input level, vs. our baseline without contextual embeddings. **A:** ELMo. **B:** BERT base. **C:** BERT large. **D:** Flair.

variance in writing style, audience, and even writer ability than a corpus of news articles, perhaps resulting in more useful contextual embeddings for GED. However, in contrast to the 0.8 billion tokens of training data available to ELMo and Flair, BERT's combination of BooksCorpus and English Wikipedia provides 3.3 billion tokens of training data. The increased volume of training data may alone suffice to explain BERT's comparatively strong performance.

Another difference is that BERT is not trained with a bi-directional LM objective. In contrast to ELMo and Flair, BERT is trained with a masked LM objective, such that it must predict the original tokens when presented with a sentence with any number of tokens masked. This training objective always provides the model access to the correct number of tokens in each sentence, which means it never needs to consider possible missing tokens. This could explain the decreased improvements on the "missing" error types compared to other error operations (Figure 3), and future work could experiment with integrating missing tokens directly into the BERT training objective.

At this point, we note that while the number of parameters, and the dimensionality of the resulting representations vary by model, extensive ablation studies (Devlin et al., 2018; Peters et al., 2018) indicate only small decreases in performance with decreasing layers or dimensionality. Future research may contrast the models considered here with those of a paired number of parameters but with randomly-initialized contextual embeddings. However, as contextual embeddings enable the integration of information captured via unsupervised learning on large general-purpose corpora, we expect that embeddings without this information (i.e. randomly-initialized) would not yield the degree of improvement detailed herein.

8 Conclusion

We have experimentally demonstrated that using contextual embeddings substantially improves GED performance, achieving a new state of the art

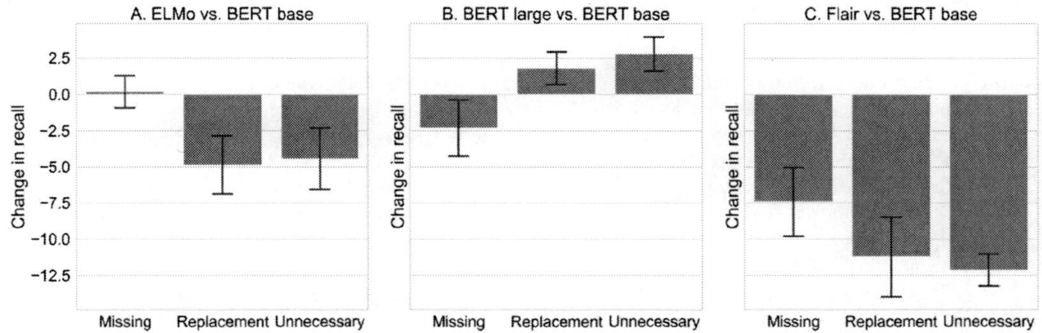

Figure 3: Mean change in recall of ERRANT-induced edit operation error types across all datasets when adding contextual embeddings at the input level, vs. the model using BERT base. **A:** ELMo. **B:** BERT large. **C:** Flair.

on a number of public datasets. We have shown that a sequence labeling architecture augmenting the input word embeddings with the BERT family (base or large) of contextual embeddings produces, overall, the best performance across datasets. In addition to improving overall performance, contextual embeddings proved to be particularly useful for improving on out-of-domain datasets.

We have also performed a detailed analysis of the strengths and weaknesses of the use of different contextual embeddings on detecting specific types of errors. We aim for the analyses presented here to facilitate future work in GED and in improving such systems further. Future work can also be directed towards investigating alternative approaches to integrating contextualized representations and fine-tuning such representations for GED.

Acknowledgments

We thank the anonymous reviewers for their valuable feedback. Marek Rei and Helen Yannakoudakis were supported by Cambridge Assessment, University of Cambridge.

References

Martín Abadi, Paul Barham, Jianmin Chen, Zhifeng Chen, Andy Davis, Jeffrey Dean, Matthieu Devin, Sanjay Ghemawat, Geoffrey Irving, Michael Isard, et al. 2016. Tensorflow: A system for large-scale machine learning. In *12th {USENIX} Symposium on Operating Systems Design and Implementation ({OSDI} 16)*, pages 265–283.

Alan Akbik, Duncan Blythe, and Vollgraf Roland. 2018. Contextual string embeddings for sequence labeling. In *Proceedings of the 27th International Conference on Computational Linguistics*, pages 1638–1649.

Christopher Bryant, Mariano Felice, Øistein E Andersen, and Ted Briscoe. 2019. The BEA-2019 shared task on grammatical error correction. In *Proceedings of the 14th Workshop on Innovative Use of NLP for Building Educational Applications*. Association for Computational Linguistics.

Christopher Bryant, Mariano Felice, and Ted Briscoe. 2017. Automatic annotation and evaluation of error types for grammatical error correction. In *Proceedings of the 55th Annual Meeting of the Association for Computational Linguistics*, pages 793–805.

Ciprian Chelba, Tomas Mikolov, Mike Schuster, Qi Ge, Thorsten Brants, Phillipp Koehn, and Tony Robinson. 2014a. One billion word benchmark for measuring progress in statistical language modeling. *Proceedings of the Annual Conference of the International Speech Communication Association, INTERSPEECH*, pages 2635–2639.

Ciprian Chelba, Tomáš Mikolov, Mike Schuster, Qi Ge, Thorsten Brants, Phillipp Koehn, and Tony Robinson. 2014b. One billion word benchmark for measuring progress in statistical language modeling. In *Fifteenth Annual Conference of the International Speech Communication Association*.

Martin Chodorow, Joel R Tetreault, and Na-Rae Han. 2007. Detection of grammatical errors involving prepositions. In *Proceedings of the fourth ACL-SIGSEM workshop on prepositions*, pages 25–30.

Rachele De Felice and Stephen G. Pulman. 2008. A classifier-based approach to preposition and determiner error correction in L2 English. In *Proceedings of the 22nd International Conference on Computational Linguistics (Coling 2008)*, pages 169–176.

Jacob Devlin, Ming-Wei Chang, Kenton Lee, and Kristina Toutanova. 2018. BERT: Pre-training of deep bidirectional transformers for language understanding. *arXiv preprint arXiv:1810.04805*.

Mariano Felice, Zheng Yuan, Øistein E Andersen, Helen Yannakoudakis, and Ekaterina Kochmar. 2014. Grammatical error correction using hybrid systems and type filtering. In *Proceedings of the Eighteenth Conference on Computational Natural Language Learning: Shared Task*, pages 15–24.

Jennifer Foster and Øisten E Andersen. 2009. GenERRate: generating errors for use in grammatical error detection. In *Proceedings of the fourth workshop on innovative use of NLP for building educational applications*, pages 82–90.

Jennifer Foster and Carl Vogel. 2004. Parsing ill-formed text using an error grammar. *Artificial Intelligence Review*, 21(3-4):269–291.

Michael Gamon. 2010. Using mostly native data to correct errors in learners' writing: A meta-classifier approach. In *Human Language Technologies: The 2010 Annual Conference of the North American Chapter of the Association for Computational Linguistics*, pages 163–171. Association for Computational Linguistics.

Sylviane Granger. 1998. The computer learner corpus: A versatile new source of data for sla research. in granger, s. (ed.). In *Learner English on Computer*, pages 3–18. Addison Wesley Longman: London & New York.

Na-Rae Han, Martin Chodorow, and Claudia Leacock. 2004. Detecting errors in English article usage with a maximum entropy classifier trained on a large, diverse corpus. In *Proceedings of the Fourth International Conference on Language Resources and Evaluation (LREC'04)*.

Na-Rae Han, Martin Chodorow, and Claudia Leacock. 2006. Detecting errors in English article usage by non-native speakers. *Natural Language Engineering*, 12(2):115–129.

Marcin Junczys-Dowmunt and Roman Grundkiewicz. 2014. The AMU system in the CoNLL-2014 shared task: Grammatical error correction by data-intensive and feature-rich statistical machine translation. In *Proceedings of the Eighteenth Conference on Computational Natural Language Learning: Shared Task*, pages 25–33.

Marcin Junczys-Dowmunt, Roman Grundkiewicz, Shubha Guha, and Kenneth Heafield. 2018. Approaching neural grammatical error correction as a low-resource machine translation task. *arXiv preprint arXiv:1804.05940*.

Sudhanshu Kasewa, Pontus Stenetorp, and Sebastian Riedel. 2018. Wronging a right: Generating better errors to improve grammatical error detection. *arXiv preprint arXiv:1810.00668*.

Claudia Leacock, Martin Chodorow, Michael Gamon, and Joel Tetreault. 2014. *Automated grammatical error detection for language learners*. Morgan & Claypool Publishers.

John Lee and Stephanie Seneff. 2008. Correcting misuse of verb forms. In *Proceedings of the 46th Annual Meeting of the Association for Computational Linguistics: Human Language Technologies*, pages 174–182.

Tomáš Mikolov, Kai Chen, Greg Corrado, and Jeffrey Dean. 2013. Efficient estimation of word representations in vector space. *arXiv preprint arXiv:1301.3781*.

Courtney Napoles, Keisuke Sakaguchi, and Joel Tetreault. 2017. JFLEG: A fluency corpus and benchmark for grammatical error correction. In *Proceedings of the 15th Conference of the European Chapter of the Association for Computational Linguistics*, pages 229–234.

Hwee Tou Ng, Siew Mei Wu, Ted Briscoe, Christian Hadiwinoto, Raymond Hendy Susanto, and Christopher Bryant. 2014. The CoNLL-2014 shared task on grammatical error correction. In *Proceedings of the Eighteenth Conference on Computational Natural Language Learning: Shared Task*, pages 1–14.

Matthew Peters, Waleed Ammar, Chandra Bhagavatula, and Russell Power. 2017. Semi-supervised sequence tagging with bidirectional language models. In *Proceedings of the 55th Annual Meeting of the Association for Computational Linguistics*, pages 1756–1765.

Matthew E. Peters, Mark Neumann, Mohit Iyyer, Matt Gardner, Christopher Clark, Kenton Lee, and Luke Zettlemoyer. 2018. Deep contextualized word representations. *arXiv preprint arXiv:1802.05365*.

Marek Rei. 2017. Semi-supervised multitask learning for sequence labeling. In *Proceedings of the 55th Annual Meeting of the Association for Computational Linguistics*, pages 2121–2130.

Marek Rei, Gamal Crichton, and Sampo Pyysalo. 2016. Attending to characters in neural sequence labeling models. In *Proceedings of COLING 2016, the 26th International Conference on Computational Linguistics: Technical Papers*, pages 309–318.

Marek Rei, Mariano Felice, Zheng Yuan, and Ted Briscoe. 2017. Artificial error generation with machine translation and syntactic patterns. *arXiv preprint arXiv:1707.05236*.

Marek Rei and Helen Yannakoudakis. 2016. Compositional sequence labeling models for error detection in learner writing. In *Proceedings of the 54th Annual Meeting of the Association for Computational Linguistics*, pages 1181–1191.

Marek Rei and Helen Yannakoudakis. 2017. Auxiliary objectives for neural error detection models. In *Proceedings of the 12th Workshop on Innovative Use of NLP for Building Educational Applications*, pages 33–43. Association for Computational Linguistics.

Alla Rozovskaya, Kai-Wei Chang, Mark Sammons, and Dan Roth. 2013. The University of Illinois system in the CoNLL-2013 shared task. In *Proceedings of the Seventeenth Conference on Computational Natural Language Learning: Shared Task*, pages 13–19.

Alla Rozovskaya, Kai-Wei Chang, Mark Sammons, Dan Roth, and Nizar Habash. 2014. The Illinois-Columbia system in the CoNLL-2014 shared task. In *Proceedings of the Eighteenth Conference on Computational Natural Language Learning: Shared Task*, pages 34–42.

Alla Rozovskaya and Dan Roth. 2016. Grammatical error correction: Machine translation and classifiers. In *Proceedings of the 54th Annual Meeting of the Association for Computational Linguistics*, pages 2205–2215. Association for Computational Linguistics.

Joel R Tetreault and Martin Chodorow. 2008. The ups and downs of preposition error detection in ESL writing. In *Proceedings of the 22nd International Conference on Computational Linguistics*, pages 865–872.

Helen Yannakoudakis, Øistein E Andersen, Ardeshir Geranpayeh, Ted Briscoe, and Diane Nicholls. 2018. Developing an automated writing placement system for esl learners. *Applied Measurement in Education*, 31(3):251–267.

Helen Yannakoudakis, Ted Briscoe, and Ben Medlock. 2011. A new dataset and method for automatically grading ESOL texts. In *Proceedings of the 49th Annual Meeting of the Association for Computational Linguistics: Human Language Technologies*, pages 180–189.

Helen Yannakoudakis, Marek Rei, Øistein E Andersen, and Zheng Yuan. 2017. Neural sequence-labelling models for grammatical error correction. In *Proceedings of the 2017 Conference on Empirical Methods in Natural Language Processing*.

Zheng Yuan and Ted Briscoe. 2016. Grammatical error correction using neural machine translation. In *Proceedings of the 2016 Conference of the North American Chapter of the Association for Computational Linguistics: Human Language Technologies*, pages 380–386.

Matthew D Zeiler. 2012. ADADELTA: an adaptive learning rate method. *arXiv preprint arXiv:1212.5701*.

Yukun Zhu, Ryan Kiros, Rich Zemel, Ruslan Salakhutdinov, Raquel Urtasun, Antonio Torralba, and Sanja Fidler. 2015. Aligning books and movies: Towards story-like visual explanations by watching movies and reading books. In *Proceedings of the IEEE international conference on computer vision*, pages 19–27.

A   Supplementary figures

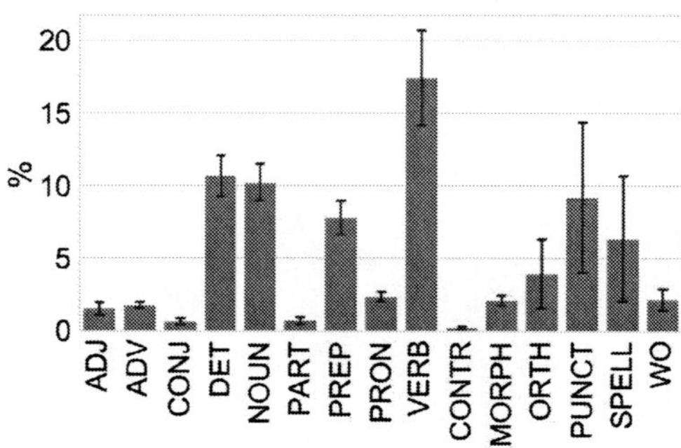

Figure 1: Mean proportion of ERRANT-induced POS-based error types across datasets (FCE test set, CoNLL 2014 test set 1 (both annotators), BEA 2019 GEC Shared Task development set and JFLEG test set). Error bars show the standard deviation.

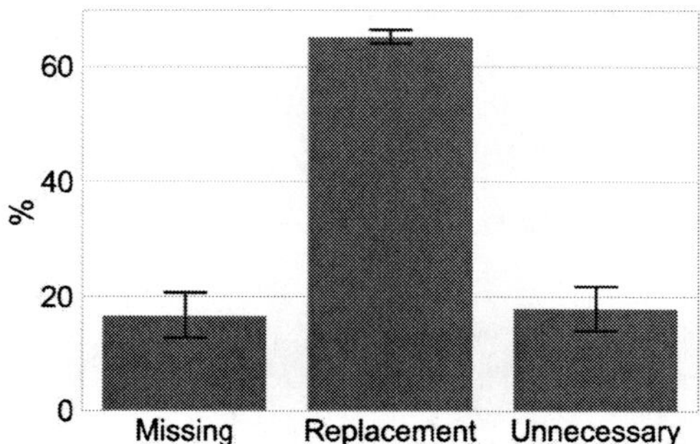

Figure 2: Mean proportion of ERRANT-induced edit operation error types across all datasets (FCE test set, CoNLL 2014 test set (both annotators), BEA 2019 GEC Shared Task development set and JFLEG test set). Error bars show the standard deviation.

B Supplementary tables

	Baseline	BERT base	R BERT large	ELMo	Flair	Frequency
ADJ	16.35	25.47	29.49	24.13	18.77	373
ADV	8.18	16.62	17.39	13.81	11.25	391
CONJ	9.63	15.56	12.59	8.89	8.15	135
CONTR	18.60	11.63	20.93	25.58	25.58	43
DET	24.78	38.11	38.02	37.28	27.30	2304
MORPH	36.34	53.12	52.69	47.53	35.48	465
NOUN	26.28	40.53	45.97	36.26	31.45	2245
ORTH	29.40	28.96	28.20	30.49	27.76	915
OTHER	18.77	29.96	31.06	27.04	20.69	4800
PART	9.62	28.85	31.41	31.41	16.67	156
PREP	10.70	34.71	35.25	31.40	20.42	1841
PRON	12.20	25.98	28.35	19.69	13.78	508
PUNCT	17.21	27.72	26.32	22.80	15.97	2504
SPELL	88.33	92.88	91.48	89.06	84.88	1362
VERB	18.63	33.75	36.80	25.40	19.32	3929
WO	13.52	23.16	22.13	19.47	14.75	488

Table 1: Overall recall of each model over all datasets broken out by ERRANT-induced POS-based error type, with frequency of occurrence of each error type.

	Baseline	BERT base	R BERT large	ELMo	Flair	Frequency
Missing	19.00	28.98	26.83	29.17	22.48	3816
Replacement	27.02	39.94	41.60	35.02	28.63	14839
Unnecessary	15.38	29.07	31.81	24.50	16.72	3804

Table 2: Overall recall of each model over all datasets broken out by ERRANT-induced edit operation error type, with frequency of occurrence of each error type.

How to account for *mispellings*:
Quantifying the benefit of character representations in neural content scoring models

Brian Riordan
ETS
briordan@ets.org

Michael Flor
ETS
mflor@ets.org

Robert Pugh[*]
Course Hero
robert.pugh@coursehero.com

Abstract

Character-based representations in neural models have been claimed to be a tool to overcome spelling variation in word token-based input. We examine this claim in neural models for content scoring. We formulate precise hypotheses about the possible effects of adding character representations to word-based models and test these hypotheses on large-scale real-world content scoring datasets. We find that, while character representations may provide small performance gains in general, their effectiveness in accounting for spelling variation may be limited. We show that spelling correction can provide larger gains than character representations, and that spelling correction improves the performance of models with character representations. With these insights, we report a new state of the art on the ASAP-SAS short content scoring dataset.

1 Introduction

Character-based representations have recently been explored in a variety of models in natural language processing, including sequence labeling (Peters et al., 2017) and machine translation (Chen et al., 2018). In educational applications such as content and essay scoring, character-based representations have been claimed to hold promise as a way to account for variation in spelling without resorting to spelling correction (Madnani et al., 2017; Horbach et al., 2017) – particularly in assessments of K-12 populations or English language learners – in part because spelling correction can introduce mistakes from bad corrections. To the extent that character-based representations can in fact help overcome noise from spelling and other errors, they could be a useful component of robust scoring models. For content scoring applications in particular, where scoring rubrics specif-

ically exclude spelling variation from consideration in scoring, it is important that credit is given for the intended words and ideas regardless of spelling.

However, the contributions of character-based representations to automated scoring performance have rarely been systematically studied. To date, no large-scale study of the effect of character representations in real-world scoring scenarios has been carried out. In particular, given the success and proliferation of neural network-based character-based representations in related tasks, there is a need to assess the potential of neural character representations for educational scoring applications.

The rationale for adoption and use of character representations, especially to augment a backbone of word representations in neural models, is typically based on enriching the input representations with morphological information (Peters et al., 2017; Chen et al., 2018), accounting for noise, out-of-vocabulary inputs (Luong and Manning, 2016), or both (Madnani et al., 2017).

We distinguish two main claims that are made for employing character representations in order to account for noise in inputs, sometimes implicitly. One claim is that including character representations in a model accounts for spelling errors in the input. The idea is that models sensitive to characters can implicitly learn the correspondence between incorrect and correct spellings of words from the character-sequence-to-score associations (as opposed to word-to-score associations) across the training data (Horbach et al., 2017). If this is the case, then models without access to character representations should perform more poorly on responses with more misspelled words, since standard word-only neural models ignore these tokens (because the tokens are unlikely to appear in sets of word embeddings and hence are typically

---

[*]Work carried out while at ETS.

Proceedings of the Fourteenth Workshop on Innovative Use of NLP for Building Educational Applications, pages 116–126
Florence, Italy, August 2, 2019. ©2019 Association for Computational Linguistics

treated as an unknown token). Therefore, one way to operationalize this claim is the following hypothesis:

- Hypothesis 1: On responses with *more* spelling errors, models with additional character representations should improve model performance relative to models with only word representations. This result should be manifested in a statistical interaction between the addition of character representations to a model and number of misspellings in the input.

A second claim, based on the first claim, is that the addition of character representations to a model's representational repertoire should be sufficient to match the use of spelling correction on the input (without adding character representations). This claim leads to two hypotheses:

- Hypothesis 2.1: Models with additional character representations should achieve performance similar to models without character representations trained on spell-corrected input.

- Hypothesis 2.2: The performance of models with additional character representations should be similar whether or not they are trained on spell-corrected input.

In this paper, we test these hypotheses on a large and diverse collection of content-based questions spanning formative and summative assessments.

We focus on *neural* models for *content* scoring. Content scoring scenarios offer a good testbed for exploring the potential contributions of character-based models because the rubrics of questions focus solely on the content of responses and ignore writing quality metrics such as spelling and mechanics errors. Neural models have seen the most active research on character-based representation and may make possible more flexible and expressive character representations compared with non-neural models. We leave a more general exploration of the contribution of character-based models across both neural and non-neural contexts to future work.

Our work makes the following contributions:

- We demonstrate that, while neural models with additional character representations show a small but durable edge over word-only models in representative real-world contexts, this improvement does not increase significantly as the number of spelling errors increases.

- We show that spell-corrected input improves model performance more than the addition of character representations, and that models with additional character representations can be improved further by using spell correction.

- We achieve a new state of the art on the ASAP-SAS dataset.

2 Related Work

Several recent works provide background on automated content scoring in educational applications (Horbach and Zesch, 2019; Burrows et al., 2015; Riordan et al., 2017). The effect of spelling errors on content scoring was investigated by Horbach et al. (2017). They generated artificial errors on the ASAP-SAS dataset and explored how the scoring performance of a non-neural model of word and character n-grams was affected by increasing amounts of artificial misspellings. They found that models with additional character representations were relatively resilient at higher rates of misspellings. Our work is complementary in that (1) we investigate neural models and (2) we analyze trends in performance on two additional large collections of real-world data.

Spelling correction has been employed in several published systems for the ASAP-SAS dataset. Tandalla (2012), the best-performing system on the ASAP-SAS shared task, employed spelling correction. Kumar et al. (2019) demonstrate strong performance on ASAP-SAS in part due to spelling correction, but use a different train and test set along with data augmentation. Recent work on neural methods for short content scoring uses word- and sentence-level representations (Kumar et al., 2017; Saha et al., 2018; Marvaniya et al., 2018); the current work examines character representations in neural content scoring and explores both short and long content scenarios.

Among neural approaches for essay scoring, Dong et al. (2017) explore a family of combinations of hierarchical CNNs and LSTMs with character-based, word-based, and combined word- and character-based representations. They find that the concatenation of word and character representations does not improve on a word-based representation. Cozma et al. (2018) describe a model that incorporates character information via string kernels. We leave to future work an exploration of the strengths of this and other non-neural character representations for capturing character-sequence-to-score correspondences that account for spelling variation in content scoring.

While spelling correction is often mentioned as a preprocessing step for content scoring, text classification, and other content-focused NLP tasks, to our knowledge, little work exists that attempts to quantify the relative contribution of spelling correction to task performance (although there are indications that general NLP tools such as morphological analyzers can have strong positive effects (Zalmout and Habash, 2017)).

3   Datasets

Table 1 shows basic statistics for each dataset.

3.1   ASAP-SAS

One of the most widely-used short answer scoring datasets is the Automated Student Assessment Prize Short Answer Scoring (ASAP-SAS) dataset. The dataset is comprised of 10 individual questions on academic subjects such as science, biology, and English Language Arts.   The questions were administered to high school students in the United States on state-level assessments. Responses were often one or a few sentences. The responses were scored by two human annotators on a scale from 0 to 2 or 0 to 3 depending on the question (Shermis, 2015). For this study, we used the official training and test data as is without any filtering of responses or manual correction.[1] Figure 1 shows a histogram of the number of misspellings per response (automatically detected). For analysis of the behavior of the models with respect to different numbers of misspellings, we manually binned the number of misspellings per response into 0, 1, and 2+ (cf. Figure 5).

3.2   Formative-K12-SAS

We collected a large sample of content-based short answer questions that have been used in a variety of formative classroom settings with middle and high school students. The questions span the

---

[1] https://www.kaggle.com/c/asap-sas. The official test set is public_leaderboard_rel_2.tsv.

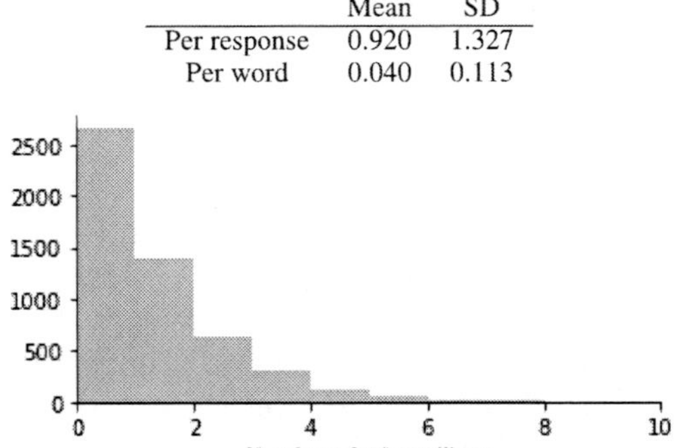

	Mean	SD
Per response	0.920	1.327
Per word	0.040	0.113

Figure 1: ASAP-SAS spelling errors.

	Mean	SD
Per response	0.414	0.997
Per word	0.026	0.093

Figure 2: Formative assessments spelling errors.

subject areas of science, ELA, and social studies. While the questions used different kinds of scoring rubrics with a variety of score ranges, all questions were content-focused. We manually binned the number of misspellings per response (Figure 2) in the same way as was done for the ASAP-SAS dataset (cf. Figure 6).

3.3   Summative-LAS

This dataset is comprised of 20 questions from a series of high-stakes, large-scale standardized tests. The tests are administered to an adult population in the United States, with individuals having completed high school and at least some post-secondary education. Test takers are typically proficient English speakers. Each test measures content knowledge of academic subject areas or elements of effective institutional leadership. Constructed response scores are assigned on a 0–3 scale. Writing proficiency is *not* part of the scoring rubric. Notably, the mean number of words per response is more than 230, making the length of responses comparable to essay questions. Hence, we dub this dataset *Summative-LAS* for *long answer*

Dataset	Number of questions	Number of responses	Score ranges	Mean number of training responses	Mean number of words (train)
ASAP-SAS	10	22,267	0/1/2(/3)	1363	48.4
Formative-K12-SAS	118	228,909	(0/)1/2(/3/4/5/6)	989	33.0
Summative-LAS	20	108,658	0/1/2/3	4346	233.9

Table 1: Overview of the datasets used in this work. The number of responses covers both the official train and test splits for ASAP-SAS. The mean number of responses and words were computed over the official training set for ASAP-SAS and over 5-fold splits of each question's data (80% train) for the remaining datasets.

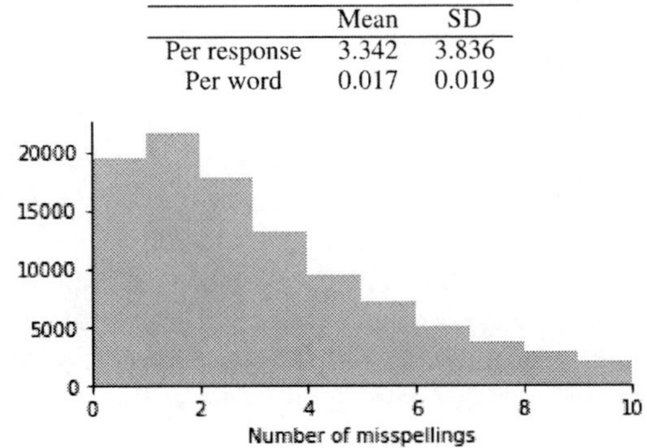

Figure 3: Summative-LAS spelling errors.

scoring. For this dataset, because of the larger spread of spelling errors (Figure 3), we elected to bin the misspellings automatically into relatively equal-sized bins: 0-1, 2-4, and 5+ (cf. Figure 7).

4 Method

4.1 Network architecture

The space of network architectures that we explored for this study is depicted in Figure 4. For a word token-only model, pretrained word embeddings are fed to a bidirectional GRU. The hidden states of the GRU are aggregated by a pooling or attention mechanism. Pooling mechanisms included mean and max pooling (Taghipour and Ng, 2016; Shen et al., 2018). The attention mechanism is an MLP-based document-level attention to combined word-character vectors (Yang et al., 2016)[2]. The output of the encoder is aggregated in a fully-connected feedforward layer with sigmoid activation that computes a scalar output for the predicted score.

For a model with additional character repre-

---

[2]A document context vector u is updated at word i with: $u_i = tanh(W h_i + b)$. The attention is computed with $\alpha_i = exp(u_i^T u)/\sum_t exp(u_i^T u)$ and $d = \sum_t \alpha_i h_i$ for a document d (response) and RNN states h.

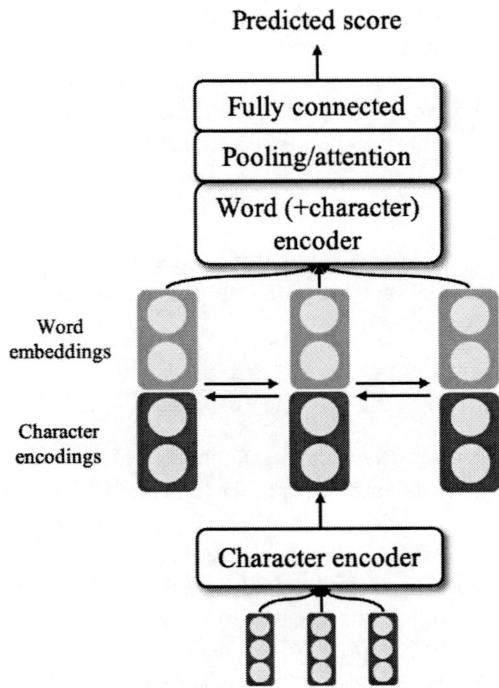

Figure 4: Neural network architectures.

sentations, each word is represented with a sequence of 25-dimensional character embeddings (randomly initialized). These sequences are encoded with a character encoder (see 4.3). The encoded outputs are concatenated with the word embeddings prior to the word-level encoder.

4.2 Data preparation and model training

The text is preprocessed with the spaCy tokenizer with limited custom postprocessing to improve the tokenization outputs. Each response is padded to uniform length, but these padding tokens are masked out during model training. Prior to training, we scale all scores of responses to [0, 1] and use these scaled scores as input to the networks. For evaluation, the scaled scores are converted back to their original range.

For the word tokens, we use GloVe 100 dimension vectors (Pennington et al., 2014) as pretrained embeddings and fine-tune these during training. Word tokens that are not found in the embeddings are mapped to a randomly initialized UNK embedding.

Networks are trained with a mean squared error loss. We carried out extensive preliminary experiments on the ASAP-SAS dev sets to find the highest-performing optimizer (RMSProp with ρ set to 0.9), learning rate (0.001), batch size (32), and gradient clipping setting (10.0).

We employ an exponential moving average of the model's weights during training. These weights w_{EMA} are updated after each batch with

$$w_{EMA} \mathrel{-}= (1.0 - d) * (w_{EMA} - w_{current}).$$

d is a decay rate that is updated dynamically at each batch taking into account the number of batches so far:

$$min(decay, \frac{1 + \#batches}{10 + \#batches}).$$

We set *decay*, the maximum decay rate, to 0.999.

For all experiments, we train models with 5-fold cross validation with train/dev/test splits. On the ASAP-SAS dataset, we split the official training data into 5 folds of 80% train and 20% dev. On all other datasets, we split the data into 5 folds of 60% train, 20% dev, and 20% test. For hyperparameter tuning, we evaluate performance only on the dev sets and record the best performance across epochs. For training final models after hyperparameter tuning, we combine the training and dev sets and stop training at the average best epoch across dev folds rounded to the nearest 5th epoch (cf. Johnson & Zhang (2017; 2015)). For ASAP-SAS, final test performance is from the official public test set. For the other datasets, final test performance is the average test performance across folds.

4.3 Hyperparameter tuning

We tuned hyperparameters for both the character and combined word-character encoders. For both encoders, we experimented with several encoder types and hyperparameter configurations on the ASAP-SAS dataset (dev sets only).

For the combined word-character encoder, we varied the encoder type in bidirectional {GRU, LSTM}. Bidirectional GRUs performed better in most cases. We varied the encoder hidden dimensions in {100, 250}, number of layers in {1, 2}, dropout on embeddings in {0.0, 0.3}, pooling/attention in {final state, mean pooling, max pooling, and attention pooling}, and dropout after pooling/attention in {0.0, 0.3}. We obtained the best results on average across the ASAP-SAS questions with 1 layer, 250 dimensions, max pooling, and no dropout.

For the character encoder, we tested a convolutional encoder and three bidirectional recurrent encoders with the same pooling/attention mechanisms: {final state, mean pooling, max pooling, and attention pooling}. For the CNN, we varied the number of filters in {50, 100} and the filter sizes in {3, 5, (3,4,5)}. For the RNNs, we varied the encoder hidden dimensions in {25, 50}. For these experiments, we used a combined word-character encoder with the best hyperparameter settings from the word-character encoder experiments. The best character encoder results were achieved with the CNN with 100 filters and filter sizes of (3,4,5) (i.e. the concatenation of filter sizes 3, 4, and 5) (Johnson and Zhang, 2015).

4.4 Spelling detection and correction

A spelling detection and correction system based on the approach described in Flor (2012) and Flor and Futagi (2012) was used in all experiments. The system employs a set of large-scale dictionaries and language models. The approach demonstrated high spelling correction accuracy on benchmark datasets of essays written on high-stakes summative assessments by both native and non-native English speakers, outperforming comparable industry and open-source spelling correction systems.

For each question in each dataset, we adapted the spelling detection algorithm by incorporating the tokens from the question text. The current work focused on *non-word* misspellings, that is, character sequences that are not valid in standard written English. We leave an examination of real-word (context-sensitive) errors (e.g., confusing *their* and *there*) to future work.

4.5 Evaluation and statistical analysis

To summarize model performance, we report mean squared error (MSE) and quadratic weighted kappa (QWK). For the ASAP-SAS dataset, we also report the Fisher-weighted mean QWK across questions, which was the official metric of the ASAP competition.

To analyze the robustness of performance improvements with character representations, we employ generalized linear mixed-effect models (GLMMs) (Harrison et al., 2018). Mixed-effect models can better capture variation across individual questions by modeling questions as random effects. In contrast with previous work in NLP that analyzes model performance with mixed-effect models, we analyze per-response prediction errors using real-valued regression model predictions. Since the prediction errors are not normally distributed, using standard linear mixed effect models (even with transformation of the dependent variable) can result in Type I errors. Analysis of the prediction error data showed that gamma distributions provided the best fit. Hence we employ gamma GLMMs with a log link function.

We investigated the interaction predicted by Hypothesis 1 with the following GLMM:

$$error \sim feat * missp + \#words + \tag{1}$$
$$score + (1|question)$$

$feat$ is the representation type (w vs. $w{+}c$), $missp$ is the misspelling bin, and $feat{*}missp$ is their interaction. $\#words$ is the number of words in the response, and $score$ is the response's human-assigned score. $(1|question)$ represents a random intercept for each question. This model estimates the effect of the representation type and the number of misspellings and their interaction, while controlling for the effect of number of words and assigned score.

Hypothesis 2 was examined with a GLMM model of the form:

$$error \sim feat * sp + (1|question) \tag{2}$$

where sp is the presence or absence of spelling correction.

For each dataset, we address Hypothesis 2 first, since the evidence relating to this hypothesis is the relative performance of the different models. Then, looking at model predictions by bins of responses for numbers of misspellings, we examine evidence for Hypothesis 1.

Condition	Mean MSE	Mean QWK	Mean$_{\text{Fisher}}$ QWK
w -sp	0.2286	0.7562	0.7652
$w{+}c$ -sp	0.2218	0.7602	0.7691
w +sp	0.2236	0.7660	0.7748
$w{+}c$ +sp	**0.2200**	**0.7705**	**0.7788**

Table 2: Human-machine agreement across models on ASAP-SAS. w = word representations, $w{+}c$ = word and character representations, $-sp$ = no spelling correction, $+sp$ = spelling correction.

	Estimate	SE	Pr($>$|z|)
(Intercept)	-1.132	0.119	$<$2e-16
feature set ($w{+}c$)	-0.028	0.020	0.168
spelling (+sp)	-0.017	0.020	0.389
feature set : spelling	0.023	0.029	0.423

Table 3: GLMM parameter estimates, standard errors, and p-values for model prediction error across all models on ASAP-SAS. *Feature set* is w vs. $w{+}c$. *Spelling* is +/- spelling correction.

5 Results

5.1 ASAP-SAS

Table 2 shows the mean MSE, mean QWK, and mean Fisher-transformed QWK across the 10 questions in the ASAP-SAS dataset. First, we see that the models with character representations outperform their word-only counterparts ($w{+}c$ vs. w; lower MSE and higher QWK). Second, the spell-corrected models outperform the corresponding uncorrected models (+sp vs. -sp) with the same representations. The spell-corrected model with character representations achieves the highest performance. The Fisher-transformed mean QWK of 0.7788 represents a new state of the art for the ASAP-SAS dataset for the official test set for single models without data augmentation.[3]

---

[3]Ramachandran et al. (2015) report a QWK of 0.78 on the ASAP-SAS dataset, but we conclude that their actual unrounded Fisher-transformed mean QWK score was 0.77696. As they note, "The mean QW Kappa achieved by our patterns is 0.78 and that achieved by Tandalla's manual regular expressions is 0.77. Although the QW Kappas are very close... their unrounded difference of 0.00530 is noteworthy." According to the Kaggle public leaderboard (https://www.kaggle.com/c/asap-sas/leaderboard), the Tandalla system's unrounded score was 0.77166. Combining this information: 0.77166 + 0.00530 = 0.77696. Moreover, elsewhere in their paper Ramachandran et al. note "The human benchmark for the dataset was 0.90. The best team achieved a score of 0.77." Because these scores match the Fisher-transformed QWK scores on the Kaggle leaderboard, we conclude that they used the Fisher-transformed mean QWK as opposed to the untransformed mean QWK.

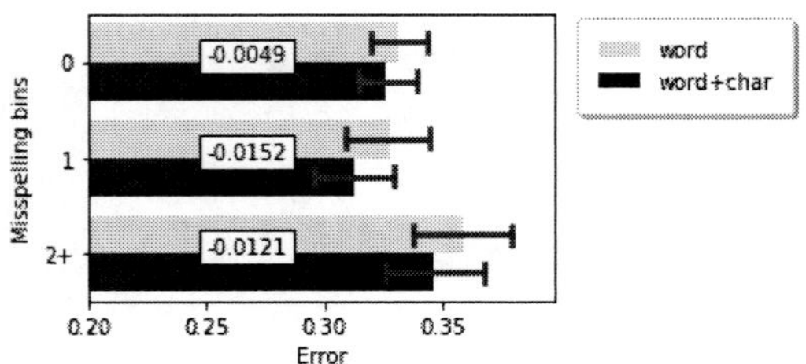

Figure 5: Mean prediction error by models without spell correction on ASAP-SAS. Numbers on the bars represent the difference between $w+c$ and w.

	Estimate	SE	Pr($>$|z|)
(Intercept)	-1.681	0.111	$<$2e-16
feature set ($w+c$)	-0.018	0.028	0.506
missp 1	0.050	0.034	0.143
missp 2+	0.138	0.037	0.0002
# words	1.947	0.142	$<$2e-16
score	0.651	0.037	$<$2e-16
feat ($w+c$) : missp 1	-0.036	0.048	0.454
feat ($w+c$) : missp 2+	-0.022	0.051	0.656

Table 4: GLMM summary for model prediction error on ASAP-SAS for the models without spelling correction. *Feature set* is w vs. $w+c$. *Missp* {*1,2+*} are bins of number of misspellings. *Score* is human-assigned response score.

With regard to Hypothesis 2.1, that character representations should improve performance as much as spell correction, the results demonstrate that adding character representations ($w+c$, -sp: mean MSE = 0.2218) can outperform spell correction of a word-only model (w, +sp: mean MSE = 0.2236) (although this is not reflected in the QWK results).

To test the strength of these results, we used the GLMM from equation (2). The model parameter estimates are shown in Table 3. Neither the effect of adding character representations ($w+c$) nor the effect of spelling correction (+sp) are statistically significant. Notably, there is no evidence for an interaction between character representations and spelling correction, suggesting relatively independent effects.

Next, we examine Hypothesis 1, that character representations should aid performance more on responses with more spelling errors. Figure 5 shows the mean error across all responses in ASAP-SAS by number of spelling errors in bins of 0, 1, and 2+ for the models without spelling correction (w -sp and $w+c$ -sp).

The mixed effect model parameter estimates are

Condition	Mean MSE	Mean QWK
w -sp	0.3220	0.7759
$w+c$ -sp	0.3190	0.7799
w +sp	0.3176	0.7815
$w+c$ +sp	**0.3140**	**0.7828**

Table 5: Human-machine agreement across models on Formative-K12-SAS.

	Estimate	SE	Pr($>$|z|)
(Intercept)	-0.962	0.024	$<$2e-16
feature set ($w+c$)	-0.010	0.002	0.0005
spelling (+sp)	-0.011	0.002	6.58e-05
feature set : spelling	0.001	0.004	0.643

Table 6: GLMM parameter estimates, standard errors, and p-values for model prediction error across all models on Formative-K12-SAS.

presented in Table 4. The main result for our investigation is that there is no significant interaction between model type and number of spelling bins. In other words, the $w+c$ models' performance did not significantly improve as the number of misspellings increased [4].

5.2 Formative-K12-SAS

The performance of the neural models on the Formative-K12-SAS dataset are shown in Table 5. The same trends that were observed for ASAP-SAS are observed here: (1) character and word representations outperform word representations alone ($w+c$ vs. w); (2) spell-corrected models outperform models without spell correction (+sp vs. -sp); (3) the spell-corrected model with character and word representations performs best. Moreover, on this dataset, the mean MSE and mean QWK trends are consistent.

Applying the statistical model from equation (2) to the prediction errors on all responses in this large dataset (Table 6), both model representations and spelling correction achieve statistical significance. No interaction was observed between representation type and spelling correction.

To analyze the differences between model representations by number of misspellings, we specified 3 bins: 0, 1, and 2+. This was because of

---

[4]The data for question 10 in the ASAP-SAS dataset suffers from preprocessing issues such that random spaces are introduced between many words. As a result, a much higher number of misspellings are detected for this question. However, refitting the GLMM model excluding the data for this question produced nearly identical trends.

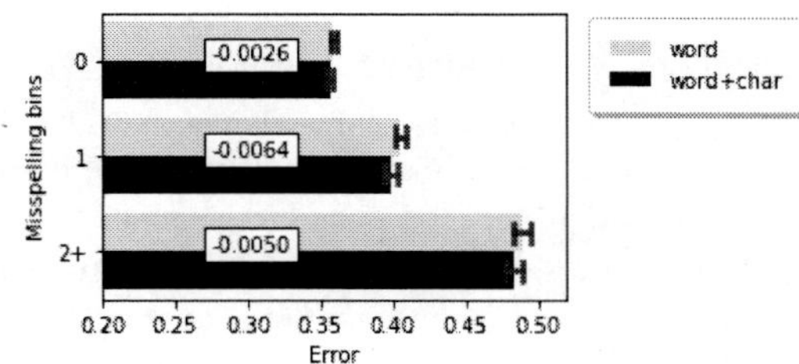

Figure 6: Mean prediction error by models without spell correction on the Formative-K12-SAS dataset. Numbers on the bars represent the difference between $w+c$ and w.

	Estimate	SE	Pr($>$|z|)
(Intercept)	-1.108	0.023	$<$2e-16
feature set ($w+c$)	-0.008	0.003	0.017
missp 1	0.077	0.005	$<$2e-16
missp 2+	0.158	0.007	$<$2e-16
# words	1.996	0.157	$<$2e-16
score	0.230	0.008	$<$2e-16
feat ($w+c$) : missp 1	-0.009	0.008	0.242
feat ($w+c$) : missp 2+	-0.004	0.010	0.703

Table 7: GLMM summary for model prediction error on Formative-K12-SAS for the models without spelling correction.

the extreme skew in the misspellings counts – the large majority of responses actually had no misspellings – which precluded specifying bins with a similar number of responses. The model mean prediction error increased across misspellings bins for both w and $w+c$ models (Figure 6). Unlike ASAP-SAS, both the difference between feature sets and between misspellings bins *was* significant even when controlling for score and number of words (Table 7). As before, however, there was not a significant interaction between misspelling bins and representation type.

5.3 Summative-LAS

Table 8 provides the MSE and QWK for the dataset of content-based questions on the summative assessment dataset. As in the other two datasets, character and word representations ($w+c$) perform best, and the best models are the models based on spell-corrected text. On this dataset, however, what is striking is the degree to which spelling correction improves model performance: QWK scores increase about 15 points.

The GLMM parameter estimates (Table 9) show that the difference between models with and without spell correction nearly reaches the 0.05 thresh-

Condition	Mean MSE	Mean QWK
w -sp	0.4768	0.5082
$w+c$ -sp	0.4766	0.5115
w +sp	0.3457	0.6590
$w+c$ +sp	**0.3441**	**0.6609**

Table 8: Human-machine agreement across models on Summative-LAS.

	Estimate	SE	Pr($>$|z|)
(Intercept)	-0.763	0.031	$<$2e-16
feature set ($w+c$)	-0.002	0.003	0.479
spelling (+sp)	-0.006	0.003	0.051
feature set : spelling	0.003	0.004	0.508

Table 9: GLMM parameter estimates, standard errors, and p-values for model prediction error across all models on Summative-LAS.

	Estimate	SE	Pr($>$|z|)
(Intercept)	-0.544	0.032	$<$2e-16
feature set ($w+c$)	-0.002	0.005	0.706
missp 2-4	0.027	0.005	6.24e-07
missp 5+	0.054	0.006	$<$2e-16
# words	0.228	0.022	$<$2e-16
score	-0.478	0.005	$<$2e-16
feat ($w+c$) : missp 2-4	9.09e-05	0.007	0.991
feat ($w+c$) : missp 5+	-0.001	0.008	0.856

Table 10: GLMM summary for model prediction error on Summative-LAS for the models without spelling correction.

old of significance, underlining the strength of the effect of building models on spell corrected text on this dataset. The addition of character representations, on the other hand, shows a negligible effect on model performance.

The mean prediction error for the w and $w+c$ models is shown in Figure 7. The results of mod-

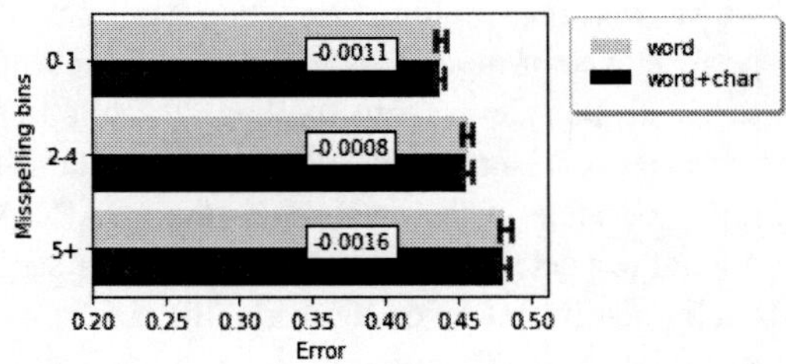

Figure 7: Mean prediction error by models without spell correction on the Summative-LAS dataset. Numbers on the bars represent the difference between $w+c$ and w.

eling the prediction errors with the model from equation (1) with these bins are given in Table 10. The mean prediction error increases significantly from bin $0-1$ to $5+$, but there is little difference between representation types and there is no interaction between representation type and misspelling bin.

6 Discussion

This study is the first large-scale examination of the contribution of character representations in neural network models for automated content scoring. We formulated three hypotheses about the effects of adding character representations to neural models and tested these hypotheses with three diverse datasets, including two large-scale real-world datasets. The results provide several new insights into the capabilities of character representations for content scoring.

First, we examined whether the addition of character representations improves scoring model performance as the number of spelling errors increases. If a model were to effectively learn character-to-score correspondences, we might expect the model to show solid gains on responses with more misspellings. While there was a small trend toward an improvement in word+character models over word-only models on such responses, this trend was not strong enough to produce a statistically significant difference between model representation types. Hence, we cannot conclude that character representations readily account for spelling variation in the training data.

Second, we showed that spelling correction can increase word-only model performance beyond what is achieved with only the addition of character representations (without spelling correction). This trend was strongest in the data with the most spelling errors (Section 5.3). Moreover, we showed that spelling correction can boost the performance of models with character representations. In fact, leveraging spelling correction and character representations contributed to establishing a new state-of-the-art result on the ASAP-SAS official test set. While both trends were not statistically significant given the variability in the prediction error data, neither of these trends are predicted by common ideas about the effectiveness of character representations in automatically learning how spelling variants correlate with scores.

We note that our results do not establish that

models with character representations do not learn about some associations between spelling variation and scores. It may be the case that larger training data would lead to more effective learning of the association between character sequence variants and scores. However, large datasets are generally not typical in training data for educational applications. Different kinds of character (or subword) representations may also prove more effective than the space of character representations considered here.

Our results show that character representations, when added to word-based neural models, consistently provide small gains in performance. Therefore, we conclude that character representations may provide some benefit in practice in neural models for content scoring, but that they are unlikely to serve as a replacement for spelling correction of the training data.

Acknowledgements

We thank Aoife Cahill, Anastassia Loukina, Beata Beigman Klebanov, Nitin Madnani and three anonymous reviewers for their helpful comments.

References

Steven Burrows, Iryna Gurevych, and Benno Stein. 2015. The Eras and Trends of Automatic Short Answer Grading. *International Journal of Artificial Intelligence in Education*, 25(1):60–117.

Huadong Chen, Shujian Huang, David Chiang, Xinyu Dai, and Jiajun Chen. 2018. Combining Character and Word Information in Neural Machine Translation Using a Multi-Level Attention. In *Proceedings of the 2018 Conference of the North American Chapter of the Association for Computational Linguistics: Human Language Technologies (NAACL-HLT)*.

Madalina Cozma, Andrei Madalin Butnaru, and Radu Tudor Ionescu. 2018. Automated essay scoring with string kernels and word embeddings. In *Proceedings of the 56th Annual Meeting of the Association for Computational Linguistics (ACL)*.

Fei Dong, Yue Zhang, and Jie Yang. 2017. Attention-based Recurrent Convolutional Neural Network for Automatic Essay Scoring. In *Conference on Natural Language Learning (CoNLL)*.

Michael Flor. 2012. Four types of context for automatic spelling correction. *Traitement Automatique des Langues (TAL)*, 53(3):61–99.

Michael Flor and Yoko Futagi. 2012. On using context for automatic correction of non-word misspellings in student essays. In *Proceedings of the 7th Workshop on Innovative Use of NLP for Building Educational Applications (BEA)*.

Xavier A. Harrison, Lynda Donaldson, Maria Eugenia Correa-Cano, Julian Evans, David N. Fisher, Cecily E. D. Goodwin, Beth S. Robinson, David J. Hodgson, and Richard Inger. 2018. A brief introduction to mixed effects modelling and multi-model inference in ecology. *PeerJ*.

Andrea Horbach, Yuning Ding, and Torsten Zesch. 2017. The Influence of Spelling Errors on Content Scoring Performance. In *Proceedings of the 4th Workshop on Natural Language Processing Techniques for Educational Applications (NLPTEA)*.

Andrea Horbach and Torsten Zesch. 2019. The Influence of Variance in Learner Answers on Automatic Content Scoring. *Frontiers in Education*, 4:28.

Rie Johnson and Tong Zhang. 2015. Effective Use of Word Order for Text Categorization with Convolutional Neural Networks. In *Proceedings of the 2015 Conference of the North American Chapter of the Association for Computational Linguistics: Human Language Technologies (NAACL-HLT)*.

Rie Johnson and Tong Zhang. 2017. Deep Pyramid Convolutional Neural Networks for Text Categorization. In *Proceedings of the 55th Annual Meeting of the Association for Computational Linguistics (ACL)*.

Sachin Kumar, Soumen Chakrabarti, and Shourya Roy. 2017. Earth Movers Distance Pooling over Siamese LSTMs for Automatic Short Answer Grading. In *International Joint Conferences on Artificial Intelligence (IJCAI)*.

Y. Anoop Kumar, Swati Aggarwal, Debanjan Mahata, Rajiv Ratn Shah, Ponnurangam Kumaraguru, and Roger Zimmermann. 2019. Get IT Scored using AutoSAS-An Automated System for Scoring Short Answers. In *9th Symposium on Educational Advances in Artificial Intelligence (EAAI-19)*.

Minh-Thang Luong and Christopher D. Manning. 2016. Achieving Open Vocabulary Neural Machine Translation with Hybrid Word-Character Models. In *Proceedings of the 54th Annual Meeting of the Association for Computational Linguistics (ACL)*.

Nitin Madnani, Anastassia Loukina, and Aoife Cahill. 2017. A Large Scale Quantitative Exploration of Modeling Strategies for Content Scoring. In *Proceedings of the 12th Workshop on Innovative Use of NLP for Building Educational Applications (BEA)*.

Smit Marvaniya, Swarnadeep Saha, Tejas I. Dhamecha, Peter Foltz, Renuka Sindhgatta, and Bikram Sengupta. 2018. Creating Scoring Rubric from Representative Student Answers for Improved Short Answer Grading. In *Conference on Information and Knowledge Management (CIKM)*.

Jeffrey Pennington, Richard Socher, and Christopher Manning. 2014. Glove: Global Vectors for Word Representation. In *Proceedings of the 2014 Conference on Empirical Methods in Natural Language Processing (EMNLP)*.

Matthew E. Peters, Waleed Ammar, Chandra Bhagavatula, and Russell Power. 2017. Semi-supervised sequence tagging with bidirectional language models. In *Proceedings of the 55th Annual Meeting of the Association for Computational Linguistics (ACL)*.

Lakshmi Ramachandran, Jian Cheng, and Peter Foltz. 2015. Identifying Patterns For Short Answer Scoring Using Graph-based Lexico-Semantic Text Matching. In *Proceedings of the 10th Workshop on Innovative Use of NLP for Building Educational Applications (BEA)*.

Brian Riordan, Andrea Horbach, Aoife Cahill, Torsten Zesch, and Chong Min Lee. 2017. Investigating neural architectures for short answer scoring. In *Proceedings of the 12th Workshop on Innovative Use of NLP for Building Educational Applications (BEA)*.

Swarnadeep Saha, Tejas I Dhamecha, Smit Marvaniya, Renuka Sindhgatta, and Bikram Sengupta. 2018. Sentence Level or Token Level Features for Automatic Short Answer Grading?: Use Both. In *19th International Conference of Artificial Intelligence in Education (AIEd)*.

Dinghan Shen, Guoyin Wang, Wenlin Wang, Martin Renqiang Min, Qinliang Su, Yizhe Zhang, Chunyuan Li, Ricardo Henao, and Lawrence Carin. 2018. Baseline Needs More Love: On Simple Word-Embedding-Based Models and Associated Pooling Mechanisms. In *Proceedings of the 56th Annual Meeting of the Association for Computational Linguistics (ACL)*.

Mark D Shermis. 2015. Contrasting state-of-the-art in the machine scoring of short-form constructed responses. *Educational Assessment*, 20(1).

Kaveh Taghipour and Hwee Tou Ng. 2016. A Neural Approach to Automated Essay Scoring. In *Proceedings of the 2016 Conference on Empirical Methods in Natural Language Processing (EMNLP)*.

Luis Tandalla. 2012. Scoring short answer essays. Technical report.

Zichao Yang, Diyi Yang, Chris Dyer, Xiaodong He, Alexander J. Smola, and Eduard H. Hovy. 2016. Hierarchical Attention Networks for Document Classification. In *Proceedings of the 2016 Conference of the North American Chapter of the Association for Computational Linguistics: Human Language Technologies (NAACL-HLT)*.

Nasser Zalmout and Nizar Habash. 2017. Don't Throw Those Morphological Analyzers Away Just

Yet: Neural Morphological Disambiguation for Arabic. In *Proceedings of the 2017 Conference on Empirical Methods in Natural Language Processing (EMNLP)*.

A   Appendix: ASAP-SAS detailed results

Prompt	Dataset-general tuning			
	w -sp	$w+c$ -sp	w +sp	$w+c$ +sp
1	0.8222	0.8310	**0.8339**	0.8301
2	0.7802	**0.8017**	0.7857	0.7913
3	0.6443	0.6311	0.6577	**0.6620**
4	0.7044	0.6934	0.7120	**0.7310**
5	0.8285	0.8272	0.8355	**0.8441**
6	0.8562	0.8477	**0.8625**	0.8610
7	0.7060	0.7250	0.7115	**0.7362**
8	0.6510	0.6662	**0.6778**	0.6641
9	0.8045	0.7942	**0.8178**	0.8087
10	0.7645	**0.7847**	0.7650	0.7766
Mean QWK	0.7561	0.7602	0.7659	**0.7705**
Mean QWK_{Fisher}	0.7652	0.7691	0.7748	**0.7788**

Table 11: Human-machine agreement on ASAP-SAS by prompt.

In Table 11 we report the performance of each prompt's model on ASAP-SAS. We used *dataset-general tuning* of hyperparameters by considering the average best performance across all prompts.

The Unreasonable Effectiveness of Transformer Language Models in Grammatical Error Correction

Dimitris Alikaniotis   **Vipul Raheja**
Grammarly
New York City, NY
`firstname.lastname@grammarly.com`

Abstract

Recent work on Grammatical Error Correction (GEC) has highlighted the importance of language modeling in that it is certainly possible to achieve good performance by comparing the probabilities of the proposed edits. At the same time, advancements in language modeling have managed to generate linguistic output, which is almost indistinguishable from that of human-generated text. In this paper, we up the ante by exploring the potential of more sophisticated language models in GEC and offer some key insights on their strengths and weaknesses. We show that, in line with recent results in other NLP tasks, Transformer architectures achieve consistently high performance and provide a competitive baseline for future machine learning models.

1 Introduction

Transformer models (Vaswani et al., 2017) trained on large-scale language modeling datasets have recently proved to be a very effective means of representing the meaning of a sentence, being put to effective use in fine-tuning both sentence-level tasks, such as the GLUE benchmark (Wang et al., 2018) and token-level tasks, such as Named Entity Recognition (Devlin et al., 2019). Recent work has also found them to produce linguistically valid representations (Goldberg, 2019), as well as to display excellent performance across multiple downstream NLP tasks (e.g., Houlsby et al. 2019).

In this work, we explore how such models perform in the task of Grammatical Error Correction (GEC). While there is a substantial amount of work on statistical (Rozovskaya and Roth, 2016; Junczys-Dowmunt and Grundkiewicz, 2014; Yannakoudakis et al., 2017) and neural (Ji et al., 2017; Xie et al., 2016; Yuan and Briscoe, 2016; Chollampatt et al., 2016; Chollampatt and Ng, 2017; Sakaguchi et al., 2017; Chollampatt and

Ng, 2018) machine translation methods for GEC, we follow the approach of Bryant and Briscoe (2018) and explore how such models would fare in this task when treated as simple language models. More specifically, Bryant and Briscoe (2018) train a 5-gram language model on the One Billion Word Benchmark (Chelba et al., 2013) dataset and find that it produces competitive baseline results without any supervised training. In our work, we extend this work by substituting the n-gram model for several publicly available implementations of state-of-the-art Transformer language models trained on large linguistic corpora and assess their performance on GEC without any supervised training. We find that Transformer language models produce results on par with supervised approaches providing a solid baseline system. This finding is of particular importance in GEC, where data collection and annotation requires substantial manual effort.

2 Related Work

The idea of using language models is quite fundamental to the task of Grammatical Error Correction, which has fed a substantial body of work over the years. More recently, with the availability of web-scale data powering the advances in language modeling, among most of the other advances in NLP, a plethora of language-modeling based approaches have been proposed for the GEC task. Gamon et al. (2008); Matthieu Hermet and Szpakowicz (2008) and Yi et al. (2008) were some of the early works to successfully leverage language models trained on large amounts of web-scale data into a GEC system, reinforcing the idea that simple models and a lot of data trump more elaborate models based on annotated data (Halevy et al., 2009).

Since then, multiple works based on language-

Proceedings of the Fourteenth Workshop on Innovative Use of NLP for Building Educational Applications, pages 127–133
Florence, Italy, August 2, 2019. ©2019 Association for Computational Linguistics

models have been proposed for the GEC task (Park and Levy, 2011; Dahlmeier and Ng, 2012a), either relying entirely on LMs or using them for fine-tuning their systems. Many of the top-ranked systems in the CoNLL-2013 and 2014 GEC shared tasks (Ng et al., 2013, 2014), were either based on language models or had them as integral parts of their systems (Kao et al., 2013; Yoshimoto et al., 2013; Xing et al., 2013; Lee and Lee, 2014; Junczys-Dowmunt and Grundkiewicz, 2014). LM-only approaches though took a backseat and were only sporadically used after the shared tasks, as Neural Machine Translation-based approaches took over, but LMs remained an integral part of the GEC systems (Junczys-Dowmunt and Grundkiewicz, 2016; Ji et al., 2017; Xie et al., 2016; Junczys-Dowmunt et al., 2018; Chollampatt and Ng, 2018). However, Bryant and Briscoe (2018) recently revived the idea, achieving competitive performance with the state-of-the-art, demonstrating the effectiveness of the approaches to the task without using any annotated data for training.

3 Methodology

In this work, we follow the setup from Bryant and Briscoe (2018) substituting the 5-gram language model for different language models based on the Transformer architecture. Specifically, we use Google's BERT (Devlin et al., 2019) and OpenAI's GPT (Radford et al., 2018) and GPT-2 (Radford et al., 2019).[1] While all these are best thought of as language models in that they have been trained to predict an element in a sequence, they use slightly different objectives which does not make them directly comparable. Specifically, GPT and GPT-2 have been trained with a classic language modeling objective, whereby they predict the next word in a sequence, whereas BERT has been trained using a *masked language modeling* objective in which the network attempts to predict masked words in the sentence.

We extract the probability of a sentence from BERT, by iteratively masking every word in the sentence and then summing the log probabilities. While this approach is far from ideal, it has been shown (Wang and Cho, 2019) that it approximates the log-likelihood of a sentence.

Test set	Sent.	Tokens	Annot.
CoNLL-2014	1,312	30k	2
FCE	2,715	47k	1

Table 1: Statistics for evaluation data

3.1 Confusion sets

Since our systems do not generate novel sequences, we follow Bryant and Briscoe (2018) and use simple heuristics to generate a confusion set of sentences that our language models score. For prepositions and determiners, the confusion set includes the set of all prepositions and determiners plus an empty string ϵ to remove unnecessary additions. For morphological errors (e.g., past tense or pluralization), we use the Automatically Generated Inflection Database (AGID) which contains different morphological forms for each word.[2] However, we notice that due to the automatic generation, AGID contains errors that might propagate into our scoring. The problem with introducing new errors and non-words is that they would be interpreted as unknown words (henceforth [UNK]s) from the model's perspective. An unknown word in some context might give higher probabilities to an erroneous sentence and cause the model not to select the correct alternative. To remedy this issue, we generate a vocabulary from all the training sets and make sure that any proposed words which do not exist in the vocabulary are replaced by [UNK]s. Note that there is no reason to re-use the vocabulary of the training sets as any large English wordlist would achieve a similar effect. Finally, for spelling mistakes, we, again, follow Bryant and Briscoe (2018) and use CyHunSpell[3] to generate alternatives for non-words.

3.2 Thresholding

Given that our confusion set is prone to errors (due to its automatic generation procedure) as well as the fact that we cannot target all potential errors (e.g., insertions), we bias our method to *prefer* the original sentence unless a much better the alternative is found. We quantify this margin by imposing a threshold above which we accept a candidate sentence as a better alternative. Concretely, let $P(s_c)$ be the probability of the candidate sentence and $P(s_o)$ the probability of the

---

[1]https://github.com/huggingface/
pytorch-pretrained-BERT/

[2]http://wordlist.aspell.net/other/
[3]https://pypi.org/project/CyHunspell/

Dataset	System	ERRANT			M2		
		P	**R**	$\mathbf{F}_{0.5}$	**P**	**R**	$\mathbf{F}_{0.5}$
CoNLL-2014	Felice et al. (2014) †	-	-	-	39.71	30.10	37.33
	Yannakoudakis et al. (2017)	-	-	-	58.79	30.63	49.66
	Chollampatt and Ng (2017)	-	-	-	62.74	32.96	53.14
	Chollampatt and Ng (2018)	-	-	-	65.49	33.14	54.79
	Ge et al. (2018)	-	-	-	**74.12**	**36.30**	**61.34**
	Bryant and Briscoe (2018)	36.62	19.93	31.37	40.56	20.81	34.09
	BERT	33.27	**27.14**	31.83	35.69	**27.99**	33.83
	GPT-1	49.58	27.06	42.5	51.08	27.45	43.57
	GPT-2	**57.73**	24.75	**45.58**	**58.51**	24.9	**46.08**
FCE	Yannakoudakis et al. (2017)	-	-	-	**65.03**	32.45	**54.15**
	Bryant and Briscoe (2018)	41.92	13.62	29.61	44.78	14.12	31.22
	BERT	29.56	**34.67**	30.46	31.97	**35.01**	32.53
	GPT-1	**62.75**	32.19	52.74	**64.01**	32.33	**53.52**
	GPT-2	61.91	33.47	**52.92**	62.64	33.74	53.48

Table 2: Results of our Transformer-Language Model approach against similar approaches (Bryant and Briscoe, 2018) and state-of-the-art on Grammatical Error Correction. For each of the datasets, we use the corresponding test set, and we do not train our models on the corpora. As BERT, we report the best performing BERT model (12 layers, retaining uppercase characters). In the top part of each dataset, we report the scores of supervised methods and in the bottom the unsupervised ones. † denotes this system won the shared task competition.

original sentence, then we accept the candidate if $P(s_c) > P(s_o) + \tau$, where τ is some threshold parameter which we fit on each development set. Note that, practically, this parameter controls the trade-off between *precision* and *recall* as higher τ values would mean that there is less chance of changing the original sentence (i.e., higher precision) and vice versa. We explore different values for $\tau \in \{0, 2, 4, 6, 8\}$ by, as above, fitting them on the corresponding development set.[4]

3.3 Search

Finally, we perform *greedy search* to find the best alternative sentence by iterating over each sentence multiple times, once for every position for which our heuristics found alternatives. If an alternative is selected for the target position, we update the original sentence and proceed to the next position. This pseudo-log-likelihood approximation makes the problem of considering every permutation more computationally tractable.

4 Experiments

We evaluate our method and report results on two standard publicly available datasets. Our evaluation is aimed to stay as true to Bryant and Briscoe (2018) as possible to ensure an even comparison. Concretely, we use the test dataset from the CoNLL-2014 (Ng et al., 2014) shared task[5] and the publicly available First Certificate in English (FCE) (Yannakoudakis et al., 2011). Unfortunately, due to licensing issues, we were unable to obtain permission to use the JFLEG (Napoles et al., 2017) corpus for evaluation. Note that in our method, we do not make use of the training sets commonly used with these datasets. However, we use the development sets used by Bryant and Briscoe (2018) to tune the hyperparameter τ. The number of sentences and tokens for the datasets we used can be found in Table 1.

Similar to Bryant and Briscoe (2018), we report results on three metrics. We use the MaxMatch (M^2) Precision, Recall and $F_{0.5}$ (Dahlmeier and Ng, 2012b) and ERRANT Precision, Recall and $F_{0.5}$ (Bryant et al., 2017).

5 Results

Table 2 presents the results of our method comparing them against recent state-of-the-art supervised models and the simple *n*-gram language model used by Bryant and Briscoe (2018). Table 3 shows some qualitative examples on how each model corrects two sentences pulled from the FCE along with the gold annotations. The reported results

---

[4]Note that the probability of each sentence is in log space.

[5]While we acknowledge the contemporaneous nature of the BEA 2019 Shared Task on GEC and would have liked to report results on the W&I+LOCNESS data, we could not do so because of license limitations.

Source	It will start by a speech from the Director of the conference, followed by a meal.
Gold	It will start **with** a speech **by** the Director of the conference, followed by a meal.
BERT	It will start **with** a speech **from** the Director of the conference, followed by a meal.
GPT	It will start **by** a speech **from** the Director of the conference, followed by a meal.
GPT-2	It will start **with** a speech **from** the Director of the conference, followed by a meal.
Source	They all knows where the conference is and when.
Gold	They all **know** where the conference is and when.
BERT	They all know where the **conferencing** is and when.
GPT	They all **knows** where the conference is and when.
GPT-2	They all **know** where the conference is and when.

Table 3: Source sentences along with the gold edits and the proposed candidates from each of our models.

come from the best performing hyperparameter τ on each dataset. For BERT, we also explored different sizes (12 vs. 24 layers) and whether retaining uppercase characters helps in performance. The best performing τ values were $\tau = 4$ for CoNLL14 for all models; for the FCE dataset: BERT $\tau = 4$, GPT $\tau = 8$, and GPT-2 $\tau = 6$. The best 'version,' of BERT was the *large, cased* (i.e., retaining the lower- /uppercase distinction).

A key result of Table 2 is that Transformer Language Models prove to be more than just a competitive baseline to legitimate Grammatical Error Correction systems on their own. Across the board, Transformer Models are able to outperform the simple *n*-gram model and even approach the performance of supervised GEC systems.

6 Discussion

Looking at the performance of the two GPT models more closely, we see that their performance is nearly identical with GPT-2 leading by a small margin in the CoNLL14 dataset. Given that the versions we used share the same number of layers (12), we attribute GPT-2's slight advantage to the fact that it was trained on considerably more data.

Another interesting result is that while BERT surpasses the *n*-gram baseline overall, it achieves worse performance than the rest in terms of precision and $F_{0.5}$ score. Considering its overall success at modeling NLP tasks, one might expect BERT to achieve better performance here. However, as mentioned above, BERT is not truly a language model in the sense that GPT and GPT-2 are but uses a quasi-language modeling objective which could explain its degraded performance in this setting. Note that framing the task differently (e.g., by masking the preposition in a sen-

tence and selecting the one with the highest probability) might give the edge to BERT as it resembles the way it was trained.

It is also worth mentioning that despite tuning τ to each dataset, we do not explore different weights for different kinds of errors (e.g., penalizing more spelling mistakes). Our key motivation was to corroborate and extend the results of Bryant and Briscoe (2018) to current state-of-the-art language models which have been trained in several languages and show that these models are tough baselines to beat for novel GEC systems.

While the results of the Transformer language models shown in Table 2 demonstrate that they are a tough baseline to beat, it is worth noting that the present approach is not without its limitations. We believe that our methodology should not be considered a panacea to GEC. For instance, being bound by the confusion sets, our system (1) cannot handle missing words (which make up about 20% of all errors), and (2) it is tuned to capture only a subset of the possible mistakes a writer can make (closed class words).

It could be argued that since our system makes use of a pre-defined confusion set (even an automatically generated one), it could not be considered as a fully unsupervised system. In principle, we agree with that statement and we believe that a system which uses, for example, corpus statistics to on-the-fly generate a confusion set would be a very interesting exercise and could yield similar results. However, the present paper is concerned with highlighting the importance of language modeling in GEC and its potential in aiding in low-resource languages where large parallel datasets are unavailable, but such confusion sets are relatively easily obtainable.

7 Conclusion

In this work, we advanced on the foundational idea that a simple language modeling-based approach to GEC with no annotated data can challenge the latest neural and machine translation approaches that rely on large quantities of annotated training data. To this end, we improve on previous work by leveraging state-of-the-art language modeling techniques and perform a thorough comparison of three state-of-the-art Transformer language models which in turn have been trained on data of the order of hundreds of millions of words. We find that merely using pre-trained, and publicly available neural language models improves the performance by a significant margin and comes within striking distance of the state-of-the-art methods.

This work reinforces the strength and robustness of language-model based methods for the task of grammatical error correction. While recent state-of-the-art GEC systems are pursuing NMT-based models with huge amounts (millions of sentences) of annotated training data, approaches like this which require no annotated training data provide great value to researchers and developers interested in building competitive GEC systems (e.g., in other languages) with limited annotated data.

Acknowledgements

The authors would like to thank Joel Tetreault for his comments on earlier drafts as well as the anonymous reviewers for their helpful suggestions.

References

Christopher Bryant and Ted Briscoe. 2018. Language model based grammatical error correction without annotated training data. In *Proceedings of the Thirteenth Workshop on Innovative Use of NLP for Building Educational Applications*, pages 247–253, New Orleans, Louisiana. Association for Computational Linguistics.

Christopher Bryant, Mariano Felice, and Ted Briscoe. 2017. Automatic annotation and evaluation of error types for grammatical error correction. In *Proceedings of the 55th Annual Meeting of the Association for Computational Linguistics (Volume 1: Long Papers)*, pages 793–805, Vancouver, Canada. Association for Computational Linguistics.

Ciprian Chelba, Tomas Mikolov, Mike Schuster, Qi Ge, Thorsten Brants, Phillipp Koehn, and Tony Robinson. 2013. One billion word benchmark for measuring progress in statistical language modeling. Technical report, Google.

Shamil Chollampatt and Hwee Tou Ng. 2017. Connecting the dots: Towards human-level grammatical error correction. In *Proceedings of the 12th Workshop on Innovative Use of NLP for Building Educational Applications*, pages 327–333, Copenhagen, Denmark. Association for Computational Linguistics.

Shamil Chollampatt and Hwee Tou Ng. 2018. A multilayer convolutional encoder-decoder neural network for grammatical error correction. In *Proceedings of the Thirty-Second AAAI Conference on Artificial Intelligence*.

Shamil Chollampatt, Kaveh Taghipour, and Hwee Tou Ng. 2016. Neural network translation models for grammatical error correction. In *Proceedings of the 25th International Joint Conference on Artificial Intelligence*, New York, USA.

Daniel Dahlmeier and Hwee Tou Ng. 2012a. A beam-search decoder for grammatical error correction. In *Proceedings of the 2012 Joint Conference on Empirical Methods in Natural Language Processing and Computational Natural Language Learning*, pages 568–578, Jeju Island, Korea. Association for Computational Linguistics.

Daniel Dahlmeier and Hwee Tou Ng. 2012b. Better evaluation for grammatical error correction. In *Proceedings of the 2012 Conference of the North American Chapter of the Association for Computational Linguistics: Human Language Technologies*, pages 568–572, Montréal, Canada. Association for Computational Linguistics.

Jacob Devlin, Ming-Wei Chang, Kenton Lee, and Kristina Toutanova. 2019. BERT: Pre-training of deep bidirectional transformers for language understanding. In *Proceedings of the 2019 Conference of the North American Chapter of the Association for Computational Linguistics: Human Language Technologies, Volume 1 (Long and Short Papers)*, pages 4171–4186, Minneapolis, Minnesota. Association for Computational Linguistics.

Mariano Felice, Zheng Yuan, Øistein E. Andersen, Helen Yannakoudakis, and Ekaterina Kochmar. 2014. Grammatical error correction using hybrid systems and type filtering. In *Proceedings of the Eighteenth Conference on Computational Natural Language Learning: Shared Task*, pages 15–24, Baltimore, Maryland. Association for Computational Linguistics.

Michael Gamon, Jianfeng Gao, Chris Brockett, Alexandre Klementiev, William B. Dolan, Dmitriy Belenko, and Lucy Vanderwende. 2008. Using contextual speller techniques and language modeling for ESL error correction. In *Proceedings of the Third International Joint Conference on Natural Language Processing: Volume-I*.

Tao Ge, Furu Wei, and Ming Zhou. 2018. Reaching human-level performance in automatic grammatical error correction: An empirical study. *CoRR*, abs/1807.01270.

Yoav Goldberg. 2019. Assessing bert's syntactic abilities. *CoRR*, abs/1901.05287.

A. Halevy, P. Norvig, and F. Pereira. 2009. The unreasonable effectiveness of data. *IEEE Intelligent Systems*, 24(2):8–12.

Neil Houlsby, Andrei Giurgiu, Stanislaw Jastrzebski, Bruna Morrone, Quentin De Laroussilhe, Andrea Gesmundo, Mona Attariyan, and Sylvain Gelly. 2019. Parameter-efficient transfer learning for NLP. In *Proceedings of the 36th International Conference on Machine Learning*, volume 97 of *Proceedings of Machine Learning Research*, pages 2790–2799, Long Beach, California, USA. PMLR.

Jianshu Ji, Qinlong Wang, Kristina Toutanova, Yongen Gong, Steven Truong, and Jianfeng Gao. 2017. A nested attention neural hybrid model for grammatical error correction. In *Proceedings of the 55th Annual Meeting of the Association for Computational Linguistics (Volume 1: Long Papers)*, pages 753–762, Vancouver, Canada. Association for Computational Linguistics.

Marcin Junczys-Dowmunt and Roman Grundkiewicz. 2014. The AMU system in the CoNLL-2014 shared task: Grammatical error correction by data-intensive and feature-rich statistical machine translation. In *Proceedings of the Eighteenth Conference on Computational Natural Language Learning: Shared Task*, pages 25–33, Baltimore, Maryland. Association for Computational Linguistics.

Marcin Junczys-Dowmunt and Roman Grundkiewicz. 2016. Phrase-based machine translation is state-of-the-art for automatic grammatical error correction. In *Proceedings of the 2016 Conference on Empirical Methods in Natural Language Processing*, pages 1546–1556, Austin, Texas. Association for Computational Linguistics.

Marcin Junczys-Dowmunt, Roman Grundkiewicz, Shubha Guha, and Kenneth Heafield. 2018. Approaching neural grammatical error correction as a low-resource machine translation task. In *Proceedings of the 2018 Conference of the North American Chapter of the Association for Computational Linguistics: Human Language Technologies, Volume 1 (Long Papers)*, pages 595–606, New Orleans, Louisiana. Association for Computational Linguistics.

Ting-hui Kao, Yu-wei Chang, Hsun-wen Chiu, Tzu-Hsi Yen, Joanne Boisson, Jian-cheng Wu, and Jason S. Chang. 2013. CoNLL-2013 shared task: Grammatical error correction NTHU system description. In *Proceedings of the Seventeenth Conference on Computational Natural Language Learning: Shared Task*, pages 20–25, Sofia, Bulgaria. Association for Computational Linguistics.

Kyusong Lee and Gary Geunbae Lee. 2014. POSTECH grammatical error correction system in the CoNLL-2014 shared task. In *Proceedings of the Eighteenth Conference on Computational Natural Language Learning: Shared Task*, pages 65–73, Baltimore, Maryland. Association for Computational Linguistics.

Alain Dsilets Matthieu Hermet and Stan Szpakowicz. 2008. Using the web as a linguistic resource to automatically correct lexico-syntactic errors. In *Proceedings of the Sixth International Conference on Language Resources and Evaluation (LREC'08)*, Marrakech, Morocco. European Language Resources Association (ELRA).

Courtney Napoles, Keisuke Sakaguchi, and Joel Tetreault. 2017. Jfleg: A fluency corpus and benchmark for grammatical error correction. In *Proceedings of the 15th Conference of the European Chapter of the Association for Computational Linguistics: Volume 2, Short Papers*, pages 229–234, Valencia, Spain. Association for Computational Linguistics.

Hwee Tou Ng, Siew Mei Wu, Ted Briscoe, Christian Hadiwinoto, Raymond Hendy Susanto, and Christopher Bryant. 2014. The CoNLL-2014 shared task on grammatical error correction. In *Proceedings of the Eighteenth Conference on Computational Natural Language Learning: Shared Task*, pages 1–14, Baltimore, Maryland. Association for Computational Linguistics.

Hwee Tou Ng, Siew Mei Wu, Yuanbin Wu, Christian Hadiwinoto, and Joel Tetreault. 2013. The CoNLL-2013 shared task on grammatical error correction. In *Proceedings of the Seventeenth Conference on Computational Natural Language Learning: Shared Task*, pages 1–12, Sofia, Bulgaria. Association for Computational Linguistics.

Y. Albert Park and Roger Levy. 2011. Automated whole sentence grammar correction using a noisy channel model. In *Proceedings of the 49th Annual Meeting of the Association for Computational Linguistics: Human Language Technologies - Volume 1*, HLT '11, pages 934–944, Stroudsburg, PA, USA. Association for Computational Linguistics.

Alec Radford, Karthik Narasimhan, Tim Salimans, and Ilya Sutskever. 2018. Improving language understanding by generative pre-training.

Alec Radford, Jeff Wu, Rewon Child, David Luan, Dario Amodei, and Ilya Sutskever. 2019. Language models are unsupervised multitask learners.

Alla Rozovskaya and Dan Roth. 2016. Grammatical error correction: Machine translation and classifiers. In *Proceedings of the 54th Annual Meeting of the Association for Computational Linguistics (Volume 1: Long Papers)*, pages 2205–2215, Berlin, Germany. Association for Computational Linguistics.

Keisuke Sakaguchi, Matt Post, and Benjamin Van Durme. 2017. Grammatical error correction with neural reinforcement learning. In *Proceedings of the Eighth International Joint Conference on Natural Language Processing (Volume 2: Short Papers)*, pages 366–372, Taipei, Taiwan. Asian Federation of Natural Language Processing.

Ashish Vaswani, Noam Shazeer, Niki Parmar, Jakob Uszkoreit, Llion Jones, Aidan N Gomez, Ł ukasz Kaiser, and Illia Polosukhin. 2017. Attention is all you need. In *Advances in Neural Information Processing Systems 30*, pages 5998–6008. Curran Associates, Inc.

Alex Wang and Kyunghyun Cho. 2019. BERT has a mouth, and it must speak: BERT as a markov random field language model. *CoRR*, abs/1902.04094.

Alex Wang, Amanpreet Singh, Julian Michael, Felix Hill, Omer Levy, and Samuel Bowman. 2018. GLUE: A multi-task benchmark and analysis platform for natural language understanding. In *Proceedings of the 2018 EMNLP Workshop BlackboxNLP: Analyzing and Interpreting Neural Networks for NLP*, pages 353–355, Brussels, Belgium. Association for Computational Linguistics.

Ziang Xie, Anand Avati, Naveen Arivazhagan, Dan Jurafsky, and Andrew Y. Ng. 2016. Neural language correction with character-based attention. *CoRR*, abs/1603.09727.

Junwen Xing, Longyue Wang, Derek F. Wong, Lidia S. Chao, and Xiaodong Zeng. 2013. UM-checker: A hybrid system for English grammatical error correction. In *Proceedings of the Seventeenth Conference on Computational Natural Language Learning: Shared Task*, pages 34–42, Sofia, Bulgaria. Association for Computational Linguistics.

Helen Yannakoudakis, Ted Briscoe, and Ben Medlock. 2011. A new dataset and method for automatically grading ESOL texts. In *Proceedings of the 49th Annual Meeting of the Association for Computational Linguistics: Human Language Technologies*, pages 180–189, Portland, Oregon, USA. Association for Computational Linguistics.

Helen Yannakoudakis, Marek Rei, Øistein E. Andersen, and Zheng Yuan. 2017. Neural sequence-labelling models for grammatical error correction. In *Proceedings of the 2017 Conference on Empirical Methods in Natural Language Processing*, pages 2795–2806, Copenhagen, Denmark. Association for Computational Linguistics.

Xing Yi, Jianfeng Gao, and William B. Dolan. 2008. A web-based English proofing system for English as a second language users. In *Proceedings of the Third International Joint Conference on Natural Language Processing: Volume-II*.

Ippei Yoshimoto, Tomoya Kose, Kensuke Mitsuzawa, Keisuke Sakaguchi, Tomoya Mizumoto, Yuta Hayashibe, Mamoru Komachi, and Yuji Matsumoto. 2013. NAIST at 2013 CoNLL grammatical error correction shared task. In *Proceedings of the Seventeenth Conference on Computational Natural Language Learning: Shared Task*, pages 26–33, Sofia, Bulgaria. Association for Computational Linguistics.

Zheng Yuan and Ted Briscoe. 2016. Grammatical error correction using neural machine translation. In *Proceedings of the 2016 Conference of the North American Chapter of the Association for Computational Linguistics: Human Language Technologies*, pages 380–386, San Diego, California. Association for Computational Linguistics.

(Almost) Unsupervised Grammatical Error Correction
using a Synthetic Comparable Corpus

Satoru Katsumata and **Mamoru Komachi**

Tokyo Metropolitan University

`katsumata-satoru@ed.tmu.ac.jp, komachi@tmu.ac.jp`

Abstract

We introduce unsupervised techniques based on phrase-based statistical machine translation for grammatical error correction (GEC) trained on a pseudo learner corpus created by Google Translation. We verified our GEC system through experiments on a low resource track of the shared task at Building Educational Applications 2019 (BEA2019). As a result, we achieved an $F_{0.5}$ score of 28.31 points with the test data.

1 Introduction

Research on grammatical error correction (GEC) has gained considerable attention recently. Many studies treat GEC as a task that involves translation from a grammatically erroneous sentence (source-side) into a correct sentence (target-side) and thus, leverage methods based on machine translation (MT) for GEC. For instance, some GEC systems use large parallel corpora and synthetic data (Ge et al., 2018; Xie et al., 2018).

We introduce an unsupervised method based on MT for GEC that does not use parallel learner data. In particular, we use methods proposed by Marie and Fujita (2018), Artetxe et al. (2018b), and Lample et al. (2018). These methods are based on phrase-based statistical machine translation (SMT) and phrase table refinements. Forward refinement used by Marie and Fujita (2018) simply augments a learner corpus with automatic corrections. We also use forward refinement for improvement of phrase table.

Unsupervised MT techniques do not require a parallel but a comparable corpus as training data. Therefore, we use comparable translated texts using Google Translation as the source-side data. Specifically, we use News Crawl written in English as target-side data and News Crawl written in another language translated into English as source-side data.

We verified our GEC system through experiments for a low resource track of the shared task at Building Educational Applications 2019 (BEA2019). The experimental results show that our system achieved an $F_{0.5}$ score of 28.31 points.

2 Unsupervised GEC

Algorithm 1 shows the pseudocode for unsupervised GEC. This code is derived from Artetxe et al. (2018b). First, the cross-lingual phrase embeddings are acquired. Second, a phrase table is created based on these cross-lingual embeddings. Third, the phrase table is combined with a language model trained by monolingual data to initialize a phrase-based SMT system. Finally, the SMT system is updated through iterative forward-translation.

Cross-lingual embeddings First, n-gram embeddings were created on the source- and target-sides. Specifically, each monolingual embedding was created based on the source- and target-sides using a variant of skip-gram (Mikolov et al., 2013) for unigrams, bigrams, and trigrams with high frequency[1] in the monolingual data. Next, the monolingual embeddings were mapped onto a shared space to obtain cross-lingual embeddings. The self-learning method of Artetxe et al. (2018a) was used for unsupervised mapping.

Phrase table induction A phrase table was created based on the cross-lingual embeddings. In particular, this involved the creation of phrase translation models and lexical translation models.

The translation candidates were limited in the source-to-target phrase translation model $\phi(\overline{f}|\overline{e})$ for each source phrase $\overline{e}$ to its 100 nearest neighbor phrases $\overline{f}$ on the target-side. The score of

---

[1] We used the most frequent 200K unigrams, 400K bigrams, and 400K trigrams in the monolingual data.

Proceedings of the Fourteenth Workshop on Innovative Use of NLP for Building Educational Applications, pages 134–138

Florence, Italy, August 2, 2019. ©2019 Association for Computational Linguistics

Algorithm 1 Unsupervised GEC

Require: language models of the target-side LM_t
Require: source training corpus C_s
Require: target training corpus C_t
Require: tuning data T
Require: iteration number N
Ensure: source-to-target phrase table $P_{s \to t}^{(N)}$
Ensure: source-to-target weights $W_{s \to t}^{(N)}$
1: $W_s^{emb} \leftarrow \text{TRAIN}(C_s)$
2: $W_t^{emb} \leftarrow \text{TRAIN}(C_t)$
3: $W_s^{cross\_emb}, W_t^{cross\_emb} \leftarrow \text{MAPPING}(W_s^{emb}, W_t^{emb})$
4: $P_{s \to t}^{(0)} \leftarrow \text{INITIALIZE}(W_s^{cross\_emb}, W_t^{cross\_emb})$
5: $W_{s \to t}^{(0)} \leftarrow \text{TUNE}(P_{s \to t}^{(0)}, LM_t, T)$
6: **for** $iter = 1, \dots, N$ **do**
7:     synthetic_data$_t$
8:     $\leftarrow \text{DECODE}(P_{s \to t}^{(iter-1)}, LM_t, W_{s \to t}^{(iter-1)}, C_s)$
9:     $P_{s \to t}^{(iter)} \leftarrow \text{TRAIN}(C_s, \text{synthetic\_data}_t)$
10:    $W_{s \to t}^{(iter)} \leftarrow \text{TUNE}(P_{s \to t}^{(iter)}, LM_t, T)$

Corpus	Sent.	Learner
Fi News Crawl	1,904,880	No
En News Crawl	2,116,249	No
One-Billion	24,482,651	No
tuning data	2,191	Yes
dev data	2,193	Yes

Table 1: Data statics: train and dev data size.

the phrase translation model was calculated based on the normalized cosine similarity between the source and target phrases.

$$\phi(\overline{f}|\overline{e}) = \frac{\exp(\cos(\overline{e}, \overline{f})/\tau)}{\sum_{\overline{f}'} \exp(\cos(\overline{e}, \overline{f}')/\tau)} \quad (1)$$

$\overline{f}'$ represents each phrase embedding on the target-side and τ is a temperature parameter that controls the confidence of prediction[2]. The backward phrase translation probability $\phi(\overline{e}|\overline{f})$ was determined in a similar manner.

The source-to-target lexical translation model $\text{lex}(\overline{f}|\overline{e})$ considers the word with the highest translation probability in a target phrase for each word in a source phrase. The score of the lexical translation model was calculated based on the product of respective phrase translation probabilities.

$$\text{lex}(\overline{f}|\overline{e}) = \prod_i \max\left(\epsilon, \max_j \phi\left(\overline{f}_i|\overline{e}_j\right)\right) \quad (2)$$

ϵ is a constant term for the case where no alignments are found. As in Artetxe et al. (2018b), the term was set to 0.001. The backward lexical translation probability $\text{lex}(\overline{e}|\overline{f})$ is calculated in a similar manner.

Refinement of SMT system The phrase table created is considered to include noisy phrase pairs. Therefore, we update the phrase table using an SMT system. The SMT system trained on synthetic data eliminates the noisy phrase pairs using

language models trained on the target-side corpus. This process corresponds to lines 6—10 in Algorithm 1. The phrase table is refined with forward refinement (Marie and Fujita, 2018).

For forward refinement, target synthetic data were generated from the source monolingual data using the source-to-target phrase table $P_{s \to t}^{(0)}$ and target language model LM_t. A new phrase table $P_{s \to t}^{(1)}$ was then created with this target synthetic corpus. This operation was executed N times.

Construction of a comparable corpus This unsupervised method is based on the assumption that the source and target corpora are comparable. In fact, Lample et al. (2018), Artetxe et al. (2018b) and Marie and Fujita (2018) use the News Crawl of source and target language as training data.

To make a comparable corpus for GEC, we use translated texts using Google Translation as the source-side data. Specifically, we use Finnish News Crawl translated into English as source-side. English News Crawl is used as the target-side as is. Finnish data is used because Finnish is not similar to English.

This translated data does not include misspelled words. To address these words, we use a spell checker as a preprocessing step before inference.

3 Experiment of low resource GEC

3.1 Experimental setting

Table 1 shows the training and development data size. Finnish News Crawl 2014—2015 translated into English was used as source training data and English News Crawl 2017 was used as target training data. To train the extra language model of the target-side (LM_t), we used training data of One Billion Word Benchmark (Chelba et al., 2014). We used `googletrans v2.4.0`[3] for Google Translation. This module did not work sometimes and thus, we obtained 2,122,714 trans-

---

[2]As in Artetxe et al. (2018b), τ is estimated by maximizing the phrase translation probability between an embedding and the nearest embedding on the opposite side.

[3]https://github.com/ssut/py-googletrans

Team	TP	FP	FN	P	R	$F_{0.5}$
UEDIN-MS	2,312	982	2,506	70.19	47.99	64.24
Kakao&Brain	2,412	1,413	2,797	63.06	46.30	58.80
LAIX	1,443	884	3,175	62.01	31.25	51.81
CAMB-CUED	1,814	1,450	2,956	55.58	38.03	50.88
UFAL, Charles University, Prague	1,245	1,222	2,993	50.47	29.38	44.13
Siteimprove	1,299	1,619	3,199	44.52	28.88	40.17
WebSpellChecker.com	2,363	3,719	3,031	38.85	43.81	39.75
TMU	1,638	4,314	3,486	27.52	31.97	28.31
Buffalo	446	1,243	3,556	26.41	11.14	20.73

Table 2: GEC results with test data.

lated sentences[4]. We sampled the 3,000,000 sentences from English News Crawl 2017 and excluded the sentences with more than 150 words for either source- and target-side data. Finally, the synthetic comparable corpus comprises processed News Crawl data listed in Table 1. The low resource track permitted to use W&I+LOCNESS (Bryant et al., 2019; Granger, 1998) development set, so we split it in half; tune data and dev data[5].

These data are tokenized by `spaCy v1.9.0`[6] and the `en_core_web_sm-1.2.0` model. We used moses truecaser for the training data; this truecaser model is learned from processed English News Crawl. We used byte-pair-encoding (Sennrich et al., 2016) learned from processed English News Crawl; the number of operations is 50K.

The implementation proposed by Artetxe et al. (2018b)[7] was modified to conduct the experiments. Specifically, some features were added; word-level Levenshtein distance, word-, and character-level edit operation, operation sequence model, (Durrani et al., 2013)[8] and 9-gram word class language model, similar to Grundkiewicz and Junczys-Dowmunt (2018) without sparse features. Word class language model was trained with One Billion Word Benchmark data; the number of classes is 200, and the word class was estimated with `fastText` (Bojanowski et al., 2017). The distortion feature was not used.

`Moses` (Koehn et al., 2007) was used to train the SMT system. `FastAlign` (Dyer et al., 2013) was used for word alignment and `KenLM` (Heafield, 2011) was used to train the 5-gram language model over each processed English News Crawl and One Billion Word Benchmark. MERT (Och, 2003) was used with the tuning data for `M^2 Scorer` (Dahlmeier and Ng, 2012). Synthetic sentence pairs with a [3, 80] sentence length were used at the refinement step. The number of iterations N was set to 5, and the embedding dimension was set to 300. We decided best iteration using the dev data and submitted the output of the best iteration model.

We used `pyspellchecker`[9] as a spell checker. This tool uses Levenshtein distance to obtain permutations within an edit distance of 2 over the words included in a word list. We made the word list from One Billion Word Benchmark and included words that occur more than five times.

We report precision, recall, and $F_{0.5}$ score based on the dev data and official test data. The output of dev data was evaluated using ERRANT scorer (Bryant et al., 2017) similarly to official test data.

3.2 Results

Table 2 shows the results of the GEC experiments with test data. The $F_{0.5}$ score for our system (TMU) is 28.31; this score is eighth among the nine teams. In particular, the number of false positives of our system is 4,314; this is the worst result of all.

4 Discussion

Table 3 shows the results of the dev data listed in Table 1. On the dev data, the system of iteration 1 is the best among all. According to the improvement of iteration from 0 to 1, it is confirmed that the refinement method works well. However, it is observed that the system is not improved after iteration 1. The source-side data is fixed, and target-side data is generated from the source-side for each iteration. Therefore, the quality of the

---

[4]Finnish News Crawl 2014—2015 have 6,360,479 sentences.

[5]Because W&I+LOCNESS data had four types of learner level, we split it so that each learner level is equal.

[6]https://github.com/explosion/spaCy

[7]https://github.com/artetxem/monoses

[8]Operation sequence model was used in refinement step.

[9]https://github.com/barrust/pyspellchecker

	iter	P	R	$F_{0.5}$
Unsupervised SMT	0	12.33	**16.13**	12.94
w/o spell check	1	**17.59**	14.63	**16.91**
	2	17.30	14.15	16.56
	3	16.04	14.17	15.63
	4	17.06	14.01	16.35
	5	15.88	13.88	15.44
spell check $\rightarrow$ SMT	1	20.58	18.04	20.01
SMT $\rightarrow$ spell check	1	19.42	16.86	18.85

Table 3: GEC results with dev data. The bold scores represent the best score without the spell checker.

	P	R	$F_{0.5}$
Top2			
SPELL	39.93	59.24	42.71
PUNCT	28.91	38.14	30.38
Bottom2			
NOUN	0.87	1.74	0.97
VERB	2.13	0.99	1.73

Table 4: Error types for which our best system corrected errors well or mostly did not correct on the dev data. Top2 denotes the top two errors, and Bottom2 denotes the lowest two errors in terms of the $F_{0.5}$[10].

source-side data is important for this refinement method. In this study, we use the automatically translated text as source-side data; thus, it is considered that the quality is not high and the refinement after iteration 1 does not work.

The results of Table 3 confirm that the spell checker works well. We also investigate the importance of the order; SMT or spell check, which is suitable for the first system for a better result? As a result, it is better to use the SMT system after using the spell checker. That is because the source-side data does not include the misspelled words as mentioned above.

Table 4 shows the error types that our system corrected well or mostly did not correct on the dev data. SPELL means the misspell errors; the correction of these errors depends only on the spell checker. PUNCT means the errors about the punctuation; e.g., 'Unfortunately when we...$\rightarrow$ Unfortunately, when we...'. It is considered that our system can correct errors such as these owing to the n-gram co-occurrence knowledge derived from the language models.

In contrast, our system struggled to correct content word errors. For example, NOUN includes an error like this; 'way $\rightarrow$ means' and VERB includes an error like this; 'watch $\rightarrow$ see'. It is considered that our system is mostly not able to correct the errors regarding word usage based on the context because the phrase table was still noisy. Although we observed some usage error examples of 'watch' in the synthetic source data, our model was not able to replace 'watch' to 'see' based on the context.

5 Related Work

Unsupervised Machine Translation Studies on unsupervised methods have been conducted for both NMT (Lample et al., 2018; Marie and Fujita, 2018) and SMT (Artetxe et al., 2018b). In this study, we apply the USMT method of Artetxe et al. (2018b) and Marie and Fujita (2018) to GEC. The UNMT method (Lample et al., 2018) was ineffective under the GEC setting in our preliminary experiments.

GEC with NMT/SMT Several studies that introduce sequence-to-sequence models in GEC heavily rely on large amounts of training data. Ge et al. (2018), who presented state-of-the-art results in GEC, proposed a supervised NMT method trained on corpora of a total 5.4 M sentence pairs. We mainly use the monolingual corpus because the low resource track does not permit the use of the learner corpora.

Despite the success of NMT, many studies on GEC traditionally use SMT (Susanto et al., 2014; Junczys-Dowmunt and Grundkiewicz, 2014). These studies apply an off-the-shelf SMT toolkit, Moses, to GEC. Junczys-Dowmunt and Grundkiewicz (2014) claimed that the SMT system optimized for BLEU learns to not change the source sentence. Instead of BLEU, they proposed tuning an SMT system using the M^2 score with annotated development data. In this study, we also tune the weights with an $F_{0.5}$ score measured by the M^2 scorer because the official score is an $F_{0.5}$ score.

6 Conclusion

In this paper, we described our GEC system for the low resource track of the shared task at BEA2019. We introduced an unsupervised approach based on SMT for GEC. This track prohibited the use of learner data as training data, so we created a synthetic comparable corpus using Google Translation. The experimental results demonstrate that

---

[10]We investigate the frequent error types; the errors occur more than one hundred times in the dev data.

our system achieved an $F_{0.5}$ score of 28.31 points with the test data.

Acknowledgments

This work was partially supported by JSPS Grant-in-Aid for Scientific Research (C) Grant Number JP19K12099.

References

Mikel Artetxe, Gorka Labaka, and Eneko Agirre. 2018a. A robust self-learning method for fully unsupervised cross-lingual mappings of word embeddings. In *Proc. of ACL*, pages 789–798.

Mikel Artetxe, Gorka Labaka, and Eneko Agirre. 2018b. Unsupervised statistical machine translation. In *Proc. of EMNLP*, pages 3632–3642.

Piotr Bojanowski, Edouard Grave, Armand Joulin, and Tomas Mikolov. 2017. Enriching word vectors with subword information. *Transactions of the Association for Computational Linguistics*, 5:135–146.

Christopher Bryant, Mariano Felice, Øistein E. Andersen, and Ted Briscoe. 2019. The BEA-2019 Shared Task on Grammatical Error Correction. In *Proc. of BEA*.

Christopher Bryant, Mariano Felice, and Ted Briscoe. 2017. Automatic annotation and evaluation of error types for grammatical error correction. In *Proc. of ACL*, pages 793–805.

Ciprian Chelba, Tomas Mikolov, Mike Schuster, Qi Ge, Thorsten Brants, Phillipp Koehn, and Tony Robinson. 2014. One billion word benchmark for measuring progress in statistical language modeling. In *Proc. of INTERSPEECH*, pages 2635–2639.

Daniel Dahlmeier and Hwee Tou Ng. 2012. Better evaluation for grammatical error correction. In *Proc. of NAACL-HLT*, pages 568–572.

Nadir Durrani, Alexander Fraser, Helmut Schmid, Hieu Hoang, and Philipp Koehn. 2013. Can Markov models over minimal translation units help phrase-based smt? In *Proc. of ACL*, pages 399–405.

Chris Dyer, Victor Chahuneau, and Noah A. Smith. 2013. A simple, fast, and effective reparameterization of IBM model 2. In *Proc. of NAACL-HLT*, pages 644–648.

Tao Ge, Furu Wei, and Ming Zhou. 2018. Reaching human-level performance in automatic grammatical error correction: An empirical study. *arXiv preprint arXiv:1807.01270*.

Sylviane Granger. 1998. The computer learner corpus: A versatile new source of data for SLA research. In Sylviane Granger, editor, *Learner English on Computer*, pages 3–18. Addison Wesley Longman, London and New York.

Roman Grundkiewicz and Marcin Junczys-Dowmunt. 2018. Near human-level performance in grammatical error correction with hybrid machine translation. In *Proc. of NAACL-HLT*, pages 284–290.

Kenneth Heafield. 2011. KenLM: Faster and smaller language model queries. In *Proc. of WMT*, pages 187–197.

Marcin Junczys-Dowmunt and Roman Grundkiewicz. 2014. The AMU system in the CoNLL-2014 shared task: Grammatical error correction by data-intensive and feature-rich statistical machine translation. In *Proc. of CoNLL*, pages 25–33.

Philipp Koehn, Hieu Hoang, Alexandra Birch, Chris Callison-Burch, Marcello Federico, Nicola Bertoldi, Brooke Cowan, Wade Shen, Christine Moran, Richard Zens, Chris Dyer, Ondrej Bojar, Alexandra Constantin, and Evan Herbst. 2007. Moses: Open source toolkit for statistical machine translation. In *Proc. of ACL Demo Sessions*, pages 177–180.

Guillaume Lample, Myle Ott, Alexis Conneau, Ludovic Denoyer, and Marc'Aurelio Ranzato. 2018. Phrase-based & neural unsupervised machine translation. In *Proc. of EMNLP*, pages 5039–5049.

Benjamin Marie and Atsushi Fujita. 2018. Unsupervised neural machine translation initialized by unsupervised statistical machine translation. *arXiv preprint arXiv:1810.12703*.

Tomas Mikolov, Kai Chen, Greg Corrado, and Jeffrey Dean. 2013. Efficient estimation of word representations in vector space. In *ICLR Workshop*.

Franz Josef Och. 2003. Minimum error rate training in statistical machine translation. In *Proc. of ACL*, pages 160–167.

Rico Sennrich, Barry Haddow, and Alexandra Birch. 2016. Neural machine translation of rare words with subword units. In *Proc. of ACL*, pages 1715–1725.

Raymond Hendy Susanto, Peter Phandi, and Hwee Tou Ng. 2014. System combination for grammatical error correction. In *Proc. of EMNLP*, pages 951–962.

Ziang Xie, Guillaume Genthial, Stanley Xie, Andrew Ng, and Dan Jurafsky. 2018. Noising and denoising natural language: Diverse backtranslation for grammar correction. In *Proc. of NAACL-HLT*, pages 619–628.

Learning to combine Grammatical Error Corrections

Yoav Kantor*   Yoav Katz*   Leshem Choshen*   Edo Cohen-Karlik
Naftali Liberman   Assaf Toledo   Amir Menczel   Noam Slonim

IBM Research AI
{yoavka,katz,leshem.choshen}@il.ibm.com
{edo.cohen,naftali.liberman,assaf.toledo}@ibm.com
{amir.menczel,noams}@il.ibm.com

Abstract

The field of Grammatical Error Correction (GEC) has produced various systems to deal with focused phenomena or general text editing. We propose an automatic way to combine black-box systems. Our method automatically detects the strength of a system or the combination of several systems per error type, improving precision and recall while optimizing F score directly. We show consistent improvement over the best standalone system in all the configurations tested. This approach also outperforms average ensembling of different RNN models with random initializations.

In addition, we analyze the use of BERT for GEC - reporting promising results on this end. We also present a spellchecker created for this task which outperforms standard spellcheckers tested on the task of spellchecking.

This paper describes a system submission to Building Educational Applications 2019 Shared Task: Grammatical Error Correction(Bryant et al., 2019).

Combining the output of top BEA 2019 shared task systems using our approach, currently holds the highest reported score in the open phase of the BEA 2019 shared task, improving $F_{0.5}$ by 3.7 points over the best result reported.

1 Introduction

Unlike other generation tasks (e.g. Machine Translation and Text Summarization), Grammatical Error Correction (GEC) contains separable outputs, edits that could be extracted from sentences, categorized (Bryant et al., 2017) and evaluated separately (Choshen and Abend, 2018a). Throughout the years different approaches were considered, some focused on specific error types (Rozovskaya et al., 2014) and others adjusted systems from other tasks (Zhao et al., 2019). While

the first receive high precision, the latter often have high recall and differ in what they correct. To benefit from both worlds, pipelines (Rozovskaya and Roth, 2016) and rescoring hybrids (Grundkiewicz and Junczys-Dowmunt, 2018) were introduced. Another suggested method for combining is average ensembling (Junczys-Dowmunt et al., 2018), used when several end to end neural networks are trained.

As single systems tend to have low recall (Choshen and Abend, 2018b), pipelining systems may propagate errors and may not benefit from more than one system per error. Rescoring reduces recall and may not be useful with many systems (Grundkiewicz and Junczys-Dowmunt, 2018). We propose a new method for combining systems (§4) that can combine many systems and relies solely on their output, i.e., it uses systems as a black-box. We show our system outperforms average ensembling, has benefits even when combining a single system with itself, and produces the new state of the art by combining several existing systems (§5).

To develop a system we trained GEC systems and gathered outputs from black-box systems (§3). One of the most frequent error types is spelling errors, we compared off of the shelf spellcheckers, systems developed for this error type specifically, to a new spellchecker (§3.1), finding that our spellchecker outperforms common spellcheckers on the task of spellchecking.

Another system tested was modifications of BERT (Devlin et al., 2018) to correct errors, allowing for less reliance on parallel data and more generalizability across domains (§3.4).

Lastly, we tested generating synthetic errors (Felice and Yuan, 2014) as a way to replace data in an unsupervised scenario. While finding that mimicking the error distribution and generating errors on the same domain is better, we did not eventually participate in the low-resource track.

---

*Contributed equally

Proceedings of the Fourteenth Workshop on Innovative Use of NLP for Building Educational Applications, pages 139–148
Florence, Italy, August 2, 2019. ©2019 Association for Computational Linguistics

2 Data

2.1 Preprocessing

Many systems assume the input is standard untokenized English sentences. In these cases, we detokenized the input data sets and then tokenized again to perform the combination and evaluation steps. For training the Nematus network, we passed the data tokenization and truecasing (Koehn et al., 2007) and trained BPE (Sennrich et al., 2015).

2.2 Synthetic Error Generation

Generating training data for the GEC problem is expensive and slow when done manually by human annotators. Most machine-learning based systems today benefit from the quantity and richness of the training data, therefore, generating synthetic data has a lot of potential, as was also shown in previous work (Felice and Yuan, 2014). We generate data with errors by applying corrections backwards. Meaning, if a correction adds a missing word X to a sentence, to produce the corresponding error we remove X from a sentence. And if a correction removes a redundant word X from a sentence, to produce the corresponding error we add word X in a random location in a sentence. And if a correction replaces word X with word Y in a sentence, to produce the corresponding error we replace word Y with word X in a sentence. In order to preserve the distribution of errors as found in the W&I+LOCNESS train data set, we analyze it and measure the distribution of corrections in it. We measure the distribution of number of corrections in a sentence and distribution of specific corrections. Using these distributions and a corpus of gold (correct) sentences we produce errors with similar distributions. We first randomly select the number of corrections in a sentence according to the distribution measured before. Then, we randomly select specific corrections according to the distribution of corrections. We then find all sentences where all corrections can be applied backwards and pick one of them randomly. Lastly, we generate the errors in the sentence and add the gold sentence and error sentence to corresponding output files.

3 Systems

3.1 Constructing a spellchecker

Many tools are available for spelling correction. Yet, with a few heuristics we managed to get a comparatively high result. As by Errant (Bryant et al., 2017), our spellchecker receives a better $F_{0.5}$ score of spelling (type R:SPELL) than other leading open-source spell-checkers. A comparison can be found at §5.1.

Our method of correcting spelling mistakes is as follows. As a preprocessing stage, we go over a large monolingual corpus - specifically a 6 million sentences corpus taken from books in project Gutenberg[1]. We count the number of occurrences of each word (in it's surface form), skipping words with less than 3 characters and words that are not composed exclusively of letters. We also use an English dictionary (both US and GB) from Libre-Office site [2] for enriching our data with English words that are not in our books corpus. When correcting a sentence, we find words that are not in our word-count (or in it and have a count below 3) nor in the Dictionary. Skipping words with digits or if it was all upper case. These words are suspected to be misspelled and we try to correct them.

For every misspelled word we try to find a replacement word by going over the words in the word-count data (words with count greater than 20) in a descending order of occurrences. For each suggested word, we check if it can be considered as a correction for the misspelled word by two methods. First, we check if the original word and the candidate correction differ from each other by swapping two characters. If not, we calculate the distance between the two words using Levenshtein distance (Levenshtein, 1966) and check if the distance is 1. We return the most frequent word that satisfies one of these conditions . If no candidate is found, we do the same with all words in the dictionary in a lexicographical order. If still no candidate is found, we check if we can split the misspelled word into two words that are in our word-count data or in the dictionary.

3.2 Nematus

We trained 4 neural machine translation systems based on Nematus (Sennrich et al., 2017) Trans-

---

[1] https://www.gutenberg.org
[2] https://cgit.freedesktop.org/ libreoffice/dictionaries/tree/en

former (Vaswani et al., 2017) implementation. All parameters used are the ones suggested for the 2017 Workshop on Machine Translation [3]. As training data we used all the restricted data, i.e., FCE (Dale and Kilgarriff, 2011), LANG8 (Mizumoto et al., 2011), NUCLE (Dahlmeier et al., 2013) and W&I+LOCNESS (Bryant et al., 2019; Granger, 1998) (upsampled 10 times). Each of the four trained models was regarded as a separate correction method and all systems were combined using our method (§4), this was especially beneficial as ensembling is not yet implemented for the transformer. See §5.4 for comparison of the two ensembling methods over RNN based Nematus.

3.3 Off the shelf

LanguageTool. LanguageTool is a free grammar correction tool mainly based on spellchecking and rules. We used language tool programmatic API to obtain all the possible corrections and applied all the suggestions.

Grammarly. Grammarly is the company owning the world leading grammar correction product, as such it is the obvious candidate to be used as a component and to assess the potential of combining black box systems. We used their free web interface to correct the dev and test sets. Grammarly does not support a programmatic API, so this process was manual. We uploaded the texts after detokenization into the web interface. For each suggested correction, we took the top prediction without human discretion. The reason to choose the top prediction was to allow combining using a single reference of Grammarly.

Spelling correction. We tested Enchant, Jam-Spell and Norvig spellcheckers, finding our spellchecker outperforms those in terms of spelling correction (See §5).

3.4 BERT

BERT (Bidirectional Encoder Representations from Transformers) (Devlin et al., 2018) is a language representation model. BERT is extremely effective in general purpose tasks, among its virtues, BERT holds a syntactic understanding of a language (Goldberg, 2019). Initial pretraining of BERT was performed over a large corpora jointly on two tasks: (1) *Masked Language Model* - randomly replace words with a predefined token, [MASK], and predict the missing word. (2) *Next Sentence Prediction* - given a pair of sentences A and B, does sentence B follow sentence A.

Our general approach for using BERT to solve the GEC task is by iteratively querying BERT as a black box language model, reminding former use of language models (Dahlmeier and Ng, 2012; Bryant and Briscoe, 2018). To detect missing words we add [MASK] between every two words, if BERT suggests a word with high confidence, we conclude that this word is missing in this gap. To detect unnecessary words, we replace words with the [MASK] token and if all the suggestions returned from BERT have a low probability, we conclude that the masked word was unnecessary. For replacing words, we perform the same procedure by replacing each word with [MASK] and checking if BERT returns a different word with high probability.

The described process produces many undesired replacements/deletions due to BERT's versatile nature, for example, given a sentence such as:

```
There are few ways to get there.
```

BERT may suggest replacing `few` with `many`. Such a replacement preserves the grammatically soundness of the sentence, but alters the semantic meaning. Hence, although possibly improving fluency, arguably the true goal of GEC (Napoles et al., 2017), this behaviour does not align with the goals of GEC requiring semantic preservation (Choshen and Abend, 2018c). In order to focus the exploration space of BERT's suggestions, we limit replacements/deletions to operate within a predefined *word set*. The word sets considered included syntactically interchangeable words, often sharing some semantic properties. When considering a removal correction, we remove a word only if the returned values from BERT are not in the same word-set as the replaced word. Replacement is allowed only within the same word set. For example, a typical mistake which occurred frequently in the dataset is wrong usage of determiners such as **a** and **an**, given the word set $\{a, an\}$ and the sentence:

```
Is that a armadillo?
```

The mechanism described limits the replacement correction options to suggest making a

---

[3] https://github.com/EdinburghNLP/
wmt17-transformer-scripts

replacement-correction of a with an to result with the corrected sentence

`Is that an armadillo?`

At each iteration of this process, a correction (addition/replacement/deletion) is performed and the resulting sentence is then used as the input to the next iteration. Each replacement/addition of the `[MASK]` token is a single candidate for a specific correction. Given an input sequence, each possible correction gives rise to a different candidate which is then sent to BERT. The most probable correction (above a minimal threshold) is then selected, this process accounts for one iteration. The resulting sentence is then processed again and the best correction is chosen until all corrections have a low probability in which case the sentence is assumed to be correct.

The above mechanism with threshold values between 0.6 and 0.98 did not yield satisfying results. For this reason, in the submitted system we limit the mechanism significantly, ignoring additions and deletions to focus solely on the replace corrections. Word sets were chosen from the most frequent errors in the training data across different error types (excluding punctuation marks R:PUNCT).

Another approach for using BERT is by fine-tuning BERT to the specific data at hand. Since the GEC task is naturally limited to specific types of errors, we fine-tuned the *Masked Language Model* task using synthetic data. Instead of randomly replacing words with the `[MASK]` token, we replace only specific words in a distribution which mimics the training data. This process should create a bias in the language model towards the prediction of words which we want to correct. Unfortunately, these efforts did not bear fruit. The authors believe a more extensive exploration of experimental settings may prove beneficial.

4 Combining systems

Combining the output of multiple systems has the potential to improve both recall and precision. Recall is increased because typically different systems focus on different aspects of the problem and can return corrections which are not identified by other systems (Bryant et al., 2017). Precision can be increased by utilizing the fact that if multiple systems predict the same annotations, we can be more confident that this correction is correct.

The outputs of Seq2Seq models, differing in training parameters, can be merged using an ensemble approach, where the predictions of the models for each possible word in the sequence are used to compute a merged prediction. It was shown that even an ensemble of models trained with the same hyperparameters but with different instances of random initialization can yield benefit (Junczys-Dowmunt et al., 2018).

The idea of automatically combining multiple system outputs is not new to other fields and was successfully used in the Named Entity Recognition (NER) and Entity linking (EL) tasks. Jiang et al. (2016) evaluated multiple NER systems and based on these results, manually selected a rule for combining the two best systems, building a hybrid system that outperformed the standalone systems. Ruiz and Poibeau (2015) used the precision calculated on a training corpus to calculate a weighted vote for each EL output on unseen data. Dlugolinský et al. (2013) used decision tree classifier to identify which output to accept. They used a feature set based on the overall text, NE surface form, the NE type and the overlap between different outputs. In GEC, combining was also proposed but was ad-hoc rather than automatic and general. Combining was done by either piping (Rozovskaya and Roth, 2016), where each system receives the output of the last system, or correction of specific phenomena per system (Rozovskaya and Roth, 2011), or more involved methods tailored to the systems used (Grundkiewicz and Junczys-Dowmunt, 2018). This required manual adjustments and refinements for every set of systems.

Evaluating by a corpus level measure such as F score renders combining systems difficult. Systems developed towards $F_{0.5}$ tend to reduce recall improving precision (Choshen and Abend, 2018b), while avoiding catastrophic errors (Choshen and Abend, 2018c) this behaviour might reduce the flexibility of the combination. It is possible to tune systems to other goals (e.g. recall) (Grundkiewicz and Junczys-Dowmunt, 2018) and thus achieve more versatile systems, but that is not the case when using black-box systems, and hence left for future inspection.

System pair. We propose a method to combine multiple systems by directly optimizing F_β for a chosen β, in the field 0.5 is usually used. We begin by considering a combination of two systems

1. Given a development set, where E are the sentences with errors and G are the gold annotations, generate M^2_{gold} file, which contains all the gold corrections to the sentences.

2. Correct E with each of the systems, to receive corrected sentences hypothesis H_i.

3. Generate M^2_i for each system i by comparing the systems' output H_i and the E input.

4. Split the annotations of the systems into three subsets: $H_{1\backslash 2}$ - all the suggested annotations of $system1$ which were not suggested by $system2$; $H_{2\backslash 1}$ - all the suggested annotations of $system2$ which were not suggested by $system1$; and $H_{1\cap 2}$ - all the suggested annotations in common.

5. Generate M^2 files for each of the three sets: $M^2_{1\backslash 2}$, $M^2_{1\backslash 2}$, $M^2_{1\cap 2}$.

6. Evaluate the performance on each of the three subsets of annotations, split by error type, by comparing M^2_{subset} with M^2_{gold}. For each subset and each error type, we obtain $TP^{error-type}_{subset}$, $FP^{error-type}_{subset}$, $FN^{error-type}_{subset}$.

7. Define selection variables $S^{error-type}_{subset}$ which determine the probability an edit of the specific error type in a specific subset of edits will be used. According to the way subsets were built, each edit corresponds to exactly one subset (e.g. $1 \backslash 2$).

8. For all error types and subset of edits, compute the optimal selection variables $S^{error-type}_{subset}$ that maximize f_β by solving

$$0 \leq S^{error-type}_{subset} \leq 1$$

$$total = \sum_{t \in error-type} TP^t_{1\cap 2} + FN^t_{1\cap 2}$$

$$TP = \sum_{t \in error-type, s \in subset} TP^t_s * S^t_s$$

$$FP = \sum_{t \in error-type, s \in subset} FP^t_s * S^t_s$$

$$FN = total - TP$$

$$Sopt = \arg\max_S f_\beta(TP, FP, FN)$$

This is a convex optimization problem with linear constraints and pose no difficulty to standard solvers.

$Sopt^{error-type}_{subset}$ need not be integer, although in practice they usually are. [4]. In our submission, for simplicity, we avoid these cases and round $Sopt^{error-type}_{subset}$ to nearest integer value (either 0 or 1). But our implementation allows sampling.

A major concern is to what extent does the precision and recall statistics per error type and subset on the development set represent the actual distribution expected during inference on unseen data. Assuming the development set and the unseen are sampled from the same distributions, the confidence is correlated with the number of samples seen for each error-type and subset.

Assuming errors come from a binomial distribution, we try to estimate the conditional probability $P\left(|prec_{test} - prec_{dev}| < 0.15 \mid prec_{dev}\right)$. Given more than 20 samples, the probability for 15% difference in development and test precision is 14.5%, and if there are 50 samples, this probability drops to 2.8%. In the experiments, we ignore error-types where there are less than 2 samples.

The process of correcting an unseen set of sentences T is as follows:

1. Correct T by every system i, to receive corrected sentences hypothesis H_i .

2. Generate M^2_i files for each system by comparing the systems' output H_i and the T input.

3. Split the annotations of the systems into three sets: $H_{1\backslash 2}$, $H_{2\backslash 1}$, and $H_{1\cap 2}$.

4. Generate M^2 files for each of the three sets: $M^2_{1\backslash 2}$, $M^2_{2\backslash 1}$, $M^2_{1\cap 2}$.

5. Remove all annotations from the M^2 files for which $Sopt^{error-type}_{subset} = 0$.

6. Merge all the annotations from the modified $M^2_{1\backslash 2}$, $M^2_{2\backslash 1}$, and $M^2_{1\cap 2}$ files to create M^2_{final}. If there are overlapping annotations - we currently select an arbitrary annotation.

7. Apply all the corrections in M^2_{final} to T and receive the final output.

In Table 1, we present the results of the most frequent error types when combining two systems,

<hr>

[4]Non integer value can occur when a 0 value yields high precision and low recall, and a 1 value yields low precision and high recall. In this case, randomly selecting a subset of the corrections will yield a medium recall and medium precision, which maximizes f_β

Nematus and Grammarly. As expected, the precision on corrections found by both systems is significantly higher than those found by a single system. For correction type 'R:OTHER', for example, the precision on common corrections is 0.67, compared to 0.17 and 0.28 of the respective standalone systems. Therefore, the optimal solution uses only the corrections produced by both systems. We can also see that in some error types (e.g., R:SPELL or R:DET) the precision of corrections identified by the Nematus system is low enough that the optimization algorithm selected only the corrections by Grammarly.

Multiple systems. When $N > 2$ systems are available, it is possible to extend the above approach by creating more disjoint subsets, which include any of the 2^N subsets of corrections. When N is large, many of these subsets will be very small, and therefore may not contain meaningful statistics. We propose an iterative approach, where at each step two systems are combined. The results of this combination can be then combined with other systems. This approach works better when the development set is small, but can also suffers from over-fitting to the dev set, because subsequent combination steps are performed on the results of the previous merges steps, which were already optimized on the same data set.

5 Experiments

As our system is based on various parts and mainly focuses on the ability to smartly combine those, we experiment with how each of the parts work separately. A special focus is given to combining strong components, black-box components and single components as combining is a crucial part of the innovation in this system.

5.1 Spell checkers' comparison

We've compared our home-brewed spell-checker with JamSpell[5], Norvig[6] and ENCHANT[7]. When comparing the results over all error categories, our spell-checker has relatively low results (See Table 2). However, when comparing the results in spelling (R:SPELL) category alone, our spell-checker excels (See Table 3).

5.2 Nematus

We trained Nematus using several different data sets. First, we trained using only the W&I train set data, we then added Lang8, FCE and Nucle data sources. Since Lang8 is significantly larger than W&I train set, inspired by Junczys-Dowmunt et al. (2018), we upsampled W&I 10 times so that it will have more significant effect on the training process. This procedure improved results significantly (See Table 4).

5.3 Synthetic Error Generation

We also tried training Nematus over synthetic errors data. We generated errors using data from two different domains. Books from project Gutenberg and gold sentences from W&I train set. Additionally, we varied data sizes and observed the effect on the results (See Table 5). These experiments show that relying on the source domain is crucial and it is best to generate data using text from similar domain. When using the synthetic W&I train set we reached a score that is just a little lower than the score when training over W&I train set directly (0.19 vs 0.23). This might suggest that there is potential in using synthetic data when combined with other data sets and promise for synthetic data methods for unsupervised GEC.

5.4 Combining

The experiments regarding combining were performed on the dev set, which was not used for training the systems. The dev set was split to two randomly. The optimal selection of error-types and subsets to combine was done on one half, and we report system results on the second half. For example, when combining the output of the Nematus and Grammarly systems under 10 different fold partitions, the average $F_{0.5}$ improvement over the best of the two systems was 6.2 points, with standard deviation of 0.28 points.

Improvement of a single tool. Even given a single system, we are able to improve the system's performance by eschewing predictions on low performing error types. This filtering procedure has a minor effect and is exemplified in Table 6. While such findings are known to exist implicitly by the cycles of development (Choshen and Abend, 2018b), and were suggested as beneficial for rule based and statistical machine translation systems when precision is 0 (Felice et al., 2014),

---

error-type	Frequency	$S_{1\backslash 2}$	$P_{1\backslash 2}$	$R_{1\backslash 2}$	$S_{1\cap 2}$	$P_{1\cap 2}$	$R_{1\cap 2}$	$S_{2\backslash 1}$	$P_{2\backslash 1}$	$R_{2\backslash 1}$
R:PUNCT	%4	1.0	0.47	0.15	0.0	0.0	0.0	1.0	0.4	0.01
U:DET	%4	1.0	0.38	0.07	1.0	0.77	0.15	1.0	0.51	0.2
R:VERB	%5	1.0	0.5	0.02	0.0	1.0	0.01	1.0	0.57	0.02
M:DET	%5	0.0	0.29	0.05	1.0	0.68	0.12	1.0	0.4	0.31
R:ORTH	%5	0.0	0.28	0.22	1.0	0.86	0.13	1.0	0.46	0.18
R:SPELL	%5	0.0	0.32	0.04	1.0	1.0	0.11	1.0	0.66	0.65
R:VERB:TENSE	%5	1.0	0.54	0.15	0.0	0.0	0.0	0.0	0.0	0.0
R:PREP	%6	1.0	0.37	0.07	1.0	0.72	0.07	1.0	0.56	0.1
R:OTHER	%11	0.0	0.17	0.02	1.0	0.67	0.02	0.0	0.28	0.04
M:PUNCT	%15	1.0	0.55	0.17	1.0	0.68	0.06	1.0	0.38	0.12

Table 1: Combination statistics of the most common error types over two systems - Nematus and Grammarly

All Categories	P	R	$F_{0.5}$
Norvig	0.5217	0.0355	0.1396
Enchant	0.2269	0.0411	0.1192
Jamspell	0.4385	0.0449	**0.1593**
our	0.5116	0.0295	0.1198

Table 2: Comparison of Grammatical Error Performance of Spellcheckers. Jamspell achieves the best score as previously suggested.

R:SPELL	P	R	$F_{0.5}$
Norvig	0.5775	0.6357	0.5882
Enchant	0.316	0.6899	0.3544
Jamspell	0.5336	0.6977	0.5599
our	0.6721	0.5297	**0.6378**

Table 3: Comparison of spellcheckers on spelling. Our method outperforms other methods.

Training Data	P	R	$F_{0.5}$
W&I train set	0.3187	0.1112	0.232
W&I train set + lang8 + FCE	0.4604	0.0742	0.225
W&I train set (upsampled X 10) + Lang8 + FCE + Nucle	0.4738	0.1529	0.333

Table 4: Nematus performance on W&I dev set by training data. The use of more data improves the system, but only when the training from the domain is upsampled.

Data Source	Size (sentences)	$F_{0.5}$
Gutenberg Books	650,000	0.1483
Gutenberg Books	7,000,000	0.1294
W&I train set	1,300,000	0.1919

Table 5: Size of synthetic datasets and Nematus scores when trained on them.

to the best of our knowledge we are the first to report those results directly, on non trivial precision with neural network based systems. In explicitly filtering corrections by error types we gain two additional benefits over the mere score improvement. First, the weak spots of the system are emphasized, and work might be directed to improving components or combining with a relevant strong system. Second, the system itself is not discouraged or changed to stop producing those corrections. So, if future enhancement would improve this type of errors enough, it will show up in results, without discouraging smaller improvements done on the way.

Restricted track. In Table 7 we present the results of our shared task restricted track submission. The submission includes four Nematus models, our spellchecker, and Bert based system ($\S$3.4). This generated a 6 point improvement on the dev set of $f_{0.5}$ when compared the best standalone Nematus model.

Off the shelf systems. As can be seen in Table 8 when we combine the system with several off the self systems, we get 3 point improvement over the restricted baseline, and a 9 point improve-

System	P	R	$F_{0.5}$
Language Tool	0.2905	0.1004	0.2107
Filtered Language Tool	0.4005	0.0889	0.2355
Grammarly	0.4846	0.1808	0.3627
Filtered Grammarly	0.5342	0.1715	0.3754
Nematus	0.52	0.1751	0.373
Filtered Nematus	0.554	0.1647	0.3761

Table 6: Change in performance when avoiding hard errors.

System	P	R	$F_{0.5}$
(1) Nematus1	0.4788	0.1544	0.3371
(2) Nematus2	0.4839	0.1583	0.3429
(3) Nematus3	0.4842	0.1489	0.3338
(4) Nematus4	0.4843	0.1502	0.3352
(5) Spellchecker	0.5154	0.0308	0.1242
(6) Bert	0.0132	0.0147	0.0135
1+2	0.4972	0.1854	0.3721
1+2+3	**0.5095**	0.1904	0.3816
1+2+3+4	0.4926	0.2017	0.3824
1+2+3+4+5	0.5039	0.2233	0.4027
1+2+3+4+5+6	0.5029	**0.2278**	**0.4051**

Table 7: Performance of systems and iterative combination of them. Combination improves both precision and recall even using low performing systems.

ment over the best standalone system. This implies there is a promise in combining existing approaches which we can't improve ourselves to harness some of their correction power. [8]

System	P	R	$F_{0.5}$
(1) Restricted-best	0.5029	0.2278	0.4051
(2) Language Tool	0.2699	0.0955	0.1977
(3) Grammerly	0.4783	0.1825	0.3612
(4) Jamspell	0.423	0.0413	0.1484
1+2	**0.5274**	0.2175	0.4105
1+2+3	0.522	**0.2656**	**0.4375**
1+2+3+4	0.5221	0.2641	0.4367

Table 8: Combining with off the shelf systems helps.

Ensemble VS Combining models results. Nematus has average ensembling built-in which enables inference over several RNN models by performing geometric average of the individual models' probability distributions. Combining outperforms the built-in ensemble by almost 4 points (See Table 9). It is also important to note that while average ensemble improves precision, it reduces recall. Combination is balancing precision and recall, improving both, in a way that maximizes $F_{0.5}$. The last observation is far from trivial as most ways to combine systems would emphasize one or the other, e.g., piping would support mainly recall perhaps reducing precision. Lastly, combining is based on the types of errors and is linguistically motivated, and hence could be fur-

<hr>

[8]Although some of the systems use only rules and non-parallel data, we did not include them in our submission to the restricted tracked, as we are not their originators.

ther improved by smart categorization and perhaps improvements of automatic detection (Bryant et al., 2017).

System	P	R	$F_{0.5}$
(1) Nematus RNN 1	0.4676	0.1157	0.2908
(2) Nematus RNN 2	0.4541	0.1223	0.2944
(3) Nematus RNN 3	0.484	0.1191	0.3002
(4) Nematus RNN 4	0.4839	0.1184	0.2991
1+2+3+4 ensemble	**0.5577**	0.1131	0.3122
1+2+3+4 combination	0.4861	**0.166**	**0.3508**

Table 9: Combining fares better compared to ensemble.

Combining the shared task systems. After the completion of the competition test phase, several teams agreed to release their outputs on the dev and test set. We combined them using the entire dev set and submitted the results to the open phase of the restricted track for evaluation. This achieves a 3.7 point improvement in $F_{0.5}$ and a 6.5 point improvement in precision over the best standalone results (See Table 10). This means this combination is the best result currently known in the field as assessed by the BEA 2019 shared task.

System	P	R	$F_{0.5}$
(1) UEDIN-MS	72.28	**60.12**	69.47
(2) Kakao&Brain	75.19	51.91	69.00
(3) Shuyao	70.17	55.39	66.61
(4) CAMB-CUED	66.75	53.93	63.72
1+2	78.31	58.00	**73.18**
3+4	74.99	54.41	69.72
1+2+3+4	**78.74**	56.04	72.84

Table 10: Test set results when combining systems from the competition used as black boxes. The combination is the new state of the art.

6 Conclusion and Future Work

In this paper, we have shown how combining multiple GEC systems, using a pure black-box approach, can improve state of the art results in the error correction task.

Additional variants of this combination approach can be further examined. The approach can work with any disjoint partition systems' corrections. We can consider combining more than 2 systems at the same time, or we can consider more refined subsets of two systems. For example, the set $H_{1\backslash 2}$ of all the suggested corrections of

$system1$ which were not suggested by $system2$, can be split to the two sets: $H_{1overlapping2}$ and $H_{1non-overlapping2}$, the former containing corrections of system 1 which have an overlapping (but different) corrections by $system2$, and the later corrections of $system1$ which have no overlap with any annotation of $system2$.

Several other approaches can be taken. The problem can be formulated as multiple-sequence to single sequence problem. The input sequences are the original text and n system corrections. The output sequence is the combined correction. During training, the gold correction is used. Given sufficient labeled data, it may be possible for such a system to learn subtle distinctions which may result in better combinations without relying on separating error types or iterative combinations.

In addition, we harnessed Bert for GEC and showed a simple spellchecking mechanism yields competitive results to the leading spellcheckers.

References

Christopher Bryant and Ted Briscoe. 2018. Language model based grammatical error correction without annotated training data. In *Proceedings of the Thirteenth Workshop on Innovative Use of NLP for Building Educational Applications*, pages 247–253, New Orleans, Louisiana. Association for Computational Linguistics.

Christopher Bryant, Mariano Felice, Øistein E. Andersen, and Ted Briscoe. 2019. The BEA-2019 Shared Task on Grammatical Error Correction. In *Proceedings of the 14th Workshop on Innovative Use of NLP for Building Educational Applications*. Association for Computational Linguistics.

Christopher Bryant, Mariano Felice, and Ted Briscoe. 2017. Automatic annotation and evaluation of error types for grammatical error correction. In *ACL*.

Leshem Choshen and Omri Abend. 2018a. Automatic metric validation for grammatical error correction. In *Proceedings of the 56th Annual Meeting of the Association for Computational Linguistics (Volume 1: Long Papers)*, pages 1372–1382.

Leshem Choshen and Omri Abend. 2018b. Inherent biases in reference-based evaluation for grammatical error correction and text simplification. In *ACL*.

Leshem Choshen and Omri Abend. 2018c. Reference-less measure of faithfulness for grammatical error correction. *arXiv preprint arXiv:1804.03824*.

Daniel Dahlmeier and Hwee Tou Ng. 2012. A beam-search decoder for grammatical error correction. In *Proceedings of the 2012 Joint Conference on Empirical Methods in Natural Language Processing and Computational Natural Language Learning*, pages 568–578. Association for Computational Linguistics.

Daniel Dahlmeier, Hwee Tou Ng, and Siew Mei Wu. 2013. Building a large annotated corpus of learner english: The nus corpus of learner english. In *Proceedings of the eighth workshop on innovative use of NLP for building educational applications*, pages 22–31.

Robert Dale and Adam Kilgarriff. 2011. Helping our own: The hoo 2011 pilot shared task. In *Proceedings of the 13th European Workshop on Natural Language Generation*, pages 242–249. Association for Computational Linguistics.

Jacob Devlin, Ming-Wei Chang, Kenton Lee, and Kristina Toutanova. 2018. Bert: Pre-training of deep bidirectional transformers for language understanding. *arXiv preprint arXiv:1810.04805*.

Štefan Dlugolinský, Peter Krammer, Marek Ciglan, Michal Laclavík, and Ladislav Hluchý. 2013. Combining named enitity recognition tools. *Making Sense of Microposts (# MSM2013)*.

Mariano Felice and Zheng Yuan. 2014. Generating artificial errors for grammatical error correction. In *Proceedings of the Student Research Workshop at the 14th Conference of the European Chapter of the Association for Computational Linguistics*, pages 116–126.

Mariano Felice, Zheng Yuan, Øistein E Andersen, Helen Yannakoudakis, and Ekaterina Kochmar. 2014. Grammatical error correction using hybrid systems and type filtering. In *Proceedings of the Eighteenth Conference on Computational Natural Language Learning: Shared Task*, pages 15–24.

Yoav Goldberg. 2019. Assessing bert's syntactic abilities. *CoRR*, abs/1901.05287.

Sylviane Granger. 1998. The computerized learner corpus: a versatile new source of data for sla research.

Roman Grundkiewicz and Marcin Junczys-Dowmunt. 2018. Near human-level performance in grammatical error correction with hybrid machine translation. *arXiv preprint arXiv:1804.05945*.

Ridong Jiang, Rafael E Banchs, and Haizhou Li. 2016. Evaluating and combining name entity recognition systems. In *Proceedings of the Sixth Named Entity Workshop*, pages 21–27.

Marcin Junczys-Dowmunt, Roman Grundkiewicz, Shubha Guha, and Kenneth Heafield. 2018. Approaching neural grammatical error correction as a low-resource machine translation task. In *NAACL-HLT*.

Philipp Koehn, Hieu Hoang, Alexandra Birch, Chris Callison-Burch, Marcello Federico, Nicola Bertoldi, Brooke Cowan, Wade Shen, Christine Moran,

Richard Zens, et al. 2007. Moses: Open source toolkit for statistical machine translation. In *Proceedings of the 45th annual meeting of the association for computational linguistics companion volume proceedings of the demo and poster sessions*, pages 177–180.

Vladimir I Levenshtein. 1966. Binary codes capable of correcting deletions, insertions, and reversals. In *Soviet physics doklady*, volume 10, pages 707–710.

Tomoya Mizumoto, Mamoru Komachi, Masaaki Nagata, and Yuji Matsumoto. 2011. Mining revision log of language learning sns for automated japanese error correction of second language learners. In *Proceedings of 5th International Joint Conference on Natural Language Processing*, pages 147–155.

Courtney Napoles, Keisuke Sakaguchi, and Joel R. Tetreault. 2017. Jfleg: A fluency corpus and benchmark for grammatical error correction. In *EACL*.

Alla Rozovskaya and Dan Roth. 2011. Algorithm selection and model adaptation for esl correction tasks. In *ACL*.

Alla Rozovskaya and Dan Roth. 2016. Grammatical error correction: Machine translation and classifiers. In *Proceedings of the 54th Annual Meeting of the Association for Computational Linguistics (Volume 1: Long Papers)*, volume 1, pages 2205–2215.

Alla Rozovskaya, Dan Roth, and Vivek Srikumar. 2014. Correcting grammatical verb errors. In *Proceedings of the 14th Conference of the European Chapter of the Association for Computational Linguistics*, pages 358–367.

Pablo Ruiz and Thierry Poibeau. 2015. Combining open source annotators for entity linking through weighted voting. In *Joint Conference on Lexical and Computational Semantics (* SEM 2015)*, pages 211–215.

Rico Sennrich, Orhan Firat, Kyunghyun Cho, Alexandra Birch, Barry Haddow, Julian Hitschler, Marcin Junczys-Dowmunt, Samuel Läubli, Antonio Valerio Miceli Barone, Jozef Mokry, and Maria Nadejde. 2017. Nematus: a toolkit for neural machine translation. In *Proceedings of the Software Demonstrations of the 15th Conference of the European Chapter of the Association for Computational Linguistics*, pages 65–68, Valencia, Spain. Association for Computational Linguistics.

Rico Sennrich, Barry Haddow, and Alexandra Birch. 2015. Neural machine translation of rare words with subword units. *arXiv preprint arXiv:1508.07909*.

Ashish Vaswani, Noam Shazeer, Niki Parmar, Jakob Uszkoreit, Llion Jones, Aidan N. Gomez, Lukasz Kaiser, and Illia Polosukhin. 2017. Attention is all you need. In *NIPS*.

Wei Zhao, Liang Wang, Kewei Shen, Ruoyu Jia, and Jingming Liu. 2019. Improving grammatical error correction via pre-training a copy-augmented architecture with unlabeled data. *arXiv preprint arXiv:1903.00138*.

Erroneous data generation for Grammatical Error Correction

Shuyao Xu   **Jiehao Zhang**   **Jin Chen**   **Long Qin**
Singsound Inc.
{xushuy,zhangjiehao,chenjin,qinlong}@singsound.com

Abstract

It has been demonstrated that the utilization of a monolingual corpus in neural Grammatical Error Correction (GEC) systems can significantly improve the system performance. The previous state-of-the-art neural GEC system is an ensemble of four *Transformer* models pretrained on a large amount of Wikipedia Edits. The Singsound GEC system follows a similar approach but is equipped with a sophisticated erroneous data generating component. Our system achieved an $F_{0.5}$ of 66.61 in the BEA 2019 Shared Task: Grammatical Error Correction. With our novel erroneous data generating component, the Singsound neural GEC system yielded an M^2 of 63.2 on the CoNLL-2014 benchmark (8.4% relative improvement over the previous state-of-the-art system).

1 Introduction

The most effective approaches to Grammatical Error Correction (GEC) task are machine translation based methods. Both Statistical Machine Translation (SMT) approaches and Neural Machine Translation (NMT) methods have achieved promising results in the GEC task.

Pretraining a decoder as a language model is an effective method to improve the performance of neural GEC systems (Junczys-Dowmunt et al., 2018). As an extension of this work, Lichtarge et al. (2018) showed pretraining on 4 billion tokens of Wikipedia edits to be beneficial for the GEC task.

In this work, we investigate a similar approach by systematically generating parallel data for pretraining. As shown in Table 1, in addition to spelling errors (price → puice), transposition errors (independent voters → voters independent) and concatenation errors (the man → theman), our

Origin	the primary is **open** to **independent voters** .
Generated	the primary is **opens** to **voters independhent** .
Origin	the **price** of alcohol is **ramped** up at every budget .
Generated	the **puice** of alchool is **ramping** up at every budget .
Origin	they say the **police** shot and killed **the man** after he had **fired** at them .
Generated	they say the **polices** shot and killed **theman** after he had **firing** at them .

Table 1: Examples of generated data.

method also introduces errors such as ramped → ramping. Our approach obtained competitive results compared to the top systems in the BEA 2019 GEC Shared Task. Both our single model and ensemble models have exceeded the previous state-of-the-art systems on the CoNLL-2014 (Ng et al., 2014) benchmark and our system reaches human-level performance on the JFLEG (Napoles et al., 2017) benchmark.

2 Related Work

Chollampatt and Ng (2018) used a convolutional sequence-to-sequence (seq2seq) model (Gehring et al., 2017) with a large language model for rescoring. Their model was the first NMT based GEC system that exceeded the strong SMT baseline system (Junczys-Dowmunt and Grundkiewicz, 2016) which combined a Phrase-based Machine Translation (PBMT) with a large language model. Then a hybrid PBMT-NMT system (Grundkiewicz and Junczys-Dowmunt, 2018) appeared to reach the new state-of-the-art on the CoNLL-2014 benchmark. Later, various pure neu-

Proceedings of the Fourteenth Workshop on Innovative Use of NLP for Building Educational Applications, pages 149–158
Florence, Italy, August 2, 2019. ©2019 Association for Computational Linguistics

Corpus	Sentences	Tokens	Anno.
WMT11	115M	2362M	No
1B words	30M	769M	No
Lang-8	1037K	12M	Yes
NUCLE	57K	1.2M	Yes
FCE	28K	455K	Yes
ABCN	34K	628K	Yes

Table 2: Statistics for training data sets.

Corpus	Sentences	Scorer
ABCN dev	4384	ERRANT
ABCN test	4477	ERRANT
JFLEG test	747	GLEU
CoNLL-2014 test	1312	M^2 Scorer

Table 3: Statistics for test and development data.

Length	Err.	Prob.	Length	Err.	Prob.
$[1, 3)$	0	0.50	$[6, 9)$	2	0.30
	1	0.50		3	0.45
$[3, 6)$	1	0.50		4	0.25
	2	0.50	$[16, 20)$	3	0.10
$[9, 16)$	3	0.15		4	0.15
	4	0.25		5	0.15
	5	0.30		6	0.30
	6	0.30		7	0.30
$[20, 30)$	4	0.10	$[30, \infty)$	5	0.10
	5	0.15		6	0.15
	6	0.15		7	0.15
	7	0.30		8	0.30
	8	0.30		9	0.30

Table 4: Probability distribution of sentence errors.

ral systems (Ge et al., 2018; Junczys-Dowmunt et al., 2018; Lichtarge et al., 2018) reported state-of-the-art results successively. Ge et al. presented the fluency boosting method which was demonstrated to be effective to improve performance of GEC seq2seq models. The system proposed by Junczys-Dowmunt et al. (2018) is an ensemble of *Transformer* models (Vaswani et al., 2017); they pretrained the decoder of transformer as a language model on a large monolingual corpus. To our best knowledge, the current state-of-the-art GEC system on both the CoNLL-2014 benchmark and the JFLEG benchmark is the system presented by Lichtarge et al. (2018), which is an ensemble of four *Transformer* models pretrained on Wikipedia revisions and then fine-tuned on Lang-8 (Mizumoto et al., 2011).

3   Data

We list the training data in Table 2. The text data used to generate parallel corpus automatically was the One Billion Words Benchmark dataset (1B words) (Chelba et al., 2013) and the WMT11 monolingual corpus (WMT11) which can be obtained from WMT11 Website[1]. Our fine-tuning data is Lang-8 (Mizumoto et al., 2011; Tajiri et al., 2012), NUS Corpus of Learner English (NUCLE) (Dahlmeier et al., 2013), FCE (Yannakoudakis et al., 2011), the Cambridge English Write & Improve (W&I) corpus and the LOCNESS corpus (ABCN) (Granger, 1998; Bryant et al., 2019) .

---

[1] `http://statmt.org/wmt11/training-monolingual.tgz`

Table 3 shows the development and test data sets in our experiments. We choose the ABCN dev set as our development set and the ABCN test, the CoNLL-2014 test, the JFLEG as our benchmark. For these benchmarks, we report precision (P), recall (R) and $F_{0.5}$ with ERRANT (Bryant et al., 2017) on the ABCN test, GLEU (Sakaguchi et al., 2016) on the JFLEG test set (Napoles et al., 2017). To compare with previous state-of-the-art systems, we provide results of MaxMatch (M^2) Scorer (Dahlmeier and Ng, 2012) on the CoNLL-2014 test set.

4   Erroneous Data Generation

In this section, we describe our error generating method. For each sentence, we assign a probability distribution (as shown in Table 4) to determine the number of errors according to the sentence length. The parameters in Table 4 are determined empirically, as well as the parameters in Table 5, Table 6 and Table 7. Because of the time limitation of the GEC competition, we did not optimize these parameters.

After the number of errors (E) in a sentence has been determined, we randomly select E tokens from all the tokens of the sentence with equal probability to be errors. And for each error, we apply a random variable (Table 5) to determine which error type it should be.

We introduce five error types:

- Concatenation: combine two consecutive tokens, *e.g.*, hello world → helloworld.

- Misspelling: introduce spelling errors into

Type	Prob.
Concatenation	0.12
Misspell	0.45
Substitution	0.40
Deletion	0.00
Transposition	0.03

Table 5: Error types.

Tok. length	Err.	Prob.
$[1, 3)$	0	1.00
$[3, 5)$	1	1.00
$[5, 10)$	1	0.80
	2	0.20
$[10, \infty)$	1	0.75
	2	0.15
	3	0.10

Table 6: Number of misspells in a token.

Type	Prob.
Deletion	0.30
Insertion	0.15
Transposition	0.25
Replacement	0.30

Table 7: Mispell types.

words, *e.g.*, computer $\rightarrow$ camputer.

- Substitution: we introduce seven different types of substitutions.

- Deletion: delete the token.

- Transposition: the token exchange position with a consecutive token.

4.1 Misspelling

To generate misspellings, we introduce a random variable to determine how many errors in the token according to the token length (parameters are shown in Table 6.), and we randomly insert errors into the token.

For each spelling error, we apply another random variable to determine which error type should be. We introduce four spelling error types (Table 7 lists the parameters.).

- Deletion: delete the character.

- Insertion: insert a random English letter into the current position.

- Transposition: exchange position with the consecutive character.

- Replacement: replace the current character with a random English character.

We only introduce spelling errors into words belonging to a vocabulary list of 32k ordinary words[2] which does not include numerals (*e.g.*, 2019), tokens that contain digits (*e.g.*, Lang8), URLs or non-word symbols (*e.g.*, $\geq \triangledown \leq$).

4.2 Substitution

We introduce seven types of substitutions according to token and its part-of-speech (POS).

- Substitution between Prepositions. *E.g.*, in, on, at, through, for, with.

- Substitution between Articles. *E.g.*, a, an, the.

- Substitution between Pronouns (Singular). *E.g.*, he, she, his, him, her, hers.

- Substitution between Pronouns (Plural). *E.g.*, their, them, they, theirs.

- Substitution between Wh words. *E.g.*, which, where, what, how, when, who, whose, whom.

- Substitution between Modal verbs. *E.g.*, will, shall, can, may, would, could, might.

- Substitution in a Word Tree (see 4.3 for details).

4.3 Word Tree

We want to make substitutions such as going $\rightarrow$ gone, useful $\rightarrow$ usable, administration $\rightarrow$ administrative. To make such substitution possible, we introduce the Word Tree.

A Word Tree represents a group of words that share the same stem but have different suffixes. Figure 1 shows an example of Word Tree of "use". A node denotes a word (*e.g.*, usable) and corresponding Extended part-of-speech (EPOS) (*e.g.*, VBP_JJ_BLE) (see 4.4 for details.), and an edge indicates the root from which the word is derived (*e.g.*, "usable" is derived from "use").

With EPOS, we can easily set rules or assign probability distributions to determine which substitutions are more likely to happen, (*e.g.*, singular $\leftrightarrow$ plural, VBD $\leftrightarrow$ VBZ $\leftrightarrow$ VBP $\leftrightarrow$ VBN $\leftrightarrow$

---

[2]We manually created this vocabulary for building the Word Tree (see 4.3 for details).

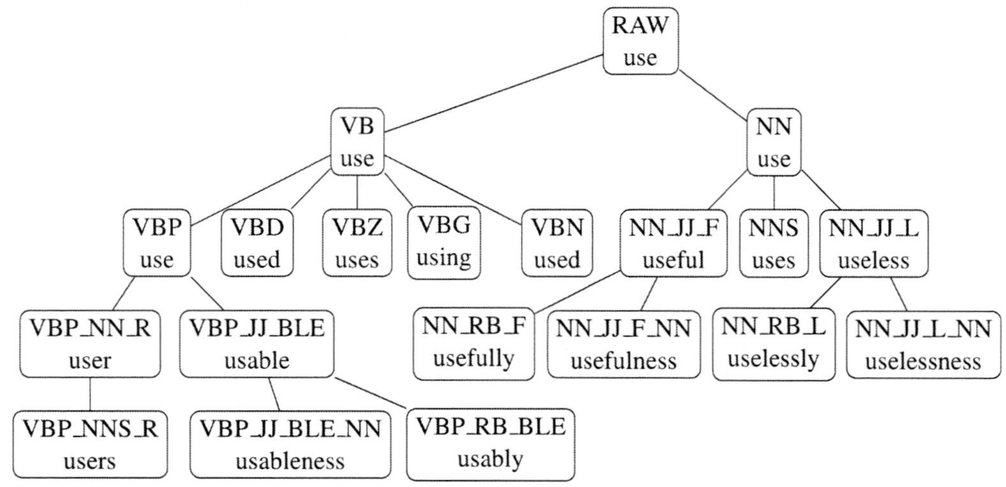

Figure 1: Word Tree: use

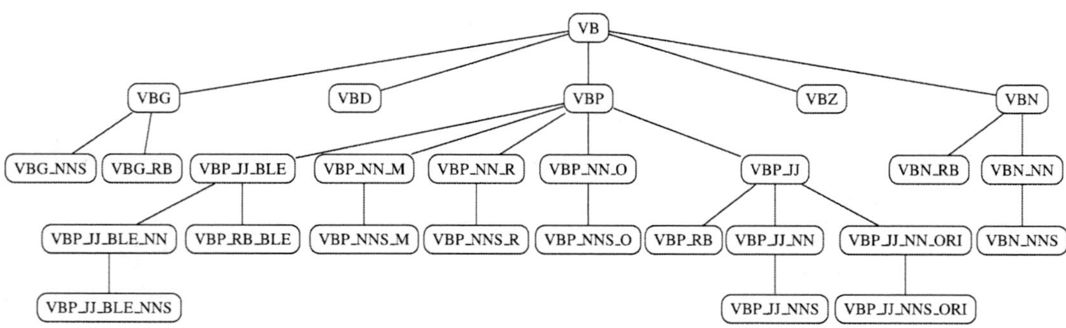

Figure 2: Verb branch of the EPOS Tree

VBG, adjective ↔ adverb), and which substitutions are less likely to happen (*e.g.*, happiest JJS ↔ happiness JJ_NN). In our experiments, due to the time limitation of the competition, we simply assigned a uniform distribution to all existing words in a Word Tree, excluding substitutions that were definitely unlikely to occur such as substitutions between the words in an NN_JJ_F branch (*e.g.*, careful) and the words in an NN_JJ_L branch (*e.g.*, carelessness).

4.4   Extended part-of-speech

A Word Tree can contain multiple words of the same POS. As shown in the example in Figure 1, use, user and usefulness can all be nouns. Therefore, in order to identify the different roles for words in a Word Tree, we propose EPOS, derived from part-of-speech (POS) and the surface form of the word.

POS explains how a word is used (mostly syn-

tactically) in a sentence. Compared to POS, EPOS also reflects some semantic role of a word in a sentence.

We define EPOS in Table 11 in the Appendix. We used NLTK (Bird, 2006) as our POS tagger, and use NLTK-style tags in this paper.

We briefly describe our method of creating word trees.

a. Extract the vocabulary from a text corpus which is tagged with NLTK POS tagger.

b. Create three tables for Noun, Verb, and Adjective respectively. The Noun table contains two columns: singular and plural; the Verb table has six columns: original verb form (VB), non-third person present (VBP), third person present (VBZ), past tense (VBD), past participle (VBN) and present participle (VBG); the Adjective table has four columns: adjective, adverb, comparative degree and superlative de-

152

#	System	P	R	$F_{0.5}$
1	UEDIN-MS	72.28	60.12	69.47
...				
4	CAMB-CLED	70.49	55.07	66.75
5	**Singsound**	70.17	55.39	66.61

Table 8: Results of BEA 2019 GEC competition.

	dev	test		
	$F_{0.5}$	P	R	$F_{0.5}$
single	52.29	66.06	56.68	63.94
w/o pretrain	44.60	50.59	43.60	49.02
4 ensemble	55.37	70.14	57.57	67.21
w/o pretrain	47.01	56.05	44.33	53.24

Table 9: Results of ABCN set. "w/o pretrain" refers to models **without** pretraining.

gree. Then we fill words into corresponding entries according to their POS tags. Words that cannot be filled in any of the above tables are filled into a list.

c. Manually check and correct all entries of the three tables, and fill missing entries as well.

d. Define EPOS as listed in Table 11 in the Appendix according to suffix transforming rules.

e. Extract a RAW list from the vocabulary according to the suffix transforming rules.

f. Create an EPOS tree structure for each token in the RAW list, and then fill each word from the vocabulary into the corresponding entry of the corresponding EPOS tree (The full structure of the EPOS Tree is described in Table 12 in the Appendix, and Figure 2 shows the Verb branch); then prune empty entries in the trees.

g. Manually check every entry of every word tree, and fix all incorrect entries.

h. Update the defined EPOS (final version in Table 11) and the EPOS tree (Table 12); recreate word trees.

i. Repeat step g and h until satisfied.

5 Experiments

In our experiments, we generated a corpus of 3 billion tokens, of which about 24% were errors.

Following Lichtarge et al. (2018), we also use *Transformer* as our encoder-decoder model, using *Tensor2Tensor* open source implementation [3].

The models are trained on words, and rare words are segmented into sub-words with the byte pair encoding (BPE) (Sennrich et al., 2015). We use 6 layers for both encoder and decoder, and 4 attention heads. The embedding size and hidden size are 1024, and the filter size for all position-wise feed forward network is 4096. We set dropout rate to 0.3, and source word dropout is set to 0.2 as a noising technique. Following Junczys-Dowmunt et al. (2018), source, target and output embeddings are tied in our models.

Following Lichtarge et al. (2018), we first trained our model on an artificially generated parallel corpus with a batch size of approximately 3072 tokens. Then we set the batch size to 2048 tokens and fine-tuned on human annotated data for 20 epochs, and we averaged the 5 best checkpoints. Finally, the averaged model was fine-tuned on the ABCN and FCE training data for 1000 steps as domain adaptation (Junczys-Dowmunt et al., 2018).

There are about 50% sentence pairs without any correction in the Lang-8 dataset, and we noticed that training with too many error-free sentence pairs had a negative effect. Therefore, we filtered out these error-free sentence pairs in the Lang-8 dataset. Since the NUCLE, FCE and ABCN datasets are much smaller than the Lang-8 set, we did not filter out the error-free sentence pairs in these datasets.

We used beam search for decoding with a beam size of 4 at evaluation time. For the ensemble, we averaged logits from 4 *Transformer* models with identical hyper-parameters at each decoding step. Following (Grundkiewicz and Junczys-Dowmunt, 2018; Junczys-Dowmunt et al., 2018; Lichtarge et al., 2018), we preprocessed the JF-LEG dataset with spell-checking. We did not apply spell-checking to the ABCN and CoNLL-2014 datasets.

6 Results and Discussion

The results of the Singsound System in the GEC competition (Table 8) were obtained by an ensemble of four models. Because of the time limitation, we only trained two independent models

---

[3] https://github.com/ tensorflow/tensor2tensor

	Model	CoNLL-2014			CoNLL-10 (SvH)			JFLEG
		P	R	$F_{0.5}$	P	R	$F_{0.5}$	GLEU
(1)	Word&Char SMT-GEC	62.7	33.0	53.1			68.3	56.8
(2)	MLConv (4 ensemble)	65.5	33.1	54.8				57.5
(3)	Transformer (single)			53.0				57.9
	Transformer (4 ensemble)	63.0	38.9	56.1				58.5
	Transformer (4 ensemble) + LM	61.9	40.2	55.8				59.9
(4)	Hybrid PBMT+NMT+LM	66.8	34.5	56.3	83.2	47.0	72.0	61.5
(5)	Transformer (single)	62.2	37.8	54.9				59.3
	Transformer (4 ensemble)	67.5	37.8	58.3				62.4
Singsound	Transformer (single)	68.3	**42.5**	60.9	83.5	55.2	75.7	60.8
	Transformer (4 ensemble)	**73.0**	41.1	**63.2**	**86.0**	53.8	**76.8**	**62.6**
	Human avg.				73.5	**69.6**	72.6	62.4

Table 10: Comparison with top performing systems on CoNLL and JFLEG datasets. (1): Chollampatt and Ng (2017) (2): Chollampatt and Ng (2018); (3): Junczys-Dowmunt et al. (2018); (4): Grundkiewicz and Junczys-Dowmunt (2018); (5): Lichtarge et al.(2018).

from scratch. The other two were based on existing trained models. Concretely, after we got a model trained from scratch, we kept training it on the generated corpus for 0.2 epoch; then fine-tuned the model on the annotated data and ABCN and FCE training sets as before.

We provide the performance of our single model and the ensemble of 4 independently trained models [4] on the ABCN dev and test datasets in Table 9. As the results shown in Table 9, models pretrained on the generated corpus significantly outperform the models without pretraining.

To compare with previous state-of-the-art GEC systems, we evaluated our systems on the CoNLL-2014 and JFLEG datasets. As the results shown in Table 10, our single model exceeded previous state-of-the-art systems on the CoNLL-2014 dataset. Our ensemble models achieved 8.4% relative improvement over the latest state-of-the-art results on the CoNLL-2014 benchmark.

We also report the results on the CoNLL-2014 10 annotation dataset (denoted as CoNLL-10) (Bryant and Ng, 2015) which is an extension of the CoNLL-2014 test set with 10 annotators. The human-level scores are calculated by averaging the scores for each annotator with regard to the remaining annotators. Following Chollampatt and Ng (2017), scores on CoNLL-10 (SvH) are calcu-

lated by removing one set of human annotations at a time and evaluating the system against the remaining sets. Our models reach human-level performance on both CoNLL-10 and JFLEG benchmarks.

7 Conclusion

In this work, we present a novel erroneous data generating method for training English GEC models. Our experiments show that *Transformer* models pretrained on generated corpus significantly outperform the previous GEC systems that are also based on *Transformer*. We also present a novel tool: the Word Tree, which represents a group of words that share the same stem but have different suffixes; and we show that one possible application of the Word Tree is generating erroneous text for training GEC models.

Acknowledgments

We thank Xiaoxue Fan, Miao Xue and Yueming Gao for their help in checking the three tables required for creating the Word Trees.

References

Steven Bird. 2006. NLTK: The natural language toolkit. *meeting of the Association for Computational Linguistics*, pages 69–72.

---

[4]The four models are trained on the same data with the same hyper-parameter set.

Christopher Bryant, Mariano Felice, Øistein E. Andersen, and Ted Briscoe. 2019. The BEA-2019 Shared Task on Grammatical Error Correction. In *Proceedings of the 14th Workshop on Innovative Use of NLP for Building Educational Applications*. Association for Computational Linguistics.

Christopher Bryant, Mariano Felice, and Edward John Briscoe. 2017. Automatic annotation and evaluation of error types for grammatical error correction. Association for Computational Linguistics.

Christopher Bryant and Hwee Tou Ng. 2015. How far are we from fully automatic high quality grammatical error correction. 1:697–707.

Ciprian Chelba, Tomas Mikolov, Mike Schuster, Qi Ge, Thorsten Brants, Phillipp Koehn, and Tony Robinson. 2013. One billion word benchmark for measuring progress in statistical language modeling. *Computer Science*.

Shamil Chollampatt and Hwee Tou Ng. 2017. Connecting the dots: Towards human-level grammatical error correction. pages 327–333.

Shamil Chollampatt and Hwee Tou Ng. 2018. A multilayer convolutional encoder-decoder neural network for grammatical error correction. In *Thirty-Second AAAI Conference on Artificial Intelligence*.

Daniel Dahlmeier and Hwee Tou Ng. 2012. Better evaluation for grammatical error correction. In *Proceedings of the 2012 Conference of the North American Chapter of the Association for Computational Linguistics: Human Language Technologies*, pages 568–572. Association for Computational Linguistics.

Daniel Dahlmeier, Hwee Tou Ng, and Siew Mei Wu. 2013. Building a large annotated corpus of learner English: The NUS corpus of learner English. In *Proceedings of the eighth workshop on innovative use of NLP for building educational applications*, pages 22–31.

Tao Ge, Furu Wei, and Ming Zhou. 2018. Fluency boost learning and inference for neural grammatical error correction. In *Proceedings of the 56th Annual Meeting of the Association for Computational Linguistics (Volume 1: Long Papers)*, pages 1055–1065.

Jonas Gehring, Michael Auli, David Grangier, Denis Yarats, and Yann N Dauphin. 2017. Convolutional sequence to sequence learning. In *Proceedings of the 34th International Conference on Machine Learning-Volume 70*, pages 1243–1252. JMLR. org.

Sylviane Granger. 1998. *The computer learner corpus: a versatile new source of data for SLA research.* na.

Roman Grundkiewicz and Marcin Junczys-Dowmunt. 2018. Near human-level performance in grammatical error correction with hybrid machine translation. *arXiv preprint arXiv:1804.05945*.

Marcin Junczys-Dowmunt and Roman Grundkiewicz. 2016. Phrase-based machine translation is state-of-the-art for automatic grammatical error correction. *arXiv preprint arXiv:1605.06353*.

Marcin Junczys-Dowmunt, Roman Grundkiewicz, Shubha Guha, and Kenneth Heafield. 2018. Approaching neural grammatical error correction as a low-resource machine translation task. *arXiv preprint arXiv:1804.05940*.

Jared Lichtarge, Christopher Alberti, Shankar Kumar, Noam Shazeer, and Niki Parmar. 2018. Weakly supervised grammatical error correction using iterative decoding. *arXiv preprint arXiv:1811.01710*.

Tomoya Mizumoto, Mamoru Komachi, Masaaki Nagata, and Yuji Matsumoto. 2011. Mining revision log of language learning SNS for automated Japanese error correction of second language learners. In *Proceedings of 5th International Joint Conference on Natural Language Processing*, pages 147–155.

Courtney Napoles, Keisuke Sakaguchi, and Joel Tetreault. 2017. JFLEG: A fluency corpus and benchmark for grammatical error correction. *arXiv preprint arXiv:1702.04066*.

Hwee Tou Ng, Siew Mei Wu, Ted Briscoe, Christian Hadiwinoto, Raymond Hendy Susanto, and Christopher Bryant. 2014. The conll-2014 shared task on grammatical error correction. In *Proceedings of the Eighteenth Conference on Computational Natural Language Learning: Shared Task*, pages 1–14.

Keisuke Sakaguchi, Courtney Napoles, Matt Post, and Joel R Tetreault. 2016. Reassessing the goals of grammatical error correction: Fluency instead of grammaticality. *Transactions of the Association for Computational Linguistics*, 4(1):169–182.

Rico Sennrich, Barry Haddow, and Alexandra Birch. 2015. Neural machine translation of rare words with subword units. *arXiv preprint arXiv:1508.07909*.

Toshikazu Tajiri, Mamoru Komachi, and Yuji Matsumoto. 2012. Tense and aspect error correction for esl learners using global context. pages 198–202.

Ashish Vaswani, Noam Shazeer, Niki Parmar, Jakob Uszkoreit, Llion Jones, Aidan N Gomez, Łukasz Kaiser, and Illia Polosukhin. 2017. Attention is all you need. In *Advances in neural information processing systems*, pages 5998–6008.

Helen Yannakoudakis, Ted Briscoe, and Ben Medlock. 2011. A new dataset and method for automatically grading ESOL texts. In *Proceedings of the 49th Annual Meeting of the Association for Computational Linguistics: Human Language Technologies-Volume 1*, pages 180–189. Association for Computational Linguistics.

A Appendix

EPOS	POS	Annotation	Examples
RAW		Root of word trees, original form	use
NN	NN	Noun	use
NNS	NNS	Plural form of Noun	uses
NN_JJ_F	JJ	NN + ful [5]	useful
NN_JJ_F_NN	NN	NN_JJ_F + ness	usefulness
NN_JJ_F_NNS	NNS	Plural form of NN_JJ_F_NN	
NN_JJ_F_NN_ORI	NN	Adjective used as Noun	dreadful
NN_JJ_F_NNS_ORI	NNS	Plural form of NN_JJ_F_NN_ORI	dreadfuls
NN_RB_F	RB	Adverb form of NN_JJ_F	usefully
NN_JJ_L	JJ	NN + less	useless
NN_JJ_L_NN	NN	NN_JJ_L + ness	uselessness
NN_JJ_L_NNS	NNS	Plural form of NN_JJ_L_NN	
NN_JJ_L_NN_ORI	NN	Adjective used as Noun	wireless
NN_JJ_L_NNS_ORI	NNS	Plural form of NN_JJ_L_NN_ORI	wirelesses
NN_RB_L	RB	Adverb form of NN_JJ_L	uselessly
NN_JJ_OUS	JJ	NN + ous	dangerous
NN_JJ_OUS_NN	NN	NN_JJ_OUS + ness	dangerousness
NN_JJ_OUS_NNS	NNS	Plural form of NN_JJ_OUS_NN	
NN_RB_OUS	RB	Adverb form of NN_JJ_OUS	dangerously
NN_JJ_AL	JJ	NN + al	rational
NN_JJ_AL_NN	NN	NN_JJ_AL + ness	rationalness
NN_JJ_AL_NNS	NNS	Plural form of NN_JJ_AL_NN	
NN_RB_AL	RB	Adverb form of NN_JJ_AL	rationally
NN_JJ_Y	JJ	NN + y	lucky
NN_JJR_Y	JJR	Comparative degree of NN_JJ_Y	luckier
NN_JJS_Y	JJS	Superlative degree of NN_JJ_Y	luckiest
NN_JJ_Y_NN	NN	NN_JJ_Y + ness	luckiness
NN_JJ_Y_NNS	NNS	Plural form of NN_JJ_Y_NN	
NN_JJ_Y_NN_ORI	NN	Adjective used as Noun	safety
NN_JJ_Y_NNS_ORI	NNS	Plural form of NN_JJ_Y_NN_ORI	safeties
NN_RB_Y	RB	Adverb form of NN_JJ_Y	luckily
NN_JJ_D	JJ	NN + ed	warmhearted
NN_JJ_D_NN	NN	NN_JJ_D + ness	warmheartedness
NN_JJ_D_NNS	NNS	Plural form of NN_JJ_D_NN	
NN_RB_D	RB	Adverb form of NN_JJ_D	warmheartedly
VB	VB	Original form of verbs	go
VBD	VBD	Past tense	went
VBZ	VBZ	Present third person singular	goes
VBN	VBN	Past participle	gone
VBN_NN	NN	VBN + ness	limitedness
VBN_NNS	NNS	Plural form of VBN_NN	
VBN_NNS_ORI	NNS	Plural form of VBN when VBN used as Noun	shots, thoughts
VBN_RB	RB	Adverb form of VBN	excitedly
VBG	VBG	Present participle	baking
VBG_NNS_ORI	NNS	Plural form of VBG when VBG used as Noun	bakings
VBG_RB	RB	Adverb form of VBG	excitingly
VBP	VBP	non-third person present	go

VBP_NN_O	NN	VBP + ion	connection
VBP_NNS_O	NNS	Plural form of VBP_NN_O	connections
VBP_NN_R	NN	VBP + er / or / ar	dancer, editor
VBP_NNS_R	NNS	Plural form of VBP_NN_R	dancers, editors
VBP_JJ_BLE	JJ	VBP + able / ible	usable
VBP_JJ_BLE_NN	NN	VBP_JJ_BLE + ness	usableness
VBP_JJ_BLE_NNS	NNS	Plural form of VBP_JJ_BLE_NN	
VBP_RB_BLE	RB	Adverb form of VBP_JJ_BLE	usably
VBP_JJ	JJ	VBP + ive	active
VBP_RB	RB	Adverb form of VBP_JJ	actively
VBP_JJ_NN	NN	VBP_JJ + ness	attractiveness
VBP_JJ_NNS	NNS	Plural form of VBP_JJ_NN	
VBP_JJ_NN_ORI	NN	VBP_JJ used as Noun	representative
VBP_JJ_NNS_ORI	NNS	Plural form of VBP_JJ_NN_ORI	representatives
VBP_NN_M	NN	VBP + ment	movement
VBP_NNS_M	NNS	Plural form of VBP_NN_M	movements
JJ	JJ	Adjectivel	happy
JJS	JJS	Superlative degree of Adjective	happiest
JJR	JJR	Comparative degree of Adjective	happier
JJ_NN	NN	JJ + ness	happiness
JJ_NNS	NNS	Plural form of JJ_NN	happinesses
RB	RB	Adverb	happily
RBR	RBR	Comparative degree of Adverb	harder
RBS	RBS	Superlative degree of Adverb	hardest
CD	CD	Cardinal digits	one
CD_JJ	JJ	Adjective form of CD	first
CD_RB	RB	Adverb form of numbers	firstly
CD_JJ_NN_ORI	NN	Adjective used as Noun	first
CD_JJ_NNS_ORI	NNS	Plural form of CD_JJ_NN_ORI	firsts
CD_RB_ORI	RB	Adverbs that are same as CD_JJ	first
CD_NNS	NNS	Plural form of CD	ones
DT	DT	Determiner	the
WRB	WRB	Wh-adverb	how, where
PRP	PRP	Personal pronoun	I, you, they
IN	IN	Preposition or subordinating conjunction	in, from, after
CC	CC	Coordinating conjunction	and
MD	MD	Modal verb	can
OFS		Any POS out of the POS column	

Table 11: EPOS table.

---

⁵By abuse notation, "+" denotes "with some suffix".

Parent	Children
RAW	NN, JJ, VB, IN, OFS, CC, MD, DT, PRP, CD, WDT, WP, WRB
NN	NNS, NN_JJ_F, NN_JJ_L, NN_JJ_Y, NN_JJ_D, NN_JJ_OUS, NN_JJ_AL
NN_JJ_D	NN_RB_D, NN_JJ_D_NN
NN_JJ_Y	NN_RB_Y, NN_JJR_Y, NN_JJS_Y, NN_JJ_Y_NN, NN_JJ_Y_NN_ORI
NN_JJ_Y_NN	NN_JJ_Y_NNS
NN_JJ_Y_NN_ORI	NN_JJ_Y_NNS_ORI
NN_JJ_F	NN_RB_F, NN_JJ_F_NN, NN_JJR_F, NN_JJS_F, NN_JJ_F_NN_ORI
NN_JJ_F_NN	NN_JJ_F_NNS
NN_JJ_F_NN_ORI	NN_JJ_F_NNS_ORI
NN_JJ_L	NN_RB_L, NN_JJ_L_NN, NN_JJR_L, NN_JJS_L, NN_JJ_L_NN_ORI
NN_JJ_L_NN	NN_JJ_L_NNS
NN_JJ_L_NN_ORI	NN_JJ_L_NNS_ORI
NN_JJ_AL	NN_RB_AL, NN_JJ_AL_NN
NN_JJ_AL_NN	NN_JJ_AL_NNS
NN_JJ_OUS	NN_RB_OUS, NN_JJ_OUS_NN
NN_JJ_OUS_NN	NN_JJ_OUS_NNS
VB	VBP, VBD, VBZ, VBG, VBN
VBP	VBP_JJ, VBP_NN_R, VBP_NN_M, VBP_NN_O, VBP_JJ_BLE
VBP_JJ	VBP_RB, VBP_JJ_NN, VBP_JJ_NN_ORI
VBP_JJ_NN	VBP_JJ_NNS
VBP_JJ_NN_ORI	VBP_JJ_NNS_ORI
VBP_JJ_BLE	VBP_RB_BLE VBP_JJ_BLE_NN
VBP_JJ_BLE_NN	VBP_JJ_BLE_NNS
VBP_NN_R	VBP_NNS_R
VBP_NN_M	VBP_NNS_M
VBP_NN_O	VBP_NNS_O
VBG	VBG_RB, VBG_NNS
VBN	VBN_RB, VBN_NN
VBN_NN	VBN_NNS
JJ	JJR, JJS, RB, JJ_NN, JJ_NN_ORI
JJ_NN	JJ_NNS
JJ_NN_ORI	JJ_NNS_ORI
RB	RBR, RBS
CD	CD_JJ, CD_JJ_NN_ORI, CD_NNS
CD_JJ	CD_RB, CD_RB_ORI
CD_JJ_NN_ORI	CD_JJ_NNS_ORI

Table 12: Structure of the EPOS Tree.

The LAIX Systems in the BEA-2019 GEC Shared Task

Ruobing Li[†]   Chuan Wang   Yefei Zha   Yonghong Yu   Shiman Guo   Qiang Wang
Yang Liu[†]   Hui Lin[†]

LAIX Inc.

[†]{ruobing.li, yang.liu, hui.lin}@liulishuo.com

Abstract

In this paper, we describe two systems we developed for the three tracks we have participated in the BEA-2019 GEC Shared Task. We investigate competitive classification models with bi-directional recurrent neural networks (Bi-RNN) and neural machine translation (NMT) models. For different tracks, we use ensemble systems to selectively combine the NMT models, the classification models, and some rules, and demonstrate that an ensemble solution can effectively improve GEC performance over single systems. Our GEC systems ranked the first in the Unrestricted Track, and the third in both the Restricted Track and the Low Resource Track.

1 Introduction

Grammatical error correction (GEC) is the task of automatically correcting grammatical errors in text. With the increasing number of language learners, GEC has gained more and more attention from educationists and researchers in the past decade. The following is a GEC example: *I [fall → fell] asleep at 11 p.m. last [nigh → night].* Here *fall* needs to be corrected to its past tense form and *nigh* is a spelling mistake.

GEC is considered as a mapping task from incorrect sentences to correct sentences. Incorrect sentences can be seen as being produced by adding noises to correct sentences. The added noise does not happen randomly, but occurs when people learn or use the language according to a certain error distribution and language usage bias. Initially, people used rule-based approaches to solve GEC problems (Naber and Miłkowski, 2005). Rules are relatively easy to make but with poor generalization. Later researchers began to treat GEC as a classification task. According to the grammatical information around the target word, classifiers can be constructed to predict the true grammatical role of the target word. One drawback of the classification methods for GEC is that training different classifiers for different error types may be resource-intensive and inefficient since there are many grammatical error types. Recently, translation methods have become the focus of research, and there is a clear trend that state-of-the-art GEC systems are being shifted from traditional NLP methods to NMT based methods.

In recent years, GEC performance has seen significant improvement in some public GEC test sets (Ge et al., 2018). In CoNLL-2013 (Ng et al., 2013) and CoNLL-2014 (Ng et al., 2014) GEC Shared Task, machine learning based GEC methods emerged with relatively good performance. Classification methods achieved the best result in CoNLL-2013 (Rozovskaya et al., 2013). After that, statistical machine translation (SMT) methods began to show better performance in CoNLL-2014 (Felice et al., 2014). (Chollampatt et al., 2016) was the first study to obtain the state-of-the-art result with neural networks. Then after (Junczys-Dowmunt and Grundkiewicz, 2016), machine translation methods became the mainstream in GEC solutions. In addition, an RNN-based context model achieved better results than previous traditional classification models (Wang et al., 2017). Using a CNN-based sequence-to-sequence architecture (Gehring et al., 2017), (Chollampatt and Ng, 2018) proposed the first end-to-end NMT model and reported the state-of-the-art result. As Transformer (Vaswani et al., 2017) plays an increasingly important role in sequence modeling, Transformer-based end-to-end NMT models began to lead the current GEC research (Junczys-Dowmunt et al., 2018; Grundkiewicz and Junczys-Dowmunt, 2018; Ge et al., 2018; Zhao et al., 2019). It is worth mentioning that (Lichtarge et al., 2019) used Wikipedia ed-

159

Proceedings of the Fourteenth Workshop on Innovative Use of NLP for Building Educational Applications, pages 159–167
Florence, Italy, August 2, 2019. ©2019 Association for Computational Linguistics

its history corpus, which is huge but noisy, and gained a result very close to the state-of-the-art result. Learning a GEC translation model from noisy data is a worthy future direction as the GEC parallel corpus is expensive to obtain.

This paper describes our two systems for the three tracks in the BEA-2019 GEC Shared Task (Bryant et al., 2019). We use two popular NMT models and two improved versions of neural classification models to train the basic models. Ensemble strategies are then used to combine outcomes from different models. Our two systems for the three tracks are described in next section. In Section 3, we evaluate the systems on the development data and show the final results on the test data. Section 4 concludes the paper and summarizes the future work.

2   System Overview

2.1   Restricted and Unrestricted Track

We submitted the same system output for the Restricted and Unrestricted tasks. The system uses several ensemble methods to combine the CNN-based and Transformer-based translation models, described in details below.

2.1.1   CNN-based translation ensemble systems

We found that CNN-based systems obtained the best results for some error types, likely due to some characteristics derived from CNN. We trained four CNN-based ensemble systems, using the model architecture in (Chollampatt and Ng, 2018), but without reranking. Four best combinations to build the ensemble systems were selected. Unlike (Chollampatt and Ng, 2018), we did not use fastText (Bojanowski et al., 2017) to initialize word embeddings because we found no improvement on the development set by doing that. We tuned parameters for the system, such as batch size, word embedding dimension, etc.

2.1.2   Transformer-based translation systems

Transformer is currently considered to be one of the most powerful models for sequence modeling. For GEC, some of the best recent results reported on CoNLL-2014 test set are obtained by Transformer-based translation models. We trained eight Transformer-based translation models in a low resource translation paradigm (Junczys-Dowmunt et al., 2018). We tuned parameters for

domain and error adaptation. We also compared the results using 2 GPUs and 4 GPUs as the authors reported the difference in their Github repository[1].

2.1.3   Ensemble methods

We expect to combine these models trained above into a more powerful system through effective ensemble methods. Our ensemble work mainly focuses on rule-based solutions. We will introduce two main modules first.

Confidence Table We can obtain the precision and $F_{0.5}$ metric on each error type through sentence alignment and error type classification by Errant (Bryant et al., 2017). Errant provides performance statistics based on 55 error types and is also the tool used to evaluate this GEC shared task, thus we use the result of *operation and error type span-level* (Bryant et al., 2017) for a model or system as the confidence table.

Conflict Solver We often encounter GEC error conflicts when combining multiple models or systems. For example, *We love played soccer.* One system corrects *played* to *playing*, while another system may correct *played* to *to play*. When two different corrections occur in the same place, we need to consider which one to choose.

We solve this problem in a unified pipeline, which can also be seen as an ensemble way:

(1) We sort each group of conflicting corrections proposed by all the systems in a reverse order of location index and confidence.

(2) We apply three sub-strategies:

- When combining outcomes from different systems, we treat the precision in a confidence table as the confidence. Each correction has its confidence obtained by looking up the precision of the corresponding type of the correction in the table. If two conflicting corrections are the same, we merge them and add α to the confidence of the correction; otherwise, the correction with a lower confidence will be discarded.

- After combining outcomes, if the confidence of a correction is lower than β, the correction is discarded.

- γ is used to distinguish when it is more important to focus on the precision or $F_{0.5}$ of

[1]https://github.com/grammatical/neural-naacl2018

160

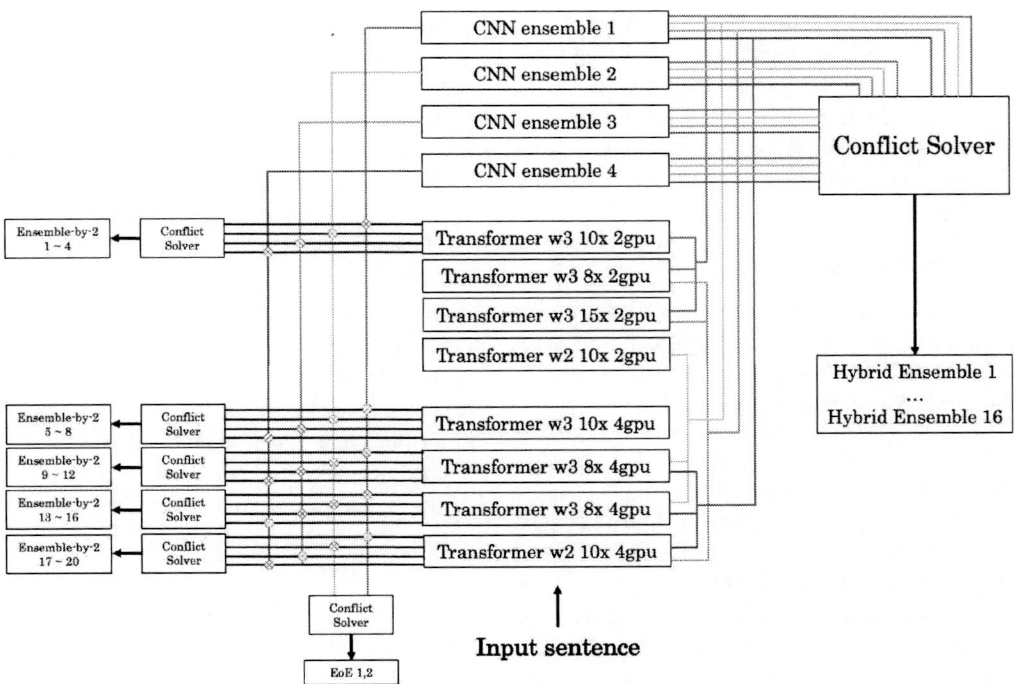

Figure 1: The architecture of the ensemble system in Restricted and Unrestricted Tracks.

a correction. When we move to the final ensemble with confidence tables of existing systems, if the confidence is larger than γ, we select the correction proposed by the system that has the best $F_{0.5}$ on the type of this correction. Otherwise, the correction by a system with the best precision is selected.

In Figure 1, $\otimes$ means the outcome is obtained by combining two systems represented by intersecting lines of two different colours. If there are multiple $\otimes$ on a line, it means the ensemble is over all of these $\otimes$ on this line. Figure 1 displays three types of ensemble methods based on all of the CNN-based and Transformer-based translation models.

- Combine each CNN-based ensemble model with each of the selected five of the Transformer-based models. This is noted as 'ensemble-by-2'.

- Perform ensemble over all of the ensemble models relating to either CNN ensemble 1 or CNN ensemble 2, noted as EoE (Ensemble over Ensemble) 1 and 2.

- Ensemble each CNN ensemble model with some selected combinations of Transformer-

based models to produce 16 strong ensemble system outcomes, represented as 'Hybrid Ensemble' in Figure 1. It is where multiple lines of the same color are merged into one line in Figure 1.

After getting all of the ensemble outcomes, we will do the final ensemble step: select the best confidence for each type from each single or ensemble system to form the strongest final outcome. In this ensemble step, we use the last aforementioned sub-strategy, and discard the error types with very low confidence to boost the final performance.

2.2 Low Resource Track

For the Low Resource Track we developed different individual systems and used an ensemble method to combine them. For the translation model, we did not obtain very strong performance because the training data is limited. We also explored the noisy Wikipedia edit history corpus for the Transformer-based translation model. However, we noticed that, for some error types with clear definitions, the classifiers trained on a large amount of native corpus have good performance. In addition, we made some grammatical rules to correct errors and adopted an off-the-shelf spelling checker (Kelly, 2006). Finally, we leverage a simple ensemble method to combine all of the classifiers, rules, spelling checker and translation models. Note that for the Restricted and Unrestricted tracks, we did not observe any gain from the classification models or the rule-based methods, therefore only the translation systems were used for those tracks.

2.2.1 Classification model

After an analysis of the development sets, we decided to build classifiers for eight common error types. Based on (Wang et al., 2017), we developed two classification model structures for the eight error types.

(A) Bi-GRU context model

Figure 2 shows the bi-directional GRU context model we use to determine the right grammatical category for a target word. The concatenated left and right source states of the target word form the contextual semantic vector representation. This is used as a query to calculate the attention weight a_t. An attention vector C_t is then computed as the weighted average, according to a_t, over all the source states. C_t is then fed through a fully connected layer and softmax layer to produce the predictive distribution.

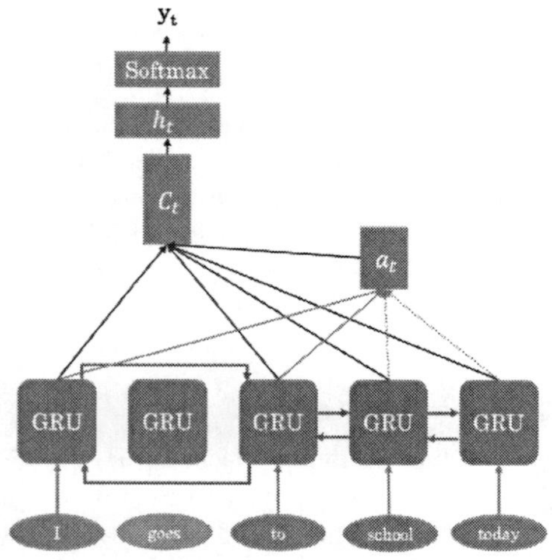

Figure 2: Bi-GRU Context model structure.

We use this to train models for the following error types: Subject-verb agreement, Article, Plural or singular noun, Verb form, Preposition substitution, Missing comma and Period comma substitution. Labels for each task were extracted automatically from the native corpus through part-of-speech tagging tools.

(B) Pointer context model

The classifiers above use the same classification labels for different target words. We also need a classification model to deal with the problem as in the Word form task, where each word has a different set of predictive labels (as shown for word 'gone' in Figure 3). Inspired by the Pointer network model (Vinyals et al., 2015), we proposed the pointer context model. Figure 3 shows the pointer context model that takes the target word's confusion set as the label candidates. The computation path is the same as the Bi-GRU model structure. We concatenate the target word's char-based embedding and C_t to obtain C_t^1, and then use it as the query to compute dot product a_t^1 with each of the word embeddings in the confusion set. a_t^1 is then fed through a softmax layer to produce the predictive distribution. This model is very effective at dealing with varying number of candidates as seen in the Word form task.

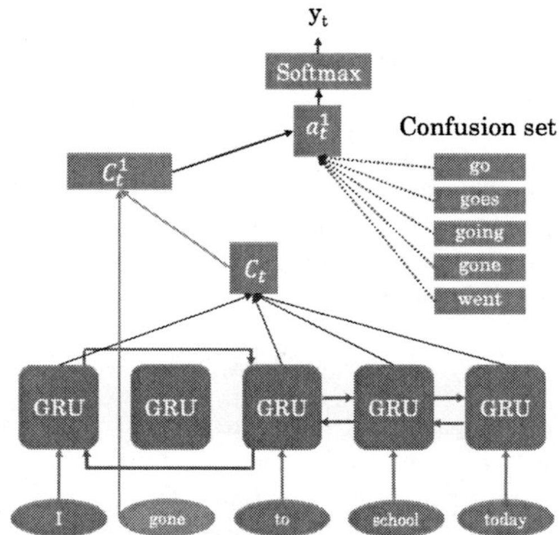

Figure 3: Pointer Context model structure.

2.2.2 NMT model

We use the same Transformer-based translation model mentioned in Subsection 3.2.2. Due to the limitation of the corpus, we leverage the Wiked (Grundkiewicz and Junczys-Dowmunt, 2014) as our training corpus for the NMT model.

2.2.3 Rules and spell checker

We have implemented the following GEC rules.

(1) **'a' and 'an' substitution**. For this problem, we made rules based on the first phoneme of the following word.

(2) **Comma deletion**. After a prepositional

Track	FCE	Lang-8	NUCLE	W&I+ LOCNESS	Common Crawl	Wiked	Wiki dumps
Restricted Track	Yes	Yes	Yes	Yes	Yes	-	-
Unrestricted Track	Yes	Yes	Yes	Yes	Yes	-	-
Low Resource Track	-	-	-	-	Yes	Yes	Yes

Table 1: Corpus used for training in corresponding track.

Seed	Batch size	Word embedding dimension	Number of input channels	Number of output channels	Number of layers	$F_{0.5}$
5001	32	128	256	256	7	0.3370
5002	32	128	256	256	7	0.3219
5003	32	128	256	256	7	0.3370
5004	32	128	256	256	7	0.3411
5005	32	128	256	256	7	0.3449
5012	32	256	512	512	10	0.3339
5102	32	128	512	512	7	0.3329
7011	16	256	512	512	7	0.3328
7205	32	256	512	512	14	0.3328

Table 2: Results of tuned single CNN-based translation models on the development set.

phrase at the beginning of a sentence, we add a comma. For example, *"Despite our differences we collaborate well."* A comma should be added after *Despite our differences*.

(3) **Orthography mistakes**. We obtain statistics of named entities that require initial capitalization and make a white list using the Wikipedia corpus. If a word is on the white list, we will force the conversion to the initial capitalization form.

In addition, we use Pyenchant as our spell checker (Kelly, 2006). The top candidate is considered to be the correction.

2.2.4 Ensemble

We use the conflict solver described above to do the ensemble for all of the outputs of the classifiers, rules, spell checker and NMT model.

3 Experiments

3.1 Data Sets

Table 1 lists the data sets used in **Restricted Track** and **Unrestricted Track**, including FCE (Yannakoudakis et al., 2011), Lang-8[2] (Mizumoto et al., 2012), NUCLE (Ng et al., 2014), W&I+LOCNESS (Bryant et al., 2019) and Common Crawl. We use Common Crawl to pretrain the decoder parameters for the Transformer-based translation model. FCE, Lang-8, NUCLE and W&I are used to train all of the translation models.

It is worth noting that we did data augmentation for W&I to train all of the translation models. The data sets used in **Low Resource Track** include Wiked, Wikipedia Dumps and Common Crawl. All of the classifiers are trained on Wikipedia Dumps and the translation model is trained on Wiked corpus. For Wiked corpus, we did some data cleaning work. We discarded some noisy sentences that include error types such as *U:OTHER*, *R:OTHER*, *R:NOUN*, etc. The development set from W&I+LOCNESS are used in all the tracks. Following the data pre-processing pipeline used to generate the data provided by the shared task, we tokenize all of the data using spaCy[3].

3.2 Restricted and Unrestricted Track

3.2.1 CNN-based translation ensemble models

We added the W&I corpus eight times to the training corpus for domain adaptation. Table 2 shows the performance of the single CNN-based translation models. All the parameters in Table 2 are tuned over the W&I+LOCNESS development set.

Table 3 shows the results of the four CNN-based ensemble systems. We use ensembles in the same way as (Chollampatt and Ng, 2018). The above results prove that the ensemble method has yielded a very large improvement in this task.

---

[2] https://lang-8.com

[3] https://spacy.io

Ensemble index	Combination	Precision	Recall	$F_{0.5}$
1	5012,5102,7011,7205	0.5076	0.2195	0.4021
2	5001,5002,5003,5004	0.5003	0.1951	0.3811
3	5005,5012,5102,7205	0.5156	0.2150	0.4029
4	5005,5012,7011,7205	0.5152	0.2159	0.4034

Table 3: Results of CNN-based ensemble systems on the development set.

Model index	Error weight	Copy number of W&I trainset	GPU number	Precision	Recall	$F_{0.5}$
1	3	10	2	0.4585	0.3525	0.4325
2	3	10	4	0.4602	0.3514	0.4333
3	3	8	2	0.4592	0.3575	0.4345
4	3	8	4	0.4641	0.3548	0.4372
5	3	15	2	0.4494	0.3479	0.4247
6	3	15	4	0.4648	0.3467	0.4352
7	2	10	2	0.4715	0.3303	0.4343
8	2	10	4	0.4868	0.3412	0.4485

Table 4: Results of Transformer-based translation models on the development set.

3.2.2 Transformer-based translation models

We trained eight Transformer-based translation models in different combinations of error adaptation, domain adaptation, and GPU set.

In Table 4, we notice that a smaller error weight yields higher precision and a slight decrease in recall. We set the copy number as 8, 10 and 15, and find that domain adaptation has no significant effect on the results. 4 GPU is obviously better than 2 GPU sets, which is probably because of the larger batch size accumulation for gradient calculation.

3.2.3 Ensemble methods

As described in Section 2.1.3, we need to ensemble all of the CNN-based and Transformer-based translation models. We have already introduced the configuration of the single models in Section 3.2.1 and Section 3.2.2. Next we will describe the configuration of the ensemble system.

For the three ensemble types: Ensemble-by-2, EoE and Hybrid Ensemble, as shown in Figure 1, we used different parameters in the conflict solver.

We did a small-scale grid search for the parameters in Table 5. When combining two models that are not strong, we expect a higher recall so β was not high. For EoE and hybrid ensemble, we expect a higher precision so that they can provide high quality single type performance. Corrections proposed by multiple models are given higher weights (controlled by α). If the confidence of a correction

Ensemble method	α	β	γ
Ensemble-by-2	0.2	0.4	-
EoE	0.15	0.8	-
Hybrid ensemble	0.15	0.62	-
Final ensemble	0.0	0.5	0.52

Table 5: Parameters in the conflict solver for the ensemble methods in **Restricted and Unrestricted Track**.

finally reaches β, the correction will be adopted. In the final ensemble, we select the best performance on each type from each single system or ensemble system and discard the corrections with low precision (controlled by β). To get higher $F_{0.5}$, in the case where the precision is greater than a predefined threshold (controlled by γ), we will choose the model with the highest $F_{0.5}$ for the corresponding error type. The final outcome of the data set is then fed through the translation models and ensemble systems again to do a second pass correction.

3.2.4 Results

Table 6 summarizes some results on the development set and gives the official test result. We can see that the individual CNN or Transformer-based translation models perform reasonably well, and the ensemble methods consistently outperform the individual systems. The second pass correction further improves the performance, and the last post-processing step boosts both recall and $F_{0.5}$.

Step	Precision	Recall	$F_{0.5}$
Best CNN-based ensemble model	0.5152	0.2159	0.4034
Best Transformer-based translation model	0.4868	0.3412	0.4485
Best ensemble-by-2	0.5281	0.3434	0.4768
Best hybrid ensemble	0.5885	0.3278	0.5078
+ Combine best performance	0.6283	0.3269	0.5305
+ Second pass	0.6272	0.3412	0.5372
Submission system (+ Post-processing, Dev set)	0.6243	0.3457	0.5376
Submission system (Test set)	0.7317	0.4950	0.6678

Table 6: Results of **Restricted and Unrestricted Track**.

Ensemble method	α	β	γ
Ensemble for all	0.15	0.3	-
Final ensemble	0.0	0.25	0.3

Table 7: Parameters for the ensemble method in **Low Resource Track**.

Table 6 also shows that there is a big gap between the performance on the development set and test set, partly because the final test set uses a combination of five annotators.

3.3 Low Resource Track

3.3.1 Classification models

We trained classifiers for seven error types: Subject-verb agreement, Article, Plural or singular noun, Verb form, Preposition substitution, Missing comma and Period comma substitution and Word form. As mentioned in Subsection 2.2.1, Word form model is trained using the Pointer Context model. The other error types are trained using Bi-GRU Context model.

3.3.2 NMT model

A Transformer-based translation model is trained on the filtered Wiked corpus. The model architecture follows that in (Junczys-Dowmunt et al., 2018). Although the performance of the NMT model is not strong, it provides good performance equivalent to the classifiers for some error types.

3.3.3 Ensemble

We use one conflict solver to combine the outputs from all of the systems in this task. Parameters for this ensemble system are shown in Table 7.

3.3.4 Results

Table 8 shows results for different systems (for classification models, different error type classifiers) on the development set, and the overall re-

Model	Precision	Recall	$F_{0.5}$
Rule	0.4497	0.0216	0.0905
Spelling	0.3188	0.0363	0.1248
Article	0.4367	0.0134	0.0597
Missing comma	0.4729	0.0503	0.1763
Period comma substitution	0.4561	0.0070	0.0328
Plural or singular noun	0.3203	0.0121	0.0524
Preposition substitution	0.3713	0.0101	0.0454
Subject-verb agreement	0.3981	0.0115	0.0517
Verb form	0.4135	0.0074	0.0344
Word form	0.4506	0.0294	0.1164
NMT	0.1279	0.1480	0.1315
Submission system (Dev set)	0.4970	0.1686	0.3577
Submission system (Test set)	0.6201	0.3125	0.5181

Table 8: Results of **Low Resource Track**.

sults on the test set. We can see that the base systems are not very strong, and the ensemble system significantly improves the performance. The difference between the development set and test set can still be observed in this task.

4 Conclusions and Future Work

We have presented two different systems for the three GEC tracks. When there is a sufficient parallel learner corpus, such as in **Restricted Track** and **Unrestricted Track**, the NMT ensemble model is the best choice to implement a GEC system. We have evaluated two kinds of NMT models: CNN-based and Transformer-based translation models. We have also explored different ensemble strategies from multiple base models to maximize the overall system performance. Finally we reached the result of $F_{0.5}$=0.6678 on the official test set in **Restricted Track** and **Unrestricted Track**, ranking the third in the Restricted track[4]. It is worth noting that there is a huge gap between the results on the development set and the test set, which suggests that there might be an unneglectable mismatch between the development set and the test set. Indeed, the development set is annotated by one annotator, while the test set is annotated by five, as announced officially.

For **Low Resource Track**, there is a lack of parallel learner corpus, and thus we rely less on the translation models. We have built eight classifiers trained on Wikipedia dumps according to different error types and an NMT model trained on the Wikipedia edits history corpus. By a simple ensemble method, we reached $F_{0.5}$=0.5181, placing our system in the third place in **Low Resource Track**.

Although GEC has reached the human level performance on some GEC test sets, there is still room for improvement. In a low resource setup, how to deal with the huge but noisy data is worth exploring. (Lichtarge et al., 2019) gave a good solution on this topic, but more work needs to be done. Second, we will investigate methods such as the reinforcement learning based method (Wu et al., 2018) to address the mismatch between the training objectives and evaluation methods in GEC.

References

Piotr Bojanowski, Edouard Grave, Armand Joulin, and Tomas Mikolov. 2017. Enriching word vectors with subword information. *Transactions of the Association for Computational Linguistics*.

Christopher Bryant, Mariano Felice, and Ted Briscoe. 2017. Automatic annotation and evaluation of error types for grammatical error correction.

Christopher Bryant, Mariano Felice, Øistein E. Andersen, and Ted Briscoe. 2019. The BEA-2019 Shared Task on Grammatical Error Correction. In *Proceedings of the 14th Workshop on Innovative Use of NLP for Building Educational Applications*. Association for Computational Linguistics.

Shamil Chollampatt and Hwee Tou Ng. 2018. A multilayer convolutional encoder-decoder neural network for grammatical error correction. *In Proceedings of the 32nd AAAI Conference on Artificial Intelligence*.

Shamil Chollampatt, Kaveh Taghipour, and Hwee Tou Ng. 2016. Neural network translation models for grammatical error correction. *In Proceedings of the 25th International Joint Conference on Artifcial Intelligence*.

Mariano Felice, Zheng Yuan, Øistein E. Andersen, Helen Yannakoudakis, and Ekaterina Kochmar. 2014. Grammatical error correction using hybrid systems and type filtering. *Eighteenth Conference on Computational Natural Language Learning*.

Tao Ge, Furu Wei, and Ming Zhou. 2018. Reaching human-level performance in automatic grammatical error correction: An empirical study. *Microsoft Research Technical Report*.

Jonas Gehring, Michael Auli, David Grangier, Denis Yarats, and Yann N. Dauphin. 2017. Convolutional sequence to sequence learning. *Proceedings of the 34th International Conference on Machine Learning*.

Roman Grundkiewicz and Marcin Junczys-Dowmunt. 2014. The wiked error corpus: A corpus of corrective wikipedia edits and its application to grammatical error correction. In *Advances in Natural Language Processing – Lecture Notes in Computer Science*, volume 8686, pages 478–490. Springer.

Roman Grundkiewicz and Marcin Junczys-Dowmunt. 2018. Near human-level performance in grammatical error correction with hybrid machine translation. *Proceedings of the 2018 Conference of the North American Chapter of the Association for Computational Linguistics*.

Marcin Junczys-Dowmunt and Roman Grundkiewicz. 2016. Phrase-based machine translation is state-of-the-art for automatic grammatical error correction. *The 2016 Conference on Empirical Methods on Natural Language Processing*.

Marcin Junczys-Dowmunt, Roman Grundkiewicz, Shubha Guha, and Kenneth Heafield. 2018. Approaching neural grammatical error correction as a low-resource machine translation task. *Proceedings of the 2018 Conference of the North American Chapter of the Association for Computational Linguistics*.

Ryan Kelly. 2006. *Pyenchant*.

Jared Lichtarge, Christopher Alberti, Shankar Kumar, Noam Shazeer, and Niki Parmar. 2019. Weakly supervised grammatical error correction using iterative decoding.

Tomoya Mizumoto, Yuta Hayashibe, Mamoru Komachi, Masaaki Nagata, and Yu Matsumoto. 2012. The effect of learner corpus size in grammatical error correction of esl writings. *In Proceedings of COLING 2012*.

Daniel Naber and Marcin Miłkowski. 2005. *LanguageTool*.

[4]`https://www.cl.cam.ac.uk/research/nl/bea2019st/#results`

Hwee Tou Ng, Siew Mei Wu, Ted Briscoe, Christian Hadiwinoto, Raymond Hendy Susanto, and Christopher Bryant. 2014. The conll-2014 shared task on grammatical error correction. *Eighteenth Conference on Computational Natural Language Learning.*

Hwee Tou Ng, Siew Mei Wu, Yuanbin Wu, Christian Hadiwinoto, and Joel Tetreault. 2013. The conll-2013 shared task on grammatical error correction. *Seventeenth Conference on Computational Natural Language Learning.*

Alla Rozovskaya, Kai-Wei Chang, Mark Sammons, and Dan Roth. 2013. The university of illinois system in the conll-2013 shared task. *Seventeenth Conference on Computational Natural Language Learning.*

Ashish Vaswani, Noam Shazeer, Niki Parmar, Jakob Uszkoreit, Llion Jones, Aidan N. Gomez, Lukasz Kaiser, and Illia Polosukhin. 2017. Attention is all you need. *31st Conference on Neural Information Processing Systems.*

Oriol Vinyals, Meire Fortunato, and Navdeep Jaitly. 2015. Pointer networks. *Proceedings of the 28th International Conference on Neural Information Processing Systems.*

Chuan Wang, RuoBing Li, and Hui Lin. 2017. Deep context model for grammatical error correction. *Proceedings of the Seventh ISCA workshop on Speech and Language Technology in Education 2017.*

Lijun Wu, Fei Tian, Tao Qin, Jianhuang Lai, and Tie-Yan Liu. 2018. A study of reinforcement learning for neural machine translation. *Proceedings of the 2018 Conference on Empirical Methods in Natural Language Processing.*

Helen Yannakoudakis, Ted Briscoe, and Ben Medlock. 2011. A new dataset and method for automatically grading esol texts. *In Proceedings of the 49th Annual Meeting of the Association for Computational Linguistics: Human Language Technologies.*

Wei Zhao, Liang Wang, Kewei Shen, Ruoyu Jia, and Jingming Liu. 2019. Improving grammatical error correction via pre-training a copy-augmented architecture with unlabeled data. *Proceedings of the 2019 Conference of the North American Chapter of the Association for Computational Linguistics.*

The CUED's Grammatical Error Correction Systems for BEA-2019

Felix Stahlberg and **Bill Byrne**
Department of Engineering
University of Cambridge
Trumpington St, Cambridge CB2 1PZ, UK
{fs439,wjb31}@cam.ac.uk

Abstract

We describe two entries from the Cambridge University Engineering Department to the BEA 2019 Shared Task on grammatical error correction. Our submission to the low-resource track is based on prior work on using finite state transducers together with strong neural language models. Our system for the restricted track is a purely neural system consisting of neural language models and neural machine translation models trained with back-translation and a combination of checkpoint averaging and fine-tuning – without the help of any additional tools like spell checkers. The latter system has been used inside a separate system combination entry in cooperation with the Cambridge University Computer Lab.

1 Introduction

The automatic correction of errors in text [*In a such situaction* → *In such a situation*] is receiving more and more attention from the natural language processing community. A series of competitions has been devoted to grammatical error correction (GEC): the CoNLL-2013 shared task (Ng et al., 2013), the CoNLL-2014 shared task (Ng et al., 2014), and finally the BEA 2019 shared task (Bryant et al., 2019). This paper presents the contributions from the Cambridge University Engineering Department to the latest GEC competition at the BEA 2019 workshop.

We submitted systems to two different tracks. The *low-resource track* did not permit the use of parallel training data except a small development set with around 4K sentence pairs. For our low-resource system we extended our prior work on finite state transducer based GEC (Stahlberg et al., 2019) to handle new error types such as punctuation errors as well as insertions and deletions of a small number of frequent words. For the *restricted track*, the organizers provided 1.2M

pairs (560K without identity mappings) of corrected and uncorrected sentences. Our goal on the restricted track was to explore the potential of purely neural models for grammatical error correction.[1] We confirm the results of Kasewa et al. (2018) and report substantial gains by applying back-translation (Sennrich et al., 2016b) to GEC – a data augmentation technique common in machine translation. Furthermore, we noticed that large parts of the training data do not match the target domain. We mitigated the domain gap by over-sampling the in-domain training corpus, and by fine-tuning through continued training. Our final model is an ensemble of four neural machine translation (NMT) models and two neural language models (LMs) with Transformer architecture (Vaswani et al., 2017). Our purely neural system was also part of the joint submission with the Cambridge University Computer Lab described by Yuan et al. (2019).

2 Low-resource Track Submission

2.1 FST-based Grammatical Error Correction

Stahlberg et al. (2019) investigated the use of finite state transducers (FSTs) for neural grammatical error correction. They proposed a cascade of FST compositions to construct a hypothesis space which is then rescored with a neural language model. We will outline this approach and explain our modifications in this section. For more details we refer to (Stahlberg et al., 2019).

In a first step, the source sentence is converted to an FST I (Fig. 1). This initial FST is augmented by composition (denoted with the ∘-operator) with various other FSTs to cover different error types. Composition is a widely used standard operation

---

[1]Models will be published at http://ucam-smt.github.io/sgnmt/html/bea19_gec.html.

Proceedings of the Fourteenth Workshop on Innovative Use of NLP for Building Educational Applications, pages 168–175
Florence, Italy, August 2, 2019. ©2019 Association for Computational Linguistics

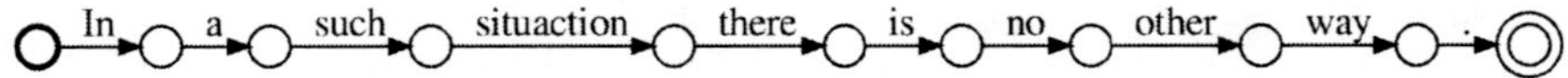

Figure 1: Input FST I representing the source sentence 'In a such situation there is no other way.'. We follow standard convention and highlight the start state in bold and the final state with a double circle.

Figure 2: Deletion FST D which can map any token in the list R from Tab. 1 to ϵ. The σ-label matches any symbol and maps it to itself.

Deletion Frequency (dev set)	Token
164	the
78	,
50	a
33	to
20	it
18	of
16	in
12	that
8	will
8	have
8	for
8	an
7	is
7	-
6	they
6	's
6	and
5	had

Table 1: List of tokens R that can be deleted by the deletion transducer D in Fig. 2.

on FSTs and supported efficiently by FST toolkits such as OpenFST (Allauzen et al., 2007). We construct the hypothesis space as follows:[2]

1. We compose the input I with the deletion transducer D in Fig. 2. D allows to delete tokens on the short list shown in Tab. 1 at a cost λ_{del}. We selected R by looking up all tokens which have been deleted in the dev set more than five times and manually filtered that list slightly. We did not use the full list of dev set deletions to avoid under-estimating λ_{del} in tuning.

2. In a next step, we compose the transducer from step 1 with the edit transducer E in Fig. 3. This step addresses substitution errors such as spelling or morphology errors.

<hr>

[2]Note that our description differs from (Stahlberg et al., 2019) in the following ways: First, we use additional FSTs to allow insertions and deletions. Second, we integrate penalties directly into the FSTs rather than using special tokens in combination with a penalization transducer.

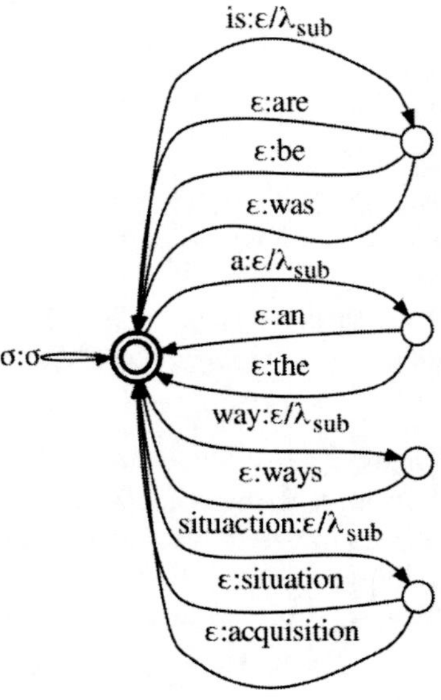

Figure 3: Edit FST E which allows substitutions with a cost of λ_{sub}. The σ-label matches any symbol and maps it to itself at no cost.

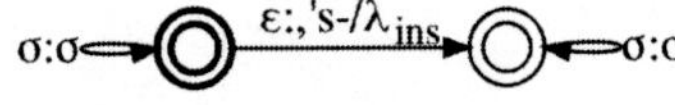

Figure 4: Insertion FST A for adding the symbols ",", "-", and "'s" at a cost of λ_{ins}. The σ-label matches any symbol and maps it to itself at no cost.

Like Stahlberg et al. (2019), we use the confusion sets of Bryant and Briscoe (2018) based on CyHunspell for spell checking (Rodriguez and Seal, 2014), the AGID morphology database for morphology errors (Atkinson, 2011), and manually defined corrections for determiner and preposition errors to construct E. Additionally, we extracted all substitution errors from the BEA-2019 dev set which occurred more than five times, and added a small number of manually defined rules that fix tokenization around punctuation symbols.

3. We found it challenging to allow insertions in LM-based GEC because the LM often prefers inserting words with high unigram probability such as articles and prepositions before

Sub	Del	Ins	LM	Beam	CoNLL-2014			BEA-2019 Dev		
					P	R	M2	P	R	ERRANT
Best published: Stahlberg et al. (2019)					54.12	25.52	44.21		n/a	
✓			1x	8	58.59	24.14	45.58	42.44	14.68	30.79
✓	✓		1x	8	59.01	26.07	47.11	41.21	16.47	31.69
✓	✓	✓	1x	8	52.89	26.68	44.20	40.09	19.97	33.36
✓	✓	✓	2x	8	54.05	26.71	44.87	40.70	20.01	33.73
✓	✓	✓	2x	16	57.05	27.22	46.80	42.02	19.76	34.29
✓	✓	✓	2x	32	58.48	28.21	48.15	42.37	19.92	34.58

Table 2: Results on the low-resource track. The λ-parameters are tuned on the BEA-2019 dev set.

less predictable words like proper names. We therefore restrict insertions to the three tokens ",", "-", and "'s" and allow only one insertion per sentence. We achieve this by adding the transducer A in Fig. 4 to our composition cascade.

4. Finally, we map the word-level FSTs to the subword-level by composition with a mapping transducer T that applies byte pair encoding (Sennrich et al., 2016c, BPE) to the full words. Word-to-BPE mapping transducers have been used in prior work to combine word-level models with subword-level neural sequence models (Stahlberg et al., 2019, 2017b, 2018b, 2017a).

In a more condensed form, we can describe the final transducer as:

$$I \circ D \circ E \circ A \circ T \tag{1}$$

with D for deletions, E for substitutions, A for insertions, and T for converting words to BPE tokens. Path scores in the FST in Eq. 1 are the accumulated penalties λ_{del}, λ_{sub}, and λ_{ins}. The λ-parameters are tuned on the dev set using a variant of Powell search (Powell, 1964). We apply standard FST operations like output projection, ϵ-removal, determinization, minimization, and weight pushing (Mohri, 1997; Mohri and Riley, 2001) to help downstream decoding. Following Stahlberg et al. (2019) we then use the resulting transducer to constrain a neural LM beam decoder.

2.2 Experimental Setup

Our LMs are Transformer (Vaswani et al., 2017) decoders (`transformer_big`) trained using the Tensor2Tensor library (Vaswani et al., 2018). We delay SGD updates (Stahlberg et al., 2018a; Saunders et al., 2018) with factor 2 to simulate 500K training steps with 8 GPUs on 4 physical GPUs. Training batches contain about 4K source and target tokens. Our LM training set comprises the monolingual *news2015-news2018* English training sets[3] from the WMT evaluation campaigns (Bojar et al., 2018) after language detection (Nakatani, 2010) (138M sentences) and subword segmentation using byte pair encoding (Sennrich et al., 2016c) with 32K merge operations. For decoding, we use our SGNMT tool (Stahlberg et al., 2017b, 2018b) with Open-FST backend (Allauzen et al., 2007).

2.3 Results

We report M2 (Dahlmeier and Ng, 2012) scores on the CoNLL-2014 test set (Ng et al., 2014) and span-based ERRANT scores (Bryant et al., 2017) on the BEA-2019 dev set (Bryant et al., 2019). On CoNLL-2014 we compare with the best published results with comparable amount of parallel training data. We refer to (Bryant et al., 2019) for a full comparison of BEA-2019 systems. We tune our systems on BEA-2019 and only report the performance on CoNLL-2014 for comparison to prior work.

Tab. 2 summarizes our low-resource experiments. Our substitution-only system already outperforms the prior work of Stahlberg et al. (2019). Allowing for deletions and insertions improves the ERRANT score on BEA-2019 Dev by 2.57 points. We report further gains on both test sets by ensembling two language models and increasing the beam size.

2.4 Differences Between CoNLL-2014 and BEA-2019 Dev

Our results in Tab. 2 differ significantly between the CoNLL-2014 test set and the BEA-2019 dev set. Allowing insertions is beneficial on BEA-2019 Dev but decreases the M2 score on CoNLL-2014. Increasing the beam size improves our system by 3.28 points on CoNLL-2014 while the im-

---

[3] `http://www.statmt.org/wmt19/translation-task.html`

	Per Sentence		Per Word	
	CoNLL	**BEA**	**CoNLL**	**BEA**
Missing	0.35	0.46	1.51%	2.30%
Replacement	1.52	1.31	6.62%	6.57%
Unnecessary	0.42	0.19	1.83%	0.98%
Total	2.29	1.96	9.95%	9.86%

Table 3: Number of correction types in CoNLL-2014 and BEA-2019 Dev references.

	BASE	BIG
T2T HParams set	trans._base	trans._big
# physical GPUs	4	4
Batch size	4,192	2,048
SGD delay factor	2	4
# training iterations	300K	400K
Beam size	4	8

Table 4: NMT setups BASE and BIG used in our experiments for the restricted track.

	Number of Sentences	
	With Identities	**W/o Identities**
FCE	28K	18K
Lang-8	1,038K	498K
NUCLE	57K	21K
W&I+LOCNESS	34K	23K
Total	1,157K	560K

Table 5: BEA-2019 parallel training data with and without removing pairs where source and target sentences are the same.

pact on BEA-2019 Dev is smaller (+0.85 points). These differences can be partially explained by comparing the error type frequencies in the reference annotations in both test sets (Tab. 3). Samples in CoNLL-2014 generally need more corrections per sentence than in BEA-2019 Dev. More importantly, the CoNLL-2014 test set contains fewer missing words, but much more unnecessary words than BEA-2019 Dev. This mismatch tempers with tuning as we explicitly tune insertion and deletion penalties.

3 Restricted Track Submission

In contrast to our low-resource submission, our restricted system entirely relies on neural models and does not use any external NLP tools, spell checkers, or hand-crafted confusion sets. For simplicity, we also chose to use standard implementations (Vaswani et al., 2018) of standard Transformer (Vaswani et al., 2017) models with standard hyper-parameters. This makes our final system easy to deploy as it is a simple ensemble of standard neural models with minimal preprocessing (subword segmentation). Our contributions on this track focus on NMT training techniques such as over-sampling, back-translation, and fine-tuning. We show that over-sampling effectively reduces domain mismatch. We found back-translation (Sennrich et al., 2016b) to be a very effective technique to utilize unannotated training data. However, while over-sampling is commonly used in machine translation to balance the number of real and back-translated training sentences, we report that using over-sampling this way for GEC hurts performance. Finally, we propose a combination of checkpoint averaging (Junczys-Dowmunt et al., 2016) and continued training to adapt our NMT models to the target domain.

3.1 Experimental Setup

We use neural LMs and neural machine translation (NMT) models in our restricted track entry.

Our neural LM is as described in Sec. 2.2. Our LMs and NMT models share the same subword segmentation. We perform exploratory NMT experiments with the BASE setup, but switch to the BIG setup for our final models. Tab. 4 shows the differences between both setups. Tab. 5 lists some corpus statistics for the BEA-2019 training sets. In our experiments without fine-tuning we decode with the average of the 20 most recent checkpoints (Junczys-Dowmunt et al., 2016). We use the SGNMT decoder (Stahlberg et al., 2017b, 2018b) in all our experiments.

In-domain corpus over-sampling The BEA-2019 training corpora (Tab. 5) differ significantly not only in size but also their closeness to the target domain. The W&I+LOCNESS corpus is most similar to the BEA-2019 dev and test sets in terms of domains and the distribution over English language proficiency, but only consists of 34K sentence pairs. To increase the importance of in-domain training samples we over-sampled the W&I+LOCNESS corpus with different rates. Tab. 6 shows that over-sampling by factor 4 (i.e. adding the W&I+LOCNESS corpus four times to the training set) improves the ERRAMT $F_{0.5}$-score by 2.2 points on the BEA-2019 dev set and does not lead to substantial losses on the CoNLL-2014 test set. We will over-sample the W&I+LOCNESS corpus by four in all subsequent experiments.

Removing identity mappings Previous works often suggested to remove unchanged sentences

W&I+LOCNESS Over-sampling Rate	Ratio	CoNLL-2014			BEA-2019 Dev		
		P	R	M2	P	R	ERRANT
1x	1:33	59.88	17.46	40.30	38.20	15.09	29.24
4x	1:8	59.16	17.20	39.76	40.40	16.67	31.44
8x	1:4	57.73	17.76	39.81	39.19	16.73	30.90

Table 6: Over-sampling the BEA-2019 in-domain corpus W&I+LOCNESS under BASE models. The second column contains the ratio of W&I+LOCNESS samples to training samples from the other corpora.

Identity Removal	CoNLL-2014			BEA-2019 Dev		
	P	R	M2	P	R	ERR.
✗	59.16	17.20	39.76	40.40	16.67	31.44
✓	53.34	28.83	45.59	33.04	23.14	30.44

Table 7: Impact of identity removal on BASE models.

(i.e. source and target sentences are equal) from the training corpora (Stahlberg et al., 2019; Zhao et al., 2019; Grundkiewicz and Junczys-Dowmunt, 2018). We note that removing these identity mappings can be seen as measure to control the balance between precision and recall. As shown in Tab. 7, removing identities encourages the model to make more corrections and thus leads to higher recall but lower precision. It depends on the test set whether this results in an improvement in $F_{0.5}$ score. For the subsequent experiments we found that removing identities in the parallel training corpora but not in the back-translated synthetic data works well in practice.

Back-translation Back-translation (Sennrich et al., 2016b) has become the most widely used technique to use monolingual data in neural machine translation. Back-translation extends the existing parallel training set by additional training samples with real English target sentences but synthetic source sentences. Different methods have been proposed to synthesize the source sentence such as using dummy tokens (Sennrich et al., 2016b), copying the target sentence (Currey et al., 2017), or sampling from or decoding with a reverse sequence-to-sequence model (Sennrich et al., 2016b; Edunov et al., 2018; Kasewa et al.,

2018). The most popular approach is to generate the synthetic source sentences with a reverse model that is trained to transform target to source sentences using beam search. In GEC, this means that the reverse model learns to introduce errors into a correct English sentence. Back-translation has been applied successfully to GEC by Kasewa et al. (2018). We confirm the effectiveness of back-translation in GEC and discuss some of the differences between applying this technique to grammatical error correction and machine translation.

Our experiments with back-translation are summarized in Tab. 8. Adding 1M synthetic sentences to the training data already yields very substantial gains on both test sets. We achieve our best results with 5M synthetic sentences (+8.44 on BEA-2019 Dev). In machine translation, it is important to maintain a balance between authentic and synthetic data (Sennrich et al., 2016b; Poncelas et al., 2018; Sennrich et al., 2016a). Over-sampling the real data is a common practice to rectify that ratio if large amounts of synthetic data are available. Interestingly, over-sampling real data in GEC hurts performance (row 3 vs. 5 in Tab. 8), and it is possible to mix real and synthetic sentences at a ratio of 1:7.9 (last three rows in Tab. 8). We will proceed with the 5M setup for the remainder of this paper.

Fine-tuning As explained previously, we over-sample the W&I+LOCNESS corpus by factor 4 to mitigate the domain gap between the training set and the BEA-2019 dev and test sets. To further adapt our system to the target domain, we fine-

Over-sampling Rate (Real Data)	Number of Synthetic Sentences	Ratio	CoNLL-2014			BEA-2019 Dev		
			P	R	M2	P	R	ERRANT
1x	0	-	53.34	28.83	45.59	33.04	23.14	30.44
1x	1M	1:1.6	56.17	31.30	48.47	37.79	23.86	33.84
1x	3M	1:4.8	61.40	34.29	53.02	42.62	25.30	37.49
1x	5M	1:7.9	64.18	34.27	54.64	44.69	25.59	38.88
3x	3M	1:1.6	57.12	32.55	49.63	40.08	24.79	35.68
6x	5M	1:1.3	59.15	33.99	51.52	41.52	25.05	36.69

Table 8: Using back-translation for GEC (BASE models). The third column contains the ratio between real and synthetic sentence pairs.

Fine-tuning (Continued Training)	Checkpoint Averaging	CoNLL-2014			BEA-2019 Dev		
		P	R	M2	P	R	ERRANT
		63.61	33.39	53.86	44.16	25.01	38.29
	✓	64.18	34.27	54.64	44.69	25.59	38.88
✓		64.98	33.05	54.46	48.62	27.19	42.00
✓	✓	66.03	34.17	55.65	48.99	26.87	42.06

Table 9: Fine-tuning through continued training on W&I+LOCNESS and checkpoint averaging with a BASE model with 5M back-translated sentences.

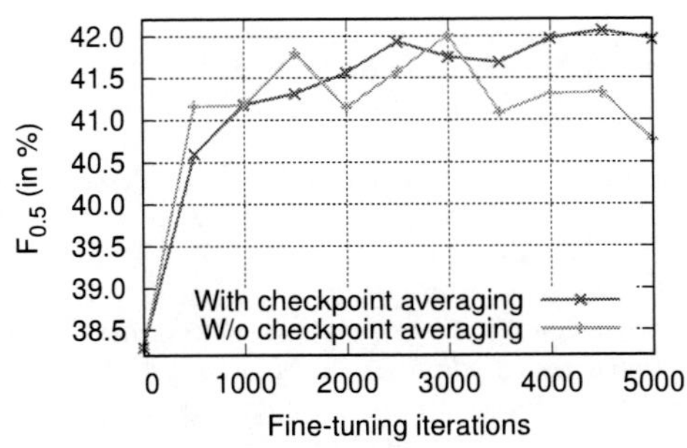

Figure 5: Span-based ERRANT $F_{0.5}$ scores on the BEA-2019 dev set over the number of fine-tuning training iterations (single GPU, SGD delay factor (Saunders et al., 2018) of 16).

tune the NMT models on W&I+LOCNESS after convergence on the full training set. We do that by continuing training on W&I+LOCNESS from the last checkpoint of the first training pass. Fig. 5 plots the $F_{0.5}$ score on the BEA-2019 dev set for two different setups. For the red curve, we average all checkpoints (Junczys-Dowmunt et al., 2016) (including the last unadapted checkpoint) up to a certain training iteration. Checkpoints are dumped every 500 steps. The green curve does not use any checkpoint averaging. Checkpoint averaging helps to smooth out fluctuations in $F_{0.5}$ score, and also generalizes better to CoNLL-2014 (Tab. 9).

Final system   Tab. 10 contains our experiments with the BIG configuration. In addition to W&I+LOCNESS over-sampling, back-translation with 5M sentences, and fine-tuning with checkpoint averaging, we report further gains by adding

the language models from our low-resource system (Sec. 2.2) and ensembling. Our best system (4 NMT models, 2 language models) achieves 58.9 M2 on CoNLL-2014, which is slightly (2.25 points) worse than the best published result on that test set (Zhao et al., 2019). However, we note that we have tailored our system towards the BEA-2019 dev set and not the CoNLL-2013 or CoNLL-2014 test sets. As we argued in Sec. 2.4, our results throughout this work suggest strongly that the optimal system parameters for these test sets are very different from each other, and that our final system settings are not optimal for CoNLL-2014. We also note that unlike the system of Zhao et al. (2019), our system for the restricted track does not use spell checkers or other NLP tools but relies solely on neural sequence models.

4   Conclusion

We participated in the BEA 2019 Shared Task on grammatical error correction with submissions to the low-resource and the restricted track. Our low-resource system is an extension of prior work on FST-based GEC (Stahlberg et al., 2019) to allow insertions and deletions. Our restricted track submission is a purely neural system based on standard NMT and LM architectures. We pointed out the similarity between GEC and machine translation, and demonstrated that several techniques which originate from MT research such as over-sampling, back-translation, and fine-tuning, are also useful for GEC. Our models have been used in a joint submission with the Cambridge University Computer Lab (Yuan et al., 2019).

NMT	Fine-tuning	LM	CoNLL-2014			BEA-2019 Dev		
			P	R	M2	P	R	ERRANT
Best published: Zhao et al. (2019)			71.57	38.65	61.15		n/a	
1x			64.04	35.74	55.28	45.86	26.46	40.00
1x	✓		66.57	35.21	56.50	51.57	27.49	43.88
1x	✓	2x	61.53	40.44	55.72	48.30	33.08	44.23
4x	✓		70.37	35.12	58.60	55.84	27.80	46.47
4x	✓	2x	66.89	39.85	58.90	53.17	32.89	47.34

Table 10: Final results on the restricted track with BIG models and back-translation.

Acknowledgments

This work was supported by the U.K. Engineering and Physical Sciences Research Council (EPSRC) grant EP/L027623/1 and has been performed using resources provided by the Cambridge Tier-2 system operated by the University of Cambridge Research Computing Service[4] funded by EPSRC Tier-2 capital grant EP/P020259/1.

References

Cyril Allauzen, Michael Riley, Johan Schalkwyk, Wojciech Skut, and Mehryar Mohri. 2007. OpenFst: A general and efficient weighted finite-state transducer library. In *Implementation and Application of Automata*, pages 11–23. Springer.

Kevin Atkinson. 2011. Automatically generated inflection database (AGID). `http://wordlist.aspell.net/other/`. [Online; accessed 24 April 2019].

Ondřej Bojar, Christian Federmann, Mark Fishel, Yvette Graham, Barry Haddow, Philipp Koehn, and Christof Monz. 2018. Findings of the 2018 conference on machine translation (WMT18). In *Proceedings of the Third Conference on Machine Translation: Shared Task Papers*, pages 272–303, Belgium, Brussels. Association for Computational Linguistics.

Christopher Bryant and Ted Briscoe. 2018. Language model based grammatical error correction without annotated training data. In *Proceedings of the Thirteenth Workshop on Innovative Use of NLP for Building Educational Applications*, pages 247–253. Association for Computational Linguistics.

Christopher Bryant, Mariano Felice, Øistein E. Andersen, and Ted Briscoe. 2019. The BEA-2019 shared task on grammatical error correction. In *Proceedings of the 14th Workshop on Innovative Use of NLP for Building Educational Applications*. Association for Computational Linguistics.

Christopher Bryant, Mariano Felice, and Ted Briscoe. 2017. Automatic annotation and evaluation of error types for grammatical error correction. In *Proceedings of the 55th Annual Meeting of the Association for Computational Linguistics (Volume 1: Long Papers)*, pages 793–805. Association for Computational Linguistics.

Anna Currey, Antonio Valerio Miceli Barone, and Kenneth Heafield. 2017. Copied monolingual data improves low-resource neural machine translation. In *Proceedings of the Second Conference on Machine Translation*, pages 148–156, Copenhagen, Denmark. Association for Computational Linguistics.

Daniel Dahlmeier and Hwee Tou Ng. 2012. Better evaluation for grammatical error correction. In *Proceedings of the 2012 Conference of the North American Chapter of the Association for Computational Linguistics: Human Language Technologies*, pages 568–572. Association for Computational Linguistics.

Sergey Edunov, Myle Ott, Michael Auli, and David Grangier. 2018. Understanding back-translation at scale. In *Proceedings of the 2018 Conference on Empirical Methods in Natural Language Processing*, pages 489–500, Brussels, Belgium. Association for Computational Linguistics.

Roman Grundkiewicz and Marcin Junczys-Dowmunt. 2018. Near human-level performance in grammatical error correction with hybrid machine translation. In *Proceedings of the 2018 Conference of the North American Chapter of the Association for Computational Linguistics: Human Language Technologies, Volume 2 (Short Papers)*, pages 284–290. Association for Computational Linguistics.

Marcin Junczys-Dowmunt, Tomasz Dwojak, and Hieu Hoang. 2016. Is neural machine translation ready for deployment? A case study on 30 translation directions. In *International Workshop on Spoken Language Translation IWSLT*.

Sudhanshu Kasewa, Pontus Stenetorp, and Sebastian Riedel. 2018. Wronging a right: Generating better errors to improve grammatical error detection. In *Proceedings of the 2018 Conference on Empirical Methods in Natural Language Processing*, pages 4977–4983, Brussels, Belgium. Association for Computational Linguistics.

Mehryar Mohri. 1997. Finite-state transducers in language and speech processing. *Computational Linguistics*, 23(2).

Mehryar Mohri and Michael Riley. 2001. A weight pushing algorithm for large vocabulary speech recognition. In *Seventh European Conference on Speech Communication and Technology*.

Shuyo Nakatani. 2010. Language detection library for Java. [Online; accessed 24 April 2019].

Hwee Tou Ng, Siew Mei Wu, Ted Briscoe, Christian Hadiwinoto, Raymond Hendy Susanto, and Christopher Bryant. 2014. The CoNLL-2014 shared task on grammatical error correction. In *Proceedings of the Eighteenth Conference on Computational Natural Language Learning: Shared Task*, pages 1–14. Association for Computational Linguistics.

Hwee Tou Ng, Siew Mei Wu, Yuanbin Wu, Christian Hadiwinoto, and Joel Tetreault. 2013. The CoNLL-2013 shared task on grammatical error correction. In *Proceedings of the Seventeenth Conference on Computational Natural Language Learning: Shared Task*, pages 1–12. Association for Computational Linguistics.

[4] `http://www.hpc.cam.ac.uk`

Alberto Poncelas, Dimitar Shterionov, Andy Way, Gideon Maillette de Buy Wenniger, and Peyman Passban. 2018. Investigating backtranslation in neural machine translation. *arXiv preprint arXiv:1804.06189.*

Michael JD Powell. 1964. An efficient method for finding the minimum of a function of several variables without calculating derivatives. *The computer journal*, 7(2):155–162.

Tim Rodriguez and Matthew Seal. 2014. Cy-Hunspell. https://github.com/MSeal/cython_hunspell. [Online; accessed 24 April 2019].

Danielle Saunders, Felix Stahlberg, Adrià de Gispert, and Bill Byrne. 2018. Multi-representation ensembles and delayed SGD updates improve syntax-based NMT. In *Proceedings of the 56th Annual Meeting of the Association for Computational Linguistics (Volume 2: Short Papers)*, pages 319–325, Melbourne, Australia. Association for Computational Linguistics.

Rico Sennrich, Barry Haddow, and Alexandra Birch. 2016a. Edinburgh neural machine translation systems for WMT 16. In *Proceedings of the First Conference on Machine Translation*, pages 371–376, Berlin, Germany. Association for Computational Linguistics.

Rico Sennrich, Barry Haddow, and Alexandra Birch. 2016b. Improving neural machine translation models with monolingual data. In *Proceedings of the 54th Annual Meeting of the Association for Computational Linguistics (Volume 1: Long Papers)*, pages 86–96, Berlin, Germany. Association for Computational Linguistics.

Rico Sennrich, Barry Haddow, and Alexandra Birch. 2016c. Neural machine translation of rare words with subword units. In *Proceedings of the 54th Annual Meeting of the Association for Computational Linguistics (Volume 1: Long Papers)*, pages 1715–1725. Association for Computational Linguistics.

Felix Stahlberg, Christopher Bryant, and Bill Byrne. 2019. Neural grammatical error correction with finite state transducers. In *Proceedings of the 2019 Conference of the North American Chapter of the Association for Computational Linguistics*. Association for Computational Linguistics.

Felix Stahlberg, Adrià de Gispert, and Bill Byrne. 2018a. The University of Cambridge's machine translation systems for WMT18. In *Proceedings of the Third Conference on Machine Translation: Shared Task Papers*, pages 504–512, Belgium, Brussels. Association for Computational Linguistics.

Felix Stahlberg, Adrià de Gispert, Eva Hasler, and Bill Byrne. 2017a. Neural machine translation by minimising the Bayes-risk with respect to syntactic translation lattices. In *Proceedings of the 15th Conference of the European Chapter of the Association for Computational Linguistics: Volume 2, Short Papers*, pages 362–368, Valencia, Spain. Association for Computational Linguistics.

Felix Stahlberg, Eva Hasler, Danielle Saunders, and Bill Byrne. 2017b. SGNMT – A flexible NMT decoding platform for quick prototyping of new models and search strategies. In *Proceedings of the 2017 Conference on Empirical Methods in Natural Language Processing: System Demonstrations*, pages 25–30. Association for Computational Linguistics.

Felix Stahlberg, Danielle Saunders, Gonzalo Iglesias, and Bill Byrne. 2018b. Why not be versatile? Applications of the SGNMT decoder for machine translation. In *Proceedings of the 13th Conference of the Association for Machine Translation in the Americas (Volume 1: Research Papers)*, pages 208–216. Association for Machine Translation in the Americas.

Ashish Vaswani, Samy Bengio, Eugene Brevdo, Francois Chollet, Aidan Gomez, Stephan Gouws, Llion Jones, Łukasz Kaiser, Nal Kalchbrenner, Niki Parmar, Ryan Sepassi, Noam Shazeer, and Jakob Uszkoreit. 2018. Tensor2tensor for neural machine translation. In *Proceedings of the 13th Conference of the Association for Machine Translation in the Americas (Volume 1: Research Papers)*, pages 193–199, Boston, MA. Association for Machine Translation in the Americas.

Ashish Vaswani, Noam Shazeer, Niki Parmar, Jakob Uszkoreit, Llion Jones, Aidan N Gomez, Łukasz Kaiser, and Illia Polosukhin. 2017. Attention is all you need. In *Advances in Neural Information Processing Systems*, pages 5998–6008.

Zheng Yuan, Felix Stahlberg, Marek Rei, Bill Byrne, and Helen Yannakoudakis. 2019. Neural and FST-based approaches to grammatical error correction. In *Proceedings of the 14th workshop on innovative use of NLP for building educational applications*. Association for Computational Linguistics.

Wei Zhao, Liang Wang, Kewei Shen, Ruoyu Jia, and Jingming Liu. 2019. Improving grammatical error correction via pre-training a copy-augmented architecture with unlabeled data. In *Proceedings of the 2019 Conference of the North American Chapter of the Association for Computational Linguistics*. Association for Computational Linguistics.

The AIP-Tohoku System at the BEA-2019 Shared Task

Hiroki Asano[12]*, **Masato Mita**[21], **Tomoya Mizumoto**[21]†, and **Jun Suzuki**[12]

[1] Graduate School of Information Sciences, Tohoku University
[2] RIKEN Center for Advanced Intelligence Project
`asano@ecei.tohoku.ac.jp, masato.mita@riken.jp`
`tomoya.mizumoto@riken.jp, jun.suzuki@ecei.tohoku.ac.jp`

Abstract

We introduce the AIP-Tohoku grammatical error correction (GEC) system for the BEA-2019 shared task in Track 1 (Restricted Track) and Track 2 (Unrestricted Track) using the same system architecture. Our system comprises two key components: error generation and sentence-level error detection. In particular, GEC with sentence-level grammatical error detection is a novel and versatile approach, and we experimentally demonstrate that it significantly improves the precision of the base model. Our system is ranked 9th in Track 1 and 2nd in Track 2.

1 Introduction

As part of the BEA-2019 shared task, we participated in Track 1 (Restricted Track) and Track 2 (Unrestricted Track). We utilized the Transformer (Vaswani et al., 2017) architecture as a base GEC model for machine translation systems as it has become a state-of-the-art approach for grammatical error correction (GEC).

In our system, the error correction model collaborates with a sentence-level error detection model. In GEC, $F_{0.5}$ is used for evaluation because precision is more important than recall. To improve the precision score on the test set, our system corrected the input sentences by detecting errors using a sentence-level error detection model (which we denote as SED). We applied the bidirectional encoder representations from transformers (BERT) model (Devlin et al., 2018) for sentence-level error detection. In order to improve the performance of SED, we propose an SED model taking the learner's proficiency into

account. To the best of our knowledge, this is the first study that has combined GEC with SED.

Because grammatical correctness is required for output sentences in GEC, the target side of parallel training corpora should not contain noisy sentences. Our correction model is trained to correct sentence pairs, which were identified by our sentence-level grammatical error detection model. We call this data cleaning process BERT-Cleaning.

For Track 1, similar to back-translation (Sennrich et al., 2016b; Edunov et al., 2018), we augmented the parallel training corpus with errors generated from monolingual data. After addition of the generated data and SED process, the $F_{0.5}$ score on the base model improved.

For Track 2, we used the EF-Cambridge Open Language Database (EFCAMDAT) (Geertzen et al., 2013) and non-public Lang-8 as the external language learner corpus.

2 Related Work

2.1 Error Detection

The field of grammatical error detection (GED) has a long history. Many previous studies have treated GED as a token-level binary classification task (Tetreault and Chodorow, 2008; Han et al., 2006; Chodorow et al., 2012; Rei and Yannakoudakis, 2016; Rei et al., 2016; Rei, 2017). Kaneko et al. (2017) improved grammatical error detection by learning word embeddings that consider grammaticality and error patterns. Yannakoudakis et al. (2017) propose an approach to N-best list re-ranking using neural sequence-labelling models.

While many studies in GED focus on token-level error detection, there are studies that perform sentence-level binary classification of sentences that need some editing (Han et al., 2006; Tetreault and Chodorow, 2008; Chodorow et al., 2012;

---

* Current affiliation: Yahoo Japan Corporation, hiroasan@yahoo-corp.jp

† Current affiliation: Future Corporation, mizumoto.tomoya.mh7@is.naist.jp

Proceedings of the Fourteenth Workshop on Innovative Use of NLP for Building Educational Applications, pages 176–182
Florence, Italy, August 2, 2019. ©2019 Association for Computational Linguistics

Schmaltz et al., 2016). Compared with token-level grammatical error correction, sentence-level grammatical error correction is a simple problem setting because there is no need to identify the location of errors.

2.2 Error Generation

In the field of machine translation, back-translation is an effective method for neural machine translation systems (Sennrich et al., 2016b; Imamura et al., 2018). Edunov et al. (2018) reported that back-translation obtained via sampling or noised beam outputs is effective for neural machine translation systems.

Recently, back-translation has been applied to grammatical error detection and correction. Rei et al. (2017) proposed artificial error generation with statistical machine translation and syntactic patterns for error detection. Kasewa et al. (2018) constructed synthetic samples using a seq2seq neural model with greedy search and temperature sampling for error detection. Xie et al. (2018) proposed certain noising methods for error generation, and Ge et al. (2018) proposed back-boost learning using fluency scores.

3 System Architecture

3.1 Base Correction Model

We used Transformer, the self-attention-based translation model, as a base GEC system (Vaswani et al., 2017). Some previous studies used Transformer to achieve high performance (Junczys-Dowmunt et al., 2018; Zhao et al., 2019).

3.2 Sentence-level Error Detection

3.2.1 Motivation

The sentence-level error detection (SED) module is one of the key components of our system, with the goal of detecting sentences with grammatical errors. The aim of introducing SED is to reduce false positive by passing only sentences that contain errors to the GEC model. We calculated the rate of a sentence that changes in the W&I+LOCNESS development set and found it to be 64.34%, i.e., almost 35% of the sentences did not require corrections.

3.2.2 Base Model

We built a base SED model using BERT (Devlin et al., 2018), which is a straightforward extension of sequence classification tasks such as

CoLA (Warstadt et al., 2018) and SST-2 (Socher et al., 2013). For setting up a training set for the base SED model, we preprocessed it to obtain binary labeled data (e.g., 0 for correct and 1 for incorrect, respectively).

3.2.3 Proposed Model

Figure 1 shows the architecture of our proposed SED model. The key ideas of our proposed model are as follows:

- There is a correlation between the error rate and the learner's level of proficiency.

- The performance of SED can be improved by fine-tuning the model according to the learners proficiency.

The first idea is based on the following observation on the W&I+LOCNESS development set: Looking at the word error rate (WER) across three different CEFR levels: A (beginner), B (intermediate), C (advanced), we can confirm that 19.49% for level A, 13.18% for level B, and 6.04% for level C. The second idea comes from previous studies on GEC (Junczys-Dowmunt and Grundkiewicz, 2016; Junczys-Dowmunt et al., 2018). They showed that better results can be achieved if the error rate of the training data is adapted to the error rate of the development set, which is called error adaptation.

Let N and M denote the total number of source words and sentences in a corpus, respectively. WER is defined as follows:

$$\text{WER} = \frac{\sum_{m=1}^{M} d(X^m, Y^m)}{\sum_{m=1}^{M} N^m}$$

where X^m denotes each source sentence, Y^m denotes each corrected sentence, and $d(X^m, Y^m)$ denotes the edit distance between X^m and Y^m.

Based on the above ideas, our SED model is developed in two steps:

1. **Building Proficiency Prediction Module (PPM):** The PPM predicts the proficiency of the learner who wrote a given sentence. Based on the above key ideas, we employed a multi-task learning approach in which the model estimates the learner's proficiency and performs sentence-level error detection simultaneously (PP&SED in Figure1), trained on labelled data obtained by simply conjoining the SED label with PP label (e.g., 1_A).

We confirmed that the PP&SED outperforms the vanilla PP by a large margin of up to 7.8 points at accuracy (from 42.2 to 50.0).

2. Fine-tuning SED model: After dividing the given text by proficiency based on the label estimated by the PPM, the SED model is fine-tuned for each level of proficiency.

Then, the SED module performs sentence-level binary classification of sentences that need editing. Table 1 shows the performance of SED on our dev set. Here, we split the official development set into test/dev set for our experiments. Our proposed SED model achieved a significant improvement both in precision and recall, by considering learner proficiency.

	Prec.	Rec.	F
Base Model	88.5	79.8	83.9
Proposed Model	**91.3**	**95.6**	**93.4**

Table 1: Performance of sent-level error detection (SED).

3.3 Error Generation

Our error generation system follows the system developed by Edunov et al. (2018). A target-to-source model is trained, and back-translation is applied to monolingual data to generate pseudo-parallel data via sampling from the distribution of the target-to-source model.

4 Experiment

4.1 Experimental Setting

We will now describe the training data and tools used to train our model.

4.1.1 Tools

We used the Transformer implemented in Fairseq[1] (Ott et al., 2019) as our GEC model. For the Transformer, we used a token embedding size of dimension 512. The hidden size is set to 512, and the filter size is set to 2048. The multi-head attention has eight individual attention heads, whereas the encoder and decoder have six layers. We use Adam optimizer with $\beta_1 = 0.9$, $\beta_2 = 0.98$, and $\epsilon = 10^{-9}$. We use inverse squared root decay. We set the dropout to 0.3. Rather than using words directly, we used byte pair encoding (BPE) (Sennrich et al., 2016a), and each

of the source and target vocabularies comprises 30K elements, which are the most frequent BPE tokens.

For building the sentence-level error detection model, we employed the model based on BERT, especially for the sequence-level tasks as described in Section 3.2. Thus, we used the PyTorch implementations for Googles BERT model [2].

For building the error generation model, we used a 7-layer convolutional seq2seq model implemented in Fairseq (Gehring et al., 2017; Chollampatt and Ng, 2018). As Chollampatt and Ng (2018), both source and target embeddings are of 500 dimensions. Each of the source and target vocabularies comprises the 30K most frequent BPE tokens. The hidden size of encoders and decoders is 1,024 with a convolution window width of 3. The output of each encoder and decoder layer is 1,024 dimensions. We set the dropout rate to 0.3. The parameters are optimized using the Nesterov Accelerated Gradient (Sutskever et al., 2013) optimizer with a momentum value of 0.99. We set the initial learning rate to 0.25, using early stopping.

For evaluating the system outputs, the ERRANT (Bryant et al., 2017) is used as a scorer. In this study, all the results shown are "span-based correction F0.5".

4.1.2 Dataset for Track-1

For training our transformer-based GEC system, we used the BEA-2019 workshop official data: the First Certificate in English corpus (FCE) (Yannakoudakis et al., 2011), the Lang-8 Corpus of Learner English (Lang-8) (Mizumoto et al., 2011; Tajiri et al., 2012), the National University of Singapore Corpus of Learner English (NUCLE) (Dahlmeier et al., 2013), and W&I+LOCNESS (Bryant et al., 2019; Granger, 1998). Our pre-processing for training data is the same as that reported previously (Chollampatt and Ng, 2018). As the result, we obtained 564,565 sentence pairs.

In generating erroneous sentences, we used Simple Wikipedia and essay scoring data sets (i.e., International Corpus of Learner English (Granger et al., 2009), and International Corpus Network of Asian Learners of English (Ishikawa, 2013), the Automated Student Assessment Prize dataset[3], ETS Corpus of Non-Native English (TOEFL

---

[1] https://github.com/pytorch/fairseq

[2] https://github.com/huggingface/ pytorch-pretrained-BERT

[3] https://www.kaggle.com/c/asap-sas

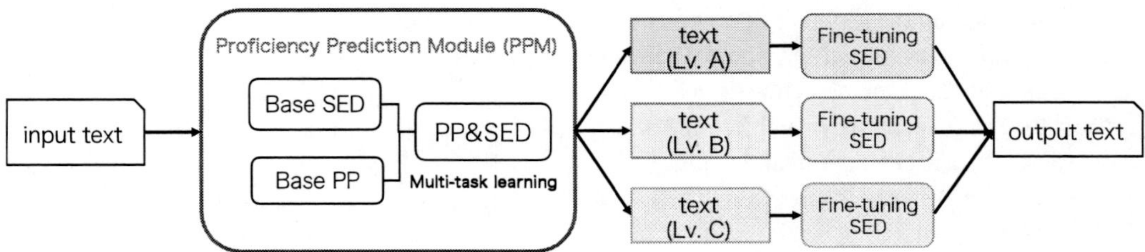

Figure 1: Architecture of proposed sentence-level error detection (SED) model. Native-level (N) is combined with C-level data.

	Prec.	Rec.	F0.5
Base	61.97	42.11	56.63
Base+SED	65.45	38.04	57.20
Base+GenData	64.57	**46.40**	59.88
Base+SED+GenData	**68.62**	42.16	**60.97**

Table 2: Track1 results

	Prec.	Rec.	F0.5
Track1	68.62	42.16	60.97
Track1 + AddData	**70.60**	**51.03**	**65.57**

Table 3: Track2 results

11) (Blanchard et al., 2013). With respect to Simple Wikipedia, we ignored sentences that were longer than 60 tokens. To remove erroneous sentences, we applied BERT-Cleaning to the essay scoring data sets. After BERT-Cleaning and pre-processing (Chollampatt and Ng, 2018), we obtained 1,426,354 sentence pairs by error generation.

4.1.3 External Dataset for Track-2

We used EFCAMDAT (Geertzen et al., 2013) and non-public Lang-8 as the external language learner corpus. The EFCAMDAT is constructed by the Department of Theoretical and Applied Linguistics at the University of Cambridge. Lo et al. (2018) were the first the researchers to use the EFCAMDAT for the GEC task. However, the system trained with the EFCAMDAT gave lower performance than the system trained with the Lang-8 Corpus. One of the causes of the lower performance is that many errors are found in the EFCAMDAT corrected sentences. Thus, we applied BERT-Cleaning to the EFCAMDAT to remove the erroneous sentences. Consequently, the number of sentence pairs of EFCAMDAT was reduced from 1,157,339 to 760,393. Finally, we used 7,739,577 sentence pairs (non-public Lang-8 + Cleand EFCAMDAT) by using pre-processing (Chollampatt and Ng, 2018) as the additional training data.

4.2 Results on Track-1

Table 2 shows the results of our systems, ensemble decoding of five independently trained models. We compared the following four systems: (1) Base (Transformer-based GEC system), (2) Base plus sentence error detection (Base+SED) described in section 3.2, (3) Base plus generated data (Base+GenData), and (4) Base plus sentence error detection and generated data (Base+SED+GenData).

Note that our system, which was composed of both SED and GenData, achieved a 60.97 $F_{0.5}$ score. Our proposed methods, the SED, and the GenData were effective for improving GEC performance. Especially, the SED is effective for a precision score, which improved from 61.97 to 65.45 (+3.48). However, the recall dropped from 42.11 to 38.04 (4.07). Nevertheless, the GenData improved both recall (from 42.11 to 46.40) and precision (from 61.97 to 64.57).

4.3 Results on Track-2

Table 3 shows the results of the model trained with additional data (Track1+AddData). The additional data improve precision and recall, and notably give a large increase in recall (improved from 42.16 to 51.03).

5 Conclusion

We described our system for the BEA-2019 Shared Task. Our system has two key components: error generation and sentence-level error detection. We input grammatically incorrect sentences predicted by the sentence-level error detection model into our correction model. Sentence-level grammatical error detection is a novel approach to grammatical error correction, and we have shown that it can significantly improve performance. Our system ranked 9th in Track-1 and 2nd in Track-2.

References

Daniel Blanchard, Joel Tetreault, Derrick Higgins, Aoife Cahill, and Martin Chodorow. 2013. TOEFL11: A Corpus of Non-Native English. Technical report.

Christopher Bryant, Mariano Felice, Øistein E. Andersen, and Ted Briscoe. 2019. The BEA-2019 Shared Task on Grammatical Error Correction. In *Proceedings of the 14th Workshop on Innovative Use of NLP for Building Educational Applications*.

Christopher Bryant, Mariano Felice, and Ted Briscoe. 2017. Automatic Annotation and Evaluation of Error Types for Grammatical Error Correction. In *Proceedings of the 55th Annual Meeting of the Association for Computational Linguistics*, pages 793–805.

Martin Chodorow, Markus Dickinson, Ross Israel, and Joel Tetreault. 2012. Problems in Evaluating Grammatical Error Detection Systems. In *Proceedings of the 24th International Conference on Computational Linguistics*, pages 611–628.

Shamil Chollampatt and Hwee Tou Ng. 2018. A Multilayer Convolutional Encoder-Decoder Neural Network for Grammatical Error Correction. In *Proceedings of the Thirty-Second AAAI Conference on Artificial Intelligence*, pages 5755–5762.

Daniel Dahlmeier, Hwee Tou Ng, and Siew Mei Wu. 2013. Building a Large Annotated Corpus of Learner English: The NUS Corpus of Learner English. In *Proceedings of the 8th Workshop on Building Educational Applications Using NLP*, pages 22–31.

Jacob Devlin, Ming-Wei Chang, Kenton Lee, and Kristina Toutanova. 2018. BERT: Pre-training of Deep Bidirectional Transformers for Language Understanding. *CoRR*, abs/1810.04805.

Sergey Edunov, Myle Ott, Michael Auli, and David Grangier. 2018. Understanding Back-Translation at Scale. In *Proceedings of the 2018 Conference on Empirical Methods in Natural Language Processing*, pages 489–500.

Tao Ge, Furu Wei, and Ming Zhou. 2018. Fluency Boost Learning and Inference for Neural Grammatical Error Correction. In *Proceedings of the 56th Annual Meeting of the Association for Computational Linguistics*, pages 1055–1065.

Jeroen Geertzen, Theodora Alexopoulou, and Anna Korhonen. 2013. Automatic linguistic annotation of large scale L2 databases: The EF-Cambridge Open Language Database (EFCAMDAT). In *Proceedings of the 31st Second Language Research Forum. Somerville, MA: Cascadilla Proceedings Project*, pages 240–254.

Jonas Gehring, Michael Auli, David Grangier, Denis Yarats, and Yann N. Dauphin. 2017. Convolutional sequence to sequence learning. *CoRR*, abs/1705.03122.

Sylviane Granger. 1998. The Computer Learner Corpus: A Versatile New Source of Data for SLA Research. In *Learner English on Computer*, pages 3–18.

Sylviane Granger, Estelle Dagneaux, Fanny Meunier, and Magali Paquot. 2009. *International Corpus of Learner English v2*. Presses universitaires de Louvain, Louvain-la-Neuve.

Na-Rae Han, Martin Chodorow, and Claudia Leacock. 2006. Detecting Errors in English Article Usage by Non-Native Speakers. *Natural Language Engineering*, 12(2):115–129.

Kenji Imamura, Atsushi Fujita, and Eiichiro Sumita. 2018. Enhancement of Encoder and Attention Using Target Monolingual Corpora in Neural Machine Translation. In *Proceedings of the 2nd Workshop on Neural Machine Translation and Generation*, pages 55–63.

Shin'ichro Ishikawa. 2013. The ICNALE and Sophisticated Contrastive Interlanguage Analysis of Asian learners of English. *Learner Corpus Studies in Asia and the World*, 1:91–118.

Marcin Junczys-Dowmunt and Roman Grundkiewicz. 2016. Phrase-based Machine Translation is State-of-the-Art for Automatic Grammatical Error Correction. In *Proceedings of the 2016 Conference on Empirical Methods in Natural Language Processing*, pages 1546–1556.

Marcin Junczys-Dowmunt, Roman Grundkiewicz, Shubha Guha, and Kenneth Heafield. 2018. Approaching Neural Grammatical Error Correction as a Low-Resource Machine Translation Task. In *Proceedings of the 2018 Conference of the North American Chapter of the Association for Computational Linguistics: Human Language Technologies*, pages 595–606.

Masahiro Kaneko, Yuya Sakaizawa, and Mamoru Komachi. 2017. Grammatical Error Detection Using Error- and Grammaticality-Specific Word Embeddings. In *Proceedings of the Eighth International Joint Conference on Natural Language Processing*, pages 40–48.

Sudhanshu Kasewa, Pontus Stenetorp, and Sebastian Riedel. 2018. Wronging a Right: Generating Better Errors to Improve Grammatical Error Detection.

In *Proceedings of the 2018 Conference on Empirical Methods in Natural Language Processing*, pages 4977–4983.

Yu-Chun Lo, Jhih-Jie Chen, Ching-Yu Yang, and Jason S. Chang. 2018. Cool English: A Grammatical Error Correction System Based on Large Learner Corpora. In *Proceedings of the 26th International Conference on Computational Linguistics: Demo*, pages 82–85.

Tomoya Mizumoto, Mamoru Komachi, Masaaki Nagata, and Yuji Matsumoto. 2011. Mining Revision Log of Language Learning SNS for Automated Japanese Error Correction of Second Language Learners. In *Proceedings of the 5th International Joint Conference on Natural Language Processing*, pages 147–155.

Myle Ott, Sergey Edunov, Alexei Baevski, Angela Fan, Sam Gross, Nathan Ng, David Grangier, and Michael Auli. 2019. FAIRSEQ: A Fast, Extensible Toolkit for Sequence Modeling. In *Proceedings of the 2019 Conference of the North American Chapter of the Association for Computational Linguistics: Human Language Technologies: Demo*, pages 48–53.

Marek Rei. 2017. Semi-supervised Multitask Learning for Sequence Labeling. In *Proceedings of the 55th Annual Meeting of the Association for Computational Linguistics*, pages 2121–2130.

Marek Rei, Gamal Crichton, and Sampo Pyysalo. 2016. Attending to Characters in Neural Sequence Labeling Models. In *Proceedings of the 26th International Conference on Computational Linguistics*, pages 309–318.

Marek Rei, Mariano Felice, Zheng Yuan, and Ted Briscoe. 2017. Artificial Error Generation with Machine Translation and Syntactic Patterns. In *Proceedings of the 12th Workshop on Innovative Use of NLP for Building Educational Applications*, pages 287–292.

Marek Rei and Helen Yannakoudakis. 2016. Compositional Sequence Labeling Models for Error Detection in Learner Writing. In *Proceedings of the 54th Annual Meeting of the Association for Computational Linguistics*, pages 1181–1191.

Allen Schmaltz, Yoon Kim, Alexander M. Rush, and Stuart Shieber. 2016. Sentence-Level Grammatical Error Identification as Sequence-to-Sequence Correction. In *Proceedings of the 11th Workshop on Innovative Use of NLP for Building Educational Applications*, pages 242–251.

Rico Sennrich, Barry Haddow, and Birc Alexandra. 2016a. Neural Machine Translation of Rare Words with Subword Units. In *Proceedings of the 54th Annual Meeting of the Association for Computational Linguistics*, pages 1715–1725.

Rico Sennrich, Barry Haddow, and Alexandra Birch. 2016b. Improving Neural Machine Translation Models with Monolingual Data. In *Proceedings of the 54th Annual Meeting of the Association for Computational Linguistics*, pages 86–96.

Richard Socher, Alex Perelygin, Jean Wu, Jason Chuang, Christopher D. Manning, Andrew Ng, and Christopher Potts. 2013. "Recursive Deep Models for Semantic Compositionality Over a Sentiment Treebank. In *Proceedings of the 2013 Conference on Empirical Methods in Natural Language Processing*, pages 1631–1642.

Ilya Sutskever, James Martens, George Dahl, and Geoffrey Hinton. 2013. On the importance of initialization and momentum in deep learning. In *Proceedings of the 30th International Conference on Machine Learning*, pages 1139–1147.

Toshikazu Tajiri, Mamoru Komachi, and Yuji Matsumoto. 2012. Tense and Aspect Error Correction for ESL Learners Using Global Context. In *Proceedings of the 50th Annual Meeting of the Association for Computational Linguistics*, pages 198–202.

Joel R Tetreault and Martin Chodorow. 2008. The Ups and Downs of Preposition Error Detection in ESL Writing. In *Proceedings of the 22nd International Conference on Computational Linguistics*, pages 865–872.

Ashish Vaswani, Noam Shazeer, Niki Parmar, Jakob Uszkoreit, Llion Jones, Aidan N Gomez, Ł ukasz Kaiser, and Illia Polosukhin. 2017. Attention is All you Need. In *Proceedings of Advances in Neural Information Processing Systems*, pages 5998–6008.

Alex Warstadt, Amanpreet Singh, and Samuel R Bowman. 2018. Neural Network Acceptability Judgments. *CoRR*, abs/1805.12471.

Ziang Xie, Guillaume Genthial, Stanley Xie, Andrew Ng, and Dan Jurafsky. 2018. Noising and Denoising Natural Language: Diverse Backtranslation for Grammar Correction. In *Proceedings of the 2018 Conference of the North American Chapter of the Association for Computational Linguistics: Human Language Technologies*, pages 619–628.

Helen Yannakoudakis, Ted Briscoe, and Ben Medlock. 2011. A New Dataset and Method for Automatically Grading ESOL Texts. In *Proceedings of the 49th Annual Meeting of the Association for Computational Linguistics: Human Language Technologies*, pages 180–189.

Helen Yannakoudakis, Marek Rei, Øistein E. Andersen, and Zheng Yuan. 2017. Neural Sequence-Labelling Models for Grammatical Error Correction. In *Proceedings of the 2017 Conference on Empirical Methods in Natural Language Processing*, pages 2795–2806.

Wei Zhao, Liang Wang, Kewei Shen, Ruoyu Jia, and
Jingming Liu. 2019. Improving Grammatical Error
Correction via Pre-Training a Copy-Augmented Architecture with Unlabeled Data. In *Proceedings of
the 2019 Conference of the North American Chapter of the Association for Computational Linguistics:
Human Language Technologies*, pages 156–165.

CUNI System for the Building Educational Applications 2019 Shared Task: Grammatical Error Correction

Jakub Náplava and **Milan Straka**

Charles University,
Faculty of Mathematics and Physics,
Institute of Formal and Applied Linguistics
{naplava,straka}@ufal.mff.cuni.cz

Abstract

In this paper, we describe our systems submitted to the Building Educational Applications (BEA) 2019 Shared Task (Bryant et al., 2019). We participated in all three tracks. Our models are NMT systems based on the Transformer model, which we improve by incorporating several enhancements: applying dropout to whole source and target words, weighting target subwords, averaging model checkpoints, and using the trained model iteratively for correcting the intermediate translations. The system in the Restricted Track is trained on the provided corpora with oversampled "cleaner" sentences and reaches 59.39 F0.5 score on the test set. The system in the Low-Resource Track is trained from Wikipedia revision histories and reaches 44.13 F0.5 score. Finally, we finetune the system from the Low-Resource Track on restricted data and achieve 64.55 F0.5 score, placing third in the Unrestricted Track.

1 Introduction

Starting with the 2013 and 2014 CoNLL Shared Tasks on grammatical error correction (GEC), much progress has been done in this area. The need to correct a variety of error types lead most researchers to focus on models based on machine translation (Brockett et al., 2006) rather than custom designed rule-based models or a combination of single error classifiers. The machine translation systems turned out to be particularity effective when Junczys-Dowmunt and Grundkiewicz (2016) presented state-of-the-art statistical machine translation system. Currently, models based on statistical and neural machine translation achieve best results: in restricted settings with training limited to certain public training sets (Zhao et al., 2019); unrestricted settings with no restrictions on training data (Ge et al., 2018); and also in low-resource track where the training data should not come from any annotated corpora (Lichtarge et al., 2018).[1]

In this paper, we present our models and their results in the restricted, unrestricted, and low-resource tracks. We start with a description of related work in Section 2. We then describe our systems together with the implementation details in Section 3. Section 4 is dedicated to our results and ablation experiments. Finally, in Section 5 we conclude the paper with some proposals on future work.

2 Related Work

Transformer (Vaswani et al., 2017) is currently one of the most popular architectures used in machine translation. Its self-attentive layers allow better gradient flow when compared to recurrent neural models and the masking in decoder provides faster training. Junczys-Dowmunt et al. (2018) propose several improvements for training Transformer on GEC: using dropout on whole input words, assigning weight to target words based on their alignment to source words, and they also propose to oversample sentences from the training set in order to have the same error rate as the test set.

Majority of work in grammatical error correction has been done in restricted area with a fixed set of annotated training datasets. Lichtarge et al. (2018), however, show that training a neural machine translation system from Wikipedia edits can lead to surprisingly good results. As the authors state, corpus of Wikipedia edits is only weakly supervised for the task of GEC, because most of the edits are not corrections of grammatical errors and also they are not human curated specifically for GEC. To overcome these issues, the authors use iterative decoding which allows for incremental corrections. In other words, the model can re-

---

[1] Note that in this settings Wikipedia revisions are allowed

Proceedings of the Fourteenth Workshop on Innovative Use of NLP for Building Educational Applications, pages 183–190
Florence, Italy, August 2, 2019. ©2019 Association for Computational Linguistics

peatedly translate its current output as long as the translation is more probable then keeping the sentence unchanged. Similar idea is also presented in (Ge et al., 2018), where the translation system is trained with respect to the incremental inference.

3 Our System

In this section, we present our three systems submitted to each track of the BEA 2019 Shared Task. We start with the Restricted Track In Section 3.1, where we present a series of improvements to the baseline Transformer model. In Section 3.2, we describe our model trained on Wikipedia revisions which was submitted to the Low-Resource Track. Finally, in Section 3.3, we describe the model submitted to the Unrestricted Track.

All our models are based on the Transformer model from Tensor2Tensor framework version 1.12.0.[2]

3.1 Restricted Track

In the Restricted Track, we use the 5 provided datasets for system development: FCE v2.1 (Yannakoudakis et al., 2011), Lang-8 Corpus of Learner English (Mizumoto et al., 2011; Tajiri et al., 2012), NUCLE (Dahlmeier et al., 2013), Write & Improve (W&I) and LOCNESS v2.1 (Bryant et al., 2019; Granger, 1998). From Lang-8 corpus, we took only the sentences annotated by annotators with ID 0 (A0) and ID 1 (A1). All but the development sets from W&I and LOCNESS datasets were used for training. The simple statistics of these datasets are presented in Table 1. The displayed error rate is computed using maximum alignment of original and annotated sentences as a ratio of non-matching alignment edges (insertion, deletion, and replacement).

We use the *transformer_base* configuration of Tensor2Tensor as our baseline solution. The training dataset consists of 1 230 231 sentences. After training, beam search decoding is employed to generate model corrections and we choose the checkpoint with the highest accuracy on a development set concatenated from the W&I and LOCNESS development sets.

3.1.1 Transformer Big

The first minor improvement was to use the *transformer_big* configuration instead of *transformer_base*. This configuration has bigger capac-

[2]https://github.com/tensorflow/tensor2tensor

Dataset		Sentences	Average error rate
Lang8	A0	1 037 561	13.33 %
	A1	67 975	25.84 %
FCE v2.1	train	28 350	11.31 %
	dev	2 191	11.67 %
	test	2 695	12.87 %
NUCLE		57 151	6.56 %
W&I	train A	10 493	18.13 %
	train B	13 032	11.68 %
	train C	10 783	5.62 %
	dev A	1 037	18.32 %
	dev B	1 290	12.46 %
	dev C	1 069	5.91 %
LOCNESS	dev N	998	4.72 %

Table 1: Statistics of available datasets. The error rate is computed as a ratio of non-matching alignment edges.

ity and as Popel and Bojar (2018) show, it reaches substantially better results on certain translation tasks.

3.1.2 Source and Target Word Dropout

Dropout (Srivastava et al., 2014) is a regularization technique that turned out to be particularly effective in the field of neural networks. It works by masking several randomly selected activations during training, which should prevent the neural network from overfitting the training data. In the area of NLP, it is a common approach to apply dropout to whole embeddings, randomly zeroing certain dimensions. As Junczys-Dowmunt et al. (2018) show, we can also apply dropout to whole source words to reduce trust in the source words. Specifically, full source word embedding vector is set to zero vector with probability p. We further note this probability as the *source_word_dropout*.

To make regularization even more effective, we decided to dropout also whole target word embeddings. We refer to the probability with which we dropout entire target word embeddings as the *target_word_dropout*.

3.1.3 Edited MLE

Compared to traditional machine translation task, whose goal is to translate one language to another, GEC operates on a single language. Together with the relatively low error rate, the translation system may converge to a local optimum, in which the model copies the input unchanged to the output. To overcome this issue, Junczys-Dowmunt et al. (2018) propose to change the maximum likelihood objective to assign bigger weights to target tokens different from the source tokens. More specifically, they start by computing the word alignment between each source $x = (x_0, x_1, ...x_N)$ and target sentence $y = (y_0, y_1, ...y_M)$. Then they set the weight λ_t of the target word y_t to 1 if it is matched, and otherwise, if it is an insertion or replacement of a source token, λ_t is set to some predefined constant. Modified log-likelihood training objective then takes following form:

$$L(x, y) = -\sum_{t=1}^{M} \lambda_t \log P(y_t | x, y_0, \ldots, y_{t-1}).$$

3.1.4 Data oversampling

It is crucial to have training data from the same domain as the test data, i.e., training data containing similar errors with similar distribution as the test data. As we can see in the Table 1, the vast majority of our training data comes from the Lang-8 corpus. However, as it is quite noisy and of low quality, it matches the target domain the least. Therefore, we decided to oversample other datasets. Specifically, we add the W&I training data 10 times, all FCE data 5 times and NUCLE corpus 5 times to the training data. The oversampled training set consists of 1 900 551.

In Table 1, we can also see token error rate of each corpus. The development error rate in W&I and LOCNESS varies from 5.91% up to 18.32%. This gives us a basic idea how the test data looks like, and since the test data does not contain annotations from which set (A, B, C, N) it comes, we decided not to optimize the training data against the token error rate any further.

3.1.5 Checkpoint Averaging

Popel and Bojar (2018) report that averaging several last Transformer model checkpoints during training leads both to lower variance results and also to slightly better performance than the baseline without averaging. They propose to save checkpoints every one hour and average either 8 or 16 last checkpoints. Since we found out that the model overfits the oversampled dataset quite quickly, we save checkpoints every 30 minutes.

3.1.6 Iterative decoding

A system for grammatical error correction should correct all errors in the text while keeping the rest

```
Data: input_sent; max_iters; threshold
for iter in [1,2,..,max_iters] do
    beam_results = decode(input_sent);
    identity_cost = +∞;
    non_identity_cost = +∞;
    non_identity_sent = None
    for beam_item in beam_results do
        text = beam_item["text"];
        cost = beam_item["cost"];
        if text == input_sent then
            identity_cost = cost;
        else if cost < non_identity_cost
          then
            non_identity_cost = cost;
            non_identity_sent = text;
    end
    if non_identity_cost ≤
      threshold · identity_cost then
        input_sent = non_identity_sent;
    else
        break;
    end
end
return input_sent;
```
Algorithm 1: Iterative decoding algorithm

of the text intact. In many situations with multiple errors in a sentence, the trained system, however, corrects only a subset of its errors. Lichtarge et al. (2018) and Ge et al. (2018) propose to use the trained system iteratively to allow the system to correct certain errors during further iterations. Iterative decoding is done as long as the cost of the correction is less than the cost of the identity translation times a predefined constant. While Lichtarge et al. (2018) use the same trained model log-likelihoods as the cost function, Ge et al. (2018) utilize an external language model for it. Because the restricted track does not contain enough training data to train a quality language model, we adopted the first approach and utilize the trained system log-likelihoods as a stopping criterion.

The iterative decoding algorithm we use is presented in Algorithm 1. Note that when the resulting beam does not contain the identical (non-modified) sentence, the correction with the lowest cost is returned regardless of the provided threshold. We adopted this approach for two reasons – efficiently obtaining the log-likelihood of the identical sentence would require non-trivial modification of the Tensor2Tensor framework, and for *threshold* > 1 (i.e., allow generating changes which are less likely than identical sentence) the results are the same.

3.1.7   Implementation Details

Apart from the first experiment in which we use *transformer_base* configuration, all our experiments are based on *transformer_big* architecture. We use Adafactor optimizer (Shazeer and Stern, 2018), linearly increasing the learning rate from 0 to 0.011 over the first 8000 steps, then decrease it proportionally to the number of steps after that.[3] We also experimented with Adam optimizer with default learning rate schedule, however, training converged poorly. We hypothesise that this was caused by the higher learning rate.

All systems are trained on 4 Nvidia P5000 GPUs for approximately 2 days. The vocabulary consists of approximately 32k most common word-pieces, batch size is 2000 word-pieces per each GPU and all sentences with more than 150 word-pieces are discarded. Model checkpoints are saved every 30 minutes. We ran a grid search to find values of all hyperparameters described in the previous sections.

At evaluation time, we run iterative decoding using a beam size of 4. Beam-search length-balance decoding hyperparameter alpha is set to 0.6. This applies to all further experiments.

3.2   Low-Resource Track

The dataset for our experiments in the Low-Resource Track consists of nearly 190M segment pairs extracted from Wikipedia XML revision dumps. To acquire these, we downloaded all English Wikipedia revision dumps (155GB in size) and processed them with the *WikiRevision* dataset problem from Tensor2Tensor. The processing pipeline extracts individual pages with chronological snapshots, removes all non-text elements and downsamples the snapshots. With low probability, additional spelling noise is added by either inserting a random character, deleting a random character, transposing two adjacent characters or replacing a character with a random one. With the same low probability, a random text substring (up to 8 characters) may also be replaced with a marker, which should force the model to learn infilling. Finally, the texts from two consecutive snapshots are aligned and sequences between matching segments are extracted to form a training pair. Only 4% of identical samples are preserved.

Despite having an enormous size compared to 1.2M sentences in the Restricted Track, the training pairs extracted from Wikipedia are extremely noisy, containing a lot of edits that are in no sense grammatical correction. It is also worth noting that the identical data modified by the spelling and infilling operations form nearly 50% of the training pairs.

Since we want to re-use the system in other scenarios, we train the model on the original (untokenized) training data. To evaluate the model on the BEA development and test data, we detokenize the data using Moses,[4] run model inference and finally tokenize corrected sentences using spaCy.[5]

The training segments may contain newline and tab symbols; therefore, we applied additional post-processing in which we replaced both these symbols with spaces.

Because overfitting should not be an issue with the Wikipedia data, we decided to use *transformer_clean_big_tpu* configuration, following Lichtarge et al. (2018). This configuration, compared to *transformer_big*, performs no dropouts. The vocabulary consists of approximately 32k most common word-pieces, batch size is 2000 word-pieces per each GPU and all sentences with more than 150 word-pieces are discarded. We train the model for approximately 10 days on 4 Nvidia P5000 GPUs. After training, the last 8 checkpoints saved in 1 hour intervals are averaged. Finally, we run a grid search to find optimal values of *threshold* and *max_iters* in iterative decoding algorithm.

3.3   Unrestricted Track

Our system submitted to the Unrestricted Track is the best system from the Low-Resource Track finetuned on the oversampled training data as described in Section 3.1.4. Since our system in the Unrestricted Track was trained on detokenized data, the training sentences for finetuning were also detokenized. The tokenization and detokenization was done in the same way as described in Section 3.2.

---

[3]We use 8000 warmup steps and learning_rate_schedule=rsqrt_decay

[4]We use mosestokenizer v1.0.0 and its detokenizer.

[5]We use spaCy v1.9.0 and the en_core_web_sm-1.2.0 model.

Track	P	R	$F_{0.5}$	Best	Rank
Restricted	67.33	40.37	59.39	69.47	10 / 21
Unrestricted	68.17	53.25	64.55	66.78	3 / 7
Low Resource	50.47	29.38	44.13	64.24	5 / 9

Table 2: Official shared task $F_{0.5}$ scores on the test set.

System	A	B	C	N	Combined
Transformer-base architecture	39.98	32.68	23.97	14.49	32.47
Transformer-big architecture	39.70	35.13	26.22	20.20	34.20
+ 0.2 src drop, 0.1 tgt drop, 3 MLE	42.06	38.25	28.72	23.80	38.15
+ Extended dataset	45.99	41.79	32.52	27.89	40.86
+ Averaging 8 checkpoints	47.90	44.13	36.19	29.05	43.29
+ Iterative decoding	48.75	45.46	37.09	30.19	44.27

Table 3: Development combined $F_{0.5}$ score of incremental improvements of our system.

We finetune the system with the Adafactor optimizer. The learning rate linearly increases from 0 to 0.0003 over the first 20 000 steps and then remains constant. We employ source word dropout, target word dropout and weighted MLE. The training data for finetuning and the rest of the training scheme are identical to Section 3.1.7.

4 Results

We now present the results of our system. Additionally, we present several ablation experiments, which are evaluated on the concatenation of W&I and LOCNESS development sets (the *Dev combined*).

4.1 Shared Task Results

The official results of our three systems on the blind test set are presented in Table 2. All our systems have substantially higher precision than recall. It is an interesting observation that the system in the unrestricted track has similar precision as the model in the restricted track while having higher recall.

4.2 Restricted Track

The first experiment we conducted is devoted to the incremental enhancements that we proposed in Section 3.1. As Table 3 indicates, applying each enhancement results in higher performance on the development set. By applying all incremental improvements, total $F_{0.5}$ score on the development set increases by 11.8%.

We improved the $F_{0.5}$ score by adding

Source word dropout	Target word dropout	MLE	Dev combined $F_{0.5}$
0	0	1	34.20
0.1			37.89
0.2			38.26
	0.1		35.43
	0.2		33.98
		2	34.56
		3	34.28
		4	34.17
0.2	0.1		37.89
0.2		3	38.68
0.2	0.1	3	38.15

Table 4: The effect of source word dropout, target word dropout, and MLE weight on development combined $F_{0.5}$ score.

source_word_dropout, *target_word_dropout* and MLE weighting by almost 4%. To find out optimal values of all three hyper-parameters, we ran a small grid search. The results of this experiment are presented in Table 4. The source-word dropout improves the results the most, MLE provides minor gains, while the influence of target-word dropout on the results is unclear.

In the next experiment, we examined the effect of checkpoint averaging. Table 5 presents results of the model without averaging and with averaging 4, 6, and 8 model checkpoints. The best results are achieved when 8 checkpoints are used and the results indicate that the more checkpoints are av-

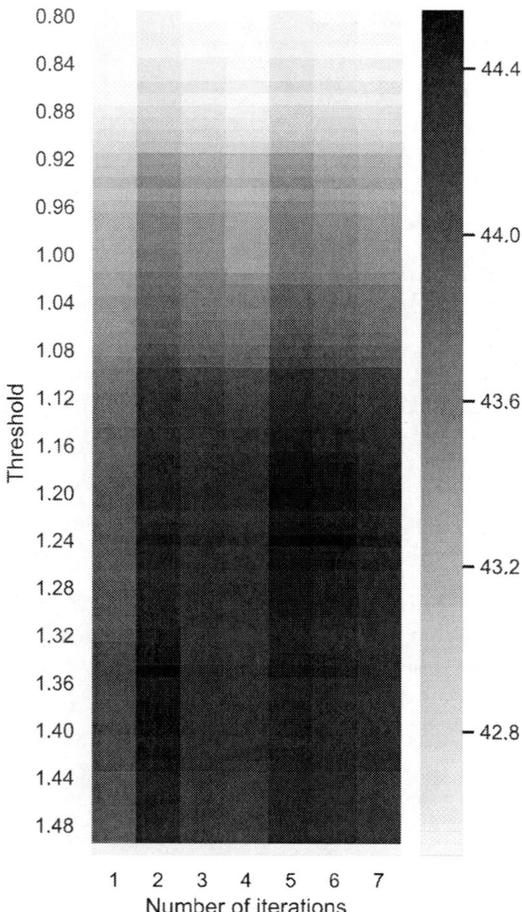

Figure 1: Performance of iterative decoding depending on number of iterations and threshold parameters.

Checkpointing	Dev combined $F_{0.5}$
No checkpointing	41.55
Averaging 4 checkpoints	43.00
Averaging 6 checkpoints	43.13
Averaging 8 checkpoints	43.29

Table 5: Maximum development combined $F_{0.5}$ score achieved by averaging the given number of checkpoints.

ID	Model	Dev combined $F_{0.5}$
1	*transformer_big* 0.2 src drop, 0.1 tgt drop	22.03
2	*transformer_clean_big_tpu* no src drop, no tgt drop	26.05
3	*transformer_clean_big_tpu* 0.2 src drop, 0.1 tgt drop	24.80
4	*transformer_clean_big_tpu* no spelling or infillment errors	21.16

Table 6: Development combined $F_{0.5}$ score achieved with different models in the Low-Resource Track.

eraged the better the results are.

Finally, we inspect the effect of iterative decoding. Specifically, we run an exhaustive grid search to find optimal values of *threshold* and *max_iters*. The results of this experimented are visualised in Figure 1. We can see that increasing *threshold* from 1 to values around 1.20 leads to substantially better results. Moreover, using more iterations also has a positive impact on the model performance. Both of these improvements are caused by the model generating more corrections which are deemed less likely to the model, i.e., we increase recall at the expense of precision.

4.3 Low-Resource Track

We train following models in the Low-Resource Track:

1. the *transformer_big* configuration with *input_word_dropout* set to 0.2 and *target_word_dropout* to 0.1 – settings similar to the best system in the Restricted Track but without edited MLE;

2. the *transformer_clean_big_tpu* configuration – this configuration uses no internal dropouts;

3. the *transformer_clean_big_tpu* configuration with *input_word_dropout* 0.2 and *target_word_dropout* 0.1;

4. the *transformer_clean_big_tpu* configuration trained on sentences extracted from Wikipedia revisions without introducing additional spelling errors and infillment marker.

All but the fourth model use the training data as described in Section 3.2 and the training scheme is in all models identical. The results of all models are presented in Table 6.

The best results are achieved with the second model which performs no dropouts. When we incorporate source and target word dropouts in the third experiment, the performance deteriorates by more than 1%. When we also add Transformer in-

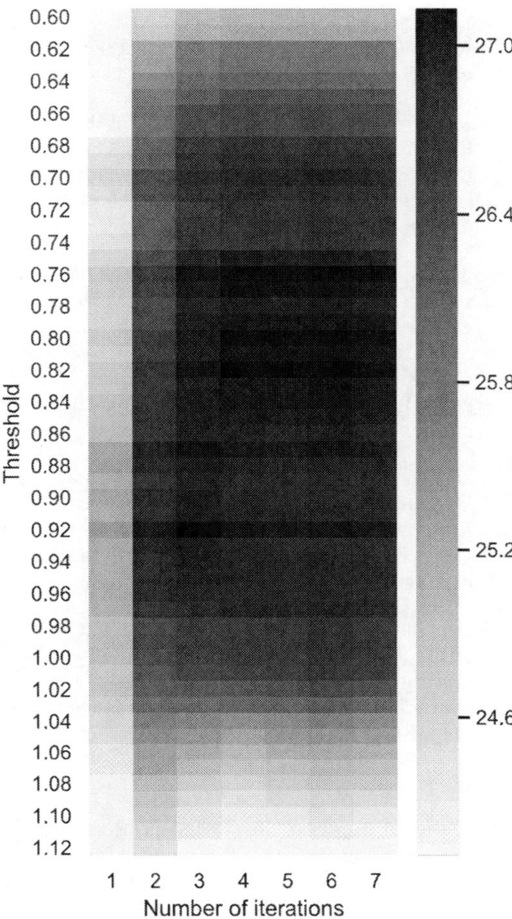

Figure 2: Performance of iterative decoding depending on number of iterations and threshold parameters.

ternal dropouts in the first experiment, the performance drops by additional 2.8%. This confirms our assumption that the enormous amount of data is strong enough regularizer and the usage of additional regularizers leads to worse performance.

The results of the fourth model, which was trained on data without additional spelling and infillment noise, are almost 5% worse than when training on data with this noise. It would be an interesting experiment to evaluate the effect of spelling and infillment noise separately, but this was not done in this paper.

We also run an exhaustive grid search to find optimal values of *threshold* and *max_iters* in iterative decoding. As we can see in Figure 2, the optimal value of *threshold* is now below 1 indicating that precision is now increased at the expense of recall. A performance gain in using more than one iteration is clearly visible.

4.4 Unrestricted Track

In the Unrestricted Track, we tried finetuning the pretrained system with two different learning rate schedules:

- linearly increase learning rate from 0 to 0.011 over the first 8000 steps, then decrease it proportionally to the number of steps after that – exactly same as while training system from scratch in the Restricted Track (see Section 3.1.7);

- linearly increase learning rate from 0 to 3e-4 then keep the learning rate constant as proposed by Lichtarge et al. (2018).

All other hyper-parameters and the training process remain the same as described in Section 3.3.

The first finetuning scheme overfitted the training corpus quite quickly while reaching score of 48.33. The second scheme converged slower and reached a higher score of 48.82.

5 Conclusion

We have presented our three systems submitted to the BEA 2019 Shared Tasks. By employing larger architecture, source and target word dropout, edited MLE, dataset extension, checkpoint averaging, and iterative decoding, our system reached 59.39 $F_{0.5}$ score in the Restricted Track, finishing 10th out of 21 participants.

In the Low Resource Track, we utilized Wikipedia revision edits as a training data, reaching 44.14 $F_{0.5}$ score. Finally, we finetuned this model using the annotated training data, obtaining 65.55 $F_{0.5}$ score in the Unrestricted Track, ranking 3rd out of 7 submissions.

As future work, we would like to explore iterative decoding algorithm more thoroughly. Specifically, we hope that allowing *threshold* parameter to change in each iteration might provide gains. We would also like to train systems on Wikipedia revisions in other languages.

Acknowledgements

The work described herein has been supported by OP VVV VI LINDAT/CLARIN project (CZ.02.1.01/0.0/0.0/16_013/0001781) and it has been supported and has been using language resources developed by the LINDAT/CLARIN project (LM2015071) of the Ministry of Education, Youth and Sports of the Czech Republic.

This research was also partially supported by SVV project number 260 453 and GAUK 578218 of the Charles University.

References

Chris Brockett, William B Dolan, and Michael Gamon. 2006. Correcting esl errors using phrasal smt techniques. In *Proceedings of the 21st International Conference on Computational Linguistics and the 44th annual meeting of the Association for Computational Linguistics*, pages 249–256. Association for Computational Linguistics.

Christopher Bryant, Mariano Felice, Øistein E. Andersen, and Ted Briscoe. 2019. The BEA-2019 Shared Task on Grammatical Error Correction. In *Proceedings of the 14th Workshop on Innovative Use of NLP for Building Educational Applications*. Association for Computational Linguistics.

Daniel Dahlmeier, Hwee Tou Ng, and Siew Mei Wu. 2013. Building a large annotated corpus of learner english: The nus corpus of learner english. In *Proceedings of the eighth workshop on innovative use of NLP for building educational applications*, pages 22–31.

Tao Ge, Furu Wei, and Ming Zhou. 2018. Reaching human-level performance in automatic grammatical error correction: An empirical study. *arXiv preprint arXiv:1807.01270*.

Sylviane Granger. 1998. The computer learner corpus: A versatile new source of data for SLA research. In Sylviane Granger, editor, *Learner English on Computer*, pages 3–18. Addison Wesley Longman, London and New York.

Marcin Junczys-Dowmunt and Roman Grundkiewicz. 2016. Phrase-based machine translation is state-of-the-art for automatic grammatical error correction. *arXiv preprint arXiv:1605.06353*.

Marcin Junczys-Dowmunt, Roman Grundkiewicz, Shubha Guha, and Kenneth Heafield. 2018. Approaching neural grammatical error correction as a low-resource machine translation task. *arXiv preprint arXiv:1804.05940*.

Jared Lichtarge, Christopher Alberti, Shankar Kumar, Noam Shazeer, and Niki Parmar. 2018. Weakly supervised grammatical error correction using iterative decoding. *arXiv preprint arXiv:1811.01710*.

Tomoya Mizumoto, Mamoru Komachi, Masaaki Nagata, and Yuji Matsumoto. 2011. Mining revision log of language learning sns for automated japanese error correction of second language learners. In *Proceedings of 5th International Joint Conference on Natural Language Processing*, pages 147–155.

Martin Popel and Ondřej Bojar. 2018. Training tips for the transformer model. *The Prague Bulletin of Mathematical Linguistics*, 110(1):43–70.

Noam Shazeer and Mitchell Stern. 2018. Adafactor: Adaptive learning rates with sublinear memory cost. *arXiv preprint arXiv:1804.04235*.

Nitish Srivastava, Geoffrey Hinton, Alex Krizhevsky, Ilya Sutskever, and Ruslan Salakhutdinov. 2014. Dropout: a simple way to prevent neural networks from overfitting. *The Journal of Machine Learning Research*, 15(1):1929–1958.

Toshikazu Tajiri, Mamoru Komachi, and Yuji Matsumoto. 2012. Tense and aspect error correction for esl learners using global context. In *Proceedings of the 50th Annual Meeting of the Association for Computational Linguistics: Short Papers-Volume 2*, pages 198–202. Association for Computational Linguistics.

Ashish Vaswani, Noam Shazeer, Niki Parmar, Jakob Uszkoreit, Llion Jones, Aidan N Gomez, Łukasz Kaiser, and Illia Polosukhin. 2017. Attention is all you need. In *Advances in neural information processing systems*, pages 5998–6008.

Helen Yannakoudakis, Ted Briscoe, and Ben Medlock. 2011. A new dataset and method for automatically grading esol texts. In *Proceedings of the 49th Annual Meeting of the Association for Computational Linguistics: Human Language Technologies-Volume 1*, pages 180–189. Association for Computational Linguistics.

Wei Zhao, Liang Wang, Kewei Shen, Ruoyu Jia, and Jingming Liu. 2019. Improving grammatical error correction via pre-training a copy-augmented architecture with unlabeled data. *arXiv preprint arXiv:1903.00138*.

Noisy Channel for Low Resource Grammatical Error Correction

Simon Flachs[1,2], Ophélie Lacroix[1], Anders Søgaard[2]
[1] Siteimprove, Denmark
[2] CoAStaL DIKU, Department of Computer Science, University of Copenhagen, Denmark
`{sfl, ola}@siteimprove.com,`
`soegaard@di.ku.dk`

Abstract

This paper describes our contribution to the low-resource track of the BEA 2019 shared task on Grammatical Error Correction (GEC). Our approach to GEC builds on the theory of the noisy channel by combining a channel model and language model. We generate confusion sets from the Wikipedia edit history and use the frequencies of edits to estimate the channel model. Additionally, we use two pre-trained language models: 1) Google's BERT model, which we fine-tune for specific error types and 2) OpenAI's GPT-2 model, utilizing that it can operate with previous sentences as context. Furthermore, we search for the optimal combinations of corrections using beam search.

1 Introduction

Grammatical Error Correction Grammatical Error Correction (GEC) is the task of automatically correcting grammatical errors in written text. The task is relevant for users producing text through text interfaces, both as assistance during the writing process and for proofreading already written work. In recent years, GEC has received increasing attention in the research community with several shared tasks on the topic, such as CoNLL 13-14 (Ng et al., 2013, 2014), HOO (Dale and Kilgarriff, 2011), and AESW (Daudaravicius et al., 2016), and most recently the BEA 2019 shared task on GEC (Bryant et al., 2019), which this work is a contribution to.

Supervised GEC Current state-of-the-art approaches to GEC use a supervised machine translation setup (Ge et al., 2018; Grundkiewicz and Junczys-Dowmunt, 2018), that relies on large amounts of annotated learner data. This means that systems do not generalize well to non-learner domains and that these approaches do not work well for low-resource languages. As most existing datasets are not freely available for commercial use, the supervised approach also limits industrial uses.

Unsupervised GEC In order to combat these problems, in recent years several approaches to GEC have used the concept of language modeling, which allows for training GEC systems without supervised data, and have so far given promising results. Bryant and Briscoe (2018) uses a 5-gram language model while Makarenkov et al. (2019) uses a bidirectional LSTM-based language model. Kaili et al. (2018) fine-tunes LSTM-based language models for specific error types.

Using a language modeling approach means that we can create models that are trained unsupervised by only being based on high quality native text corpora. This means that our systems will only require a small amount of labeled data for tuning purposes. We can therefore build GEC systems for any language given enough native text.

The Noisy Channel The core idea that these language modeling approaches are using for GEC is that low probability sequences are more likely to contain grammatical errors than high probability sequences. However this formulation does not take into account the writer's likelihood of making particular errors. For example, "then" → "than" is much more common than "then" → "the" due to an underlying similarity in phonetics.

In order to take this into account we utilize the concept of the noisy channel model, which allows for modeling the users likelihood of making particular errors, instead of only relying on which sequences of words are more probable.

Contributions In the following, we present our low-resource approach to GEC, which ranked as the 6th best performing system in the low-resource

Proceedings of the Fourteenth Workshop on Innovative Use of NLP for Building Educational Applications, pages 191–196
Florence, Italy, August 2, 2019. ©2019 Association for Computational Linguistics

track of the BEA 2019 shared task. We utilize confusion sets and edit statistics gathered from the Wikipedia edit history, as well as unsupervised language models in a noisy channel setting.

Our contributions are 1) formalizing GEC in the noisy channel framework, 2) generating confusion sets from the Wikipedia edit history, 3) estimating a channel model based on frequencies of edits from the confusion sets, 4) combining existing pre-trained language models, with each their own strength, 5) specializing models for specific grammatical error types, and 6) using beam search to find the optimal combination of corrections.

2 The Noisy Channel

The intuition of the noisy channel model (Kernighan et al., 1990; Mays et al., 1990) is that for any given word in a sentence, we have a true underlying word, that has been passed through a noisy communication channel, which potentially has modified the word into an erroneous surface form.

Our goal is to build a model of the channel. With this, given a confusion set, we can pass every candidate correction through this noisy channel to see which one is most likely to have produced the surface word.

The noisy channel model can be formulated as a form of Bayesian inference. Given a potentially erroneous surface word, x, we want to find the hidden word, c^*, from all candidates $c \in C$, that generated x.

$$\hat{c} = \arg\max_{c \in C} P(c|x)$$

Using Bayes' rule this can be restated as

$$\hat{c} = \arg\max_{c \in C} P(x|c) * P(c)$$

where $P(x|c)$ is the likelihood of the noisy channel producing a particular x. This is referred to as the channel model. The prior probability of a hidden word, $P(c)$, is modeled by a language model (Jurafsky and Martin, 2009).

3 System

Our system is a combination of several components: a PoS tagger, the channel model, two language models (BERT and GPT-2) and beam search. We first PoS tag the sentence. Then, the sentence is processed from left to right, and for every word x, we identify the set C of possible correction candidates, based on the PoS tag and our

generated confusion sets. We then pick the $c \in C$ with the highest $P(c|x)$ estimated using our components in the following formula:

$$P(c|x) = P_{Channel} * P_{BERT} * P_{GPT-2}$$

We allow the system to consider multiple hypotheses by using beam search, which continuously keeps track of a beam of the most likely hypotheses.

In the following, we describe the different components that make up our GEC system in more detail.

3.1 Channel Model

We estimate the channel model in two ways, depending if the written word is in our vocabulary (real-word error) or not (non-word error).

Real-word errors In order to estimate the channel model $P(x|c)$ for real-word errors, we first make a simplifying assumption that a human only makes a mistake for 1 in 20 words. This means that there is a 5% probability (denoted as α) of the surface word x being wrong. This probability can be distributed between the candidate corrections taken from the confusion set. For a given candidate word c_i we can calculate the channel probability using frequency counts of edits for all candidates in C. We gather frequency counts from the Wikipedia edit history (§ 4.1).

$$P(x|c_i) = \alpha * \frac{|x \rightarrow c_i|}{\sum_{j=1}^{|C|} |x \rightarrow c_j|}$$

Non-word errors For non-word errors we assume that any x not in our vocabulary and not a named entity[1] is an error. Assuming a list of candidate corrections, we use the inverse Levenshtein distance to distribute the error probability between the candidates. Hereby, candidates which are lexically closer to the original word are made more likely.

3.2 Language Models

For language modeling we use a combination of two pre-trained models that have recently given good results: BERT (Devlin et al., 2018) and GPT-2 (Radford et al., 2019).

---

[1] as estimated by Spacy, https://spacy.io

BERT BERT is a Transformer-based (Vaswani et al., 2017) language model pre-trained on a large text corpus. It estimates probabilities by jointly conditioning on both left and right context. We use the pre-trained BERT-Base Uncased model as a starting point for several models, which are each fine-tuned for specific error types on sentences extracted from a Wikipedia dump. We do three types of fine-tuning, using the default hyperparameters of BERT.

- PoS-based fine-tuning, where a word is removed and the model predicts its PoS tag. This is used to classify which word category should be at the position for verb form errors and noun number errors.

- Word-based fine-tuning, where a word is removed and the model predicts the word from a vocabulary of the most common 40.000 words from the Wikipedia dump. This is used to estimate probabilities for words in our confusion sets.

- Comma prediction, where we remove all commas and let the model predict where to insert commas. Any discrepancies between the produced and original sentence is used as comma edits, if the model is more than 95% certain.

GPT-2 GPT-2 is another Transformer-based language model trained on a dataset of 8 million web pages. GPT-2 only looks at the previous context to estimate probabilities. We take advantage of the fact that GPT-2 is trained using previous sentences as context by including the previous sentence when estimating probabilities.

3.3 Beam Search

Since our error correction models make a decision separately for every word, sometimes conflicting corrections can be made, e.g., "the cats is big." might be corrected to "the cat are big". Therefore we utilize beam search in order to efficiently explore combinations of corrections in order to find the optimal output sentence. We utilize a beam width of 3.

4 Confusion Sets

The first step in correcting a sentence is to identify the potentially erroneous tokens (or groups of tokens) and determine a set of possible corrections for each. We use several methods for deducing these confusion sets according to different error types.

4.1 Wikipedia Edit History

We utilize the WikEd Error Corpus (Grund-kiewicz and Junczys-Dowmunt, 2014) generated from Wikipedia revision histories to create confusion sets. We only retain edits of sentences where only a single word has been changed. We first end up with a list of confused token pairs which includes all types of edits, i.e., semantic or grammatical. We set up a set of rules to filter the edits not adapted to the task (e.g., the semantic replacements), and infrequent ones. We thus remove confusion pairs which define: (i) the replacement of a verb form (e.g., tense/subject–verb agreement errors); (ii) noun number errors; (iii) replacement of numbers or dates; (iv) synonyms and antonyms (using Wordnet[2] (Miller, 1995)); (v) replacement of pronouns with determiners; (vi) insertion/deletion of content words (e.g., nouns) and numbers; (vii) spelling errors.

We end up with a list of 348 edit pairs and their corresponding frequency counts in the WikedEd Error Corpus (ranging from 741 to 60,184 instances). The list includes, for instance, determiner replacements (e.g., "a"→"an") and frequently confused tokens (e.g. "to"→"too"). It covers most replacement error types but mostly closed-class words replacements such as R:DET or R:PREP.

4.2 Misspelled Words

Given a misspelled word (which we refer as non-word in the channel model) we use the Enchant library[3] to derive a set of suggestions for corrections. It mostly covers the R:SPELL error type but can also include other replacement types (such as content word replacements).

4.3 Specialized Models

For fine-tuned models on specific error types, we define specific rules (mainly based on Part-of-Speech tags) to detect the corresponding tokens and their possible replacements. We use the Spacy[4] library to PoS-tag the sentences.

---

[2] https://wordnet.princeton.edu/
[3] Wrapper for various spell checker engines.
[4] https://spacy.io/

Noun number model We detect the nouns by their PoS-tags: NN (singular) and NNS (plural) and use a list of matching singular/plural nouns derived from Wiktionary[5] to suggest a correction. It covers the R:NOUN:NUM and R:NOUN:INFL error types.

Verb forms model We detect all forms of verbs through their PoS-tags and derive a list of potential corrections (i.e., all possible inflections) using the list of English verb inflections from the Unimorph project (Kirov et al., 2016). Here, we mainly cover the R:VERB:FORM and R:VERB:SVA error types but also cases of R:VERB:INFL and R:VERB:TENSE error types.

5 Discussion

5.1 Results

Results on the BEA 2019 shared task test dataset are listed per edit and error type in Table 1. It is evident, that out approach deals with a wide array of error types, but with varying quality. The model performs particularly well on spelling errors, subject–verb agreement errors and inserting missing commas. However, the model performs rather poorly on the replacement of adjectives, adverbs and conjunctions which are based on confusion sets derived from Wikipedia edits suggesting that more filtering would be necessary.

5.2 Ablation analysis

We do an ablation analysis of the different components of our model to see how each part contributes to the performance. The global results are shown in Table 2. Detailed results per error type are shown in Appendix A for all models.

Beam search removing the beam search results in a considerable drop in $F_{0.5}$ by 2.73. This shows that figuring out how to optimally combine multiple local edits is important.

GPT-2 removing GPT-2 results in the largest drop in $F_{0.5}$ score of 5.09. The drop is large for most error types but the ablation is especially damaging on the precision of verb form errors.

BERT dropping BERT results in a 1.11 drop in $F_{0.5}$ score. This indicates that GPT-2 is pulling most of the weight.

<hr>

[5] https://www.wiktionary.org/

Error type	#	P	R	$F_{0.5}$
M:PUNCT	422	80.10	38.15	65.66
R:ADJ	24	12.50	4.17	8.93
R:ADV	17	33.33	5.88	17.24
R:CONJ	5	2.22	20.00	2.70
R:DET	129	20.48	52.71	23.34
R:MORPH	128	46.15	18.75	35.71
R:NOUN	70	50.00	8.57	25.42
R:NOUN:INFL	19	42.86	31.58	40.00
R:NOUN:NUM	290	43.79	68.31	47.18
R:ORTH	349	10.20	1.43	4.59
R:OTHER	618	20.43	6.15	13.95
R:PART	15	38.89	46.67	40.23
R:PREP	292	39.49	58.56	42.24
R:PRON	50	34.15	56.00	37.04
R:SPELL	321	76.51	75.08	76.22
R:VERB	134	25.00	2.99	10.10
R:VERB:FORM	169	47.96	55.62	49.32
R:VERB:INFL	7	100.00	85.71	96.77
R:VERB:SVA	146	74.39	83.56	76.06
R:VERB:TENSE	160	42.50	10.62	26.56
U:PUNCT	118	34.90	88.14	39.69
All error types	4498	44.52	28.88	40.17

Table 1: Span-level correction results of our system. We do not show results for the error types we do not predict.

Channel model we ablate the channel model by dividing out probabilities by uniform distribution over the candidates instead of using the frequency counts of the confusion sets and reverse Levenshtein distance. It results in a drop in $F_{0.5}$ score by 0.44.

	P	R	$F_{0.5}$
Chan + BERT + GPT	40.29	29.19	37.44
Chan + BERT + beam	37.03	28.98	35.08
Chan + GPT + beam	42.31	29.89	39.06
BERT + GPT + beam	43.50	29.49	39.73
Chan + BERT + GPT + beam	44.52	28.88	40.17

Table 2: Span-level correction results of the ablated models.

6 Conclusions

In this work we have presented our system for the BEA 2019 shared task on Grammatical Error Correction, which ranked as the 6th best in the low resource track.

Our ablation analysis showed that each of the components of our system has a positive effect on the overall performance, meaning that the combination of all of our components leads to the best score.

Future work could explore using more advanced

channel models, such as using phonetic features to determine the similarity of words. Furthermore our approach could also be adapted to handle insertions and deletions. Additionally, there are several parameters that could be tuned for better performance, including for example, α, the probability that the channel inserts an error, and the beam width.

Acknowledgements

This project was supported by Siteimprove and the Innovation Fund of Denmark through an industrial PhD grant.

References

Christopher Bryant and Ted Briscoe. 2018. Language model based grammatical error correction without annotated training data. In *Proceedings of the Thirteenth Workshop on Innovative Use of NLP for Building Educational Applications*, pages 247–253, New Orleans, Louisiana. Association for Computational Linguistics.

Christopher Bryant, Mariano Felice, Øistein E. Andersen, and Ted Briscoe. 2019. The BEA-2019 Shared Task on Grammatical Error Correction. In *Proceedings of the 14th Workshop on Innovative Use of NLP for Building Educational Applications*. Association for Computational Linguistics.

Robert Dale and Adam Kilgarriff. 2011. Helping Our Own: The HOO 2011 Pilot Shared Task. In *Proceedings of the 13th European Workshop on Natural Language Generation*, ENLG '11.

Vidas Daudaravicius, Rafael E. Banchs, Elena Volodina, and Courtney Napoles. 2016. A Report on the Automatic Evaluation of Scientific Writing Shared Task. In *Proceedings of BEA 2016*.

Jacob Devlin, Ming-Wei Chang, Kenton Lee, and Kristina Toutanova. 2018. BERT: Pre-training of Deep Bidirectional Transformers for Language Understanding. *arXiv preprint arXiv:1810.04805*.

Tao Ge, Furu Wei, and Ming Zhou. 2018. Reaching Human-level Performance in Automatic Grammatical Error Correction: An Empirical Study. *CoRR*, abs/1807.01270.

Roman Grundkiewicz and Marcin Junczys-Dowmunt. 2014. The WikEd Error Corpus: A Corpus of Corrective Wikipedia Edits and its Application to Grammatical Error Correction. In *Advances in Natural Language Processing – Lecture Notes in Computer Science*, volume 8686, pages 478–490. Springer.

Roman Grundkiewicz and Marcin Junczys-Dowmunt. 2018. Near Human-Level Performance in Grammatical Error Correction with Hybrid Machine Translation. *CoRR*, abs/1804.05945.

Daniel Jurafsky and James H. Martin. 2009. *Speech and Language Processing*, 2nd edition. Pearson London.

Zhu Kaili, Chuan Wang, Ruobing Li, Yang Liu, Tianlei Hu, and Hui Lin. 2018. A Simple but Effective Classification Model for Grammatical Error Correction. *CoRR*, abs/1807.00488.

Mark Kernighan, Kenneth Church, and William A. Gale. 1990. A Spelling Correction Program Based on a Noisy Channel Model. In *Proceedings of the 13th conference on Computational linguistics*.

Christo Kirov, John Sylak-Glassman, Roger Que, and David Yarowsky. 2016. Very-large Scale Parsing and Normalization of Wiktionary Morphological Paradigms. In *Proceedings of LREC 2016*.

Victor Makarenkov, Lior Rokach, and Bracha Shapira. 2019. Choosing the Right Word: Using Bidirectional LSTM Tagger for Writing Support Systems. *CoRR*, abs/1901.02490.

Eric Mays, Fred J. Damerau, and Robert Mercer. 1990. Context Based Spelling Correction. *Information Processing Management*, 27:517–522.

George A Miller. 1995. WordNet: a Lexical Database for English. *Communications of the ACM*, 38(11).

Hwee Tou Ng, Siew Mei Wu, Ted Briscoe, Christian Hadiwinoto, Raymond Hendy Susanto, and Christopher Bryant. 2014. The CoNLL-2014 Shared Task on Grammatical Error Correction. In *Proceedings of CoNLL 2014: Shared Task*.

Hwee Tou Ng, Siew Mei Wu, Yuanbin Wu, Christian Hadiwinoto, and Joel Tetreault. 2013. The CoNLL-2013 Shared Task on Grammatical Error Correction. In *Proceedings of CoNLL 2013: Shared Task*.

Alec Radford, Jeff Wu, Rewon Child, David Luan, Dario Amodei, and Ilya Sutskever. 2019. Language Models are Unsupervised Multitask Learners. *OpenAI Blog*.

Ashish Vaswani, Noam Shazeer, Niki Parmar, Jakob Uszkoreit, Llion Jones, Aidan N Gomez, Łukasz Kaiser, and Illia Polosukhin. 2017. Attention Is All You Need. In *Proceedings of Advances in neural information processing systems (NIPS 2017)*.

A Results per error type

Error type	#	All models	C+B+G	C+B+beam	C+G+beam	B+G+beam
M:PUNCT	422	65.66	65.86	65.54	64.15	65.65
R:ADJ	24	8.93	7.69	8.20	7.81	15.38
R:ADV	17	17.24	12.20	17.24	16.67	13.16
R:CONJ	5	2.70	1.92	2.65	2.65	2.36
R:DET	129	23.34	19.92	23.15	22.24	23.29
R:MORPH	128	35.71	29.48	28.12	31.18	35.09
R:NOUN	70	25.42	23.81	25.21	23.08	23.81
R:NOUN:INFL	19	40.00	38.46	37.31	69.57	46.67
R:NOUN:NUM	290	47.18	43.82	42.59	47.11	46.46
R:ORTH	349	4.59	4.58	4.57	4.61	4.60
R:OTHER	618	13.95	13.30	14.24	13.29	15.07
R:PART	15	40.23	44.12	38.89	33.98	41.67
R:PREP	292	42.24	39.47	41.46	40.46	42.01
R:PRON	50	37.04	34.25	32.22	34.04	35.48
R:SPELL	321	76.22	73.66	75.59	70.85	75.02
R:VERB	134	10.10	9.76	9.35	11.57	10.47
R:VERB:FORM	169	49.32	44.53	17.86	46.58	48.03
R:VERB:INFL	7	96.77	96.77	96.77	96.77	96.77
R:VERB:SVA	146	76.06	72.73	72.66	73.16	74.88
R:VERB:TENSE	160	26.56	26.88	26.61	31.73	30.03
U:PRON	21	0.00	20.00	0.00	18.52	20.00
U:PUNCT	118	39.69	39.13	39.91	39.79	39.91
All types	4498	40.17	37.44	35.08	39.06	39.73

Table 3: Span-level correction results ($F_{0.5}$) for different error types (we do not show results for the error types that we do not predict). **C**: Channel Model, **B**: BERT, **G**: GPT-2.

The BLCU System in the BEA 2019 Shared Task

Liner Yang[†], Chencheng Wang[‡], Tianxin Liao[†], Erhong Yang[†]
[†]Beijing Language and Culture University, Beijing, China
[‡]Beijing University of Technology, China
`lineryang@gmail.com, hsamswang@gmail.com,`
`dubhe98@163.com, yerhong@126.com`

Abstract

This paper describes the BLCU Group submissions to the Building Educational Applications (BEA) 2019 Shared Task on Grammatical Error Correction (GEC). The task is to detect and correct grammatical errors that occurred in essays. We participate in 2 tracks including the Restricted Track and the Unrestricted Track. Our system is based on a Transformer model architecture. We integrate many effective methods proposed in recent years, such as Byte Pair Encoding, model ensemble, checkpoints average and spell checker. We also corrupt the public monolingual data to further improve the performance of the model. On the test data of the BEA 2019 Shared Task, our system yields $F_{0.5}$ = 58.62 for the Restricted Track and 59.50 for the Unrestricted Track, ranking twelfth and fourth respectively.

1 Introduction

The GEC task has attracted wide interest in recent years. The goal of GEC is to detect and correct errors in essays made by English as a Second Language (ESL) learners. Since the end of both CoNLL2013 (Ng et al., 2013) and CoNLL2014 (Ng et al., 2014), many GEC researchers have used the two test sets as benchmark evaluation sets. Because of using different training sets, such as Lang-8, NUCLE, FCE, the performance of the systems are not comparable, even though they are evaluated on the same test sets. The Building Educational Applications 2019 Shared Task provides a forum for participating teams to evaluate on the same blind test set using the same training sets and evaluation metric.

Unlike previous GEC shared tasks, new corpus provided by the organizers has different CEFR[1]

---

[1]`https://www.cambridgeenglish.org/`
`exams-and-tests/cefr/`

	A	B	C	N	Total
Train	10,493	13,032	10,783	-	34,308
Dev	1,037	1,290	1,069	998	4,384
Test	1,107	1,330	1,010	1,030	4,477
Total	29.3%	36.3%	29.8%	4.6%	43,169

Table 1: Statistics for the sentence pairs of W&I+L corpus. A, B and C represent different CEFR levels for describing language ability, from beginner to proficient user. N denotes essays written by native English students.

levels. The distribution of different levels is shown in Table 1. The training set includes essays at different levels of language ability, but no articles written by native students. There are three tracks in this shared task: Restricted Track, Unrestricted Track and Low Resource Track. Each sub-task restricts the error-corrected corpus that can be used except the Unrestricted Track. It means that the model needs to learn useful information from a large number of data written by ESL in order to correct the errors written by native learners.

In this paper, we describe the submissions from the group of Beijing Language and Culture University (BLCU) in the first two tracks. This shared task aims to tackle the full set of grammar errors, classified into 56 kinds of errors. More types of errors represent an increase in difficulty. Subtask one of the shared task (Restricted Track) restricts participants to use only the learner corpus provided by the organizers. We believe that effective use of monolingual data will enable the model to achieve better performance. Therefore, we propose a data augmentation method to corrupt a monolingual corpus with a fixed probability according to the proportion of errors in the development set and integrate many techniques proposed in recent years. We also participate in the second subtask (Unrestricted Track) which allows participants to use any learner corpus.

Proceedings of the Fourteenth Workshop on Innovative Use of NLP for Building Educational Applications, pages 197–206
Florence, Italy, August 2, 2019. ©2019 Association for Computational Linguistics

Example	Source	Target
A	I think that **the** public transport will always **be** in the future .	I think that public transport will always **exist** in the future .
B	When the concert finished , we went to **cloakroom** to get **signatures** from musicians .	When the concert finished , we went to **the dressing room** to get **autographs** from musicians .
C	Nevertheless , **you have** another side to this reality .	Nevertheless , **there is** another side to this reality .
N	All professional boxers are at risk from being killed in **his** next fight .	All professional boxers are at risk from being killed in **their** next fight .

Table 2: Example of sentence pairs with different CEFR levels. **Bold font** represents the difference between the source and the target.

The paper is structured as follows: we present the related work in the next section. In Section 3, we describe the details of our system features. Section 4, we describe the training procedure for our system. Section 5 we specify the data sets and experiments settings. We draw our conclusions in Section 6.

2 Related Work

To our knowledge, Helping Our Own (HOO) 2011 (Dale and Kilgarriff, 2011) is the first shared task on grammatical error correction. The aim of HOO2011 is to correct errors in papers written by non-native authors (NNS), which have been published in the proceedings of ACL. Dahlmeier et al. (2011) use different open-source tools to detect spelling mistakes, prepositional errors and article errors and correct them with rule-based methods. Except for the group of University of Illinois, all participants score below 20.

Therefore, the HOO2012 shared task (Dale et al., 2012) focus more specifically on the preposition and determiner errors made by NNS who are learning English. Dahlmeier et al. (2012) treat the error correction as a classification problem and build different classifiers for determiner errors and preposition errors. Their system achieves the highest score.

The Conference on Computational Natural Language Learning (CoNLL) 2013 (Ng et al., 2013) believes that the GEC community is ready for dealing with more error types, including the two types in HOO2012, noun number, verb form and subject-verb agreement errors. Although the number of error types has increased, the most effective way at that time is still to use a pipeline of processes that combines the results from multiple systems, like Rozovskaya et al. (2013).

The CoNLL 2014 shared task (Ng et al., 2014) is the extension of CoNLL 2013, which requires participants to correct all 28 error types. Felice et al. (2014) present a hybrid approach, using statistical machine translation (SMT) as part of their pipeline system. Junczys-Dowmunt and Grundkiewicz (2014) combine Lang-8 large-scale corpus (Mizumoto et al., 2011) with the Moses (Koehn et al., 2007) SMT system. These two studies perform well, ranking first and third respectively.

Yuan and Briscoe (2016) present the first study using neural machine translation (NMT) for grammatical error correction. Xie et al. (2016a) use a character level RNN structure with attention. But all their results are worse than SMT at the same period. Chollampatt and Ng (2018) use a multilayer convolutional encoder-decoder neural network with embeddings that make use of character N-gram information. It is the first neural approach that outperforms the current state-of-the-art statistical machine translation-based approach. In the same year, Grundkiewicz and Junczys-Dowmunt (2018) combine the RNN with a phrase-based SMT system to achieve a similar score to Chollampatt and Ng (2018).

On the other hand, many scholars are committed to using additional monolingual corpora to improve the effectiveness of the models. Sennrich et al. (2016a) argue that the decoder of an NMT model is equivalent to a language model. They explore strategies to train with monolingual data without changing the NMT architecture. Yuan and Felice (2013) explore ways of generating pairs

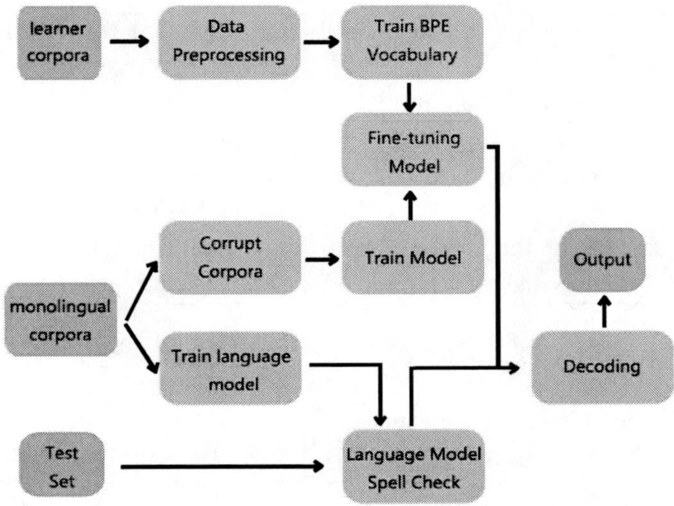

Figure 1: The pipeline of our grammatical error correction system

of incorrect and correct sentences automatically from other existing learner corpora. Both Rei et al. (2017) and Xie et al. (2018) add noise to monolingual data using Back-translation mechanism based on SMT and NMT. Wang et al. (2018) randomly replace words in both the source and target sentence with other random words from their corresponding vocabularies.

3 System Features

In this section, we will describe the features of our grammatical error correction system.

Figure 1 shows the general pipeline of the system. The training steps are shown as follows:

1) Pre-processing the learner corpora provided by the organizers.

2) Training Byte Pair Encoding (BPE) on the corpora.

3) Corrupting the One Billion Word Benchmark monolingual corpus.

4) Training model using corrupted data.

5) Fine-tuning model using the learner corpora.

The error correction steps for evaluation are:

1) Using monolingual corpus to train a language model as the spell check model.

2) Using the spell check model to correct spelling errors in the test set.

3) Decoding the output of the previous step with the grammar error correction model.

The final output after the last step forms our submission to the shared task. The following sections describe each of these components in detail.

3.1 Pre-processing and sub-words

In track one, we use four learner corpora provided by the organizers and an additional monolingual corpus.

NUCLE - This corpus is collected by the National University of Singapore and release in CoNLL shared task (Dahlmeier et al., 2013).

Lang-8 - This corpus is collected from the website called Lang-8. It is the largest publicly available learner corpus (Mizumoto et al., 2011).

FCE - The First Certificate in English corpus is collected by the University of Cambridge (Yannakoudakis et al., 2011).

W&I+L - It consists of two corpora, including Write & Improve (Bryant et al., 2019) and LOCNESS (Granger, 1998). The Write & Improve is collected by the University of Cambridge with W&I system (Yannakoudakis et al., 2018)

Source	Target
said that two Tele involved the case had been disciplined .	It said that two officers involved in the case had been disciplined .
That y to have been com their model til stat now .	That seems to have been their model up til now .
Why does sp everything have to become such a issue	Why does everything have to become such a big issue ?
Ch majority will be of the standard 6X6 configuration for carrying personnel k	The majority will be of the standard 6X6 configuration for carrying personnel .

Table 3: Example of sentence pairs made by corruption method.

and is one of the key contributions of this shared task.

One Billion - One Billion Word Benchmark dataset is a public monolingual corpus (Chelba et al., 2013), consisting of close to one billion words of English taken from news articles on the web.

All learner corpora use M2 format. For each sentence, the start and end token offsets of the wrong text range are marked and the corresponding corrections are provided.

Firstly, we extract the original sentences and modified sentences from the M2 files and write them into two files. Like in previous works (Zhao et al., 2019), we remove the unchanged sentence pairs from the original sentences and the modified sentences. We use spaCy v1.9.0[2] and the en_core_web_sm-1.2.0 model as a serializer based on the organizers' recommendations.

By analyzing the data, we find that there are many instances containing URLs in NUCLE, character encoding errors and emojis in Lang-8. So we removed the sentence pairs containing the previously mentioned case from all training sets.

In track two, we use an additional Non-public Lang-8 corpus besides all the corpora used in track one. The pre-processing method is the same as before.

In order to solve the large vocabulary and out-of-vocabulary (OOV) problem, we adopt the recommendation of Junczys-Dowmunt et al. (2018) to use the Byte Pair Encoding (BPE) algorithm (Sennrich et al., 2016b). All of the corpora are used to train the BPE vocabulary except the One Billion monolingual corpus. We split the training set, development set and the

[2]https://spacy.io/

test set into sub-words using the learned BPE code. The sub-words in the test set will be merged before evaluating.

3.2 Corrupting Corpora

Many resent work regard grammatical error correction as a low-resource neural machine translation task (Junczys-Dowmunt et al., 2018; Zhao et al., 2019; Lichtarge et al., 2019). Both Grundkiewicz and Junczys-Dowmunt (2014) and Lichtarge et al. (2019) use the Wikipedia revision histories to generate additional corpora. Junczys-Dowmunt and Grundkiewicz (2016); Junczys-Dowmunt et al. (2018) utilize the Common Crawl corpus to train the language model and pre-train part of the NMT model. Inspired by these studies, we also try to use a monolingual corpus for data augmentation.

First, we define the error rate of the corpus as:

$$Er(C) = \frac{1}{n} \sum_{i=0}^{n} \frac{\text{levenshtein}(src, trg)}{\text{length}(trg)} \quad (1)$$

where n is the number of sentence pairs in corpus, src refers to the sentence to be modified, trg is the modification of src. levenshtein(src, trg) means the shortest edit distance for the src and trg in terms of tokens. length(trg) refers to the number of token in trg.

Secondly, we assume that errors in the corpus can be divided into three types (Bryant et al., 2017):

- Missing type (**M**)

  src : w_0 ... w_{i-1} $\quad$ w_{i+1} ... w_n

  trg : w_0 ... w_{i-1} w_i w_{i+1} ... w_n

  Token w_i is a missing type.

- Unnecessary type (**U**)

  src : w_0 ... w_{i-1} w_i w_{i+1} ... w_n

  trg : w_0 ... w_{i-1} w_{i+1} ... w_n

  Token w_i is an unnecessary type.

- Replacement type (**R**)

  src : w_0 ... w_{i-1} $w_{i'}$ w_{i+1} ... w_n

  trg : w_0 ... w_{i-1} w_i w_{i+1} ... w_n

  Token w_i is a replacement type.

Counting all of the training sets, we find that the error rate is 30% and the ratio of M : U : R is 1:1:1. We apply this to corrupt the monolingual corpus. It means that 30% tokens in the training set will be corrupted. The steps of corruption are shown as follows:

- Delete the token with a probability of 33%.

- Randomly add a token in the vocabulary with a probability of 33%.

- Randomly replace a token in the vocabulary with a probability of 34%.

This process produces a large number of wrong sentences. Finally, the original One Billion Word Benchmark corpus sentence is the target sentence and the output of the corruption system is the corresponding source sentence.

3.3 Transformer

As mentioned in the previous section, neural machine translation has become the state-of-the-art approach for Grammatical Error Correction. We adopt the attention-based NMT model proposed by Vaswani (Vaswani et al., 2017).

The embedding layer is divided into two embeddings, including token and position embedding. The token embedding contains the vector corresponding to each token, and the position embedding contains the vector of each absolute position. The embedding layer encodes each token S_i^{src} of the input sentence S^{src} into a vector $h_{S_i}^{src}$ by looking up in a token embedding matrix and adding a position vector, as shown in Eq (2).

$$h_{S_i}^{src} = Token\_emb(S_i^{src}) + Position\_emb(i) \tag{2}$$

The Encoder has N identical attention blocks, each block containing a Multi-Head attention and a linear layer. The Multi-Head is the concatenation of the N attention heads. The Encoder produces the input context-aware hidden state, shown in the Eq (3,4).

$$MultiHead(h_S^{src}, h_S^{src}, h_S^{src}) =$$
$$Concat(Attention(h_S^{src}, h_S^{src}, h_S^{src})) \tag{3}$$

$$HS_S^{src} = Encoder(h_S^{src}) \tag{4}$$

The structure of the decoder is similar to that of the encoder, with N identical attention blocks. The only difference is that the decoder's attention block has an extra Multi-Head attention which attends over the encoder's context-aware hidden state. The decoder updates the hidden state of the current layer based on the attention output from the encoder and the hidden states of previous layer:

$$HS_{S_{i+1}}^{trg} = Decoder(HS_S^{src}, HS_{S_i}^{trg}) \tag{5}$$

The final decoder layer output vector HS_S^{trg} is dot-multiplied with the output embedding. Applying softmax on the inner product's output can get the predicted probability of each word, like Eq (6). Words with the highest predicted probability are chosen as the final output.

$$p(S_{i+1}|S_1, ..., S_i, S) =$$
$$softmax(OutEmbedding(HS_S^{trg})) \tag{6}$$

The model can be trained with maximum likelihood estimation, as shown in Eq(7):

$$L(S^{trg}) = -\sum_{i=1}^{T} log(p(S_i^{trg})) \tag{7}$$

For the grammatical error correction task, the model copy correct tokens in most cases. But what the model really needs to learn is to translate the wrong tokens into the right ones. Therefore, we add the Edit-weighted MLE objective (Junczys-Dowmunt et al., 2018) into the loss function to give the wrong tokens greater penalty. Details of the implementation are shown as follows:

$$L(S^{trg}) = -\sum_{i=1}^{T} A(S_j^{src}, S_i^{trg})log(p(S_i^{trg}))$$

$$A(S_j^{src}, S_i^{trg}) = \begin{cases} \Lambda \ \ if \ S_j^{src} \neq S_i^{trg} \\ 1 \ \ otherwise \end{cases} \quad (8)$$

where $A(S_j^{src}, S_i^{trg})$ is an alignment between source token and target token. It means that if the source token is inconsistent with the target, the loss value will be multiplied by Λ.

3.4 Language Model based Spell Checker

As mentioned in Xie et al. (2016b) and Chollampatt and Ng (2017), a token-based neural machine translation model is not designed to correct spelling mistakes. To address this issue, we have adopted a language model based spell checker.

We use Kenlm[3] to build a 5-gram language model from the Billion Word Benchmark dataset. Based on this language model, we use CyHunspell[4] which is a Python wrapper for Hunspell to correct spelling errors in corpora.

Algorithm 1 describes the process of correcting the corpus using the spell check model.

Algorithm 1 Language Model based Spell Checker

Input: Language Model LM, corpus with errors E, error correction threshold η, CyHunspell spell checker $Spell$
Output: corrected corpus C
  Initialize $C = \{\}$
  for all sentences s_i in E **do**
     score = LM.score(s_i)
     for all tokens t_j in s_i **do**
        candidate = $Spell$.suggest(t_j)
        temp = s_i.apply(candidate)
        tempscore = LM.score(temp)
        if tempscore/score $> \eta$ **then**
           $s_i = s_i$.apply(candidate)
        end if
     end for
     Add s_i to C
  end for
  return C

For each sentence in E, record the language model score. The modification will be applied

[3]https://github.com/kpu/kenlm
[4]https://pypi.org/project/CyHunspell/

only if the ratio of *tempscore* to *score* is greater than η. Finally, the output of the program is the corrected result.

4 Training procedure

Augmentation data for corruption is collected from articles on news sites. The Lang-8 corpus used in training is written by many second language learners about their daily life. Corrupted corpus and learner corpus belong to different domains. Moreover, the errors contained in the augmentation data are not common errors for second language learners.

Based on this situation, we train on the augmentation corpus and the learner corpus separately. Firstly, we pre-train the corrupted corpus for 5 epochs. We use the arithmetic mean of the last three epochs as the final weighed result of the pre-training.

Next, we fine-tune the pre-trained model using the learner corpus consisting of (Non-public) Lang-8, NUCLE, FCE and W&I+L datasets and evaluate on the development set at each end of epoch. For each single model, we calculate the arithmetic mean of the five epochs with the best cross-entropy cost on the development set as the final model.

Our model is composed of the ensemble of 8 single models. The hyper-parameters and the training procedure used in each single model are the same except the random seed.

5 Data sets and Experiments

In this section, we will detail the data sets, the hyper-parameters and the open source tools we use.

5.1 Data sets

The statistics for the data we use in this shared task are shown in Table 6. We implement the pre-processing method mentioned in Section 3.1 for both tracks. The first four rows list the fine-tuning datasets we use in track one. The fifth line summaries the above datasets. The Non-public Lang-8 in the sixth line is the additional corpus we collect from Lang-8[5]. It is worth mentioning that some instances of Non-public Lang-8 also exist in Lang-8. We use the union of all learner corpora as the training data for track two, including 6 million

[5]https://lang-8.com/

Model	without LM Spell Checker			with LM Spell Checker		
	Precision	Recall	$F_{0.5}$	Precision	Recall	$F_{0.5}$
transformer single	43.11	24.98	37.65	43.61	26.87	38.78
transformer single + CC	46.14	27.66	40.71	46.23	29.50	41.52
transformer ensemble + CC	48.83	26.39	41.79	48.96	28.29	42.72

Table 4: The evaluation of our system on the track one development set. Transformer single refers to the single model, while transformer ensemble denotes the ensemble of 8 single models. *CC* means use additional corrupted corpus.

	Restricted Track			Unrestricted Track		
	Precision	Recall	$F_{0.5}$	Precision	Recall	$F_{0.5}$
A	64.26	49.89	60.76	68.29	54.18	64.91
B	61.83	48.71	58.67	61.89	53.87	60.10
C	60.75	55.84	59.70	56.31	64.04	57.71
N	49.02	58.86	50.71	44.25	62.58	47.00
ALL	60.81	51.22	58.62	60.32	56.42	59.50

Table 5: The evaluation of our system on the test set.

Corpus	Before process	After process
NUCLE	56,670	21,242
FCE	32,844	20,552
Lang-8	1,112,513	560,542
W&I+L	34,308	22,544
Track One	1,236,335	624,880
Non-public Lang-8	8,655,173	6,230,606
Track Two	9,891,508	6,456,889
One Billion*	30,301,028	20,032,188
W&I+L(dev)	4,384	-
W&I+L(test)*	4,477	-

Table 6: Number of the sentence pair for different dataset. Track one summaries the statistic of all of the data we use in track one, and so does Track Two. Non-public Lang-8 is the additional corpus we use in track two. W&I+L(dev,test) is provided by the organizers. * indicates that this corpus has no target available.

sentence pairs. The last two rows in the table show the size of the development and test set.

5.2 Experimental settings

In this shared task, we use the Transformer model (Vaswani et al., 2017) implemented by FAIR[6] as the GEC model. The detailed parameters of the model are as follows: model BPE embeddings are trained for 50,000 steps (Junczys-Dowmunt et al., 2018) on the error-annotated data by the subword algorithm[7]. Both the source embedding and the target embeddings have 512 dimensions and use the same vocabulary. We share the weights of decoder input and output embeddings. Both of the encoder and decoder have 6 multi-head layers and 8 attention heads. The size of the inner layer at each layer is 2048.

We use the Adam optimizer (Kingma and Ba, 2014) to train transformer with inverse squared root schedule which decays the learning rate based on the inverse square root of the warm-up steps. The initial learning rate is 5×10^{-4} and the warm-up step is set to be 4000. We use a batch size of approximately 32,000 tokens and fine-tune the model on learner corpus for 50,000 steps. Dropout is applied at a ratio of 0.3. The loss factor Λ is set to 1.2.

The ensemble model is composed of 8 identical Transformers trained and fine-tuned separately. The only difference between them is that they use different random seeds.

During model inference, we run beam search with the emsemble model and set the beam size to 12. We use ERRANT[8] (Bryant et al., 2017) to evaluate the decoding results.

5.3 Experiment result and analysis

Table 4 shows the performance of our model with different settings. For the *without LM Spell Checker* columns, we do not use language model based spell checker to correct spelling mistakes,

---

[6]https://github.com/pytorch/fairseq
[7]https://github.com/rsennrich/subword-nmt

[8]https://github.com/chrisjbryant/errant

while *with LM Spell Checker* is the opposite. The first two lines report the result with a single Transformer model, and the last line with the ensemble model. + *CC* means that we pretrain the transformer model using the corrupted corpus and then fine-tune with learner corpus. We submit the best model, namely the ensemble model, for the shared task.

In Table 4, we can see that the main contribution comes from the corruption method. About 20 million monolingual data have brought about an increase of 3.06 in terms of F-measure on a single model. The spell checker based on the language model improves the performance of the model by about one point. We use an ensemble of identical models (except for the random seed), but we will attempt to use different types of models in future work.

Table 5 shows the result on the test set which is evaluated by the organizers. Comparing the results of the two tracks, we find that training with the Non-public Lang-8 data can significantly improve the recall about 5-10 points. However, in terms of $F_{0.5}$, the performance of the model has only been significantly improved on the test data at A and B levels, and has dropped by about two points in C and N. One possible explanation is that the errors contained in the Non-public Lang-8 belong to the lower CEFR level. Overtraining in a large amount of data containing beginner errors has reduced the performance of our system at C and N levels.

6 Conclusions

In this paper, we have described the submission to the BEA 2019 shared task on Grammatical Error Correction. Our approach combines a method of data augmentation with a pipeline system based on the Transformer model. We first corrupt the monolingual corpus and pre-train a single model on it. Then we fine-tune on the learner corpora and ensemble eight single Transformer models to further improve the performance.

The results of our best system on the blind test set are $F_{0.5}$ = 58.62 for the Restricted Track and $F_{0.5}$ = 59.50 for the Unrestricted Track, placing our system in the twelfth and fourth place respectively.

Acknowledgments

This research project is supported by Science Foundation of Beijing Language and Culture University (supported by "the Fundamental Research Funds for the Central Universities") (18YBB20), and the National Natural Science Foundation of China (61872402).

References

Christopher Bryant, Mariano Felice, Øistein E. Andersen, and Ted Briscoe. 2019. The BEA-2019 Shared Task on Grammatical Error Correction. In *Proceedings of the 14th Workshop on Innovative Use of NLP for Building Educational Applications*. Association for Computational Linguistics.

Christopher Bryant, Mariano Felice, and Ted Briscoe. 2017. In *Proceedings of the 55th Annual Meeting of the Association for Computational Linguistics*. Association for Computational Linguistics.

Ciprian Chelba, Tomas Mikolov, Mike Schuster, Qi Ge, Thorsten Brants, Phillipp Koehn, and Tony Robinson. 2013. One billion word benchmark for measuring progress in statistical language modeling. *arXiv preprint arXiv:1312.3005*.

Shamil Chollampatt and Hwee Tou Ng. 2017. Connecting the dots: Towards human-level grammatical error correction. In *Proceedings of the 12th Workshop on Innovative Use of NLP for Building Educational Applications*.

Shamil Chollampatt and Hwee Tou Ng. 2018. A multilayer convolutional encoder-decoder neural network for grammatical error correction. In *Thirty-Second AAAI Conference on Artificial Intelligence*.

Daniel Dahlmeier, Hwee Tou Ng, and Eric Jun Feng Ng. 2012. Nus at the hoo 2012 shared task. In *Proceedings of the Seventh Workshop on Building Educational Applications Using NLP*.

Daniel Dahlmeier, Hwee Tou Ng, and Thanh Phu Tran. 2011. Nus at the hoo 2011 pilot shared task. In *Proceedings of the Generation Challenges Session at the 13th European Workshop on Natural Language Generation*. Association for Computational Linguistics.

Daniel Dahlmeier, Hwee Tou Ng, and Siew Mei Wu. 2013. Building a large annotated corpus of learner english: The nus corpus of learner english. In *Proceedings of the eighth workshop on innovative use of NLP for building educational applications*.

Robert Dale, Ilya Anisimoff, and George Narroway. 2012. Hoo 2012: A report on the preposition and determiner error correction shared task. In *Proceedings of the Seventh Workshop on Building Educational Applications Using NLP*. Association for Computational Linguistics.

Robert Dale and Adam Kilgarriff. 2011. Helping our own: The hoo 2011 pilot shared task. In *Proceedings of the 13th European Workshop on Natural Language Generation*. Association for Computational Linguistics.

Mariano Felice, Zheng Yuan, Oistein E. Andersen, Helen Yannakoudakis, and Ekaterina Kochmar. 2014. Grammatical error correction using hybrid systems and type filtering. In *Proceedings of the Eighteenth Conference on Computational Natural Language Learning: Shared Task*. Association for Computational Linguistics.

Sylviane Granger. 1998. The computer learner corpus: A versatile new source of data for SLA research. In Sylviane Granger, editor, *Learner English on Computer*, pages 3–18. Addison Wesley Longman, London and New York.

Roman Grundkiewicz and Marcin Junczys-Dowmunt. 2014. The wiked error corpus: A corpus of corrective wikipedia edits and its application to grammatical error correction. In *International Conference on Natural Language Processing*. Springer.

Roman Grundkiewicz and Marcin Junczys-Dowmunt. 2018. Near human-level performance in grammatical error correction with hybrid machine translation. In *Proceedings of the 2018 Conference of the North American Chapter of the Association for Computational Linguistics: Human Language Technologies*. Association for Computational Linguistics.

Marcin Junczys-Dowmunt and Roman Grundkiewicz. 2014. The amu system in the conll-2014 shared task: Grammatical error correction by data-intensive and feature-rich statistical machine translation. In *Proceedings of the Eighteenth Conference on Computational Natural Language Learning: Shared Task*.

Marcin Junczys-Dowmunt and Roman Grundkiewicz. 2016. Phrase-based machine translation is state-of-the-art for automatic grammatical error correction. *arXiv preprint arXiv:1605.06353*.

Marcin Junczys-Dowmunt, Roman Grundkiewicz, Shubha Guha, and Kenneth Heafield. 2018. Approaching neural grammatical error correction as a low-resource machine translation task. In *Proceedings of the 2018 Conference of the North American Chapter of the Association for Computational Linguistics: Human Language Technologies*. Association for Computational Linguistics.

Diederik P Kingma and Jimmy Ba. 2014. Adam: A method for stochastic optimization. *arXiv preprint arXiv:1412.6980*.

Philipp Koehn, Hieu Hoang, Alexandra Birch, Chris Callison-Burch, Marcello Federico, Nicola Bertoldi, Brooke Cowan, Wade Shen, Christine Moran, Richard Zens, et al. 2007. Moses: Open source toolkit for statistical machine translation. In *Proceedings of the 45th annual meeting of the association for computational linguistics companion volume proceedings of the demo and poster sessions*.

Jared Lichtarge, Chris Alberti, Shankar Kumar, Noam Shazeer, Niki Parmar, and Simon Tong. 2019. Corpora generation for grammatical error correction. *arXiv preprint arXiv:1904.05780*.

Tomoya Mizumoto, Mamoru Komachi, Masaaki Nagata, and Yuji Matsumoto. 2011. Mining revision log of language learning sns for automated japanese error correction of second language learners. In *Proceedings of 5th International Joint Conference on Natural Language Processing*.

Hwee Tou Ng, Siew Mei Wu, Ted Briscoe, Christian Hadiwinoto, Raymond Hendy Susanto, and Christopher Bryant. 2014. The conll-2014 shared task on grammatical error correction. In *Proceedings of the Eighteenth Conference on Computational Natural Language Learning: Shared Task*. Association for Computational Linguistics.

Hwee Tou Ng, Siew Mei Wu, Yuanbin Wu, Christian Hadiwinoto, and Joel Tetreault. 2013. The conll-2013 shared task on grammatical error correction. In *Proceedings of the Seventeenth Conference on Computational Natural Language Learning: Shared Task*. Association for Computational Linguistics.

Marek Rei, Mariano Felice, Zheng Yuan, and Ted Briscoe. 2017. Artificial error generation with machine translation and syntactic patterns. In *Proceedings of the 12th Workshop on Innovative Use of NLP for Building Educational Applications*.

Alla Rozovskaya, Kai-Wei Chang, Mark Sammons, and Dan Roth. 2013. The university of illinois system in the conll-2013 shared task. In *Proceedings of the Seventeenth Conference on Computational Natural Language Learning: Shared Task*. Association for Computational Linguistics.

Rico Sennrich, Barry Haddow, and Alexandra Birch. 2016a. Improving neural machine translation models with monolingual data. In *Proceedings of the 54th Annual Meeting of the Association for Computational Linguistics*. Association for Computational Linguistics.

Rico Sennrich, Barry Haddow, and Alexandra Birch. 2016b. Neural machine translation of rare words with subword units. In *Proceedings of the 54th Annual Meeting of the Association for Computational Linguistics*. Association for Computational Linguistics.

Ashish Vaswani, Noam Shazeer, Niki Parmar, Jakob Uszkoreit, Llion Jones, Aidan N Gomez, Łukasz Kaiser, and Illia Polosukhin. 2017. Attention is all you need. In *Advances in neural information processing systems*.

Xinyi Wang, Hieu Pham, Zihang Dai, and Graham Neubig. 2018. Switchout: an efficient data augmentation algorithm for neural machine translation. In *Proceedings of the 2018 Conference on Empirical Methods in Natural Language Processing*.

Ziang Xie, Anand Avati, Naveen Arivazhagan, Dan Jurafsky, and Andrew Y Ng. 2016a. Neural language correction with character-based attention. *arXiv preprint arXiv:1603.09727*.

Ziang Xie, Anand Avati, Naveen Arivazhagan, Dan Jurafsky, and Andrew Y Ng. 2016b. Neural language correction with character-based attention. *arXiv preprint arXiv:1603.09727*.

Ziang Xie, Guillaume Genthial, Stanley Xie, Andrew Ng, and Dan Jurafsky. 2018. Noising and denoising natural language: Diverse backtranslation for grammar correction. In *Proceedings of the 2018 Conference of the North American Chapter of the Association for Computational Linguistics: Human Language Technologies*.

Helen Yannakoudakis, Øistein E Andersen, Ardeshir Geranpayeh, Ted Briscoe, and Diane Nicholls. 2018. Developing an automated writing placement system for esl learners. *Applied Measurement in Education*, 31(3):251–267.

Helen Yannakoudakis, Ted Briscoe, and Ben Medlock. 2011. A new dataset and method for automatically grading esol texts. In *Proceedings of the 49th Annual Meeting of the Association for Computational Linguistics: Human Language Technologies*. Association for Computational Linguistics.

Zheng Yuan and Ted Briscoe. 2016. Grammatical error correction using neural machine translation. In *Proceedings of the 2016 Conference of the North American Chapter of the Association for Computational Linguistics: Human Language Technologies*.

Zheng Yuan and Mariano Felice. 2013. Constrained grammatical error correction using statistical machine translation. In *Proceedings of the Seventeenth Conference on Computational Natural Language Learning: Shared Task*.

Wei Zhao, Liang Wang, Kewei Shen, Ruoyu Jia, and Jingming Liu. 2019. Improving grammatical error correction via pre-training a copy-augmented architecture with unlabeled data. In *Proceedings of the 2019 Conference of the North American Chapter of the Association for Computational Linguistics: Human Language Technologies*. Association for Computational Linguistics.

TMU Transformer System Using BERT for Re-ranking at BEA 2019 Grammatical Error Correction on Restricted Track

Masahiro Kaneko   **Kengo Hotate**   **Satoru Katsumata**   **Mamoru Komachi**
Tokyo Metropolitan University, Japan
{kaneko-masahiro@ed, hotate-kengo@ed,
katsumata-satoru@ed, komachi@}.tmu.ac.jp

Abstract

We introduce our system that is submitted to the restricted track of the BEA 2019 shared task on grammatical error correction[1] (GEC). It is essential to select an appropriate hypothesis sentence from the candidates list generated by the GEC model. A re-ranker can evaluate the naturalness of a corrected sentence using language models trained on large corpora. On the other hand, these language models and language representations do not explicitly take into account the grammatical errors written by learners. Thus, it is not straightforward to utilize language representations trained from a large corpus, such as Bidirectional Encoder Representations from Transformers (BERT), in a form suitable for the learner's grammatical errors. Therefore, we propose to fine-tune BERT on learner corpora with grammatical errors for re-ranking. The experimental results of the W&I+LOCNESS development dataset demonstrate that re-ranking using BERT can effectively improve the correction performance.

1 Introduction

Grammatical error correction (GEC) systems may be used for language learning to detect and correct grammatical errors in text written by language learners. GEC has grown in importance over the past few years due to the increasing need for people to learn new languages. GEC has been addressed in the Helping Our Own (HOO) (Dale and Kilgarriff, 2011; Dale et al., 2012) and Conference on Natural Language Learning (CoNLL) (Ng et al., 2013, 2014) shared tasks between 2011 and 2014.

Recent research has demonstrated the effectiveness of the neural machine translation model for GEC. There are three main types of neural network models for GEC, namely, recurrent neural networks (Ge et al., 2018), a multi-layer convolutional model based on convolutional neural networks (Chollampatt and Ng, 2018a) and a transformer model based on self-attention (Junczys-Dowmunt et al., 2018). We follow the best practices to develop our system based on the transformer model, which has achieved better performance for GEC (Zhao et al., 2019).

Re-ranking using a language model trained on large-scale corpora contributes to the improved hypotheses of the GEC model (Chollampatt and Ng, 2018a). Typically, a language model is trained by maximizing the log-likelihood of a sentence. Hence, such models observe only the positive examples of a raw corpus. However, these models may not be sufficient to take into account the grammatical errors written by language learners. Therefore, we fine-tune these models trained from large-scale raw data on learner corpora to explicitly take into account grammatical errors to re-rank the hypotheses for the GEC tasks.

Bidirectional Encoder Representations from Transformer (BERT) (Devlin et al., 2019) can consider information of large-scale raw corpora and task specific information by fine-tuning on the target task corpora. Moreover, BERT is known to be effective in the distinction of grammatical sentences from ungrammatical sentences (Kaneko and Komachi, 2019). They proposed a grammatical error detection (GED) model based on BERT that achieved state-of-the-art results in word-level GED tasks. Therefore, we use BERT, pre-trained with large-scale raw corpora, and fine-tune it with learner corpora for re-ranking the hypotheses of our GEC model to utilize not only the large-scale raw corpora but also a set of information on grammatical errors.

The main contribution of this study is that

---

[1] https://www.cl.cam.ac.uk/research/nl/
bea2019st/

Proceedings of the Fourteenth Workshop on Innovative Use of NLP for Building Educational Applications, pages 207–212
Florence, Italy, August 2, 2019. ©2019 Association for Computational Linguistics

the experimental results demonstrate that BERT, which considers both the representations trained on large-scale and learners corpora, is effective for re-ranking the hypotheses for GEC tasks. Additionally, we demonstrated that BERT based on self-attention can re-rank sentences corrected from the GEC model by capturing long distance information.

2 TMU System

Our system is a GEC model that is combined with a re-ranker. The GEC model is given a source sentence as input and generates hypothesis sentences. These hypothesis sentences are given as input to the re-ranker, which selects the final corrected sentence form the hypothesis sentences.

We use the transformer (Vaswani et al., 2017) architecture for the GEC model because it is a state-of-the-art model in the GEC task (Zhao et al., 2019). The transformer architecture comprises multiple layers of `transformer_block`. The layers of the encoder and decoder have position-wise feedforward layers over the tokens of input sentences. The decoder has an extra attention layer over the encoder's hidden states. This GEC model is optimized by minimizing the label smoothed cross-entropy loss.

The re-ranker uses five features. We use BERT fine-tuned on learner corpora to predict the grammatical quality as a feature of re-ranking.

2.1 Architecture and training of BERT for re-ranking

We used BERT (Devlin et al., 2019) as a feature for re-ranking the hypotheses of the GEC system. BERT is designed to learn deep bidirectional representations by jointly conditioning both the left and right contexts in all layers, based on `transformer_block` with multi-head self-attention and fully connected layers. The parameters of BERT were pre-trained using a masked language model and the prediction of the next sentence.

We fine-tuned the pre-trained BERT on learner corpora to judge the grammatical quality of the input sentence, i.e., to distinguish between a sentence with and without grammatical errors on a sentence-level. We annotated sentences from parallel learner corpora having incorrect and correct sentences with 0 (incorrect) and 1 (correct) labels. Hence, using the above, we can take advantage of

Corpus	Train	Dev	Test
FCE	28,350	2,191	2,695
Lang-8	1,037,561	-	-
NUCLE	57,151	-	-
W&I+LOCNESS	34,308	4,384	4,477

Table 1: Number of sentences in corpora on GEC shared task for restricted track.

both the large-scale raw data and learner corpora by using BERT. The model was optimized during fine-tuning by minimizing the sentence-level cross-entropy loss.

2.2 Re-ranking

We used the following set of features for re-ranking, which are the same as those in a previously reported approach (Chollampatt and Ng, 2018a), except for BERT:

- **GEC model**: The score of the hypothesis sentence from the GEC model is computed using the log probabilities of predictions normalized by sentence length on a token-level.

- **Language model**: A 5-gram language model score is computed by normalizing the log probabilities of the hypothesis sentence by sentence length.

- **BERT**: The predicted score for the grammatical quality of the hypothesis sentence.

- **Edit operations**: Three token level features, namely, denoting the number of substitutions, deletions, and insertions between the source sentence and the hypothesis sentence.

- **Hypothesis sentence length**: The number of words in the hypothesis sentence to penalize short hypothesis sentences.

Feature weights are optimized by minimum error rate training (MERT) (Och, 2003) on the development set.

3 Experiments

3.1 Dataset

In the restricted track, we only used the corpora listed in Table 1. The First Certificate in English (FCE) corpus (Yannakoudakis et al., 2011), Lang-8 learner corpus (Mizumoto et al., 2011), National University of Singapore Corpus of Learner

Parameter	Value
Word embedding size	500
Multi-head number	10
Layer size	6
Hidden size	2,048
Optimizer	Adam
Adam β_1	0.9
Adam β_2	0.98
Learning rate	0.0005
Learning rate scheduler	inverse square root
Warmup steps	4,000
Minimum learning rate	1e-09
Dropout	0.3
Weight decay	0.0001
Label smoothing	0.1
Max token size	4,096
Ensemble size	3

Table 2: Hyperparameter values of our transformer GEC model.

#	Team Name	P	R	$F_{0.5}$
1	UEDIN-MS	72.28	60.12	**69.47**
2	Kakao&Brain	**75.19**	51.91	69.00
7	ML@IITB	65.70	**61.12**	64.73
14	TMU	53.91	51.65	53.45

Table 3: Results of GEC systems with the highest P, R and $F_{0.5}$ overall vs TMU on restricted track on official W&I test data.

English (NUCLE) (Dahlmeier et al., 2013) and Write & Improve (W&I)+LOCNESS corpus (Yannakoudakis et al., 2018; Granger, 1998) were used for this shared task. W&I+LOCNESS corpus was a new corpus released for this shared task and the shared task systems were evaluated on a gold test set of the overall W&I+LOCNESS dataset.

We used FCE (official split of train, dev, and test set), Lang-8, NUCLE, and W&I+LOCNESS training set as training data and we split the W&I+LOCNESS development set into development and test data by random selection from each Common European Framework of Reference for Languages (CEFR) levels (beginner, intermediate, advanced, native) for the transformer and BERT. The development and test data sizes were 2,191 and 2,193, respectively.

Model	P	R	$F_{0.5}$
TMU system	37.79	**28.08**	**35.35**
w/o BERT	**38.75**	23.76	34.41
w/o language model	37.85	26.41	34.83
w/o re-ranking	36.46	22.91	32.60

Table 4: Effectiveness of re-ranking without different features.

3.2 Setup

We implemented the transformer model based on the *Fairseq* tool[2]. The hyperparameters used in our transformer GEC model are listed in Table 2. The parameters of the ensemble models were initialized with different values. We initialized the embedding layers of the encoder and decoder with the embeddings pre-trained on the English Wikipedia using *fastText* tool[3] (Bojanowski et al., 2017).

We used a publicly available pre-trained BERT model[4], namely the $\text{BERT}_{\text{BASE}}$ uncased model, which was pre-trained on large-scale BooksCorpus and English Wikipedia corpora. This model had 12 layers, 768 hidden sizes, and 16 heads of self-attention. Our model's hyperparameters for re-ranking were similar to the default ones described by Devlin et al. (2019). We used the same learner corpora with incorrect and correct sentences used for training our GEC model to fine-tune BERT.

The 5-gram language model for re-ranking was trained on a subset of the Common Crawl corpus (Chollampatt and Ng, 2018a).[5] We used a Python spell checker tool[6] on the GEC model hypothesis sentences.

3.3 Evaluation

The systems submitted to the shared task were evaluated using the ERRANT[7] scorer (Felice et al., 2016; Bryant et al., 2017). This metric is an improved version of the MaxMatch scorer (Dahlmeier and Ng, 2012) originally used in the

---

[2] https://github.com/pytorch/fairseq
[3] https://github.com/facebookresearch/fastText
[4] https://github.com/google-research/bert
[5] https://github.com/nusnlp/mlconvgec2018
[6] https://pypi.org/project/pyspellchecker/
[7] https://github.com/chrisjbryant/errant

(a)	Source	The range of public services will be expanded to remote areas , **it become** much more convenient .
	Gold	The range of public services will be expanded to remote areas , <u>and it will become</u> much more convenient .
	w/o BERT	The range of public services will be expanded to remote areas , *has become* much more convenient .
	TMU system	The range of public services will be expanded to remote areas , *and it will become* much more convenient .
(b)	Source	Her sister is 6 years old and you should **look after every weekend** .
	Gold	Her sister is 6 years old and you would have to <u>look after her every weekend</u> .
	w/o BERT	Her sister is 6 years old and you should *look after it every weekend* .
	TMU system	Her sister is 6 years old and you should *look after it every weekend* .

Table 5: (a) Successful and (b) unsuccessful examples of TMU system for long distance errors. **Bold** indicates the erroneous part of the source sentence; <u>Underline</u> indicates the corrected part of the gold sentence; *Italic* represents the corrected output of the GEC system.

CoNLL shared tasks (Ng et al., 2013, 2014). The scorer reported the performance in terms of span-based and token-based detection. The system performance was primarily measured with regard to span-based correction using the $F_{0.5}$ metric, which assigned twice as much weight to the precision. In this study, we report on precision, recall, and $F_{0.5}$ based on the ERRANT score.

3.4 Results

Table 3 presents the results of our system (TMU) and others on precision (P), recall (R) and $F_{0.5}$ on W&I+LOCNESS test data for the BEA 2019 GEC shared task on the restricted track. Our system was ranked 14 out of 21 teams.

4 Discussions

We investigated whether using BERT as a feature for re-ranking can improve the corrected results. Table 4 presents the experimental results of removing the following re-ranking features: BERT (w/o BERT); language model (w/o language model); and all features (w/o re-ranking). The recall and $F_{0.5}$ of the complete model (TMU system) is higher than those of w/o BERT, indicating that using BERT for re-ranking can improve the accuracy; especially, the recall is significantly improved. We conclude that BERT uses the advantage of large-scale raw data to acquire general linguistic expressions and learn grammatical error information from learner corpora, thus detecting and re-ranking errors more effectively.

Additionally, we analyzed the type of grammatical errors that were corrected by using BERT for re-ranking. Table 5 presents the output examples of our system with and without BERT. Example (a) demonstrates that our system can correct long distance verb tense errors, matching Gold in this case, where after stating that *"... services will be expanded ..."* in the first half, our system prop-

erly corrected *"... it become ..."* to *"... it will become ..."* in the second part of the given sentence. On the other hand, w/o BERT created a sentence with inconsistent verb tense by changing *"... it become ..."* to *"... it has become ..."*. Example (b) demonstrates that neither of the systems, i.e., with and without BERT, could properly correct the coreference resolution error. They both failed to trace the reference of *"it"* to *"her sister"*. By using BERT based on self-attention for re-ranking, which is effective for long distance information, our system became better at solving long distance errors; however, there is a room for improvement.

5 Related Work

Re-ranking using a language model trained on large-scale raw data significantly improved the results in numerous GEC studies (Junczys-Dowmunt and Grundkiewicz, 2016; Chollampatt and Ng, 2018a; Grundkiewicz and Junczys-Dowmunt, 2018; Junczys-Dowmunt et al., 2018; Zhao et al., 2019). However, their models do not explicitly consider grammatical errors of language learners.

Yannakoudakis et al. (2017) utilized the score from a GED model as a feature to consider grammatical errors for re-ranking. Chollampatt and Ng (2018b) proposed a neural quality estimator for GEC. Their models predict the quality score when given a source sentence and its corresponding hypothesis. They consider representations of grammatical errors of learners for re-ranking. However, their models did not use large-scale raw corpora.

Rei and Søgaard (2018) used a sentence-level GED model based on bidirectional long short-term memory (LSTM). The goal of their study was to predict the token-level labels on a sentence-level using the attention mechanism for zero-shot sequence labeling.

Kaneko and Komachi (2019) proposed a model of applying attention to each layer of BERT for GED and achieved state-of-the-art results in word-level GED tasks. Our BERT model predicts grammatical quality on a sentence-level for re-ranking.

6 Conclusion

In this paper, we described our TMU system, which is based on the GEC transformer model using BERT for re-ranking. We evaluated our TMU system on the restricted track of the BEA 2019 GEC shared task. The experimental results demonstrated that using BERT for re-ranking can improve the correction quality.

In this work, we only considered the information of the hypothesis sentence. In our future work, we will analyze the re-ranker, allowing BERT to utilize the information of the source sentence of the GEC model as well, given both source and hypothesis sentences.

7 Acknowledgments

We thank Yangyang Xi of Lang-8, Inc. for kindly allowing us to use the Lang-8 learner corpus. This work was partially supported by JSPS Grant-in-Aid for Scientific Research (C) Grant Number JP19K12099.

References

Piotr Bojanowski, Edouard Grave, Armand Joulin, and Tomas Mikolov. 2017. Enriching Word Vectors with Subword Information. *TACL*, 5:135–146.

Christopher Bryant, Mariano Felice, and Ted Briscoe. 2017. Automatic Annotation and Evaluation of Error Types for Grammatical Error Correction. In *ACL*, pages 793–805, Vancouver, Canada. Association for Computational Linguistics.

Shamil Chollampatt and Hwee Tou Ng. 2018a. A Multilayer Convolutional Encoder-Decoder Neural Network for Grammatical Error Correction. In *AAAI*, pages 5755–5762, New Orleans, Louisiana. Association for the Advancement of Artificial Intelligence.

Shamil Chollampatt and Hwee Tou Ng. 2018b. Neural Quality Estimation of Grammatical Error Correction. In *EMNLP*, pages 2528–2539, Brussels, Belgium. Association for Computational Linguistics.

Daniel Dahlmeier and Hwee Tou Ng. 2012. Better Evaluation for Grammatical Error Correction. In *NAACL*, pages 568–572, Montreal, Canada. Association for Computational Linguistics.

Daniel Dahlmeier, Hwee Tou Ng, and Siew Mei Wu. 2013. Building a Large Annotated Corpus of Learner English: The NUS Corpus of Learner English. In *BEA*, pages 22–31, Atlanta, Georgia. Association for Computational Linguistics.

Robert Dale, Ilya Anisimoff, and George Narroway. 2012. HOO 2012: A Report on the Preposition and Determiner Error Correction Shared Task. In *BEA*, pages 54–62, Montreal, Canada. Association for Computational Linguistics.

Robert Dale and Adam Kilgarriff. 2011. Helping Our Own: The HOO 2011 Pilot Shared Task. In *ENLG*, pages 242–249, Nancy, France. Association for Computational Linguistics.

Jacob Devlin, Ming-Wei Chang, Kenton Lee, and Kristina Toutanova. 2019. BERT: Pre-training of Deep Bidirectional Transformers for Language Understanding. In *NAACL*, Minneapolis, USA. Association for Computational Linguistics.

Mariano Felice, Christopher Bryant, and Ted Briscoe. 2016. Automatic Extraction of Learner Errors in ESL Sentences Using Linguistically Enhanced Alignments. In *COLING*, pages 825–835, Osaka, Japan. The COLING 2016 Organizing Committee.

Tao Ge, Furu Wei, and Ming Zhou. 2018. Fluency Boost Learning and Inference for Neural Grammatical Error Correction. In *ACL*, pages 1055–1065, Melbourne, Australia. Association for Computational Linguistics.

Sylviane Granger. 1998. The Computer Learner Corpus: A Versatile New Source of Data for SLA Research. pages 3–18. Learner English on Computer.

Roman Grundkiewicz and Marcin Junczys-Dowmunt. 2018. Near Human-Level Performance in Grammatical Error Correction with Hybrid Machine Translation. In *NAACL*, pages 284–290, New Orleans, Louisiana. Association for Computational Linguistics.

Marcin Junczys-Dowmunt and Roman Grundkiewicz. 2016. Phrase-based Machine Translation is State-of-the-Art for Automatic Grammatical Error Correction. In *EMNLP*, pages 1546–1556, Austin, Texas. Association for Computational Linguistics.

Marcin Junczys-Dowmunt, Roman Grundkiewicz, Shubha Guha, and Kenneth Heafield. 2018. Approaching Neural Grammatical Error Correction as a Low-Resource Machine Translation Task. In *NAACL*, pages 595–606, New Orleans, Louisiana. Association for Computational Linguistics.

Masahiro Kaneko and Mamoru Komachi. 2019. Multi-Head Multi-Layer Attention to Deep Language Representations for Grammatical Error Detection. In *CICLing*, La Rochelle, France.

Tomoya Mizumoto, Mamoru Komachi, Masaaki Nagata, and Yuji Matsumoto. 2011. Mining Revision Log of Language Learning SNS for Automated Japanese Error Correction of Second Language Learners. In *IJCNLP*, pages 147–155, Chiang Mai, Thailand. Asian Federation of Natural Language Processing.

Hwee Tou Ng, Siew Mei Wu, Ted Briscoe, Christian Hadiwinoto, Raymond Hendy Susanto, and Christopher Bryant. 2014. The CoNLL-2014 Shared Task on Grammatical Error Correction. In *CoNLL*, pages 1–14, Baltimore, Maryland. Association for Computational Linguistics.

Hwee Tou Ng, Siew Mei Wu, Yuanbin Wu, Christian Hadiwinoto, and Joel Tetreault. 2013. The CoNLL-2013 Shared Task on Grammatical Error Correction. In *CoNLL*, pages 1–12, Sofia, Bulgaria. Association for Computational Linguistics.

Franz Josef Och. 2003. Minimum Error Rate Training in Statistical Machine Translation. In *ACL*, pages 160–167, Sapporo, Japan. Association for Computational Linguistics.

Marek Rei and Anders Søgaard. 2018. Zero-Shot Sequence Labeling: Transferring Knowledge from Sentences to Tokens. In *NAACL*, pages 293–302, New Orleans, Louisiana. Association for Computational Linguistics.

Ashish Vaswani, Noam Shazeer, Niki Parmar, Jakob Uszkoreit, Llion Jones, Aidan N Gomez, Łukasz Kaiser, and Illia Polosukhin. 2017. Attention is All you Need. In *NIPS*, pages 5998–6008. Curran Associates, Inc.

Helen Yannakoudakis, Øistein E. Andersen, Ardeshir Geranpayeh, Ted Briscoe, and Diane Nicholls. 2018. Developing an Automated Writing Placement System for ESL Learners. pages 251–267. Applied Measurement in Education 31:3.

Helen Yannakoudakis, Ted Briscoe, and Ben Medlock. 2011. A New Dataset and Method for Automatically Grading ESOL Texts. In *NAACL*, pages 180–189, Portland, Oregon, USA. Association for Computational Linguistics.

Helen Yannakoudakis, Marek Rei, Øistein E. Andersen, and Zheng Yuan. 2017. Neural Sequence-Labelling Models for Grammatical Error Correction. In *EMNLP*, pages 2795–2806, Copenhagen, Denmark. Association for Computational Linguistics.

Wei Zhao, Liang Wang, Kewei Shen, Ruoyu Jia, and Jingming Liu. 2019. Improving Grammatical Error Correction via Pre-Training a Copy-Augmented Architecture with Unlabeled Data. In *NAACL*, Minneapolis, USA. Association for Computational Linguistics.

A Neural Grammatical Error Correction System Built On
Better Pre-training and Sequential Transfer Learning

Yo Joong Choe[*]
Kakao
yj.c@kakaocorp.com

Jiyeon Ham[*]
Kakao Brain
jiyeon.ham@kakaobrain.com

Kyubyong Park[*]
Kakao Brain
kyubyong.park@kakaobrain.com

Yeoil Yoon[*]
Kakao Brain
yeoil.yoon@kakaobrain.com

Abstract

Grammatical error correction can be viewed as a low-resource sequence-to-sequence task, because publicly available parallel corpora are limited. To tackle this challenge, we first generate erroneous versions of large unannotated corpora using a realistic noising function. The resulting parallel corpora are subsequently used to pre-train Transformer models. Then, by sequentially applying transfer learning, we adapt these models to the domain and style of the test set. Combined with a context-aware neural spellchecker, our system achieves competitive results in both restricted and low resource tracks in ACL 2019 BEA Shared Task. We release all of our code and materials for reproducibility. [1]

1 Introduction

Grammatical error correction (GEC) is the task of correcting various grammatical errors in text, as illustrated by the following example:

[Travel → **Travelling**] by bus is [exspensive → **expensive**], [bored → **boring**] and annoying.

While the dominant approach following the CoNLL-2014 Shared Task (Ng et al., 2014) has been different adaptations of phrase-based and statistical machine translation (PBSMT) models (Junczys-Dowmunt and Grundkiewicz, 2016), more recent work on GEC increasingly adopted partial (Grundkiewicz and Junczys-Dowmunt, 2018) or exclusive (Junczys-Dowmunt et al., 2018; Chollampatt and Ng, 2018a) use of deep sequence-to-sequence (seq2seq) architectures (Sutskever et al., 2014; Cho et al., 2014), which showed immense success in neural machine translation (NMT) (Bahdanau et al., 2015; Gehring et al., 2017; Vaswani et al., 2017).

In GEC, unlike NMT between major languages, there are not enough publicly available corpora (GEC's hundreds of thousands to NMT's tens of millions). This motivates the use of pre-training and transfer learning, which has shown to be highly effective in many natural language processing (NLP) scenarios in which there is not enough annotated data, notably in low-resource machine translation (MT) (Lample et al., 2018b; Ruder, 2019). As a result, recent GEC systems also include pre-training on various auxiliary tasks, such as language modeling (LM) (Junczys-Dowmunt et al., 2018), text revision (Lichtarge et al., 2018), and denoising (Zhao et al., 2019).

In this paper, we introduce a neural GEC system that combines the power of pre-training and transfer learning. Our contributions are summarized as follows:

- We pre-train our model for the denoising task using a novel noising function, which gives us a parallel corpus that includes realistic grammatical errors;

- We leverage the idea of sequential transfer learning (Ruder, 2019), thereby effectively adapting our pre-trained model to the domain as well as the writing and annotation styles suitable for our final task.

- We introduce a context-aware neural spellchecker, which improves upon an off-the-shelf spellchecker by incorporating context into spellchecking using a pre-trained neural language model (LM).

2 Background

2.1 Transformers

Transformers (Vaswani et al., 2017) are powerful deep seq2seq architectures that rely heavily on the

---

[*]Equal contribution. Listed alphabetically.
[1]https://github.com/kakaobrain/helo_word

Proceedings of the Fourteenth Workshop on Innovative Use of NLP for Building Educational Applications, pages 213–227
Florence, Italy, August 2, 2019. ©2019 Association for Computational Linguistics

attention mechanism (Bahdanau et al., 2015; Luong et al., 2015). Both the encoder and the decoder of a Transformer are stacks of Transformer blocks, each of which consists of a multi-head self-attention layer followed by a position-wise feed-forward layer, along with residual connection (He et al., 2016) and layer normalization (Ba et al., 2016). Each decoder block also attends (Luong et al., 2015) to the encoder outputs, in between its self-attention and feed-forward layers. Each input token embedding in a Transformer is combined with a positional embedding that encodes where the token appeared in the input sequence.

2.2 Copy-Augmented Transformers

Copy-augmented Transformers (Zhao et al., 2019) are a class of Transformers that also incorporate an attention-based copying mechanism (Gu et al., 2016; See et al., 2017; Jia and Liang, 2016) in the decoder. For each output token y_t at output position t, the output probability distribution of a copy-augmented Transformer is a mixture of the decoder's generative distribution p^{gen} and a copy distribution p^{copy}, which is defined as an encoder-decoder attention layer that assigns a distribution over tokens appearing in the source sentence. By defining a mixture weight parameter α_t^{copy} per each decoding step, the output distribution can be compactly represented as follows:

$$p(y_t) = (1 - \alpha_t^{\text{copy}}) \cdot p^{\text{gen}}(y_t) + \alpha_t^{\text{copy}} \cdot p^{\text{copy}}(y_t) \tag{1}$$

The mixture weight balances between how likely it is for the model to simply copy a source token, rather than generating a possibly different token.

2.3 Denoising Autoencoders

Denoising autoencoders (DAEs) (Vincent et al., 2008) are a class of neural networks that learns to reconstruct the original input given its noisy version. Given an input $\mathbf{x}$ and a (stochastic) noising function $\mathbf{x} \mapsto \tilde{\mathbf{x}}$, the encoder-decoder model of a DAE minimizes the reconstruction loss:

$$L(\mathbf{x}, \text{dec}(\text{enc}(\tilde{\mathbf{x}}))) \tag{2}$$

where L is some loss function.

Within the NLP domain, DAEs have been for pre-training in seq2seq tasks that can be cast as a denoising task. For example, in GEC, pre-trained DAEs have been used for correcting erroneous sentences (Xie et al., 2018; Zhao et al., 2019). Another example is low-resource machine translation (MT) (Lample et al., 2018b), pre-trained DAEs were used to convert word-by-word translations into natural sentences.

3 Related Work

Many recent neural GEC models (Junczys-Dowmunt et al., 2018; Lichtarge et al., 2018; Zhao et al., 2019) made use of the Transformer (Vaswani et al., 2017) architecture and saw results nearly as good as or better than convolutional (Chollampatt and Ng, 2018a,b) and recurrent (Grundkiewicz and Junczys-Dowmunt, 2018; Ge et al., 2018a) architectures. Recently, Zhao et al. (2019) further incorporated a copying mechanism (Gu et al., 2016; See et al., 2017; Jia and Liang, 2016) to the Transformer, highlighting the fact that most (from 83% in Lang-8 to 97% in CoNLL-2013) of the target tokens are exact copies of the corresponding source tokens.

Several prior results, both early (Brockett et al., 2006; Felice and Yuan, 2014) and recent (Ge et al., 2018a; Xie et al., 2018; Zhao et al., 2019), introduced different strategies for generating erroneous text that can in turn be used for model (pre-)training. One major direction is to introduce an additional "back-translation" model (Ge et al., 2018a; Xie et al., 2018), inspired by its success in NMT (Sennrich et al., 2016a), and let this model learn to generate erroneous sentences from correct ones. While these back-translation models can learn naturally occurring grammatical errors from the parallel corpora in reverse, they also require relatively large amounts of parallel corpora, which are not readily available in low resource scenarios. The other direction, which can avoid these issues, is to incorporate a pre-defined noising function, which can generate pre-training data for a denoising task (Zhao et al., 2019). Compared to (Zhao et al., 2019), our work introduces a noising function that generates more realistic grammatical errors.

4 Pre-training a Denoising Autoencoder on Realistic Grammatical Errors

Given the relative lack of parallel corpora for the GEC task, it is important to define a realistic pre-training task, from which the learned knowledge can transfer to an improved performance.

When pre-training a seq2seq model on an auxiliary denoising task, the choice of the noising function is important. For instance, in low-resource MT, Lample et al. (2018a,b) made use of a noising function that randomly insert/replace/remove tokens or mix up nearby words at uniform probabilities. They showed that this approach is effective in translating naive word-by-word translations into correct ones, both because the coverage of word-to-word dictionaries can be limited and because word order is frequently swapped between languages (e.g., going from SVO to SOV).

In GEC, Zhao et al. (2019) used a similar noising function to generate a pre-training dataset. However, we find that this noising function is less realistic in GEC than in low-resource MT. For example, randomly mixing up nearby words can be less effective for GEC than for low-resource MT, because word order errors occur less frequently than other major error categories, such as missing punctuations and noun numbers. Also, replacing a word to any random word in the vocabulary is a less realistic scenario than only replacing it with its associated common error categories, such as prepositions, noun numbers and verb tenses.

To generate realistic pre-training data, we introduce a novel noising function that captures in-domain grammatical errors commonly made by human writers.

4.1 Constructing Noising Scenarios

We introduce two kinds of noising scenarios, using a token-based approach and a type-based approach.

In the token-based approach, we make use of extracted human edits from annotated GEC corpora, using automated error annotation toolkits such as ERRANT (Bryant et al., 2017). We first take a subset of the training set, preferably one that contains in-domain sentences with high-quality annotations, and using an error annotation toolkit, we collect all edits that occurred in the parallel corpus as well as how often each edit was made. We then take edits that occur in for at least k times, where k is a pre-defined threshold (we fix $k = 4$ in our experiments), in order to prevent overfitting to this (possibly small) subset. These extracted edits include errors commonly made by human writers, including missing punctuations (e.g., adding a comma), preposition errors (e.g., $of \rightarrow at$), and verb tenses (e.g., $has \rightarrow have$). As a result, we

obtain an automatically constructed dictionary of common edits made by human annotators on the in-domain training set. Then, we can define a realistic noising scenario by randomly applying these human edits, in reverse, to a grammatically correct sentence.

In the type-based approach, we also make use of *a priori* knowledge and construct a noising scenario based on token types, including prepositions, nouns, and verbs. For each token type, we define a noising scenario based on commonly made errors associated with that token type, but without changing the type of the original token. In particular, we replace prepositions with other prepositions, nouns with their singular/plural version, and verbs with one of their inflected versions. This introduces another set of realistic noising scenarios, thereby increasing the coverage of the resulting noising function.

4.2 Generating Pre-training Data

Our goal is to come up with an error function that introduces grammatical errors that are commonly made by human writers in a specific setting (in this case, personal essays written by English students). Given sets of realistic noising scenarios, we can generate large amounts of erroneous sentences from high-quality English corpora, such as the Project Gutenberg corpus (Lahiri, 2014) and Wikipedia (Merity et al., 2016).

We first check if a token exists in the dictionary of token edits. If it does, a token-based error is generated with the probability of 0.9. Specifically, the token is replaced by one of the associated edits with the probabilities proportional to the frequency of each edit. For example, the token *for* may be replaced with *during, in, four*, and also *for* (coming from a *noop* edit).

If a token is not processed through the token-based scenario, we then examine if it belongs to one of the pre-defined token types: in our case, we use prepositions, nouns, and verbs. If the token belongs to one such type, we then apply the corresponding noising scenario.

5 Sequential Transfer Learning

5.1 Transferring Pre-trained DAE Weights

As discussed in (Zhao et al., 2019), an important benefit of pre-training a DAE is that it provides good initial values for both the encoder and the decoder weights in the seq2seq model. Given a pre-trained DAE, we initialize our seq2seq GEC model using the learned weights of the DAE and train on all available parallel training corpora with smaller learning rates. This model transfer approach (Wang and Zheng, 2015) can be viewed as a (relatively simple) version of sequential transfer learning (Ruder, 2019).

5.2 Adaptation by Fine-tuning

As noted in (Junczys-Dowmunt et al., 2018), the distribution of grammatical errors occurring in text can differ across the domain and content of text. For example, a Wikipedia article introducing a historical event may involve more rare words than a personal essay would. The distribution can also be affected significantly by the writer's style and proficiency, as well as the annotator's preferred style of writing (e.g., British vs. American styles, synonymous word choices, and Oxford commas).

In this work, given that the primary source of evaluation are personal essays at various levels of English proficiency – in particular the W&I+LOCNESS dataset (Yannakoudakis et al., 2018) – we adapt our trained models to such characteristics of the test set by fine-tuning the model only on the training portion of W&I, which largely matches the domain of the development and test sets.[2] Similar to our training step in §5.1, we use (even) smaller learning rates. Overall, this sequential transfer learning framework can also be viewed as an alternative to oversampling in-domain data sources, as proposed in (Junczys-Dowmunt et al., 2018).

6 A Context-Aware Neural Spellchecker

Many recent GEC systems include an off-the-shelf spellchecker, such as the open-source package `enchant` (Sakaguchi et al., 2017; Junczys-Dowmunt et al., 2018) and Microsoft's Bing spellchecker (Ge et al., 2018a,b). While the idea of incorporating context into spellchecking has been repeatedly discussed in the literature (Flor and Futagi, 2012; Chollampatt and Ng, 2017), popular open-sourced spellcheckers such as `hunspell` primarily operate at the word level. This fundamentally limits their capacity, because it is often difficult to find which word is intended for without context. For example, given the input sentence *This is an esay about my favorite sport.*,

Source	Public?	# Sent.	# Annot.
Gutenberg	Yes	11.6M	n/a
Tatoeba	Yes	1.17M	n/a
WikiText-103	Yes	3.93M	n/a
FCE	Yes	33.2K	1
Lang-8	Yes	1.04M	1-8
NUCLE	Yes	57.2K	1
W&I-Train	Yes	34.3K	1
W&I+L-Dev	Yes	4.38K	1
W&I+L-Test	Yes	4.48K	5

Table 1: Summary of datasets. The first three datasets are unannotated English corpora, from which we generate parallel data for pre-training using a pre-defined noising function.

`hunspell` invariably suggests *easy* as its top candidate for *esay*, which should actually be corrected as *essay*.

Our spellchecker incorporates context to `hunspell` using a pre-trained neural language model (LM). Specifically, we re-rank the top candidates suggested by `hunspell` through feeding each, along with the context, to the neural LM and scoring them.

7 Experiments

Throughout our experiments, we use `fairseq`[3] (Ott et al., 2019), a publicly available sequence-to-sequence modeling toolkit based on PyTorch (Paszke et al., 2017). Specifically, we take `fairseq-0.6.1` and add our own implementations of a copy-augmented transformer model as well as several GEC-specific auxiliary losses.

7.1 Datasets & Setups

In Table 1, we summarize all relevant data sources, their sizes, whether they are public, and the number of annotators.

For pre-training, we use the Gutenberg dataset (Lahiri, 2014), the Tatoeba[4] dataset, and the WikiText-103 dataset (Merity et al., 2016). We learned through initial experiments that the quality of pre-training data is crucial to the final model's performance, because our DAE model assumes §4 that these unannotated corpora contain little grammatical errors. Our choice of corpora is based on both the quality and diversity of text: Guten-

---

[2]This is analogous to the NUCLE dataset matching "perfectly" with the CoNLL dataset, as noted in (Junczys-Dowmunt et al., 2018).

[3]`https://github.com/pytorch/fairseq`
[4]`https://tatoeba.org/eng/downloads`

	Restricted (§7.5)	**Low Resource (§7.6)**	**CoNLL-2014 (§7.7)**
Error Extraction	W&I Train	W&I+L Dev-3K	NUCLE
Pre-training	Gutenberg, Tatoeba, WikiText-103		
Training	FCE, Lang-8, NUCLE, W&I Train	W&I+L Dev-3K	FCE, Lang-8, NUCLE
Fine-tuning	W&I Train	n/a	NUCLE
Validation	W&I+L Dev	W&I+L Dev-1K	CoNLL-2013
Test	W&I+L Test	W&I+L Test	CoNLL-2014

Table 2: Datasets used for each set of results. For the W&I+L development set, Dev-3K and Dev-1K respectively indicate a 3:1 train-test random split of the development set, such that the original proportions of English proficiency (A, B, C, N) are kept the same in each split. See Table 1 for more information about each dataset.

Sequential Transfer Learning Using (copy) Transformers

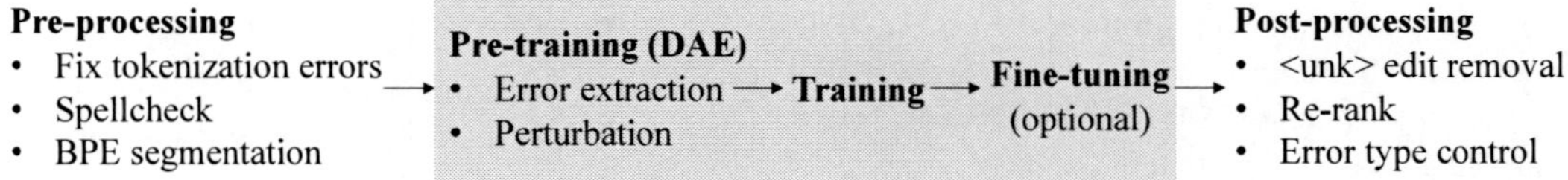

Figure 1: Overall pipeline for our approach. Gray shaded box includes the training steps for a seq2seq model.

berg contains clean novel writings with minimal grammatical errors, Tatoeba contains colloquial sentences used as sample sentences in dictionaries, and WikiText-103 contains "Good" and "Featured" articles from Wikipedia. Our final pre-training data is a collection of 45M (perturbed, correct) sentence pairs based on these datasets, with our noising approach (§4) applied multiple times to each dataset to approximately balance data from each source (1x Gutenberg, 12x Tatoeba, and 5x WikiText-103).

Our default setup is the "Restricted Track" scenario (§7.5) for the BEA 2019 Shared Task, where we use four data sources: the FCE dataset (Bryant et al., 2019), the Lang-8 dataset[5] (Mizumoto et al., 2011; Tajiri et al., 2012), the NUCLE (v3.3) dataset (Dahlmeier et al., 2013), and the newly released Write & Improve and LOCNESS (W&I+L) datasets (Yannakoudakis et al., 2018).[6] For the "Low Resource Track" (§7.6), we use a 3:1 train-test random split of the W&I+L development set, keeping the proportions of proficiency levels the same. In both tracks, we report our final results on the W&I+L test set, which contains 5 annotations. Further, because the W&I+L dataset is relatively

new, we also include results on the CoNLL-2014 (Ng et al., 2014) dataset, with and without using the W&I+L dataset during training (§7.7). In Table 2, we summarize which datasets were used in each setup.

7.2 Pre-processing

As part of pre-processing, we first fix minor tokenization issues in the dataset using regular expressions. We use spaCy v1.9 (Honnibal and Montani, 2017) to make tokenization consistent with the final evaluation module (ERRANT).

This tokenized input is then fed to our context-aware neural spellchecker (§6). For the neural LM, we use a gated convolutional neural network language model (Dauphin et al., 2017) pre-trained on WikiText-103 (Merity et al., 2016).

During spellchecking, we also found it beneficial to fix casing errors within our context-aware spellchecking process. To fix case errors, we extract a list of words used in the capital form much more than their lower-case version (more than 99 times) in WikiText-103 (Merity et al., 2016). We then include a capitalized version of the word as a candidate in the LM re-scoring process if it appears in its capitalized form is in the extracted list of common capital words.

Before feeding spellchecked text into our seq2seq model, we apply byte-pair encoding

---

[5]As in previous results, we remove all duplicates but take multiple annotations (if available) the Lang-8 dataset, leaving only 575K parallel examples.

[6]See Appendix B for an exploratory data analysis.

(BPE) (Sennrich et al., 2016b) using Sentence-Piece (Kudo and Richardson, 2018). We first train a SentencePiece model with 32K vocabulary size on the original Gutenberg corpus, and apply this model to all input text to the model. This allows us to avoid <unk> tokens in most training and validation sets, including the W&I+L development set.

7.3 Model & Training Details

Throughout our experiments, we use two variants of the Transformer model: the "vanilla" Transformer (Vaswani et al., 2017) and the copy-augmented Transformer (Zhao et al., 2019). We use two configurations for the vanilla Transformer: a *base* model with 6 blocks of 512-2048 units with 8 attention heads, and a *large* model with 6 blocks of 1024-4096 units with 16 attention heads and pre-attention layer normalization. We only use the large model for Restricted Track (§7.5) and for the CoNLL-2014 comparison (§7.7). For the *copy*-augmented Transformer, we follow the default configuration from (Zhao et al., 2019): 6 blocks of 512-4096 units with 8 attention heads, along with an 8-head copy attention layer. For each model configuration, we train two independent models using different seeds.

Our model training is a three-stage process, as illustrated in Figure 1: DAE pre-training, training, and fine-tuning, except in Low Resource Track where there is no fine-tuning data (see Table 2). At each step, we train a model until its ERRANT score on the development set reaches convergence, and use the learned weights as initial values for the next step. In all training steps, we used the Adam (Kingma and Ba, 2015) optimizer.

Our final model is an ensemble among the different model configurations and seeds. Among the six (four for Low Resource Track) best models, we greedily search for the best combination, starting with the best-performing single model.

7.4 Post-processing

Our post-processing phase involves three steps. First, we find any <unk> tokens found in the original input text, and using ERRANT, we remove any edits associated with the token. Next, since many of the model's corrections can still be unnatural, if not incorrect, we re-rank candidate corrections within each sentence using a pre-trained neural LM (Dauphin et al., 2017). Specifically, we remove any combination of up to 7 edits per sentence, and choose the combination that yields the highest LM score. Finally, we noticed that, as in many previous results, our neural system performs well on some error categories (e.g., M:PUNCT) but poorly on others (e.g., R:OTHER). Because ERRANT provides a fine-grained analysis of model performance based on error types, we found it beneficial to remove edits belonging to certain categories in which the model performs too poorly. Given our final model, we randomly remove all edits from a subset of (at most N) categories for repeated steps, and choose to remove the subset of error categories that gave the highest score on the development set.

7.5 Restricted Track Results

In Table 3, we summarize our results on Restricted Track. The results illustrate that each step in our approach substantially improves upon the previous model, both on the W&I+L development and test sets. We highlight that our pre-training step with realistic human errors already gets us at a 54.82 $F_{0.5}$ score on span-based correction in ERRANT for the test set, even though we only indirectly used the W&I training set for error extraction and no other parallel corpora. This suggests that pre-training on a denoising task with realistic and common errors can already lead to a decent GEC system.

Our final ensemble model is a combination of five independent models – one base model, two large models, and two copy-augmented models – achieving 69.06 $F_{0.5}$ score on the test set.

7.6 Low Resource Track Results

In Table 4, we summarize our results on Low Resource Track. Similar to Restricted Track, each step in our approach improves upon the previous model significantly, and despite the lack of parallel data (3K for training, 1K for validation), our pre-training step already gets us at 51.71 $F_{0.5}$ score on the test set. Compared to Restricted Track, the only difference in pre-training is that the reverse dictionary for the noising function was constructed using much fewer parallel data (3K), but we see that this amount of parallel data is already enough to get within 3 points of our pre-trained model in Restricted Track.

Our final model is an ensemble of two independent models – one base model and one copy model – achieving 61.47 $F_{0.5}$ score on the test set.

Steps	W&I+L Dev				W&I+L Test			
	P	**R**	**F0.5**	Δ	**P**	**R**	**F0.5**	Δ
Spellcheck	59.28	5.27	**19.43**	n/a	68.77	10.55	**32.69**	n/a
+ DAE Pre-train	48.58	24.92	**40.82**	+21.39	58.33	44.20	**54.82**	+22.13
+ Train	54.30	28.67	**46.07**	+ 5.25	66.05	50.72	**62.28**	+ 7.46
+ Fine-tune	54.34	32.15	**47.75**	+ 1.68	66.02	53.41	**63.05**	+ 0.77
+ Ensemble (5)	63.54	31.48	**52.79**	+ 5.04	76.19	50.25	**69.06**	+ 6.01

Table 3: ACL 2019 BEA Workshop **Restricted Track** results. For each training step, we only list results from the model configuration that achieved the best $F_{0.5}$ test set score. All evaluation is done using ERRANT's span-based correction scorer. Pre-processing and post-processing are included in the first step and last steps, respectively.

Steps	W&I+L Dev-1K				W&I+L Test			
	P	**R**	**F0.5**	Δ	**P**	**R**	**F0.5**	Δ
Spellcheck	61.88	5.29	**19.72**	n/a	68.77	10.55	**32.69**	n/a
+ DAE Pre-train	46.26	19.84	**36.53**	+16.81	57.14	37.46	**51.71**	+19.02
+ Train	47.97	30.91	**43.20**	+ 6.67	58.60	47.47	**55.98**	+ 4.27
+ Ensemble (4)	58.89	26.68	**47.02**	+ 5.75	69.69	41.76	**61.47**	+ 5.49

Table 4: ACL 2019 BEA Workshop **Low Resource Track** results. For each training step, we only list results from the model configuration that achieved the best $F_{0.5}$ test set score. All evaluation is done using ERRANT's span-based correction scorer. Note that 3K examples from the W&I+Locness development set ("W&I+L Dev-3K") were used for the training step and is excluded during evaluation. Pre-processing and post-processing are included in the first step and last steps, respectively.

7.7 CoNLL-2014 Results

In Table 5, we show the performance of our approach on the CoNLL-2014 (Ng et al., 2014) dataset, with and without the newly released W&I+L dataset.[7] We also list some of the state-of-the-art[8] results prior to the shared task: copy-augmented Transformers pre-trained on random error denoising (Zhao et al., 2019), Transformers pre-trained on Wikipedia revisions and round-trip translations (Lichtarge et al., 2019), hybrid statistical and neural machine translation systems (Junczys-Dowmunt et al., 2018), and convolutional seq2seq models with quality estimation (Chollampatt and Ng, 2018b).

The results show that our approach is competitive with some of the recent state-of-the-art results that achieve around 56 MaxMatch (M^2) scores and further achieves 60+ M^2 score when the W&I+L dataset is used. This illustrates that our approach can also achieve a "near human-level performance" (Grundkiewicz and Junczys-Dowmunt, 2018). We also note that the 60.33 M^2 score was obtained by the final ensemble model

from §7.5, which includes a fine-tuning step to the W&I model. This suggests that "overfitting" to the W&I dataset does not necessarily imply a reduced performance on an external dataset such as CoNLL-2014.

8 Analysis & Discussion

8.1 Error Analysis

Here, we give an analysis of our model's performance on some of the major ERRANT error categories on the W&I test set. Detailed information is available in Tabel 10. We observe that our model performs well on syntax relevant error types, i.e., subject-verb agreement (VERB:SVA) (84.09 $F_{0.5}$), noun numbers (NOUN:NUM) (72.19), and prepositions (PREP) (64.27), all of which are included as part of our type-based error generation in the pre-training data (§4.2). Our model also achieves 77.26 on spelling errors (SPELL) and 75.83 on orthographic errors (ORTH), both of which are improvements made mostly by our context-aware neural spellchecker. Our model also achieves 77.86 on punctuation errors (PUNCT), which happen to be the most common error category in the

---

[7]See Appendix F for a step-by-step training progress.

[8]`http://nlpprogress.com/english/grammatical_error_correction.html`.

Models	Pre-training	W&I+L	CoNLL-2014		
			P	R	F0.5
Our Models					
Transformers	DAE with Realistic Errors	No	71.11	32.56	**57.50**
(Vanilla + Copy-Aug.)		Yes	74.76	34.05	**60.33**
Previous Results					
Copy-Aug. Transformers	DAE with Random Errors	No	71.57	38.65	**61.15**
Transformers	Revisions + Round-Trip Translations	No	66.70	43.90	60.40
ConvS2S + QE	LM (Decoder Pre-training)	No	n/a	n/a	56.52
SMT + BiGRU	LM (Ensemble Decoding)	No	66.77	34.49	56.25

Table 5: Results on CoNLL-2014 as point of comparison. "W&I+L" indicates whether the approach made use of the (newly released) W&I+L dataset. Evaluation is done using the MaxMatch (M^2) scorer, rather than ERRANT. Pre-processing & post-processing are included before the first step and after the last step, respectively. See §7.7 for details and references.

Step	Ours	Random	Δ
DAE	**54.82**	32.25	+22.57
+ Train	**62.28**	57.00	+ 5.28
+ Fine-tune	**63.05**	60.22	+ 2.83

Table 6: Comparison of realistic and random error generation on Restricted Track. Δ means the difference between **Ours** and **Random**.

Step	Ours	Random	Δ
DAE	**51.71**	32.01	+19.70
+ Train	**55.98**	35.44	+20.54

Table 7: Comparison of realistic and random error generation on Low Resource Track. Δ means the difference between **Ours** and **Random**.

W&I+L dataset. This may be due to both our use of extracted errors from the W&I dataset during pre-training and our fine-tuning step. Finally, we find it challenging to match human annotators' "naturalness" edits, such as VERB (26.76), NOUN (41.67), and OTHER (36.53). This is possibly due to the variability in annotation styles and a lack of large training data with multiple human annotations.

8.2 Effect of Realistic Error Generation

To see how effective our realistic error based pre-training is, we compare it with (Zhao et al., 2019)'s method. According to them, random insertion, deletion, and substitution occur with the probability of 0.1 at every word, and words are re-ordered with a certain probability. As seen in Table 6 and 7, our pre-training method outperforms the random based one in both Restricted and Low Resource Tracks by 22.57 and 19.70, respectively. And it remains true for each step of the following transfer learning. The performance gap, however, decreases to 5.3 after training and to 3.2 after fine-tuning in Restricted Track. On the other hand, the gap in Low Resource Track slightly increases to 20.54 after training. This leads to the conclusion that our pre-training functions as proxy for training, for our generated errors resemble the human errors in the training data more than the random errors do.

8.3 Effect of Context-Aware Spellchecking

We further investigate the effects of incorporating context and fixing casing errors to the off-the-shelf `hunspell`, which we consider as a baseline. We test three spellchecker variants: `hunspell`, `hunspell` using a neural LM, and our final spellchecker model.

On the original W&I+L test set, our LM-based approach improves upon the ERRANT F0.5 score by 5.07 points, and fixing casing issues further improves this score by 4.02 points. As a result, we obtain 32.69 F0.5 score just by applying our context-aware spellchecker model.

9 Conclusion & Future Work

We introduced a neural GEC system that leverages pre-training using realistic errors, sequential transfer learning, and context-aware spellchecking with a neural LM. Our system achieved competitive results on the newly released W&I+L dataset in both standard and low-resource settings.

Spellchecker	W&I+L Test			
	P	**R**	**F0.5**	Δ
Hunspell	53.59	7.29	**23.60**	n/a
Hunspell + LM	65.14	8.85	**28.67**	+5.07
Ours	68.77	10.55	**32.69**	+4.02

Table 8: Effect of incorporating context into a standard spellchecker.

There are several interesting future directions following our work. One is to extend sentence-level GEC systems to multi-sentence contexts, for example by including the previous sentence, to better cope with complex semantic errors such as collocation. Because the W&I+L dataset is also a collection of (multi-)paragraph essays, adding multi-sentence contexts can improve these GEC systems. Also, to better understand the role of several components existing in modern GEC systems, it is important to examine which components are more necessary than others.

References

Jimmy Lei Ba, Jamie Ryan Kiros, and Geoffrey E Hinton. 2016. Layer normalization. arXiv preprint arXiv:1607.06450.

Dzmitry Bahdanau, Kyunghyun Cho, and Yoshua Bengio. 2015. Neural machine translation by jointly learning to align and translate. In ICLR.

Chris Brockett, William B Dolan, and Michael Gamon. 2006. Correcting esl errors using phrasal smt techniques. In Proceedings of the 21st International Conference on Computational Linguistics and the 44th annual meeting of the Association for Computational Linguistics, pages 249–256. Association for Computational Linguistics.

Christopher Bryant, Mariano Felice, Øistein E. Andersen, and Ted Briscoe. 2019. The BEA-2019 Shared Task on Grammatical Error Correction. In Proceedings of the 14th Workshop on Innovative Use of NLP for Building Educational Applications. Association for Computational Linguistics.

Christopher Bryant, Mariano Felice, and Edward John Briscoe. 2017. Automatic annotation and evaluation of error types for grammatical error correction. In ACL.

Kyunghyun Cho, Bart van Merrienboer, Caglar Gulcehre, Dzmitry Bahdanau, Fethi Bougares, Holger Schwenk, and Yoshua Bengio. 2014. Learning phrase representations using rnn encoder–decoder for statistical machine translation. In EMNLP.

Shamil Chollampatt and Hwee Tou Ng. 2017. Connecting the dots: Towards human-level grammatical error correction. In Proceedings of the 12th Workshop on Innovative Use of NLP for Building Educational Applications, pages 327–333.

Shamil Chollampatt and Hwee Tou Ng. 2018a. A multilayer convolutional encoder-decoder neural network for grammatical error correction. In Proceedings of the Thirty-Second AAAI Conference on Artificial Intelligence, (AAAI-18), the 30th innovative Applications of Artificial Intelligence (IAAI-18), and the 8th AAAI Symposium on Educational Advances in Artificial Intelligence (EAAI-18), New Orleans, Louisiana, USA, February 2-7, 2018, pages 5755–5762.

Shamil Chollampatt and Hwee Tou Ng. 2018b. Neural quality estimation of grammatical error correction. In Proceedings of the 2018 Conference on Empirical Methods in Natural Language Processing, pages 2528–2539.

Daniel Dahlmeier, Hwee Tou Ng, and Siew Mei Wu. 2013. Building a large annotated corpus of learner english: The nus corpus of learner english. In Proceedings of the eighth workshop on innovative use of NLP for building educational applications, pages 22–31.

Yann N. Dauphin, Angela Fan, Michael Auli, and David Grangier. 2017. Language modeling with gated convolutional networks. In Proceedings of the 34th International Conference on Machine Learning, volume 70 of Proceedings of Machine Learning Research, pages 933–941, International Convention Centre, Sydney, Australia. PMLR.

Mariano Felice and Zheng Yuan. 2014. Generating artificial errors for grammatical error correction. In Proceedings of the Student Research Workshop at the 14th Conference of the European Chapter of the Association for Computational Linguistics, pages 116–126, Gothenburg, Sweden. Association for Computational Linguistics.

Michael Flor and Yoko Futagi. 2012. On using context for automatic correction of non-word misspellings in student essays. In Proceedings of the seventh workshop on building educational applications Using NLP, pages 105–115. Association for Computational Linguistics.

Tao Ge, Furu Wei, and Ming Zhou. 2018a. Fluency boost learning and inference for neural grammatical error correction. In Proceedings of the 56th Annual Meeting of the Association for Computational Linguistics (Volume 1: Long Papers), volume 1, pages 1055–1065.

Tao Ge, Furu Wei, and Ming Zhou. 2018b. Reaching human-level performance in automatic grammatical error correction: An empirical study. arXiv preprint arXiv:1807.01270.

Jonas Gehring, Michael Auli, David Grangier, Denis Yarats, and Yann N Dauphin. 2017. Convolutional sequence to sequence learning. In Proceedings of the 34th International Conference on Machine Learning-Volume 70, pages 1243–1252. JMLR. org.

Roman Grundkiewicz and Marcin Junczys-Dowmunt. 2018. Near human-level performance in grammatical error correction with hybrid machine translation. In Proceedings of the 2018 Conference of the North American Chapter of the Association for Computational Linguistics: Human Language Technologies, Volume 2 (Short Papers), volume 2, pages 284–290.

Jiatao Gu, Zhengdong Lu, Hang Li, and Victor O.K. Li. 2016. Incorporating copying mechanism in sequence-to-sequence learning. In Proceedings of the 54th Annual Meeting of the Association for Computational Linguistics (Volume 1: Long Papers), pages 1631–1640, Berlin, Germany. Association for Computational Linguistics.

Kaiming He, Xiangyu Zhang, Shaoqing Ren, and Jian Sun. 2016. Identity mappings in deep residual networks. In European conference on computer vision, pages 630–645. Springer.

Matthew Honnibal and Ines Montani. 2017. spacy 2: Natural language understanding with bloom embeddings, convolutional neural networks and incremental parsing. To appear.

Robin Jia and Percy Liang. 2016. Data recombination for neural semantic parsing. In Proceedings of the 54th Annual Meeting of the Association for Computational Linguistics (Volume 1: Long Papers), pages 12–22, Berlin, Germany. Association for Computational Linguistics.

Marcin Junczys-Dowmunt and Roman Grundkiewicz. 2016. Phrase-based machine translation is state-of-the-art for automatic grammatical error correction. In Proceedings of the 2016 Conference on Empirical Methods in Natural Language Processing, pages 1546–1556, Austin, Texas. Association for Computational Linguistics.

Marcin Junczys-Dowmunt, Roman Grundkiewicz, Shubha Guha, and Kenneth Heafield. 2018. Approaching neural grammatical error correction as a low-resource machine translation task. In Proceedings of the 2018 Conference of the North American Chapter of the Association for Computational Linguistics: Human Language Technologies, Volume 1 (Long Papers), volume 1, pages 595–606.

Diederik P Kingma and Jimmy Ba. 2015. Adam: A method for stochastic optimization. ICLR.

Taku Kudo and John Richardson. 2018. Sentencepiece: A simple and language independent subword tokenizer and detokenizer for neural text processing. arXiv preprint arXiv:1808.06226.

Shibamouli Lahiri. 2014. Complexity of Word Collocation Networks: A Preliminary Structural Analysis. In Proceedings of the Student Research Workshop at the 14th Conference of the European Chapter of the Association for Computational Linguistics, pages 96–105, Gothenburg, Sweden. Association for Computational Linguistics.

Guillaume Lample, Alexis Conneau, Ludovic Denoyer, and Marc'Aurelio Ranzato. 2018a. Unsupervised machine translation using monolingual corpora only. In International Conference on Learning Representations.

Guillaume Lample, Myle Ott, Alexis Conneau, Ludovic Denoyer, and Marc'Aurelio Ranzato. 2018b. Phrase-based & neural unsupervised machine translation. In Proceedings of the 2018 Conference on Empirical Methods in Natural Language Processing, pages 5039–5049, Brussels, Belgium. Association for Computational Linguistics.

Jared Lichtarge, Chris Alberti, Shankar Kumar, Noam Shazeer, Niki Parmar, and Simon Tong. 2019. Corpora generation for grammatical error correction. arXiv preprint arXiv:1904.05780.

Jared Lichtarge, Christopher Alberti, Shankar Kumar, Noam Shazeer, and Niki Parmar. 2018. Weakly supervised grammatical error correction using iterative decoding. arXiv preprint arXiv:1811.01710.

Thang Luong, Hieu Pham, and Christopher D. Manning. 2015. Effective approaches to attention-based neural machine translation. In EMNLP.

Stephen Merity, Caiming Xiong, James Bradbury, and Richard Socher. 2016. Pointer sentinel mixture models. arXiv preprint arXiv:1609.07843.

Tomoya Mizumoto, Mamoru Komachi, Masaaki Nagata, and Yuji Matsumoto. 2011. Mining revision log of language learning sns for automated japanese error correction of second language learners. In Proceedings of 5th International Joint Conference on Natural Language Processing, pages 147–155.

Hwee Tou Ng, Siew Mei Wu, Ted Briscoe, Christian Hadiwinoto, Raymond Hendy Susanto, and Christopher Bryant. 2014. The conll-2014 shared task on grammatical error correction. In Proceedings of the Eighteenth Conference on Computational Natural Language Learning: Shared Task, pages 1–14.

Myle Ott, Sergey Edunov, Alexei Baevski, Angela Fan, Sam Gross, Nathan Ng, David Grangier, and Michael Auli. 2019. fairseq: A fast, extensible toolkit for sequence modeling. arXiv preprint arXiv:1904.01038.

Adam Paszke, Sam Gross, Soumith Chintala, Gregory Chanan, Edward Yang, Zachary DeVito, Zeming Lin, Alban Desmaison, Luca Antiga, and Adam Lerer. 2017. Automatic differentiation in pytorch. In NIPS-W.

Sebastian Ruder. 2019. Neural Transfer Learning for Natural Language Processing. Ph.D. thesis, NATIONAL UNIVERSITY OF IRELAND, GALWAY.

Keisuke Sakaguchi, Matt Post, and Benjamin Van Durme. 2017. Grammatical error correction with neural reinforcement learning. In Proceedings of the Eighth International Joint Conference on Natural Language Processing (Volume 2: Short Papers), volume 2, pages 366–372.

Abigail See, Peter J. Liu, and Christopher D. Manning. 2017. Get to the point: Summarization with pointer-generator networks. In Proceedings of the 55th Annual Meeting of the Association for Computational Linguistics (Volume 1: Long Papers), pages 1073–1083, Vancouver, Canada. Association for Computational Linguistics.

Rico Sennrich, Barry Haddow, and Alexandra Birch. 2016a. Improving neural machine translation models with monolingual data. In Proceedings of the 54th Annual Meeting of the Association for Computational Linguistics (Volume 1: Long Papers), pages 86–96, Berlin, Germany. Association for Computational Linguistics.

Rico Sennrich, Barry Haddow, and Alexandra Birch. 2016b. Neural machine translation of rare words with subword units. In ACL.

Ilya Sutskever, Oriol Vinyals, and Quoc V Le. 2014. Sequence to sequence learning with neural networks. In NIPS.

Toshikazu Tajiri, Mamoru Komachi, and Yuji Matsumoto. 2012. Tense and aspect error correction for esl learners using global context. In Proceedings of the 50th Annual Meeting of the Association for Computational Linguistics: Short Papers-Volume 2, pages 198–202. Association for Computational Linguistics.

Ashish Vaswani, Noam Shazeer, Niki Parmar, Llion Jones, Jakob Uszkoreit, Aidan N Gomez, and Ł ukasz Kaiser. 2017. Attention is all you need. In NIPS.

Pascal Vincent, Hugo Larochelle, Yoshua Bengio, and Pierre-Antoine Manzagol. 2008. Extracting and composing robust features with denoising autoencoders. In Proceedings of the 25th international conference on Machine learning, pages 1096–1103. ACM.

Dong Wang and Thomas Fang Zheng. 2015. Transfer learning for speech and language processing. In 2015 Asia-Pacific Signal and Information Processing Association Annual Summit and Conference (APSIPA), pages 1225–1237. IEEE.

Ziang Xie, Guillaume Genthial, Stanley Xie, Andrew Ng, and Dan Jurafsky. 2018. Noising and denoising natural language: Diverse backtranslation for grammar correction. In Proceedings of the 2018 Conference of the North American Chapter of the Association for Computational Linguistics: Human Language Technologies, Volume 1 (Long Papers), pages 619–628, New Orleans, Louisiana. Association for Computational Linguistics.

Helen Yannakoudakis, Øistein E Andersen, Ardeshir Geranpayeh, Ted Briscoe, and Diane Nicholls. 2018. Developing an automated writing placement system for esl learners. Applied Measurement in Education, 31(3):251–267.

Wei Zhao, Liang Wang, Kewei Shen, Ruoyu Jia, and Jingming Liu. 2019. Improving grammatical error correction via pre-training a copy-augmented architecture with unlabeled data. In NAACL.

A Copy-Augmented Transformers: Formal Derivation

Copy-augmented Transformers (Zhao et al., 2019) incorporate an attention-based copying mechanism (Gu et al., 2016; See et al., 2017; Jia and Liang, 2016) in the decoder of Transformers. For each output token y_t at output position t, given source token sequence $\mathbf{x} = (x_1, \ldots, x_{T'})$, the output probability distribution over token vocabulary V is defined as:

$$\mathbf{H}^{\text{enc}} = \text{enc}(\mathbf{x}) \tag{3}$$

$$\mathbf{h}_t^{\text{dec}} = \text{dec}\left(y_{1:t-1}; \mathbf{H}^{\text{enc}}\right) \tag{4}$$

$$p^{\text{gen}}(y_t \mid y_{1:t-1}; \mathbf{x}) = \text{softmax}\left(\mathbf{W}^{\text{gen}}\mathbf{h}_t^{\text{dec}}\right) \tag{5}$$

where enc denotes the encoder that maps the source token sequence $\mathbf{x}$ to a sequence of hidden vectors $\mathbf{H}^{\text{enc}} \in \mathbb{R}^{d \times T'}$, dec denotes the decoder that takes output tokens at previous time steps along with encoded embeddings and produces a hidden vector $\mathbf{h}_t^{\text{dec}} \in \mathbb{R}^d$, and $\mathbf{W}^{\text{gen}} \in \mathbb{R}^{|V| \times d}$ is a learnable linear output layer that maps the hidden vector to a pre-softmax output probabilities ("logits"). We denote the resulting distribution as the (token) generative distribution, denoted as p^{gen}.

A copy attention layer can be defined as an additional (possibly multi-head) attention layer between the encoder outputs and the final-layer hidden vector at the current decoding step. The attention layer yields two outcomes, the layer output $\mathbf{o}_t$ and the corresponding attention scores $\mathbf{s}_t$:

$$\mathbf{s}_t = \text{softmax}\left(\frac{(\mathbf{h}_t^{\text{dec}})^T \mathbf{H}^{\text{enc}}}{\sqrt{d}}\right) \tag{6}$$

$$\mathbf{o}_t = \mathbf{H}^{\text{enc}}\mathbf{s}_t \tag{7}$$

The copy distribution is then defined as the attention scores in (6) themselves[9]:

$$p^{\text{copy}}(y_t \mid y_{1:t-1}; \mathbf{x}) = \mathbf{s}_t \qquad (8)$$

The final output of a copy-augmented Transformer as a mixture of both generative and copy distributions. The mixture weight[10] α_t^{copy} is defined at each decoding step as follows:

$$\alpha_t^{\text{copy}} = \text{sigmoid}\left((\mathbf{w}^{\text{alpha}})^T \mathbf{o}_t \right) \qquad (9)$$

$$p(y_t) = (1 - \alpha_t^{\text{copy}}) \cdot p^{\text{gen}}(y_t) + \alpha_t^{\text{copy}} \cdot p^{\text{copy}}(y_t) \qquad (10)$$

where $\mathbf{w}^{\text{alpha}} \in \mathbb{R}^d$ is a learnable linear output layer. (For simplicity, we omit the dependencies of all probabilities in (10) on both $y_{1:t-1}$ and $\mathbf{x}$.) The mixture weight balances between how likely it is for the model to simply copy a source token, rather than generating a possibly different token.

B   Exploratory Data Analysis

B.1   Data Sizes

Figure 2 illustrates the number of available parallel corpora (counting multiple annotations) across data sources. Note that the vertical axis is capped at 100K for a better visual comparison among other sources.

For the Lang-8 dataset, we count all available (ranging from 1 to 8) annotations for each of 1.04M original sentences. Also note that we only use the subset of Lang-8 whose source and target sentences are different, leaving only 575K sentences instead of 1.11M.

B.2   Sentence Length vs. Number of Edits

Figure 3 illustrates the distribution of sentence lengths and the number of edits per sentence across different data sources.

Table 9 includes our permutation test[11] results on the number of edits per sentence, normalized

---

[9]In practice, this involves adding up the copy scores defined for each source token into a $|V|$-dimensional vector, using commands such as `scatter_add()` in PyTorch.

[10]When computing the mixture weight α_t^{copy}, Zhao et al. (2019) applies a linear layer to $\mathbf{H}^{\text{enc}} \tilde{\mathbf{s}}_t$, where $\tilde{\mathbf{s}}_t$ are the attention scores in (6) *before* taking softmax. Our formulation gives essentially the same copying mechanism, while being more compatible to standard Transformer implementations.

[11]We used the off-the-shelf `mlxtend` package to run permutation tests. See `http://rasbt.github.io/mlxtend/user_guide/evaluate/permutation_test/`.

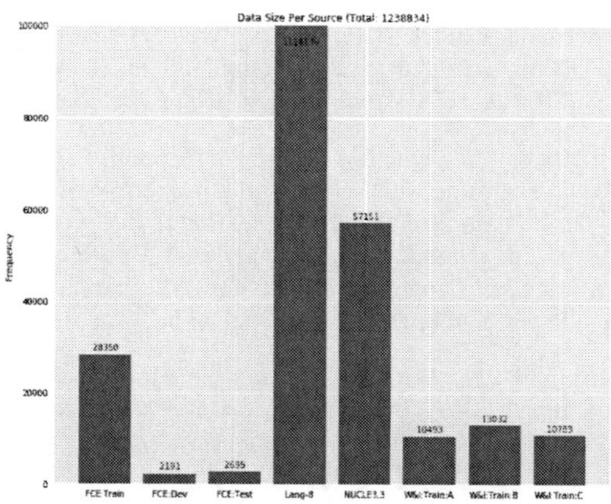

Figure 2: Data size per source for all Restricted Track training data. Number includes multiple annotations for Lang-8. Vertical axis is capped at 100K for a better visual comparison among the smaller sources. The three FCE splits (train, dev, test) are collectively used for training, and the three W&I+L splits correspond to three English proficiency levels ("A", "B", "C"). After duplicate removal, only 575K of the Lang-8 parallel corpus are actually used for training.

by sentence length (i.e., number of word-level tokens), between training data sources. Using an approximate permutation test with 10k simulations and a significant level of $\alpha = 0.05$, we find that there is a statistical difference in the normalized edit count per sentence between the W&I training set and each of FCE, NUCLE, and Lang-8. This serves as a preliminary experiment showing how the distribution of grammatical errors can be significantly different across different sources – even when they belong to a roughly similar domain.

C   Full Noising Algorithm

Algorithms 1 and 2 detail our noising scenarios.

D   Results on error categories

Table 10 shows the result on error categories.

E   CoNLL-2014 Full Results (Without Using W&I+L)

In Table 11, we include the training progress for our result for CoNLL-2014.

A noticeable difference between this result and our results for Restricted Track and Low Resource Track is that adaptation via fine-tuning is not necessarily effective here. We hypothesize that this is mostly due to the fact that the training subset to which we fine-tune our model (NUCLE) comes

Algorithm 1 Pseudocode for constructing noise dictionary

---

function CONSTRUCTNOISEDICTIONARY(ParallelCorpus, min_count)

    Initialize a dictionary dict

    for (CorToken, OriToken) in ParallelCorpus **do**

        dict[CorToken] += OriToken

    end for

    for CorToken, OriTokenList in dict **do**

        for OriToken in OriTokenList **do**

            if count(OriToken) < min_count **then**

                delete OriToken from dict[CorToken]

            end if

        end for

        if length(OriTokenList)==1 and CorToken==OriTokenList[0] **then**

            delete OriToken from dict

        end if

    end for

    return dict

end function

Algorithm 2 Pseudocode for generating noisy sentences

---

function CHANGE_TYPE(word, prob)

    preposition_set = [$\emptyset$, for, to, at, $\cdots$]

    if random[0, 1] > prob **then return** word

    else

        if word in preposition_set **then**

            random_choose_one_from(preposition_set)

        else if word is Noun **then** change_number(word)

        else if word is Verb **then** change_form(word)

        end if

    end if

    return word

end function

function MAKE_NOISE(sentence, prob)

    dict = ConstructNoiseDictionary(ParallelCorpus, min_count)

    noised = []

    for word in sentence **do**

        if word in dict and random[0, 1] > prob **then**

            candidates = dict[word]

            noise = random_choose_one_from(candidates)

        else

            noise = change_type(word)

        end if

        noised += noise

    end forreturn noised

end function

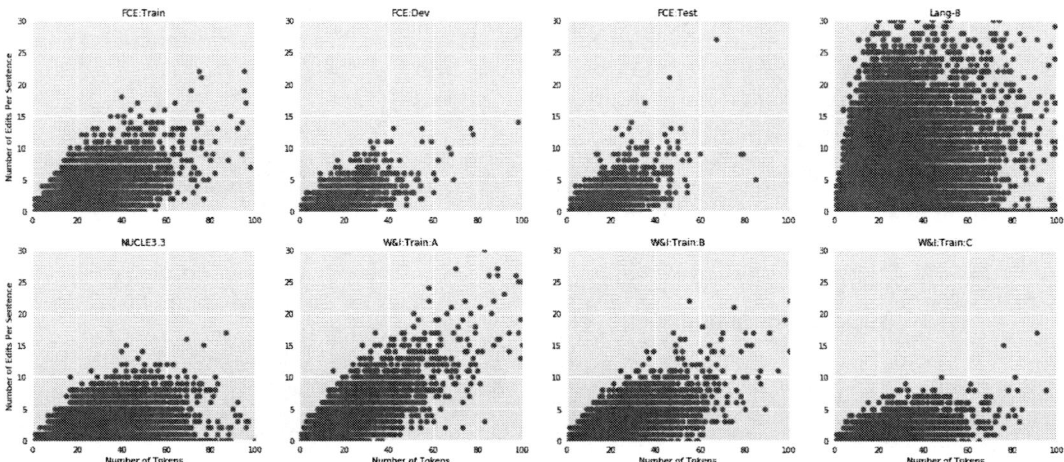

Figure 3: Sentence length versus the number of edits made in each sentence, across all training data sources for the Restricted Track. The horizontal axis is capped at 100 words (less than 0.02% of all sentences contain more than 100 words). The vertical axis is capped at 40 edits (less than 0.02% of all sentences contain more than 30 edits).

Source	# Sent.	# Edits / Length	Perm. Test vs. W&I
W&I-Train	34.3K	0.0922	n/a
FCE	33.2K	0.0898	$p = .002$
NUCLE	57.2K	0.0318	$p < .001$
Lang-8	1.11M	0.1357	$p < .001$

Table 9: Comparing the average number of edits per sentence, normalized by sentence length, between the W&I training set and other available training data sources for the Restricted Track. "vs. W&I" refers to the result of an approximate permutation test (10k rounds) against that in the W&I training set. Under the significance level of $\alpha = 0.05$, the number for FCE, NUCLE, and Lang-8 are all significantly different from that for the W&I training set.

from a different source than the actual test set (CoNLL-2014) – despite the fact that both datasets have similar domains (personal essays from English students), they can still have many other different characteristics, including the writer's English proficiency and annotation styles.

F Training Details

Our model training is a three-stage process: DAE pre-training, training, and fine-tuning, except in Low Resource Track where there is no fine-tuning data. At each step, we train a model until its ERRANT score on the development set reaches convergence, and use the learned weights as ini-

Error types	P	R	F0.5
ADJ	71.43	28.57	54.95
ADJ:FORM	100.00	40.00	76.92
ADV	70.59	22.22	49.18
CONJ	100.00	4.76	20.00
CONTR	100.00	91.67	98.21
DET	78.95	47.04	69.52
MORPH	81.18	49.29	71.88
NOUN	64.52	17.24	41.67
NOUN:INFL	100.00	41.18	77.78
NOUN:POSS	81.82	48.21	71.81
ORTH	87.38	49.60	75.83
OTHER	55.93	15.30	36.53
PART	76.19	55.17	70.80
PREP	69.69	49.01	64.27
PRON	78.67	43.70	67.82
PUNCT	79.95	70.48	77.86
SPELL	76.07	82.41	77.26
VERB	66.67	7.88	26.76
VERB:FORM	72.45	73.20	72.60
VERB:INFL	100.00	85.71	96.77
VERB:SVA	83.77	85.43	84.09
VERB:TENSE	71.43	45.64	64.18
WO	67.74	25.61	50.97

Table 10: Results on error types.

Steps	CoNLL-2014		
	P	**R**	**F0.5**
Spellcheck	54.75	5.75	**20.25**
+ Pre-train (b)	54.76	15.09	**35.89**
+ Train (b)	60.43	34.22	**52.40**
+ Fine-tune (b)	60.81	33.32	**52.20**
+ Pre-train (c)	65.81	24.17	**48.95**
+ Train (c)	61.38	30.97	**51.30**
+ Fine-tune (c)	60.82	32.50	**51.79**
+ Ensemble (b+c)	71.11	32.56	**57.50**

Table 11: Training progress on CoNLL-2014. *No W&I+Locness datasets were used in these results.* 'b' and 'c' refer to the base and copy configurations of the Transformer, respectively. Evaluation is done using the MaxMatch (M^2) scorer. Pre-processing & post-processing are included before the first step and after the last step, respectively.

tial values for the next step. For pre-training, we used a learning rate of $5 \cdot 10^{-4}$ for the base and copy-augmented Transformers and 10^{-3} for the large Transformer. For training, we reset the optimizer and set the learning rate to 10^{-4}. For fine-tuning (if available), we again reset the optimizer and set the learning rate to $5 \cdot 10^{-5}$. In all training steps, we used the Adam (Kingma and Ba, 2015) optimizer with the inverse square-root schedule and a warmup learning rate of 10^{-7}, along with a dropout rate of 0.3.

G   Further Analysis

G.1   Effect of Copying Mechanisms & Ensembles

One of our contributions is to highlight the benefit of ensembling multiple models with diverse characteristics. As shown in Table 3, the final ensemble step involving different types of models was crucial for our model's performance, improving the test score by over 6 $F_{0.5}$ points. We first no-

ticed that the copy-augmented Transformer learns to be more conservative – i.e., higher precision but lower recall given similar overall scores – in its edits than the vanilla Transformer, presumably because the model includes an inductive bias that favors copying (i.e., not editing) the input token via its copy attention scores. Table 12 shows this phenomenon for Restricted Track.

Given multiple models with diverse characteristics, the choice of models for ensemble can translate to controlling how conservative we want our final model to be. For example, combining one vanilla model with multiple independent copy-augmented models will result in a more conservative model. This could serve as an alternative to other methods that control the precision-recall ratio, such as the edit-weighted loss (Junczys-Dowmunt et al., 2018).

Model (Config.)	W&I+L Test		
	P	**R**	**F0.5**
Vanilla (Large)	63.66	56.82	62.17
Copy (Copy)	66.02	53.41	63.05
Δ	+2.36	-3.41	+0.88

Table 12: Single-model ERRANT scores for Restricted Track, using a large Transformer and a copy-augmented Transformer.

Neural and FST-based approaches to grammatical error correction

Zheng Yuan[♠♢] **Felix Stahlberg**[♣] **Marek Rei**[♠♢] **Bill Byrne**[♣] **Helen Yannakoudakis**[♠♢]

[♠]Department of Computer Science & Technology, University of Cambridge, United Kingdom
[♢]ALTA Institute, University of Cambridge, United Kingdom
[♣]Department of Engineering, University of Cambridge, United Kingdom

{zheng.yuan, marek.rei, helen.yannakoudakis}@cl.cam.ac.uk,
{fs439, bill.byrne}@eng.cam.ac.uk

Abstract

In this paper, we describe our submission to the BEA 2019 shared task on grammatical error correction. We present a system pipeline that utilises both error detection and correction models. The input text is first corrected by two complementary neural machine translation systems: one using convolutional networks and multi-task learning, and another using a neural Transformer-based system. Training is performed on publicly available data, along with artificial examples generated through back-translation. The n-best lists of these two machine translation systems are then combined and scored using a finite state transducer (FST). Finally, an unsupervised re-ranking system is applied to the n-best output of the FST. The re-ranker uses a number of error detection features to re-rank the FST n-best list and identify the final 1-best correction hypothesis. Our system achieves 66.75% $F_{0.5}$ on error correction (ranking 4th), and 82.52% $F_{0.5}$ on token-level error detection (ranking 2nd) in the restricted track of the shared task.

1 Introduction

Grammatical error correction (GEC) is the task of automatically correcting grammatical errors in written text. In this paper, we describe our submission to the restricted track of the BEA 2019 shared task on grammatical error correction (Bryant et al., 2019), where participating teams are constrained to using only the provided datasets as training data. Systems are expected to correct errors of all types, including grammatical, lexical and orthographical errors. Compared to previous shared tasks on GEC, which have primarily focused on correcting errors committed by non-native speakers (Dale and Kilgarriff, 2011; Dale et al., 2012; Ng et al., 2013, 2014), a new annotated dataset is introduced, consisting of essays produced by native and non-native English language learners, with a wide coverage of language proficiency levels for the latter, ranging from elementary to advanced.

Neural machine translation (NMT) systems for GEC have drawn growing attention in recent years (Yuan and Briscoe, 2016; Xie et al., 2016; Ji et al., 2017; Sakaguchi et al., 2017; Chollampatt and Ng, 2018; Junczys-Dowmunt et al., 2018), as they have been shown to achieve state-of-the-art results (Ge et al., 2018; Zhao et al., 2019). Within this framework, error correction is cast as a monolingual translation task, where the source is a sentence (written by a language learner) that may contain errors, and the target is its corrected counterpart in the same language.

Due to the fundamental differences between a "true" machine translation task and the error correction task, previous work has investigated the adaptation of NMT for the task of GEC. Byte pair encoding (BPE) (Chollampatt and Ng, 2018; Junczys-Dowmunt et al., 2018) and a copying mechanism (Zhao et al., 2019) have been introduced to deal with the "noisy" input text in GEC and the non-standard language used by learners. Some researchers have investigated ways of incorporating task-specific knowledge, either by directly modifying the training objectives (Schmaltz et al., 2017; Sakaguchi et al., 2017; Junczys-Dowmunt et al., 2018) or by re-ranking machine-translation-system correction hypotheses (Yannakoudakis et al., 2017; Chollampatt and Ng, 2018). To ameliorate the lack of large amounts of error-annotated learner data, various approaches have proposed to leverage unlabelled native data within a number of frameworks, including artificial error generation with back translation (Rei et al., 2017; Kasewa et al., 2018), fluency boost learning (Ge et al., 2018), and pre-training with denoising autoencoders (Zhao et al., 2019).

Previous work has shown that a GEC system

Proceedings of the Fourteenth Workshop on Innovative Use of NLP for Building Educational Applications, pages 228–239
Florence, Italy, August 2, 2019. ©2019 Association for Computational Linguistics

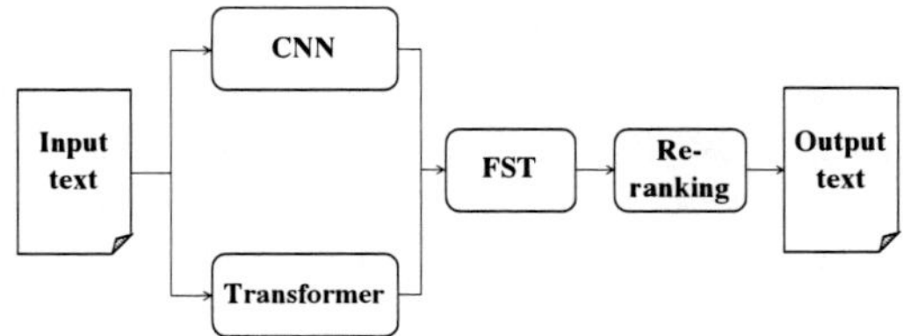

Figure 1: Overview of our best GEC system pipeline.

targeting all errors may not necessarily be the best approach to the task, and that different GEC systems may be better suited to correcting different types of errors, and can therefore be complementary (Yuan, 2017). As such, hybrid systems that combine different approaches have been shown to yield improved performance (Felice et al., 2014; Rozovskaya and Roth, 2016; Grundkiewicz and Junczys-Dowmunt, 2018). In line with this work, we present a hybrid approach that 1) employs two NMT-based error correction systems: a neural convolutional system and a neural Transformer-based system; 2) a finite state transducer (FST) that combines and further enriches the n-best outputs of the NMT systems; 3) a re-ranking system that re-ranks the n-best output of the FST based on error detection features.

The remainder of this paper is organised as follows: Section 2 describes our approach to the task; Section 3 describes the datasets used and presents our results on the shared task development set; Section 4 presents our official results on the shared task test set, including a detailed analysis of the performance of our final system; and, finally, Section 5 concludes the paper and provides an overview of our findings.

2 Approach

We approach the error correction task using a pipeline of systems, as presented in Figure 1. In the following sections, we describe each of these components in detail.

2.1 The convolutional neural network (CNN) system

We use a neural sequence-to-sequence model and an encoder–decoder architecture (Cho et al., 2014; Sutskever et al., 2014). An encoder first reads and encodes an entire input sequence $\mathbf{x} = (x_1, x_2, ..., x_n)$ into hidden state representations. A decoder then generates an output sequence $\mathbf{y} = (y_1, y_2, ..., y_m)$ by predicting the next token y_t

based on the input sequence $\mathbf{x}$ and all the previously generated tokens $\{y_1, y_2, ..., y_{t-1}\}$:

$$p(\mathbf{y}) = \prod_{t=1}^{m} p(y_t | \{y_1, ..., y_{t-1}\}, \mathbf{x}) \qquad (1)$$

Our convolutional neural system is based on a multi-layer convolutional encoder–decoder model (Gehring et al., 2017), which employs convolutional neural networks (CNNs) to compute intermediate encoder and decoder states. The parameter settings follow Chollampatt and Ng (2018) and Ge et al. (2018). The source and target word embeddings have size 500, and are initialised with fastText embeddings (Bojanowski et al., 2017) trained on the native English Wikipedia corpus ($2, 405, 972, 890$ tokens). Each of the encoder and decoder is made up of seven convolutional layers, with a convolution window width of 3. We apply a left-to-right beam search to find a correction that approximately maximises the conditional probability in Equation 1.

BPE is introduced to alleviate the rare-word problem, and rare and unknown words are split into multiple frequent subword tokens (Sennrich et al., 2016b). NMT systems often limit vocabulary size on both source and target sides due to the computational complexity during training. Therefore, they are unable to translate out-of-vocabulary (OOV) words, which are treated as unknown tokens, resulting in poor translation quality. As noted by Yuan and Briscoe (2016), this problem is more serious for GEC as non-native text contains, not only rare words (e.g., proper nouns), but also misspelled words (i.e., spelling errors).

In our model, each of the source and target vocabularies consist of the 30K most frequent BPE tokens from the source and target side of the parallel training data respectively. The same BPE operation is applied to the Wikipedia data before being used for training of our word embeddings.

Copying mechanism is a technique that has led to performance improvement on various monolingual sequence-to-sequence tasks, such as text summarisation, dialogue systems, and paraphrase generation (Gu et al., 2016; Cao et al., 2017). The idea is to allow the decoder to choose between simply copying an original input word and outputting a translation word. Since the source and target sentences are both in the same language (i.e., monolingual translation) and most words in the source sentence are correct and do not need to change, GEC seems to benefit from the copying mechanism.

Following the work of Gu et al. (2016), we use a dynamic target vocabulary, which contains a fixed vocabulary learned from the target side of the training data plus all the unique tokens introduced by the source sentence. As a result, the probability of generating any target token $p(y_t|\{y_1, ..., y_{t-1}\}, \mathbf{x})$ in Equation 1 is defined as a "mixture" of the generation probability $p(y_t, g|\{y_1, ..., y_{t-1}\}, \mathbf{x})$ and the copy probability $p(y_t, c|\{y_1, ..., y_{t-1}\}, \mathbf{x})$:

$$p(y_t|\{y_1, ..., y_{t-1}\}, \mathbf{x}) = p(y_t, g|\{y_1, ..., y_{t-1}\}, \mathbf{x}) + p(y_t, c|\{y_1, ..., y_{t-1}\}, \mathbf{x}) \quad (2)$$

Multi-task learning has found success in a wide range of tasks, from natural language processing (NLP) (Collobert and Weston, 2008) and speech recognition (Deng et al., 2013) to computer vision (Girshick, 2015). Multi-task learning allows systems to use information from related tasks and learn from multiple objectives, which leads to performance improvement on individual tasks. Recently, Rei (2017) and Rei and Yannakoudakis (2017) investigated the use of different auxiliary objectives for the task of error detection in learner writing.

In addition to our primary error correction task, we propose two related auxiliary objectives to boost model performance:

- **Token-level labelling**

  We jointly train an error detection and error correction system by providing error detection labels. Instead of only generating a corrected sentence, we extend the system to additionally predict whether a token in the source sentence is correct or incorrect.

- **Sentence-level labelling**

  A binary classification task is also introduced to predict whether the original source sentence is grammatically correct or incorrect. We investigate the usefulness of sentence-level classification as an auxiliary objective for training error correction models.

Labels for both auxiliary error detection tasks are generated automatically by comparing source and target tokens using the ERRANT automatic alignment tool (Bryant et al., 2017). We first align each token x_i in the source sentence $\mathbf{x}$ with a token y_j in the target sentence $\mathbf{y}$. If $x_i = y_j$, the source token x_i is correct; while if $x_i \neq y_j$, the source token x_i is incorrect. Similarly, the source sentence $\mathbf{x}$ is correct if $\mathbf{x} = \mathbf{y}$, and incorrect otherwise.

Artificial error generation is the process of injecting artificial errors into a set of error-free sentences. Compared to standard machine translation tasks, GEC suffers from the limited availability of large amounts of training data. As manual error annotation of learner data is a slow and expensive process, artificial error generation has been applied to error correction (Felice and Yuan, 2014) and detection (Rei et al., 2017) with some success. Following the work of Rei et al. (2017), we treat error generation as a machine translation task, where a grammatically correct sentence is translated to an incorrect counterpart. We built an error generation system using the same network architecture as the one described here, with error-corrected sentences as the source and their corresponding uncorrected counterparts written by language learners as the target. The system is then used to collect the n-best outputs: $\mathbf{y}_o^1, \mathbf{y}_o^2, ..., \mathbf{y}_o^n$, for a given error-free native and/or learner sentence $\mathbf{y}$. Since there is no guarantee that the error generation system will inject errors into the input sentence $\mathbf{y}$ to make it less grammatically correct, we apply "quality control". A pair of artificially generated sentences $(\mathbf{y}_o^k, \mathbf{y})$, for $k \in \{1, 2, ..., n\}$, will be added to the training set of the error correction system if the following condition is met:

$$\frac{f(\mathbf{y})}{f(\mathbf{y}_o^k)} \leq \sigma \quad (3)$$

where $f(\mathbf{y})$ is the normalised log probability of $\mathbf{y}$:

$$f(\mathbf{y}) = \frac{\sum_{t=1}^{m} \log(P(y_t|\mathbf{y}_{<t}))}{m} \quad (4)$$

This ensures that the quality of the artificially generated sentence, as estimated by a language model, is lower compared to the original sentence. We use a 5-gram language model (LM) trained on the One Billion Word Benchmark dataset (Chelba et al., 2014) with KenLM (Heafield, 2011) to compute $P(y_t|\mathbf{y}_{<t})$.

The σ in Equation 3 is a threshold used to filter out sentence pairs with unnecessary changes; e.g., [*I look forward to hearing from you.* → *I am looking forward to hearing from you.*]. It is an averaged score learned on the development set:

$$\sigma = \frac{\sum_{i=1}^{N} \frac{f(\mathbf{y}_i)}{f(\mathbf{x}_i)}}{N} \tag{5}$$

where $(\mathbf{x}, \mathbf{y})$ is a pair of parallel sentences in the development set, and N is the total number of pairs.

2.2 The neural Transformer-based system

Besides the convolutional system from the previous section, we also use the purely neural Transformer-based system of Stahlberg and Byrne (2019). They use an ensemble of four Transformer (Vaswani et al., 2017) NMT and two Transformer LM models in Tensor2Tensor (Vaswani et al., 2018) `transformer_big` configuration. The NMT models are trained with back-translation (Sennrich et al., 2016a; Rei et al., 2017; Kasewa et al., 2018) and fine-tuning through continued training. For a detailed description of this system we refer the reader to Stahlberg and Byrne (2019).

2.3 FST-based system combination

Stahlberg et al. (2019) demonstrated the usefulness of FSTs for grammatical error correction. Their method starts with an input lattice I which is generated with a phrase-based statistical machine translation (SMT) system. The lattice I is composed with a number of FSTs that aim to enrich the search space with further possible corrections. Similarly to Bryant and Briscoe (2018), they rely on external knowledge sources like spell checkers and morphological databases to generate additional correction options for the input sentence. The enriched lattice is then mapped to the subword level by composition with a mapping transducer, and re-scored with neural machine translation models and neural LMs.

In this work, rather than combining SMT and neural models, we use the framework of Stahlberg et al. (2019) to combine and enrich the outputs of two neural systems. The input lattice I is now the union of two n-best lists – one from the convolutional system (Section 2.1), and one from the Transformer-based system (Section 2.2). After composition, we re-score the enriched input lattice I with the system described in Section 2.2. The FST-based system combination uses 7 different features: the convolutional system score, the LM and NMT scores from the Transformer-

based system, the edit distance of hypotheses in I to the input sentence, substitution and deletion penalties for the additional correction options from the FST framework, and the word count. Following Stahlberg et al. (2019); Stahlberg and Byrne (2019), we scale these features and tune the scaling weights on the BEA-2019 development set using a variant of Powell search (Powell, 1964). We use OpenFST (Allauzen et al., 2007) as backend for FST operations, and the SGNMT decoder (Stahlberg et al., 2017, 2018) for neural decoding under FST constraints.

2.4 Re-ranking FST output

Yannakoudakis et al. (2017) found that grammatical error detection systems can be used to improve error correction outputs. Specifically, they re-rank the n-best correction hypotheses of an SMT system based on error detection predictions. Following this work, we also deploy a re-ranking component which re-ranks the n-best correction hypotheses of the FST system (Section 2.3) based on error detection predictions output by an error detection system.

Error detection. Our system for grammatical error detection is based on the model described by Rei (2017).[1] The task is formulated as a sequence labeling problem – given a sentence, the model assigns a probability to each token, indicating the likelihood of that token being incorrect in the given context (Rei and Yannakoudakis, 2016). The architecture maps words to distributed embeddings, while also constructing character-based representations for each word with a neural component. These are then passed through a bidirectional LSTM, followed by a feed-forward layer and a softmax layer at the output.

In addition to neural text representations, we also include several external features into the model, designed to help it learn more accurate error detection patterns from the limited amounts of training data available:

- Two binary features indicating whether two publicly available spell-checkers – HunSpell[2] and JamSpell[3] – identify the target word as a spelling mistake.

---

[1] `https://github.com/marekrei/sequence-labeler`
[2] `http://hunspell.github.io/`
[3] `https://github.com/bakwc/JamSpell`

- The POS tag, NER label and dependency relation of the target word based on the Stanford parser (Chen and Manning, 2014).

- The number of times the unigram, bigram, or trigram context of the target word appears in the BNC (Burnard, 2007) and in ukWaC (Ferraresi et al., 2008).

- Contextualized word representations from ELMo (Peters et al., 2018).

The discrete features are represented as 10-dimensional embeddings and, together with the continuous features, concatenated to each word representation in the model. The overall architecture is optimized for error detection using cross-entropy. Once trained, the model returns the predicted probabilities of each token in a sentence being correct or incorrect.

Re-ranker. We generate the list of the 8 best correction hypotheses from our FST system, and then use the following set of error detection-based features to assign a new score to each hypothesis and determine a new ranking:

1. Sentence correctness probability: the error detection model outputs a probability indicating whether a token is likely to be correct or incorrect in context. We therefore use as a feature the overall FST sentence probability, calculated based on the probability of each of its tokens being correct: $\sum_{w} \log P(w)$

2. Levenshtein distance (LD): we first use LD to identify 1) which tokens in the original/uncorrected sentence have been corrected by the FST candidate hypothesis, and 2) which tokens in the original/uncorrected sentence our detection model predicts as incorrect (i.e., the probability of being incorrect is > 0.5). We then convert these annotations to binary sequences – i.e., 1 if the token is identified as incorrect, and 0 otherwise – and use as a feature the LD between those binary representations. Specifically, we would like to select the candidate FST sentence that has the smallest LD from the binary sequence created by the detection model, and therefore use as a feature the following: $\frac{1.0}{LD+1.0}$

3. False positives: using the binary sequences described above, we count the number of false positives (FP) on token-level error detection by treating the error detection model as the "gold standard". Specifically, we count how many times the candidate FST hypothesis disagrees with the detection model on the tokens identified as incorrect, and use as a feature the following: $\frac{1.0}{FP+1.0}$

We use a linear combination of the above three features together with the original score given by the FST system for each candidate hypothesis to re-rank the FST system's 8-best list in an unsupervised way. The new 1-best correction hypothesis c^* is then the one that maximises:

$$c^* = \arg\max_{c} \sum_{i=1}^{K} \lambda_i\, h_i(c) \qquad (6)$$

where h represents the score assigned to candidate hypothesis c according to feature i; λ is a weighting parameter that controls the effect feature i has on the final ranking; and $K = 4$ as we use a total of four different features (three features based on the detection model, and one which is the original score output by the FST system). λs are tuned on the development set and are set to $\lambda = 2.0$ for features 1. and 2., $\lambda = 3.0$ for feature 3. and $\lambda = 1.5$ for the original FST score.

3 Experiments and results

3.1 Datasets and evaluation

In the restricted track, participating teams were constrained to use only the provided learner datasets:[4]

- **Cambridge English W&I corpus**

  Cambridge English Write & Improve (W&I)[5] (Yannakoudakis et al., 2018) is an online web platform that assists non-native English learners with their writing. Learners from around the world submit letters, stories, articles and essays for automated assessment in response to various prompts. The W&I corpus (Bryant et al., 2019) contains $3,600$ annotated submissions across 3 different CEFR[6] levels: A (beginner), B (intermediate), and C (advanced). The data has been

---

[4]We note that there are no restrictions on the use of NLP tools (e.g., POS taggers, parsers, spellcheckers, etc.), nor on the amount of unannotated data that can be used, so long as such resources are publicly available.

[5]https://writeandimprove.com/

[6]https://www.cambridgeenglish.org/exams-and-tests/cefr/

split into training ($3,000$ essays), development (200 essays), and test (200 essays) partitions.

- **LOCNESS**

  The LOCNESS[7] corpus (Granger, 1998) consists of essays written by native English students. A subsection of 100 essays has been manually annotated, and equally partitioned into development and test sets.

- **FCE**

  The First Certificate in English (FCE) corpus (Yannakoudakis et al., 2011) is a subset of the Cambridge Learner Corpus (CLC) that consists of $1,244$ exam scripts written by learners of English sitting the FCE exam.

- **NUCLE**

  The National University of Singapore Corpus of Learner English (NUCLE) (Dahlmeier et al., 2013) contains $1,400$ essays written by undergraduate students at the National University of Singapore who are non-native English speakers.

- **Lang-8 Corpus of Learner English**

  Lang-8[8] is an online language learning website which encourages users to correct each other's grammar. The Lang-8 Corpus of Learner English (Mizumoto et al., 2011; Tajiri et al., 2012) refers to an English subsection of this website (can be quite noisy).

Additional resources used in our system include:

- **English Wikipedia corpus**

  The English Wikipedia corpus ($2,405,972,890$ tokens in $110,698,467$ sentences) is used to pre-train word embeddings for the convolutional neural system. We also use it as error-free native data for artificial error generation (see Section 2.1).

- **One Billion Word Benchmark dataset**

  A LM is trained on the One Billion Word Benchmark dataset, which consists of close to a billion words of English taken from news articles on the web, to evaluate the quality of artificially generated sentence pairs. A filtered version ($768,646,526$ tokens in $30,301,028$ sentences) is used as input to the error generation model in Section 2.1.

In order to cover the full range of English levels and abilities, the official development set consists of 300 essays from W&I (A: 130, B:100, and C:70) and 50 essays from LOCNESS ($86,973$ tokens in $4,384$ sentences).

The ERRANT scorer (Bryant et al., 2017) is used as the official scorer for the shared task. System performance is evaluated in terms of span-level correction using $F_{0.5}$, which emphasises precision twice as much as recall.

3.2 Training details

The convolutional NMT model is trained with a hidden layer size of $1,024$ for both the encoder and the decoder. Dropout at a rate of 0.2 is applied to the embedding layers, convolutional layers and decoder output. The model is optimized using Nesterov's Accelerated Gradient Descent (NAG) with a simplified formulation for Nesterov's momentum (Bengio et al., 2013). The initial learning rate is set to 0.25, with a decaying factor of 0.1 and a momentum value of 0.99. We perform validation after every epoch, and select the best model based on the performance on the development set. During beam search, we keep a beam size of 12 and discard all other hypotheses.

The grammatical error detection system was optimized separately as a sequence labeling model. Word embeddings were set to size 300 and initialized with pre-trained Glove embedding (Pennington et al., 2014). The bi-LSTM has 300-dimensional hidden layers for each direction. Dropout was applied to word embeddings and LSTM outputs with probability 0.5. The model was optimized with Adam (Kingma and Ba, 2015), using a default learning rate 0.001. Training was stopped when performance on the development set did not improved over 7 epochs.

3.3 Individual system performance

Individual system performance on the development set is reported in Table 1, where 'CNN' refers to the convolutional neural system, and 'Transformer' refers to the Transformer-based neural system. These results are based on the 1-best output from each system, although the n-best

---

[7]https://uclouvain.be/en/
research-institutes/ilc/cecl/locness.
html
[8]https://lang-8.com/

System	TP	FP	FN	P	R	$F_{0.5}$
CNN	1697	2371	5858	41.72	22.46	35.61
Transformer	2455	2162	5006	53.17	32.90	47.34

Table 1: Span-level correction results for individual systems on the development set. TP: true positives, FP: false positives, FN: false negatives, P: precision, R: recall.

lists are used later for system combination.

3.4 Pipelines

Since corrections made by the convolutional neural system and the Transformer-based system are often complementary, and re-scoring has been proven to be useful and effective for error correction, we investigated ways to combine corrections generated by both systems. Table 2 shows results for different combinations, where 'CNN' refers to the convolutional neural system, 'Transformer' refers to the Transformer-based system, subscript '10-best' indicates the use of the 10-best list of correction candidates from the system, '+' indicates a combination of corrections from different systems, and '>' indicates a pipeline where the output of one system is the input to the other.

4 Official evaluation results

Our submission to the shared task is the result of our best hybrid system, described in Section 2 and summarised in Figure 1. Similar to the official development set, the test set comprises 350 texts ($85,668$ tokens in $4,477$ sentences) written by native and non-native English learners.

Systems were evaluated using the ERRANT scorer, with span-based correction $F_{0.5}$ as the primary measure. In the restricted track, where participants were constrained to use only the provided training sets, our submitted system ranked fourth[9] out of 21 participating teams. The official results of our submission in terms of span-level correction, span-level detection and token-level detection, including our system rankings, are reported in Table 3. It is worth noting that our correction system yielded particularly high performance on error detection tasks, ranking third on span-level detection and second on token-level detection. We believe that much of the success in error detection can be credited to the error detection auxiliary objectives introduced in the convolutional neural sys-

tem (see Section 2.1) and the error detection features used in our final re-ranking system (see Section 2.4).

We also report span-level correction performance in terms of different CEFR levels (A, B, and C),[10] as well as on the native texts only (N) in Table 4. Our final error correction system performs best on advanced learner data (C), achieving an $F_{0.5}$ score of 73.28, followed by intermediate learner data (B), native data (N), and lastly beginner learner data (A). The difference between the highest and lowest $F_{0.5}$ scores is 8.12 points. We also note that the system seems to be handling errors made by native students effectively even though it has not been trained on any native parallel data. Overall, we observe that our system generalises well across native and non-native data, as well as across different proficiency/CEFR levels.

In order to better understand the performance of our hybrid error correction system, we perform a detailed error analysis. This helps us understand the strengths and weaknesses of the system, as well as identify areas for future work. Error type-specific performance is presented in Table 5. We can see that our system achieves the highest results on *VERB:INFL* (verb inflection) errors with an $F_{0.5}$ of 93.75. However, the result is not truly representative as there are only 8 verb inflection errors in the test data, and our system successfully corrects 6 of them. The error type that follows is *ORTH* (orthography), which comprises case and/or whitespace errors. A high precision score of 89.11 is observed, suggesting that our system is particularly suitable for these kind of errors. We also observe that our system is effective at correcting *VERB:SVA* (subject–verb agreement) errors, achieving an $F_{0.5}$ of 80.08. Results for *ADJ:FORM* (adjective form; $F_{0.5}$=78.95) and *CONTR* (contraction; $F_{0.5}$=77.92) are high; however, these error types only account for small fractions of the test set (0.188% and 0.245% respectively).

The worst performance is observed for type *CONJ* (conjunction), with an $F_{0.5}$ of 28.46. Our system successfully corrected 7 conjunction errors, while missed 20 and made 17 unnecessary changes. We note that our system is less effective at correcting open-class errors

---

[9]The system is tied for third place as the difference in $F_{0.5}$ is negligible.

[10]https://www.cambridgeenglish.org/exams-and-tests/cefr/

Pipeline	TP	FP	FN	P	R	$F_{0.5}$
$CNN_{10\text{-best}}$ + $Transformer_{10\text{-best}}$ > FST	2416	1798	5045	57.33	32.38	49.68
$CNN_{10\text{-best}}$ + $Transformer_{10\text{-best}}$ > $FST_{8\text{-best}}$ > Re-ranking	2502	1839	4959	57.64	33.53	50.39

Table 2: Span-level correction results for different system pipelines on the development set.

Evaluation	TP	FP	FN	P	R	$F_{0.5}$	#
Span-level correction	2924	1224	2386	70.49	55.07	66.75	4
Span-level detection	3383	774	2181	81.38	60.80	76.22	3
Token-level detection	4098	470	2461	89.71	62.48	82.52	2

Table 3: Official results of our submitted system on the test set.

Level	TP	FP	FN	P	R	$F_{0.5}$
A	1272	573	1108	68.94	53.45	65.16
B	905	368	806	71.09	52.89	66.51
C	425	131	251	76.44	62.87	73.28
N	322	152	221	67.93	59.30	66.01

Table 4: Proficiency level-specific span-level correction performance of our submitted system on the test set. A: CEFR beginner; B: CEFR intermediate; C: CEFR advanced; N: native.

such as *NOUN* (noun; $F_{0.5}$=34.75), *OTHER* (other;[11] $F_{0.5}$=38.95); *VERB* (verb; $F_{0.5}$=39.80); *ADJ* (adjective; $F_{0.5}$=41.94) and *ADV* (adverb; $F_{0.5}$=51.65) errors. As noted by Kochmar (2016), such error types are quite challenging for error detection and correction systems: content words express meaning, and their semantic properties should be taken into account. Unlike errors in function words, content word errors are often less systematic; e.g., [*person → people, ambulate → walk, big → wide, speedily → quickly*].

5 Conclusion

In this paper, we have presented a hybrid approach to error correction that combines a convolutional and a Transformer-based neural system. We have explored different combination techniques involving sequential pipelines, candidate generation and re-ranking. Our best hybrid system submitted to the restricted track of the BEA 2019 shared task yields a span-level correction score of $F_{0.5} = 66.75$, placing our system in the fourth place out of 21 participating teams. High results were observed for both span-level and token-level error detection (ranking our system third and second respectively), suggesting that our error correction system can also effectively detect errors. De-

Error type	TP	FP	FN	P	R	$F_{0.5}$
ADJ	13	15	30	46.43	30.23	41.94
ADJ:FORM	6	1	4	85.71	60.00	78.95
ADV	25	19	41	56.82	37.88	51.65
CONJ	7	17	20	29.17	25.93	28.46
CONTR	12	4	1	75.00	92.31	77.92
DET	421	149	228	73.86	64.87	71.87
MORPH	91	20	60	81.98	60.26	76.47
NOUN	36	63	86	36.36	29.51	34.75
NOUN:INFL	7	1	13	87.50	35.00	67.31
NOUN:NUM	199	85	64	70.07	75.67	71.12
NOUN:POSS	29	10	25	74.36	53.70	69.05
ORTH	229	28	162	89.11	58.57	80.69
OTHER	160	181	530	46.92	23.19	38.95
PART	24	8	10	75.00	70.59	74.07
PREP	262	125	193	67.70	57.58	65.40
PRON	59	20	82	74.68	41.84	64.55
PUNCT	636	192	291	76.81	68.61	75.02
SPELL	204	47	108	81.27	65.38	77.51
VERB	57	64	175	47.11	24.57	39.80
VERB:FORM	157	52	45	75.12	77.72	75.63
VERB:INFL	6	0	2	100.00	75.00	93.75
VERB:SVA	127	32	30	79.87	80.89	80.08
VERB:TENSE	122	64	137	65.59	47.10	60.82
WO	35	27	49	56.45	41.67	52.71

Table 5: Error type-specific span-level correction performance of our submitted system on the test set.

tailed analyses show that our system generalises well across different language proficiency levels (CEFR) and native / non-native domains. An error-type analysis showed that our system is particularly good at correcting verb inflection, orthography and subject–verb agreement errors, but less effective at correcting open-class word errors which are less systematic.

Acknowledgments

We thank the anonymous reviewers for their valuable feedback. Zheng Yuan, Marek Rei and Helen Yannakoudakis were supported by Cambridge Assessment, University of Cambridge. Felix Stahlberg and Bill Byrne acknowledge support for this work by the U.K. Engineering and Physical Sciences Research Council (EPSRC) grant EP/L027623/1 and grant EP/P020259/1 which provided Cambridge Tier-2 resources operated by the University of Cambridge Research Computing

[11]Errors that do not fall into any other category (e.g., paraphrasing).

Service.[12] We thank the NVIDIA Corporation for the donation of the Titan X Pascal GPU used in this research.

References

Cyril Allauzen, Michael Riley, Johan Schalkwyk, Wojciech Skut, and Mehryar Mohri. 2007. OpenFst: A general and efficient weighted finite-state transducer library. In *Implementation and Application of Automata*, pages 11–23. Springer.

Yoshua Bengio, Nicolas Boulanger-lew, and Razvan Pascanu. 2013. Advances in optimizing recurrent networks. In *Proceedings of the 2013 IEEE International Conference on Acoustics, Speech and Signal Processing*, pages 8624–8628, Vancouver, BC, Canada. IEEE.

Piotr Bojanowski, Edouard Grave, Armand Joulin, and Tomas Mikolov. 2017. Enriching word vectors with subword information. *Transactions of the Association for Computational Linguistics*, 5:135–146.

Christopher Bryant and Ted Briscoe. 2018. Language model based grammatical error correction without annotated training data. In *Proceedings of the Thirteenth Workshop on Innovative Use of NLP for Building Educational Applications*, pages 247–253. Association for Computational Linguistics.

Christopher Bryant, Mariano Felice, Øistein E. Andersen, and Ted Briscoe. 2019. The BEA-2019 Shared Task on Grammatical Error Correction. In *Proceedings of the 14th Workshop on Innovative Use of NLP for Building Educational Applications*, Florence, Italy. Association for Computational Linguistics.

Christopher Bryant, Mariano Felice, and Ted Briscoe. 2017. Automatic annotation and evaluation of error types for grammatical error correction. In *Proceedings of the 55th Annual Meeting of the Association for Computational Linguistics (Volume 1: Long Papers)*, pages 793–805, Vancouver, Canada. Association for Computational Linguistics.

Lou Burnard. 2007. Reference Guide for the British National Corpus (XML Edition). Technical report.

Ziqiang Cao, Chuwei Luo, Wenjie Li, and Sujian Li. 2017. Joint copying and restricted generation for paraphrase. In *Proceedings of the Thirty-First AAAI Conference on Artificial Intelligence (AAAI-17)*, pages 3152–3158, San Francisco, California, USA. Association for the Advancement of Artificial Intelligence.

Ciprian Chelba, Tomas Mikolov, Mike Schuster, Qi Ge, Thorsten Brants, Phillipp Koehn, and Tony Robinson. 2014. One billion word benchmark for measuring progress in statistical language modeling. In *Proceedings of INTERSPEECH 2014*, pages 2635–2639, Singapore. International Speech Communication Association.

Danqi Chen and Christopher Manning. 2014. A fast and accurate dependency parser using neural networks. In *Proceedings of the 2014 conference on empirical methods in natural language processing (EMNLP)*, pages 740–750.

Kyunghyun Cho, Bart van Merrienboer, Caglar Gulcehre, Dzmitry Bahdanau, Fethi Bougares, Holger Schwenk, and Yoshua Bengio. 2014. Learning phrase representations using RNN encoder–decoder for statistical machine translation. In *Proceedings of the 2014 Conference on Empirical Methods in Natural Language Processing (EMNLP)*, pages 1724–1734, Doha, Qatar. Association for Computational Linguistics.

Shamil Chollampatt and Hwee Tou Ng. 2018. A multilayer convolutional encoder-decoder neural network for grammatical error correction. In *Proceedings of the Thirty-Second AAAI Conference on Artificial Intelligence (AAAI-18)*, pages 5755–5762, New Orleans, Louisiana, USA. Association for the Advancement of Artificial Intelligence.

Ronan Collobert and Jason Weston. 2008. A unified architecture for natural language processing: Deep neural networks with multitask learning. In *Proceedings of the 25th International Conference on Machine Learning*, pages 160–167. ACM.

Daniel Dahlmeier, Hwee Tou Ng, and Siew Mei Wu. 2013. Building a large annotated corpus of learner English: The NUS corpus of learner English. In *Proceedings of the Eighth Workshop on Innovative Use of NLP for Building Educational Applications*, pages 22–31, Atlanta, Georgia. Association for Computational Linguistics.

Robert Dale, Ilya Anisimoff, and George Narroway. 2012. HOO 2012: A report on the preposition and determiner error correction shared task. In *Proceedings of the Seventh Workshop on Building Educational Applications Using NLP*, pages 54–62, Montréal, Canada. Association for Computational Linguistics.

Robert Dale and Adam Kilgarriff. 2011. Helping our own: The HOO 2011 pilot shared task. In *Proceedings of the Generation Challenges Session at the 13th European Workshop on Natural Language Generation*, pages 242–249, Nancy, France. Association for Computational Linguistics.

Li Deng, Geoffrey Hinton, and Brian Kingsbury. 2013. New types of deep neural network learning for speech recognition and related applications: an overview. In *Proceedings of the 2013 IEEE International Conference on Acoustics, Speech and Signal Processing*, pages 8599–8603, Vancouver, BC, Canada. IEEE.

---

[12]http://www.hpc.cam.ac.uk

Mariano Felice and Zheng Yuan. 2014. Generating artificial errors for grammatical error correction. In *Proceedings of the Student Research Workshop at the 14th Conference of the European Chapter of the Association for Computational Linguistics*, pages 116–126, Gothenburg, Sweden. Association for Computational Linguistics.

Mariano Felice, Zheng Yuan, Øistein E. Andersen, Helen Yannakoudakis, and Ekaterina Kochmar. 2014. Grammatical error correction using hybrid systems and type filtering. In *Proceedings of the Eighteenth Conference on Computational Natural Language Learning: Shared Task*, pages 15–24, Baltimore, Maryland. Association for Computational Linguistics.

Adriano Ferraresi, Eros Zanchetta, Marco Baroni, and Silvia Bernardini. 2008. Introducing and evaluating ukwac, a very large web-derived corpus of english. In *Proceedings of the 4th Web as Corpus Workshop (WAC-4) Can we beat Google*, pages 47–54.

Tao Ge, Furu Wei, and Ming Zhou. 2018. Reaching human-level performance in automatic grammatical error correction: An empirical study. Technical report, Microsoft Research.

Jonas Gehring, Michael Auli, David Grangier, Denis Yarats, and Yann N Dauphin. 2017. Convolutional sequence to sequence learning. In *Proceedings of the 34th International Conference on Machine Learning*, pages 1243–1252, Sydney, Australia.

Ross Girshick. 2015. Fast r-cnn. In *Proceedings of the 2015 IEEE International Conference on Computer Vision*, pages 1440–1448, Santiago, Chile. IEEE.

Sylviane Granger. 1998. The computer learner corpus: A versatile new source of data for SLA research. In Sylviane Granger, editor, *Learner English on Computer*, pages 3–18. Addison Wesley Longman, London and New York.

Roman Grundkiewicz and Marcin Junczys-Dowmunt. 2018. Near human-level performance in grammatical error correction with hybrid machine translation. In *Proceedings of the 2018 Conference of the North American Chapter of the Association for Computational Linguistics: Human Language Technologies, Volume 2 (Short Papers)*, pages 284–290, New Orleans, Louisiana. Association for Computational Linguistics.

Jiatao Gu, Zhengdong Lu, Hang Li, and Victor O.K. Li. 2016. Incorporating copying mechanism in sequence-to-sequence learning. In *Proceedings of the 54th Annual Meeting of the Association for Computational Linguistics (Volume 1: Long Papers)*, pages 1631–1640, Berlin, Germany. Association for Computational Linguistics.

Kenneth Heafield. 2011. KenLM: Faster and smaller language model queries. In *Proceedings of the Sixth Workshop on Statistical Machine Translation*, pages 187–197, Edinburgh, Scotland. Association for Computational Linguistics.

Jianshu Ji, Qinlong Wang, Kristina Toutanova, Yongen Gong, Steven Truong, and Jianfeng Gao. 2017. A nested attention neural hybrid model for grammatical error correction. In *Proceedings of the 55th Annual Meeting of the Association for Computational Linguistics (Volume 1: Long Papers)*, pages 753–762, Vancouver, Canada. Association for Computational Linguistics.

Marcin Junczys-Dowmunt, Roman Grundkiewicz, Shubha Guha, and Kenneth Heafield. 2018. Approaching neural grammatical error correction as a low-resource machine translation task. In *Proceedings of the 2018 Conference of the North American Chapter of the Association for Computational Linguistics: Human Language Technologies, Volume 1 (Long Papers)*, pages 595–606, New Orleans, Louisiana. Association for Computational Linguistics.

Sudhanshu Kasewa, Pontus Stenetorp, and Sebastian Riedel. 2018. Wronging a right: Generating better errors to improve grammatical error detection. In *Proceedings of the 2018 Conference on Empirical Methods in Natural Language Processing*, pages 4977–4983, Brussels, Belgium. Association for Computational Linguistics.

Diederik P. Kingma and Jimmy Lei Ba. 2015. Adam: a Method for Stochastic Optimization. In *International Conference on Learning Representations*.

Ekaterina Kochmar. 2016. Error detection in content word combinations. Technical Report UCAM-CL-TR-886, Computer Laboratory, University of Cambridge.

Tomoya Mizumoto, Mamoru Komachi, Masaaki Nagata, and Yuji Matsumoto. 2011. Mining revision log of language learning SNS for automated Japanese error correction of second language learners. In *Proceedings of 5th International Joint Conference on Natural Language Processing*, pages 147–155, Chiang Mai, Thailand. Asian Federation of Natural Language Processing.

Hwee Tou Ng, Siew Mei Wu, Ted Briscoe, Christian Hadiwinoto, Raymond Hendy Susanto, and Christopher Bryant. 2014. The CoNLL-2014 shared task on grammatical error correction. In *Proceedings of the Eighteenth Conference on Computational Natural Language Learning: Shared Task*, pages 1–14, Baltimore, Maryland. Association for Computational Linguistics.

Hwee Tou Ng, Siew Mei Wu, Yuanbin Wu, Christian Hadiwinoto, and Joel Tetreault. 2013. The CoNLL-2013 shared task on grammatical error correction. In *Proceedings of the Seventeenth Conference on Computational Natural Language Learning: Shared Task*, pages 1–12, Sofia, Bulgaria. Association for Computational Linguistics.

Jeffrey Pennington, Richard Socher, and Christopher D Manning. 2014. GloVe : Global Vectors for Word Representation. In *Proceedings of the Empirical Meth- ods in Natural Language Processing (EMNLP 2014)*.

Matthew E. Peters, Mark Neumann, Mohit Iyyer, Matt Gardner, Christopher Clark, Kenton Lee, and Luke Zettlemoyer. 2018. Deep contextualized word representations. In *Proc. of NAACL*.

Michael JD Powell. 1964. An efficient method for finding the minimum of a function of several variables without calculating derivatives. *The computer journal*, 7(2):155–162.

Marek Rei. 2017. Semi-supervised multitask learning for sequence labeling. In *Proceedings of the 55th Annual Meeting of the Association for Computational Linguistics (Volume 1: Long Papers)*, pages 2121–2130, Vancouver, Canada. Association for Computational Linguistics.

Marek Rei, Mariano Felice, Zheng Yuan, and Ted Briscoe. 2017. Artificial error generation with machine translation and syntactic patterns. In *Proceedings of the 12th Workshop on Innovative Use of NLP for Building Educational Applications*, pages 287–292, Copenhagen, Denmark. Association for Computational Linguistics.

Marek Rei and Helen Yannakoudakis. 2016. Compositional Sequence Labeling Models for Error Detection in Learner Writing. In *Proceedings of the 54th Annual Meeting of the Association for Computational Linguistics*.

Marek Rei and Helen Yannakoudakis. 2017. Auxiliary objectives for neural error detection models. In *Proceedings of the 12th Workshop on Innovative Use of NLP for Building Educational Applications*, pages 33–43, Copenhagen, Denmark. Association for Computational Linguistics.

Alla Rozovskaya and Dan Roth. 2016. Grammatical error correction: Machine translation and classifiers. In *Proceedings of the 54th Annual Meeting of the Association for Computational Linguistics (Volume 1: Long Papers)*, pages 2205–2215, Berlin, Germany. Association for Computational Linguistics.

Keisuke Sakaguchi, Matt Post, and Benjamin Van Durme. 2017. Grammatical error correction with neural reinforcement learning. In *Proceedings of the Eighth International Joint Conference on Natural Language Processing (Volume 2: Short Papers)*, pages 366–372, Taipei, Taiwan. Asian Federation of Natural Language Processing.

Allen Schmaltz, Yoon Kim, Alexander Rush, and Stuart Shieber. 2017. Adapting sequence models for sentence correction. In *Proceedings of the 2017 Conference on Empirical Methods in Natural Language Processing*, pages 2807–2813, Copenhagen, Denmark. Association for Computational Linguistics.

Rico Sennrich, Barry Haddow, and Alexandra Birch. 2016a. Improving neural machine translation models with monolingual data. In *Proceedings of the 54th Annual Meeting of the Association for Computational Linguistics (Volume 1: Long Papers)*, pages 86–96, Berlin, Germany. Association for Computational Linguistics.

Rico Sennrich, Barry Haddow, and Alexandra Birch. 2016b. Neural machine translation of rare words with subword units. In *Proceedings of the 54th Annual Meeting of the Association for Computational Linguistics (Volume 1: Long Papers)*, pages 1715–1725, Berlin, Germany. Association for Computational Linguistics.

Felix Stahlberg, Christopher Bryant, and Bill Byrne. 2019. Neural grammatical error correction with finite state transducers. In *Proceedings of the 2019 Conference of the North American Chapter of the Association for Computational Linguistics*. Association for Computational Linguistics.

Felix Stahlberg and Bill Byrne. 2019. The CUED's grammatical error correction systems for BEA19. In *Proceedings of the 14th Workshop on Innovative Use of NLP for Building Educational Applications*, Florence, Italy. Association for Computational Linguistics.

Felix Stahlberg, Eva Hasler, Danielle Saunders, and Bill Byrne. 2017. SGNMT – A flexible NMT decoding platform for quick prototyping of new models and search strategies. In *Proceedings of the 2017 Conference on Empirical Methods in Natural Language Processing: System Demonstrations*, pages 25–30. Association for Computational Linguistics.

Felix Stahlberg, Danielle Saunders, Gonzalo Iglesias, and Bill Byrne. 2018. Why not be versatile? Applications of the SGNMT decoder for machine translation. In *Proceedings of the 13th Conference of the Association for Machine Translation in the Americas (Volume 1: Research Papers)*, pages 208–216. Association for Machine Translation in the Americas.

Ilya Sutskever, Oriol Vinyals, and Quoc V Le. 2014. Sequence to sequence learning with neural networks. In Z. Ghahramani, M. Welling, C. Cortes, N. D. Lawrence, and K. Q. Weinberger, editors, *Advances in Neural Information Processing Systems 27*, pages 3104–3112. Curran Associates, Inc.

Toshikazu Tajiri, Mamoru Komachi, and Yuji Matsumoto. 2012. Tense and aspect error correction for ESL learners using global context. In *Proceedings of the 50th Annual Meeting of the Association for Computational Linguistics (Volume 2: Short Papers)*, pages 198–202, Jeju Island, Korea. Association for Computational Linguistics.

Ashish Vaswani, Samy Bengio, Eugene Brevdo, Francois Chollet, Aidan Gomez, Stephan Gouws, Llion Jones, Łukasz Kaiser, Nal Kalchbrenner, Niki Parmar, Ryan Sepassi, Noam Shazeer, and Jakob

Uszkoreit. 2018. Tensor2tensor for neural machine translation. In *Proceedings of the 13th Conference of the Association for Machine Translation in the Americas (Volume 1: Research Papers)*, pages 193–199, Boston, MA. Association for Machine Translation in the Americas.

Ashish Vaswani, Noam Shazeer, Niki Parmar, Jakob Uszkoreit, Llion Jones, Aidan N Gomez, Łukasz Kaiser, and Illia Polosukhin. 2017. Attention is all you need. In *Advances in Neural Information Processing Systems*, pages 5998–6008.

Ziang Xie, Anand Avati, Naveen Arivazhagan, Dan Jurafsky, and Andrew Y. Ng. 2016. Neural language correction with character-based attention. *arXiv*, abs/1603.09727.

Helen Yannakoudakis, Øistein E Andersen, Ardeshir Geranpayeh, Ted Briscoe, and Diane Nicholls. 2018. Developing an automated writing placement system for esl learners. *Applied Measurement in Education*, 31(3):251–267.

Helen Yannakoudakis, Ted Briscoe, and Ben Medlock. 2011. A new dataset and method for automatically grading ESOL texts. In *Proceedings of the 49th Annual Meeting of the Association for Computational Linguistics: Human Language Technologies*, pages 180–189, Portland, Oregon, USA. Association for Computational Linguistics.

Helen Yannakoudakis, Marek Rei, Øistein E. Andersen, and Zheng Yuan. 2017. Neural sequence-labelling models for grammatical error correction. In *Proceedings of the 2017 Conference on Empirical Methods in Natural Language Processing*, pages 2795–2806, Copenhagen, Denmark. Association for Computational Linguistics.

Zheng Yuan. 2017. Grammatical error correction in non-native english. Technical Report UCAM-CL-TR-904, Computer Laboratory, University of Cambridge.

Zheng Yuan and Ted Briscoe. 2016. Grammatical error correction using neural machine translation. In *Proceedings of the 2016 Conference of the North American Chapter of the Association for Computational Linguistics: Human Language Technologies*, pages 380–386, San Diego, California. Association for Computational Linguistics.

Wei Zhao, Liang Wang, Kewei Shen, Ruoyu Jia, and Jingming Liu. 2019. Improving grammatical error correction via pre-training a copy-augmented architecture with unlabeled data. In *Proceedings of the 2019 Conference of the North American Chapter of the Association for Computational Linguistics*. Association for Computational Linguistics.

Improving Precision of Grammatical Error Correction with a Cheat Sheet

Mengyang Qiu[†‡*]   Xuejiao Chen[†*]

Maggie Liu[†]   Krishna Parvathala[§]   Apurva Patil[§]   Jungyeul Park[†]

[†] Department of Linguistics
[‡] Department of Communicative Disorders and Sciences
[§] Department of Computer Science and Engineering
State University of New York at Buffalo
{mengyang,xuejiaoc,mliu22,leelasai,acpatil,jungyeul}@buffalo.edu

Abstract

In this paper, we explore two approaches of generating error-focused phrases and examine whether these phrases can lead to better performance in grammatical error correction for the restricted track of BEA 2019 Shared Task on GEC. Our results show that phrases directly extracted from GEC corpora outperform phrases from a statistical machine translation phrase table by a large margin. Appending error+context phrases to the original GEC corpora yields comparably higher precision. We also explore the generation of artificial syntactic error sentences using error+context phrases for the unrestricted track. The additional training data greatly facilitates syntactic error correction (e.g., verb form) and contributes to better overall performance.

1 Introduction

Grammatical Error Correction (GEC) is a natural language processing (NLP) task of automatically detecting and correcting grammatical errors in the text. With the ever-growing number of second language learners of English and demand to facilitate their learning with timely feedback, GEC has become increasingly popular and attracted much attention in both academia and industry in recent years. In a typical GEC task, for example, *Travel* and *bored.* in the sentence ***Travel** by bus is expensive and **bored*** needs to be first detected as incorrect and then be modified to their correct forms (*Travelling* and *boring*). Various approaches have been proposed to solve this problem including language modeling, rule-based classifiers, machine-learning based classifiers, machine translation (MT), and etc. (Ng et al., 2013, 2014). In the past few years, both GEC-tuned statistical machine translation (SMT) and neural machine translation (NMT) using sequence-to-sequence (seq2seq) learning have demonstrated to be more effective in grammatical error correction than other approaches (Chollampatt and Ng, 2017, 2018; Ge et al., 2018; Zhao et al., 2019).

Just as in other machine translation tasks, the quantity anfd quality of data play an important role in the MT approach to grammatical error correction. While several recent studies have focused on generating artificial grammatical error sentences (e.g. Rei et al., 2017; Kasewa et al., 2018), the current study explores how error-focused phrases influence the performance of grammatical error correction. There are slightly over half million error-contained sentences in the training data provided by the BEA 2019 Shared Task, and the total number of errors is over 1.3 million, which means there are on average 2 or 3 errors in each error sentence. Our intuition is that multiple errors in one sentence can be challenging for MT models to learn and generalize, especially when the amount of training data is limited. Thus, by augmenting the training data with error-focused phrases, which we term "cheat sheet", MT models can directly "see" the errors and their corrections. We predict that this will lead to better overall performance and precision in particular. We examine two ways of creating a cheat sheet–one extracting errors and surrounding context and the other one extracting from a SMT phrase table (§2). Phrases extracted from the first method are also used to generate artificial **syntactic** error sentences for the unrestricted track of the shared task (§3). We run both SMT using Moses (Koehn et al., 2007) and multi-layer CNN seq2seq NMT (Chollampatt and Ng, 2018) for our training data in restricted (original training + cheat sheet) and unrestricted (original training + cheat sheet + syntactic pseudo corpus) settings (§4). In general, our results show that a cheat sheet created with errors and surrounding context does lead to an improvement in precision. However, compared

---

*Equally contributed authors

Proceedings of the Fourteenth Workshop on Innovative Use of NLP for Building Educational Applications, pages 240–245
Florence, Italy, August 2, 2019. ©2019 Association for Computational Linguistics

to current state-of-the-art results, the recall of our models is considerably lower. These results and future work are discussed in the last section.

2 Cheat Sheet

2.1 Error+Context Dictionary

Artificial Error Generation has been a long-studied technique for creating more training data for Grammatical Error Correction systems. In previous studies, there are two types of methods of generating an artificial error, one making use of the real learner data statistics and the other treats all types of errors uniformly. Through experiments, it has been shown that accuracy improves when training and test data are more similar to each other (Felice, 2016). This observation is one reason that motivates us to use directly the extracted parallel phrase dictionary from the combined m2 files as part of our training data since the dictionary preserves the original error distribution. In the dictionary, each pair of the phrases contains one edit in the m2 file and contains one context word on both sides of the edit (one context word if the edit is at the start of the end of the sentence). The instances in the dictionary have shorter lengths compared to the parallel sentences.

2.2 SMT Phrase Translation Table

Generating a large table of phrase pairs is an integral part of statistical machine translation. These phrase pairs and their corresponding scores (e.g., translation probability and lexical weighting) are the knowledge source during translation/decoding. These phrases are not linguistically well-formed (e.g., noun phrases and prepositional phrases). Rather, they are just sequences of words of arbitrary length. One major difference between the error+context approach and this one is that error is always centered in the former approach, while an error can appear in any position in a phrase in this one.

The Moses SMT system (Koehn et al., 2007) was used to generate a phrase translation table. We used Giza++ (Och and Ney, 2003) for word alignment, and a 3-gram language model trained on 2 million sentences from the AFP news corpus[1] with KenLM (Heafield, 2011). Our input and output sentence length was limited to 40 to ensure the quality of the phrase table, as longer sentences are

---

[1]From *English Gigaword*, https://catalog.ldc.upenn.edu/LDC2003T05

harder to train using SMT because of their complex syntax and long dependency structures (Bach, 2012). We then extracted phrase pairs with five or more words and the direct translation probability over 95%. Phrase pairs that were same on the error and correct side were also discarded.

3 Pseudo Corpus with Syntactic Errors

We can define syntactic errors as errors that are grammatically incorrect but in most cases, the meaning is still conveyed as compared to semantic errors where the learner fails to convey the desired meaning across to the reader but the sentence structure is correct. Observing syntactic errors is crucial in improving grammatical error correction since they have a direct correlation to grammatical errors since syntactic errors produce grammatically incorrect sentences.

Learners usually make these errors mostly due to overgeneralizations and simplifications (Heydari and Bagheri, 2012). The learner will overgeneralize and apply the grammatical rule to a place where it does not apply. For simplification, the learner will omit the rule in the context when the rule is supposed to apply. Most of this is due to the learner not having a frame of reference for that rule in their native language. For example, Chinese does not use article or determiners so they tend to overgeneralize or simplify and some times insert or omit an article or determiner (Robertson, 2000). Table 1 shows examples of a syntactic error and a semantic error. In the syntactic error example, the use of the form of the verb is incorrect. *Working* should be changed to *to work*. In the semantic example, *Lately* should be changed to *Recently*.

For the unrestricted track, we created a pseudo corpus by using the syntactic errors from the dictionary described in the previous section. We used 6 types of syntactic errors based on the ERRANT annotation (Bryant et al., 2017), including ADJ:FORM (*is **good** for our health than – is **better** for our health than*), MORPH (*the everyday **invents** – the everyday **inventions***), NOUN:INFL (***TVs** companies – **TV** companies*), VERB:FORM (*make my dream **comes** true – make my dream come true*), VERB:INFL (*he **thinked** – he **thought***) and VERB:SVA (*there **are** a – there **is** a*). The total number of syntactic error pairs we extracted from the dictionary is around 100K entries. The clean corpus we use has around 2 million sen-

Syntactic Error: *I want **working** in our cafe.*
Semantic Error: ***Lately** I have seen a very interesting TV show.*

Table 1: Examples of a syntactic error and a semantic error

tences from the AFP news corpus. Each error in the syntactic error dictionary can be used at most once. We keep the numbers of different types of errors the same and thirty percent of the sentences in the pseudo learner corpus contains exactly one error. For each sentence, the search of the phrase starts from the longest length. Once we find an n-gram that appeared in the correct side of the dictionary, we replace it with the incorrect counterpart. The cheat sheet and the pseudo syntactic error corpus improved our results by emphasizing the learners' errors and their contexts.

4 Experiments and Results

4.1 Experiment settings

We used all the four datasets — FCE, NUCLE, W&I+LOCNESS and Lang-8 — provided in the BEA 2019 Shared Task[2] as our baseline data (1,171,078 sentence pairs). For the restricted track, we appended the baseline data with our cheat sheet (in total over 2M sentence / phrase pairs), and for the unrestricted track, the additional syntactic pseudo corpus was supplemented on top of the training data in the restricted track (over 4M sentences in total). The official W&I+LOCNESS development set and test set were used as development and evaluation[3]. We did not use any spell check to pre- or post-process our data, which could affect our results negatively (Chollampatt and Ng, 2017).

For the SMT approach to GEC, we used the same Moses (Koehn et al., 2007) setup as in §2.2, except for the sentence length, which we changed to the default value $(1 - 80)$. The standard Minimum Error Rate Training (MERT) algorithm (Och, 2003) was used for tuning. For the NMT approach, we used a 7-layer convolutional seq2seq model[4] as described in Chollampatt and Ng (2018) with similar hyper-parameters, such as the top 30K BPE tokens as the input and output vocabularies, 1,024 (hidden size) $\times$ 3 (convolution window

		Prec.	**Recall**	$F_{0.5}$
Baseline	SMT	52.68	16.42	36.54
Restricted	SMT	51.48	17.85	37.39
	NMT	**63.31**	15.43	**39.06**
Unrestricted	SMT	56.03	15.85	37.18
	NMT	**65.14**	17.63	**42.33**

Table 2: Baseline result and results submitted to the BEA 2019 Shared Task

size) in the encoders and decoders, Nesterov Accelerated Gradient as the optimizer with a momentum of 0.99, dropout rate of 0.2 and an adaptive learning rate (initially 0.25, minimum 10^{-4}). Unlike Chollampatt and Ng (2018), we set the word embedding dimensions in both encoders and decoders to 300 rather than 500, and we trained the word embeddings separately using the error and correct side training data instead of external corpora. During inference, we used a beam size of 10.

4.2 Results

Table 2 shows the baseline result and the results we submitted to the BEA 2019 Shared Task. The submitted results were all from the versions with an error+context cheat sheet because our phrase table cheat sheet yielded much worse results. Overall, our models with an error+context cheat sheet achieved higher precision and $F_{0.5}$ in both restricted and unrestricted tracks than the baseline model. Within our own models, GEC-tuned NMT, as expected, consistently outperformed the generic SMT models. In the unrestricted setting, for example, the gap in $F_{0.5}$ was over 5%. When comparing the two NMT models across the two tracks, our results clearly show that the additional pseudo corpus contributed to better performance in precision, recall and $F_{0.5}$.

5 Conclusion and Future Work

In this study, we explored two error-focused approaches to grammatical error correction. One was to extract parallel error-correct phrases (error + surrounding context) from the GEC corpora and append them to our training data direct. Extracting

---

[2] https://www.cl.cam.ac.uk/research/nl/bea2019st/
[3] https://competitions.codalab.org/competitions/21922
[4] https://github.com/pytorch/fairseq

error phrases is not a new method per se, as previous studies have used these phrases to generate artificial errors (e.g., Felice, 2016). However, we purposefully included these phrases in our training in order for our models to pay attention to these errors and to focus on one error at a time. As a result, the precision of our GEC models gained much improvement.

The second approach was to incorporate phrases from SMT-generated phrase translation table. In the current study, we extracted parallel phrases with five or more words and the direct translation probability (from error to correct) over 95%. Contrary to our prediction, appending these phrases to our training data dramatically decreased the performance. A closer examination of the phrases shows that there are many partial redundancies, which may have caused our models to miss focus. Thus, we plan to investigate various techniques to prune the phrase table (e.g. Johnson et al., 2007; Zens et al., 2012) so that errors are truly highlighted as in the error+context approach.

In the unrestricted track, we injected syntactic errors from our error+context dictionary to a clean corpus and appended the artificial error corpus to the training data for the restricted track. When training with SMT, there was no performance gain overall and at the syntactic error type level. For example, the precision of the VERB:FORM error type was only 48.98% and the $F_{0.5}$ was 35.40%. However, when the same data was trained with NMT, the benefit of additional data was evident. The precision and $F_{0.5}$ of VERB:FORM almost doubled in this setting, compared to that in SMT. These results, again, demonstrate the limitations of the generic SMT approach to grammatical error correction (e.g. Yuan and Felice, 2013).

The recall of our models stayed low across all the settings, which indicates our models were too conservative. The conservativeness can be mainly attributed to the large proportion of unchanged sentences in the training data. Indeed, our pseudo corpus generation process was constrained as only 30% of the two million sentences were applied error injection. We will further explore the relationship between recall and proportion of unchanged sentences in GEC.

Finally, our current study only focused on syntactic errors, which should be easier for MT models to detect and correct compared to semantic errors, because semantic errors require knowledge about meaning in addition to structure. Given the complexity of language, the individual meaning of a word in a sentence changes according to the context. A simple example, *She kicked the bucket.* and *He filled the bucket with soda.* both contain the word *bucket*, but the meanings are drastically different. Traditional word embeddings such as word2vec (Mikolov et al., 2013), GloVe (Pennington et al., 2014) and fastText (Bojanowski et al., 2017) only have one representation per word. As the meaning of each word changes based on the surrounding context, in which previous methods fail. Therefore, we require a model that is capable of understanding the variations in meaning of the given word based on its surrounding text in the sentence. ELMo is another method for text embedding (Peters et al., 2018) which uses a deep, bi-directional LSTM model that takes contextual information into account and achieves state-of-the-art results in many NLP tasks. ELMo analyses words within the context that they are used, hence the way ELMo is used is quite different to word2vec or fastText. As opposed to having a dictionary of words and their corresponding vectors, ELMo instead creates vectors on-the-fly by passing text through the deep learning model. The model is character based and hence forms representations of out-of-vocabulary words. We will investigate whether incorporating ELMo in our NMT model can improve the performance of correcting semantic errors in the near future.

References

Nguyen Bach. 2012. *Dependency Structures for Statistical Machine Translation.* Ph.D. thesis, Carnegie Mellon University.

Piotr Bojanowski, Edouard Grave, Armand Joulin, and Tomas Mikolov. 2017. Enriching Word Vectors with Subword Information. *Transactions of the Association for Computational Linguistics*, 5:135–146.

Christopher Bryant, Mariano Felice, and Ted Briscoe. 2017. Automatic Annotation and Evaluation of Error Types for Grammatical Error Correction. In *Proceedings of the 55th Annual Meeting of the Association for Computational Linguistics (Volume 1: Long Papers)*, pages 793–805, Vancouver, Canada. Association for Computational Linguistics.

Shamil Chollampatt and Hwee Tou Ng. 2017. Connecting the dots: Towards human-level grammatical error correction. In *Proceedings of the 12th Workshop on Innovative Use of NLP for Building Educational Applications*, Copenhagen, Denmark. Association for Computational Linguistics.

Shamil Chollampatt and Hwee Tou Ng. 2018. A Multilayer Convolutional Encoder-Decoder Neural Network for Grammatical Error Correction. In *Proceedings of The Thirty-Second AAAI Conference on Artificial Intelligence (AAAI-18)*, New Orleans, Louisiana.

Mariano Felice. 2016. Artificial error generation for translation-based grammatical error correction. Technical Report UCAM-CL-TR-895, University of Cambridge, Computer Laboratory.

Tao Ge, Furu Wei, and Ming Zhou. 2018. Fluency Boost Learning and Inference for Neural Grammatical Error Correction. In *Proceedings of the 56th Annual Meeting of the Association for Computational Linguistics (Volume 1: Long Papers)*, pages 1055–1065, Melbourne, Australia. Association for Computational Linguistics.

Kenneth Heafield. 2011. KenLM: Faster and Smaller Language Model Queries. In *Proceedings of the Sixth Workshop on Statistical Machine Translation*, pages 187–197, Edinburgh, Scotland. Association for Computational Linguistics.

Pooneh Heydari and Mohammad S Bagheri. 2012. Error analysis: Sources of l2 learners' errors. *Theory & Practice in Language Studies*, 2(8).

Howard Johnson, Joel Martin, George Foster, and Roland Kuhn. 2007. Improving Translation Quality by Discarding Most of the Phrasetable. In *Proceedings of the 2007 Joint Conference on Empirical Methods in Natural Language Processing and Computational Natural Language Learning (EMNLP-CoNLL)*, pages 967–975, Prague, Czech Republic. Association for Computational Linguistics.

Sudhanshu Kasewa, Pontus Stenetorp, and Sebastian Riedel. 2018. Wronging a Right: Generating Better Errors to Improve Grammatical Error Detection. In *Proceedings of the 2018 Conference on Empirical Methods in Natural Language Processing*, pages 4977–4983, Brussels, Belgium. Association for Computational Linguistics.

Philipp Koehn, Hieu Hoang, Alexandra Birch, Chris Callison-Burch, Marcello Federico, Nicola Bertoldi, Brooke Cowan, Wade Shen, Christine Moran, Richard Zens, Chris Dyer, Ondrej Bojar, Alexandra Constantin, and Evan Herbst. 2007. Moses: Open Source Toolkit for Statistical Machine Translation. In *Proceedings of the 45th Annual Meeting of the Association for Computational Linguistics Companion Volume Proceedings of the Demo and Poster Sessions*, pages 177–180, Prague, Czech Republic. Association for Computational Linguistics.

Tomas Mikolov, Kai Chen, Greg Corrado, and Jeffrey Dean. 2013. Efficient Estimation of Word Representations in Vector Space. *http://arxiv.org/abs/1301.3781*.

Hwee Tou Ng, Siew Mei Wu, Ted Briscoe, Christian Hadiwinoto, Raymond Hendy Susanto, and Christopher Bryant. 2014. The CoNLL-2014 Shared Task on Grammatical Error Correction. In *Proceedings of the Eighteenth Conference on Computational Natural Language Learning: Shared Task*, pages 1–14, Baltimore, Maryland. Association for Computational Linguistics.

Hwee Tou Ng, Siew Mei Wu, Yuanbin Wu, Christian Hadiwinoto, and Joel Tetreault. 2013. The CoNLL-2013 Shared Task on Grammatical Error Correction. In *Proceedings of the Seventeenth Conference on Computational Natural Language Learning: Shared Task*, pages 1–12, Sofia, Bulgaria. Association for Computational Linguistics.

Franz Josef Och. 2003. Minimum Error Rate Training in Statistical Machine Translation. In *Proceedings of the 41st Annual Meeting of the Association for Computational Linguistics*, pages 160–167, Sapporo, Japan. Association for Computational Linguistics.

Franz Josef Och and Hermann Ney. 2003. A Systematic Comparison of Various Statistical Alignment Models. *Computational Linguistics*, 29(1):19–51.

Jeffrey Pennington, Richard Socher, and Christopher D. Manning. 2014. GloVe: Global Vectors for Word Representation. In *Proceedings of the 2014 Conference on Empirical Methods in Natural Language Processing (EMNLP)*, pages 1532–1543, Doha, Qatar. Association for Computational Linguistics.

Matthew Peters, Mark Neumann, Mohit Iyyer, Matt Gardner, Christopher Clark, Kenton Lee, and Luke Zettlemoyer. 2018. Deep Contextualized Word Representations. In *Proceedings of the 2018 Conference of the North American Chapter of the Association for Computational Linguistics: Human Language Technologies, Volume 1 (Long Papers)*, pages 2227–2237, New Orleans, Louisiana. Association for Computational Linguistics.

Marek Rei, Mariano Felice, Zheng Yuan, and Ted Briscoe. 2017. Artificial Error Generation with Machine Translation and Syntactic Patterns. In *Proceedings of the 12th Workshop on Innovative Use of NLP for Building Educational Applications*, pages 287–292, Copenhagen, Denmark. Association for Computational Linguistics.

Daniel Robertson. 2000. Variability in the use of the english article system by chinese learners of english. *Second language research*, 16(2):135–172.

Zheng Yuan and Mariano Felice. 2013. Constrained grammatical error correction using statistical machine translation. In *Proceedings of the Seventeenth Conference on Computational Natural Language Learning: Shared Task*, pages 52–61, Sofia, Bulgaria. Association for Computational Linguistics.

Richard Zens, Daisy Stanton, and Peng Xu. 2012. A systematic comparison of phrase table pruning techniques. In *Proceedings of the 2012 Joint Conference on Empirical Methods in Natural Language Processing and Computational Natural Language Learning*, pages 972–983, Jeju Island, Korea. Association for Computational Linguistics.

Wei Zhao, Liang Wang, Kewei Shen, Ruoyu Jia, and Jingming Liu. 2019. Improving Grammatical Error Correction via Pre-Training a Copy-Augmented Architecture with Unlabeled Data. In *Proceedings of the 2019 Conference of the North {A}merican Chapter of the Association for Computational Linguistics: Human Language Technologies, Volume 1 (Long and Short Papers)*, pages 156–165, Minneapolis, Minnesota. Association for Computational Linguistics.

Multi-headed Architecture Based on BERT for Grammatical Errors Correction

Julia Shaptala
WebSpellChecker LLC
julia@webspellchecker.net

Bohdan Didenko
NLP Research, WebSpellChecker LLC
bogdan@webspellchecker.net

Abstract

During last years we have seen tremendous progress in the development of NLP-related solutions and area in general. It happened primarily due to emergence of pre-trained models based on the Transformer (Vaswani et al., 2017) architecture such as GPT (Radford et al., 2018) and BERT (Devlin et al., 2019). Fine-tuned models containing these representations can achieve state-of-the-art results in many NLP-related tasks. Given this, the use of pre-trained models in the Grammatical Error Correction (GEC) task seems reasonable.

In this paper, we describe our approach to GEC using the BERT model for creation of encoded representation and some of our enhancements, namely, "Heads" are fully-connected networks which are used for finding the errors and later receive recommendation from the networks on dealing with a highlighted part of the sentence only. Among the main advantages of our solution is increasing the system productivity and lowering the time of processing while keeping the high accuracy of GEC results.

1 Introduction

Modern state-of-the-art GEC models use the sequence-to-sequence (seq2seq) approach and Transformer Encoder-Decoder architecture (Ge et al., 2018). The core idea of seq2seq approach for GEC is the following: tokens from the source sequence are sent to the model input, and a similar sequence without errors is expected as an output. Transformer Decoder is auto-regressive, meaning that it predicts tokens one by one. Though this approach can represent the following challenges: (i) the sequence is reconstructed entirely, regardless of errors number; (ii) sentences are processed at low speed during inference; (iii) errors tend to accumulate since a failure in prediction of a single token can lead to a rupture of the entire chain in the network.

In this paper, we suggest an alternative approach for GEC with "Multi-headed" architecture that uses BERT as Encoder and specialized "Heads" networks enabling additional text processing based on particular error types. In addition, particular Heads let us discover the error placement and come out with error correction. When we can create an effective dictionary for different types of errors suggested in ERRor ANnotation Toolkit (Bryant et al., 2017), such Heads as Punctuation, Articles and Case will be used. Otherwise, if we cant create an effective dictionary, we are going to use a special **"highlight and decode" technique** in a bundle with Transformer Decoder to suggest a correction.

Also, we used Boosting Approach (Ge et al., 2018) as an auxiliary step to improve the GEC within the framework of this competition.

2 Data and Text Pre-processing

The data sets which we used for the network training were in the m2 format (Dahlmeier and Ng, 2012). This data obviously has its issues; not all the data sets can be considered the perfect ones and may require pre-processing before they can be used for neural networks training. Thus, before using given data sets we performed a number of operations to filter out irrelevant data and improve its quality by simplifying its form. The main problem of such data format is that each edit made is recorded separately, and it is not possible to display the related changes.

The data and text pre-processing phases are described below.

Phase 1. Adjusting form of the information in data sets (by combining related changes). Below is an example of a sentence in m2 format which

Proceedings of the Fourteenth Workshop on Innovative Use of NLP for Building Educational Applications, pages 246–251
Florence, Italy, August 2, 2019. ©2019 Association for Computational Linguistics

displays our approach to grammatical errors correction:

```
S I think that you have to bring with you winter clothes because
here there is a really cold weather !
    A 7 11|||R:OTHER|||winter|||REQUIRED|||-NONE-|||0
    A 11 11|||M:OTHER|||clothes with you|||REQUIRED|||-NONE-|||0
    A 13 14|||R:OTHER|||it|||REQUIRED|||-NONE-|||0
    A 15 16|||U:DET||||||REQUIRED|||-NONE-|||0
    A 18 19|||U:NOUN||||||REQUIRED|||-NONE-|||0
Result - I think that you have to bring winter clothes with you
because here it is really cold !
```

As you can see, the related changes in the sentence are divided into a number of edit operations U (Unnecessary), M (Missing) and in some cases R (Replacement), M, and even R, R. To combine related changes, we find $R \cap I$ where R removed tokens, I inserted tokens from all edits. In addition, we have combined edits with a non-zero intersection into one edit. As a result, we get an example with only one edit which is MOVE.

```
S I think that you have to bring with you winter clothes because here
it is really cold !
A 7 11|||MOVE|||winter clothes with you|||REQUIRED|||-NONE-|||0
```

Phase 2. Using Textual Semantic Similarity (Yang and Tar, 2018) analysis to filter noisy data. For example, to filter noise in the data like this:

```
S It was very spicy .
A 0 1|||R:OTHER|||Delete|||REQUIRED|||-NONE-|||0
A 1 4|||R:OTHER|||this sentence|||REQUIRED|||-NONE-|||0
```

Textual Semantic Similarity analysis was used to define the similarity between a source sequence and a sequence after applying corrections and discarded the sentences with the similarity below 0.87.

The original sentence containing a mistake is a vector as well as the meaning of a corrected sentence. Textual Semantic Similarity is calculated using the scalar multiplication of vectors (vector size equals 512), each of them is output of the Universal Sentence Encoder[1]. As a result we have one number ranging from 0 to 1 which is the ratio of semantic similarity of the two sentences. The higher the scalar multiplication number is, the higher Textual Semantic Similarity of the two sentences.

After we have processed 600K sentences from the data sets used for this competition[2], we realised that most part of sentences before the number of 0.87 are not acceptable for usage and change the meaning or not valid at all.

Thus, our assumption is that the sentences that equal 0.87 and above are usable, and we will train our model on it. All the other sentences are filtered as noise as in the example in m2 format above.

Phase 3. Flattening the data by extending the number of sentences for training. Our next step is to enlarge the amount of data for training and convert the sentence with N edits to N sentences with one edit. Conventionally, we called it "flatten m2 blocks".

Example below represents a sentence in m2 format with 2 edits: we replace the verb (R:VERB:SVA) and add missing adjective (M:ADJ). As a result we have two sentences with one edit, one for a replaced verb (R:VERB:SVA) and the second for an added missing adjective (M:ADJ).

Example of the original sentence in m2 format:

```
S This are a sentence .
A 1 2|||R:VERB:SVA|||is|||-REQUIRED-|||NONE|||0
A 3 3|||M:ADJ|||good|||-REQUIRED-|||NONE|||0
Result - This is a good sentence.
```

Result sentence after the first edit:

```
S This are a sentence .
A 1 2|||R:VERB:SVA|||is|||-REQUIRED-|||NONE|||0
Result - This is a sentence.
```

Result sentence after the second edit:

```
S This is a sentence .
A 3 3|||M:ADJ|||good|||-REQUIRED-|||NONE|||0
Result - This is a good sentence.
```

Our assumption is that one epoch (or the process of training of a neural network) on the "flatten" of data should have a better result than a few epochs on the original data and reduce the effect of network overfitting.

3 The Model

The main architectural advantage of our approach is using trained "Heads". Heads are the fully-connected networks that receive the BERT output

---

[1] https://tfhub.dev/google/universal-sentence-encoder/2

[2] https://www.cl.cam.ac.uk/research/nl/bea2019st/

result embedding as input and have an output of the Head dictionary size. Each Head is classified by error type given in Errant Error Type Token Tier (Bryant et al., 2017).

We distinguish the following Heads types depending on their usage and based on their context:

- By the type of operation: Replace, Insert, Range Start and Range End;

- By the type of error: Punctuation, Articles, Case, Noun Number, Spelling, Verbs;

- By the type of correction method: ByDictionary (Punctuation, Articles, Case), ByDecoder (Noun Number, Spelling, Verbs). Output of ByDictionary Heads will be a suggestion from the dictionary. Output of ByDecoder Heads which only detect errors positions will be represented as a "Head type mask" (e.g. Spelling Head mask). For example, Punctuation offers suggestions from its dictionary while Verbs points the place of the error to generate a suggestion by Decoder.

Figure 1 below outlines the number of the parameters of each Head. The dark grey color represents the output which is processed by Decoder, and light grey - the results provided from a Head dictionary.

Error Types / Operations	Punctuation	Articles	Case	Noun Number	Spelling	Verbs
Replace	BES * PDS	BES * ADS	BES * CDS	BES * HDS		
Insert	2 * BES * (PDS - 1)	2 * BES * (ADS - 1)	-	-	-	-
Range Start	BES * RDS					
Range End	BES * RDS					

Figure 1: Number of parameters for each Head type.

The following Head dictionary sizes are used: BERT embedding size (BES) 768; Punctuation dictionary size (PDS) 36; Articles dictionary size (ADS) 5; Case dictionary size (CDS) 3; Highlighting dictionary size (HDS) 2; Range dictionary size (RDS) 2. RDS is applicable for Range Start and Range End Hands. The size of the dictionary for both equals 2; one for *skip* and the other for *start position* or *end position* accordingly. Additionally, for the Insert operation, Delete is eliminated action, thus, we use "-1".

Since a BERT output is the encoded representation of each token from the input sequence, Heads analyze each token from the BERT output, detect an error in it and depending on its type, either immediately provide a correction or highlight this error position for further correction by the Decoder as shown in Figure 2 below.

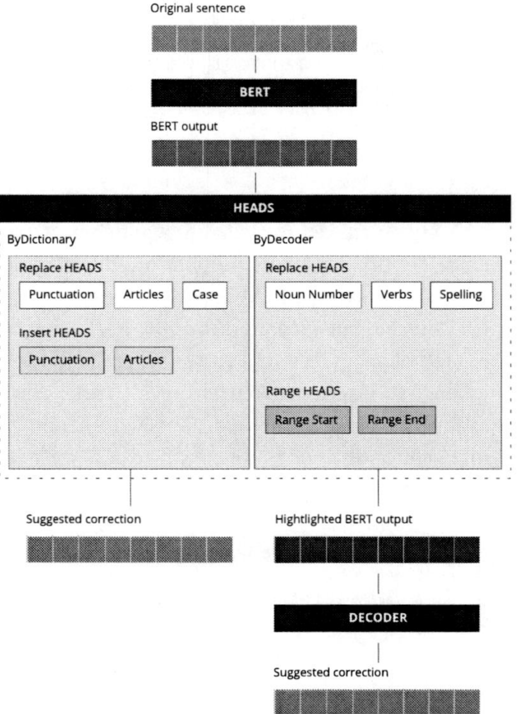

Figure 2: The Multi-headed model architecture.

Also, Heads networks are distinguished by the type of the operation performed such as Replace and Insert. Replace Heads are the Heads performing the Replace operation, and it can either provide a suggestion from its dictionary (ByDictionary), or provide a Head type mask for further processing by the Decoder (ByDecoder) as shown in Figure 3 below.

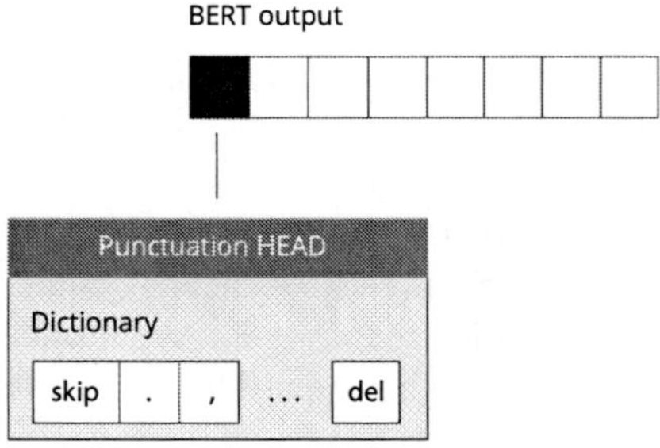

Figure 3: Example of the Replace operation.

During the Insert operation, an Insert Head takes two BERT output embeddings which have the dimension of 768 located nearby, concatenates to one embedding with dimension 2*768, processes it and outputs the result with the dimension which equals the dictionary size of a particular Head type.

Thus, we have probability distribution of a particular Head. Position with highest probability in a dictionary is what should be inserted. If the probability equals 0, nothing should be done. An example of the Insert operation is shown in Figure 4 below.

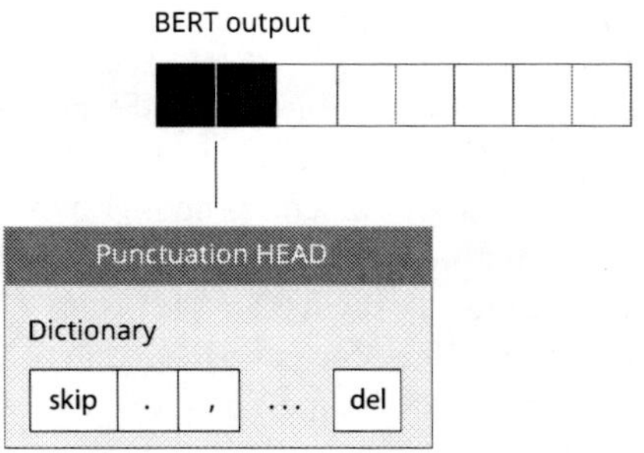

Figure 4: Example of the Insert operation.

Range Heads, Range Start, and Range End are used to define the range (start and end position) of an error for the Decoder. Each Range Head uses an approach similar to the Replace ByDictionary Head, thus, the length of its dictionary equals 2. As an output from two Heads, we receive Range Start mask and Range End mask. Using these masks we receive a resulting Range mask that will be used in the highlight and decode technique as shown in Figure 5 below. Thus, Range Head enables detection of those parts of the sentence which need to be either replaced or paraphrased.

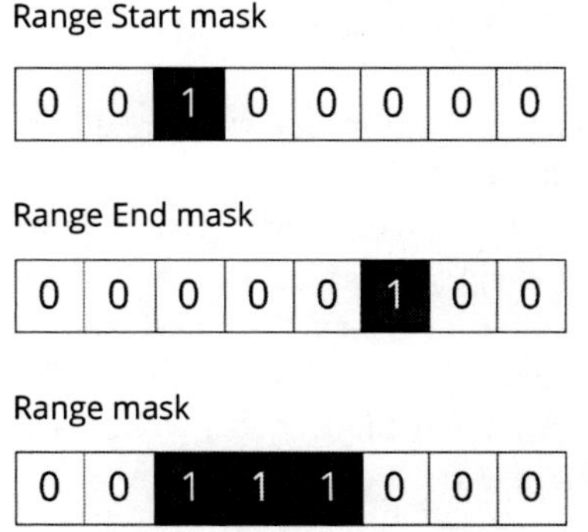

Figure 5: Example of the Range Start and Range End operation.

4 Highlight and Decode Technique

Since there are different types of errors, and it is not possible to compile effective dictionaries as the number of correction options is too large, we used classic Transformer Decoder (Vaswani et al., 2017) and the entire BERT vocabulary. We developed a special "highlight and decode" technique to generate a suggestion for a particular place, determined by one of the Heads, and, thus, managed to avoid the reconstruction of the entire sentence (see Figure 6 below).

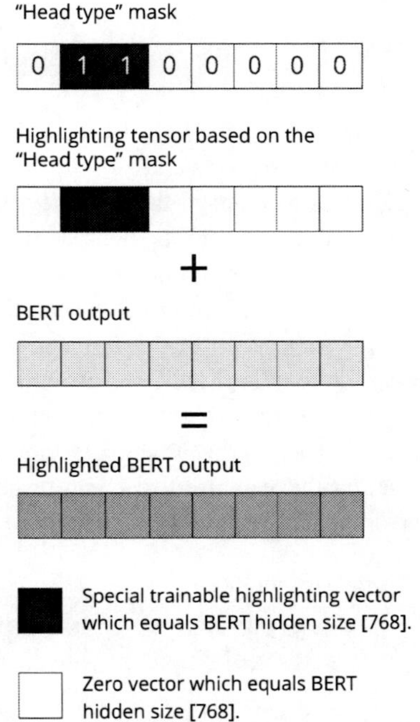

Figure 6: Obtaining of the highlighted BERT output.

The highlighted BERT output, a Decoder input, in Figure 6 above is a summary of the BERT output and the highlighting tensor, consisting of special embeddings (based on Head type mask) in place of errors detected by one of the ByDecoder Heads (such as Spelling), and zero vectors in other places. Such approach allows the Decoder to learn how to predict a suggestion only for the highlighted place in the sentence. The various types of Heads and "highlight and decode" technique let the network find and offer suggestions for any error types.

5 Training Process and Setup

We trained our neural networks using Google Colab TPU resources. A total of 100,000 iterations were performed on "flatten" data from the Cambridge English Write & Improve (W&I) corpus and the LOCNESS corpus dataset[3]. The learning rate *5e-5* which is recommended in the BERT approach (Devlin et al., 2019) was implemented. However, for the layers of the BERT itself, a layer-by-layer multiplier was used for the learning rate which decreases from the last layers to the first. We calculated the learning rate of a specific layer using the logarithmic formula:

$$lr_i = LR * \log_2\left(1 + \frac{1}{(BL + 1) - i}\right),$$

where BL is number of the BERT layers; LR is model learning rate, e.g.: 5e-5.

It helped us to manage the accuracy of the results adjusting their weights, thus, helping to sort out the errors and improving the results quality by 15% according to our empirical observations.

Also, for each Head of the Replace operation, a special "protection mask" was used to reveal an error only for tokens that can be changed by the given Head. The approach which is shown in Figure 7 below the was used to create a protection mask (for details, see the Spacy library [4]).

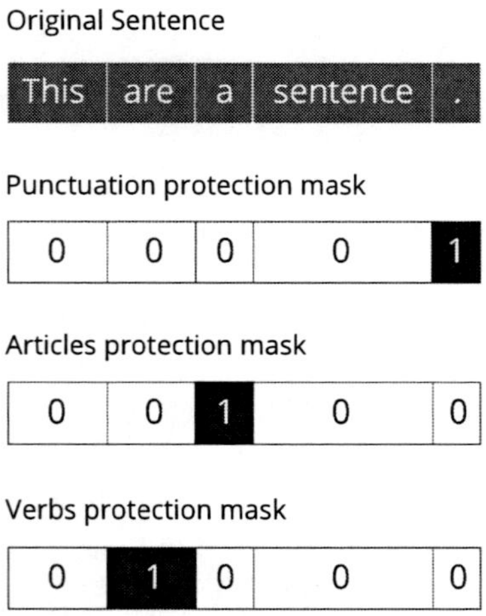

Original Sentence

This	are	a	sentence	.

Punctuation protection mask

0	0	0	0	1

Articles protection mask

0	0	1	0	0

Verbs protection mask

0	1	0	0	0

Figure 7: The protection masks examples for three Head types, namely Punctuation, Articles, and Verbs.

Unlike the Replace operation, the protection masks are not used for the Insert operation as it is equal to a protection mask with all values equaling 1. Thus, Insert can be done to any place between the tokens.

6 Post Processing and Model Output

At the inference stage, iterative sentences corrections were applied. Each sentence passes through the model, and we get the probability distribution for each Head as an output. During each iteration, the Head with the highest "confidence rate" is chosen from all the Heads as the code below shows:

max_class = argmax(prob) confidence_rate = prob[max_class] if max_class != 0 else 0. # Index 0 means skip in all dictionaries.

Similar to the training stage, the probabilities for the Replace operation are multiplied by the protection mask. The edit proposed by the Head with maximal confidence rate is applied to the sentence, preliminary saving it to the history of previous changes. The process is looped until the following conditions are met: (i) probabilities of edits in all Heads reach zero (0), e.g. all errors have been fixed; (ii) length of the history is more than ten (10) meaning the network tried to improve the original sentence more than 10 times.

Also during each stage, we calculate Textual Semantic Similarity between the current version and the original sentence. This is also a part of our architecture concept. If the similarity is below 0.87, the loop stops, and we use the most recent sentence from the iterations history. Thus, we intended to perform the most effective correction for all grammatical errors in a sentence.

7 Concept Analysis and Roadmap

We have achieved the following results[5] within the framework of BEA 2019 competition. Let us now summarize the main challenges we faced when developing the suggested concept:

- Each Head type has a different learning speed due to different sizes and quality of dictionaries. When some Heads have not been trained yet, others start overfitting. For example, Spelling, Articles, and Punctuation Heads were trained faster than the Range Head and the Decoder itself. Thus, the results have worsened.

---

[3] https://www.cl.cam.ac.uk/research/nl/bea2019st
[4] https://spacy.io/

[5] https://competitions.codalab.org/my/competition/submission/563950/detailed_results/

- All Heads work independently. This is an issue for sentences where errors depend on each other, for example, in a sentence where the tense of one verb relies on the tense of another one. In the approach proposed in this article, each Head gives the probability of an error without taking into account the probabilities for other Heads in other networks. The same is true for the suggestion prediction. Thus, all results should be revised, and assessment should be made.

- The Decoder learned to predict the "End Of Sequence" (EOS) token as the first one to remove the token. Since EOS is the most frequently encountered token, position of the maximum probability on the Decoder prediction was often EOS. As a result, our solution has mistakenly eliminated tokens from the sentence, thus, lowering the quality of neural network and final output result .

To address the above-mentioned issues, we plan the following changes for our proposal:

- Choosing a unique learning rate for each Head separately. A different approach to consider in our case is to freeze the change in Head weights after it reaches the maximum accuracy for the validation dataset.

- Redesigning the architecture so that the Heads can share information among themselves.

- Using a separate token for deletion, as an option to use one of [unused1-100] tokens from the BERT vocabulary. According to our research and test results, it can improve the accuracy in two times.

References

Christopher Bryant, Mariano Felice, and Ted Briscoe. 2017. Universal sentence encoder. *ERRor ANnotation Toolkit: Automatically extract and classify grammatical errors in parallel original and corrected sentences.*

Daniel Dahlmeier and Hwee Tou Ng. 2012. Better evaluation for grammatical error correction. *In Proceedings of the 2012 Conference of the North American Chapter of the Association for Computational Linguistics: Human Language Technologies*, pages 568–572.

Jacob Devlin, Ming-Wei Chang, Kenton Lee, and Kristina Toutanova. 2019. Bert: Pre-training of deep bidirectional transformers for language understanding. *arXiv preprint arXiv:1810.04805v2 [cs.CL] 24 May 2019.*

Tao Ge, Furu Wei, and Ming Zhou. 2018. Reaching human-level performance in automatic grammatical error correction: An empirical study;. *Microsoft Research Technical Report.*

Alec Radford, Karthik Narasimhan, Tim Salimans, Jakob Uszkoreit, and Ilya Sutskever. 2018. Improving language understanding by generative pre-training. *OpenAI Blog.*

Ashish Vaswani, Noam Shazeer, Niki Parmar, Jakob Uszkoreit, Llion Jones, Aidan N. Gomez, Lukasz Kaiser, and Illia Polosukhin. 2017. Attention is all you need. *arXiv preprint arXiv:1706.03762v5 [cs.CL] 6 Dec 2017.*

Yinfei Yang and Chris Tar. 2018. Advances in semantic textual similarity. *Google AI Blog.*

Neural Grammatical Error Correction Systems with Unsupervised Pre-training on Synthetic Data

Roman Grundkiewicz[†] Marcin Junczys-Dowmunt[‡] Kenneth Heafield[†]
[†] University of Edinburgh, Scotland, EU
[‡] Microsoft, Redmond, USA
{rgrundki,kheafiel}@inf.ed.ac.uk, marcinjd@microsoft.com

Abstract

Considerable effort has been made to address the data sparsity problem in neural grammatical error correction. In this work, we propose a simple and surprisingly effective unsupervised synthetic error generation method based on confusion sets extracted from a spellchecker to increase the amount of training data. Synthetic data is used to pre-train a Transformer sequence-to-sequence model, which not only improves over a strong baseline trained on authentic error-annotated data, but also enables the development of a practical GEC system in a scenario where little genuine error-annotated data is available. The developed systems placed first in the BEA19 shared task, achieving 69.47 and 64.24 $F_{0.5}$ in the restricted and low-resource tracks respectively, both on the W&I+LOCNESS test set. On the popular CoNLL 2014 test set, we report state-of-the-art results of 64.16 M^2 for the submitted system, and 61.30 M^2 for the constrained system trained on the NUCLE and Lang-8 data.

1 Introduction

For the past five years, machine translation methods have been the most successful approach to automated Grammatical Error Correction (GEC). Work started with statistical phrase-based machine translation (SMT) methods (Junczys-Dowmunt and Grundkiewicz, 2016; Chollampatt and Ng, 2017) while sequence-to-sequence methods adopted from neural machine translation (NMT) lagged in quality until recently (Chollampatt and Ng, 2018; Junczys-Dowmunt et al., 2018b). These two papers established a number of techniques for neural GEC, such as transfer learning from monolingual data, strong regularization, model ensembling, and using a large-scale language model.

Subsequent work highlighted two challenges in neural GEC, data sparsity and multi-pass decoding:

Data sparsity: parallel training data has been enlarged by generating additional parallel sentences during training (Ge et al., 2018a,b), synthesizing noisy sentences (Xie et al., 2018), or pre-training a neural network on a large-scale but out-of-domain parallel corpus from Wikipedia (Lichtarge et al., 2018).

Multi-pass decoding: the correction process has been improved by incrementally correcting a sentence multiple times through multi-round inference using a model of one type (Ge et al., 2018a; Lichtarge et al., 2018), involving right-to-left models (Ge et al., 2018b), or by pipelining SMT and NMT-based systems (Grundkiewicz and Junczys-Dowmunt, 2018).

Motivated by the problems identified in these papers but concerned by the complexity of their methods, we sought simpler and more effective approaches to both challenges. For data sparsity, we propose an unsupervised synthetic parallel data generation method exploiting confusion sets from a spellchecker to augment training data used for pre-training sequence-to-sequence models. For multi-pass decoding, we use right-to-left models in rescoring, similar to competitive neural machine translation systems.

In the Building Educational Application (BEA) 2019 Shared Task on Grammatical Error Correction[1] (Bryant et al., 2019), our GEC systems ranked first in the restricted and low-resource tasks.[2] This confirms the effectiveness of the proposed methods in scenarios with and without readily-available large amounts of error-annotated data.

The rest of the paper is organized as follows:

---

[1] https://www.cl.cam.ac.uk/research/nl/bea2019st/

[2] Incidentally, our restricted system also outperformed all submissions to the unrestricted task to which we did not submit.

Proceedings of the Fourteenth Workshop on Innovative Use of NLP for Building Educational Applications, pages 252–263
Florence, Italy, August 2, 2019. ©2019 Association for Computational Linguistics

Section 2 briefly describes the BEA19 shared task and Section 3 presents related work. In Section 4 we demonstrate components of our neural GEC systems: transformer models, unsupervised synthetic data generation, ensembling and rescoring methods. Section 5 provides details of the experiments. The results are discussed in Sections 6 and 7, and we summarize in Section 8.

2   BEA19 shared task

The object of the BEA 2019 shared task was to automatically correct errors in written text, including grammatical, lexical, and orthographic errors. The shared task introduced two new annotated datasets for development and evaluation: Cambridge English Write & Improve (W&I) and the LOCNESS corpora (Bryant et al., 2019; Granger, 1998). These represent a more diverse cross-section of English language levels and domains than previous datasets.

There were three tracks that varied in the amount of admissible annotated learner data for system development. In the restricted track, participants were provided with four learner corpora containing 1.2 million sentences in total: the public FCE corpus (Yannakoudakis et al., 2011), NU-CLE (Dahlmeier et al., 2013), Lang-8 Corpus of Learner English (Mizumoto et al., 2012), and the mentioned W&I+LOCNESS datasets. No restriction was placed on publicly available unannotated data or NLP tools such as spellcheckers. The low-resource track was limited to the use of the W&I+LOCNESS development set. The organizers further clarified that automatically extracted parallel data, e.g. from Wikipedia, could be used only to build low-resource and unrestricted systems; it was inadmissible in the restricted track. We participated in the restricted and low-resource tracks; the third track allowed unrestricted data.

The performance of participating systems was evaluated using the ERRANT scorer (Bryant et al., 2017) which reports a $F_{0.5}$ over span-based corrections.

3   Related work

Many recent advances in neural GEC aim at overcoming the mentioned data sparsity problem. Ge et al. (2018a) proposed fluency-boost learning that generates additional training examples during training from an independent backward model or the forward model being trained. Xie et al. (2018) supplied their model with noisy examples synthesized from clean sentences. Junczys-Dowmunt et al. (2018b) utilized a large amount of monolingual data by pre-training decoder parameters with a language model, and Lichtarge et al. (2018, 2019), on the other hand, used a large-scale out-of-domain parallel corpus extracted from Wikipedia revisions to pre-train their models. We also pre-train a neural sequence-to-sequence model, but we do so solely on synthetic data.

Although our unsupervised method for synthesising parallel data by means of an (inverted) spellchecker is novel, the idea of generating artificial errors has been explored in the literature before, as summarized by Felice (2016). Previously proposed methods usually require a error-annotated corpus as a seed to generate artificial errors reflecting linguistic properties and error distributions observed in natural-error corpora (Foster and Andersen, 2009; Felice and Yuan, 2014). Artificial error generation methods spanned conditional probabilistic models for specific error types only (Rozovskaya and Roth, 2010; Rozovskaya et al., 2014; Felice and Yuan, 2014), statistical or neural MT systems trained on reversed source and target sides (Rei et al., 2017; Kasewa et al., 2018) or neural sequence transduction models (Xie et al., 2018). None of these methods is unsupervised.

Other recent work focuses on improving model inference. Ge et al. (2018a) proposed correcting a sentence more than once through multi-round model inference. Lichtarge et al. (2018) introduced iterative decoding to incrementally correct a sentence with a high-precision system. The multi-round correction approach has been further extended (Ge et al., 2018b) by interchanging decoding of a standard left-to-right model with a right-to-left model. The authors claim that the two models display unique advantages for specific error types as they decode with different contexts. Inspired by this finding, we adapt a common technique from NMT (Sennrich et al., 2016, 2017) that reranks with a right-to-left model, but without multiple rounds. We contend that multiple rounds are only necessary if the system has low recall.

4   System overview

4.1   Transformer models

Our neural GEC systems are based on Transformer models (Vaswani et al., 2017) that have been recently adapted to grammatical error correction with

Word	Confusion set
has	Haas HS Hans hats gas had Ha ha As as
is	IRS ISO OS US us Si its
island	islands Iceland slant
issued	issues issue used issuers eased sued assumed assured missed
student	students strident stunt
walking	talking whaling
large	larger lag lake barge Lodge lodge
largest	latest longest

Table 1: Examples of confusion sets generated from a spellchecker.

very good results (Junczys-Dowmunt et al., 2018b; Lichtarge et al., 2018).

We apply GEC-specific adaptations proposed by Junczys-Dowmunt et al. (2018b) with some modifications. Following the paper, we use extensive regularization to avoid overfitting to the limited labelled data, including dropping out entire source embeddings (Sennrich et al., 2016), and additional dropout on attention and feed-forward network transformer layers. For the sake of simplicity, we replace averaging the best four model checkpoints with exponential smoothing (Gardner, 1985). We increase the size of mini-batches as this improved the performance in early experiments. Parameters of the full model are pre-trained on synthetic parallel data, instead of pre-training only the decoder parameters (Ramachandran et al., 2017). We also experiment with larger Transformer models as described in Section 5.3.

4.2 Synthetic data generation

Synthetic parallel training examples for GEC could be generated by substituting random words in an error-free sentence and using the pair of artificial and original sentences as a new training example. In a naïve approach, words can be replaced randomly within a vocabulary, but this may result in unrealistic error patterns that do not resemble those observed in the genuine data. More accurate errors can be generated by replacing words only within confusion sets if such a confusion set consists of words that are commonly confused with each other (Rozovskaya and Roth, 2010; Rozovskaya et al., 2014; Bryant and Briscoe, 2018).

Instead of applying a supervised probabilistic method to learn error distributions (Felice and

Yuan, 2014; Rei et al., 2017; Xie et al., 2018; Kasewa et al., 2018; Bryant and Briscoe, 2018), we propose generating confusion sets with the help of a spellchecker. For each word in the vocabulary[3] that consists of only alphabetic characters, including correct words, we extract suggestions from the Aspell spellchecker to create the confusion set of that word. Aspell sorts suggestion lists[4] by a score that is the weighted average of the weighted edit distance of the proposed word to the input word and the distance between their phonetic equivalents generated by the metaphone algorithm (Philips, 2000). Confusion sets are limited to top 20 suggestions. Table 1 presents examples of generated confusion sets.

Synthetic errors are introduced into an error-free text in the following manner. For each sentence, we sample an error probability p_{err} from a normal distribution with mean 0.15, chosen to resemble the word error rate of the development set, and arbitrary standard deviation 0.2. This is multiplied by sentence length and rounded to a number of words to change. Exactly that many words in the sentence are chosen by sampling uniformly without replacement. Next, for each chosen word, we perform one of the following operations with a given probability: substituting w_i with a random word from its confusion set, deleting w_i, inserting a random word after w_i, or swapping it with an adjacent word w_{i+1}. The probability for word substitution is set arbitrarily to 0.7 and the three remaining operations are chosen with a probability of 0.1 each.

Furthermore, to make our models more capable of correcting spelling errors, similarly to Lichtarge et al. (2018), we introduce additional noise in source words. We randomly perturb characters in 10% of words using the same operations as above for the word level operations, i.e. substitution, deletion, insertion or transposition of characters, with the same probabilities. An example of a synthetic sentence is presented in Table 2.

The proposed method does not generate context-aware errors, but is simple and can be applied to any alphabetic language with existing spell-checkers. In preliminary experiments, confusion sets generated using a spellchecker led to better performance during pre-training than methods based on the Levenshtein edit distance (Levenshtein, 1966) or word-

---

[3]We add noise into the subword-segmented texts, so the vocabulary here is the same as the training vocabulary.

[4]http://aspell.net/0.50-doc/man-html/8_How.html

Type	Output
Original input	*But they have left their exam rooms and come out the streets to joining hands with the public and to fight for the country under the guidance of the monks .*
+ Synthetic errors	*But they have lift their exam rooms <u>end</u> <s>come</s> out the streets to joining <u>lands</u> with the public <u>band</u> to fight for country the <u>unity</u> the guidance of the <u>monos</u> .*
+ Spelling errors	*But they have lift their <u>exm</u> rooms end out the streets to joining lands with the public band to fight for <u>counrty</u> the unity the guidance of the monos .*

Table 2: An example of an artificially generated erroneous sentence.

embedding similarities (Mikolov et al., 2013).

4.3 Model pre-training and fine-tuning

We generate synthetic errors from 100 million sentences sampled from the English part of the WMT News Crawl corpus (Bojar et al., 2018) and use pairs of synthetic and authentic sentences exclusively to pre-train transformer models. A pre-trained model can be used with the actual in-domain error-annotated data by fine-tuning (Hinton and Salakhutdinov, 2006; Miceli Barone et al., 2017). We experimented with two fine-tuning strategies:

1. Initialising the neural network weights with the pre-trained model and starting a new training run on new data. This resets learning rate scheduling and optimizer parameters. We further refer to this procedure as *re-training*.

2. Continuing training the existing model with new data preserving the learning rate, optimizer parameters and historic weights for exponential smoothing. We refer to this scheme as *fine-tuning*.

The main difference between re-training and fine-tuning is resetting the training state after pre-training. The latter strategy worked best in our experiments.

4.4 Ensembling

Similarly to Junczys-Dowmunt et al. (2018b), we build a heterogeneous ensemble of independently trained sequence-to-sequence models and a language model (LM). Sequence-to-sequence models are weighted equally, while the weight for the LM is grid-searched on the development set.

4.5 Right-to-left re-ranking

A common approach to improve the performance of NMT systems is re-ranking with right-to-left

Corpus	Track	Sentences
FCE Train	R	28,350
NUCLE	R	57,113
Lang-8	R	1,041,409
W&I Train	R	34,308
W&I+LOCNESS Dev	L,R	4,384
WikEd	L	2,000,000
News Crawl	L,R	100M

Table 3: Parallel and monolingual training data. R denotes datasets used to develop our restricted systems, L — low-resource systems.

models that have been trained on the reversed word direction (Sennrich et al., 2016, 2017). In GEC, Ge et al. (2018b) use a right-to-left model for multi-round error correction where models following opposite sequence direction are run recursively one followed by another. The motivation is that both models use different contexts, so can be more capable of correcting errors of different types.

We adapt the re-ranking technique. We first generate n-best lists using the ensemble of standard left-to-right models and the language model, then re-score sentence pairs with right-to-left models using length-normalized scores, and re-rank the hypotheses. We have experimented with different weighting strategies during re-scoring, but found that weighting all sequence-to-sequence models equally with 1.0 and grid-searching the weight of the language model again works best. Tuning all ensemble weights independently with MERT (Och, 2003) lead to overfitting to the development set.

5 Experiments

5.1 Datasets

Error-annotated data The restricted models are trained on data provided in the shared task: the

FCE corpus (Yannakoudakis et al., 2011), NUCLE (Dahlmeier et al., 2013), W&I+LOCNESS data sets (Bryant et al., 2019; Granger, 1998), and a pre-processed version of the Lang-8 Corpus of Learner English (Mizumoto et al., 2012).

We clean Lang-8 using regular expressions[5] to 1) filter out sentences with a low ratio of alphabetic to non-alphabetic tokens, 2) clear sentences from emoticons and sequences of repeated single non-alphanumeric characters longer than 3 elements e.g. repeated question or exclamation marks, and 3) remove trailing brackets with comments from the target sentences. If a sentence has alternative corrections, we expand them to separate training examples.

Our final training set in the restricted setting contains 1,953,554 sentences, assembled from the cleaned Lang-8 corpus and oversampled remaining corpora: FCE and the training portion of W&I are oversampled 10 times, NUCLE 5 times. Table 3 summarizes all data sets used for training. W&I+LOCNESS Dev is used solely as a development set in both tracks.

Monolingual data We use News Crawl[6] — a publicly available corpus of monolingual texts extracted from online newspapers released for the WMT series of shared tasks (Bojar et al., 2018) — as our primary monolingual data source. We uniformly sampled 100 million English sentences from de-duplicated crawls in years 2007 to 2018 to produce synthetic parallel data for model pre-training. Another subset of 2 million sentences was selected to augment the training data during fine-tuning.

The Enchant spellchecker[7] with the Aspell back-end and a British English dictionary were used to generate confusion sets.

Wikipedia edits In the low-resource setting, we use a filtered subset of the WikEd corpus (Grundkiewicz and Junczys-Dowmunt, 2014). The original corpus contains 56 million automatically extracted edited sentences from Wikipedia revisions and is quite noisy.

We clean the data using cross-entropy difference filtering by Moore and Lewis (2010). W&I+LOCNESS Dev is used as an in-domain seed corpus. All sentence pairs in WikEd are sorted w.r.t

an average score from two language models: an n-gram probabilistic word-level language model estimated from target sentences, and a simplified operation sequence model built on edits between source and target sentences.[8] We use KenLM (Heafield, 2011) to build 5-gram language models. The top 2 million sentence pairs with the highest scores are used as training data in place of the error-annotated ESL learner data to train models for the low-resource system.

5.2 Data preprocessing

Following the preprocessing methods of the data provided in the shared task, we tokenize other data sets with spaCy.[9] We also normalize Unicode punctuation to ASCII with a script included in the Moses SMT toolkit[10] (Koehn et al., 2007).

To handle the open vocabulary issue, we split tokens into 32,000 subword units trained on 10 million randomly sampled sentences from News Crawl using the default unigram-LM segmentation algorithm (Kudo, 2018) from SentencePiece (Kudo and Richardson, 2018).

5.3 Model architecture

We experiment with different variants of Transformer models (Vaswani et al., 2017). The "Transformer Base" architecture has 6 blocks of self-attention/feed forward sub-layers in the encoder and decoder, 8-head self-attention layers, and embeddings vector size of 512. The ReLU activation function (Nair and Hinton, 2010) is used between filters of size 2048. We tie output layer, decoder and encoder embeddings (Press and Wolf, 2017).

We choose the "Transformer Big" architecture as our final models for the restricted track. They differ from Transformer Base by the number of heads in multi-head attention components (16 heads instead for 8), larger embeddings vector size of 1024 and filter size of 4096.

The architecture of the language models corresponds to the structure of the decoder of the sequence-to-sequence model, either Transformer Base or Big.

---

[5]Cleaning Lang-8 led to minor improvements during the preliminary experiments when no pre-training was used.

[6]http://data.statmt.org/news-crawl/

[7]https://abiword.github.io/enchant/

[8]For example, a sentence pair (*„I think that the public transport will always be in the future .", „I think that public transport will always exist in the future ."*) is first converted into the sequence „`<del> the <sub> be <to> exist`", and then a standard n-gram probabilistic language model is built on such edit operation sequences.

[9]https://spacy.io/

[10]https://github.com/moses-smt/
mosesdecoder/blob/master/scripts/
tokenizer/normalize-punctuation.perl

	Restricted systems				Low-resource systems			
	W&I+LOCNESS			FCE	W&I+LOCNESS			FCE
System	P	R	$F_{0.5}$	$F_{0.5}$	P	R	$F_{0.5}$	$F_{0.5}$
Baseline	47.1	30.2	42.37	47.46	37.3	18.3	30.89	30.53
Baseline + LM pretraining	47.2	30.9	**42.69**	47.61	39.7	20.2	33.14	34.46
Pre-training on synthetic data	43.2	10.6	26.76	34.00	43.2	10.6	26.76	34.00
→ Re-training	53.2	35.8	**48.44**	51.53	44.2	20.8	36.11	35.91
→ Fine-tuning	**54.8**	34.2	48.92	52.69	49.6	21.0	38.97	41.79
+ 2M synthetic data	56.1	34.8	50.01	53.64	53.6	18.9	39.16	42.23
Ensemble Base×8	58.4	34.8	51.42	53.92	55.0	20.8	41.37	43.75
+ LM Base	57.3	37.7	51.88	53.33	51.1	26.5	43.11	44.04
+ LM Big	56.9	38.9	52.04	53.17	52.0	26.7	43.69	45.68
+ RL rescoring Base×4	57.7	38.3	52.42	55.03	55.0	26.0	**44.95**⋆	47.42
Ensemble Big×4 + LM Big	58.5	36.8	52.30	54.57			—	
+ RL rescoring Base×4	59.1	36.8	**53.00**⋆	55.81			—	

Table 4: Results for restricted and low-resource systems on W&I+LOCNESS Dev and FCE Test. Stars (⋆) indicate the submitted systems.

Method	P	R	$F_{0.5}$
Ensemble×4 +LM	58.5	36.8	52.30
→ Second pass	58.2	37.3	52.36
→ Round-way right-left	55.7	40.0	51.64
→ Iterative decoding	58.3	37.2	52.37
→ Right-left rescoring	59.1	36.8	53.00

Table 5: Comparison of different methods for inference optimization for the final restricted system on W&I+LOCNESS Dev.

5.4 Training settings

We train all models with the Marian toolkit[11] (Junczys-Dowmunt et al., 2018a), and generally follow the configuration proposed by Junczys-Dowmunt et al. (2018b).

Transformer models are trained using Adam (Kingma and Ba, 2014) with a learning rate of 0.0003 and linear warm-up for the first 16k updates, followed by inverted squared decay. For the larger models, we decrease the learning rate to 0.0002 and warm-up to 8k first updates. We train with synchronous SGD (Adam) and dynamically sized mini-batches fitted into 48GB GPU RAM memory across 4 GPUs, accumulating gradients for 3 iterations before making an update (Bogoychev et al., 2018). This results in mini-batches consisting of ca. 2,700 sentences. The maximum length of a training sentence is limited to 150 subword units. Strong regularization via dropout (Gal and Ghahramani, 2016) is used to dissuade the model from simply copying the input: we use a dropout probability between transformer layers of 0.3, for transformer self-attention and filters of 0.1, and for source and target words of 0.3 and 0.1 respectively. For source and target words we dropout entire embedding vectors, not just single neurons. We also use label smoothing with a weight of 0.1, and exponential averaging of model parameters with a smoothing factor of 0.0001.

During fine-tuning, we use the the cross-entropy training objective with edits up-weighted by a factor of $\Lambda = 2$ (Junczys-Dowmunt et al., 2018b).

The model is validated every 5000 updates on W&I+LOCNESS Dev using the ERRANT $F_{0.5}$ score. Models are trained with early stopping with a patience of 10. Pre-training is additionally limited to 5 epochs. We decode with beam search with a beam size of 12, and normalize scores for each hypothesis by sentence length. The checkpoint with the highest $F_{0.5}$ score on the development set is selected as a final model.

Right-to-left models are trained with exactly the same settings, the only difference is the reversed word order in source and target sentences[12] with no further data processing requirements.

---

[11] https://marian-nmt.github.io/

[12] Training right-to-left models is built into Marian and can be enabled with the `-right-left` option.

Language models are trained with the same settings as sequence-to-sequence models, but validated every 10,000 updates on the target side of the development set.

6 Results on the development set

Table 4 summarizes the results of the experiments on the W&I+LOCNESS Dev and FCE Test in the restricted and low-resource settings.

Restricted systems   We compare our models to two Transformer-based baselines trained solely on the original error-annotated data without and with transfer learning from the language model. Surprisingly, for the restricted system, pre-training the decoder parameters (Baseline + LM pretraining) does not yield much improvement. A major improvement is achieved, however, by pre-training of the entire neural network on the synthetic data (Re-training).

The fine-tuning strategy generally leads to better results than re-training, mostly due to increased precision. Adding 2 million of synthetic sentences to the error-annotated data — resulting approximately in an 1:1 ratio of genuine and artificial training examples (Sennrich et al., 2017) — further improves the performance.

Ensembling eight Transformer models with a language model and re-ranking the n-best lists with four right-to-left models leads to consistent improvements. The quality of the language model is important as using a stronger language model (LM Big) generally improves the scores.

The systems with bigger models (Ensemble Big×4 + LM Big) have a higher precision and thus perform better on both datasets. Interestingly, re-ranking using smaller and relatively weaker right-to-left Transformer Base models is still beneficial. We have found that re-ranking works best for our high-recall system, better than other methods for multi-pass decoding as presented in Table 5.

The final system with four Transformer Big models constitutes our submission to the restricted track for the official evaluation in the shared task.

Low-resource systems   For the low-resource task, we follow the same experiments as for the restricted task, replacing the error-annotated training data with a subset of the filtered WikEd corpus of comparable size. Using out-of-domain data in place of the high-quality ESL learner data reduces the performance substantially in the low-resource

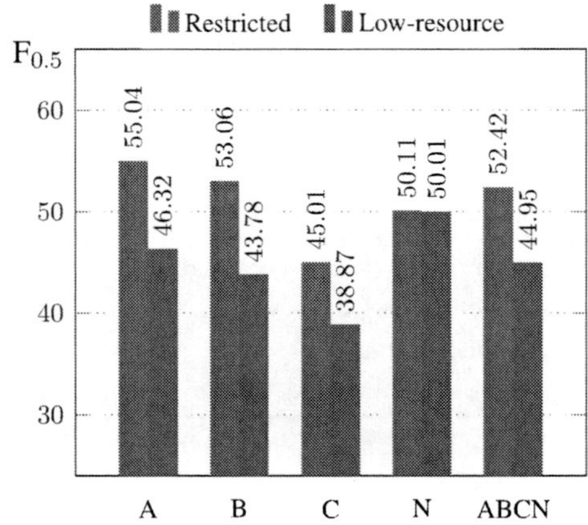

Figure 1: Comparison of restricted and low-resource systems on different parts of W&I+LOCNESS Dev.

baseline, but the gap is reduced in the final systems. Ensembling and re-ranking lead to larger relative improvements than for the restricted systems.

Due to a tight time frame, the final system submitted to the low-resource track uses eight Transformer Base models.

6.1 Proficiency levels and error types

The key contribution of the BEA19 shared task is the introduction of the W&I+LOCNESS dataset that consists of texts written by students of different English skill levels (A, B and C represents beginner, intermediate and advanced levels, respectively), including native texts (N). Figure 1 compares $F_{0.5}$ scores of the corresponding restricted and low-resource ensemble systems for distinct parts of W&I+LOCNESS Dev.

Generally the higher the proficiency level of ESL texts, the lower the advantage of the systems trained on real error-annotated ESL learner data. Interestingly, the performance of restricted and low-resourcse systems on native texts is identical. It remains to be investigated if pre-training (the common part for those systems) is responsible for this.

As can be seen in Figure 2, the restricted and low-resource systems achieve similar performance on specific error types, for instance, morphology and subject-verb agreement errors, some errors within nouns, or misspellings.

6.2 Comparison to the state of the art

To compare with the current state of the art, we evaluate our best systems on other popular GEC benchmarks in Table 6. We report $F_{0.5}$ scores on

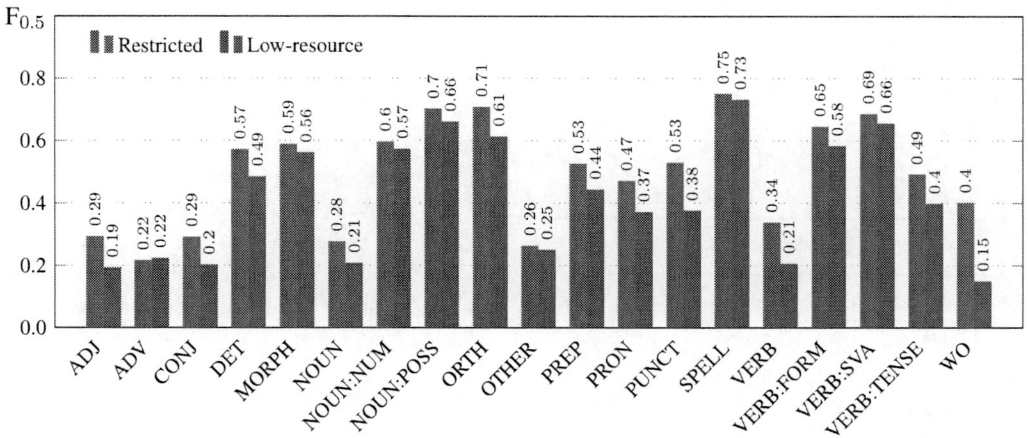

Figure 2: Comparison of restricted and low-resource systems ($F_{0.5}$) on a selection of error types from ERRANT on W&I+LOCNESS Dev.

the CoNLL 2014 test set (Dahlmeier et al., 2013) calculated with the official M2Scorer (Dahlmeier and Ng, 2012). We also report results on the JFLEG test set (Napoles et al., 2017) using GLEU (Napoles et al., 2015). Following other works (Sakaguchi et al., 2017; Junczys-Dowmunt et al., 2018b), we correct spelling errors in JFLEG using Enchant before decoding.

On CoNLL-2014, our best GEC system achieves 64.16 M^2, which is the highest score reported on this test set so far, including the systems trained on non-publicly available resources (Ge et al., 2018a,b). Although comparing to prior work, the improvement is impressive, our submitted system uses the public FCE corpus and the new W&I Train sets and should not be directly contrasted with systems trained on the NUCLE and Lang-8 corpora only. In contrastive experiments, we have trained a system with four Transformer Base models using the NUCLE and Lang-8 data from Junczys-Dowmunt et al. (2018b). That system achieves 61.30 $F_{0.5}$, which is the state-of-the-art result for a constrained GEC system, and it is comparable to the results reported by Ge et al. (2018b) for their system trained on non-public data. We expect even higher scores if our system would consist of larger Transformer models as in our submission.

7   Official results

The evaluation in the shared task was performed on the blind W&I+LOCNESS test set consisting of 350 student essays and 4,477 sentences. Excerpts

System	CoNLL	JFLEG
Chollampatt and Ng (2018)	54.79	57.47
Junczys-Dowmunt et al. (2018b)	55.80	59.90
Grundkiewicz and Junczys-Dowmunt (2018)	56.25	61.50
Lichtarge et al. (2018)	58.30	62.40
Stahlberg et al. (2019)	58.40	58.63
Lichtarge et al. (2019)	60.4	63.3
Zhao et al. (2019)	61.15	61.00
Ge et al. (2018b)	61.34	62.42
Our low-resource system	52.44	58.07
Our restricted system	64.16	61.16
Constrained system	61.30	61.22

Table 6: Comparison with other works on the CoNLL-2014 and JFLEG test sets. The results for the constrained system are reported for best systems according to CoNLL-2013 and JFLEG Dev.

of the official rankings are presented in Table 7.[13]

Our final GEC system achieves an official result of 69.47 F-score, which ranks it first among 21 systems participating in the main track. The top two systems perform significantly better than the remaining systems. We outperform the second system mainly due to higher recall and better performance on non-native parts of the test set: our system is +1.7 better on texts written by beginner English learners and -1.1 worse on native texts.

[13]Full rankings with detailed results: https://www.cl.cam.ac.uk/research/nl/bea2019st/#results

#	Team	P	R	$F_{0.5}$
1	UEdin-MS	72.28	60.12	69.47
2	Kakao&Brain	75.19	51.91	69.00
3	LAIX	73.17	49.50	66.78
4	CAMB-CLED	70.49	55.07	66.75
5	Shuyao	70.17	55.39	66.61

(a) Restricted track.

#	Team	P	R	$F_{0.5}$
1	UEdin-MS	70.19	47.99	64.24
2	Kakao&Brain	63.06	46.30	58.80
3	LAIX	62.01	31.25	51.81
4	CAMB-CUED	55.58	38.03	50.88
5	UFAL	50.47	29.38	44.13

(b) Low-resource track.

Table 7: Official results for top 5 systems in the BEA19 shared task in the restricted (top) and low-resource (bottom) tracks. UEdin-MS is our submission.

Our low-resource GEC system is also ranked first among 9 participating teams achieving 64.24 $F_{0.5}$ and outperforming the second best system significantly by +5.4. Interestingly, this system achieves the highest F-score of 72.25 on the part of the test set written by native speakers, comparing to the best result of 71.94 $F_{0.5}$ by Kakao&Brain in the restricted track.

We did not submit a system to the unrestricted track, however our best system outperforms all systems in this track.

8 Summary

We presented an unsupervised synthetic error generation method based on confusion sets generated from an inverted spellchecker. With this method we increased the amount of training data for a grammatical error correction system. The generated synthetic parallel corpus was used to pre-train the sequence-to-sequence model and then fine-tuned on authentic data, which improved the performance of the adapted Transformer model in comparison to a model trained on authentic data alone. We also demonstrated the effectiveness of this approach in a scenario where little genuine error-annotated ESL learner data is available. Our final systems[14] consist of ensembles of sequence-to-sequence Transformer models and a Transformer-based language model re-ranked with right-to-left models.

The presented GEC systems form our submissions to the BEA19 shared task as the UEdin-MS team. They are ranked first in the restricted and low-resource tracks achieving 69.47 and 64.24 $F_{0.5}$ score on the W&I+LOCNESS test set respectively. On the popular CoNLL 2014 test set, we report state-of-the-art results of 64.16 M^2 for the best submitted system, and 61.30 M^2 for a system trained on the NUCLE and Lang-8 data.

Acknowledgments

This work was performed using resources provided by the Cambridge Service for Data Driven Discovery (CSD3) operated by the University of Cambridge Research Computing Service (`http://www.csd3.cam.ac.uk/`), provided by Dell EMC and Intel using Tier-2 funding from the Engineering and Physical Sciences Research Council (capital grant EP/P020259/1), and DiRAC funding from the Science and Technology Facilities Council (`www.dirac.ac.uk`).

References

Nikolay Bogoychev, Marcin Junczys-Dowmunt, Kenneth Heafield, and Alham Fikri Aji. 2018. Accelerating asynchronous stochastic gradient descent for neural machine translation. In *Proceedings of the 2018 Conference on Empirical Methods in Natural Language Processing*, EMNLP'18, pages 2991–2996, Brussels, Belgium.

Ondřej Bojar, Christian Federmann, Mark Fishel, Yvette Graham, Barry Haddow, Philipp Koehn, and Christof Monz. 2018. Findings of the 2018 conference on machine translation (WMT18). In *Proceedings of the Third Conference on Machine Translation: Shared Task Papers*, pages 272–303, Belgium, Brussels. Association for Computational Linguistics.

Christopher Bryant and Ted Briscoe. 2018. Language model based grammatical error correction without annotated training data. In *Proceedings of the Thirteenth Workshop on Innovative Use of NLP for Building Educational Applications*, pages 247–253, New Orleans, Louisiana. Association for Computational Linguistics.

Christopher Bryant, Mariano Felice, Øistein E. Andersen, and Ted Briscoe. 2019. The BEA-2019 Shared Task on Grammatical Error Correction. In *Proceedings of the 14th Workshop on Innovative Use of NLP for Building Educational Applications*. Association for Computational Linguistics.

---

[14]Models, system configurations and outputs are available from `https://github.com/grammatical/pretraining-bea2019`

Christopher Bryant, Mariano Felice, and Ted Briscoe. 2017. Automatic annotation and evaluation of error types for grammatical error correction. In *Proceedings of the 55th Annual Meeting of the Association for Computational Linguistics (Volume 1: Long Papers)*, pages 793–805, Vancouver, Canada. Association for Computational Linguistics.

Shamil Chollampatt and Hwee Tou Ng. 2017. Connecting the dots: towards human-level grammatical error correction. In *Proceedings of the 12th Workshop on Innovative Use of NLP for Building Educational Applications*, pages 327–333, Copenhagen, Denmark. Association for Computational Linguistics.

Shamil Chollampatt and Hwee Tou Ng. 2018. A multi-layer convolutional encoder-decoder neural network for grammatical error correction. In *Proceedings of the Thirty-Second AAAI Conference on Artificial Intelligence*.

Daniel Dahlmeier and Hwee Tou Ng. 2012. Better evaluation for grammatical error correction. In *Proceedings of the 2012 Conference of the North American Chapter of the Association for Computational Linguistics: Human Language Technologies*, pages 568–572, Montréal, Canada. Association for Computational Linguistics.

Daniel Dahlmeier, Hwee Tou Ng, and Siew Mei Wu. 2013. Building a large annotated corpus of learner English: The NUS corpus of learner English. In *Proceedings of the Eighth Workshop on Innovative Use of NLP for Building Educational Applications*, pages 22–31, Atlanta, Georgia. Association for Computational Linguistics.

Mariano Felice. 2016. Artificial error generation for translation-based grammatical error correction. Technical report, University of Cambridge, Computer Laboratory.

Mariano Felice and Zheng Yuan. 2014. Generating artificial errors for grammatical error correction. In *Proceedings of the Student Research Workshop at the 14th Conference of the European Chapter of the Association for Computational Linguistics*, pages 116–126, Gothenburg, Sweden. Association for Computational Linguistics.

Jennifer Foster and Øistein E Andersen. 2009. Generrate: generating errors for use in grammatical error detection. In *Proceedings of the fourth workshop on innovative use of nlp for building educational applications*, pages 82–90. Association for Computational Linguistics.

Yarin Gal and Zoubin Ghahramani. 2016. A theoretically grounded application of dropout in recurrent neural networks. In *Advances in neural information processing systems*, pages 1019–1027.

Everette Gardner. 1985. Exponential smoothing: The state of the art. *Journal of forecasting*, 4(1):1–28.

Tao Ge, Furu Wei, and Ming Zhou. 2018a. Fluency boost learning and inference for neural grammatical error correction. In *Proceedings of the 56th Annual Meeting of the Association for Computational Linguistics (Volume 1: Long Papers)*, pages 1055–1065, Melbourne, Australia. Association for Computational Linguistics.

Tao Ge, Furu Wei, and Ming Zhou. 2018b. Reaching human-level performance in automatic grammatical error correction: An empirical study. Technical report, Microsoft Research Technical Report.

Sylviane Granger. 1998. The computer learner corpus: A versatile new source of data for SLA research. In Sylviane Granger, editor, *Learner English on Computer*, pages 3–18. Addison Wesley Longman, London and New York.

Roman Grundkiewicz and Marcin Junczys-Dowmunt. 2014. The WikEd error corpus: A corpus of corrective Wikipedia edits and its application to grammatical error correction. In *Advances in Natural Language Processing – Lecture Notes in Computer Science*, volume 8686, pages 478–490. Springer.

Roman Grundkiewicz and Marcin Junczys-Dowmunt. 2018. Near human-level performance in grammatical error correction with hybrid machine translation. In *Proceedings of the 2018 Conference of the North American Chapter of the Association for Computational Linguistics: Human Language Technologies, Volume 2 (Short Papers)*, pages 284–290, New Orleans, Louisiana. Association for Computational Linguistics.

Kenneth Heafield. 2011. KenLM: Faster and smaller language model queries. In *Proceedings of the Sixth Workshop on Statistical Machine Translation*, WMT '11, pages 187–197, Stroudsburg, USA. Association for Computational Linguistics.

Geoffrey E Hinton and Ruslan R Salakhutdinov. 2006. Reducing the dimensionality of data with neural networks. *science*, 313(5786):504–507.

Marcin Junczys-Dowmunt and Roman Grundkiewicz. 2016. Phrase-based machine translation is state-of-the-art for automatic grammatical error correction. In *Proceedings of the 2016 Conference on Empirical Methods in Natural Language Processing*, pages 1546–1556, Austin, Texas. Association for Computational Linguistics.

Marcin Junczys-Dowmunt, Roman Grundkiewicz, Tomasz Dwojak, Hieu Hoang, Kenneth Heafield, Tom Neckermann, Frank Seide, Ulrich Germann, Alham Fikri Aji, Nikolay Bogoychev, André F. T. Martins, and Alexandra Birch. 2018a. Marian: Fast neural machine translation in C++. In *Proceedings of ACL 2018, System Demonstrations*, pages 116–121, Melbourne, Australia. Association for Computational Linguistics.

Marcin Junczys-Dowmunt, Roman Grundkiewicz, Shubha Guha, and Kenneth Heafield. 2018b. Approaching neural grammatical error correction as a low-resource machine translation task. In *Proceedings of the 2018 Conference of the North American Chapter of the Association for Computational Linguistics: Human Language Technologies, Volume 1 (Long Papers)*, pages 595–606, New Orleans, Louisiana. Association for Computational Linguistics.

Sudhanshu Kasewa, Pontus Stenetorp, and Sebastian Riedel. 2018. Wronging a right: Generating better errors to improve grammatical error detection. In *Proceedings of the 2018 Conference on Empirical Methods in Natural Language Processing*, pages 4977–4983, Brussels, Belgium. Association for Computational Linguistics.

Diederik Kingma and Jimmy Ba. 2014. Adam: A method for stochastic optimization. *Proceedings of the 3rd International Conference on Learning Representations (ICLR)*.

Philipp Koehn, Hieu Hoang, Alexandra Birch, Chris Callison-Burch, Marcello Federico, Nicola Bertoldi, Brooke Cowan, Wade Shen, Christine Moran, Richard Zens, Chris Dyer, Ondrej Bojar, Alexandra Constantin, and Evan Herbst. 2007. Moses: Open source toolkit for statistical machine translation. In *Annual Meeting of the Association for Computational Linguistics*. The Association for Computer Linguistics.

Taku Kudo. 2018. Subword regularization: Improving neural network translation models with multiple subword candidates. In *Proceedings of the 56th Annual Meeting of the Association for Computational Linguistics (Volume 1: Long Papers)*, pages 66–75, Melbourne, Australia. Association for Computational Linguistics.

Taku Kudo and John Richardson. 2018. SentencePiece: A simple and language independent subword tokenizer and detokenizer for neural text processing. In *Proceedings of the 2018 Conference on Empirical Methods in Natural Language Processing: System Demonstrations*, pages 66–71, Brussels, Belgium. Association for Computational Linguistics.

Vladimir I Levenshtein. 1966. Binary codes capable of correcting deletions, insertions, and reversals. In *Soviet physics doklady*, volume 10, pages 707–710.

Jared Lichtarge, Chris Alberti, Shankar Kumar, Noam Shazeer, Niki Parmar, and Simon Tong. 2019. Corpora generation for grammatical error correction. In *Proceedings of the 2019 Conference of the North American Chapter of the Association for Computational Linguistics: Human Language Technologies, Volume 1 (Long and Short Papers)*, pages 3291–3301, Minneapolis, Minnesota. Association for Computational Linguistics.

Jared Lichtarge, Christopher Alberti, Shankar Kumar, Noam Shazeer, and Niki Parmar. 2018. Weakly supervised grammatical error correction using iterative decoding. *CoRR*, abs/1811.01710.

Antonio Valerio Miceli Barone, Barry Haddow, Ulrich Germann, and Rico Sennrich. 2017. Regularization techniques for fine-tuning in neural machine translation. In *Proceedings of the 2017 Conference on Empirical Methods in Natural Language Processing*, pages 1489–1494, Copenhagen, Denmark. Association for Computational Linguistics.

Tomas Mikolov, Ilya Sutskever, Kai Chen, Greg S Corrado, and Jeff Dean. 2013. Distributed representations of words and phrases and their compositionality. In C. J. C. Burges, L. Bottou, M. Welling, Z. Ghahramani, and K. Q. Weinberger, editors, *Advances in Neural Information Processing Systems 26*, pages 3111–3119. Curran Associates, Inc.

Tomoya Mizumoto, Yuta Hayashibe, Mamoru Komachi, Masaaki Nagata, and Yu Matsumoto. 2012. The effect of learner corpus size in grammatical error correction of ESL writings. In *Proceedings of COLING 2012*, pages 863–872.

Robert C. Moore and William Lewis. 2010. Intelligent selection of language model training data. In *Proceedings of the ACL 2010 Conference Short Papers*, pages 220–224, Uppsala, Sweden. Association for Computational Linguistics.

Vinod Nair and Geoffrey E Hinton. 2010. Rectified linear units improve restricted boltzmann machines. In *Proceedings of the 27th international conference on machine learning (ICML-10)*, pages 807–814.

Courtney Napoles, Keisuke Sakaguchi, Matt Post, and Joel Tetreault. 2015. Ground truth for grammatical error correction metrics. In *Proceedings of the 53rd Annual Meeting of the Association for Computational Linguistics and the 7th International Joint Conference on Natural Language Processing (Volume 2: Short Papers)*, pages 588–593, Beijing, China. Association for Computational Linguistics.

Courtney Napoles, Keisuke Sakaguchi, and Joel Tetreault. 2017. JFLEG: A fluency corpus and benchmark for grammatical error correction. In *Proceedings of the 2017 Conference of the European Chapter of the Association for Computational Linguistics*, Valencia, Spain. Association for Computational Linguistics.

Franz Josef Och. 2003. Minimum error rate training in statistical machine translation. In *Proceedings of the 41st Annual Meeting on Association for Computational Linguistics - Volume 1*, ACL '03, pages 160–167, Stroudsburg, USA. Association for Computational Linguistics.

Lawrence Philips. 2000. The double metaphone search algorithm. *C/C++ Users J.*, 18(6):38–43.

Ofir Press and Lior Wolf. 2017. Using the output embedding to improve language models. In *Proceedings of the 15th Conference of the European Chapter of the Association for Computational Linguistics: Volume 2, Short Papers*, pages 157–163, Valencia, Spain. Association for Computational Linguistics.

Prajit Ramachandran, Peter Liu, and Quoc Le. 2017. Unsupervised pretraining for sequence to sequence learning. In *Proceedings of the 2017 Conference on Empirical Methods in Natural Language Processing*, pages 383–391, Copenhagen, Denmark. Association for Computational Linguistics.

Marek Rei, Mariano Felice, Zheng Yuan, and Ted Briscoe. 2017. Artificial error generation with machine translation and syntactic patterns. In *Proceedings of the 12th Workshop on Innovative Use of NLP for Building Educational Applications*, pages 287–292, Copenhagen, Denmark. Association for Computational Linguistics.

A. Rozovskaya, D. Roth, and V. Srikumar. 2014. Correcting grammatical verb errors. In *European Chapter of the Association for Computational Linguistics*.

Alla Rozovskaya and Dan Roth. 2010. Generating confusion sets for context-sensitive error correction. In *Proceedings of the 2010 Conference on Empirical Methods in Natural Language Processing*, pages 961–970, Cambridge, MA. Association for Computational Linguistics.

Keisuke Sakaguchi, Matt Post, and Benjamin Van Durme. 2017. Grammatical error correction with neural reinforcement learning. In *Proceedings of the Eighth International Joint Conference on Natural Language Processing (Volume 2: Short Papers)*, pages 366–372, Taipei, Taiwan. Asian Federation of Natural Language Processing.

Rico Sennrich, Alexandra Birch, Anna Currey, Ulrich Germann, Barry Haddow, Kenneth Heafield, Antonio Valerio Miceli Barone, and Philip Williams. 2017. The university of Edinburgh's neural MT systems for WMT17. In *Proceedings of the Second Conference on Machine Translation*, pages 389–399, Copenhagen, Denmark. Association for Computational Linguistics.

Rico Sennrich, Barry Haddow, and Alexandra Birch. 2016. Edinburgh neural machine translation systems for WMT16. In *Proceedings of the First Conference on Machine Translation*, pages 371–376, Berlin, Germany. Association for Computational Linguistics.

Felix Stahlberg, Christopher Bryant, and Bill Byrne. 2019. Neural grammatical error correction with finite state transducers. In *Proceedings of the 2019 Conference of the North American Chapter of the Association for Computational Linguistics: Human Language Technologies, Volume 1 (Long and Short Papers)*, pages 4033–4039, Minneapolis, Minnesota. Association for Computational Linguistics.

Ashish Vaswani, Noam Shazeer, Niki Parmar, Jakob Uszkoreit, Llion Jones, Aidan N Gomez, Łukasz Kaiser, and Illia Polosukhin. 2017. Attention is all you need. In *Advances in neural information processing systems*, pages 5998–6008.

Ziang Xie, Guillaume Genthial, Stanley Xie, Andrew Ng, and Dan Jurafsky. 2018. Noising and denoising natural language: Diverse backtranslation for grammar correction. In *Proceedings of the 2018 Conference of the North American Chapter of the Association for Computational Linguistics: Human Language Technologies, Volume 1 (Long Papers)*, pages 619–628, New Orleans, Louisiana. Association for Computational Linguistics.

Helen Yannakoudakis, Ted Briscoe, and Ben Medlock. 2011. A new dataset and method for automatically grading ESOL texts. In *Proceedings of the 49th Annual Meeting of the Association for Computational Linguistics: Human Language Technologies*, pages 180–189, Portland, Oregon, USA. Association for Computational Linguistics.

Wei Zhao, Liang Wang, Kewei Shen, Ruoyu Jia, and Jingming Liu. 2019. Improving grammatical error correction via pre-training a copy-augmented architecture with unlabeled data. In *Proceedings of the 2019 Conference of the North American Chapter of the Association for Computational Linguistics: Human Language Technologies, Volume 1 (Long and Short Papers)*, pages 156–165, Minneapolis, Minnesota. Association for Computational Linguistics.

Evaluation of automatic collocation extraction methods for language learning

Vishal Bhalla
Department of Informatics
Technical University of Munich
Arcisstraße 21, 80333
München, Germany
vishal.bhalla@tum.de

Klara Klimcikova
Department of English and American Studies
Ludwig Maximilian University of Munich
Schellingstrae 3, 80799
München, Germany
k.klimcikova@lmu.de

Abstract

A number of methods have been proposed to automatically extract collocations, i.e., conventionalized lexical combinations, from text corpora. However, the attempts to evaluate and compare them with a specific application in mind lag behind. This paper compares three end-to-end resources for collocation learning, all of which used the same corpus but different methods. Adopting a gold-standard evaluation method, the results show that the method of dependency parsing outperforms regex-over-pos in collocation identification. The lexical association measures (AMs) used for collocation ranking perform about the same overall but differently for individual collocation types. Further analysis has also revealed that there are considerable differences between other commonly used AMs.

1 Introduction

Collocations, as the most common manifestation of formulaic language, have attracted a great deal of research in the last decade (Wray, 2012). Most of the research on collocations has been connected to their definition (section 2.1) and extraction (section 2.2), but also to their acquisition, and consequently teaching. Herbst and Schmid (2014) argue, "Any reflection upon what is important in the learning and, consequently, also in the teaching of a foreign language will have to take into account the crucial role of conventionalized but unpredictable collocations. Any attempt by a learner to achieve some kind of near-nativeness will have to include facts of language such as the fact that it is *lay* or *set the table* in English, but *Tisch decken* in German, and *mettre la table* in French" (p. 1).

Collocation learning comes down to three main benefits for language learners: accurate production, efficient comprehension and increased fluency of processing (e.g., Men, 2017; Durrant and Mathews-Aydınlı, 2011). To increase their language proficiency, beginners and advanced learners often look up for words and it's common collocates online, using a mobile app or web browser and it benefits to provide personalized items, tailored to the user's interest and proficiency. Examples of using collocations for building educational applications include question generation (e.g., Lin et al., 2007), distractor generation (e.g., Liu et al., 2005; Lee and Seneff, 2007) for multiple choice cloze items and an online collocation writing assistant - Collocation Inspector (Wu et al., 2010a) in the form of a web service.

Despite their widely recognized importance and ubiquity in language use, collocations pose a great challenge for language learners thanks to their arbitrary nature and the learner's insufficient experience with the target language (Ellis, 2012). Thus, there is a pressing need to create resources for language learners to support their explicit collocation learning. Given the vast amount of collocations and the different goals of language learners, various methods have been proposed to extract them automatically from text. Yet it is still not conclusive which one performs the best for language learning and "the selection of one or another seems to be somewhat arbitrary" (González Fernández and Schmitt, 2015) (p. 96).

This paper[1] attempts to evaluate three end-to-end resources of collocations built for language learning: Sketch Engine[2] (Kilgarriff et al., 2014), Flexible Language Acquisition (FLAX)[3] (Wu, 2010) and Elia (Bhalla et al., 2018). They use the same British Academic Written English (BAWE) corpus (Nesi, 2011), but different meth-

---

[1]Code, data and evaluation results are available at https://github.com/vishalbhalla/autocoleval
[2]https://www.sketchengine.eu/
[3]http://flax.nzdl.org/greenstone3/flax

Proceedings of the Fourteenth Workshop on Innovative Use of NLP for Building Educational Applications, pages 264–274
Florence, Italy, August 2, 2019. ©2019 Association for Computational Linguistics

ods for collocation identification, i.e., regex-over-pos, n-grams combined with regex-over-pos and dependency parsing, respectively, and also different association measures for collocation ranking, i.e., Log Dice, raw frequency and Formula Teaching Worth (FTW). On top of that, we compare other widely used lexical association measures of MI, MI2, MI3, t-score, log-likelihood, Salience and Delta P using the data from the best performing candidate identification method as a baseline. For our evaluation, we use the expert-judged Academic Collocation List (ACL) (Ackermann and Chen, 2013) as a reference set (section 3.1), and calculate the recall and precision metrics separately for collocation identification and ranking.

2 Theoretical Background

2.1 Notion of Collocation

Among the many different interpretations of collocations in the literature, three leading approaches can be distinguished: psychological, phraseological and distributional (Men, 2017).

The psychological approach envisages collocations as lexical associations in the mental lexicon of language users underlying their fluent and meaningful language use (e.g., Ellis et al., 2008). This perspective on collocations is supported by the evidence from psycholinguistic research using reaction time tasks, free associations tasks, self-paced reading and eye-tracking which suggests that collocations are holistically stored as chunks and thus processed faster (Wray, 2012). However, as found out by Meara (2009), the storage of word associations in the mental lexicon of native speakers is different from that of nonnative speakers.

The phraseological approach focuses predominantly on delimiting collocations (*call a meeting*) from free word combinations with a predictable meaning (*call a doctor*), on the one hand, and fixed idioms with an unpredictable meaning (*call it a day*) on the other (e.g., Cowie, 1998) by defining a set of criteria related to the compositionality of meaning and fixedness of form. Schmitt (2010) argues that such approach is rather problematic for the identification task as it is not clear how to operationalize such criteria without making it subjective and labor-intensive.

The distributional approach, also called Firthian or frequency-based, shifts the focus from the semantic aspects of collocations to structural. As Sinclair (1991) put it, "Collocation is the co-occurrence of two or more words within a short space of each other in a text. The usual measure of proximity is a maximum of four words intervening" (p. 170). Following this definition, various criteria have been considered for identifying collocation, e.g., distance, frequency, exclusivity, directionality, dispersion, type-token distribution and connectivity (Brezina et al., 2015). However, some researchers (e.g., Bartsch, 2004) argue that because of the little account of syntactic features of the words, it fails to capture certain collocations, e.g., the collocation *collect stamps* in the sentence *They collect many things, but chiefly stamps,* or vice versa, captures false collocations, such as *things but.*

Despite the obvious differences, there is considerable overlap between the three approaches as Durrant and Mathews-Aydnl (2011) rightly point out, "Non-compositionality and high frequency of occurrence can both be cited as evidence for holistic mental storage, and non-substitutability of parts can be evidenced in terms of co-occurrence frequencies in a corpus" (p. 59). It is precisely this extended notion of two-word collocations which was adopted by the collocation references under investigation in this study.

2.2 Automatic Extraction of Collocations

The task of collocation extraction is usually split into two steps, that of candidate identification which automatically generates a list of potential collocations from a text according to some criteria, and that of candidate ranking, which ranks the list to keep the best collocations on top according to some association measure (Seretan, 2008).

2.2.1 Candidate Identification

In the candidate identification step, four prominent methods can be distinguished based on the proximity of words and the amount of linguistic information used: window, n-gram, regex-over-pos and parsing. The first two are based on linear proximity whereas the other two are on syntactic proximity.

The window-based method (e.g., Brezina et al., 2015) identifies collocations within a window of n words before and after the target word. It belongs to the most commonly known and used and directly follows the Firthian definition of collocations. Similarly, the n-gram method (e.g., Smadja and McKeown, 1990), extracts sequences of adjacent n words including the target word. The application of these two methods can vary along several dimensions, e.g., the nature of words considered, such as word forms, lemmas or word families (Seretan, 2008), the context span on the left and right or the number of grams, part-of-speech filtering, etc. However, due to the lack of linguistic information used, these methods are prone to many recall and precision errors (for a detailed discussion, see Lehmann and Schneider, 2009).

In contrast to the previous two methods, the regex-over-pos method takes into account the grammatical relations between words (e.g., Wu, 2010). It identifies collocations in text via regular expressions over part-of-speech tags which match a certain grammatical pattern of the collocation. An alternative, though less frequent, method identifies collocations in a syntactic relation via parsing (Seretan, 2008), and thus accounts for the syntactic flexibility feature of collocations. Bartsch and Evert (2014) found out that collocation extraction using parsing method improved the results in comparison to the window method. However, they also caution that the success depends on the accuracy of the parser and the set of grammatical relations used.

2.2.2 Candidate Ranking

The next step of candidate ranking entails measuring the strength of association between the two words, hence association measure (AMs). In principle, AMs compare the observed and expected frequencies of collocations in different ways, and thus differ in how much they highlight or downplay different features of collocations (for a detailed overview, see Pecina, 2010). There is no single best performing AM but rather the choice of an appropriate measure depends on the particular purpose and theoretical criteria. In language learning research and practice, the following AMs have received most attention: raw frequency, MI, MI2, MI3, Log Dice, t-score, log-likelihood, Salience, FTW and Delta P.

The Mutual Information (MI) measure prioritizes rare exclusivity of collocations which is strongly linked to predictability (Gablasova et al., 2017). However, it is also biased towards low-frequency combinations which can be circumvented by setting a minimum frequency threshold or giving extra weight to the collocation frequency by squaring (MI2) or cubing (MI3).

The Log Dice score is similar to MI2 and highlights the exclusivity of word combinations without putting too much weight to rare combinations. However, Log Dice, in contrast to MI2, is suitable for comparing scores from different corpora and has been described as a "lexicographer-friendly association score" (Rychlỳ, 2008, p. 6-9). Another measure adjusted for lexicographic purposes is Salience, the forerunner of Log Dice, which combines the strengths of MI and log frequency (Kilgarriff and Tugwell, 2002).

The t-score represents the strength of association between words by calculating the probability that a certain collocation will occur without considering the level of significance (Pecina, 2010). It prioritizes the frequency of the whole collocation, and hence there is a tendency for frequent collocations to rank higher.

The only measure created specifically for pedagogical purposes is the Formula Teaching Worth (FTW) which is again a combined measure of MI and the raw frequency with more weight given to the former. It was derived from an empirical research using both statistical measures and instructor judgments. Basically, the score represents "a prediction of how instructors would judge their teaching worth" (Simpson-Vlach and Ellis, 2010, p. 496).

In contrast to the previous measures, log-likelihood is a statistic which determines whether the word combination occurs more frequently than chance or not. In particular, the score does not provide information on "how large the difference is" but rather "whether we have enough evidence in the data to reject the null hypothesis" (Brezina et al., 2015, p. 161).

The last measure is Delta P which takes directionality into account and calculates the strength of the attraction between two words for each word separately. Therefore, in contrast to all the previous measures, it does not treat the collocational relationship as symmetrical (Gries, 2013).

3 Methodology

3.1 Reference Set

The recently compiled Academic Collocation List (ACL) (Ackermann and Chen, 2013) was selected as the reference set (gold standard) to be compared against the test sets. Five main considerations drove this decision: First, it needed to be in line with the nature of the BAWE[4] corpus that was cho-

---

[4] https://www.coventry.ac.uk/
research/research-directories/

sen as a source input for extracting collocations. BAWE contains around 3000 good-standard student assignments (with 6,506,995 words), evenly distributed across four broad disciplinary areas (Arts and Humanities, Social Sciences, Life Sciences and Physical Sciences) and across four levels of study (undergraduate and taught masters level). Since BAWE is a collection of academic writing of university students, the baseline set should also consist of academic collocations. Second, it should contain collocations consisting of two words as all the three resources focus on two-word collocations. Third, the collocations should preferably be grouped into collocation types based on their word classes or syntactic functions as in the test sets. Fourth, the reference set should be human-made or human-judged to ensure the quality of collocations. And finally, it should be compiled for pedagogical purposes.

The ACL comprises of 2,469 lexical collocations in written academic English and is based on a written part of the Pearson International Corpus of Academic English (PICAE) of around 25 million words. It was carefully compiled using the combination of automatic computational analysis to ensure an adequate recall and human judgment to ensure the quality and relevance of the collocations for pedagogical purposes. Consisting of the most frequent and pedagogically relevant entries, ACL can therefore be immediately operationalized by English for Academic Purposes (EAP) teachers and students. By highlighting the most important cross-disciplinary collocations, the ACL can help learners increase their collocational competence and thus their proficiency in academic English. The collocations are grouped into eight collocation types: adjective + noun, noun + noun, verb + noun, verb + adjective, adverb + verb, verb + adverb, adverb + verb past participle, adverb + adjective.

To make it comparable to the test sets, we lemmatized all its inflected word forms using an automatic lemmatization tool from SpaCy[5] and then manually checked all the errors. Next, it was organized by headwords with the POS tags *noun*, *adjective* and *verb*, grouped by possible collocation types, and with the respective collocates appended resulting in a list of 1,455 headwords, 11 collocation types and 4,626 collocations as presented in

Collocation Type	Headwords	Collocations
n1_n2	39	62
n2_n1	52	62
n2_v1	156	306
n2_adj1	483	1769
v1_n2	107	306
v1_adj2	8	30
v1_adv2	19	29
v2_adv1	79	139
adj1_n2	416	1769
adj2_v1	23	30
adj2_adv1	73	124
Total	1455	4626

Table 1: Reference set grouped by collocation types starting with a headword where noun is *n*, adjective is *adj*, verb is *v*, adverb is *adv* and the numbers *1* and *2* indicate their positions in the collocation pair.

Table 1. For example, the notation of the collocation type *n2_adj1* indicates that the headword is a noun (*n*) in the 2nd position in the collocation pair, and the collocate is an adjective (*adj*) in the 1st position, so when the learner searches the adjectival collocates for the word *feature*, it gives him the collocate *distinguishing* among others.

3.2 Tests sets

3.2.1 Sketch Engine

Sketch Engine (SE) is an online corpus software with a wide range of functions and preloaded corpora which can be used for pedagogical purposes either indirectly, in the creation of textbooks and dictionaries, or directly in the classroom (Kilgarriff et al., 2014). One of its functions is the Word Sketch for extracting collocations in a range of grammatical patterns, and one of its corpora is BAWE. The corpus is automatically POS-tagged using CLAWS 7[6] and the collocations are identified with the help of their embedded Sketch Grammar[7] which is a set of regular expressions over POS tags. The retrieved collocates are then organized based on the grammatical relation to the headword and within each relation sorted by the Log Dice measure (alternatively, raw frequency).

The SE collocations were extracted using web scraping wherein, firstly, the URL was built us-

[5] https://spacy.io/
current-projects/2015/
british-academic-written-english-corpus-bawe
[6] https://www.sketchengine.eu/
english-claws7-part-of-speech-tagset/
[7] For a full list of Sketch Grammar, see https://the.sketchengine.co.uk/corpus/wsdef?
corpname=preloaded/bawe2

ACL	Sketch Engine	FLAX	Elia
n1_n2	modifies	n-nn	NOUN + NOUN
n2_n1	modifier	n-nn	NOUN + NOUN
n2_v1	object_of	n-vn	VERB + NOUN
n2_adj1	modifier	n-an	ADJ + NOUN
v1_n2	object	v-vn	VERB + NOUN
v1_adj2	adj_comp np_adj_comp	v-vppa	VERB + ADJ
v1_adv2	modifier	v-vr	VERB + ADV
v2_adv1	modifier	v-rv	VERB + ADV
adj1_n2	modifies	a-an	ADJ + NOUN
adj2_v1	adj_comp_of np_adj_comp_of	a-vppa	VERB + ADJ
adj2_adv1	modifier	a-ra	ADV + ADJ

Table 2: Mapping of collocation types between the reference set (ACL) and test sets (Sketch Engine, FLAX, Elia)

ing the lemma and POS tag of each word and then the eleven collocation types from the reference set were mapped to the collocation types used at SE to pickup the collocations of interest (Table 2). Picking up all the headwords (lemmas) from the reference set, the count and score of each collocate was stored in an intermediate file for each lemma in order to generate SE files[8] for the final evaluation.

3.2.2 FLAX

FLAX (Flexible Language Acquisition) is an online library and tool specifically created for collocation learning (Wu, 2010). It consists of large collections of collocations and phrases extracted from different corpora, one of which is BAWE, and can be used for searching collocations for a particular word or for automatic generation of a variety of collocation exercises and games. The collocations are extracted using the combination of n-gram and regex over-pos methods which involved the following steps. Firstly, n-grams (n=5) are extracted from the corpus and tagged with the OpenNLP[9] tagger. The tagged 5-grams are then matched against a set of regular expressions based on predefined collocation types[10]. Finally, the individual collocations organized by collocation types are then sorted by raw frequency within each collocation type (Wu, 2010, p. 98).

For the evaluation, all FLAX collocations[11]

were extracted using the same web scraping process as for SE. However, as FLAX operates on word forms in contrast to the reference set operating on lemmas, all lemmas from the reference set had to be converted to their word forms using Pattern[12] (Smedt and Daelemans, 2012) to get the corresponding collocations from FLAX for each headword in the reference set and then remapped back to its lemma to continue with the same evaluation flow as in SE.

3.2.3 Elia

Elia[13] is an intelligent personal assistant for language learning which provides immediate assistance for English learners when they use English online (Bhalla et al., 2018). One of its design features is to provide a learner with a list of collocates for a given word, which are in line with the learner's proficiency level. It is based on BAWE where, firstly, all the dependency relations using the SpaCy parser[14] are extracted and mapped to a predefined set of 15 collocation types and then run for the Academic Vocabulary List (Gardner and Davies, 2013) of 20,000 most frequent academic words from the Corpus of Contemporary American English (COCA)[15]. Subsequently, the collocations are organized for each headword (lemma)

---

[8]Code and data in the 'sketchengine' folder of the Supplementary Material.

[9]http://opennlp.apache.org/

[10]For a full list of the collocation types with examples, see Wu et al. (2010b, p. 9).

[11]Code and data in the 'flax' folder of the Supplementary Material.

[12]https://github.com/clips/pattern

[13]Elia is not available online yet, however, the code to generate the database of collocations can be accessed at https://drive.google.com/open?id=1FGFy_yp797saphx8-wzcLkMxQbkCVZlp

[14]https://spacy.io/usage/linguistic-features#section-dependency-parse

[15]https://corpus.byu.edu/coca/

and collocation type and ranked according to the Teaching Worth Formula (Simpson-Vlach and Ellis, 2010).

For the evaluation, only the collocations for the headwords and collocation type present in the reference set were filtered out from Elia after running the code from the link shared previously. On running this setup, intermediate files for each headword containing all its collocates along with the chosen metric were generated. These are in line with the web scraping files from Sketch Engine and FLAX in order to generate the final evaluation files[16].

4 Results and Discussion

For the comparative evaluation of the three test sets, the standard metric recall and precision were calculated separately for identification and ranking of collocations grouped into collocation types. On top of that, additional evaluation was performed on the best performing test set as a baseline to compare different collocation ranking measures introduced in section 2.2.2.

4.1 Candidate Identification

Table 3 clearly shows that the method of dependency parsing used by Elia resulted in higher overall recall (99%) than the method of regex-over-pos used by Sketch Engine (91%) and FLAX (84%). It seems that some dependency parsers have reached a sufficiently high accuracy to be used for collocation extraction or other NLP tasks (Levy et al., 2015). At the same time, there are obvious differences between Sketch Engine and FLAX, despite using the same method (regex-over-pos), which leads to the conclusion that manual mappings of collocation types and syntactic patterns might be as important as the method itself. Another plausible explanation could be the fact that FLAX used regex patterns over 5-grams extracted from the corpus whereas Sketch Engine over full sentences.

Turning to individual collocation types (CTs), all of them achieved a high recall of above 80% in all three test sets, except for *v1_adj2* and *adj2_v1* in FLAX with a recall of only 13% and 7% respectively. Tempting as it might seem, this does not explain the lowest overall recall for FLAX as they account for only 7% (54 out of 710) of all missed collocations. FLAX performed especially

---

[16]Code and data in the 'elia' folder of the Supplementary Material.

Collocation Type	SE		FL		EL	
	R	P	R	P	R	P
n1_n2	89	6	82	2	98	1
n2_n1	89	5	81	1	98	0
n2_v1	94	8	88	3	99	1
n2_adj1	88	10	86	4	99	2
v1_n2	92	4	84	2	99	1
v1_adj2	90	10	13	2	100	1
v1_adv2	90	5	100	4	100	1
v2_adv1	92	9	90	5	99	2
adj1_n2	93	6	84	5	99	2
adj2_v1	90	40	7	9	100	7
adj2_adv1	87	10	89	8	99	5
Total	91	**7**	84	4	**99**	2

Table 3: Candidate identification comparison of Sketch Engine (SE), FLAX (FL) and Elia (EL) across collocation types with the recall (R) and precision (P) values in percentages.

well for *v1_adv2* (100%) in comparison to its other CTs starting from 90% *(v2_adv1)* downwards to 7% *(adj2_v1)*. On the other hand, the results for Sketch Engine are rather consistent across individual CTs ranging from 87% *(adj2_adv1)* to 94% *(n2_v1)*. The same applies for Elia ranging from 98% *(n1_n2, n2_n1)* to 100% *(v1_adj2, adj2_v1, v1_adv2)*.

Looking closer at the results for Elia, we found out that exactly one half (19) of all the missed collocations (38) was due to parsing or tagging errors whereas the other half was due to different type classification; for example, the collocation *learning activity* was grouped under *n2_adj1* in the reference set whereas, in Elia, it was assigned to *n1_n2*, and thus missed. This might as well be the case for some of the missed collocations in Sketch Engine and FLAX.

The precision, on the other hand, is very low for all (the highest 7% reached by Sketch Engine) at the expense of high recall. This, however, is not that important at this stage since the next step of ranking should shift all the irrelevant collocations to the bottom.

4.2 Candidate Ranking

For candidate ranking, recall and precision values were calculated for three samples of *n*-best candidates per headword for each test set: Top 4,626 where *n* refers to the exact number of collocates

Collocation Type	Top 4,626			Top 14,550						Top 29,100					
	SE	FL	EL	SE		FL		EL		SE		FL		EL	
	R=P	R=P	R=P	R	P	R	P	R	P	R	P	R	P	R	P
n1_n2	19	15	10	58	10	52	8	37	6	77	8	73	6	68	5
n2_n1	31	23	19	69	10	61	7	56	7	82	8	68	4	69	4
n2_v1	42	44	48	73	15	70	14	83	16	87	10	75	8	90	9
n2_adj1	36	41	39	50	18	52	19	50	18	68	13	66	12	65	12
v1_n2	37	31	35	55	16	47	14	52	15	68	10	57	8	64	9
v1_adj2	47	0	43	73	28	3	4	63	24	80	17	7	5	73	14
v1_adv2	48	34	34	86	13	86	13	83	13	90	8	97	8	86	7
v2_adv1	46	52	37	81	15	79	15	80	14	91	11	86	9	90	8
adj1_n2	36	43	44	40	18	47	21	49	20	57	13	61	14	64	14
adj2_v1	70	3	33	90	29	7	9	97	15	90	29	7	9	100	10
adj2_adv1	37	54	28	80	16	82	17	80	14	87	11	85	11	89	8
Total	37	**41**	40	51	**17**	52	**17**	**54**	**17**	67	**12**	65	11	**68**	11

Table 4: Candidate ranking comparison of Sketch Engine (SE), FLAX (FL) and Elia (EL) across collocation types for three samples: Top 4,626 (*n*-best collocates per headword where *n* refers to the number of collocations per headword in the reference set), Top 14,550 (10-best collocates per headword) and Top 29,100 (20-best collocates per headword) with the recall (R) and precision (P) values in percentages. Note that the recall and precision results for the top 4,626 are the same (i.e. R=P) because the number of missed collocations (false negatives) and unwanted collocations (false positives) is the same. And this is because the number of the TOP collocations in the first test sample (4,626) is the same as the total number of collocations in the reference set (4,626).

per each headword in the reference set, Top 14,550 to the 10-best collocates per headword, and Top 29,100 to the 20-best collocates per headword.

As illustrated in Table 4, the association measure Log Dice used by Sketch Engine performed slightly worse (37%) overall than Elia (40%) using FTW, a combination of MI and frequency, and FLAX (41%) using raw frequency for the Top 4,626 sample. As the sample increased to 14,550, Elia with a recall of 54% outperformed FLAX (52%) and Sketch Engine (51%). In the even larger sample of 29,100, Elia was still marginally better reaching 68% whereas Sketch Engine outperformed FLAX with a recall of 67% and 65% respectively. It seems that Log Dice improves its performance as more of the data is examined whereas raw frequency acts in quite the opposite way. However, it should also be pointed out that the differences between all of the scores are very subtle, less than 4% in all the samples. This is even more pronounced in the overall precision results which, for all three resources, are the same (17%) in Top 14,550 and almost the same (12%, 11%, 11%) in Top 29,100.

Looking at the individual CTs, an interesting picture of differences emerges. Sketch Engine's

measure performed consistently better for *n1_n2*, *n2_n1*, *v1_n2* and *v1_adj2* in all three samples. Elia's measure performs consistently better for *n2_v1* and *adj1_n2*. FLAX seems to perform better only for *v2_adv1* and *adj2_adv1* for Top 4,626 but it is not consistent for the other samples. Variability can be found not only among individual resources but also among individual CTs within one resource. For example, in Top 4,626, Sketch Engine reaches a recall of 19% for *n1_n2* and of as high as 70% for *adj2_v1*. Recall values for Elia range from 37% (*n1_n2*) to 97% (*adj2_v1*) and for FLAX from 7% (*adj2_v1*) to 86% (*v1_adv2*) in Top 14,550. The syntactic structure underlying collocations seems to have a great impact on the results, and thus should always be considered and specified as already suggested in some previous studies (e.g., Evert and Krenn, 2001; Bartsch and Evert, 2014).

To sum it up, despite the apparent similarities in the overall recall and precision values, it would be misleading to conclude that the three measures are equally efficient since they had a different data from the identification step to start with. It becomes clear when looking at the individual collocation types, for example *v1_adj1* where Elia

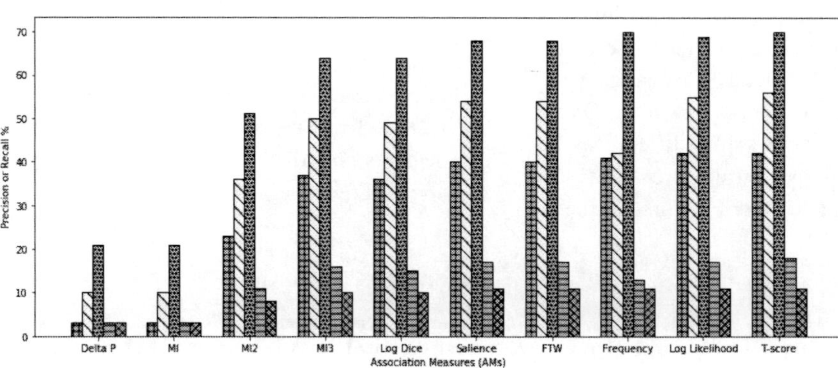

Figure 1: Comparison of different association measures (AMs) using Elia as a baseline.

reached 43% as compared to 0% by FLAX. This could have been caused by the low recall (13%) of FLAX in the identification part. The issue with credit assignment is that it is not clear how much of the success can be attributed to the identification method discussed in the previous section and how much to the metric itself. To exclude the identification method as a factor, we decided to perform another analysis: the comparison of different AMs using the best-performing data from the candidate identification step, that is Elia, as a baseline to find out the differences when all things being equal.

4.2.1 Comparison of Different AMs with Elia as a Baseline

Using Elia collocations as a baseline, we have computed recall and precision for ten different ranking measures described in section 2.2.2. As in the previous section, we have computed it separately for the three samples of Top 4,626, Top 14,550 and Top 29,100, however, this time not for all individual CTs separately. The formulas used to compute each of the different AMs can be found in Brezina et al. (2015, p. 169-170).

The results on candidate ranking, arranged progressively by the best measures in Figure 1, show that recall curves for all AMs increase whereas precision curves decrease with the increased sample sizes as expected. In terms of coverage, the best performing measures are t-score and log likelihood across all samples with the recall values of 42%, 56%, 70% and 42%, 55%, 69% respectively. They are followed by Salience and FTW with the same values of 40%, 54%, 68%. All of these four measures exhibit a consistent behavior increasing by about 14% with the increased samples. On the other hand, the raw frequency mea-

sure, even though reaching similarly high scores for Top 4,262 (41%) and Top 29,100 (70%), increases only by 1% for Top 14,550. The next two measures MI3 and Log Dice lag slightly behind with the scores of 36%, 50%, 64% and 36%, 49%, 64% respectively, consistently increasing by about 14%. The MI2 score performs significantly worse with a recall of 23%, 36%, 51%. The most collocations are missed by the measures Delta P and MI both reaching only a recall of 3%, 10%, 21%.

The precision values defining quality of the collocations point to very similar tendencies with t-score and log likelihood reaching the highest precision in all three samples with the scores of 42%, 18%, 11% and 42%, 17%, 11% respectively and with the FTW and Salience measures right behind, both with 40%, 17%, 11%. MI3 and Log Dice performs about the same with 37%, 16%, 10% and 36%, 15%, 10% respectively. Again, the MI2 score misses significantly more collocations than the previous measures reaching a precision of 23%, 11%, 8%. Surprisingly enough, MI and Delta P, both reached the lowest precision score of 3% for all samples. Thus, it can be concluded that the sample size does not affect the precision of the MI and Delta P association measures which, in the case of MI, is consistent with the previous findings by Evert and Krenn (2001).

These results question the dominant role of MI for collocation extraction (Gablasova et al., 2017), at least for language learning purposes. It also questions the assumption that Log Dice is fairly similar to MI or MI2 as our results suggests that it is actually more similar to MI3 (Gablasova et al., 2017). Furthermore, Delta P did not fulfill the expectations as expressed by Gries (2013). However, in defense of Delta P, it must be pointed out that the reference list did not indicate the direction of attraction for collocations, which is the underlying assumption of the Delta P measure, which might be the reason for the poor results. On the other hand, there are only subtle differences between some of the best-performing measures, such as log likelihood and t-score or FTW and Salience.

5   Conclusion

The aim of this study was to evaluate three collocation learning resources namely Sketch Engine, FLAX and Elia on a pedagogical reference - Academic Collocational List, where all of them use the same corpus of academic writings of university students but different methods for collocation identification and different lexical association measures for collocation ranking.

The findings indicate that using dependency parsing (Elia) for collocation identification led to much better results than using regular expressions over tagged corpus (Sketch Engine and FLAX). However, the success does not depend on the specific method entirely, but also on the quality of the set of syntactic structures. Using the same method with differently designed collocation types might lead to very different results, as was the case for Sketch Engine and FLAX.

The evaluation of collocation ranking has revealed that, overall, some of the association measures perform equally well, such as t-score, log-likelihood, FTW (used by Elia) and Salience. Raw frequency (used by FLAX) was also found to perform well but acting inconsistently across different sample sizes. The Log Dice measure (used by Sketch Engine) worked best for the majority of individual collocation types in comparison to raw frequency and FTW. On the other hand, the widely used MI and newly introduced Delta P were relatively poor in comparison to other AMs, but exhibited consistency in precision across varying sample sizes.

It has also become apparent that there are considerable differences between individual collocation types, and therefore should always be considered as a factor in collocation extraction. However, a future line of work is required to substantiate the consistency of these results on different reference lists and corpora.

Acknowledgments

We would like to thank Mrs. Wu for her insights on FLAX extraction, Aisulu for preparing the COCA list, Ivet for the help in large scale experiments and all the anonymous reviewers for their critical feedback.

References

Kirsten Ackermann and Yu-Hua Chen. 2013. Developing the Academic Collocation List (ACL)–A corpus-driven and expert-judged approach. *Journal of English for Academic Purposes*, 12(4):235–247.

Sabine Bartsch. 2004. *Structural and functional properties of collocations in English: A corpus study of lexical and pragmatic constraints on lexical co-occurrence*. Gunter Narr Verlag.

Sabine Bartsch and Stefan Evert. 2014. Towards a Firthian notion of collocation. *Network Strategies, Access Structures and Automatic Extraction of Lexicographical Information. 2nd Work Report of the Academic Network Internet Lexicography, OPAL–Online publizierte Arbeiten zur Linguistik. Institut für Deutsche Sprache, Mannheim, to appear*.

Vishal Bhalla, Klara Klimcikova, and Aisulu Rakhmetullina. 2018. The missing link between learners' language use and their language learning - Elia. In *Proceedings of the 13th Teaching and Language Corpora Conference*.

Vaclav Brezina, Tony McEnery, and Stephen Wattam. 2015. Collocations in context: A new perspective on collocation networks. *International Journal of Corpus Linguistics*, 20(2):139–173.

Anthony Paul Cowie. 1998. *Phraseology: Theory, analysis, and applications*. OUP Oxford.

Philip Durrant and Julie Mathews-Aydınlı. 2011. A function-first approach to identifying formulaic language in academic writing. *English for Specific Purposes*, 30(1):58–72.

Nick C Ellis. 2012. Formulaic language and second language acquisition: Zipf and the phrasal teddy bear. *Annual Review of Applied Linguistics*, 32:17–44.

Nick C Ellis, RITA Simpson-Vlach, and Carson Maynard. 2008. Formulaic language in native and second language speakers: Psycholinguistics, corpus linguistics, and TESOL. *Tesol Quarterly*, 42(3):375–396.

Stefan Evert and Brigitte Krenn. 2001. Methods for the qualitative evaluation of lexical association measures. In *Proceedings of the 39th Annual Meeting on Association for Computational Linguistics*, pages 188–195. Association for Computational Linguistics.

Dana Gablasova, Vaclav Brezina, and Tony McEnery. 2017. Collocations in Corpus-Based Language Learning Research: Identifying, Comparing, and Interpreting the Evidence. *Language Learning*, 67(S1):155–179.

Dee Gardner and Mark Davies. 2013. A new academic vocabulary list. *Applied Linguistics*, 35(3):305–327.

Beatriz González Fernández and Norbert Schmitt. 2015. How much collocation knowledge do L2 learners have? *ITL-International Journal of Applied Linguistics*, 166(1):94–126.

Stefan Th Gries. 2013. 50-something years of work on collocations. *International Journal of Corpus Linguistics*, 18(1):137–166.

Thomas Herbst, Hans-Jörg Schmid, and Susen Faulhaber. 2014. *Constructions Collocations Patterns*, volume 282. Walter de Gruyter GmbH & Co KG.

Adam Kilgarriff, Vít Baisa, Jan Bušta, Miloš Jakubíček, Vojtěch Kovář, Jan Michelfeit, Pavel Rychlỳ, and Vít Suchomel. 2014. The Sketch Engine: ten years on. *Lexicography*, 1(1):7–36.

Adam Kilgarriff and David Tugwell. 2002. Sketching words. *Lexicography and natural language processing: a festschrift in honour of BTS Atkins*, pages 125–137.

John Lee and Stephanie Seneff. 2007. Automatic generation of cloze items for prepositions. In *Eighth Annual Conference of the International Speech Communication Association*.

Hans Martin Lehmann and Gerold Schneider. 2009. Parser-based analysis of syntax-lexis interactions. *Language and computers studies in practical linguistics*, 68:477.

Omer Levy, Yoav Goldberg, and Ido Dagan. 2015. Improving distributional similarity with lessons learned from word embeddings. *Transactions of the Association for Computational Linguistics*, 3:211–225.

Yi-Chien Lin, Li-Chun Sung, and Meng Chang Chen. 2007. An automatic multiple-choice question generation scheme for english adjective understanding. In *Workshop on Modeling, Management and Generation of Problems/Questions in eLearning, the 15th International Conference on Computers in Education (ICCE 2007)*, pages 137–142.

Chao-Lin Liu, Chun-Hung Wang, Zhao-Ming Gao, and Shang-Ming Huang. 2005. Applications of lexical information for algorithmically composing multiple-choice cloze items. In *Proceedings of the second workshop on Building Educational Applications Using NLP*, pages 1–8. Association for Computational Linguistics.

Paul Meara. 2009. Simulating word associations in an l2: approaches to lexical organisation. *International Journal of English Studies*, 7(2):1–20.

Haiyan Men. 2017. *Vocabulary Increase and Collocation Learning: A Corpus-Based Cross-sectional Study of Chinese Learners of English*. Springer.

Hilary Nesi. 2011. BAWE: An introduction to a new resource. *New trends in corpora and language learning*, pages 213–228.

Pavel Pecina. 2010. Lexical association measures and collocation extraction. *Language resources and evaluation*, 44(1-2):137–158.

Pavel Rychlỳ. 2008. A lexicographer-friendly association score. *Proceedings of Recent Advances in Slavonic Natural Language Processing, RASLAN*, 2008:6–9.

Norbert Schmitt. 2010. *Researching vocabulary: A vocabulary research manual*. Springer.

Violeta Seretan. 2008. *Collocation extraction based on syntactic parsing*. Ph.D. thesis, Ph. D. thesis, University of Geneva.

Rita Simpson-Vlach and Nick C Ellis. 2010. An academic formulas list: New methods in phraseology research. *Applied linguistics*, 31(4):487–512.

John Sinclair. 1991. *Corpus, concordance, collocation*. Oxford University Press.

Frank A Smadja and Kathleen R McKeown. 1990. Automatically extracting and representing collocations for language generation. In *Proceedings of the 28th annual meeting on Association for Computational Linguistics*, pages 252–259. Association for Computational Linguistics.

Tom De Smedt and Walter Daelemans. 2012. Pattern for python. *Journal of Machine Learning Research*, 13(Jun):2063–2067.

Alison Wray. 2012. What do we (think we) know about formulaic language? An evaluation of the current state of play. *Annual Review of Applied Linguistics*, 32:231–254.

Jian-Cheng Wu, Yu-Chia Chang, Teruko Mitamura, and Jason S Chang. 2010a. Automatic collocation suggestion in academic writing. In *Proceedings of the ACL 2010 Conference Short Papers*, pages 115–119. Association for Computational Linguistics.

Shaoqun Wu. 2010. *Supporting collocation learning*. Ph.D. thesis, University of Waikato.

Shaoqun Wu, Margaret Franken, and Ian H Witten. 2010b. Supporting collocation learning with a digital library. *Computer assisted language learning*, 23(1):87–110.

A Formulas

The formulas for all the Association Measures (AMs) tried out for Elia can be found at p. 169-170 of (Brezina et al., 2015).

B Supplemental Material

The authors have also released the code, reference data, evaluation results and plots with a Readme document on Github at `https://github.com/vishalbhalla/autocoleval` to assist the incremental research in the ACL-NLP community. It contains the code for web scraping of both Sketch Engine and FLAX, as well as extracting the filtered collocations for Elia. Since, the Data and Evaluation files for all the three test sets (Sketch Engine, FLAX and Elia) are large, these files can be accessed from `https://drive.google.com/open?id=17eydi0KkviG2VxB121_oNt5LAhuQ6FR0`.

Anglicized Words and Misspelled Cognates
in Native Language Identification

Ilia Markov[1], Vivi Nastase[2], Carlo Strapparava[3]

[1]CLiPS, University of Antwerp, Antwerp, Belgium
[2]University of Heidelberg, Heidelberg, Germany
[3]Fondazione Bruno Kessler, Trento, Italy
`ilia.markov@uantwerpen.be`, `nastase@cl.uni-heidelberg.de`,
`strappa@fbk.eu`

Abstract

In this paper, we present experiments that estimate the impact of specific lexical choices of people writing in a second language (L2). In particular, we look at misspelled words that indicate lexical uncertainty on the part of the author, and separate them into three categories: misspelled cognates, "L2-ed" (in our case, anglicized) words, and all other spelling errors. We test the assumption that such errors contain clues about the native language of an essay's author through the task of native language identification. The results of the experiments show that the information brought by each of these categories is complementary. We also note that while the distribution of such features changes with the proficiency level of the writer, their contribution towards native language identification remains significant at all levels.

1 Introduction

Producing an utterance in a language, be it the native, second or n-th one, relies in large part on the vocabulary range of the speaker. When dealing with a second language L2, this range may be correctly or incorrectly expanded through commonalities or similarities of form with the vocabulary of the native language L1. Examples of this process are cognates, which are words that have the same ancestors or were derived from the same sources, that we often approximate in computational approaches as words having similar forms and similar meaning in L1 and L2, for example, SPA. *religión* and ENG. *religion*. Research in psycholinguistics and native language identification have shown that using cognates when producing L2 is common and shared across native speakers of the same L1 to the degree that a quite accurate phylogenetic language tree can be reconstructed (Rabinovich et al., 2018).

In this paper, we analyze in parallel three of the phenomena responsible for the *incorrect* expansion of L2's vocabulary using L1 material: misspelled cognates, L2-ed words, and all other spelling errors. Misspelled cognates are words that are misspellings from the point of view of L2, but have a very close form in L2 and L1. L2-ed words are something like false cognates (not in the sense of false friends): words in L1 that were "adjusted" to seem and sound like legitimate L2 words. For example, a Spanish native speaker could use the incorrectly anglicized word *lentaly* instead of *slowly* (SPA. *lentamente*). From the point of view of the L2 vocabulary, L2-ed words are spelling errors, but they are special because they have a very similar L1 form. Chen et al. (2017) have shown that spelling errors, represented as character n-grams, are also very indicative of an author's L1, as they may capture language-specific sound-to-spelling mappings.

The experiments presented in this paper aim to analyze how much each of these phenomena reveal about the L2 speaker's native language. We analyze misspelled words and split them into cognates, L2-ed words or all other misspellings, and analyze their impact through the task of native language identification (NLI). The goal of NLI is to identify the native language (L1) of a person based on his/her writing in the second language (L2). The underlying hypothesis is that the L1 influences learners' second language writing as a result of the language transfer effect (Odlin, 1989). NLI is usually approached as a multi-class classification problem of assigning class labels representing L1s to essays written in L2. The state-of-the-art results for this task are usually in the 80%–90% accuracy range, depending on the number of languages being considered, amount of data, etc. NLI is an interesting example of a task which is hard to perform for humans: the study of human per-

Proceedings of the Fourteenth Workshop on Innovative Use of NLP for Building Educational Applications, pages 275–284
Florence, Italy, August 2, 2019. ©2019 Association for Computational Linguistics

formance in NLI (Malmasi et al., 2015) showed that automated systems significantly outperform human annotators (73% vs. 37% accuracy, respectively).

We test the impact of the three phenomena – misspelled cognates, L2-ed words, spelling errors – on the subsets of the TOEFL (Blanchard et al., 2013) and ICLE (Granger et al., 2009) datasets that cover languages that use the Latin script. The results of the multi-class classification experiments show that the role of all these phenomena is significant. Higher results are achieved when features representing each of these are combined, indicating that they are complementary for the NLI task. Experiments on data split by proficiency levels show that the L2-ed based features have a higher impact the lower the proficiency level, while the influence of the cognates grows with the proficiency level. This is not surprising, but it reveals an interesting phenomenon – when people do not know a word in a target language, they may make a "false cognate", and while the vocabulary of a proficient speaker is larger, they still resort occasionally to this incorrect lexicon expansion. Understanding the source and effects of lexical choice in L2 speakers, and how this changes with proficiency levels, could have direct applications in second language teaching.

2   Related Work

Cognates. Cognates are words that have the same ancestor, or were derived from the same "borrowed" sources. The "cognatehood" of word pairs may be obscured by phonological and spelling changes in different languages, and by the drift in their meaning from the common source: e.g., *milk* (ENG.), *latte* (ITA.), *gala* (GER.) are all cognates despite their current different forms, while *journey* (ENG.) and *journeé* (FRA. *day*) have a common etymological ancestor but their current meaning has lost this connection (*journey* used to mean *a day's travelling*). Because of the lack of computational resources on word etymologies until relatively recently, cognates have been approximated in computational linguistics as words that have similar form and meaning. The influence of cognates as indicators of an author's

native language has been explored in various ways through the task of native language identification.[1]

Nicolai et al. (2013) add cognate-based features to frequently used ones (e.g., character and word n-grams, syntax production rules, misspelling features) for the NLI shared task 2013 (Tetreault et al., 2013). Cognates were detected by identifying misspelled words whose form is closer to an L2 word w_{L2} than to w_{L2}'s translation in L1. The authors report that cognate features, in spite of being extracted just for 4 out of 11 languages, improved the accuracy by 0.7% and reduced the relative error rate by about 4%.

Rabinovich et al. (2018) investigate the cognate effect on lexical choice in L2 of advanced non-native speakers. They construct a *focus set* of more than 1,000 words, that have synonyms (provided by WordNet) with different etymologies (provided by the Etymological WordNet), thus potentially leading to different patterns of usage for speakers with different L1s. The influence of cognates on lexical choice is measured through frequency of usage with respect to this list of words. Aggregated evidence for all texts belonging to the same L1 can be used to build a relatively accurate phylogenetic language tree for the Indo-European language family (31 languages).

Nastase and Strapparava (2017) did not look specifically at cognates, but used etymological information to build etymological ancestor profiles for sets of English essays written by different L1 speakers. This representation quantified the influence of different etymological ancestors when producing texts in L2, and showed that these influences are different depending on L1.

From the previous studies it is hard to see the quantitative impact of cognates on the NLI task: in the study by Nicolai et al. (2013) cognates were used in combination with a large number of features (including words and word 2-grams), while in (Nastase and Strapparava, 2017; Rabinovich et al., 2018) the authors were mostly concerned with reconstructing language family tree and not with the role of cognates in the task of NLI.

Spelling errors. Spelling errors were used in one of the first studies on NLI (Koppel et al., 2005). The authors focused on syntax errors and eight types of spelling errors, e.g., missing let-

---

[1]Distinguishing between actual cognates and false friends is not being done, so when we refer to cognates in the related literature or in our own work, we mean both.

ters, repeated letters, double letters appearing only once, among others. The relative frequency of each error type to the length of the essay was used as the corresponding feature value. When combining these with commonly used features, i.e., function words, the authors obtained 80.2% accuracy on a 5-way subset of the ICLE dataset.

Nicolai et al. (2013) focused on the misspelled part of a word and used pairs of correct and misspelled parts as character n-gram features. Misspelling features contributed 0.4% accuracy to their NLI shared task system when used in combination with other commonly used NLI features.

Chen et al. (2017) also explored spelling errors, testing the hypothesis that spelling errors capture L1-biased sound-to-spelling mappings. Spelling errors were represented as character n-grams, and added to other commonly used features (word, lemma, and character n-grams). Including these typo-based features leads to an increase in NLI accuracy of 1.2% on the TOEFL11 test set.

Flanagan and Hirokawa (2018) classified five L1s from the lang-8 dataset (Japanese, Chinese, Korean, Taiwanese, and Spanish) using 15 automatically identified types of writing errors, achieving higher results than when using unbiased words.

These studies clearly show that spelling errors are influenced by an author's L1. The source of such errors was not of interest though, and they may hide interesting linguistic phenomena, like cognates and L2-ed words.

L2-ed words. The combination of languages within one text has been studied before, under the name of code switching or code mixing, e.g., (Solorio et al., 2014). This switching/mixing though happens at the word level, and lexical items in the text belong fully to one language. In the phenomenon we study here, the switching/mixing happens below the word level, where the word in a language L1 is inflected or adjusted to "fit" language L2.

3 Methodology

To investigate the impact of L2-ed words and cognates, we use the native language identification task: we perform multi-class classification of essays written in L2 (English in our case) by people with different native languages (L1s) – with L1 as the class labels – using a representation of these essays through features that capture these

phenomena. We use two datasets – TOEFL and ICLE – previously used for NLI, and extract the subsets that cover languages that use a Latin script.

3.1 Datasets

We use two datasets commonly used in NLI research:

TOEFL (Blanchard et al., 2013): the ETS Corpus of Non-Native Written English (TOEFL11) contains 1,100 essays in English for 11 native languages. We used a 4-language subset of the corpus, focusing on the languages that use the Latin script: French, German, Italian, and Spanish. This subset, to which we refer as TOEFL4, contains 1,100 essays (with an average of 353 tokens per essay) for each of the four languages.

ICLE (Granger et al., 2009): consists of essays written by highly-proficient non-native college-level students of English. We used a 4-language subset of the corpus that represents the same languages as included in TOEFL4: French (347 essays), German (437), Italian (392), and Spanish (251). Overall, this subset, to which we refer as ICLE4, contains 1,427 essays with avg. 690 tokens/essay.

The four languages represented in the TOEFL4 and ICLE4 datasets have shared etymological ancestors and therefore shared cognates, which is a complicating factor in the classification.

3.2 Experiment setup

We used the (pre-)tokenized version of the TOEFL4 dataset and tokenized ICLE4 with the Natural Language Toolkit (NLTK) tokenizer[2], removing metadata in pre-processing. Each essay was represented through the sets of features described below, using term frequency (tf) weighting scheme and the liblinear scikit-learn (Pedregosa et al., 2011) implementation of Support Vector Machines (SVM) with OvR (one vs. the rest) multi-class strategy. We report classification accuracy on 10-fold cross-validation experiments.

3.3 Features

Following previous studies on NLI, e.g., (Markov et al., 2018a,b), we evaluate the impact of L2-ed words and cognates in combination with the part-

---

[2]http://www.nltk.org

of-speech (POS) tag and function word (FW) representations. POS tags and function words (FWs) are considered core features in NLI research (Malmasi and Dras, 2015), not susceptible to topic bias, unlike word and character n-grams (Brooke and Hirst, 2011).

An essay will be represented through various combinations of the feature sets we consider: POS & FW n-grams; n-grams from POS & FW sequences including word-level L1 information; character n-grams that represent misspelled words.

3.3.1 Part-of-speech tags and function words

POS features capture the morpho-syntactic patterns in a text, and are indicative of the L1, especially when used in combination with other types of features (Cimino and Dell'Orletta, 2017; Markov et al., 2017). POS tags were obtained with TreeTagger (Schmid, 1999), which uses the Penn Treebank tagset (36 tags).

FWs clarify the relationships between the content-carrying elements of a sentence, and introduce syntactic structures like verbal complements, relative clauses, and questions (Smith and Witten, 1993). The FW feature set consists of 318 English FWs from the scikit-learn package (Pedregosa et al., 2011).

3.3.2 Misspelled cognates, L2-ed words and other misspellings

We build features that gather information from misspelled words in the essays in the data. The information about which L1 a cognate or L2-ed word hints to is used as an attribute of the word.

Misspelled cognates. Several studies applied discriminative string similarity to the task of cognate identification (Mann and Yarowsky, 2001; Bergsma and Kondrak, 2007; Nicolai et al., 2013). Following the work by Nicolai et al. (2013), we detect cognates by identifying the cases where the closest correctly spelled L2 word w_e to the misspelled word w_m has a translation in an L1 w_f to which it is close in form, and w_m is closer to w_f than to w_e. Formally:

1. For each misspelled English word w_m identify the intended word w_e using a spell-checking tool.[3]

2. For each L1:

   (a) Look up the translation w_f of the intended word w_e in L1.[4]

   (b) Replace diacritics in w_f with the corresponding Latin equivalent (e.g., "é" $\rightarrow$ "e").

   (c) Compute the Levenshtein distance D between w_e and w_f.

   (d) If $D(w_e, w_f) < 3$ then w_f is assumed to be a cognate of w_e.[5]

   (e) If w_f is a cognate and $D(w_m, w_f) < D(w_e, w_f)$ then consider the L1 as a clue of the native language of the author.[6]

L2-ed words. To identify the L2-ed, in our case anglicized, words we take a misspelled word and look for forms close to it in the L1 vocabularies. The idea is that a misspelled word may be an L1 word that got anglicized, which is a clue for the L1 of the author.

We use the freely available lists of expressions provided by the OmegaWiki project[7] and extract vocabularies for each of the L1 languages represented in our datasets. The statistics for each language in terms of the number of expressions and the extracted vocabularies is provided in Table 2.

We apply the following algorithm:

1. For each misspelled English word w_m identify its closest word in some L1:

2. For w_f in each L1:

   (a) Replace diacritics in w_f with the corresponding Latin equivalent (e.g., "é" $\rightarrow$ "e").

   (b) Compute the Levenshtein distance $D(w_m, w_f)$.

   (c) Identify the L1 with the smallest $D(w_m, w_f)$ value, and if $D(w_m, w_f) < 5$ then take w_m to be an L2-ed version

---

[3] We use the Enchant spellchecking library: https://www.abisource.com/projects/enchant/; 14,176 unique misspelled words were identified in TOEFL4 and 6,912 in ICLE4.

[4] We use Python's translation tool: https://pypi.org/project/translate/

[5] Following Mann and Yarowsky (2001) we consider a word pair (w_e, w_f) to be cognate if their Levenshtein distance (Levenshtein, 1966) is less than three.

[6] If $D(w_m, w_f) < D(w_e, w_f)$ was for several L1s, we opted for the one with the lowest $D(w_m, w_f)$ value. If the lowest $D(w_m, w_f)$ value was the same for several L1s, the word was discarded.

[7] http://www.omegawiki.org/Meta:Main_Page

L1	TOEFL4						ICLE4					
	Misspelled	Ratio, %	Cognates	Ratio, %	L2-ed	Ratio, %	Misspelled	Ratio, %	Cognates	Ratio, %	L2-ed	Ratio, %
French	8,150	2.31	884	0.25	3,457	0.98	3,038	1.34	281	0.12	1,211	0.53
German	7,544	1.99	425	0.11	2,869	0.76	3,913	1.69	244	0.11	1,259	0.54
Italian	8,403	2.58	585	0.18	3,249	1.00	3,223	1.43	267	0.12	1,105	0.49
Spanish	10,224	2.82	617	0.17	3,988	1.10	5,899	2.96	613	0.31	2,323	1.16
Total	**34,321**	**2.41**	**2,511**	**0.18**	**13,563**	**0.95**	**16,072**	**1.82**	**1,405**	**0.16**	**5,898**	**0.67**
Unique	**14,176**		**580**		**5,754**		**6,912**		**414**		**2,770**	

Table 1: Statistics (absolute number and ratio (%) to the total number of words) of misspelled words, cognates, and L2-ed words for each language in the TOEFL4 and ICLE4 datasets.

Language	No. of expressions	No. of unique words (vocabulary)
French	32,184	21,433
German	31,450	28,378
Italian	26,764	18,561
Spanish	39,566	27,321

Table 2: Statistics of the number of expressions and the extracted vocabularies for each of the languages.

of w_f, and consider w_m as a clue for the native language of the author. [8]

Table 1 presents the statistics of misspelled words, cognates, and L2-ed words for each language in the TOEFL4 and ICLE4 datasets, respectively. The number of L2-ed words is much larger than the number of cognates: in both datasets around 40% were assigned the corresponding L1 (5,754 out of the 14,176 unique misspelled words in TOEFL4 and 2,770 out of 6,912 in ICLE4). This could be because of the tight constraint for "cognatehood" we followed (Mann and Yarowsky, 2001). In TOEFL4, the cognate and the L2-ed word lists have 350 elements in common (310 of which have the same identified L1), while there are 230 cognates that were not identified as L2-ed words and 5,404 L2-ed words that were not identified as cognates. In ICLE4, the cognate and the L2-ed word lists have 266 elements in common (231 of which have the same identified L1), while there are 148 cognates that were not identified as L2-ed words and 2,504 L2-ed words that were not identified as cognates.

We combine the L1s of misspelled cognates and L2-ed words with the POS & FW representation. As an example consider the two phrases: `have a happy ancianity` and `a good inocent man`.[9] The identified L2-ed words and cognates

---

[8] If the lowest $D(w_m, w_f)$ value was the same for several L1s, the word was discarded.

[9] Extracted from the training essays in the data we work with (ICLE4: SPM04022.txt and TOEFL4: 00284.txt, respectively).

are *ancianity* (ENG. old age) → SPA. ancian-idad → L2-ed and *inocent* (ENG. innocent) → SPA. inocente → cognate. The phrases are represented through POS & FW & cognates & L2-ed words as `have a JJ SPA-L2-ed` and `a JJ SPA-cognate NN`, respectively. Then n-grams (n = 1–3) from this representation are extracted.

Spelling errors. Spelling errors may capture language specific transcriptions of sound sequences, as influenced by the native language (Chen et al., 2017): e.g., Spaniards often use c instead of q, writing *cuestion* instead of *question*. Following (Chen et al., 2017) we represent misspelled words through character n-grams (n = 1–3). When used, these features are added as a separate subset of the feature vector representing an essay.

4 Results and Discussion

The impact of features based on misspelled cognates, L2-ed words and character n-grams from all misspellings is evaluated using the NLI task. We report accuracy on 10-fold cross-validation experiments on the full data sets. The set-ups consist of various combinations of these features. Tests on the TOEFL dataset split by proficiency levels will allow us to assess how these features change with higher language competency.

Results on the TOEFL4 and ICLE4 datasets
We first examine only the features obtained from misspelled words – cognates, L2-ed, spelling error (SE) character n-grams – and verify whether they are informative for NLI: (i) we use just the aggregated information about identified L1s as features; (ii) we use them in combination with the spelling error character n-grams (n = 1–3). We compare the obtained results with the majority baselines of 25.00% and 30.62% accuracy for TOEFL4 and ICLE4, respectively. We then use as a baseline the POS and FW features, to which we add the cognates, L2-ed words, and spelling error character

Features	TOEFL4			ICLE4		
	Acc.%	diff	No.	Acc.%	diff	No.
Majority baseline	25.00			30.62		
Cognates	37.34	**12.34***	4	38.55	**7.93***	4
L2-ed	36.05	**11.05***	4	44.85	**14.23***	4
Cognates & L2-ed	39.84	**14.84***	8	46.18	**15.56***	8
Cognates & L2-ed & SE	54.55	**29.55***	7,347	56.33	**25.71***	6,391
POS & FW 1–3-grams	74.45		231,737	80.58		189,622
POS & FW 1–3-grams & cognates	75.50	**1.05***	236,716	80.72	**0.14**	192,572
POS & FW 1–3-grams & L2-ed	75.80	**1.35***	247,814	81.56	**0.98**	198,469
POS & FW 1–3-grams & cognates & L2-ed	76.20	**1.75***	253,175	81.77	**1.19**	201,623
POS & FW 1–3-grams & SE	78.23	**3.78***	238,929	82.75	**2.17***	195,869
POS & FW 1–3-grams & cognates & L2-ed & SE	78.80	**4.35***	260,367	82.61	**2.03***	207,870

Table 3: 10-fold cross-validation accuracy for cognates, L2-ed words, their combination, and when combined with spelling error (SE) character n-grams on the TOEFL4 and ICLE4 datasets, and for POS & FW 1–3-grams combined with the cognate and L2-ed features and in combination with SE character n-grams. Diff stands for difference: gain/drop; '*' marks statistically significant differences.

Features	Low			Medium			High		
	Acc.%	diff	No.	Acc.%	diff	No.	Acc.%	diff	No.
Majority baseline	51.09			28.64			35.35		
Cognates	56.49	**5.40***	4	39.81	**11.17***	4	40.23	**4.88***	4
L2-ed	58.12	**7.03***	4	38.39	**9.75***	4	36.24	**0.89**	4
Cognates & L2-ed	59.24	**8.15***	8	42.57	**13.93***	8	40.18	**4.83***	8
Cognates & L2-ed &SE	60.79	**9.70***	3,241	55.26	**26.62***	6,031	45.95	**10.60***	5,366
POS & FW 1–3-grams	62.92		34,970	74.33		148,878	67.71		152,105
POS & FW 1–3-grams & cognates	62.38	**−0.54**	35,609	75.57	**1.24***	152,158	68.08	**0.37**	154,318
POS & FW 1–3-grams & L2-ed	65.16	**2.24**	37,214	76.17	**1.84***	159,508	68.03	**0.32**	160,025
POS & FW 1–3-grams & cognates & L2-ed	64.54	**1.62**	37,922	77.09	**2.76***	163,057	68.55	**0.84**	162,419
POS & FW 1–3-grams & SE	66.09	**3.17**	38,114	78.14	**3.81***	154,774	70.07	**2.36***	157,346
POS & FW 1–3-grams & cognates & L2-ed & SE	69.13	**6.21***	41,066	79.25	**4.92***	168,953	71.28	**3.57***	167,660

Table 4: 10-fold cross-validation accuracy for cognates, L2-ed words, their combination, and when combined with spelling error (SE) character n-grams for each proficiency level, and for POS & FW 1–3-grams combined with the cognate and L2-ed features and in combination with SE character n-grams. Diff stands for difference: gain/drop; '*' marks statistically significant differences.

L1	Low		Medium		High	
	No.	%	No.	%	No.	%
French	63	19.6	577	26.5	460	24.2
German	15	4.7	412	18.9	673	35.3
Italian	164	51.1	623	28.6	313	16.4
Spanish	79	24.6	563	25.9	458	24.1
Total	**321**	**7.3**	**2,175**	**49.4**	**1,904**	**43.3**

Table 5: Data statistics for the three English proficiency levels in TOEFL4.

n-grams. The POS tags of the cognates and L2-ed words are replaced by the identified L1, and we then build n-grams from this representation. SE character n-grams are represented through separate feature vectors (as explained in Section 3).

The result for this experiment is shown in Table 3. The number of features (No.) is included. Statistically significant gains with respect to the baseline according to McNemar's statistical significance test (McNemar, 1947) with $\alpha < 0.05$ are marked with '*'.

The improvement in terms of accuracy over the majority baselines by more than 10 percentage points achieved when using the proposed features in isolation confirms that these features are highly relevant for NLI. Combining these features further boosts the results, showing that their L1 signal is strengthened with each additional source of information. The combination of L2-ed words and misspelled cognates provide statistically significant improvement in the majority of cases. Spelling error character n-grams further enhance the obtained results. Replacing the POS tags of the misspelled words by the corresponding L1s, and using word n-grams of such features (n = 1–3) provides improvement on both datasets.

On the TOEFL4 dataset, the result for the combination of the proposed features is similar to the performance of the bag-of-words (BoW) approach, while on the ICLE4 dataset the BoW approach outperforms our representation by around 5% accuracy. The BoW approach covers a multitude of linguistic particularities, while the goal of this work is to identify which particular characteristics skew the language production in an L2.

As mentioned above, a complicating factor in this classification is the fact that the four languages represented in the dataset have shared etymological ancestors and thus shared cognates. Furthermore, three of these languages are Romance languages, and thus are even closer, and may confound the Levenshtein distance computation.

Proficiency-level experiments The TOEFL dataset contains information concerning the proficiency levels of the students (low, medium, high). We evaluated the impact of cognates and L2-ed words within each proficiency level. It is expected that the impact (as well as the frequency) of L2-ed words will decrease with an increase in proficiency.

The statistics for the number of essays per language within each proficiency level is shown in Table 5. The statistics for the misspelled words, cognates, and L2-ed words (as a percentage of the total number of tokens) for each language within each proficiency level is provided in Figure 1. As all these phenomena are gathered from misspelled words, it is not surprising that their overall frequency decreases with the proficiency level. The number of L2-ed words is still higher than the number of cognates throughout all proficiency levels and L1s. Analysis of the identified L2-ed words reveal that many of them do have a common etymological ancestor as a word from L2, but they are written in such a way that their Levenshtein distance from the L2 version is greater than their distance from the L1 version. Using information about shared etymologies could help make the separation between words with shared etymologies and "corrupted" L1 words clearer.

The results for each proficiency level when cognates and L2-ed words are evaluated separately and in combination with spelling error (SE) 1–3-grams, as well as when these features are combined with the POS & FW representation, are presented in Table 4.

The results presented in Table 4 indicate that, in the majority of cases, the influence of L2-ed words gets weaker from low to high proficiency, while the influence of the cognates grows with the proficiency level, despite the fact that even for higher levels of proficiency the number of L2-ed words is higher than the number of cognates. This shows that even high-proficiency language users are prone to extend their vocabulary in L2 incorrectly, but following cognate principles, when no fitting lexical item is readily available to them.

High improvement achieved for medium proficiency can be related to a larger number of essays for this level.[10] Moreover, it can be noted that higher results are usually achieved when these features are combined, regardless of the proficiency level.

Discussion In the experiments presented above, we exploited only misspelled words to extract L1-indicative features. While we do not expect to find L2-ed words among the correctly spelled words, there will be correct cognates. In order to detect properly spelled cognates, we used etymological information obtained from the Etymological WordNet (de Melo and Weikum, 2010). We identify "perfect" cognates if the lemma occurs in the Etymological WordNet's L1 vocabulary, while "not perfect" cognates are identified as words (lemmas) that share an etymological ancestor and their Levenshtein distance < 3 (diacritics removed). The Levenshtein distance was used since the ancestor can have multiple descendants.

When the L1s of the identified correct cognates are used as features in isolation, they perform by around 3 percentage points above the majority baseline, but do not enhance the results when combined with misspelled cognates and L2-ed words. This could be related to the fact that correct cognates are either closest to their L1 form, or are part of a more basic vocabulary that all learners have to master. We design features that capture the distance between cognates in L2 and some L1 – for correct cognates we use the average of the Levenshtein distances for each L1 as a numeric feature. These features outperform the majority baseline by around 4% on TOEFL4 and 6% on ICLE4. When combined with L2-ed words, misspelled cognates, or POS & FW 1–3 gram representations, the improvement on ICLE4 (1%–5% improvement depending on the setting) is higher than on TOEFL4 (1%–3% improvement depending on the setting), which could be due to the top-

---

[10]We do not balance the dataset by proficiency levels for this experiment, because the dataset will become too small.

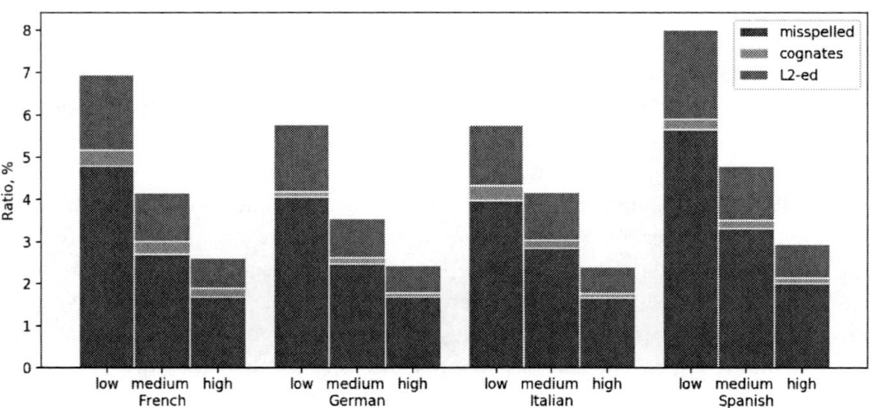

Figure 1: Ratio (%) of the misspelled words, cognates, and L2-ed words to the total number of words for each language within each proficiency level.

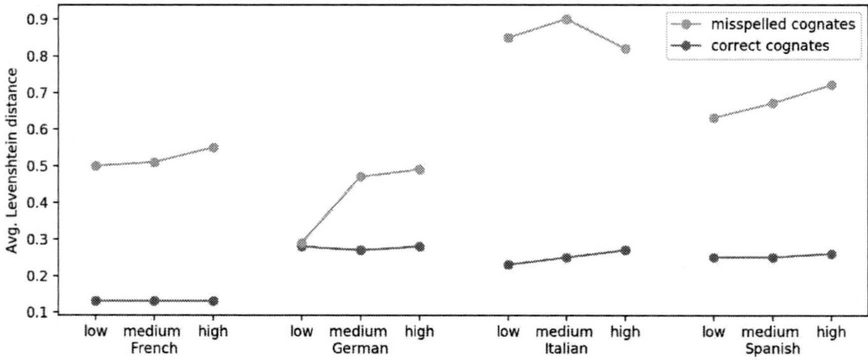

Figure 2: Average Levenshtein distances for correct and misspelled cognates for each language within each proficiency level.

ics or the high proficiency level of the ICLE essays.

Analysis of the average Levenshtein distances in our datasets and within each proficiency level for correct and misspelled cognates reveal that the average Levenshtein distance is lower for correct cognates (Figure 2), which indicates that learners tend to correctly use cognates when they are closer to the form they are familiar with in their L1. This distance increases with the proficiency level, which can be due to the fact that learners with high proficiency use more complex vocabulary, with cognates that have a form that is more distant from the one in L1.

Another factor to consider are false friends. Since words are judged outside of their context and based only on their form, false friends are not distinguished from proper cognates. The word *became* may appear correct, unless the larger context is taken into account: *I became a letter.* Such a usage would reveal the writer to be a native German speaker, where *bekommen* means *to receive.* Detecting false friends though is a more difficult problem.

Gathering all such information would provide additional insight on how the L1 vocabularies influence lexical choice in L2, and we plan to address some of these issues in future work.

5   Conclusions

In this paper, we analyzed misspellings for particular clues about an essay author's native language. In particular, we identified misspelled cognates and L2-ed (here, anglicized) words and analyzed the information they provided separately and combined with other misspellings. Experiments on native language identification (NLI) showed that all three phenomena provide useful information for identifying the native language of the author.

An analysis of these phenomena at different levels showed that although the frequency of misspellings in general – and of L2-ed words – decreases with an increase in proficiency, as expected, their contribution to the NLI task remains strong for all levels. When combined, the results increase in most tested scenarios, showing that the L1 signal is boosted by considering all these phenomena together. We find it particularly interesting that L2-ed words are still frequent at the high proficiency level, showing that the impulse of using cognates is so strong that people make them when they are not available.

In future work, we plan to explore deeper the usefulness of cognates and L2-ed words, by distinguishing them from false friends, which we think may be even more telling about the author's L1. We also plan to examine these phenomena – cognates, L2-ed words, and misspelled words – on datasets with other L2s, and include in the analysis languages that do not use the Latin script.

References

Shane Bergsma and Grzegorz Kondrak. 2007. Alignment-based discriminative string similarity. In *Proceedings of the 45th Annual Meeting of the Association of Computational Linguistics*, pages 656–663, Prague, Czech Republic. ACL.

Daniel Blanchard, Joel Tetreault, Derrick Higgins, Aoife Cahill, and Martin Chodorow. 2013. TOEFL11: A corpus of non-native English. *ETS Research Report Series*, 2013(2):i–15.

Julian Brooke and Graeme Hirst. 2011. Native language detection with 'cheap' learner corpora. In *Proceedings of the Conference of Learner Corpus Research*, pages 37–47, Louvain-la-Neuve, Belgium. Presses universitaires de Louvain.

Lingzhen Chen, Carlo Strapparava, and Vivi Nastase. 2017. Improving native language identification by using spelling errors. In *Proceedings of the 55th Annual Meeting of the Association for Computational Linguistics*, pages 542–546, Vancouver, Canada. ACL.

Andrea Cimino and Felice Dell'Orletta. 2017. Stacked sentence-document classifier approach for improving native language identification. In *Proceedings of the 12th Workshop on Building Educational Applications Using NLP*, pages 430–437, Copenhagen, Denmark. ACL.

Brendan Flanagan and Sachio Hirokawa. 2018. An automatic method to extract online foreign language learner writing error characteristics. *International Journal of Distance Education Technologies*, 16(4):15–30.

Sylviane Granger, Estelle Dagneaux, Fanny Meunier, and Magali Paquot. 2009. *International Corpus of Learner English v2 (ICLE)*. Presses Universitaires de Louvain, Louvain-la-Neuve, Belgium.

Moshe Koppel, Jonathan Schler, and Kfir Zigdon. 2005. Determining an author's native language by mining a text for errors. In *Proceedings of the Eleventh ACM SIGKDD International Conference on Knowledge Discovery in Data Mining*, pages 624–628, New York, NY, USA. ACM.

Vladimir Levenshtein. 1966. Binary codes capable of correcting deletions, insertions, and reversals. *Soviet Physics Doklady*, 10(8):707–710.

Shervin Malmasi and Mark Dras. 2015. Multilingual native language identification. *Natural Language Engineering*, 23(2):163–215.

Shervin Malmasi, Joel Tetreault, and Mark Dras. 2015. Oracle and human baselines for native language identification. In *Proceedings of the Tenth Workshop on Innovative Use of NLP for Building Educational Applications*, pages 172–178, Denver, CO, USA. ACL.

Gideon Mann and David Yarowsky. 2001. Multipath translation lexicon induction via bridge languages. In *Proceedings of the Second Meeting of the North American Chapter of the Association for Computational Linguistics*, pages 151–158, Pittsburgh, PA, USA. ACL.

Ilia Markov, Lingzhen Chen, Carlo Strapparava, and Grigori Sidorov. 2017. CIC-FBK approach to native language identification. In *Proceedings of the 12th Workshop on Building Educational Applications Using NLP*, pages 374–381, Copenhagen, Denmark. ACL.

Ilia Markov, Vivi Nastase, and Carlo Strapparava. 2018a. Punctuation as native language interference. In *Proceedings of the 27th International Conference on Computational Linguistics*, pages 3456–3466, Santa Fe, New Mexico, USA. The COLING 2018 Organizing Committee.

Ilia Markov, Vivi Nastase, Carlo Strapparava, and Grigori Sidorov. 2018b. The role of emotions in native language identification. In *Proceedings of the 9th Workshop on Computational Approaches to Subjectivity, Sentiment and Social Media Analysis*, pages 123–129, Brussels, Belgium. ACL.

Quinn McNemar. 1947. Note on the sampling error of the difference between correlated proportions or percentages. *Psychometrika*, 12(2):153–157.

Gerard de Melo and Gerhard Weikum. 2010. Towards universal multilingual knowledge bases. In *Principles, Construction, and Applications of Multilingual Wordnets. Proceedings of the 5th Global WordNet Conference*, pages 149–156, New Delhi, India. Narosa Publishing.

Vivi Nastase and Carlo Strapparava. 2017. Word etymology as native language interference. In *Proceedings of the 2017 Conference on Empirical Methods in Natural Language Processing*, pages 2692–2697, Copenhagen, Denmark. ACL.

Garrett Nicolai, Bradley Hauer, Mohammad Salameh, Lei Yao, and Grzegorz Kondrak. 2013. Cognate and misspelling features for natural language identification. In *Proceedings of the Eighth Workshop on Innovative Use of NLP for Building Educational Applications*, pages 140–145, Atlanta, GA, USA. ACL.

Terence Odlin. 1989. *Language Transfer: cross-linguistic influence in language learning.* Cambridge University Press, Cambridge, UK.

Fabian Pedregosa, Gaël Varoquaux, Alexandre Gramfort, Vincent Michel, Bertrand Thirion, Olivier Grisel, Mathieu Blondel, Peter Prettenhofer, Ron Weiss, Vincent Dubourg, Jake Vanderplas, Alexandre Passos, David Cournapeau, Matthieu Brucher, Matthieu Perrot, and Édouard Duchesnay. 2011. Scikit-learn: Machine learning in Python. *Journal of Machine Learning Research*, 12:2825–2830.

Ella Rabinovich, Yulia Tsvetkov, and Shuly Wintner. 2018. Native language cognate effects on second language lexical choice. *Transactions of the Association for Computational Linguistics*, 6:329–342.

Helmut Schmid. 1999. *Improvements In Part-of-Speech Tagging With an Application to German*, pages 13–25. Springer.

Tony C. Smith and Ian H. Witten. 1993. Language inference from function words. Working papers, https://hdl.handle.net/10289/9927.

Thamar Solorio, Elizabeth Blair, Suraj Maharjan, Steven Bethard, Mona Diab, Mahmoud Ghoneim, Abdelati Hawwari, Fahad AlGhamdi, Julia Hirschberg, Alison Chang, and Pascale Fung. 2014. Overview for the first shared task on language identification in code-switched data. In *Proceedings of the First Workshop on Computational Approaches to Code Switching*, pages 62–72, Doha, Qatar. ACL.

Joel Tetreault, Daniel Blanchard, and Aoife Cahill. 2013. A report on the first native language identification shared task. In *Proceedings of the Eighth Workshop on Innovative Use of NLP for Building Educational Applications*, pages 48–57, Atlanta, GA, USA. ACL.

Linguistically-Driven Strategy for Concept Prerequisites Learning on Italian

Alessio Miaschi[*,◇], Chiara Alzetta[•,◇], Franco Alberto Cardillo[◇], Felice Dell'Orletta[◇]
[*]Dipartimento di Informatica, Università di Pisa
[•]DIBRIS, Università degli Studi di Genova
[◇]Istituto di Linguistica Computazionale "Antonio Zampolli" (ILC-CNR), Pisa
ItaliaNLP Lab – *www.italianlp.it*
`alessio.miaschi@phd.unipi.it,`
`chiara.alzetta@edu.unige.it,`
`{francoalberto.cardillo, felice.dellorletta}@ilc.cnr.it`

Abstract

We present a new concept prerequisite learning method for Learning Object (LO) ordering that exploits only linguistic features extracted from textual educational resources. The method was tested in a cross- and in-domain scenario both for Italian and English. Additionally, we performed experiments based on a incremental training strategy to study the impact of the training set size on the classifier performances. The paper also introduces ITA-PREREQ, to the best of our knowledge the first Italian dataset annotated with prerequisite relations between pairs of educational concepts, and describe the automatic strategy devised to build it.

1 Introduction

Learning Objects (LO) are digital or non-digital educational resources deliverable over the Internet that can be employed in technology–supported learning (Wiley, 2000). According to the Learning Technology Standards Committee, being small and re-usable educational elements (e.g. lecture notes, multimedia content, presentations) is what mostly distinguishes LOs form other educational resources (IEEE, 2002). Recommendations for creating LOs in fact suggest that, although there is no standard LO structure, the content should be direct, succinct and homogeneous (Thompson and Yonekura, 2005). Grounded in the notion of object-oriented computing and programming, LO are designed according to the idea that combining small chunks of knowledge is what builds up an effective learning path. In order to promote sharing and re-usability, LO repositories were made available on the web, where LOs are stored, collected and can be searched by means of metadata provided by their authors (Tzikopoulos et al., 2009). Teachers and instructional designers can highly benefit from LO repositories since they can use them to build educational materials such as textbooks, courses or, more in general, learning paths by combining various LOs of the same subject.

Being able to give a pedagogical meaning to the content of a set of LOs by ordering them respecting their pedagogical precedence is not trivial: uncovering educational relationship between LOs is a difficult and time consuming practice usually performed by domain experts (Gordon et al., 2017). Among all pedagogical relations, the most fundamental is the prerequisite relation, which best describes pedagogical precedence since it defines what one needs to know before approaching a new content.

Previous work in course and LO sequencing and knowledge tracing infers prerequisite relation between LOs based on their metadata and/or students' preferences and competences (De-Marcos et al., 2009; Vuong et al., 2011; Piech et al., 2015; Méndez et al., 2016). Educational Data Mining methods usually rely also on graph information of ontologies, university programs or Wikipedia graph structure (Scheines et al., 2014; Chen et al., 2016).

In this paper we present a novel method based on deep learning applied to the task of automatic prerequisite relations identification between concepts to automatically create pedagogically motivated sequences of LOs. To the best of our knowledge, this is the first method that exploits exclusively linguistic feature extracted from textual resources. Considering only textual content is possibly the most complex condition to infer relationships between educational concepts since it cannot rely on any structured information. At the same time this is also the closest condition to a real world scenario, hence we aim to demonstrate that textual content can be sufficient to infer a pedagogically motivated ordering of LO pairs.

To verify the effectiveness of our strategy, we

Proceedings of the Fourteenth Workshop on Innovative Use of NLP for Building Educational Applications, pages 285–295
Florence, Italy, August 2, 2019. ©2019 Association for Computational Linguistics

performed experiments on the AL-CPL dataset (Liang et al., 2018b), an English dataset manually annotated with prerequisite relations between educational concepts, and on an Italian dataset we created. Hence, we introduce ITA-PREREQ[1], the first Italian dataset, to the best of our knowledge, annotated with prerequisite relations between pairs of concepts, built completely automatically.

Along the paper, we use the terms *Learning Object* (LO) and *Wikipedia page* interchangeably: in a broad sense, Wikipedia entries can be considered Ls (Nash, 2005), moreover previous work in related fields represent educational units as Wikipedia pages (Gasparetti et al., 2018). This fits our needs since a Wikipedia page consists of textual content pertaining to a single unit of learning. The term *concept* is also frequently used in the literature referring to educational units in general, and annotated dataset are usually described as identifying prerequisite relations between concepts. In this paper we use the term *concept* relying on the same sense of Liang et al. (2018b) as equivalent to the term *LO*.

The remaining part of the paper is organised as follows. First we present related work (Sec 2), then, after briefly presenting our approach (Sec. 3), we describe in more detail the data (Sec. 3.1), used features (3.2) and the classifier (Sec. 3.3). We also provide an insight of feature analysis in Sec 3.2.1. Experiments, results and incremental training tests are described in Section 4. In Section 5 we conclude the paper.

Our Contribution. In this paper, we present: (i) the first system based on neural network which exploits only linguistic features extracted from LO content and does not rely on Wikipedia graph or LO metadata information; (ii) the first Italian dataset annotated with prerequisite relations between pairs of concepts (ITA-PREREQ) and the automatic strategy devised to construct it; (iii) the first system for prerequisite relations extraction on Italian.

2   Related Work

Identifying prerequisite relations between educational materials is a task that has recently gained much attention both in the NLP community, aided by the fact that it is applicable to many contexts, such as curriculum planning (Agrawal, 2016), course sequencing (Vuong et al., 2011), reading list generation (Gordon et al., 2017), automatic assessment (Wang and Liu, 2016) and domain ontology construction (Zouaq et al., 2007; Larranaga et al., 2014).

NLP techniques usually exploit structured information (e.g. hyperlinks, citations, DBpedia structure) combined with content-based information extracted from educational materials, like scientific literature (Gordon et al., 2016; Li et al., 2019), knowledge units in courses (Yang et al., 2015; Chaplot et al., 2016; Pan et al., 2017; Li et al., 2019) or Learning Objects (Gasparetti et al., 2018), often understood as Wikipedia pages (Gasparetti et al., 2015). Talukdar and Cohen (2012) presented the first work on predicting prerequisite structure of concepts using Wikipedia, which eventually became the most widely used resource for this task. They collected a manually annotated dataset of page pairs using crowd-sourcing and then trained a MaxEnt classifier using Wikipedia graph features, page content and edits to reproduce the prerequisite structure between pages. The classifier was tested both in and across domains, obtaining higher results in terms of accuracy if compared against a random baseline. The same dataset was used by (Liang et al., 2015) to test the RefD metric, that models the prerequisite relation by measuring how differently two concepts refer to each other using the tf-idf measure. Results are comparable with the MaxEnt classifier but the metric does not take into account all the available information in the resource so we argue that it could be improved further. The RefD metric was also used by (Wang et al., 2016) in a method that jointly extracts relevant concepts and prerequisite structure from textbooks exploiting also external knowledge from Wikipedia. Relying on textbooks but not on structured resources, Adorni et al. (2019) describe a method to infer prerequisite relations between concepts using burst analysis of concept occurrences in text and patterns based on temporal reasoning to identify possible propaedeutic relations.

Machine and deep learning techniques have been applied only recently to the prerequisite learning task. In (Liang et al., 2018b,a), the authors investigated the effects of integrating an active learning strategy in automatic extraction of prerequisites using a Random Forest classifier.

Gasparetti et al. (2018) proposed a ML methods based on Multilayer Perceptron exploiting LOs, Wikipedia pages of concepts mentioned in the LOs and Wikipedia hierarchical category structure. Roy et al. (2018) presented a supervised learning method using a Siamese Network to predict prerequisite relations between University and MOOC courses.

The above methods strictly rely on Wikipedia graph information, which they report as highly informative, but that is not available when applying the method on different educational materials. We show how comparable results can be obtained considering only textual information.

Another acknowledged limit of the above methods is the need of large annotated datasets. Manual annotation by domain experts is the most commonly adopted strategy to build such resources, regardless the knowledge unit considered (Wang et al., 2016; Pan et al., 2017; Liang et al., 2017; Alzetta et al., 2018; Fabbri et al., 2018), with the notable exception of the crowd-sourcing strategy of Talukdar and Cohen (2012). The dataset we present in this paper is the first dataset annotated with prerequisite relations between concepts for Italian build completely automatically.

3 Our Approach

We tackle the problem of LO ordering as a task of automatic prerequisite relationship identification between LOs, here defined as follows: given a pair of LOs (A, B), we predict whether or not B is a prerequisite of A. As mentioned above, we define a LO as a concept corresponding to a Wikipedia page.

We trained deep learning models to predict whether or not two concepts are in a prerequisite relationship using a pre-trained word embedding lexicons and a set of linguistic features extracted from the pages of the concepts in the pair. The model was tested on two datasets: ITA-PREREQ, an Italian dataset annotated with prerequisite relations, and, to prove the effectiveness of the model, also on AL-CPL, an English dataset already used for the task of automatic prerequisite identification. In particular, the AL-CPL dataset was used both in its original and reduced version, as described in the next Section.

AL-CPL			
Domain	**Concepts**	**Pairs**	**Prerequisites**
Data Mining	120	826	292
Geometry	89	1,681	524
Physics	153	1,962	487
Precalculus	224	2,060	699
Total	586	6,529	2,002
ITA-PREREQ / English Reduced			
Domain	**Concepts**	**Pairs**	**Prerequisites**
Data Mining	75	429	154
Geometry	73	1,338	430
Physics	131	1,651	409
Precalculus	176	1,504	502
Total	455	4,922	1,495

Table 1: Number of concepts, pairs, pairs showing a prerequisite relation for each domain of each dataset and total values considering all domains for each dataset.

3.1 Dataset

For our experiments on the English language, we relied on the AL-CPL Dataset (Liang et al., 2018b), which is in turn based on the Wiki Concept Map dataset (Wang et al., 2016).

The Wiki Concept Map dataset is a manually constructed dataset consisting of binary-labelled concept pairs collected from textbooks on different educational domains: data mining, geometry, physics and precalculus. Concepts mentioned in the textbooks and appearing in the title of a Wikipedia page were considered domain concepts. Among them, key concepts and prerequisite relationships between them were annotated by experts for each domain, resulting in a concept map, a specific type of knowledge graph where each node is a scientific concept and edges represent pedagogical relations. Pairs not having prerequisite relation were also annotated, therefore the final dataset consists of both positive and negative pairs.

In Liang et al. (2018b) the dataset was expanded by adding (i) irreflexive and (ii) transitive relations: considering A, B and C as distinct concepts, (i) add (B, A) as a negative sample of (A, B); (ii) add (A, C) as positive sample if (A, B) and (B, C) are positive samples.

The AL-CPL dataset was also used by us to build ITA-PREREQ, the first Italian dataset annotated with prerequisite relation between pair of concepts, which we used to test our model on Italian. Considering the concepts of the AL-CPL dataset, we retrieved their Italian Wikipedia pages by matching the page title with the concept name. If the Italian page of a concept was not available,

287

the concept was excluded from the dataset. At the end of this process, we obtained an automatically constructed version of the AL-CPL dataset for Italian with a subset of 418 concepts (77.40% of the original dataset).

Note that the dataset only provides concept names (i.e. page titles), which means that downloading the pages from Wikipedia at different times might results in a slightly different corpus, since Wikipedia pages are frequently edited. In our case, we used the latest Wikipedia dump at the time of the experiments (February 2019).

Considering such Wikipedia impact factors (i.e. editing and differences between languages), we created a third dataset, again generated starting from AL-CPL. We call this version *English Reduced* since it is built excluding all those English Wikipedia pages that do not have a corresponding Italian one. Therefore, the size of English Reduced is the same of ITA-PREREQ. The aim of having this dataset is to check the real impact of languages differences by balancing the number of pages taken into account, as we will discuss further in the next Section.

Table 1 summarises the statistics of the three datasets. Although ITA-PREREQ and English Reduced resulted in smaller datasets in terms of both concepts and relations, their sizes are suited for training our systems.

3.2 Features

For each concept pair, we extracted two different sets of linguistic features: (*i*) *lexical features*, i.e. features that pertain to a single concept/page, and (*ii*) *global features*, i.e. features derived from the combination of concepts in pairs. All features were extracted for the AL-CPL, ITA-PREREQ and English Reduced datasets.

Hereafter, we denote by A and B the content of the Wikipedia page A or B; (A, B) is how we refer to the concept pair, while A_t/B_t refers to the title of the corresponding page.

Lexical features. The first type of feature corresponds to pre-trained word embeddings (WE) computed for the first 400 words of each Wikipedia page. Specifically, we used a WE lexicon with 128 dimensions built with word2vec (Mikolov et al., 2013) both for Italian and English. We generated the two lexicons using the itWac and ukWac corpora, two collections of approximately 2 billion words constructed from web pages under,

respectively, the .it and .uk domains (Baroni et al. 2009, Ferraresi et al. 2008).

Global features. The second type of feature was devised to extract linguistic information from both A and B Wikipedia pages. Specifically, for each pair (A, B), we extracted the following set of 16 text-based features:

- In text (#1, #2): if B_t/A_t appears in A/B.

- Count (#3, #4): how many times B_t/A_t is mentioned in A/B.

- In first line (#5, #6): if B_t/A_t appears in A/B's first line, i.e. A/B definition.

- In title (#7): If B_t appears in A_t.

- Length (#8, #9): the number of words of A/B.

- Jaccard Sim. (#10): the Jaccard similarity between A and B.

- Jaccard Sim. (Nouns) (#11): the Jaccard similarity between nouns appearing in A and B.

- RefD (#12): the RefD metric between A and B (Liang et al., 2015).

- LDA Entropy (#13, #14): the Shannon entropy of the LDA vector of A/B. Note that we trained three different LDA (Deerwester et al., 1990) topic models, one for each dataset.

- LDA Cross Entropy (#15, #16): the cross entropy between the LDA vector of A/B and B/A.

Features from #1 to #6, #8, #9 and form #13 to #16 were used also in Liang et al. (2018a), but we expanded their set of features considering mentions in titles and Jaccard Similarities between both whole page contents and nouns only. Our set of linguistic features includes also the RefD metric (Liang et al., 2015), a feature usually considered a graph-based feature, that we adapted in order to be applicable also to those contexts where no structured information (i.e. hyperlinks) is provided. In fact, contrary to Liang et al. (2015) where the RefD value is computed considering hyperlinks between Wikipedia pages, we computed the metric using the mention of concept B/A in the page content of A/B, regardless the association of an hyperlink to that mention. Specifically, we implemented RefD as follows:

$$RefD(A, B) = \frac{\sum_{i=1}^{N} r(c_i, B) \cdot w(c_i, A)}{\sum_{i=1}^{N} w(c_i, A)} -$$
$$\frac{\sum_{i=1}^{N} r(c_i, A) \cdot w(c_i, B)}{\sum_{i=1}^{N} w(c_i, B)}$$

where c_i is a concept from our concept space C (all the Wikipedia articles in the domain); $r(c_i, B)$ is a binary indicator showing whether c_i is mentioned in the content of page B; $w(c_i, A)$ is a weight indicator of the importance of c_i to page A (measured in terms of tf-idf).

3.2.1 Feature Analysis

In order to understand the relevance and behaviour of the *global features* in different domains and languages, we decided to perform feature analysis.

Following Liang et al. (2018a), we computed the feature importance by "mean decrease impurity" using an Extra-Trees Classifier, an implementation of a decision tree classifier. We decided also to perform the analysis using both the ITA-PREREQ and English Reduced dataset in order to compare the results in a cross-lingual scenario.

As we can see in Table 2, the results obtained from the English Reduced dataset show that, despite the ranking positions, there are many features that are common to all four domains. Specifically, the top features are RefD, LDA (entropy and cross-entropy), Length of B and B_t in first line of A. Moreover, we can notice that, except for graph features, our results are comparable to those obtained by Liang et al. (2018a). Nevertheless, the two rankings present some differences: e.g. Length of *A/B* tends to be more significant for our dataset. This could be to the fact that, as mentioned, the Wikipedia version used for our experiments could be different if compared to the one used by Liang et al. (2018b). It is also important to notice that the English Reduced dataset contains less concept pairs with respect to the original one.

Comparing the results according to the two languages, we can notice that the most important features tend to be quite similar. We can, however, identify some differences. For instance, we observe that Data Mining in ITA-PREREQ is the only domain for which RefD is not the most significant feature. Interestingly enough, the first 4 positions in the English Reduced dataset for Geometry, Physics and Precalculus seem to be more homogeneous when compared to the Italian ones.

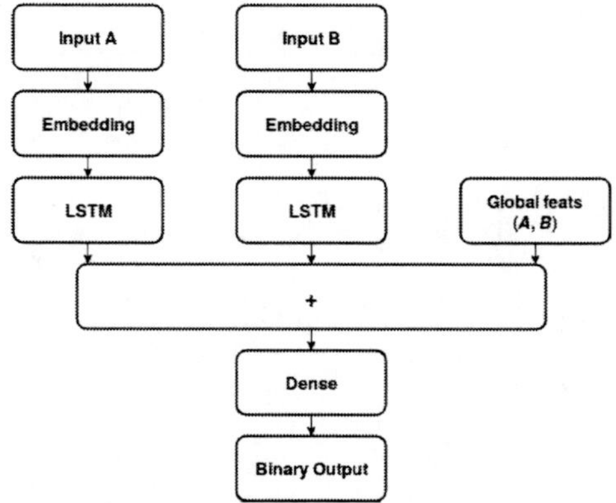

Figure 1: M3 architecture. M1 roughly corresponds to the left part of the architecture.

3.3 Classifier

For our LOs ordering experiments, we tested three different neural network models: (**M1**) one that learns to classify the binary labels using only pretrained WE, (**M2**) one that learns using the global features automatically extracted and (**M3**) the last one which merges M1 with the input of M2.

M1 is composed of two identical LSTM-based sub-networks with 32 units, whose outputs are concatenated and classified by the outer Dense Layer. Each sub-network receive as input the WE of the first 400 words of the corresponding Wikipedia page of a given concept pair (A, B). The two LSTM outputs are then concatenated ($V_A \oplus V_B$) and passed to a last Dense Layer.

M2 is based on a feedforward neural network that takes as input the global features of the pair (A, B) and passes them to a multilayer perceptron neural network (3 layers with ReLU activation).

M3 (represented in Figure 1) combines the previous two, joining the two sub-networks of M1 with the input of M2.

Each output layer of the three models consists of a single dense unit with sigmoid activation function.

The models are trained maximising the F-Score on the validation set, which corresponds to the 30% of the training data. The training stops after a certain number of epochs without improvement.

4 Experiments

We tested our approach predicting in-domain and cross-domain prerequisite relationships. Since the majority of (A, B) pairs do not present a prerequisite relation, we balanced the training and test sets

ITA-PREREQ

Data Mining	Geometry	Physics	Precalculus
Length of B	RefD	RefD	RefD
Length of A	B_t in text of A	Length of B	Length of B
RefD	Length of B	LDA entropy of B	B_t in first line of A
Jaccard Sim.	LDA entropy of B	Length of A	LDA entropy of B
Jaccard Sim. (Nouns)	B_t in first line of A	LDA cross-entropy of B/A	Length of A
LDA entropy of B	A_t in text of B	LDA cross-entropy of A/B	Jaccard Sim.
LDA entropy of A	Length of A	LDA entropy of A	B_t in text of A
LDA cross-entropy of B/A	LDA entropy of A	Jaccard Sim.	Jaccard Sim. (Nouns)
LDA cross-entropy of A/B	LDA cross-entropy of A/B	Jaccard Sim. (Nouns)	LDA cross-entropy of A/B
B_t in first line of A	LDA cross-entropy of B/A	B_t in first line of A	LDA entropy of A

English Reduced

Data Mining	Geometry	Physics	Precalculus
RefD	RefD	RefD	RefD
Length of B	B_t in first line of A	B_t in first line of A	B_t in first line of A
LDA entropy of B	LDA entropy of B	Length of B	Length of B
LDA entropy of A	Length of B	LDA entropy of B	LDA entropy of B
LDA cross-entropy of B/A	A_t in text of B	Length of A	A_t in first line of B
Lenght of A	LDA cross-entropy of B/A	LDA cross-entropy of A/B	Length of A
LDA cross-entropy of A/B	LDA entropy of A	Count of B_t in text of A	LDA entropy of A
Jaccard Sim.	B_t in text of A	LDA cross-entropy of B/A	Jaccard Sim. (Nouns)
Jaccard Sim. (Nouns)	Jaccard Sim.	Jaccard Sim. (Nouns)	Jaccard Sim.
B_t in first line of A	Jaccard Sim. (Nouns)	A_t in text of B	LDA cross-entropy of A/B

Table 2: Rankings of the first 10 features for each domain in the ITA-PREREQ and English Reduced datasets.

by oversampling the minority class.

All experiments were performed on AL-CPL, ITA-PREREQ and English Reduced datasets. As baseline, we used the Zero Rule algorithm, and F-Score as evaluation metric.

4.1 Experimental Settings

We run experiments using the three classifiers presented in Sec 3.3 on each dataset, considering each of the four domains independently (i.e Data Mining, Geometry, Physics and Precalculus). Each classifier was tested both in a in-domain and cross-domain scenario.

To perform in-domain experiments, we trained and tested the classifiers on concept pairs belonging to the same domain. The evaluation is performed using a 5-fold cross validation. Cross-domain experiments were performed in a leave-one-domain-out manner: classifiers were trained on three domains and tested on the fourth.

4.2 Results and Discussion

In-domain. As it can be noted in Table 3, our systems performs extremely well for the in-domain setting, achieving high scores for both English and Italian pages. Note that our results always outperform both the Zero Rule baseline and the results obtained by Liang et al. (2018a) for all domains. This confirms our hypothesis: it is possible to identify prerequisite relations between edu-

cational materials using linguistic information extracted from textual content alone.

Best results are obtained using M3, the classifier that exploits both lexical and global features. Interestingly, M1 model performs are constantly better than M2, especially for the Data Mining domain: this suggests that lexical information from the WE lexicon contributes significantly.

Although comparable, the AL-CPL dataset is the one obtaining best results, with an average F-Score of 92.21%. This is probably due to the fact that the other two datasets are smaller than AL-CPL in terms of number of Wikipedia pages. However, comparing the results obtained with ITA-PREREQ and English Reduced we notice that ITA-PREREQ is the one that achieves lower results. This could be due to differences in the composition of the two datasets. For example, we noticed that there is a high difference in the average page length (number of tokens) of the two languages: for English Wikipedia pages it is about twice the Italian ones (2,728 and 1,073 tokens respectively). The impact of this characteristic can be twofold, both on the lexical and global features. For what concerns the lexical features, since we considered WE of the first 400 tokens of each Wikipedia page this means that if a page is shorter then that our network can acquire less information. As proof, the number of pages shorter than 400 tokens is higher in ITA-PREREQ (138)

In-domain					
		Data Mining	**Geometry**	**Physics**	**Precalculus**	**Avg.**
ITA-PREREQ	Baseline	66.66	67.86	75.22	66.66	69.1
	M1	72.45	86.89	79.28	90.53	82.28
	M2	64.25	85.27	76.26	89.02	78.7
	M3	**77.91**	**90.01**	**85.08**	**93.91**	**86.72**
English Reduced	Baseline	66.66	67.86	75.22	66.66	69.1
	M1	85.36	92.03	84.4	90.84	88.15
	M2	70.78	89.05	78.52	89.62	81.99
	M3	**85.6**	**94.1**	**88.49**	**95.22**	**90.85**
AL-CPL	Baseline	66.66	68.82	75.17	66.66	69.32
	M1	88.81	92.43	83.49	92.48	89.30
	M2	73.29	89.66	80.72	90.9	83.64
	M3	**89.66**	**95.69**	**88.54**	**94.95**	**92.21**
Liang et al. (2018a)	RF	76.7	89.5	69.9	88.6	81.17
Cross-domain					
		Data Mining	**Geometry**	**Physics**	**Precalculus**	**Avg.**
ITA-PREREQ	Baseline	**66.66**	67.86	**75.22**	66.66	**69.1**
	M1	28.07	62.99	45.34	59.88	49.07
	M2	37.09	**79.53**	71.56	**83.66**	67.96
	M3	30.36	76.33	69.6	83.4	64.92
English Reduced	Baseline	**66.66**	67.86	**75.22**	66.66	69.1
	M1	47.83	69.17	28.97	69.18	53.78
	M2	59.91	75.8	75.05	**85.81**	**74.14**
	M3	41.9	**80.24**	58.33	79.52	64.99
AL-CPL	Baseline	**66.66**	68.82	**75.17**	66.66	69.32
	M1	37.89	70.04	39.31	71.98	54.80
	M2	50.89	80.41	74.74	**87.14**	**73.29**
	M3	38.78	**82.53**	63.67	84.41	67.34

Table 3: In- and cross-domain results in terms of F-Score obtained by the three models and the baseline on each domain for each dataset. The in-domain setting also shows results obtained by Liang et al. (2018a) using a Random Forest (RF) classifier.

than English Reduced (8). Additionally, global features could be affected by the fact that English Wikipedia pages tend to be linguistically richer than their Italian counterparts containing more information and mentions to related concepts.

Cross-domain. Observing the results obtained in the cross-domain setting, we notice a significant performance drop if compared to in–domain results (see Table 3). The reason might be due to differences in the topic coverage of some domains in Wikipedia. Following (Wang et al., 2016), we believe that fundamental and broad subjects, such as precalculus and geometry, have more clear learning dependencies expressed through Wikipedia, while Data Mining, which obtained the lowest scores with our models, being a specific and relatively newer topic presents shorter pages, which means less information. Another possible explanation could be that pages belonging to the same domain are more homogeneous internally in terms of content structure, so it is easier for the networks to identify regularities.

Interestingly, contrary to what happens for the in-domain setting, Table 3 shows that the main contribution to the cross-domain results is given by the global features, most likely because they can detect domain-independent properties. Word embedding lexicon alone (M1 model) is not sufficient to exceed the baseline, with the only exception of Geometry ad Precalculus. Since these two domains share more lexicon than the others, we assumed that our model could perform better if trained only on a single domain that is lexically close to the testing one.

To test this hypothesis, we computed the Jaccard similarity between pairs of domains using all their Wikipedia pages in order to define lexically close pairs and use them to perform cross-domain experiments, i.e. one domain for training and one for testing.

Despite low results still below the baseline, we identified a correlation between lexical similarity between domains and obtained scores. For instance, results achieved using two domains with high Jaccard similarity (0.35) such as Precalculus and Geometry are much higher that those obtained comparing two domains with low Jaccard similarity (0.28), such as Precalculus and Physics

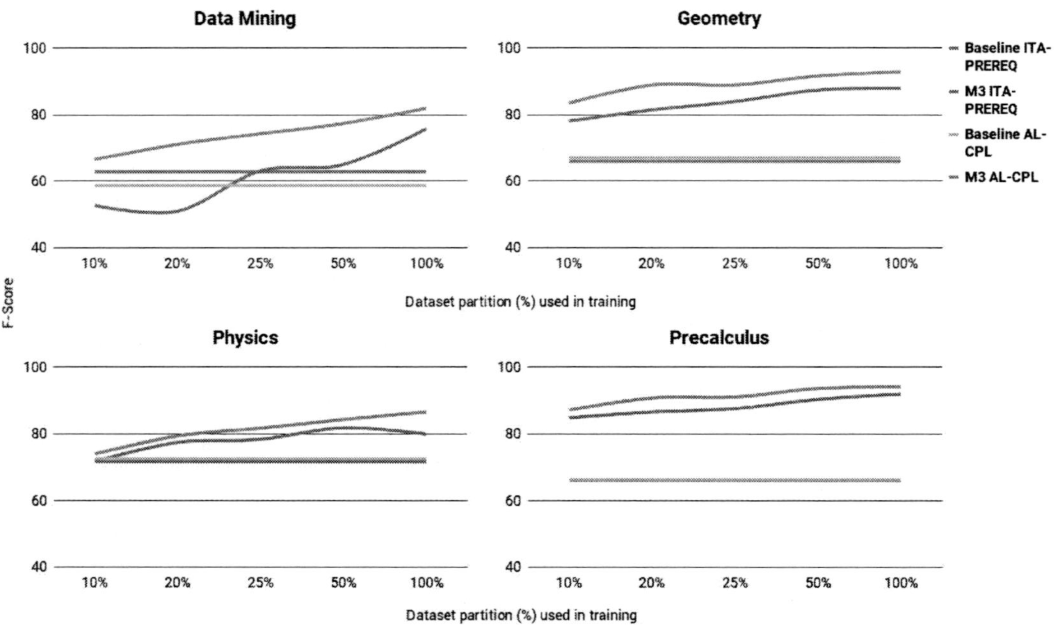

Figure 2: Incremental training strategy results for ITA-PREREQ and AL-CPL compared to the respective baselines.

(70.01% and 44.49% respectively).

However, considering that cross-domain experiments prove that further work needs to be done with this respect, in the next Section (4.2.1) we present another in-domain strategy based on incremental training with the aim of studying the impact of the training set size on the classifier performances.

4.2.1 Incremental Training Strategy

For the purposes of this paper, we describe incremental training strategy as the process of adding incrementally new concept pairs examples into the training set. Specifically, for each domain in the ITA-PREREQ and AL-CPL datasets we split the dataset in training and test set with 70% and 30% of the total examples, respectively.

We performed 5 experiments, feeding the M3 neural network model with different runs of 10%, 20%, 25%, 50% and 100% of the training set. All experiments, excluding the one with 100% of training samples, were performed using a k-fold cross validation strategy, with k equal to 10, 5, 4 and 2 according to the percentages of data samples previously defined.

Figure 2 reports results obtained for both ITA-PREREQ and AL-CPL datasets. As we can see, our model achieves good results even using limited portions of the ITA-PREREQ training data.

Specifically, for Geometry and Precalculus, even using only 10% of the training data the results we obtained are much higher than the baseline and they improve as the percentage of data samples in the training set increases. In respect to the Physics domain, we outperform the baseline by feeding our model with 20% of the training data. Using instead only 10% of the training data we obtained results comparable to those obtained by the baseline algorithm (71.78% and 71.79% respectively).

Data Mining is the only domain for which our classifier needs more training examples in order to obtain acceptable results. In fact, even if with 25% of the training set we can outperform the baseline outcomes, it is only with 100% of the examples that we are able to achieve satisfying results. This could be due to the fact that, as said previously, Data Mining is a more specialised topic with less clear prerequisite relations. Moreover, since Data Mining contains fewer concept pairs, it could be that a training set with only 10% or 20% of the concept pairs (38 and 77 respectively) is not sufficient for the network to identify regularities.

Results obtained for the AL-CPL dataset behave quite similarly, although we notice a faster increase in performances, especially for those domains that achieved lower results in the previous experiments (Data Mining and Physics).

5 Conclusion

In this paper we presented the results obtained on automatic prerequisite identification between LOs using a novel system based on neural network which exploits only linguistic features and does not rely on Wikipedia graph or LO metadata information. We performed our experiments on English and on a new Italian dataset, both in a in- and cross- domain scenario for four different domains.

The experiments demonstrated the effectiveness of our deep learning model and offer important insights into the exclusive use of linguistic feature on the task. The neural network achieved very good results for the in-domain setting, while we noticed a significant drop in performance for the cross-domain scenario. In the cross-domain setting, lexical features proved to be not well suited for the task, while global features obtained much better results, despite their simplicity. We thus think that further work needs to be done to investigate whether or not complex global features could improve the effectiveness of concept prerequisite learning models.

In the paper we also presented ITA-PREREQ, the first dataset annotated with prerequisite relation between concepts for Italian built starting from an English corpus (AL-CPL) with a completely automatic strategy.

The final goal would be to integrate this system as part of a educational design process, suggesting personalised learning paths, possibly in very distant domains from those used here, such as the humanities. We will address this lines of research in future work.

Acknowledgments

The work reported in the paper was partially supported by the 2year project (2018-2020) SchoolChain, *Soluzioni innovative per la creazione, la certificazione, il riuso e la condivisione di unità didattiche digitali allinterno del sistema Scuola*. Project funded by Regione Toscana (BANDO POR FESR 2014-2020).

References

Giovanni Adorni, Chiara Alzetta, Frosina Koceva, Samuele Passalacqua, and Ilaria Torre. 2019. Towards the identification of propaedeutic relations in textbooks. In *International Conference on Artificial Intelligence in Education (AIED)*. Springer.

Golshan B. & Papalexakis E. Agrawal, R. 2016. Toward data-driven design of educational courses: A feasibility study. *Journal of Educational Data Mining (JEDM)*, 8(1):1–21.

Chiara Alzetta, Forsina Koceva, Samuele Passalacqua, Ilaria Torre, and Giovanni Adorni. 2018. Pret: Prerequisite-enriched terminology. a case study on educational texts. In *Proceedings of the Fifth Italian Conference on Computational Linguistics CLiC-it 2018*.

Marco Baroni, Silvia Bernardini, Adriano Ferraresi, and Eros Zanchetta. 2009. The wacky wide web: a collection of very large linguistically processed web-crawled corpora. *Language resources and evaluation*, 43(3):209–226.

Devendra Singh Chaplot, Yiming Yang, Jaime G Carbonell, and Kenneth R Koedinger. 2016. Data-driven automated induction of prerequisite structure graphs. In *EDM*, pages 318–323.

Yetian Chen, José P González-Brenes, and Jin Tian. 2016. Joint discovery of skill prerequisite graphs and student models. In *EDM*, pages 46–53.

Luis De-Marcos, José J Martínez, José A Gutiérrez, Roberto Barchino, and José M Gutiérrez. 2009. A new sequencing method in web-based education. In *2009 IEEE Congress on Evolutionary Computation*, pages 3219–3225. IEEE.

Scott Deerwester, Susan T Dumais, George W Furnas, Thomas K Landauer, and Richard Harshman. 1990. Indexing by latent semantic analysis. *Journal of the American society for information science*, 41(6):391–407.

Alexander R Fabbri, Irene Li, Prawat Trairatvorakul, Yijiao He, Wei Tai Ting, Robert Tung, Caitlin Westerfield, and Dragomir R Radev. 2018. Tutorialbank: A manually-collected corpus for prerequisite chains, survey extraction and resource recommendation. *arXiv preprint arXiv:1805.04617*.

Adriano Ferraresi, Eros Zanchetta, Marco Baroni, and Silvia Bernardini. 2008. Introducing and evaluating ukwac, a very large web-derived corpus of english. In *Proceedings of the 4th Web as Corpus Workshop (WAC-4) Can we beat Google*, pages 47–54.

Fabio Gasparetti, Carlo De Medio, Carla Limongelli, Filippo Sciarrone, and Marco Temperini. 2018. Prerequisites between learning objects: Automatic extraction based on a machine learning approach. *Telematics and Informatics*, 35(3):595–610.

Fabio Gasparetti, Carla Limongelli, and Filippo Sciarrone. 2015. Exploiting wikipedia for discovering prerequisite relationships among learning objects. In *2015 International Conference on Information Technology Based Higher Education and Training (ITHET)*, pages 1–6. IEEE.

Jonathan Gordon, Stephen Aguilar, Emily Sheng, and Gully Burns. 2017. Structured generation of technical reading lists. In *Proceedings of the 12th Workshop on Innovative Use of NLP for Building Educational Applications*, pages 261–270.

Jonathan Gordon, Linhong Zhu, Aram Galstyan, Prem Natarajan, and Gully Burns. 2016. Modeling concept dependencies in a scientific corpus. In *Proceedings of the 54th Annual Meeting of the Association for Computational Linguistics (Volume 1: Long Papers)*, volume 1, pages 866–875.

IEEE. 2002. Ieee standard for learning object metadata (draft). ieee standard 1484.12.1.

Mikel Larranaga, Angel Conde, Inaki Calvo, Jon A Elorriaga, and Ana Arruarte. 2014. Automatic generation of the domain module from electronic textbooks: method and validation. *IEEE transactions on knowledge and data engineering*, 26(1):69–82.

Irene Li, Alexander R Fabbri, Robert R Tung, and Dragomir R Radev. 2019. What should i learn first: Introducing lecturebank for nlp education and prerequisite chain learning. *Proceedings of AAAI 2019*.

Chen Liang, Zhaohui Wu, Wenyi Huang, and C Lee Giles. 2015. Measuring prerequisite relations among concepts. In *Proceedings of the 2015 Conference on Empirical Methods in Natural Language Processing*, pages 1668–1674.

Chen Liang, Jianbo Ye, Shuting Wang, Bart Pursel, and C Lee Giles. 2018a. Investigating active learning for concept prerequisite learning. *Proc. EAAI*.

Chen Liang, Jianbo Ye, Zhaohui Wu, Bart Pursel, and C Lee Giles. 2017. Recovering concept prerequisite relations from university course dependencies. In *AAAI*, pages 4786–4791.

Chen Liang, Jianbo Ye, Han Zhao, Bart Pursel, and C Lee Giles. 2018b. Active learning of strict partial orders: A case study on concept prerequisite relations. *arXiv preprint arXiv:1801.06481*.

Nestor D Duque Méndez, Valentina Tabares Morales, and Rosa M Vicari. 2016. Learning object metadata mapping with learning styles as a strategy for improving usability of educational resource repositories. *IEEE Revista Iberoamericana de Tecnologias del Aprendizaje*, 11(2):101–106.

Tomas Mikolov, Kai Chen, Greg Corrado, and Jeffrey Dean. 2013. Efficient estimation of word representations in vector space. *arXiv preprint arXiv:1301.3781*.

Susan Nash. 2005. Learning objects, learning object repositories, and learning theory: Preliminary best practices for online courses. *Interdisciplinary Journal of E-Learning and Learning Objects*, 1(1):217–228.

Liangming Pan, Xiaochen Wang, Chengjiang Li, Juanzi Li, and Jie Tang. 2017. Course concept extraction in moocs via embedding-based graph propagation. In *Proceedings of the Eighth International Joint Conference on Natural Language Processing (Volume 1: Long Papers)*, volume 1, pages 875–884.

Chris Piech, Jonathan Bassen, Jonathan Huang, Surya Ganguli, Mehran Sahami, Leonidas J Guibas, and Jascha Sohl-Dickstein. 2015. Deep knowledge tracing. In *Advances in neural information processing systems*, pages 505–513.

Sudeshna Roy, Meghana Madhyastha, Sheril Lawrence, and Vaibhav Rajan. 2018. Inferring concept prerequisite relations from online educational resources. *31st AAAI Conference on Innovative Applications of Artificial Intelligence (IAAI-19)*.

Richard Scheines, Elizabeth Silver, and Ilya M Goldin. 2014. Discovering prerequisite relationships among knowledge components. In *EDM*, pages 355–356.

Partha Pratim Talukdar and William W Cohen. 2012. Crowdsourced comprehension: predicting prerequisite structure in wikipedia. In *Proceedings of the Seventh Workshop on Building Educational Applications Using NLP*, pages 307–315. Association for Computational Linguistics.

Kelvin Thompson and Francisca Yonekura. 2005. Practical guidelines for learning object granularity from one higher education setting. *Interdisciplinary Journal of E-Learning and Learning Objects*, 1(1):163–179.

Argiris Tzikopoulos, Nikos Manouselis, and Riina Vuorikari. 2009. An overview of learning object repositories. In *Database Technologies: Concepts, Methodologies, Tools, and Applications*.

Annalies Vuong, Tristan Nixon, and Brendon Towle. 2011. A method for finding prerequisites within a curriculum. In *EDM*, pages 211–216.

Shuting Wang and Lei Liu. 2016. Prerequisite concept maps extraction for automatic assessment. In *Proceedings of the 25th International Conference Companion on World Wide Web*, pages 519–521. International World Wide Web Conferences Steering Committee.

Shuting Wang, Alexander Ororbia, Zhaohui Wu, Kyle Williams, Chen Liang, Bart Pursel, and C Lee Giles. 2016. Using prerequisites to extract concept maps from textbooks. In *Proceedings of the 25th acm international on conference on information and knowledge management*, pages 317–326. ACM.

David Arnim Wiley. 2000. *Learning object design and sequencing theory*. Ph.D. thesis, Brigham Young University.

Yiming Yang, Hanxiao Liu, Jaime Carbonell, and Wanli Ma. 2015. Concept graph learning from educational data. In *Proceedings of the Eighth ACM International Conference on Web Search and Data Mining*, pages 159–168. ACM.

Amal Zouaq, Roger Nkambou, and Claude Frasson. 2007. An integrated approach for automatic aggregation of learning knowledge objects. *Interdisciplinary Journal of E-Learning and Learning Objects*, 3(1):135–162.

Grammatical-Error-Aware Incorrect Example Retrieval System for Learners of Japanese as a Second Language

Mio Arai   **Masahiro Kaneko**   **Mamoru Komachi**

Tokyo Metropolitan University

Hino City, Tokyo, Japan

{arai-mio@ed., kaneko-masahiro@ed., komachi@}tmu.ac.jp

Abstract

Existing example retrieval systems do not include grammatically incorrect examples, or only present a few examples, if any. Even if a retrieval system has a wide coverage of incorrect examples along with the correct counterparts, learners need to know whether their query includes errors. Considering the usability of retrieving incorrect examples, our proposed method uses a large-scale corpus and presents correct expressions along with incorrect expressions using a grammatical error detection system so that the learner does not need to be aware of how to search for examples. Intrinsic and extrinsic evaluations indicate that our method improves the accuracy of example sentence retrieval and the quality of a learner's writing.

1 Introduction

Grammatical error detection for learners of English as a second language (ESL) is widely studied. However, there are few studies on grammatical error detection for learners of Japanese as a second language (JSL). Most studies on grammatical error detection in Japanese focus on a learner's particular error types, mainly with particles (Suzuki and Toutanova, 2006; Imamura et al., 2012). Among others, there are studies using phrase-based statistical machine translation (PB-SMT), which does not limit the types of grammatical errors made by a learner (Mizumoto et al., 2011). However, PBSMT-based grammatical error detection cannot consider long-distance relationships because it relies on either character or word n-grams.

A standard method that supports the effort of learning a second language is the use of examples. Example retrieval systems such as Rakhilina et al. (2016) and Kilgarriff et al. (2004) in particular check for the appropriate use of words based on

the context in which they are written. However, in such a system, if the query word is incorrect, finding appropriate examples is impossible using ordinary search engines, such as Google. Even if learners have access to an incorrect example retrieval system, such as Kamata and Yamauchi (1999) and Nishina et al. (2014), they do not know how to search for the examples because they do not know whether their query includes errors. Moreover, they are often unable to rewrite a composition in the absence of correct versions of the incorrect examples. These systems are primarily developed for use by Japanese teachers. As such, they are not as helpful for learners who do not have a strong background in Japanese.

Considering this, our study develops an example sentence retrieval system[1] with grammatical error detection using the large-scale Lang-8[2] dataset for JSL by focusing on the usability of automatic incorrect example retrieval. The main contributions of this work are as follows:

- This is the first study that tackles grammatical error detection in Japanese using a neural network. It shows the state-of-the-art F score on the Lang-8 dataset and establishes a new baseline.

- To the best of our knowledge, our system is the first incorrect example sentence retrieval system using neural grammatical error detection. This function allows a user to recognize which part of the query is wrong.

- Our system seamlessly shows the incorrect sentences, and the corresponding sentences corrected by a native speaker. Thus, learners

---

[1] http://cl.sd.tmu.ac.jp/sakura/v3

[2] Multi-lingual language learning and language exchange social networking service. http://lang-8.com/

Proceedings of the Fourteenth Workshop on Innovative Use of NLP for Building Educational Applications, pages 296–305

Florence, Italy, August 2, 2019. ©2019 Association for Computational Linguistics

Name	Correct Sent.	Incorrect Sent.	Revised Sent.	Error Detection
Learners' Error Corpora of Japanese Searching Platform	✓	✓	✓	×
Tagged KY corpus	✓	✓	×	×
Proposed system	✓	✓	✓	✓

Table 1: Features of example retrieval systems for Japanese language learners. "Correct Sent." indicates whether the system can display the correct sentences; "Incorrect Sent." indicates whether the system can display the incorrect sentences; "Revised Sent." indicates whether the system can display the revised sentence corresponding to the incorrect sentence; and "Error Detection" denotes whether the system has a grammatical error detection system.

can rectify their mistakes while writing the composition.

- Our intrinsic evaluation shows that our system is good at correcting lexical choice and misformation errors in a learner's writing. Our extrinsic evaluation also shows that our example sentence retrieval system improves the quality of a learner's writing.

2 Related Works

2.1 Grammatical Error Detection

In the grammatical error detection task in English, neural methods such as Bi-LSTM in particular have been actively used (Rei et al., 2016; Rei and Yannakoudakis, 2016; Kaneko et al., 2017; Kasewa et al., 2018). Most studies on grammatical error detection/correction in Japanese limit the target learner's error types, mainly to particles (Imaeda et al., 2003; Suzuki and Toutanova, 2006; Imamura et al., 2012; Oyama et al., 2013). Among others, there are studies in Japanese grammatical error correction using statistical machine translation which do not limit the type of errors from the learner (Mizumoto et al., 2011). On the other hand, in Japanese, there are few studies on grammatical error detection and correction using neural networks.

In this study, we constructed an error detection system using a neural network without limiting the target error type. Although phrase-based statistical machine translation cannot consider long-distance relationships because it is n-gram based, neural networks using Bi-LSTM can consider long-distance relationships because they can maintain input history. Recently, neural network-based approaches outperformed PBSMT-based methods in grammatical error correction (Junczys-Dowmunt et al., 2018; Chollampatt and Ng, 2018); they are expected to be effective in grammatical error detection as well.

2.2 Example Retrieval System for Japanese as a Second Language

Various Japanese example retrieval systems were proposed in recent times. However, in practice, learners find them difficult to use. We explain herein the reasons why these systems are not effective when used by JSL learners.

Table 1 lists the features of each system. Our proposed system, Sakura, employs a large-scale Japanese JSL corpus for correct and incorrect example sentences along with revisions for the incorrect example.

First, the "Learner's Error Corpora of Japanese Searching Platform"[3] was constructed by the Corpus-based Linguistics and Language Education at Tokyo University of Foreign Studies. This system displays sentences in the keyword in context (KWIC) format based on the learner's information, such as native language, age, and gender. Japanese language teachers can identify the features of the learner's mistakes using this system. However, this system is primarily intended for educators rather than learners. As such, learners might find it confusing to use. In addition, this system has few examples. Also, the users may not know whether their query includes errors because it does not perform grammatical error detection. Therefore, they do not know how to search for the examples.

Second, the "KY corpus" is a transcribed speech corpus for JSL learners. "Tagged KY corpus" (Kamata and Yamauchi, 1999) supersedes the "KY corpus" with a search engine using POS. It displays correct and incorrect examples for text written by learners. However, it has the drawback that often, no results are provided, even for high-frequency words, because the number of incorrect examples is small; therefore, it is difficult for language learners to use the limited set of examples as a reference.

---

[3]http://ngc2068.tufs.ac.jp/corpus_ja/

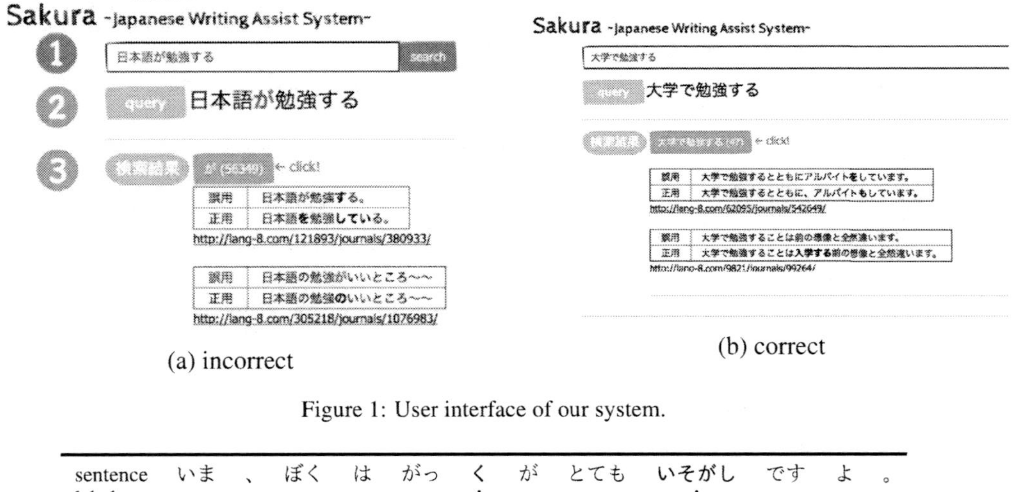

(a) incorrect   (b) correct

Figure 1: User interface of our system.

sentence	いま	、	ぼく	は	がっ	く	が	とても	いそがし	です	よ	。
label	c	c	c	c	c	i	c	c	i	c	c	c

Table 2: Example of incorrect and correct labels. The c indicates that the target word is correct. The i indicates that the target word is incorrect. The meaning of this sentence is "I am very busy at school now."

2.3 Example Retrieval System for English as a Second Language

Web-based search engines are the most common search systems that can be used to search for example sentences. However, these search engines are not intended to retrieve examples for language learners; therefore, the search engines neither show example sentences nor the correct version of a given incorrect sentence to aid learners.

Language learners can use several example retrieval systems. All of them provide special features for writing assistance, but none of them offers grammatical error detection and incorrect examples to support learners.

FLOW (Chen et al., 2012) is a system that displays some candidates for English words when ESL learners write a sentence in their native language using candidate paraphrases with bilingual pivoting. By contrast, our system suggests incorrect examples and their counterparts based on corrections from the learner corpus.

Another system, called StringNet (Wible and Tsao, 2010), displays the patterns in which a query is used, along with their frequency. The noun and the preposition are substituted by their parts of speech, in place of the words themselves, to eliminate data sparseness.

The ESCORT (Matsubara et al., 2008) system shows example sentences to learners based on the grammatical relations of queries. The syntactic structures of the English sentences are stored in the database of a raw corpus. ESCORT analyzes the dependency relations of the input queries and only displays appropriate examples that match the relations. Our system displays the examples in descending order of the cosine similarity of the input vector and vectors of the examples to avoid data sparseness.

Furthermore, ESL learners can check examples while writing an English sentence using WriteAhead (Yen et al., 2015). This system shows pattern suggestions based on collocation and syntax. For example, when the user writes "We discussed," the system displays the patterns for the use of the word "discussed."

Sketch Engine (Kilgarriff et al., 2004) displays the grammar constructs associated with words along with the thesaurus information. As previously mentioned, our system presents incorrect examples using a learner corpus apart from the correct examples extracted from a raw corpus.

3 Incorrect Example Retrieval System using Grammatical Error Detection for JSL

This section describes our incorrect example retrieval system with grammatical error detection. It combines grammatical error detection and example sentence retrieval. We assume that language learners put queries that may contain errors so that we will perform grammatical error detection on the users' input. If errors are detected, it will be passed to the incorrect example sentence search; otherwise, it will be processed by the correct example sentence search.

This section is organized as follows. Section 3.1 shows the typical use case of our system. The user interface illustrated in Section 3.2 allows learners to search for incorrect examples. The grammatical error detection algorithm is explained in Section 3.3. Our example sentence retrieval algorithm is explained in Section 3.4.

3.1 Use Case

One of the obstacle in learning Japanese as a second language is to learn the use of particles. Particles in Japanese indicate grammatical relations between verbs and nouns. For example, the sentence, "日本語を勉強する。", which means "I study Japanese." includes an accusative case marker "を", which introduces the direct object of the verb. However, in this case, Japanese learners often make mistakes, such as "日本語が勉強する。", which means "Japanese language studies." Thus, the appropriate use of particles is not obvious for non-native speakers of Japanese. Particle errors and word choice are the most common Japanese grammatical errors (Oyama et al., 2013), both of which require a sufficient number of correct and incorrect examples to understand the usage in context. A word n-gram search provides only a few or no examples for a phrase because Japanese is a relatively free word order language, in which a syntactically dependent word may appear in a distant position.

Ideally, Our system can deal with these particle errors. Figure 1 (a) illustrates an example of the search result obtained using our system. Suppose a learner wants to view examples for the usage of "日本語が勉強する (*nihongo ga benkyousuru*, which include an incorrect usage "が"(*ga*))". As can be seen in No.2 of Figure 1, our system indicates the query with "が" written in red. The learner can recognize that "が" is wrong. As can be seen in No.3 of Figure 1, our system displays correct examples using "日本語を勉強する。(*nihongo wo benkyousuru*, which is the correct euphonic form of "I study Japanese")". The learner can then identify that "が" is the incorrect word, and "を" is the correct word.

If the query returns that learner input is correct, our system shows the examples that match the query. For example, Figure 1 (b) displays the examples using "大学で勉強する (*daigaku de benkyou suru*, meaning "I study at university.")" which is the correct sentence.

3.2 User Interface

Figure 1 shows the user interface of our system. There are two types of user interfaces. Figure 1 (a) and Figure 1 (b) show the example search interfaces used when searching for incorrect and correct examples, respectively. The components of the user interface are explained below.

1. Query Input the words to be searched for. The input query is assumed to be a sentence or several words (a sequence of words).

2. Grammatical error detection The system detects errors. If errors are detected, the part with errors is displayed in red.

3. Retrieval result The retrieval results that match the query are displayed. The incorrect sentences written by learners are shown in the upper part, paired with the correct examples revised by native speakers. The revised part is represented in bold.

3.3 Grammatical Error Detection

In this study, grammatical error detection is treated as a sequence labeling task and each word in the input sentence is assigned an incorrect or correct label. Table 2 shows the example of labels. We labeled detection tags using dynamic programming from incorrect sentences and correct sentences.

We used the character- and word-level Bi-LSTM models for grammatical error detection, proposed by Rei et al. (2016). As with Rei et al. (2016), we construct a concatenation-based character-level Bi-LSTM and word-level Bi-LSTM for error detection. Our code is available on GitHub[4]. Figure 2 is the construction of our model. The system receives words $[w_1...w_T]$ as input and predicts labels for each word. A word w_t is converted to word vector e_t^w and character vector e_t^c using word-leve Bi-LSTM and character-level Bi-LSTM, respectively. The character vector is created by combining the hidden states of the beginning and the end of character-level Bi-LSTM, which takes one character as input.

---

[4]https://github.com/kanekomasahiro/japanese_error_detection

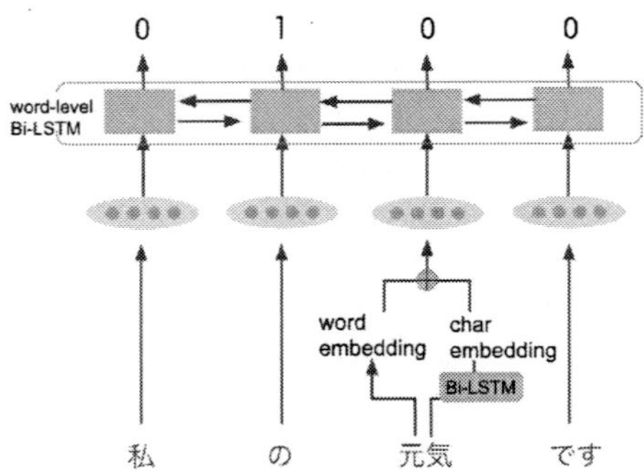

Figure 2: Architecture of our grammatical error detection.

The t-th input vector $\tilde{x}_t$ is created by combining e_t^{w} and e_t^{c}. The input vector calculates the hidden states h_t as follows using a character- and word-level Bi-LSTM (Hochreiter and Schmidhuber, 1997):

$$\overrightarrow{h}_t = LSTM(\tilde{x}_t, \overrightarrow{h}_{t-1}) \qquad (1)$$
$$\overleftarrow{h}_t = LSTM(\tilde{x}_t, \overleftarrow{h}_{t+1}) \qquad (2)$$
$$h_t = [\overrightarrow{h}_t; \overleftarrow{h}_t] \qquad (3)$$

$\overrightarrow{h}_t$ is forward LSTM, $\overleftarrow{h}_t$ is backward LSTM, and h_t is a combination of hidden states in both directions. We calculate an additional hidden layer d_t to mitigate the dimensionality difference between Bi-LSTM and the output layer using the full connected layer:

$$d_t = \tanh(W_\mathrm{d} h_t) \qquad (4)$$

W_d is a weight matrix. We make predictions using the output layer and the softmax function:

$$P(y_t | w_1 ... w_T) = \mathrm{softmax}(W_\mathrm{o} d_t) \qquad (5)$$

W_o is an output weight matrix and y_t is a prediction label.

3.4 Example Sentence Retrieval Algorithm

The input queries can be either sentences or words. Once the user enters a query, examples of incorrect sentences written by language learners and their corresponding correct sentences are retrieved from the learner corpus and displayed in pairs. The search strategy is described below:

1. The error detection model processes an input query.

2. If an error is detected, the error part of the query is searched from examples of incorrect sentences. The incorrect examples are displayed along with their correct examples in descending order of the cosine similarity[5] of the input vector and vectors of the examples of incorrect sentences.

3. If no error is detected, the entire query is searched among the examples of correct sentences. The system displays the incorrect examples along with their correct versions in descending order of the cosine similarity of the input vector and vectors of the examples of correct sentences.

4 Experiments

4.1 Dataset

In this study, we use the Lang-8 Learner Corpora created by Mizumoto et al. (2011). The developers of the dataset used it for Japanese grammatical error correction, whereas we used it as an example retrieval database for JSL.

Each learner's sentence has at least one revised sentence. A learner's sentence is combined with a revised sentence to make a sentence pair. If a learner's sentence has more than one revised sentence, each of the revised sentences is paired with the learner's sentence as separate sentence pairs. Sentences with a length of more than 100 words or with a Levenshtein distance of more than 7 are eliminated to remove the noise in the corpus.

We extracted 1.4 million pairs of learner sentences written by Japanese language learners and revised sentences corrected by Japanese native speakers. The total number of included Japanese essays was 185,991.

The learner sentences and the revised sentences were tokenized by the morphological analyzer, MeCab (ver. 0.996)[6] with UniDic (ver. 2.2.0). We used `gensim`[7] to create the sentence vectors.

4.2 Grammatical Error Detection

For the experiments with error detection, we use the dataset described in Section 4.1. We split the corpus into 720,000 sentences for training data, 1,000 sentences for development data, and 1,000

---

[5]We use word2vec (Mikolov et al., 2013) to obtain the word vectors. The average of the word vectors is taken as a sentence vector.

[6]https://github.com/taku910/mecab

[7]https://github.com/RaRe-Technologies/gensim

model	precision	recall	F-value$_{0.5}$
SMT system	0.599	0.121	0.202
proposed system	**0.615**	**0.304**	**0.407**

Table 3: Accuracy of detection of writing errors made by Japanese learner.

error type	TP	FN	FP
all	294	263	106
particle choice	**75**	60	
alternating form	16	38	
lexical choice	22	77	
omission	**33**	18	
misformation	**53**	14	
redundant	**40**	27	
pronunciation	**55**	25	
others	0	4	

Table 4: Number of true positives, false negatives, and false positives. "TP", "FN", and "FP" indicate true positive, false negative, and false positive, respectively.

sentences for test data, respectively. We used automatically converted error tags as the gold label for grammatical error detection.

Setting For hyper parameter settings, the dimension of the word embedding and the word-level LSTM are 300, and the dimension of the character embedding and the character-level LSTM are 100. The Bi-LSTM models are optimized using Adadelta with a learning rate of 1.0 and a batch size of 64 sentences. These word and character embeddings are updated during training.

We reimplemented the word-wise phrase-based statistical machine translation system of Mizumoto et al. (2011) as a baseline system. We used minimum error rate training (MERT) (Och, 2003) for the model.

Result The results are shown in Table 3. It can be seen that all of the precision, recall, and F-values are better than the baseline. As Nagata and Nakatani (2010) suggested, a high precision error detection system can be used to help learners write essays. We will verify this hypothesis in the next subsection.

Table 4 lists the number of true positives and false negatives by error type. Particle choice, pronunciation, and misformation are easy to detect. Lexical choice and alternating form are hard to detect. The number of false negatives for particle choice is large because it forms the majority of all the errors.

Table 5 shows the example sentences detected as true positives and false negatives by our method. Because of the neural network, our method can detect a long-distance error such as the column of "true positive" in Table 5. "お願い" (meaning, "Please.") is at the beginning of the sentence, because of which this sentence is not considered to be of future tense; instead, it is considered as expressing desire. Therefore, it can be seen that it is appropriate to use "〜たい" to mark desire explicitly. LSTM can deal with this kind of long-distance dependency; hence, our method can detect such errors. On the other hand, the column of "false negative" on Table 5 shows that the learner has incorrectly input "家康" as "家安". "家康" is the name of a famous historical personage, and its misspelled variant, "家安", is not in the data. The column of "false positive" on Table 5 is an example of misdetection. "名刺" is a noun and the corpus has only two instances of "名刺", which co-occur with a different particle "に" (dative case marker). Such errors cannot be detected owing to lack of data.

4.3   Incorrect Example Retrieval System

Intrinsic Evaluation We randomly extracted 55 incorrect phrases and 55 correct phrases from the learner's sentences in the Lang-8 dataset, which are not included in the corpus of the retrieval system. We classified each incorrect example into seven types: alternating form (A), lexical choice (L), omission (O), misformation (M), redundant (R), pronunciation (P), and others (X). Table 6 lists the examples of the test phrases.

Table 7 shows the frequency of each error type and the relevance of each system per error type. An example is judged relevant if it matches the auto-tagged results annotated to the data; otherwise, it is judged irrelevant. Because the user needs to select whether to search correct examples or incorrect examples in previous work, both the baseline correct example retrieval system (BC) and the baseline incorrect example retrieval system (BI) are used as the baseline systems. We searched for these phrases in each system (BC, BI, and ours) and counted the number of hits for each system that led to the top-1 correct expressions to measure relevance. The proposed system searches either the correct or incorrect sentences including the target phrase depending on whether the query contains errors while it searches for the phrase cor-

true positive	incorrect	おねがい 、 しあわせ に なる ！		
	correct	おねがい 、 しあわせ に なりたい ！		
	meaning	Please, I hope to be happy!		
false negative	incorrect	定刻 に なると 、 徳川 家**安** が 出 て き ます 。		
	correct	定刻 に なると 、 徳川 家**康** が 出 て き ます 。		
	meaning	When the time comes, Tokugawa Ieyasu will be coming.		
false positive	correct	これ 、 私 の 名刺 で ござい ます 。		
	meaning	This is my business card.		

Table 5: Examples of true positive, false negative, and false positive.

incorrect phrase	pronunciation	correct phrase	pronunciation	BC	BI	**Ours**	type
おねさん	onesan	おねえさん (sister)	oneesan	×	×	✓	O
ニュージランド	nyu-jirando	ニュージーランド (New Zealand)	nyu-ji-rando	×	✓	✓	O
みんなさん	min'nasan	みなさん (eveybody)	minasan	×	✓	✓	R
大体に	daitaini	大体 (roughly)	daitai	×	×	✓	R
疑問をして	gimonwoshite	疑問に思って (in doubt)	gimon'niomotte	×	×	✓	M
驚い	odoroi	驚き (surprise)	odoroki	×	✓	×	M
がもらえる	gamoraeru	しかもらえない (only get this)	shikamoraenai	×	×	×	A
稼ぐ	kasegu	稼いだ (earned)	kaseida	×	✓	×	A
ちさい	chisai	少ない (few)	sukunai	×	✓	×	L
助けられる	tasukerareru	できる (can)	dekiru	×	×	✓	L
しましだ	shimashida	いました (there was)	imashita	×	×	×	P
死んちゃう	shincha	死んじゃう (will die)	shinjau	×	✓	✓	P
ハウス	hausu	家 (house)	ie	×	✓	✓	X

Table 6: Examples of test results. The column "Incorrect phrase" contains the phrases written by the learner. These are extracted from the Lang-8 test set. The column "Ours" shows whether our system was able to find the correct answer for that phrase.The column "type" shows the error type of each phrase.

error type	frequency	relevance		
		BC	BI	Ours
incorrect all	55	0.00	**0.45**	0.44
alternating form	19		**0.37**	0.32
lexical choice	16		**0.38**	0.19
omission	8		**0.75**	**0.75**
misformation	6		0.40	**0.67**
redundant	3		0.67	**1.00**
pronunciation	2		**0.50**	**0.50**
others	1		**1.00**	**1.00**
correct	55	**0.90**	0.15	0.85
average	110	0.45	0.30	**0.65**

Table 7: Frequency and relevance of each system (intrinsic evaluation).

responding each system.

The BC system has the highest relevance for correct phrases, but has no matches for incorrect phrases; therefore, the relevance becomes 0.00 in the incorrect example retrieval task. BI, on the other hand, finds almost no examples when searching for correct phrases, while high relevance is obtained with incorrect phrases. In our proposed system, although the overall relevance of incorrect phrases is little lower than that of BI, the user has to switch between the incorrect retrieval and the correct retrieval in the baseline systems. The proposed system determines whether the query is correct by using error detection. This system gets the highest overall relevance, including for both the incorrect phrase and correct phrase retrieval tasks.

In contrast to the baseline system, the proposed system can detect misformation well. Because the erroneous expression is explicit in this error type, the accuracy of error detection is high and it presents relevant sentences at the top. In addition, obvious errors such as omission and redundancy are easily detected, so it receives a high relevance rate.

On the other hand, searching for a lexical choice is difficult. If the sentences written by the learner are syntactically correct but semantically incorrect, the system cannot detect errors. Additionally, because the recall of error detection is not sufficient, it sometimes misses an incorrect input query and searches through correct examples.

Extrinsic Evaluation In the extrinsic evaluation, we compared the writing scores of compo-

No.	Prompt
1	Introduce the city you live in.
2	Which do you like better, summer or winter?
3	Which aspects of Japanese do you find difficult?
4	What is the difference between televised and printed news?
5	What would you like to experience overseas?
6	If you have free time, what would you like to do?
7	Introduce the charm of your country.
8	Is it a good thing to tell a lie?
9	What are you doing for your health?
10	What was the most enjoyable thing in university life?

Table 8: Prompts for extrinsic evaluation.

Learner	BC w/o ED	BC+BI w/o ED	BC+BI w/ ED
A	14	20	**21**
B	26	27	**29**
C	15	**16**	**16**
D	**28**	25	26
E	22	**25**	**25**
F	20	23	**28**
ave.	20.8	22.7	**24.2**

Table 9: Result of extrinsic evaluation.

error type	frequency	#	relevance
incorrect all	44	9	0.20
alternating form	6	1	0.17
lexical choice	14	4	**0.29**
omission	7	1	0.14
misformation	6	2	**0.33**
redundant	9	1	0.11
pronounciation	2	0	0.00
other	0	0	0.00

Table 10: Frequency and relevance of our system for an actual learner's composition (extrinsic evaluation).

sitions using three systems. All systems used the data constructed in Section 4.1.

- BC w/o ED: Perform no error detection and search correct examples only.

- BC+BI w/o ED: Perform no error detection and search correct examples and incorrect examples according to the user's choice.

- BC+BI w/ ED: Perform error detection and search for correct and incorrect examples automatically.

We compare the writing score of the composition using the BC system w/o ED against the that of the BC+BI system w/o ED to confirm the usability of incorrect examples. We compare the writing score of the composition using BC+BI systems with and without ED to check the practicality of the error detection module.

We recruited six Japanese non-native speakers majoring in computer science in a graduate school in Japan to complete 10 Japanese composition exercises. The prompts of the 10 Japanese composition exercises are shown in Table 8. Chinese was the native language of all participants. Five of the participants had passed the N1 (advanced) Japanese-Language Proficiency Test, while the other had passed the N2 (intermediate) level. We divided the prompts into five prompts each and asked each learner to write either of the halve using the BC system w/o ED and the other half using BC+BI system w/o ED. After that, they were asked to use the BC+BI system w/ ED to revise the composition. The number of sentences in each exercise was three to ensure a fair comparison. The composition exercise was given a score by deducting points, and each participant was assigned 30 points at the beginning. One point was deducted per error. The total score of each system was taken over five exercises.

The results of the extrinsic evaluation are shown in Table 9. We confirmed that the highest score was achieved using the proposed system, and 5 out of the 6 people achieved the highest score using the proposed system.

Table 10 shows the ratio of errors that could be corrected when the compositions were first written using the BC+BI system w/o ED and then revised using the BC+BI system w/ ED. We manually checked all errors and classified them as relevant or irrelevant. As with intrinsic evaluation, misformation was corrected at the highest rate. Unlike intrinsic evaluation, lexical choice was corrected well, but it can be seen from the breakdown that function words can also be corrected at a high rate. The relevance of suggestion of lexical choice for content words was 0.17 whereas that for function words was 0.38. It was not clear from the intrinsic evaluation because function words such as particles are not the targets of evaluation, but it is understood that a neural grammatical error detection method can cope with lexical choice errors for function words such as particles frequently found in writings by learners.

303

5 Conclusion

We constructed a large-scale incorrect example retrieval system with grammatical error detection for JSL learners. Our proposed system switches between incorrect example sentence retrieval and correct example sentence retrieval automatically by using grammatical error detection and then displays incorrect examples along with the revised sentences and example sentences. The results of our experiment showed that our system was useful for JSL learners in writing Japanese compositions. Each example includes incorrect sentences; hence, language teachers can identify the difficulty faced by learners and use this information for language education.

Although this system was constructed for JSL learners, it can easily be customized for other languages. We plan to extend our system to support ESL learners (Tajiri et al., 2012).

Acknowledgements

We would like to thank the Lang-8 web organizer for providing the text data for our system. This work was partially supported by JSPS Grant-in-Aid for Scientific Research (C) Grant Number JP19K12099.

References

Mei-Hua Chen, Shih-Ting Huang, Hung-Ting Hsieh, Ting-Hui Kao, and Jason S. Chang. 2012. FLOW: A first-language-oriented writing assistant system. In *Proceedings of the ACL 2012 System Demonstrations*, pages 157–162.

Shamil Chollampatt and Hwee Tou Ng. 2018. A multi-layer convolutional encoder-decoder neural network for grammatical error correction. In *Proceedings of AAAI*, pages 5755–5762.

Sepp Hochreiter and Jürgen Schmidhuber. 1997. Long short-term memory. In *Neural Computation, 9*.

Koji Imaeda, Atsuo Kawai, Yuji Ishikawa, Ryo Nagata, and Fumito Masui. 2003. Error detection and correction of case particles in Japanese learner's composition. In *Proceedings of the Information Processing Society of Japan SIG*, pages 39–46.

Kenji Imamura, Kuniko Saito, Kugatsu Sadamitsu, and Hitoshi Nishikawa. 2012. Grammar error correction using pseudo-error sentences and domain adaptation. In *Proceedings of ACL*, pages 388–392.

Marcin Junczys-Dowmunt, Roman Grundkiewicz, Shubha Guha, and Kenneth Heafield. 2018. Approaching neural grammatical error correction as a low-resource machine translation task. In *Proceedings of ACL*, pages 595–606.

Osamu Kamata and Hiroyuki Yamauchi. 1999. KY corpus version 1.1. Report, Vocaburary Acquisition Study Group.

Masahiro Kaneko, Yuya Sakaizawa, and Mamoru Komachi. 2017. Grammatical error detection using error- and grammaticality-specific word embeddings. In *Proceedings of IJCNLP*, pages 40–48.

Sudhanshu Kasewa, Pontus Stenetorp, and Sebastian Riedel. 2018. Wronging a right: Generating better errors to improve grammatical error detection. In *Proceedings of EMNLP*, pages 4977–4983.

Adam Kilgarriff, Pavel Rychly, Pavel Smrž, and David Tugwell. 2004. The sketch engine. In *Proceedings of EURALEX*, pages 105–116.

Shigeki Matsubara, Yoshihide Kato, and Seiji Egawa. 2008. ESCORT: example sentence retrieval system as support tool for English writing. *Journal of Information Processing and Management*, 51(4):251–259.

Tomas Mikolov, Kai Chen, Greg Corrado, and Jeffrey Dean. 2013. Efficient estimation of word representations in vector space. In *Proceedings of ICLR*.

Tomoya Mizumoto, Mamoru Komachi, Masaaki Nagata, and Yuji Matsumoto. 2011. Mining revision log of language learning SNS for automated Japanese error correction of second language learners. In *Proceedings of IJCNLP*, pages 147–155.

Ryo Nagata and Kazuhide Nakatani. 2010. Evaluating performance of grammatical error detection to maximize learning effect. In *Proceedings of COLING*, pages 894–900.

Kikuko Nishina, Bor Hodošček, Yutaka Yagi, and Takeshi Abekawa. 2014. Construction of a learner corpus for Japanese language learners: Natane and Nutmeg. *Acta Linguistica Asiatica*, 4(2):37–51.

Franz Josef Och. 2003. Minimum error rate training in statistical machine translation. In *Proceedings of ACL*, pages 160–167.

Hiromi Oyama, Mamoru Komachi, and Yuji Matsumoto. 2013. Towards automatic error type classification of Japanese language learners' writing. In *Proceedings of PACLIC*, pages 163–172.

Ekaterina Rakhilina, Anastasia Vyrenkova, and Elmira Mustakimova. 2016. Building a learner corpus for Russian. In *Proceedings of the Joint Workshop on NLP for Computer Assisted Language Learning and NLP for Language Acquisition*, pages 66–75.

Marek Rei, Gamal K.O. Crichton, and Sampo Pyysalo. 2016. Attending to characters in neural sequence labeling models. In *Proceedings of COLING*, pages 309–318.

Marek Rei and Helen Yannakoudakis. 2016. Compositional sequence labeling models for error detection in learner writing. In *Proceedings of ACL*, pages 1181–1191.

Hisami Suzuki and Kristina Toutanova. 2006. Learning to predict case markers in Japanese. In *Proceedings of ACL*, pages 1049–1056.

Toshikazu Tajiri, Mamoru Komachi, and Yuji Matsumoto. 2012. Tense and aspect error correction for ESL learners using global context. In *Proceedings of ACL*, pages 198–202.

David Wible and Nai-Lung Tsao. 2010. StringNet as a computational resource for discovering and investigating linguistic constructions. In *Proceedings of the NAACL HLT Workshop on Extracting and Using Constructions in Computational Linguistics*, pages 25–31.

Tzu-Hsi Yen, Jian-Cheng Wu, Jim Chang, Joanne Boisson, and Jason Chang. 2015. WriteAhead: Mining grammar patterns in corpora for assisted writing. In *Proceedings of ACL-IJCNLP 2015 System Demonstrations*, pages 139–144.

Toward Automated Content Feedback Generation for Non-native Spontaneous Speech

Su-Youn Yoon, Ching-Ni Hsieh, Klaus Zechner,
Matthew Mulholland, Yuan Wang, and Nitin Madnani
Educational Testing Service
660 Rosedale road, Princeton, USA
{syoon, chsieh, kzechner, mmulholland, ywang, nmadnani}@ets.org

Abstract

In this study, we developed an automated algorithm to provide feedback about the specific content of non-native English speakers' spoken responses. The responses were spontaneous speech, elicited using integrated tasks where the language learners listened to and/or read passages and integrated the core content in their spoken responses. Our models detected the absence of key points considered to be important in a spoken response to a particular test question, based on two different models: (a) a model using word-embedding based content features and (b) a state-of-the art short response scoring engine using traditional n-gram based features. Both models achieved a substantially improved performance over the majority baseline, and the combination of the two models achieved a significant further improvement. In particular, the models were robust to automated speech recognition (ASR) errors, and performance based on the ASR word hypotheses was comparable to that based on manual transcriptions. The accuracy and F-score of the best model for the questions included in the train set were 0.80 and 0.68, respectively. Finally, we discussed possible approaches to generating targeted feedback about the content of a language learner's response, based on automatically detected missing key points.

1 Introduction

In this study, we propose an automated algorithm which provides feedback about the specific content of non-native English speakers' spoken responses. It is designed to help language learners preparing for a speaking test that is part of an assessment of English proficiency for academic purposes. The speaking test includes questions eliciting spontaneous speech. In particular, the items require language learners to read and/or listen to stimulus materials and then integrate and reproduce the key content from the source materials into their speaking performances (hereafter, integrated tasks). Research in integrated task performance (Brown et al., 2005; Cotos, 2011; Frost et al., 2012; Xi, 2010) has shown that human raters pay substantial attention to test-takers' speech content. A speaker's performance is evaluated by the content completeness and accuracy of the reproduced information, in addition to linguistic criteria including fluency, pronunciation, grammar, and vocabulary.

The current study investigated automated feedback through the dimension of content completeness. This content-aspect of speech performance refers to the degree to which an individual can process, select, integrate, and reproduce key source information into a subsequent oral response. The ability to reproduce complete content represents a critical aspect of integrated speaking task performance and is evaluated by the number of key points reproduced from the input materials (Frost et al., 2012). Key points are brief descriptions of content elements that test developers determine to be important in responses to a particular test question.

Providing feedback on content aspects of speech can help language learners discern the quality of their speech performance beyond linguistic dimensions such as fluency or grammar. This type of feedback is particularly relevant and crucial when we consider integrated task performance, because the ability to accurately and adequately recreate the source materials is an essential language skill required in real-world academic or workplace contexts.

Despite the importance of content as a component of speech, few studies have explored automated content feedback. To address this gap, we aim to develop a content feedback algorithm. In

Proceedings of the Fourteenth Workshop on Innovative Use of NLP for Building Educational Applications, pages 306–315
Florence, Italy, August 2, 2019. ©2019 Association for Computational Linguistics

this study, we trained automated models to detect the absence of key points that are the core content expected in correct answers. Next, we discussed possible ways to generate content feedback based on the output of the automated models.

2 Previous studies

In the past two decades, feedback has become a central issue for second language education research, and language teachers and researchers have continued to identify guidelines and best practices for providing learners with effective feedback (Lyster et al., 2013). Advances in technology have led to increased research efforts in developing automated feedback systems that can support language learners (Xi, 2010). Automated feedback systems can provide practical benefits, such as making teaching and learning more individualized, efficient, and cost effective. However, research on automated feedback is still scarce and primarily focused on aspects of learners' writing performance, rather than speech (Cotos, 2011). In automated feedback for spoken responses, previous studies focused on pronunciation (Franco et al., 2010) and prosody (Eskenazi et al., 2007) from restricted speech.

Automated scoring of, or automated feedback generation about content in spontaneous speech is a challenging task for a variety of reasons. First, an automated speech recognition (ASR) system is used to generate an automated transcription of a spoken response as an input of the content feature generator. Errors at the ASR stage may negatively affect the content features such that they are noisy and distorted to some extent. Secondly, and more importantly, spontaneous speech, unlike read speech, is highly variable, and particular aspects of content can be expressed in many different ways by different speakers. Consequently, relatively few studies have explored content of spontaneous spoken responses. Xie et al. (2012) and Cheng et al. (2014) assessed content using similarity scores between test responses and highly proficient sample responses, based on content vector analysis (CVA). Loukina and Cahill (2016) used a content-scoring engine based on many sparse features, such as unigrams and bigrams, trained on a large corpus of existing responses. These studies were based on traditional character or word n-grams. Recently, significant improvement in ASR systems, semantic modeling technology based on

more advanced deep-neural networks (DNN), and larger training data sets encouraged researchers in the automated scoring field to explore content-modeling for spoken responses. For instance, Chen et al. (2018) and Qian et al. (2018) developed automated oral proficiency scoring models using diverse neural models and achieved comparable or superior performance to sophisticated linguistic feature-based systems. In addition, Yoon et al. (2018) and Rei and Cummins (2016) used similarity scores between the prompt texts and test responses based on word embeddings. Compared to the traditional word-matching based method, they have the advantage of capturing topical relevance that is not based on specific, identical words. However, these studies have focused only on scoring, and based on our knowledge, no study has explored content feedback for spontaneous speech.

3 Overview of the approach

In order to address this gap, we developed an automated algorithm which provides feedback about content completeness for non-native speakers' spontaneous speech. Distinct from previous content scoring approaches that look at correctness of overall content by calculating similarity scores with high-scoring responses, our algorithm first determines absence of *individual* key points. The absence of a key point signals an issue in the content completeness of a spoken response. Next, we provide a list of missing key points with feedback about how to improve content completeness to the speakers. Our approach is able to provide much more fine-grained and targeted feedback about the content of a response, as compared to a traditional holistic approach.

In order to determine the absence of the key points, we calculated similarity scores between a spoken response and a key point using a short response scoring engine (Heilman and Madnani, 2013) and new word-embedding based features. The short response scoring engine generally requires a sizable amount of response data for each question to achieve a reliable performance. Collecting question-specific data is a difficult task. Thus, the word-embedding features, that do not require any sample responses for each question for the feature training, have a strong advantage for practical systems. We evaluated the algorithm in two different conditions (questions in the training data vs. questions not in the training data) and explored the impact of a question-specific training dataset.

4 Data

We used a collection of spoken responses from an English proficiency assessment. 395 non-native speakers with a wide range of proficiency levels[1] and from 52 different native language backgrounds produced a total of $1,185$ responses. Each response consisted of around one minute of spontaneous speech. We used four forms[2], and each student responded to the questions on one form. We collected approximately 100 speakers' responses per form.

When producing the integrated speaking tasks that were used for the current study, expert assessment developers first generated a list of key points to guide the creation of the reading and listening passages. These key points were provided to and used by human raters to evaluate content completeness of the spoken responses. Six key points were generated for each speaking task (henceforth, Key Point 1 to Key Point 6).

Each key point generally consisted of one complete sentence. Key Point 1 and 2 were about the mentioning of the concepts introduced in the source materials or the general opinions voiced (i.e., agree or disagree with a situation/change/proposal). Depending on the nature of the task questions, Key Point 3, 4, 5, and 6 involved brief definitions of the concepts, reasons provided for the opinions voiced, or detailed examples that illustrated the topics or concepts discussed. Key Point 1 and 2 were relatively straightforward whereas Key Point 3 to 6 contained more elaborated content.

To give an idea of what the key points look like, we provide one sample in Figure 1. Originally, a question, a reading material, and a listening material were one set, and there were three Key Points for the reading material and three Key Points for the listening material. Due to the page limit, we provide only the question, the reading material, and three Key Points relevant to the reading material.

The human transcripts of the audio files were

Figure 1: Question, reading material, and KPs

analyzed by three annotators who had backgrounds in linguistics and language education. In order to identify the Key Points that the students included or omitted in their responses, a binary scale, with 1 representing presence and 0 representing absence of each Key Point for the entire response[3], was used. The annotators paid attention to the ideas rather than the particular wording in Key Points and assigned a score of 1 (presence of Key Point) when students' conveyed the Key Points in semantically legitimate variations, not necessarily using identical expressions. The three annotators went through multiple rounds of training and calibration in order to establish inter-rater reliability. In the initial rounds of training, when there were disagreements in the annotation, the three annotators resolved the problematic cases through discussions until exact agreements were reached. After that, each annotator independently annotated roughly even numbers of responses. The inter-rater agreement was relatively strong, and Cohen's kappa based on the 22% of double-scored responses was 0.72. However, there were large variations across different Key Points and kappa ranged from 0.61 to 0.85. The number of responses and distribution of Key Point score

---

[1] We selected approximately 100 speakers per A2, B1, B2, and C1 levels based on Common European Framework of Reference for Languages (CEFR).

[2] A form is a set of three questions, and we used four forms. There were no question overlaps among different forms. Thus, we used a total of 12 questions.

[3] The annotators were not indicating the specific location of the Key Points in the responses.

are presented in Table 1.

5 Method

We used two different approaches to detect the absence of a Key Point in a spoken response. First, we trained classifiers using a set of features that calculate similarity scores between a student's response and a Key Point. Next, we trained automated models used for short response scoring.

5.1 Models based on word-embedding features

First, both Key Points and transcriptions of students' responses were normalized by removing stop words and disfluencies. After the normalization process, the length of the Key Points and responses were reduced into 60% and 40% of the original texts on average. After removing stop words, the average number of words in responses was 50.9 (based on the manual transcriptions) and 51.3 (based on the ASR hypotheses), respectively.

The number of words in the Key Point after the normalization was 3.85 on average. In particular, Key Point 1 and Key Point 2 were shorter than the other Key Points; the average number of words for Key Point 1 was 2.08, while it was 5.58 for Key Point 6. For each Key Point, we first created a word list containing all words (ALL) after the normalization. While some words (e.g., the topic or the concept name) appeared in multiple Key Points in the same question, some words were unique to a particular Key Point. Under the assumption that these unique words may be more important for detecting the absence of the specific Key Point, we created two additional word lists for each Key Point: a unique word list (Unique) [4] and a shared word list (Shared) that contained words not in the unique list.

The response was segmented into a sequence of word n-grams [5] with 5 words overlap between two consecutive n-grams. For each n-gram, the similarity with a particular Key Point was calculated using the following three word-embedding based metrics:

- Word Mover's Distance (WM-distance): This calculates a sum of the minimum distances between words in the two compared strings (a key-point and an n-gram of the response) where the distance between two words was the Euclidean distance between the two corresponding word vectors in the embedding space (Kusner et al., 2015).

- Weighted word embeddings: This calculates a cosine similarity score between a Key Point vector and a response n-gram vector. The Key Point vector was an average of the corresponding embedding vector with a tf-idf weight for each word in the Key Point. The n-gram vector was generated using the same process.

- Query-document Similarity (QD): Responses are generally much longer than Key Points and WM-distance may assign unfairly low similarity scores to responses with extra information. To address this issue, we use metrics designed for information retrieval (Kim et al., 2016). For each word in the Key Point, the algorithm finds the word with the maximum similarity from a response n-gram, where the similarity score is the cosine similarity between two corresponding word embeddings. Finally, this metric uses a sum of all maximum similarity scores normalized by the Key Point length.

Next, we generated response-level features by selecting the minimum and the maximum values among all n-grams in a response. From 9 n-gram-based features (3 Key Point word lists * 3 metrics), 18 values were selected for each response. We used the publicly available word embedding vectors trained on the Google News corpus by Mikolov et al. (2013) for all word-embedding based features, and WM-distance implementation in the gensim package (Rehurek and Sojka, 2010) for WM-distance calculation.

Finally, we trained a binary classifier using response-level features with human Key Point scores as class labels. A total of 6 binary classifiers (one per Key Point) were trained using the random forest classifier algorithm[6] in scikit-learn (Pedregosa et al., 2011).

---

[4]words unique to the particular Key Point when comparing the 6 Key Points for a given question

[5]n = the number of words in a Key Point after the normalization

[6]During a pilot experiment, multiple machine learning algorithms such as decision tree, Support Vector Machine, AdaBoost were tested, and the random forest classifier was selected based on the consistently high performance.

CEFR	# speakers	# responses	# ratings	Percentage of Key Point absence (score = 0)						
				All	KP1	KP2	KP3	KP4	KP5	KP6
A2	95	285	1710	63	48	60	60	65	71	73
B1	100	300	1800	43	32	39	38	49	48	51
B2	100	300	1800	28	21	28	17	34	32	37
C1	100	300	1800	19	22	20	11	19	15	26
Total	395	1185	7110	31	37	31	42	41	47	38

Table 1: Data size and Key Point (KP) distribution by proficiency levels

5.2 Models based on the content scoring engine

We used an automated scoring system that achieved state-of-the-art performance in scoring content of short text responses (Heilman and Madnani, 2013) (hereafter, c-rater). This is also the same system used in Loukina and Cahill (2016).

The system first generated sparse lexicalized features including word and character n-gram features and syntactic dependency features. Unlike the word-embedding features, we used an entire spoken response as an input for the feature generator. Finally, we trained a Support Vector Regressor with a radial basis function kernel for each Key Point, resulting in a total of 6 regression models. Each model was a generic model that was trained on all 12 questions[7].

6 Experiment

The speakers were partitioned into two sets: train (49%), and test sets (51%). All responses from the same speaker belonged to one set, and thus the train and test sets did not share any speakers. The percentage of each form and speakers' proficiency levels were similar in each set. In order to investigate the impact of a question-specific training dataset, we conducted 4-fold cross-validation. As described in Section 4, the data was comprised of four forms (with three questions on each form). For each fold, three forms were used as the "seen form", and the remaining form was used as the "unseen form". The model was trained only on the seen form responses in the training partition.

During evaluation, the model was evaluated on the seen form responses and the unseen form responses, separately. In the results section, we report the average of the four-folds.

We used two different transcription methods: manual transcriptions by professional transcribers and automated transcriptions by an ASR system trained on non-native speakers' speech. We used a gender-independent acoustic model (AM) trained on 800 hours of spoken responses covering over 100 native languages across 8,900 speakers using the Kaldi toolkit (Povey et al., 2011). A DNN-HMM model was adapted to test takers with fMLLR and i-vectors. The language model (LM) was a trigram model trained using the same dataset used for AM training. This ASR system achieved a Word Error Rate of 18.5% on 600 held-out responses. Detailed information about the ASR system is provided in Qian et al. (2016). In order to compare the performance of the content features with c-rater, we trained three models: EMB (model based on word-embedding features), c-rater (model based on the c-rater engine), and CMB (combination of two models). For CMB, we averaged the probabilities generated by EMB and c-rater with 0.5 as a decision boundary. Finally, for each transcription mode, we trained 18 binary classifiers.

7 Results

7.1 Performance on Seen form

Table 2 provides performance of the models on the seen forms where all questions in the test set appeared in the train set. The models were evaluated in terms of accuracy, F-score, and Cohen's kappa for detecting absence of the Key Points. We reported the average performance for 6 Key Points. In this study, the accuracy of the majority class baseline (classifying all responses as the Key Point presented) was 64% since the proportion of the responses without Key Point was 36% on av-

---

[7]We also trained a separate regression model for each question of each Key Point, resulting in $6 \times 12 = 72$ models (question-specific models). Because the overall performance of the question-specific models were not superior to the generic models, we reported only the generic model-based results. In a future study using a much larger numbers of questions, we will conduct more rigorous comparisons between the generic models and the question-specific models and select the final models.

erage.

	Model	accuracy	F-score	κ
	EMB	0.77	0.65	0.47
Manual	c-rater	0.76	0.65	0.43
	CMB	0.79	0.69	0.51
	EMB	0.77	0.64	0.46
ASR	c-rater	0.75	0.63	0.42
	CMB	0.80	0.68	0.51

Table 2: Average performance of six Key Points on seen form

For the experiment using the manual transcriptions, both the EMB and c-rater models achieved substantial improvement over the majority baseline. The performance of the EMB model was comparable to the c-rater model, and the combination of the two models resulted in further improvement. The accuracy and F-score of the CMB model were 0.79 and 0.69, respectively.

The results based on the ASR word hypotheses were comparable to those based on the manual transcriptions; the accuracy of the CMB model was 0.80 (0.79 for the manual transcription-based results) and F-score was 0.68 (0.69 for the manual transcription-based results). The EMB model achieved a slightly better performance than the c-rater model.

7.2 Performance on Unseen form

Table 3 provides the performance of the models on the unseen form where all questions in the test set did not appear in the train set.

	Model	accuracy	F-score	κ
	EMB	0.71	0.56	0.35
Manual	c-rater	0.61	0.56	0.23
	CMB	0.71	0.61	0.37
	EMB	0.71	0.54	0.33
ASR	c-rater	0.61	0.55	0.23
	CMB	0.71	0.60	0.36

Table 3: Average performance of six Key Points on unseen form

The performance of models for the unseen forms was substantially lower than that for the seen forms. For the manual transcription-based results, the accuracy and the F-score of the CMB model were 0.71 and 0.61, respectively, approximately 0.07 ~ 0.08 lower than the results on the seen form. Notably, the performance drop of the c-rater model was much larger than that of the EMB model, and the accuracy of the c-rater model was lower than the majority baseline. The performance of the EMB model was relatively better than the c-rater model, but it was still substantially lower than the performance on the seen forms. Finally, the combination of the two models resulted in a slight improvement in the F-score, but not in accuracy. The results based on the ASR word hypotheses were comparable to those based on the manual transcriptions.

The low performance of the c-rater models for the unseen form was somewhat expected. The models learned characteristic n-grams of specific Key Points from the training data. The Key Points in this study were largely different by questions, and these characteristic n-grams for one question may not be useful for other questions. The EMB models, however, did not directly use the n-gram patterns in the training data. Instead, they calculated the similarity scores between Key Points and responses using the word-embeddings-based metrics and the train set was only used to determine the relationships between these features. This difference resulted in the performance difference between the two models on the unseen forms.

In summary, the models were relatively robust to the ASR errors, and performance based on the ASR hypotheses was comparable to the manual-transcription-based performance when using a high performing ASR system. Feedback that relies on manual transcription may be a critical challenge, or not even a feasible option, for automated feedback systems used for large-scale learning programs. Therefore, the robustness to the ASR errors is an important advantage of our method. In contrast, unseen questions had a strong negative impact on the models, and the performance of the best performing model (CMB model) decreased substantially when using the unseen questions. This may raise an important challenge to adding new questions in an operational learning program; in order to add new questions without lowering system performance, a sizable amount of responses may need to be annotated for each question.

8 Discussion

The proposed models achieved promising performance in detecting missing Key Points from responses to the questions included in the training set. However, their performance was meaningfully lower than the performance of human raters; the κ between the algorithm and the human rater was 0.52, while the κ between two human raters was 0.72.

In this study, the raters did not penalize students who did not use the exact wordings in the Key Points; if a response contained a semantically comparable sentence to a Key Point, then the Key Point was considered to be present in the response. This approach may increase the difficulty of automated detection. In order to investigate how frequently students used expressions different from Key Points, we calculated a ratio of Key Point words that appeared in a response to all words in a particular Key Point (hereafter, Key Point ratio). For instance, if a Key Point is comprised of 5 words and only 2 words appear in a response, then the Key Point ratio is 0.4, and it roughly suggests that 3 words in the Key Point are realized in different expressions. If the Key Point ratios are generally low for the Key Point-present responses, then it suggests that students frequently use expressions other than those in the Key Point. We calculated Key Point ratio for each response using the manual transcription after the normalization process. Table 4 presents the average of the Key Point ratio.

Key Point type	Proportion of Key Point words in responses
Key Point 1	0.69
Key Point 2	0.54
Key Point 3	0.60
Key Point 4	0.49
Key Point 5	0.41
Key Point 6	0.51

Table 4: Average of the Key Point ratios for the Key Point-present responses

The average of the ratios for Key Point-present responses was 0.54. It ranged from 0.41 to 0.69. This suggests that around half of the words in the Key Points were realized in the different wordings in these responses.

In order to understand the reason for the relatively low use of the exact wordings, we selected a subset of Key Point-present responses with low Key Point ratio and analyzed how the Key Points were expressed. Figure 2 shows one Key Point and two sample responses. For the responses, we provide only the segments that are relevant to the

specific Key Point.

Key Point
- original: "Students use the books for papers and need to refer to them over a longer period of time."
- after normalization: "students use books papers need refer longer period time"

Example 1: "... you actually need it for a long amount of time mostly research assignments because you need the reference from the books ..."
Example 2: "the student writing a paper or something so he will be will need to go back to the book to do it his or hers research for a long time"

Figure 2: Sample Key Point and responses

Example 1 contained 3 Key Point words ("need", "time", "books"), and "reference", "longer" were realized in their morphological variations ("refer", "long"). "papers", "students", "use", and "period" were replaced with contextually legitimate expressions (e.g., "research assignments" for "papers") or omitted. In example 2, the Key Point was realized in very different wordings. For instance, the core concepts, "use books for papers" and "need the reference", were expressed as "writing a paper" and "need to go back to the book", respectively. In particular, spontaneous non-native speech includes frequent grammatical or vocabulary usage errors, and this results in even wider variations in the realization of Key Points in their responses. The Key Point in this study was generally short and 38 Key Point (53%) contained less than 3 content word types. The short Key Point length may increase the difficulty of automated detection further, since the impact of replacing one Key Point word with different wordings is large.

This analysis further motivates use of the word-embedding based features. In contrast to traditional lexical similarity features, which are limited to a reliance on exact word matching, the word embedding features have the advantage of capturing topically relevant words that are not identical. The students' responses frequently included semantically legitimate expressions that were not same words with Key Points, and this has resulted in improvements over systems using only traditional lexical similarity features.

9 Targeted feedback based on the missing Key Points

In this section, we will discuss our future plan about how to generate targeted feedback based on the automated Key Point scores. There are several reasons that language learners may miss the key information from the source materials. When a student misses a key point, it may be an issue of reading and/or listening comprehension difficulty, or it could be an indication of lower speaking proficiency. When a language learner processes, selects, and synthesizes the key information from the source materials, the individual will need to recreate the key points using their linguistic knowledge to generate the speech content. If a speaker does not possess the required linguistic knowledge to produce a full response, a speaker may reproduce inaccurate or inadequate key points. In addition, previous research has suggested that reading and/or listening to source materials and reproducing them in an assessment context is a cognitively taxing task, especially for lower-proficiency students (Brown et al., 2005). This implies that some learners may not have the necessary linguistic working memory capacity to retain all the detailed information they read or heard that would enable them to reproduce the key information satisfactorily. Thus, providing feedback about missing key points can be helpful and revealing because it indicates the gaps in spoken summaries or responses.

To address this need, our preliminary feedback algorithm provides targeted feedback about the missing Key Points. Specifically, the feedback is comprised of four parts: (a) source materials, (b) a language learner's response, (c) actionable instructions, and (d) sample responses.

The first part (source materials) provides the listening passage and/or the reading passage of the question. The expert assessment developers annotate sentences relevant to each Key Point from the source materials, and the algorithm stores this information in advance. During feedback generation, the algorithm first automatically identifies Key Points missing from a response and displays the source materials relevant to the missing Key Points.

The second part (a language learner's response) provides a function for the language learner to replay their own responses. Listening to his or her own responses while paying attention to the missing Key Points provided in the first part may help the test taker to understand the gaps in the response better. Optionally, the algorithm provides the ASR-based transcriptions of the responses.

For the third part, the algorithm first classifies a response into a sub-group based on the automated Key Point scores and provides feedback prepared for the particular group. The Key Points in this study were designed in a highly structured way, and each Key Point was tied to specific skill areas (e.g., listening and reading) or tasks (e.g., define a concept, express his/her position about the proposal). Thus, the combination of the Key Point scores for each response may reveal specific weaknesses of the language learner. For instance, a high proportion of missing Key Points related to the listening passage may indicate that the language learner has a weakness with regard to listening or integrating information from listening into speaking. The algorithm stores actionable instructions prepared based on these language learners' characteristics for each group. In addition, when applying the feedback algorithm with an automated proficiency scoring system, it further classifies a response into a sub-group based on an automatically detected proficiency level and provides feedback prepared for the particular proficiency level. The algorithm may provide different instructions for different proficiency levels, and this enables us to provide simpler and easier instructions for beginners while more complicated and sophisticated instructions are provided for the intermediate or advanced learners.

Finally, the fourth part (samples) provides representative samples from highly proficient language learners. The algorithm also provides explanations about how Key Points are expressed in their responses and what their strengths are. Optionally, the algorithm may provide some samples from low proficiency language learners with explanations about their weaknesses.

10 Conclusions

In this study, we aim to develop an automated content feedback algorithm for spontaneous speech from non-native English speakers. The algorithm was designed for integrated tasks where language learners listen to and/or read the passages and integrate the key content in their spoken responses. Focusing on the content completeness, the algorithm generated automated Key Point scores and provided targeted feedback about the missing Key Points. It achieved promising performance for questions included in the training data and also was robust to ASR errors. In future work, we will conduct a user study and investigate whether our content feedback system could lead to improvement in learners integrated speaking task performance.

Acknowledgments

We thank Aoife Cahill, Keelan Evanini, Lin Gu, Beata Beigman Klebanov, and two anonymous reviewers for their comments and suggestions. We also thank Patrick Houghton for his careful edits.

References

Annie Brown, Noriko Iwashita, and Tim McNamara. 2005. An examination of rater orientations and test-taker performance on English-for-academic-purposes speaking tasks. *ETS Research Report Series*, 2005(1):i–157.

Lei Chen, Jidong Tao, Shabnam Ghaffarzadegan, and Yao Qian. 2018. End-to-end neural network based automated speech scoring. In *2018 IEEE International Conference on Acoustics, Speech and Signal Processing (ICASSP)*, pages 6234–6238. IEEE.

Jian Cheng, Yuan Zhao D'Antilio, Xin Chen, and Jared Bernstein. 2014. Automatic assessment of the speech of young English learners. In *Proceedings of the Workshop on Innovative Use of NLP for Building Educational Applications*, pages 12–21.

Elena Cotos. 2011. Potential of automated writing evaluation feedback. *CALICO Journal*, 28(2):420–459.

Maxine Eskenazi, Angela Kennedy, Carlton Ketchum, Robert Olszewski, and Garrett Pelton. 2007. The $NativeAccent^{TM}$ pronunciation tutor: measuring success in the real world. In *Workshop on Speech and Language Technology in Education*.

Horacio Franco, Harry Bratt, Romain Rossier, Venkata Rao Gadde, Elizabeth Shriberg, Victor Abrash, and Kristin Precoda. 2010. EduSpeak®: A speech recognition and pronunciation scoring toolkit for computer-aided language learning applications. *Language Testing*, 27(3):401–418.

Kellie Frost, Catherine Elder, and Gillian Wigglesworth. 2012. Investigating the validity of an integrated listening-speaking task: A discourse-based analysis of test takers oral performances. *Language Testing*, 29(3):345–369.

Michael Heilman and Nitin Madnani. 2013. ETS: Domain adaptation and stacking for short answer scoring. In *Proceedings of the Seventh International Workshop on Semantic Evaluation (SemEval 2013)*, volume 2, pages 275–279.

Sun Kim, W John Wilbur, and Zhiyong Lu. 2016. Bridging the gap: a semantic similarity measure between queries and documents. *arXiv preprint arXiv:1608.01972*.

Matt Kusner, Yu Sun, Nicholas Kolkin, and Kilian Weinberger. 2015. From word embeddings to document distances. In *International Conference on Machine Learning*, pages 957–966.

Anastassia Loukina and Aoife Cahill. 2016. Automated scoring across different modalities. In *Proceedings of the Workshop on Innovative Use of NLP for Building Educational Applications*, pages 130–135.

Roy Lyster, Kazuya Saito, and Masatoshi Sato. 2013. Oral corrective feedback in second language classrooms. *Language teaching*, 46(1):1–40.

Tomas Mikolov, Ilya Sutskever, Kai Chen, Greg S Corrado, and Jeff Dean. 2013. Distributed representations of words and phrases and their compositionality. In *Advances in neural information processing systems*, pages 3111–3119.

F. Pedregosa, G. Varoquaux, A. Gramfort, V. Michel, B. Thirion, O. Grisel, M. Blondel, P. Prettenhofer, R. Weiss, V. Dubourg, J. Vanderplas, A. Passos, D. Cournapeau, M. Brucher, M. Perrot, and E. Duchesnay. 2011. Scikit-learn: Machine learning in Python. *Journal of Machine Learning Research*, 12:2825–2830.

Daniel Povey, Arnab Ghoshal, Gilles Boulianne, Lukas Burget, Ondrej Glembek, Nagendra Goel, Mirko Hannemann, Petr Motlicek, Yanmin Qian, Petr Schwarz, et al. 2011. The kaldi speech recognition toolkit. In *IEEE 2011 workshop on automatic speech recognition and understanding*, EPFL-CONF-192584. IEEE Signal Processing Society.

Yao Qian, Rutuja Ubale, Matthew Mulholland, Keelan Evanini, and Xinhao Wang. 2018. A prompt-aware neural network approach to content-based scoring of non-native spontaneous speech. In *Proceedings of the 2018 Workshop on Spoken Language Technology*.

Yao Qian, Xinhao Wang, Keelan Evanini, and David Suendermann-Oeft. 2016. Self-adaptive dnn for improving spoken language proficiency assessment. In *INTERSPEECH*, pages 3122–3126.

Radim Rehurek and Petr Sojka. 2010. Software framework for topic modelling with large corpora. In *In Proceedings of the LREC 2010 Workshop on New Challenges for NLP Frameworks*.

Marek Rei and Ronan Cummins. 2016. Sentence similarity measures for fine-grained estimation of topical relevance in learner essays. In *Proceedings of the 11th Workshop on Innovative Use of NLP for Building Educational Applications*, pages 283–288.

Xiaoming Xi. 2010. Automated scoring and feedback systems: Where are we and where are we heading? *Language Testing*, 27(3):291–300.

Shasha Xie, Keelan Evanini, and Klaus Zechner. 2012. Exploring content features for automated speech scoring. In *Proceedings of NAACL*, pages 103–111.

Su-Youn Yoon, Anastassia Loukina, Chong Min Lee, Matthew Mulholland, Xinhao Wang, and Ikkyu Choi. 2018. Word-embedding based content features for automated oral proficiency scoring. In *Proceedings of the Third Workshop on Semantic Deep Learning*, pages 12–22.

Analytic Score Prediction and Justification Identification
in Automated Short Answer Scoring

Tomoya Mizumoto[1,2*] **Hiroki Ouchi**[1,2] **Yoriko Isobe**[1] **Paul Reisert**[1,2]
Ryo Nagata[3,1] **Satoshi Sekine**[1] **Kentaro Inui**[2,1]
[1]RIKEN AIP, [2]Tohoku University, [3]Konan University
{tomoya.mizumoto, hiroki.ouchi, yoriko.isobe, paul.reisert, satoshi.sekine}@riken.jp,
nagata-bea2019@ml.hyogo-u.ac.jp., inui@ecei.tohoku.ac.jp

Abstract

This paper provides an analytical assessment of student short answer responses with a view to potential benefits in pedagogical contexts. We first propose and formalize two novel analytical assessment tasks: analytic score prediction and justification identification, and then provide the first dataset created for analytic short answer scoring research. Subsequently, we present a neural baseline model and report our extensive empirical results to demonstrate how our dataset can be used to explore new and intriguing technical challenges in short answer scoring. The dataset is publicly available for research purposes.

1 Introduction

Short answer scoring (SAS) is the task of assessing short, written, free-text student responses to a given prompt. Typically, a prompt is a text which either elicits recall of information that was given in a reading passage, asks for a summary of a reading passage, or asks students to draw on knowledge they already have. The task is to assess the responses based on context and writing quality, in accordance with the criteria prespecified for each assessment by a *scoring rubric*. Automation of this process has the potential to significantly reduce the workload of human raters and has attracted a considerable amount of attention from both academia and industry (Riordan et al., 2017; Zhao et al., 2017; Sultan et al., 2016; Heilman and Madnani, 2015; Pulman and Sukkarieh, 2005; Leacock and Chodorow, 2003; Vigilante, 1999, etc.).

It should be emphasized that, in admissions tests and other tests, such as writing proficiency tests, large groups of students receive and respond to the exact same set of problems, for which

---

Current affiliation: Future Corporation, mizumoto.tomoya.mh7@is.naist.jp

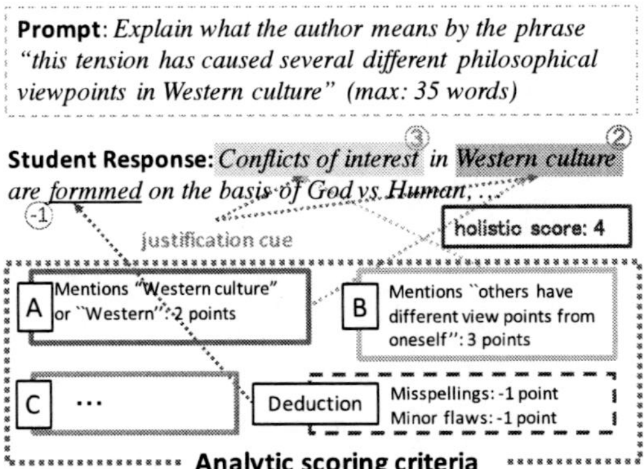

Figure 1: Example of short answer scoring with several analytic criteria.

rubrics have been prepared in advance. In other words, rubrics are normally available in the SAS setting as they are in preset paper assignments. Additionally, at least a small amount of training data is also available because responses are scored by human raters in any case.

This paper examines the issue of analytical assessment of short answer responses. Typically, in a short answer setting, a scoring rubric comprises multiple analytic criteria, each of which stipulates different aspects of the conditions necessary for a response to receive points, and the overall score (referred to as the *holistic score*) of a given student response is determined by some predefined function (e.g., summation) of the score gained for each analytic criterion (*analytic score*).

Consider the example illustrated in Figure 1, where a student response is assessed according to multiple analytic scoring rubrics (denoted by A, B, C, etc.). The response gains two points for analytic criterion A (denoted by the red circled "2") and three points for B (yellow circled "3"), and the holistic score is given by the total of the analytic scores (+2 for A, +3 for B, and −1 for the mis-

Proceedings of the Fourteenth Workshop on Innovative Use of NLP for Building Educational Applications, pages 316–325
Florence, Italy, August 2, 2019. ©2019 Association for Computational Linguistics

spelling).

Assessing student responses by analytic scores as well as holistic scores is essential in pedagogical contexts because (i) for teachers, analytic scores are useful for a precise assessment of student proficiency, and (ii) for students, analytic scores can be used as informative feedback indicating what has been achieved and what remains to be learned next. To the best of our knowledge, however, no prior study on automatic SAS has ever addressed this task.

Motivated by this background, we propose and formalize two analytical assessment tasks of SAS, (i) *analytic score prediction* and (ii) *justification identification*. Analytic score prediction is the task of predicting the analytic score for each analytic scoring criterion, whereas justification identification is the task of identifying the *justification cue* for each analytic score. By justification cue, we refer to the segment of the response (a subsequence of words) that causes the response to be awarded points in the analytic score. In Figure 1, for example, the phrase *Western culture* is identified as a justification for criterion A, whereas the phrase *Conflicts of interest* is a justification for criterion B. Justification cues not only explain the model's prediction but also help students learn how to improve their responses.

One crucial issue in addressing such analytical assessment tasks is the lack of data. The datasets that are presently available for SAS research (Mohler et al., 2011; ASAP-SAS; Dzikovska et al., 2013; Basu et al., 2013, etc.) are all accompanied by annotations of holistic scores alone. In this study, we developed a new dataset with annotated analytic scores and justification cues as well as holistic scores. The dataset contains 2,100 sample student responses for each of six distinct reading comprehension test prompts, collected from commercial achievement tests for Japanese high school students. The dataset is publicly available for research purposes.[1]

SAS requires content-based, prompt-specific rubrics, which means that one needs to create a labeled dataset to train a model for each given prompt. This nature of the task raises the issue of how one can reduce the required labelling costs while achieving sufficient performance. This challenge is even more critical in analytical assess-

ment because annotating student responses with analytic scores and justification cues tends to be much more costly than when only holistic scores are used. This study explores several situations with limited amounts of analytic scores and justification cues as well as large numbers of holistic scores. We show that analytical assessment performance for analytic score prediction and justification identification can be improved by compensating for a lack of data with these different types of annotations.

The contributions of this work are three-fold. First, we propose and formalize two analytical assessment tasks: analytic score prediction and justification identification. Second, we have created the first dataset for analytic SAS and released it for research. Third, we present a neural baseline model and report some of the empirical results to demonstrate how our dataset can be used to address new amd intriguing technical challenges in SAS.

2 Task

2.1 Analytic criteria

We assume that each prompt is provided with a scoring rubric which comprises several (typically two to four) analytic criteria. Each analytic criterion stipulates the conditions under which a student response will gain an analytic score, typically in the form of "if it includes the content $\langle \ldots \rangle$, the response gains x points."

A response may lose a few points owing to misspellings or other minor flaws (referred to as *deductions*). We also regard the criteria for such deductions as special analytic scoring rubrics which are allotted negative points.

The holistic (total) score of a response is assumed to be the sum of all the item scores including the deductions.

2.2 Analytic score prediction

Analytic score prediction is the task of predicting the score of a given student response for each analytic criterion. Given a student response that consists of T words $w_{1:T} = (w_1, \cdots, w_T)$, the goal is to predict the analytic score $y^{(m)} \in \mathbb{R}$ for each criterion $m \in \mathcal{M}$, where $\mathcal{M}$ is a given set of analytic criteria.

As an evaluation metric, we use quadratic weighted kappa (QWK) (Cohen, 1968), which is commonly used in the SAS literature.

---

[1] https://aip-nlu.gitlab.io/resources/sas-japanese

2.3 Justification identification

Justification identification is the task of identifying a justification cue in a given student response for each analytic score. A justification cue is the segment of a response that causes that response to gain points in the analytic score. For a content-based criterion (i.e., a criterion of the form "if it includes the content $\langle\ldots\rangle$, the response gains x points"), the fragment that explicitly expresses the required content is a justification cue. Justification cues not only explain the model's prediction but also help students learn how to improve their responses.

Formally, given a student response $w_{1:T} = (w_1, \cdots, w_T)$, the goal is to identify the phrase $w_{i:j}^{(m)} = (w_i, \cdots, w_j)$, where $1 \leq i \leq j \leq T$, for each criterion m. As an evaluation metric, we use precision, recall and F1 scores based on the overlaps between gold-standard (henceforth "gold") and predicted justification cues (phrases). Consider the following example.

> *A carbon filament was used.*
> [gold   ]
>   [pred   ]

Here, the gold justification is *A carbon filament*, and the predicted one is *filament was*. The number of true positives (TP) is 1 (*filament*), that of false positives (FP) is 1 (*was*), and that of false negatives (FN) is 2 (*A carbon*). Thus we can calculate the precision, $1/(1 + 1) = 0.50$, and the recall, $1/(1 + 2) = 0.33$. F1 score is then $2 \times 0.50 \times 0.33/(0.50 + 0.33) = 0.398$.

3 Dataset

This section provides an overview of our dataset.

3.1 Original dataset

Table 1 shows the statistics of our dataset. The dataset consists of six prompts and 2,100 student responses for each prompt. Those prompts and their rubrics were collected from commercial achievement tests provided by a long-standing leading education company, where problems and rubrics are carefully generated by professional experts. All the prompts are for reading comprehension tests and are of the type that requires recall of information that has been given (either explicitly or implicitly) in a reading passage.

Responses (6 prompts × 2,100 responses) were originally annotated with holistic scores by professional raters employed by the education company (not by those employed for this research). Before the scoring, the raters were carefully instructed about the rubrics and conducted a trial annotation on the same sample response set for calibration.

3.2 Analytical assessment annotation

Each prompt in this dataset has three or four analytic criteria. The stipulation of each criterion is provided in the rubric. However, the responses in the dataset were originally annotated only with holistic scores and not with analytic scores. This is often the case in the real-world answer scoring business because (i) the manual annotation of individual analytic scores tends to be very costly, and (ii) proficient human assessors can efficiently grade a student response with a holistic score taking analytic scores into account "implicitly". Accordingly, we employed expert annotators and conducted additional annotation of all the responses with analytic scores and justification cues.

Before instructing the annotators to work on the dataset, we first investigated the difficulty of annotation. For each prompt, we randomly sampled 100 responses from the 2,100 responses and used them to train and calibrate the annotators. During this calibration process, we instructed the annotators to identify analytic scores so that, for each given student response, the sum of the analytic scores would be equal to the holistic score given in the original dataset. Then, using 100 additional exclusively sampled responses, we measured the inter-annotator agreement.

Table 2 shows the inter-annotator agreement of analytic scores for each prompt in Kappa (Cohen, 1960) and QWK. The results are reasonably high. This means that the annotation of analytic scores is not too difficult for expert human annotators. Given this observation, the remaining 1,900 responses for each prompt were annotated by a single annotator with self-double checking. To avoid inconsistency across annotators, we assigned all 1,900 responses to each prompt to the same annotator. Furthermore, if an annotator was not confident about scoring a given response, the annotator was instructed to discuss the response with person who prepared the the exam to reach a consensus. As a result, we obtained 12,600 student responses (6 prompts × 2,100 responses) with ana-

	Q1	Q2	Q3	Q4	Q5	Q6
Max holistic score	16	12	12	15	15	14
Average holistic score	6.8	4.0	5.3	5.5	4.6	5.5
Standard deviation	3.5	1.8	2.1	2.7	2.6	3.1
# analytic criteria	4	4	4	3	3	3
length (char.) limit	70	50	60	70	70	60
Average length (char.)	62.86	45.15	54.13	65.53	64.83	55.44

Table 1: Statistics of our dataset.

	Q1	Q2	Q3	Q4	Q5	Q6	Ave.
Kappa	.93	.92	.79	.70	.83	.82	.84
QWK	.96	.94	.76	.84	.82	.90	.87

Table 2: Inter-annotator agreement of analytic scores in Kappa (Cohen, 1960) and Quadratic Weighted Kappa (QWK) (Cohen, 1968). The scores are calculated by averaging the agreement scores for each analytic criterion.

lytic scores and justification cues for each prompt.

In the future, we intend to extend the dataset by adding a wider variety of prompts. In fact, we have already started the annotation for three additional prompts and plan to extend the dataset to a far larger scale. However, our current dataset is already as large as the biggest existing datasets available for SAS research (ASAP-SAS), and furthermore, no prior dataset has been annotated with analytical assessment.

4 A Neural Baseline Model

The goal of the rest of the paper is to demonstrate how our dataset can be used to address intriguing but as yet unexplored challenges in analytic SAS. To this end, we first present our neural network baseline model in this section and then report some of the experimental results withwe have obtained using the model in the next section.

4.1 Overall architecture

Figure 2 illustrates the overall architecture of our baseline model. The idea is three-fold: (i) build a distinct model of analytic score prediction for each analytic criterion based on Riordan et al. (2017)'s model for holistic SAS, (ii) train the analytic score prediction models jointly with the holistic score prediction model, and (iii) use supervised attention for justification identification.

The model includes $|\mathcal{M}|$ analytic score models and an addition layer. First, the input student response $w_{1:T} = (w_1, w_2, \cdots, w_T)$ is mapped to word embeddings. Second, these embeddings are

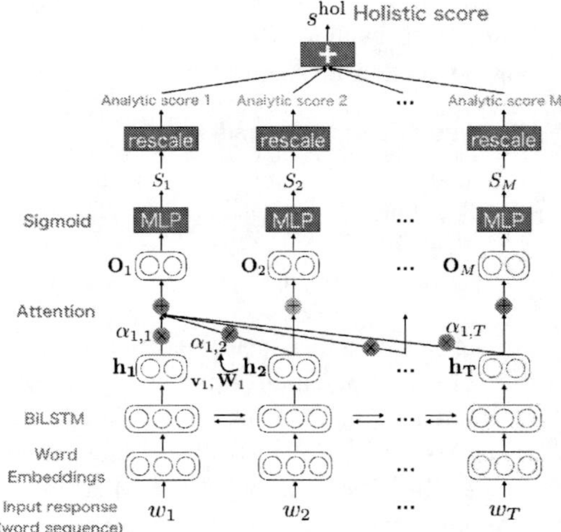

Figure 2: Overview of the baseline model for analytic short answer scoring.

fed to the BiLSTM layer. Third, through an attention mechanism associated with each analytic criterion $m \in \mathcal{M}$, an analytic scoring model outputs the analytic score s_m. Finally, the addition layer sums up the analytic scores to calculate the holistic score s_{hol},

Formally, the holistic score s_{hol} is calculated by summing all the analytic scores $\{s_m \mid m \in \mathcal{M}\}$.

$$s_{\text{hol}} = \max\left(\sum_{m \in \mathcal{M}} \text{rescale}(s_m), 0 \right) , \quad (1)$$

$$s_m = f_m(w_{1:T}) . \quad (2)$$

Here, we use $\max(\cdot, 0)$ to prevent negative scoring in the event that no scoring rubric criteria are met, misspellings, and other minor flaws. The function "rescale$(\cdot)$" scales the analytic score back to the original score range. As Equation 3 in Section 4.2 shows, we use the sigmoid function to compute each analytic score. This means that each analytic score takes a value from 0 to 1, i.e., $s_m \in [0, 1]$. We thus re-scale the 0-1 ranged score to the original scaled score. Consider a case in which the analytic scoring model outputs $s_m = 0.7$ for an analytic criterion assigned 3 points. The rescale func-

319

tion multiplies 3 by the score $s_m = 0.7$, and the resulting score is 2.1. This score of 2.1 is then rounded off, and 2 is summed into the holistic score.

One advantage of this architecture is that the connection between the holistic and analytic scoring models enables the loss of the holistic score to back-propagate to the analytic scoring models. This means that without analytic score annotations, each analytic scoring model can still be trained with holistic score signals.

4.2 Analytic scoring model

Each analytic scoring model f_m in Equation 2 is defined as follows:

$$f_m(w) = \text{sigmoid}(\mathbf{w}_m \cdot \mathbf{o}_m + b_m) \ , \quad (3)$$

, where $\mathbf{w}_m$ is a parameter vector and b_m is a bias value. An attention vector $\mathbf{o}_m$ is calculated by an attention mechanism, i.e., $\mathbf{o}_m = f_m^{\text{att}}(\mathbf{h}_{1:T})$, where a sequence of the hidden states $\mathbf{h}_{1:T} = (\mathbf{h}_1, \cdots, \mathbf{h}_T)$ is output by a BiLSTM layer.

As mentioned above, owing to the use of the sigmoid function, each analytic score takes a value from 0 to 1, i.e., $s_m \in [0, 1]$. In the training phase, we also scale gold analytic scores to match the scale. In the evaluation phase, the predicted scores are re-scaled back to their original range.

4.3 Attention mechanism

An attention mechanism f_m^{att} is defined as follows:

$$f_m^{\text{att}}(\mathbf{h}_{1:T}) = \sum_{t=1}^{T} \alpha_{m,t} \mathbf{h}_t \quad (4)$$

An attention value $\alpha_{m,t}$ denotes the importance weight, which represents relative importance of the t-th word for predicting analytic score s_m.

4.4 Justification identification method

The attention mechanism is used not only for analytic score prediction but also for justification identification. Specifically, based on the attention scores α, we extract a set of justification cues C.

$$\alpha_{\max} = \max_{t=1,\cdots,T} \alpha_t \ ,$$
$$C = \{t \in [1, T] \mid \alpha_{\max} - \alpha_t < \beta\} \ .$$

Here, we first calculate the maximum attention score $\alpha_{\max}$ among all the attention scores. We then extract the word indices t if the difference between the maximum score $\alpha_{\max}$ and its score α_t is less than the threshold β. As a result, we can obtain a set of justification cues C. The threshold β is a hyperparameter, which is selected by using the development set.

4.5 Training

Training with analytic scores. To train each analytic scoring model, we minimize the mean squared error (MSE) as the loss function,

$$\frac{1}{N} \sum_{n=1}^{N} \sum_{i \in \mathcal{I}^{(n)}} (s_i^{(n)} - \hat{s}_i^{(n)})^2 \ , \quad (5)$$

where N is the number of training instances, and $s_i^{(n)}$ and $\hat{s}_i^{(n)}$ are the predicted score and gold score, respectively.

Training with holistic scores. To train the whole network on holistic score annotations, we minimize the MSE calculated with gold and predicted holistic scores (Equation 1) as follows:

$$\frac{1}{N} \sum_{n=1}^{N} (s_{\text{hol}}^{(n)} - \hat{s}_{\text{hol}}^{(n)})^2 \ , \quad (6)$$

where N is the number of training instances, and $s_{\text{hol}}^{(n)}$ and $\hat{s}_{\text{hol}}^{(n)}$ are the predicted score and gold score, respectively.

Supervised attention. We further train the attention mechanism for each criterion in a supervised manner, called supervised attention (Mi et al., 2016; Liu et al., 2016; Kamigaito et al., 2017). In supervised attention, attention is learned from the difference between the span where the attention is focused and the given gold signal of a justification cue. Following a previous study by Liu et al. (2016), we add a soft constraint method to obtain the following objective function:

$$\sum_{i \in \mathcal{I}} \{ \frac{1}{N} \sum_{n=1}^{N} (s_i^{(n)} - \hat{s}_i^{(n)})^2$$
$$+ \frac{\lambda}{N} \sum_{n=1}^{N} \sum_{t=1}^{T} (\alpha_{i,t}^{(n)} - \hat{\alpha}_{i,t}^{(n)})^2 \} \quad (7)$$

where $\alpha_{i,t}^{(n)}$ denotes an attention weight, $\hat{\alpha}_{i,t}$ is the supervision of attention that corresponds to the justification cue annotated by human assessors, and $\lambda > 0$ is a hyper-parameter. If the t-th word is part of a gold justification cue (e.g., the phrase

"Western culture" in Figure 1), $\hat{\alpha}_{i,t}^{(n)}$ is 1, otherwise it is 0.

If an analytic score is zero, all the attention weights $\{\hat{\alpha}_{i,t}^{(n)}\}_{t=1}^{T}$ take zero values. To solve this problem, we explicitly encode the information that there is no justification cue by appending a dummy token to an input sequence. Specifically, we add $\hat{\alpha}_{i,T+1}$ to $\{\hat{\alpha}_{i,t}\}_{t=1}^{T}$ and set its value to 1 if an analytic score is zero and to 0 otherwise.

5 Experiments

5.1 Settings

Dataset We first split our dataset into three subsets for each prompt: 1,600 responses for training, 250 responses for development, and 250 responses for testing. To tokenize the response texts, we employed an off-the-shelf morphological analyzer, MeCab 0.98 (Kudo et al., 2004), with default settings.

Implementation We implemented the neural baseline model with Keras and TensorFlow. The code will be made publicly available at *an anonymous URL* once the paper is accepted. We chose the same hyperparameters and training settings as in Riordan et al. (2017)'s holistic scoring model.

SVR Baseline We also implemented another simpler baseline model based on the support vector regression model (SVR) following Sakaguchi et al. (2015) to provide sparse feature-based baseline results. We adopted the feature set proposed by Sakaguchi et al. (2015), which includes word 1-gram, word 2-gram, and predicate-argument structure features[2]. We used KNP 4.16 (Kawahara and Kurohashi, 2006) to extract Japanese predicate-argument structure features.

5.2 Experimental scenarios

As argued in Sections 1 and 3.2, one crucial issue in analytic SAS is that the annotation of analytic scores and justification cues is far more expensive than holistic score annotation. One of our primary concerns, therefore, is finding ways to reduce the required labeling costs while achieving sufficient performance. To explore this issue, we consider three experimental scenarios:

---

[2]We excluded response length and character n-gram features because the performance was worse on the development set.

	Q1	Q2	Q3	Q4	Q5	Q6	Ave.
Analytic/Justification: 25							
SVR	.55	.60	.20	.54	.58	.45	.486
NN base	.60	.62	.19	.58	.64	.47	.516
+just.	.74	.73	.29	.64	.74	.53	.610
+hol.	.94	.84	.48	.72	.86	.75	.764
Analytic/Justification: 50							
SVR	.69	.73	.29	.64	.68	.56	.596
NN base	.77	.78	.29	.68	.72	.59	.638
+just.	.83	.85	.38	.71	.78	.64	.700
+hol.	.95	.93	.59	.71	.87	.79	.806
Analytic/Justification: 100							
SVR	.77	.80	.35	.72	.73	.66	.670
NN base	.87	.84	.40	.74	.79	.67	.719
+just.	.90	.88	.52	.76	.81	.72	.767
+hol.	.96	.93	.67	.81	.87	.82	.844
Analytic/Justification: 200							
SVR	.85	.87	.44	.77	.78	.71	.735
NN base	.92	.91	.57	.78	.83	.76	.794
+just.	.95	.92	.65	.80	.84	.78	.822
+hol.	.97	.94	.72	.82	.88	.83	.859
human	.96	.94	.76	.84	.82	.90	.873

Table 3: Performance in QWK for analytic score prediction. "SVR" denotes the SVR baseline model described in Section 5.1. "NN base", "+just. ", and "+hol. " denote the models trained in the three hypothetical situations, Situations (i) to (iii), described in Section 5.2., respectively.

Scenario (i): Basic setting (analytic score signals only) The first scenario assumes that we only have analytic scores annotated to a small set of responses. Thus we can train a model on these annotations for each task. We consider this scenario as our baseline scenario. We refer to the model for this scenario as "NN base."

Scenario (ii): (i) + justification signals In addition to the analytic score annotations, the second scenario assumes that we have justification cues annotated to the same set of responses. We can thus train a model on both the analytic score and justification annotations.

Scenario (iii): (ii) + holistic score signals In addition to the analytic scores and justification cues, the third scenario assumes that we have holistic scores annotated to a relatively large set of responses. In addition to implementing supervised learning, we can train models in a weakly supervised manner using holistic scores.

All the reported results are the average of ten distinct trials with the use of ten different random seeds.

5.3 Analytic score prediction

Scenario (i) Table 3 shows the results of each model. Here we vary the numbers of analytic scores and justification cues used for training each model. "Analytic/Justification: N" denotes that we used $N \in \{25, 50, 100, 200\}$ analytic scores and justification cues, respectively.[3] In all the settings, the base analytic scoring model (NN base) consistently outperformed the SVR. Also, compared with human performance, the analytic scoring models yields reasonably strong results.

Scenario (ii) Here, we are interested in the effects of gold justification signals on analytic score prediction. In Table 3, "+just." denotes the models trained on N analytic scores and the same number of justification signals. Comparing the base model (NN base) with the justification-added model (+just.), we observed that gold justification signals consistently improved the base model in all the settings. This result reveals that gold justification signals are useful for analytic score prediction.

Scenario (iii) Another issue is the effects of holistic score signals on analytic score prediction. In Table 3, "+hol." denotes the models trained on N analytic score signals, N justification signals, and 1,600 holistic scores signals. Comparing the justification-added model (+just) with the holistic-score-added model (+hol.), we observed that extra holistic score signals contributed to further performance improvement. This result suggests that holistic score signals are useful for analytic score prediction.

Summary These results suggest that our scenarios (ii) and (iii) are both worth considering in order to improve the performance of analytic score prediction. Note that the gains achieved by incorporating scenarios (ii) and (iii) are both statistically significant ($p < 0.01$ by a paired bootstrap test (Koehn, 2004)). Specifically, the performance of the "+just." model was significantly better than that of the "NN base" model for all the prompts. The performance of the "+hol." model was also significantly better than that of the "+just." model for all the prompts.

	Prec.	Rec.	F1
NN base (100)	.332	.491	.349
+just. (100)	.837	.703	.758
+hol.	.807	.692	.738

Table 4: Performance of justification identification.

5.4 Justification identification

Scenario (i) Table 4 shows the results for justification identification. The "NN base" model is trained on analytic scores of 100 responses. This means that we used no justification signals for training. Nevertheless, the model was able to identify some phrases that appeared in the training responses frequently and that were strongly associated with analytic scores (e.g., the phrase "Western culture" in Figure 1). This result suggests that, although this model's performance was not very strong, some useful information relevant to justification identification can be exploited from the analytic score signals alone.

Scenario (ii) In Table 4, "+just." denotes the model trained on analytic scores as well as the justification cues of 100 responses. Naturally, the model's performance was drastically improved when we fed it the gold justification signals (0.349 to 0.758 in F1).

Scenario (iii) In Table 4, "+hol." denotes the model trained on 100 analytic score signals, 100 justification signals, and 1,600 holistic score signals. Interestingly, the model's performance was not improved by the incorporation of the extra holistic score signals (0.758 vs. 0.738 in F1). This is in contrast to the case of analytic score prediction task, which was improved by the extra holistic score signals. A more in-depth analysis of this matter is needed, but our findings do raise the nontrivial question of which architecture is optimal to maximize the gain that results from including justification identification from holistic score signals.

Additional analysis Another interesting question deals with how well the accuracy of analytic score prediction correlates with the accuracy of justification identification. We observed that the neural baseline models showed strong performance for justification identification. These results raise the simple question of whether the sys-

---

[3]Since our dataset is entirely annotated with analytic scores, one could conduct experiments with more training signals.

tem is able to correctly predict the analytic scores for each response with the same high performance seen in justification identification. To answer this question, we created two subgroups from among the responses to Q3[4]: (i) responses with higher precision ($>$ .70) and (ii) those with lower precision ($<$ .50) on the justification identification task. We then calculated the QWK for each of these groups. We obtained QWK values of 0.835 and 0.182 (averaged across all the criteria) for responses with higher and lower precision, respectively. This strong correlation between analytic scoring and justification empirically indicates the feasibility of simultaneously pursuing the two analytical assessment tasks because one benefits from the other.

5.5 Holistic score prediction

Our dataset can, of course, be used to conduct experiments on holistic SAS as well. One unique advantage of our dataset is that it contains analytic scores and justification cues, and thus one can draw more profound insights using these new types of annotations. For example, we can investigate the effects of analytic score signals on holistic score prediction.

Table 5 shows the results for holistic score prediction. The first thing to note here is the comparison between the SVR model and the "hol." model trained on only the holistic score signals. We can observe that the "SVR" model consistently outperformed the "hol." model, that the difference in their performance was smaller with a larger training set, and that the two models have nearly comparable QWK (0.848 vs. 0.844) for $n = 1600$. The second issue is the comparison between the "hol." model and the "analytic" model trained on only the analytic score signals. In all the settings, the "analytic" model considerably outperformed the "hol." model. This indicates that analytic score signals are very informative for training a holistic score prediction model as well. The third issue is the comparison between the "NN base" model and the "+just." model trained on both the analytic score and justification signals. We can observe that using justification signals as well as analytic score signals for training further boosts the performance at holistic score prediction, particularly when the training set is smaller.

---

[4]To simplify the analysis, we selected Q3, which exhibited the lowest performance.

n	100	200	400	800	1600
SVR (n)	.724	.772	.810	.832	.848
hol. (n)	.671	.733	.782	.815	.844
NN base (n)	.738	.803	.841	.869	.891
+just. (n)	.776	.827	.856	.876	.892

Table 5: The performances of holistic score prediction. n denotes the number of training instances (responses). "hol. (n)" denotes the model trained with n holistic score signals only. "NN base (n)" denotes the model trained with the analytic score signals of n responses. "+just. (n)" denotes the model trained with both analytic scores and justification signals of n responses.

Summary These results imply that, when only a limited number of responses is available for training a holistic scoring model, it may well be worth annotating them with analytic scores and justification cues as well as with holistic scores. Note that this findings regarding the correlation between holistic and analytic score predictions has never previously been reported in the context of SAS. Our dataset containing analytic score and justification annotations opens up several potential directions of research in the field of SAS.

6 Related Work

Short answer scoring Previous research on SAS has solely focused on holistic score prediction. We believe that this is partly because, to date, the publicly available datasets for SAS have contained holistic scores only (Mohler et al., 2011; Dzikovska et al., 2012, 2013; ASAP-SAS) . To the best of our knowledge, our dataset is the first to provide both annotated analytic scores and their justification cues.

Analytical assessment Analytical assessment has been studied in the context of automated essay scoring (Persing and Ng, 2016, 2015, etc.). The analytic criteria adopted in essay scoring tend to be more general, e.g., organization, clarity, and argument strength. In contrast, analytic criteria in SAS are typically *prompt-specific* as in our examples in Figure 1. Thus, the analytic criteria need to be learned by the model separately for each individual prompt. It is an interesting open question whether the insights gained from essay scoring research can be applicable to analytic SAS research.

Interpretability of neural models In recent years, the interpretability of neural models has received widespread attention. Some research on interpretability has been conducted in the image processing field (Bach et al., 2015; Shrikumar et al., 2017). In NLP, researchers have attempted to interpret the model by analyzing the focus of attention of neural networks (Ghader and Monz, 2017; Vinyals et al., 2015). In these previous studies, however, the attention was qualitatively rather than quantitatively analyzed. In contrast, we quantitatively evaluated the justifications by examining the extent to which justification cues correspond to the span on which the system focuses to predict the analytic score. To the best of our knowledge, this is the first evaluation of the performance of justifications (i.e., interpretability) in SAS.

7 Conclusion

In this paper, we have examined analytical assessment for SAS. We proposed and formalized two analytic tasks: (i) analytic score prediction and (ii) justification identification. For these tasks, we developed a new dataset with analytic score and justification cue annotations. We then designed a neural model that predicts analytic scores simultaneously with a holistic score and trained the model with only a small number of analytic score signals and a larger number of holistic score signals. Through our extensive experiments, we have provided intriguing research scenarios and questions on the correlations between analytic and holistic scores.

One interesting line of future research is the possibility of developing datasets in other languages. It is worth examining scoring models in multilingual settings, although we plan to start by creating and releasing an English-language dataset. Another line of future research could include the development of more sophisticated models. In this paper, analytic scoring models calculate scores independently, yet there are some interdependencies between analytic score criteria. Accordingly, we plan to develop a model that incorporates this interdependency.

Acknowledgements

We thank Tomoya Okubo for helping to obtain the data for Japanese short answer scoring and Takamiya Gakuen Yoyogi Seminar for providing the data.

References

ASAP-SAS. 2012. Scoring short answer essays. ASAP short answer scoring competition system description.

Sebastian Bach, Alexander Binder, Grégoire Montavon, Frederick Klauschen, Klaus-Robert Müller, and Wojciech Samek. 2015. On Pixel-Wise Explanations for Non-Linear Classifier Decisions by Layer-Wise Relevance Propagation. *PloS one*, 10(7).

Sumit Basu, Chuck Jacobs, and Lucy Vanderwende. 2013. Powergrading: a Clustering Approach to Amplify Human Effort for Short Answer Grading. *Transactions of the Association for Computational Linguistics*, 1:391–402.

Jacob Cohen. 1960. A Coefficient of Agreement for Nominal Scales. *Educational and Psychological Measurement*, 20(1):37–46.

Jacob Cohen. 1968. Weighted Kappa: Nominal Scale Agreement with Provision for Scaled Disagreement or Partial Credit. *Psychological bulletin*, 70(4):213–220.

Myroslava O. Dzikovska, Rodney D. Nielsen, and Chris Brew. 2012. Towards Effective Tutorial Feedback for Explanation Questions: A Dataset and Baselines. In *Proceedings of the 2012 Conference of the North American Chapter of the Association for Computational Linguistics: Human Language Technologies (NAACL-HLT)*, pages 200–210.

Myroslava O. Dzikovska, Rodney D. Nielsen, Chris Brew, Claudia Leacock, Danilo Giampiccolo, Luisa Bentivogli, Peter Clark, Ido Dagan, and Hoa Trang Dang. 2013. SemEval-2013 Task 7: The Joint Student Response Analysis and 8th Recognizing Textual Entailment Challenge. In *Proceedings of the Seventh International Workshop on Semantic Evaluation (SemEval)*, pages 263–274.

Hamidreza Ghader and Christof Monz. 2017. What does Attention in Neural Machine Translation Pay Attention to? In *Proceedings of the 8th International Joint Conference on Natural Language Processing (IJCNLP)*, pages 30–39.

Michael Heilman and Nitin Madnani. 2015. The Impact of Training Data on Automated Short Answer Scoring Performance. In *Proceedings of the 10th Workshop on Building Educational Applications Using NLP (BEA)*, pages 81–85.

Hidetaka Kamigaito, Katsuhiko Hayashi, Tsutomu Hirao, Hiroya Takamura, Manabu Okumura, and Masaaki Nagata. 2017. Supervised Attention for Sequence-to-Sequence Constituency Parsing. In *Proceedings of the 8th International Joint Conference on Natural Language Processing (IJCNLP)*, pages 7–12.

Daisuke Kawahara and Sadao Kurohashi. 2006. A Fully-Lexicalized Probabilistic Model for Japanese Syntactic and Case Structure Analysis. In *Proceedings of Human Language Technologies: The 2006 Annual Conference of the North American Chapter of the Association for Computational Linguistics (NAACL-HLT)*, pages 176–183.

Philipp Koehn. 2004. Statistical Significance Tests for Machine Translation Evaluation. In *Proceedings of the 2004 Conference on Empirical Methods in Natural Language Processing (EMNLP)*, pages 388–395.

Taku Kudo, Kaoru Yamamoto, and Yuji Matsumoto. 2004. Applying Conditional Random Fields to Japanese Morphological Analysis. In *Proceedings of the 2004 Conference on Empirical Methods in Natural Language Processing (EMNLP)*, pages 230–237.

Claudia Leacock and Martin Chodorow. 2003. C-rater: Automated Scoring of Short-Answer Questions. *Computer and the Humanities*, 37:389–405.

Lemao Liu, Masao Utiyama, Andrew Finch, and Eiichiro Sumita. 2016. Neural Machine Translation with Supervised Attention. In *Proceedings of the 26th International Conference on Computational Linguistics (COLING)*, pages 3093–3102.

Haitao Mi, Zhiguo Wang, and Abe Ittycheriah. 2016. Supervised Attentions for Neural Machine Translation. In *Proceedings of the 2016 Conference on Empirical Methods in Natural Language Processing (EMNLP)*, pages 2283–2288.

Michael Mohler, Razvan Bunescu, and Rada Mihalcea. 2011. Learning to Grade Short Answer Questions using Semantic Similarity Measures and Dependency Graph Alignments. In *Proceedings of the 49th Annual Meeting of the Association for Computational Linguistics: Human Language Technologies (ACL-HLT)*, pages 752–762.

Isaac Persing and Vincent Ng. 2015. Modeling Argument Strength in Student Essays. In *Proceedings of the 53rd Annual Meeting of the Association for Computational Linguistics and the 7th International Joint Conference on Natural Language Processing (ACL-IJCNLP)*, pages 543–552.

Isaac Persing and Vincent Ng. 2016. Modeling Stance in Student Essays. In *Proceedings of the 54th Annual Meeting of the Association for Computational Linguistics (ACL)*, pages 2174–2184.

Stephen G. Pulman and Jana Z. Sukkarieh. 2005. Automatic Short Answer Marking. In *Proceedings of the Second Workshop on Building Educational Applications Using NLP (BEA)*, pages 9–16.

Brian Riordan, Andrea Horbach, Aoife Cahill, Torsten Zesch, and Chong Min Lee. 2017. Investigating Neural Architectures for Short Answer Scoring. In *Proceedings of the 12th Workshop on Building Educational Applications Using NLP (BEA)*, pages 159–168.

Keisuke Sakaguchi, Michael Heilman, and Nitin Madnani. 2015. Effective Feature Integration for Automated Short Answer Scoring. In *Proceedings of the 2015 Conference of the North American Chapter of the Association for Computational Linguistics: Human Language Technologies (NAACL-HLT)*, pages 1049–1054.

Avanti Shrikumar, Peyton Greenside, and Anshul Kundaje. 2017. Learning Important Features Through Propagating Activation Differences. In *Proceedings of the Thirty-fourth International Conference on Machine Learning (ICML)*, pages 3145–3153.

Md Arafat Sultan, Cristobal Salazar, and Tamara Sumner. 2016. Fast and Easy Short Answer Grading with High Accuracy. In *Proceedings of the 2016 Conference of the North American Chapter of the Association for Computational Linguistics: Human Language Technologies (NAACL-HLT)*, pages 1070–1075.

Richard Vigilante. 1999. Online Computer Scoring of Constructed-response Questions. *Journal of information technology impact*, 1(2):57–62.

Oriol Vinyals, Lukasz Kaiser, Terry Koo, Slav Petrov, Ilya Sutskever, and Geoffrey Hinton. 2015. Grammar As a Foreign Language. In *Proceedings of Advances in Neural Information Processing Systems 28 (NIPS)*, pages 2773–2781.

Siyuan Zhao, Yaqiong Zhang, Xiaolu Xiong, Anthony Botelho, and Neil T. Heffernan. 2017. A Memory-Augmented Neural Model for Automated Grading. In *Proceedings of Fourth ACM Conference on Learning @ Scale*, pages 189–192.

Content Customization for Micro Learning using Human Augmented AI Techniques

Ayush Shah[1], Tamer Abuelsaad[2], Jae-Wook Ahn[2], Prasenjit Dey[2],
Ravi Kokku[2], Ruhi Sharma Mittal[1], Aditya Vempaty[2], Mourvi Sharma[1]
[1]IBM Research - India, [2]IBM Research - Yorktown Heights, NY, USA
`ayush13027@iiitd.ac.in`, {`tamera, jaewook.ahn`}`@us.ibm.com`
{`prasenjit.dey, ruhi.sharma`}`@in.ibm.com`, `aditya.vempaty@ieee.org`
{`ravi.kokku, mourvi`}`@gmail.com`

Abstract

Visual content has been proven to be effective for micro-learning compared to other media. In this paper, we discuss leveraging this observation in our efforts to build audio-visual content for young learners' vocabulary learning. We attempt to tackle two major issues in the process of traditional visual curation tasks. Generic learning videos do not necessarily satisfy the unique context of a learner and/or an educator, and hence may not result in maximal learning outcomes. Also, manual video curation by educators is a highly labor-intensive process. To this end, we present a customizable micro-learning audio-visual content curation tool that is designed to reduce the human (educator) effort in creating just-in-time learning videos from a textual description (learning script). This provides educators with control of the content while preparing the learning scripts. As a use case, we automatically generate learning videos with British National Corpus' (BNC) frequently spoken vocabulary words and evaluate them with experts. They positively recommended the generated learning videos with an average rating of 4.25 on a Likert scale of 5 points. The inter-annotator agreement between the experts for the video quality was substantial (Fleiss Kappa=0.62) with an overall agreement of 81%.

1 Introduction

Various studies have shown that learning with audio-visual content leads to better retention and engagement than just reading text or listening to spoken content (Parkinson, 2012; Lankow et al., 2012). The flipped-classroom model (Bishop and Verleger, 2013) makes a case for increased use of videos in learning, where students can use audio-visual content to learn concepts at their own pace, freeing up the educator's time to prepare for other personalized one-on-one interactions with their students. This approach is especially attractive for micro-learning that deals with relatively small learning units and short-term learning activities. As much as educators (including parents and caregivers) desire to use audio-visual content to make learning more engaging, customized content production is often difficult to scale and cost prohibitive. While instructors could create their own customized content, this is labor-intensive, given the wide variety of concepts and domain areas children need to be exposed to. Every educator may have a different learning-objective in mind. To teach a vocabulary word, instructors provide a definition of the word highlighting the important characteristics of it along with some contextual information (Beck et al., 2013). For instance, if a teacher wants to teach about "Elephant" focusing on its habitat she may want to show Elephant in Forests, and Grasslands. However, a generic video obtained from the web may emphasize on the different body parts of the Elephant. Moreover, the student's age is an important factor. If teaching a concept to a small child, educators would want to avoid violent or inappropriate images. Similarly, a slightly grown up learner may not resonate with cartoons being shown for learning. Hence, the educator should have an option to customize scripts to reflect their intended learning objective and be able to control the appropriateness of visuals. To this end, we explore a human-augmented approach that leverages AI techniques for creating customized content by a just-in-time combination of contextual image content mined from the Internet, along with appropriate voice-over. This human-machine semi-automated approach has high potential to address the instructional needs of young learners who are in the process of acquiring basic conceptual ideas across domains for the first time, particularly in areas that need identification and recall.

Proceedings of the Fourteenth Workshop on Innovative Use of NLP for Building Educational Applications, pages 326–335
Florence, Italy, August 2, 2019. ©2019 Association for Computational Linguistics

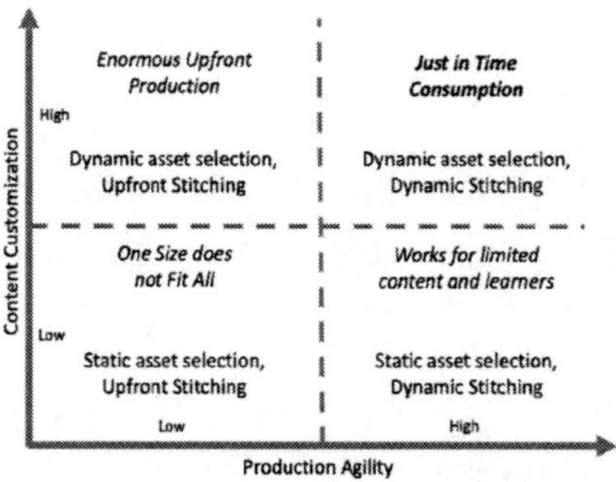

Figure 1: Framework for Content Creation

The trade-off between the agility of content production and content customization exposes a wide design space (as depicted in Figure 1). Most learner-oblivious content falls into the bottom left quadrant, which works well when the content does not require customization (like content including hard facts such as the place or year an event occurred, the name of an inventor etc.). Solutions in the bottom right quadrant enable flexible and efficient creation of content at run-time, allowing for more flexibility of content presentation, although it requires upfront planning of all the content. Solutions in the top left quadrant require content to be curated upfront for many possible customized scenarios (which could be prohibitively expensive), so that they can be just selected at run-time. For young learners, especially, high content customization is desirable, which often cannot be generated upfront since the context in which a learning moment occurs cannot be known a priori. Our ideal goal is to be able to operate in the top right quadrant to ensure maximal learning outcomes. To this end, we explore a solution that enables just-in-time production of audio-visual content for vocabulary learning when supplied with learning scripts. Our system processes a *learning script* in natural language (selected by the educator based on their learning requirements), along with an image library, to semi-automatically generate a multi-modal *learning video*: with voice-over and contextual images synchronized in a way that the video is coherent and easily comprehended by young children. A learning-script is the textual manuscript for the learning-video. The voice-over is generated using a text-to-speech engine and hence can be customized to different requirements of a friendly or familiar speech model (e.g. that of a favourite cartoon character) for a child to maximize engagement. Using an audio-visual format, the same concept can be presented in a multitude of ways customized to each child's unique learning trajectory, context, and interests. Educators are familiar with a child's learning trajectory and areas of interest, and hence our solution allows customizing a default textual script or write a new script. The system takes this customized textual script, uses NLP techniques to extract relevant features and their representative images, uses human assistance to *verify* images, and finally creates a video. Since this content is created for children, human verification process is critical to ensure that no inappropriate image content has inadvertently crept in as the system automatically pulls relevant images from the image repository based on textual features of the script. As automatic safe image search becomes more readily feasible, human assistance could be reduced further. More importantly, this approach achieves our main goal of reducing the content creation load for educators because it is much easier to *verify* created content than to *create* new content from scratch.

The rest of the paper is organized as follows. We review the related work in Section 2. In Section 3, we explain our proposed system and all the system components. In Section 4, we describe the experiment and evaluation results of our model. In Section 5, we present the future work and finally, we conclude in Section 6.

2   Related Work

Our goal is to create just-in-time learning-videos using textual input and an image library mined from the Internet. In this section, we discuss prior work related to these different aspects.

Word Concreteness: Using NLP techniques with word-concreteness we derive meaningful search phrases from textual scripts which help curate visuals for aptly representing the script. Many previous studies have shown the importance of word-concreteness as a measure and come up with ways to compute this score (Hessel et al., 2018; Kiela et al., 2018). Also, some work has been done in assisting and evaluating creative writing (Roemmele and Gordon, 2018; Somasundaran et al., 2018).

Personalized Learning: Prior work has explored various dimensions of dynamic personalized learning. Jovanovic et al.(2006) demonstrate how semantic-web based learning objectives can be decomposed into content units, which on reassembly produce content-sequence personalized to the needs of each student. This serves as a valuable complimentary effort to scale our approach based on the semantic web and learner models. Our focus remains on generating learning-videos by combining various available media, when provided with scripts.

Automated Visual Generation: There have been some efforts aimed at creating slideshows given a script, like My Simple Slideshow[1]. This tool identifies keywords from the text corresponding to which they have images. These image cutouts are brought together on the screen to create a visual description similar to the text. However, the combination of different individual images may not convey the overall intended meaning of the sentence. Hence, it is important to contextualize the images based on the sentence context or bring in images which represent multiple connected keywords. Scene construction has also been considered in a project 'Imagine This'(Gupta et al., 2018). The authors have identified various entities and actions present in a script, and then used those to create a scene by combining image segments. This is based on first training over a database consisting of the constituent scene objects and actions from a densely annotated video dataset. Since we focus on building slideshows, and not complete motion videos we circumvent the problem of generating continuous frames. Rather than creating or combining images and scenes, we construct search terms to get the most relevant images.

3   Solution Overview

We explore human-assisted just-in-time curation of learning content for micro-learning. Our solution enables educators to generate learning videos for vocabulary words very easily: First, we automatically create sample scripts for a vocabulary word based on definitions and usage sentences from Simple English Wiktionary[2] and allow educators to edit them. Alternatively, they can also write their own scripts if they are not satisfied with the generated script. Once a script is chosen, the system uses a set of natural language processing (NLP) techniques to derive a list of relevant search terms or concepts. The search terms are then used

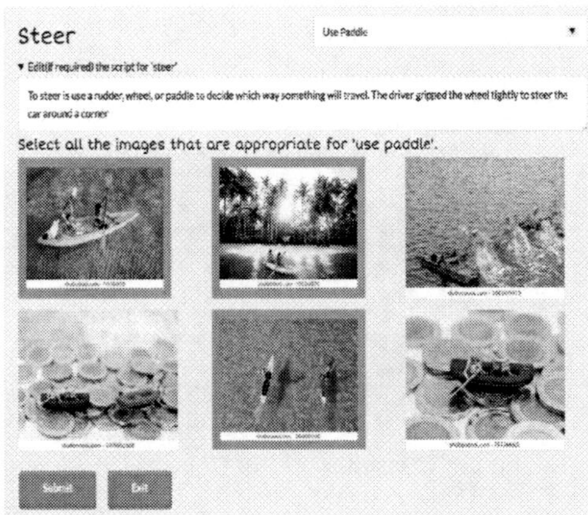

Figure 2: Sample screen for Script and Image Verification. The green boxes represent selected images.

to fetch images from an image repository (such as Shutterstock[3]) and display them to the educator for validation. During the validation phase, the educator selects the images they prefer for each search term. With time, the educator preferences are learned and the images presented for validation are ranked in a personalized manner.

A sample screen for script and image verification is shown in Figure 2 for the word 'steer'. The available script, can be edited, and the corresponding search terms drop down (top right) gets populated accordingly. The screen shows Image Verification for the search term 'use paddle' extracted from the script. The educators can simply tap on the images which look appropriate. Once the image validation phase is completed, the system aligns and stitches selected images along with the speech synthesized script. The output is a learning video personalized to the given script. Notably, the tasks of mining and ranking relevant visual content (which is heavy-weight for humans) are relatively easily done by the machine, and the tasks of verifying the appropriateness of the content (which is often heavy-weight for machines) is done by humans.

3.1   Terminology

- A *learning-script* is the manuscript for the *learning-video*. It can be a textual/contextual description or definition of a vocabulary word/concept. We often refer to a learning-script as *script*, and to the learning-video as *video*.

- A *vocabulary-word* is the word/concept for which given a script, the system generates a learning-video.

- Image *labels* are the words or phrases assigned to images to describe them. Image repositories often assign multiple labels/keywords for every image.

- A *slice* is a part of the learning-script that maps to a search term. A learning-script can have multiple slices.

- *Concreteness* refers to how palpable a word is or how much is it perceptible through senses. The *concreteness score* of a word measures its concreteness, the higher the value the more concrete a word is.

- A *concrete word* is a word that has a concreteness score exceeding a given threshold. We use concreteness scores from (Brysbaert et al., 2014)

- *Grammar templates* are templates derived from Dependency Parsing and Part of Speech (POS). We construct grammar templates to extract terms related to concrete words.

- A *search tree* consists of search terms. Each child node in the tree is a substring of the parent search term.

- The *prioritized search terms* are the Level Order Traversal of the Search Tree.

Word Concreteness: Word concreteness is an established term in the field of psychology (Paivio et al., 1968; Kounios and Holcomb, 1994). Some studies have relied on crowd-sourcing to compute average concreteness scores for a majority of the commonly used words in the English language (Brysbaert et al., 2014). Multi-modal machine learning techniques also utilize concreteness scores for improving performance (Young et al., 2014).

3.2 System Architecture

An educator selects a vocabulary-word to be taught. The available scripts are displayed. The educator selects a script and optionally edits it. The script is then passed to the NLP Layer. Figure 3 shows the system architecture and layer-wise components, with a face indicating the components requiring human intervention.

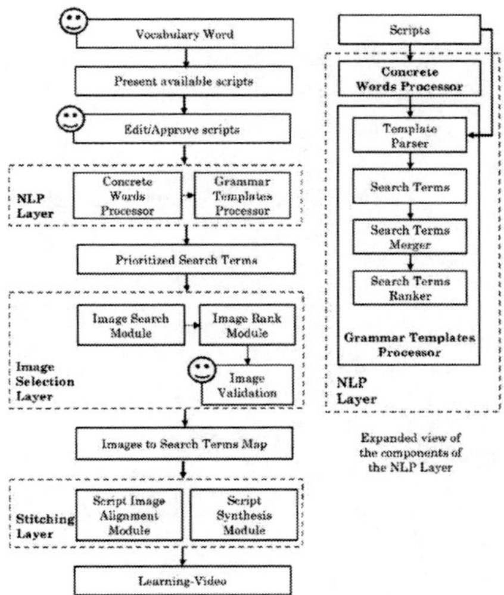

Figure 3: System Architecture

3.2.1 NLP Layer

The NLP layer processes the learning-script to provide prioritized search terms on a sentence level. First, sentence tokenization is performed. Next, each sentence is examined, using the *Concrete Words Processor*, to identify any concrete words present. Concrete words imply a higher likelihood of finding appropriate images in an image repository. However, the concrete words by themselves might not adhere to script usage context and therefore make for poor search terms. For example consider the script *"Many people prefer to commute to work via public transport as it is cheaper than having a car"*. The concrete words obtained from the Concrete Words Processor are shown in Figure 5. If a concrete word like 'work' was solely used, it will produce images that are not contextually appropriate to the sentence. However, if 'commute work' is used, it could yield more contextual results. Therefore, to construct contextually appropriate search terms, it is important that some context from the script is used to support the concrete words. To this end, we construct grammar templates, such as Noun Templates and Prepositional Templates. The expanded view of the NLP layer components is shown in the Figure 3.

Grammar Templates Processor: The dependency relations and POS are determined for the words in the script and then the script is passed to the *Template Parser* along with the Concrete Words. Every template match is extracted and

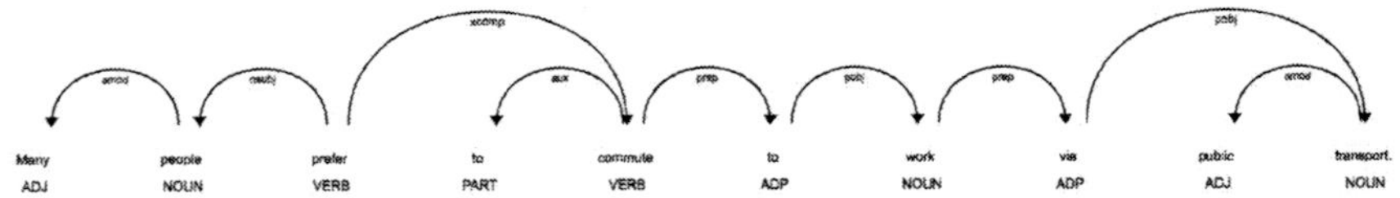

Figure 4: Dependency relations for a part of the script snippet for 'commute'.

Figure 5: Script snippet processing for 'commute'

added to the Search Terms. Each match must include one or more of the identified Concrete Words. Stop-words are omitted from all the Search Terms. Figure 5 shows a detailed example of the script for the word 'commute' as it is processed through the NLP Layer.

Grammatical Relationships: We use a 3-tuple representation of the form *(arrow tail POS, dependency relation, arrow head POS)* for expressing the grammatical relationship between two words (represented by arcs in Figure 4). For instance consider the two words 'public' (arrow head of the relation arc) and 'transport' (arrow tail of the relation arc) from Figure 4. In this case the 3-tuple relationship is represented as *(Noun, amod, Adj)*. A three word relationship is considered a combination of two two-word relationships. Therefore we extend the notation to represent a three word relationship using a 5-tuple representation in the form *(POS, Dependency Relation, POS, Dependency Relation, POS)*. In this case the middle POS is the head of the first dependency relation and the tail of the second. Consider the example of 'commute to work' from the Figure 4. The corresponding representation becomes *(Verb, prep, Adp, pobj, Noun)*.

Template Parser: In this paper, we discuss two grammar templates that we implemented, however, others can be constructed and utilized by our framework. We construct templates in the 3-tuple and 5-tuple format defined above. In the tuple we fix a few elements and put '*' in the rest of them to represent an any element match. This indicates that any value in position of '*' is acceptable.

Our generic *Noun Templates* are *(Noun, *, *)* and *(*, *, Noun)*. If a concrete word is a noun, then the Noun Template checks if it is part of a Noun Phrase. If so, the Noun Phrase is added to the Search Terms. Further, the Dependency Parser is used to check the relations of the Noun or Noun Phrase. A sample dependency relation is shown in Figure 4. This was obtained using an online visualization tool Displacy[4].

The related terms are added along with the Noun or Noun Phrase to the Search Terms. For example in Figure 4, for the noun term 'people', a search term constructed is 'people prefer'. The relation *(Noun, nsubj, Verb)* matches the template *(Noun, *, *)*. nsubj refers to the nominal subject relationship. Similarly for the noun term 'transport' the search term 'public transport' is added. This acts as a noun phrase and *(Noun, amod, Adj)* also matches the template *(Noun, *, *)*. Here amod refers to the adjectival modifier relationship. The Search Terms coming from the Noun Templates have been shown in Figure 5 as Noun Search Terms.

Prep refers to the prepositional modifier dependency. For *Prep Templates* the adjectives, verbs and nouns having the prep relations are considered along with their corresponding object relationships. If these contain a concrete word then they are added to the Search Terms. We define the prep templates in the 5-tuple format *(*, prep, *, obj, *)* and *(*, obj, *, prep, *)*. Words are added to the search terms for any relations that match these templates. For example, in the Figure 4 the relation 'commute to work' has the form *(Verb, prep, Adp, pobj, Noun)*, which passes the first prep template. Please note that pobj (object of preposition), belongs to the obj (object) relationship. Removing 'to' which is a stop word, we add 'commute work' to the Search Terms. The Search Terms contributed by the Prep Templates

―――――――――
[4]https://explosion.ai/demos/displacy

are shown in Figure 5 as Prep Search Terms.

In *Search Terms Merger* (Figure 3), the Search Terms are checked for overlap. The merged terms are added to the Merged Search Terms. For example, for search terms 'commute work transport' and 'public transport'. In this case these would be merged into 'commute work public transport' (Figure 5). Further, all the remaining concrete words which were not part of any templates are individually added as search terms. For example, in the commute example, 'car' does not have any matching templates and is added as such to the Merged Search Terms. We believe that chains of contextually related words represent the intent of a given sentence much better than individual words. The merged chains shape the Prioritized Search Terms.

In *Search Terms Ranker* (Figure 3) the Merged Search Terms are used to create a Search Tree, where each child search term in the tree is a substring of the parent search term. A Level Order Traversal (or Breadth First Traversal) of this tree would yield the Prioritized Search Terms.The search terms which are substrings of other search terms are given less priority (lower level in the tree). These Prioritized Search Terms are provided as the output of the NLP Layer. For example in the Search Tree shown in Figure 5 the search terms at L1 (Level-1) are the Search Terms which do not have any other larger encapsulating Search Terms. The L2 (Level-2) search terms are put after L1 search terms in the Prioritized Search List, and similarly the later levels follow.

3.2.2 Image Selection Layer

This layer takes the Prioritized Search Terms as its input. The search terms are used to retrieve images from the image repository. The images for every search term are ranked in an order personalized to the validator's preferences. These ranked images are then rendered on the tool for validation. The Image Rank Module is implemented using a Random Forest binary classifier (classes: accept, reject), which is trained on image labels and whether they were approved or rejected by a validator (human). After enough training samples are received (for our case approx 100-200 images across 20 vocabulary words), the recall probability is used to rank future image search results for each search term in descending order. The classifier learns over time and thereby improves its ranking. With the aforementioned training set we were able to repeatedly achieve a recall accuracy of 0.86 or higher in identifying images which are likely to be selected by the validator. The validator looks through the images and selects the ones which he/she thinks is appropriate considering the script and search term (Figure 2). A search term without valid images is considered irrelevant and is ignored. Once the validation is completed, the verification step concludes. The output of this layer is a mapping between the Prioritized Search Terms and the verified images. An example mapping for 'steer' is shown in Figure 6.

3.2.3 Stitching Layer

This layer is responsible for the final production of the learning-video (Figure 3). First, the Script Image Alignment Module aligns the images to the script based on the Search Terms' script ordinal positions. Second, the Script Synthesis Module prepares a Text-to-Speech (TTS) audio for all the Script Slices. An example of Script Slices is shown in Figure 6. Finally, this layer combines the synthesized audio with the image ordering, producing a Learning Video.

Script Image Alignment Module: The sentences from the script are further sliced based on the Image-to-Search Terms Map received from the Image Selection Layer. If a sentence has multiple slices, i.e. multiple search terms mapped to it, this module combines the images derived from these slices into an ordered grid (Figure 6). This is important because when a sentence contains multiple keywords, the narrative needs to move from image to image promptly and sequentially. In this scenario, maximum relevant images are rendered/grouped together in a grid for maximum concept comprehension. In case there are two search terms, and thereby two slices in a sentence, two images are shown for each slice in a 2x2 grid. For example, in Figure 6, two images are shown each for the search terms 'use rudder wheel' and 'use paddle'. If a sentence has three or more search terms, then one image per slice is shown in a grid. For each search term, the first word of the search term which has not been covered by any of the preceding search terms is used as the point to insert images (mapped to that search term). For the first search term 'use rudder wheel', the corresponding image appears on utterance of the word 'use' (or the start of the sentence if it is the first search term in a sentence). While, for the second search term 'use paddle' the image appears on utterance of the word 'paddle'. However, it should be noted that the exact slicing rules and grid formation could easily be changed keeping the overall flow intact.

Timestamps are assigned for the appearance of each image in the grid based on the timestamps obtained from the corresponding audio of the slices. The stitching layer combines all the images based on the timestamps. The audio obtained using TTS is added to the video. Background music is also added to make the experience more engaging. The output of the stitching layer is a learning-video for the given script.

4 Experiment and Evaluation

In this section, we first present the setup of the experiment we conducted for evaluating our approach. The result & discussion follows in the further subsections.

4.1 Experimental Setup

We selected ten vocabulary words from the British National Corpus (BNC) frequently spoken list. The words were: *Barrier, Clinic, Commute, Customer, Facility, Pedestrian, Serve, Steer, Stir,* and *Weave*. We obtained the definitions and usage sentences from Simple English Wiktionary. These were combined to form sample scripts. For Example, the script for *Steer* derived was: *"To steer is use a rudder, wheel, or paddle to decide which way something will travel. The driver gripped the wheel tightly to steer the car around a corner."*

As described in the Approach Section, we derived the Prioritized Search Terms from the NLP Layer. These Search Terms were then used to search for images from Shuterstock. These images were sent for human verification using our authoring tool (Figure 2). The verified images constituted the verified image library. These were then combined using our approach to generate learning videos for all ten words. The layer-wise outputs for *Steer* is shown in Figure 6.

4.2 Experiment Design

In our experiment, we sent out Google Forms to participants, asking them to rate the generated videos and provide comments. The participants were proficient in using the English language and included native and non-native English speakers. The study included diverse professionals; including educators, college students, engineers, doc-

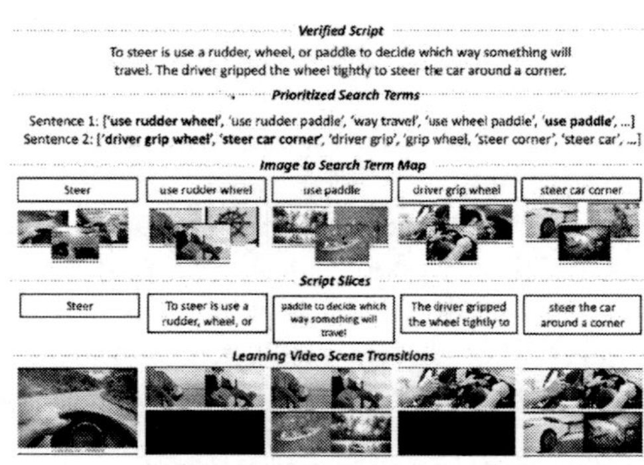

Figure 6: Creation of learning video for 'steer'

tors and information technology researchers. Each form took feedback on one of the ten generated videos. The participants were allowed to provide feedback on as many words as they liked. We posed the same question for every word. For example, for the word 'steer' we asked 'Would you recommend this video to someone who does not know "steer"?' The responses were taken on a Likert scale of five points, where five indicated strong affirmation, and one indicated strong reluctance.

4.3 Results and Discussion

We received a total of 210 responses from a total of 28 unique participants. The distribution of the scores received are in Table 1

Word	Likert rating counts					Total Responses
	1	**2**	**3**	**4**	**5**	
Weave	1	4	2	6	9	22
Facility	0	3	2	8	8	21
Clinic	1	1	5	5	11	23
Customer	0	2	3	5	10	20
Stir	0	0	3	9	9	21
Barrier	0	0	2	10	10	22
Serve	0	0	2	8	10	20
Commute	0	1	1	8	12	22
Pedestrian	0	1	1	4	14	20
Steer	0	0	1	6	12	19
Total	2	12	22	69	105	210

Table 1: Likert Score distribution for learning videos

Since our survey asked participants if they are likely to recommend a given learning-video, we chose to use Net Promoter Score (NPS) to measure participant satisfaction with the generated learning-videos. NPS (Reichheld, 2003) is an aggregate-level measure derived from scores on likely to recommend a utility/service. NPS is widely used in the service industries.

We consider ratings of 4 and 5 as *promoters*. The promoter ratings amount to 82.8% of the total responses. The ratings of 1 and 2 we consider as *detractors* and these amount to 6.7%. The 3 rating is considered as *neutral*. Neutral rating is given by 10.4% of total responses.

$$NPS = \%promoters - \%detractors \quad (1)$$

Using the Net Promoter Score (NPS) formula above, our NPS is 76%. Per video summarized measures have been reported in Table 2. Also, the overall average Likert rating was 4.25 out of 5 when combined across all videos.

Word	Avg. Score (Likert)	#Responses	SD	#Images	#Search Terms
Weave	3.82	22	1.30	6	3
Facility	4.00	21	1.05	3	2
Clinic	4.04	23	1.15	3	2
Customer	4.15	20	1.04	3	2
Stir	4.29	21	0.72	3	2
Barrier	4.36	22	0.66	3	2
Serve	4.40	20	0.68	6	3
Commute	4.41	22	0.80	6	3
Pedestrian	4.55	20	0.83	3	2
Steer	4.58	19	0.61	9	4
Averages	**4.25**	**21**	**0.93**	**4.50**	**2.50**

Table 2: Feedback on learning videos

17 unique participants gave feedback on all words, contributing 10 responses each. For the 17 people who provided feedback on all 10 videos, we computed the inter-annotator agreement using Fleiss Kappa (Fleiss et al., 2013). Since the rating on the Likert scale of 5 can be subjective and a rating of 4 may be the same as a rating of 5 for someone else, we classify the responses into two classes 'yes' and 'no'. The class 'yes' indicates that the reviewers would indeed recommend the video for learning a vocabulary word, and the class 'no' indicates otherwise. We consider the rating of 4, and, 5 in the 'yes' class and 1, and, 2 in the 'no' class. The responses with rating of 3 were equally distributed at random between the two classes. The free-marginal Kappa value came out to be 0.62, with an overall percentage agreement of 81%.

An observation we make from Table 2, besides the word *weave*, there is a correlation between the number of images and the average rating; the higher the number of images the higher the average score. The number of images is correlated to the number of search terms identified in the script. We plan to take this under advisement for future work in this domain. The participants raised some concerns about the videos. The following is a summary of their comments regarding the scripts and the images.

Script Related Comments: For our experiment, we used the scripts as obtained from Simple English Wiktionary i.e. the combination of the definition and usage sentence. Hence, a common observation was that at times the usage sentence did not coherently follow the definition sentence. This could be addressed in one of two ways, a careful refinement of scripts by educators or video content presentation changes. An example of the content presentation changes could be to divide the video into two logical sections: 'Definition' and 'Sample usage sentence'. Before the definition is presented the video would explicitly say 'Definition' and 'Example sentence' for sample usage sentence(s).

Visual Related Comments: The scripts we used for words like 'weave' happen to describe a process. Processes are not easily represented by showing a sequence of images, and rather necessitate the need to have small video clips. We plan to incorporate this suggestion, and discuss it further in Section 5. The number of images that people preferred for a given script were also variable. This again, would be addressed when the educators use our tool and perform the Image Verification task themselves. They would then simply pick the images for the search terms they find most suitable for their learning environment. Accordingly the number of images would change based on the search terms.

5 Future Work

We believe that the problem of reducing human effort in learning content creation, and hence fostering dynamic contextual content creation, is applicable in multiple domains. To explore this broad applicability, our future work will be focused on several topics:

Personalized script recommendation: In our current approach, we receive a learning-script as an input from either the educator or the Simple English Wiktionary. As a continuation of this work, we would like to use a learner model and concept-graph to generate a personalized script targeted at teaching a concept or a neighborhood of concepts (e.g., neighborhood of conceptual words are words related to and/or supporting a given word in a semantic sense). The script can explore the relationships with related words such as examples of a higher level category (e.g. mites, spiders, and scorpions are relevant in teaching the concept of arachnid). If a curriculum of vocabulary words to be taught, is available, a recommendation system could be leveraged for selection of the next best video for a learner (Mbipom et al., 2018).

Visual curation: Harvesting images from the open Web, or even a curated image repository, has drawbacks, especially for learning and age appropriateness. Unless a human inspects each image, it could be deemed inappropriate for learning or for a particular learner age group. Utilizing work from image scene identification (Vailaya et al., 2001; Bosch et al., 2006) and image understanding (Eakins, 2002), could help reduce the human effort for flagging inappropriate images. Further image scene identification could pair image concepts with learning-script concepts or vocabulary word supporting concepts (for example, Amphibian and Frog).

Once labeled images are retrieved, personalizing the selection of images based on learner likes and dislikes is an area of interest. As humans, we individually gravitate towards certain things, which can have an impact on learning. For example, a student that has arachnophobia might benefit from images of plush toy Arachnids rather than real Arachnids (or a balance between real versus illustrated).

Further, knowing words a learner mastered versus words struggling with, based on learner model, can be powerful in selecting images that link multiple concepts for the learner. For example, the learner mastered the word *spider*, but is struggling with the word *arachnid*. Purposefully choosing *spider* image(s) as a way to explain *arachnids* can help accelerate mastery. Using reading complexity tests, such as Flesch-Kincaid[5], script reading complexity scores can be exposed in our tool (Figure 2) to allow the educator to select/craft age-appropriate scripts.

Script understanding: A better understanding of the script (by the system) can help to improve the search and curation for visuals. Hill and Anna have looked at concreteness as a dimension of lexical meaning (2014) and have used multi-modal models for concrete and abstract concept meanings (Hill et al., 2014). Recent advances have tried to come up with adaptive algorithms to quantify visual concreteness of words and topics in these multi-modal datasets (Hessel et al., 2018). Adaptive concreteness scores for words, in context with the scripts can help refine search terms generated by our system. This in turn, would reduce the human effort in the validation step.

Audio: Attributes of a voice can be captivating or repulsive to the human ear. Identifying the right voice and tone to synthesize the learning-script with can play a significant role in learning. Achieving this will rely on collecting learner behavioral data or external input sources, such as teacher selection.

Interactive Learning: Learning videos do not have to be a one-way street; rather they can also be used to assess the learner's knowledge and/or engagement. Injecting assessment/engagement questions can help drive a point to the learner as well as assess the learner's connections with the generated content. Feedback collected can shape creation of the next learning video. The key here is inserting such content at the opportune moment of the learning script.

6 Conclusion

Creating customized and just-in-time learning content in an agile manner completely shifts the paradigm of micro-learning. Our solution approach is generic enough to be used in any content creation scenario where it is possible to have scripted text, and there is a repository of images (or open Internet) to choose from. The key direction of this research is to provide the right system in the hands of learning designers so that they can be more efficient and agile with their essential role of making learning effective, engaging, and fun.

References

Isabel L Beck, Margaret G McKeown, and Linda Kucan. 2013. *Bringing words to life: Robust vocabulary instruction*. Guilford Press.

Jacob Lowell Bishop and Matthew A Verleger. 2013. The flipped classroom: A survey of the research. In *ASEE National Conference Proceedings, Atlanta, GA*, volume 30, pages 1–18.

Anna Bosch, Andrew Zisserman, and Xavier Muñoz. 2006. Scene classification via plsa. In *Computer Vision – ECCV 2006*, pages 517–530.

Marc Brysbaert, Amy Beth Warriner, and Victor Kuperman. 2014. Concreteness ratings for 40 thousand generally known english word lemmas. *Behavior research methods*, 46(3):904–911.

---

[5]https://en.wikipedia.org/wiki/
Flesch-Kincaid_readability_tests

John P. Eakins. 2002. Towards intelligent image retrieval. *Pattern Recognition*, 35(1):3 – 14.

Joseph L Fleiss, Bruce Levin, and Myunghee Cho Paik. 2013. *Statistical methods for rates and proportions*. John Wiley & Sons.

Tanmay Gupta, Dustin Schwenk, Ali Farhadi, Derek Hoiem, and Aniruddha Kembhavi. 2018. Imagine this! scripts to compositions to videos. In *The European Conference on Computer Vision (ECCV)*.

Jack Hessel, David Mimno, and Lillian Lee. 2018. Quantifying the visual concreteness of words and topics in multimodal datasets. In *Proceedings of the 2018 Conference of the North American Chapter of the Association for Computational Linguistics: Human Language Technologies, Volume 1 (Long Papers)*, pages 2194–2205. Association for Computational Linguistics.

Felix Hill and Anna Korhonen. 2014. Concreteness and subjectivity as dimensions of lexical meaning. In *Proceedings of the 52nd Annual Meeting of the Association for Computational Linguistics (Volume 2: Short Papers)*, volume 2, pages 725–731.

Felix Hill, Roi Reichart, and Anna Korhonen. 2014. Multi-modal models for concrete and abstract concept meaning. *Transactions of the Association of Computational Linguistics*, 2(1):285–296.

Jelena Jovanović, Dragan Gašević, and Vladan Devedžić. 2006. Dynamic assembly of personalized learning content on the semantic web. In *The Semantic Web: Research and Applications*, pages 545–559.

Douwe Kiela, Alexis Conneau, Allan Jabri, and Maximilian Nickel. 2018. Learning visually grounded sentence representations. In *Proceedings of the 2018 Conference of the North American Chapter of the Association for Computational Linguistics: Human Language Technologies, Volume 1 (Long Papers)*, pages 408–418. Association for Computational Linguistics.

John Kounios and Phillip J Holcomb. 1994. Concreteness effects in semantic processing: Erp evidence supporting dual-coding theory. *Journal of Experimental Psychology: Learning, Memory, and Cognition*, 20(4):804.

Jason Lankow, Josh Ritchie, and Ross Crooks. 2012. *Infographics: The power of visual storytelling*. John Wiley & Sons.

Blessing Mbipom, Stewart Massie, and Susan Craw. 2018. An e-learning recommender that helps learners find the right materials.

Allan Paivio, John C Yuille, and Stephen A Madigan. 1968. Concreteness, imagery, and meaningfulness values for 925 nouns. *Journal of experimental psychology*, 76(1p2):1.

Mike Parkinson. 2012. The power of visual communication. *Billion Dollar Graphics*.

Frederick F Reichheld. 2003. The one number you need to grow. *Harvard business review*, 81(12):46–55.

Melissa Roemmele and Andrew Gordon. 2018. Linguistic features of helpfulness in automated support for creative writing. In *Proceedings of the First Workshop on Storytelling*, pages 14–19.

Swapna Somasundaran, Michael Flor, Martin Chodorow, Hillary Molloy, Binod Gyawali, and Laura McCulla. 2018. Towards evaluating narrative quality in student writing. *Transactions of the Association for Computational Linguistics*, 6:91–106.

A. Vailaya, M. A. T. Figueiredo, A. K. Jain, and Hong-Jiang Zhang. 2001. Image classification for content-based indexing. *IEEE Transactions on Image Processing*, 10(1):117–130.

Peter Young, Alice Lai, Micah Hodosh, and Julia Hockenmaier. 2014. From image descriptions to visual denotations: New similarity metrics for semantic inference over event descriptions. *Transactions of the Association for Computational Linguistics*, 2:67–78.

Curio SmartChat : A system for Natural Language Question Answering for Self-Paced K-12 Learning

Srikrishna Raamadhurai   Ryan S Baker*   Vikraman Poduval
Saal.ai, Al Bateen Offices, Abu Dhabi 112230
*University of Pennsylvania, PA 19104
{srikrishna, vikram} @saal.ai,   ryanshaunbaker@gmail.com

Abstract

During learning, students often have questions which they would benefit from responses to in real time. In class, a student can ask a question to a teacher. During homework, or even in class if the student is shy, it can be more difficult to receive a rapid response. In this work, we introduce Curio SmartChat, an automated question answering system for middle school Science topics. Our system has now been used by around 20,000 students who have so far asked over 100,000 questions. We present data on the challenge created by students' grammatical errors and spelling mistakes, and discuss our system's approach and degree of effectiveness at disambiguating questions that the system is initially unsure about. We also discuss the prevalence of student "small talk" not related to science topics, the pluses and minuses of this behavior, and how a system should respond to these conversational acts. We conclude with discussions and point to directions for potential future work.

1   Introduction

Question asking is an important part of students' classroom learning. Through asking questions, students can clarify their confusions, address their doubts, and explore a topic in greater depth. Student questions, when framed appropriately, can form an important tool for learning in Science and other domains (Chin & Brown, 2002).

However, this same type of learning support is not available when students are working at home. Even in a classroom setting, teachers may not be able to answer all student questions, much less to say about some shy students who do not even register their questions in class. Increasing numbers of students now spend class time working one-on-one with adaptive learning platforms (Baker, 2016), and in these contexts, multiple students may have questions at the same time, and teachers may not be able to answer all questions at the same time (Schofield, 1995).

This challenge has led to the idea of automated question answering systems in education (Louwerse et al., 2002; Corbett et al., 2005; Milik et al., 2006; Jin et al., 2018), where students can ask questions in natural language. Different than simply a search engine, educational question answering systems attempt to provide answers focused on current content, set at an appropriate level for the student's current stage of learning. An 8th grader with a question about the Krebs Cycle needs different types of information than an undergraduate Biology major, for example.

However, despite research into the possibility of automated question answering in education, there has been little effort to scale these systems, with considerably more energy going into tutor-led tutorial dialogue systems (Wolfe et al., 2013; Ventura et al., 2018).

Building such a system is non-trivial for several reasons, first and foremost the complexity that arises from handling unforeseen queries that represent considerable variability in the use of human language. Several challenges must be solved in order for an automated question answering system to be optimally effective. It must recognize which questions are germane and which are off-topic (see, for instance, Corbett et al., 2005), and decide how to respond. It must be able to handle students' grammatical errors and spelling mistakes (a challenge in all NLP-based learning systems – see Chollampatt & Ng, 2017). It must be able to map from often ill-formed questions to the content in those questions. It must provide content at the right educational level.

Proceedings of the Fourteenth Workshop on Innovative Use of NLP for Building Educational Applications, pages 336–342
Florence, Italy, August 2, 2019. ©2019 Association for Computational Linguistics

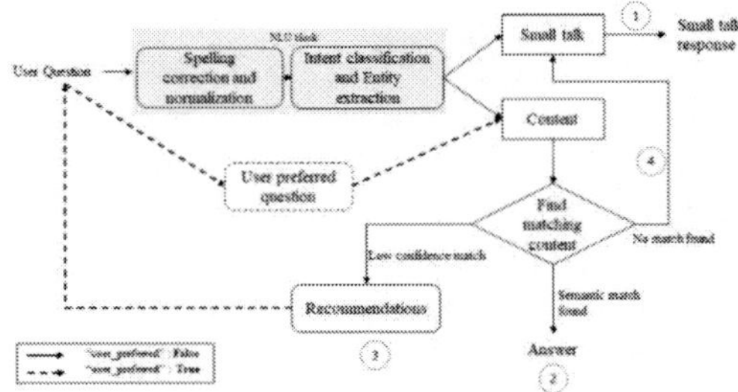

Figure 1: Architecture of QA Engine

In this paper, we discuss our system, Curio SmartChat for self-paced K-12 learning through Question Answering as a mode and is currently being used by around 20,000 students, who have asked over 100,000 questions, in the domain of middle school Science. K-12 stands for Kindergarten through 12th grade in many countries while some others refer to this as "All-through-school". While we only present our system in practice for middle school which forms a part of K-12 system, we believe the exact framework can be extended to serve across other grades provided the content is available in a similar format, as the focus of our system is more technology oriented (Question Answering) rather than content oriented. Within this paper, we will present data on the challenge created by students' grammatical errors and spelling mistakes, and discuss our system's approach and degree of effectiveness at disambiguating questions that the system is initially unsure about. We also discuss the prevalence of student "small talk" not related to Science topics, the pluses and minuses of this behavior, and how a system should respond to these conversational acts. We focus on our efforts to address these challenges, towards developing a system that can effectively give the right response to a student question, and thereby help them to progress rather than becoming frustrated or stuck (Beck & Rodrigo, 2014).

In the next section we will describe our system architecture and the QA engine's workflow in more detail. Section 3 will explain the challenges faced. Section 4 will present the discussion, followed by potential directions for future work.

2   System Description

Our system architecture comprises of three blocks: a semantic match engine (referred to as the QA engine), a content library and a web browser-based client for user interaction. The client is a simple chat interface with a text input field. The content library is where our entire collection of curriculum based text documents, metadata of pictures and other media exist. Our QA engine handles all the information processing tasks.

Let us go through a typical work flow and possible outcome scenarios. The user inputs his or her query in the text field. Based on the system's understanding of the user query, it tries to retrieve the *Answer* from the content library. When the system encounters complex user queries which are difficult to comprehend, it alternates to offering *recommendations*, to try to disambiguate what the student is asking. *Recommendations*, unlike *Answer* are a list of possible questions from the question bank that closely matches the initial user query. However, when a query has no potential recommendations with sufficiently high probability, the system responds with small talk: off-topic exchanges such as system level guidance, greetings, weather, sports and so on. The level of our small talk content has been designed to suit our target users, who are around 13-16 years old. At the moment, our small talk service is simple and stateless, meaning it does not remember the sequence of exchanges to respond to the query at hand.

2.1   Content library

The content library in this study pertains to middle school Science topics. The library includes a compilation of text documents and quick definitions collected based on the curriculum. This library also contains questions and answers tagged according to three levels of Bloom's (1956) Taxonomy: *Knowledge, Understanding* and *Application*. Content such as definitions are labeled as *Knowledge* since they could be understood without any other prerequisite (ex: *"What is energy?"*). *Understanding* level content are those where the students can relate to what they learned from *Knowledge* (ex: *"Cutting a tree with an axe is very easy. Why?"*). *Application* level content allow the students to test their understanding by way of more practical scenarios (ex: *"How do we separate oil from water?"*).

2.2   QA Engine

Figure 1shows the architecture of the QA engine which is the main component of our system. When a user asks a questions, the engine checks for spelling mistakes and does spelling correction and spelling normalization including replacing contractions in informal English. For example, *'What's energy?'* is converted into *'What is energy?'*. As a next step the system predicts if the user is interested in the content or small talk.

We have trained our own custom taggers for intent and entity extraction by extending SpaCy taggers (https://spacy.io/). The intent classifier decides which service will provide the response, small talk or content library, while the entity extractor will retrieve the entities the user is interested in. For example, if the query is *"What is photosynthesis?"*, then the tagged JSON would look like {"intent": *"content"*, "entity": [*"photosynthesis"*]}. There could also be more than one desired entity but only one intent per query. If the query is assessed to be content related, the system then will look to retrieve the answer from the content library through a combination of semantic matches. Our main search methodology includes a Vector Space approach to look for related concepts in our content library to find out candidate responses.

A naive, search system would look for keywords (entities), however those methods suffer from out-of-vocabulary problem and cannot detect paraphrases. More recent Information Retrieval systems have moved to employing word vectors. Popular word vectors such as Word2Vec (Mikolov et al., 2013a) and GloVe (Pennington et al., 2014) provide a fixed size representation for words, in a sense attempting to capture their *meaning* in the language space by providing synonymous words with similar vectors. Word vectors have been shown to be superior to simple keyword approaches towards understanding syntactic similarities (Mikolov et al., 2013b). However, there are still some shortcomings in terms of processing unknown words. A heuristic approach has been suggested to handle this problem by way of randomly initializing such unknown words (Sutskever et al., 2014). There are still concerns with respect to word sense disambiguation, however. For example, the word "mean" could be a Verb, Adjective or a Noun based on the sentence structure. Word vectors usually only offer one representation towards a word. To address the problem of polysemy, a model called sense2vec was trained as a deep bidirectional language model (Trask et al., 2015).

In our work we have used sentence level encoders instead of word level encoders. Sentence level encoders, similar to word vectors, provide a fixed size representation for an entire sentence instead of individual words. In principle, the embedding of a sentence and its paraphrase should be vectorially similar in a target language space even if those two sentences use different words to convey the same idea. In our system, we use a pretrained model released by Google called Universal Sentence Encoder (Cer et al., 2018) to detect paraphrases. We also use a combination of hash map lookups besides paraphrase detection to make the retrieval faster and scalable.

If the probability of our candidate response does not pass the confidence check, the system dynamically offers recommendations to the student that are conceptually related to that particular query. As our system consists of a Deep Learning model in production, we have made use of the Tensorflow framework and Docker containerization which are best practices in the industry for developing scalable, production grade software.

3   Data

Since the time of launching the service, the system has served over 100,000 questions from around 20,000 students, mostly 13-16 years old. We focus our analyses on the quality of the served responses. User logs comprising the input user query, the response (either direct answer or small talk) and/or the recommendations have been collected.

Any user query could have one of the three possible outcomes as shown in Figure 2; (i) A direct answer obtained through exact or semantic match, (ii) Recommendations, (iii) Small talk exchange.

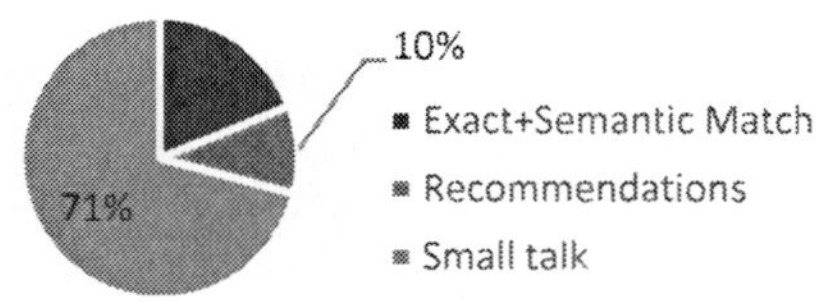

Figure 2: Distribution of Responses

Assessing the correctness of (i) is straightforward and it means that the query was understood by the system and had passed all the necessary confidence checks. Given our architecture's two-step

Content Available	Count	Mean valid recommendation (count) Rater 1	Mean valid recommendation (count) Rater 2
No	28	0.70 (19)	0.64 (18)
Yes	107	0.55 (59)	0.73 (78)
Query not clear	65	0.49 (31)	0.47 (29)
	200	0.55	0.63

Table 1: Quality of Recommendations

winnowing approach as shown in Figure 1, a drop in confidence for direct answers alternates to recommendations and an even lower confidence defaults to small talk. Thanks to our carefully chosen parameters for checks, we have hardly ever found the system presented a wrong answer to the user. Hence we are only left with (ii) and (iii) to be evaluated as follows.

To evaluate the quality of recommendations, we randomly chose 200 sample queries and employed two human raters to independently rate the recommendations. As for small talk analysis, we analyze only the misspelt queries linguistically and share our findings.

3.1 Analyses of quality of recommendations

The purpose of our analyses is to check the validity of our recommendations. The raters were asked to rate every single recommendation for each query as valid/ invalid depending on what was asked by the user. For a given user query even if one recommendation from the list of recommendations was validated by the rater, we count that as valid and represent the mean grouped by content availability in Table 1.

The reader is required to note that recommendations could happen due to two primary reasons; either the user asked a query where the system lacked content about or the query could not be clearly disambiguated by the system. We have observed that the system very rarely responded with wrong answers when it lacked content, instead it responded with recommendation, thanks to the confidence check.

With the above method of estimation, the average quality of recommendations by both raters is around 60% which could already offer a good level of user engagement. It is also important to note that despite human raters finding it difficult to precisely understand the purpose of 65 out of 200 user queries (32.5%), the system had offered valid recommendations to retain the users' interest. Such a situation in class would have required the student having to rephrase the question until the teacher

Category	User Query
Insertion	you are frome wich contry
	can you tell me what acide are the produce
	what is nonpoar moleculens
Omission	what is mixtur
	wate is a substsnce with a sour taste
	wat is meen saturated solution
Substitution	what is a substence
	what are the eyeglasses called that habe both concave and convex lenses
	yas i neeed halp
Inversion	waht is meen pressure
	waht maen acid ph
Duplication	can u tell me about definning solubility?
	wich termes deescribe a substance that has an equal amount of hydronium and hydroxide ions
Phonetic errors	but i don't find the anser
	Hi. Wat your name
	were you are

Table 2: Analyses of Spelling mistakes

was confident of responding. For example, a user query as *"as the pressure increases, the solubility of solids and liquids"* is vague but also implies that the student is interested in knowing more about *solubility* and *saturated solution*. The system offered recommendations along these lines.

3.2 Analyses of Spelling mistakes

We present the analysis of common spelling mistakes our users make by manually categorizing at a character level. Our scheme for categorization follows linguistic cues such as insertion, omission, substitution, inversion and so on.

We find that a majority of students tend to heavily depend on phonetics to spell words, with examples of student misspellings such as *"anser"*, *"meen"*, *"wich"*. Among these queries, it appears that the silent characters have almost consistently been dropped such as *"w"* and *"h"* in *"anser"* and *"wich"* respectively. Since "a" and "e" have different forms of phonetic presence in the English language, students tend to interchangeably use these characters. Learning to correctly spell words is lacking with our users which makes serving

User 1 says	Curio SmartChat responds
What is a mammal?	Mammals are animals that give birth to babies rather than laying eggs and feed their young with milk. Examples of mammals include human beings, dogs, whales and bears.
What is an animal?	An animal is a living organism that feeds on organic matter. It typically has specialized sense organs and a nervous system, which makes it able to respond rapidly to stimuli.
I want to just chill	Please ask me about middle school topics in Science.
fine	Okay.
can you explain bird	A bird is a warm-blooded vertebrate with feathers.
User 2 says	**Curio SmartChat responds**
Dim	Dim means not shining brightly or clearly.
good	Let's just try again, we'll get it right eventually.
:(	! You are not too nice.
i mean :)	Never mind. Just kidding.
what does meiosis mean	The chromosome number is halved from diploid to haploid, resulting in genetically different cells. This process of reduction division is called meiosis.

Table 3: Good examples episodes of small talk and default response

User 3 says	Curio SmartChat responds
I am nicer than u	I would have to agree.
U should agree	I guess I can appreciate that.
no ur not	Are we debating?
ya we r	Please ask me about middle school topics in Science.
b bbbbdjv cvmnsnv vdklv sd ,bfvheeubrh	Please ask me about middle school topics in Science.
User 4 says	**Curio SmartChat responds**
Hello! How can I help you?	Hey! That's my line!
Hey! That's my line!	Please ask me about middle school topics in Science.
v	Please ask me about middle school topics in Science.
;vojoevjverfd	Please ask me about middle school topics in Science.

Table 4: Bad example episodes of small talk and default response

answers a lot more challenging. In practice, smarter text input devices correct user input in real time, although depriving the users of learning from their mistakes. Please see Table 2 for more analyses on spelling mistakes.

3.3 Analyses of small talk

Although the primary focus of Curio SmartChat is to talk about content, our work follows recommendations from Bickmore and Cassell (2000) to use small talk as a means to create student-system rapport that ultimately builds student willingness to engage in learning with the system. While education researchers have long argued that off-topic conversation takes time away from learning (Carroll, 1963), there is evidence that small talk is associated with more effective collaboration in human-human learning (Kreijns, 2004). Similar rapport has been created by conversational agents (Crossley & Kostyuk, 2017). In our work we employed small talk along with recommendations to gently nudge the user into content. Though users of Curio SmartChat do engage in small talk with the system, they have continued to produce content-based queries as well. So far we have observed that roughly one in every three queries are still content based as shown in Figure 2.

As seen in systems that use wizard of oz approaches to generate small talk (e.g. Crossley & Kostyuk, 2017), students develop social relationships with the system, explicitly asking Curio SmartChat questions about its family, friends and hobbies. When a question is beyond the capacity of Curio SmartChat to answer, a default response- *"Please ask me about middle school topics in Science"* is provided. This default response has seen mixed follow-up reactions from the students. Some students gracefully react to this default response by returning to asking about the content (~22.97%) as shown by examples in Table 3 while other students appear to become upset or respond with nonsense strings of letters (~29.66%) as shown by examples in Table 4. Given the scope of this paper, we will not psycho-analyze the user behavior, hence we simply report our findings.

4 Challenges

There are several technical challenges involved in developing and maintaining a chat service of this nature for students. Students do not always provide grammatically correct queries. Especially in the UAE where Curio SmartChat is primarily used, English is the language of instruction for Science but is not the native language. Hence good modules for spelling correction and spelling normalization are necessary to handle misspelt user queries. Every student has his or her own way of phrasing a question, however the response to a particular question has to be consistent across all students unless the input is irrecoverably broken. Even after spelling correction and normalization, there are still inputs that cannot be even understood by human raters. Some of these appear to represent nonsense strings that were never intended to communicate (see Table 4) but others may represent difficulty in communicating ideas, sometimes due to lack of mastery in English-language communication, and sometimes due to the difficulty of the Science content and ideas. These utterances would be difficult for any system to parse accurately. It would be better to develop a mechanism where the students learn to properly spell alongside auto-correction rather than the system overriding the user with correct replacements.

Our system as of now either offers recommendations or responds with small talk when it does not completely understand what the user is asking. It is not very clear as to what is the best way to serve more content based queries as against small talk between building user models or developing stateful dialog managers at this scale. As with any chat service, some users tend to use profanity and insults. There are still some doubts about how to best deal with such inputs in the context of an education chat agent.

5   Conclusion

We introduced Curio SmartChat, our Natural Language Question Answering system for K-12 learning and analyzed its performance while serving over 100,000 queries for around 20,000 middle school students on Science topics. Curio SmartChat is capable of performing both content based and off topic conversations with students. Given the scope of the system we have analyzed the user queries for spelling mistakes, off topic chats and validity of offered recommendations. The system is able to either directly answer or at the very least offer relevant recommendations to the users at least 60% of the time. We showed that even when humans were not able to precisely understand the queries, the system was still able to provide relevant recommendations 50% of the time thereby saving the time for both students and teachers alike. We only expect such benefits to grow with more content and better spelling correction mechanisms added to our system as future work. As we have shown the most common forms of spelling mistakes students make, developing such systems could be crucial for improved quality of answer retrieval. The pluses and minus of having a default response appear to be roughly similar, in other words not very

harmful. Perhaps there are smarter ways of nudging the student back into content that could make the experience more productive.

Acknowledgments

We would like to extend our heartfelt thanks to our content team, the independent raters and our linguist towards ensuring a successful, timely submission.

References

Baker, R.S. 2016. *Stupid Tutoring Systems, Intelligent Humans.* International Journal of Artificial Intelligence and Education, 26 (2), 600-614.

Beck, J., & Rodrigo, M. M. T. 2014, June. *Understanding wheel spinning in the context of affective factors.* In International conference on intelligent tutoring systems (pp. 162-167). Springer, Cham.

Bickmore, T., & Cassell, J. 2000. *"How about this weather?" Social dialogue with embodied conversational agents.* Proceedings from the American Association for Artificial Intelligence (AAAI) Fall Symposium. North Falmouth, MA: AAAI Press.

Bloom, B. S. 1956. *Taxonomy of educational objectives. Vol. 1: Cognitive domain.* New York: McKay, 20-24.

Carroll, J. 1963. *A Model For School Learning.* Teachers College Record, 64, 723-733.

Cer, Daniel, et al. 2018. *"Universal sentence encoder."* arXiv preprint arXiv:1803.11175.

Chin, C., & Brown, D. E. 2002. *Student-generated questions: A meaningful aspect of learning in science.* International Journal of Science Education, 24(5), 521-549.

Chollampatt, S., & Ng, H. T. 2017, September. *Connecting the dots: Towards human-level grammatical error correction.* In Proceedings of the 12th Workshop on Innovative Use of NLP for Building Educational Applications (pp. 327-333).

Corbett, A., Wagner, A., Chao, C. Y., Lesgold, S., Stevens, S., & Ulrich, H. 2005, May. *Student questions in a classroom evaluation of the ALPS learning environment.* In Proceedings of the 2005 conference on Artificial Intelligence in Education: Supporting Learning through Intelligent and Socially Informed Technology (pp. 780-782). IOS Press.

Crossley, S., & Kostyuk, V. 2017. *Letting the Genie out of the Lamp: Using Natural Language Processing tools to predict math performance*. In International Conference on Language, Data and Knowledge (pp. 330-342). Springer, Cham.

Jin, L., King, D., Hussein, A., White, M., & Danforth, D. 2018. *Using Paraphrasing and Memory-Augmented Models to Combat Data Sparsity in Question Interpretation with a Virtual Patient Dialogue System*. In Proceedings of the Thirteenth Workshop on Innovative Use of NLP for Building Educational Applications (pp. 13-23).

Kreijns, K. 2004. *Sociable CSCL environments: Social Affordances, Sociability, and Social Presence*. Unpublished doctoral dissertation, Open University of the Netherlands, The Netherlands.

Louwerse, M. M., Graesser, A. C., Olney, A., & Tutoring Research Group. 2002. *Good computational manners: Mixed-initiative dialog in conversational agents*. In Etiquette for Human-Computer Work, Papers from the 2002 Fall Symposium, Technical Report FS-02-02 (pp. 71-76).

Mikolov, Tomas, et al. 2013. *"Distributed representations of words and phrases and their compositionality."* Advances in neural information processing systems.

Mikolov, Tomas, et al. 2013. *"Efficient estimation of word representations in vector space."* arXiv preprint arXiv:1301.3781.

Milik, N., Marshall, M., & Mitrovic, A. 2006, June. *Responding to free-form student questions in ERM-Tutor*. In International Conference on Intelligent Tutoring Systems (pp. 707-709). Springer, Berlin, Heidelberg.

Pennington, Jeffrey, Richard Socher, and Christopher Manning. 2014. *"Glove: Global vectors for word representation."* Proceedings of the 2014 conference on empirical methods in natural language processing (EMNLP).

Schofield, J. W. 1995. *Computers and classroom culture*. Cambridge University Press
Sutskever, Ilya, Oriol Vinyals, and Quoc V. Le. 2014. *"Sequence to sequence learning with neural networks."* Advances in neural information processing systems.

Trask, Andrew, Phil Michalak, and John Liu. 2015. *"sense2vec-a fast and accurate method for word sense disambiguation in neural word embeddings."* arXiv preprint arXiv:1511.06388.

Ventura, M., Chang, M., Foltz, P., Mukhi, N., Yarbro, J., Salverda, A. P., ... & Marvaniya, S. 2018, June. *Preliminary Evaluations of a Dialogue-Based Digital Tutor*. In International Conference on Artificial Intelligence in Education (pp. 480-483). Springer, Cham.

Wolfe, C. R., Widmer, C. L., Reyna, V. F., Hu, X., Cedillos, E. M., Fisher, C. R., ... & Weil, A. M. 2013. *The development and analysis of tutorial dialogues in AutoTutor Lite*. Behavior research methods, 45(3), 623-636.

Supporting content evaluation of student summaries by Idea Unit embedding

Marcello Gecchele[†]   **Hiroaki Yamada**[‡]   **Takenobu Tokunaga**[‡]   **Yasuyo Sawaki**[◦]

[†]University of Trento
Trento, Italy

[‡]School of Computing
Tokyo Institute of Technology
Tokyo, Japan

[◦]School of Education
Waseda University
Tokyo, Japan

marcello.gecchele@pm.me   yamada.h.ax@m.titech.ac.jp   take@c.titech.ac.jp   ysawaki@waseda.jp

Abstract

This paper discusses the computer-assisted content evaluation of summaries. We propose a method to make a correspondence between the segments of the source text and its summary. As a unit of the segment, we adopt "Idea Unit (IU)" which is proposed in Applied Linguistics. Introducing IUs enables us to make a correspondence even for the sentences that contain multiple ideas. The IU correspondence is made based on the similarity between vector representations of IU. An evaluation experiment with two source texts and 20 summaries showed that the proposed method is more robust against rephrased expressions than the conventional ROUGE-based baselines. Also, the proposed method outperformed the baselines in recall. We implemented the proposed method in a GUI tool "Segment Matcher" that aids teachers to establish a link between corresponding IUs across the summary and source text.

1 Introduction

Summary writing is a complex task involving various linguistic operations, and as such it is useful for developing student linguistic proficiency including text comprehension and composition (Graham and Perin, 2007). The quality of a summary is a good indicator of language proficiency. Therefore, teachers can use summaries to evaluate a student's proficiency. To evaluate the quality of a summary, a teacher has to assess if the summary conveys the important ideas of the source text, as well as the grammatical and lexical correctness. However, finding the corresponding information between the summary and source text is not an easy task for humans.

Another important aspect of summarization is rephrasing. This practice is encouraged as it is a core skill to master, especially for scholars, to avoid plagiarism (Keck, 2014). Rephrasing, however, often obfuscates the bonds between the contents of the source and summary texts and it represents one of the reasons why summary evaluation is such a complex activity.

This paper proposes a support tool for evaluating student summaries in terms of their contents by suggesting the links between the ideas of a source text and its summary. We divide texts into Idea Units (IUs) in order to deal with complex sentences that convey multiple ideas. The IU is defined as a minimal fragment of a text that conveys an "idea" or "thought" coherently (Kroll, 1977). We make correspondence between IUs instead of sentences across the source text and its summary. To circumvent inaccurate IU pairing due to rephrasing we adopt word embedding for the calculation of IU similarity.

2 Related Work

Evaluation is one of the important aspects of the automated text summarization research (Lin and Hovy, 2003). BLEU (Papineni et al., 2002) delivers a similarity score by analyzing n-grams that appear both in the source and summary texts in terms of precision. ROUGE (Lin, 2004) expands on BLEU by providing recall-oriented statistics with n-grams and Longest Common Subsequence. As these measures are based on string matching of n-grams, they fail in making a correspondence between rephrased expressions.

The Pyramid approach (Passonneau, 2009) divides the texts into text fragments named Summary Content Units (SCU). Assuming a set of summaries for a source text, SCUs are weighted based on their frequency over the summary set. The rationale is that frequent SCUs contain important ideas. The score of a summary is calculated by summing up the weight of every SCU in

Proceedings of the Fourteenth Workshop on Innovative Use of NLP for Building Educational Applications, pages 343–348
Florence, Italy, August 2, 2019. ©2019 Association for Computational Linguistics

the summary.

Automatic summary evaluation tools based on the Pyramid approach, such as PEAK (Yang et al., 2016) and PyrEval (Gao et al., 2018), are not suitable in educational environments as we cannot expect a number of reliable summaries large enough to certify a proper weighting. In addition, the quality of summaries is not guaranteed due to insufficient student proficiency in comprehension or composition. Their summaries might overlook obscure yet paramount information. These facts lead to imprecise SCU weighting. Lastly, writing a Gold Standard summary is a time-consuming task; therefore we are forced to compare the summaries against the source text directly.

FRESA (Torres-Moreno et al., 2010) is a framework for the evaluation of summaries that relies on the Jensen-Shannon divergence between n-gram probabilities. It scores summaries directly against the source text without reference summaries. A high correlation was reported between the Jensen-Shannon divergence against the source text and the ROUGE or Pyramid-based scores, which are based on the reference summaries. However, as the metric relies on n-grams, such high correlation cannot be guaranteed when summaries use a lot of rephrasing.

3   Segmentation

We divide the summaries and source text into Idea Unit (IU) and make a correspondence between them. The reason why segmentation is necessary can be found in Keck (2014). In Keck's study, the level of rephrasing of student summaries was manually graded by matching sentences that shared some words. This implies that rephrased sentences in the summary borrow at least one term from their source text. Keck mentions that Gist statements were particularly difficult to analyze as they expressed the information described in multiple sentences in a few words. Such constructs are desirable, as they are an indication of an advanced understanding of the language, but finding the corresponding sentences in the source text is difficult. Shorter units than sentences would be more versatile for making a correspondence between the summaries and source text.

Foster et al. (2000) analyzed several segmentation units from the viewpoint of intonation, syntax and semantics. For our purpose, we consider three kinds of syntactic units: IU, T-Unit (Hunt, 1965,

1966, 1970) and C-Unit (Loban, 1963). Despite being a popular approach, the T-Unit is too generous as it includes subordinate clauses in a single unit. Furthermore, the T-Unit is purely a syntactic unit, while IUs and C-Units also serve as a semantic unit. Despite being readopted by multiple scholars over the years, the C-Unit is rather vague in its definition and still retains the T-Unit feature of allowing multiple clauses in a unit. On the other hand, IUs tend to be shorter in length. For instance, it separates relative clauses in different units (Figure 1). Moreover, its rather strict definition suggests a smooth transition into an automatic segmentation algorithm in the future.

C-unit concerns the identification of units. The T-unit and C-unit use orthographic sentences as the unit of analysis. However, identifying orthographic sentences could be a problem in analyzing student summaries, particularly those written by second language learners, due to grammatical errors and punctuation.

In Applied Linguistics, IUs have been employed for in-depth analyses of the content of student summaries in the second language learning and assessment literature (Johns and Mayes, 1990). Accordingly, adopting the IU enables us to interpret our study results in reference to such previous investigations of summary content.

4   Ranking Method

To link two corresponding IUs across the summary and source text, we calculate the similarity between the units based on word embedding. A vector representing an IU is constructed by averaging the vector representation of the words appearing in the unit. We use the GloVe word vectors (Pennington et al., 2014) that have been pretrained with the Wikipedia + Gigaword data. We ignored the words that are not included in the word vector model when constructing the IU vector. We call an IU in a summary "Summary IU" and one in the source text "Source IU" hereafter. Given a Summary IU, its cosine similarity to every Source IU is calculated to create a ranking list of Source IUs that are arranged in descending order of similarity. We called this list "Prediction Ranking".

As a baseline, we use ROUGE-1, ROUGE-2 and ROUGE-L-based rankings. We selected ROUGE as it has proven to be effective in evaluating short summaries of single documents (Lin, 2004).

> 1. a subject and verb counted as one idea unit together with (when present) a (a) direct object, (b) prepositional phrase, (c) adverbial element, (d) mark of subordination, *or (e) a combination of the above*
> 2. full relative clauses counted as one idea unit when the relative pronoun was present
>   - (a) *phrases that are set off by a complementizer are counted as an Idea Unit*
>   - (b) *subordinate conjunctions and relative pronouns are always attached to the subordinate clause*
> 3. phrases which occurred in sentence initial position followed by a comma or which were set off from the sentence with commas were counted as separate idea units
>   - (a) *adverbial conjunctions (e.g.: "However,") are not to be split into separate Idea Units*
>   - (b) *citations are counted as separeted idea units only when they are set off from the sentence in their entirety*
> 4. verbs whose structure requires or allows a verbal element as object were counted with both verbal elements as one idea unit
> 5. reduced clauses in which a subordinator was followed by a non-finite verb element were counted as one idea unit
> 6. post-nominal -ing phrases used as modifiers counted as one idea unit
> 7. other types of elements counted as idea units were (a) absolutes, (b) appositives, and (c) verbals
> 8. *An idea unit can be discontinuous*

Figure 1: Extended definition of IU based on Kroll (1977). Our edits are presented in *italics*.

5 Evaluation

5.1 Data set

Our data set is comprised of two source texts and ten student summaries for each. The sources were taken from the questions in the comprehension section of the IELTS English proficiency test and their topic is "the preservation of endangered languages" and "the impact of noise on cognitive abilities". The summaries were composed by ten Ph.D. students of the University of Cambridge. They were instructed to summarize each source text to about one-fourth of the original length in 15 minutes while maintaining every piece of information they deemed necessary to the correct understanding of the source text. Table 1 illustrates the stats of the data set. The column "Summary" shows the averaged figures of ten summaries.

	Source 1	Summary	Source 2	Summary
Words	996	185.5	807	204.5
IUs	111	20.6	89	24.6
Links	—	18.0	—	21.3

Table 1: Statistics of data set

We manually segmented all texts into IUs according to an extended version of Kroll (1977)'s specification. Our version includes some addenda to define an IU as strictly and as clearly as possible (Figure 1). The extended parts are italicized in Figure 1. Syntactical and grammatical corrections were deemed out of scope and as such the texts were left unedited.

We also manually aligned the corresponding Summary IUs and Source IUs to make a set of correct IU links, pairs consisting of a Summary IU and a corresponding Source IU. No link was assigned to a Summary IU in cases where its content contradicts the source or was entirely fabricated by the student. Our data set includes such linkless IUs since the number of links is less than that of Summary IUs as shown in Table 1. A Summary IU can have multiple links to Source IUs as long as it contains information from those Source IUs. These gold IU links were used in the evaluation of our ranking method.

5.2 Evaluation Metric

For each IU in our set of summaries, we calculated a Prediction Ranking based on four ranking methods: the proposed Vector-based ranking and three ROUGE-based baselines (ROUGE-1, ROUGE-2 and ROUGE-L). We then studied the precision and recall of these rankings to evaluate the effectiveness of our Vector-based model.

The recall and precision are calculated as follows.

$$Precision^{(n)}(s) = \frac{|PR^{(n)}(s) \cap GL(s)|}{|PR^{(n)}(s)|}, \quad (1)$$

$$Recall^{(n)}(s) = \frac{|PR^{(n)}(s) \cap GL(s)|}{|GL(s)|}, \quad (2)$$

where s is a summary, $PR^{(n)}(s)$ is the Prediction Ranking sliced at the top n links for summary s and $GL(s)$ is the set of Gold links for summary s.

We further averaged recall and precision values over all summaries. Figure 2 and Figure 3 show the averaged precision and the averaged recall against the rank threshold n.

5.3 Results

Figure 2 and Figure 3 indicate that our Vector-based method shows comparable performance to the three ROUGE-based baselines in terms of precision but our method outperforms the others in recall. The difference in recall becomes larger according to the increase of the rank threshold n. This result is promising, as the final decision on

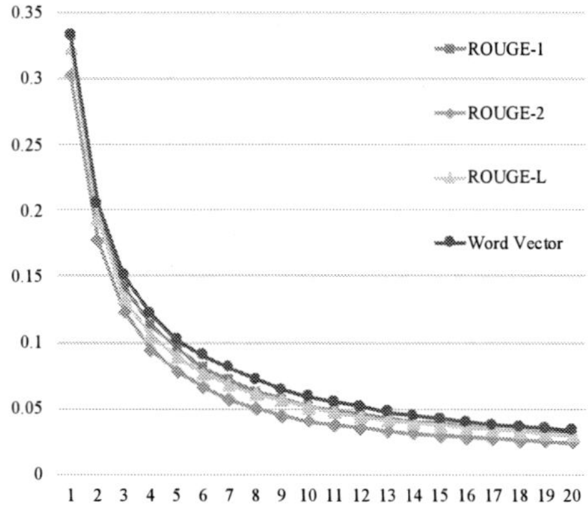

Figure 2: Averaged precision at at rank threshold n

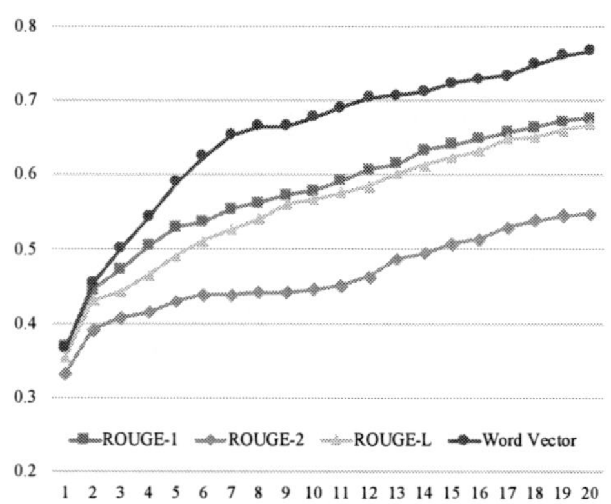

Figure 3: Averaged recall at rank threshold n

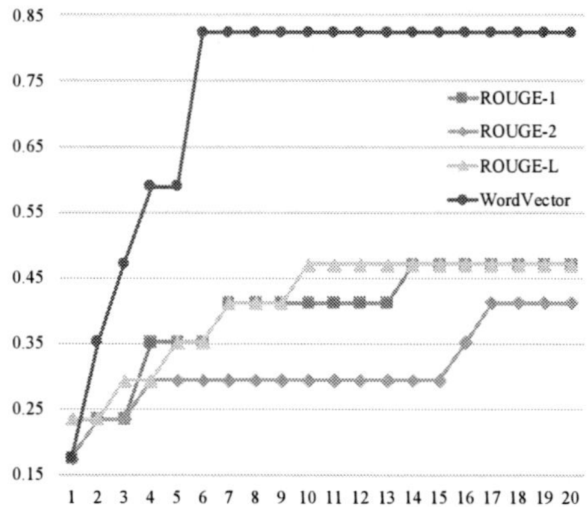

Figure 4: Recall at rank threshold n for summary 4B

Summary 4B
... A large factor is not the volume,\but the predictability of a noise,\as those exposed to quiet unpredictable noises performed worse than those listening to a loud predictable one. ...

Source text 2
... Probably the most significant finding from research on noise is \that its predictability is more important than how loud it is.\We are much more able to 'tune out' chronic, background noise, ...

Figure 5: IU samples with rephrasing.

similarities in Table 2.

what IUs should be linked is left to the end user, i.e. we favor recall.

The recall curve for summary 4B (Figure 4) is an example that shows a particularly big difference between our method and the others. When the ranking threshold is 6, the recall of our model is saturated at 0.82, which is more than the double of the recall of other baselines.

Figure 5 shows an example of the robustness of our method against rephrasing. The Source IU *"that its predictability is more important than how loud it is"* was linked to the Summary IU *"A large factor is not the volume"* by our raters. These two IUs share very few words, but they are close in meaning. Our Vector-based ranking method was able to capture this correspondence while the baselines could not. Indeed, the Vector model ranked the Source IU as the 5th most probable candidate for the Summary IU, while ROUGE-1 and ROUGE-L ranked it as 27th and 26th respectably. ROUGE-2 failed altogether to match the two segments. This data is shown along with the relative

6 Segment Matcher: A visual helper for Idea Unit alignment

We built a tool named "Segment Matcher" to aid teachers to establish links between Summary IUs and Source IUs through a graphical user interface. The tool consists of a front end developed entirely in JavaScript to ensure platform independence and a back end Python server to calculate the similarity between IU vecors. The back end server was built in Python inside a Docker container[1] for portability reasons.

The front end presents three different modes of use: Match, Edit and Compare. In the Match mode, the user firstly selects a summary file and its source file that adhere to our data format. Each text should presents one IU per line, with discontinuous IUs having a number prefix followed by a control character. These files are uploaded to the server and Prediction Rankings are returned for every Summary IUs. When the segment rankings have been successfully received, Segment Matcher moves to the link editor.

[1] https://www.docker.com/

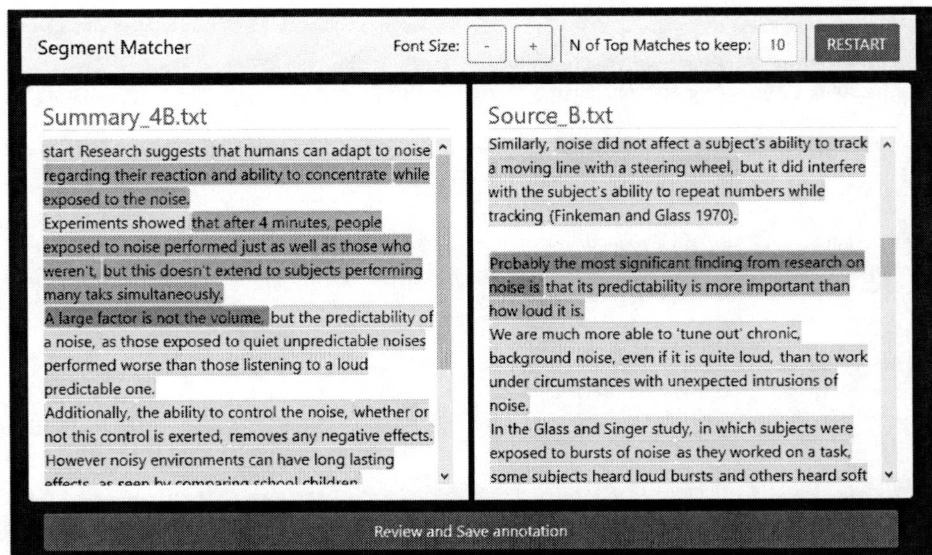

Figure 6: Screenshot of Segment Matcher

	Vector	R-1	R-2	R-L
Rank	5	27	—	26
Similarity	0.91	0.12	0	0.11

Table 2: Rank and similarity for IUs in Figure 5

Figure 6 shows a summary and the source text side by side, with IUs encircled in balloons, signalling that they are clickable elements. The user can link two IUs by first selecting a Summary IU from the left panel and then clicking the relevant Source IU in the right panel. To simplify the user experience, we colored the IU balloons as follows. When a Summary IU is firstly selected, it turns into yellow and the top N most likely candidates for the Summary IU are colored in a different shade of red, from the darkest indicating the most likely candidate to the lightest indicating the least likely one. When the user clicks a Source IU to be linked, the current Summary IU turns into dark green and the linked Source IU turns into blue as shown in Figure 6. The already linked Summary IUs are indicated in light green. The user can choose how many candidates to highlight, with the default being five.

Once the user is satisfied with their work, they can review the alignment by listing the IU links and save the alignment in a CSV file. This CSV file can be modified later via the Edit mode.

The Compare mode allows users to compare the alignments of two different raters, where two alignment CSV files can be selected along with their source texts to show the IU links side by side.

7 Conclusion and Future Work

In this paper, we introduced the Idea Unit (IU) (Kroll, 1977) for the content evaluation of student summaries and proposed a method for aligning IUs across a source text and its summaries. Our aligning method adopts the word embedding technique to deal with rephrased expressions. The experiment with 20 summaries for two source texts confirmed that our proposed method is more robust against rephrasing than the ROUGE-based baselines. The experiment also showed that our method outperformed the baselines in recall. The high recall is favorable as the final decision on the IU alignment is left to the end user.

Adopting the proposed aligning method, we built "Segment Matcher" to aid teachers to establish links between the IUs in a summary and the source text through a graphical user interface. We believe our tool contributes to making the content evaluation of student summaries by teachers more efficient.

In the future, we plan to further improve our work by implementing an automatic segmentation algorithm. This will allow teachers to evaluate summaries without having to segment them into IUs beforehand. We believe this to be a mission-critical feature that has to be implemented before the tool can be considered complete. We also plan to conduct tests in real world scenarios before releasing our tool to the public.

References

Pauline Foster, Alan Tonkyn, and Gillian Wigglesworth. 2000. Measuring spoken language: A unit for all reasons. *Applied linguistics*, 21(3):354–375.

Yanjun Gao, Andrew Warner, and Rebecca Passonneau. 2018. Pyreval: An automated method for summary content analysis. In *Proceedings of the 11th Language Resources and Evaluation Conference*, Miyazaki, Japan. European Language Resource Association.

Steve Graham and Dolores Perin. 2007. A meta-analysis of writing instruction for adolescent students. *Journal of Educational Psychology - J EDUC PSYCHOL*, 99.

Kellogg W Hunt. 1965. *Grammatical structures written at three grade levels*. 3. National Council of Teachers of English Champaign, IL.

Kellogg W Hunt. 1966. Recent measures in syntactic development. *Elementary English*, 43(7):732–739.

Kellogg W Hunt. 1970. Syntactic maturity in schoolchildren and adults. *Monographs of the society for research in child development*, 35(1):iii–67.

Ann M Johns and Patricia Mayes. 1990. An analysis of summary protocols of university esl students. *Applied linguistics*, 11(3):253–271.

Casey Keck. 2014. Copying, paraphrasing, and academic writing development: A re-examination of l1 and l2 summarization practices. *Journal of Second Language Writing*, 25:4 – 22.

Barbara Kroll. 1977. Combining ideas in written and spoken english: a look at subordination and coordination. In Elinor Ochs and Tina Bennett-Kastor, editors, *Discourse across time and space*, volume 5 of *S.C.O.P.I.L.* Los Angeles, Calif.: Dept. of Linguistics, University of Southern California.

Chin-Yew Lin. 2004. Rouge: A package for automatic evaluation of summaries. In *Text Summarization Branches Out: Proceedings of the ACL-04 Workshop*, pages 74–81, Barcelona, Spain. Association for Computational Linguistics.

Chin-Yew Lin and Eduard Hovy. 2003. Automatic evaluation of summaries using n-gram co-occurrence statistics. In *Proceedings of the 2003 Human Language Technology Conference of the North American Chapter of the Association for Computational Linguistics*, pages 150–157.

Walter Loban. 1963. The language of elementary school children.

Kishore Papineni, Salim Roukos, Todd Ward, and Wei-Jing Zhu. 2002. Bleu: a method for automatic evaluation of machine translation. In *Proceedings of 40th Annual Meeting of the Association for Computational Linguistics*, pages 311–318, Philadelphia, Pennsylvania, USA. Association for Computational Linguistics.

Rebecca J. Passonneau. 2009. Formal and functional assessment of the pyramid method for summary content evaluation. *Natural Language Engineering*, 16(2):107–131.

Jeffrey Pennington, Richard Socher, and Christopher D. Manning. 2014. Glove: Global vectors for word representation. In *Empirical Methods in Natural Language Processing (EMNLP)*, pages 1532–1543.

Juan-Manuel Torres-Moreno, Horacio Saggion, Iria da Cunha, Eric SanJuan, and Patricia Velázquez-Morales. 2010. Summary evaluation with and without references. *Polibits*, (42):13–20.

Qian Yang, Rebecca J Passonneau, and Gerard De Melo. 2016. Peak: Pyramid evaluation via automated knowledge extraction. In *Thirtieth AAAI Conference on Artificial Intelligence*.

On Understanding the Relation between Expert Annotations of Text Readability and Target Reader Comprehension

Sowmya Vajjala
National Research Council, Canada
sowmya.vajjala@nrc-cnrc.gc.ca

Ivana Lučić
Iowa State University, USA
ilucic@iastate.edu

Abstract

Automatic readability assessment aims to ensure that readers read texts that they can comprehend. However, computational models are typically trained on texts created from the perspective of the text writer, not the target reader. There is little experimental research on the relationship between expert annotations of readability, reader's language proficiency, and different levels of reading comprehension. To address this gap, we conducted a user study in which over a 100 participants read texts of different reading levels and answered questions created to test three forms of comprehension. Our results indicate that more than readability annotation or reader proficiency, it is the type of comprehension question asked that shows differences between reader responses - inferential questions were difficult for users of all levels of proficiency across reading levels. The data collected from this study is released with this paper[1], which will, for the first time, provide a collection of 45 reader bench marked texts to evaluate readability assessment systems developed for adult learners of English. It can also potentially be useful for the development of question generation approaches in intelligent tutoring systems research.

1 Introduction

Readability assessment refers to the task of predicting the reading difficulty of a text and its suitability to a target user's reading abilities. However, a typical computational approach relies on standard corpora that are created based on the writer's perception of what is difficult for a reader, and not on the target readers' comprehension data. While it is difficult to create such validated corpora in large samples sufficient to build automated models, lack of such data also raises a question

about the validity of such models (Valencia et al., 2014; Williamson et al., 2014; Cunningham and Mesmer, 2014). A reasonably sized corpus of readers' comprehension scores for texts of varying reading levels can be a starting point in this direction, as it can enable evaluating the suitability of an existing readability assessment system for that target group as well as look for the validity of the labeled dataset.

This issue then raises a question of how we should evaluate comprehension. There is a significant body of research on forming questions to assess different levels of comprehension in educational and tutoring systems research (e.g., Day and Park, 2005; Adamson et al., 2013; Mazidi and Nielsen, 2015). Readability is not considered as a factor in such studies. In the few user studies that do consider readability (Rayner et al., 2006; Crossley et al., 2014; Vajjala et al., 2016), differences between different levels of comprehension were not considered.

In this paper, we take first steps towards understanding the relation between expert annotations, reader proficiency and comprehension for automatic readability assessment research by conducting a web-based reading study with over 100 participants in a natural reading environment. Participants read six newspaper texts, and answered six questions on each text, covering three levels of comprehension. We analyzed our results by using methods from educational assessment research. We are releasing the data from this study, which for the first time, creates a freely available reader response based dataset for evaluating readability assessment systems. While it is not a large dataset and we cannot claim to have solved the problem of validating the readability annotations against target user groups, we believe this study is a first step in a much needed direction.

Our paper's contributions can be summarized as

---

[1] https://github.com/nishkalavallabhi/BEA19UserstudyData

Proceedings of the Fourteenth Workshop on Innovative Use of NLP for Building Educational Applications, pages 349–359
Florence, Italy, August 2, 2019. ©2019 Association for Computational Linguistics

follows: we conducted a user study with over 100 participants by,

- asking questions of different forms (short answer, T/F) that target three levels of comprehension (literal, re-organization, inference) for the first time,

- using a web-based reading setup where the readers read the full text in a normal computer based interaction setting, which can make the results potentially more relevant to practical, non-lab scenarios.

- using methods from educational assessment to show the differences in user responses for different levels of comprehension.

The rest of this paper is organized as follows: Section 2 summarizes related research. Sections 3 and 4 describe the study and results. Section 5 summarizes the insights gained from this study.

2   Related Work

Reading is the primary means of learning and knowing. Thus, readability or complexity of a text affects the comprehension process. Considering its important role in learning and assessment, text complexity has been extensively studied in the form of user studies, theories of comprehension, and computational approaches.

User studies on the impact of text complexity on reading comprehension have been done in Cognitive Psychology research since the 70s (Evans, 1972; Kintsch and van Dijk, 1978; Walmsley et al., 1981; Green and Olsen, 1988; Smith, 1988; Britton and Gülgöz, 1991). Eye-tracking was also used in the past to understand reading processes and comprehension difficulties (Just and Carpenter, 1980; Rayner, 1998; Jr et al., 2007). Attempting to study the problem from a second language reading perspective, Crossley et al. (2014) conducted a sliding-window based reading study where participants read texts word by word, using a collection of news articles written at three reading levels by language teachers. Comprehension was assessed by means of yes/no questions. More recently, Vajjala et al. (2016) combined both eye-tracking and second language reading perspectives by doing an eye-tracking study using texts from the same source (but not full text), asking readers to respond to two types of questions - factual and yes/no questions. They concluded that developing

questions that address different forms of comprehension may lead to a better understanding of the text-reader interaction.

Though there has been some work on creating questions that aim at testing different levels of comprehension (Day and Park, 2005, e.g.,), it was not utilized in these studies. Further, eye-tracking and sliding window approaches are closer to a lab environment than real-world reading, which makes it difficult to conduct larger-scale studies which can yield more reader response data, which is needed for evaluating computational approaches.

Unrelated to such user studies, there is a large body of research on readability assessment in the past century. Some of the early research on assessing readability relied on asking readers comprehension questions to evaluate text difficulty (Dale and Tyler, 1934). Such approaches were also criticized in terms of what is the right way to assess comprehension and how the nature of questions asked may influence readers' performance (Lorge, 1939). However, modern day research on readability assessment over the past decade largely ignored this aspect in creating and evaluating readability models. Since we don't have access to the data from such older studies, there is a need for the creation of new reader response based corpora to evaluate modern computational models.

Computational models of automatic readability assessment (ARA) (Collins-Thompson, 2014) and automatic text simplification (ATS) (Siddharthan, 2014) were proposed in the past 15 years. Unlike early research in this direction, such approaches generally rely on the presence of corpora that are either manually annotated for grade level/readability score. These are typically written by teachers or other experts, without a direct input from target readers. Evaluation of ARA and ATS systems is also typically done either automatically by splitting the data into train-test set or, occasionally, by asking a small group of human raters to evaluate the texts in terms of their grammaticality, and simplicity - not by actually testing for comprehension with target population. Except for some systems specifically developed for addressing certain intellectual disabilities (Carroll et al., 1998; Canning et al., 2003), there is very little research in this direction. Considering this background, to our knowledge, this is the first study in the recent past which conducted a user study with a goal of supporting the development and validation of computational models of readability assessment.

3   Methods and Experiment Procedure

Texts: We randomly selected 15 texts from the OneStopEnglish corpus (Vajjala and Lucic, 2018), consisting of manually simplified news articles from The Guardian, by English teachers, to suit beginner, intermediate, and advanced readers of English as Second Language (ESL). This corpus was also used in past user studies related to readability assessment (Crossley et al., 2014; Vajjala et al., 2016).[2]

Participants: 112 non-native English speaking participants were recruited for this study from among the student population of an American university by means of an internal email advertisement. Participants were compensated for their participation with Amazon.com gift coupons.

Questions: The   onestopenglish.com   news lessons included comprehension questions at the end of each article. However, these questions were primarily fill-in-the-blank and multiple choice questions, and they were not the same across all the reading levels for the same article. Further, they did not cover different forms of comprehension we wanted to check. Hence, the questions (and appropriate responses) for this study were created by an experienced language instructor following the guidelines of (Day and Park, 2005), and manually checked by the authors.

Questions covered three levels of comprehension: **literal**, **re-organization**, and **inferential**. Literal comprehension questions require learner's understanding of the straightforward meaning of the text. Therefore, the answers to such questions can be found directly and explicitly in the text. Reorganization questions require similar understanding, but learners are required to combine information from various portions of the text in order to provide a correct answer. Inference questions require a deeper understanding of the text, as the answer to such questions is not explicitly stated. The correct answer requires a combination of literal understanding of the text, learner's background knowledge and the ability to infer from what is written.

Questions were created such that answers are the same for all three reading level versions of a given text (i.e., content deleted or added between versions will not affect answering these questions). Six questions were created per text, covering three levels of comprehension, and two question forms (True-False, short answer).[3]

Proficiency Test: All the participants completed a free English language proficiency test provided by the British Council[4] after they completed reading all the texts and answering all the questions. The test gave a percentage score, and hence was on a scale of 0–100.

Study Procedure: After IRB approval, the first step involved developing a web-based application for setting up the reading study. We developed a Python and MySQL based web application that allowed users to log in and read the displayed texts and their responses were stored. Each reader read 6 of the 15 texts randomly chosen balancing for reading level i.e., each user read two texts per reading level, and without reading the same text in multiple versions. After reading each text, they first saw two questions dealing with factual comprehension. The text was not visible while answering these questions. The next page had the text along with reorganization questions and the third page had the text along with inference questions. Reading time was calculated based on the time taken to click on the next page but was not used in our analysis. After finishing reading all texts and answering questions, the participants did the proficiency test. [5].

3.1   Data Analysis:

In order to test whether the reported comprehension scores (total and across levels) can be predicted from learner's reading proficiency and text readability, a variety of regression analyses were performed using SPSS (Corp, 2013).

To compare comprehension question types and the two question forms (T/F, short-answer) and find possible difficulty levels among them, Multi-

---

[2]An example of the degree of simplification and summary statistics about the texts we used can be found in Appendix in Table 8 and Table 9 respectively, and all the used texts are provided in the supplementary material.

[3]The texts, questions and participant responses will be released with this paper and are provided as supplemental material for the submission.

[4]https://learnenglish.britishcouncil.org/en/content

[5]The code for this web-study will be released with the paper for reproducibility. It can potentially be re-used and enhanced to create a framework for testing larger, future studies in this direction.

Facet Rasch Measurement (MFRM) models were employed using the software package FACETS (Linacre, 2012). MFRM is typically used in psychometric and educational assessment research to examine different facets of question-answer data and their inter-relationships (Eckes, 2011). These relationships can include differences between participants, texts, question difficulty etc. In our case, the primary MFRM model used was a three facet model. The facets of measurement included the participants, three question types (based on comprehension) and two question forms (T/F and short answer questions). Assumptions required for all statistical analyses used were confirmed for both the analyses.

The data collected through this study is available on github at: `https://github.com/nishkalavallabhi/BEA19UserstudyData`.

4 Results

Post-study, we analyzed the responses from all the readers, and scored them manually using the question-answer key created while forming the questions.[6] The proficiency score was obtained automatically from the British Council test. Since we asked two questions per level of comprehension, each individual comprehension category had a score between 0–2 and total comprehension had a score between 0–6. Proficiency was on a score range 0–100. Table 1 shows descriptive statistics about the range of scores for our data set.

Score	Mean	S.D
Proficiency	76.6	10.25
Literal comp.	1.47	0.61
Reorganization comp.	1.45	0.67
Inferential comp.	1.33	0.65
Total comp.	4.26	1.19

Table 1: Summary of participant responses

Purely in terms of mean scores, readers generally seemed to do poorer on inferential comprehension than on the other two question types. The proficiency score was in the range of $[52 - 100]$ with a mean of 76.6. Table 2 shows the correlation between the scores for different comprehension question types and the overall comprehension score.

<hr>

[6]provided in the supplementary material.

	Lit.	Reorg.	Inf.	Total
Lit.	1	-0.28	0.101	0.553
Reorg.		1	0.134	0.622
Inf.			1	0.672
Total				1

Table 2: Correlations between participant scores for different comprehension types

Clearly, while different comprehension scores had very low correlation among each other, they (as expected) had a higher correlation with the total comprehension score. This shows that the questions were indeed different in terms of what they are testing.

4.1 Regression Analyses

We estimated regression models to predict the different reading comprehension scores based on proficiency, reading level, and an interaction between proficiency and reading level. Table 3 shows the summary of a multiple regression model to predict the total comprehension score, in terms of the co-efficient, standard error, and the significance of the predictor variables. The results show that this model has a low R^2 of 5.3%. This indicates that proficiency and reading level can explain only 5.3% of the variance in participants' reading comprehension scores. Also, only proficiency was a significant predictor, albeit with a low unstandardized coefficient (B). This is clearly not useful information in a practical scenario to use as a basis to build predictive models to recommend appropriate texts for language learners based on their proficiency and text's complexity.

Table 3: Regression model with full data

	B	S.E.	t	Sig.
total comp.	1.902	.890	2.137	0.33
proficiency	.031	.012	2.715	0.007
reading level	.164	.412	.399	.690
prof. and reading level interaction	-.002	.005	-.444	.657
$R^2 = .053$				

Vajjala et al. (2016) in their eye-tracking study with texts of two reading levels concluded that low proficiency readers fixate more for difficult texts compared to easy texts. To verify if that cognitive effort is also reflected in their comprehension performance, another multiple linear regression was calculated only with those participants who scored less than the median score (75) on the proficiency test. This additional analysis was conducted to investigate possible specific relationships of the same variables for low proficiency participants. The results are summarized in Table 4 and do not result in a different conclusion compared to the model with full data above in Table 3.

	B	S.E.	t	Sig.
total comp.	3.321	1.760	1.887	0.60
proficiency	.010	.026	.375	0.708
reading level	-.309	.815	-.379	.705
prof. and reading level interaction	.005	.012	.433	.665
R^2= .014				

Table 4: Regression model with low proficiency data

Regression models with these variables turned out to be poor fits for predicting scores for the three levels of comprehension separately as well, explaining less than 3% of the variance for all the three models (where literal, reorganization, and inference scores were the predictor variables respectively instead of total comprehension score). Proficiency had a statistically significant relation with only the literal comprehension score, and reading level was not significant in any of the models. Therefore, we are not discussing these analyses in further detail.

From what we see so far, it appears that we cannot predict reader comprehension based on an expert annotated measure of text readability, and/or a test of language proficiency. However, considering that the labels are given from the perspective of an instructor/writer and not the actual target reader, and considering that the texts did result in different scores from users, it is possible that there could be some other linguistic characteristics of text beyond the manually assigned readability label which relate to different forms of comprehension. One approach to explore this could be using the feature extraction modules from existing ARA systems. These methods extract a wide range of language features from texts, and there is evidence that, based on these features, texts can be successfully divided into different levels (Nelson et al., 2012). We would leave this exploration for future research.

4.2   MFRM Models:

To compare reader responses to different types and forms of questions, we constructed three three-facet MFRM models. The first model used participants, reading levels, and comprehension types (literal, reorganization, and inferential) as the three facets, and it was conducted to reveal possible difficulty levels of the three question types. The three facets for the second model were participants, reading levels, and question form (true/false and short answer), and this analysis was used to evaluate the comparability of the question form. Finally, the third model combined literal and reorganization comprehension into one group factual comprehension, and had the facets as participants, reading levels, and comprehension-question type combinations.

MFRM model calibrations from FACETS can be visualized by a vertical ruler known as **Wright map** or **variable map**. The first column in this map is the measurement scale with logits as measurement units. The second column shows the estimates of the participants' scores on the reading comprehension questions. This facet is positively oriented, so higher scoring participants appear on the upper portion of the ruler, while lower scoring participants appear at the bottom. The third column compares the reading levels in terms of difficulty. This facet is negatively oriented, and that means that more difficult levels would appear on the top of the ruler, while less difficult ones would appear at the bottom. The fourth column is discussed in more detail in paragraphs below for each model, and the fifth column maps the rating scale to the logit scale (first column).

In the associated summary tables for these three models (Tables 5–7), the reliability statistic is the ratio of true to observed variance for the elements of a given facet. It has a value between 0 to 1 (values closer to 1 are preferred) and this shows how reproducible is the ordering, and how reliably different are the values on the scale.

MFRM for levels of comprehension: Figure 1 shows the MFRM summary showing the distance between reading levels and comprehension levels.

As seen in the figure, the "levels" column does not show any differences between the reading levels. All the three levels are placed horizontally,

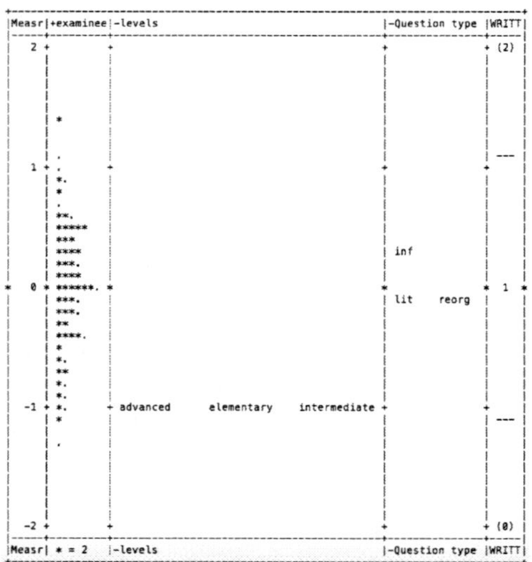

Figure 1: MFRM variable map comparing different types of comprehension

indicating there are no differences in terms of comprehension difficulty per reading level. The "Question Type" column in the ruler displays difficulty information about question type, and it is negatively oriented. This means that inferential comprehension questions were somewhat harder than literal and reorganization comprehension questions which seem to be the same level of difficulty.

The difference in logits (Table 5) is at 0.38, which is about 10% of the logit spread observed for the participants' reading comprehension. Small standard errors associated with the logit values indicate less variation from the mean. These values, along with other score averages for each comprehension type, are presented in Table 5.

comp. type	observed raw score average	average proficiency measure (logits)	S.E.
lit.	1.48	-0.13	0.07
reorg.	1.48	-0.12	0.07
inf.	1.33	0.25	0.06
Mean	1.43	0.00	0.06
S.D.	0.09	0.22	0.00
Separation = 3.26, Reliability = 0.91			

Table 5: MFRM for types of comprehension

The reliability statistic (given by $= separation^2/(1 + separation^2)$) for this model is 0.91, which indicates that there is a good separation between the two levels of questions - literal and reorganization grouped at one level, and inferential comprehension at the other level. Since literal and re-organization are two forms of factual comprehension, we can interpret this result as supporting evidence for inference questions being more difficult than factual questions.

MFRM for question types: The second MFRM model checked for the differences in comprehension scores between the two forms of questions - T/F and short answer. Figure 2 shows the summary of this model. The "question form" column in this summary indicates that short answer questions are more difficult to answer than true/false questions.

The difference in logits, presented in Table 6, is about 10% (0.42 logits) of the logit scale spread observed for the participants' reading comprehension. Again, small standard errors are observed. In terms of the reading level, as seen in column 3 of Figure 2, there are negligible differences between the three reading levels, with intermediate level being slightly more difficult than the other two. Table 6 shows the reliability statistic as 0.97, indicating that the participants showed a good degree of differences between the two forms of questions.

ans. type	observed raw score average	average proficiency measure (logits)	S.E.
short	2.03	0.21	0.05
T/F	2.25	-0.21	0.05
Mean	2.14	0.00	0.05
S.D.	0.16	0.30	0.00
Separation = 5.41, Reliability = 0.97			

Table 6: MFRM for forms of questions

MFRM for question types and forms: Since we saw two levels of difficulty among three levels of comprehension in the first MFRM model (Figure 1) and two levels of difficulty between question types, we evaluated a third MFRM model to understand the interaction between question form and the level of comprehension. Figure 3 shows the vertical ruler for this model, where literal and reorganization comprehension are grouped to-

Figure 2: MFRM variable map comparing the two forms of questions

```
+--------------------------------------------------+
|Measr|+examinee|-levels                |-QForm|WRITT|
|-----+---------+----------------------+------+-----|
|  2 +         +                       +      + (3) |
|     |         |                       |      |     |
|     |    .    |                       |      |     |
|     |         |                       |      | --- |
|     |    .    |                       |      |     |
|     |         |                       |      |     |
|     |    *    |                       |      |     |
|  1 +         +                       +      +     |
|     |   **    |                       |      |     |
|     |    *    |                       |      |  2  |
|     |    *    |                       |      |     |
|     |   **.   |                       |      |     |
|     | *****.  |                       |      |     |
|     |   *.    |                       |      |     |
|     |  ***    |                       |      |     |
|     | *****   |                       |  SA  |     |
|     |  **.    |                       |      |     |
*  0 * ******* *                       *      * --- *
|     |  ***    |                       |      |     |
|     |  ***    |                       |  TF  |     |
|     |  **.    |                       |      |     |
|     | ****    |                       |      |     |
|     |  **.    |                       |      |     |
|     |   *.    |                       |      |     |
|     |   **    |                       |      |  1  |
|     |    *    |                       |      |     |
|     |    *    |                       |      |     |
| -1 +  **    + intermediate          +      +     |
|     |    .    | advanced    elementary|      |     |
|     |    .    |                       |      |     |
|     |    .    |                       |      |     |
|     |    .    |                       |      |     |
|     |         |                       |      |     |
|     |         |                       |      |     |
|     |         |                       |      | --- |
| -2 +         +                       +      + (0) |
|-----+---------+----------------------+------+-----|
|Measr| * = 2   |-levels                |-QForm|WRITT|
+--------------------------------------------------+
```

```
+----------------------------------------------------------+
|Measr|+examinee|-levels                        |-tasks    |WRITT|
|-----+---------+------------------------------+----------+-----|
|  2 +         +                               +          + (2) |
|     |         |                               |          | --- |
|     |         |                               |  SAInf   |     |
|     |         |                               |  TFInf   |     |
|     |    *    |                               |          |     |
|     |    .    |                               |          |     |
|  1 + .       +                               +          +     |
|     |         |                               |          |     |
|     |  ***    |                               |          |     |
|     |   *.    |                               |          |     |
|     |  **     |                               |          |     |
|     | ****.   |                               |          |     |
|     |  **.    |                               |          |     |
|     | *****   |                               |          |     |
|     | ***.    |                               |          |     |
|     | ***.    |                               |          |     |
*  0 * *****. *                               *          * 1 * |
|     | ****.   |                               |          |     |
|     |   *.    | intermediate                  |          |     |
|     | ****    | advanced       elementary     |          |     |
|     | ****    |                               |          |     |
|     |    *    |                               |          |     |
|     |   *.    |                               |          |     |
|     |    *    |                               |          |     |
|     |   **    |                               |          |     |
|     |    .    |                               |          |     |
| -1 +  *.     +                               +          +     |
|     |   *.    |                               | SALitReorg|    |
|     |    .    |                               |          |     |
|     |    .    |                               |          |     |
|     |    .    |                               | TFLitReorg| ---|
| -2 +         +                               +          + (0) |
|-----+---------+------------------------------+----------+-----|
|Measr| * = 2   |-levels                        |-tasks    |WRITT|
+----------------------------------------------------------+
```

Figure 3: MFRM variable map comparing 2 forms of questions with respect to factual and inferential comprehension

gether into one (i.e., factual comprehension). The "Tasks" column in this summary shows that both types short answer and T/F inference questions were more difficult than Literal/Reorganization questions of both forms. This is further demonstrated by a pretty large difference in logit values which is presented in Table 10 7.

ques. type/form	observed raw score average	average proficiency measure (logits)	S.E.
T/F, fact.	1.56	-1.83	0.08
short, fact.	1.39	-1.16	0.08
T/F, inf.	0.69	1.42	0.07
short, inf.	0.65	1.57	0.07
Mean	1.43	0.00	0.06
S.D.	0.09	0.22	0.00
Separation = 23.08, Reliability = 1.00			

Table 7: MFRM for forms of questions and factual versus inferential comprehension

The difference between the lowest point of inference (T/F) and the highest point of literal and reorganization comprehension (short-answer), as displayed on the ruler (Figure 3), is 2.58 logits, which is 64.5% of the total logit spread. This means that the difference in difficulty is compelling. Additionally, within a given level of comprehension, short answer questions are more difficult to answer compared to T/F questions. For factual comprehension the difference in logits is 0.67, and for inferential comprehension, this difference is much lower at 0.15 logits. This accounts for 16.75% and 3.75% of the logit spread, respectively. This model shows that short answer questions are more difficult than T/F questions within a given level of comprehension.

5 Conclusions and Discussion

In this paper, we started out with the goal of understanding the relationship between expert annotations of readability, reader's language proficiency, and their reading comprehension, while also aiming to create a dataset which is useful for benchmarking computational models of readability assessment. To achieve this, we conducted a user study, and built a range of models on the data from this study.

The initial regression models were built to understand how much of reader comprehension scores can be explained by text's reading level, and the reader's language proficiency. These resulted in a poor fit for the data with neither reading level, nor proficiency score contributing much to predicting reader comprehension. As it was seen in related studies, reader proficiency had a statistically significant correlation with the comprehension score. However, it did not convert into actual predictive power despite the fact that we had over 100 users and almost 700 data points for the regression model. This result, while questioning the validity of expert annotations to target population's comprehension, also leads us to speculate that single measures of readability level and user proficiency by themselves may not be sufficient to match texts to readers in terms of predicted comprehension. We may have consider a broader set of linguistic features, and go beyond a single proficiency measure.

The results of first MFRM model (Figure 1 and Table 5) lead us to a conclusion that the participants had difficulty answering inference questions compared to literal and re-organization questions, irrespective of the reading level. There are no differences between the scores for responses to literal and reorganization questions though, indicating that the separation is between factual (which includes both literal and reorganization) and inferential comprehension, rather than the three levels. The results from the second MFRM model (Figure 2 and Table 6) show that there are differences between question types with or without considering comprehension levels separately. Short answer questions were generally difficult to answer correctly compared to T/F questions. As the results from the third MFRM model (Figure 3 and Table 7) showed, even within a given level of comprehension, short answer questions remained more difficult than T/F questions.

5.1 Discussion

Overall, the results from our study are mixed. It did not provide any evidence in the direction of using expert annotation of text readability and reader's language proficiency information to be able to predict reader comprehension and recommend linguistically appropriate texts to language learners. On one hand, this may indicate that the level of simplification performed in the texts is not substantial enough to merit differences in comprehension, and such an experiment may hold more value in scenarios that aim at content simplification, along with form. On the other hand, it may also question the validity of expert annotations of text readability.

However, we know it is possible to automatically distinguish between these levels in this corpus using machine learning models (Ambati et al., 2016; Vajjala and Meurers, 2016; Vajjala and Lucic, 2018). Whether the variation between texts of any specific linguistic property (e.g., lexical richness, syntactic complexity, coherence) can be correlated with the differences in comprehension scores instead of "reading level" assigned by the teachers should be explored as a part of future work.

The MFRM results provide evidence in the direction of different questions resulting in different responses, and hence, call for the need to focus on methods to automatically generate questions that target multiple levels of comprehension. Asking the right kind of questions is important in various scenarios that relate to the application of Artificial Intelligence in education such as - learning support in tutoring systems, and the assessment of comprehension in both self-learning and test taking scenarios.

Limitations: The study has been conducted in a relatively less-controlled manner compared to, say, an eye-tracking study, so there is no way to know whether the participants actually read the texts. Additionally, the study did not consider how much the readers' background knowledge helped them in answering the questions. While these factors may have affected the outcome of this study (as they will for most studies of this nature), it would not also be possible to conduct a study with over 100 participants while controlling for both these aspects. One aspect that was not considered in this analysis was the variation within different texts used in the study (random variation). This can perhaps be addressed in future considering it as another facet that affects the outcome.

Finally, the results of this study could be specific to the texts or the proficiency test or the questions used. Consequently, we believe more such studies are needed in future to establish the relation between expert annotations and reader comprehension in the context of readability assessment. Conducting such studies with texts from different sources, and with texts that are validated more thoroughly (e.g., pedagogical texts, which are perhaps created with increasing levels of comprehension in mind) will be a useful direction to pursue to overcome this limitation.

Outlook: As mentioned earlier, an immediate extension to this work would be to study what linguistic properties that differ across reading levels (if any) correlate with reader comprehension of the text. Additionally, expanding the study to other forms of comprehension, collecting information about more than one form of proficiency as was done in (Crossley et al., 2014), and evaluating different readability assessment systems using this data could lead us in the right direction in terms of matching texts to target readers in future.

Acknowledgments

We thank the three anonymous reviewers for their useful comments. This study was funded through an Iowa State University's internal grant, when the first author was employed there.

References

David Adamson, Divyanshu Bhartiya, Biman Gujral, Radhika Kedia, Ashudeep Singh, and Carolyn P Rosé. 2013. Automatically generating discussion questions. In *International Conference on Artificial Intelligence in Education*, pages 81–90. Springer.

Bharat Ram Ambati, Siva Reddy, and Mark Steedman. 2016. Assessing relative sentence complexity using an incremental ccg parser. In *HLT-NAACL*, pages 1051–1057.

Bruce K. Britton and Sami Gülgöz. 1991. Using kintsch's computational model to improve instructional text: Effects of repairing inference calls on recall and cognitive structures. *Journal of Educational Psychology*, 83:329–345.

Yvonne Canning, John Tait, Jackie Archibald, and Ros Crawley. 2003. Cohesive generation of syntactically simplified newspaper text. In *Text, Speech and Dialogue: Third International Workshop, TSD 2000 Brno, Czech Republic, September 13-16, 2000 Proceedings*, page 145. Springer.

John Carroll, Guido Minnen, Yvonne Canning, Siobhan Devlin, and John Tait. 1998. Practical simplification of english newspaper text to assist aphasic readers. In *Proceedings of the AAAI-98 Workshop on Integrating Artificial Intelligence and Assistive Technology*, pages 7–10.

Kevyn Collins-Thompson. 2014. Computational assessment of text readability: A survey of current and future research. *ITL-International Journal of Applied Linguistics*, 165(2):97–135.

IBM Corp. 2013. Ibm spss statistics for macintosh.

Scott A. Crossley, Hae Sung Yang, and Danielle S. McNamara. 2014. Whats so simple about simplified texts? a computational and psycholinguistic investigation of text comprehension and text processing. *Reading in a Foreign Language*, 26(1):92–113.

James W. Cunningham and Heidi Anne Mesmer. 2014. Quantitative measurement of text difficulty: Whats the use? *The Elementary School Journal*, 115(2):pp. 255–269.

Edgar Dale and Ralph W. Tyler. 1934. A study of the factors influencing the difficulty of reading materials for adults of limited reading ability. *The Library Quarterly*, 4:384–412.

Richard R. Day and Jeong-Suk Park. 2005. Developing reading comprehension questions. *Reading in a Foreign Language*, 17(1):60–73.

Thomas Eckes. 2011. Introduction to many-facet rasch measurement. *Frankfurt: Peter Lang.*

Ronald V. Evans. 1972. The effect of transformational simplification on the reading comprehension of selected high school students. In *Journal of Literacy Research*, pages 273–281.

Georgia M. Green and Margaret S. Olsen. 1988. *Linguistic Complexity and Text Comprehension: Readability Issues Reconsidered*, chapter 5. Preferences for and Comprehension of Original and Readability Adapted Materials. Lawrence Erlbaum Associates.

Charles Clifton Jr, Adrian Staub, and Keith Rayner. 2007. *Eye movement research: A window on mind and brain*, chapter Eye movements in reading words and sentences. Oxford:Elsevier Ltd.

M.A. Just and P.A. Carpenter. 1980. A theory of reading: From eye fixations to comprehension. *Psychological Review*, 87:329–355.

Walter Kintsch and Teun A van Dijk. 1978. Toward a model of text comprehension and productions. *Pschological Review*, 85(5):363–394.

John M Linacre. 2012. Facets computer program for many-facet rasch measurement, version 3.70. 0. *Beaverton, Oregon: Winsteps. com.*

Irving Lorge. 1939. Predicting reading difficulty of selections for children. *The Elementary English Review*, 16(6):229–233.

Karen Mazidi and Rodney Nielsen. 2015. Leveraging multiple views of text for automatic question generation. In *Proceedings of the 17th International Conference on Artificial Intelligence in Education (AIED 2015)*, pages 257–266. Springer International Publishing.

J. Nelson, C. Perfetti, D. Liben, and M. Liben. 2012. Measures of text difficulty: Testing their predictive value for grade levels and student performance. Technical report, The Council of Chief State School Officers.

K. Rayner. 1998. Eye movements in reading and information processing: 20 years of research. *Psychological Bulletin*, 124:372–422.

Keith Rayner, Kathryn H. Chace, Timothy J. Slattery, and Jane Ashby. 2006. Eye movements as reflections of comprehension processes in reading. *Scientific Studies of Reading*, 10(3):241–255.

Advaith Siddharthan. 2014. A survey of research on text simplification. *ITL-International Journal of Applied Linguistics*, 165(2):259–298.

Carlota S. Smith. 1988. *Linguistic Complexity and Text Comprehension: Readability Issues Reconsidered*, chapter Chapter 10: Factors of Linguistic Complexity and Performance. Lawrence Erlbaum Associates.

Sowmya Vajjala and Ivana Lucic. 2018. Onestopenglish corpus: A new corpus for automatic readability assessment and text simplification. In *Proceedings of the Thirteenth Workshop on Innovative Use of NLP for Building Educational Applications*, pages 297–304. Association for Computational Linguistics.

Sowmya Vajjala and Detmar Meurers. 2016. Readability-based sentence ranking for evaluating text simplification. *arXiv preprint arXiv:1603.06009*.

Sowmya Vajjala, Detmar Meurers, Alexander Eitel, and Katharina Scheiter. 2016. Towards grounding computational linguistic approaches to readability: Modeling reader-text interaction for easy and difficult texts. *Proceedings of the Workshop on Computational Linguistics for Linguistic Complexity*, pages 38–48.

Sheila W. Valencia, Karen K. Wixson, and P. David Pearson. 2014. Putting text complexity in context: Refocusing on comprehension of complex text. *The Elementary School Journal*, 115(2):pp. 270–289.

Sean A. Walmsley, Kathleen M. Scott, and Richard Lehrer. 1981. Effects of document simplification on the reading comprehension of the elderly. *Journal of Literacy Research*, 13(3):237–248.

Gary L. Williamson, Jill Fitzgerald, and A. Jackson Stenner. 2014. Student reading growth illuminates the common core text-complexity standard: Raising both bars. *The Elementary School Journal*, 115(2):pp. 230–254.

A Supplemental Material

Table 8: Example texts for three reading levels

Reading Level	Example
Advanced	*Amsterdam still looks liberal to tourists, who were recently assured by the Labour Mayor that the city's marijuana-selling coffee shops would stay open despite a new national law tackling drug tourism. But the Dutch capital may lose its reputation for tolerance over plans to dispatch nuisance neighbours to scum villages made from shipping containers.*
Intermediate	*To tourists, Amsterdam still seems very liberal. Recently the city's Mayor assured them that the city's marijuana-selling coffee shops would stay open despite a new national law to prevent drug tourism. But the Dutch capitals plans to send nuisance neighbours to scum villages made from shipping containers may damage its reputation for tolerance.*
Elementary	*To tourists, Amsterdam still seems very liberal. Recently the city's Mayor told them that the coffee shops that sell marijuana would stay open, although there is a new national law to stop drug tourism. But the Dutch capital has a plan to send antisocial neighbours to scum villages made from shipping containers, and so maybe now people wont think it is a liberal city any more.*

Table 9: Summary Statistics for Texts

	Elementary			Intermediate			Advanced		
	WC	AWL	ASL	WC	AWL	ASL	WC	AWL	ASL
Text 1	474	4.57	20.22	482	4.80	22.55	484	4.88	23.74
Text 2	607	4.11	16.46	660	4.13	20.32	661	4.19	21.03
Text 3	589	4.19	16.88	641	4.21	19.47	657	4.27	20.03
Text 4	662	4.73	16.44	681	4.8	18.72	736	4.89	20.37
Text 5	527	4.5	17.53	561	4.6	19.31	599	4.72	20.68
Text 6	691	4.51	17.08	707	4.66	19	769	4.8	19.5
Text 7	627	4.65	20.7	646	4.82	22.07	714	4.9	23.9
Text 8	273	4.21	18.71	327	4.28	22.57	376	4.33	26.77
Text 9	596	4.58	17.26	658	4.71	19.63	703	4.74	21.71
Text 10	500	4.65	21.57	580	4.76	25.13	609	4.75	25.65
Text 11	445	4.40	18.27	536	4.54	20.28	554	4.61	22.86
Text 12	578	4.46	16.03	655	4.67	24.97	690	4.76	27.35
Text 13	472	4.55	19.13	552	4.73	22.54	586	4.77	23.17
Text 14	535	4.38	12.71	610	4.52	14.24	673	4.57	16.38
Text 15	437	3.97	17.52	547	4.01	19.83	599	4.09	20.9

Measuring Text Complexity for Italian as a Second Language Learning Purposes

Luciana Forti[1], Alfredo Milani[2], Luisa Piersanti[2],
Filippo Santarelli[1], Valentino Santucci[1], Stefania Spina[1]

[1]Department of Humanities and Social Sciences,
University for Foreigners of Perugia, Perugia (Italy)
[2]Department of Mathematics and Computer Science,
University of Perugia, Perugia (Italy)
{luciana.forti,valentino.santucci,stefania.spina}@unistrapg.it
luisa.piersanti@studenti.unipg.it, alfredo.milani@unipg.it
filippo.santarelli@unicam.it

Abstract

The selection of texts for second language learning purposes typically relies on teachers' and test developers' individual judgment of the observable qualitative properties of a text. Little or no consideration is generally given to the quantitative dimension within an evidence-based framework of reproducibility. This study aims to fill the gap by evaluating the effectiveness of an automatic tool trained to assess text complexity in the context of Italian as a second language learning. A dataset of texts labeled by expert test developers was used to evaluate the performance of three classifier models (decision tree, random forest, and support vector machine), which were trained using linguistic features measured quantitatively and extracted from the texts. The experimental analysis provided satisfactory results, also in relation to which kind of linguistic trait contributed the most to the final outcome.

1 Introduction

The task of automatically classifying a text according to its different levels of complexity has had various applications in a number of different fields. It is key in mood and sentiment analysis, in the detection of hate speech, in text simplification, and also in the assessment of text readability in relation to both native and non-native readers.

Being able to select a text and compare it with others is a central concern in the field of second language learning. When choosing a text to be used in a lesson or as part of a language test, a teacher and/or language test developer will generally assess the suitability of that text on the basis of several aspects: the need to adhere to a specific syllabus and curriculum, as well as general guidelines and test specifications. Other aspects that are considered include learner-related variables such as their linguistic needs, their educational background, and their age, all elements involving other aspects such as text genre, text type, tasks to be assigned to the text, and so on.

According to the literature, there is wide consensus on specific characteristics that can influence the difficulty of a text in the context of a reading comprehension task. These characteristics have a role in terms of the cognitive demands that a text will impose on its reader (Bachman and Palmer, 2010)(Purpura, 2014). These characteristics are text length, grammatical complexity, word frequency, cohesion, rhetorical organization, genre, text abstractness, subject knowledge and cultural knowledge. All these aspects relate to readability, and are often evaluated intuitively and subjectively by individual experienced teachers, who will then use a given text deemed to be representative of a certain proficiency level in a lesson or as part of a test.

Although this kind of sensitivity to the text is extremely valuable, especially when adapting a lesson or test item to the specific needs of a group of learners, its limitations are evident for at least two reasons: the evaluation is performed by single teachers or test developers at the one time and it is not reproducible; the evaluation is conducted solely on the basis of observable qualitative features of a text.

In the context of language assessment, text selection for the purposes of a reading comprehension task has considerable implications with regard to the interpretation of test scores: a text subjectively deemed suitable for a given proficiency level, which would have objectively been deemed otherwise, will inevitably hinder the validity of the overall testing process. The same can be argued for text selection aimed at lesson planning: an in-

Proceedings of the Fourteenth Workshop on Innovative Use of NLP for Building Educational Applications, pages 360–368
Florence, Italy, August 2, 2019. ©2019 Association for Computational Linguistics

adequate text chosen for a given class will hinder the whole learning process.

As a result, an automatic system able to used extract objective and reproducible information about a text, combining qualitative and quantitative data, is highly desirable in the field of second language learning, though still largely lacking, especially for the Italian language and in relation to different proficiency levels. The Common European Framework of Reference for Languages (CEFR) descriptors are unable to provide this kind of support in relation to the readability of a text.

In this study, we assess the effectiveness of an automatic classification tool for the evaluation of text complexity in Italian. We used a dataset of texts used at CVCL, Centro Valutazione Certificazioni Linguistiche, one of the main Italian language testing centres with sections all over the world, based at the University for Foreigners of Perugia. Each text in the dataset was labeled by test development experts according to the CEFR descriptors. The dataset was used to train a classification model, enabling it to automatically predict the proficiency level of any text in input. The dataset was used to test three different classifiers: decision tree, random forest and support vector machine. The main difference between this study and the related work in the field that will be described in the following paragraph is that a set of linguistic features is used to distinguish texts from the perspective of CEFR levels. Therefore, linguistic features measured quantitatively and extracted from the texts are used to train the classification models that, in turn, allow to predict the proficiency level of an unseen text.

The rest of the article is organized as follows. The literature related to this work is described in Section 2. The architecture of the system is introduced in Section 3, while the definitions of the linguistic features adopted in the study are provided in Section 4. Experiments are discussed in Section 5, while the conclusions are drawn in Section 6 together with future lines of research.

2   Related Work

The assessment of text readability in relation to its complexity has been a central research topic for many decades now. In particular, advances in computational linguistics and the development of corpora, along with the availability of sophisticated language technologies, allow the capturing of a wide variety of increasingly complex linguistic features that are able to affect the readability of a text.

A number of studies aimed at developing automatic readability measures have focused on the English language, both for the simplification of administrative texts and for the purposes of first and second language learning. In more recent years, these studies have also involved other languages, such as French, Swedish, Dutch, German and Portuguese.

The texts used as a gold standard to train the classification models vary. For French, the corpus of texts was a second language coursebook corpus, containing texts developed by expert teachers and materials' designers (François and Fairon, 2012). A similar approach has been used for Swedish (Pilán et al., 2016), with the subsequent addition of a corpus of texts produced by second language learners (Pilán and Volodina, 2018). Other studies have used exams texts (Branco et al., 2014) or a combination of exam texts and native texts (Xia et al., 2011). One study on the readability of Dutch texts (Velleman and Van der Geest, 2014) uses a set of reference texts calibrated in order to represent a range of reading skills, while another one tailored for English (Vajjala and Meurers, 2016) includes a wide range graded corpora to cater for both natives' and learners' reading skills in both general and specialist language needs.

In terms of features, a number of systems have been developed, such as the Flesch-Kincaid (Kincaid and Lieutenant Robert, 1975), Coh-metrix (Graesser et al., 2004) and CTAP (Xiaobin and Meurers, 2016). In relation to the Italian language, three main approaches have been explored: the Flesch-Vacca formula, an adaptation of the Flesch-Kincaid formula for English (Franchina and Vacca, 1986), the GulpEase index (Lucisano and Piemontese, 1988), and READ-IT (Dell'Orletta et al., 2011).

In the Flesch-Kincaid formula, and its Italian counterpart, text complexity is measured with reference to the average length of words, based on syllables, and the average length of sentences, based on words. In addition to this, the formula provides an output indicating the approximate number of years spent in the education system that are necessary to comprehend a given text. The GulpEase index provides information that is similar to the Flesch-Kincaid formula, though it is based on considerably different characteristics. First, it is created directly on and for the Italian language. Second, though it includes the average length of words as well as the average length of sentences, the former is calculated on the basis of letters, not syllables, which aids the automatic treatment of the text.

For both of these measures, values range from 1 to 100, namely the highest and lowest textual complexity levels respectively. READ-IT, on the other hand, is based on a number of raw text, lexical, morpho-syntactic, and syntactic features, based on Support Vector Machines. This set of features is used together with a training corpus in order to develop a statistical model that is able to assess the complexity of newly inputted texts. The training corpus is formed by newspaper articles and a simplified reader of newspaper articles.

The aim of these measures developed for the Italian language have so far concerned the requirements of text simplification of administrative texts or other typically complex texts, in order to meet the needs of people with low literacy levels or with mild cognitive disorders. To the best of our knowledge, this study represents the first attempt to automatically classify Italian texts on the basis of a wide set of linguistic features, and in relation to the CEFR levels. In this respect, it lays the groundwork for a new resource in the context of Italian as a second language learning and teaching.

3 The System's Architecture

The problem of automatically measuring text complexity through the CEFR proficiency levels has been cast to a supervised classification problem.

We collected a dataset of texts labeled by the experts of the CVCL center of the University for Foreigners of Perugia. This dataset is used to train a classification model that, in turn, allows to automatically predict the proficiency level of any text in input.

As it is possible to see from the system's architecture depicted in Figure 1, the classification model does not directly work with the texts in their pure form. Indeed, any text is converted to a vector of numeric features and then passed on to the classification model (both for training or level prediction).

This scheme allows, on the one hand to adopt the most common classification models available

in the machine learning literature (Shalev-Shwartz and Ben-David, 2014) and, on the other hand, to build a classification model based only on the linguistic features of the text that, we think, are what discriminate texts from the point-of-view of proficiency classes.

Therefore, the most important part of our system is the component performing the "Linguistic Features Extraction" phase. This component has been implemented on top of Natural Language Processing (NLP) tools for the Italian language. In particular, we have adopted the NLP pipeline tools provided by Tint (Palmero Aprosio and Moretti, 2016), i.e., the Italian counterpart of the widely known Stanford CoreNLP tool (Manning et al., 2014). The linguistic features used in this work are detailed in Section 4.

Although most of the recently proposed works in NLP use semantically based features (Santucci et al., 2018), such as the well known word embeddings system introduced in (Mikolov et al., 2013) and (Bojanowski et al., 2016), it is worthwhile to note that here we chose lexical and syntactic features because they are the key linguistic traits for distinguishing different CEFR levels.

Regarding the classification model, we ran experiments on our system with three widely known models: decision tree (DT), random forest (RF), and support vector machine (SVM)[1]. While DT and RF provide more interpretable models, that can be analyzed ex post by linguistic scholars, we expect that SVM should reach a larger accuracy.

In our prototypical system, we have used the implementations of DT, RF and SVM available in the widely adopted "Sci-Kit Learn" library (Pedregosa et al., 2011).

4 Linguistic Features

The features used for predicting the text level are inspired by those adopted in (Dell'Orletta et al., 2011). These linguistics features have been divided into four main categories, and are described as follows.

4.1 Raw text features

Raw text features are the most elementary type of features considered here and they were computed through the tokenization of the text in input. In particular, they are:

---

[1] See (Shalev-Shwartz and Ben-David, 2014) for a description of the models employed here

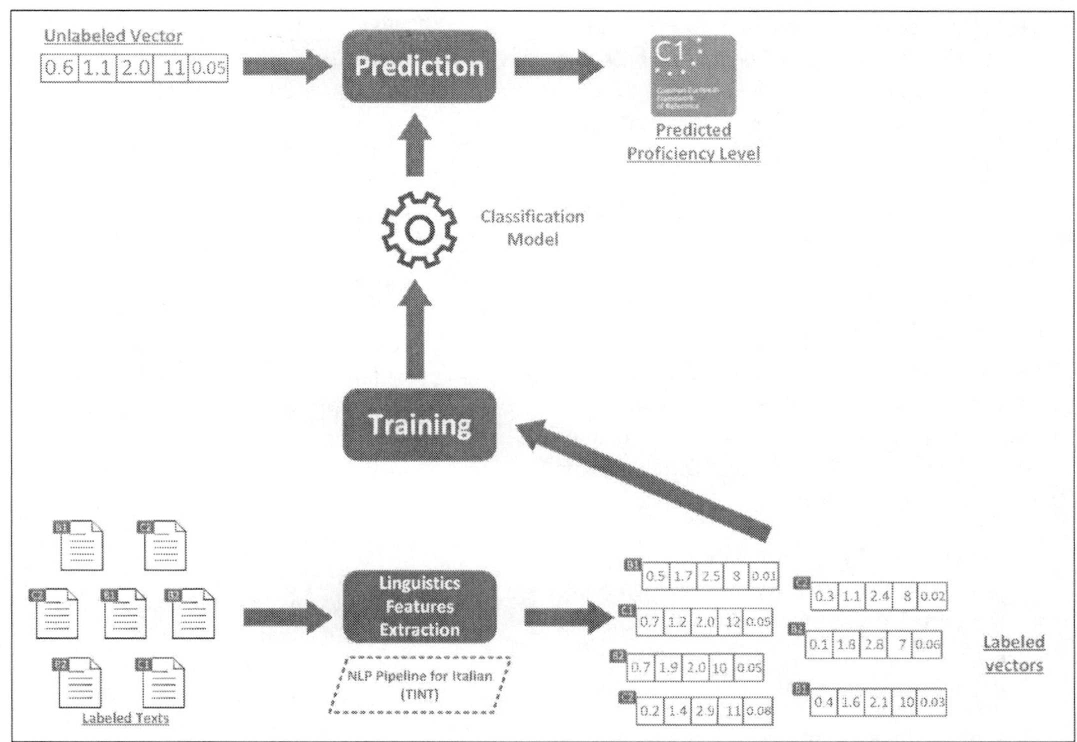

Figure 1: Architecture of the System

- *Word Length*, computed as the average number of characters per word, and

- *Sentence Length*, i.e., the average number of tokens per sentence.

4.2 Lexical Features

Lexical features are mainly computed through the lemmatization of the text's tokens and with reference to the New Basic Italian Vocabulary (NBIV) (De Mauro and Chiari, forthcoming) which includes the following three reference wordlists:

- fundamental (F) words (i.e.: the first 2000 most frequent words), such as *cane, gatto*;

- high usage (HU) words (i.e: occurring between frequency ranks 2000 and 4300) , such as *accademia, incapace, orribile*;

- high availability (HA) words (i.e.: identified in De Mauro and Chiari (forthcoming) through a native speaker judgment questionnaire), such as *affannato, mandarino, salvadanaio*.

Therefore, the considered lexical features are:

- *Lemmas in NBIV*, i.e., the percentage of text's lemmas belonging to NBIV;

- *Lemmas' distribution with respect to NBIV*, i.e., the distribution of the text's lemmas in the previous point among the three subsets F, HU and HA of NBIV (this feature is a vector of three numbers);

- *Type Token Ratio* (TTR), computed as the ratio between the number of different lemmas and the number of tokens in the text; however, since TTR is highly influenced by the text length, we restricted the computation to the first 100 tokens of every text in input.

4.3 Morpho-syntactic features

Morpho-syntactic features are computed basing on the Part-of-speech (POS) tagging and the morphological analysis performed on the text in input. In particular, we have considered the following features:

- *POS Tags Distribution*, i.e., for each POS tag p, it is computed the ratio between the number of tokens with type p and the total number of tokens in the text;

- *Lexical Density*, computed as the ratio between the number of content words (i.e., words tagged as nouns, adjectives, adverbs or verbs) and the total number of tokens in the text;

- *Verbal Moods Distribution*, i.e., the distribution of the seven verbal moods among the verbal tokens of the text.

4.4 Syntactic Features

The text in input is syntactically parsed by Tint and, for each sentence of the text, a dependency parse tree is produced. The syntactic features, described in the following, are then computed through dependency trees.

- *Dependency Types Distribution*, i.e., for each possible dependency type d, we computed the ratio between the number of dependencies with type d and the total number of dependencies, considering all the parse trees.

- *Depth of the Parse Trees*, computed as the maximum depth among all the parse trees.

- *Length of non-Verbal Chains*, i.e., the average length of the paths without verbal nodes in the parse trees.

- *Verbal Roots*, i.e., the percentage of parse trees with a verbal root.

- *Average Verbal Arity*, where the verbal arity of a verbal node v is the number of dependency links with v as a head.

- *Subordinates*, i.e., the number of subordinate clauses in the parse trees.

- *Average Length of the Dependency Links*, where the length of a dependency link between two tokens t_1 and t_2 is the distance, in terms of number of tokens, between t_1 and t_2 in the syntagmatic dimension of the sentence.

5 Experiments

Experiments have been held in order to: analyze the effectiveness and the robustness of the prototypical classification system here proposed, and gain useful insights about which features discriminate more the texts.

The rest of the section is organized as follows. Section 5.1 describes the corpus of texts and the

	B1	**B2**	**C1**	**C2**	**Total**
2C	0	129	0	97	226
4C	194	129	103	97	523

Table 1: Distribution of proficiency levels across datasets 2C and 4C.

datasets used in our experimentation. The experimental design is described in Section 5.2. The effectiveness of our system is analyzed in Section 5.3, while its robustness is discussed in Section 5.4. Finally, Section 5.5 analyzes the contribution of the different features selected for this work.

5.1 Corpus and Datasets

An important preliminary step to the experiments was the creation of a reliable corpus of labeled texts. In regard to this, we collected 523 texts with CEFR levels manually marked by expert language test developers. The corpus contains texts for the four CEFR levels B1, B2, C1 and C2.

Two different datasets, namely *4C* and *2C*, have been extracted from the corpus. While *4C* (i.e., four classes) corresponds to the whole corpus, the smaller dataset *2C* (i.e., two classes) contains the subset of 226 texts belonging to the levels B2 and C2. Table 1 provides the distribution of the different levels for both datasets.

Two main reasons motivated the introduction of the smaller dataset *2C*. First, the distribution of the proficiency levels in 4C is unbalanced, therefore a smaller and more balanced dataset such as 2C can be more reliable in terms of representativeness. Second, as the classification models do not treat the four levels as part of an ordinal scale, thus ignoring the natural ordering characterizing them, choosing two levels instead of four eliminates this issue.

5.2 Experimental Design

We tested three classifier models, namely, Decision Tree (DT), Random Forest (RF) and SVM, on both the datasets *2C* and *4C*.

For each dataset, the effectiveness and robustness of each model was evaluated using the nested cross-validation scheme (Varma and Simon, 2006). Two nested cross-validation loops were performed: the outer loop aims at estimating the effectiveness of the model setting which is calibrated in the inner loop. Both loops use 5 stratified folds. The inner loop performs an exhaustive

Parameters Name	Values
Feature-wise normalization	NN, SS, L2, RS
Split quality measure (`criterion`)	GI, IE
Min. impurity decrease (`min_impurity_decrease`)	0, 2
Min. samples to split (`min_samples_split`)	$2, 10, \dfrac{N_S}{10}$
Min. samples per leaf (`min_samples_leaf`)	1, 5, 10
Max. number of features (`max_features`)	$\sqrt{N_F}, N_F$
Max. number of leaf nodes (`max_leaf_nodes`)	2, 5
Weights associated with classes (`class_weight`)	$1, \dfrac{N_S}{N_C \cdot n_k}$

Table 2: Parameters space for the Decision Tree and the Random Forest classifiers. The original name of each parameter in the Sci-Kit documentation is in typewriter font within brackets. The function used to measure the quality of a split can either be the Gini impurity (GI) or the Information entropy (IE). N_F is the number of features, N_S and N_C are the number of samples and the number of classes in the dataset, respectively; n_k is the number of samples in the k-th class of the dataset.

Parameters Name	Values
Penalty parameter (`c`)	0.5, 0.75, 1.0, 1.25, 1.5
Kernel coefficient γ (`gamma`)	$10^{-3}, 10^{-4}$
One-vs-rest or one-vs-one (`decision_function_shape`)	OvO, OvR
Weights associated with classes (`class_weight`)	$1, \dfrac{N_S}{N_C \cdot n_k}$

Table 3: Parameters space for the SVM classifier. The original name of each parameter in the Sci-Kit documentation is in typewriter font within brackets.

2C	A	P	R	F_1
DT	0.9292	0.9265	**0.9303**	0.9281
RF	0.9292	0.9278	0.9278	0.9278
SVM	**0.9336**	**0.9355**	0.9291	**0.9318**

4C	A	P	R	F_1
DT	0.7189	0.6908	0.6888	0.6885
RF	0.7495	0.7136	0.7186	0.7130
SVM	**0.7725**	**0.7400**	**0.7407**	**0.7398**

Table 4: Accuracy A, precision P, recall R and F_1-score for Decision Tree (D.T.), Random Forest (R.F.) and Support Vector Machine (SVM) on 2C (upper table) and 4C (lower table). Such measures are first computed for each class, then their unweighted mean is computed.

grid search on the hyper-parameters space, cross-validated on the training and validation sets obtained by the outer loop. Every grid search returns the setting of hyper-parameters which maximizes the (macro-averaged) F_1-score. Then, the generalization ability of the selected model setting is assessed on the test sets generated by the outer loop and using the classic metrics accuracy, precision, recall and F_1-score.

The linguistic features described in Section 4 may have different scales, hence we introduced a preprocessing step to normalize them. Four normalization methods were considered: no normalization at all (NN), L^2 normalization (L2), standardization (SS), and robust standardization (RS) (which, with respect to SS, do not consider the outlier values). Hence, the choice of the normalization method is a further hyper-parameter which is tuned by the grid search.

The calibrated hyper-parameters and their ranges are provided in Table 2 for DT and RF, and Table 3 for SVM.

Finally, in order to reduce the computational ef-fort, we fixed the following hyper-parameters:

- the maximum tree depth of DT and RF has been set to $\lfloor\sqrt{N_F}\rfloor$, where N_F is the number of features;

- the number of trees in RF has been set to 100;

- the SVM uses the radial basis function as kernel type.

5.3 Results

For each dataset we tested all three classifiers, and we report the results, in terms of accuracy, precision, recall and F_1-score, in Table 4 for datasets 2C and 4C.

For the 2C dataset the differences between Decision Trees and Random Forests are irrelevant, indeed the precision slightly increases, the recall decreases comparably, and the F_1-score consequently remains pretty much the same. SVMs

Actual \ Predicted	B1	B2	C1	C2
B1	174	20	0	0
B2	13	95	20	1
C1	0	29	45	29
C2	0	3	16	78

Table 5: Confusion Matrix for Random Forests on 4C.

achieve better results, although the performances are satisfactory for all classifiers.

For the 4C dataset the situation is different: there is an improvement switching from Decision Trees to Random Forests, as is expected, and also from these ones to SVMs, that outperform the other models by 2.3% in terms of accuracy. However, as can be expected, the performances obtained on the 2C dataset are generally better than those obtained on 4C.

As previously reported, our models do not take into account the levels' ordering. Hence, we analyze how much this aspect influenced the performances. In particular, we analyze the results obtained by the RF model on the 4C dataset. With this aim, Table 5 shows the confusion matrix (for RF on 4C) with the levels ordered according to their natural ordering. From these data, it is evident that only four misclassified texts are two classes away from the actual class. Therefore, the classifier model does not seem to be very sensitive to the levels' ordering.

5.4 Robustness Analysis

Here we analyze the robustness of the RF model by considering the differences among the five settings of hyper-parameters obtained by the calibrations performed in the outer-loop of the nested cross-validation.

Most notably, every setting has the same assignment for the hyper-parameters `criterion`, `min_impurity_decrease` and `max_leaf_nodes`. Moreover, the hyper-parameters `class_weight`, `min_samples_leaf`, `max_features` and `min_samples_split` have been assigned to the same value in three settings out of five. The only unstable parameter is the normalization method which assumes all the possible values.

These results, despite some minor differences, shows the robustness of the proposed approach.

5.5 Analysis of Linguistic Features

The choice of Random Forests classifiers come in handy when we want to analyze how the classifier works internally, how the linguistic features are used and how they contribute to the final result.

The importance of a feature used by the Random Forests classifier can be quantified by means of the loss of Gini impurity due to each node where the splitting is performed according to that feature.

As already pointed out, a single run of nested cross-validation for Random Forests provides 5 different sets of parameters for each dataset; we analyzed them all separately, however, due to space constraints, in Figure 2, we only show the features' importance for one of them. The importance of linguistic features remains quite steady across the different 5 folds of the nested cross-validation both for 2C and 4C, thus proving the robustness of our architecture, and providing a sound assessment of the contribution of a feature to the final outcome.

6 Conclusion and Future Work

In this work we introduced an automatic classification system for assessing the proficiency level of an Italian text used for second language learning purposes.

A dataset of texts labeled by expert test developers was used to evaluate the performance of three classifier models (decision tree, random forest, and support vector machine), which were trained using linguistic features measured quantitatively and extracted from the texts.

Experiments were held in order to analyze the effectiveness and robustness of the proposed prototypical classification system, and to gain useful insight about which features contribute the more to discriminate the texts from the point of view of CEFR levels.

Overall, considering the preliminary nature of the work, the classification accuracy we obtained is satisfactory. Moreover, we derived interesting indications about the contribution of the different linguistic features we considered.

This work can be extended along several future research avenues: integrating more linguistic features, considering the natural ordering among the proficiency levels, including more classification models, and artificially augmenting the dataset of texts.

References

L. Bachman and A.S. Palmer. 2010. *Language Assessment in Practice*. Oxford University Press.

Piotr Bojanowski, Edouard Grave, Armand Joulin, and Tomas Mikolov. 2016. Enriching word vectors with subword information. *arXiv preprint arXiv:1607.04606*.

António Branco, João Rodrigues, Francisco Costa, João Silva, and Rui Vaz. 2014. Rolling out text categorization for language learning assessment supported by language technology. *Computational Processing of the Portuguese Language*, pages 256–261.

T. De Mauro and I. Chiari. forthcoming. *Il Nuovo Vocabolario di Base della Lingua Italiana*.

Felice Dell'Orletta, Simonetta Montemagni, and Giulia Venturi. 2011. Read–it: Assessing readability of italian texts with a view to text simplification. In *Proceedings of the Second Workshop on Speech and Language Processing for Assistive Technologies*, pages 73–83, Edinburgh, Scotland, UK. Association for Computational Linguistics.

V. Franchina and R. Vacca. 1986. Adaptation of flesh readability index on a bilingual text written by the same author both in italian and english languages. *Linguaggi*, 3:47–49.

Thomas François and Cedrik Fairon. 2012. An "ai readability" formula for french as a foreign language. *Proceedings of the 2012 Joint Conference on Empirical Methods in Natural Language Processing and Computational Natural Language Learning*, pages 466–477.

A.C. Graesser, D.S. McNamara, M.M. Louwerse, and Z. Cai. 2004. Coh-metrix: Analysis of text on cohesion and language. *Behavior Research Methods, Instruments, And Computers*, 36:193–202.

P.J. Kincaid and Fishburne R. Lieutenant Robert, P. 1975. Derivation of new readability formulas for navy enlisted personnel. *Research Branch Report, Millington, TN: Chief of Naval Training*, pages 8–75.

P. Lucisano and M.E. Piemontese. 1988. Gulpease: una formula per la predizione della difficoltà dei testi in lingua italiana. *Scuola e città*, 31(3):110–124.

Christopher D. Manning, Mihai Surdeanu, John Bauer, Jenny Finkel, Steven J. Bethard, and David McClosky. 2014. The Stanford CoreNLP natural language processing toolkit. In *Association for Computational Linguistics (ACL) System Demonstrations*, pages 55–60.

Tomas Mikolov, Ilya Sutskever, Kai Chen, Greg S Corrado, and Jeff Dean. 2013. Distributed representations of words and phrases and their compositionality. In C. J. C. Burges, L. Bottou, M. Welling,

Z. Ghahramani, and K. Q. Weinberger, editors, *Advances in Neural Information Processing Systems 26*, pages 3111–3119. Curran Associates, Inc.

A. Palmero Aprosio and G. Moretti. 2016. Italy goes to Stanford: a collection of CoreNLP modules for Italian. *ArXiv e-prints*.

F. Pedregosa, G. Varoquaux, A. Gramfort, V. Michel, B. Thirion, O. Grisel, M. Blondel, P. Prettenhofer, R. Weiss, V. Dubourg, J. Vanderplas, A. Passos, D. Cournapeau, M. Brucher, M. Perrot, and E. Duchesnay. 2011. Scikit-learn: Machine learning in Python. *Journal of Machine Learning Research*, 12:2825–2830.

Ildiko Pilán and Elena Volodina. 2018. Predicting proficiency levels in learner writings by transferring a linguistic complexity model from expert-written coursebooks. *Proceedings of the Workshop on Linguistic Complexity and Natural Language Processing*, pages 49–58.

Ildikó Pilán, Sowmya Vajjala, and Elena Volodina. 2016. A readable read: Automatic assessment of language learning materials based on linguistic complexity. *International Journal of Computational Linguistics and Applications, 7 (1)*, pages 143–159.

J.E. Purpura. 2014. Cognition and language assessment. In *The Companion to Language Assessment volume III*, pages 1,453–1,476.

Valentino Santucci, Stefania Spina, Alfredo Milani, Giulio Biondi, and Gabriele Di Bari. 2018. Detecting hate speech for italian language in social media. In *EVALITA 2018, co-located with the Fifth Italian Conference on Computational Linguistics (CLiC-it 2018)*, volume 2263.

Shai Shalev-Shwartz and Shai Ben-David. 2014. *Understanding machine learning: From theory to algorithms*. Cambridge university press.

Sowmya Vajjala and Detmar Meurers. 2016. Readability-based sentence ranking for evaluating text simplification. *Int. Jour. of Applied Linguistics*, pages 194–222.

Sudhir Varma and Richard Simon. 2006. Bias in error estimation when using cross-validation for model selection. *BMC Bioinformatics*, 7(1):91.

Eric Velleman and Thea Van der Geest. 2014. Online test tool to determine the cefr reading comprehension level of text. *Procedia Computer Science*, pages 350–358.

Menglin Xia, Ekaterina Kochmar, and Ted Briscoe. 2011. Text readability assessment for second language learners. *Proc. of the 11th Works. on Innov. Use of NLP for Building Educ. Appl.*, pages 12–22.

C. Xiaobin and D. Meurers. 2016. Ctap: A web-based tool supporting automatic complexity analysis. *Proc. of the Workshop on Computational Linguistics for Linguistic Complexity*, pages 113–119.

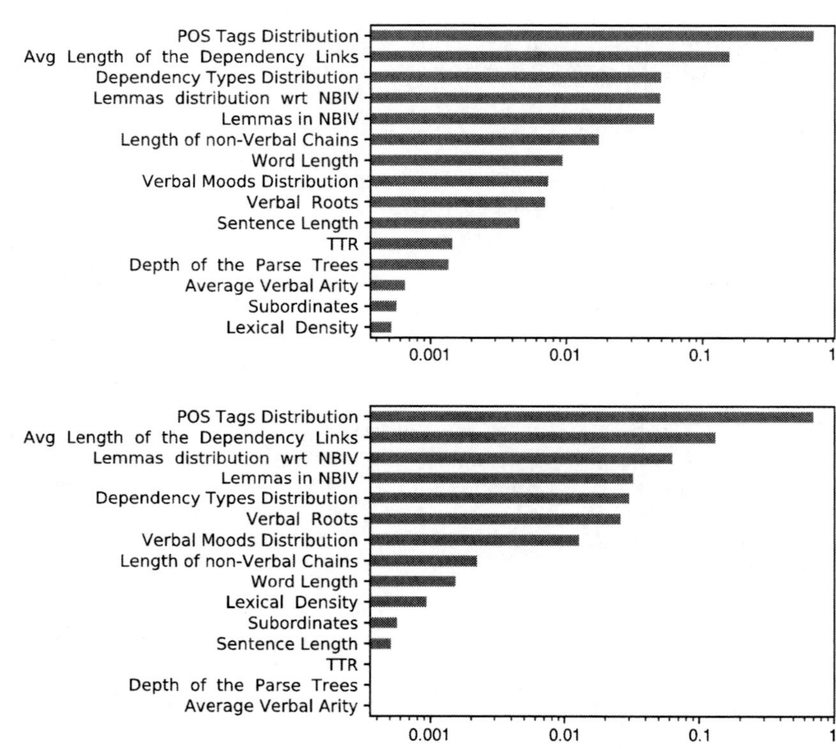

Figure 2: Relative importance of the features used by the Random Forest classifier trained on 2C (top plot) and 4C (bottom plot), in logarithmic scale.

Simple Construction of Mixed-Language Texts
for Vocabulary Learning

Adithya Renduchintala and **Philipp Koehn** and **Jason Eisner**
Center for Language and Speech Processing
Johns Hopkins University
{adi.r,phi}@jhu.edu jason@cs.jhu.edu

Abstract

We present a machine foreign-language teacher that takes documents written in a student's native language and detects situations where it can replace words with their foreign glosses such that new foreign vocabulary can be learned simply through reading the resulting mixed-language text. We show that it is possible to design such a machine teacher without any supervised data from (human) students. We accomplish this by modifying a cloze language model to incrementally learn new vocabulary items, and use this language model as a proxy for the word guessing and learning ability of real students. Our machine foreign-language teacher decides which subset of words to replace by consulting this language model.

We evaluate three variants of our student proxy language models through a study on Amazon Mechanical Turk (MTurk). We find that MTurk "students" were able to guess the meanings of foreign words introduced by the machine teacher with high accuracy for both function words as well as content words in two out of the three models. In addition, we show that students are able to retain their knowledge about the foreign words after they finish reading the document.

1 Introduction

Proponents of using extensive reading for language acquisition, such as Krashen (1989), argue that much of language acquisition takes place through *incidental learning*, where a reader infers the meaning of unfamiliar vocabulary or structures using the surrounding (perhaps more familiar) context. Unfortunately, when it comes to learning a foreign language (L2), considerable fluency is required before seeing the benefits of incidental learning. But it may be possible to use a student's native language (L1) fluency to introduce new L2 vocabulary. The student's L1 fluency can provide sufficient "scaffolding" (Wood

et al., 1976), which we intend to exploit by finding the "zone of proximal development" (Vygotskiĭ, 2012) in which the learner is able to comprehend the text but only by stretching their L2 capacity.

As an example of such *mixed-language* incidental learning, consider a native speaker of English (learning German) presented with the following sentence: **Der** Nile is a **Fluss** in Africa. With a little effort, one would hope a student can infer the meaning of the German words because there is sufficient contextual information. Perhaps with repeated exposure, the student may eventually learn the German words. Our goal is to create a machine teacher that can detect and exploit situations where incidental learning can occur in narrative text (stories, articles etc.). The machine teacher will take a sentence in the student's native language (L1) and replace certain words with their foreign-language (L2) translations, resulting in a mixed-language sentence. We hope that reading mixed-language documents does not feel like a traditional vocabulary learning drill even though novel L2 words can be picked up over time. We envision our method being used *alongside* traditional foreign-language instruction.

Typically, a machine teacher would require supervised data, meaning data on student behaviors and capabilities (Renduchintala et al., 2016; Labutov and Lipson, 2014). This step is expensive, not only from a data collection point of view, but also from the point of view of students, as they would have to give feedback (i.e. generate labeled data) on the actions of an initially untrained machine teacher. However, our machine teacher requires no supervised data from human students. Instead, it uses a cloze language model trained on corpora from the student's native language as a proxy for a human student. Our machine teacher consults this proxy to guide its construction of mixed-language data. Moreover, we create an evaluation dataset that allows us to determine whether students can actually

369

Proceedings of the Fourteenth Workshop on Innovative Use of NLP for Building Educational Applications, pages 369–379
Florence, Italy, August 2, 2019. ©2019 Association for Computational Linguistics

Sentence	The	Nile	is	a	river	in	Africa
Gloss	Der	Nil	ist	ein	Fluss	in	Afrika
Mixed-Lang	Der	Nile	ist	a	river	in	Africa
Configurations	The	Nile	is	a	Fluss	in	Africa
	Der	Nil	ist	ein	river	in	Africa

Table 1: An example English (L1) sentence with German (L2) glosses. Using the glosses, several possible mixed-language configurations are possible. Note that the glosses do not form fluent L2 sentences.

understand our generated texts and learn from them.

We present three variants of our machine teacher, by varying the underlying language models, and study the differences in the mixed-language documents they generate. We evaluate these systems by asking participants on Amazon Mechanical Turk (MTurk) to read these documents and guess the meanings of L2 words as and when they appear (the participants are expected to use the surrounding words to make their guesses). Furthermore, we select the best performing variant and evaluate if participants can actually *learn* the L2 words by letting participants read a mixed-language passage and give a L2 vocabulary quiz at the *end* of passage, where the L2 words are presented in isolation.

2   Approach

Will a student be able to infer the meaning of the L2 tokens I have introduced? This is the fundamental question that a machine teacher must answer when deciding on which words in an L1 sentence should be replaced with L2 glosses. The machine teacher must decide, for example, if a student would correctly guess the meanings of **Der**, **ist**, **ein**, or **Fluss** when presented with this mixed-language *configuration*: **Der** Nile **ist ein Fluss** in Africa.[1] The machine teacher must also ask the same question of many other possible mixed-language configurations. Table 1 shows an example sentence and three mixed-language configurations from among the exponentially many choices. Our approach assumes a 1-to-1 correspondence (i.e. gloss) is available for each L1 token. Clearly, this is not true in general, so we only focus on mixed-language configurations when 1-to-1 glosses *are* possible. If a particular L1 token does not have a gloss, we only consider configurations where that token is always represented in L1.

---

[1] By "meaning" we mean the L1 token that was originally in the sentence before it was replaced by an L2 gloss.

2.1   Student Proxy Model

Before we address the aforementioned question, we must introduce our student proxy model. Concretely, our student proxy model is a cloze language model that uses bidirectional LSTMs to predicts L1 words from their surrounding context (Mousa and Schuller, 2017; Hochreiter and Schmidhuber, 1997). We refer to it as the cLM (cloze language model). Given a L1 sentence $[x_1, x_2, ..., x_T]$, the model defines a distribution $p(x_t \mid [\mathbf{h}^f : \mathbf{h}^f])$ at each position in the sentence. Here, $\mathbf{h}^f$ and $\mathbf{h}^b$ are D−dimensional hidden states from forward and backward LSTMs.

$$\mathbf{h}^f{}_t = \text{LSTM}^f([\mathbf{x}_1, ..., \mathbf{x}_{t-1}]; \boldsymbol{\theta}^f) \quad (1)$$
$$\mathbf{h}^b{}_t = \text{LSTM}^b([\mathbf{x}_{t+1}, ..., \mathbf{x}_T]; \boldsymbol{\theta}^b) \quad (2)$$

The cLM assumes a fixed L1 vocabulary of size V, and the vectors $\mathbf{x}_t$ above are embeddings of these word types, which correspond to the rows of a matrix $\mathbf{E} \in \mathbb{R}^{V \times D}$. The output distribution (over V word types) is obtained by concatenating the hidden states from the forward and backward LSTMs and projecting the resulting $2D$-dimensional state down to D-dimensions using a projection layer $h(\cdot; \boldsymbol{\theta}^h)$. Finally, a softmax operation is performed:

$$p(\cdot \mid [\mathbf{h}^f : \mathbf{h}^b]) = \text{softmax}(\mathbf{E} \cdot h([\mathbf{h}^f : \mathbf{h}^b]; \boldsymbol{\theta}^h)) \quad (3)$$

Note that the softmax layer also uses the word embedding matrix $\mathbf{E}$ when generating the output distribution (Press and Wolf, 2017). This cloze language model encodes left-and-right contextual dependence rather than the typical sequence dependence of standard (unidirectional) language models.

We train the parameters $\boldsymbol{\theta} = [\boldsymbol{\theta}^f; \boldsymbol{\theta}^b; \boldsymbol{\theta}^h; \mathbf{E}]$ using Adam (Kingma and Ba, 2014) to maximize $\sum_{\mathbf{x}} \mathcal{L}(\mathbf{x})$, where the summation is over sentences $\mathbf{x}$ in a large L1 training corpus.

$$\mathcal{L}(\mathbf{x}) = \sum_t \log p(x_t \mid [\mathbf{h}^f{}_t : \mathbf{h}^b{}_t]) \quad (4)$$

We assume that the resulting model represents the entirety of the student's L1 knowledge, and that the L1 parameters $\boldsymbol{\theta}$ will not change further.

2.2   Incremental L2 Vocabulary Learning

The model so far can assign probability to an L1 sentence such as The Nile is a river in Africa, (using Eq. (4)) but what about a mixed-language sentence such as **Der** Nile **ist ein Fluss** in Africa? To accommodate the new L2 words, we use another word-embedding matrix, $\mathbf{F} \in \mathbb{R}^{V' \times D}$ and modify Eq 3 to consider both the L1 and L2 embeddings:

$$p(\cdot \mid [\mathbf{h^f} : \mathbf{h^b}]) = \text{softmax}([\mathbf{E};\mathbf{F}] \cdot h([\mathbf{h^f} : \mathbf{h^b}];\boldsymbol{\theta^h}))$$

We also restrict the softmax function above to produce a distribution not over the full bilingual vocabulary of size $|V| + |V'|$, but only over the bilingual vocabulary consisting of the V L1 types together with only the $v' \subset V'$ L2 types that actually appear in the mixed-language sentence $\mathbf{x}$. In the above example mixed-language sentence, $|v'|$ is 4. We initialize $\mathbf{F}$ by drawing its elements IID from Uniform$[-0.01,0.01]$. Thus, all L2 words initially have random embeddings $[-0.01,0.01]^{1 \times D}$.

These modifications lets us compute $\mathcal{L}(\mathbf{x})$ for a mixed-language sentence $\mathbf{x}$. We assume that when a human student reads a mixed-language sentence $\mathbf{x}$, they update their L2 parameters $\mathbf{F}$ (but not their L1 parameters $\boldsymbol{\theta}$) to increase $\mathcal{L}(\mathbf{x})$. Specifically, we assume that $\mathbf{F}$ will be updated to maximize

$$\mathcal{L}(\mathbf{x};\boldsymbol{\theta^f},\boldsymbol{\theta^b},\boldsymbol{\theta^h},\mathbf{E},\mathbf{F}) - \lambda \|\mathbf{F} - \mathbf{F^{prev}}\|^2 \qquad (5)$$

Maximizing Eq. (5) adjusts the embeddings of each L2 word in the sentence so that it is more easily predicted from the other L1/L2 words, and also so that it is more helpful at predicting the other L1/L2 words. Since the rest of the model's parameters do not change, we expect to find an embedding for **Fluss** that is similar to the embedding for `river`. However, the regularization term with coefficient $\lambda > 0$ prevents $\mathbf{F}$ from straying too far from from $\mathbf{F^{prev}}$, which represents the value of $\mathbf{F}$ before this sentence was read. This limits the degree to which our simulated student will change their embedding of an L2 word such as **Fluss** based on a *single* example. As a result, the embedding of **Fluss** reflects *all* of the past sentences that contained **Fluss**, although (realistically) with some bias toward the most recent such sentences. We do not currently model spacing effects, i.e., forgetting due to the passage of time.

In principle, λ should be set based on human-subjects experiments, and might differ from human to human. In practice, in this paper, we simply took $\lambda = 1$. We (approximately) maximized the objective above using 5 steps of gradient ascent, which gave good convergence in practice.

2.3 Scoring L2 embeddings

The incremental vocabulary learning procedure (Section 2.2) takes a mixed-language configuration and generates a new L2 word-embedding matrix by applying gradient updates to a previous version of the L2 word-embedding matrix. The new matrix represents the proxy student's L2 knowledge after observing the mixed-language configuration.

Thus, if we can score the new L2 embeddings, we can, in essence, score the mixed-language configuration that generated it. The ability to score configurations affords search (Sections 2.4 and 2.5) for high-scoring configurations. With this motivation, we design a scoring function to measure the "goodness" of L2 word-embeddings, $\mathbf{F}$.

The machine teacher evaluates $\mathbf{F}$ with reference to all correct word-gloss pairs from the *entire document*. For our example sentence, the word pairs are $\{(\texttt{The}, \textbf{Der}), (\texttt{is},\textbf{ist}), (\texttt{a},\textbf{ein}),$ $(\texttt{river},\textbf{Fluss})\}$. But the machine teacher also has access to, for example, $\{(\texttt{water},\textbf{Wasser}),$ $(\texttt{stream}, \textbf{Fluss}) \ldots\}$, which come from elsewhere in the document. Thus, if $\mathcal{P}$ is the set of word pairs, $\{(x_1,f_1),\ldots(x_{|\mathcal{P}|},f_{|\mathcal{P}|})\}$, we compute:

$$\tilde{r}_p = R(x_p,\mathbf{cs}(\mathbf{F}_{f_p},\mathbf{E})) \qquad (6)$$

$$r_p = \begin{cases} \tilde{r}_p & \text{if } \tilde{r}_p < r_{\max} \\ \infty & \text{otherwise} \end{cases}$$

$$\text{MRR}(\mathbf{F},\mathbf{E},r_{\max}) = \frac{1}{|\mathcal{P}|}\sum_p \frac{1}{r_p} \qquad (7)$$

where $\mathbf{cs}(\mathbf{F}_f,\mathbf{E})$ denotes the vector of cosine similarities between the embedding of an L2 word f and the entire L1 vocabulary. $R(x,\mathbf{cs}(\mathbf{E},\mathbf{F}_f))$ queries the rank of the correct L1 word x that pairs with f. r can take values from 1 to $|V|$, but we use a rank threshold $r_{\max}$ and force pairs with a rank worse than $r_{\max}$ to ∞. Thus, given a word-gloss pairing $\mathcal{P}$, the current state of the L2 embedding matrix $\mathbf{F}$, and the L1 embedding matrix $\mathbf{E}$, we obtain the Mean Reciprocal Rank (MRR) score in (7).

We can think of the scoring function as a "vocabulary test" in which the proxy student gives (its best) $r_{\max}$ guesses for each L2 word type and receives a numerical grade.

2.4 Mixed-Language Configuration Search

So far we have detailed our simulated student that would learn from a mixed-language sentence, and a metric to measure how good the learned L2 embeddings would be. Now the machine teacher only has to search for the best mixed-language configuration of a sentence. As there are exponentially many possible configurations to consider, exhaustive search is infeasible. We use a simple left-to-right greedy search to approximately find the highest scoring configuration for a given sentence. Algorithm 1 shows the pseudo-code for the search process. The inputs to the search algorithm are the initial L2 word-embeddings matrix $\mathbf{F}^{\mathbf{prev}}$, the scoring function MRR(), and the student proxy model SPM(). The algorithm proceeds left to right, making a binary decision at each token: Should the token be replaced with its L2 gloss or left as is? For the first token, these two decisions result in the two configurations: (i) `Der Nile...` and (ii) `The Nile...` These configurations are given to the student proxy model which updates the L2 word embeddings. The scoring function (section 2.3) computes a score for each L2 word-embedding matrix and caches the best configuration (i.e. the configuration associated with the highest scoring L2 word-embedding matrix). If two configurations result in the same MRR score, the number of L2 word types exposed is used to break ties. In Algorithm 1, $\rho(\mathbf{c})$ is the function that counts the number of L2 word types exposed in a configuration $\mathbf{c}$.

Algorithm 1 Mixed-Lang. Config. Search

Require: $\mathbf{x} = [x_1, x_2, ..., x_T]$ ▷ L1 tokens
Require: $\mathbf{f} = [f_1, f_2, ..., f_T]$ ▷ L2 glosses
Require: E   ▷ L1 emb. matrix
Require: $\mathbf{F}^{\mathbf{prev}}$ ▷ initial L2 emb. matrix
Require: SPM   ▷ Student Proxy Model
Require: MRR, r_{max} ▷ Scoring Func., threshold
1: **function** SEARCH($\mathbf{x}, \mathbf{f}, \mathbf{F}^{\mathbf{prev}}$)
2:      $\mathbf{c} \leftarrow \mathbf{x}$ ▷ initial configuration is the L1 sentence
3:      $\mathbf{F} \leftarrow \mathbf{F}^{\mathbf{prev}}$
4:      $s = \text{MRR}(\mathbf{E}, \mathbf{F}, r_{max})$
5:      **for** $i = 1; i \leq T; i++$ **do**
6:          $\mathbf{c}' \leftarrow c_1 \cdots c_{i-1} f_i x_{i+1} \cdots x_T$
7:          $\Phi' = \text{SPM}(\mathbf{F}^{\mathbf{prev}}, \mathbf{c}')$
8:          $s' = \text{MRR}(\mathbf{E}, \Phi', r_{max})$
9:          **if** $(s', -\rho(\mathbf{c}')) \geq (s, -\rho(\mathbf{c}))$ **then**
10:             $\mathbf{c} \leftarrow \mathbf{c}', \mathbf{F} \leftarrow \mathbf{F}', s \leftarrow s'$
11:          **end if**
12:      **end for**
13:      **return** c, F   ▷ Mixed-Lang. Config.
14: **end function**

2.5 Mixed-Language document creation

Our idea is that a sequence of mixed-language configurations is good if it drives the student proxy model's L2 embeddings toward an MRR score close to 1 (maximum possible). Note that we do *not* change the sentence order (we still want a coherent document), just the mixed-language *configuration* of each sentence. For each sentence in turn, we greedily search over mixed-language configurations using Algorithm 1, then choose the configuration

that learns the best $\mathbf{F}$, and proceed to the next sentence with $\mathbf{F}^{\mathbf{prev}}$ now set to this learned $\mathbf{F}$.[2] This process is repeated until the end of the document. The pseudo-code for generating an entire document of mixed-language content is shown in Algorithm 2.

Algorithm 2 Mixed-Lang. Document Gen.

Require: $\mathcal{D} = [(\mathbf{x_1}, \mathbf{f_1}), ..., (\mathbf{x_N}, \mathbf{f_N})]$ ▷ Document
Require: E   ▷ L1 emb. matrix
Require: $\mathbf{F}^{\mathbf{0}}$ ▷ initial L2 emb. matrix
1: **function** DOCGEN($\mathcal{D}, \mathbf{F}^{\mathbf{0}}$)
2:      $\mathcal{C} = []$ ▷ Configuration List
3:      **for** $i = 1; i \leq N; i++$ **do**
4:          $\mathbf{x_i}, \mathbf{f_i} = \mathcal{D}[i]$
5:          $\mathbf{c_i}, \mathbf{F_i} = \text{SEARCH}(\mathbf{x_i}, \mathbf{f_i}, \mathbf{F_{i-1}})$
6:          $\mathcal{C} \leftarrow \mathcal{C} + [\mathbf{c_i}]$
7:      **end for**
8:      **return** $\mathcal{C}$ ▷ Mixed-Lang. Document
9: **end function**

In summary, our machine teacher is composed of (i) a student proxy model which is a contextual L2 word learning model (Sections 2.1 and 2.2) and (ii) a configuration sequence search algorithm (Sections 2.4 and 2.5), which is guided by (iii) an L2 vocabulary scoring function (Section 2.3). In the next section, we describe two variations for the student proxy models.

3 Variations in Student Proxy Models

We developed two variations for the student proxy model to compare and contrast the mixed-language documents that can be generated.

3.1 Unidirectional Language Model

This variation restricts the bidirectional model (from Section 2.1) to be unidirectional (uLM) and follows a standard recurrent neural network (RNN) language model (Mikolov et al., 2010).

$$\log p(\mathbf{x}) = \sum_t \log p(x_t \mid \mathbf{h^f}_t) \tag{8}$$

$$\mathbf{h^f}_t = \text{LSTM}^{\mathbf{f}}(\mathbf{x}_0, ..., \mathbf{x}_{t-1}; \theta^{\mathbf{f}}) \tag{9}$$

$$p(\cdot \mid \mathbf{h^f}) = \text{softmax}(\mathbf{E} \cdot \mathbf{h^f}) \tag{10}$$

Once again, $\mathbf{h^f} \in \mathbb{R}^{D \times 1}$ is the hidden state of the LSTM recurrent network, which is parameterized by $\theta^{\mathbf{f}}$, but unlike the model in Section 2.1, no backward LSTM and no projection function is used.

The same procedure from the bidirectional model is used to update L2 word embeddings (Section 2.2). While this model does not explicitly encode context

---

[2]For the first sentence, we initialize $\mathbf{F}^{\mathbf{prev}}$ to have values randomly between $[-0.01, 0.01]$.

from "future" tokens (i.e. words to the right of x_t) , there is still pressure from right-side tokens $x_{t+t:T}$ because the new embeddings will be adjusted to explain the tokens to the right as well. Fixing all the L1 parameters further strengthens this pressure on L2 embeddings from words to their right.

3.2 Direct Prediction Model

The previous two models variants adjust L2 embeddings using gradient steps to improve the pseudo-likelihood of the presented mixed-language sentences. One drawback of such an approach is computation speed caused by the bottleneck introduced by the softmax operation.

We designed an alternate student prediction model that can "directly" predict the embeddings for words in a sentence using contextual information. We refer to this variation as the *Direct Prediction* (DP) model. Like our previous student proxy models, the DP model also uses bidirectional LSTMs to encode context and an L1 word embedding matrix $\mathbf{E}$. However, the DP model does not attempt to produce a distribution over the output vocabulary; instead it tries to predict a real-valued vector using a feed-forward highway network (Srivastava et al., 2015). The DP model's objective is to minimize the mean square error (MSE) between a predicted word embedding and the *true embedding*. For a time-step t, the predicted word embedding $\hat{\mathbf{x}}_t$, is generated by:

$$\mathbf{h^f}_t = \mathrm{LSTM^f}([\mathbf{x}_1,...,\mathbf{x}_{t-1}];\boldsymbol{\theta^f}) \quad (11)$$

$$\mathbf{h^b}_t = \mathrm{LSTM^b}([\mathbf{x}_{t+1},...,\mathbf{x}_T];\boldsymbol{\theta^b}) \quad (12)$$

$$\hat{\mathbf{x}}_t = \mathrm{FF}([\mathbf{x}_t:\mathbf{h^f}_t:\mathbf{h^b}_t];\boldsymbol{\theta^w}) \quad (13)$$

$$\mathcal{L}(\boldsymbol{\theta^f},\boldsymbol{\theta^b},\boldsymbol{\theta^w}) = \sum_t (\hat{\mathbf{x}}_t - \mathbf{x}_t)^2 \quad (14)$$

where $FF(.;\boldsymbol{\theta^w})$ denotes a feed forward highway network with parameters $\boldsymbol{\theta^w}$. Thus, the DP model training requires that we already have the "true embeddings" for all the L1 words in our corpus. We use pretrained L1 word embeddings from FastText as "true embeddings" (Bojanowski et al., 2017). This leaves the LSTM parameters $\boldsymbol{\theta^f},\boldsymbol{\theta^b}$ and the highway feed-forward network parameters $\boldsymbol{\theta^w}$ to be learned. Equation 14 can be minimized by simply copying the input $\mathbf{x}_t$ as the prediction (ignoring all context). We use *masked training* to prevent the model itself from trivially copying (Devlin et al., 2018). We randomly "mask" 30% of the input embeddings during training. This masking operation replaces the original embedding with either (i) 0 vectors, or (ii) vectors of a random word in vocabulary, or

(iii) vectors of a "neighboring" word from the vocabulary. [3] The loss, however, is always computed with respect to the correct token embedding.

With the L1 parameters of the DP model trained, we turn to L2 learning. Once again the L2 vocabulary is encoded in $\mathbf{F}$, which is initialized to $\mathbf{0}$ (i.e. before any sentence is observed). Consider the configuration: `The Nile is a Fluss in Africa.` The tokens are converted into a sequence of embeddings: $[\mathbf{x}_0 = \mathbf{E}_{x_0}, ... , \mathbf{x}_t = \mathbf{F}_{f_t},...,\mathbf{x}_T = \mathbf{E}_{x_T}]$. Note that at time-step t the L2 word-embedding matrix is used ($t=4, f_t=$`Fluss` for the example above). A prediction $\hat{\mathbf{x}}_t$ is generated by the model using Equations 11-13. Our hope is that the prediction is a "refined" version of the embedding for the L2 word. The refinement arises from considering the context of the L2 word. If `Fluss` was not seen before, $\mathbf{x}_t = \mathbf{F}_{f_t} = \mathbf{0}$, forcing the DP model to only use contextual information. We apply a simple update rule that modifies the L2 embeddings based on the direct predictions:

$$\mathbf{F}_{f_t} \leftarrow (1-\eta)\mathbf{F}_{f_t} + \eta\hat{\mathbf{x}}_t \quad (15)$$

where η controls the interpolation between the old values of a word embedding and the new values which have been predicted based on the current mixed sentence. If there are multiple L2 words in a configuration, say at positions i and j (where $i < j$), we can still follow Eq 11–13. However, to allow the predictions $\hat{\mathbf{x}}_i$ and $\hat{\mathbf{x}}_j$ to jointly influence each other, we need to execute multiple prediction iterations.

Concretely, let $\mathbf{X} = [\mathbf{x}_0,...,\mathbf{F}_{f_i},...,\mathbf{F}_{f_j},...,\mathbf{x}_T]$ be the sequence of word embeddings for a mixed-language sentence. The DP model generates predictions $\hat{\mathbf{X}} = [\hat{\mathbf{x}}_0,...,\hat{\mathbf{x}}_i,...,\hat{\mathbf{x}}_j,...,\hat{\mathbf{x}}_T]$. We only use its predictions at time-steps corresponding to L2 tokens since the L2 words are those we want to update (Eq 16).

$$\mathbf{X}^1 = \mathrm{DP}(\mathbf{X}^0)$$
$$\mathrm{Where,} \mathbf{X}^0 = [\mathbf{x}_1,...,\mathbf{F}_{f_i},...,\mathbf{F}_{f_j},...,\mathbf{x}_T]$$
$$\mathbf{X}^1 = [\mathbf{x}_1,...,\hat{\mathbf{x}}_i^1,...,\hat{\mathbf{x}}_j^1,...,\mathbf{x}_T] \quad (16)$$
$$\mathbf{X}^k = \mathrm{DP}(\mathbf{X}^{k-1}) \; \forall 0 \le k < K-1 \quad (17)$$

where $\mathbf{X}^1$ contains predictions at i and j and the original L1 word-embeddings in other positions. We then pass $\mathbf{X}^1$ as input again to the DP model. This is executed for K iterations (Eq 17). With

---

[3] We precompute 20 neighboring words (based on cosine-similarity) for each word in the vocabulary using FastText embeddings before training.

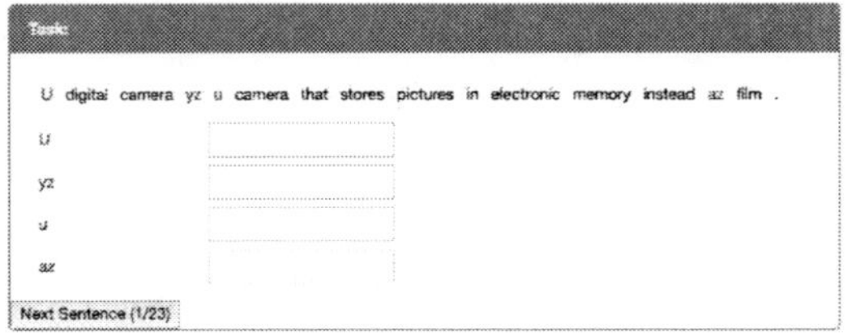

Figure 1: A screenshot of a mixed-language sentence presented on Mechanical Turk.

Metric	Model	$r_{max}=1$	$r_{max}=4$	$r_{max}=8$
Replaced	cLM	0.25	0.31	0.35
	uLM	0.20	0.25	0.25
	DP	0.19	0.22	0.21
Guess Accuracy	cLM	86.00($\pm$0.87)	74.00($\pm$1.10)	55.13($\pm$2.54)
	uLM	84.57($\pm$0.56)	73.89($\pm$1.72)	72.83($\pm$1.58)
	DP	88.44($\pm$0.73)	81.07($\pm$1.03)	70.85($\pm$1.49)

Table 3: Results from MTurk data. The first section shows the percentage of tokens that were replaced with L2 glosses under each condition. The Accuracy section shows the percentage token accuracy of MTurk participants' guesses along with 95% confidence interval calculated via bootstrap resampling.

each iteration, our hope is that the DP model's predictions $\hat{\mathbf{x}}_i$ and $\hat{\mathbf{x}}_j$ get refined by influencing each other and result in embeddings that are well-suited to the sentence context. A similar style of imputation has been studied for one dimensional time-series data by Zhou and Huang (2018). Finally, after $K-1$ iterations, we use the predictions of $\hat{\mathbf{x}}_i$ and $\hat{\mathbf{x}}_j$ from $\mathbf{X}^K$ to update the L2 word-embeddings in $\mathbf{F}$ corresponding to the L2 tokens f_i and f_j. η was set to 0.3 and the number of iterations $K=5$.

$$\mathbf{F}_{f_i} \leftarrow (1-\eta)\mathbf{F}_{f_i} + \eta\hat{\mathbf{x}}_i^K$$
$$\mathbf{F}_{f_j} \leftarrow (1-\eta)\mathbf{F}_{f_j} + \eta\hat{\mathbf{x}}_j^K \tag{18}$$

4 Experiments

We first investigate the patterns of word replacement produced by the machine teacher under the influence of the different student proxy models and how these replacements affect the guessability of L2 words. To this end, we used the machine teacher to generate mixed-language documents and asked MTurk participants to guess the foreign words. Figure 1 shows an example screenshot of our guessing interface. The words in blue are L2 words whose meaning (in English) is guessed by MTurk participants. For our study, we created a synthetic L2 language by randomly replacing characters from English word types. This step lets us safely assume that all MTurk participants are "absolute beginners." We tried to ensure that the resulting synthetic words

are pronounceable by replacing vowels with vowels, stop-consonants with other stop-consonants, etc. We also inserted or deleted one character from some of the words to prevent the reader from using the length of the synthetic word as a clue. While our evaluation required use of a synthetic foreign language, we provide as an example mixed-language documents with real L2 languages in Appendix A.1.

We studied the three student proxy models (cLM , uLM , and DP) while keeping the rest of the machine teacher's components fixed (i.e. same scoring function and search algorithms). All three models were constructed to have roughly the same number of L1 parameters ($\approx 20M$). The uLM model used 2 unidirectional LSTM layers instead of a single bidirectional layer. The L1 and L2 word embedding size and the number of recurrent units D were set to 300 for all three models (to match the size of FastText's pretrained embeddings). We trained the three models on the Wikipedia-103 corpus (Merity et al., 2016).[4] All models were trained for 8 epochs using the Adam optimizer (Kingma and Ba, 2014). We limit the L1 vocabulary to the $60k$ most frequent English types.

4.1 MTurk Setup

We selected 6 documents from Simple Wikipedia to serve as the input for mixed-language content.[5] To keep our study short enough for MTurk, we selected documents that contained $20 - 25$ sentences. A participant could complete up to 6 HITs (Human Intelligence Tasks) corresponding to the 6 documents. Participants were given 25 minutes to complete each HIT (on average, the participants took 12 minutes to complete the HITs). To prevent typos, we used a $20k$ word English dictionary, which includes all the word types from the 6 Simple Wikipedia documents. We provided no feedback regarding the correctness of guesses. We recruited 128 English speaking MTurk participants and obtained 162 responses, with each response encompassing a participant's guesses over a full document.[6] Participants were compensated $4 per HIT.

4.2 Experiment Conditions

We generated 9 mixed-language versions (3 models {cLM ,uLM ,DP } in combination with 3 rank

---

[4]FastText pretrained embeddings were trained on more data.

[5]https://dumps.wikimedia.org/simplewiki/20190120/

[6]Participants self-reported their English proficiency, only native or fluent speakers were allowed to participate. Our HITs were only available to participants from the US.

Model	$r_{\max}=1$	$r_{\max}=8$
cLM	**Hu** Nile (``an-nı̄l'') **ev** a river **um** Africa. **Up** is **hu** longest river **iñ** Earth (about 6,650 km or 4,132 miles), though other rivers carry more water... Many **ozvolomb** types **iv emoner** live in or near **hu** waters **iv hu** Nile, including crocodiles, birds, fish **ñb** many others. Not only do animals depend **iñ hu** Nile for survival, but also people who live there need **up zi** everyday use like washing, as **u jopi** supply, keeping crops watered **ñb** other jobs...	**Hu** Nile (``an-nı̄l'') **ev u** river **um** Africa. **Up ev** the longest river on Earth (about 6,650 km or 4,132 miles), though other rivers carry more water... **Emu ozvolomb** types of **emoner** live **um** or **iul** the waters of **hu Uro**, including crocodiles, **ultf, yvh** and **emu** others. **Ip** only do animals depend **iñ** the Nile **zi** survival, but also **daudr** who live there need **up zi** everyday use like washing, **ez** a **jopi** supply, keeping crops watered **ñb** other jobs...
uLM	The Nile (``an-nı̄l'') **ev** a river **um** Africa. It **ev hu** longest river on Earth (about 6,650 km or 4,132 miles), though other rivers carry more **jopi**... Many different **pita** of **emoner** live in or near **hu** waters **iv hu** Nile, including crocodiles, **ultf**, fish and many others. Not **mru** do **emoner** depend **iñ hu** Nile for survival, but also people who live there need it for everyday use like washing, as a **jopi** supply, keeping crops watered **ñb** other jobs...	**Hu** Nile (``an-nı̄l'') **ev u** river **um** Africa. **Up ev** the longest river **iñ** Earth (about 6,650 km or 4,132 miles), though other rivers carry more **jopi**... Many different **pita** of **emoner** live **um** or near **hu** waters **iv hu** Nile, including crocodiles, **ultf**, fish and many others. Not **mru** do **emoner** depend on the Nile for survival, **id** also people who live there need it **zi** everyday use like washing, as **u** water supply, keeping crops watered **ñb** other jobs...
DP	**Hu** Nile (``an-nı̄l'') **ev** a river **um** Africa. **Up ev hu** longest river on Earth (about 6,650 km or 4,132 miles), though other rivers carry more water... Many different types **iv** animals live in or near **hu** waters **iv hu** Nile, including crocodiles, birds, fish and many others. Not only do animals depend **iñ hu** Nile for survival, but also people who live there need it for everyday use like washing, as **u** water supply, keeping crops watered and other jobs...	**Hu** Nile (``an-nı̄l'') **ev** a river **um** Africa. **Up ev hu** longest river on Earth (about 6,650 km or 4,132 miles), though **udho** rivers carry more water... Many different **pita** of animals live in or near **hu** waters of **hu** Nile, including crocodiles, birds, fish and many others. Not **mru** do animals depend **iñ hu** Nile **zi** survival, **id** also people who live there need it **zi** everyday use like washing, **ez** a water supply, keeping crops watered and **udho** jobs...

Table 2: Portions of one of our Simple Wikipedia articles. The document has been converted into a mixed-language document by the machine teacher using the three student proxy models. Our experiments use a synthetic L2 language, see Appendix A.1 for examples with real L2 language (German and Spanish) on two stories. The two columns show the effect of the rank threshold $r_{\max}$. Note that this mixed-language document is 25 sentences long; here, we only show the first 2 sentences and another middle 2 sentences to save space.

thresholds $r_{\max} \in \{1,4,8\}$) for each of the 6 Simple Wikipedia documents. For each HIT, an MTurk participant was randomly assigned one of the 9 mixed-language versions. Table 2 shows the output at two settings of $r_{\max}$ for one of the documents. We see that $r_{\max}$ controls the number of L2 words the machine teacher deems guessable, which affects text readability. The increase in L2 words is most noticeable with the cLM model. We also see that the DP model differs from the others by favoring high frequency words almost exclusively. While the cLM and uLM models similarly replace a number of high frequency words, they also occasionally replace lower frequency word classes like nouns and adjectives (**emoner**, **Emu**, etc.). Table 3 summarizes our findings. The first section of 3 shows the percentage of tokens that were deemed guessable by our machine teacher. The cLM model replaces more words as $r_{\max}$ is increased to 8, but we see that MTurkers had a hard time guessing the meaning of the replaced tokens: their guessing accuracy drops to 55% at $r_{\max} = 8$ with the cLM model. The uLM model, however, displays a reluctance to replace too many tokens, even as $r_{\max}$ was increased to 8.

We further analyzed the replacements and MTurk guesses based on word-class. We tagged the L1 tokens with their part-of-speech and categorized tokens into open or closed class following Universal Dependency guidelines (Nivre et al.).[7] Table 4 summarizes our analysis of model and human behavior when the data is separated by word-class. The pink bars indicate the percentage of tokens replaced per word-class. The blue bars represent the percentage of tokens from a particular word-class that MTurk users *guessed correctly*. Thus, an ideal machine teacher should strive for the highest possible pink bar while ensuring that the blue bar is as close as possible to the pink. Our findings suggest that the uLM model at $r_{\max} = 8$ and the cLM model at $r_{\max} = 4$ show the desirable properties – high guessing accuracy and more representation of L2 words (particularly open-class words).

---

[7] https://universaldependencies.org/u/pos/

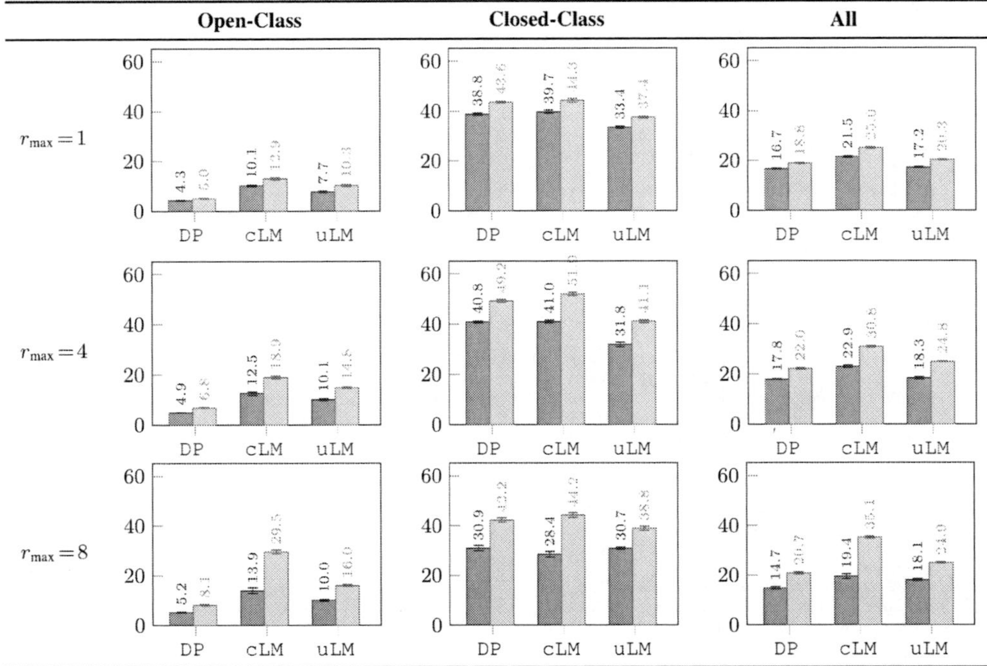

Table 4: Results of MTurk results split up by word-class. The y-axis is percentage of tokens belonging to a word-class. The pink bar (right) shows the percentage of tokens (of a particular word-class) that were *replaced* with an L2 gloss. The blue bar (left) and indicates the percentage of tokens (of a particular word-class) that were *guessed correctly* by MTurk participants. Error bars represent 95% confidence intervals computed with bootstrap resampling. For example, we see that only 5.0% (pink) of open-class tokens were replaced into L2 by the DP model at $r_{max} = 1$ and 4.3% of all open-class tokens were guessed correctly. Thus, even though the guess accuracy for DP at $r_{max} = 1$ for open-class is high (86%) we can see that participants were not exposed to many open-class word tokens.

Metric	Model	Closed	Open
Types Replaced	random	59	524
	cLM	33	149
Guess Accuracy	random	62.06(±1.54)	39.36(±1.75)
	cLM	**74.91(±0.94)**	**61.96(±1.24)**

Table 5: Results comparing our student proxy based approach to a random baseline. The first part shows the number of L2 word types exposed by each model for each word-class. The second part shows the average guess accuracy percentage for each model and word-class. 95% confidence intervals (in brackets) were computed using bootstrap resampling.

4.3 Random Baseline

So far we've compared different student proxy models against each other, but is our student proxy based approach required at all? How much better (or worse) is this approach compared to a *random* baseline? To answer these questions, we compare the cLM with $r_{max} = 4$ model against a randomly generated mixed-language document. As the name suggests, word replacements are decided randomly for the random condition, but we ensure that the number of tokens replaced in each sentence equals that from the cLM condition.

We used the 6 Simple Wikipedia documents from Section 4.1 and recruited 64 new MTurk partipants who completed a total of 66 HITs (compensation was $4 per HIT). For each HIT, the participant was given either the randomly generated or the cLM based mixed-language document. Once again, participants were made to enter their guess for each L2 word that appears in a sentence. The results are summarized in Table 5.

We find that randomly replacing words with glosses exposes more L2 word types (59 and 524 closed-class and open-class words respectively) while the cLM model is more conservative with replacements (33 and 149). However, the random mixed-language document is much harder to comprehend, indicated by significantly lower average guess accuracies than those with the cLM model. This is especially true for open-class words. Note that Table 5 shows the number of word types replaced across all 6 documents.

Model	Closed	Open
random	9.86($\pm$0.94)	4.28($\pm$0.69)
cLM	**35.53($\pm$1.03)**	**27.77($\pm$1.03)**

Table 6: Results of our L2 learning experiments where MTurk subjects simply read a mixed-language document and answered a vocabulary quiz at the end of the passage. The table shows the average guess accuracy percentage along with 95% confidence intervals computed from bootstrap resampling.

4.4 Learning Evaluation

Our mixed-language based approach relies on incidental learning, which states that if a novel word is repeatedly presented to a student with sufficient context, the student will eventually be able to learn the novel word. So far our experiments test MTurk participants on the "guessability" of novel words in context, but not learning. To study if students can actually learn the L2 words, we conduct an MTurk experiment where participants are simply required to read a mixed-language document (one sentence at a time). At the end of the document an L2 vocabulary quiz is given. Participants must enter the meaning of every L2 word type they have seen during the reading phase.

Once again, we compare our cLM ($r_{max} = 4$) model against a random baseline using the 6 Simple Wikipedia documents. 47 HITs were obtained from 45 MTurk participants for this experiment. Participants were made aware that there would be a vocabulary quiz at the end of the document. Our findings are summarized in Table 6. We find the accuracy of guesses for the vocabulary quiz at the end of the document is considerably lower than guesses with context. However, subjects still managed to retain 35.53% and 27.77% of closed-class and open-class L2 word types respectively. On the other hand, when a random mixed-language document was presented to participants, their guess accuracy dropped to 9.86% and 4.28% for closed and open class words respectively. Thus, even though more word types were exposed by the random baseline, fewer words were retained.

5 Related Work

Our work does not require any supervised data collection from students. This departure makes our work easier to deploy in diverse settings (i.e. for different document genres, and different combinations of L1/L2 languages etc). While there are numerous self-directed language learning applications such as Duolingo (von Ahn, 2013), our approach uses a different style of "instruction". Furthermore, reading L2 words in L1 contexts is also gaining popularity in commercial applications like Swych (2015) and OneThirdStories (2018).

Most recently, Renduchintala et al. (2016) attempt to model a student's ability to guess the meaning of foreign language words (and phrases) when prompted with a mixed language sentence. One drawback of this approach is its need for large amounts of training data, which involves prompting students (in their case, MTurk users) with mixed language sentences created randomly. Such a method is potentially inefficient, as random configurations presented to users (to obtain their guesses) would not reliably match those that a beginner student would encounter. Labutov and Lipson (2014) also use a similar supervised approach. The authors required two sets of annotations, first soliciting guesses of missing words in a sentences and then obtaining another set of annotations to judge the guesses.

6 Conclusion

We are encouraged by the ability to generate mixed-language documents without the need of expensive data collection from students. Our MTurk study shows that students can guess the meaning of foreign words in context with high accuracy and also retain the foreign words.

For future work, we would like to investigate ways to smoothly adapt our student proxy models into personalized models. We also recognize that our approach may be "low-recall," i.e., it might miss out on teaching possibilities. For example, our machine teacher may not realize that cognates can be replaced with the L2 and still understood, even if there are no contextual clues (**Afrika** can likely be understood without much context). Incorporating spelling information into our language models (Kim et al., 2016) could help the machine teacher identify more instances for incidental learning. Additionally, we would like to investigate how our approach could be extended to enable phrasal learning (which should consider word-ordering differences between the L1 and L2). As the cLM and uLM models showed the most promising results in our experiments, we believe these models could serve as the baseline for future work.

References

Luis von Ahn. 2013. Duolingo: Learn a language for free while helping to translate the web. In *Proceedings of the 2013 International Conference on Intelligent User Interfaces*, pages 1–2.

Piotr Bojanowski, Edouard Grave, Armand Joulin, and Tomas Mikolov. 2017. Enriching word vectors with subword information. *Transactions of the Association for Computational Linguistics*, 5:135–146.

Jacob Devlin, Ming-Wei Chang, Kenton Lee, and Kristina Toutanova. 2018. Bert: Pre-training of deep bidirectional transformers for language understanding. *arXiv preprint arXiv:1810.04805*.

Sepp Hochreiter and Jürgen Schmidhuber. 1997. Long short-term memory. *Neural computation*, 9(8):1735–1780.

Yoon Kim, Yacine Jernite, David Sontag, and Alexander M Rush. 2016. Character-aware neural language models. In *Thirtieth AAAI Conference on Artificial Intelligence*.

Diederik P Kingma and Jimmy Ba. 2014. Adam: A method for stochastic optimization. *arXiv preprint arXiv:1412.6980*.

Stephen Krashen. 1989. We acquire vocabulary and spelling by reading: Additional evidence for the input hypothesis. *The Modern Language Journal*, 73(4):440–464.

Igor Labutov and Hod Lipson. 2014. Generating code-switched text for lexical learning. In *Proceedings of ACL*, pages 562–571.

Stephen Merity, Caiming Xiong, James Bradbury, and Richard Socher. 2016. Pointer sentinel mixture models. *arXiv preprint arXiv:1609.07843*.

Tomas Mikolov, Martin Karafiát, Lukas Burget, Jan Cernockỳ, and Sanjeev Khudanpur. 2010. Recurrent neural network based language model. In *INTERSPEECH 2010, 11th Annual Conference of the International Speech Communication Association, Makuhari, Chiba, Japan, September 26-30, 2010*, pages 1045–1048.

Amr El-Desoky Mousa and Björn Schuller. 2017. Contextual bidirectional long short-term memory recurrent neural network language models: A generative approach to sentiment analysis. In *Proceedings EACL*.

Joakim Nivre, Marie-Catherine De Marneffe, Filip Ginter, Yoav Goldberg, Jan Hajic, et al. Universal dependencies v1: A multilingual treebank collection.

OneThirdStories. 2018. Onethirdstories. https://onethirdstories.com/. Accessed: 2019-02-20.

Ofir Press and Lior Wolf. 2017. Using the output embedding to improve language models. In *Proceedings of the 15th Conference of the European Chapter of the Association for Computational Linguistics, EACL 2017, Valencia, Spain, April 3-7, 2017, Volume 2: Short Papers*, pages 157–163.

Adithya Renduchintala, Rebecca Knowles, Philipp Koehn, and Jason Eisner. 2016. User modeling in language learning with macaronic texts. In *Proceedings of the 54th Annual Meeting of the Association for Computational Linguistics (Volume 1: Long Papers)*, pages 1859–1869, Berlin, Germany. Association for Computational Linguistics.

Rupesh Kumar Srivastava, Klaus Greff, and Jürgen Schmidhuber. 2015. Highway networks. *arXiv preprint arXiv:1505.00387*.

Swych. 2015. Swych. http://swych.it/. Accessed: 2019-02-20.

Lev Vygotskiï. 2012. *Thought and Language (Revised and Expanded Edition)*. MIT Press.

David Wood, Jerome S. Bruner, and Gail Ross. 1976. The role of tutoring in problem solving. *Journal of Child Psychology and Psychiatry*, 17(2):89–100.

Jingguang Zhou and Zili Huang. 2018. Recover missing sensor data with iterative imputing network. In *Workshops at the Thirty-Second AAAI Conference on Artificial Intelligence*.

Sense **y** Sensibility
CHAPTER **1**

    La family **de** Dashwood **llevaba** long been settled **en** Sussex. Their estate **era** large, and their residence was **en** Norland Park, **en el** centre **de** their **propiedad**, where, **por** many generations, **ellos** had lived **en** so respectable a manner as **a** engage the general **buena** opinion of their surrounding acquaintance. **El** late owner **de esta** estate was a single man, who lived to **una** very advanced age, and who for many **años de su** life, had **una** constant companion **y** housekeeper in **su** sister. But her death, which happened ten **años** before **su** own, produced a great alteration **en** his home; for **para** supply her loss, he invited **y** received into his house the family of his nephew Mr. **Henry** Dashwood, the legal inheritor **de** the Norland estate, **y** the person to whom **se** intended to bequeath it. **En la** society of his nephew and niece, and their children, **el** old Gentleman's days **fueron** comfortably spent. **Su** attachment **a** them all increased. **La** constant attention **de** Mr. **y** Mrs. Henry Dashwood **a sus** wishes, which proceeded not merely from interest, but from goodness **de** heart, **dio** him every degree **de** solid comfort which his age could receive; **y la** cheerfulness **de los** children added **un** relish to his existence.

    Por a former marriage, Mr. **Henry** Dashwood had one **hijo**: by **su** present lady, **tres** daughters. **El** son, **un** steady respectable young man, **tenía** amply provided for by **la** fortune **de su** mother, which **había** been large, **y** half **de** which devolved on him on **su** coming **de** age. **Por** his own marriage, likewise, which happened soon afterwards, he added **a su** wealth. **Para** him therefore **la** succession **a la** Norland estate **era** not so really important **como para** his sisters; **para su** fortune, independent of what might arise **a** them **de su** father's inheriting that **propiedad**, could **ser** but small. **Su madre** had nothing, and their father only seven thousand pounds **en su** own disposal; **porque** the remaining moiety of **su** first wife's fortune **era** also secured **a su** child, **y** he had only a life-interest **en** it.

Table 7: Example of mixed-language output for Jane Austen's "Sense and Sensibility". We used the uLM with $r_{\max}=8$.

A Appendices

A.1 Mixed-Language Examples

While our experiments necessitated use of synthetic L2 words, our methods are compatible with real L2 learning. For a more "real-world" experience of how our methods could be deployed, we present the first few paragraphs of mixed-language novels generated using the uLM model with $r_{\max} = 8$. First example is from Jane Austin's "Sense and Sensibility" (Table 7), and for the second example, as we are transforming text from one language into a "strange hybrid creature" (i.e mixed-language) it seems appropriate to use Franz Kafka's "Metamorphosis" (Table 8). For these examples, glosses were obtained from a previous MTurk data collection process from bilingual speakers. Glosses for

Metamorphosis
I

    One morning, when Gregor Samsa woke from troubled dreams, **er** found himself transformed **in** his bed into **einem** horrible vermin. **Er** lay **auf** his armour-like back, **und** if **er** lifted **seinen** head a **wenig** he could see his brown belly, slightly domed **und** divided **von** arches into stiff sections. **das** bedding was hardly able **zu** cover it and seemed ready to slide off any moment. His many legs, pitifully thin compared **mit der** size of **dem** rest of him, waved about helplessly **als** he looked.

    ``What's happened **mit** me?'' **er** thought. His room, **ein** proper human room although a **wenig** too small, lay peacefully between **seinen** four familiar walls. **Eine** collection of textile samples lay spread out on **dem** table – Samsa was **ein** travelling salesman – **und** above it there hung **ein** picture that **er** had recently cut out **von** an illustrated magazine and housed **in** a nice, gilded frame. It showed **eine** lady fitted out with **einem** fur hat **und** fur boa who sat upright, raising **einen** heavy fur muff that covered the whole of her lower arm towards **dem** viewer.

    Gregor **dann** turned to look out the window at the dull weather. Drops of rain could **sein** heard hitting the pane, which **machte** him feel quite sad. ``How about if I sleep **ein** little bit longer and forget all this nonsense,'' **er** thought, but that **war** something **er war** unable **zu** do because he **war** used **zu** sleeping on **seiner** right, **und** in **seinem** present state couldn't get into **diese** position. However hard he threw himself onto **seine** right, **er** always rolled **zurück** to where he was. **Er** must **haben** tried it **ein** hundred times, shut **seine** eyes so **dass er** wouldn't have to look at **die** floundering legs, **und** only stopped when **er** began to feel **einen** mild, dull pain there that **er** had **nie** felt before.

    ``Oh, God,'' **er** thought, ``what a strenuous career it **ist** that I've chosen! Travelling day in **und** day out. Doing business like **diese** takes much **mehr** effort than doing your own **Geschäft** at home, **und auf** top of that there's **der** curse **des** travelling, worries about making train connections, bad and irregular food, contact with **verschiedenen** people all **die** time so **das** you **kannst** never get to know anyone or become friendly **mit** them. **es** can all **gehen** to Hell!'' **Er** felt a slight itch up **auf seinem** belly ; pushed himself slowly up on **seinen** back towards the headboard so **dass** he **konnte** lift **seinen** head better ; found where **das** itch was, **und** saw **dass** it was **besetzt** with lots of little white spots which **er** didn't know what to make of ; **und** when **er** tried to feel **die** place with one of his legs **er** drew **es** quickly back because as soon as he touched it **er** was overcome by **einem** cold shudder.

Table 8: Example of mixed-language output for the English translation (by David Wyllie) of Franz Kafka's "Metamorphosis". We used the uLM with $r_{\max}=8$.

each English (L1) token was obtained from 3 MTurkers, if a majority of them agree on the gloss it is considered by our machine teacher as a possible L2 gloss. If no agreement was obtained we restrict that token to always remain as L1.

Analyzing Linguistic Complexity and Accuracy in Academic Language Development of German across Elementary and Secondary School

Zarah Weiss and **Detmar Meurers**
University of Tübingen
Department for General and Computational Linguistics
`{zweiss,dm}@sfs.uni-tuebingen.de`

Abstract

We track the development of writing *complexity* and *accuracy* in German students' early academic language development from first to eighth grade. Combining an empirically broad approach to linguistic complexity with the high-quality error annotation included in the Karlsruhe Children's Text corpus (Lavalley et al., 2015) used, we construct models of German academic language development that successfully identify the student's grade level. We show that classifiers for the early years rely more on accuracy development, whereas development in secondary school is better characterized by increasingly complex language in all domains: linguistic system, language use, and human sentence processing characteristics. We demonstrate the generalizability and robustness of models using such a broad complexity feature set across writing topics.

1 Introduction

We model the development of linguistic complexity and accuracy in German early academic language and writing acquisition from first to eighth grade. Complexity and Accuracy are well-established notions from Second Language Acquisition (SLA) research. Together with Fluency, they form the CAF triad that has successfully be used to characterize second language development (Housen et al., 2012). Accuracy here is defined as a native-like production error rate (Wolfe-Quintero et al., 1998) and Complexity as the elaborateness and variation of the language which may be assessed across various linguistic domains (Ellis and Barkhuizen, 2005).

While there has been substantial research on the link between linguistic complexity analysis and second language proficiency and writing development for English (cf., e.g., Bulté and Housen, 2014; Kyle, 2016), much less is known about academic language development for other languages, such as the morphologically richer German. In this article, we target this gap with three contributions. We build classification models for early academic language development in German from first to eighth grade, based on a uniquely broad set of linguistically informed measures of complexity and accuracy. Our results indicate that two phases of academic language development can be distinguished: Initial academic language and writing acquisition focusing on the writing process itself, best characterized in terms of accuracy development, with little development in terms of complexity. A second stage is characterized by the increasing linguistic complexity, in particular in the domains of lexis and syntactic complexity at the phrasal level. We demonstrate the robustness and generalizability of the models informed by the broad range of linguistic characteristics – a major concern not only for obtaining practically relevant approaches for real-life use, but also for characterizing machine learning going beyond focused task to approaches capable of capturing general language characteristics.

The article is structured as follows: We first give a brief overview of research on writing development in terms of complexity and accuracy. We then present the *Karlsruhe Children's Text* corpus used as empirical basis of our work. In Section 4, we spell out our approach to assessing writing in terms of complexity and accuracy, before sections 5, 6, and 7 report on three studies designed to address the research issues introduced above.

2 Related Work

The main strand of research analyzing the complexity and accuracy constructs targets the assessment of second language development. Linguistic complexity measures have been successfully used to model the language acquisition of English

Proceedings of the Fourteenth Workshop on Innovative Use of NLP for Building Educational Applications, pages 380–393
Florence, Italy, August 2, 2019. ©2019 Association for Computational Linguistics

as a Second Language (ESL) learners (Bulté and Housen, 2014; Crossley and McNamara, 2014). Work on first language writing development for English has also been conducted, but it is less common (Crossley et al., 2011) The same holds for the development of accuracy (Larsen-Freeman, 2006; Yoon and Polio, 2016). Most studies focus on adult ESL learners' development during periods of instruction. Vercellotti (2015) finds an increase in syntactic and lexical complexity, overall accuracy, and fluency in adult ESL speech over the course of several months. Crossley and McNamara (2014) find that advanced adult ESL learners phrasal and clausal complexity significantly increases over the course of one semester of writing instruction in particular with regard to nominal modification and number of clauses. These findings are corroborated by Bulté and Housen (2014). For uninstructed settings, however, this does not hold. Knoch et al. (2014, 2015) study university students' ESL development over 12 months and three years without instruction in an immersion context and found that only fluency but not grammatical and lexical complexity developed.

Research on languages other than English is starting to appear (Hancke et al., 2012; Velleman and van der Geest, 2014; Pilán and Volodina, 2016; Reynolds, 2016). As for English, research on German writing development has predominantly focused on German as a Second Language (GSL) in instructed settings (Byrnes, 2009; Byrnes et al., 2010; Vyatkina, 2012). Their findings suggest that as for ESL learners' writing, clausal complexity progressively increases. For lexical complexity results have been more mixed depending on the proficiency of GSL learners' proficiency level. The development of writing accuracy has also been assessed in some corpus studies using automated or manual error annotation (Lavalley et al., 2015; Göpferich and Neumann, 2016). In Weiss et al. (2019) we analyze the impact of linguistic complexity and accuracy on teacher grading behavior.

One challenge for the assessment of language performance in terms of complexity that is starting to receive attention is the influence of the task. Alexopoulou et al. (2017) demonstrate task effects, specifically task complexity and task type, on the complexity of English as a Second Language writers in the EF-Cambridge Open Language Database (EFCAMDAT) and show mixed results for accuracy. This is in line with findings by Yoon and Polio (2016), who investigate the effect of genre differences on CAF constructs. Yoon (2017) focuses on the effect of topic on the syntactic, lexical, and morphological complexity of ESL learners' writings and shows a significant influence on the complexity of writings of the same learners, similar to findings in Yang et al. (2015). Such task effects have mostly been discussed from a theoretical perspective, considering their implications for the development of CAF constructs and the two main task frameworks (Robinson, 2001; Skehan, 1996). From a more practical perspective, task, genre, and topic effects have been recognized as an important issue for machine learning for readability assessment or Automatic Essay Scoring (AES). For the real-world applicability of such approaches it is crucial for them to account for differences due to genre or topic. In their readability assessment system *READ-IT* for Italian, Dell'Orletta et al. (2014) use this issue to motivate favoring a ranking-based over a classification-based approach. A recent AES approach discussing the issue is the placement system for ESL by Yannakoudakis et al. (2018).

3 Data

Our studies are based on the *Karlsruhe Children's Text* (KCT) corpus by Lavalley et al. (2015).[1] It is a cross-sectional collection of 1,701 German texts produced by students in German elementary and secondary school students from first to eighth grade. The secondary school students in the corpus attended one of two German school tracks, either a basic school track (*Hauptschule*) or an intermediate school track (*Realschule*). The texts were written on a topic chosen by the students from a set of age-appropriate options: Elementary school students were asked to continue one of two stories, one about children playing in a park, and the other about a wolf who learns how to read. Secondary school students wrote about a hypothetical day spent with their idol or their life in 20 years. All student texts in the corpus are made available in the original, including all student errors, and a normalized version, where errors and misspellings were corrected. The data is enriched with error annotations covering word splitting, incorrect word choices and repetitions, grammar, and legibility.

For our studies analyzing writing development

---

[1] https://catalog.ldc.upenn.edu/LDC2015T22

in terms of development across the grade levels, we made use of the normalized texts and the error annotation. Some grade levels in the corpus include only few texts, such as the 42 cases of first grade writings compared to the other grade levels with 189 to 283 writings. We thus grouped adjacent grade levels, i.e., grades 1 and 2 together, grades 3 and 4, etc., to obtain a data set with a substantial number of instances for each class.

4 Assessment of Writing Performance

To assess writing performance in terms of complexity and accuracy, we operationalized these SLA concepts in terms of several features which we automatically computed or derived from the error annotation of the KCT corpus.

4.1 Complexity

The analysis of complexity is based on our implementation of a broad range of complexity features for German (Weiss, 2017; Weiss and Meurers, 2018, in press). The features cover clausal and phrasal syntactic complexity, lexical complexity, discourse complexity, and morphological complexity. Complementing the measures of complexity of the linguistic system, we also compute two cognitively-motivated features: a characterization of language use based on word frequencies, and measures of human language processing (HLP). Table 1 summarizes the features designed to capture the elaborateness and variability in the respective domain, with more details provided in Weiss (2017) and Weiss and Meurers (in press). Overall, the studies in the current paper make use of a comprehensive set of 308 complexity features for the assessment of academic language development.[2]

4.2 Accuracy

The second dimension of language performance that we are interested in is writing accuracy. In SLA research accuracy has predominantly been assessed in terms of types of error rates or error-free T-units (Wolfe-Quintero et al., 1998; Verspoor et al., 2012). We exploited the KCT corpus' elaborate error annotation to extract a broad range of accuracy measures. Annotations on the level of individual letters and words mark (ill)legibility, word splitting errors, repetition errors, foreign words,

and grammatical errors. Annotations at the sentence level mark content deletions, insertions, and incorrect word choices. In addition, we developed an approach to automatically derive additional error types by comparing the original student writings with their normalized sentence-aligned target hypotheses. This procedure allowed us to extract counts for punctuation errors, incorrect quotation marks, spelling mistakes, and word capitalization errors. The last item is a particular challenge of German orthography, given that capitalization in German is governed by a complex set of rules and conventions relating to syntactic structure.[3]

Overall, we extracted 20 accuracy counts which we aggregated and normalized by the total number or errors or the total number of words in the text as counted by the complexity analysis described in the previous subsection. The feature set measuring writing accuracy and an example feature is included as the last row in Table 1.[4]

5 Study 1: Predicting Grade-Levels across School Types

5.1 Set up

We extracted the text data from the KCT corpus, removing all texts containing less than ten words and excluding texts written by children younger than seven years and older than 15 years. This resulted in a corpus of N$=1,633$ texts, for which we computed the features of linguistic complexity and error rates. Table 2 shows the distribution of texts across grade levels and school tracks.

From the analyzed data set, we eliminated all complexity and error rate features that did not exhibit enough variability to be of interest for the analysis. Specifically, we excluded all features whose most common value occurred more than 90% of the time. For the remaining 262 features, we computed their z-score, centered around zero.

On this data, we performed ten iterations of 10-fold cross-validation (CV) generating different splits each time, i.e., 100 training and testing runs in total, using an SMO classifier with a linear kernel (Platt, 1998). This outperformed models using random forests or linear regression. Similarly, introducing non-linearity did not improve the clas-

---

[2]We are making the complexity code available as part of a multilingual version of CTAP: `https://github.com/zweiss/multilingual-ctap-feature`

[3]The Python script used to identify accuracy features in the KCT annotation is available at `https://github.com/zweiss/KCTErrorExtractor`

[4]Here and in the following, we will refer to this feature set as the *error rate* measures to avoid confusion with the term accuracy used as a classification performance metric.

Feature Set	Size	Description
Lexical complexity	31	measures vocabulary range (lexical density and variation) and sophistication, measures of lexical relatedness; e.g., type token ratio
Discourse complexity	64	measures the use of cohesive devices such as connectives; e.g., connectives per sentence
Phrasal complexity	47	measures of phrase modification; e.g., NP modifiers per NP
Clausal complexity	27	measures of subordination or clause constituents; e.g., subordinate clauses per sentence
Morphological complexity	41	measures inflection, derivation, and composition; e.g., average compound depth per compound noun
Language Use	33	measures word frequencies based on frequency data bases; e.g., mean word frequency in Subtlex-DE (Brysbaert et al., 2011)
Human Language Processing	24	measures of cognitive load during human sentence processing, mostly based on Dependency Locality Theory (Gibson, 2000) e.g., average total integration cost at the finite verb
Error Rate	41	measures ratios of error types per error or word; e.g., spelling mistakes per word

Table 1: Overview over the feature sets used to capture linguistic complexity and accuracy

	1/2	3/4	5/6	7/8	all
Elementary	203	524	0	0	727
Realschule	0	0	297	236	533
Hauptschule	0	0	165	208	373
all	203	524	462	444	1633

Table 2: Text distribution across grades & school tracks

sification. For each feature set introduced in Section 4, we trained a separate classifier to support a comparison of the different complexity and error feature sets. In addition, we built one classifier based on the combination of all complexity feature sets and one combining all feature sets including error rate. Finally, we built a classifier also including the meta information about the school track and topic chosen, to investigate their influence on the complexity features and the comparability of grade-levels across school types.

As reference for evaluating classifier performance, we use a majority baseline assigning always the most common grade level, and a second baseline inspired by traditional readability formulas, for which we trained a classifier using text length and average word length features.

5.2 Results & Discussion

Table 3 shows the performance of the classifiers in terms of mean accuracy and standard deviation across iterations and folds, and the feature set size. The majority baseline and the tradi-

tional readability feature baseline displayed above the dashed line are both around 32%. All linguistically informed classifiers clearly outperform these two baselines. The best performing model with an accuracy of 72.68% combines linguistic complexity features and error rate with information on topic and school track.[5] Adding this meta-information, which in most real-life application contexts is readily available, accounts for an 1.72% increase in accuracy. But also without this meta-information, the combination of linguistic complexity features and error rate is highly successful with an accuracy of 70.96%.

Let us take a look at the individual contributions of the different feature sets. The overall linguistic complexity classifier clearly outperforms the one informed by the error rate features. This comparison may be biased towards the linguistic complexity classifier because it is informed by six times more features. However, the impression that complexity features are more indicative for writing development as a function of grade level is supported by the classifiers based on individual domains of linguistic complexity, which are more comparable in size to the error rate based classifier. The lexical complexity, discourse complexity, and phrasal complexity classifiers all clearly outperform the classifier informed by error rate with accuracies between 60.10% and 61.29% compared to 54.47%. The same holds for morphological

---

[5] The confusion matrix for all ten iterations of the 10-CV may be found in Table 10 in the Appendix.

	Size	μ-Acc.	SD-Acc.
Majority baseline	1	32.08	0.14
Traditional baseline	2	32.56	0.80
All Features + Meta	264	**72.68**	1.94
All Features	262	**70.96**	2.01
Complexity	225	**68.35**	2.25
Error Rate	37	54.47	2.11
Lexical	31	60.10	1.69
Discourse	48	60.10	1.66
Phrasal	41	61.29	1.73
Clausal	26	52.95	1.56
Morphological	27	56.45	1.47
Language Use	30	45.45	1.28
Human processing	20	42.18	1.55

Table 3: Grade-level classification of elementary & secondary school texts, ten iterations of 10-fold CV, distinguishing levels 1st/2nd, 3rd/4th, 5th/6th, 7th/8th

complexity (56.45%), although the difference is less pronounced. However, not all dimensions of linguistic complexity outperform error rate. This holds only for features measuring the linguistic system. While psycho-linguistic measures of language use and human language processing clearly outperform the baselines, they are performing significantly worse than the error rate features. Language experience and cognitive measures of the complexity in processing language does not seem to be the factor limiting academic writing performance, which is intuitively plausible considering that, especially in the early school years, the language experience and language processing will be mostly shaped by spoken language interaction.

6 Study 2: Writing Development in Elementary vs. Secondary School

6.1 Set-Up

Having established that linguistic complexity and error rate successfully predict writing performance across academic writing development, let us compare the development in early writing with that in secondary school. For this, we split the KCT data into two subsets: one containing only elementary school writing ($N = 727$), the other the secondary school writing from the different school tracks ($N = 906$). We applied the same pre-processing steps described in Section 5.1 including feature reduction and scaling of all predictor variables, obtaining 256 features for the elementary school and 255 for the secondary school data set (with num-

bers differing slightly since the feature reduction is performed separately on each data set).

We then followed a two-fold approach: First, we again tested and trained the same SMO classifiers as in Study 1 with linear kernels and 10 iterations of 10-fold CV (Section 6.2). Although the classifiers were informed by the same feature sets, due to the reduction of the sample size some sets were reduced more in the aforementioned pre-processing step which may result in slightly deviating feature set sizes across tables. For the elementary school data set, only topic was added as meta information, because there are no different elementary school tracks in Germany.

Then, for both data sets we selected the most informative features of each feature set in order to zoom in on how they differ across grade-levels (Section 6.3). This more fine grained analysis allows us to complement the broader perspective gained form the classification experiments with a more concrete sense of which features matter and how they change. For the selection, we ranked all features by their information gain for the distinction of grade-levels in the respective data set and selected the most informative feature of each feature set resulting in overall 16 features chosen for closer inspection. We then conducted two-tailed t-tests to test for significant differences across grade-levels in both data sets. To avoid redundancy in our comparison, if the most informative feature for a given feature set in both data subsets assessed the same concept, we chose the next-most informative feature.[6]

6.2 Results & Discussion

Table 4 shows the classifiers performance on the elementary school data subset.

Unlike in the previous study, the majority baseline for this binary classification task is relatively high with 71.72% given that there is less data for the first and second grade. As in the first study, the second baseline using the traditional readability formula features text length and average word length performs only at the level of the majority baseline. The classifier combining evi-

---

[6] For example, the most informative feature of lexical complexity is in both subsets a measure of lexical diversity (Yule's k and root type-token ratio). Due to its higher ranking (overall most informative for secondary school) and its reduced sensitivity to text length, we chose to keep Yule's k and included the second most informative lexical complexity feature for elementary school: corrected verb variation (measuring lexical variation).

	Size	μ-Acc.	SD-Acc.
Majority baseline	1	71.72	0.35
Traditional baseline	2	71.72	0.35
All Features + Meta	256	**82.81**	2.11
All Features	255	**82.60**	1.97
Complexity	218	77.93	2.42
Error Rate	37	**81.56**	1.27
Lexical	31	77.32	1.92
Discourse	46	75.18	1.71
Phrasal	39	76.77	2.18
Clausal	26	72.44	0.49
Morphological	27	71.72	0.35
Language Use	30	71.72	0.35
Human processing	19	71.72	0.35

Table 4: Grade-level classification of elementary school texts, ten iterations of 10-fold CV, distinguishing levels *1st/2nd* and *3rd/4th*

dence from linguistic complexity features and error rate clearly outperforms the baselines with an accuracy of 82.60%.[7] Adding meta-information, which here means adding the writing topic, does not make a significant contribution.

Looking at the classifiers for the subsets of features, we see that error rate features make a significant contribution. While the difference in performance still is significant,[8] the classifier informed only by error rate features with an accuracy of 81.56% performs close to the combined model with an accuracy of 82.60%. The classifier using only complexity features performs worse, with an accuracy of 77.93%, even though this classifier is informed by considerably more features. When looking at the individual domains of linguistic complexity, again lexical complexity, discourse complexity, and phrasal complexity are the most informative features, but they perform significantly lower than the error rate features. The other domains of linguistic complexity seem to be uninformative for the grade level distinction in elementary school student writings – clausal and morphological complexity, language use, and human language processing all perform at baseline level.

Our findings show that early writing and academic language development predominantly focuses on establishing writing correctness rather than language complexification. However, in certain domains writing performance also advances in terms of complexity, namely the lexicon, discourse, and phrase complexity. Systematic improvements in the domains of clausal and morphological complexity or language use and human language processing, however, do not take place.

Turning to the secondary school data set, Table 5 shows the classification results for that subset.

	Size	μ-Acc.	SD-Acc.
Majority baseline	1	51.15	0.27
Traditional baseline	2	51.56	1.75
All Features + Meta	258	**65.66**	2.13
All Features	255	**63.71**	1.82
Complexity	220	**64.16**	1.63
Error Rate	35	54.34	2.48
Lexical	30	62.74	1.58
Discourse	45	57.13	1.75
Phrasal	41	57.64	2.10
Clausal	25	58.70	2.37
Morphological	27	54.31	2.39
Language Use	30	55.73	2.34
Human processing	18	52.67	1.90

Table 5: Grade-level classification on secondary school texts, ten iterations of 10-fold CV, distinguishing levels: *5th/6th* and *7th/8th*

The data set is more balanced across grouped grade levels, with a majority baseline of 51.15%. Traditional readability features again perform at the same level as the majority baseline. The best performing classifier again combines the features encoding linguistic complexity and error rate with information on topic and school track. It reaches an accuracy of 65.66%, performing nearly 2% better than the model without the meta-information.[9] Different from the elementary school data classifier, we here also distinguish the two secondary school tracks, which apparently differ in the complexity of the texts written in a given grade level.

A comparison of the classifiers based on error rate features versus the complexity features shows that for secondary school grade levels linguistic complexity is more indicative for differentiating grade levels. The classifiers differ in terms of their accuracy by nearly 10%. When comparing the performance of error rate features with the individual domains of linguistic complexity, we see that this difference cannot merely be explained by

---

[7] The confusion matrix for all ten iterations of the 10-CV may be found in Table 11 in the Appendix.

[8] One-sided t-test: t = −4.3978, df = 169.34, p = 9.63e-06

[9] The confusion matrix for all ten iterations of the 10-CV may be found in Table 12 in the Appendix.

the difference in feature set size. Lexical complexity, in particular, but also discourse complexity, phrasal complexity, and clausal complexity significantly outperform error rate features. This clear development of clausal complexity in secondary school writing is another difference to the development of writing of elementary school students. Language use and morphological complexity also show more development and significantly outperform the baselines. Human language processing features do not show a significant development.

Summarizing the findings from Table 4 and Table 5, we saw that the early writing and academic language development seemed to predominantly focus on establishing writing correctness rather than complexification. However, despite this focus on correctness, writing performance exhibits also in early stages of writing acquisition advances in terms of linguistic complexity in the domains of lexicon, discourse, and phrasal complexity. Systematic improvements in the other domains of linguistic complexity only take place at later stages of writing development. The beginning of this trend may be seen in the evidence from secondary school writings, for which clausal complexity and to some extent also morphological complexity and language use become increasingly relevant. Lexical complexity, phrasal complexity, and discourse complexity develop throughout all stages of writing acquisition.

6.3 Zooming in on Individual Features

Table 6 shows the most informative features from each feature set, their group means across grade-levels in elementary and secondary school, and the results of the t-tests.[10] In the first step (Section 6.2), we found that error rate as well as lexical, phrasal, and discourse complexity develop in both, elementary and secondary school writing. Zooming in on these domains, we see that some features systematically develop throughout grade-levels. Overall error rate and capitalization errors are highly informative in both data sets and decrease significantly across all grade-levels. Similarly, for lexical complexity, lexical diversity measured by Yule's k significantly decreases with progressing grade-levels (from 217 in grade-level 1/2 to 128 in grade-level 7/8). However, not in all

cases the results are as clear. Lexical variation measured as corrected verb ratio significantly increases from grade-levels 1/2 to 3/4 and 5/6 to 7/8. Yet, the lexical variation of grade-level 7/9 writing is closer to that of grade-level 3/4 than 5/6, leaving unclear to which extent we see systematic development in this subdomain of lexical complexity.

For discourse complexity, the transition probability of dropping the subject in a following sentence, i.e., not repeating it as, e.g., the subject or object, significantly decreases with increasing grade-level in elementary school, i.e., the discourse becomes more coherent. The probability remains stable at a low level in secondary school. There, discourse complexity seems to develop rather in terms of use of connectives such as temporal connectives which significantly increase with progressing grade-level, while showing inconclusive results for elementary school. The two most informative features from the domain of phrasal complexity behave similarly: The coverage of noun phrase modifiers for elementary school which significantly increases from grades 1/2 to grades 3/4 from 0.31 to 0.42 but stagnates around 0.52 in secondary school. For secondary school, it is represented by the ratio of verb modifiers per verb, which significantly increases across all grade-levels from 0.29 to 0.65.

In contrast to phrasal complexity, clausal complexity represented by conjunction clauses per sentence and verbs per t-unit does not significantly change throughout elementary school. However, it significantly increases in secondary school from 0.13 conjunction clauses per sentence to 0.18 and from 1.69 verbs per t-unit to 1.8. This is in line with our previous observation that elementary school writing rather develops in terms of phrasal but not clausal complexity, while clausal complexity gains importance in secondary school.

The same holds for morphological complexity and language use, which we found to only play a role in the development of secondary school writing. Accordingly, we do not see a significant difference in either across elementary school grade-levels for the most informative features of these domains. For secondary school writing, however, the number of derived nouns per noun significantly increases, indicating a stronger nominal style in students writing and we see a significant increase in vocabulary overlap with dlexDB, which consists of frequencies from news

---

[10] The appendix contains the information gain ranking for the 16 most informative features for both data sets, see Tables 15 and 16 as well as boxplots visualizing of all features across grade-levels, see Figures 2 to 1.

Feature name	Set	Elementary school				Secondary school			
		1/2	3/4	t	p	5/6	7/8	t	p
Overall errors / W	Error Rate	0.68	0.37	11.53	.000	0.28	0.22	5.60	.000
Corrected verb variation	Lexical	1.62	2.13	-11.55	.000	1.88	2.01	-3.03	.003
P(Subject → Nothing)	Discourse	0.15	0.10	3.40	.001	0.05	0.06	-1.35	.177
Avg. NP modifier types	Phrasal	0.31	0.42	-8.93	.000	0.52	0.52	-0.21	.831
Conjunction clauses / S	Clausal	0.11	0.13	-0.96	.339	0.13	0.18	-3.47	.001
Finite verbs / verb	Morph.	0.82	0.81	1.63	.105	0.71	0.70	0.88	.381
Pct. LW in Subtlex	Language Use	0.04	0.05	-1.71	.089	.085	.077	1.82	.069
DLT-IC (M) / finite verb	Human Processing	1.09	1.11	-1.96	.051	1.22	1.25	-1.65	.099
Capitalization errors / W	Error Rate	0.15	0.07	9.87	.000	0.05	0.04	5.61	.000
Yule's K	Lexical	217.	153.	7.21	.000	152.	128.	5.60	.000
Temp. connectives / S	Discourse	0.73	0.63	1.85	.066	0.47	0.62	-4.10	.000
Verb modifiers / VP	Phrasal	0.29	0.49	-4.85	.000	0.55	0.65	-2.86	.004
Verbs / t-unit	Clausal	1.67	1.57	-0.97	.333	1.69	1.81	-3.18	.002
Derived nouns / noun	Morph.	0.02	0.02	-0.38	.708	0.04	0.05	-2.66	.008
Pct. LW in dlexDB	Language Use	0.62	0.60	1.60	.111	0.60	0.63	-3.27	.001
($\sum$ max. dep.) / S	Human Processing	5.12	5.60	-2.64	.009	6.30	6.97	-4.59	.000

Table 6: Across-grade level group means of the most informative features of each feature set for distinguishing grade-levels in elementary school (above dashed line) and secondary school (below dashed line).

texts. This might indicate that language use becomes more similar to news language in secondary school, as dlexDB is based on news paper data.

Interestingly, for human language processing, there seems to be a marginally significant increase in DLT processing costs at the finite verb (with decreased modifier weight as defined in Shain et al. 2016) and a significant increase in the mean maximal dependency length per sentence across all grade-levels in elementary and secondary school.

7 Study 3: Cross-Topic Testing of Academic Language Development Across Topics

7.1 Set Up

In our final study, we want to test whether the results we obtained generalize across topics. Elementary school and secondary school students were both allowed to freely choose from two different topics for their writing as spelled out in Section 3. We used the two data subsets from Study 2, but additionally split them by topics, obtaining four data sets: i) elementary school: *Wolf* topic, ii) elementary school *Park* topic, iii) secondary school: *Future* topic, and iv) secondary school *Idol* topic. Table 7 shows the distribution of texts across grade levels and topics.

We used the data sets of *Wolf* topic writings and *Future* topic writings as training data sets and tested the resulting model on *Park* topic and *Idol*

	1/2	3/4	5/6	7/8	all
Wolf	133	353	0	0	466
Park	90	171	0	0	261
Future	0	0	332	333	665
Idol	0	0	130	111	241
all	203	524	462	444	1,663

Table 7: Distribution of grade levels across topics

topic texts, respectively. We chose this set-up since the two test data sets are too small to allow for training and testing with reversed data sets. We do not use cross-validation here, because we specifically want to study transfer across different topics rather than just different folds. In the new set-up, we cross-topic trained and tested the SMO classifiers based on the combination of complexity and error rate features and separately for the error rate and for the complexity features. We compared the results against the majority baseline and the traditional readability baseline containing measures of text and word length. For the secondary school data, we trained one model with and one without meta information on school tracks.

7.2 Results & Discussion

Table 8 shows the cross-topic classification performance on elementary school students' writings.

Feature Set	Train	Test	Acc.
Majority baseline	*n.a.*	Park	65.52
Traditional baseline	Wolf	Park	65.52
All Features	Wolf	Park	76.63
Complexity	Wolf	Park	68.58
Error Rate	Wolf	Park	81.61

Table 8: Cross-topic results for elementary school data

The majority baseline for elementary school writings' on the *Park* topic is more balanced than the one for the *Wolf* topic. For both topics, 3rd/4th grade was the most common grade-level. Training on *Wolf* texts and testing on *Park* texts with the SMO classifier yields an accuracy of 76.63%. While this does constitute a drop in accuracy as compared to Study 2, which may at least partially be explained by the reduced size of the training data set, the model clearly generalizes across topics. When taking a closer look at the difference between the purely error rate-based informed classifier and the complexity feature based classifier, we see that both generalize across topics. However, error rate clearly outperforms the complexity features and in fact hardly drops in performance when compared to the results obtained in Study 2.[11] The better performance of the classifier informed by error rate compared to both complexity-based classifiers indicates that error rate is more robust across topics than complexity. It also further corroborates the particular importance of writing correctness for early writing and academic language development.

Table 9 shows the results of the classifiers for the secondary school writing.

Feature Set	Train	Test	Acc.
Majority baseline	*n.a.*	Idol	50.01
Traditional baseline	Future	Idol	43.15
All Features + Meta	Future	Idol	62.66
All Features	Future	Idol	59.33
Complexity	Future	Idol	59.34
Error Rate	Future	Idol	55.19

Table 9: Cross-topic results for secondary school data

Unlike for the elementary school data, grade-levels are more or less balanced across topics for

this data set, leading to a majority baseline around 50%. As before, we see that all SMO classifier generalize across topics when training on the larger data set (*Future*) and testing on the smaller one (*Idol*). In line with their relative importance for this school level established in the second study, the complexity features play more of a role and interestingly generalize well, while the error rate measures known to play less of a role at this level of development are also less robust.[12]

8 Conclusion and Outlook

We presented the first approach modeling the linguistic complexity and accuracy in German academic language development across grades one to eight in elementary and secondary school. Our models are informed by a conceptually broad feature set of linguistic complexity measures and accuracy features extracted from error annotations. The computational linguistic analysis made it possible to empirically identify a shift in the developmental focus from accuracy as the primary locus of development in elementary school to the increasing complexity of the linguistic system in secondary school. Our results also show where both domains advance in parallel, in particular in the lexical complexity domain, which plays an important role throughout. Despite the emerging focus on complexity throughout secondary school, accuracy also continues to play a role. Investigating the generalizability of our results and the approach to complexity and accuracy development, we demonstrated the cross-topic robustness of our classifiers. The use of cross-topic testing to establish the robustness of machine learning models thus supports the applicability of language development modeling in real life.

These first results provide insights into the complexity and accuracy development of academic writing across the first eight years in German. Yet, they are based on the quasi-longitudinal operationalization of writing development as a function of grade level. Tracking genuine longitudinal develop of individual students across extended periods of time is a natural next step, which will make it possible to study individual differences and learning trajectories rather than overall group characteristics. We plan to follow up on this in future work.

---

[11] The confusion matrix for all ten iterations of the 10-CV may be found in Table 13 in the Appendix.

[12] The confusion matrix for all ten iterations of the 10-CV may be found in Table 14 in the Appendix.

References

Theodora Alexopoulou, Marije Michel, Akira Murakami, and Detmar Meurers. 2017. Task effects on linguistic complexity and accuracy: A large-scale learner corpus analysis employing natural language processing techniques. *Language Learning*, 67:181–209.

Marc Brysbaert, Matthias Buchmeier, Markus Conrad, Arthur M. Jacobs, Jens Bölte, and Andrea Böhl. 2011. The word frequency effect: A review of recent developments and implications for the choice of frequency estimates in German. *Experimental Psychology*, 58:412–424.

Bram Bulté and Alex Housen. 2014. Conceptualizing and measuring short-term changes in L2 writing complexity. *Journal of Second Language Writing*, 26(0):42 – 65. Comparing perspectives on L2 writing: Multiple analyses of a common corpus.

Heidi Byrnes. 2009. Emergent L2 German writing ability in a curricular context: A longitudinal study of grammatical metaphor. *Linguistics and Education*, 20(1):50 – 66.

Heidi Byrnes, Hiram H. Maxim, and John M. Norris. 2010. Realizing advanced foreign language writing development in collegiate education: Curricular design, pedagogy, assessment. *The Modern Language Journal*, 94.

Scott A Crossley and Danielle S McNamara. 2014. Does writing development equal writing quality? a computational investigation of syntactic complexity in L2 learners. *Journal of Second Language Writing*, 26:66–79.

Scott A. Crossley, Jennifer L. Weston, Susan T. McLain Sullivan, and Danielle S. McNamara. 2011. The development of writing proficiency as a function of grade level: A linguistic analysis. *Written Communication*, 28(3):282–311.

Felice Dell'Orletta, Simonetta Montemagni, and Giulia Venturi. 2014. Assessing document and sentence readability in less resourced languages and across textual genres. *Recent Advances in Automatic Readability Assessment and Text Simplification. Special issue of the International Journal of Applied Linguistics*, 165(2):163–193.

Rod Ellis and Gary Barkhuizen. 2005. *Analysing learner language*. Oxford University Press.

Edward Gibson. 2000. The dependency locality theory: A distance-based theory of linguistic complexity. In Alec Marantz, Yasushi Miyashita, and Wayne O'Neil, editors, *Image, language, brain: papers from the First Mind Articulation Project Symposium*, pages 95–126. MIT.

Susanne Göpferich and Imke Neumann. 2016. Writing competence profiles as an assessment grid? – students' L1 and L2 writing competences and their development after one semester of instruction. In *Developing and Assessing Academic and Professional Writing Skills*, pages 103–140. Peter Lang, Bern, Switzerland.

Julia Hancke, Sowmya Vajjala, and Detmar Meurers. 2012. Readability classification for German using lexical, syntactic, and morphological features. In *Proceedings of the 24th International Conference on Computational Linguistics (COLING)*, pages 1063–1080, Mumbay, India.

Alexis Housen, Folkert Kuiken, and Ineke Vedder. 2012. Complexity, accuracy and fluency: Definitions, measurement and research. In Alex Housen, Folkert Kuiken, and Ineke Vedder, editors, *Dimensions of L2 Performance and Proficiency*, Language Learning & Language Teaching, pages 1–20. John Benjamins.

Ute Knoch, Amir Roushad, Su Ping oon, and Neomy Storch. 2015. What happens to ESL students' writing after three years of study at an English medium university? *Journal of Second Language Writing*, 28:39–52.

Ute Knoch, Amir Roushad, and Neomy Storch. 2014. Does the writing of undergraduate ESL students develop after one year of study in an english-medium university? *Assessing Writing*, 21:1–17.

Kristopher Kyle. 2016. *Measuring Syntactic Development in L2 Writing: Fine Grained Indices of Syntactic Complexity and Usage-Based Indices of Syntactic Sophistication*. Ph.D. thesis, Georgia State University.

Diane Larsen-Freeman. 2006. The emergence of complexity, fluency, and accuracy in the oral and written production of five Chinese learners of English. *Applied Linguistics*, 27(4):590–619.

Rémi Lavalley, Kay Berkling, and Sebastian Stüker. 2015. Preparing children's writing database for automated processing. In *LTLT@ SLaTE*, pages 9–15.

Ildikó Pilán and Elena Volodina. 2016. Classification of language proficiency levels in swedish learners' texts. In *Proceedings of Swedish language technology conference*.

John C. Platt. 1998. Sequential minimal optimization: A fast algorithm for training support vector machines. Technical Report MSR-TR-98-14, Microsoft Research.

Robert Reynolds. 2016. *Russian natural language processing for computer-assisted language learning: capturing the benefits of deep morphological analysis in real-life applications*. Ph.D. thesis, UiT - The Arctic University of Norway.

Peter Robinson. 2001. Task complexity, task difficulty, and task production: exploring interactions in a componential framework. *Applied Linguistics*, 22(1):27–57.

Cory Shain, Marten van Schijndel, Richard Futrell, Edward Gibson, and William Schuler. 2016. Memory access during incremental sentence processing causes reading time latency. In *Proceedings of the Workshop on Computational Linguistics for Linguistic Complexity (CL4LC)*, pages 49–58, Osaka.

Peter Skehan. 1996. A framework for the implementation of task-based instruction. *Applied Linguistics*, 17(1):38.

Eric Velleman and Thea van der Geest. 2014. Online test tool to determine the cefr reading comprehension level of text. *Procedia computer science*, 27:350–358.

Mary Lou Vercellotti. 2015. The development of complexity, accuracy, and fluency in second language performance: A longitudinal study. *Applied Linguistics*, 38(1):90–111.

Marjolijn Verspoor, Monika S. Schmid, and Xiaoyan Xu. 2012. A dynamic usage based perspective on L2 writing. *Journal of Second Language Writing*, 21(3):239–263.

Nina Vyatkina. 2012. The development of second language writing complexity in groups and individuals: A longitudinal learner corpus study. *The Modern Language Journal*, 96(4):576–598.

Zarah Weiss. 2017. Using measures of linguistic complexity to assess German L2 proficiency in learner corpora under consideration of task-effects. Master's thesis, University of Tübingen, Germany.

Zarah Weiss and Detmar Meurers. 2018. Modeling the readability of German targeting adults and children: An empirically broad analysis and its cross-corpus validation. In *Proceedings of the 27th International Conference on Computational Linguistics (COLING)*, Santa Fe, New Mexico, USA.

Zarah Weiss and Detmar Meurers. in press. Broad linguistic modeling is beneficial for German L2 proficiency assessment. In *Widening the Scope of Learner Corpus Research. Selected Papers from the Fourth Learner Corpus Research Conference*, Louvain-La-Neuve. Presses Universitaires de Louvain.

Zarah Weiss, Anja Riemenschneider, Pauline Schröter, and Detmar Meurers. 2019. Computationally modeling the impact of task-appropriate language complexity and accuracy on human grading of German essays. In *Proceedings of the 14th Workshop on Innovative Use of NLP for Building Educational Applications (BEA)*, Florence, Italy.

Kate Wolfe-Quintero, Shunji Inagaki, and Hae-Young Kim. 1998. *Second Language Development in Writing: Measures of Fluency, Accuracy & Complexity*. Second Language Teaching & Curriculum Center, University of Hawaii at Manoa, Honolulu.

Weiwei Yang, Xiaofei Lu, and Sara Cushing Weigle. 2015. Different topics, different discourse: Relationships among writing topic, measures of syntactic complexity, and judgments of writing quality. *Journal of Second Language Writing*, 28:53–67.

Helen Yannakoudakis, Øistein E. Andersen, Ardeshir Geranpayeh, Ted Briscoe, and Diane Nicholls. 2018. Developing an automated writing placement system for ESL learners. *Applied Measurement in Education*, 31(3):251–267.

Hyung-Jo Yoon. 2017. Linguistic complexity in L2 writing revisited: Issues of topic, proficiency, and construct multidimensionality. *System*, 66:130–141.

Hyung-Jo Yoon and Charlene Polio. 2016. The linguistic development of students of English as a second language in two written genres. *TESOL Quarterly*, pages 275–301.

A Appendices

↓Obs/Pred→	1/2	3/4	5/6	7/8	∑
1/2	**1217**	813	0	0	2030
3/4	430	**4810**	0	0	5240
5/6	0	0	**3029**	1591	4620
7/8	0	0	1590	**2850**	4440
∑	1647	5623	4619	4441	16330

Table 10: Confusion matrix for the best model in study 1 (all feat. + meta) summed across iterations

↓Obs/Pred→	1/2	3/4	∑
1/2	**1232**	798	2030
3/4	449	**4791**	5240
∑	1681	5589	7270

Table 11: Confusion matrix for best elementary school model in study 2 (all feat. + meta) summed across iterations

↓Obs/Pred→	5/6	7/8	∑
5/6	**3049**	1571	4620
7/8	1497	**2943**	4440
∑	4546	4514	9060

Table 12: Confusion matrix for best secondary school model in study 2 (all feat. + meta) summed across iterations

↓Obs/Pred→	1/2	3/4	∑
1/2	**51**	39	90
3/4	9	**162**	171
∑	60	201	261

Table 13: Confusion matrix for the best model for elementary school in study 3 (Error rate)

↓Obs/Pred→	5/6	7/8	∑
5/6	**91**	39	130
7/8	51	**60**	111
∑	142	99	241

Table 14: Confusion matrix for the best model for secondary school in study 3 (all feat. + meta)

Feature name	Set	Merit
Overall errors / W	Error rate	.166
Root type-token ratio	Lexical	.150
Corrected type-token ratio	Lexical	.150
Number of words	Clausal	.137
Capitalization errors / W	Error rate	.128
HDD	Lexical	.124
Corrected verb variation	Lexical	.110
Squared verb variation	Lexical	.110
Word splitting + hyphenation errors / W	Error rate	.108
P(Subject→Nothing)	Discourse	.106
P(Nothing→Nothing)	Discourse	.104
P(Nothing→Subject)	Discourse	.099
Number of sentences	Clausal	.094
P(Nothing→Object)	Discourse	.093
Yule's K	Lexical	.091
MTLD	Lexical	.088

Table 15: Top features in information gain ranking for grade-level distinction in elementary school

Feature name	Set	Merit
Yule's K	Lexical	.030
Capitalization errors / W	Error rate	.029
($\sum$ max. dep.) / S	Human processing	.026
MTLD	Lexical	.023
Verbs / t-unit	Clausal	.023
Verbs / S	Clausal	.023
HDD	Lexical	.022
Overall errors / W	Error rate	.022
Nouns / W	Lexical	.021
$\sum$ Non-terminal nodes / tree	Clausal	.021
W / S	Clausal	.021
to infinitives / S	Lexical	.020
Uber index	Lexical	.020
Temporal connectives / S	Discourse	.019
$\sum$ Non-terminal nodes / W	Clausal	.019
Clauses / S	Clausal	.017

Table 16: Top features in information gain ranking for grade-level distinction in secondary school

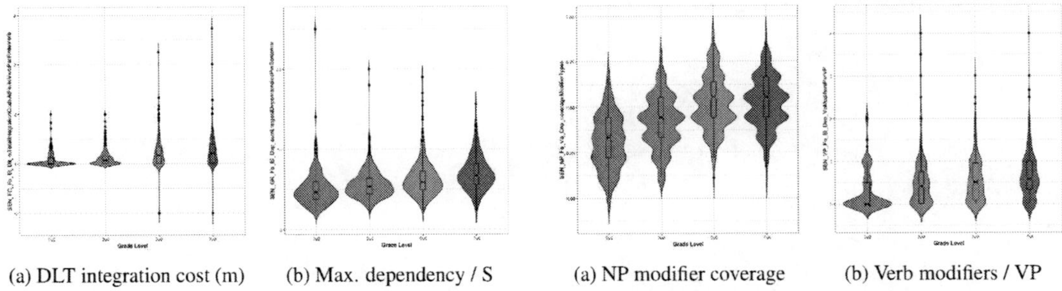

(a) DLT integration cost (m)   (b) Max. dependency / S

Figure 1: Most informative human processing features

(a) NP modifier coverage   (b) Verb modifiers / VP

Figure 5: Most informative phrasal features.

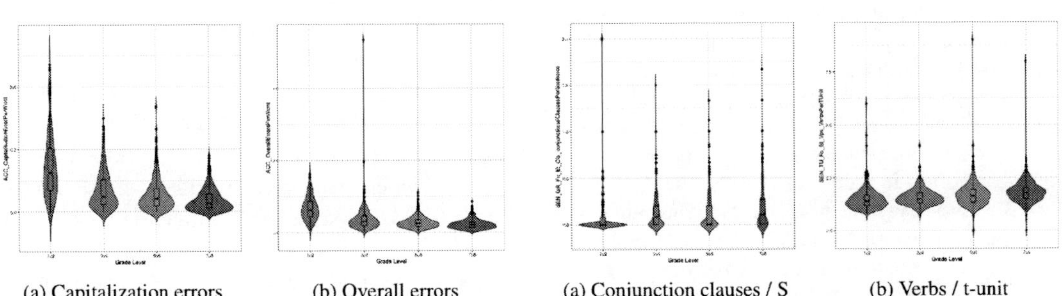

(a) Capitalization errors   (b) Overall errors

Figure 2: Most informative error rate features

(a) Conjunction clauses / S   (b) Verbs / t-unit

Figure 6: Most informative clausal features.

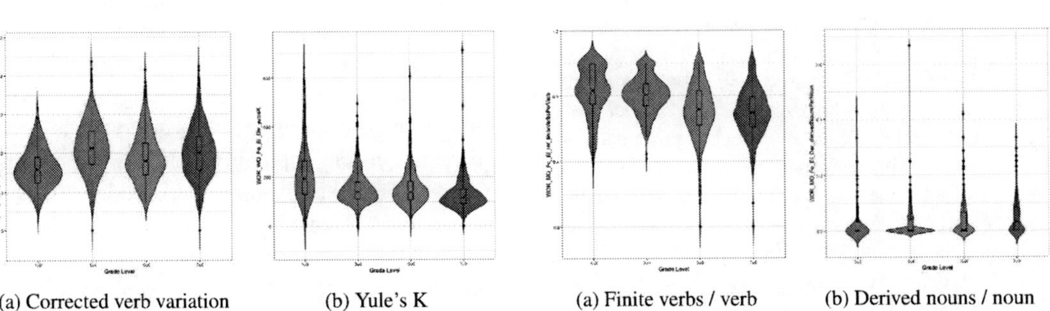

(a) Corrected verb variation   (b) Yule's K

Figure 3: Most informative lexical features

(a) Finite verbs / verb   (b) Derived nouns / noun

Figure 7: Most informative morphology features.

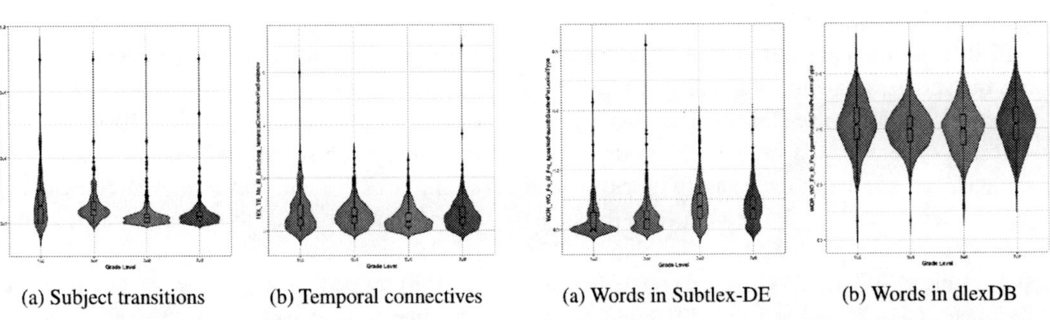

(a) Subject transitions   (b) Temporal connectives

Figure 4: Most informative discourse features.

(a) Words in Subtlex-DE   (b) Words in dlexDB

Figure 8: Most informative language use features

Content Modeling for Automated Oral Proficiency Scoring System

Su-Youn Yoon and Chong Min Lee
Educational Testing Service / 660 Rosedale road, Princeton, USA
`{syoon,clee001}@ets.org`

Abstract

We developed an automated oral proficiency scoring system for non-native English speakers' spontaneous speech. Automated systems that score holistic proficiency are expected to assess a wide range of performance categories, and the content is one of the core performance categories. In order to assess the quality of the content, we trained a Siamese convolutional neural network (Siamese CNN) to model the semantic relationship between key points generated by experts and a test response. The correlation between human scores and Siamese CNN scores was comparable to human-human agreement ($r = 0.63$), and it was higher than the baseline content features. The inclusion of Siamese CNN-based feature to the existing state-of-the-art automated scoring model achieved a small but statistically significant improvement. However, the new model suffered from score inflation for long atypical responses with serious content issues. We investigated the reasons of this score inflation by analyzing the associations with linguistic features and identifying areas strongly associated with the score errors.

1 Introduction

We developed an automated scoring model for an oral proficiency assessment of non-native English speakers. In particular, the system was designed to score spontaneous speech, elicited using questions where the test takers summarized the core content of a reading and/or listening passages. A system for scoring holistic proficiency of spontaneous speech is expected to assess a wide range of areas such as fluency (Cucchiarini et al., 2000; Zechner et al., 2009), pronunciation (Witt and Young, 1997), prosody, grammar (Chen and Zechner, 2011; Yoon and Bhat, 2018) and vocabulary (Yoon and Bhat, 2012). Content is also one of the core performance categories in holistic oral proficiency scoring. In particular, automated scoring systems without content scoring capabilities may show sub-optimal performance when scoring responses with mismatched proficiency levels between content and other areas. For instance, some responses have critical content issues but good delivery skills, while some responses have good content but issues in other areas. Furthermore, in large-scale oral proficiency assessments, some responses may have sub-optimal characteristics. The types of these problematic responses (hereafter, atypical responses) for the tests eliciting spontaneous speech frequently have severe content issues. For instance, some test takers may try to game the system by citing memorized responses for unrelated topics (e.g., off-topic responses). Even state-of-the-art automated scoring systems face challenges in scoring these atypical responses, and automated scoring systems without content scoring capability may assign inaccurate scores for these responses. To address these issues, more researchers started to actively explore content scoring in the context of oral proficiency scoring (Xie et al., 2012; Evanini et al., 2013; Yoon et al., 2018).

Recently, deep neural networks (DNN) and word embeddings have been applied successfully to various natural language processing tasks. In the automated scoring area, several researchers have explored the use of diverse neural networks for essay scoring (Farag et al., 2018; Alikaniotis et al., 2016; Dong and Zhang, 2016) and spontaneous speech scoring (Chen et al., 2018a; Qian et al., 2018a,b) and they achieved comparable or superior performance to the sophisticated linguistic feature-based system. In particular, Qian et al. (2018b) trained an automated scoring model covering the content aspect and achieved a further improvement over the generic model without content modeling.

Proceedings of the Fourteenth Workshop on Innovative Use of NLP for Building Educational Applications, pages 394–401
Florence, Italy, August 2, 2019. ©2019 Association for Computational Linguistics

The content relevance of a response is a concept relative to the question, and thus, it is important that the neural network learns the semantic relevance between a question-response pair. Siamese networks are characterized by shared weights between two subnetworks modeling inputs and are effective in calculating semantic similarity between sentence pairs (Mueller and Thyagarajan, 2016; Yin et al., 2015; Hu et al., 2014).

In order to address the strong need for content scoring and based on the promising performance of the Siamese CNN in the semantic relevance modeling, we developed a Siamese CNN-based content model. In particular, we make the following two contributions:

- We developed a new feature, based on the Siamese CNN by modeling the semantic distance between the core content and the test takers' responses. The new Siamese CNN-based feature outperformed the baseline content features, and the inclusion of the new feature further improved the performance of a state-of-the-art automated speech scoring model.

- We examined whether the automated scoring model including the new Siamese CNN-based feature could assign accurate scores for atypical responses. Differing from previous studies (Higgins and Heilman, 2014; Yannakoudakis and Briscoe, 2012; Lee et al., 2017) using synthesized atypical responses in their evaluations, we used authentic atypical responses collected from a large number of test administrations.

2 Data

We used a large collection of spoken responses from an English proficiency assessment. It was composed of $109,894$ responses from $37,830$ speakers. For each question, test takers read and/or listened to a passage and then provided answers consisting of around one minute of spontaneous speech based on the given passage. We used 80 questions, covering a wide range of topics such as education, entertainment, health, and policies. For each question, the data included $1,374$ responses on average, but there were large variations ranging from 305 to $3,013$.

During the question generation, expert assessment developers first generated a list of key points

to guide the creation of the reading and listening passages. These key points were provided to and used by human raters to evaluate content of the spoken responses. Three key points were generated for each question, and the responses with the perfect content coverage were expected to include all three key points. We concatenated three key points into one text and used it during the content model building. The key points contained on average 93 words.

All responses were scored by the trained raters using a 4-point scoring scale from 1 to 4 with 4 indicating the highest proficiency. In addition, raters provided a score of 0 when test takers did not show any intention of directly responding to the question. The rubrics consisted of three major performance categories: delivery (pronunciation, prosody, and fluency), language use (vocabulary and grammar), and topic development (content and coherence). Both the Pearson correlation and quadratic weighted kappa between two human raters based on 10% double-scored data[1] were 0.61.

The average of the human scores was 2.58, and the most frequent score was 3 (48%), followed by 2 (39%), 4 (8%), 1 (4%), and 0 (1%). The number of words in the transcriptions generated by an automated speech recognition (ASR) system (*numwds*) ranged from 11 to 248 (129 on average).

The characteristics of responses with score of 0 were widely varied, but some of the most frequent categories included (a) response in a non-target language; (b) off-topic; (c) canned responses[2]; (d) no-response including no speech other than fillers or simple sentences (e.g., "I don't know"); and (e) repetition of the question. These responses had serious problems in content. We used the responses with score of 0 as atypical responses and used them for an additional evaluation.

However, due to the low percentage of the score 0 responses, it was difficult to analyze the model accuracy for them. In order to address this issue, we constructed a separate atypical dataset by extracting a large number of responses with a score of 0 from the same English proficiency assessment, but much larger administrations. The size of dataset is presented in Table 1.

---

[1] The double-scored data included responses with scores of 1 to 4.

[2] Responses that only included memorized segments from external sources. The sources were irrelevant to the question, and the responses were likely to be off-topic.

Partition	Purpose	N. of responses
Train	Training of content features and a Siamese CNN model	54,051
LR Train	Training of linear regression models	25,706
Test	Evaluation	28,497
Atypical responses	Evaluation	1,640

Table 1: Number of responses for each partition

3 Method

3.1 Siamese Convolutional Neural Network (Siamese CNN)

We used a Siamese convolutional neural network (CNN) consisting of an input modeling step using two weight-sharing CNNs (one CNN was for modeling the key points and the other was for modeling responses), a similarity distance calculation layer, and a neural network layer. Figure 1 illustrates the overall architecture of our Siamese CNN.

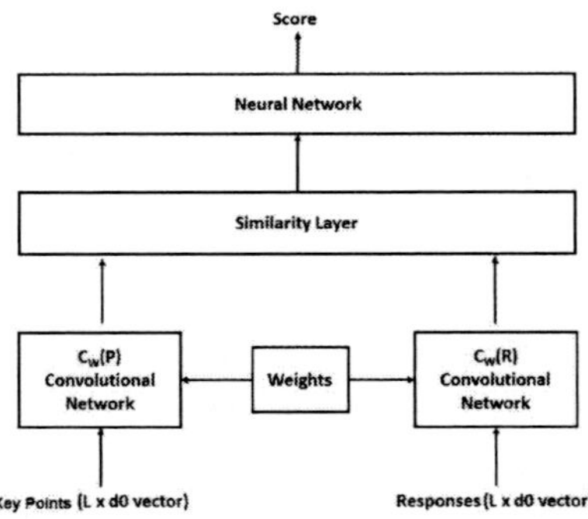

Figure 1: Diagram of Siamese Convolutional Neural Network

An input, a pair of a response and a text composed of three key points, was converted into a 2D tensor with a shape of $L \times d0$, where $L = 100$[3] and $d0 = 300$. $d0$ was the dimension of the word embedding vector, and we used Google word embedding vectors (Mikolov et al., 2013) with 300 dimensions.

The converted vector was fed into the convolution layer with the filter numbers $d1$ and filter width w; each filter created concatenated embedding vectors of w consecutive words. We trained models using different $d1$ (16, 64, 128, 256) and w (3, 4, 5, 6), and they were optimized using hyperopt software (Bergstra et al., 2013). This was followed by an averaging pooling layer, and two vectors (one for the key points and one for the response) were generated.

Next, a cosine similarity between the two vectors was calculated at the similarity layer. Finally, we stacked a neural network as the output layer, and it generated a score. The mean squared error (MSE) between the output scores and human scores was the learning metric and Adaptive Grad Optimizer was the optimizer. The model had a similar architecture to the 'basic Bi-CNN' model in Yin et al. (2015) with the final layer and different learning metric for the regression task.

3.2 Features from an automated proficiency scoring system

We used 38 features generated by a state-of-the-art automated proficiency scoring system for non-native speakers' spontaneous speech (Chen et al., 2018b). For a given spoken response, the system performed speech processing including speech recognition and forced-alignment and generated 38 features in five groups: (a) speech rate features, (b) pronunciation quality features[4], (c) pause pattern features, (d) prosody features[5], and (e) content features.

In particular, we generated 3 content features to assess the content accuracy and completeness. The first feature was designed to assess lexical similarity with high-scoring responses. It calculated a term frequency-inverse document frequency (tf-idf) weighted cosine similarity score between a test response vector and the question-specific tf vector. The question-specific tf vector was a vector whose elements were the frequency of each word in the entire sample responses with a score of 4 that answered the same question. The question-specific vector was trained on the Train partition.

---

[3]Typically, L is the maximum length of the input, but we used $L = 100$ due to the consistently superior performance in the pilot experiments using varying L. For key points or responses shorter than 100 words, we added zeros to the end. On the contrary, for key points or responses longer than 100, we selected the initial 100 words.

[4]This group of features measures how much the test takers' pronunciation deviates from the native norms.

[5]This group of features measures patterns of variation in time intervals between syllables or phonemes.

The remaining two features were designed to measure similarity with the key points created by the assessment developers. We created an average embedding vector and an idf weighted average embedding vector for the key-points. Next, we created two vectors for a test response using the same process. Finally, we calculated two cosine similarity scores between the key-point embedding vector and response embedding vector: one score for the average embedding vectors and one score for the idf weighted average embedding vectors. The detailed description of features used in this study is provided in Yoon et al. (2018).

3.3 Scoring Model Training

We trained linear regression models to generate a proficiency score for each response. In order to evaluate the impact of the Siamese CNN based feature, we classified features into 4 groups:

- content: three content features in Section 3.2

- all-features: all 38 features in Section 3.2

- Siamese CNN: output score of the Siamese CNN model

- CMB: combination of all-feature and the output score of the Siamese CNN model

Finally, we trained 4 linear regression models (one model for each feature group) using a human score as a dependent variable using the RSMTool (Madnani and Loukina, 2016).

4 Experiment

We generated transcriptions of a spoken response using an ASR system composed of a gender-independent acoustic model and a trigram language model trained on 800 hours of spoken responses extracted from the same English proficiency test using the Kaldi toolkit (Povey et al., 2011). The ASR system achieved a Word Error Rate of 23% on 600 held-out responses (Tao et al., 2016).

Next, we normalized both key points and ASR-based transcriptions by tokenizing and removing stop words and disfluencies. After the normalization process, the length of the key points and responses were reduced to 60% and 40% of the original texts.

We trained a Siamese CNN model using the normalized texts of the Train partition and the key-points. The model was implemented using Tensorflow (Abadi et al., 2015). The parameters were optimized using the hyperopt software, and the final model used $L = 100$, $d = 300$, $d1 = 256$, $w = 4$, and the learning rate $l = 0.0001$. In addition, the automated scoring system using the same ASR engine generated 38 features. Finally, we trained linear regression models on the LR Train partition.

5 Results

5.1 Scoring of normal responses

We first evaluated the performance of the automated scoring models on the Test partition in terms of its strength in the associations with proficiency scores assigned by human raters. Table 2 presents the agreement between the human scores and the automated scores for each model.

	Correlation	κ	RMSE
Siamese CNN	0.634	0.588	0.601
content	0.452	0.499	0.663
all-feature	0.672	0.620	0.565
CMB	0.686	0.631	0.555

Table 2: Correlations, quadratic weighted kappas (κ), and root mean squared error (RMSE) between the automated scores and human scores

The performance of the Siamese CNN model was substantially better than the content feature-based model; the correlation and quadratic weighted kappa increased approximately 0.18 and 0.09, respectively. On the contrary, the performance of the Siamese CNN model was significantly lower than the performance of the all-feature model, and this difference was also statistically significant ($p < 0.01$) based on the Steigers Z-test for dependent correlations.

The combination of the Siamese CNN and all-feature achieved a small improvement. The correlation and quadratic weighted kappa of the CMB model were 0.686 and 0.631, respectively. There was approximately 0.01 increase over the best performing individual model (all-feature model). This improvement was statistically significant at 0.01 level ($p < 0.01$).

5.2 Scoring of the atypical responses

Next, we evaluated whether the automated scoring models assign accurate scores for atypical responses using the Atypical response set. Table 3 compares the mean and standard deviation (STD) of the automated scores for each model. In general, the models with the lower average score are more accurate than those with the higher average score because the human scores for all responses in this set were 0.

	Mean	STD
Siamese CNN	1.129	0.344
content	0.545	0.500
all-feature	0.969	0.845
CMB	0.732	0.490

Table 3: Comparison of the automated scores for the atypical responses

In general, the average scores of the automated models were low. The average scores of the feature-based models (both content and all-feature) were lower than 1.0, and this was lower than the lowest scale score for the normal responses; our scoring scale for normal responses (excluding atypical responses) ranged from 1 to 4 with 1 indicating the lowest proficiency. The average score of the Siamese CNN model was slightly higher, at 1.13. Finally, the average score of the CMB model was lower than both Siamese CNN and all-feature models. The combination of the two groups of features resulted in assigning more accurate scores for the atypical responses and improved the robustness of the automated scoring system.

In general, automated scoring models tend to assign high scores for long responses, and thus the automated models in this study may assign even higher scores for the long atypical responses. In the Atypical response set, the percentage of short responses was high (atypical responses with less than 20 words was 59%). Therefore, despite the low average score, there was a possibility that the automated models assigned high scores for a subset of atypical responses. Figure 2 presents the average automated scores by the response length.

The automated scores for the Siamese CNN model were relatively low for the short responses, and they increased substantially as the response length increased; it sharply increased

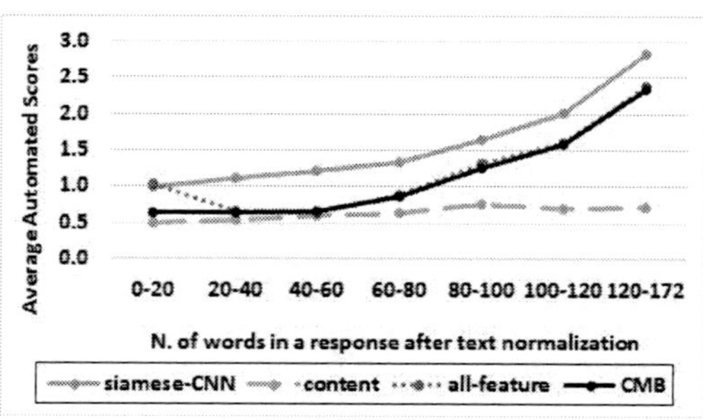

Figure 2: Average score predicted by the scoring models.

when the responses contained more than 60 words. The average Siamese CNN score for the responses longer than 120 words was 2.84. In contrast, the automated scores for the content model were consistently lower than 1.0.

The all-feature model also showed a similar trend to the Siamese CNN model; as the response length increased, the automated scores increased substantially. However, the average scores were substantially lower than those of the Siamese CNN model. Finally, the combination of the Siamese CNN and the all-feature (CMB model) resulted in the improvement in the short atypical responses; the average score of the responses containing 0-20 words was 0.64, and it was 0.4 lower than the all-feature model. However, no large difference was found from the longer atypical responses.

6 Discussion

From the atypical response scoring experiment, we found that the Siamese CNN model had a tendency to inflate scores for the long atypical responses. The long atypical responses in this study tended to be associated with the salient content issues such as off-topic responses from the test takers who cited answers for unrelated topics. The score inflation of these responses suggested that the Siamese CNN model may not have strong power in identifying responses with the severe content abnormality.

In order to get better understanding about which performance areas (e.g., content, fluency, vocabulary) the Siamese CNN model assessed mainly, we analyzed the relationships between the Siamese CNN score and three features from the automated proficiency scoring system: (a) speaking rate (fluency), (b) an average of the frequencies of the words used in a response (vocabulary), and (c) a cosine similarity score between a question-specific content vector and a response (content). These features assess fluency, vocabulary, and content skills. Table 4 presents the correlation analysis calculated from the Atypical response set.

	vocabulary	content	fluency
r	0.395	0.430	0.706

Table 4: Correlation of the Siamese CNN score with the features from the oral proficiency scoring system: Pearson correlation coefficients in absolute values

All human scores in this set were 0. Therefore, the associations between the features and the holistic proficiency had no effect on the correlations showed in Table 4.

All correlations were statistically significant at 0.01 level. However, the Siamese CNN score showed the strongest correlation with the fluency feature, and the correlation with the content feature was much weaker than that with the fluency feature.

Next, we randomly selected an atypical response with a high Siamese CNN score; the Siamese CNN score was 3.3 while the score of the all-feature model was 2.2. Thus, the Siamese CNN model showed a stronger score inflation than the all-feature model. The response included 53 words after the text normalization. The response was clearly off-topic; the question was in the "entertainment life at the university" domain, while the answer was about "science, nature." Similar to Zeiler and Fergus (2014)'s occlusion experiment, we systematically removed n-words ($n = 1, 2, ..., 5$) from the response and generated scores for the new responses by the Siamese CNN model to identify the areas associated with high score inflation. Figure 3 presents the relationship between the score changes and the removed n-words.

There were approximately 5 points with substantial score drops (marked with red square in the Figure). The words at these points were "plankton," "swam," "microsoft," "semester," and "nice." These words were strongly associated with the score inflation and removal of these words resulted in substantially lower scores. Among them, first three words were relatively low frequency words but not topically relevant. The word frequencies in language learners' responses have been consistently identified as one of the strong predictors of vocabulary skill. These analyses supported the notion that the current Siamese CNN model might be paying strong attention to the fluency and vocabulary aspect.

7 Conclusion

We trained a Siamese CNN to model the semantic distance between the key points generated by the experts and the test takers' responses. The Siamese CNN model achieved a high performance without sophisticated feature engineering. For scoring normal responses, it achieved substantially better performance than the model using the content features from the existing automated speech scoring system. The inclusion of the Siamese CNN based feature to the existing state-of-the-art automated speech scoring system resulted in a small but statistically significant improvement. Furthermore, it improved the validity and robustness of the automated scoring system by assigning more accurate scores for short atypical responses. However, the Siamese CNN model suffered from score inflation during scoring long atypical responses. In the current human scoring scenario, the percentage of these long atypical responses was extremely low and they were correctly scored by human raters. However, this may be an important challenge that we need to overcome for the use of an automated scoring model as a sole scorer.

In this study, we explored the linear combination of the Siamese-CNN and linguistic features. The reviewers commented that there may be a further improvement by using non-linear algorithms to combine them. In particular, one of the reviewer suggested a possibility to train a Siamese CNN with linguistic features as additional inputs. In a future study, we will explore these points. In addition, we will also explore developing separate binary classifiers to filter out atypical responses and prevent an automated scoring model from generating erroneous scores.

Acknowledgments

We thank Rene Lawless, Patrick Houghton, Klaus Zechner, Michael Flor, Xinhao Wang, and anonymous reviewers for their comments and suggestions.

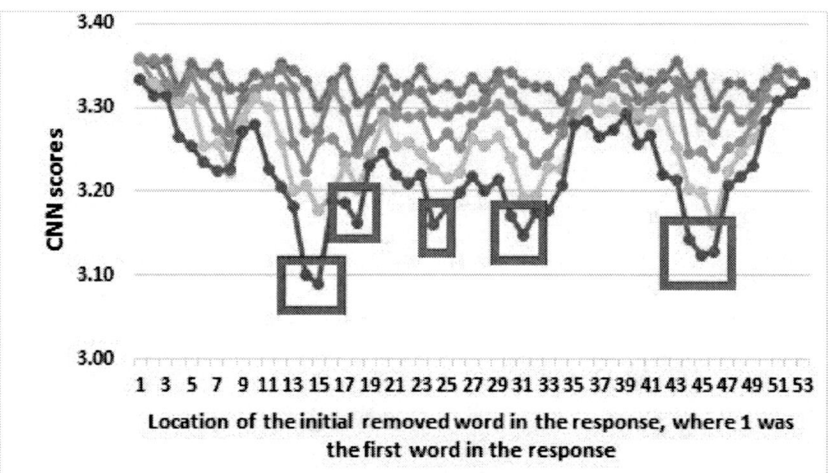

Figure 3: Siamese CNN scores for the responses excluding n-words by 1-word (green), 2-words (orange), 3-words (grey), 4-words (yellow), and 5-words (blue)

References

Martín Abadi, Ashish Agarwal, Paul Barham, Eugene Brevdo, Zhifeng Chen, Craig Citro, Greg S. Corrado, Andy Davis, Jeffrey Dean, Matthieu Devin, Sanjay Ghemawat, Ian Goodfellow, Andrew Harp, Geoffrey Irving, Michael Isard, Yangqing Jia, Rafal Jozefowicz, Lukasz Kaiser, Manjunath Kudlur, Josh Levenberg, Dan Mané, Rajat Monga, Sherry Moore, Derek Murray, Chris Olah, Mike Schuster, Jonathon Shlens, Benoit Steiner, Ilya Sutskever, Kunal Talwar, Paul Tucker, Vincent Vanhoucke, Vijay Vasudevan, Fernanda Viégas, Oriol Vinyals, Pete Warden, Martin Wattenberg, Martin Wicke, Yuan Yu, and Xiaoqiang Zheng. 2015. TensorFlow: Large-scale machine learning on heterogeneous systems. Software available from tensorflow.org.

Dimitrios Alikaniotis, Helen Yannakoudakis, and Marek Rei. 2016. Automatic text scoring using neural networks. *arXiv preprint arXiv:1606.04289*.

James Bergstra, Daniel Yamins, and David Daniel Cox. 2013. Making a science of model search: Hyperparameter optimization in hundreds of dimensions for vision architectures.

Lei Chen, Jidong Tao, Shabnam Ghaffarzadegan, and Yao Qian. 2018a. End-to-end neural network based automated speech scoring. In *2018 IEEE International Conference on Acoustics, Speech and Signal Processing (ICASSP)*, pages 6234–6238. IEEE.

Lei Chen, Klaus Zechner, Su-Youn Yoon, Keelan Evanini, Xinhao Wang, Anastassia Loukina, Jidong Tao, Lawrence Davis, Chong Min Lee, Min Ma, et al. 2018b. Automated scoring of nonnative speech using the speechrater sm v. 5.0 engine. *ETS Research Report Series*, 2018(1):1–31.

Miao Chen and Klaus Zechner. 2011. Computing and evaluating syntactic complexity features for automated scoring of spontaneous non-native speech. In *Proceedings of ACL*, pages 722–731.

Catia Cucchiarini, Helmer Strik, and Lou Boves. 2000. Quantitative assessment of second language learners fluency by means of automatic speech recognition technology. *The Journal of the Acoustical Society of America*, 107(2):989–999.

Fei Dong and Yue Zhang. 2016. Automatic features for essay scoring–an empirical study. In *Proceedings of the 2016 Conference on Empirical Methods in Natural Language Processing*, pages 1072–1077.

Keelan Evanini, Shasha Xie, and Klaus Zechner. 2013. Prompt-based content scoring for automated spoken language assessment. In *Proceedings of the eighth workshop on innovative use of NLP for building educational applications*, pages 157–162.

Youmna Farag, Helen Yannakoudakis, and Ted Briscoe. 2018. Neural automated essay scoring and coherence modeling for adversarially crafted input. *arXiv preprint arXiv:1804.06898*.

Derrick Higgins and Michael Heilman. 2014. Managing what we can measure: Quantifying the susceptibility of automated scoring systems to gaming behavior. *Educational Measurement: Issues and Practice*, 33(3):36–46.

Baotian Hu, Zhengdong Lu, Hang Li, and Qingcai Chen. 2014. Convolutional neural network architectures for matching natural language sentences. In Z. Ghahramani, M. Welling, C. Cortes, N. D. Lawrence, and K. Q. Weinberger, editors, *Advances in Neural Information Processing Systems 27*, pages 2042–2050. Curran Associates, Inc.

Chong Min Lee, Su-Youn Yoon, Xihao Wang, Matthew Mulholland, Ikkyu Choi, and Keelan Evanini. 2017. Off-topic spoken response detection using siamese convolutional neural networks. In *INTERSPEECH*, pages 1427–1431.

Nitin Madnani and Anastassia Loukina. 2016. Rsmtool: collection of tools building and evaluating automated scoring models. *The Journal of Open Source Software*, 2016.

Tomas Mikolov, Ilya Sutskever, Kai Chen, Greg S Corrado, and Jeff Dean. 2013. Distributed representations of words and phrases and their compositionality. In *Advances in neural information processing systems*, pages 3111–3119.

Jonas Mueller and Aditya Thyagarajan. 2016. Siamese recurrent architectures for learning sentence similarity. In *Proceedings of the Thirtieth AAAI Conference on Artificial Intelligence*, AAAI'16, pages 2786–2792. AAAI Press.

Daniel Povey, Arnab Ghoshal, Gilles Boulianne, Lukas Burget, Ondrej Glembek, Nagendra Goel, Mirko Hannemann, Petr Motlicek, Yanmin Qian, Petr Schwarz, et al. 2011. The kaldi speech recognition toolkit. In *IEEE 2011 workshop on automatic speech recognition and understanding*, EPFL-CONF-192584. IEEE Signal Processing Society.

Yao Qian, Rutuja Ubale, Matthew Mulholland, Keelan Evanini, and Xinhao Wang. 2018a. A prompt-aware neural network approach to content-based scoring of non-native spontaneous speech. In *Proceedings of the Spoken Language Technology Workshop*.

Yao Qian, Rutuja Ubale, Matthew Mulholland, Keelan Evanini, and Xinhao Wang. 2018b. A prompt-aware neural network approach to content-based scoring of non-native spontaneous speech. In *Proceedings of the 2018 Workshop on Spoken Language Technology*.

Jidong Tao, Shabnam Ghaffarzadegan, Lei Chen, and Klaus Zechner. 2016. Exploring deep learning architectures for automatically grading non-native spontaneous speech. In *Proceedings of ICASSP*, pages 6140–6144.

Silke Witt and Steve Young. 1997. Performance measures for phone-level pronunciation teaching in CALL. In *Proceedings of STiLL*, pages 99–102.

Shasha Xie, Keelan Evanini, and Klaus Zechner. 2012. Exploring content features for automated speech scoring. In *Proceedings of NAACL*, pages 103–111.

Helen Yannakoudakis and Ted Briscoe. 2012. Modeling coherence in ESOL learner texts. In *Proceedings of the Seventh Workshop on Building Educational Applications Using NLP*, pages 33–43. Association for Computational Linguistics.

Wenpeng Yin, Hinrich Schütze, Bing Xiang, and Bowen Zhou. 2015. ABCNN: Attention-based convolutional neural network for modeling sentence pairs. *arXiv preprint arXiv:1512.05193*.

Su-Youn Yoon and Suma Bhat. 2012. Assessment of esl learners' syntactic competence based on similarity measures. In *Proceedings of EMNLP*, pages 600–608.

Su-Youn Yoon and Suma Bhat. 2018. A comparison of grammatical proficiency measures in the automated assessment of spontaneous speech. *Speech Communication*, 99:221–230.

Su-Youn Yoon, Anastassia Loukina, Chong Min Lee, Matthew Mulholland, Xinhao Wang, and Ikkyu Choi. 2018. Word-embedding based content features for automated oral proficiency scoring. In *Proceedings of the Third Workshop on Semantic Deep Learning*, pages 12–22.

Klaus Zechner, Derrick Higgins, Xiaoming Xi, and David M. Williamson. 2009. Automatic scoring of non-native spontaneous speech in tests of spoken English. *Speech Communication*, 51(10):883–895.

Matthew D Zeiler and Rob Fergus. 2014. Visualizing and understanding convolutional networks. In *European conference on computer vision*, pages 818–833. Springer.

Learning Outcomes and Their Relatedness in a Medical Curriculum

Sneha Mondal[1], Tejas Indulal Dhamecha[1], Shantanu Godbole[1], Smriti Pathak[2], Red Mendoza[3],
K Gayathri Wijayarathna[3], Nabil Zary[3], Swarnadeep Saha[1], Malolan Chetlur[1]
[1]IBM Research - India
[2]Imperial College, London
[3]Lee Kong Chian School of Medicine, Nanyang Technological University, Singapore
{snmondal, tidhamecha, shantanugodbole, swarnads, mchetlur}@in.ibm.com,
smriti.pathak@kcl.ac.uk, {mendozaredante, gwkumari, nabil.zary}@ntu.edu.sg

Abstract

A typical medical curriculum is organized in a hierarchy of instructional objectives called Learning Outcomes (LOs); a few thousand LOs span five years of study. Gaining a thorough understanding of the curriculum requires learners to recognize and apply related LOs across years, and across different parts of the curriculum. However, given the large scope of the curriculum, manually labeling related LOs is tedious, and almost impossible to scale. In this paper, we build a system that learns relationships between LOs, and we achieve up to human-level performance in the LO relationship extraction task. We then present an application where the proposed system is employed to build a map of related LOs and Learning Resources (LRs) pertaining to a virtual patient case. We believe that our system enables building educational tools to help medical students grasp the curriculum better, within classroom and Intelligent Tutoring Systems (ITS) settings.

1 Introduction

Learning Outcomes (LOs) encapsulate discrete knowledge components and provide a framework for curriculum planning, teaching, learning, and assessment. In this work, we study the curriculum of the Lee Kong Chian School of Medicine, Nanyang Technological University, Singapore. At the highest level, their curriculum is organized into major *Themes*, which branch into *Fundamentals*, and further into *Fundamental Units*. A Fundamental Unit is comprised of multiple related *Topics*, and each topic constitutes several LOs. Thus, related LOs get grouped together at multiple levels of increasing granularity. This hierarchy is hand-curated by medical experts and represents a well-formed, well-understood body of knowledge.

However, qualitative evidence suggests that sig-

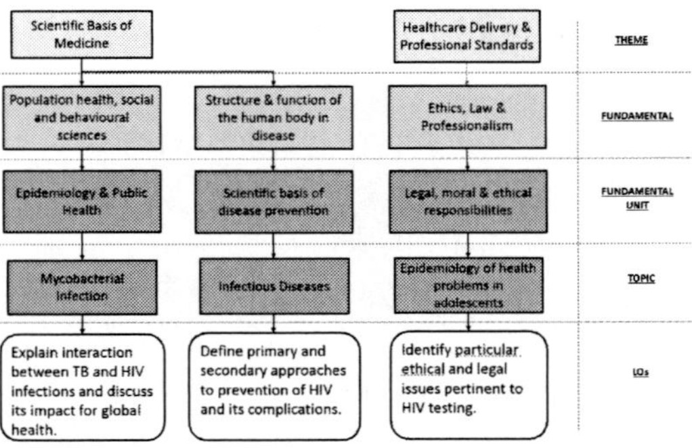

Figure 1: Related Learning Outcomes placed far apart in the expert-curated curriculum hierarchy.

nificant relationships exist between LOs placed far apart in the curriculum; these relationships cannot be uncovered without explicit expert intervention. Figure 1 illustrates one such instance, where LOs drawn from disjoint sections of the curriculum hierarchy are related as they address multiple aspects of HIV treatment.

Our main motivation in this work is to automatically discover LO relationships that cannot be accessed by a straightforward navigation of the curriculum. Extracting such LO relationships can help build a knowledge-base that can be foundational to various educational tools. To this end, we propose looking into the semantic content of disparate LOs, in addition to their relatedness specified by the curriculum hierarchy. We formulate this as a three-class classification task. Given a pair of LOs, they are categorized as being either strongly related or weakly related, or unrelated.

Although the current study is limited to a medical curriculum, our approach is general. Techniques reported in this paper would extend to any curricula that take a 'design down' approach (Harden, 2002), where related LOs are nested in a hierarchical order. An LO-relationship extraction tool that utilizes both semantic and curricu-

Proceedings of the Fourteenth Workshop on Innovative Use of NLP for Building Educational Applications, pages 402–411
Florence, Italy, August 2, 2019. ©2019 Association for Computational Linguistics

lum cues, can be exploited by Intelligent Tutoring Systems (ITS) to suggest useful interventions to both learners and instructors. Potential applications include: a) improved content recommendation, by proactively suggesting pre-requisites or guiding the learner to discover LOs that are related across disjoint sections of the curriculum; b) designing better assessment items which test a learner on closely related LOs; and c) accurate learner modeling, by taking into account all related LOs when tracking the progress of a learner's mastery of an LO. Building upon these motivations, this work documents our efforts to answer the following research questions :

RQ1: *Which features determine relatedness between LOs?* Information available to us is both structured (by way of a well-defined curriculum hierarchy), as well as unstructured (by way of free text descriptions of LOs). We aim to devise a method to appropriately integrate the two in order to compare two LOs.

RQ2: By design, LOs are crisp and compact. A drawback of their conciseness is that they do not provide enough information to ascertain relatedness with other, similarly concise LOs. So, we ask, *can the resources linked to LOs be suitably leveraged to improve the quality of LO-relationship extraction?*

RQ3: *Are there any latent factors beyond curriculum and semantic similarity establishing relatedness among LOs?* If so, are they exploited by the proposed approach?

RQ4: *Can LO relatedness be used to understand a virtual patient case?* Disparate LOs of disease and symptoms could be related in the context of a case. We leverage the LO relationship extraction system to understand the context of a case, and build a case map from relevant concepts.

2   Related Work

Intelligent Tutoring Systems (ITS) greatly improve students' user experience, even in comparison to human tutors (Aleven et al., 2004; Van-Lehn, 2011). Automated methods for creating domain ontology from text have been explored in (Zouaq and Nkambou, 2008). While most previous work employ semantic networks with frames and production rules (Stankov et al., 2008), we tap into state-of-the-art AI - based techniques to *learn* semantic relationship between LOs, as opposed to enumerating rules to generate them. Our work comes close in spirit to that of (John et al.,

2015), that seek to generate knowledge graphs for closely related math word problems. They employ a random-walk paradigm on a graph whose edges are weighed by tf-idf based cosine similarity. Unlike them, we exploit the existing medical curriculum hierarchy, and use a suite of semantic features extending beyond tf-idf.

Graphs have been widely used to establish prerequisite relationships between domain knowledge concepts (Chen et al., 2015; Käser et al., 2014), where a link between concepts indicates a prerequisite-outcome relation. Guerra et al. (2015) represent a student model as a graph where links are gradually added between pairs of knowledge concepts when a student is able to work with aforementioned pairs in the same context. Similarly, Rihák and Pelánek (2017) group similar knowledge concepts using learners' performance data and response time metadata. However, missing here are relations between knowledge concepts already encoded in the curriculum and its textual content.

There is a parallel thread of work on Semantic Textual Similarity (STS), which measures the degree of equivalence in the underlying semantics of paired snippets of text (Agirre et al., 2015, 2016, 2012). This aligns with our work since it is also posed as a natural language understanding problem. However, techniques explored within the ambit of STS are agnostic to any domain specific ontology. This is a major drawback for our application, as the medical curriculum embodies pertinent domain information, which, as we later show, goes a long way in establishing accurate relationships between LOs.

To the best of our knowledge, we are the first to exploit expert-annotated data from an extensively detailed medical curriculum for the LO-relationship extraction task. By establishing semantic relationships among the curriculum concepts, we bridge the gulf between hand-curated domain-specific ontologies and state-of-the-art data driven textual similarity measures, and show its utility in understanding a patient case.

3   Curriculum and Problem Statement

In this section, we briefly describe the organization of LOs in the medical curriculum, and formulate the problem statement.

Medical Curriculum :   The curriculum content is designed around 3 *Themes* that run throughout the programme: 1) Scientific Basis of Medicine,

Relation with Ref. LO	LO	Fundamental unit	Fundamental
-	**Reference LO:** Explain the normal development of the embryonic heart	Embryology	Human Structure & Function
Strong	**LO1:** Explain how the pulmonary and systemic circulations are linked in fetal life	Embryology	Human Structure & Function
Weak	**LO2:** Explain the mechanisms underlying Starling's Law of the Heart	Anatomy/ Physiology	Human Structure & Function
None	**LO3:** List the clinical uses of pulse oximetry	History, Exam. and MSE	Integrated Clinical Practice

Table 1: Example LO relationships along with their placement in curriculum hierarchy.

2) Clinical Management and Patient Centred Care, and 3) Healthcare Delivery and Professional Standards. The themes correspond to cognition, attitude, and skills of the spiral curriculum, as suggested by Harden (1999).

Figure 1 depicts the organization of LOs into themes that consist of *Fundamentals*, branching in order into *Fundamental Units* and *Topics*. Additionally, an LO is not constrained to belong to a unique fundamental unit, and may span a small *set* of relevant themes, fundamentals and fundamental units. Overall, our curriculum contains $4,251$ LOs, organized into 670 Topics, 81 Fundamental Units, and 16 Fundamentals.

Learning Outcomes and Resures : In addition, curriculum designers have manually linked a majority of the LOs to relevant study material, termed Learning Resource (LR). These LRs could be selected pages from textbooks, transcripts of video lectures, links to online reading material, or extracts from presentations. In this work, we restrict ourselves to LRs that are well-curated slide decks, in the form of pdf files. We also note that all LOs and corresponding LRs are authored in English.

3.1 Problem Statement

Since our goal is to predict the degree of relatedness between a pair of LOs, we define our problem statement as follows: Given two LOs and their positions in the curriculum, classify the relationship between them as Strong, Weak, or None. More precisely, we seek to learn a function that, for a pair of LOs p and q, maps them to one of three possible classes, i.e.,

$$f : (p, q) \rightarrow \{\texttt{Strong}, \texttt{Weak}, \texttt{None}\}$$

Such a function could then be employed to predict relationships between any unseen pair of LOs.

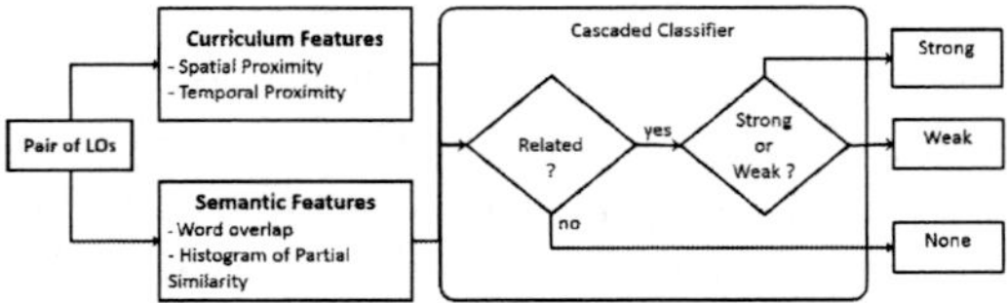

Figure 2: Proposed approach to classify an LO pair.

Expert-annotated Data : Annotations are obtained from Subject Matter Experts (SMEs), who are both doctors and faculty. The annotated data consists of pairs of LOs, each pair labeled as Strong, Weak, or None. Additionally, SMEs were requested to provide guided comments to help us understand their mechanism for coping with ambiguity. For a subset of LO-pairs, annotations were obtained separately from two SMEs to ascertain inter-annotator agreement.

4 Proposed Solution

Our approach for LO-relationship extraction is summarized in the block diagram in Figure 2. The pipeline involves choosing features meaningful for the task, followed by a cascaded classifier design. In sections that follow, we detail and motivate individual components of the pipeline. Subsequently, we investigate the benefit of employing LRs and additional metadata in our task.

4.1 Features

Observations from data indicate that two classes of features, curriculum and semantic, are critical for LO-relationship extraction. Thus, final representation for a pair of LOs is the concatenation of their curriculum and semantic features.

4.1.1 Curriculum-based Features

Curriculum-based features characterize the relative position of LOs within the curriculum hierarchy, which is used to obtain spatial and temporal proximity estimates, as follows:

Spatial Proximity: We hypothesize that the closer LOs are located in the curriculum hierarchy, the more likely they are to be related. In Table 1, we compare a reference LO against LOs that are placed gradually farther in the curriculum (same fundamental unit, separate fundamental units within the same fundamental, and separate fundamentals, respectively). In this specific example, we note that the degree of relatedness decreases with decreasing spatial proximity from the reference LO.

As discussed in previously, each LO may span multiple fundamentals, fundamental units, and themes. For LOs p and q, let their set of themes, fundamentals, and fundamental units be $T_{i \in \{p,q\}}$, $F_{i \in \{p,q\}}$, and $U_{i \in \{p,q\}}$, respectively. Proximity of the LO pair is represented as:

$$SP(p, q) = [J(T_p, T_q), J(F_p, F_q), J(U_p, U_q)]$$

where Jaccard similarity J between sets A and B is defined as $J(A, B) = |A \cap B| / |A \cup B|$.

Temporal Proximity: Related concepts are taught successively within a course curriculum, hence, the time of delivery of LOs is an indicator of their relatedness. For LOs p and q, let $y_{i \in \{p,q\}}$ and $w_{i \in \{p,q\}}$ be their year and week of delivery, respectively. Temporal proximity is then encoded as

$$TP(p, q) = [|y_p - y_q|, |w_p - w_q|]$$

The year information is encoded separately since curriculum focus differs year-wise, i.e., content taught in the last week of year 1 may not always be related to first week of year 2.

4.1.2 Semantic Features

While curriculum hierarchy encodes one paradigm for grouping related LOs, it misses the rich semantic information contained in the text of the LO. Revisiting our example, consider the LOs : 1) *Identify the particular ethical and legal issues pertinent to HIV testing.* and 2) *List some of the common HIV indicator conditions and HIV-related opportunistic infections.* They are far apart in the hierarchy, however there exists a `Strong` relationship between them as they are related in the context of treating an HIV-infected patient. Thus

we explore features that encode semantic similarity between LOs.

Embedding based Features: Semantic relatedness between LOs is often encapsulated by the similarity of their constituent tokens. As an example, the LOs : 1) *List the common symptoms of sudden cardiac arrest*, and 2) *List the common symptoms of myocardial infarction*, are related since term pairs (*cardiac, myocardial*) and (*arrest, infarction*) refer to similar entities. Since exact token matching (as in Eq. 2) is deficient in modelling such semantic overlap, we utilize word embeddings (Chiu et al., 2016) to represent individual tokens, which are further used to compute the following similarity measures.

- **Word Overlap:** Each LO text is treated as a bag-of-words. We define that a word w_i in LO p overlaps with a word w_j in LO q, if their cosine similarity in the word embedding space exceeds a certain threshold δ. Based on this *soft* matching of words, we define semantic word overlap to be the fraction of matching word pairs across the two bags-of-words, as:

$$WO(p, q) = \frac{\sum_{w_i \in p} \sum_{w_j \in q} \mathbf{1}\left[\cos(\mathbf{w_i}, \mathbf{w_j}) \geq \delta\right]}{|p||q|} \quad (1)$$

where $\mathbf{1}[\cdot]$ is an operator that evaluates to 1 if corresponding condition is True, and 0 otherwise.

- **Histogram of Partial Similarities (HoPS):** We employ HoPS (Saha et al., 2018) to model the *similarity profile* between two LOs. For each word w_i in LO p, first its similarity score is computed with respect to LO q as:

$$S(w_i, q) = \max_{w_j \in q} \cos\left(\mathbf{w_i}, \mathbf{w_j}\right), \text{ where } w_i \in p$$

This strategy pairs each word in LO p with its closest matching counterpart in LO q. These similarity scores are then partitioned into N bins and normalized, resulting in a histogram of scores for p. We obtain another normalized histogram by binning the similarity scores for each word in q with respect to p.

$$HoPS(p, q) = [\text{Histogram}\left(\{S(w_i, q) | w_i \in p\}\right), \\ \text{Histogram}\left(\{S(w_j, p) | w_j \in q\}\right)]$$

Unlike word overlap, HoPS considers all tokens in the LO text without thresholding on a similarity score, and hence provides a more granular similarity profile between LOs.

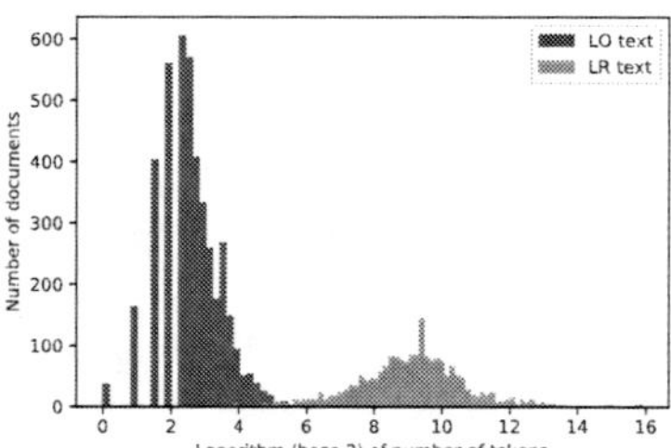

Figure 3: Distribution of the length of LO and LR texts on a logarithmic scale.

TF-IDF based Feature: For LOs p and q, let $\mathbf{p} \in R^{|v|}$ and $\mathbf{q} \in R^{|v|}$ be their respective representations as tf-idf vectors (Ramos et al., 2003); where v is the vocabulary set. Then tf-idf based similarity is encoded as their absolute difference and Hadamard product

$$TI(p,q) = [|\mathbf{p} - \mathbf{q}|, \mathbf{p} \circ \mathbf{q}] \qquad (2)$$

Essentially, our representation encodes the information gap between LOs in a pair, in terms of their exact token overlap weighed by importance of said token in the LO corpus.

The final feature representation for an LO pair is the concatenation of spatial proximity, temporal proximity, word-overlap, and HoPS features. As explained in Section 5, we drop the tf-idf based feature owing to its poor performance. Instead, it serves as a useful baseline for comparison with word-overlap and HoPS based semantic features.

4.2 Learning Resources

What makes "understanding" the curriculum particularly challenging is the diversity of curriculum documents. The length of an LO text varies considerably, as does the scope of its underpinning concept. While a few LOs are independent, most are better understood in the context of their LRs, which elaborate on the dense information contained in the LO. In fact, Figure 3 depicts that most LOs are pithy, comprising fewer than 50 tokens (median token length = 6). In sharp contrast, LRs are lengthy documents with extensive detail (median token length = 578).

Whenever an LO is linked to an LR, we can obtain features from both of them. As mentioned in Section 3, LRs are well-curated slide decks. Inspired from Query Expansion (Vechtomova and Wang, 2006), we append the bold text from all slides of the linked LR to the LO text. Various semantic features, as detailed in Section 4.1.2, are

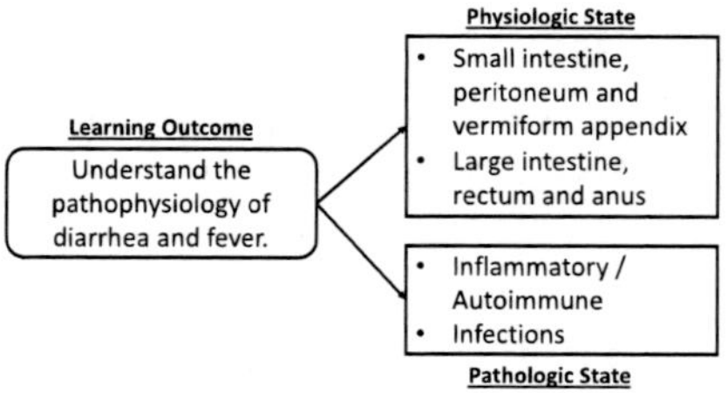

Figure 4: An LO annotated with relevant Physiologic and Pathologic states.

then extracted from the expanded LO text and utilized in the proposed pipeline.

4.3 Expert Medical Codes (EMC)

To further enrich the feature space, we incorporate additional domain specific knowledge. For each LO, SMEs added a medical code indicating its 1) location or physiologic (Phys.) state, and/or 2) disease or pathologic (Patho.) state.

The physiologic code of an LO indicates the organ system it deals with, whereas the pathologic code specifies the nature of the disease or dysfunction covered by the LO. Experts hand-curated a total of 13 distinct physiologic states and 7 distinct pathologic states. Each LO could pertain to multiple physiologic and pathologic states, as depicted in Figure 4. Overlap between the EMCs of an LO pair is encoded as:

Categorical Similarity: Jaccard indices are obtained between 1) pathologic states and 2) physiologic states of the LOs in a pair, to ascertain overlap between their respective medical codes.

Semantic Similarity: While categorical similarity treats each physiologic and pathologic code as a distinct label, closer inspection reveals that there is inherent relatedness among the codes. For instance, the physiologic state "Pulmonary/Lung and Pleura" is closer in meaning to the state "Larynx, trachea, bronchi and alveoli", than it is to state "Renal/Kidney". Thus, while comparing two LOs, we encode the word overlap of their respective medical codes as detailed in Eq. 1.

The final representation for the EMCs of an LO-pair is the concatenation of categorical similarity and semantic similarity features of the codes.

4.4 Cascaded Classification

A crucial aspect of this dataset is its extreme class imbalance. As Tables 2 and 3 demonstrate, LO pairs with `None` relationship vastly outnumber `Strong` or `Weak` pairs. This is to be expected, since the medical curriculum is extensive, and a

Confusion Matrix		Annotator 1			Total
		`Strong`	`Weak`	`None`	
Annotator 2	`Strong`	54	24	1	79
	`Weak`	38	64	25	127
	`None`	1	22	323	346
	Total	93	110	349	552
Macro-Average F1= 69.9, Accuracy= 79.9					

Table 2: Inter-Annotator agreement between two experts on the test set (note the substantial disagreement in annotating LO pairs as `Strong` and `Weak`).

Dataset	`Strong`	`Weak`	`None`	Total
Train	235 (14%)	344 (20%)	1,145 (66%)	1,724
Test	79 (14%)	127 (23%)	346 (63%)	552
Total	314 (14%)	471 (21%)	1,491 (65%)	2,276

Table 3: Train-Test splits. Note the class imbalance.

particular LO is likely to be related only to a small number of other LOs scattered in the curriculum.

While the priors of `Strong` and `Weak` classes are low, the risk in missclassifying them is high. Failure to identify a `Strong` LO pair is more detrimental than failure to identify a `None` pair. When we fail to recommend an LO strongly related to the one that a student is currently pursuing, it leads to a gap in their knowledge acquisition, whereas recommending an unrelated LO only leads to a degradation in user experience.

Additionally, we believe that the semantic gap between the three class labels is not identical. While it is relatively easier to distinguish `None` from `Strong` or `Weak`, the separation between `Strong` and `Weak` pairs is not as discernible. This is borne out further by the inter-annotator agreement in Table 2; for a large number of LO pairs, expert annotators disagree between `Strong` and `Weak` labels.

Aforementioned factors prompt us to split the 3-way classification task into two sequential binary classification tasks, as illustrated in Figure 2. The first classifier is trained on all input LO pairs, and classifies them as `Related` or `Unrelated`. In the next step, `Related` LO pairs are passed to the second classifier, which learns the degree of the relationship and further classifies them as `Strong` or `Weak`. LO pairs classified as `Unrelated` by the first classifier are directly labeled as `None`.

5 Experiments and Results

In all our experiments, we use NLTK for stop-word removal and scikit-learn for the classifiers. We use $N = 20$ bins for HoPS features and set similarity threshold $\delta = 0.6$ for embedding-based features. We trained an SVM and Random For-

est model for our task. Owing to space constraints and sub-par performance of the SVM, we report results for a Random Forest classifier with 100 estimators; all other parameters of the model are tuned using 5-fold cross validation on the training data. We use macro-F1 of the classifier on held out test data as our metric. Mean and standard deviations of macro-F1 are reported over 10 runs of the random forest. We use `BioNLP`(Chiu et al., 2016) word-embeddings.

For a subset of 552 LO-pairs, we obtain separate annotations from two SMEs. Inter-annotator performance (Table 2) on this held-out test set serves as a *skyline* for comparative evaluation. Owing to data-labeling constraints, only a subset of LOs could be linked to respective LRs by the SMEs. Similarly, tagging LOs with one of several possible physiologic/pathologic states entails significant cognitive engagement, and could be done only for a subset of LOs. For uniformity, we ensured that both subsets have a class label distribution identical to the total distribution in Table 3.

We perform three sets of experiments to 1) evaluate the effectiveness of the proposed approach, 2) evaluate the utility of LRs, and 3) evaluate utility of expert medical codes (EMC).

5.1 Evaluation

We compare five feature variants in an ablated study. Since the proposed approach stipulates curriculum and semantic features (CR+SM), we perform a comparison when individual curriculum (CR) or semantic features (SM) are used. To gauge the efficacy of tf-idf based features, experiments are performed using these features alone (TF), and along with curriculum features (CR+TF). For each feature variant, we contrast results obtained with a baseline 3-way monolithic classifier, and the proposed cascaded classifier. In the monolithic classifier, we ensure that the misclassification penalty for each class is inversely proportional to its frequency in the training data. This accounts for class imbalance, and ensures fair comparison against the cascaded classifier. Results of experiments are reported in Table 4. Our the key observations are :
Exact vs Embedding-based Features: Tf-idf features (TF) perform exact token matching which gets derailed whenever similar concepts are addressed differently (such as *myocardial* and *cardiac*). Instead, embedding-based features (SM) are more adept at capturing semantic relatedness as by construction, context vectors for related con-

Features	Classifiers	
	Baseline	Cascaded
CR	57.6±2.5	58.8±2.9
TF	43.1±0.9	49.8±1.2
CR+TF	53.2±1.3	55.9±2.0
SM	58.4±2.0	59.9±1.8
CR+SM	**63.6±1.1**	**66.1±2.3**
Inter-annotator agreement: 69.9		

Table 4: Macro-F1 (mean±std) values on the test set for two classifier variants and different features.

Features	Classifiers	
	Baseline	Cascaded
CR+SM without LR	63.3±1.5	65.9±1.3
CR+SM with LR	65.1±2.2	**67.2±1.7**
Inter-annotator agreement: 70.0		

Table 5: Macro-F1 (mean±std) on LR-linked test set.

Features	Classifiers	
	Baseline	Cascaded
CR	65.8±2.3	68.1±2.1
SM	64.8±3.2	68.3±2.9
CR+SM	**70.5±2.4**	**72.6±2.0**
CR+SM+EMC	69.9±2.5	72.9± 2.3

Table 6: Macro-F1 (mean±std) values on ten random splits comparing the baseline, and inclusion of EMCs.

cepts are closely located in the embedding space. Similarly, CR+SM outperforms CR+TF.

Importance of Feature Concatenation: A combination of both curriculum and semantic features (CR+SM) significantly outperforms their individual performance. Answering **RQ1**, we conclude that curriculum and semantics encode distinct aspects of an LO-pair's relatedness, and our system improves when information encoded in each feature class is jointly represented.

Effectiveness of Cascaded Classifier: For all feature combinations, the cascaded classifier outperforms the monolithic baseline. This supports our hypothesis that the decision boundary between `Related` (`Strong + Weak`) and `Unrelated` pairs is more discernible than the decision boundary between `Strong` and `Weak`.

For the rest of our experiments, we utilize CR+SM features with a cascaded classifier, since this combination yields best results, and approaches near human performance (refer Table 4). The proposed pipeline can now be used to establish LO relationships on the whole curriculum. This effectively circumvents the scale problem that manual annotation of all LO-pairs ($\sim$1 million) in the curriculum entails, while maintaining the accuracy of an expert.

5.2 Utility of Learning Resources

As reported in Table 5, it is clear that using LR text along with LO text improves LO-relationship extraction. This satisfactorily answers the question raised in **RQ2**. The dearth of adequate information and context in a concise LO poses a challenge for data-driven methods to ascertain semantic relatedness. LRs help plug this gap since they are

more detailed and help expand the scope of both of our algorithms.

5.3 Utility of EMCs

Using features extracted from EMCs (detailed in Section 4.3), we compare the following combinations : curriculum (CR), semantic (SM), proposed concatenation of both (CR+SM), and subsequent concatenation with features from EMCs (CR+SM+EMC). Table 6 reports comparative results over 10 random 75-25% train-test splits.

We note that contrary to expectation, inclusion of EMC features (CR+SM+EMC) does *not* improve over CR+SM. We hypothesize that this may be because the classifier trained over CR+SM features learns an intermediate representation that correlates closely with the patho and physio states, thus their explicit inclusion provides no additional information to the classifier. While we may not know precisely what form the internal representation takes, it is interesting to note that our handcrafted features (CR+SM) and cascaded classifier design are both powerful enough to uncover underlying patterns of similarity between LOs. To answer **RQ3**, our approach does exploit latent patterns in the data.

6 Case Map Generation

The LO relationship extraction system can be applied to uncover LOs relevant to a virtual patient case (thus addressing **RQ4**). A virtual patient case describes a real-life scenario where a patient presents at the clinic with certain symptoms, and is administered specific tests. The medical student is expected to assume the role of a health-care professional and develop clinical skills such as making diagnoses and therapeutic decisions.

Figure 5 depicts part of a clinical case that has been annotated by SMEs. Crucial aspects of the case are highlighted as clinical factors, which may be symptoms (fever, hypotension, etc.) as well as diagnostic and screening tests. Each clinical factor is further linked to few pertinent *anchor* LOs. Successfully addressing a virtual patient case involves understanding these LOs, which may be

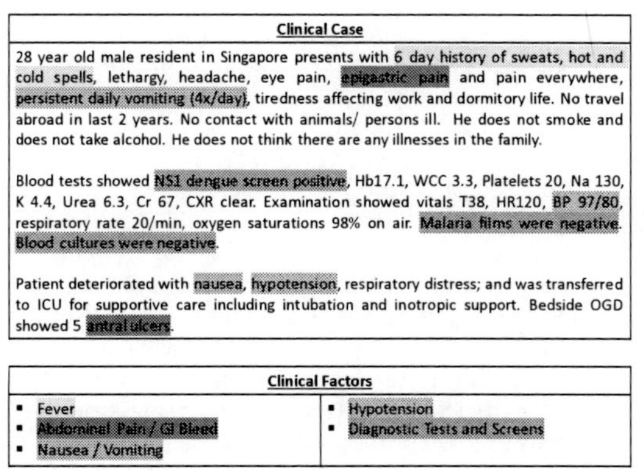

Clinical Case

28 year old male resident in Singapore presents with 6 day history of sweats, hot and cold spells, lethargy, headache, eye pain, epigastric pain and pain everywhere, persistent daily vomiting (4x/day), tiredness affecting work and dormitory life. No travel abroad in last 2 years. No contact with animals/ persons ill. He does not smoke and does not take alcohol. He does not think there are any illnesses in the family.

Blood tests showed NS1 dengue screen positive, Hb17.1, WCC 3.3, Platelets 20, Na 130, K 4.4, Urea 6.3, Cr 67, CXR clear. Examination showed vitals T38, HR120, BP 97/80, respiratory rate 20/min, oxygen saturations 98% on air. Malaria films were negative. Blood cultures were negative.

Patient deteriorated with nausea, hypotension, respiratory distress; and was transferred to ICU for supportive care including intubation and inotropic support. Bedside OGD showed 5 antral ulcers.

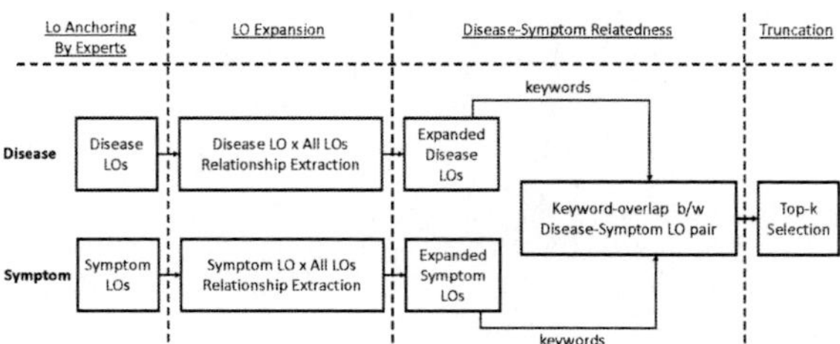

Clinical Factors

- Fever
- Abdominal Pain / GI Bleed
- Nausea / Vomiting
- Hypotension
- Diagnostic Tests and Screens

Figure 5: Annotated clinical case.

Figure 6: An approach to generate case map based on proposed LO-relationship extraction.

LO ID	LO Text
LO_6704	Recall the clinical presentation and management of Dengue fever and Chikungunya infection
LO_4880	Describe how the presence of a viral infection may trigger off production of endogenous pyrogens leading to development of fever
LO_4881	Describe how bacterial infections may produce exogenous pyrogens resulting in the development of fever
LO_4882	Briefly describe how fever complements the immune response in infection
LO_6170	List the other abdominal organs that maybe responsible for abdominal pain
LO_6174	Explain the pathways controlling vomiting and nausea
LO_6175	Recall the use of vomiting patterns in differential diagnosis
LO_7793	Describe the role of relevant investigations for fever, including: Blood tests - hematology, chemistries, serology; Clinical samples - blood, respiratory, stool, urine, body fluids; Microbiology tests - cultures, PCR, serology; Imaging - Xrays, CT, MRI, ultrasound
LO_7794	Describe the role of relevant investigations for common infections, specific pathogens including dengue, malaria, typhoid, HIV, TB, MRSA
LO_7834	Define (and perform if relevant) appropriate resuscitation , immediate life support and acute management of: septic shock, neutropenic sepsis, dengue shock syndrome, severe malaria, acute bacterial meningitis

Table 7: Identifiers and text of the LOs that are part of the generated case graph in Figure 7 .

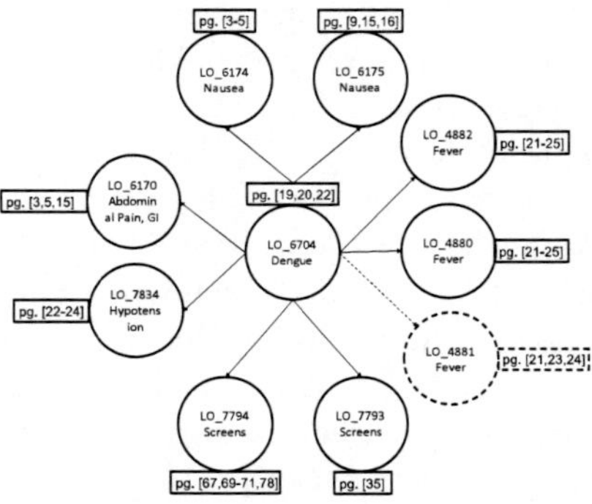

Figure 7: Case map extracted using proposed approach (see Table 7 for LO text corresponding to the LO IDs).

drawn from different years and disjoint sections of the curriculum. We aim to construct a *case map* that provides learners with a comprehensive view of the clinical case, in terms of its constituent LOs and their relationships. The map is envisioned as a graph, where nodes represent LOs, and edges establish relationships between them.

In attempting this, we encounter two primary challenges: 1) While SMEs can annotate a few anchor LOs, it is not feasible to manually enumerate all LOs related to the virtual patient case. This calls for an accurate LO-relationship extraction system that does not rely on expert intervention. 2) We must guarantee that these LOs are related within the context of the case. Since LOs by themselves do not provide enough textual content, we must look to LRs to ascertain whether LOs proposed by the system are appropriate in the context of the case at hand.

Given a disease, its symptoms, and diagnostic tests, we assume the availability of anchor LOs pertaining to each of them, and propose an approach outlined in Figure 6.

LO Expansion: The LO-relationship extraction system sequentially pairs an anchor LO with every LO in the curriculum, and classifies the rela-tionship between them. For our purpose, we retain LOs that are labeled `Strong`, and disregard the rest. Thus, starting with a small set of anchor LOs, we obtain an expanded set of LOs that is strongly related to them.

Disease-Symptom Relatedness: We pair a disease-specific LO with a symptom (or diagnosis) specific LO, and measure the semantic overlap between their linked LRs. Higher the overlap, more relevant is the symptom (or diagnosis) LO to the disease LO. Thus, for each symptom (or diagnosis), their LOs are ranked by relevance to the disease LOs.

Truncation: The ranked list can be pruned to select the topmost k symptom (or diagnosis) LOs. Truncation ensures that for each symptom (or diagnosis), we select high-precision relationships with the disease specific LOs (characterized by overlap between their LRs). In the case map, this translates to at most k edges between a disease and each of its symptoms.

Figure 7 depicts the constructed case map for

the dengue clinical case presented in Figure 5. Of the five clinical factors, four correspond to symptoms, namely : 1) Fever, 2) Abdominal Pain and GI bleed, 3) Nausea and Vomiting, and 4) Hypotension. The last factor corresponds to diagnostic tests and screens for dengue. We set $k = 3$, permitting at most 3 edges between dengue and each clinical factor. The generated case map was evaluated by an SME; one LO (LO_4881) is found to be spuriously a part of the map, whereas rest of the connections are deemed valid, thus establishing the efficacy of our approach.

7 Conclusion and Future Work

This work summarizes our effort to extract LO relationships using both semantic and curriculum cues. Owing to its human-level performance, our system serves as a reliable building block in constructing a case map from a virtual patient case.

Going forward, we would like to generate a concept map for all five years of the curriculum. We could then employ network analysis tools to uncover central LOs that drive most of the linkages. Secondly, we would like to *characterize* relationships between edges. Given a pair of related LOs, a simple characterization would be to assert if one of them is a pre-requisite to the other. Besides, we have observed that the classifier learns an intermediate representation that corresponds closely to EMCs. We could investigate if this can be harnessed to *predict* the states, thereby enriching curriculum metadata.

References

Eneko Agirre, Carmen Banea, Claire Cardie, Daniel Cer, Mona Diab, Aitor Gonzalez-Agirre, Weiwei Guo, Inigo Lopez-Gazpio, Montse Maritxalar, Rada Mihalcea, et al. 2015. Semeval-2015 task 2: Semantic textual similarity, english, spanish and pilot on interpretability. In *Proceedings of the 9th international workshop on semantic evaluation (SemEval 2015)*, pages 252–263.

Eneko Agirre, Carmen Banea, Daniel Cer, Mona Diab, Aitor Gonzalez-Agirre, Rada Mihalcea, German Rigau, and Janyce Wiebe. 2016. Semeval-2016 task 1: Semantic textual similarity, monolingual and cross-lingual evaluation. In *Proceedings of the 10th International Workshop on Semantic Evaluation (SemEval-2016)*, pages 497–511.

Eneko Agirre, Mona Diab, Daniel Cer, and Aitor Gonzalez-Agirre. 2012. Semeval-2012 task 6: A pilot on semantic textual similarity. In *Proceedings of the First Joint Conference on Lexical and Computational Semantics-Volume 1: Proceedings of the main conference and the shared task, and Volume 2: Proceedings of the Sixth International Workshop on Semantic Evaluation*, pages 385–393. Association for Computational Linguistics.

Vincent Aleven, Amy Ogan, Octav Popescu, Cristen Torrey, and Kenneth Koedinger. 2004. Evaluating the effectiveness of a tutorial dialogue system for self-explanation. In *International Conference on Intelligent Tutoring Systems*, pages 443–454. Springer.

Yang Chen, Pierre-Henr Wuillemin, and Jean-Marc Labat. 2015. Discovering prerequisite structure of skills through probabilistic association rules mining. *International Educational Data Mining Society*.

Billy Chiu, Gamal Crichton, Anna Korhonen, and Sampo Pyysalo. 2016. How to train good word embeddings for biomedical NLP. In *Proceedings of the 15th workshop on biomedical natural language processing*, pages 166–174.

Julio Guerra, Yun Huang, Roya Hosseini, and Peter Brusilovsky. 2015. Graph analysis of student model networks. In *CEUR Workshop Proceedings*, volume 1446. University of Pittsburgh.

R.M. Harden. 1999. What is a spiral curriculum? *Medical Teacher*, 21(2):141–143. PMID: 21275727.

R.M. Harden. 2002. Learning outcomes and instructional objectives: is there a difference? *Medical Teacher*, 24(2):151–155. PMID: 12098434.

Rogers Jeffrey Leo John, Thomas S McTavish, and Rebecca J Passonneau. 2015. Semantic graphs for mathematics word problems based on mathematics terminology. In *EDM (Workshops)*.

Tanja Käser, Severin Klingler, Alexander Gerhard Schwing, and Markus Gross. 2014. Beyond knowledge tracing: Modeling skill topologies with bayesian networks. In *International Conference on Intelligent Tutoring Systems*, pages 188–198. Springer.

Juan Ramos et al. 2003. Using tf-idf to determine word relevance in document queries. In *Proceedings of the first instructional conference on machine learning*, volume 242, pages 133–142.

Jirí Rihák and Radek Pelánek. 2017. Measuring similarity of educational items using data on learners' performance. In *Proceedings of the 10th International Conference on Educational Data Mining (EDM)*, pages 16–23.

Swarnadeep Saha, Tejas I Dhamecha, Smit Marvaniya, Renuka Sindhgatta, and Bikram Sengupta. 2018. Sentence level or token level features for automatic short answer grading?: Use both. In *International Conference on Artificial Intelligence in Education*, pages 503–517. Springer.

Slavomir Stankov, Marko Rosić, Branko Žitko, and Ani Grubišić. 2008. Tex-sys model for building intelligent tutoring systems. *Computers & Education*, 51(3):1017–1036.

Kurt VanLehn. 2011. The relative effectiveness of human tutoring, intelligent tutoring systems, and other tutoring systems. *Educational Psychologist*, 46(4):197–221.

Olga Vechtomova and Ying Wang. 2006. A study of the effect of term proximity on query expansion. *Journal of Information Science*, 32(4):324–333.

Amal Zouaq and Roger Nkambou. 2008. Building domain ontologies from text for educational purposes. *IEEE Transactions on learning technologies*, 1(1):49–62.

Measuring text readability with machine comprehension: a pilot study

Marc Benzahra[1,2] and **François Yvon**[1]
[1]LIMSI, CNRS, Université Paris-Saclay, F-91405 Orsay, France
[2]Glose, 53 rue du rocher, F-75008 Paris, France
{marc.benzahra,francois.yvon}@limsi.fr

Abstract

This article studies the relationship between text readability levels and automatic machine understanding systems. Our hypothesis is that the simpler a text is, the better it should be understood by a machine. We thus expect a strong correlation between readability levels on the one hand, and performance of automatic reading systems on the other hand. We test this hypothesis with several understanding systems based on language models of varying strengths, measuring this correlation on two corpora of journalistic texts. Our results suggest that this correlation is quite small and that existing comprehension systems are far to reproduce the gradual improvement of their performance on texts of decreasing complexity.

1 Introduction

The automatic evaluation of the readability of texts is an old subject (see, for example, (DuBay, 2007) for an historical account), which continues to arouse great interest from the Natural Language Processing (NLP) community; a recent analysis of the state-of-the-art is given by Collins-Thompson (2014). Checking that a written document is expressed in a language that is accessible to its target audience is essential in many situations: for instance to ensure that the information conveyed by the text is properly understood or to allow sufficient engagement of the reader in the reading activity (Dietrich, 2004). These issues are relevant both for the dissemination of general purpose information (e.g. news articles) and more targeted information such as drug leaflets, administrative texts or legal documents. They apply to various readerships: children in first or second language learning situations, adults with varying levels of education or with disabilities, etc.

The classical measures of readability are based on crude approximations of the syntactic complexity (using the average sentence length as a proxy) and lexical complexity (average length in characters or syllables of words in a sentence). One of the most well-known measure along these lines is the Flesch-Kincaid readability index (Kincaid et al., 1975), which combines these two measures into a global score. This approach has recently been renewed by the use of supervised statistical learning methods capable of integrating into the prediction of readability a very large number of linguistic characteristics (Schwarm and Ostendorf, 2005; Petersen and Ostendorf, 2009; Vajjala and Meurers, 2012; François and Fairon, 2012; Vajjala and Meurers, 2014; Brunato et al., 2018) aimed at capturing readability indices at the lexical, syntactic, semantic and even discursive levels. It can be argued that these enhanced feature sets are able to take into account so-called *cognitive* factors (Feng et al., 2009).

However, these approaches depend on the availability of texts annotated with their difficulty levels, which are often defined in relation to a particular task or readership. The elicitation of these annotations is a complex operation, which requires either the implementation of understanding measurement protocols on controlled populations, using for example cloze tests to evaluate understanding (Taylor, 1953; Oller Jr., 1973); or the work of highly qualified experts, at the risk of observing disagreements between annotators (Petersen and Ostendorf, 2009). They also require automatically extracting linguistic features from texts, which existing NLP tools only partially achieve, for a limited number of languages.

In this paper, we study an alternative method that could help assess the readability level of texts in an unsupervised manner. Our main hypothesis, developed in § 2, is that automatic text understanding systems (*machine reading*) having made remarkable progress (Hermann et al., 2015; Dhin-

Proceedings of the Fourteenth Workshop on Innovative Use of NLP for Building Educational Applications, pages 412–422
Florence, Italy, August 2, 2019. ©2019 Association for Computational Linguistics

gra et al., 2017; Yu et al., 2018),[1] it might become possible to use them to assess the readability of texts. The preliminary question of interest here is therefore whether *the ability of automatic comprehension systems to respond to gap-filling questions correlates with the difficulty of the text, and can be help to measure readability*. To answer this question, we study several simplistic machine understanding systems, described in § 2.4 and empirically examine the correlation between their performance and the actual complexity of texts, measured by humans (see § 3). Our main findings are that when comprehension is evaluated using cloze tests, all the systems make very little difference, if any, between texts of varying complexities, suggesting that we should reconsider our evaluation scheme, or our set of comprehension systems, or both, to achieve a behavior that would be more similar to human's performance.

2   Simulating human comprehension

2.1   The design of readability scores

From a bird's eye view, the construction of measures of text readability involves two steps: (a) having human subjects perform controlled comprehension tests on texts of interest, which determine the *empirical readability* of the texts for the concerned population of readers (typically characterized by a level of education, or a level of language proficiency for second language learners); (b) measuring a set of indices in texts that effectively predict empirical readability values and learning the parameters of a function relating these surface cues with difficulty.

The approach we explore relies on the assumption that automatic comprehension systems having greatly improved, it should become possible to use them to simulate step (a) above, and thus to use the results of machine comprehension tests on a given text to directly evaluate its empirical readability, dispensing with the need to perform step (b).

As a first step in this direction, we need to check whether that performance of machine comprehension systems should exhibit a form of dependency to the actual readability of the text: the simpler the text, the better they should be understood by a machine. This is the main question that we empirically address below, using an automatic understanding architecture based on statistical Language Models (LMs), and evaluating the task of automatic comprehension using cloze tests.

A second important question will concern our ability to build comprehension systems that accurately simulate the understanding ability of a target population (of children, of language learners, of people with disabilities, etc). We delay the systematic study of this question for further work, but contend that our methodology is compatible with this objective, as it can handle, as will be seen, the design of comprehension systems of varying strengths.

To reiterate, our objective is to study the performance of comprehension systems as a possible measure of text readability: our final goal is not so much to improve comprehension systems but to see how they could be used as proxies of human comprehension.

2.2   Testing machine comprehension

The measurement of automatic comprehension of texts is an old and difficult issue. By analogy with measures of human understanding, two main methods are commonly used: comprehension questions (Richardson et al., 2013; Rajpurkar et al., 2016) and cloze tests.

The use of cloze tests to assess the performance of comprehension systems has for instance been proposed by Hill et al. (2016), which studies the ability of various neural models to fill in blanks in sentences from children's stories, introducing the CBT (*Children Book Tests*) corpus.

This technique has also been used in several previous studies (Bimbot et al., 2001; Zweig and Burges, 2012) to evaluate language models: the former reference establishes a direct link between perplexity and filling-the-gap tests; the latter introduces the *Sentence Completion Challenge* in which gaps and distractors are carefully selected.

One of the challenges of recent work on this issue is the development of realistic test sets, which can only be answered by a deep understanding of the text (Paperno et al., 2016; Xie et al., 2018), using for instance information regarding words part-of-speech or syntactic role of the deleted word.

---

[1]See however the work of Jia and Liang (2017) or Kaushik and Lipton (2018), who claim that quantitative progresses, measured on standard question answering tasks, mainly reflect an improvement in the ability of these systems to perform surface matches between questions and answers.

Cloze test	Prediction	Ground truth
Herring is a type of fish ____ it swims closer to San Francisco than before. Herring is a favorite food of sea ____ , so they might have followed those fish to ____ . Sea lions might also like the pier because ...	, otters San	, lions shore
They have twin daughters named Barbara and Jenna ____ The family has a dog ____ Barney and a ____ named India.	. **named** **cat**	. **named** **cat**
Neil Armstrong was the first man to step onto the moon . ____ put an American flag up on the moon . ____ brought moon rocks back to ____ .	. **He** **Earth**	He **He** **Earth**

Table 1: Cloze test examples filled with a GPT-2 language model.

2.3 Cloze test generation, completion and evaluation

We stick here to a much simpler form of cloze testing, based on a uniform random strategy to select the deleted words. We leave for future work the use of more sophisticated methods specifically designed to generate difficult tests.

In practice, each test document is automatically divided into N passages of the same size; in each passage, M positions are randomly selected uniformly and correspond to the words that will be blanked out. These words will have to be recovered by the comprehension system, which has access to the complete left context of the gap since the beginning of the passage. In our experiments, we use $N = 5$ and $M = 3$.

One interesting property of cloze tests is that they provide ways to analyze the complexity of gap fillings with respect to arbitrary linguistic lexical descriptors; they also provide ways to compute difficulty levels separately for each sentence and check for instance its dependency with respect to the length of the context. Table 1 shows examples of Cloze tests given to our language models.

Gap filling performance is measured as the average number of words that are correctly predicted in a text (noted p@1) in the tables below. This metric being very strict, we also report the number of times the correct word appears in the first 5, 25, and 50 candidates. Many other techniques could be entertained to weaken the p@1 metric, for example by considering the similarity (formal or distributional) between the predicted word and the reference. Again, we leave the study of these alternative metrics to future work.

2.4 A comprehension architecture based on language models

Our comprehension systems are neural language models based on recurrent structures (RNN) (Elman, 1990; Mikolov et al., 2010) with LSTM cells (Hochreiter and Schmidhuber, 1997), which continue to deliver (near) state-of-the-art results for statistical language modelling (Melis et al., 2018). Once trained, the prediction of a missing word is performed by only looking at its left context, ordering the candidate words w at position t according to $P(w_t = w|w_{<t})$.[2]

Among all the degrees of freedom of the method, we simply varied (a) the quality of models using the same architecture, and (b) the training data. We acknowledge that it would also be possible to use other architectures for language models (e.g. n-grams models (Chen and Goodman, 1999)); to use character-based models (Sutskever et al., 2011; Kim et al., 2016) or subword-based models that could accommodate open vocabularies; or to train more sophisticated RNN models (Yang et al., 2018).

It would likewise be possible to use more complex algorithms to predict missing words (e.g. by using left and right contexts), or even by testing text understanding systems that are more representative to the current state of-the-art (Dhingra et al., 2017; Yu et al., 2018).

As a first step in this direction, we also experiment with a self-attentional language-model (Al-Rfou et al., 2018; Liu et al., 2018) using the Transformer architecture (Vaswani et al., 2017), from

____

[2]In this respect, our use of LMs for readability continues the work of Collins-Thompson and Callan (2004); Petersen and Ostendorf (2009) and many others who used LM scores as a predictor of the complexity level.

	WikiText-2			WikiText-103			Wiki-Simple		
	#params	#epochs	ppl	#params	#epochs	ppl	#params	#epochs	ppl
RNN	19M	100	90	113M	3	87	44M	50	51
AWD	19M	100	78	113M	3	137	44M	50	65

Table 2: Basic statistics regarding language models

the implementation of Radford et al. (2019). Such models are capable to effectively handle very long range dependencies and have been able to achieve good performance on some recent machine comprehension benchmarks.

3 Experiments

In this section, we compare the automatic comprehension measures produced by our language models with readability scores produced by humans, as well as with other automatic standard indices of readability. We start with details regarding the implementation of our language models.

3.1 Language Model Training

3.1.1 Corpora

To train our language models, we use two standard corpora of articles from the English Wikipedia:[3] `WikiText-2` and `WikiText-103`, that have already been used as benchmarks in language modeling tasks (Merity et al., 2017). As can be seen from the statistics in Table 3, these corpora mostly differ in their size and vocabulary.

We also use an additional set of articles from the English version of the simplified Wikipedia:[4] `Wiki-Simple`.[5] Following Merity et al. (2017), this "simple" dataset is pre-processed as follow: tokens with less than 3 occurrences are replaced by the "<unk>" token as in `WikiText-2` and `WikiText-103`.

Source	Docs	Tokens	Types
Wiki-2	720	2.5M	33K
Wiki-103	28 591	103M	260K
Wiki-Simple	60K	7.9M	96K

Table 3: Language model training corpora

All language modelling corpora in Table 3 are tokenized by splitting text for each space separator

(" ") encountered. It is expected that training models on the `Wiki-Simple` corpora should yield poorer gap-filling systems than the other two corpora, as these systems will be exposed to simpler sentence structures and a more basic vocabulary.

3.1.2 LM Implementation issues

Our own RNN language models use the following architecture: 3 hidden layers, each containing 512 recurrent cells. Training starts with randomly initialized embeddings, and is performed using SGD (Robbins and Monro, 1951), dividing by 4 the learning rate (initialized to 30) every 5 epochs if the loss does not decrease. We use a drop-out of 0.1 for the embedding layer, 0.3 for the LSTM layers and 0.4 for the output layer ; the batch size is 64, and backpropagation context is 64. We borrow two additional techniques from Merity et al. (2018): the use of variable-length backpropagation sequences and the use of two regularization terms penalizing the parameters of the output layers: activation regularization and temporal activation regularization (see reference for details). The weight matrices at the output of LSTM after the linear projection and the word embedding are shared to avoid overfitting (Inan et al., 2017; Press and Wolf, 2017) and to reduce the number of parameters. This implementation is referred to as RNN below.

We contrast our implementation with that of Merity et al. (2018)[6] trained with the same parameter values as our RNN implementation, random seed value is 1882. This implementation is referred to as AWD below. Basic statistics regarding these models (size, test set perplexity) are in Table 2, suggesting that we were able to have a diverse set of models of varying strengths[7].

Last, we also report results obtained with a self-attentional architecture, directly using the smaller version (context size is 768 and number of param-

---

[3] https://en.wikipedia.org

[4] https://simple.wikipedia.org/

[5] Version 2.0 http://www.cs.pomona.edu/~dkauchak/simplification/

[6] https://github.com/salesforce/awd-lstm-lm

[7] Note that the perplexity score do not directly compare across training corpus, as the underlying event space is slightly different for each training corpus.

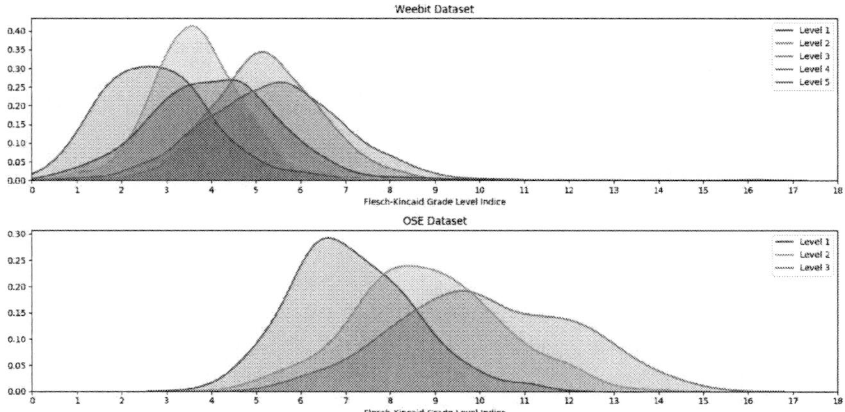

Figure 1: Distribution of the Flesch-Kincaid index by complexity level

eters $117M$ against a context size of 1600 units and $1.5B$ parameters for the largest and closed source version) of the trained models of Radford et al. (2019)[8], referred to as GPT-2 in the Tables below. This model uses a vocabulary of 50K variable length subword units (Sennrich et al., 2016) and is trained on a corpus of 8M documents; according to its authors, it achieves a perplexity of respectively 29 and 37 on `WikiText-2` and `WikiText-103`. As this model is based on sub-word units, it can not directly be used to fill gaps. Our greedy heuristic gap-filling procedure is the following: (a) first generate a list of K most likely subword units; (b) greedily expend rightwards these K hypotheses until one word is generated for at most t time steps. We use $t = 10$ in our experiments.

3.2 Test data and evaluation

The reference annotations used to validate our method mostly come from two sources: `Weebit` (Vajjala and Meurers, 2012) and `OneStopEnglish` (OSE for short) (Vajjala and Lucic, 2018). The first identifies 5 levels of complexity in educational news articles published online (on the WeeklyReader and BBC-Bitesize Web sites), covering learners aged from 7 to 16. As a merger of two sources, the distribution of categories is quite unbalanced, with more texts for the fifth level than for all the other categories taken together.

The second test set[9] also contains extracts of journalistic texts originally from the newspaper *The Guardian*. Each document has been rewritten twice by experts to correspond to two less advanced reading levels, and thus distinguishes three levels of readability. Statistics on these test corpora are in Table 4.

Source	Docs	Tokens	Gaps	Levels
`Weebit`	10 486	3.9M	157K	5
`OSE`	567	450K	8.5K	3

Table 4: Basic statistics of test corpora

Figure 1 displays the distribution of the Flesch-Kincaid Grade Level (FKGL) for these two corpora. Complexity levels are distributed nearly as expected for the Weebit corpus apart from levels 3 and 4 where the latter seems simpler than foreseen, with large overlapping spans. It was already noted by (Vajjala and Meurers, 2012) that the actual readability level of each test was difficult to predict accurately based on the sole FKGL. OSE complexity levels are also in agreement with the Flesch-Kincaid index, and in agreement with the numbers reported in (Vajjala and Lucic, 2018); again we see a large overlap between levels for this index. Overall, OSE texts are somewhat more complex than Weebit's, with OSE level 1 comparable in difficulty to Weebit level 4.

Both sources were pre-processed with regular expressions to discard bits of text that were recurrent such as advertisement footers for companies (BBC, WeeklyReader, MetaMetrics) and material

---

[8]Taken with their associated API from `https://github.com/huggingface/pytorch-pretrained-BERT`

[9]See `https://zenodo.org/record/1219041`.

p@...	WikiText-2				WikiText-103				Wiki-Simple			
	1	5	25	50	1	5	25	50	1	5	25	50
RNN (1)	0.10	0.21	0.33	0.39	0.12	0.24	0.37	0.44	0.12	0.27	0.40	0.47
RNN (2)	0.09	0.20	0.29	0.35	0.11	0.23	0.34	0.41	0.11	0.23	0.36	0.43
RNN (3)	0.08	0.19	0.28	0.34	0.10	0.22	0.33	0.39	0.10	0.22	0.33	0.39
RNN (τ)	0.05	0.06	0.11	0.12	0.06	0.06	0.09	0.10	0.11	0.13	0.17	0.19
AWD (1)	0.11	0.22	0.34	0.40	0.12	0.23	0.35	0.42	0.12	0.25	0.36	0.43
AWD (2)	0.10	0.20	0.31	0.37	0.11	0.21	0.32	0.37	0.11	0.22	0.32	0.38
AWD (3)	0.09	0.19	0.30	0.35	0.10	0.21	0.31	0.37	0.10	0.21	0.30	0.36
AWD (τ)	0.05	0.08	0.09	0.11	0.06	0.07	0.09	0.11	0.11	0.11	0.15	0.17

Table 5: Completion rates broken down per readability level for gap filling systems of variable strength tested on the OSE dataset. Kendall tau-b correlation is reported as τ.

p@...	WikiText-2				WikiText-103				Wiki-Simple			
	1	5	25	50	1	5	25	50	1	5	25	50
RNN (1)	0.07	0.18	0.28	0.34	0.10	0.23	0.34	0.40	0.15	0.28	0.40	0.46
RNN (2)	0.08	0.21	0.33	0.39	0.11	0.24	0.36	0.43	0.13	0.27	0.38	0.46
RNN (3)	0.09	0.21	0.33	0.39	0.12	0.25	0.36	0.43	0.13	0.26	0.39	0.45
RNN (4)	0.05	0.15	0.26	0.31	0.08	0.18	0.28	0.35	0.09	0.20	0.32	0.40
RNN (5)	0.06	0.15	0.24	0.29	0.09	0.19	0.28	0.33	0.10	0.20	0.31	0.37
RNN (τ)	0.07	0.11	0.11	0.12	0.07	0.12	0.15	0.14	0.15	0.19	0.16	0.16
AWD (1)	0.09	0.21	0.30	0.35	0.11	0.22	0.32	0.38	0.15	0.27	0.37	0.43
AWD (2)	0.09	0.22	0.33	0.40	0.12	0.23	0.35	0.41	0.13	0.25	0.36	0.42
AWD (3)	0.10	0.22	0.34	0.40	0.12	0.24	0.35	0.41	0.13	0.24	0.35	0.41
AWD (4)	0.06	0.17	0.27	0.33	0.08	0.18	0.26	0.31	0.09	0.19	0.27	0.34
AWD (5)	0.08	0.17	0.26	0.31	0.09	0.18	0.27	0.31	0.10	0.19	0.28	0.34
AWD (τ)	0.06	0.12	0.10	0.11	0.10	0.12	0.14	0.16	0.15	0.17	0.19	0.18

Table 6: Completion rates broken down per readability level for gap filling systems of variable strength tested on the Weebit dataset. Kendall tau-b correlation is reported as τ.

from automatic scraping (e.g. "Your web browser does not have JavaScript switched on at the moment."). Empty and duplicate documents were removed (around 400 texts), moreover, we used `spacy-cld`[10] (which uses CLD2 from Google) to detect the main language of a document and get rid of documents that were not written in English (around 60 texts in French, German, Spanish and Gaelic). In all our test and evaluation datasets, word tokenization and POS tags inference are performed with SpaCy.[11] Following this processing and as described in Section 2.3, passages and cloze positions are selected and fixed for all experiments to have a deterministic experimental setup. All the results presented below are computed using 500 randomly chosen texts for each readability level.

Since our objective is to study the correlation between gap filling performance and readability level, we compute two main metrics for each of the experimental conditions below: (a) the precision of comprehension systems broken down by complexity group; (b) the correlation (Kendall's Tau) between complexity classes and completion rates.[12]

3.3 Results

Our main results are presented in Table 5, 6 and 7 where we report the completion rates and correlations for all the systems compared in our experiments.

A first observation is that completion rates (especially p@1) are overall distributed as expected across models/training corpora. Training on `WikiText-2` yields results that are consistently worse than for the other two corpora; for both RNN implementations, the average success rate for `WikiText-2` and `WikiText-103` are very comparable. Interestingly, results for the easiest readability levels (Weebit 1 and 2) are higher for models trained on `Wiki-Simple` than on `WikiText-103` and `WikiText-2`. Regarding models, for `WikiText-2` and `WikiText-103` the RNN implementation of (Merity et al., 2018)

---

[10]`https://github.com/nickdavidhaynes/spacy-cld`

[11]`http://spacy.io`

---

[12]We use the Tau-b statistic which makes adjustments for ties (documents in the same complexity class).

is slightly better than ours, while our model performance is better for `Wiki-Simple`, which is consistent with the perplexity scores in Table 2

p@...	WebText	
	1	5
OSE (1)	0.22	0.42
OSE (2)	0.21	0.42
OSE (3)	0.20	0.40
OSE (τ)	0.05	0.04
Weebit (1)	0.18	0.35
Weebit (2)	0.18	0.37
Weebit (3)	0.21	0.39
Weebit (4)	0.13	0.27
Weebit (5)	0.13	0.29
Weebit (τ)	0.13	0.14

Table 7: Completion rates broken down per readability level for the GPT-2 gap filling system pre-trained on WebText and tested on the Weebit and OSE datasets. Kendall tau-b correlation is reported as τ.

As expected, GPT-2 scores in Table 7 vastly outperform all RNN-based approaches, with completion rates (p@1 / p@5) that approximately double the completion rates of the other systems.

We can conclude that our set of models is quite diverse, even though we would have expected to get more diversity across training corpora from our RNNs, suggesting that we may have to move away from the Wikipedia domain in future experiments.

If we now look at the variance of completion rates across difficulty levels, the overall picture is less clear. Overall, the most consistent results are obtained with OSE than with Weebit: for the former we almost always see better completion rates for simpler texts, across systems, training corpus and metrics, even though the differences are often small. Results for Weebit are more difficult to analyze: all RNN models seem to achieve their best completion rates for Weebit level 3, which is consistently higher than levels 4 and 5 (which is fine), but also higher than for level 1 and 2 (which is contradictory to our expectations). In fact, these easiest texts seem difficult to predict for all models; as mentioned above, for RNNs, training on the simpler `Wiki-Simple` gives a slight hedge over the other language models, which we also see as a positive sign. Overall however, the observed correlation scores remain small and insignificant, for all systems and metrics. Our best results are in the region $[0.1, 0.2]$ for OSE and Weebit. In comparison, the correlation for Flesh-Kincaid grade level score is 0.48 for OSE and 0.61 for Weebit.

A first conclusion is that with current machine comprehension systems, as implemented in this study, we show gap filling performances that are not significantly impacted by the actual readability level of texts. Therefore, their performance in cloze tests can not reliably be used to infer the difficulty of a text.

4 Discussion

4.1 Cloze tests and morphological tags

The results in Section 3 were obtained with a naive cloze test generation strategy, where deleted tokens are selected uniformly at random. There are several ways in which this approach can be problematic. Indeed, it is already a well documented fact that RNNs are far better at correctly predicting determiners, prepositions, or even verbs, than at predicting nouns (common or proper) that often require a much larger textual context (Hill et al., 2016).

This is also what we observe in Table 8 where we give the completion rate averaged over all texts in OSE corpora, broken down by part-of-speech (POS),[13] for all our models.

	verb	noun	punct	det
RNN-WT2 (λ)	0.03	0.08	0.76	0.61
RNN-WTSIMPLE (λ)	0.05	0.14	0.81	0.66
RNN-WT103 (λ)	0.04	0.11	0.82	0.59
RNN-WT2 (τ)	0.02	0.06	0	0
RNN-WTSIMPLE (τ)	0.03	0.08	0.04	0.05
RNN-WT103 (τ)	0.01	0.03	0.01	0
AWD-WT2 (λ)	0.02	0.08	0.81	0.61
AWD-WTSIMPLE (λ)	0.05	0.1	0.81	0.66
AWD-WT103 (λ)	0.05	0.09	0.81	0.6
AWD-WT2 (τ)	-0.01	0.06	0.02	0.01
AWD-WTSIMPLE (τ)	0.03	0.07	0.03	0.01
AWD-WT103 (τ)	-0.03	0.06	0.02	-0.03
GPT2 (λ)	0.24	0.39	0.87	0.64
GPT2 (τ)	0.04	0	0.01	-0.02

Table 8: Completion rates (λ with p@5) broken down per model and POS tag and Kendall-Tau (τ) correlation between completion rates and their respective level on the OSE dataset.

A first consequence is that easy-to-predict tokens, such as punctuations or determiners, will artificially increase the completion rate, even for texts that should be difficult to complete.

This would not be so much of a problem if the distribution of POS was constant across readability levels, an assumption that is also well known to be unrealistic - in fact, POS ratios have repeatedly

---

[13] Again, we use SpaCy to compute part-of-speech tags.

Level	Title	CR
K0	Goldilocks and the Three Bears	0
K1	The Courage of Sarah Noble	0
K1	Flat Stanley	0
K2	The Velveteen Rabbit	0.07
K2	Ribsy	0.07
K3	Stuart Little	0.20
K3	Peter Pan	0.33
K4	Prince Caspian	0.07
K4	Alice's Adventures in Wonderland	0.07
K5	Robinson Crusoe	0.13
K5	The Voyage of the Dawn Treader	0.07
K6	The Red Badge of Courage	0.13
K6	The Last Battle	0.07
K7	The Count of Monte Cristo	0.07
K7	The Black Arrow	0.27
K8	Hamlet	0
K8	The Sword in the Stone	0.07
K+	The Art of War	0.07

Table 9: A literary test set with completion rates from our RNN implementation trained on WikiText-2 using p@1 and 5 chunks of text per document.

been found to yield useful features when predicting readability (e.g. François and Fairon (2012)). The main consequence for our argument is that randomly selecting gaps will yield uneven POS distribution across readability levels, therefore biaising the overall result.

As suggested by the variance of the results in Table 8, this confounding factor cannot be ignored. Part-of-speech tags with the best rank correlation between their completion rate and their text's level are nouns and verbs; their occurrences are however lesser than punctuations and determiners, which means that an uniformly random gap selection strategy is biased by morphological tags that are worse predictors of text readability for our models.

4.2 Experiment with literary texts

The test datasets used in this study are quite similar in content, and all correspond to news articles intended for readers with variable levels of proficiency. In this subsection, we run a small confirmation study with an alternative test set based on literary texts. We use extracts from classical fictional books (see list in Table 9 where we also report the associated readability level and completion rate).

Kendall rank coefficient between these rates and their respective levels is equal to -0.28.

Here again, levels are not distinguishable based on the observed completion rates. However, as seen above in section § 3.3 our systems perform better when we release the exact match constraint

for the precision@N metrics. We expect to increase the Kendall rank metric on larger experiments with this dataset in our future work.

5 Conclusion and outlook

In this paper, we have ran a preliminary study regarding the ability of basic reading comprehension systems, here implemented as mere neural language models, to recognize variance in the difficulty of their input texts. Using randomly uniformly generated cloze tests to measure comprehension, we found that completion rates seem to deliver a small, yet insufficient, signal regarding the readability level of a text. Our strongest comprehension system, based on the recent GPT-2 model, is the worst of all, and does not help to distinguish between simple and more complex texts. Complementary experiments show that better controlling for POS distribution across corpora is likely to improve, albeit by a small margin our results: and that testing with other genre of texts might yield similar conclusions.

This pilot study only scratches at the surface of the problem, and we intend to continue this research in several directions. First, we need to continue the exploration of comprehension systems of controllable strength, using either more sophisticated language modelling architectures, or even considering full-fledge machine comprehension systems. A second line of study will consider alternative procedures for generating and filling cloze tests: generation could for instance restrict to specific gap types, based on their morphosyntactic properties or blank word parts instead of complete words; filling could for instance increase the context rightwards. Finally, we feel that it will also be crucial to make more direct experiments of the ability of automatic system to consistently reproduce the performance of human subjects, notably in the context of the evaluation of educational material, and we aim to develop experimental protocols involving controlled populations of language learners.

References

Rami Al-Rfou, Dokook Choe, Noah Constant, Mandy Guo, and Llion Jones. 2018. Character-level language modeling with deeper self-attention. In *Proceedings of the Thirty-Third AAAI Conference on Artificial Intelligence*, AAAI, Honolulu, Hawaï.

Frédéric Bimbot, Marc El-Bèze, Stéphane Igounet,

Michèle Jardino, Kamel Smaili, and Imed Zitouni. 2001. An alternative scheme for perplexity estimation and its assessment for the evaluation of language models. *Computer Speech & Language*, 15(1):1–13.

Dominique Brunato, Lorenzo De Mattei, Felice Dell'Orletta, Benedetta Iavarone, and Giulia Venturi. 2018. Is this sentence difficult? do you agree? In *Proceedings of the 2018 Conference on Empirical Methods in Natural Language Processing*, pages 2690–2699, Brussels, Belgium.

Stanley F Chen and Joshua Goodman. 1999. An empirical study of smoothing techniques for language modeling. *Computer Speech & Language*, 13(4):359–394.

Kevyn Collins-Thompson. 2014. Computational assessment of text readability: A survey of current and future research. *ITL-International Journal of Applied Linguistics*, 165(2):97–135.

Kevyn Collins-Thompson and James P. Callan. 2004. A language modeling approach to predicting reading difficulty. In *HLT-NAACL 2004: Main Proceedings*, pages 193–200, Boston, Massachusetts, USA.

Bhuwan Dhingra, Hanxiao Liu, Zhilin Yang, William Cohen, and Ruslan Salakhutdinov. 2017. Gated-attention readers for text comprehension. In *Proceedings of the 55th Annual Meeting of the Association for Computational Linguistics (Volume 1: Long Papers)*, pages 1832–1846, Vancouver, Canada.

Arne Dietrich. 2004. Neurocognitive mechanisms underlying the experience of flow. *Consciousness and Cognition*, 13(4):746 – 761.

William H DuBay. 2007. Smart language. *Readers, Readability, and the Grading of Text. Costa Mesa: Impact Information*.

Jeffrey L. Elman. 1990. Finding structure in time. *Cognitive Science*, 14(2):179–211.

Lijun Feng, Noémie Elhadad, and Matt Huenerfauth. 2009. Cognitively motivated features for readability assessment. In *Proceedings of the 12th Conference of the European Chapter of the ACL*, EACL 2009, pages 229–237, Athens, Greece.

Thomas François and Cédrick Fairon. 2012. An AI readability formula for French as a foreign language. In *Proceedings of the 2012 Joint Conference on Empirical Methods in Natural Language Processing and Computational Natural Language Learning*, pages 466–477.

Karl Moritz Hermann, Tomas Kocisky, Edward Grefenstette, Lasse Espeholt, Will Kay, Mustafa Suleyman, and Phil Blunsom. 2015. Teaching machines to read and comprehend. In *Advances in Neural Information Processing Systems 28*, pages 1693–1701. Curran Associates, Inc.

Felix Hill, Antoine Bordes, Sumit Chopra, and Jason Weston. 2016. The Goldilocks principle: reading children's books with explicit memory representations. In *Proceedings of the International Conference on Learning Representations*, ICLR, San Juan, Puerto Rico.

Sepp Hochreiter and Jürgen Schmidhuber. 1997. Long short-term memory. *Neural computation*, 9(8):1735–1780.

Hakan Inan, Khashayar Khosravi, and Richard Socher. 2017. Tying word vectors and word classifiers: A loss framework for language modeling. In *Proceedings of the International Conference on Representation Learning*, ICLR, Toulon, France.

Robin Jia and Percy Liang. 2017. Adversarial examples for evaluating reading comprehension systems. In *Proceedings of the 2017 Conference on Empirical Methods in Natural Language Processing*, pages 2021–2031.

Divyansh Kaushik and Zachary C. Lipton. 2018. How much reading does reading comprehension require? a critical investigation of popular benchmarks. In *Proceedings of the 2018 Conference on Empirical Methods in Natural Language Processing*, pages 5010–5015, Brussels, Belgium.

Yoon Kim, Yacine Jernite, David A Sontag, and Alexander M. Rush. 2016. Character-aware neural language models. In *Proceedings of the Annual Meeting of the American Association for Artificial Intelligence*, AAAI 16.

J Peter Kincaid, Robert P Fishburne Jr, Richard L Rogers, and Brad S Chissom. 1975. Derivation of new readability formulas (automated readability index, fog count and Flesch reading ease formula) for navy enlisted personnel. Technical report, Institute for Simulation and Training, University of Central Florida.

Peter J. Liu, Mohammad Saleh, Etienne Pot, Ben Goodrich, Ryan Sepassi, Lukasz Kaiser, and Noam Shazeer. 2018. Generating wikipedia by summarizing long sequences. In *Proceedings of the International Conference on Learning Representations*, ICLR, Vancouver, BC, Canada.

Gábor Melis, Chris Dyer, and Phil Blunsom. 2018. On the state of the art of evaluation in neural language models. In *Proceedings of the International Conference on Learning Representations*, ICLR, Vancouver, BC, Canada.

Stephen Merity, Nitish Shirish Keskar, and Richard Socher. 2018. Regularizing and optimizing LSTM language models. In *Proceedings of the International Conference on Learning Representations*, ICLR.

Stephen Merity, Caiming Xiong, James Bradbury, and Richard Socher. 2017. Pointer sentinel mixture models. In *Proceedings of the International Conference on Learning Representations*, ICLR, Toulon, France.

Tomáš Mikolov, Martin Karafiát, Lukáš Burget, Jan Černocký, and Sanjeev Khudanpur. 2010. Recurrent neural network based language model. In *Eleventh Annual Conference of the International Speech Communication Association (InterSpeech)*, pages 1045–1048, Makuhari, Chiba, Japan.

John W. Oller Jr. 1973. Cloze tests of second language proficiency and what they measure. *Language Learning*, 23(1):105–118.

Denis Paperno, Germán Kruszewski, Angeliki Lazaridou, Ngoc Quan Pham, Raffaella Bernardi, Sandro Pezzelle, Marco Baroni, Gemma Boleda, and Raquel Fernandez. 2016. The LAMBADA dataset: Word prediction requiring a broad discourse context. In *Proceedings of the 54th Annual Meeting of the Association for Computational Linguistics (Volume 1: Long Papers)*, pages 1525–1534, Berlin, Germany.

Sarah E. Petersen and Mari Ostendorf. 2009. A machine learning approach to reading level assessment. *Computer Speech & Language*, 23(1):89 – 106.

Ofir Press and Lior Wolf. 2017. Using the output embedding to improve language models. In *Proceedings of the 15th Conference of the European Chapter of the Association for Computational Linguistics: Volume 2, Short Papers*, pages 157–163, Valencia, Spain.

Alec Radford, Jeffrey Wu, Rewon Child, David Luan, Dario Amodei, and Ilya Sutskever. 2019. Language models are unsupervised multitask learners. Technical report, OpenAI.

Pranav Rajpurkar, Jian Zhang, Konstantin Lopyrev, and Percy Liang. 2016. Squad: 100,000+ questions for machine comprehension of text. In *Proceedings of the 2016 Conference on Empirical Methods in Natural Language Processing*, pages 2383–2392, Austin, Texas.

Matthew Richardson, Christopher J.C. Burges, and Erin Renshaw. 2013. MCTest: A challenge dataset for the open-domain machine comprehension of text. In *Proceedings of the 2013 Conference on Empirical Methods in Natural Language Processing*, pages 193–203, Seattle, Washington, USA.

Herbert Robbins and Sutton Monro. 1951. A stochastic approximation method. *The Annals of Mathematical Statistics*, 22(3):400–407.

Sarah Schwarm and Mari Ostendorf. 2005. Reading level assessment using support vector machines and statistical language models. In *Proceedings of the 43rd Annual Meeting of the Association for Computational Linguistics (ACL'05)*, pages 523–530, Ann Arbor, Michigan.

Rico Sennrich, Barry Haddow, and Alexandra Birch. 2016. Neural machine translation of rare words with subword units. In *Proceedings of the 54th Annual Meeting of the Association for Computational Linguistics (Volume 1: Long Papers)*, pages 1715–1725, Berlin, Germany.

Ilya Sutskever, James Martens, and Geoffrey Hinton. 2011. Generating text with recurrent neural networks. In *Proceedings of the 28th International Conference on International Conference on Machine Learning*, ICML'11, pages 1017–1024.

Wilson L. Taylor. 1953. Cloze procedure: A new tool for measuring readability. *Journalism Quarterly*, 30:415–433.

Sowmya Vajjala and Ivana Lucic. 2018. Onestopenglish corpus: A new corpus for automatic readability assessment and text simplification. In *Proceedings of the Thirteenth Workshop on Innovative Use of NLP for Building Educational Applications*, pages 297–304, New Orleans, Louisiana.

Sowmya Vajjala and Detmar Meurers. 2012. On improving the accuracy of readability classification using insights from second language acquisition. In *Proceedings of the seventh workshop on building educational applications using NLP*, pages 163–173.

Sowmya Vajjala and Detmar Meurers. 2014. Exploring measures of "readability" for spoken language: Analyzing linguistic features of subtitles to identify age-specific tv programs. In *Proceedings of the 3rd Workshop on Predicting and Improving Text Readability for Target Reader Populations (PITR)*, pages 21–29.

Ashish Vaswani, Noam Shazeer, Niki Parmar, Jakob Uszkoreit, Llion Jones, Aidan N Gomez, Łukasz Kaiser, and Illia Polosukhin. 2017. Attention is all you need. In *Advances in Neural Information Processing Systems*, pages 5998–6008.

Qizhe Xie, Guokun Lai, Zihang Dai, and Eduard Hovy. 2018. Large-scale Cloze test dataset created by teachers. In *Proceedings of the 2018 Conference on Empirical Methods in Natural Language Processing*, pages 2344–2356, Brussels, Belgium.

Zhilin Yang, Zihang Dai, Ruslan Salakhutdinov, and William W. Cohen. 2018. Breaking the softmax bottleneck: A high-rank RNN language model. In *Proceedings of the International Conference on Learning Representations*, ICLR.

Adams Wei Yu, David Dohan, Minh-Thang Luong, Rui Zhao, Kai Chen, Mohammad Norouzi, and Quoc V. Le. 2018. QANet: Combining local convolution with global self-attention for reading comprehension. In *Proceedings of the International Conference on Learning Representations*, ICLR.

Geoffrey Zweig and Chris J.C. Burges. 2012. A challenge set for advancing language modeling. In *Proceedings of the NAACL-HLT 2012 Workshop: Will*

We Ever Really Replace the N-gram Model? On the *Future of Language Modeling for HLT*, pages 29–36, Montréal, Canada.

Metaphors in Text Simplification:
To change or not to change, that is the question

Yulia Clausen
Linguistics Department, SFB 1287
University of Potsdam
Potsdam, Germany
yulia.clausen@uni-potsdam.de

Vivi Nastase
Department of Computational Linguistics
University of Heidelberg
Heidelberg, Germany
nastase@cl.uni-heidelberg.de

Abstract

We present an analysis of metaphors in news text simplification. Using features that capture general and metaphor specific characteristics, we test whether we can automatically identify which metaphors will be changed or preserved, and whether there are features that have different predictive power for metaphors or literal words. The experiments show that the Age of Acquisition is the most distinctive feature for both metaphors and literal words. Features that capture Imageability and Concreteness are useful when used alone, but within the full set of features they lose their impact. Frequency of use seems to be the best feature to differentiate metaphors that should be changed and those to be preserved.

1 Introduction

Metaphor is ubiquitous in everyday language and central to human thought (Lakoff and Johnson, 1980). We find manifestations of it in colloquial and academic discourse, newspaper, school textbooks, political discourse and probably anywhere language is used. There are conflicting views though on whether metaphors are a useful communication device. Golden (2010) found that metaphors present in school textbooks can make the overall content comprehension more difficult. On the other hand, the essence of metaphor is to make abstract concepts, which are often hard to grasp, more easily understandable through concrete descriptions (e.g. Kövecses, 2017).

In this paper we investigate metaphors in the context of news texts simplification. On a corpus of parallel sentences from news articles and their simplified version (to grade 4 level, which corresponds to 9-10 years of age), we analyze metaphors that are kept, changed or added in the simplified version. Our aim is to verify

whether we can characterize and automatically detect metaphors that help or do not help text understanding in the context of news articles.

The task of automatic text simplification has received a considerable amount of attention within NLP research. The proposed systems have, for the most part, addressed lexical and syntactic transformations, such as substitution of difficult words with simpler equivalents or altering the structure of sentences to make them more easily understandable (e.g. Barlacchi and Tonelli, 2013; De Belder and Moens, 2010; Drndarević and Saggion, 2012; Torunoğlu-Selamet et al., 2016; Vu et al., 2014).

The automatic handling of metaphorical language has also been researched extensively. However, the studies have mainly investigated the possibilities of automatic metaphor identification. Simplification of metaphorical language has not been explicitly addressed yet. This could be attributed to the fact that metaphor simplification is a challenging task for automatic implementation (cf. Drndarević and Saggion, 2012). Some approaches have considered the problem of automatic metaphor interpretation (e.g. Bollegala and Shutova, 2013; Shutova, 2013), which aims to find literal paraphrases for metaphorical expressions. It is not clear though whether the literal version is easier to understand than the original metaphor. Sometimes lexical simplifications for complex words can be too basic to convey the original meaning (cf. Vu et al., 2014).

We take a step towards filling the gap in metaphor simplification research. We combine information (in the form of features) from text simplification, and characteristics of metaphors to investigate whether there are specific features that can predict whether metaphors should be changed, and if these are different from features that are pre-

Proceedings of the Fourteenth Workshop on Innovative Use of NLP for Building Educational Applications, pages 423–434
Florence, Italy, August 2, 2019. ©2019 Association for Computational Linguistics

dictive of lexical simplification in general. We use parallel versions ("raw" and simplified) of news data from Newsela[1], a company that produces professionally simplified news texts, in which we annotate metaphors. In experiments that predict whether a target word will be changed or not, we analyze the performance of the features used w.r.t. the type of the target word – metaphoric or literal (the full set of features is described in Section 4.2). We find that the Age of Acquisition is the strongest feature overall, for both metaphoric and literal words. Imageability, Familiarity and Concreteness are useful when used alone, but within the context of the full set of features they lose their impact. Frequency of use is an important feature for distinguishing metaphors that should be changed from those to be preserved.

2   Related work

Text simplification has numerous facets, and can be approached from different angles. The general need for simplification can be predicted based on the readability of a text, from the point of view of sentence complexity (Štajner et al., 2017) or a combination of lexical, syntactic and semantic text characteristics (De Clercq and Hoste, 2016). Simplification can be targeted by identifying complex words (e.g. Paetzold and Specia, 2016; Yimam et al., 2018), and then performing lexical simplification (e.g. Glavaš and Štajner, 2015; Glavaš and Vulić, 2018; Horn et al., 2014; Kriz et al., 2018).

Lexical simplification systems often build on sentence-aligned simplification corpora and propose substitutes for complex words from a number of synonyms based on the words' frequency, length and suitability for the original context (De Belder and Moens, 2010; Drndarević and Saggion, 2012; Vu et al., 2014). Approaches influenced by machine translation have also been explored, as lexical simplification can be viewed as monolingual translation (e.g. Nisioi et al., 2017; Xu et al., 2016; Zhu et al., 2010). Other neural based models have also been developed, which exploit word embeddings and their closeness in the vector space as clues for substitution candidates. Glavaš and Štajner (2015) produce word simplifications in a large regular corpus using word embeddings to perform lexical substitution tasks. The simplification candidates are ranked based on features such as semantic and context similarity, and

information load.

Our focus in this paper is narrower. We aim to explore metaphors in text simplification, and check if there are specific features that predict whether a metaphor should be changed or not. To represent the instances in our data we use features that previous work on text simplification have shown to be beneficial, as well as features useful in metaphor identification tasks.

3   Data

The data for this study comes from Newsela, a company that provides professionally simplified news texts for school reading activities. The editors follow simplification guidelines and are assisted by a tool in detecting difficult words. There is no description of the criteria used by the tool to detect such words. Regarding metaphors, the instructions are brief and seem to draw attention to idioms rather than metaphors: "be literal in lower versions. No straight out metaphors, as in no 'paint into a corner' in 5th grade or below.".

Each Newsela article has five versions of different difficulty levels determined based on the Lexile[2] readability scores, which are used to measure the complexity of texts and assign them to appropriate grade levels. Using these parallel news texts allows for the quick identification of changed items to produce a dataset to which metaphor information is then added (Wolska and Clausen, 2017).

3.1   The dataset

We use a parallel corpus of 1,130 Newsela articles by Xu et al. (2015), where each original article has been aligned with its four simplified versions at the sentence level based on Jaccard similarity. For our study we look at the original (V0) and the most simplified (V4) versions, as between them we expect the most differences w.r.t. simplification strategies. From this corpus, we automatically sampled original sentences along with their equivalents from the chosen simplified version.

Each Newsela version covers several, unevenly distributed, grade levels. Because of the potential differences between the grade levels within versions, we sampled only articles at grade level 12 from the original version and grade level 4 from the most simplified version. The selected grade levels correspond to the largest subsets within the

---

respective versions. The sampling was randomized across documents to counter author and editor bias. The final dataset contains 582 documents, each consisting of one original sentence and one or more sentences in the corresponding simplified version.[3] All alignments were manually checked and corrected where necessary either by inserting missing sentences or by replacing wrong alignments with the correct ones. This resulted in 278 corrections, exemplified below ("m" indicates the manually inserted sentence, initially missing from the alignment):

> V0 A year ago, [Shaw] Mychal suffered a concussion in a game that rendered him temporarily unable to walk or speak.
> V4 Shaw suffered a concussion in a game last year.
> V4-m Shaw could not walk or speak for a while.

3.2 Metaphor annotation

We focus on the two most common word classes – nouns and verbs. In the sampled documents, we annotated their occurrences in the original sentences as either metaphoric or not by following the guidelines of the metaphor identification procedure MIPVU (Steen et al., 2010).[4]

The annotation in this study builds on Wolska and Clausen (2017), where it was carried out as follows: one author initially identified metaphoric items in a smaller subset of the data. All unclear cases were then discussed with the second author and either resolved or left unannotated. The annotation was completed by the initial annotator. In this study, we use a version of the dataset with expanded annotations – every noun/verb left unannotated in the previous study was annotated for metaphoricity by the same annotator as in the initial study.

In MIPVU, metaphoricity is identified by examining a text on a word-for-word basis and determining the context and the basic senses of each word. "Words" are considered to be lexical units provided with separate part of speech tags.[5] A word is used metaphorically if its context sense

can be sufficiently contrasted to and understood in comparison with its basic sense. The context sense of a word is "the meaning it has in the situation in which it is used", whereas the basic sense is taken to be "more concrete, specific, and human-oriented" (Steen et al., 2010, p. 33-35).

The senses are determined by means of a dictionary; we consult the Macmillan Dictionary[6], which is a standard reference used by the authors of the procedure. Different senses of a word correspond to separate, numbered descriptions within its grammatical category in a dictionary.

In an example from our dataset, given in (1), the verb *struggling* is used metaphorically, as there exists a more basic sense ("to use your strength to fight against someone or something"), which is contrasted to and compared with the contextual sense ("to try hard to do something that you find very difficult").[7]

(1) But now she's *struggling* to obtain documents required by the new law.

The quantitative information on the annotated dataset is summarized in Table 1.

Measure		Count
No. of sentences		566
No. of sentences containing metaphors		350
Mean No. of metaphors per sentence		1.7
No. of annotated metaphors		587
	Verbs	354
	Nouns	233
No. of annotated non-metaphors		2,952
	Verbs	852
	Nouns	2,100
No. of unique lexemes		2,261
	Metaphoric	433
	Non-metaphoric	1,828

Table 1: Statistics on the annotated dataset.

3.3 Simplification types

For each annotated word we marked its equivalent in the simplified version and determined the simplification type chosen by an editor.[8] There

---

[3] Documents where original and simplified versions were identical based on string comparison were excluded.

[4] The annotation was done with the tool BRAT (Stenetorp et al., 2012): http://brat.nlplab.org/

[5] In MIPVU, phrasal verbs and compound nouns are regarded as single lexical units. Although we annotated them, in this paper we experiment only with the single words due to the non-availability of various features for multi-item words.

[6] https://www.macmillandictionary.com/

[7] The definitions of the basic and contextual senses: https://www.macmillandictionary.com/dictionary/american/struggle_1

[8] We encountered cases of clauses, such as coordinate and subordinate, not retained in the simplified version. These clauses were not annotated, as they might have been removed

	Simplification	Original sentence	Simplified sentence
metaphoric	same metaphor	*... like the magnetized nails, unable to resist a powerful magnetic* **force** *in the galactic bulge ...*	*Like the magnetized nails, they would have been unable to resist a powerful magnetic* **force** *in the galactic bulge ...*
	other metaphor	*Obama also has* **grappled** *publicly with reconciling King's teachings on nonviolence ...*	*Obama has* **wrestled** *publicly with living up to King's teachings on nonviolence ...*
	changed to non-metaphor	*In exchange for a 4 percent* **piece** *of their companies, entrepreneurs in the program will gain access ...*	*... people in the program will give up a 4 percent* **share** *of their companies. In exchange they will get ...*
	phrase with metaphor(s)	*But now she's* **struggling** *to obtain documents required by the new law.*	*But now she's* **having a hard time** *getting the papers that the new law requires.*
	phrase w/o metaphor(s)	*Utah officials say that since 2008, highway crashes have* **dropped** *annually on stretches of rural Interstate ...*	*They say there have* **been fewer** *accidents where the speed limit was raised.*
	word removed	*Our goal is to provide Internet service to people in areas that can't afford to* **throw down** *fiber lines ...*	*Our goal is to provide Internet service to people in areas that can't afford* Ø *usual Internet lines ...*
non-metaphoric	same non-metaphor	*"In the past several hundred* **years**, *people have cultivated the habit of smoking wherever they want," she said.*	*"In the past several hundred* **years**, *people have "gotten used to" smoking wherever they want," she said.*
	other non-metaphor	*With nothing less at stake than the future of planet Earth, NASA has decided to crowdsource ideas to* **detect** *and track asteroids ...*	*NASA wants to* **find** *and track asteroids, but it needs help. It is asking people around the world for ideas ...*
	changed to metaphor	*That information could help the team's trainers* **implement** *practice plans that keep him spry the rest of the season.*	*That could help the team's trainers* **make** *plans that keep him healthy for the season.*
	phrase with metaphor(s)	*"Even after the Holocaust, our minority still encounters racism and discrimination," he said, noting that they are Europe's last* **hired**, *first fired.*	*His people still suffer unfair and insulting treatment, he said. They are the last in Europe* **to get jobs**. *They are also the first to be fired.*
	phrase w/o metaphor(s)	*On Thursday, the snowpack was a paltry 25 percent of* **average** *for this time of year.*	*The snowpack was just one-quarter of* **what it usually is** *for this time of year.*
	word removed	*SnapDragon is a cross of Honeycrisp with a Jonagold-like hybrid that's easier for* **farmers** *to manage.*	*SnapDragon is a cross of the tasty Honeycrisp apple and another kind that's easier* Ø *to grow.*

Table 2: Simplification types for metaphoric and non-metaphoric lexical items.

are six simplification options that were identified for metaphoric items in Wolska and Clausen (2017), which we now apply to non-metaphoric items as well. A word can be preserved (*same metaphor/same non-metaphor*)[9], replaced by another word of the same metaphorical status (*other metaphor* for metaphoric items and *other non-metaphor* for literal items), replaced by a word of opposite metaphorical status (*changed to non-metaphor* for metaphors and *changed to metaphor* for literal items), rephrased with metaphorical language (*phrase with metaphors*) or without (*phrase without metaphors*), or removed (*word removed*). See Table 2 for an overview with examples.

The annotation of the simplification types in Wolska and Clausen (2017) was done as follows: on a smaller subset of sentences annotated for metaphoricity, two authors identified and discussed the simplification choices. Once these were finalized, one author annotated the remainder of

the dataset and the second author 99 instances.[10] Inter-annotator agreement on the common subset was $\kappa = .87$. In the present study, one author extended the annotations.

The quantitative information on the annotated simplification types is summarized in Table 3.[11] The statistics show that metaphors can be both useful and confusing for communication: 62% of the phrases that contained metaphors in the original article version contain a metaphor (the same or another one) in the simplified version. A small number of non-metaphors (2.3%) were replaced with metaphors in the simplified version.

With respect to the two word classes – nouns and verbs – we note considerable variation in the dataset (see Table 4). 93% of the verbs (186 metaphoric and 368 literal) appear less than five times; 67% (143 metaphoric and 256 literal) only once. The most frequent verbs annotated as metaphoric are *have* (22), *make* (18) and *take*

---

due to various reasons, e.g. complex syntactic structure. This is to be differentiated from the option *word removed*, where the changes are performed on the word level and which we annotate.

[9]Morphological deviations are considered the same word.

[10]One erroneous instance had to be excluded.

[11]30 of the annotated words are not included in the counts; they were excluded from the experiment part, as most of the features we use were not available for them.

Simplification type	Count
Metaphoric	584
same metaphor	299
other metaphor	43
changed to non-metaphor	101
phrase with metaphor(s)	20
phrase without metaphor(s)	14
word removed	107
Non-metaphoric	2,925
same non-metaphor	1,933
other non-metaphor	418
changed to metaphor	34
phrase with metaphor(s)	32
phrase without metaphor(s)	77
word removed	431

Table 3: Distribution of the simplification types.

(13). The verbs *say* (86) and *use* (16) are mostly used literally. Nouns behave similarly: 95% (167 metaphoric and 1,049 literal) appear less than five times; 68% (131 metaphoric and 746 literal) with frequency 1. The most frequent nouns are *drone* (9) (metaphoric), and *year* (47) and *school* (22) (literal). About 10% (65) verb types and 4% (56) noun types are used both metaphorically and literally, indicating that features that combine information about the word and its context are needed.

	Metaphoric		Literal	
	V	N	V	N
Min	1	1	1	1
Max	22	9	86	47
Mean	1.8	1.37	2.12	1.86
No. of types	196	169	401	1118

Table 4: Frequency distribution of metaphoric and literal verb/noun types.

4 Experiments

The purpose of these experiments is to test whether there are distinguishable characteristics that indicate whether a metaphoric/literal word should/should not be changed to make the text easier to understand, and also whether there are features that are particular to metaphoric or literal words with respect to simplification. We conducted two sets of experiments: on the full dataset (metaphoric and literal items), and on the metaphoric part of the data. Through the experiments on the full dataset we investigate whether

there are different features indicative of metaphor and literal word simplification, respectively. In the second set of experiments we perform a more in depth exploration of the metaphoric part of the data and look at the changes within the fine-grained simplification types.

4.1 Experimental setup

For the first set of experiments, we group the simplification types in two classes: *preserved* and *changed*. Unchanged items (i.e. *same metaphor* and *same non-metaphor*) were assigned the *preserved* class. All other simplification types were combined as *changed*. The quantitative information on the items used in the experiments is provided in Table 5.

Simplification type	Count
Preserved	2,232
metaphoric	299
non-metaphoric	1,933
Changed	1,277
metaphoric	285
non-metaphoric	992

Table 5: Statistics on the coarse-grained simplification types.

The experiments were done with a Linear Support Vector Machine classifier using 10-fold cross-validation startegy.[12] The feature values were standardized prior to the experiments.[13] We report the results of the random baseline, and the distribution of the different phenomena in the data.

4.2 Features

Data analysis has shown that both metaphors and literal words can be changed to help comprehension, and either can be replaced with metaphoric or literal expressions. To determine whether there are identifiable characteristics that could make this distinction automatable, we compile a number of features that have been shown to be useful for text simplification and metaphor identification. The metaphor-sensitive features are *Imageability, Concreteness, WordNet senses* and *word's context*; the

---

[12]We use the SVM implementation in *scikit-learn* (Pedregosa et al., 2011): `https://scikit-learn.org/stable/modules/generated/sklearn.svm.LinearSVC.html`

[13]Standardization was performed with the StandardScaler in *scikit-learn*: `http://scikit-learn.org/stable/modules/generated/sklearn.preprocessing.StandardScaler.html`

general features are *part of speech, vector space word representations, Age of Acquisition, word frequency* and *Familiarity*. The feature types used and their coverage in our dataset are described below.

Part of speech: The part of speech (POS) tagging was done using the NLTK toolkit[14] (Bird et al., 2009). The POS tags were then manually corrected where necessary. The two possible values are noun and verb.

Vector space word representations: We obtained vector space representations for each annotated word using Google's pre-trained *word2vec* model (Mikolov et al., 2013).[15]

Word embeddings have been successfully used in metaphor identification (e.g. Dinh and Gurevych 2016; Gutiérrez et al. 2016) as well as in lexical simplification tasks (e.g. Glavaš and Štajner 2015; Glavaš and Vulić 2018).

Age of Acquisition: Age of Acquisition (AoA) ratings were obtained from the AoA norms database of 51,715 English words (Kuperman et al., 2012). AoA denotes the approximate age at which a word is learned. The simplified news articles used in this study are intended for classroom use by 9-10 year old children. Words usually acquired after this age should be more readily changed/removed in the simplified version.

We extracted the AoA ratings by matching both word forms and lemmas (e.g. noun *testing/testing* vs. verb *testing/test*).

Imageability, Familiarity and Concreteness: Imageability stands for the ability of a word to evoke mental images; Familiarity refers to the frequency of exposure to a word; Concreteness describes the level of abstraction associated with the concept a word represents. The connection of these variables to metaphor comprehension has been shown in multiple studies (e.g. Marschark et al. 1983; Paivio et al. 1968; Ureña and Faber 2010). Concrete words are more easily learned, processed and remembered than the abstract ones (Paivio et al., 1968). It is quite likely then that abstract words will be discarded during simplification. Marschark et al. (1983) found a link between high imageability and easier processing for certain

metaphor types. These features were successfully used in lexical simplification (e.g. Jauhar and Specia 2012; Vajjala and Meurers 2014).

Imageability and Familiarity ratings were obtained from the MRC Psycholinguistic Database (Wilson, 1988). This database contains up to 26 (psycho)linguistic attributes for 150,837 words. Concreteness ratings were extracted from a collection of English Abstractness/Concreteness ratings (Köper and Schulte im Walde, 2017).

We extracted the values for the word forms if present in the databases and for the respective lemmas otherwise. For a number of words, the values are missing (see Table 6). De Hertog and Tack (2018) use the third and first quartile values for Imageability and Concreteness, respectively, following an assumption that rarer words tend to have lower imageability and concreteness, while Gooding and Kochmar (2018) use the null value. We decided to assign instead a "neutral" value: the median value for each feature based on the ratings in the MRC.

	Available	**Missing**	
Imag	2,288	1,221	(35%)
Fam	2,293	1,216	(35%)
Concr	3,509	0	(0%)

Table 6: Counts for Imageability, Familiarity and Concreteness ratings.

Word frequency: In lexical simplification systems, it is common to substitute infrequent words with their more frequent synonyms (e.g. De Belder and Moens, 2010). As Kriz et al. (2018), we assume that highly frequent words are easier to understand, whereas infrequent words are more difficult and therefore will be removed/changed in the process of simplification.

We use word frequency counts from the SUBTLEX$_{US}$ database (Brysbaert and New, 2009), a corpus of subtitles for American English of 51M words. The frequencies are given per million words. We extracted the values based on the word forms in our data (3,503 words); 6 words (.2%) have frequency 0.

WordNet sense: The WordNet (Fellbaum, 1998) sense feature approximates a word's meaning in context. The values are the synset numbers representing the sense of a word in the original sentence. MIPVU uses sense information and comparison with a "basic" sense of a word

---

[14] https://www.nltk.org/

[15] The model can be downloaded from here: https://code.google.com/archive/p/word2vec/

to assign metaphoricity. The WordNet sense number could be an indication whether a word is metaphoric or not: the first sense is the more frequent, and could thus be considered basic, while the higher the sense number, the more likely it could be that the word is used metaphorically.

We use a Lesk-like (Lesk, 1986) method to disambiguate a target word relative to WordNet: a vector representation of the context of an annotated word (i.e. V0 sentence) is compared to a representation for each of the word's definitions in WordNet. The representations are generated using Google's pre-trained *word2vec* model. The context and each definition are compared using Word Mover's Distance (Kusner et al., 2015).[16] We chose the synset number whose definition is most similar to the word's context. The lookup in WordNet was done based on the word forms and matching POS tags. For 9 words (.3%) not found in WordNet the values are missing.

Word's context: This feature reflects the discrepancy between the level of abstractness of a metaphoric word and its context. It was operationalized with ratings of Concreteness (Köper and Schulte im Walde, 2017) and Imageability from the MRC database.

Turney et al. (2011) have shown that a word's degree of abstractness, relative to the context it appears in, can be successfully used to distinguish between literal and metaphoric meanings. Broadwell et al. (2013) used Imageability ratings to discover metaphors based on the assumption that they stand out of their context as being highly imageable.

We considered a symmetrical seven-word window centered on the target word. A word w's Concreteness context (CC) value is computed as:

$$CC_w = C\lceil n/2 \rceil - \left(\sum_{i=1}^{\lfloor n/2 \rfloor} C_i + \sum_{i=\lceil n/2 \rceil+1}^{n} C_i \right)$$

where n is the size of the window. The Imageability context (IC) is calculated in the same way.

In the computation we used the context words with available Concreteness and Imageability scores in the database. If ratings for the target word itself or for all context words were not found, the value for the feature was set to missing. The overview of the value counts is given in Table 7.

	Available	Missing	
IC	2,258	1,251	(36%)
CC	3,503	6	(.2%)

Table 7: Counts for the words' context features: Imageability context (IC) and Concreteness context (CC).

4.3 Experiment 1: Metaphoric vs. literal words

To assess the impact of the different features on predicting whether a word should or should not be changed, we group the features based on the type of information they capture:

- *IFC* (Imageability + Familiarity + Concreteness) – informative for metaphoric words

- *WN+IC/CC* (WordNet sense + word's context) – different aspect of metaphor relevance

- *Freq+AoA* (word frequency + Age of Acquisition) – relevant for both metaphoric and literal items

The F-score results on the full dataset (1,277 changed, 2,232 preserved instances) for different feature combinations are presented in Figure 1.[17]

AoA has the highest Precision for the class *changed* in both metaphoric and literal cases. This shows that whereas this feature might be good in accurately detecting items that need simplification, it does not differentiate between metaphoric and literal usages in the current setting. Previous studies have shown that some correlation exists between the AoA and frequency of usage (e.g. Ghyselinck et al., 2004), but in this case the AoA feature and the Frequency feature have different effects when used alone (see Figure 1). In particular, the Frequency feature is not useful to determine whether a word should be changed or not, contrary to our expectations.

We expected the "metaphor-specific" features (IFC) to have a higher impact on the metaphoric than on the literal words. When used alone they do lead to better prediction for changing metaphoric words compared to literal ones, but within the context of the full feature set, their impact is minimal (all, all-IFC/I/F/C). The imbalance in the data set could explain why, when using other features which can pick up on characteristics of literal

---

[16]We used the implementation in Gensim Python library (Řehůřek and Sojka, 2010).

[17]We report only the F-scores for this experiment due to space limitations.

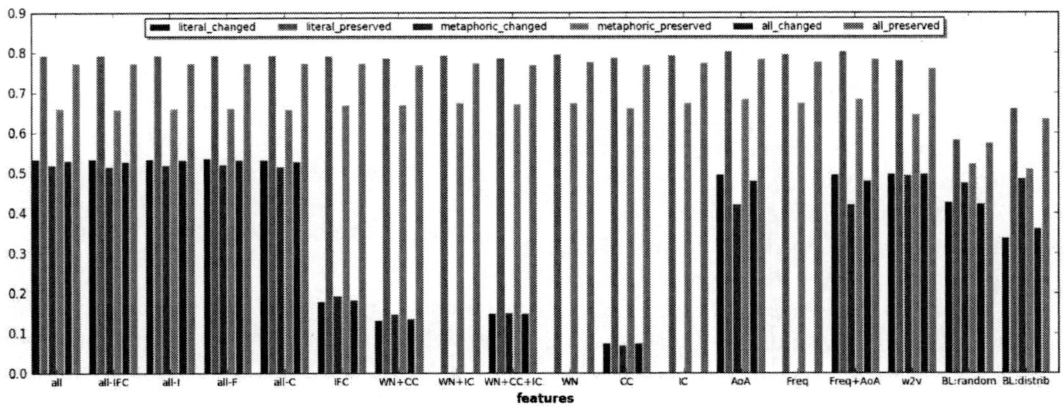

Figure 1: F-scores on learning changed vs. preserved on the full dataset, with results on all data and the metaphoric and literal subsets when using different feature combinations.

words (or both), the effect of Familiarity, Concreteness and Imageability is lost.

The WN and context features also behave in an interesting manner. Alone, neither of these has much impact on distinguishing words that should be changed or not (WN/CC/IC). But when combined, their predictive power grows, particularly considering the approximate 1:5 ratio between metaphoric and literal target words. We tested a binary representation of the WN feature: is the disambiguated sense the first one (the "basic" one) or not. This set-up led to worse results. This could mean that assuming that the first sense in WordNet is the "basic" sense is erroneous, even though it is the most frequent one.

	Changed		Preserved	
Feature(s)	Verbs	Nouns	Verbs	Nouns
all	.562	.515	.784	.770
IFC	.199	.175	.766	.779
WN+CC	.206	.093	.752	.780
WN+IC	.004	.000	.771	.779
WN+CC+IC	.220	.107	.750	.780
Freq+AoA	.480	.482	.803	.777
random	.424	.408	.523	.556
majority	.000	.000	.773	.780

Table 8: F-scores: changed vs. preserved on the full dataset, for nouns (833 changed, 1474 preserved) and verbs (444 changed, 758 preserved).

Looking at the results on the subsets corresponding to nouns and verbs (see Table 8), we note that there are differences in terms of the useful features. Predicting that nouns should be preserved is consistent w.r.t. the features used, and close to the majority baseline. Using all features leads to the best results overall, for both nouns and verbs, whether they should be changed or preserved. Metaphor-relevant features (IFC and contextual information) are not helpful in predicting verbs and nouns that need to be changed. However, they appear to be more relevant for verbs. The Frequency and Age of Acquisition combination seems to be more important for verbs than for nouns.

4.4 Experiment 2: Metaphoric words

We use the subset of 285 changed and 299 preserved metaphors to test the impact of different subsets of features for predicting change/preserve for metaphoric target words. The results are given in Table 9 for the complete metaphoric dataset.

We further analyze the results of classifying originally metaphoric words as changed or preserved in the simplified texts. We look into the data subsets corresponding to the different metaphor simplification phenomena, and produce the recall results shown in Table 10. We cannot compute precision because all instances in each subset belong to one class (i.e. either *changed* or *preserved*).

The results for the metaphoric data preserve some of the tendencies seen on the complete dataset, and they also reveal some new insights. AoA leads to the highest Precision score for the class *changed* and has high Recall and F-score for the class *preserved*. Frequency of use appears to be the most useful in distinguishing between metaphors that should be changed or preserved. This is quite intuitive, as metaphors that are less common are more difficult to understand. Contrary to its impact in the first experiment – classifying whether a word should be changed or not,

Feature(s)	Changed			Preserved		
	P	R	F_1	P	R	F_1
all	.573	.561	.567	.590	.602	.596
all-IFC	.568	.558	.563	.586	.595	.590
all-I	.568	.554	.561	.585	.599	.592
all-F	.571	.561	.566	.589	.599	.594
all-C	.573	.561	.567	.590	.602	.596
IFC	.576	.519	.546	.581	.635	.607
WN+CC	.522	.505	.513	.542	.559	.550
WN+IC	.513	.540	.526	.539	.512	.525
WN+CC+IC	.540	.519	.530	.558	.579	.568
WN	.497	.554	.524	.523	.465	.492
CC	.495	.319	.388	.515	**.689**	.589
IC	.438	.186	.261	.499	**.773**	.606
AoA	**.602**	.530	.563	.598	**.666**	**.630**
Freq	.548	**.884**	**.677**	**.734**	.304	.430
Freq+AoA	.594	.586	.590	.611	.619	.615
w2v	.576	.572	.574	.595	.599	.597
random	.489	.463	.476	.513	.538	.525
majority	.000	.000	.000	.512	1.00	.677

Table 9: Results on learning changed vs. preserved on the subset of metaphoric items (285 changed / 299 preserved instances). Best results are given in bold.

regardless of whether it is metaphoric or literal – when analyzing metaphoric words and classifying them into changed/preserved, Frequency is the best feature. This effect is apparent also when looking at the subsets corresponding to the different simplification types (see Table 10).

Feature(s)	Changed to					Pres.
	other met	phr. with met	lit.	phr. no met	rem.	same
all	.651	.600	.515	.500	.570	.602
all-IFC	.674	.600	.515	.500	.551	.595
all-I	.651	.600	.505	.500	.651	.599
all-F	.698	.600	.505	.500	.561	.599
all-C	.585	.560	.582	.500	.570	.602
IFC	.535	**.850**	.545	.286	.548	.635
WN+CC	.581	.500	.525	.500	.458	.559
WN+IC	.605	.550	.515	.571	.533	.512
WN+CC+IC	.488	.650	.545	.500	.486	.579
WN	.581	.450	.545	**.643**	.561	.465
CC	.326	.450	.327	.286	.290	**.689**
IC	.186	.200	.188	.143	.187	**.773**
w2v	.674	.600	.495	.571	.598	.599
w2v+IFC	.674	.600	.495	.571	.589	.605
AoA	.605	.600	.535	.571	.477	.666
Freq	**.884**	**.950**	**.931**	**.929**	**.822**	.304
Freq+AoA	.651	.650	.604	.643	.523	.619
random	.419	.450	.475	.357	.514	.518

Table 10: Recall: changed vs. preserved on the subset of metaphoric items (285 changed / 299 preserved instances) for each fine-grained simplification type. Best results are given in bold.

The word's context features (IC/CC) have the highest Recall scores for the preserved cases, but in combination with the WordNet senses feature they stop being useful for differentiating between the two classes. Just as in the first experiment, when used alone the IFC features are clearly useful, but within the full set of features they lose their predictive power. For the preserved items, the context features (IC/CC) show the best results. Those metaphors that were rephrased with metaphorical content are best described with the IFC features, whereas the WN senses feature is good when identifying paraphrases without metaphors.

5 Conclusion

The analysis of metaphor usage in original and simplified versions of the same news texts has shown that not all metaphors are alike, from the point of view of text comprehension. A large percentage of metaphors in our dataset were either preserved or replaced using metaphorical language, while a (much) smaller number of literally used words was replaced with a metaphoric expression.

The evaluation of the features most frequently used in literature for text simplification and metaphor identification has shown that for both metaphors and literal words, the most informative feature is the Age of Acquisition. Features that capture the imageability, familiarity and concreteness of a word have similar performance in predicting change/no change for both metaphorical and literal words when used alone. When used together with our other features, their predictive power diminishes. While not useful to separate changed and preserved words in the full dataset, for metaphoric words the frequency of usage is a telling feature, even at a fine-grained level.

One factor that could have influenced the results of these experiments is the incomplete coverage provided by the Imageability and Familiarity features. In future work we plan to improve the assignment of missing values by deriving a value using the scores assigned to the most similar words. We will further explore features that capture the interaction between a target word and its context, including contextual embeddings and the word's syntactic role.

Acknowledgements

We thank the reviewers for the interesting comments. Yulia Clausen's research was partially funded by the Deutsche Forschungsgemeinschaft (DFG, German Research Foundation) – project number 317633480 – SFB 1287, project A03.

References

G. Barlacchi and S. Tonelli. 2013. ERNESTA: A sentence simplification tool for children's stories in italian. In *Proceedings of the 14th International Conference on Computational Linguistics and Intelligent Text Processing - Volume 2*, CICLing'13, pages 476–487, Berlin, Heidelberg. Springer-Verlag.

S. Bird, E. Klein, and E. Loper. 2009. *Natural Language Processing with Python*, 1st edition. O'Reilly Media, Inc.

D. Bollegala and E. Shutova. 2013. Metaphor interpretation using paraphrases extracted from the web. *PLoS ONE*, 8(9):e74304.

G. A. Broadwell, U. Boz, I. Cases, T. Strzalkowski, L. Feldman, S. Taylor, S. Shaikh, T. Liu, K. Cho, and N. Webb. 2013. Using imageability and topic chaining to locate metaphors in linguistic corpora. In *Proceedings of the 6th International Conference on Social Computing, Behavioral-Cultural Modeling and Prediction*, SBP'13, pages 102–110, Berlin, Heidelberg. Springer-Verlag.

M. Brysbaert and B. New. 2009. Moving beyond Kučera and Francis: A critical evaluation of current word frequency norms and the introduction of a new and improved word frequency measure for American English. *Behavior Research Methods, Instruments & Computers*, 41(4):977–990.

J. De Belder and M.-F. Moens. 2010. Text simplification for children. In *SIGIR: Workshop on Accessible Search Systems*, pages 19–26.

O. De Clercq and V. Hoste. 2016. All mixed up? Finding the optimal feature set for general readability prediction and its application to English and Dutch. *Computational Linguistics*, 42(3):457–490.

D. De Hertog and A. Tack. 2018. Deep learning architecture for complex word identification. In *Proceedings of the Thirteenth Workshop on Innovative Use of NLP for Building Educational Applications*, pages 328–334.

E.-L. Do Dinh and I. Gurevych. 2016. Token-level metaphor detection using neural networks. In *Proceedings of the Fourth Workshop on Metaphor in NLP*, pages 28–33.

B. Drndarević and H. Saggion. 2012. Towards automatic lexical simplification in Spanish: An empirical study. In *Proceedings of the First Workshop on Predicting and Improving Text Readability for target reader populations*, pages 8–16.

Christiane Fellbaum, editor. 1998. *WordNet: An Electronic Lexical Database*. MIT Press, Cambridge, MA.

M. Ghyselinck, M. B. Lewis, and M. Brysbaert. 2004. Age of acquisition and the cumulative-frequency hypothesis: A review of the literature and a new multi-task investigation. *Acta psychologica*, 115 (1):43–67.

G. Glavaš and S. Štajner. 2015. Simplifying lexical simplification: Do we need simplified corpora? In *Proceedings of the 53rd Annual Meeting of the Association for Computational Linguistics and the 7th International Joint Conference on Natural Language Processing (Volume 2: Short Papers)*, pages 63–68.

G. Glavaš and I. Vulić. 2018. Explicit retrofitting of distributional word vectors. In *Proceedings of the 56th Annual Meeting of the Association for Computational Linguistics (Volume 1: Long Papers)*, pages 34–45.

A. Golden. 2010. Grasping the point: A study of 15-year-old students' comprehension of metaphorical expressions in schoolbooks. In Graham Low, Zazie Todd, Alice Deignan, and Lynne Cameron, editors, *Researching and Applying Metaphor in the Real World*, pages 35–62. John Benjamins B. V.

S. Gooding and E. Kochmar. 2018. CAMB at CWI shared task 2018: Complex word identification with ensemble-based voting. In *Proceedings of the Thirteenth Workshop on Innovative Use of NLP for Building Educational Applications*, pages 184–194.

E. D. Gutiérrez, E. Shutova, T. Marghetis, and B. Bergen. 2016. Literal and metaphorical senses in compositional distributional semantic models. In *Proceedings of the 54th Annual Meeting of the Association for Computational Linguistics (Volume 1: Long Papers)*, pages 183–193.

C. Horn, C. Manduca, and D. Kauchak. 2014. Learning a lexical simplifier using Wikipedia. In *Proceedings of the 52nd Annual Meeting of the Association for Computational Linguistics (Volume 2: Short Papers)*, pages 458–463.

S. K. Jauhar and L. Specia. 2012. UOW-SHEF: SimpLex - lexical simplicity ranking based on contextual and psycholinguistic features. In **SEM 2012: The First Joint Conference on Lexical and Computational Semantics – Volume 1: Proceedings of the main conference and the shared task, and Volume 2: Proceedings of the Sixth International Workshop on Semantic Evaluation (SemEval 2012)*, pages 477–481.

M. Köper and S. Schulte im Walde. 2017. Improving verb metaphor detection by propagating abstractness to words, phrases and individual senses. In *Proceedings of the 1st Workshop on Sense, Concept and Entity Representations and their Applications*, pages 24–30.

Z. Kövecses. 2017. *The Routledge Handbook of Metaphor and Language*, chapter Conceptual Metaphor Theory. Routledge.

R. Kriz, E. Miltsakaki, M. Apidianaki, and Ch. Callison-Burch. 2018. Simplification using paraphrases and context-based lexical substitution. In *Proceedings of the 2018 Conference of the North*

American Chapter of the Association for Computational Linguistics: Human Language Technologies (Volume 1: Long Papers), pages 207–217.

V. Kuperman, H. Stadthagen-Gonzalez, and M. Brysbaert. 2012. Age-of-acquisition ratings for 30,000 english words. *Behavior Research Methods*, 44(4):978–990.

M. J. Kusner, Y. Sun, N. I. Kolkin, and K. Q. Weinberger. 2015. From word embeddings to document distance. In *Proceedings of the 32nd International Conference on Machine Learning (ICML 2015)*, volume 37, pages 957–966.

G. Lakoff and M. Johnson. 1980. *Metaphors We Live By*. University of Chicago Press, Chicago.

M. Lesk. 1986. Automatic sense disambiguation using machine readable dictionaries: How to tell a pine cone from an ice cream cone. In *Proceedings of the 5th Annual International Conference on Systems Documentation*, SIGDOC '86, pages 24–26.

M. Marschark, A. N. Katz, and A. Paivio. 1983. Dimensions of metaphor. *Journal of Psycholinguistic Research*, 12(1):17–40.

T. Mikolov, G. Corrado, K. Chen, and J. Dean. 2013. Efficient estimation of word representations in vector space. In *Proceedings of Workshop at ICLR*, pages 1–12.

S. Nisioi, S. Štajner, S. Paolo Ponzetto, and L. P. Dinu. 2017. Exploring neural text simplification models. In *Proceedings of the 55th Annual Meeting of the Association for Computational Linguistics (Volume 2: Short Papers)*, pages 85–91.

G. Paetzold and L. Specia. 2016. SemEval 2016 task 11: Complex word identification. In *Proceedings of the 10th International Workshop on Semantic Evaluation (SemEval-2016)*, pages 560–569.

A. Paivio, J. C. Yuille, and S. A. Madigan. 1968. Concreteness, imagery, and meaningfulness values for 925 nouns. *Journal of Experimental Psychology, Monograph Supplement*, 76(3, Pt. 2):1–25.

F. Pedregosa, G. Varoquaux, A. Gramfort, V. Michel, B. Thirion, O. Grisel, M. Blondel, P. Prettenhofer, R. Weiss, V. Dubourg, J. Vanderplas, A. Passos, D. Cournapeau, M. Brucher, M. Perrot, and É. Duchesnay. 2011. Scikit-learn: Machine learning in Python. *Journal of Machine Learning Research*, 12:2825–2830.

R. Řehůřek and P. Sojka. 2010. Software framework for topic modelling with large corpora. In *Proceedings of the LREC 2010 Workshop on New Challenges for NLP Frameworks*, pages 45–50.

E. Shutova. 2013. Metaphor identification as interpretation. In *Second Joint Conference on Lexical and Computational Semantics (*SEM), Volume 1: Proceedings of the Main Conference and the Shared Task*, pages 276–285.

G. Steen, L. Dorst, J. B. Herrmann, A. Kaal, T. Krennmayr, and T. Pasma. 2010. *A method for linguistic metaphor identification: From MIP to MIPVU*. John Benjamins B.V.

P. Stenetorp, S. Pyysalo, G. Topić, T. Ohta, S. Ananiadou, and J. Tsujii. 2012. brat: a web-based tool for NLP-assisted text annotation. In *Proceedings of the Demonstrations at the 13th Conference of the European Chapter of the Association for Computational Linguistics*, pages 102–107.

D. Torunoğlu-Selamet, T. Pamay, and G. Eryiğit. 2016. Simplification of Turkish sentences. In *Proceedings of The First International Conference on Turkic Computational Linguistics*, pages 55–59.

P. D. Turney, Y. Neuman, D. Assaf, and Y. Cohen. 2011. Literal and metaphorical sense identification through concrete and abstract context. In *Proceedings of the Conference on Empirical Methods in Natural Language Processing*, EMNLP '11, pages 680–690.

J. M. Ureña and P. Faber. 2010. Reviewing imagery in resemblance and non-resemblance metaphors. *Cognitive Linguistics*, 21:123–149.

S. Vajjala and D. Meurers. 2014. Readability assessment for text simplification: From analyzing documents to identifying sentential simplifications. *International Journal of Applied Linguistics, Special Issue on Recent Advances in Automatic Readability Assessment and Text Simplification*, 165(2):194–222.

S. Štajner, S. Paolo Ponzetto, and H. Stuckenschmidt. 2017. Automatic assessment of absolute sentence complexity. In *Proceedings of the 26th International Joint Conference on Artificial Intelligence*, IJCAI '17, pages 4096–4102.

Tu Thanh Vu, Giang Binh Tran, and Son Bao Pham. 2014. Learning to simplify children stories with limited data. In *9th Asian Conference on Intelligent Information and Database Systems*, pages 31–41.

M. Wilson. 1988. MRC psycholinguistic database: Machine-usable dictionary, version 2.00. *Behavior Research Methods, Instruments, & Computers*, 20(1):6–10.

M. Wolska and Y. Clausen. 2017. Simplifying metaphorical language for young readers: A corpus study on news text. In *Proceedings of the 12th Workshop on Innovative Use of NLP for Building Educational Applications*, pages 313–318.

W. Xu, Ch. Callison-Burch, and C. Napoles. 2015. Problems in current text simplification research: New data can help. *Transactions of the Association for Computational Linguistics*, 3:283–297.

W. Xu, C. Napoles, E. Pavlick, Q. Chen, and Ch. Callison-Burch. 2016. Optimizing statistical machine translation for text simplification. *Transactions of the Association for Computational Linguistics*, 4:401–415.

S. M. Yimam, Ch. Biemann, S. Malmasi, G. Paetzold, L. Specia, S. Štajner, A. Tack, and M. Zampieri. 2018. A report on the complex word identification shared task 2018. In *Proceedings of the Thirteenth Workshop on Innovative Use of NLP for Building Educational Applications*, pages 66–78.

Z. Zhu, D. Bernhard, and I. Gurevych. 2010. A monolingual tree-based translation model for sentence simplification. In *Proceedings of the 23rd International Conference on Computational Linguistics (Coling 2010)*, pages 1353–1361.

Application of an Automatic Plagiarism Detection System in a Large-scale Assessment of English Speaking Proficiency

Xinhao Wang[1], **Keelan Evanini**[2], **Matthew Mulholland**[2], **Yao Qian**[1], **James V. Bruno**[2]
Educational Testing Service
[1]90 New Montgomery St #1450, San Francisco, CA 94105, USA
[2]660 Rosedale Road, Princeton, NJ 08541, USA
`{xwang002, kevanini, mmulholland, yqian, jbruno}@ets.org`

Abstract

This study aims to build an automatic system for the detection of plagiarized spoken responses in the context of an assessment of English speaking proficiency for non-native speakers. Classification models were trained to distinguish between plagiarized and non-plagiarized responses with two different types of features: text-to-text content similarity measures, which are commonly used in the task of plagiarism detection for written documents, and speaking proficiency measures, which were specifically designed for spontaneous speech and extracted using an automated speech scoring system. The experiments were first conducted on a large data set drawn from an operational English proficiency assessment across multiple years, and the best classifier on this heavily imbalanced data set resulted in an F1-score of 0.761 on the plagiarized class. This system was then validated on operational responses collected from a single administration of the assessment and achieved a recall of 0.897. The results indicate that the proposed system can potentially be used to improve the validity of both human and automated assessment of non-native spoken English.

1 Introduction

Plagiarism of spoken responses has become a vexing problem in the domain of spoken language assessment, in particular, the evaluation of non-native speaking proficiency, since there exists a vast amount of easily accessible online resources covering a wide variety of topics that test takers can use to prepare responses prior to the test. In the context of large-scale, standardized assessments of spoken English for academic purposes, such as the TOEFL iBT test (ETS, 2012), the Pearson Test of English Academic (Longman, 2010), and the IELTS Academic assessment

(Cullen et al., 2014), some test takers may utilize content from online resources or other prepared sources in their spoken responses to test questions that are intended to elicit spontaneous speech. These responses that are based on canned material pose a problem for both human raters and automated scoring systems, and can reduce the validity of scores that are provided to the test takers; therefore, research into the automated detection of plagiarized spoken responses is necessary.

In this paper, we investigate a variety of features for automatically detecting plagiarized spoken responses in the context of a standardized assessment of English speaking proficiency. In addition to examining several commonly used text-to-text content similarity features, we also use features that compare various aspects of speaking proficiency across multiple responses provided by a test taker, based on the hypothesis that certain aspects of speaking proficiency, such as fluency, may be artificially inflated in a test taker's canned responses in comparison to non-canned responses. These features are designed to be independent of the availability of the reference source materials. Finally, we evaluate the effectiveness of this system on a data set with a large number of control (non-plagiarized) responses in an attempt to simulate the imbalanced distribution from an operational setting in which only a small number of the test takers' responses are plagiarized. In addition, we further validate this system on operational data and show how it can practically assist both human and automated scoring in a large scale assessment of English speaking proficiency

2 Previous Work

Previous research related to automated plagiarism detection for natural language has mainly focused on written documents. For example, a

Proceedings of the Fourteenth Workshop on Innovative Use of NLP for Building Educational Applications, pages 435–443
Florence, Italy, August 2, 2019. ©2019 Association for Computational Linguistics

series of shared tasks has enabled a variety of NLP approaches for detecting plagiarism to be compared on a standardized set of texts (Potthast et al., 2013), and several plagiarism detection services are available online.[1] Various techniques have been employed in this task, including *n*-gram overlap (Lyon et al., 2006), document fingerprinting (Brin et al., 1995), word frequency statistics (Shivakumar and Garcia-Molina, 1995), information retrieval-based metrics (Hoad and Zobel, 2003), text summarization evaluation metrics (Chen et al., 2010), WordNet-based features (Nahnsen et al., 2005), stopword-based features (Stamatatos, 2011), features based on shared syntactic patterns (Uzuner et al., 2005), features based on word swaps detected via dependency parsing (Mozgovoy et al., 2007), and stylometric features (Stein et al., 2011), among others. In general, for the task of monolingual plagiarism detection, these methods can be categorized as either external plagiarism detection, in which a document is compared to a body of reference documents, or intrinsic plagiarism detection, in which a document is evaluated independently without a reference collection (Alzahrani et al., 2012). This task is also related to the widely studied task of paraphrase recognition, which benefits from similar types of features (Finch et al., 2005; Madnani et al., 2012). The current study adopts several of these features that are designed to be robust to the presence of word-level modifications between the source and the plagiarized text; since this study focuses on spoken responses that are reproduced from memory and subsequently processed by a speech recognizer, metrics that rely on exact matches are likely to perform sub-optimally.

Little prior work has been conducted on the task of automatically detecting similar spoken responses, although research in the field of Spoken Document Retrieval (Hauptmann, 2006) is relevant. Due to the difficulties involved in collecting corpora of actual plagiarized material, nearly all published results of approaches to the task of plagiarism detection have relied on either simulated plagiarism (i.e., plagiarized texts generated by experimental human participants in a controlled environment) or artificial plagiarism (i.e., plagiarized texts generated by algorithmically modifying

---

[1]For example, `http://turnitin.com/en_us/what-we-offer/feedback-studio`,`http://www.grammarly.com/plagiarism`, and `http://www.paperrater.com/plagiarism_checker`.

a source text) (Potthast et al., 2010). These results, however, may not reflect actual performance in a deployed setting, since the characteristics of the plagiarized material may differ from actual plagiarized responses.

In previous studies (Evanini and Wang, 2014; Wang et al., 2016), we conducted experiments on a simulated data set from an operational, large-scale, standardized English proficiency assessment and obtained initial results with an F1-measure of 70.6% using an automatic system to detect plagiarized spoken responses (Wang et al., 2016). Based on these previous findings, we extend this line of research and contribute in the following ways: 1) an improved automatic speech recognition (ASR) system based on Kaldi was introduced, and an unsupervised language model adaptation method was employed to improve the ASR performance on spontaneous speech elicited by new, unseen test questions; 2) an improved set of text-to-text content similarity features based on *n*-gram overlap and Word Mover's Distance was investigated; 3) in addition to evaluating the system on a simulated imbalanced data set, we also validated the developed automatic system using all of the responses from a single operational administration of the English speaking assessment in order to obtain a reliable estimate of the system's performance in a practical deployment.

3 Data

The data used in this study was drawn from a large-scale, high-stakes assessment of English for non-native speakers, which assesses English communication skills for academic purposes. The Speaking section of this assessment contains six tasks designed to elicit spontaneous spoken responses: two of them require test takers to provide an opinion or preference based on personal experience, which are referred to as independent tasks; and the other four tasks require test takers to summarize or discuss material provided in a reading and/or listening passage, which are referred to as integrated tasks.

In general, the independent tasks ask questions on topics that are familiar to test takers and are not based on any stimulus materials. Therefore, test takers can provide responses containing a wide variety of specific examples. In some cases, test takers may attempt to game the assessment by memorizing canned material from an external source and adapting it to the questions presented in the independent tasks. This type of plagiarism can affect the validity of a test taker's speaking score and can be grounds for score cancellation. However, it is often difficult even for trained human raters to recognize plagiarized spoken responses, due to the large number and variety of external sources that are available to test takers.

In order to identify the plagiarized spoken responses from the operational test, human raters need to first flag spoken responses that contained potentially plagiarized material, then trained experts subsequently review them to make the final decision. In the review process, the responses were transcribed and compared to external source materials obtained through manual internet searches; if it was determined that the presence of plagiarized material made it impossible to provide a valid assessment of the test taker's performance on the speaking task, the response was labeled as a plagiarized response and assigned a score of 0. In this study, a total of 1,557 plagiarized responses to independent test questions were collected from the operational assessment across multiple years.

During the process of reviewing potentially plagiarized responses, the raters also collected a data set of external sources that appeared to have been used by test takers in their responses. In some cases, the test taker's spoken response was nearly identical to an identified source; in other cases, several sentences or phrases were clearly drawn from a particular source, although some modifications were apparent. Table 1 presents a sample source that was identified for several of the responses in the data set along with a sample plagiarized response that apparently contains extended sequences of words directly matching idiosyncratic features of this source, such as the phrases "how romantic it can ever be" and "just relax yourself on the beach." In general, test takers typically do not reproduce the entire source material in their responses; rather, they often attempt to adapt the source material to a specific test question by providing some speech that is directly relevant to the prompt and combining it with the plagiarized material. An example of this is shown by the opening and closing non-italicized portions of the sample plagiarized response in Table 1. In total, human raters identified 224 different source materials while reviewing the potentially plagiarized responses, and their statistics information is

as follows: the average number of words is 95.7 (std. dev. = 38.5), the average number of clauses is 10.3 (std. dev. = 5.1), and the average number of words per clause is 9.3 (std. dev. = 7.1).

In addition to the source materials and the plagiarized responses, a set of non-plagiarized control responses was also obtained in order to conduct classification experiments between plagiarized and non-plagiarized responses. Since the plagiarized responses were collected over the course of multiple years, they were drawn from many different test forms, and it was not practical to obtain control data from all of the test forms that were represented in the plagiarized set. So, only the 166 test forms that appear most frequently in the canned data set were used for the collection of control responses, and 200 test takers were randomly selected from each form, without any overlap with speakers in the plagiarized set. The two spoken responses from the two independent questions were collected from each speaker; in total, 66,400 spoken responses from 33,200 speakers were obtained as the control set. Therefore, the data set used in this study is quite imbalanced: the number of control responses is larger than the number of plagiarized responses by a factor of 43.

4 Methodology

This study employed two different types of features in the automatic detection of plagiarized spoken responses: 1) similar to human raters' behavior in identifying the canned spoken responses, a set of features is developed to measure the content similarities between a test response and the source materials that were collected; 2) to deal with this particular task of plagiarism detection for spontaneous spoken responses, a set of features is introduced based on the assumption that the production of spoken language based on memorized material is expected to differ from the production of non-plagiarized speech in aspects of a test taker's speech delivery, such as fluency, pronunciation, and prosody.

4.1 Content Similarity

Previous work (Wang et al., 2016; Evanini and Wang, 2014) has demonstrated the effectiveness of using content-based features for the task of automatic plagiarized spoken response detection. Therefore, this study investigates the use of improved features based on the measurement of text-

Table 1: A sample source passage and the transcription of a sample plagiarized spoken response that was apparently drawn from the source. The test question/prompt used to elicit this response is also included. The overlapping word sequences between the source material and the transcription of the spoken response are indicated in italics.

Sample source passage: Well, the place I enjoy the most is a small town located in France. I like this small town because it *has very charming ocean view.* I mean *the sky there is so blue and the beach is always full of sunshine. You know how romantic it can ever be, just relax yourself on the beach, when the sun is* setting *down,* when the ocean breeze is blowing and *the seabirds are singing. Of course* I like this small French town *also because there are many great French restaurants. They offer the best seafood in the world like lobsters and tuna fishes.* The most important, I have been benefited a lot from this trip to France because I made friends with some gorgeous French girls. One of them even gave me a little watch as a souvenir of our friendship.	**Prompt:** Talk about an activity you enjoyed doing with your family when you were a kid. **Transcription of a plagiarized response:** family is a little trip to France when I was in primary school ten years ago I enjoy this activity first because we visited a small French town located by the beach the town *has very charming ocean view* and in *the sky is so blue and the beach is always full of sunshine you know how romantic it can ever be just relax yourself on the beach when the sun is* settling *down the sea birds are singing of course* I enjoy this activity with my family *also because there are many great French restaurants they offer the best sea food in the world like lobsters and tuna fishes* so I enjoy this activity with my family very much even it has passed several years

to-text content similarity. Given a test response, a comparison is made with each of the 224 reference sources using the following two content similarity metrics: word n-gram overlap and Word Mover's Distance. Then, the maximum similarity or the minimum distance is taken as a single feature to measure the content relevance between the test responses and the source materials.

4.1.1 N-gram Overlap

Features based on the BLEU metric have been proven to be effective in measuring the content appropriateness of spoken responses in the context of English proficiency assessment (Zechner and Wang, 2013) and in measuring content similarity in the detection of plagiarized spoken responses (Wang et al., 2016; Evanini and Wang, 2014). In this study, we first design a new type of feature, known as n-gram overlap, by simulating and improving the previous BLEU-based features. Word n-grams, with n varying from 1 word to 11 words, are first extracted from both the test response and each of the source materials, and then the number of overlapping n-grams are counted, where both n-gram types and tokens are counted separately. The intuition behind decreasing the maximum order is to increase the classifier's recall by evaluating the overlap of shorter word sequences, such

as individual words in the unigram setting. On the other hand, the motivation behind increasing the maximum order is to boost the classifier's precision, since it will focus on matches of longer word sequences. Here, the maximum order of 11 was experimentally decided in consideration of the average number of words per clause in source materials, which is 9.3 as described in Section 3.

In order to calculate the maximum similarity across all source materials, the 11 n-gram overlap counts are combined together to generate one weighted score between a test and each source as in Equation 1, and then the maximum score across all sources is calculated as a feature to measure the similarity between a test and the set of source materials. Meanwhile, the 11 n-gram overlap counts calculated using the source with the maximum similarity score are also taken as features.

$$\sum_{i=1}^{n} \frac{i}{(n \cdot (n+1)/2)} \text{count\_overlap}(i\text{-gram}) \quad (1)$$

Furthermore, the n-gram based feature set can be enlarged by: 1) normalizing the n-gram counts by either the number of n-grams in the test response or the number of n-grams in each of the sources; 2) combining all source materials together into a single document for comparison (11 features based on n-gram overlap with the combined source), which is designed based on the assumption that test takers may attempt to use content from multiple sources. Similarly, this type of features can be further normalized by the number of n-grams in the test response. Based on all of these variations, a total of 116 n-gram overlap features is generated for each spoken response.

4.1.2 Word Mover's Distance

More recently, various approaches based on deep neural networks (DNN) and word-embeddings trained on large corpora have shown promising performance in document similarity detection (Kusner et al., 2015). In contrast to traditional similarity features, which are limited to a reliance on exact word matching, as the above n-gram overlap features, these new approaches have the advantage of capturing topically relevant words that are not identical. In this study, we employ Word Mover's Distance (WMD) (Kusner et al., 2015) to measure the distance between a test response and a source material based on word-embeddings.

Embeddings of words are first represented as vectors, and then the distance between each word appearing in a test response and each word in a source can be measured using the Euclidean distance in the embedding space. WMD represents the sum of the minimum values among the Euclidean word distances between words in the two compared documents. This minimization problem is a special case of Earth Mover's Distance (Rubner et al., 1998), for which efficient algorithms are available. Kunsner et al. (Kusner et al., 2015) reported that WMD outperformed other distance measures on document retrieval tasks and that the embeddings trained on the Google News corpus consistently performed well across a variety of contexts. For this work, we used the same word embeddings used in weighted embedding features as the input for the WMD calculation.

4.2 Difference in Speaking Proficiency

The performance of the above content similarity features greatly depends on the availability of a comprehensive set of source materials. If a test taker uses unseen source materials as the basis for a plagiarized response, the system may fail to detect it. Accordingly, a set of features that do not rely on a comparison with source materials has been proposed previously (Wang et al., 2016). The current study also examined this type of features.

As described in Section 3, the Speaking section of the assessment includes both independent and integrated tasks. In a given test administration, test takers are required to respond to all six questions; however, plagiarized responses are more likely to appear in the two independent tasks, since they are not based on specific reading and/or listening passages and thus elicit a wider range of variation across responses. Since the plagiarized responses are mostly constructed based on memorized material, they may be delivered in a more fluent and proficient manner compared to the responses that contain fully spontaneous speech. Based on this assumption, a set of features can be developed to capture the difference between various speaking proficiency features extracted from the canned and the fully spontaneous speech produced by the same test taker, where an automated spoken English assessment system, SpeechRater® (Zechner et al., 2007, 2009), can be used to provide the automatic proficiency scores along with 29 features measuring fluency, pronunciation, prosody, rhythm, vocabulary, and grammar. Since most plagiarized responses are expected to occur in the independent tasks, we assume the integrated responses are based on spontaneous speech. A mismatch between the proficiency scores and the feature values from the independent responses and the integrated responses from the same speaker can potentially indicate the presence of both prepared speech and spontaneous speech, and, therefore, the presence of plagiarized spoken responses.

Given an independent response from a test taker, along with the other independent response and four integrated responses from the same test taker, 6 features can be extracted according to each of the proficiency scores and 29 SpeechRater features. First, the difference of score/feature values between two independent responses was calculated as a feature, which was used to deal with the case in which only one independent response was canned and the other one contained spontaneous speech. Then, basic descriptive statistics, including mean, median, min, and max, were obtained across the four integrated responses. The differences between the score/feature value of the independent response and these four basic statistics were extracted as additional features. Finally, another feature was also extracted by standardizing the score/feature value of the independent response with the mean and standard deviation from the integrated responses. In total, a set of 180 features were extracted, referred as *SpeechRater* in the following experiments.

5 Experiments and Results

5.1 ASR Improvement

In this study, spoken responses need to be transcribed into text so that they can be compared with the source materials to measure the text-to-text similarity. However, due to the large amount of spoken responses considered in this study, it is not practical to manually transcribe all of them; therefore, a Kaldi[2]-based automatic speech recognition engine was employed. The training set used to develop the speech recognizer consists of similar responses (around 800 hours of speech) drawn from the same assessment and do not overlap with the data sets included in this study.

When using an ASR system to recognize spoken responses from new prompts that are not seen in the ASR training data, a degradation in recognition accuracy is expected because of the mismatch between the training and test data. In this study, we used an unsupervised language model (LM) adaptation method to improve the ASR performance on unseen data. In this method, two rounds of language model adaptation were conducted with the following steps: first, out-of-vocabulary (OOV) words from the prompt materials were added to the pronunciation dictionary and the baseline models were adapted with the prompts; second, the adapted models were applied to spoken responses from these new prompts to produce the recognized texts along with confidence scores corresponding to each response; third, automatically transcribed texts with confidence scores higher than a predefined threshold of 0.8 were selected; finally, these high-confident recognized texts were used to conduct another round of language model adaptation. We evaluated this unsupervised language model adaptation method on a stand-alone data set with 1,500 responses from 250 test speakers, where the prompts used to elicit these responses were unseen in the baseline recognition models. In this experiment, supervised language model adaptation with human transcriptions was also examined for comparison. As shown in Table 2, the overall word error rate

[2] http://kaldi-asr.org/

Table 2: Word error rate (WER %) reduction with an unsupervised language model adaptation method, where the WERs on Independent items (IND), Integrated items (INT), as well as all items (ALL), are reported. The WER with the supervised adaptation method based on human transcriptions is also listed for comparison.

ASR Systems	IND	INT	ALL
Baseline	22.5	26.6	25.5
Unsupervised	21.5	23.5	22.9
Supervised	21.2	22.1	21.8

(WER) is 25.5% for the baseline models. By applying the unsupervised LM adaptation method, the overall WER can be reduced to 22.9%; in comparison, the overall WER can be reduced to 21.8% by using supervised LM adaptation. The unsupervised method can achieve very similar results to the supervised method especially for responses to the independent prompts, i.e., with WER of 21.5% (unsupervised) vs 21.2% (supervised). These results indicate the effectiveness of the proposed unsupervised adaptation method, which was employed in the subsequent automatic plagiarism detection work.

5.2 Experimental Setup

Due to ASR failures, a small number of responses were excluded from the experiments; finally, a total of 1,551 canned and 66,257 control responses were included in the simulated data. Since this work was conducted on a very imbalanced data set and only 2.3% of the responses in the simulated data are authentic plagiarized ones confirmed by human raters, 10-fold cross-validation was performed first on the simulated data. Afterward, the classification model built on the simulated data set was further evaluated on a corpus with real operational data.

We employed the machine learning tool of scikit-learn[3] (Pedregosa et al., 2011), for training the classifier. It provides various classification methods, such as decision tree, random forest, AdaBoost, etc. This study involves a variety of features from two different categories, and preliminary experiments demonstrated that the random forest model can achieve the overall better perfor-

[3] SKLL, a python tool making the running of scikit-learn experiments simpler, was used. Downloaded from `https://github.com/EducationalTestingService/skll`.

mance. Therefore, the random forest method is used to build classification models in the following experiments, and the precision, recall, as well as F1-score on the positive class (plagiarized responses) are used as the evaluation metrics.

5.3 Experimental Results

First, in order to verify the effectiveness of the newly developed n-gram overlap features, a preliminary experiment was conducted to compare this set of features with BLEU-based features, since they had been shown to be effective in previous research (Wang et al., 2016). The results as shown in Table 3 indicate that the F1-Measure of the n-gram features outperforms the BLEU features (0.761 vs. 0.748), and the recall of the n-gram features is higher than the BLEU features (0.716 vs. 0.683); inversely, the BLEU features result in higher precision (0.83 vs. 0.814). Accordingly, the n-gram features are used to replace the BLEU ones, since it is more important to reduce the number of false negatives, i.e., improve the recall, for our task.

Table 3: Comparison of n-gram and BLEU features.

Features	Precision	Recall	F1
BLEU	0.83	0.683	0.748
n-gram	0.814	0.716	0.761

Furthermore, each individual type of feature and their combinations were examined in the classification experiments described above. As shown in Table 4, each feature set alone was used to build classification models. The n-gram overlap features result in the best performance with an F1-score of 0.761, and the WMD features capturing the topical relevance between word pairs result in a much lower F1-score of 0.649. Furthermore, the combination of both types of content similarity features, i.e., n-gram and WMD, slightly reduces the F1-score to 0.76. These results indicate that for this particular task, the exact match of certain expressions appearing in both the test response and a source material plays a critical role.

As to the speaking proficiency related features, they can lead to a promising precision of 0.8 but with a very low recall of 0.009. After reexamining the assumption that human experts may be able to differentiate prepared speech from fully spontaneous speech based on the way how the speech is delivered, it turns out that it is quite challenging

Table 4: Classification performance using each individual feature set and their combinations.

Features	Precision	Recall	F1
1. n-gram	0.814	0.716	0.761
2. WMD	0.663	0.636	0.649
3. SpeechRater	0.8	0.009	0.018
1 + 2	0.812	0.716	0.76
1 + 2 + 3	0.821	0.696	0.752

for human experts to make a reliable judgment of plagiarism just based on the speech delivery without any reference to the source materials, in particular, within the context of high-stakes language assessment. Accordingly, the features capturing the difference in speaking proficiency of prepared and spontaneous speech can be used as contributory information to improve the accuracy of an automatic detection system, but they are unable to achieve promising performance alone. Also as shown in Table 4, By adding the speaking proficiency features, the precision can be improved to 0.821, but the recall is reduced; finally, the F1-score is reduced to 0.752.

6 Employment in Operational Test

6.1 Operational Use

In order to obtain a more accurate estimate of how well the automatic plagiarism detection system might perform in a practical application in which the distribution is expected to be heavily skewed towards the non-plagiarized category, all test-taker responses to independent prompts were collected from a single administration of the speaking assessment. In total, 13,516 independent responses from 6,758 speakers were extracted for system evaluation. We collected 39 responses confirmed as plagiarized through the human review process, which represents 0.29% of the data set.

In this particular task, automatic detection systems can be applied to support human raters, where all potentially plagiarized responses can be first automatically identified and then human experts can be involved to review flagged responses and make the final decision about potential instances of plagiarism. In this scenario, it is more important to increase the number of true positives flagged by the automated system; thus, recall of plagiarized responses was used as the evaluation metric, i.e., how many responses can be successfully detected among these 39 confirmed instances of plagiarism.

6.2 Results and Discussion

In order to maximize the recall of plagiarized responses for this review, several models were built with either different types of features or different types of classification models, for example, random forest and Adaboost with decision tree as the weak classifier, and then they were combined in an ensemble manner to flag potentially plagiarized responses, i.e., a response is flagged if any of the models detects it as a plagiarized response. This ensemble system flagged 850 responses as instances of plagiarism in total and achieved a recall of 0.897, i.e., 35 of the confirmed plagiarized responses were successfully identified by the automatic system and 4 of them were missed.

These results prove that the developed system can provide a substantial benefit to both human and automated assessment of non-native spoken English. Manual identification of plagiarized responses can be a very difficult and time-consuming task, where human experts need to memorize hundreds of source materials and compare them to thousands of responses. By applying an automated system, potentially plagiarized responses can first be filtered out of the standard scoring pipeline; subsequently, experts can review these flagged responses to confirm whether they actually contain plagiarized material. Accordingly, instead of reviewing all 13,516 responses in this administration for plagiarized content, human effort is required only for the 850 flagged responses, thus substantially reducing the overall human effort. Thus, optimizing recall is appropriate in this targeted use case, since the number of false positives is within an acceptable range for the expert review. In addition, the source labels indicating which source materials were likely used in the preparation of each response are automatically generated by the automatic system for each suspected response; this information can help to accelerate the manual review process.

7 Conclusion and Future Work

This study proposed a system which can benefit a high-stakes assessment of English speaking proficiency by automatically detecting potentially plagiarized spoken responses, and investigated the empirical effectiveness of two different types of features. One is based on automatic plagiarism detection methods commonly applied to written texts, in which the content similarity between a test response and a set of source materials collected from human raters were measured. In addition, this study also adopted a set of features which do not rely on the human effort involved in source material collection and can be easily applied to unseen test questions. This type of feature attempts to capture the difference in speech patterns between prepared responses and fully spontaneous responses from the same speaker in a test. Finally, the classification models were evaluated on a large set of responses collected from an operational test, and the experimental results demonstrate that the automatic detection system can achieve an F1-measure of 0.761. Further evaluation on the real operational data also shows the effectiveness of the automatic detection system.

The task of applying an automatic system in a large-scale operational assessment is quite challenging since typically only a small number of plagiarized responses are distributed among a much larger amount of non-plagiarized responses to a wide range of different test questions. In the future, we will continue our research efforts to improve the automatic detection system along the following lines. First, since deep learning techniques have recently shown their effectiveness in the fields of both speech processing and natural language understanding, we will further explore various deep learning techniques to improve the metrics used to measure the content similarity between test responses and source materials. Next, further analysis will be conducted to determine the extent of differences between canned and spontaneous speech, and additional features will be explored based on the findings. In addition, another focus is to build automatic tools to regularly update the pool of source materials. Besides internet search, new sources can also be detected by comparing all candidate responses from the same test question, since different test takers may use the same source to produce their canned responses.

References

S. M. Alzahrani, N. Salim, and A. Abraham. 2012. Understanding plagiarism linguistic patterns, textual features, and detection methods. *IEEE Transaction on Systems, Man, and Cybernetics-Part C: Applications and Reviews*, 42(2):133–149.

S. Brin, J. Davis, and H. Garcia-Molina. 1995. Copy

detection mechanisms for digital documents. In *Proceedings of the ACM SIGMOD Annual Conference*, pages 398–409.

C. Chen, J. Yeh, and H. Ke. 2010. Plagiarism detection using ROUGE and WordNet. *Journal of Computing*, 2(3):34–44.

P. Cullen, A. French, and V. Jakeman. 2014. *The Official Cambridge Guide to IELTS*. Cambridge University Press.

ETS. 2012. *The Official Guide to the TOEFL® Test, Fourth Edition*. McGraw-Hill.

Keelan Evanini and Xinhao Wang. 2014. Automatic detection of plagiarized spoken responses. In *Proceedings of the Ninth Workshop on Innovative Use of NLP for Building Educational Applications*, pages 22–27.

A. Finch, Y. Hwang, and E. Sumita. 2005. Using machine translation evaluation techniques to determine sentence-level semantic equivalence. In *Proceedings of the Third International Workshop on Paraphrasing*, pages 17–24.

A. Hauptmann. 2006. Automatic spoken document retrieval. In Ketih Brown, editor, *Encylclopedia of Language and Linguistics (Second Edition)*, pages 95–103. Elsevier Science.

T. C. Hoad and J. Zobel. 2003. Methods for identifying versioned and plagiarised documents. *Journal of the American Society for Information Science and Technology*, 54:203–215.

Matt Kusner, Yu Sun, Nicholas Kolkin, and Kilian Weinberger. 2015. From word embeddings to document distances. In *Proceedings of the 32nd International Conference on Machine Learning*, volume 37 of *Proceedings of Machine Learning Research*, pages 957–966, Lille, France.

P. Longman. 2010. *The Official Guide to Pearson Test of English Academic*. Pearson Education ESL.

C. Lyon, R. Barrett, and J. Malcolm. 2006. Plagiarism is easy, but also easy to detect. *Plagiary*, 1:57–65.

N. Madnani, J. Tetreault, and M. Chodorow. 2012. Re-examining machine translation metrics for paraphrase identification. In *Proceedings of the 2012 Conference of the North American Chapter of the Association for Computational Linguistics: Human Language Technologies*, pages 182–190, Montréal, Canada. Association for Computational Linguistics.

M. Mozgovoy, T. Kakkonen, and E. Sutinen. 2007. Using natural language parsers in plagiarism detection. In *Proceedings of the ISCA Workshop on Speech and Language Technology in Education (SLaTE)*.

T. Nahnsen, Ö. Uzuner, and B. Katz. 2005. Lexical chains and sliding locality windows in content-based text similarity detection. CSAIL Technical Report, MIT-CSAIL-TR-2005-034.

Fabian Pedregosa, Gaël Varoquaux, Alexandre Gramfort, Vincent Michel, Bertrand Thirion, Olivier Grisel, Mathieu Blondel, Peter Prettenhofer, Ron Weiss, Vincent Dubourg, et al. 2011. Scikit-learn: Machine learning in python. *Journal of machine learning research*, 12(Oct):2825–2830.

M. Potthast, M. Hagen, T. Gollub, M. Tippmann, J. Kiesel, P. Rosso, E. Stamatatos, and B. Stein. 2013. Overview of the 5th International Competition on Plagiarism Detection. In *CLEF 2013 Evaluation Labs and Workshop – Working Notes Papers*.

M. Potthast, B. Stein, A. Barrón-Cedeño, and P. Rosso. 2010. An evaluation framework for plagiarism detection. In *Proceedings of the 23rd International Conference on Computational Linguistics*.

Y. Rubner, C. Tomasi, and L. J. Guibas. 1998. A metric for distributions with applications to image databases. In *Proceedings of the Sixth International Conference on Computer Vision*.

N. Shivakumar and H. Garcia-Molina. 1995. SCAM: A copy detection mechanism for digital documents. In *Proceedings of the Second Annual Conference on the Theory and Practice of Digital Libraries*.

E. Stamatatos. 2011. Plagiarism detection using stopword n-grams. *American Society for Information Science and Technology*, 62(12):2512–2527.

B. Stein, N. Lipka, and P. Prettenhofer. 2011. Intrinsic plagiarism analysis. *Language Resources and Evaluation*, 45(1):63–82.

Ö. Uzuner, B. Katz, and T. Nahnsen. 2005. Using syntactic information to identify plagiarism. In *Proceedings of the 2nd Workshop on Building Educational Applications using NLP. Ann Arbor*.

X. Wang, K. Evanini, J. Bruno, and M. Mulholland. 2016. Automatic plagiarism detection for spoken responses in an assessment of english language proficiency. In *Proceedings of the IEEE Spoken Language Technology Workshop*, pages 121–128.

K. Zechner, D. Higgins, and X. Xi. 2007. Speechrater[SM]: A construct-driven approach to scoring spontaneous non-native speech. In *Proceedings of the International Speech Communication Association Special Interest Group on Speech and Language Technology in Education*, pages 128–131.

K. Zechner, D. Higgins, X. Xi, and D. M. Williamson. 2009. Automatic scoring of non-native spontaneous speech in tests of spoken English. *Speech Communication*, 51(10):883–895.

K. Zechner and X. Wang. 2013. Automated content scoring of spoken responses in an assessment for teachers of english. In *Proceedings of the Eighth Workshop on Innovative Use of NLP for Building Educational Applications*, page 73–81.

Equity Beyond Bias in Language Technologies for Education

Elijah Mayfield[1]*, **Michael Madaio**[2], **Shrimai Prabhumoye**[1], **David Gerritsen**[3],
Brittany McLaughlin[4], **Ezekiel Dixon-Román**[5], and **Alan W Black**[1]
[1]Language Technologies Institute, [2]Human-Computer Interaction Institute, and
[3]Eberly Center for Teaching Excellence, Carnegie Mellon University;
[4]ScribbleUp Learning; [5]School of Social Policy and Practice, University of Pennsylvania
* Corresponding author: elijah@cmu.edu

Abstract

There is a long record of research on equity in schools. As machine learning researchers begin to study fairness and bias in earnest, language technologies in education have an unusually strong theoretical and applied foundation to build on. Here, we introduce concepts from culturally relevant pedagogy and other frameworks for teaching and learning, and identify future work on equity in NLP. We present case studies in a range of topics like intelligent tutoring systems, computer-assisted language learning, automated essay scoring, and sentiment analysis in classrooms, and provide an actionable agenda for research.

1 Introduction

Researchers across machine learning applications are finding unintended outcomes from their systems, with inequitable or even unethical impacts (Barocas and Selbst, 2016). We are at an inflection point in the study of fair machine learning; popular science publications are shedding light on the widespread impacts of algorithmic bias (Noble, 2018; Eubanks, 2018; Angwin et al., 2016) and specialized technical conferences like ACM FAT*[1] and FATML[2] now provide methods and examples of research addressing ethics in model bias, the design of datasets, and user interfaces for algorithmic interventions. "Impact" investing in educational technology[3] has grown (Gates Foundation and Chan Zuckerberg Initiative, 2019) and these machine learning tools are now pervasive in educational decision-making (Wan, 2019). Yet in recent literature reviews of NLP in edtech, the focus has been on narrowly scoped technical topics, like speech (Eskenazi, 2009) or text and chat data (Litman, 2016), but crucially, do not address equity issues more broadly. NLP applications are

---

[1]https://fatconference.org/2019/

[2]http://www.fatml.org/

[3]From this point forward, abbreviated as "edtech."

mainstays in schools and have great reach, a trend poised to accelerate with the adoption of interactive, language-enabled devices like Alexa, both at home and in the classroom (Ziegeldorf et al., 2014; Horn, 2018; Boccella, 2019). As a field, we risk unwittingly contributing to harm for learners if we don't understand the ethical consequences of our research – but we don't have to start from scratch.

Education philosophers have long advocated for equity in schooling for all learners (Dewey, 1923; Freire, 1970), and over decades, have built rich pedagogies to accomplish goals of social justice for students (Ladson-Billings, 1995); this work has flourished in progressive schools (Morrell, 2015; Paris and Alim, 2017). Developers of edtech have already moved from technological innovation for its own sake, to a focus on efficacy and learning analytics, tying educational data mining to specific student outcomes (Baker and Inventado, 2014). This paper presents a roadmap for now incorporating equity into the design, evaluation, and implementation of those systems.

In sections 2 and 3 we give overviews of existing research, first on fair machine learning, then on social justice pedagogies in education. The bulk of our new contributions are in section 4-7, where we describe key problem areas for NLP researchers in education. We conclude with practical recommendations in section 8.

2 Primer on Fair Machine Learning

The topic of ethics in technology dates back to decades ago (Winner, 1989); but uptake of conversations about building equitable algorithmic systems is fairly recent. The existing literature prioritizes topics of bias and fairness, mostly based on what some have called *"allocational harm"* (Crawford, 2017). Researchers measure the distribution of outcomes produced by automated decision-making, and evaluate whether subgroups received proportional shares of a resource being

Proceedings of the Fourteenth Workshop on Innovative Use of NLP for Building Educational Applications, pages 444–460
Florence, Italy, August 2, 2019. ©2019 Association for Computational Linguistics

distributed - bail release recommendations, approval for a mortgage, high test scores, and so on. Over and over, differential outcomes have been tied to biased modeling along demographic lines like gender, race, and age (Friedler et al., 2019).

Some have questioned the value of fairness research, arguing that machine learning may simply reproduce existing distributions, rather than cause harm in itself (see Mittelstadt et al. (2016) for an overview of this debate). But high-profile research has repeatedly shown an *amplifying* effect of machine learning on concrete real-world outcomes, like racial bias in recidivism prediction in judicial hearings (Corbett-Davies et al., 2017), or disproportionate error from facial recognition for dark skin tones, particularly among individuals identifying as female (Buolamwini and Gebru, 2018).

Fairness work in NLP has focused particularly in dense semantic representations at the lexical or sentence level. In learned embeddings of meaning, bias exists along race and gender lines (Caliskan et al., 2017; Garg et al., 2018) and is passed downstream, producing biased outcomes for tasks like coreference resolution (Zhao et al., 2018a), sentiment analysis (Kiritchenko and Mohammad, 2018), search (Romanov et al., 2019), and dialogue systems (Voigt et al., 2018; Henderson et al., 2018). Research beyond metrics, analyzing the broader social impact of biased NLP, has also begun (Hovy and Spruit, 2016).

Many of these problems stem from training data selection; models trained on standard written professional English, like the Penn Treebank (Marcus et al., 1993), fail to transfer to other writing styles, especially online where research suggests that NLP performance is degraded for underrepresented language groups, like African American English (Petrov and McDonald, 2012; Blodgett et al., 2017). Early work on "de-biasing" NLP has begun, seeking to reduce the amplification of bias in dense word embeddings (Bolukbasi et al., 2016; Zhao et al., 2017, 2018b); but early results still leave room for improvement (Gonen and Goldberg, 2019). Accounting for dialects and other language variation has been moderately more successful, with examples in speech recognition (Kraljic et al., 2008), parsing (Gimpel et al., 2011), and classification (Jurgens et al., 2017).

There are many open questions. Chouldechova (2017) and Corbett-Davies and Goel (2018) work to even *define* fairness, giving several proposals;

but related research has shown these definitions are brittle. Classifiers may trivially fail to maintain fairness properties when the output from one classifier is used as input for another, for instance (Dwork and Ilvento, 2018), or even worsen disparate outcomes after iterating on algorithmic predictions over time (Liu et al., 2018). Research in computational ethics (Hooker and Kim, 2018) may give some guidelines for the NLP community broadly, and work on richer formal systems of guarantees on fairness is underway (Kearns et al., 2019); but while this research is ongoing, developers continue to build systems. For NLP researchers working in education, specifically, a key resource will be the long tradition of educational equity research and praxis that exists today, and is being practiced in schools already.

3 Equity in Education Research

Machine learning research in general tends to focus on recent publication; to counteract this and set a longer-term context, in the following section we explain the historical background on learning science research that considers socio-cultural dimensions of learning and their implications for equity, work that motivates our recommendations for technologists building educational interventions.

3.1 Sociocultural and Critical Perspectives

While much of the earliest work on learning science was purely behaviorist, the field's expansion into sociocultural factors that affect learning is old, beginning nearly a century ago. Driven by Marxist philosopher and psychologist Lev Vygotsky, the gaze of research shifted from inner processes of the mind to interactions between students and their cultural context and practices (Moll, 1992). This tradition drove research into individual development via socially-mediated processes of learning (Chaiklin, 2003). The mediated learning experience is done via a process of scaffolding what the learner knows and what they need help on, in their "zone of proximal development" (Hammond and Gibbons, 2005). This work also acknowledged the connection between formal school education and informal education in the world (Scribner and Cole, 1973), and introduced the idea of learning as a social process in which students build identity (Wenger, 2010). This conceptual framework now dominate the scientific discourse on sociocultural research in edtech systems (Aleven et al., 2016).

The sociocultural paradigm from Vygotsky has humanized education compared to purely behaviorist approaches; meanwhile, parallel work in the emerging field of *critical pedagogy* was taking more aggressive steps. Led by Brazilian educational and social philosopher Freire (1970), this work argued that formal schooling was an ideological system for preserving existing power structures, that treats students as receptacles to be filled with culturally dominant views (*i.e.* a "banking" model), rather than giving students the opportunity to learn topics of intrinsic meaning to them. This alternate approach led to unprecedented gains in adult literacy during the twentieth century, particularly in Brazil (Kirkendall, 2010) and in Cuba (Samuel and Williams, 2016), demonstrating what pedagogical theorists described as liberatory education and critical consciousness (Freire, 1985). This, and later work by critical theorists like hooks (2003), critiqued the banking model where learning is viewed as providing neutral information to students. Critical pedagogy instead views teaching as a fundamentally political process, where students may engage with topics from their life, ask questions about their contexts, and identify systemic power relations and institutions. When applied in school contexts, this approach successfully reaches students typically left behind in more mainstream pedagogies (Morrell, 2015).

Multiculturalist approaches to education build on this, drawing from cultural, ethnic, and womens studies to teach by drawing on students' own cultural history and practices. The goal is to promote equity through learning within a student's community and culture, producing a *culturally sustaining pedagogy* (Ladson-Billings, 1995). This approach necessitates educators who come from, or are deeply competent in, the cultural norms and expressions of their students, creating content and opportunities that allow students to connect with learning in an affirming way. By giving students tools to engage with and critique society, the most recent approaches continue to enable student growth (Paris and Alim, 2017).

3.2 Application to Algorithms in Edtech

These perspectives can be hard to align with technological interventions. As direct critiques of dominant ideologies and institutions that legitimate and maintain inequality for students, their language is more forceful than most machine learning research. Unlike fairness literature in computer science venues, these works explicitly describe existing practices as based in white supremacist patriarchy, heteronormativity, and colonialism. This makes these pedagogies more expressive, capable of defining a path forward for equitable technologies; but it also makes them more suspicious of interventions that scale without local context and cultural knowledge.

However, educators have successfully applied these principles in technology-oriented work. Mislevy et al. (2009) shows how critical analysis can support and define assessment; Morris and Stommel (2018) uses them to develop a digital pedagogy. The Gordon Commission shows how critical work can be a basis for development of adaptive learning systems (Armour-Thomas and Gordon, 2013). Across these and other applications, some principles are immediately clear:

- A shift in the goal of assessment, from measuring *static knowledge* to assessing *formative process*, acknowledging student growth at least as much as facts they have "banked."

- A vocabulary and willingness to describe existing systems as oppressive for students, on lines of race, economic class, gender, physical abilities, and other aspects of identity.

- A demand for cultural competence from the teachers and designers of learning systems, aligning the creators of educational environments with the students they teach.

The remainder of our paper summarizes key recommendations that lead from these principles. We reference them in the hope that researchers will move their conversations about equity in machine learning beyond model bias and allocational harm for subgroups. Such work is vital and the task of bias measurement is not solved yet, but researchers are already racing to build tools for these problems. Madnani et al. (2017), for instance, presents a capable tool for evaluating fair outcomes in automated essay scoring. It would be a mistake to focus on bias alone Given existing pedagogical work on equity and its focus on learning through dialogue, critical discourse, and action, we can propose broader mindset shifts for researchers. Our goal is to avoid harm to students and prevent expenditure of resources on research that maintains inequity rather than closing gaps in achievement across student populations.

4 Avoiding Representational Harms

First, beyond allocational harm, there are *"representational harms"* in machine learning (Crawford, 2017). This class of issues includes the ways in which technologies represent groups of people or cultures. This may take the form of search results returning stereotypical images of minorities (Noble, 2018) or other algorithmic stereotyping (Abbasi et al., 2019); much of the work in word embeddings falls into this category (Caliskan et al., 2017), though research on downstream tasks and outcomes often have more allocational focus. Machine learning may also marginalize groups by simply *not* representing their culture, resulting in educational systems where learners do not see themselves in the texts selected by instructors.

These harms can exist even when no disparate outcomes are observed, and even if there is no measured gap in predictive accuracy of models (Binns, 2018). Students whose cultural background is in the minority in a classroom are less prone to participate in teacher-student interactions (Tatum et al., 2013) and in student group discussion (White, 2011); these variations are predictable by gender, race, and nationality (Eddy et al., 2015). We also know that instructor credibility is tied to demographics (Bavishi et al., 2010), as are student evaluations of a teacher's trustworthiness and caring (Finn et al., 2009).

4.1 Case Study: Agent-based Intelligent Tutoring Systems

In intelligent tutoring systems (ITS), a human-like agent or visual avatar engages with students through text or speech. These systems now pair natural language instruction with parasocial features (Lubold et al., 2018) and mimicking nuanced human behaviors like finding "teachable moments" (Nye et al., 2014). They are used individually or with groups of students (Kumar et al., 2007) and to provide narrowly targeted support for Autistic students (Nojavanasghari et al., 2017) and deaf students (Scassellati et al., 2018).

When these pedagogical agents are used with students, regardless of if they play the role of tutors, coaches, or peers (Baylor and Kim, 2005), representation matters. Decisions for agents' appearance, language, and behavior may impact learners' perceptions of the cultural identity of the agents (Haake and Gulz, 2008), and may impact learners perceptions of their *own* belongingness

and identity (*cf.* (Fordham and Ogbu, 1986)). Past work on agent representation also lacks alignment with modern understanding of identity, relying on binary definitions of gender (West and Zimmerman, 1987; Keyes, 2018) and failing to account for identities at the intersection of multiple marginalized groups (Crenshaw, 1990), especially in less developed countries (Wong-Villacres et al., 2018).

Incorporating representation improves embodied tutors, with improved student outcomes (Finkelstein et al., 2013). One of the simplest, most valuable steps for developers of ITS agents is to view the choice of the agent's identity presentation (identity factors such as race, appearance, voice, language, gender) as a non-neutral, political choice. The agents designed by researchers express to students beliefs about what a "model teacher" or "model student" look and sound like. Practitioners and researchers alike often have great flexibility, at no additional expense, to intentionally design of the characters and content of the applications they create. This is different from the models themselves in a machine learning system, which rely on expensive training data, and which are often pretrained before development even begins, making it an attractive and high-leverage point for technologists to intervene.

5 Culturally Relevant Pedagogy

A lack of representation more broadly has contributed to an educational curriculum that privileges dominant cultures and which actively harms student engagement. The consequences are concrete - for instance, in recent bans on Chicano texts in the Southwest United States (Wanberg, 2013). One can draw a straight line back to historical policies that have devalued cultures, particularly for indigenous populations (Adams, 1995) and descendants of Black slaves (Alim et al., 2016; Lanehart, 1998). Historically, students coming from marginalized cultures have been measured by a "deficit model" (Brannon et al., 2008), where their home culture was viewed merely as a lack of knowledge about the dominant majority culture.

But there are alternatives in the existing pedagogy literature, like Moll et al. (2005)'s "funds of knowledge" model. This approach defines the accumulated and culturally developed bodies of information and skills that students learn at home and in their communities, essential to their functioning and well-being. An equitable approach treats cultural knowledge instead as an asset, and allows students to build on what they know. This extends to technologies used in the everyday lives, homes, and communities of students - influencing their ability to impact student learning outcomes.

5.1 Case Study: Reading Comprehension

For early readers, speech recognition systems have been developed for children's voice and language (Gerosa et al., 2009) and are used to improve students' early reading skills (Mostow et al., 2003), or for speech-based vocabulary practice (Kumar et al., 2012). Yet these systems are often unable to generate questions for texts from nonstandard linguistic groups (*e.g.* with the syntactic and morphological transformations in African-American English (Siegel, 2001)). Systems today may also fail to recognize speech from students speaking certain dialects or accents, though progress in recognition for marginalized language variation is improving rapidly (Blodgett et al., 2016; Stewart, 2014; Jørgensen et al., 2015).

After basic literacy skills are acquired, NLP tools for language understanding are widely used to generate reading comprehension questions (Heilman and Smith, 2010). NLP is also used in related tasks like the measurement of readability (Aluisio et al., 2010; Vajjala and Meurers, 2012), and generation of simplified texts to differentiate homework based on student ability (Xu et al., 2015). But from a pedagogy perspective, content from these systems may be inappropriate - for instance, the questions generated are often factual rather than encouraging critical thinking (Rickford, 2001). This format does not measure student skills equally across cultures, and particularly under-reports progress in students of color, who tend to thrive when assessed through naturalistic narrative (Fagundes et al., 1998).

In pursuit of more reliable automated assessment, comprehension tasks may also fail to prioritize growth in student ability. Struggling readers understand texts more effectively when they are given chances to initiate dialogues and ask questions about texts, with teachers acting as listeners rather than ask their own questions about texts (Yopp, 1988). Teachers have difficulty creating these interactions (Allington, 2005), and intelligent agents have at least the potential for scaffolding tasks through real-time support for students as they perform their own tasks (Adamson et al., 2014). But to date, work has primarily focused on factoid assessment (Mostow and Jang, 2012; Zesch and Melamud, 2014; Wojatzki et al., 2016). This is an opportunity for future equitable NLP research at the intersection of ITS agents and reading comprehension. Additionally, coaching teachers to perform these dialogues has potential to fill in gaps in professional development and preservice training (Gerritsen et al., 2018), further incentivizing development of culturally responsive reading comprehension.

5.2 Case Study: Automated Writing Feedback and Scoring

Algorithmic assessment of student writing has taken many forms, from summative use in standardized testing (Shermis and Hamner, 2012) and the GRE (Chen et al., 2016) to formative use for classroom feedback (Woods et al., 2017; Wilson and Roscoe, 2019). This trend has led to sophisticated NLP analyses like argument mining (Nguyen and Litman, 2018) and rhetorical structure detection (Fiacco et al., 2019). Automated scoring has seen some more limited use in higher education, as well (Cotos, 2014; Johnson et al., 2017). For writers who are proficient or already working in professional settings, language technologies provide scaffolds like grammatical error detection and correction (Ng et al., 2014). These systems are enabled by rubrics, which give consistent and clear goals for writers (Reddy and Andrade, 2010). Rubric-based writing has drawbacks like rigid formulation of tasks (Warner, 2018), and many applications of rubrics are rooted in a racialized history difficult for technology to escape (Dixon-Román et al., 2019).

Bias creeps into rubric writing and scoring of training data, unless extensive countermeasures are taken to maintain reliability across student backgrounds and varied response types (Loukina et al., 2018; West-Smith et al., 2018). It also limits flexibility in task choice and response type from students, limiting students to writing styles that mirror the norms of the dominant school culture. Developers have an opportunity for equity work here, to the extent that they have leverage over task definition and training data collection (Lehr and Ohm, 2017; Holstein et al., 2018). Automated feedback systems may be improved through tasks that are flexible, and give culturally aligned opportunities for topic selection and choice; feedback on rubrics that align to student "funds of knowledge" rather than the often-racialized language of deficits; and collaborative opportunities to share their work, receiving feedback that extends beyond algorithmic response.

6 Avoiding Linguistic Imperialism

Beyond selection of which content to teach, a broader issue is the focus of most language education globally on English and other prestige languages. This creates a privileged medium of communication and learning, and is rooted in colonialism; see for instance English's position over regional languages in India (Hornberger and Vaish, 2009) and the similar role of Afrikaans in South Africa (Heugh, 1995; Alim and Haupt, 2017); as well as how this extends to modern geopolitics in regions like Asia, with Han Chinese (He, 2013). In presumed-monolingual environments where students already speak the dominant language at home, this same effect plays out in dialects; examples include the privileging of white American or British dialects over stigmatized dialects like African-American Vernacular English in America (Henderson, 1996; Siegel, 2001), or the role of Classical Arabic as a prestige language over regional variants across the Arab world (Haeri, 2000). In language policy, this privileged position of a dominant language has been described as "linguistic imperialism" (Phillipson, 1992).

This dominant position of specific languages, especially English, comes despite cognitive science findings that bilingualism and code-switching ability has a marked positive effect on cognitive function (Petitto et al., 2012; Kroll and Bialystok, 2013) and may even have a positive economic effect on lifetime earnings (Agirdag, 2014). Moreover, language learning can promote new language acquisition while preserving respect for the learner's home language (or "heritage" language), helping learners to selectively choose when and how to communicate in each. Pedagogies exist which value pragmatic, socially conscious use of code-switching in mixed linguistic environments (Wang and Mansouri, 2017); these techniques are applicable to NLP.

6.1 Case Study: Computer-Assisted Language Learning

Computer-Assisted Language Learning, or CALL (Thomas et al., 2012), is an effective use of language technologies for vocabulary-building, pronunciation training, and practice through speech recognition, and other less common tasks (Witt, 2012; Levy and Stockwell, 2013). Language learning is a convenient fit for quantification, rapid experimentation (Presson et al., 2013), large dataset collection through "learner corpora" (Meurers, 2015), and fine-grained descriptions of progress through second language acquisition modeling (Settles et al., 2018). For second language teachers, NLP can improve their language awareness and skills (Burstein et al., 2014); for individual learners, language learning is highly personalizable and can be gamified for motivation and engagement (Munday, 2016). Machine learning models are also a good fit for summative assessment of student skill, and is used both in speech (Chen et al., 2018) and writing (Ghosh et al., 2016), including on high-stakes exams like the TOEFL (Chodorow and Burstein, 2004).

These systems make numerous design choices to implicitly or explicitly reject the grammar and lexicon of minority dialects. Typically, code-switching is neither taught as a skill nor supported as input. The relative sparsity of data for these variations may have resulted in unacceptable modeling accuracy in the past (Blodgett et al., 2016), but we are now closing that gap (Dalmia et al., 2018; Sitaram et al., 2019). For this field, an equitable language technologies agenda would seek to support rather than penalize these pragmatic skills. Such work can take place at multiple levels, beginning in early vocabulary work but particularly excelling in more sophisticated, scenario-driven practice for intermediate and advanced learners.

7 Surveillance Capitalism in Edtech

If we accept the premise that dominance hierarchies play a key role in education, it follows to acknowledge large-scale edtech that tracks students' activity in real time as one instantiation of "surveillance capitalism" in schools (Zuboff, 2015). Recent evaluations suggest that when students are aware of such systems in use, they report being anxious, paranoid, and afraid of long-term repercussions for undesirable behavior (Yujie, 2019). This may lead to short-term undesirable changes in students' behavior or expression to "game" algorithmic systems (*cf.* (Baker et al., 2008)). Effects may be greater in the long-term, with potential consequences to students' mental health from always-on affect monitoring.

This presents an intersection for NLP to collaborate with information security and privacy researchers. Those fields are active in education, and the field has developed deep protections for students' personally identifiable data, enforced in America through laws like COPPA and FERPA (Regan and Jesse, 2018). While these laws do have gaps (Parks, 2017), they are largely robust and respected by technologists. More recent actions like the EU General Data Protection Regulation (GDPR) have also had meaningful impact on NLP research and data collection (Lewis et al., 2017). Legally, aggregating student data in order to develop and improve edtech provides a benefit to students and thus does not violate any law (Brinkman, 2013) — but scholars continue to ask ethical questions on how to account for student privacy and control (Morris and Stommel, 2018), and what data is being collected (Mieskes, 2017).

As always-on systems monitor students throughout their school day and beyond, these questions of student privacy and control become compounded in scope and complexity. Additionally, continuous monitoring impacts students' behavior and well-being: behavioral science has established that people change their actions when they are being observed (Harris and Lahey, 1982). Now, we must understand the impact when the observer is algorithmic.

7.1 Case Study: Student Engagement and Sentiment Analysis

One of the most common tasks in NLP research, for education and elsewhere, is sentiment and emotion recognition. This is important for education, both for design of affect-oriented curriculum (Taylor et al., 2017) and funding for socioemotional skills (Chan Zuckerberg Initiative, 2018). This recent turn is driven by promising initial results of efficacy from socioemotional interventions in schools (Dougherty and Sharkey, 2017). Measuring instantaneous student affective states is not only possible to reliably annotate, but also appears broadly possible to automatically infer (Yu et al., 2017); affect-aware tutoring systems are the subject of widespread research (Woolf et al., 2009; DMello and Graesser, 2012). In text-only settings online, sentiment has been a key part of prediction of attrition rates in MOOCs (Yang et al., 2013; Wen et al., 2014), especially when combined with

micro-level instantaneous data like clickstream events (Crossley et al., 2016). These systems are now moving from data collected in text-only or tech-only environments, to multimodal data collected by always-on platforms like Alexa (Boccella, 2019) and emerging video monitoring platforms like the "Class Care System" (Yujie, 2019).

With this broad trend, we should question the implications of these systems as part of a move towards surveillance and monitoring, and their potential for impact on learners' well-being and behavior. Multimodal data are increasingly used to inform sentiment and affect detection algorithms (Yu et al., 2017; DMello and Graesser, 2012; Woolf et al., 2009), but these algorithms are known to produce discriminatory results, with disparate outcomes by gender (Volkova et al., 2013), race (Kiritchenko and Mohammad, 2018), and age (Díaz et al., 2018), perpetuating a quantifiable trend of disproportionate surveillance impact for people of color (Voigt et al., 2017). In a particularly illuminating example of bias introduced during corpus creation, Okur et al. (2018) found that experts from one culture radically misclassify affective states when they do not share the same cultural background as their subjects. A primary question for educational affect-detection systems will be to identify whether and how these discriminatory results replicate in educational systems, and will only become more urgent as real-time data from cameras, microphones, and other technologies become ubiquitous in the classroom.

8 An Equity Agenda

8.1 Representation on Teams

A theme of our review is that cultural representations should be built into NLP systems; here, though, we refer back to critical pedagogy's demand for cultural competence on the *builders* of these systems. Digital embodiment of characters from marginalized identities, developed by technologists without a background in those communities' culture and practices, runs significant risks of negative impacts and appropriation, or "digital Blackface" (Green, 2006). When NLP interventions mirror student cultures in purely performative ways, that representation is unlikely to be meaningful; indeed, it may worsen student engagement with agent-based systems. But these downfalls can be avoided through teams with "cultural competence" through lived experience and group membership shared with the students they are building applications for.

A lack of diversity on research teams is a key contributor to discriminatory outcomes of machine learning systems in practice (West et al., 2019). Representational harms can be avoided by bringing those voices directly into the development of systems. Many of the challenges we have laid out are second nature to researchers with a cultural background in the communities that they seek to serve; having those voices in empowered positions during development can help make these issues salient before they are implemented - provided these voices are heard and empowered during the design process (*cf.* Holstein et al. (2018)).

8.2 Intentional Science Communication

As researchers, our work always has the potential to "go viral" and reshape public discourse. To illustrate, we can look to early language acquisition. In Hart and Risley (1995), researchers prominently reported findings of a "30-million word gap" for children raised in lower-class, predominantly Black households, hindering their literacy development. Later research showed this gap was likely overstated by an order of magnitude (Gilkerson et al., 2017), and likely excluded race-related environmental factors like bystander talk (Sperry et al., 2018). The discourse that emerged was largely discriminatory towards poor parents from minority backgrounds (Avineri et al., 2015).

But scientists can also cautiously understate results in public - most prominently in climate change policy and climate denialism (Dunlap, 2013). In other fields, collective action by researchers has produced unified stands on how their technology should be used ethically, as in the use of gene-editing tool CRISPR to modify unborn children - an action that evoked unified condemnation from governments (Collins, 2018), public figures (Lovell-Badge, 2019), and peer researchers in China[4]. Understanding the wider implications of research findings on NLP in education and positioning that work to have maximal impact is part of the job of effective science writing. Each circumstance is specific and there are no universal best practices - the key is to emphasize findings that are well-grounded in results, and to be intentional in how researchers encourage stories to evolve from those findings.

8.3 Transparency and Regulation

If we do not take collective stances on ethical NLP in education from within our community, enforcement may instead come from external regulation. Some have argued this is a useful tool for enforcing accountability on algorithmic systems. Prior work has proposed regulatory frameworks that may serve as guidance (Whittaker et al., 2018); legal frameworks for these questions are already being developed (Kroll et al., 2016); bills are being introduced into the US Senate (Farivar, 2019). Potential outcomes include waiving trade secrecy for data science companies, or applying "truth-in-advertising" laws to AI systems. These may be general, or may prioritize specific focus areas like affect recognition.

Should we move in this direction, research will need to support regulation, improving transparency and governance of algorithmic predictions. NLP researchers have aggressively studied interpretability, offering explanation of results rather than predictions alone (Guidotti et al., 2018) - linguistic information is captured by newer neural language models of text (Conneau et al., 2018; Sommerauer and Fokkens, 2018) and speech (Elloumi et al., 2018; Krug and Stober, 2018), reading comprehension (Kaushik and Lipton, 2018), and machine translation (Shi et al., 2016; Raganato and Tiedemann, 2018; Belinkov and Glass, 2019). Other work focuses on replication, allowing consistent tying of modeling choices to changes in behavior (Dror et al., 2017, 2018).

But the connection to liability is rarely made explicit, and is worth emphasis. These tools are not just useful for error analysis and optimization of model performance; they will also be a critical step towards liability for harmful decisions made by algorithms, which cannot alter behavior if it cannot be traced and enforced (Ananny and Crawford, 2018). Governance can also come from somewhere in between collective action and national-level regulation. Some have proposed best practices for ethical industry research in NLP, mirroring IRB processes in universities (Leidner and Plachouras, 2017). This approach would assign responsibility during research, limiting experiments on users of commercial products. Either unregulated software will cause harm to students and teachers, or regulation and accountability to prevent inequitable use will come from somewhere. There is a spectrum of options for NLP, from interpretability and self-governance to top-down regulation. It would be better for researchers to be at the forefront of that conversation.

8.4 Defining Boundaries for Software

As our last recommendation, researchers should acknowledge the "solutionism" trap endemic in technical research, which assumes that there is a methodological change that could fix any problem while maintaining the primacy of our algorithmic solutions (Selbst et al., 2019). Some activists advocate for leaving certain problems unresearched entirely, due to their intrinsic and systemic risk of harm for marginalized populations — see for instance this discussion in the case of facial recognition software, in Whittaker et al. (2018). Sometimes, machine learning systems will not be the right way to solve problems. A valuable contribution of future work will be to better lay out the taxonomies of ethics and equity that apply to NLP research, following work that has begun in algorithmic systems more broadly (Ananny, 2016). This will allow researchers to make consistent choices about which problems are tractable with technological solutions, rather than addressing each new problem in an ad hoc fashion (Chancellor et al., 2019). This can only improve the quality of the products we do choose to build.

9 Conclusion

Machine learning has made many promises that are going to be difficult to fulfill. Throughout the 1960s and 1970s, science fiction author Arthur C. Clarke described the aim of technology in education to be: *"Any teacher that can be replaced by a machine should be."* (Bayne, 2015). As late as 2015, adaptive learning companies like Knewton argued in favor of *"robot tutors in the sky that can semi-read your mind"* to replace traditional teachers (Westervelt, 2015). While this language has become more muted in recent years, the promise of AI and attached hype for our work is at an all-time peak. Language technologies in education have the potential to enable equity in the "pedagogical troika" of teaching, learning, and assessment (Gordon and Rajagopalan, 2016). While that potential is great, reifying existing power hierarchies is easy to do by accident or by choice; we hope researchers will resist simple answers, and build equity into future work from the start.

References

Mohsen Abbasi, Sorelle A Friedler, Carlos Scheidegger, and Suresh Venkatasubramanian. 2019. Fairness in representation: quantifying stereotyping as a representational harm. *arXiv preprint arXiv:1901.09565*.

David Wallace Adams. 1995. *Education for Extinction: American Indians and the Boarding School Experience, 1875-1928*. ERIC.

David Adamson, Gregory Dyke, Hyeju Jang, and Carolyn Penstein Rosé. 2014. Towards an agile approach to adapting dynamic collaboration support to student needs. *International Journal of Artificial Intelligence in Education*, 24(1):92–124.

Orhan Agirdag. 2014. The long-term effects of bilingualism on children of immigration: student bilingualism and future earnings. *International Journal of Bilingual Education and Bilingualism*, 17(4):449–464.

Vincent Aleven, Elizabeth A McLaughlin, R Amos Glenn, and Kenneth R Koedinger. 2016. Instruction based on adaptive learning technologies. *Handbook of research on learning and instruction. Routledge.*

H Samy Alim and Adam Haupt. 2017. reviving soul (s) with afrikaaps. *Culturally Sustaining Pedagogies: Teaching and Learning for Justice in a Changing World*, page 157.

H Samy Alim, John R Rickford, and Arnetha F Ball. 2016. *Raciolinguistics: How Language Shapes Our Ideas About Race*. Oxford University Press.

Richard L Allington. 2005. *What Really Matters for Struggling Readers: Designing Research-Based Programs (What Really Matters Series)*. Boston, MA: Allyn & Bacon.

Sandra Aluisio, Lucia Specia, Caroline Gasperin, and Carolina Scarton. 2010. Readability assessment for text simplification. In *Proceedings of the NAACL HLT 2010 Fifth Workshop on Innovative Use of NLP for Building Educational Applications*, pages 1–9. Association for Computational Linguistics.

Mike Ananny. 2016. Toward an ethics of algorithms: Convening, observation, probability, and timeliness. *Science, Technology, & Human Values*, 41(1):93–117.

Mike Ananny and Kate Crawford. 2018. Seeing without knowing: Limitations of the transparency ideal and its application to algorithmic accountability. *New Media & Society*, 20(3):973–989.

Julia Angwin, Jeff Larson, Surya Mattu, and Lauren Kirchner. 2016. Machine bias. *ProPublica, May*, 23.

Eleanor Armour-Thomas and Edmund W Gordon. 2013. Toward an understanding of assessment as a dynamic component of pedagogy. *The Gordon Commission, Princeton NJ*.

Netta Avineri, Eric Johnson, Shirley Brice-Heath, Teresa McCarty, Elinor Ochs, Tamar Kremer-Sadlik, Susan Blum, Ana Celia Zentella, Jonathan Rosa, Nelson Flores, et al. 2015. Invited forum: Bridging the language gap. *Journal of Linguistic Anthropology*, 25(1):66–86.

Ryan Baker, Jason Walonoski, Neil Heffernan, Ido Roll, Albert Corbett, and Kenneth Koedinger. 2008. Why students engage in gaming the system behavior in interactive learning environments. *Journal of Interactive Learning Research*, 19(2):185–224.

Ryan Shaun Baker and Paul Salvador Inventado. 2014. Educational data mining and learning analytics. In *Learning analytics*, pages 61–75. Springer.

Solon Barocas and Andrew D Selbst. 2016. Big data's disparate impact. *Calif. L. Rev.*, 104:671.

Anish Bavishi, Juan M Madera, and Michelle R Hebl. 2010. The effect of professor ethnicity and gender on student evaluations: Judged before met. *Journal of Diversity in Higher Education*, 3(4):245.

Amy L Baylor and Yanghee Kim. 2005. Simulating instructional roles through pedagogical agents. *International Journal of Artificial Intelligence in Education*, 15(2):95–115.

Sian Bayne. 2015. Teacherbot: interventions in automated teaching. *Teaching in Higher Education*, 20(4):455–467.

Yonatan Belinkov and James Glass. 2019. Analysis methods in neural language processing: A survey. *Transactions of the Association for Computational Linguistics*, 7:49–72.

Reuben Binns. 2018. Fairness in machine learning: Lessons from political philosophy. In *Conference on Fairness, Accountability and Transparency*, pages 149–159.

Su Lin Blodgett, Lisa Green, and Brendan O'Connor. 2016. Demographic dialectal variation in social media: A case study of african-american english. In *Proceedings of the 2016 Conference on Empirical Methods in Natural Language Processing*, pages 1119–1130.

Su Lin Blodgett, Johnny Wei, and Brendan O'Connor. 2017. A dataset and classifier for recognizing social media english. In *Proceedings of the 3rd Workshop on Noisy User-generated Text*, pages 56–61.

Kathy Boccella. 2019. Alexa, can you help kids learn and teachers manage a classroom? at garnet valley, the answer is: Yes. https://www.philly.com/news/alexa-amazon-garnetvalley-school–20190213.html. Accessed 2019-04-13.

Tolga Bolukbasi, Kai-Wei Chang, James Y Zou, Venkatesh Saligrama, and Adam T Kalai. 2016. Man is to computer programmer as woman is to homemaker? debiasing word embeddings. In D. D. Lee, M. Sugiyama, U. V. Luxburg, I. Guyon, and R. Garnett, editors, *Advances in Neural Information Processing Systems 29*, pages 4349–4357. Curran Associates, Inc.

Lil Brannon, Jennifer Pooler Courtney, Cynthia P Urbanski, Shana V Woodward, Jeanie Marklin Reynolds, Anthony E Iannone, Karen D Haag, Karen Mach, Lacy Arnold Manship, and Mary Kendrick. 2008. Ej extra: The five-paragraph essay and the deficit model of education. *The English Journal*, 98(2):16–21.

Bo Brinkman. 2013. An analysis of student privacy rights in the use of plagiarism detection systems. *Science and engineering ethics*, 19(3):1255–1266.

Joy Buolamwini and Timnit Gebru. 2018. Gender shades: Intersectional accuracy disparities in commercial gender classification. In *Conference on Fairness, Accountability and Transparency*, pages 77–91.

Jill Burstein, Jane Shore, John Sabatini, Brad Moulder, Jennifer Lentini, Kietha Biggers, and Steven Holtzman. 2014. From teacher professional development to the classroom: How nlp technology can enhance teachers' linguistic awareness to support curriculum development for english language learners. *Journal of Educational Computing Research*, 51(1):119–144.

Aylin Caliskan, Joanna J Bryson, and Arvind Narayanan. 2017. Semantics derived automatically from language corpora contain human-like biases. *Science*, 356(6334):183–186.

Seth Chaiklin. 2003. The zone of proximal development in vygotskys analysis of learning and instruction. *Vygotskys educational theory in cultural context*, 1:39–64.

The Chan Zuckerberg Initiative. 2018. Chan zuckerberg initiative announces support to advance student development and success. https://chanzuckerberg.com/newsroom/chan-zuckerberg-initiative-announces-support-to-advance-student-development-and-success/. Accessed 2018-04-13.

Stevie Chancellor, Michael L Birnbaum, Eric D Caine, Vincent Silenzio, and Munmun De Choudhury. 2019. A taxonomy of ethical tensions in inferring mental health states from social media. In *Proceedings of the 2nd ACM Conference on Fairness, Accountability, and Transparency (Atlanta GA*.

Jing Chen, James H Fife, Isaac I Bejar, and André A Rupp. 2016. Building e-rater® scoring models using machine learning methods. *ETS Research Report Series*, 2016(1):1–12.

Lei Chen, Jidong Tao, Shabnam Ghaffarzadegan, and Yao Qian. 2018. End-to-end neural network based automated speech scoring. In *2018 IEEE International Conference on Acoustics, Speech and Signal Processing (ICASSP)*, pages 6234–6238. IEEE.

Martin Chodorow and Jill Burstein. 2004. Beyond essay length: evaluating e-rater®'s performance on toefl® essays. *ETS Research Report Series*, 2004(1):i–38.

Alexandra Chouldechova. 2017. Fair prediction with disparate impact: A study of bias in recidivism prediction instruments. *Big data*, 5(2):153–163.

Francis S. Collins. 2018. Statement on claim of first gene-edited babies by chinese researcher. https://www.nih.gov/about-nih/who-we-are/nih-director/statements/statement-claim-first-gene-edited-babies-chinese-researcher. Accessed 2019-04-13.

Alexis Conneau, German Kruszewski, Guillaume Lample, Loïc Barrault, and Marco Baroni. 2018. What you can cram into a single vector: Probing sentence embeddings for linguistic properties. *arXiv preprint arXiv:1805.01070*.

Sam Corbett-Davies and Sharad Goel. 2018. The measure and mismeasure of fairness: A critical review of fair machine learning. *Synthesis of tutorial presented at ICML 2018*.

Sam Corbett-Davies, Emma Pierson, Avi Feller, Sharad Goel, and Aziz Huq. 2017. Algorithmic decision making and the cost of fairness. In *Proceedings of the 23rd ACM SIGKDD International Conference on Knowledge Discovery and Data Mining*, pages 797–806. ACM.

Elena Cotos. 2014. *Genre-based automated writing evaluation for L2 research writing: From design to evaluation and enhancement*. Springer.

Kate Crawford. 2017. The trouble with bias, 2017. *URL http://blog. revolutionanalytics. com/2017/12/the-trouble-with-bias-by-kate-crawford. html. Invited Talk by Kate Crawford at NIPS*.

Kimberle Crenshaw. 1990. Mapping the margins: Intersectionality, identity politics, and violence against women of color. *Stan. L. Rev.*, 43:1241.

Scott Crossley, Luc Paquette, Mihai Dascalu, Danielle S McNamara, and Ryan S Baker. 2016. Combining click-stream data with nlp tools to better understand mooc completion. In *Proceedings of the sixth international conference on learning analytics & knowledge*, pages 6–14. ACM.

Siddharth Dalmia, Ramon Sanabria, Florian Metze, and Alan W Black. 2018. Sequence-based multilingual low resource speech recognition. In *2018 IEEE International Conference on Acoustics, Speech and Signal Processing (ICASSP)*, pages 4909–4913. IEEE.

John Dewey. 1923. *Democracy and education: An introduction to the philosophy of education*. Macmillan.

Mark Díaz, Isaac Johnson, Amanda Lazar, Anne Marie Piper, and Darren Gergle. 2018. Addressing age-related bias in sentiment analysis. In *Proceedings of the 2018 CHI Conference on Human Factors in Computing Systems*, page 412. ACM.

Ezekiel Dixon-Román, T. Philip Nichols, and Ama Nyame-Mensah. 2019. The racializing forces of/in ai educational technologies. *Learning, Media & Technology Special Issue on AI and Education: Critical Perspectives and Alternative Futures*.

Danielle Dougherty and Jill Sharkey. 2017. Reconnecting youth: Promoting emotional competence and social support to improve academic achievement. *Children and Youth Services Review*, 74:28–34.

Rotem Dror, Gili Baumer, Marina Bogomolov, and Roi Reichart. 2017. Replicability analysis for natural language processing: Testing significance with multiple datasets. *Transactions of the Association for Computational Linguistics*, 5:471–486.

Rotem Dror, Gili Baumer, Segev Shlomov, and Roi Reichart. 2018. The hitchhikers guide to testing statistical significance in natural language processing. In *Proceedings of the 56th Annual Meeting of the Association for Computational Linguistics (Volume 1: Long Papers)*, pages 1383–1392.

Riley E Dunlap. 2013. Climate change skepticism and denial: An introduction. *American behavioral scientist*, 57(6):691–698.

Cynthia Dwork and Christina Ilvento. 2018. Fairness under composition. In *10th Innovations in Theoretical Computer Science Conference (ITCS 2019)*. Schloss Dagstuhl-Leibniz-Zentrum fuer Informatik.

Sidney DMello and Art Graesser. 2012. Dynamics of affective states during complex learning. *Learning and Instruction*, 22(2):145–157.

Sarah L Eddy, Sara E Brownell, Phonraphee Thummaphan, Ming-Chih Lan, and Mary Pat Wenderoth. 2015. Caution, student experience may vary: social identities impact a students experience in peer discussions. *CBELife Sciences Education*, 14(4):ar45.

Zied Elloumi, Laurent Besacier, Olivier Galibert, and Benjamin Lecouteux. 2018. Analyzing learned representations of a deep asr performance prediction model. In *Blackbox NLP Workshop and EMLP 2018*.

Maxine Eskenazi. 2009. An overview of spoken language technology for education. *Speech Communication*, 51(10):832–844.

Virginia Eubanks. 2018. *Automating inequality: How high-tech tools profile, police, and punish the poor*. St. Martin's Press.

Deana D Fagundes, William O Haynes, Nancy J Haak, and Michael J Moran. 1998. Task variability effects on the language test performance of southern lower socioeconomic class african american and caucasian five-year-olds. *Language, Speech, and Hearing Services in Schools*, 29(3):148–157.

Cyrus Farivar. 2019. New bill aims to stamp out bias in algorithms used by companies. Accessed 2019-04-27.

James Fiacco, Elena Cotos, and Carolyn Rosé. 2019. Towards enabling feedback on rhetorical structure with neural sequence models. In *Proceedings of the 9th International Conference on Learning Analytics & Knowledge*, pages 310–319. ACM.

Samantha Finkelstein, Evelyn Yarzebinski, Callie Vaughn, Amy Ogan, and Justine Cassell. 2013. The effects of culturally congruent educational technologies on student achievement. In *International Conference on Artificial Intelligence in Education*, pages 493–502. Springer.

Amber N Finn, Paul Schrodt, Paul L Witt, Nikki Elledge, Kodiane A Jernberg, and Lara M Larson. 2009. A meta-analytical review of teacher credibility and its associations with teacher behaviors and student outcomes. *Communication Education*, 58(4):516–537.

Signithia Fordham and John U Ogbu. 1986. Black students' school success: Coping with the burden of acting white. *The urban review*, 18(3):176–206.

Paulo Freire. 1970. *Pedagogy of the oppressed*. Bloomsbury publishing USA.

Paulo Freire. 1985. *The politics of education: Culture, power, and liberation*. Greenwood Publishing Group.

Sorelle A Friedler, Carlos Scheidegger, Suresh Venkatasubramanian, Sonam Choudhary, Evan P Hamilton, and Derek Roth. 2019. A comparative study of fairness-enhancing interventions in machine learning. In *Proceedings of the Conference on Fairness, Accountability, and Transparency*, pages 329–338. ACM.

Nikhil Garg, Londa Schiebinger, Dan Jurafsky, and James Zou. 2018. Word embeddings quantify 100 years of gender and ethnic stereotypes. *Proceedings of the National Academy of Sciences*, 115(16):E3635–E3644.

Bill & Melinda Gates Foundation and the Chan Zuckerberg Initiative. 2019. Education research & development: Learning from the field.

Matteo Gerosa, Diego Giuliani, Shrikanth Narayanan, and Alexandros Potamianos. 2009. A review of asr technologies for children's speech. In *Proceedings of the 2nd Workshop on Child, Computer and Interaction*, page 7. ACM.

David Gerritsen, John Zimmerman, and Amy Ogan. 2018. Towards a framework for smart classrooms that teach instructors to teach. In *International Conference of the Learning Sciences*, volume 3.

Debanjan Ghosh, Aquila Khanam, Yubo Han, and Smaranda Muresan. 2016. Coarse-grained argumentation features for scoring persuasive essays. In *Proceedings of the 54th Annual Meeting of the Association for Computational Linguistics (Volume 2: Short Papers)*, volume 2, pages 549–554.

Jill Gilkerson, Jeffrey A Richards, Steven F Warren, Judith K Montgomery, Charles R Greenwood, D Kimbrough Oller, John HL Hansen, and Terrance D Paul. 2017. Mapping the early language environment using all-day recordings and automated analysis. *American Journal of Speech-Language Pathology*, 26(2):248–265.

Kevin Gimpel, Nathan Schneider, Brendan O'Connor, Dipanjan Das, Daniel Mills, Jacob Eisenstein, Michael Heilman, Dani Yogatama, Jeffrey Flanigan, and Noah A Smith. 2011. Part-of-speech tagging for twitter: Annotation, features, and experiments. In *Proceedings of the 49th Annual Meeting of the Association for Computational Linguistics: Human Language Technologies: short papers-Volume 2*, pages 42–47. Association for Computational Linguistics.

Hila Gonen and Yoav Goldberg. 2019. Lipstick on a pig: Debiasing methods cover up systematic gender biases in word embeddings but do not remove them. *arXiv preprint arXiv:1903.03862*.

Edmund W Gordon and Kavitha Rajagopalan. 2016. Assessment for teaching and learning, not just accountability. In *The Testing and Learning Revolution*, pages 9–34. Springer.

Joshua Lumpkin Green. 2006. *Digital Blackface: The Repackaging of the Black Masculine Image*. Ph.D. thesis, Miami University.

Riccardo Guidotti, Anna Monreale, Salvatore Ruggieri, Franco Turini, Fosca Giannotti, and Dino Pedreschi. 2018. A survey of methods for explaining black box models. *ACM computing surveys (CSUR)*, 51(5):93.

Magnus Haake and Agneta Gulz. 2008. Visual stereotypes and virtual pedagogical agents. *Journal of Educational Technology & Society*, 11(4):1–15.

Niloofar Haeri. 2000. Form and ideology: Arabic sociolinguistics and beyond. *Annual review of anthropology*, 29(1):61–87.

Jennifer Hammond and Pauline Gibbons. 2005. What is scaffolding? *Teachers voices*, 8:8–16.

Francis C Harris and Benjamin B Lahey. 1982. Subject reactivity in direct observational assessment: A review and critical analysis. *Clinical Psychology Review*, 2(4):523–538.

Betty Hart and Todd R Risley. 1995. *Meaningful differences in the everyday experience of young American children*. Paul H Brookes Publishing.

Baogang He. 2013. The power of chinese linguistic imperialism and its challenge to multicultural education.

Michael Heilman and Noah A Smith. 2010. Good question! statistical ranking for question generation. In *Human Language Technologies: The 2010 Annual Conference of the North American Chapter of the Association for Computational Linguistics*, pages 609–617. Association for Computational Linguistics.

Lyn Henderson. 1996. Instructional design of interactive multimedia: A cultural critique. *Educational technology research and development*, 44(4):85–104.

Peter Henderson, Koustuv Sinha, Nicolas Angelard-Gontier, Nan Rosemary Ke, Genevieve Fried, Ryan Lowe, and Joelle Pineau. 2018. Ethical challenges in data-driven dialogue systems. In *Proceedings of the 2018 AAAI/ACM Conference on AI, Ethics, and Society*, pages 123–129. ACM.

Kathleen Heugh. 1995. Disabling and enabling: Implications of language policy trends in south africa. *Language and social history: Studies in South African sociolinguistics*, pages 329–350.

Kenneth Holstein, Jennifer Wortman Vaughan, Hal Daumé III, Miro Dudík, and Hanna Wallach. 2018. Improving fairness in machine learning systems: What do industry practitioners need? *arXiv preprint arXiv:1812.05239*.

John N Hooker and Tae Wan N Kim. 2018. Toward non-intuition-based machine and artificial intelligence ethics: A deontological approach based on modal logic. In *Proceedings of the 2018 AAAI/ACM Conference on AI, Ethics, and Society*, pages 130–136. ACM.

bell hooks. 2003. *Teaching community: A pedagogy of hope*, volume 36. Psychology Press.

Michael B Horn. 2018. Hey alexa, can you help kids learn more? *Education Next*, 18(2).

Nancy Hornberger and Viniti Vaish. 2009. Multilingual language policy and school linguistic practice: globalization and english-language teaching in india, singapore and south africa. *Compare*, 39(3):305–320.

Dirk Hovy and Shannon L Spruit. 2016. The social impact of natural language processing. In *Proceedings of the 54th Annual Meeting of the Association for Computational Linguistics (Volume 2: Short Papers)*, volume 2, pages 591–598.

Adam C Johnson, Joshua Wilson, and Rod D Roscoe. 2017. College student perceptions of writing errors, text quality, and author characteristics. *Assessing Writing*, 34:72–87.

Anna Jørgensen, Dirk Hovy, and Anders Søgaard. 2015. Challenges of studying and processing dialects in social media. In *Proceedings of the Workshop on Noisy User-generated Text*, pages 9–18.

David Jurgens, Yulia Tsvetkov, and Dan Jurafsky. 2017. Incorporating dialectal variability for socially equitable language identification. In *Proceedings of the 55th Annual Meeting of the Association for Computational Linguistics (Volume 2: Short Papers)*, pages 51–57.

Divyansh Kaushik and Zachary C Lipton. 2018. How much reading does reading comprehension require? a critical investigation of popular benchmarks. *arXiv preprint arXiv:1808.04926*.

Michael Kearns, Seth Neel, Aaron Roth, and Zhiwei Steven Wu. 2019. An empirical study of rich subgroup fairness for machine learning. In *Proceedings of the Conference on Fairness, Accountability, and Transparency*, pages 100–109. ACM.

Os Keyes. 2018. The misgendering machines: Trans/hci implications of automatic gender recognition. *Proceedings of the ACM on Human-Computer Interaction*, 2(CSCW):88.

Svetlana Kiritchenko and Saif M Mohammad. 2018. Examining gender and race bias in two hundred sentiment analysis systems. *NAACL HLT 2018*, page 43.

Andrew J Kirkendall. 2010. *Paulo Freire and the cold war politics of literacy*. Univ of North Carolina Press.

Tanya Kraljic, Susan E Brennan, and Arthur G Samuel. 2008. Accommodating variation: Dialects, idiolects, and speech processing. *Cognition*, 107(1):54–81.

Joshua A Kroll, Solon Barocas, Edward W Felten, Joel R Reidenberg, David G Robinson, and Harlan Yu. 2016. Accountable algorithms. *U. Pa. L. Rev.*, 165:633.

Judith F Kroll and Ellen Bialystok. 2013. Understanding the consequences of bilingualism for language processing and cognition. *Journal of cognitive psychology*, 25(5):497–514.

Andreas Krug and Sebastian Stober. 2018. Introspection for convolutional automatic speech recognition. In *Proceedings of the 2018 EMNLP Workshop BlackboxNLP: Analyzing and Interpreting Neural Networks for NLP*, pages 187–199, Brussels, Belgium. Association for Computational Linguistics.

Anuj Kumar, Pooja Reddy, Anuj Tewari, Rajat Agrawal, and Matthew Kam. 2012. Improving literacy in developing countries using speech recognition-supported games on mobile devices. In *Proceedings of the SIGCHI Conference on Human Factors in Computing Systems*, pages 1149–1158. ACM.

Rohit Kumar, Carolyn Penstein Rosé, Yi-Chia Wang, Mahesh Joshi, and Allen Robinson. 2007. Tutorial dialogue as adaptive collaborative learning support. *Frontiers in artificial intelligence and applications*, 158:383.

Gloria Ladson-Billings. 1995. Toward a theory of culturally relevant pedagogy. *American educational research journal*, 32(3):465–491.

Sonja L Lanehart. 1998. African american vernacular english and education: The dynamics of pedagogy, ideology, and identity. *Journal of English linguistics*, 26(2):122–136.

David Lehr and Paul Ohm. 2017. Playing with the data: What legal scholars should learn about machine learning. *UCDL Rev.*, 51:653.

Jochen L Leidner and Vassilis Plachouras. 2017. Ethical by design: ethics best practices for natural language processing. In *Proceedings of the First ACL Workshop on Ethics in Natural Language Processing*, pages 30–40.

Mike Levy and Glenn Stockwell. 2013. *CALL dimensions: Options and issues in computer-assisted language learning*. Routledge.

Dave Lewis, Joss Moorkens, and Kaniz Fatema. 2017. Integrating the management of personal data protection and open science with research ethics. In *Proceedings of the First ACL Workshop on Ethics in Natural Language Processing*, pages 60–65.

Diane Litman. 2016. Natural language processing for enhancing teaching and learning. In *Thirtieth AAAI Conference on Artificial Intelligence*.

Lydia T Liu, Sarah Dean, Esther Rolf, Max Simchowitz, and Moritz Hardt. 2018. Delayed impact of fair machine learning. In *Proceedings of the 35th International Conference on Machine Learning*.

Anastassia Loukina, Klaus Zechner, James Bruno, and Beata Beigman Klebanov. 2018. Using exemplar responses for training and evaluating automated speech scoring systems. In *Proceedings of the Thirteenth Workshop on Innovative Use of NLP for Building Educational Applications*, pages 1–12.

Robin Lovell-Badge. 2019. Crispr babies: a view from the centre of the storm. *Development*, 146(3):dev175778.

Nichola Lubold, Erin Walker, Heather Pon-Barry, and Amy Ogan. 2018. Automated pitch convergence improves learning in a social, teachable robot for middle school mathematics. In *International Conference on Artificial Intelligence in Education*, pages 282–296. Springer.

Nitin Madnani, Anastassia Loukina, Alina von Davier, Jill Burstein, and Aoife Cahill. 2017. Building better open-source tools to support fairness in automated scoring. In *Proceedings of the First ACL Workshop on Ethics in Natural Language Processing*, pages 41–52.

Mitchell P Marcus, Mary Ann Marcinkiewicz, and Beatrice Santorini. 1993. Building a large annotated corpus of english: The penn treebank. *Computational linguistics*, 19(2):313–330.

Detmar Meurers. 2015. Learner corpora and natural language processing. *The Cambridge handbook of learner corpus research*, pages 537–566.

Margot Mieskes. 2017. A quantitative study of data in the nlp community. In *Proceedings of the First ACL Workshop on Ethics in Natural Language Processing*, pages 23–29.

Robert J Mislevy, Pamela A Moss, and James P Gee. 2009. On qualitative and quantitative reasoning in validity. *Generalizing from educational research: Beyond qualitative and quantitative polarization*, pages 67–100.

Brent Daniel Mittelstadt, Patrick Allo, Mariarosaria Taddeo, Sandra Wachter, and Luciano Floridi. 2016. The ethics of algorithms: Mapping the debate. *Big Data & Society*, 3(2):2053951716679679.

Luis Moll, Cathy Amanti, Deborah Neff, and Norma Gonzalez. 2005. Funds of knowledge for teaching: Using a qualitative approach to connect homes and classrooms. *Funds of knowledge: Theorizing practices in households, communities, and classrooms*, pages 71–87.

Luis C Moll. 1992. *Vygotsky and education: Instructional implications and applications of sociohistorical psychology*. Cambridge University Press.

Ernest Morrell. 2015. *Critical literacy and urban youth: Pedagogies of access, dissent, and liberation*. Routledge.

Sean Michael Morris and Jesse Stommel. 2018. *An urgency of teachers: The work of critical digital pedagogy*. Hybrid Pedagogy Incorporated.

Jack Mostow, Greg Aist, Paul Burkhead, Albert Corbett, Andrew Cuneo, Susan Eitelman, Cathy Huang, Brian Junker, Mary Beth Sklar, and Brian Tobin. 2003. Evaluation of an automated reading tutor that listens: Comparison to human tutoring and classroom instruction. *Journal of Educational Computing Research*, 29(1):61–117.

Jack Mostow and Hyeju Jang. 2012. Generating diagnostic multiple choice comprehension cloze questions. In *Proceedings of the Seventh Workshop on Building Educational Applications Using NLP*, pages 136–146. Association for Computational Linguistics.

Pilar Munday. 2016. The case for using duolingo as part of the language classroom experience. *RIED: revista iberoamericana de educación a distancia*, 19(1):83–101.

Hwee Tou Ng, Siew Mei Wu, Ted Briscoe, Christian Hadiwinoto, Raymond Hendy Susanto, and Christopher Bryant. 2014. The conll-2014 shared task on grammatical error correction. In *Proceedings of the Eighteenth Conference on Computational Natural Language Learning: Shared Task*, pages 1–14.

Huy V Nguyen and Diane J Litman. 2018. Argument mining for improving the automated scoring of persuasive essays. In *Thirty-Second AAAI Conference on Artificial Intelligence*.

Safiya Umoja Noble. 2018. *Algorithms of oppression: How search engines reinforce racism*. nyu Press.

Behnaz Nojavanasghari, Charles E Hughes, and Louis-Philippe Morency. 2017. Exceptionally social: Design of an avatar-mediated interactive system for promoting social skills in children with autism. In *Proceedings of the 2017 CHI Conference Extended Abstracts on Human Factors in Computing Systems*, pages 1932–1939. ACM.

Benjamin D Nye, Arthur C Graesser, and Xiangen Hu. 2014. Autotutor and family: A review of 17 years of natural language tutoring. *International Journal of Artificial Intelligence in Education*, 24(4):427–469.

Eda Okur, Sinem Aslan, Nese Alyuz, Asli Arslan Esme, and Ryan S Baker. 2018. Role of sociocultural differences in labeling students affective states. In *International Conference on Artificial Intelligence in Education*, pages 367–380. Springer.

Django Paris and H Samy Alim. 2017. *Culturally sustaining pedagogies: Teaching and learning for justice in a changing world*. Teachers College Press.

Cecelia Parks. 2017. Beyond compliance: Students and ferpa in the age of big data. *Journal of Intellectual Freedom and Privacy*, 2(2):23.

Laura-Ann Petitto, Melody S Berens, Ioulia Kovelman, Matt H Dubins, K Jasinska, and M Shalinsky. 2012. The perceptual wedge hypothesis as the basis for bilingual babies phonetic processing advantage: New insights from fnirs brain imaging. *Brain and language*, 121(2):130–143.

Slav Petrov and Ryan McDonald. 2012. Overview of the 2012 shared task on parsing the web.

Robert Phillipson. 1992. Linguistic imperialism. *The Encyclopedia of Applied Linguistics*, pages 1–7.

Nora Presson, Colleen Davy, and Brian MacWhinney. 2013. Experimentalized call for adult second language learners. *Innovative research and practices in second language acquisition and bilingualism*, 38:139.

Alessandro Raganato and Jörg Tiedemann. 2018. An analysis of encoder representations in transformer-based machine translation. In *Proceedings of the 2018 EMNLP Workshop BlackboxNLP: Analyzing and Interpreting Neural Networks for NLP*, pages 287–297, Brussels, Belgium. Association for Computational Linguistics.

Y Malini Reddy and Heidi Andrade. 2010. A review of rubric use in higher education. *Assessment & evaluation in higher education*, 35(4):435–448.

Priscilla M Regan and Jolene Jesse. 2018. Ethical challenges of edtech, big data and personalized learning: twenty-first century student sorting and tracking. *Ethics and Information Technology*, pages 1–13.

Angela Rickford. 2001. The effect of cultural congruence and higher order questioning on the reading enjoyment and comprehension of ethnic minority students. *Journal of education for students placed at risk*, 6(4):357–387.

Alexey Romanov, Maria De-Arteaga, Hanna Wallach, Jennifer Chayes, Christian Borgs, Alexandra Chouldechova, Sahin Geyik, Krishnaram Kenthapadi, Anna Rumshisky, and Adam Tauman Kalai. 2019. What's in a name? reducing bias in bios without access to protected attributes. In *Proceedings of ACL*.

Noah Oluwafemi Samuel and Kate Williams. 2016. An english-language bibliography of the 1961 cuban literacy campaign. Technical report.

Brian Scassellati, Jake Brawer, Katherine Tsui, Setareh Nasihati Gilani, Melissa Malzkuhn, Barbara Manini, Adam Stone, Geo Kartheiser, Arcangelo Merla, Ari Shapiro, et al. 2018. Teaching language to deaf infants with a robot and a virtual human. In *Proceedings of the 2018 CHI Conference on Human Factors in Computing Systems*, page 553. ACM.

Sylvia Scribner and Michael Cole. 1973. Cognitive consequences of formal and informal education. *Science*, 182(4112):553–559.

Andrew D Selbst, Danah Boyd, Sorelle A Friedler, Suresh Venkatasubramanian, and Janet Vertesi. 2019. Fairness and abstraction in sociotechnical systems. In *Proceedings of the Conference on Fairness, Accountability, and Transparency*, pages 59–68. ACM.

Burr Settles, Chris Brust, Erin Gustafson, Masato Hagiwara, and Nitin Madnani. 2018. Second language acquisition modeling. In *Proceedings of the Thirteenth Workshop on Innovative Use of NLP for Building Educational Applications*, pages 56–65.

Mark D Shermis and Ben Hamner. 2012. Contrasting state-of-the-art automated scoring of essays: Analysis. In *Annual national council on measurement in education meeting*, pages 14–16.

Xing Shi, Inkit Padhi, and Kevin Knight. 2016. Does string-based neural mt learn source syntax? In *Proceedings of the 2016 Conference on Empirical Methods in Natural Language Processing*, pages 1526–1534.

J Siegel. 2001. Pidgins, creoles, and minority dialect in education. *Concise Encyclopedia of Sociolinguistics, Elsevier, Oxford*, pages 747–749.

Sunayana Sitaram, Khyathi Raghavi Chandu, Sai Krishna Rallabandi, and Alan W Black. 2019. A survey of code-switched speech and language processing. https://arxiv.org/abs/1904.00784. ArXiv preprint. Accessed 2019-04-13.

Pia Sommerauer and Antske Fokkens. 2018. Firearms and tigers are dangerous, kitchen knives and zebras are not: Testing whether word embeddings can tell. In *Proceedings of the 2018 EMNLP Workshop BlackboxNLP: Analyzing and Interpreting Neural Networks for NLP*, pages 276–286, Brussels, Belgium. Association for Computational Linguistics.

Douglas E Sperry, Linda L Sperry, and Peggy J Miller. 2018. Reexamining the verbal environments of children from different socioeconomic backgrounds. *Child development*.

Ian Stewart. 2014. Now we stronger than ever: African-american english syntax in twitter. In *Proceedings of the Student Research Workshop at the 14th Conference of the European Chapter of the Association for Computational Linguistics*, pages 31–37.

Holly E Tatum, Beth M Schwartz, Peggy A Schimmoeller, and Nicole Perry. 2013. Classroom participation and student-faculty interactions: does gender matter? *The Journal of Higher Education*, 84(6):745–768.

Rebecca D Taylor, Eva Oberle, Joseph A Durlak, and Roger P Weissberg. 2017. Promoting positive youth development through school-based social and emotional learning interventions: A meta-analysis of follow-up effects. *Child development*, 88(4):1156–1171.

Michael Thomas, Hayo Reinders, and Mark Warschauer. 2012. *Contemporary computer-assisted language learning*. A&C Black.

Sowmya Vajjala and Detmar Meurers. 2012. On improving the accuracy of readability classification using insights from second language acquisition. In *Proceedings of the seventh workshop on building educational applications using NLP*, pages 163–173. Association for Computational Linguistics.

Rob Voigt, Nicholas P Camp, Vinodkumar Prabhakaran, William L Hamilton, Rebecca C Hetey, Camilla M Griffiths, David Jurgens, Dan Jurafsky, and Jennifer L Eberhardt. 2017. Language from police body camera footage shows racial disparities in officer respect. *Proceedings of the National Academy of Sciences*, 114(25):6521–6526.

Rob Voigt, David Jurgens, Vinodkumar Prabhakaran, Dan Jurafsky, and Yulia Tsvetkov. 2018. Rtgender: A corpus for studying differential responses to gender. In *LREC*.

Svitlana Volkova, Theresa Wilson, and David Yarowsky. 2013. Exploring demographic language variations to improve multilingual sentiment analysis in social media. In *Proceedings of the 2013 Conference on Empirical Methods in Natural Language Processing*, pages 1815–1827.

Tony Wan. 2019. Us edtech investments peak again with $1.45 billion raised in 2018. https://www.edsurge.com/news/2019-01-15-us-edtech-investments-peak-again-with-1-45-billion-raised-in-2018. Accessed 2019-04-13.

Kyle Wanberg. 2013. Pedagogy against the state: The ban on ethnic studies in arizona. *Journal of Pedagogy/Pedagogický Casopis*, 4(1):15–35.

Hao Wang and Behzad Mansouri. 2017. Revisiting code-switching practice in tesol: A critical perspective. *The Asia-Pacific Education Researcher*, 26(6):407–415.

John Warner. 2018. *Why They Can't Write: Killing the Five-Paragraph Essay and Other Necessities*. JHU Press.

Miaomiao Wen, Diyi Yang, and Carolyn Rose. 2014. Sentiment analysis in mooc discussion forums: What does it tell us? In *Educational data mining 2014*. Citeseer.

Etienne Wenger. 2010. Communities of practice and social learning systems: the career of a concept. In *Social learning systems and communities of practice*, pages 179–198. Springer.

Candace West and Don H Zimmerman. 1987. Doing gender. *Gender & society*, 1(2):125–151.

Sarah Myers West, Meredith Whittaker, and Kate Crawford. 2019. Discriminating systems: Gender, race and power in ai. *AI Now Institute*.

Patti West-Smith, Stephanie Butler, and Elijah Mayfield. 2018. Trustworthy automated essay scoring without explicit construct validity. In *Proceedings of the AAAI Spring Symposium on AI and Society: Ethics, Safety and Trustworthiness in Intelligent Agents*.

Eric Westervelt. 2015. Meet the mind-reading robo tutor in the sky. http://tinyurl.com/y3l4jk4a. NPR Morning Edition. Accessed 2019-04-13.

John Wesley White. 2011. Resistance to classroom participation: Minority students, academic discourse, cultural conflicts, and issues of representation in whole class discussions. *Journal of Language, Identity & Education*, 10(4):250–265.

Meredith Whittaker, Kate Crawford, Roel Dobbe, Genevieve Fried, Elizabeth Kaziunas, Varoon Mathur, Sarah Mysers West, Rashida Richardson, Jason Schultz, and Oscar Schwartz. 2018. *AI now report 2018*. AI Now Institute at New York University.

Joshua Wilson and Rod D Roscoe. 2019. Automated writing evaluation and feedback: Multiple metrics of efficacy. *Journal of Educational Computing Research*, page 0735633119830764.

Langdon Winner. 1989. *The whale and the reactor: A search for limits in an age of high technology*. University of Chicago Press.

Silke M Witt. 2012. Automatic error detection in pronunciation training: Where we are and where we need to go. *Proc. IS ADEPT*, 6.

Michael Wojatzki, Oren Melamud, and Torsten Zesch. 2016. Bundled gap filling: A new paradigm for unambiguous cloze exercises. In *Proceedings of the 11th Workshop on Innovative Use of NLP for Building Educational Applications*, pages 172–181.

Marisol Wong-Villacres, Arkadeep Kumar, Aditya Vishwanath, Naveena Karusala, Betsy DiSalvo, and Neha Kumar. 2018. Designing for intersections. In *Proceedings of the 2018 on Designing Interactive Systems Conference 2018*, pages 45–58. ACM.

Bronwyn Woods, David Adamson, Shayne Miel, and Elijah Mayfield. 2017. Formative essay feedback using predictive scoring models. In *Proceedings of the 23rd ACM SIGKDD International Conference on Knowledge Discovery and Data Mining*, pages 2071–2080. ACM.

Beverly Woolf, Winslow Burleson, Ivon Arroyo, Toby Dragon, David Cooper, and Rosalind Picard. 2009. Affect-aware tutors: recognising and responding to student affect. *International Journal of Learning Technology*, 4(3-4):129–164.

Wei Xu, Chris Callison-Burch, and Courtney Napoles. 2015. Problems in current text simplification research: New data can help. *Transactions of the Association for Computational Linguistics*, 3:283–297.

Diyi Yang, Tanmay Sinha, David Adamson, and Carolyn Penstein Rosé. 2013. Turn on, tune in, drop out: Anticipating student dropouts in massive open online courses. In *Proceedings of the 2013 NIPS Data-driven education workshop*, volume 11, page 14.

RE Yopp. 1988. Questioning and active comprehension. *Questioning Exchange*, 2(3):231–238.

Hongliang Yu, Liangke Gui, Michael Madaio, Amy Ogan, Justine Cassell, and Louis-Philippe Morency. 2017. Temporally selective attention model for social and affective state recognition in multimedia content. In *Proceedings of the 25th ACM international conference on Multimedia*, pages 1743–1751. ACM.

Xue Yujie. 2019. Camera above the classroom. https://www.sixthtone.com/news/1003759/camera-above-the-classroom. *Sixth Tone*. Accessed 2019-04-27.

Torsten Zesch and Oren Melamud. 2014. Automatic generation of challenging distractors using context-sensitive inference rules. In *Proceedings of the Ninth Workshop on Innovative Use of NLP for Building Educational Applications*, pages 143–148.

Jieyu Zhao, Tianlu Wang, Mark Yatskar, Vicente Ordonez, and Kai-Wei Chang. 2017. Men also like shopping: Reducing gender bias amplification using corpus-level constraints. In *Proceedings of the 2017 Conference on Empirical Methods in Natural Language Processing*, pages 2979–2989.

Jieyu Zhao, Tianlu Wang, Mark Yatskar, Vicente Ordonez, and Kai-Wei Chang. 2018a. Gender bias in coreference resolution: Evaluation and debiasing methods. In *Proceedings of the 2018 Conference of the North American Chapter of the Association for Computational Linguistics: Human Language Technologies*, volume 2.

Jieyu Zhao, Yichao Zhou, Zeyu Li, Wei Wang, and Kai-Wei Chang. 2018b. Learning gender-neutral word embeddings. In *Proceedings of the 2018 Conference on Empirical Methods in Natural Language Processing*, pages 4847–4853.

Jan Henrik Ziegeldorf, Oscar Garcia Morchon, and Klaus Wehrle. 2014. Privacy in the internet of things: threats and challenges. *Security and Communication Networks*, 7(12):2728–2742.

Shoshana Zuboff. 2015. Big other: surveillance capitalism and the prospects of an information civilization. *Journal of Information Technology*, 30(1):75–89.

From Receptive to Productive: Learning to Use Confusing Words through Automatically Selected Example Sentences

Chieh-Yang Huang[1], Yi-Ting Huang[2], Mei-Hua Chen[3] and Lun-Wei Ku[2]
[1] IST, Pennsylvania State University, USA, [2] IIS, Academia Sinica, Taiwan
[3] FLLD, Tunghai University, Taiwan
[1] chiehyang@psu.edu, [2] {ythuang, lwku}@iis.sinica.edu.tw
[3] mhchen@thu.edu.tw

Abstract

Knowing how to use words appropriately has been a key to improving language proficiency. Previous studies typically discuss how students learn receptively to select the correct candidate from a set of confusing words in the fill-in-the-blank task where specific context is given. In this paper, we go one step further, assisting students to learn to use confusing words appropriately in a productive task: sentence translation. We leverage the GiveMe-Example system, which suggests example sentences for each confusing word, to achieve this goal. In this study, students learn to differentiate the confusing words by reading the example sentences, and then choose the appropriate word(s) to complete the sentence translation task. Results show students made substantial progress in terms of sentence structure. In addition, highly proficient students better managed to learn confusing words. In view of the influence of the first language on learners, we further propose an effective approach to improve the quality of the suggested sentences.

1 Introduction

In second or foreign language learning, learning synonyms is not uncommon in vocabulary learning (Hashemi and Gowdasiaei, 2005; Webb, 2007). However, clear differentiation and proper use of near-synonyms poses a challenge to many language learners (Laufer, 1990; Tinkham, 1993; Waring, 1997). Researchers have investigated language learners' lexical use problems, e.g., (Chen and Lin, 2011; Hemchua et al., 2006; Yanjuan, 2014; Laufer, 1990; Tinkham, 1993; Waring, 1997; Yeh et al., 2007; Zughoul, 1991) and suggested that discriminating among semantically similar items presents difficulties for learners (Laufer, 1990). For example, Zughoul (1991) analyzed the writings of Arab EFL college students and found that misapplication of near-

synonyms was the most common type of word choice error made by his students. Likewise, Hemchua and Schmitt (2006) investigated lexical error types in the writings of Thai college students and found that the use of near-synonyms was the most common error made by their students.

Learners are prone to assuming that synonyms behave identically in all contexts (Martin, 1984). Actually, even though two words may share similar meanings, they may not be fully substitutable in certain scenarios (Edmonds and Hirst, 2002; Karlsson, 2014; Liu and Zhong, 2014; Martin, 1984; Webb, 2007). Synonyms are highly likely to confuse learners (Martin, 1984). For example, both *emphasis* and *stress* describe "special attention or importance". The verbs *lay*, *place*, and *put* can collocate with "emphasis on" and "stress on"; however, "place stress on" is a rare expression (it occurs only once in the British National Corpus). For ESL/EFL learners, correct word usage necessitates not only knowledge of the meaning of a word but also knowledge of its paradigmatic and syntagmatic association. Without usage information, synonyms "usually leave the student mystified" (Martin, 1984). Verbs *construct* and *establish* illustrate the fact that synonyms do not always have the same collocates (Webb, 2007). Although both words share the same meaning of "build", in practice, they are not interchangeable in the collocations "establish contact" and "construct system". Learners must grasp the collocational and syntactic differences to use synonyms effectively in a productive mode (Martin, 1984).

For language learners, to facilitate the use of near-synonyms, confusing words, or collocations, it is not enough to just learn the senses of a single confusing word. This has led to the design of learning materials such as thesauri and dictionaries for confusing and easily-misused words (Room, 1988; Ragno, 2016). Although the

Proceedings of the Fourteenth Workshop on Innovative Use of NLP for Building Educational Applications, pages 461–471
Florence, Italy, August 2, 2019. ©2019 Association for Computational Linguistics

information these reference tools provide is appropriate and instructive, the contents – especially example sentences – are neither rich nor constantly updated.

In view of this, artificial intelligence techniques recently have been widely applied to assist language learning. Applications such as grammar correction (Ng et al., 2014; Napoles and Callison-Burch, 2017) and essay scoring (Alikaniotis et al., 2016; Dong and Zhang, 2016; Zhang and Litman, 2018) are relatively mature. Research on the lexical substitution (McCarthy and Navigli, 2007, 2009; Mihalcea et al., 2010; Melamud et al., 2015) and the detection and correction of collocation errors (Futagi, 2010; Alonso Ramos et al., 2014) have also shown the potential of helping ESL learn similar words, near-synonyms or synonyms. Lexical substitution task try to determine a substitute for a word in a context and preserving its meaning and is possible to help language learners understand the correct meaning of a target word by selecting a lexical substitute. The detection and correction, on the other hand, is an inevitable assistance for ESL learners since, as we know, collocation error is one of the most common lexical misuse problem. However, as interpretation is still challenging for AI models, especially deep learning models (Ribeiro et al., 2016; Doshi-Velez and Kim, 2017), there are fewer applications for tasks involving comparisons and explanations, which is the key to learning confusing words.

GiveMeExample (Huang et al., 2017) is one of the few systems. It offers students suggestions of example sentences for confusing words and helps them to choose proper words for fill-in-the-blank multiple-choice questions. GiveMeExample aims to provide opportunities for learners to self-learn the nuances between confusing words by comparing and contrasting the suggested example sentences. However, the fill-in-the-blank multiple-choice format has its limitations. First, it decreases learning efficiency: students look for hints (such as prepositions or collocations) from the example sentences to match the words adjacent to the blank instead of reading and comparing these example sentences thoroughly. Also, as answering multiple-choice questions is a discriminative task, students attempt to select the most possible candidate among all choices instead of learning to properly use the confusing words in question.

To improve the learning effect, we adopt Give-MeExample but deploy it using a carefully designed sentence translation task. Studies (Uzawa, 1996; Prince, 1996; Laufer and Girsai, 2008) have investigated the effect of using translation tasks in language learning. With the integration of the translation task, learners were asked to produce a second language (L2) text conditioned on a given first language (L1) sentence. It is one of effective ways to learn word usage by producing a good translation. In other words, we intentionally move from a receptive to a productive learning task. Generating sentences using confusing words requires a better understanding of the words: with this task we hope to discover how to better assist language learners to learn to differentiate confusing words.

2 Automatic Example Sentence Selection

In this study, we seek to use the GiveMeExample system (Huang et al., 2017) as a basis to improve the automatic example sentence selection task which aims to select sentences that clarify the differences between confusing words. GiveMeExample proposes a clarification score to represent the ability of a sentence to clear up confusion between the given words. In this section, we describe the three main steps to build the automatic example sentence selection model: the definition of the clarification score, the word usage model, and the dictionary-like sentence classifier.

2.1 Problem Definition

Here we define the task more clearly. Given a confusing word set $W = \{w_1, w_2, ..., w_n\}$ and their corresponding sentence sets $\{S_1, S_2, ..., S_n\}$, each sentence set contains a set of sentences $S_t = \{s_{t1}, s_{t2}, ..., s_{tm}\}$. The target is to choose k sentences from each sentence set that clarify the differences among the words in the confusing word set. The desired results are thus sentence sets which clarify W, $\{S'_1, S'_2, ..., S'_n\}$, where $S'_t = \{s'_1, s'_2, ..., s'_k\}$.

2.2 Workflow

Given a word set and the corresponding sentence sets, GiveMeExample selects sentences by (1) building a word usage model for each word, (2) selecting learning-suitable sentences using a dictionary-like sentence classifier, and (3) ranking sentences by computing clarification scores with the help of the word usage model. The top

Number	Word	Example sentence
1	refuse	I was expecting you to <u>refuse</u> to leave the house.
2	refuse	She declined to serve as an informant and <u>refused</u> his request that she keep their meeting secret.
3	reject	In July, a judge in Australia <u>rejected</u> his request for a suppression order.

Table 1: Example sentences that illustrate clarification

five sentences for each word are selected to show learners.

2.3 Clarification Score

To understand the definition of clarification, we start from the confusing word set {*refuse, reject*} in Table 1. The first sentence clarifies the differences better than the second sentence, as the usage of *refuse* in "refused his request" from the second sentence is the same as that for *reject* in "rejected his request" in the third sentence. This illustrates two properties of clarification: the fitness score and the relative closeness score. The fitness score measures how well a sentence s illustrates the usage of word w_1: in this sentence the word should be used in a common way instead of a rare way. The relative closeness score, in turn, measures how well a sentence s for word w_1 highlights the difference between w_1 and the other words $\{w_2, ..., w_n\}$: it must be appropriate for w_1 but inappropriate for $\{w_2, ..., w_n\}$. Namely, when we replace w_1 with $\{w_2, ..., w_3\}$ in s, this sentence should become a wrong sentence. As a result, given a function $P(s|w)$ that estimates the fitness between a sentence s and a word w, we define the clarification score as

$$score(s|w_i) = P(s|w_i) * (\sum_{w_j \in W - w_i} P(s|w_i) - P(s|w_j))$$

$$\tag{1}$$

which is the multiplication of the fitness score and the relative closeness score.

2.4 Word Usage Model

The word usage model represents the distribution of the usage and the context for a given word, that is, the fitness score $P(s|w)$. GiveMeExample includes two word usage models: a Gaussian mixture model (GMM) and a bidirectional long-short-term-memory model (BiLSTM), described as follows. Notice that the word usage model is trained as a classifier per word.

2.4.1 GMM with Local Contextual Features

The idea of the GMM is to turn words around the target word, namely, its context, into embeddings and then model the distribution with a Gaussian mixture model (Xu and Jordan, 1996). Empirically, taking words within a window of size two provides the best results. Therefore, given a sentence $s = \{w_1 \cdots w_t \cdots w_n\}$ where w_t is the target word, the features are $f = \{e_{w_{t-2}}, e_{w_{t-1}}, e_{w_{t-2}} + e_{w_{t-1}}, e_{w_{t+1}}, e_{w_{t+2}}, e_{w_{t+1}} + e_{w_{t+2}}\}$. Note that the features contain not only the corresponding word embeddings, but also the summation of two adjacent words to leverage the meaning. Since the word embedding contains both word identity information and semantic information, the GMM model[1] therefore learns the distribution of both usage and semantic meaning.

2.4.2 BiLSTM

As the confusing words can diverge widely from the target word itself, or could involve long-term dependencies, GMM with local contextual features do not always capture enough information. The BiLSTM model thus utilizes the whole sentence as a feature. The BiLSTM model consists of a forward LSTM and a backward LSTM, which take the words preceding and following the target word as features respectively. The output vectors of these two LSTMs are concatenated to form a sentence embedding. After passing through two dense layers, the BiLSTM model is then built as a binary classifier that decides whether the given sentence is the sentence of the target word or not. In contrast to the generative GMM model, negative samples are needed to train the BiLSTM. As a result, sentences from the corpus are randomly sampled as negative samples[2].

2.5 Dictionary-like Sentence Classification

The given sentences are not always suitable for language learning. For example, a 40-word-long sentence could be too complicated and distracting to learn, and a short sentence such as "It is sophisticated" is not suitable for language learning due to its lack of information. GiveMeExample is equipped with a dictionary-like sentence classifier to select sentences that are simple but informa-

---

[1]Each GMM model is trained on 5,000 instances.
[2]Each BiLSTM model is trained on 5,000 positive instances and 50,000 negative instances.

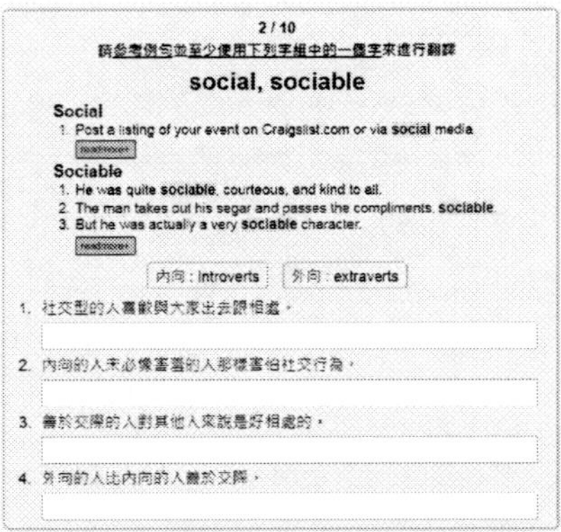

Figure 1: Example questions for translation experiment. Participants click the readmore button to retrieve more example sentences (the maximum number of sentences for each word is five). Also, *introverts* and *extraverts* are two tips that we provide, as they are more difficult but not directly related to *social* and *sociable*.

tive. GiveMeExample collects sentences from the COBUILD English Usage Dictionary (Sinclair, 1992) to train the dictionary-like sentence classifier with syntactic features (Pilán et al., 2014) and a logistic regression model (Walker and Duncan, 1967). Hence, it tends to select sentences similar to those in the COBUILD dictionary.

3　Deployment: Sentence Translation

The sentence translation experiment was separated into a pre-test and a post-test. In both of the tests, participants were asked to translate ten sets of questions from Mandarin to English. In each set, there were four translation questions corresponding to a specific set of confusing words. In addition to answering the question, participants could refer to the example sentences suggested by Give-MeExample in the post-test. In the following paragraph, we describe the experiment in detail.

3.1　Building Translation Questions

In the sentence translation task were 15 confusing word sets selected from Collins COBUILD English Usage (Sinclair, 1992) and the Longman Dictionary of Common Errors (Turton and Heaton, 1996). These two books identify errors in word usage commonly made by language learners and then clear up the confusion. Thus the word sets provided in the books were used as the desired confusing words. A word set contained two or three words. After selecting the confusing word set, we extracted sentences that contain these words from the parallel corpora Chinese English

News Magazine Parallel Text (LDC2005T10) and Hong Kong Parallel Text (LDC2004T08). These sentences were used as candidate questions. Since many sentences in the parallel corpora were long and complicated, we removed sentences whose Chinese translation contains more than 40 words. In the last step, we manually chose appropriate sentences for testing the confusing words. In the end, 15 confusing word sets were determined, each of which contains four questions to be translated resulting a total of 60 questions. Note that some difficult words in the question, such as "introverts" and "extraverts" in Figure 1, were provided as they were unrelated to testing learner use of confusing words.

3.2　Recommending Example Sentences

To recommend sentences, we first collected sentences from Vocabulary[3], an online dictionary. The example sentences in Vocabulary mainly come from formally-written news articles. We collected 5,000 sentences for each word and used all of them to train the GMM and BiLSTM word usage models. When recommending example sentences, we used only the qualified sentences which were filtered by the dictionary-like sentence classifier. The pretrained 300-dimension GloVe (Pennington et al., 2014) embeddings were used in both GMM and BiLSTM. We selected the last five sentences from Vocabulary as a baseline setting.

3.3　Experimental Setup

Sixteen college students were recruited for this translation experiment. As the translation of total 60 questions may not be done in one class, each participants was asked to complete ten randomly-assigned question sets, each of which contained four questions. Thus a total of 40 translation questions were given. This process guarantees that every questions is translated by the same number of participants. The testing period was about 45 minutes, leaving participants about five minutes for each question set. In addition to translating, five example sentences were provided for each word in the post-test. To ensure the students read the suggested sentences, only one example sentence was displayed in the beginning, a "readmore" button was designed for retrieving more example sentences (the maximum number of example sentences is five for each word). The "read-

---

[3]https://www.vocabulary.com/

Category	Example	Grade
Appropriateness	There is a small ~~opportunity~~ **possibility** that she had actually met such a person.	0
Local grammar	What are you going to do if we <u>refuse</u> to ~~following~~ **follow** you?	3
Global grammar	This building ~~is~~ **was** destroyed by the earthquake.	3
Structure	The accident was caused ~~by error~~. (The error is made by human, so it should be "by human error.")	1
Meaning	To a <u>skillful</u> pilot, ~~it's lucky to say that landing in torrential rain.~~ (The meaning is wired and the correct sentence should be "Landing safely in torrential rain can only be a matter of luck for the most skilled pilot.")	1

Table 2: Examples of grade criteria. The underlined word is the target confusing word.

more" activities were logged for further investigation. The pre- and post-tests were administered in two different weeks to reduce short-term memory effects. Figure 1 shows a screen-shot of a post-test with the confusing word set *social* and *sociable*.

The example sentences provided were suggested by the GMM and BiLSTM models or selected from the Vocabulary website. Note that to discourage participants from guessing specific patterns, the example sentences from one of the three sources were presented randomly. For instance, as GMM takes contexts within a window as features, the most significant difference exists only within this window. However, we do not expect participants to look only at this small piece of text. Also, sentences from Vocabulary are generally more difficult than those from GMM or BiLSTM, but participants who are consistently presented with difficult sentences may stop considering these example sentences to be useful resources. As the source is assigned randomly for each proposed example sentence, the total number of sentences for each source is set to the number that can best distribute sentences from different sources evenly.

3.4 Grading

Grading was done by an English native speaker who is professional in language learning and teaching. The grading criteria takes into account appropriateness, grammar, and completeness. Appropriateness measures whether the correct word is used or not, so the score here is either zero or one point. Grammar involves local grammar as well as global grammar. All the grammar errors relating directly to the target confusing word belong to local grammar; the remaining grammar errors throughout the sentence belong to global grammar. The initial points for both grammar parts are four points; each grammar error results in a one-point deduction. Completeness, which eval-

uates whether the student's translation represents all of the meanings, takes into account structure and meaning. If a student missed content such as adverbial phrases, points were deducted in terms of structure. Similarly, if a student's translation was different from the original meaning, points were deducted in terms of meaning. Both structure and meaning started with two points. Examples are listed in Table 2. Given our focus on examining whether students can learn how to differentiate and use confusing words, we computed a weighted sum for reference as follows:

$$WeightedSum = 5*Appropriateness+LocalGrammar \tag{2}$$

which is the sum of the appropriateness scores, weighted by 5, and the local grammar scores.

4 Results and Discussions

The pre and post scores for the grading categories are summarized in Table 3. Student are separated into Highly proficient group and Less proficient group evenly by an external collocation test score (Chen and Lin, 2011). In general, the suggested example sentences helped students make substantial progress in terms of sentence structure. It is worth noting that students were able to comprehend the meaning of confusing words in the given sentences selected from both of the BiLSTM and GMM models. Students performed significantly better in *appropriateness*, *local grammar*, and *structure* when the sentences were suggested by BiLSTM; while the GMM model was good at presenting the structures of sentences and demonstrating the meaning of confusing words.

Highly proficient students learned confusing words better from the suggested example sentences. The findings showed that BiLSTM helped them gain a better understanding of *appropriateness*, *local grammar*, and *structure*, and GMM

Group	Model	Appropriateness			Local grammar			Weighted sum			Global grammar			Structure			Meaning		
		pre	post	t-test	pre	post	t-test	pre	post	t-test	pre	post	t-test	pre	post	t-test	pre	post	t-test
H	Vocabulary	**0.714**	0.571	0.302	**3.429**	3.143	0.178	**7.000**	6.000	0.237	**2.429**	2.143	0.229	0.714	**1.000**	0.229	1.000	1.000	0.500
H	GMM	0.444	0.444	0.500	2.444	**3.000**	0.123	4.667	**5.222**	0.347	**1.667**	1.556	0.364	0.667	**1.222**	0.025*	0.333	**1.111**	0.004*
H	BiLSTM	0.273	**0.545**	0.041*	2.364	**3.273**	0.008*	3.727	**6.000**	0.011*	**1.545**	1.364	0.276	0.818	**1.182**	0.052	0.545	**0.909**	0.052
L	Vocabulary	0.182	**0.364**	0.170	2.182	**2.909**	0.098	3.091	**4.727**	0.056	0.818	**1.091**	0.247	0.364	**1.000**	0.013*	0.455	**0.636**	0.220
L	GMM	0.417	**0.583**	0.169	2.333	**2.917**	0.066	4.417	**5.833**	0.072	0.750	**1.500**	0.028*	0.500	**1.167**	0.012*	0.333	**1.083**	0.010*
L	BiLSTM	0.429	**0.524**	0.165	2.667	**2.714**	0.443	4.810	**5.333**	0.169	1.238	**1.571**	0.116	0.762	**1.143**	0.004*	0.524	**0.857**	0.025*

Table 3: Result of translation experiment. The number of translated questions for each model ranges from 7 to 21, with the average number 11.8, depending on the number of early leave and absence we encountered in the experiment day. The pre- and post- numbers correspond to the average score for pre-test and post-test respectively and the t-test stars represent significance. The participants were separated into highly proficient (H) and less proficient (L) groups.

helped with *structure* and *meaning*. Although it was difficult for less-proficient students to recognize the difference (small improvement in *appropriateness* and *local grammar*), the GMM model significantly facilitated their comprehension in terms of *structure*, *global grammar* and *meaning*.

The "readmore" logs show that most of the students clicked the button and expand all the example sentences immediately. This might imply that students did read all the example sentences and could refer to them when producing translations.

We analyzed the translation tasks to identify possible problems. Below we discuss three possible explanations in terms of test items, learner behavior, and the suggested example sentences.

First, in the proposed translation task, participants sometimes focused on the wrong segment of the test item to translate with the confusing words. This may be because in this productive testing process, we do not specifically tell participants which source word should be aligned to the target confusing word. For instance, in "For a person to become so poor, if it's not because they didn't work hard in their youth then its because they have truly had hard luck", participants should have translated the source words "hard luck" to English using the appropriate word in the confusing word set. However, the students showed confusion in their focusing on translating the source word *poor* into one of *hard*, *difficult*, and *tough* as opposed to the source word *hard* in *hard luck*. One example translation made by a participant is "The reason why a person's life is tough might because he/she was lazy when he/she was young or he/she had a bad luck". In such cases, the learning effect cannot be correctly evaluated.

We seek to find the best example sentences for word sets where the words are confusing for learners. Hence regarding the suggested example sentences, the example sentences were extracted as long as the confusing words shared the least familiar senses. However, this led to words being chosen in example sentences with different senses and/or even different parts of speech, which is how we wanted to compare them. The words *hard* and *difficult* exemplify these issues. First, according to WordNet, *hard* in this case indicates "resisting weight or pressure" in the example sentence "Such uncertainty can be hard on families, too", whereas *difficult* means "needing skill or effort" in the sentence "But other stories are more difficult to explain". On the other hand, *hard* is an adverb in "Banks will have to work harder to make profits", while *difficult* is an adjective in "But other stories are more difficult to explain".

Student behavior also affected the performance of this study. Some highly proficient students were observed skipping the example sentences and thus not learning from them how to differentiate the confusing words, which led to inappropriate translations similar to those made in the pre-test. It could be that these highly proficient students were more confident of their command of certain confusing words. For example, when required to choose from *beat*, *defeat*, and *win* to translate "Emmanuel Macron beats Marine Le Pen in both rounds of the French presidential election", one highly proficient student made these translations in the pre- and post-tests, respectively: "Emmanuel Macron won over Marine Le Pen for two rounds of presidential election", and "Emmanuel Macron won over Marine Le Pen for presidential election for two rounds", whereas *win over* is not a usage suggested by example sentences. In addition, from this example we can see that though they rarely read example sentences, they did try to translate in other words in the post-test, which results in the unstable scores of *global grammar* that are less relevant to the near-synonym recognition but to the translation instead.

These three limitations partially explain learner performance in the translation task. Thus we attempted to refine the method for example sentence extraction. Improving the test items and controlling student learning behavior is beyond the scope of this study.

5 Leveraging First Language for Better Example Sentence Selection

From the results of the translation experiment, we observed that some words were confusing to students due to language transfer from L1 (native language) to L2 (foreign language). Some students learn English such that they only remember how to spell words and their L1 definitional glosses, rather than understanding their context or usage. For example, the confusing words *hard* and *difficult* are very similar and almost interchangeable. If these words are memorized only by memorizing the L1 definitional glosses, *not easy*, students may fail to recognize the slight difference between them. In other words, example sentences containing words that translate into similar glosses in L1 are the sentences that indeed contain confusing senses, and thus are the target candidates for the GiveMeExample system to consider for suggestion. We follow this line of thinking to improve the example sentences.

In the new setting, the GiveMeExample system groups example sentences by the L1 definitional glosses of confusing words before proceeding to automatic sentence selection with the BiLSTM or GMM word usage model. When a word has multiple senses, this step helps to identify the confusing sense, under the assumption that words with similar L1 definitions are confusing. Take for example *hard* and *difficult*: *hard* as an adjective has multiple meanings – "not easy, requiring great physical or mental effort to accomplish, resisting weight or pressure, hard to bear", etc; whereas *difficult* has the meanings "not easy, requiring great physical or mental effort to accomplish, and hard to control". The common sense in L1 is *not easy, requiring great physical or mental effort to accomplish.* Sentences containing confusing words whose L1 translations share these two senses are selected for later processing and suggestion.

To identify these sentences, we need each word in the sentence and its corresponding L1 translation. For this purpose, parallel texts from two corpora – Chinese English News Magazine Paral-

lel Text (LDC2005T10) and Hong Kong Parallel Text (LDC2004T08), that is, a total of 2,682,129 English-Chinese sentence pairs – are utilized to learn the word alignment between L1 and L2 parallel sentences. To align example sentences from Vocabulary, first they were all translated into Traditional Chinese using Googletrans[4]. Then we used NLTK[5] to tokenize English sentences and CKIP (Chen and Liu, 1992) to segment Chinese sentences respectively. After that, the word alignment model GIZA++ (Och and Ney, 2003), a toolkit that implements several statistical word alignment models, was adopted to align English words to their corresponding Chinese words. After alignment, the L1 translations of confusing words were recognized, after which the sentences in the example sentence pool of the confusing words in the same set were clustered with respect to their L1 translation. There were 12 confusing word sets with more than one common L1 translation. Only words in three confusing word sets (*possibility* vs. *opportunity*, *social* vs. *sociable*, and *unusual* vs. *strange*) had all different L1 translations. When a common L1 translation was found for a set of confusing words, GiveMeExample passed through only those sentences containing confusing words with the same L1 translation to the sentence selection component.

5.1 Human Evaluation

We employed Amazon Mechanical Turk crowd-workers to give their perspectives on the suggested sentences considering the L1 of learners. Twelve sets of confusing words with common L1 translations were evaluated. GiveMeExample in both the original and the new settings suggested respectively five sentences using the BiLSTM and GMM models for each word in the twelve sets. In this new setting, six words – (*briefly*, *duty*, *ordinary*, *sight*, *shortly*, and *unusual*) – had less than five sentences.

Figure 2 shows a screenshot of two versions of the suggested example sentences presented side-by-side. Crowd-workers were given no information about the settings or the sentence selection models (BiLSTM or GMM). For each task, participants were to read several sentences suggested by the two versions of the GiveMeExample system and then answer the following four questions.

---

[4]https://pypi.org/project/googletrans/
[5]https://www.nltk.org/

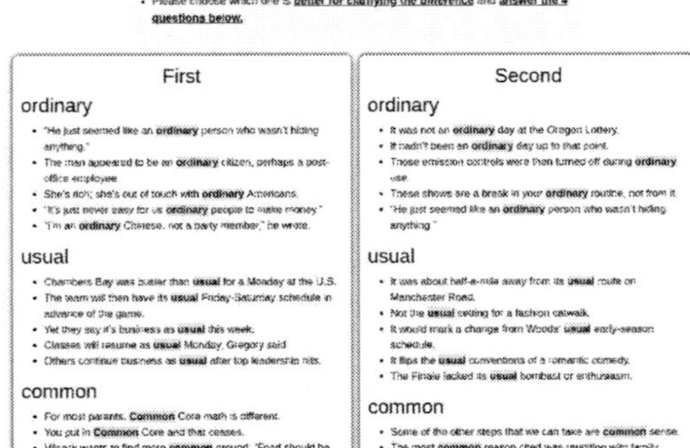

Figure 2: An example survey for crowd-workers to compare GiveMeExample with different settings. In this specific example, *first* represents sentences suggested by the new setting; *second* represents those from the original.

Q1: Is Mandarin your first language (y/n)?

Q2: Are these words confusing to you (y/n)?

Q3: Which set of example sentences you think is more useful for learning these words (1/2)?

Q4: In what aspect you think they are more useful (choose one)? (a) clarifying their meaning (e.g., *social* encounter vs. *sociable character*) (b) demonstrate their usage (e.g., *as usual* but not *as common*) (c) showing correct grammar (e.g., *The proposal was narrowly defeated in a January election*, but *Obviously we want to continue to win games.*)

The purpose of Q1 and Q2 is to understand the background of turkers, Q3 is to compare the new setting with old setting among two models, and Q4 is to investigate the effect of considering L1 translation. We also consulted a native speaker who works as an expert editor. This expert completed the surveys under the same conditions as the crowd-workers.

5.2 Results and Analysis

Sixty-one crowd-workers participated in the evaluation. Mandarin was the first language of 12 (19.67%) of them. On average, each worker completed six tasks (SD=8.17). For each set out of 12 sets, 15 workers were asked to answer the questions. We tested the example sentences suggested by both GMM and BiLSTM models, collecting in total 360 ratings from workers. It was an interesting finding that only 5% of the confusing word sets were labeled by workers as confusing no matter they were native speakers or not [6]. Details are shown in Table 4.

Table 4 shows the feedback on Q3 and Q4 from workers and the expert on each confusing word set. Results from the expert confirm that when considering L1, our approach could provide better example sentences. However, results from the crowd-workers were mixed.

Several interesting observations were gleaned from this experiment. First, when considering the L1 translation and grouping sentences by their L1 sense, the example sentences containing confusing words with different senses were excluded. Therefore, learners could focus more on the confusing sense to be learned. For example, *work hard* is a commonly seen phrase in the example sentences suggested by the original setting. When students learned the confusion set containing *hard*, *difficult*, and *tough*, the sentences containing *work hard* were of little help, as the meanings were irrelevant to the confusing sense in this set. However, in the new setting, the example sentences for *hard* were more semantically related to *difficult* and *tough*. We can say that in this task, consideration of L1 amounted to implicitly performing word sense disambiguation (WSD).

The exclusion of sentences that did not contain words with the confusing sense has additional benefit. That is, the suggested sentences are more likely to focus on the demonstration of the confusing sense. This has the advantage that the confusing words in the suggested sentences are diverse in their part of speech and pragmatic domain. For instance, in the confusion set *defeat*, *win*, and *beat*, the common L1 sense among them is "to conquest" and "victory". Under these certain meanings, only *win* can be used as a verb or a noun whereas the other two words can only function as a verb. This illustrates the power of grouping sentences by L1 translation Another example is *destroy* in the confusion set *destroy*, *ruin*, and *spoil*. In the original setting, *destroy* is used in only the military domain and thus is misleading. When using the GMM model which considers only the local context, the issue is even more serious. This is mitigated in the new setting, especially for the GMM model.

Following the above, in some cases workers indeed tended to prefer example sentences of some

---

[6]The expert had a clear understanding of these words.

Confusing word set	Q2 (turkers)		Q3 (turkers)		Q3 (expert)		Q4 (turkers)					
							BiLSTM			GMM		
	No	Yes	BiLSTM	GMM	BiLSTM	GMM	(a)	(b)	(c)	(a)	(b)	(c)
ordinary / usual / common	97%	3%	N	N	O	N	46%	40%	14%	46%	40%	14%
skillful / skilled	93%	7%	O	O	O	N	46%	46%	6%	34%	46%	20%
alternative / alternate	97%	3%	O	O	N	O	34%	60%	6%	26%	46%	26%
destroy / ruin / spoil	100%	0%	O	N	N	N	40%	40%	20%	20%	74%	6%
scarce / rare / unusual	97%	3%	O	O	O	O	14%	74%	14%	0%	74%	26%
defeat / win / beat	100%	0%	N	N	N	N	40%	46%	14%	20%	60%	20%
sight / landscape / scenery	93%	7%	N	O	N	O	40%	46%	14%	34%	46%	20%
briefly / shortly / concisely	97%	3%	O	N	O	O	14%	66%	20%	14%	60%	26%
hard / difficult / tough	90%	10%	O	N	O	O	14%	80%	6%	20%	54%	26%
error / mistake / oversight	90%	10%	O	N	N	N	26%	60%	14%	20%	66%	14%
duty / job / task	97%	3%	N	N	O	N	46%	46%	6%	14%	66%	20%
obligation / responsibility / commitment	93%	7%	N	N	N	N	26%	66%	6%	46%	40%	14%
Mean	95%	5%	42%(N)	67%(N)	50%(N)	58%(N)	32%	56%	12%	24%	56%	20%

Table 4: Results from the human evaluation. N represents the example sentences from the new setting, and O are from the original one. In addition, the expert annotated that ALL of the suggested sentences were useful for demonstrating their usage (b).

pattern. For example, in the set *scarce*, *rare*, and *unusual*, confusing words in the example sentences that shared the L1 translation *very hardly* resulted in example sentences containing confusing words functioning as adverb, adjective, and adjective, respectively; however, in the original setting where context is considered before sense, they all function as adjectives. This interesting result reveals that there is overhead when learning from materials without patterns, which could also be why only highly proficient students can learn the appropriateness.

6 Conclusion

In this paper, we leverage GiveMeExample, an AI system which automatically suggests example sentences to help ESL learners better learn to differentiate confusing words. To evaluate the system effectiveness, we designed a sophisticated sentence translation task around the problem of students not really learning via the previously designed receptive task, i.e., multiple-choice selection. This approach was evaluated using college students; results show that students made substantial progress with assistance of the system. Specifically, after learning the example sentences, students produced more structural sentences. However, learning to use appropriate words is a demanding task which requires higher language proficiency.

The learner's first language may lead to confusion in different areas: this is also taken into account with a novel approach. Overall, the example sentences in the refined list were considered more useful for learning by Amazon mechanical turkers and the expert English editor. However, for ESL learners such as students and some of the turkers, they tended to prefer example sentences with similar patterns to mitigate cognitive overhead. Thus, future work will focus on providing example sentences with similar patterns but diverse contexts.

Acknowledgments

This research is partially supported by Ministry of Science and Technology, Taiwan under Grant No. MOST108-2634-F-002-008- and MOST108-2634-F-001-004-.

References

Dimitrios Alikaniotis, Helen Yannakoudakis, and Marek Rei. 2016. Automatic text scoring using neural networks. *arXiv preprint arXiv:1606.04289*.

Margarita Alonso Ramos, Marcos García Salido, and Orsolya Vincze. 2014. Towards a collocation writing assistant for learners of spanish.

Keh-Jiann Chen and Shing-Huan Liu. 1992. Word identification for Mandarin Chinese sentences. In *Proceedings of the 14th Conference on Computational linguistics (COLING '92) - Volume 1*, pages 101–107.

Mei-Hua Chen and Maosung Lin. 2011. Factors and analysis of common miscollocations of college students in Taiwan. *Studies in English Language and Literature*, (28):57–72.

Fei Dong and Yue Zhang. 2016. Automatic features for essay scoring–an empirical study. In *Proceedings of the 2016 Conference on Empirical Methods in Natural Language Processing*, pages 1072–1077.

Finale Doshi-Velez and Been Kim. 2017. Towards a rigorous science of interpretable machine learning. *arXiv preprint arXiv:1702.08608*.

Philip Edmonds and Graeme Hirst. 2002. Near-synonymy and lexical choice. *Computational linguistics*, 28(2):105–144.

Yoko Futagi. 2010. The effects of learner errors on the development of a collocation detection tool. In *Proceedings of the fourth workshop on Analytics for noisy unstructured text data*, pages 27–34. ACM.

Mohammad Reza Hashemi and Farah Gowdasiaei. 2005. An attribute-treatment interaction study: Lexical-set versus semantically-unrelated vocabulary instruction. *RELC journal*, 36(3):341–361.

Saengchan Hemchua, Norbert Schmitt, et al. 2006. An analysis of lexical errors in the English compositions of Thai learners.

Chieh-Yang Huang, Mei-Hua Chen, and Lun-Wei Ku. 2017. Towards a better learning of near-synonyms: Automatically suggesting example sentences via fill in the blank. In *Proceedings of the 26th International Conference on World Wide Web Companion*, pages 293–302. International World Wide Web Conferences Steering Committee.

Monica Karlsson. 2014. Advanced Students' L1 and L2 Mastery of Lexical Fields of Near Synonyms. *World Journal of English Language*, 4(3):1.

Batia Laufer. 1990. Ease and difficulty in vocabulary learning: Some teaching implications. *Foreign Language Annals*, 23(2):147–155.

Batia Laufer and Nany Girsai. 2008. Form-focused instruction in second language vocabulary learning: A case for contrastive analysis and translation. *Applied linguistics*, 29(4):694–716.

Dilin Liu and Shouman Zhong. 2014. L2 vs. L1 use of synonymy: An empirical study of synonym use/acquisition. *Applied linguistics*, 37(2):239–261.

Marilyn Martin. 1984. Advanced vocabulary teaching: The problem of synonyms. *The Modern Language Journal*, 68(2):130–137.

Diana McCarthy and Roberto Navigli. 2007. SemEval-2007 task 10: English lexical substitution task. In *Proceedings of the Fourth International Workshop on Semantic Evaluations (SemEval-2007)*, pages 48–53, Prague, Czech Republic. Association for Computational Linguistics.

Diana McCarthy and Roberto Navigli. 2009. The english lexical substitution task. *Language resources and evaluation*, 43(2):139–159.

Oren Melamud, Omer Levy, and Ido Dagan. 2015. A simple word embedding model for lexical substitution. In *Proceedings of the 1st Workshop on Vector Space Modeling for Natural Language Processing*, pages 1–7.

Rada Mihalcea, Ravi Sinha, and Diana McCarthy. 2010. Semeval-2010 task 2: Cross-lingual lexical substitution. In *Proceedings of the 5th international workshop on semantic evaluation*, pages 9–14. Association for Computational Linguistics.

Courtney Napoles and Chris Callison-Burch. 2017. Systematically adapting machine translation for grammatical error correction. In *Proceedings of the 12th Workshop on Innovative Use of NLP for Building Educational Applications*, pages 345–356.

Hwee Tou Ng, Siew Mei Wu, Ted Briscoe, Christian Hadiwinoto, Raymond Hendy Susanto, and Christopher Bryant. 2014. The CoNLL-2014 shared task on grammatical error correction. In *Proceedings of the Eighteenth Conference on Computational Natural Language Learning: Shared Task*, pages 1–14.

Franz Josef Och and Hermann Ney. 2003. A systematic comparison of various statistical alignment models. *Computational Linguistics*, 29(1):19–51.

Jeffrey Pennington, Richard Socher, and Christopher Manning. 2014. GloVe: Global vectors for word representation. In *Proceedings of the 2014 Conference on Empirical Methods in Natural Language Processing (EMNLP)*, pages 1532–1543.

Ildikó Pilán, Elena Volodina, and Richard Johansson. 2014. Rule-based and machine learning approaches for second language sentence-level readability. In *Proceedings of the Ninth Workshop on Innovative Use of NLP for Building Educational Applications*, pages 174–184.

Peter Prince. 1996. Second language vocabulary learning: The role of context versus translations as a function of proficiency. *The modern language journal*, 80(4):478–493.

Nancy Ragno. 2016. *Use the Right Word: Your Quick & Easy Guide to 158 Words Most Often Confused or Misused*. Nancy Ragno.

Marco Tulio Ribeiro, Sameer Singh, and Carlos Guestrin. 2016. Why should I trust you?: Explaining the predictions of any classifier. In *Proceedings of the 22nd ACM SIGKDD International Conference on Knowledge Discovery and Data Mining*, pages 1135–1144. ACM.

Adrian Room. 1988. *Dictionary of confusing words and meanings*. Dorset Press.

John Sinclair. 1992. *Collins COBUILD English Usage*. Collins.

Thomas Tinkham. 1993. The effect of semantic clustering on the learning of second language vocabulary. *System*, 21(3):371–380.

Nigel D Turton and John Brian Heaton. 1996. *Longman Dictionary of Common Errors*. Longman.

Kozue Uzawa. 1996. Second language learners' processes of l1 writing, l2 writing, and translation from l1 into l2. *Journal of second language writing*, 5(3):271–294.

Strother H Walker and David B Duncan. 1967. Estimation of the probability of an event as a function of several independent variables. *Biometrika*, 54(1-2):167–179.

Robert Waring. 1997. The negative effects of learning words in semantic sets: A replication. *System*, 25(2):261–274.

Stuart Webb. 2007. The effects of synonymy on second-language vocabulary learning. *Reading in a Foreign Language*, 19(2):120–136.

Lei Xu and Michael I Jordan. 1996. On convergence properties of the EM algorithm for Gaussian mixtures. *Neural computation*, 8(1):129–151.

HUO Yanjuan. 2014. BNC-Based Design of College English Vocabulary Teaching for Chinese College Students. *Studies in Literature and Language*, 8(3):122–125.

Yuli Yeh, Hsien-Chin Liou, and Yi-Hsin Li. 2007. Online synonym materials and concordancing for EFL college writing. *Computer Assisted Language Learning*, 20(2):131–152.

Haoran Zhang and Diane Litman. 2018. Co-attention based neural network for source-dependent essay scoring. In *Proceedings of the Thirteenth Workshop on Innovative Use of NLP for Building Educational Applications*, pages 399–409.

Muhammad Raji Zughoul. 1991. Lexical choice: Towards writing problematic word lists. *International Review of Applied Linguistics*, 29(1):45–60.

Equipping Educational Applications with Domain Knowledge

Tarek Sakakini[*]   **Hongyu Gong**[*]   **Jong Yoon Lee**[*]
Robert Schloss[†]   **Jinjun Xiong**[†]   **Suma Bhat**[*]
[*]University of Illinois at Urbana-Champaign, USA
[†]T. J. Watson Research Center, IBM, USA
[*]{sakakini, hgong6, jlee642, spbhat2}@illinois.edu
[†]{rschloss, jinjun}@us.ibm.com

Abstract

One of the challenges of building natural language processing (NLP) applications for education is finding a large domain-specific corpus for the subject of interest (e.g., history or science). To address this challenge, we propose a tool, Dexter, that extracts a subject-specific corpus from a heterogeneous corpus, such as Wikipedia, by relying on a small seed corpus and distributed document representations. We empirically show the impact of the generated corpus on language modeling, estimating word embeddings, and consequently, distractor generation, resulting in a better performance than while using a general domain corpus, a heuristically constructed domain-specific corpus, and a corpus generated by a popular system: BootCaT.

1 Introduction

Educational applications tend to target a specific subject, in other words, a specific domain, such as the medical domain in the case of (Jin et al., 2018). Thus, building these applications with underlying NLP algorithms, would typically require a large domain-specific corpus. Example uses of these large corpora are estimating language models (Rosenfeld, 2000), estimating word embeddings (Mikolov et al., 2013), and estimating document embeddings (Le and Mikolov, 2014). These estimations are central to several downstream applications including automatic speech recognition (Katz, 1987), machine translation (Koehn et al., 2003), and text categorization (Tang et al., 2015).

Previous findings, such as (McClosky, 2010), have shown that training NLP applications on a domain different from the target domain could prove detrimental to the performance of these applications. In order to help educational applications in specific disciplines such as science and history create a large, yet domain-specific corpus,

we propose a domain extraction tool, Dexter[1], that extracts a domain-specific corpus from Wikipedia.

The algorithm, elaborated in Section 2, retrieves a set of documents from Wikipedia that are closest in discipline to a user-supplied small seed corpus. The size of this extracted set is a user-defined hyperparameter, and thus controls the trade-off between the specificity of the output corpus and its size. We empirically determine the favorable configuration of Dexter, demonstrate its benefits towards estimating word embeddings, and consequently distractor generation, as well as language models. We also show how, on the aforementioned tasks, Dexter outperforms BootCaT, a popular toolkit to automatically create an Internet-derived corpus (Baroni and Bernardini, 2004). Datasets used in this research are released for public use[2].

2 Method

Dexter's algorithm builds on the assumption that the distributed representation of two documents covering similar topics are closer in the vector space than two documents covering different topics. To test this assumption qualitatively, we embed all Wikipedia articles in $\mathbb{R}^{300}$ using Doc2Avg[3], and then map them to $\mathbb{R}^2$ using t-SNE (Maaten and Hinton, 2008) as shown in Figure 1. We see that the subset of science Wikipedia articles form a cluster, thus validating our assumption. Details on how science Wikipedia articles were identified are provided in Section 3.1. Building on this observation, Dexter takes a seed set of articles representing the target domain (e.g., science), then sorts Wikipedia articles in increasing order of distance to seed set, then returns the first k documents as the extracted in-domain corpus.

---

[1]Publicly available at http://bit.ly/dexter-acl
[2]http://bit.ly/dexter-dataset-acl
[3]By averaging embeddings of words in document.

Proceedings of the Fourteenth Workshop on Innovative Use of NLP for Building Educational Applications, pages 472–477
Florence, Italy, August 2, 2019. ©2019 Association for Computational Linguistics

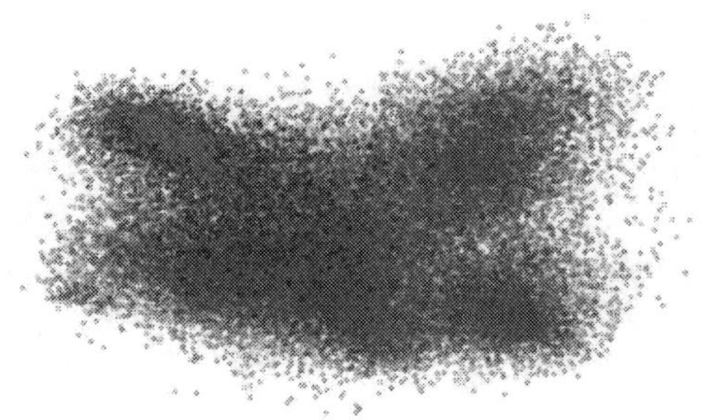

Figure 1: Clustering of science (red) Wikipedia articles among all (blue) Wikipedia articles in 2D.

Multiple design choices need to be considered carefully and are decided empirically in Section 3.2. These decisions are: The document representation method, the distance function to the seed set, and the seed corpus size. For the document representation, we consider: Doc2Vec (Le and Mikolov, 2014), Doc2Avg, Doc2wAvg[4], TFIDF (Leskovec et al., 2014), and LSA (Dumais, 2004). For the distance function, we consider: Mean, Min, Max, 90th percentile, and 10th percentile (the last two being robust to outliers). For the seed corpus size, we experiment with: 10, 10^2, and 10^3.

3 Experiments

We perform three main experiments. The first is an intrinsic evaluation of Dexter, guiding our design choices. Second, we check the effect of the domain-specificity of the resulting word embeddings on the downstream educational task of distractor generation for science questions. Third, we evaluate the effect of Dexter on language modeling. Before we delve on the experimental details, we describe the process of labeling Wikipedia articles as science or not, and describe our competitive baseline: BootCaT.

3.1 Experimental Setup

Dataset Preparation: Wikipedia does not clearly partition its articles into different domains, but instead assigns a set of categories to each article. Wikipedia also organizes its categories as a directed graph, where, if category b is a subcategory of category a, then there exists an edge (a, b) (Schönhofen, 2009). Although it might seem natural to consider all descendants of a category (domain in a broad sense) to belong to that category, upon inspection we found the need for setting a

depth limit. For example, "Stalking" is a third descendant of "Biology", although "Stalking" is not considered a "Biology"-related subject. Based on similar observations, we set the depth limit to two.

To identify science articles, we consider a list of science root categories, and all their subcategories up to a depth of 2. All articles labeled with any category in this list are considered science articles, amounting to 176,905 articles. This collected science corpus will be referred to as C_D, while the general Wikipedia corpus will be referred to as C.

We note that the corpus C_D is created using heuristics on Wikipedia's taxonomy. In order to assess the extent to which the articles in C_D belong to the discipline of science, we do the following. Two annotators assess the quality of C_D by taking a subset of 1000 articles equally spread across depths: 0, 1, 2, and 3. Each article (depth anonymized) was given an integer score between 0 and 5 to reflect how much the content of the article is related to science. The inter-annotator agreement on the scores had a Pearson's correlation coefficient of 0.77 suggesting a reasonably high agreement on the scores. Upon comparing the average scores of articles at different depths, we found the score to be inversely proportional to the depth, with scores 4.35, 3.58, 3.21, and 2.4 for articles at depth 0, 1, 2, and 3 respectively. This further justifies our depth limit of 2, below which the average score suddenly drops below 3.

Also, for the purposes of our experiments, we split C_D (176,905 articles) into three corpora: (1) C_{seed} (1,000 articles having a depth of 0), used as the seed corpus for Dexter and the BootCaT baselines, (2) C_{ho} (40,000 articles), which is a held-out dataset to be used for testing language models, and (3) $C_{silver}{}^5$ (136,905 articles) = $C_D - C_{ho}$, our training subset of C_D to be used in language modeling experiments. C_D reflects the quality of such a corpus heuristically-constructed using Wikipedia's taxonomy.

Baseline: One popular system used by researchers to extract a domain-specific corpus is BootCaT (Baroni and Bernardini, 2004), which operates on the World Wide Web. BootCaT generates queries to a search engine from user-supplied key phrases and parses the first n pages retrieved for each query, where n is set by the user.

Since Dexter requires seed articles instead of

---

[4]The embedding of a document is the average of its words' embeddings weighted by a word's TFIDF score

[5]The term silver is used, rather than gold, since we rely on heuristics rather than direct human supervision.

key phrases, we bridge the gap by a key phrase extraction algorithm (Rose et al., 2010) on the set of seed articles, by utilizing a publicly available implementation[6] with default parameters. We thus take C_{seed} and extract the top-100 key phrases with less than 4 words, then feed them to Boot-CaT, leading to a domain-specific corpus (referred to as BootCat-KE). To avoid any possible noise introduced by the keyword extraction algorithm we consider another version of the BootCaT baseline but now with a manual set of 100 key phrases describing the domain of science. We take a list of science key phrases available online[7], and then randomly select 100 phrases. The corpus generated by this algorithm is referred to as BootCat-M.

3.2 Intrinsic Evaluation

Before we analyze Dexter's performance on downstream tasks and compare it to BootCaT, we study the intrinsic performance of Dexter under several design choices and conditions. Our evaluation of Dexter is based on the precision of the extracted articles averaged over 5 runs. Since we would be manipulating the seed set size, and to ensure Dexter's robustness under randomness, we artificially construct our seed set by taking a random subset of C_D instead of using C_{seed}. That seed set is then used to algorithmically extract the rest of C_D via Dexter. Accordingly, precision is calculated as the percentage of articles extracted, which belong to $C_D - C_{seed}$. As for recall, it is not measured since precision is sufficient as a comparison between methods assuming same number of documents extracted.

Document representation: We vary the document representation method while fixing the seed corpus size at 10^3, and the distance function as Mean (c.f. Figure 2a). We observe that LSA and TFIDF are initially superior, but perform comparably to Doc2Avg and Doc2wAvg as k increases. LSA is chosen due to its low-dimensionality, and superiority for modest k values.

Distance function: We vary the distance function used while fixing the document representation to LSA and the seed corpus size to 1000 (c.f. Figure 2b). We observe that the 10th percentile distance function leads to the best precision. We hypothesize that this is due to the 10th percentile being robust to noise, and requiring closeness to only one

subdomain of science rather than all at once.

Seed corpus size: We vary the seed corpus size while fixing the document representation to LSA and the distance function as 10th percentile (c.f. Figure 2c). We observe that a size of 100 was equally sufficient to 1000. This shows that Dexter does not require an unfeasibly large seed corpus size, which would have defeated the purpose.

3.3 Distractor generation

To better assess the impact of the extracted corpus by Dexter, we consider the task of distractor generation for multiple-choice questions (MCQs) (Stasaski and Hearst, 2017). Educators spend significant amount of time choosing suitable distractors for MCQs, where the distractors are the incorrect choices in an MCQ. Moreover, distractor generation is an essential task for automatic question generation. The choice of distractors is critical to the learning outcomes of students, since a misinformed selection of easy distractors could render questions non-challenging (Araki et al., 2016). The main aspect of the distractors' quality is their semantic similarity to the correct answer. The distractor cannot be a synonym of the answer and if too distant, it can be easily eliminated by the learner.

To automate this process, one considered methodology is relying on word embeddings to capture the semantics of the answer, and retrieve the distractors closest semantically to the answer (Araki et al., 2016). An essential component to the quality of these word embeddings is the domain of the training corpus, as any shift in domain would lead to a decrease in performance as noted in (Bollegala et al., 2015). To illustrate this further, we take the corpora C ($\sim$2.3B words) and C_D ($\sim$150M words), as described in Section 3.1, as well as the science corpus extracted by Dexter at size 150K ($\sim$187M words) along with the corpora BootCaT-KE ($\sim$986K words), and BootCaT-M ($\sim$1.2M words). Also, to eliminate any effects of corpus size between Dexter and the BootCaT baselines, we downsample Dexter's corpus to the size of the BootCaT corpora (986K words). We then train six sets of word embeddings using FastText (Bojanowski et al., 2017), on each of the six aforementioned corpora. The quality of these word embeddings at capturing the semantics of science words is then measured on the task of distractor generation. Taking all questions from

---

[6]https://github.com/csurfer/rake-nltk
[7]http://sci2.esa.int/glossary/

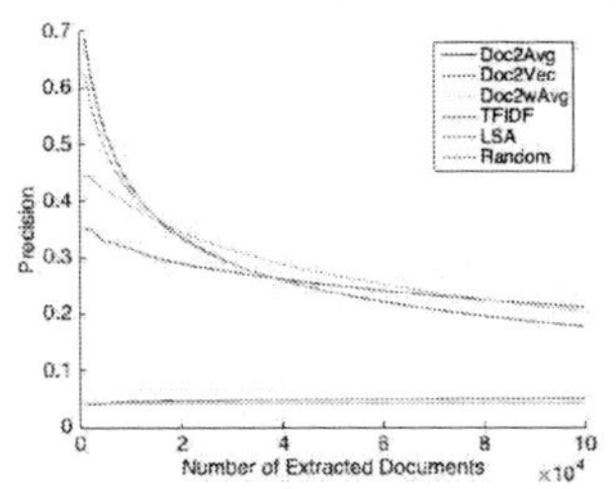

(a) Effect of Document Representation

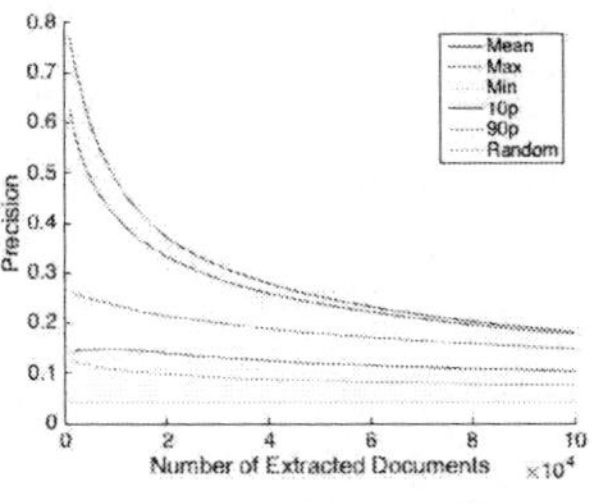

(b) Effect of Distance Function

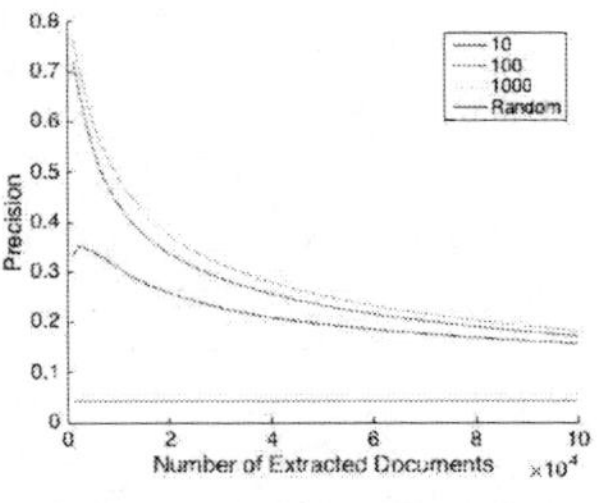

(c) Effect of Seed Corpus Size

Figure 2: Effect of design choices on accuracy of extracted domain

Corpus	Recall	Perplexity
C	17.43%	431.78
C_{silver}	N/A	334.57
C_D	20.47%	N/A
BootCaT-KE	15.28%	3199.30
BootCaT-M	13.82%	4586.80
Dexter-Downsampled	18.86%	1117.34
Dexter	22.71%	294.20

Table 1: Distractor recall@100 for word embeddings (middle) and perplexity of language models (right) trained on corpora of varying domain specificity.

three science questions datasets – 7,787 questions from ARC (Clark et al., 2018), 13,679 questions from SciQ (Johannes Welbl and Gardner, 2017), and 5059 questions from AI2-ScienceQuestions (Allen Institute for AI, 2017) – we check the recall of the distractors[8] in the top 100 most similar words to the answer of each question. Results are reported in Table 1.

As hypothesized, we notice that science-specific word embeddings trained on C_D (20.47%) perform better than when trained on all of Wikipedia (17.43%). But it was surprising to observe that training on the science corpus generated by Dexter led to an even better performance (22.71%) than C_D (20.47%). Since C_D was heuristically constructed from human categorization, it might be the case that Dexter was able to capture the language characteristics of the science seed corpus better than heuristic methods operating on Wikipedia's taxonomy. The same two annotators mentioned in 3.1 manually labeled the extracted corpus (top 500 articles) using the same scale. The scores of the two annotators had a Pearson's correlation coefficient of 0.66. Indeed the quality of the extracted

corpus turned out higher than that of C_D, with an average score of 4.712. A less surprising result was Dexter's outperformance (22.71%) of both BootCaT baselines (15.28% and 13.82%) even when Dexter was downsampled (18.86%). This is expected as the automatic scraping of webpages by BootCaT introduces noisy artifacts into the corpus.

To qualitatively understand why word embeddings trained on domain-specific corpora outperform general ones we take a look at examples of polysemous words, and their word embeddings when trained on different corpora (c.f. Table 2). For example, the closest neighbors to the word "Force" when trained on C are: "Forces", "Troops", and "Army", which reflect the military sense to the word "Force". When trained on C_D, the closest neighbors become: "Deflection", "Torque", and "Gravity", reflecting the scientific sense of the word "Force". Similarly, the closest neighbors to the word "Field", when trained on C, are: "Fields", "Football", and "Professional-sized", reflecting a sports field sense. Whereas, when trained on the extracted corpus by Dexter, neighbors of "Field" become: "Fields", "Magnetobiology", and "Ambipolar", reflecting a scientific sense of the word "Field".

3.4 Language modeling

Similar to the previous experiment, except for using C_{silver} instead of C_D, we train 6 different trigram language models (Brown et al., 1992) on each corpus using kenlm (Heafield et al., 2013) and under default parameters[9]. We then test the perplexity of these language models on C_{ho}. The same pattern of comparative performances (c.f. Table 1) is noticed in language modeling, which reflects the impact of the quality of the domain-specific corpus on the variety of resources (language models and word embeddings) trained on

---

[8] We checked the recall of only one-word distractors since there is no straightforward method to retrieve phrases, as distractors, using distance over word embeddings. This does not affect our comparison study of different word embeddings.

[9] https://kheafield.com/code/kenlm/

Word	Neighbors (General)			Neighbors (Science)		
Force	Forces	Troops	Army	Deflection	Torque	Gravity
Digest	Review	Guide	Supplement	Digested	Extract	Metabolize
Matter	Matters	Subject	Debate	Particles	Materials	Universe
Field	Fields	Football	Professional-sized	Fields	Magnetobiology	Ambipolar
Rock	Punk	Pop	Indie	Rocks	Shoegazing	Screamo
Cellular	Cell	Signalling	Apoptosis	Cell	Organelle	Automata

Table 2: Neighbors of polysemous scientific words when trained on the general Wikipedia (left), trained on C_D (top right), and trained on the extracted science corpus by Dexter bottom right).

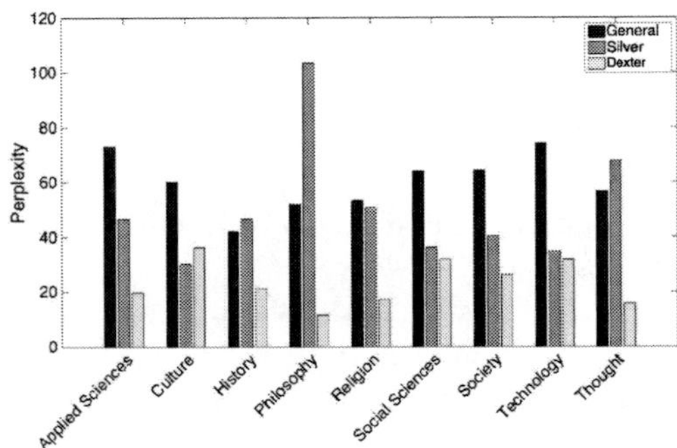

Figure 3: Perplexity scores for language models trained on General, Silver, and Dexter corpora across different domains.

it. We thus conclude that educational NLP applications in science can benefit from Dexter if their algorithm relies on a monolingual corpus. An example of an educational NLP application utilizing language models would be a machine translator for science webpages.

4 Generalization to other domains

To ensure Dexter's applicability to other educational domains, we repeated the experiment in Section 3.4 for educational domains other than science and show the results in Figure 3. We notice that the extracted corpus by Dexter is capable of training a significantly better language model than that trained on either the respective silver corpus or all of Wikipedia. The ineffectiveness of the general corpus is expected as the extracted corpus offers a more domain-specific training data. As for the more surprising outcome of inefficacy of the respective silver corpora, the reason seems to be the size of the silver corpus for most of these domains owing to the lack of articles in Wikipedia. The extracted corpus does not suffer from this limitation as its size is a hyperparameter set by the

user, 100K in this case. With fewer than 100K in-domain articles, Dexter continues extracting articles that are close to but not in the domain leading to an extrapolated language model combining the benefits of the specificity of the small in-domain corpus and the generality of the large corpus.

5 Conclusion

Relying on off-the-shelf resources reduces the quality of educational NLP applications. To address this challenge, we offer to the community an aiding tool, Dexter, to extract a domain-specific corpus from Wikipedia. We show that our simple method outperforms in-domain corpora constructed heuristically using Wikipedia's taxonomy, or those constructed using popular systems scraping the World Wide Web.

Acknowledgment

This work is supported by IBM-ILLINOIS Center for Cognitive Computing Systems Research (C3SR) - a research collaboration as part of the IBM AI Horizons Network.

References

Allen Institute for AI. 2017. AI2 Science Questions v2.1. Accessed: 2019-04-16.

Jun Araki, Dheeraj Rajagopal, Sreecharan Sankaranarayanan, Susan Holm, Yukari Yamakawa, and Teruko Mitamura. 2016. Generating questions and multiple-choice answers using semantic analysis of texts. In *Proceedings of COLING 2016, the 26th International Conference on Computational Linguistics: Technical Papers*, pages 1125–1136, Osaka, Japan. The COLING 2016 Organizing Committee.

Marco Baroni and Silvia Bernardini. 2004. Bootcat: Bootstrapping corpora and terms from the web. In *LREC*, page 1313.

Piotr Bojanowski, Edouard Grave, Armand Joulin, and Tomas Mikolov. 2017. Enriching word vectors with subword information. *Transactions of the Association for Computational Linguistics*, 5:135–146.

Danushka Bollegala, Takanori Maehara, and Ken-ichi Kawarabayashi. 2015. Unsupervised cross-domain word representation learning. *arXiv preprint arXiv:1505.07184*.

Peter F Brown, Peter V Desouza, Robert L Mercer, Vincent J Della Pietra, and Jenifer C Lai. 1992. Class-based n-gram models of natural language. *Computational linguistics*, 18(4):467–479.

Peter Clark, Isaac Cowhey, Oren Etzioni, Tushar Khot, Ashish Sabharwal, Carissa Schoenick, and Oyvind Tafjord. 2018. Think you have solved question answering? try arc, the ai2 reasoning challenge. *arXiv preprint arXiv:1803.05457*.

Susan T Dumais. 2004. Latent semantic analysis. *Annual review of information science and technology*, 38(1):188–230.

Kenneth Heafield, Ivan Pouzyrevsky, Jonathan H. Clark, and Philipp Koehn. 2013. Scalable modified Kneser-Ney language model estimation. In *Proceedings of the 51st Annual Meeting of the Association for Computational Linguistics*, pages 690–696, Sofia, Bulgaria.

Lifeng Jin, David King, Amad Hussein, Michael White, and Douglas Danforth. 2018. Using paraphrasing and memory-augmented models to combat data sparsity in question interpretation with a virtual patient dialogue system. In *Proceedings of the Thirteenth Workshop on Innovative Use of NLP for Building Educational Applications*, pages 13–23.

Nelson F. Liu Johannes Welbl and Matt Gardner. 2017. Crowdsourcing multiple choice science questions. In *Workshop on Noisy User-generated Text*.

Slava Katz. 1987. Estimation of probabilities from sparse data for the language model component of a speech recognizer. *IEEE transactions on acoustics, speech, and signal processing*, 35(3):400–401.

Philipp Koehn, Franz Josef Och, and Daniel Marcu. 2003. Statistical phrase-based translation. In *Proceedings of the 2003 Conference of the North American Chapter of the Association for Computational Linguistics on Human Language Technology-Volume 1*, pages 48–54. Association for Computational Linguistics.

Quoc Le and Tomas Mikolov. 2014. Distributed representations of sentences and documents. In *Proceedings of the 31st International Conference on Machine Learning (ICML-14)*, pages 1188–1196.

Jure Leskovec, Anand Rajaraman, and Jeffrey David Ullman. 2014. *Mining of massive datasets*. Cambridge university press.

Laurens van der Maaten and Geoffrey Hinton. 2008. Visualizing data using t-sne. *Journal of Machine Learning Research*, 9(Nov):2579–2605.

David McClosky. 2010. *Any domain parsing: automatic domain adaptation for natural language parsing*. Ph.D. thesis, Brown University.

Tomas Mikolov, Kai Chen, Greg Corrado, and Jeffrey Dean. 2013. Efficient estimation of word representations in vector space. *arXiv preprint arXiv:1301.3781*.

Stuart Rose, Dave Engel, Nick Cramer, and Wendy Cowley. 2010. Automatic keyword extraction from individual documents. *Text Mining: Applications and Theory*, pages 1–20.

Ronald Rosenfeld. 2000. Two decades of statistical language modeling: Where do we go from here? *Proceedings of the IEEE*, 88(8):1270–1278.

Peter Schönhofen. 2009. Identifying document topics using the wikipedia category network. *Web Intelligence and Agent Systems: An International Journal*, 7(2):195–207.

Katherine Stasaski and Marti A. Hearst. 2017. Multiple choice question generation utilizing an ontology. In *Proceedings of the 12th Workshop on Innovative Use of NLP for Building Educational Applications*, pages 303–312, Copenhagen, Denmark. Association for Computational Linguistics.

Duyu Tang, Bing Qin, and Ting Liu. 2015. Document modeling with gated recurrent neural network for sentiment classification. In *EMNLP*, pages 1422–1432.

The Unbearable Weight of Generating Artificial Errors for Grammatical Error Correction

Phu Mon Htut[*]
Center for Data Science
New York University
pmh330@nyu.edu

Joel Tetreault
Grammarly
joel.tetreault@grammarly.com

Abstract

In recent years, sequence-to-sequence models have been very effective for end-to-end grammatical error correction (GEC). As creating human-annotated parallel corpus for GEC is expensive and time-consuming, there has been work on artificial corpus generation with the aim of creating sentences that contain realistic grammatical errors from grammatically correct sentences. In this paper, we investigate the impact of using recent neural models for generating errors to help neural models to correct errors. We conduct a battery of experiments on the effect of data size, models, and comparison with a rule-based approach.

1 Introduction

Grammatical error correction (GEC) is the task of automatically identifying and correcting the grammatical errors in the written text. Recent work treats GEC as a translation task that use sequence-to-sequence models (Sutskever et al., 2014; Bahdanau et al., 2015) to rewrite sentences with grammatical errors to grammatically correct sentences. As with machine translation models, GEC models benefit largely from the amount of parallel training data. Since it is expensive and time-consuming to create annotated parallel corpus for training, there is research into generating sentences with artificial errors from grammatically correct sentences with the goal of simulating human-annotated data in a cost-effective way (Yuan and Briscoe, 2016; Xie et al., 2016; Chollampatt and Ng, 2018).

Recent work in artificial error generation (AEG) is inspired by the back-translation approach of machine translation systems (Sennrich et al., 2016; Poncelas et al., 2018). In this framework, an intermediate model is trained to translate correct sentences into errorful sentences. A new parallel corpus is created using the largely available grammatically correct sentences and the corresponding synthetic data generated by this intermediate model. The newly created corpus with the artificial errors is then used to train a GEC model (Rei et al., 2017; Xie et al., 2018; Ge et al., 2018).

To date, there is no work that compares how different base model architectures perform in the AEG task. In this paper, we investigate how effective are different model architectures in generating artificial, parallel data to improve a GEC model. Specifically, we train four recent neural models (and one rule-based model (Bryant and Briscoe, 2018)), including two new syntax-based models, for generating as well as correcting errors. We analyze which models are effective in the AEG and correction conditions as well as by data size. Essentially, we seek to understand how effective are recent sequence-to-sequence (seq2seq) neural model as AEG mechanisms "out of the box."

2 Related Work

Before the adoption of neural models, early approaches to AEG involved identifying error statistics and patterns in the corpus and applying them to grammatically correct sentences (Brockett et al., 2006; Rozovskaya and Roth, 2010). Inspired by the back-translation approach, recent AEG approaches inject errors into grammatically correct input sentences by adopting methods from neural machine translation (Felice and Yuan, 2014; Kasewa et al., 2018). Xie et al. (2018) propose an approach that adds noise to the beam-search phase of an back-translation based AEG model to generate more diverse errors. They use the synthesized parallel data generated by this method to train a multi-layer convolutional GEC model and achieve a 5 point $F_{0.5}$ improvement on the CoNLL-2014 test data (Ng et al., 2014).

---

[*]Work done during internship at Grammarly

478

Proceedings of the Fourteenth Workshop on Innovative Use of NLP for Building Educational Applications, pages 478–483
Florence, Italy, August 2, 2019. ©2019 Association for Computational Linguistics

Ge et al. (2018) propose a fluency-boosting learning method that generates less fluent sentences from correct sentences and pairs them with correct sentences to create new error-correct sentence pairs during training. Their GEC model trained with artificial errors approaches human-level performance on multiple test sets.

3 Approach

3.1 Correction and Generation Tasks

We train our models on the two tasks—error correction and error generation. In *error correction*, the encoder of the sequence-to-sequence model takes an errorful sentence as input and the decoder outputs the grammatically correct sentence. The process is reversed in the *error generation* task, where the model takes a correct sentence as input and produces an errorful sentence as the output of the decoder.

We investigate four recent neural sequence-to-sequence models—(i) multi-layer convolutional model (MLCONV; Chollampatt and Ng, 2018), (ii) Transformer (Vaswani et al., 2017), (iii) Parsing-Reading-Predict Networks (PRPN; Shen et al., 2018), (iv) Ordered Neurons (ON-LSTM; Shen et al., 2019)—as error correction models as well as error generation models. The PRPN and ON-LSTM models are originally designed as recurrent language models that jointly learn to induce latent constituency parse trees. We use the adaption of PRPN and ON-LSTM models as decoders of machine translation systems (UnderReview, 2019): In this setting, a 2-layer LSTM is used as the encoder of the syntactic seq-to-seq models, and the PRPN and ON-LSTM are implemented as the decoders with attention (Bahdanau et al., 2015). We hypothesize that syntax is important in GEC and explore whether models that incorporate syntactic bias would help with GEC task. We provide a brief description of each model in §3.2 and refer readers to the original work for more details.

3.2 Models

Multi-layer Convolutional Model We use the multi-layer convolutional encoder-decoder base model (MLCONV) of Chollampatt and Ng (2018) using the publicly available code from the authors.[1] As our aim is to only compare the performance of different architectures and not to achieve state-of-the-art performance, we make few changes to their code. The model of Chollampatt and Ng (2018) produces 12 possible correct sentences for each input sentences with error. They also train an N-gram language model as a re-ranker to score the generated sentences and pick the corrected sentence with the best score as final output. We did not use this re-ranking step in our model, nor did we perform ensembling or use the pre-trained embeddings as in the original work. We do not observe improvement in models like transformer and PRPN using re-ranking with an N-gram language model. Additionally, there's only a slight improvement in MLCONV using re-ranking. The reason might be because the N-gram language model is not very powerful.

Transformer Model We use the publicly available Fairseq framework which is built using Pytorch for training the Transformer model. We apply the same hyper-parameters used for training the IWSLT'14 German-English translation model in the experiments of Vaswani et al. (2017).

PRPN Model is a language model that jointly learns to parse and perform language modeling (Shen et al., 2018). It uses a recurrent module with a self-attention gating mechanism and the gate values are used to construct the constituency tree. We use the BiLSTM model as the encoder and PRPN as the decoder of the sequence-to-sequence model.

ON-LSTM Model is follow-up work of PRPN, which incorporates syntax-based inductive bias to the LSTM unit by imposing hierarchical update order on the hidden state neurons (Shen et al., 2019). ON-LSTM assumes that different nodes of a constituency trees are represented by the different chunks of adjacent neurons in the hidden state, and introduces a master forget gate and a master input gate to dynamically allocate the chunks of hidden state neurons to different nodes. We use a BiLSTM model as encoder and ON-LSTM model as decoder.

4 Experiments

4.1 Data

We use the NUS Corpus of Learner English (NUCLE; Dahlmeier et al., 2013) and the Cambridge Learner Corpus (CLC; Nicholls, 2003) as base data for training both the correction and generation models. We remove sentence pairs that do

---

[1] https://github.com/nusnlp/mlconvgec2018

not contain errors during preprocessing resulting in 51,693 sentence pairs from NUCLE and 1.09 million sentence pairs from the CLC . We append the CLC data to the NUCLE training set (henceforth NUCLE-CLC) to use as training data for both AEG and correction. We use the standard NUCLE development data as our validation set and we early-stop the training based on the cross-entropy loss of the seq-to-seq models for all models. For the generation of synthetic errorful data, we use the 2017 subsection of the LDC New York Times corpus also employed in the error generation experiments of Xie et al. (2018) which contains around 1 million sentences.[2]

4.2 Setup

We conduct four experiments in this paper. In **Exp1**, we train all the AEG models and intermediate GEC models on NUCLE-CLC. We use the NYT dataset as input to the AEG models to generate sentences with artificial errors. We then create new parallel training sets for correction by combining the sentences from CLC and NUCLE with the errorful sentences generated by each model. We then train the GEC models using these parallel datasets.

The three other experiments are variants of the first. In **Exp2** we train all correction models on artificial errors generated by the top neural AEG systems and a rule-based system for comparison. In **Exp3**, we train the GEC models on NUCLE to analyze models built on real data. Finally, in **Exp4**, we train all GEC models on artificial data to determine how well correction models can perform without any real data.

All our experiments are tested on the CoNLL-2014 test set and we use the sentence-level $F0.5$ score from the MaxMatch (M^2) scorer (Dahlmeier and Ng, 2012) for evaluation. All models are implemented using the Fairseq framework.[3]

4.3 Results

Exp1: Figure 1 shows the performance of GEC models trained on the base NUCLE-CLC set and then retraining with various amounts of artificial data. We first observe that PRPN performs substantially higher than the rest of the models when trained only with the base CLC-NUCLE

data. However, its performance drops when artificial data generated by the corresponding PRPN AEG model is added. As for ON-LSTM, the performance improves slightly when the amount of added data is less than 100k but the performance drops drastically otherwise. Conversely, the performance of MLCONV and Transformer improves with the added artificial data but the improvement is not linear with the amount of added data.

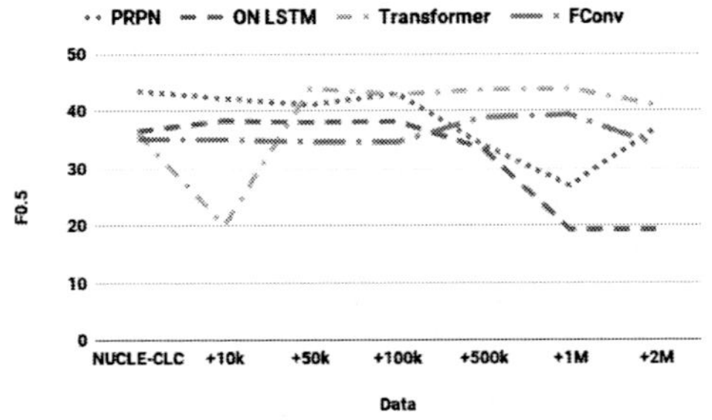

Figure 1: (Exp1) Models trained on the artificial data generated by the corresponding AEG model. The X-axis represents the amount of artificial data added to NUCLE-CLC during training.

Exp2: Since the performance of MLCONV and Transformer GEC models improve with the addition of artificial data generated by corresponding AEG models, we hypothesize that the artificial error generated by these models are useful. To test this hypothesis, we train all the GEC models with various amount of artificial error generated by MLCONV and Transformer AEG models. We also compare these AEG models to a rule-based one inspired by the confusion set generation method in Bryant and Briscoe (2018). We subsequently score each sentence with a language model (GPT-2 (Radford et al., 2018)) in order not to select the most probable sentence. This method generates a confusion set for prepositions (set of prepositions plus an empty element), determiners, and morphological alternatives (cat → cats).

The results of these experiments are found in Table 1. Nearly all correction models improve when using MLCONV or Transformer AEG data with the biggest performances yielded using the Transformer model. Interestingly, when using 1M or 2M samples, performance starts to decline. We believe that over 1M samples, the noisiness of the artificial data overwhelms the contributions of the real data (roughly over 1M samples). The performance of all models drops when trained with

<hr>

[2]https://catalog.ldc.upenn.edu/LDC2008T19

[3]https://github.com/pytorch/fairseq

GEC Model	AEG model	NUCLE-CLC	10K	50K	100K	500K	1M	2M
MLCONV	MLCONV	35.2	35.1	34.7	34.6	38.9	39.4	34.0
Transformer	MLCONV	36.3	43.9	**44.1**	**45.4**	44.4	**45.5**	**42.0**
PRPN	MLCONV	**43.6**	**45.4**	42.8	43.2	39.6	38.6	31.7
ON-LSTM	MLCONV	36.6	39.8	35.6	38.4	36.9	24.2	20.1
MLCONV	Transformer	35.2	36.1	35.2	39.4	36.6	36.6	36.1
Transformer	Transformer	36.3	20.1	**43.9**	**42.9**	**43.7**	**44.0**	**41.0**
PRPN	Transformer	**43.6**	**43.1**	40.9	40.6	41.4	29.4	31.7
ON-LSTM	Transformer	36.6	39.8	38.2	39.6	24.0	21.3	20.1
MLCONV	Rule-based	35.2	6.0	7.8	10.5	13.7	13.9	–
Transformer	Rule-based	36.3	**13.5**	**14.4**	**21.8**	**14.5**	**21.6**	–
PRPN	Rule-based	**43.6**	2.8	4.9	2.6	3.9	8.9	–
ON-LSTM	Rule-based	36.6	4.7	3.9	5.5	4.2	5.3	–

Table 1: (Exp2) Evaluating the impact of MLCONV, Transformer and the rule-based AEG systems. NUCLE-CLC column represents the F0.5 score of GEC models trained on the base NUCLE-CLC data. *10K, 50K, 100K, 500K, 1M, and 2M* represents the amount of artificial data added to the NUCLE-CLC during training.

the errors generated by the rule-based model. It is interesting to observe that the performance drops significantly just by adding 10K artificial sentences to the base data.

Exp3: Table 2 shows the performance of the models trained on NUCLE dataset with additional artificial data generated by corresponding AEG models trained on NUCLE-CLC. We can see that the performance of all models, except ON-LSTM, improves significantly when 1 million artificial sentence pairs are added to the NUCLE training data, even though the errors in these sentences do not resemble natural errors. This contrasts with the result in Figure 1 where the performance of the GEC models trained with the combination of artificial error and CLC-NUCLE base data drops. This suggests that artificial data is helpful when the base data size is relatively small.

Model	NUCLE	+10K	+50K	+1M
MLCONV	10.1	12.3	12.9	16.1
Transformer	11.2	**28.1**	**16.9**	22.8
PRPN	8.3	6.9	12.5	**26.2**
ON-LSTM	9.4	11.3	11.8	6.0

Table 2: (Exp3) Using only NUCLE as base training for correction. The AEG models are trained using NUCLE-CLC data as in other experiments.

Exp4: The GEC models trained only on artificial data perform very poorly. The best setups, Transformer and MLCONV, achieve F0.5 scores of 12.8 and 12.4 respectively when trained with 2 million sentences generated by the corresponding AEG model. This outcomes suggests that AEG data should be paired with some sample of real data to be effective.

4.4 Manual Evaluation

We performed a manual analysis of the generated error sentences and found that many of the errors did not always resemble those produced by humans. For example, *The situation with other types is not much (better → downward)*. This shows that despite the noisiness of the error-generated data, some models (namely MLCONV and Transformer) were robust enough to improve. This also suggests that we may achieve better improvement by controlling artificial errors to resemble the errors produced by humans. The performance of syntax-based models goes down significantly with the addition of artificial errors, which indicates that these models may be sensitive to poor artificial data.

5 Conclusion

We investigated the potential of recent neural architectures, as well as rule-based one, to generate parallel data to improve neural GEC. We found that the Multi-Layer Convolutional and Transformer models tended to produce data that could improve several models, though too much of it would begin to dampen performance. The most substantial improvements could be found when the size of the real data for training was quite small. We also found that the syntax-based models, PRPN and ONLSTM, are very sensitive to the quality of artificial errors and their performance drops substantially with the addition of artificial error data. Our experiments suggest that, unlike in machine translation, it is not very straightforward to use a simple back-translation approach for GEC as unrealistic errors produced by back-translation can hurt the correction performance substantially.

We believe this work shows the promise of using recent neural methods in an out-of-the-box framework, though with care. Future work will focus on ways of improving the quality of the synthetic data. Ideas include leveraging recent developments in powerful language models or better controlling for diversity and frequency of specific error types.

Acknowledgements

We would like to thank the Grammarly Research Team, especially Maria Nadejde, Courtney Napoles, Dimitris Alikaniotis, Andrey Gryschuck, Maksym Bezva and Oleksiy Syvokon. We would also like to thank Sam Bowman, Kyunghyun Cho, and the three anonymous reviewers for their helpful discussion and feedback.

References

Dzmitry Bahdanau, Kyunghyun Cho, and Yoshua Bengio. 2015. Neural machine translation by jointly learning to align and translate. In *3rd International Conference on Learning Representations, ICLR 2015, San Diego, CA, USA, May 7-9, 2015, Conference Track Proceedings*.

Chris Brockett, William B. Dolan, and Michael Gamon. 2006. Correcting ESL errors using phrasal SMT techniques. In *ACL 2006, 21st International Conference on Computational Linguistics and 44th Annual Meeting of the Association for Computational Linguistics, Proceedings of the Conference, Sydney, Australia, 17-21 July 2006*.

Christopher Bryant and Ted Briscoe. 2018. Language model based grammatical error correction without annotated training data. In *BEA@NAACL-HLT*.

Shamil Chollampatt and Hwee Tou Ng. 2018. A multilayer convolutional encoder-decoder neural network for grammatical error correction. In *Proceedings of the Thirty-Second AAAI Conference on Artificial Intelligence*.

Daniel Dahlmeier and Hwee Tou Ng. 2012. Better evaluation for grammatical error correction. In *Human Language Technologies: Conference of the North American Chapter of the Association of Computational Linguistics, Proceedings, June 3-8, 2012, Montréal, Canada*, pages 568–572.

Daniel Dahlmeier, Hwee Tou Ng, and Siew Mei Wu. 2013. Building a large annotated corpus of learner english: The NUS corpus of learner english. In *Proceedings of the Eighth Workshop on Innovative Use of NLP for Building Educational Applications, BEA@NAACL-HLT 2013, June 13, 2013, Atlanta, Georgia, USA*, pages 22–31.

Mariano Felice and Zheng Yuan. 2014. Generating artificial errors for grammatical error correction. In *Proceedings of the 14th Conference of the European Chapter of the Association for Computational Linguistics, EACL 2014, April 26-30, 2014, Gothenburg, Sweden*, pages 116–126.

Tao Ge, Furu Wei, and Ming Zhou. 2018. Reaching human-level performance in automatic grammatical error correction: An empirical study. *CoRR*, abs/1807.01270.

Sudhanshu Kasewa, Pontus Stenetorp, and Sebastian Riedel. 2018. Wronging a right: Generating better errors to improve grammatical error detection. In *Proceedings of the 2018 Conference on Empirical Methods in Natural Language Processing, Brussels, Belgium, October 31 - November 4, 2018*, pages 4977–4983.

Hwee Tou Ng, Siew Mei Wu, Ted Briscoe, Christian Hadiwinoto, Raymond Hendy Susanto, and Christopher Bryant. 2014. The CoNLL-2014 shared task on grammatical error correction. In *Proceedings of the Eighteenth Conference on Computational Natural Language Learning: Shared Task*, pages 1–14, Baltimore, Maryland. Association for Computational Linguistics.

Diane Nicholls. 2003. The cambridge learner corpus - error coding and analysis for lexicography and elt. In *Proceedings of the Corpus Linguistics 2003 conference*.

Alberto Poncelas, Dimitar Shterionov, Andy Way, Gideon Maillette de Buy Wenniger, and Peyman Passban. 2018. Investigating backtranslation in neural machine translation. *CoRR*, abs/1804.06189.

Alec Radford, Jeffrey Wu, Rewon Child, David Luan, Dario Amodei, and Ilya Sutskever. 2018. Language models are unsupervised multitask learners.

Marek Rei, Mariano Felice, Zheng Yuan, and Ted Briscoe. 2017. Artificial error generation with machine translation and syntactic patterns. In *Proceedings of the 12th Workshop on Innovative Use of NLP for Building Educational Applications, BEA@EMNLP 2017, Copenhagen, Denmark, September 8, 2017*, pages 287–292.

Alla Rozovskaya and Dan Roth. 2010. Training paradigms for correcting errors in grammar and usage. In *Human Language Technologies: Conference of the North American Chapter of the Association of Computational Linguistics, Proceedings, June 2-4, 2010, Los Angeles, California, USA*, pages 154–162.

Rico Sennrich, Barry Haddow, and Alexandra Birch. 2016. Improving neural machine translation models with monolingual data. In *Proceedings of the*

54th Annual Meeting of the Association for Computational Linguistics, ACL 2016, August 7-12, 2016, Berlin, Germany, Volume 1: Long Papers.

Yikang Shen, Zhouhan Lin, Chin wei Huang, and Aaron Courville. 2018. Neural language modeling by jointly learning syntax and lexicon. In International Conference on Learning Representations.

Yikang Shen, Shawn Tan, Alessandro Sordoni, and Aaron Courville. 2019. Ordered Neurons: Integrating tree structures into recurrent neural networks. In International Conference on Learning Representations.

Ilya Sutskever, Oriol Vinyals, and Quoc V. Le. 2014. Sequence to sequence learning with neural networks. In Advances in Neural Information Processing Systems 27: Annual Conference on Neural Information Processing Systems 2014, December 8-13 2014, Montreal, Quebec, Canada, pages 3104–3112.

UnderReview. 2019. Unknown title.

Ashish Vaswani, Noam Shazeer, Niki Parmar, Jakob Uszkoreit, Llion Jones, Aidan N. Gomez, Lukasz Kaiser, and Illia Polosukhin. 2017. Attention is all you need. In Advances in Neural Information Processing Systems 30: Annual Conference on Neural Information Processing Systems 2017, 4-9 December 2017, Long Beach, CA, USA, pages 6000–6010.

Ziang Xie, Anand Avati, Naveen Arivazhagan, Dan Jurafsky, and Andrew Y. Ng. 2016. Neural language correction with character-based attention. CoRR, abs/1603.09727.

Ziang Xie, Guillaume Genthial, Stanley Xie, Andrew Y. Ng, and Dan Jurafsky. 2018. Noising and denoising natural language: Diverse backtranslation for grammar correction. In Proceedings of the 2018 Conference of the North American Chapter of the Association for Computational Linguistics: Human Language Technologies, NAACL-HLT 2018, New Orleans, Louisiana, USA, June 1-6, 2018, Volume 1 (Long Papers), pages 619–628.

Zheng Yuan and Ted Briscoe. 2016. Grammatical error correction using neural machine translation. In NAACL HLT 2016, The 2016 Conference of the North American Chapter of the Association for Computational Linguistics: Human Language Technologies, San Diego California, USA, June 12-17, 2016, pages 380–386.

Automated Essay Scoring with Discourse-Aware Neural Models

Farah Nadeem[1], Huy Nguyen[2], Yang Liu[2], and Mari Ostendorf[1]

[1]Department of Electrical and Computer Engineering, University of Washington
{farahn, ostendor}@uw.edu
[2]LAIX Inc.
{huy.nguyen, yang.liu}@liulishuo.com

Abstract

Automated essay scoring systems typically rely on hand-crafted features to predict essay quality, but such systems are limited by the cost of feature engineering. Neural networks offer an alternative to feature engineering, but they typically require more annotated data. This paper explores network structures, contextualized embeddings and pre-training strategies aimed at capturing discourse characteristics of essays. Experiments on three essay scoring tasks show benefits from all three strategies in different combinations, with simpler architectures being more effective when less training data is available.

1 Introduction

In the context of large scale testing and online learning systems, automated essay scoring (AES) is an important problem. There has been work on both improving the performance of these systems and on validity studies (Shermis, 2014). The ability to evaluate student writing has always been important for language teaching and learning; now it also extends to science, since the focus is shifting towards assessments that can more accurately gauge construct knowledge as compared to multiple choice questions (Shermis, 2014). Most existing systems for automatic essay scoring leverage hand crafted features, ranging from word-counts to argumentation structure and coherence, in linear regression and logistic regression models (Chodorow and Burstein, 2004; Shermis and Burstein, 2013; Klebanov et al., 2016; Nguyen and Litman, 2018). Improving feature-based models requires extensive redesigning of features (Taghipour and Ng, 2016). Due to high variability in types of student essays, feature-based systems are often individually designed for specific prompts (Burstein et al., 2013). This poses a challenge for building essay scoring systems.

These problems (and the success of deep learning in other areas of language processing) have led to the development of neural methods for automatic essay scoring, moving away from feature engineering. A variety of studies (mostly LSTM-based) have reported AES performance comparable to or better than feature-based models (Taghipour and Ng, 2016; Cummins and Rei, 2018; Wang et al., 2018; Jin et al., 2018; Farag et al., 2018; Zhang and Litman, 2018). However, the current state-of-the-art models still use a combination of neural models and hand-crafted features (Liu et al., 2019).

While vanilla RNNs, particularly LSTMs, are good at representing text sequences, essays are longer structured documents and less well suited to an RNN representation. Thus, our work looks at advancing AES by exploring other architectures that incorporate document structure for longer documents. Discourse structure and coherence are important aspects of essay writing and are often explicitly a part of grading rubrics. We explore methods that aim at discourse-aware models, through design of the model structure, use of discourse-based auxiliary pretraining tasks, and use of contextualized embeddings trained with cross-sentence context (Devlin et al., 2018). In order to better understand the relative advantages of these methods, we compare performance on three essay scoring tasks with different characteristics, contrasting results with a strong feature-based system.

Our work makes two main contributions. First, we demonstrate that both discourse-aware structures and discourse-related pre-training (via auxiliary tasks or contextualized embeddings) benefit performance of neural network systems. In a TOEFL essay scoring task, we obtain a substantial improvement over the state-of-the-art. Second, we show that complex contextualized embedding

Proceedings of the Fourteenth Workshop on Innovative Use of NLP for Building Educational Applications, pages 484–493
Florence, Italy, August 2, 2019. ©2019 Association for Computational Linguistics

models are not useful for tasks with small annotated training sets. Simpler discourse-aware neural models are still useful, but they benefit from combination with a feature-based model.

2 Method

2.1 Neural Models

The overall system involves a neural network to map an essay to a vector, which is then used with ordinal regression (McCullagh, 1980) for essay scoring. For this work we consider two neural models that incorporate document structure:

- Hierarchical recurrent network with attention (HAN) (Yang et al., 2016)
- Bidirectional context with attention (BCA) (Nadeem and Ostendorf, 2018)

Both models are LSTM based. HAN captures the hierarchical structure within a document, by using two stacked layers of LSTMs. The first layer takes word embeddings as input and outputs contextualized word representations. Self attention is used to compute a sentence vector as a weighted average of the contextualized word vectors. The second LSTM takes sentence vectors as input and outputs a document vector based on averaging using self attention at the sentence level.

BCA extends HAN to account for cross sentence dependencies. For each word, using the contextualized word vectors output from the first LSTM, a look-back and look-ahead context vector is computed based on the similarity with words in the previous and following sentence, respectively. The final word representation is then created as a concatenation of the LSTM output, the look-back and look-ahead context vectors, and then used to create a sentence vector using attention weights, which feeds into the second LSTM. The representation of cross-sentence dependencies makes this model discourse aware.

2.2 Auxiliary Training Tasks

Neural networks typically require more training data than feature-based models, but unlike these models, neural networks can make use of related tasks to improve performance through pretraining. We use additional data chosen with the idea that having related tasks for pretraining can help the model learn aspects that impact the main classification problem. We use the following tasks:

- Natural language inference (NLI): given a pair of sentences, predict their relation as neutral, contradictory, or entailment.
- Discourse marker prediction (DM): given a pair of sentences, predict the category of discourse marker that connects them, e.g. "however" (corresponding to the idea opposition category).

The NLI task has been shown to improve performance for several NLP tasks (Cozma et al., 2018). The DM prediction task is used since discourse structure is an important aspect for essay writing. Both tasks involve sentence pairs, so they impact the first-level LSTM of the HAN and BCA models.

The use of contextualized embeddings can also be thought of as pre-training with an auxiliary task of language modeling (or masked language modeling). In this work, we chose the bidirectional transformer architecture (BERT) embeddings (Devlin et al., 2018), which uses a transformer architecture trained on two tasks, masked language model and next sentence prediction. We hypothesized that the next sentence prediction would capture aspects of discourse coherence.

2.3 Training Methods

All HAN models and a subset of BCA models are initialized with pretrained Glove word embeddings[1] (Pennington et al., 2014). All models are trained with the essay training data.

For models that are pretrained, the word-level LSTM and bidirectional context with attention (for BCA), are common for all tasks used in training. Given the word-level representations, the model computes attention weights over words for the target task (DM, NLI or essay scoring). The sentence representation is then computed by averaging the word representations using task-specific attention weights. For the pretraining tasks, the sentence representations the two sentences in the pair are concatenated, passed through a feedforward neural network, and used with task-specific weights and biases to predict the label. For pretraining the BCA with the auxiliary tasks, the forward context vector is computed for the first sentence and the backward context vector is computed for the second sentence. This allows the model to learn the similarity projection matrix during pretraining.

---

[1] http://nlp.stanford.edu/data/glove.42B.300d.zip

For the essay scoring task there is another sentence-level LSTM on top of the word-level LSTM, with sentence-level attention, followed by task-specific weights and biases. Pretraining is followed by training with the essay data, with all model parameters updated during training, except for the auxiliary task-specific word-level attention, feedforward networks, weights and biases. The network used for BCA with pretraining tasks is shown in Figure 1. The hyper-parameters were tuned for the auxiliary tasks and the essay scoring task. To incorporate BERT embeddings in our model, we freeze the BERT model, and learn contextualized token embeddings for our data using the base uncased model. The tokens are from the second-to-last hidden layer, since we are not fine-tuning the model and the last layer is likely to be more tuned to the original BERT training tasks. These embeddings are then used as input to the BCA model (BERT-BCA), which is then trained on the essay scoring task.

3 Experiments

3.1 Data

The first set of essay data is the ETS Corpus of Non-Native Written English from the Linguistic Data Consortium (LDC) (Blanchard et al., 2013) consisting of 12,100 TOEFL essays.[2]

The data has essay scores given as high, medium or low. Two train/test splits are used:

- Split 1 from LDC, 11,000 training essays and 1100 test essays

- Split 2 from (Klebanov et al., 2016), 6074 training essays and 2023 test essays

Split 1 is a larger publicly available set, and split 2 is used in the prior published work on this data. The data distribution is shown in Table 1. The data is skewed, with the medium score being the majority class.

To evaluate model performance on smaller data sets, we use essays in Sets 1 and 2 of the Automated Student Assessment Prize (ASAP) Competition.[3] We chose the first two sets from the ASAP data, since they are persuasive essays, and are likely to benefit more from discourse-aware pretraining. The two essay sets have topics in computer usage and library censorship, respectively. Data statistics of the two essay sets are

Data set	Essays	High	Medium	Low
Train/dev	11,000	3,835	5,964	1,202
Test	1,100	367	604	129
Train/dev	6,074	2,102	3,318	655
Test	2,023	700	1,101	222

Table 1: Label distribution in LDC TOEFL dataset. Data is split into training and test sets: split 1 (upper part) and split 2 (lower part).

Data set	Essays	Avg. len	Score range
1	1783	350	2-12
2	1800	350	1-6

Table 2: Data statistics for essay sets 1 and 2 of ASAP corpus.

shown in Table 2. Since only the training samples are available for both sets, we report results for 5-fold cross-validation using the same splits as (Taghipour and Ng, 2016).

Pretraining tasks use two data sets. The NLI task uses the Stanford natural language inference (SNLI) data set (Bowman et al., 2015). We cast our NLI task as a four-way classification task, because a subset of the data does not have gold labels. Unlabeled examples were used with an "X" label. While tuning on the main task, we found that including the fourth NLI label gave better performance on the essay scoring than not using it.

The DM task is based on a collection of over 13K free books from `www.smashwords.com` – an online book distribution platform.[4] Labeled discourse marker data was created by identifying sentence pairs that had a discourse marker at the start of the second sentence. We used 87 discourse markers, which were then mapped to seven groups, for a total of 581,650 sentence pairs. A set of randomly-selected 95,450 consecutive sentence pairs without discourse markers was added to the data set as negative examples, leading to an eight way classification task. Example discourse marker categories include:

- **Idea opposition**: nonetheless, on the other hand, however

- **Idea justification**: in other words, for example, alternatively

- **Time relation**: meanwhile, in the past, simultaneously

---

[2] https://catalog.ldc.upenn.edu/LDC2014T06
[3] http://www.kaggle.com/c/asap-aes

[4] The data set published by (Zhu et al., 2015) is no longer available, so we compiled our own data set.

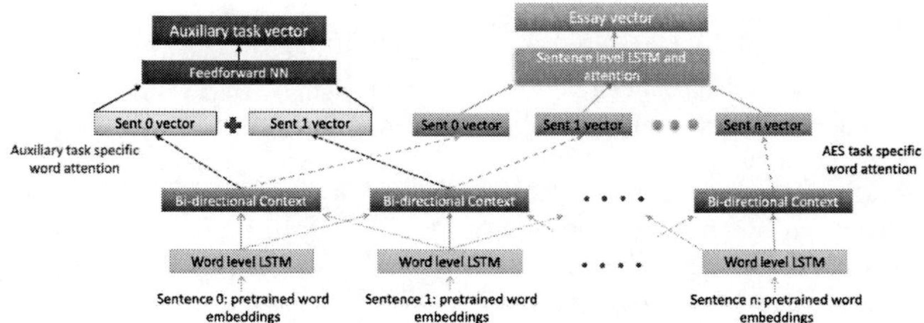

Figure 1: Network structure for BCA with pretraining tasks.

The complete set of labels, number of samples and mapping scheme are given in Appendix A.

3.2 Training Configurations

We explore the following setups to train AES models for the LDC-TOEFL essays:

1. Training using only LDC essay data;

2. Pretraining with one task (either NLI or DM prediction), followed by training with the essay data;

3. Pretraining alternating between the two auxiliary tasks (NLI-DM), followed by training with the essay data; and

4. Training the BCA model with only the essay data, using static BERT token embeddings as input to the model.

For the ASAP data, we used the third training configuration.

For the pretraining tasks, 10% of the training data is used as a held out development set. On pretraining tasks, the BCA model achieves accuracy 0.60 (8 classes) on the development set of DM data, and accuracy 0.78 (4 classes) on the dedicated test set of SNLI data (Bowman et al., 2015).

Ten-fold cross validation was used for the LDC essay data, five-fold for the ASAP data. A vocabulary size of 75000 was used for all the experiments, except those trained with BERT token embeddings. Dropout and early stopping was used for regularization, including variational recurrent dropout (Gal and Ghahramani, 2016) at both LSTM layers. Hyper-parameter training was used to find the optimal dropout and determine early stopping. Network sizes, dropout and number of epochs over the training data are listed in Table 3.[5]

---

[5]Trained models and code is available at https://github.com/Farahn/AES

Shared parameters	
Word level LSTM	150
Word level attention weight size	75
Sentence level LSTM	150
Sentence level attention weight size	50
Dropout rate	0.25-0.5
BERT embedding size	768
Auxiliary task parameters	
Feed-forward network layer 1	500
Feed-forward network layer 2	250
Training epochs	
Essay data	35-45
NLI data	15-25
DM data	5-7

Table 3: Hyper-parameters

3.3 Baselines

We develop a feature-based model that combines text readability (Vajjala and Meurers, 2014; Vajjala, 2018) and argument mining features (Nguyen and Litman, 2018). In our implementation, we remove one set of basic features, e.g., word counts, spelling errors etc., since they are present in both models and keep the set from (Vajjala and Meurers, 2014). Given the extracted features, a gradient boosting algorithm is used to learn a regression model. Predicted scores are scaled and rounded to calculate Quadratic Weighted Kappa (QWK) against the true scores. These two feature sets are chosen because they incorporate discourse features in AES. In (Vajjala and Meurers, 2014), the authors used the addDiscourse toolkit (Pitler et al., 2009), which takes as input the syntactic tree of the sentence, and tags the discourse connectives, e.g., therefore, however, and their senses, e.g., CONTINGENCY.Cause, COMPARISON.Contrast. These automated annotations are then used to calculate connective based features,

487

e.g., number of discourse connectives per sentence, number of each sense. In (Nguyen and Litman, 2018), an end-to-end pipeline system was built to parse input essays for argument structures. The system identifies argument components, e.g., claims, premises, in essay sentences, and determines if a support relation is present between each pair of components. Based on that, the authors extract 33 argumentative features used for their AES model.

In addition, we build neural baselines using existing sentence representations as input to a document level LSTM. Specifically, we compare: i) the *BERT sentence encoder*, taking the sentence representation from the second-to-last hidden layer of BERT (as in BERT-BCA) and ii) the *Universal sentence encoder* (USE) (Cer et al., 2018), which is trained on multiple down-stream tasks including classification and sentiment analysis. Unlike for BERT, there are no sequential sentence tasks used in training USE, so we claim that USE is not discourse-aware. The vectors output from the LSTM are then averaged using attention weights to generate a document representation, as in the HAN and BCA models, so these baselines are also hierarchical models and will be referred to as *BERT-HAN* and *USE-HAN*, respectively. For both setups, the sentence vectors are frozen and not updated during training; initial experiments found no performance gain from fine-tuning.

3.4 Results

3.4.1 LDC TOEFL Essays

The results are shown in Table 4, together with previously reported results for feature-based automatic essay scoring systems from (Klebanov et al., 2016) (Klebanov16) and (Nguyen and Litman, 2018) (Nguyen18). Significance testing was done on the test set using bootstrap.

All neural models outperform previously reported results on split 2, with the exception of USE-HAN, as does the augmented feature-based baseline implemented here. Using the new feature-based system as the baseline for significance testing, only the results from BERT-BCA give a statistically significant improvement ($p < 0.01$). The two models that do not explicitly use discourse cues, HAN and USE-HAN, have the lowest scores of the neural models. The best result is obtained when we combine contextualized token level embeddings from BERT with the cross-

Model	Split 1	Split 2
Arg (Klebanov16)	-	0.344
Length (Klebanov16)	-	0.518
Arg + Len (Klebanov16)	-	0.540
Nguyen18	-	0.622
Feature baseline	0.659	0.642
USE-HAN	0.626	0.618
BERT-HAN	0.688	0.680
HAN	0.635	0.623
NLI-HAN	0.643	0.630
DM-HAN	0.651	0.654
NLI-DM-HAN	0.655	0.644
BCA	0.637	0.636
NLI-BCA	0.652	0.647
DM-BCA	0.661	0.661
NLI-DM-BCA	0.659	0.663
BERT-BCA	0.729	0.715

Table 4: Results for the essay scoring task on LDC TOEFL corpus for both splits reported in QWK.

sentence attention in BCA. This indicates that the two methods are complementary and useful for writing evaluation.

Figure 2 shows the confusion matrices for the USE-HAN baseline, DM-BCA and BERT-BCA systems for the LDC TOEFL split 1. The confusion matrices indicate that both USE-HAN and DM-BCA over-predict the essay scores compared to BERT-BCA, i.e. assign a higher scoring category than the true score. The problem is most severe for USE-HAN, which correctly labels only 40% of the low test samples.

3.4.2 ASAP Essays

Results are reported for 5-fold CV. For each of the splits, 20% data is used to tune the dropout rate, learning rate and number of iterations. Since there was a small variation in the optimal parameters for the 5 folds, we used the average of the parameters from the first two sets for training all five folds. The test QWK is computed by taking the true labels and predictions for all 5 test sets. For the ASAP data set, we report performances of our feature baseline, the best sentence representation model, and the best pretrained BCA model. In addition, we present a simple combination of the feature-based and BCA model, averaging the scores predicted by the two models. The results are shown in table 5.

For both ASAP sets, feature based models perform better than the neural models. We hypoth-

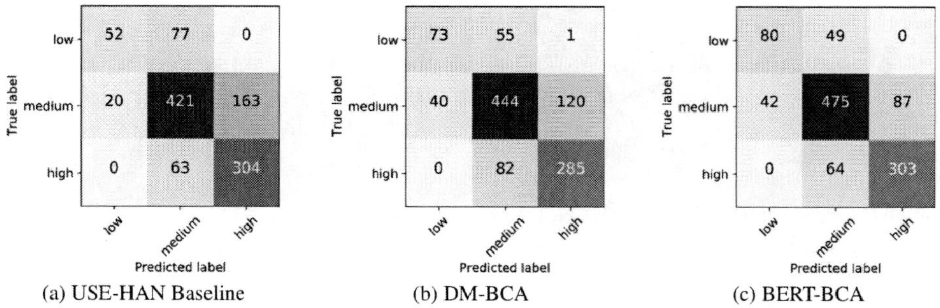

(a) USE-HAN Baseline   (b) DM-BCA   (c) BERT-BCA

Figure 2: Confusion matrices for the USE-HAN baseline vs. the best neural models on LDC TOEFL split 1.

Model	ASAP 1	ASAP 2
TSLF (Liu 2019)	0.852	0.736
Feature baseline	0.833	0.692
BERT-HAN	0.748	0.627
NLI-DM-BCA	0.800	0.671
NLI-DM-BCA+features	0.840	0.711

Table 5: Results for the essay scoring task for ASAP sets 1 and 2 reported in QWK.

Model	sim_2 Min	σ	sim_{all} Min	σ
USE-HAN	-0.180	0.214	-0.440	0.400
BERT-HAN	-0.012	0.013	-0.047	-0.005
HAN	0.021	-0.023	0.069	-0.051
DM-HAN	-0.414	0.365	-0.437	0.460
BCA	-0.394	0.362	**-0.571**	**0.632**
DM-BCA	**-0.448**	**0.433**	-0.554	0.589
BERT-BCA	0.052	-0.071	0.186	-0.153

Table 6: Correlation of sim_2 and sim_{all} with the true essay scores for LDC TOEFL split 1.

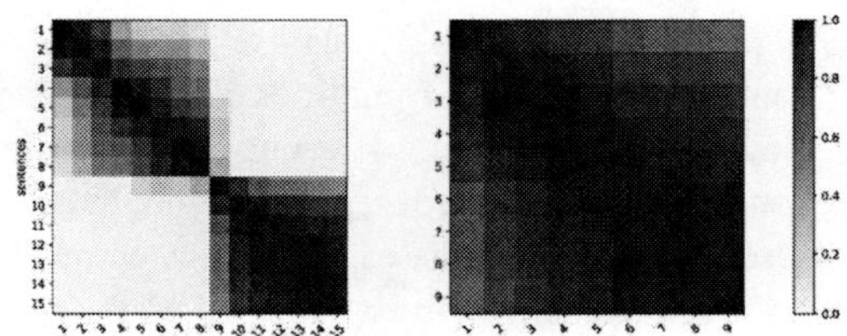

Figure 3: Sentence similarity for DM-BCA, left is a high scoring essay (ID 108264), right is a low scoring essay (ID 10226).

esize that this is due to having less training data than for the TOEFL essays. Using the pretrained BERT-HAN model does significantly worse than the pretrained NLI-DM-BCA model. Combining the best neural and feature-based model gives a small, but insignificant performance gain. A more sophisticated combination would likely yield better results.

The current state-of-the art is the two stage learning framework (TSLF) (Liu et al., 2019). The model has two components, one using sentence representation from BERT input to an RNN (similar to our BERT-HAN), and the second component uses hand crafted features. The BERT sentence representations are used to learn an essay score, a prompt-relevance score and a "coherence" score, trained on original and permuted essays. Document representations from the neural network and the hand crafted features are then used together in a gradient-boosting decision tree to predict the final essay score.

4 Analysis and Discussion

We hypothesized that good quality essays would be more coherent. To see if this is captured by the learned sentence representations, we examined sentence similarities in the TOEFL essays in relation to the essay score. Taking the sentence vector outputs from the second LSTM layer for essay i for a particular model for LDC split 1, we compute the cosine similarity of each sentence with its neighboring sentence sim_2 and with all other sentences sim_{all}. We then compute the correlation of the mean, min and standard deviation of both sim_2 and sim_{all} with the true labels. The mean gave no meaningful differences between models, but there were differences for the min and standard deviation (σ), which are presented in Table 6.

In terms of correlation between essay scores and min/variance of sentence similarity, the highest correlations are associated with the models that use explicit discourse-aware approaches: DM pre-training and/or the BCA architecture (with-

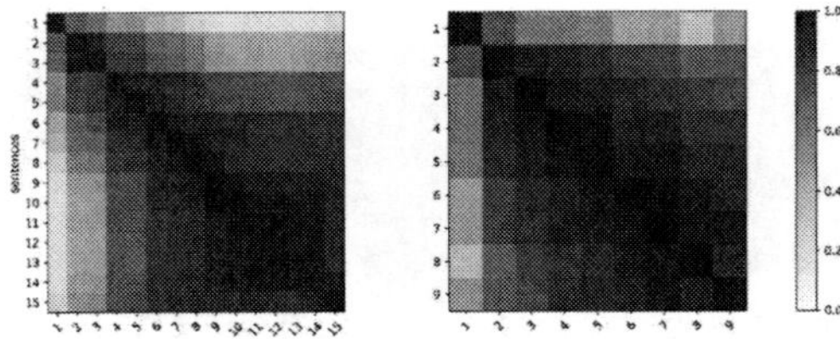

Figure 4: Sentence similarity for BERT-HAN, left is a high scoring essay (ID 108264), right is a low scoring essay (ID 10226).

out BERT). The correlation values indicate that these sentence representations capture aspects of text structure that are reflected in a positive trend for the variance and negative trends for minimum sentence similarity. This suggests that discussion on multiple topics/aspects, as opposed to a single theme, tends to result in high scoring essays, as visualized in Figure 3 for DM-BCA. The fact that low-scoring essays have higher cross-sentence similarity likely reflects a less varied use of vocabulary than higher coherence.

Both BERT-HAN and BERT-BCA lead to representations for which sentence similarity has lower variance and lower correlation of the standard deviation with essay quality. The BERT-BCA sentence embedding similarities, illustrated for the same essays in Figure 4, seem to be learning a fundamentally different representation, but clearly also useful. In both cases, the BERT embeddings are learned using the next sentence prediction objective (together with the masked language model objective). We hypothesize that AES performance improvement with BERT, i.e., BERT-HAN and BERT-BCA, may be due to contextualized word representations (within and cross-sentence), reducing the need for BCA cross-sentence attention, as seen by the good performance of the BERT-HAN model, which has no explicit cross-sentence dependencies.

An initial investigation of sentence-level attention weights suggests that weights tend to be more uniform for low scoring essays and show more variation for higher scoring ones. However we observe no meaningful difference between the different models.

For both BERT-HAN and BERT-BCA, we froze the sentence and token embeddings (respectively) for use in our models. Our experiments indicated that it is hard to fine-tune the BERT model with the limited training data available for the LDC TOEFL and ASAP training sets. Experiments showed that freezing the model and using tokens as input to the model gave similar performance as fine-tuning BERT, and was much easier to optimize. For the ASAP data, initial experiments using BERT token embeddings as input to BCA gave significantly worse performance than the best BCA model. Fine tuning in this case also proved more challenging, and results indicated that it did not perform better than freezing sentence embeddings.

5 Related Work

Neural networks have already shown promising results for AES. Our work differs from prior efforts primarily in the particular architecture that we use. Most prior work uses LSTMs (Farag et al., 2018; Wang et al., 2018; Cummins and Rei, 2018) or a combination LSTMs and CNNs (Taghipour and Ng, 2016; Zhang and Litman, 2018), cast as linear or logistic regression problems. In contrast, we use a hierarchically structured model with ordinal regression. The work by (Farag et al., 2018) is similar in that they model local text coherence, though the coherence features are for detecting adversarial examples and not used directly in essay scoring. The neural essay scoring system presented in (Cummins and Rei, 2018) also uses a multitask framework, but the auxiliary task is grammatical error detection. In our work, we found that adding grammatical error features improved an existing feature-based system, and we expect that grammar error detection would be a useful auxiliary task for our neural model as well.

There is no single data set that all systems report on, which makes it difficult to compare results. For the TOEFL data, where prior published work uses feature-based systems (Klebanov et al., 2016; Nguyen and Litman, 2018), our system provides state-of-the-art results. For the ASAP data, where there are published studies using neural networks, the best scoring systems use ensembling and/or combine neural and feature-based approaches (Liu et al., 2019; Taghipour and Ng, 2016). Such methods would likely also benefit our model, but the focus here was on the use of auxiliary pretraining tasks.

Our study explored the hierarchical attention network (HAN) (Yang et al., 2016) and bidirectional context with attention (BCA) network (Nadeem and Ostendorf, 2018). Other neural network architectures for document classification could also be explored, e.g., (Le and Mikolov, 2014; Ji and Smith, 2017; Card et al., 2018). Numerous previous studies have looked at using external data to improve performance of neural classifiers. One study that influenced our work is (Jernite et al., 2017), which showed that discourse-based tasks such as sentence order and conjunction prediction can improve neural sentence representations for several NLP tasks. This study used the Book Corpus data (Zhu et al., 2015) and the Gutenberg data (Stroube, 2003) for discourse-based tasks. Our task is similar, but we use a larger set of discourse markers.

Representations from pretrained models including (Devlin et al., 2018; Cer et al., 2018; Peters et al., 2018) have led to performance improvements across a variety of downstream NLP tasks. As shown in the previous section, token and sentence embeddings from BERT (Devlin et al., 2018) were useful for the essay scoring task, for which more data was available. In contrast to our work, which did not find the BERT sentence embeddings as useful for the ASAP data (when used in a hierarchical document model), BERT was found to be useful for ASAP in (Liu et al., 2019), where neural and hand-crafted features are used jointly in classification. While we experimented with both freezing and fine-tuning BERT, we observed no difference in model performance with fine-tuning. Work by (Peters et al., 2019) has shown that fine tuning BERT vs. freezing can give significant performance improvements for textual similarity tasks, but it is not significant for natural language inference tasks.

6   Conclusions

In this work we show that using a neural model with cross-sentence dependencies and having a discourse-based training task can improve performance on automatic essay scoring over both the feature-based state-of-the-art models and hierarchical LSTMs for the LDC TOEFL essay data. The natural language inference task, although useful for other text classification tasks, does not contribute as much to essay scoring. Using pretrained BERT tokens can further improve performance on the TOEFL data, indicating that other discourse-aware tasks, such as next sentence prediction, help essay scoring. For the ASAP data sets, our augmented feature-based system outperforms our best neural models, which may be due to the small amount of training data. The better results in (Liu et al., 2019) are achieved with a model that learns the combination of hand-crafted features and the neural document representation. Thus, for tasks with limited labeled data, there is still a place for hand-crafted features.

Like other neural models, our approach suffers from a lack of interpretability. While our analysis of sentence similarity with the DM-BCA model provides some useful insights into differences between high and low scoring TOEFL essays, the best scoring model did not have the same behavior. This remains an open problem.

References

Daniel Blanchard, Joel Tetreault, Derrick Higgins, Aoife Cahill, and Martin Chodorow. 2013. Toefl11: A corpus of non-native english. *ETS Research Report Series*, 2013(2):i–15.

Samuel R Bowman, Gabor Angeli, Christopher Potts, and Christopher D Manning. 2015. A large annotated corpus for learning natural language inference. *arXiv preprint arXiv:1508.05326.*

Jill Burstein, Joel Tetreault, and Nitin Madnani. 2013. The e-rater automated essay scoring system. *Handbook of automated essay evaluation: Current applications and new directions*, pages 55–67.

Dallas Card, Chenhao Tan, and Noah A Smith. 2018. Neural models for documents with metadata. In *Proceedings of the 56th Annual Meeting of the Association for Computational Linguistics (Volume 1: Long Papers)*, volume 1, pages 2031–2040.

Daniel Cer, Yinfei Yang, Sheng-yi Kong, Nan Hua, Nicole Limtiaco, Rhomni St John, Noah Constant, Mario Guajardo-Cespedes, Steve Yuan, Chris Tar, et al. 2018. Universal sentence encoder. *arXiv preprint arXiv:1803.11175.*

Martin Chodorow and Jill Burstein. 2004. Beyond essay length: evaluating e-rater®'s performance on toefl® essays. *ETS Research Report Series*, 2004(1):i–38.

Mădălina Cozma, Andrei M Butnaru, and Radu Tudor Ionescu. 2018. Automated essay scoring with string kernels and word embeddings. *arXiv preprint arXiv:1804.07954.*

Ronan Cummins and Marek Rei. 2018. Neural multi-task learning in automated assessment. *arXiv preprint arXiv:1801.06830.*

Jacob Devlin, Ming-Wei Chang, Kenton Lee, and Kristina Toutanova. 2018. Bert: Pre-training of deep bidirectional transformers for language understanding. *arXiv preprint arXiv:1810.04805.*

Youmna Farag, Helen Yannakoudakis, and Ted Briscoe. 2018. Neural automated essay scoring and coherence modeling for adversarially crafted input. *arXiv preprint arXiv:1804.06898*.

Yarin Gal and Zoubin Ghahramani. 2016. A theoretically grounded application of dropout in recurrent neural networks. In *Advances in neural information processing systems*, pages 1019–1027.

Yacine Jernite, Samuel R Bowman, and David Sontag. 2017. Discourse-based objectives for fast unsupervised sentence representation learning. *arXiv preprint arXiv:1705.00557*.

Yangfeng Ji and Noah Smith. 2017. Neural discourse structure for text categorization. *arXiv preprint arXiv:1702.01829*.

Cancan Jin, Ben He, Kai Hui, and Le Sun. 2018. Tdnn: a two-stage deep neural network for prompt-independent automated essay scoring. In *Proceedings of the 56th Annual Meeting of the Association for Computational Linguistics (Volume 1: Long Papers)*, volume 1, pages 1088–1097.

Beata Beigman Klebanov, Christian Stab, Jill Burstein, Yi Song, Binod Gyawali, and Iryna Gurevych. 2016. Argumentation: Content, structure, and relationship with essay quality. In *Proceedings of the Third Workshop on Argument Mining (ArgMining2016)*, pages 70–75.

Quoc Le and Tomas Mikolov. 2014. Distributed representations of sentences and documents. In *International Conference on Machine Learning*, pages 1188–1196.

Jiawei Liu, Yang Xu, and Lingzhe Zhao. 2019. Automated essay scoring based on two-stage learning. *arXiv preprint arXiv:1901.07744*.

Peter McCullagh. 1980. Regression models for ordinal data. *Journal of the royal statistical society. Series B (Methodological)*, pages 109–142.

Farah Nadeem and Mari Ostendorf. 2018. Estimating linguistic complexity for science texts. In *Proceedings of the Thirteenth Workshop on Innovative Use of NLP for Building Educational Applications*, pages 45–55.

Huy V Nguyen and Diane J Litman. 2018. Argument mining for improving the automated scoring of persuasive essays. In *Proc. AAAI*, pages 5892–5899.

Jeffrey Pennington, Richard Socher, and Christopher Manning. 2014. Glove: Global vectors for word representation. In *Proceedings of the 2014 conference on empirical methods in natural language processing (EMNLP)*, pages 1532–1543.

Matthew Peters, Mark Neumann, Mohit Iyyer, Matt Gardner, Christopher Clark, Kenton Lee, and Luke Zettlemoyer. 2018. Deep contextualized word representations. In *Proceedings of the 2018 Conference of the North American Chapter of the Association for Computational Linguistics: Human Language Technologies, Volume 1 (Long Papers)*, pages 2227–2237.

Matthew Peters, Sebastian Ruder, and Noah A Smith. 2019. To tune or not to tune? adapting pretrained representations to diverse tasks. *arXiv preprint arXiv:1903.05987*.

Emily Pitler, Annie Louis, and Ani Nenkova. 2009. Automatic sense prediction for implicit discourse relations in text. In *Proceedings of the Joint Conference of the 47th Annual Meeting of the ACL and the 4th International Joint Conference on Natural Language Processing of the AFNLP: Volume 2-Volume 2*, pages 683–691. Association for Computational Linguistics.

Mark D. Shermis. 2014. State-of-the-art automated essay scoring: Competition, results, and future directions from a united states demonstration. *Assessing Writing*, 20:53 – 76.

Mark D Shermis and Jill Burstein. 2013. *Handbook of automated essay evaluation: Current applications and new directions*. Routledge.

Bryan Stroube. 2003. Literary freedom: Project gutenberg. *Crossroads*, 10(1):3–3.

Kaveh Taghipour and Hwee Tou Ng. 2016. A neural approach to automated essay scoring. In *Proceedings of the 2016 Conference on Empirical Methods in Natural Language Processing*, pages 1882–1891.

Sowmya Vajjala. 2018. Automated assessment of nonnative learner essays: Investigating the role of linguistic features. *International Journal of Artificial Intelligence in Education*, 28(1):79–105.

Sowmya Vajjala and Detmar Meurers. 2014. Readability assessment for text simplification: From analysing documents to identifying sentential simplifications. *ITL-International Journal of Applied Linguistics*, 165(2):194–222.

Yucheng Wang, Zhongyu Wei, Yaqian Zhou, and Xuanjing Huang. 2018. Automatic essay scoring incorporating rating schema via reinforcement learning. In *Proceedings of the 2018 Conference on Empirical Methods in Natural Language Processing*, pages 791–797.

Zichao Yang, Diyi Yang, Chris Dyer, Xiaodong He, Alex Smola, and Eduard Hovy. 2016. Hierarchical attention networks for document classification. In *Proceedings of the 2016 Conference of the North American Chapter of the Association for Computational Linguistics: Human Language Technologies*, pages 1480–1489.

Haoran Zhang and Diane Litman. 2018. Co-attention based neural network for source-dependent essay scoring. In *Proceedings of the Thirteenth Workshop on Innovative Use of NLP for Building Educational Applications*, pages 399–409.

Yukun Zhu, Ryan Kiros, Rich Zemel, Ruslan Salakhutdinov, Raquel Urtasun, Antonio Torralba, and Sanja Fidler. 2015. Aligning books and movies: Towards story-like visual explanations by watching movies and reading books. In *Proceedings of the IEEE international conference on computer vision*, pages 19–27.

A   Discourse marker data

The data for discourse marker prediction task was created using over 13,000 books from `www.smashwords.com`. Sentence pairs with 87 discourse markers were selected, mapped to seven groups. The distribution of labels is shown in Table 7.

The mapping of labels to groups is given below:

- **Idea justification**: in other words, in particular, this means that, in fact, for example, alternatively, for instance, to exemplify, specifically, instead, indeed, as an example, as an alternative, actually, as an illustration, as a matter of fact

- **Time relation**: meanwhile, in the past, simultaneously, thereafter, after a while, by then, in turn, in the future, at the same time, previously, in the meantime

- **Idea support**: for this reason, therefore, thus, consequently, hence, as a consequence, as a result, that is the reason why, the reason is that, accordingly, this shows that, for that reason, thereby, one of the main reasons

- **Idea opposition**: nonetheless, on the other hand, however, conversely, on the contrary, in comparison, by contrast, in opposition, in contrast, still, by comparison, nevertheless

- **Idea expansion**: in like manner, likewise, in addition, also, moreover, equally important, what is more, additionally, in the same way, furthermore, besides, in addition to this, similarly

- **Alternative**: else, otherwise

- **Conclusion**: ultimately, in the end, in closing, finally, in brief, last but not least, in sum, to summarize, lastly, at the end of the day, in short, after all, in conclusion, to conclude, overall, eventually, at last, all in all, on the whole, briefly, in summary

Category	Number of samples
Idea justification	144022
Time relation	24600
Idea support	67223
Idea opposition	181949
Idea expansion	67800
Alternative	7203
Conclusion	88853
Negative samples	95450

Table 7: Categories and data distribution for the discourse marker prediction task.

Modeling language learning using specialized Elo ratings

†**Jue Hou**, †**Maximilian W. Koppatz**, †**José María Hoya Quecedo**,
⋆**Nataliya Stoyanova**, ‡**Mikhail Kopotev** and †**Roman Yangarber**
†University of Helsinki, Department of Computer Science, Finland
‡University of Helsinki, Department of Modern Languages, Finland
`first.last@helsinki.fi`
⋆University of Milan, Department of Foreign Languages and Literatures, Italy
`first.last@unimi.it`

Abstract

Automatic assessment of the proficiency levels of the learner is a critical part of Intelligent Tutoring Systems. We present methods for assessment in the context of language learning. We use a specialized Elo formula used in conjunction with educational data mining. We simultaneously obtain ratings for the proficiency of the learners and for the difficulty of the linguistic concepts that the learners are trying to master. From the same data we also learn a graph structure representing a domain model capturing the relations among the concepts. This application of Elo provides ratings for learners and concepts which correlate well with subjective proficiency levels of the learners and difficulty levels of the concepts.

1 Introduction

A key goal of Intelligent Tutoring Systems (ITS) is to provide students with individualized learning, and thus support their learning process. Several systems for various subjects have proven to be effective, (Ritter et al., 2007; Arroyo et al., 2014; Klinkenberg et al., 2011). Our work is part of an international collaborative effort to developing large-scale Intelligent Computer-Aided Language Learning (ICALL) systems for use in real-world environments. Our system, Revita (Katinskaia et al., 2018), is in use in official university-level curricula at several major universities, to enhance language learning and teaching.[1]

To develop automated methods for personalized tutoring, robust models for assessing the current proficiency of learners are required. Such models enable quantitative evaluation and comparison of teaching methods with respect to the rate of development of the learners, which enables us to evaluate the performance of the ICALL system.

Several approaches for modeling knowledge have been proposed, such as Bayesian Knowledge Tracing (Corbett and Anderson, 1994), Learning Factor Analysis (Cen et al., 2006), and its more advanced variant—Performance Factor Analysis, (Pavlik Jr et al., 2009). These models, however, are complex and time-consuming to implement for ITS, and require large amounts of data for each learner, (Pelánek, 2016).

In this work, we present a simple and effective method for assessing the proficiency of language learners, as well as the difficulty of linguistic concepts, by utilizing the Elo formula, (Elo, 1978)—in an unsupervised fashion. The result is a set of rated concepts and a method for assessing the current and historical proficiency of each learner. We also present a concept graph—learned from the educational data—representing the dependencies between concepts.

We use educational data, collected from real language learners, in two assessment contexts. One context is where learners take language proficiency tests. During the test the system samples questions from a database, each question linked to a specific linguistic concept. Examples of concepts are collocations, certain type of verb inflection, certain word-order rules, etc. In the second context, learners do exercises based on "authentic" texts—chosen based on the learners' interests— that have a difficulty estimate, assigned by a statistical model. In each context, the result is a numeric Elo-based rating describing learners' proficiency in the target language.

The paper is organized as follows. Section 2 outlines out data generation process. In Section 3, we describe the Elo rating system, and discuss our modifications to the formulas in the two assessment contexts. In Section 4, we discuss our approach for building a domain model, represented by a concept graph. Section 5 describes simula-

---

[1] `https://revita.cs.helsinki.fi/`

Proceedings of the Fourteenth Workshop on Innovative Use of NLP for Building Educational Applications, pages 494–506
Florence, Italy, August 2, 2019. ©2019 Association for Computational Linguistics

tions and experiments on obtaining Elo ratings for concepts and for assessing learner competency. In Section 6, we discuss preliminary results on correlation between Elo ratings in different assessment contexts, and the correlation between the Elo ratings and the performance levels assigned by teachers. We also demonstrate a graph of concepts, each with Elo difficulty estimates. In Section 7, we discuss current problems. Section 8 concludes with current directions of research.

2 Data

This work builds on educational data we have collected through a collaborative effort with language teachers at several universities. In this paper, we focus on students learning Russian as a second language (L2) at different levels on the CEFR scale, ranging from A1 to C2, (Little, 2007). The students yield data in two assessment contexts:

Language tests: In the testing context, the students take online language tests on a platform provided by the system. Each test is time-limited, and comprised of approximately 300 test items, sampled from a database of 3390 multiple-choice questions. The questions were prepared by language teachers and linguistic experts over a period of 20 years, (Kopotev, 2012, 2010). Each question is linked to one of 140 linguistic "concepts," also predefined by the experts. At the time of this writing, the response data consists of 600 000 test answers, by approximately 1000 learners. For each answer we record to which concept the question belongs, whether the answer was correct, as well as timestamps.

Language practice: In the practice context, students practice the language by doing exercises based on a text. The response data consists of student answers to the exercises: one set of exercises is associated with a *snippet* of text (e.g, one paragraph). The system offers various types of exercises, including multiple-choice questions, "cloze" quizzes (fill-in-the-blank), and listening comprehension, which are generated automatically based on the text chosen by the learner. Each text has been assigned a difficulty rating by a linear model, described in 3.4. Currently, we do not use information about to which linguistic concepts each exercise belong. For each attempted set of exercises, we use the percentage of correct answers, text difficulty, and the timestamp.

3 Rating methods

This section describes how we calculate and update ratings of users and linguistic concepts. We cover the two assessment contexts in which the data were generated: first, the testing context, and second, the practice context. The estimator of text difficulty is described at the end of this section.

3.1 Elo ratings

The Elo rating, introduced by Arpad Elo, (Elo, 1978), was originally used for rating the skills of chess players, and evolved versions of it are now widely used in a variety of domains, ranging from video-games to Tinder.

The Elo formula defines the *expected* result of actor A in a match against actor B according to:

$$E_A = \frac{1}{1 + 10^{\frac{R_B - R_A}{\sigma}}} \tag{1}$$

E_A is a value between 0 and 1, indicating the expectation (probability) of success/win. R_X refers to the current rating of actor X, and σ is a scale variable. The scale is traditionally set to 400 (in chess). This controls the spread of the resulting ratings. In the present work, we used $\sigma = 600$.[2]

The rating of actor A *after* a match with another actor is completed is updated according to:

$$R'_A = R_A + K(S_A - E_A) \tag{2}$$

The factor K controls the maximum rating adjustment that is possible at one time. We use a static K value of 32. S_A denotes the outcome, or the score of a match for actor A: loss, draw and win for A is denoted as 0, 0.5 and 1, respectively.

The Elo rating method has three important properties. First, the formulas are symmetric: A and B switch places when calculating with respect to B. This leads to the zero-sum property of the Elo rating distribution, when K is static—the amount of Elo lost by the losing actor is transferred to the winning one. As a result, the mean of the ratings of all actors will be whatever the initial rating is set to. We initially set the rating of all players (concepts and learners) to 1500.

Second, the magnitude of the rating update depends on the difference between the outcome S_A

---

[2]The reason for this is largely aesthetic; the number of users is currently small (about 1000), which results in a somewhat narrow spread of the rating distribution. A larger spread is more comparable to actual chess ratings, which is more familiar and easier to conceptualize.

and the expected score E_A. This means that a highly rated actor failing against a significantly lower rated one will have a severe loss in Elo, approaching the value of K. Conversely, the success of a higher rated actor is expected, thus it yields a small update in the rating. If the actors are evenly matched the update is between the two extremes.

Finally, the final, or "*current*," distribution of Elo ratings in a system *depends on the order* of the matches. This implies that the Elo rating is a representation of an actor's *current* proficiency. Consider an actor who fails in the first half of 100 matches, and succeeds in the second half, and compare the result to the reverse order. Because the rating updates decrease toward the expected extremes, and are exaggerated at the unexpected extremes, the resulting rating of the actor will be high when his successes are in the second half of the matches and low in the reverse case—even though the two sequences are events are the same, and differ only in their ordering.

3.2 Language test ratings

In (Klinkenberg et al., 2011; Pelánek, 2016), it was shown that Elo ratings can be adapted for use in educational systems, to model the proficiency of students and the difficulty of questions. In our system, in the testing context, the analogue of an outcome of a "game" is a student attempting an exercise; the two rated "actors" are the student and the exercise. S_A represents whether a student has answered the question correctly. The rating R_Q of a question Q captures the difficulty of the question.

An adjustment is made for *multiple-choice* problems to account for the fact that students have some chance of guessing correctly, even if they do not know the correct answer. For this, we adopt an approach recommended by Pelánek (2016), penalizing the expected value by the probability that a random guess is correct. A similar expectation formula is proposed in Item Response Theory (Embretson and Reise, 2013).

In (Klinkenberg et al., 2011; Pelánek, 2016), the focus was assessing the difficulty of each particular *question*. In our system, we model the concept category to which the questions belong; every question from a concept is a representative for the concept in the calculations. In our data, each question is linked to one linguistic concept. The formula for the expectation of student S having a correct response on a question from Concept C

adjusted for guessing is:

$$E_A = \frac{1}{k} \cdot 1 + \left(1 - \frac{1}{k}\right) \cdot \frac{1}{1 + 10^{\frac{R_C - R_S}{\sigma}}}, \quad (3)$$

where k is the number of choices in the multiple-choice question. We expect the Elo ratings for concepts to approach their true value after a large number of data points ("games" or exercise attempts) have been sampled. To obtain concept ratings of better quality, they are learned by re-adjusting all ratings by re-playing all games/attempts in chronological order over several epochs. We call this the Elo "*burn-in*" period, and describe it in Section 5.1. This is used to obtain "stable" concept ratings.

3.3 Language practice ratings

In the practice context, the exercises are different from the test context. Our method therefore differs in the two contexts in several ways. Here, the exercises sets that the learners have answered are composed of a variety of exercises, some of which may not be linked to a specific linguistic concept (recall, each test item is linked to a concept). This means we cannot share the ratings directly between the two learning contexts.

To address this problem, we make the simplifying assumption that *on average* the exercises in a given text correspond to the *difficulty* rating of the text. The method for estimating the difficulty of a text is described in the following subsection.[3]

Concretely, we define S_A as the percentage of correct responses in a given set of exercises. E_A for a set of exercises is set to the Elo rating of the *entire text* from which the exercises are drawn.

We update the learner's Elo after *each* set of exercises, but update the text's Elo only after an entire iteration through the text. Crucially, the system updates the Elo for the text only with respect to the *specific user* who practiced it. This models the notion that as I practice with the same text over and over, the text becomes "easier" for me—but not for other players.

3.4 Estimator of text difficulty

Modeling and characterizing the readability of texts is a well-studied problem with a long history, (Dubay, 2009). Experiments with lexical and

---

[3]This means that A. our difficulty model should return an accurate estimate of the complexity of the text, and B. that these difficulty estimates should be properly calibrated to the desired rating scale.

grammatical features have been conducted, (Chen and Meurers, 2016; Heilman et al., 2008).

We use a simple linear model for estimating the difficulty of a given text. The output of this model is scaled onto the Elo rating scale. This enables us to calculate the expected result of any rated learner solving exercises from any rated text.

Lexical frequency is known to be a powerful predictor of text readability, (Chen and Meurers, 2016). We use the normalized mean of the lexical frequencies of the tokens in a text as a feature. Additionally, we use **mean token length** and **mean sentence length**, as they are also used in classic readability measurements, (Kincaid et al., 1975; Flesch, 1979). These three features are scaled for a simple 3-variable regression model.

Currently, data for training this model are partitioned into two types: texts from sources with simplified language vs. texts from difficult sources. We label simple texts with a value of 0.2 and difficult texts with 0.8.[4] We aim for a model that produces a correct ordering of texts with respect to their difficulty. We do not need an exact estimate. If the learner Elo ratings based on these estimates correlate well with the ratings from the testing context, we consider this estimator accurate enough. In Section 5 we show that so far, this indeed seems to be the case.

The model outputs typically range between 0 and 1. We scale these values to Elo ratings according to formula 4. This transformation is based on the Elo rating distribution acquired in the testing context. The bounds are clamped at $(0, 1)$, as some texts may get a high difficulty value (sometimes even > 2, in extreme cases).

$$f(x) = \begin{cases} 600, & \text{if } x < -0.4 \\ 1000x + 1000, & \text{if } -0.4 \leq x \leq 1.4 \\ 2400, & \text{if } x > 1.4 \end{cases}$$

(4)

4 Concept graph

We are interested in finding a model for the "natural" order in which learners acquire linguistic concepts—directly from learner data. Learners will find some orders more natural than others—

e.g., when some concept is a requirement for another. The fact that one concept "precedes" another is called the *surmise* relation in Knowledge Space Theory (Doignon and Falmagne, 1999).

Often the domain model in ITS is built by eliciting domain knowledge from experts. We devised a baseline model to infer such relations from user data, without supervision. As we mentioned, each test question is mapped to a certain linguistic concept, and we store all test results from all students. Based on these results, we know to what extent which users have mastered which concepts; from this, we can try to tell apart the more basic concepts from the more advanced ones.

The aim is to build a partial order over the set of all concepts C, which specifices which concepts are related—i.e., we write $c_2 \rightarrow c_1$ to mean concept c_2 *presupposes* (or implies) concept c_1.[5]

Given a set of users U, we build a matrix of "mastery" scores M, of dimension $|U| \times |C|$. Every element M_{ij} is the proportion of correct answers that user u_i has given for concept c_j. In the current implementation, we consider each "user" to be a single *test session*. If the same person completes the test at different times, they will be treated as different users for the purpose of computing consistency. This is done to take into account the fact that a user's level of proficiency changes over time.

For every pair $c_1, c_2 \in C$, we check whether $c_2 \rightarrow c_1$, $c_1 \rightarrow c_2$ or $c_1 \perp c_2$. We compare all columns of M pairwise. Let c_j denote column j of M and c_k column k. To check whether $c_k \rightarrow c_j$ is true, we define a logical function CON_u which checks that user u is consistent with this relation:

M_{uk}	M_{uj}	$CON_u(c_k \rightarrow c_j)$
0	0	1
1	0	0
0	1	1
1	1	1

Again, here c_k is the "harder" concept than c_j. Thus, if $M_{uk} = 0$ (user u knows nothing about concept c_k), that is consistent with $c_k \rightarrow c_j$ regardless of the value of c_j. Conversely if $M_{uj} = 1$ (user u mastered concept c_k perfectly), that is consistent with $c_k \rightarrow c_j$ regardless of the value of c_k.

In practice, the values in M are fractions between 0 and 1. Therefore we introduce two thresh-

---

[4]This is a simplification, which does not reflect reality accurately, as not all texts from a given source are of equal difficulty. However, simply fitting a low dimensional, high-bias estimator such as this yields a reasonable baseline model that generalizes well enough to other texts. We will explore more sophisticated models in the future.

[5]We would like to say that c_1 is a *prerequisite* for c_2, but that may be too strong a claim. However we *may* be able to learn from the data that *typically* c_1 is mastered before c_2.

old parameters to map M_{ij} to zeroes and ones: we believe that a user u really does not know the (harder) concept c_k if $M_{uk} \leqslant \overline{\theta}_{guess}$: the "guessing" upper bound, below which we believe that the user does not know the concept, while sometimes only guessing the correct answer. Analogously, we say that a user u has mastered quite well the (easier) concept c_j if $M_{uj} \geqslant \underline{\theta}_{master}$: the "mastery" lower bound, above which we believe that the user knows the concept, while sometimes making a few mistakes.

To check whether $c_k \to c_j$, we compute the proportion σ of all users who are consistent with this relation $c_k \to c_j$, as follows:

$$\sigma(c_k \to c_j) = \frac{1}{n} \sum_{u \in U} CON_u(M_{uk}, M_{uj})$$

where:

$$CON_u(M_{uk}, M_{uj}) = \begin{cases} 1 & \text{if } M_{uk} \leqslant \overline{\theta}_{guess} \\ 1 & \text{if } M_{uj} \geqslant \underline{\theta}_{master} \\ 0 & otherwise \end{cases}$$

n is the total number of users. θ_{guess} and θ_{master} refer to the thresholds of guessing and mastering respectively. That is, we ignore all users where the level of proficiency in c_1 and c_2 suggests that user only partially understands both concepts, since they do not support to the consistency from $c_k \to c_j$.

We then apply a *consistency* threshold θ such that, if $\sigma(c_2 \to c_1) > \theta$, we add the relation $c_2 \to c_1$ to our partial order.

Finally, we represent the partial order as a directed acyclic graph (DAG), where each path in the graph represents a possible prerequisite route toward learning a concept. For example, if we wish to obtain a complete syllabus for a language course, then we can find a total order compatible with our partial order (i.e., a linear extension) by topologically sorting the nodes in the graph.

We tested this approach with a set of over 620K answers gathered from 700 users, and manually evaluated the results, setting $\theta = .7$.

Our domain experts confirm that the resulting graph provides a plausible model for the relations between the concepts in the language.

5 Experiments

5.1 Elo burn-in

In conventional Elo rating systems, the ratings of both actors are updated after each match. Our goal

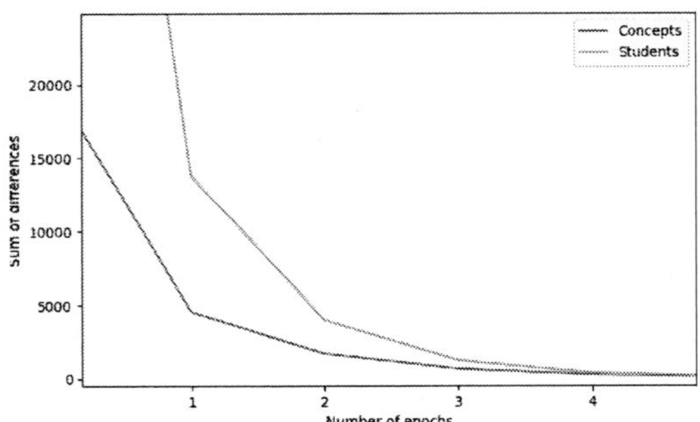

Figure 1: Learning concept Elo ratings with burn-in

is to learn a stable rating for each language concept, which we can keep unchanged as learners take further tests and improve. The rationale behind this is that the concepts don't become less difficult for everyone if a learner masters it.

To achieve this, we perform a burn-in simulation based on the user data we have collected. Specifically, we take the entire collection of data and calculate the Elo updates for each data point— user U doing exercise E—in chronological order. We do this for repeated epochs until the sum of differences between epochs nears zero. This is illustrated in Figure 1.

Once convergence is achieved, we reset the student ratings, and recalculate them from scratch with the *fixed* concept ratings. This yields a system where the learners' ratings are comparable and independent for any learner, including future ones.

5.2 Test and exercise simulation

To verify that one test (of 300 items) is sufficient for a learner to reach her current "true" rating, we performed simulation experiments. Concretely, we measured how many test items a new learner (e.g., with a rating of 1800 Elo) must answer in order to settle on her rating.

In this simulation, each student is initially rated as 1500, and complete some test items. We use the Elo expectation formula to get the response accuracy for the simulated actors. We perform randomized simulations of actors performing one 300-item test with this average response accuracy and observe the results, shown in Figure 2. The actors' responses—correct or false—are sampled randomly according to her supposed correct rate. We also add a small amount of normally distributed random noise. As Figure 2 shows, in this case, one 300-item test is enough to reach one's "true" rating.

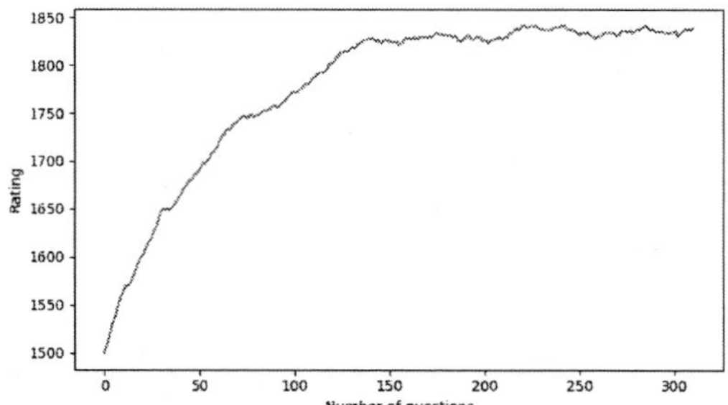

Figure 2: Simulation: test items

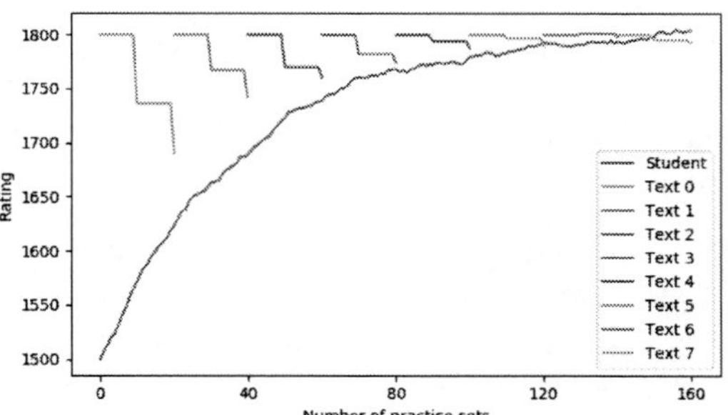

Figure 3: Simulation: exercises based on texts

In contrast to the test item context, in the context of text-based exercises, the Elo ratings will be updated over time both for for learners and practice texts. We conducted a simulation to visualize the rating trends.

In the exercise simulation, the simulated actor has the same starting point as in the simulation for tests—1500. We fix her rate of correct responses, e.g., as 50%, and the actor is practicing only simulated texts rated at 1800. This means that the theoretical upper bound of the actors' rating is, by definition, under 1800.[6] The same normally distributed noise is introduced in this simulation as above. The data in our system shows that texts typically contain 10 snippets (exercise sets) or fewer. After a full pass through a text, namely, 10 problem sets, the ratings for the text are updated with respect to this particular actor. In this simulation each text is to be practiced twice. Figure 3 shows the result of this simulation. We stopped the simulation after 8 texts (each practiced twice) because the rating of the actor had converged to 1800. Since the student begins far below 1800, the first several problem sets will have a substantial drop in their rating, due to the large initial dif-

---

[6]50% success rate in a competition setting means the players are perfectly matched; since the text is rated 1800, the learner's Elo rating should also reach 1800 and remain there.

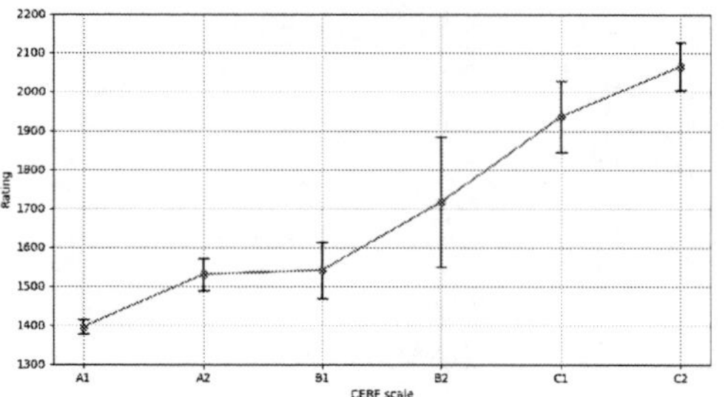

Figure 4: Expert annotated CEFR groups vs. mean Elo rating for each CEFR level

ference between student's rating and text's difficulty estimate. This initial burn-in process soon ends, after the student practice several snippets. As we can observe in Figure 3, the initial burn-in process ends after 3 texts—10 snippets/practice sets per text, each text practiced twice, yielding 60 snippets—the subsequent ones showing only a slight change. The simulation is based on the assumption that the student will go though every problem set in strict order. In reality, this is not very likely. We can therefore infer that this student can reach a rating around 1800 rating after practicing with less than 140 snippets/problem sets.

6 Results

The result of primary interest is how well the Elo ratings given by our system correspond to CEFR levels assigned to the learners by the expert teachers, who estimate the learners' proficiency based on a wide range of assessment criteria, including written essays and oral exams. The relationship between Elo and CEFR is illustrated in Figure 4.

The figure shows the means and 95% confidence intervals of the Elo ratings for the CEFR levels of students, assigned subjectively by the teachers. The numbers of students at each CEFR level in our experiments are given in Table 1. The data in Figure 4 comes from 142 students whose CEFR levels were established *independently* of these tests by the teachers. Although language competency encompasses several skills—reading, writing, aural comprehension, speaking—and the learner may be at different levels in different skills, we normally expect that the competencies across different sills are fairly well correlated. The correlation om Figure 4 is 0.90. Thus, the data in the figure indicate good correlation between our rating method and actual proficiency.

While assessing and modeling the improvement

CEFR	Students
A1	48
A2	31
B1	18
B2	6
C1	17
C2	22
Total	142

Table 1: Number of CEFR rated students in Figure 4

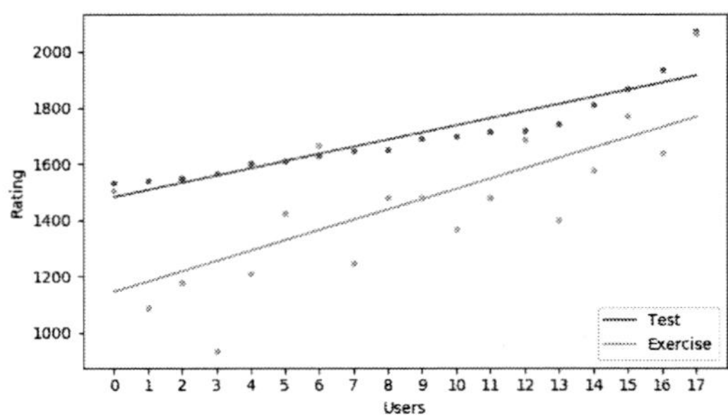

Figure 6: Correlation between test and text-based exercise ratings ($\rho = 0.79$)

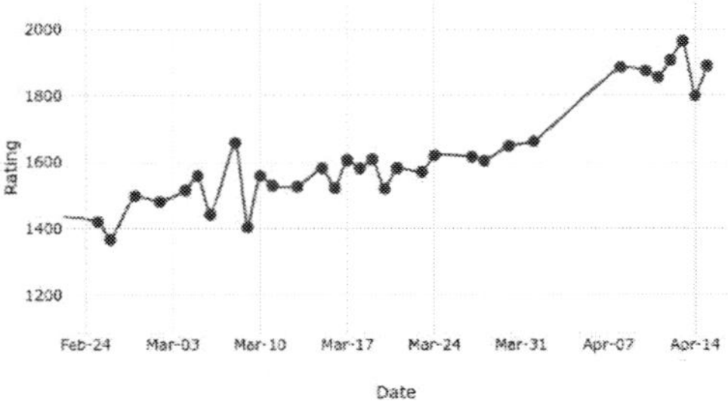

Figure 5: A representative student test Elo progress

of learners is largely in the realm of future work, we have interesting preliminary data of learners' improvement. Figure 5 shows an example of the progress of a typical actual learner taking tests. The learner takes (randomized) tests over a period of time, with the rating improving consistently. In this example, we see an increase of almost 300 in average Elo during the periods. The improvement is attributed to the fact that the learner has covered new material during the period, mastered more of the concepts in the test, and consequently scoring better on those questions.

Another crucial question is how well our Elo estimates from the exercise context correlate with Elo ratings from the testing context. For this we also have initial results, shown in Figure 6. We have so far collected only a modest amount of learner data, and therefore the conclusions drawn from the data are preliminary. Investigating this correlation requires substantial data from learners who have worked in both contexts: practicing with exercises based on texts, and completing tests. The figure shows results for the top 17 students, who have completed at least 1000 exercise sets (text snippets, in orange) and at least 300 test items (in blue)—sorted according to their *test* rating. The figure shows good correlation between the two rat-

ings for the students. At present, the correlation between test and practice Elo score is 0.79.

The last goal in our work is to investigate the relationship between the concept graph and the Elo ratings. Figure 7 shows a small sub-graph of the concept graph. The complete concept graph 8 can found in the Appendix. From Figures 7 and 8, we can see that typically (though not always), if concept A surmises concept B, A will have a higher Elo rating than B. This makes sense, as more difficult concepts should surmise easier ones. The Elo ratings and the graph structure do not correspond perfectly. Expecting that real-valued linear ratings can accurately describe the natural order of concepts is unreasonable. Since the graph and the Elo ratings describe different processes, it is not surprising to find inversions in the graph, such as between concepts 98 and 93, in Figure 7. The structure of the graph, its relation to the difficulty of concepts, and the natural learning order of concepts is an key future research topic.

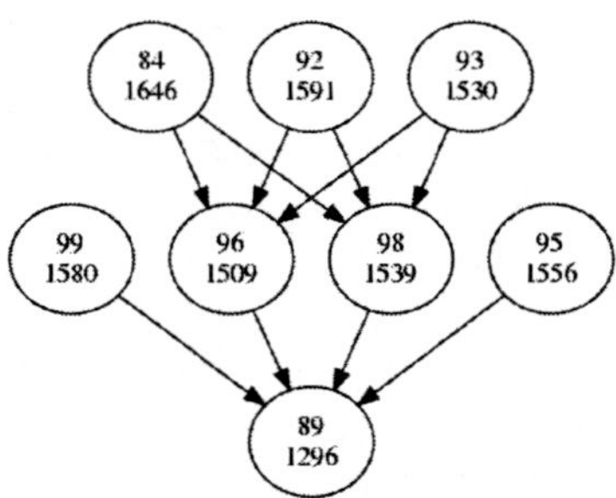

Figure 7: Sub-graph of the complete concept graph (see Supplementary Materials). Arrows denote implication. Top number: ID of the concept (appendix A); bottom number: Elo score of the concept (appendix B).

7 Current problems

We are in the process of collecting user data and evaluating the methods of assessment presented in this paper. Subjective CEFR ratings are being collected from the teachers for some of the students. While the number of hand-labeled CEFR ratings is modest at the time of writing, it is sufficient to indicate that using Elo-based ratings for measuring language proficiency shows promise. Building domain models based on the concept precedence graph is another direction of research.

Comparing our ratings and expert-annotated proficiency levels in larger quantities will raise the confidence of our method. We must note that a single value cannot be expected to describe the language proficiency of a learner completely, as there are several aspects of the language to master.

We plan to compare other Elo-based models, such as Glicko (Glickman, 1999), and TrueSkill (Herbrich et al., 2007), with our Elo rating formula. Robust methods for obtaining numerical estimates of skills enables us to develop ICALL systems, by facilitating the quantitative evaluation of skills, and the resulting improvement of the learners.

8 Conclusions

The main contributions of this paper are:

- We adapt and evaluate Elo-based rating formulas for modeling language learners' proficiency, as well as the difficulty of texts and linguistic concepts, not only the difficulty of questions/test items.
- We obtain static difficulty ratings for the linguistic concepts by performing an initial burn-in for the Elo ratings based on a large amount of learner data, and then assess students' proficiency using the learned Elo ratings. Feedback from language teachers/experts indicates that the ratings correlate with their estimates of learner competency.
- We use a linear-regression model of text difficulty as an estimator, to obtain Elo ratings for the texts. This enables us to rate the performance of learners, who practice with exercises generated from the texts. Preliminary results indicate that there is a positive correlation between ratings in the exercise and the test contexts.

- We build a partial order over all concepts found in the domain, and visualize the partial order as a DAG over concepts. The concept graph is not linear as the Elo ratings. The structure of the concept graph and the Elo ratings of the concepts generally agree in that the graph displays a strong tendency of decreasing rating from the more complex concepts to the more fundamental concepts, as indicated by the actual data collected from the learning process.

In sum, the proposed methods enable us to rate the proficiency of the current and future language learners, which is a fundamental goal in ITS and ICALL.

Acknowledgements

Work was supported in part by the Academy of Finland, Project *FinUgRevita*, Grant No. 267097, and by HIIT—Helsinki Institute for Information Technology.

References

Ivon Arroyo, Beverly Park Woolf, Winslow Burelson, Kasia Muldner, Dovan Rai, and Minghui Tai. 2014. A multimedia adaptive tutoring system for mathematics that addresses cognition, metacognition and affect. *International Journal of Artificial Intelligence in Education*, 24(4):387–426.

Hao Cen, Kenneth Koedinger, and Brian Junker. 2006. Learning factors analysis – a general method for cognitive model evaluation and improvement. In *Intelligent Tutoring Systems*, pages 164–175, Berlin, Heidelberg. Springer Berlin Heidelberg.

Xiaobin Chen and Detmar Meurers. 2016. Characterizing text difficulty with word frequencies. In *Proceedings of the 11th Workshop on Innovative Use of NLP for Building Educational Applications*, pages 84–94.

Albert T Corbett and John R Anderson. 1994. Knowledge tracing: Modeling the acquisition of procedural knowledge. *User modeling and user-adapted interaction*, 4(4):253–278.

Jean-Paul Doignon and Jean-Claude Falmagne. 1999. *Knowledge Spaces*.

William Dubay. 2009. Unlocking language: The classic readability studies. *Professional Communication, IEEE Transactions on*, 51:416 – 417.

Arpad E. Elo. 1978. *The rating of chessplayers, past and present*. Arco Pub., New York.

Susan E Embretson and Steven P Reise. 2013. *Item response theory*. Psychology Press.

Rudolf Flesch. 1979. How to write plain English: Let's start with the formula. *University of Canterbury*.

Mark E Glickman. 1999. Parameter estimation in large dynamic paired comparison experiments. *Journal of the Royal Statistical Society: Series C (Applied Statistics)*, 48(3):377–394.

Michael Heilman, Kevyn Collins-Thompson, and Maxine Eskenazi. 2008. An analysis of statistical models and features for reading difficulty prediction. In *Proceedings of the third workshop on innovative use of NLP for building educational applications*, pages 71–79. Association for Computational Linguistics.

Ralf Herbrich, Tom Minka, and Thore Graepel. 2007. Trueskill^{TM}: A Bayesian skill rating system. In B. Schölkopf, J. C. Platt, and T. Hoffman, editors, *Advances in Neural Information Processing Systems 19*, pages 569–576. MIT Press.

Anisia Katinskaia, Javad Nouri, and Roman Yangarber. 2018. Revita: a language-learning platform at the intersection of ITS and CALL. In *Proceedings of LREC: 11th International Conference on Language Resources and Evaluation*, Miyazaki, Japan.

J Peter Kincaid, Robert P Fishburne Jr, Richard L Rogers, and Brad S Chissom. 1975. Derivation of new readability formulas (automated readability index, fog count and Flesch reading ease formula) for Navy enlisted personnel.

Sharon Klinkenberg, Marthe Straatemeier, and Han LJ van der Maas. 2011. Computer adaptive practice of maths ability using a new item response model for on-the-fly ability and difficulty estimation. *Computers & Education*, 57(2):1813–1824.

Mikhail Kopotev. 2010. Система прогрессивного тестирования **Karttu** (описание и первые результаты). Русский язык за рубежом, (3):23–29.

Mikhail Kopotev. 2012. Karttu: результаты языкового тестирования в школе и вузе. Формирование и оценка коммуникативной компетенции билингвов в процессе двуязычного образования: Сб. ст./Под ред. ЕЕ Юркова и др. СПб.: МИРС, pages 312–339.

David Little. 2007. The common European framework of reference for languages: Perspectives on the making of supranational language education policy. *The Modern Language Journal*, 91(4):645–655.

Philip I Pavlik Jr, Hao Cen, and Kenneth R Koedinger. 2009. Performance factors analysis–a new alternative to knowledge tracing. *Online Submission*.

Radek Pelánek. 2016. Applications of the Elo rating system in adaptive educational systems. *Computers & Education*, 98:169–179.

Steven Ritter, John R. Anderson, Kenneth R. Koedinger, and Albert Corbett. 2007. Cognitive tutor: Applied research in mathematics education. *Psychonomic Bulletin & Review*, 14(2):249–255.

A List of concepts

ID	Rating	Name of concept
6	1602	Lexicology. Lexical semantics
7	1860	Collocations
8	1679	Lexicology. Coordination of words
9	1382	Verb. Case government
10	1541	Verb. Prepositional government
11	1550	Adjectives
12	1509	Nouns
19	1471	Impersonal verbs (except verba meteorologica) and their government
20	1482	Predicative adverbs and their government. Existence, state, time
21	1480	Predicative adverbs and their government. Necessity, possibility, impossibility
22	1577	Negative constructions with predicative 'be' (and synonyms), genitive of negation
23	1423	Sentences with dative subject: 'Кате 25 лет'
24	1445	Expressions of time, place and manner. Preposition-free expressions
25	1621	Constructions with cardinal numerals
26	1470	Constructions with collective numerals
27	1652	Genitive plural of Pluralia tantum words
28	1630	I declension. Type 'музей-музеи, воробей-воробьи'
29	1595	I declension. Type 'санаторий'
30	1662	I declension. Fleeting vowels and alternations я, е, ё / й ('заяц-зайца, заём-займа')
31	1608	I declension. Type 'карандаш'
32	1671	I declension. Type 'адрес-адреса'
33	1562	I declension. Type 'солдат-много солдат, сапог-пара сапог'
34	1586	I declension. Type '-анин/-янин, -ин'
35	1518	I declension. Type 'дерево-деревья'
36	1616	II declension. Type 'армия'
37	1603	II declension. Type на -ня
38	1713	II declension. Type 'статья'
39	1616	Fleeting vowel in genitive plural
40	1504	Nouns with prepositions в/на ending in -у/-ю in prepositional singular
41	1619	Nouns ending in -у/-ю in prepositional singular and -а in nominative plural
42	1644	Possessive adjectives. Type 'лисий'
43	1601	Ordinal numbers. Type 'третий'
44	1612	Possessive adjectives. Type 'мамин'
45	1543	Cardinal numbers. 'Сто' vs. 'пятьсот, шестьсот, семьсот, девятьсот'
46	1608	Quantifiers. Collective quantifiers in oblique cases
47	1528	Quantifiers. Collective quantifiers 'оба, обе'
48	1594	I conjugation. Type 'плакать'
49	1511	I conjugation. Type 'рисовать'
51	1560	II conjugation. Type 'молчать'
52	1674	Preterite. Type 'исчезнуть'
54	1570	Regular verbs with vowel alternation
55	1512	Resultative
56	1553	Iterative / potential iterative / qualities
57	1507	Expression of duration - 'за какое время'
58	1416	Factual meaning of verbs
59	1817	Aspect, expression of action completed in the past
60	1648	Aspect, expression of capability/incapability. ('Тебе этого не понимать/понять!')
61	1509	Inception of action
62	1525	'Забыть, успеть, удаться' + infinitive
63	1539	'Уметь, нравиться, любить' etc. + infinitive
64	1651	'Пора, скорее' + infinitive
65	1553	'Нельзя, невозможно, не могу' + infinitive
66	1499	'Не' + infinitive
67	1501	Negative sentences
68	1411	Imperative
69	1559	Proximal future
70	1674	Impersonal sentences. Infinitival sentences. Subordinate sentences ('если / прежде чем' + infinitive)
71	946	Impersonal sentences. Infinitival sentences. Modal expressions
72	1580	Impersonal sentences. Infinitival sentences. Sentences, with negative pronouns and adverbs
73	1701	Generis-personal sentences
75	1516	Passive and its relation to indefinite-personal sentences (equivalent of Finnish impersonal passive)
76	1800	Stress: forms of verbal preterite
77	1706	Stress: short adjectives
78	1736	Stress: participles
79	1548	Nouns. Type A: stress on the stem
80	1719	Nouns. Type B, B1, B2: stress on the ending

B Concept graph

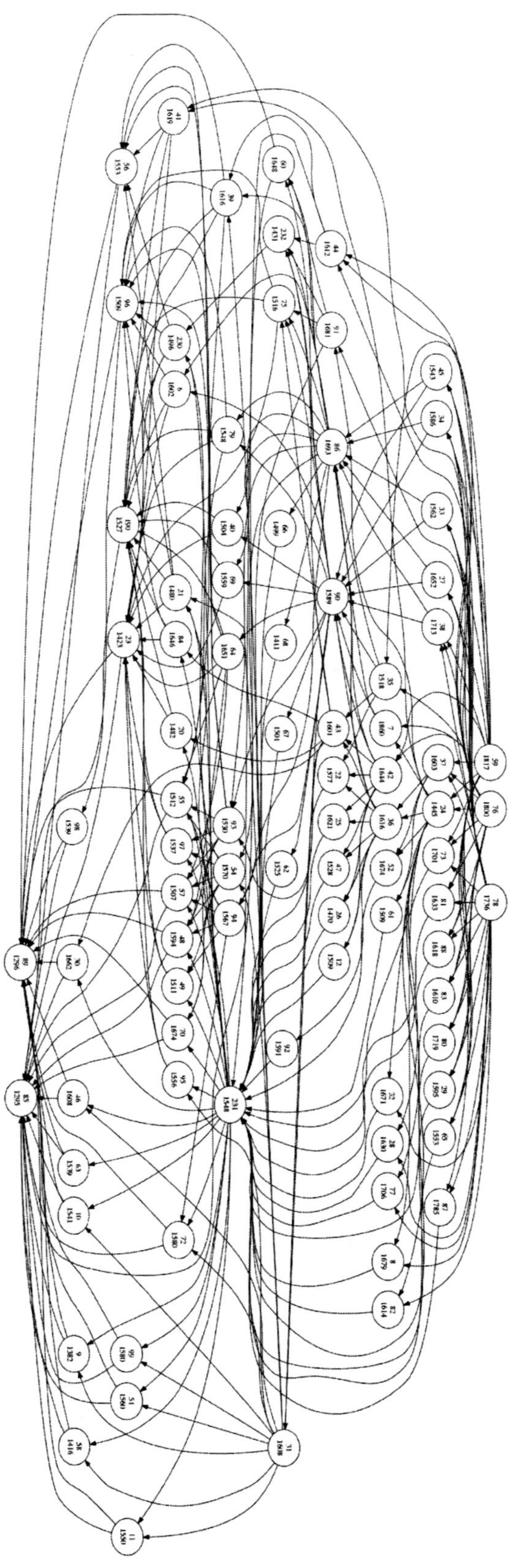

Figure 8: The full concept graph.

Rubric Reliability and Annotation of Content and Argument in Source-Based Argument Essays

Yanjun Gao[*] and **Alex Driban**[*] and **Brennan Xavier McManus**[**] and **Elena Musi**[†]
Patricia M. Davies[‡] and **Smaranda Muresan**[**] and **Rebecca J. Passonneau**[*]

[*]Department of Computer Science and Engineering
Penn State University
{yug125, akd524, rjp49}@cse.psu.edu

[**]Department of Computer Science, Columbia University
{bm2530, smara}@columbia.edu

[†]Department of Communication and Media, University of Liverpool
Elena.Musi@liverpool.ac.uk

[‡]College of Sciences and Human Studies, Prince Mohammad Bin Fahd University
pdavies@pmu.edu.sa

Abstract

We present a unique dataset of student source-based argument essays to facilitate research on the relations between content, argumentation skills, and assessment. Two classroom writing assignments were given to college students in a STEM major, accompanied by a carefully designed rubric. The paper presents a reliability study of the rubric, showing it to be highly reliable, and initial annotation on content and argumentation annotation of the essays.

1 Introduction

Researchers in education have long recommended the use of rubrics to assess student writing and to inform instruction, especially regarding feedback to students (Graham et al., 2016; Jonsson and Svingby, 2007). Writing is important not only as a means to demonstrate knowledge, but also to acquire understanding of subject matter, including in STEM (Sampson et al., 2013; Klein and Rose, 2010; Gunel et al., 2007; Norris and Phillips, 2003). Argumentative writing plays a key role in such learning (Hand et al., 2015). It is difficult, however, for instructors in subject areas to provide writing instruction alongside the disciplinary content (Gillespie et al., 2014; Graham et al., 2014; Kiuhara et al., 2009). We are investigating the use of rubrics to support instruction in argumentation writing, with two goals in mind. Our first goal is to investigate effective instruction of argument writing skills, including the design and application of rubrics. Our second goal is to investigate how natural language processing techniques can facilitate instructors' use of rubrics.

The study described here is a collaboration among three computer science faculty: one specializing in educational technology, and two in natural language processing (NLP), who apply NLP to educational data. To investigate how a rubric can support instruction in argument writing, we designed a sequence of two argument essay assignments and rubrics. The collaborator in educational technology gave the assignments to college freshman enrolled in her academic skills class in their first semester. Both assignments asked students to do a critical analysis of source material, and write an argumentative essay in response to a prompt by stating a claim, providing arguments in support of their claim, as well as counterarguments, before reaching a conclusion. The instruction, and therefore the rubrics, emphasized students' ability to understand source material (content), to write a coherent essay (coherence), and to construct an argument (argumentation).

The assignments asked students to summarize the source material before writing the argument. To support a fine-grained analysis of the students' essays and provide data for evaluating NLP techniques, the students' essays are manually annotated for content and argument. The following sections present the assignments and rubrics, the essay data set, the reliability study, and the annotation methods for content and argumentation. We present initial findings on the comparison of grades assigned in the class to those assigned by reliable raters, and on the relation of the annotation to the reliable grades. We discuss questions that can be investigated about student learning, and about the interdependence of students' ability to articulate content and construct an argument.

2 Related Work

Previous work has looked at automated methods to support rubric-based writing (Passonneau

507

Proceedings of the Fourteenth Workshop on Innovative Use of NLP for Building Educational Applications, pages 507–518
Florence, Italy, August 2, 2019. ©2019 Association for Computational Linguistics

et al., 2018). Rubric-based writing assessment has recently been brought to researchers' attention, particularly on designing automated assessment methods. Gerard et al. (2016); Gerard and Linn (2016) have demonstrated that automated assessment using rubrics successfully identifies the students at risk of failing, and facilitates effective guidance and meaningful classroom interactions. Agejev and Šnajder (2017) uses ROUGE and BLEU in assessing summary writing from college L2 students. Santamaría Lancho et al. (2018) show that using G-Rubric, an LSA-based tool applying rubric assessment, helps the instructors grade the short text answers to open-ended questions, and proves to be reliable, with a Pearson correlation between human graders and G-Rubric of 0.72.

Recent work investigates fine-grained writing assessment, especially on content quality evaluation by diving into linguistic phenomena and structures, combined with various NLP techniques. Klebanov et al. (2014) investigated the correlations between essays scores with a content importance model. Another line of research has studied the role of argumentative features in predicting the overall essay quality (Ong et al., 2014; Song et al., 2014; Klebanov et al., 2016; Ghosh et al., 2016; Persing and Ng, 2015). For example, Klebanov et al. (2016) and Ghosh et al. (2016) examine the relations between argumentation structure features and the holistic essay quality (low, medium and high) applied to TOEFL essays. In this paper, we use the argumentative features introduced by Ghosh et al. (2016), but correlate them with the rubric related to the quality of the argument on a scale of 0-5.

3 Assignments and Rubrics

Two argument essays were assigned in fall 2018 to computer science freshman in a university in the United Kingdom. In the first of these (Essay 1, assigned early in the semester), students were asked to choose one of three articles on a current technology topic, with the number of students per article capped at one third of the class comprising 141 students. These students are enrolled in a variety of degree programs, ranging from information technology to computer engineering, offered by a department of mathematics and computer science. They form a heterogeneous group, both in educational background and age, since many are admitted through the university's mission to provide learning opportunities for the whole community.

The first part of the assignments required that students **summarize** the readings in one hundred and fifty to two hundred and fifty words. The second part elicited a three to five hundred-word **argument essay** addressing a given question. The list of topics and associated questions is shown below. Students were allowed to use external sources to back up their arguments, but had to reference these.

1. Autonomous Vehicles: will these change how we travel today?
2. Cybercrime: will education and investment provide the solution?
3. Cryptocurrencies: are they the currencies of the future?

For the second assignment (Essay 2), all students were provided with the same three journal articles relating to uses of AI in education. They were asked to **summarize**, in one hundred and fifty to two hundred and fifty words, key issues relating to the use of AI in teaching and learning as stated in the articles. Then, they had to write a three to five hundred word **argument essay** addressing the question: *Should artificial intelligence be used in teaching and learning?* Both essays were assessed using a rubric designed by the three collaborators, based on existing rubrics: SRI's Source-Based Argument Scoring Attributes (AWC) (Gallagher et al., 2015) and Ferretti's well known argument rubric (Ferretti et al., 2000). The four dimensions and their weights (in parentheses) are shown below. Each dimension or subdimension was rated on a 6-point scale ([0 to 5]; see Appendix A which gives the rubric for Essay 1.)

1. Content (3/7) - quality, coverage, coherence;
2. Argument (2/7) - claims, support, counterargument;
3. Conventions (1/7) - lexis and grammar;
4. Referencing (1/7) - sources and citations.

For Essay 2, some of the details of the Content-quality and the Referencing dimensions of the rubric were revised in recognition of the fact that in the second essay, students were not allowed to use external sources.

Students received three hours of preparatory instruction prior to the essays being assigned. The first two hours focused on how to write argument essays - engaging with the prompt, formulating a claim, developing arguments and counterarguments, and concluding the essay - as prescribed by Simon Black (2018) in his text, *Crack the Essay: Secrets of Argumentative Writing Revealed.*

The third hour of instruction, given later in the course, provided students with feedback, exemplified by student submissions for the first essay. During this lecture, they were shown good and poor examples of essay writing through an application of the rubric to several anonymized examples. These were later made available for their reference. Using the rubric to provide formative feedback may have resulted in better performance by students on Essay 2. Many of the students performed better on the second assignment.

Of the 141 enrolled students, 123 completed Essay 1, 101 completed Essay 2, and 97 completed both. Essay 2 was due 4 weeks following the submission of Essay 1, which made it possible for students to receive feedback on Essay 1 before submitting Essay 2. The framework used in designing the instruction is the cyclical process suggested by Jonassen (2008). Grading of Essay 1 was done by three of the five tutors teaching the course; each tutor graded all the essays for one of the three topics. The two remaining tutors split the Essay 2 submissions between them. To ensure consistency between the graders, the instructor moderated the grading by randomly selecting one-tenth of each set to regrade.

Using rubrics in higher education is well documented (Reddy and Andrade, 2010). Although mainly used for defining and grading assignments, rubrics can also be incorporated into instruction. Here, the feedback provided following the scoring of Essay 1 using the rubric was part of a developmental process, which culminated in Essay 2. For many of these students, it was their first attempt at writing an argument essay. A large proportion of them reported that the rubric helped them to understand the assignment better, and that they used it as a guide. In a survey examining how students used the rubric for Essay 1, 84 students responded, and 34% believed they achieved a good mark because they used the rubric. Only 11.3% felt the rubric made them lose marks.

Over 65% of students who submitted both essays received the same or a better grade on the second essay. Most who received the same grade on both essays ranked in the 95th percentile on both. The students had very positive things to say about what they learned from the assignment. These included: how to read critically; recognizing and questioning an author's argument; how to structure and write an argument; how to support a claim with evidence; and how to analyze complex issues. All of these competencies underpin critical thinking and problem solving, which are the fundamental skills taught to STEM majors.

4 Essay Dataset

The composition of the dataset supports simultaneous investigation of summary content analysis and argumentation mining: the former reflects the skills of reading comprehension and summarization, and the latter includes logical reasoning, argumentation, and writing skills. While summary and argument serve distinct roles, the combination into a single writing assignment allows us to assess the interdependence between reading comprehension and argument writing.

Below, we present descriptive statistics of the dataset. Table 1 shows the sample sizes for essays on the given topics Cybercrime (CyberCri) with 44, Autonomous Vehicles (AutoV) with 42, and CryptoCurrencies (CrypCurr) with 37. In the second assignment, there are 101 essays about AI. Table 2 shows that the second assignment had a higher average of tokens per sentence across summary, argument and overall. The vocabulary size of the whole dataset is 5,923.

Assignment1			Assignment2
CyberCri	AutoV	CrypCurr	AI
44	42	37	101

Table 1: Sample size given each assignment and topic; the total number of essays is 224.

In contrast to other data sets investigated for argument mining, here the assignments are from a single course with the same set of students. The size of our data set is comparable to one used in (Ghosh et al., 2016) (TOEFL essays), but smaller than those used in (Stab and Gurevych, 2014; Klebanov et al., 2016). In addition, the data set we collected has multiple essays for four topics, based on source readings. This gives us the opportunity to investigate students' reliance on source material in their argumentation.

Sum	CyberCri	AutoV	CrypCurr	AI
Sents	7.43	7.24	8.62	7.30
Tk/Sents	34.21	32.84	28.52	36.08
Arg	CyberCri	AutoV	CrypCurr	AI
Sents	17.36	19.66	19.51	19.05
Tk/Sents	31.96	32.32	33.20	34.79
Overall	CyberCri	AutoV	CrypCurr	AI
Sents	24.78	27.04	28.14	26.34
Tk/Sent	32.46	32.90	32.04	36.17
Vocabulary Size			5923	

Table 2: Dataset statistics of average numbers of sentences (Sents) and average tokens per sentence (Tk/Sents) from summaries (Sum) and arguments (Arg) across topics. The total vocabulary size is also given.

5 Rubric Reliability

Educational intervention studies where researchers investigate the potential benefit of a proposed intervention apply rubrics whose reliability has been assessed. For example, in their meta-analysis of educational interventions, Graham and Perin (2007) exclude interventions whose reliability is below 0.60. We also test the reliability of the rubric used in the classroom assignments discussed here. The reliability study we present has two purposes. First, it provides insight into the difficulty of graders' use of a multi-dimensional content and argument rubric under ordinary classroom conditions where there is time pressure to assign grades. Second, it provides a measure of the quality of the gold standard against which to evaluate the automated NLP techniques we will develop. Our reliability study addressed the content and argument dimensions of the rubric, and achieved high inter-rater reliability.

Two advanced undergraduates were recruited for the reliability study. They were trained by a team consisting of the collaborators and their research assistants during a period of seven weeks, with each rater devoting 10 hours per week. Each rater then graded half the essays (apart from six used in training).

The raters' training consisted of activities in which they learned about the structure of argument writing and carried out the assignment, used the rubric to assess different topics and writers, and participated in webinars where they received feedback and further training. Figure 1 shows the seven-week training regimen. During weeks 1-2, they became familiar with all three writing prompts through their own essay writing, and grading the other rater's essays. There were two

rounds in which they independently assessed three Cryptocurrency essays (weeks 4, 6; six distinct essays), with webinar feedback in between (weeks 5, 7). The week 5 webinar involved all three researchers, the two raters, and a PhD student on the project. All other webinars with the raters were presented by the instructor co-author. A final webinar (week 7) pointed to minor differences between the two assignments and rubrics pertaining to use of open-ended external sources in Essay 1 and not Essay 2.

For the assessment tasks in weeks 4 and 6, three Cryptocurrency essays representing high, medium and low students' scores were selected. The raters did not know there was a difference in the students' original grades, and no one on the project other than the instructor knew how the three were originally graded. As a result of the discussion from the week 5 webinar, a consensus was reached on the three initial Cryptocurrency essays. The raters were instructed to use these as a model for applying the rubric in a consistent manner.

Rater agreement was assessed using Pearson correlation on the content and argument components of the rubric. Content quality, content coverage, and content coherence were each independently rated on a six-point scale (0 to 5). Argument was rated on an eleven-point scale (0 to 10). After the raters applied the rubric to the first three Cryptocurrency essays, their correlations with each other and with the assigned grades varied widely, from negative correlation to high correlation. After the second round of three essays, the correlation between the two raters was perfect on two, and poor on the third. After a brief discussion, we decided that this was sufficient agreement for the raters to work indepen-

Week	Activity
1	Webinar to review argument writing, assignment #1, and rubric #1
2	Each rater writes one essay on AV, and one on Crypto or Cyber; raters apply rubric to the other rater's two essays
3	Webinar on their essays and assessments
4	Raters each assess the same three Crypto
5	Webinar on their first round of assessment with detailed discussion among raters and all researchers
6	Raters each assess three additional Crypto
7	Feedback on the second round of assessment; webinar on assignment and rubric #2

Figure 1: Seven-week rater training

Essay	CQual	CCov	CCoher	Arg	Conven	Ref	Cont/Arg	Total
AutoV	0.38	0.52	0.29	0.32	0.19	0.56	0.63	0.52
Crypto	0	0.12	0	0.48	0.47	0.56	0.72	0.36
Cyber	0.36	0.33	0.12	0.44	0.30	0.84	0.59	0.50
All Essay 1	0.23	0.40	0.14	0.41	0.31	0.69	0.62	0.47
Essay 2 (AI and Ed)	0.32	0.44	0.42	0.36	0.44	0.61	0.54	0.47
All	0.25	0.38	0.25	0.34	0.38	0.69	0.55	0.42

Table 3: Correlations of the reliable grades with the tutors' grades

dently to apply the rubric to the remaining essays.

To complete the gold standard rubric scores, each rater worked on 28 essays per week for three weeks, and 31 in the fourth week. A random selection of 10 essays were assessed by both raters. The correlation for the content and argument dimensions on the ten essays ranged from one low outlier of -0.52 to 1.0. The average was 0.75, and on all but the outlier it was 0.89.

The reliability study shows that the rubric can be applied reliably, but also highlights the difficulty of incorporating a fine-grained rubric into classroom use, where tutors have little time to engage in training. The assessments from the reliable raters generally have moderate correlation with the tutors' grades, ranging from 0.72 for the Cryptocurrency essays to 0.54 for the AI Education essays for the complete rubric. Table 3 gives the correlations between the raters and the tutors who did the grading on each component of the rubric, the sum of the four content and argument dimensions, and the total. In addition to providing the correlations for all the essays as a whole, the table also gives the breakdown for each assignment, and for the three topics in assignment 1.

6 Annotation of Essay Content

Here we describe the annotation of the content of the summary portion and argument portion of students' essays. This comprises three annotation tasks: identification of summary content units (SCUs) in the summary; identification of elementary discourse units (EDUs) in the argument; and alignment of EDUs with SCUs.

To annotate the summary content, we use Pyramid annotation (Nenkova et al., 2007), a summary content annotation that has been shown to correlate with a main ideas rubric used in an educational intervention with community college students (Passonneau et al., 2018). As in that study, we collect five reference summaries written by more advanced students, referred to as a wise crowd. The wise crowd summaries are first an-

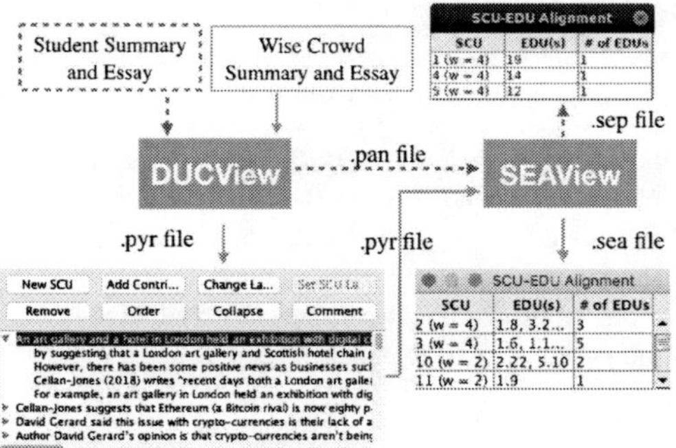

Figure 2: Workflow diagram for content annotation: from DUCView to SEAView. The green box and arrows indicate the flow of the wise crowd summaries and essays, and the box and arrows in dashed red lines are show the flow of a student summary and essay.

notated with DUCView[1] to create a list of summary content units (SCUs) (see Figure 2), where each SCU appears in at least one wise crowd summary and at most in all five. An SCU is roughly a proposition, but need not be expressed as a full clause. SCUs are ranked by their frequency in the wise crowd summaries to provide an importance measure of the SCU. Content scores given to student summaries are based on matches from the student summary to SCUs in the pyramid. Pyramid scores measure the inherent quality of a student's summary (relative proportion of high-weighted SCUs), and the content coverage (proportional representation of average SCU weights in wise crowd summaries). Pyramid annotation has been found to be highly reliable (Passonneau, 2010). Agreement measured by Krippendorf's alpha (scores in [-1,1]) on ten pairs of pyramids created by different annotators, for five topics from each of two distinct datasets, ranged from 0.75 to 0.89. For sixteen peer summarizers on three topics each, average alpha for annotation of pyramid SCUs in summaries was 0.78. Due to the exten-

---

[1] We made some modifications to the original DUCView; the new version is available from `https://github.com/psunlpgroup/DUCView`.

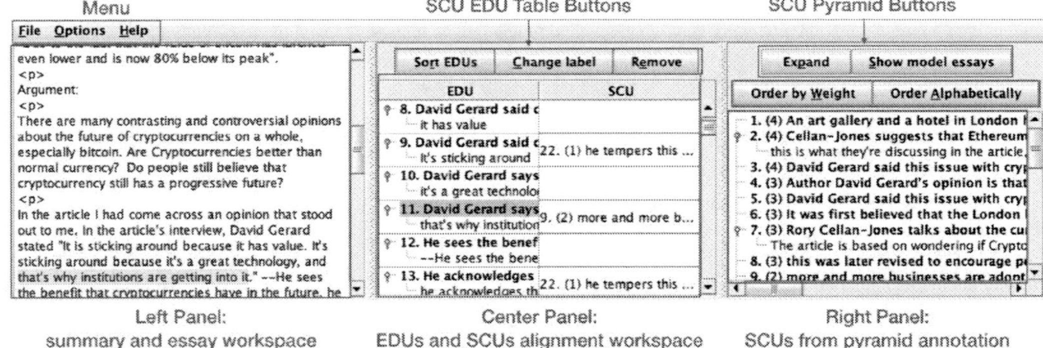

Figure 3: SEAView interface. Left panel as the workspace of summary and essay: users could select the span of text, drag and drop to the center panel as an EDU then change the label; center panel for EDUs and SCUs alignments; right panel for displaying list of SCUs from manual pyramid. The text highlighted by yellow color in left panel is the current selected EDU annotated and labeled as blue highlighted text in EDU and SCU alignment table, as shown in center panel, with EDU ID as 11 and a match of SCU weighted 2 and ID as 9, corresponding to the pyramid in right panel.

sive reliability measures in past work on pyramid annotation, we did not re-assess its reliability here.

To annotate the content of the argument portion of the essay, we identify all distinct Elementary Discourse Units (EDU). Identifying (segmenting) EDUs from text and representing their meanings play a key role in discourse parsing (Marcu, 2000; Li et al., 2016; Braud et al., 2017). Definitions of EDUs vary, thus Prasad et al. (2008) consider the full range of clause types, including verb arguments and non-finite clauses. To simplify the annotation, we restrict EDUs to propositions derived from tensed clauses that are not verb arguments (such as *that* complements of verbs of belief). In (Gao et al., 2019), we report the iterative development of reliable annotation guidelines for untrained annotators.[2] Annotators first identify the start and end of tensed clauses, omitting discourse connectives from the EDU spans, which can be discontinuous. Annotators then provide a paraphrase of the EDU span as an independent simple sentence. The EDU annotation is illustrated in a subsection below along with the annotation tool developed for this purpose.

6.1 Content annotation workflow

To follow the principles of pyramid annotation applied to education (Passonneau et al., 2018), we collected wise crowd essays written by sophomores who took the academic skills course in the previous year and by the trained raters on the project (advanced undergraduates), to constitute

five references per topic. We used the guidelines from DUC 2006 (Passonneau, 2006), and an enhanced annotation tool (see above). As shown in Figure 2, the annotation workflow begins with pyramid content annotation, which takes wise crowd summaries as input to DUCView. The annotator creates SCUs and exports the pyramid XML file (*.pyr). A pyramid file and a student summary are then the input for the annotator to match phrases in the student summary to pyramid SCUs, which is also exported as XML (*.pan).

6.2 SEAView

We designed a tool to annotate EDUs in the wise crowd essays and the student essays, and to align EDUs with SCUs.[3] As shown in Figure 3, SEAView (for **SCU** and **EDU** Alignment) takes as input two-part essays that contain a summary and an argument, where the summary has already been annotated in DUCView. To annotate the wise crowd essays, a .pyr file is loaded into SEAView. The input files must contain document separator lines between the essays, and another header line between the summary and argument of each essay. The annotator identifies EDUs in each of the wise crowd essays. To annotate a student essay, a .pan file is loaded into SEAView. Annotators perform the annotation in two steps: identification of all the EDUs in the argument text; alignment of EDUs with any SCUs that share the same meaning. The final output from SEAView includes a list

---

[2]Currently in submission to another venue.

[3]Available for download: `https://github.com/psunlpgroup/SEAView`.

of EDUs, a list of SCUs matched with the EDUs, and an alignment table. Depending on the type of input, SEAView will generate SCU-EDU alignment for wise crowd essays (.sea files), or SCU-EDU alignments for student essays (.sep files).

7 Initial Content Annotation Results

We first present preliminary content annotation results on topic Cryptocurrencies and Autonomous Vehicle. Two manual pyramids are annotated, with statistics shown in Table 4. The total number of SCUs are 34 and 41 for Cryptocurrencies and Autonomous Vehicle respectively. Neither topic has found SCUs weighted 5 (number of wise crowd). Both found 8 SCUs that are weighted 4 and 3, and a long tail distribution of low-weighted SCUs (26 for Cryptocurrencies; 33 for Autonomous Vehicles).

Table 5 presents statistics of content annotation of essays, from both wise crowd submissions and students submissions, on EDU-SCU alignment between manual pyramid and essays. In wise crowds, the average weight of SCUs matched in essays is 2.60 (Cryptocurrencies) and 2.37 (Autonomous Vehicle). Autonomous Vehicle has more EDUs on average (N=35.00) than Cryptocurrencies (N=23.80), while Cryptocurrencies has longer length of EDU than Autonomous Vehicle, respectively 17.39 and 15.18 words. Finally, the SCU weights normalized by the total number of EDUs are 0.11 and 0.7, and by the number of matched EDUs are 1.07 and 0.62, for Cryptocurrencies and Autonomous Vehicles, respectively. For student submissions, the Autonomous Vehicles set has slightly higher numbers except for total EDUs, which is 36.70 for Autonomous Vehicle and 36.76 for Cryptocurrencies. Autonomous Vehicle has 2.75 as average weight of SCUs and Cryptocurrencies has 2.07. Cryptocurrencies has shorter length of EDUs compared to Autonomous Vehicle, as 13.62 and 14.00. For the normalized SCU by total number of EDUs and number of matched EDUs, Autonomous Vehicle shows more with 0.08 and 0.84, while Cryptocurrencies has

Topic	Total SCUs	w=5	w=4	w=3	w ≤ 2
CrypCurr	34	0	3	5	26
AutoV	41	0	6	2	33

Table 4: Distributions of SCUs with weights from manual pyramids annotation of Cryptocurrencies and Autonomous Vehicle

0.06 and 0.70. This indicates that more important content is mentioned in Autonomous Vehicle submissions than Cryptocurrencies.

Table 5 also lists the average (reliable) total grade, and the breakdown for content quality and content coverage. Students' grades on Autonomous Vehicle and Cryptocurrencies are similar in all three aspects, as 23.48, 3.68 and 3.83 for Autonomous Vehicle, and 23.16, 3.81 and 3.39 in Cryptocurrencies.

8 Annotation of Argument Structure

To annotate the argumentative part of the essays, we used the coarse-grained argumentative structure proposed by Stab and Gurevych (2014): argument components (major claim, claim, premises) and argument relations (support/attack). Similar to Hidey et al. (2017), we took as annotation unit the proposition instead of the clause, given that premises are frequently propositions that conflate multiple clauses. For this pilot annotation task we labeled the 37 Cryptocurrency essays and used two expert annotators with background in linguistics and/or argumentation. We used Brat as annotation tool.[4] The set contains 36 main claims, 559 claims, 277 premises, 560 support relations and 101 attack relations.

Ghosh et al. (2016) proposed a set of argumentative features and showed that they correlate well with the holistic essay scores (low, medium and high) when applied to TOEFL persuasive essays: 1) features related to *argument components* (AC) such as the number of claims, number of premises, fraction of sentences containing argument components; 2) features related to *argument relations* (AR), such as the number and percentage of supported claims, and the number and percentage of dangling claims (i.e., claims with no supporting premises), the number of attack relations and attacks against the major claim; and 3) features related to the *typology of argument structures* (TS) such as the number of argument chains, number of argument trees. In this study, we wanted to see whether these proposed features correlate well with the 6 scale rubric that rate the "quality" of the argument. The scored used were the one obtained in our reliability study. Table 6 summarizes the features (for details see (Ghosh et al., 2016)).

Given the manual annotation of the essays, to measure the effectiveness of the argumenta-

---

[4] https://brat.nlplab.org.

Stat	CrypCurr$_{Wise}$	AutoV$_{Wise}$	CrypCurr$_{Peer}$	AutoV$_{Peer}$
Weight$_{SCU}$	2.60	2.37	2.07	2.75
Total EDUs	23.80	35.00	36.76	36.70
Tokens per EDU	17.39	15.18	13.62	14.00
NormSCUEDU$_{Total}$	0.11	0.07	0.06	0.08
NormSCUEDU$_{Matched}$	1.07	0.62	0.70	0.84
Final Scores$_{Rubric}$	-	-	23.16	23.48
Content Quality$_{Rubric}$	-	-	3.81	3.68
Content Coverage$_{Rubric}$	-	-	3.39	3.83

Table 5: Statistics of annotated wise crowd summaries and essays form Cryptocurrencies (CrypCurr$_{Wise}$) and Autonomous Vehicle (AutoV$_{Wise}$), and student submissions (CrypCurr$_{Peer}$ and AutoV$_{Peer}$): average matched SCU weights (Weight$_{SCU}$), average numbers of EDUs (Total EDUs), average tokens per EDU (Tokens per EDU), weighted SCU normalized by total number of EDUs (NormSCUEDU$_{Total}$), weighted SCU normalized by the number of matched EDUs (NormSCUEDU$_{Matched}$). We also provide the scores from rubrics here (bottom of the table): Final scores across 6 categories (Final Scores$_{Rubric}$), content quality (Content Quality$_{Rubric}$) and content coverage (Content Coverage$_{Rubric}$).

Feature Group	Argumentation Feature Description		
AC	# of Claims		
	# of Premises		
	# and fraction of sentences containing argument components		
AR	# and % of supported Claims		
	# and % of dangling Claims		
	# of Claims supporting Major Claim		
	# of total Attacks and Attacks against Major Claim		
TS	# of Argument Chains		
	# of Argument Trees (hight=1 or >1)		

Table 6: Argumentation Features

Features	Correlations
bl	0.15
AC	0.27
AR	0.35
TS	0.17
bl + AC	0.21
bl + AR	0.26
bl + TS	0.33
AC + AR + TS	0.41
bl + AC + AR + TS	0.26

Table 7: Correlation of LR (5 fold CV) with argument quality scores.

tive features in predicting the quality of argument scores (0-5) we use Logistic Regression (LR) learners and evaluate the learners using quadratic-weighted kappa (QWK) against the human scores, a methodology generally used for essay scoring (Farra et al., 2015; Ghosh et al., 2016). QWK corrects for chance agreement between the system prediction and the human prediction, and it takes into account the extent of the disagreement between labels. Since the number of essays is very small we did a five-fold cross validation. Table 7 reports the performance for the three feature groups as well as their combination. The baseline feature (bl) is the number of sentences in the essay, since essay length has been shown to be generally highly correlated with essay scores (Chodorow and Burstein, 2004).

As seen in Table 7 out of the individual features groups the higher correlation is obtained by the Argument Relation group. The best correlation is obtained when using all the argumentative features (AC+Ar+TS). Unlike Ghosh et al. (2016), we found that adding the baseline feature to the argument features did not help, except when combin-

ing with the typology of argument structure features. We also looked at what features are associated with different rubric scores based on the the regression coefficients. As expected, the tree structure features (TS) correlated with high score essays (4 and 5). In addition, high scoring essays (5) have a higher number of "attack" relations to the main claim, showing that the essays contain counterarguments (presenting both sides of the issue). Number of supported claims correlated negatively with lower scoring essays (meaning that the low scoring essays has more unsupported claims). Moreover, number of claims supporting the main claim was negatively correlated with low scoring essays. In those essays, the students, although advancing arguments, they failed to connect them to their main claim. Looking at the different between high scoring essays (4 vs. 5) we noticed an interesting aspect: for the essays scored with 5 the ratio of argumentative sentences w.r.t total number of sentence was higher than for the essays with a 4 score, while the essays with a 4 scores tend to be longer. In general our correlations scores were much lower than the ones reported by Ghosh et al. (2016). There are several explanations for that. First, the number of essays is smaller (37 compared to 107) and we have a 6-point scale rather than a 3 point scale. In addition, our scale reflected the argument quality and not a holistic essays score; looking just at argumentative discourse structure might not be enough, we need to look both at structure and the semantics of arguments (content) to more reliably distinguish essays based on their argument quality (Klebanov et al., 2016). Our annotation of content and argument will allow us to pursue this line of inquiry in our future work.

9 Conclusion

We have presented the collection of a rich data set of essays written by college freshman in an academic skills class. We conducted a reliability assessment of the rubric used to explain the assignment expectations. The moderate correlation of the raters' scores with the grades assigned by tutors, combined with the lengthy investment in time to train the raters, shows that high reliability can be achieved at a cost that cannot be sustained in ordinary classrooms. One of the questions our future work will address is the degree to which rubrics could be partly automated using NLP techniques. Partial automation could free instructors from the demands of managing a team of graders, and potentially lead to greater consistency in student feedback.

Our future work will investigate the interdependence of the content and argument annotations presented here, and the ramifications for student learning. Two teams of annotators working completely independently performed the content annotation (SCUs, EDUs) and the argument annotation. We will investigate the correspondence between EDUs and argument components, both of which are simple propositions. Depending on how well they correspond, it is possible that providing EDU annotation as input to argument annotation could improve the argument annotation reliability. Ultimately we aim to help instructors provide students with better feedback on their ability to summarize the main ideas of source material, the role that these ideas play in their arguments, and the overall quality of their essays.

Acknowledgments

This work is supported by NSF IIS 1847842. We thank two undergraduate REUs, Connor Heaton and Annie Qin Sui, who participated in the reliability studies and other project activities. Finally, we thank the reviewers for the valuable feedback.

References

Tamara Sladoljev Agejev and Jan Šnajder. 2017. Using analytic scoring rubrics in the automatic assessment of college-level summary writing tasks in l2. In *Proceedings of the Eighth International Joint Conference on Natural Language Processing (Volume 2: Short Papers)*, pages 181–186.

Simon Black. 2018. *Crack the Essay: Secrets of Argumentative Writing Revealed*. Gramercy House Publishing.

Chloé Braud, Maximin Coavoux, and Anders Søgaard. 2017. Cross-lingual RST discourse parsing. In *Proceedings of the 15th Conference of the European Chapter of the Association for Computational Linguistics: Volume 1, Long Papers*, volume 1, pages 292–304.

Martin Chodorow and Jill Burstein. 2004. Beyond essay length: Evaluating e-rater®'s performance on toefl® essays. *ETS Research Report Series*, 2004(1):i–38.

Noura Farra, Swapna Somasundaran, and Jill Burstein. 2015. Scoring persuasive essays using opinions and their targets. In *Proceedings of the Tenth Workshop on Innovative Use of NLP for Building Educational Applications*, pages 64–74, Denver, Colorado. Association for Computational Linguistics.

Ralph P. Ferretti, Charles A. MacArthur, and Nancy S. Dowdy. 2000. The effects of an elaborated goal on the persuasive writing of students with learning disabilities and their normally achieving peers. *Journal of Educational Psychology*, 92(4):694–702.

H. A. Gallagher, K. R. Woodworth, and N. L. Arshan. 2015. Impact of the national writing projects college-ready writers program on teachers and students.

Yanjun Gao, Kenneth Huang, and Rebecca J. Passonneau. 2019. AESOP: Annotated elementary discourse units from student opinion essays. In submission.

Libby Gerard, Marcia C Linn, and Jacquie Madhok. 2016. Examining the impacts of annotation and automated guidance on essay revision and science learning. Singapore: International Society of the Learning Sciences.

Libby F Gerard and Marcia C Linn. 2016. Using automated scores of student essays to support teacher guidance in classroom inquiry. *Journal of Science Teacher Education*, 27(1):111–129.

Debanjan Ghosh, Aquila Khanam, Yubo Han, and Smaranda Muresan. 2016. Coarse-grained argumentation features for scoring persuasive essays. In *Proceedings of the 54th Annual Meeting of the Association for Computational Linguistics*, pages 549–554.

Amy Gillespie, Steve Graham, Sharlene Kiuhara, and Michael Hebert. 2014. High school teachers use of writing to support students learning: a national survey. *Reading and Writing*, 27(6):1043–1072.

Steve Graham, Andrea Capizzi, KarenR Harris, Michael Hebert, and Paul Morphy. 2014. Teaching writing to middle school students: a national survey. *Reading and Writing*, 27(6):1015–1042.

Steve Graham, Jill Fitzgerald, Linda D. Friedrich, Katie Greene, James S. Kim, and Carol Booth Olson. 2016. Teaching secondary students to write effectively. Technical Report NCEE 2017-4002, National Center for Education Evaluation and Regional Assistance (NCEE), Institute of Education Sciences, U.S. Department of Education, Washington, DC.

Steve Graham and Dolores Perin. 2007. A meta-analysis of writing instruction for adolescent students. *Journal of Educational Psychology*, 99:445476.

Murat Gunel, Brian Hand, and Vaughan Prain. 2007. Writing for learning in science: A secondary analysis of six studies. *International Journal of Science and Mathematics Education*, 5(4):615–637.

Brian Hand, Lori A. Norton-Meier, Murat Gunel, and Recai Akkus. 2015. Aligning teaching to learning: A three-year study examining the embedding of language and argumentation into elementary science classrooms. *International Journal of Science and Mathematics Education*.

Christopher Hidey, Elena Musi, Alyssa Hwang, Smaranda Muresan, and Kathy McKeown. 2017. Analyzing the semantic types of claims and premises in an online persuasive forum. In *Proceedings of the 4th Workshop on Argument Mining*.

D. H. Jonassen. 2008. Instructional design as design problem solving: An iterative process. *Educational Technology*, 48(3):21–26.

Anders Jonsson and Gunilla Svingby. 2007. The use of scoring rubrics: Reliability, validity and educational consequences. *Educational Research Review*, 2(2):130 – 144.

Sharlene A. Kiuhara, Steve Graham, and Leanne S. Hawken. 2009. Teaching writing to high school students: A national survey. *Journal of Educational Psychology*, 101(1):136–160.

Beata Beigman Klebanov, Nitin Madnani, Jill Burstein, and Swapna Somasundaran. 2014. Content importance models for scoring writing from sources. In *Proceedings of the 52nd Annual Meeting of the Association for Computational Linguistics (Volume 2: Short Papers)*, volume 2, pages 247–252.

Beata Beigman Klebanov, Christian Stab, Jill Burstein, Yi Song, Binod Gyawali, and Iryna Gurevych. 2016. Argumentation: Content, structure, and relationship with essay quality. In *Proceedings of the Third Workshop on Argument Mining (ArgMining2016)*, pages 70–75.

Perry D. Klein and Mary A. Rose. 2010. Teaching argument and explanation to prepare junior students for writing to learn. *Reading Research Quarterly*, 45(4):433–461.

Qi Li, Tianshi Li, and Baobao Chang. 2016. Discourse parsing with attention-based hierarchical neural networks. In *Proceedings of the 2016 Conference on Empirical Methods in Natural Language Processing*, pages 362–371.

Daniel Marcu. 2000. *The theory and practice of discourse parsing and summarization*. MIT press.

Ani Nenkova, Rebecca Passonneau, and Kathleen McKeown. 2007. The pyramid method: Incorporating human content selection variation in summarization evaluation. *ACM Trans. Speech Lang. Process.*, 4(2).

Stephen P. Norris and Linda M. Phillips. 2003. How literacy in its fundamental sense is central to scientific literacy. *Science Education*, 87(2):224–240.

Nathan Ong, Diane Litman, and Alexandra Brusilovsky. 2014. Ontology-based argument mining and automatic essay scoring. *ACL 2014*, page 24.

Rebecca J Passonneau. 2006. Pyramid annotation guide: Duc 2006.

Rebecca j. Passonneau. 2010. Formal and functional assessment of the pyramid method for summary content evaluation*. *Nat. Lang. Eng.*, 16(2):107–131.

Rebecca J. Passonneau, Ananya Poddar, Gaurav Gite, Alisa Krivokapic, Qian Yang, and Dolores Perin. 2018. Wise crowd content assessment and educational rubrics. *International Journal of Artificial Intelligence in Education*, 28(1):29–55.

Isaac Persing and Vincent Ng. 2015. Modeling argument strength in student essays. In *Proceedings of the 53rd Annual Meeting of the Association for Computational Linguistics and the 7th International Joint Conference on Natural Language Processing (Volume 1: Long Papers)*, pages 543–552.

Rashmi Prasad, Nikhil Dinesh, Alan Lee, Eleni Miltsakaki, Livio Robaldo, Aravind K Joshi, and Bonnie L Webber. 2008. The Penn Discourse Treebank 2.0. In *LREC*.

Y. Maline Reddy and Heidi Andrade. 2010. A review of rubric use in higher education. *Assessment Evaluation in Higher Education*, 35(4):435–448.

Victor Sampson, Patrick Enderle, Jonathon Grooms, and Shelbie Witte. 2013. Writing to learn by learning to write during the school science laboratory: Helping middle and high school students develop argumentative writing skills as they learn core ideas. *Science Education*, 97(5):643–670.

Miguel Santamaría Lancho, Mauro Hernández, Ángeles Sánchez-Elvira Paniagua, José María Luzón Encabo, and Guillermo de Jorge-Botana. 2018. Using semantic technologies for formative assessment and scoring in large courses and MOOCs. *Journal of Interactive Media in Education*, 2018(1).

Yi Song, Michael Heilman, Beata Beigman Klebanov, and Paul Deane. 2014. Applying argumentation schemes for essay scoring. In *Proceedings of the First Workshop on Argumentation Mining*, pages 69–78.

Christian Stab and Iryna Gurevych. 2014. Annotating argument components and relations in persuasive essays. In *Proceedings of the 25th International Conference on Computational Linguistics (COLING 2014)*, pages 1501–1510.